Suez: The Twice-Fought War

SUEZ

The Twice-Fought War

A HISTORY BY

KENNETT LOVE

McGRAW-HILL BOOK COMPANY
NEW YORK / TORONTO

PW

DESIGNED BY RONALD FARBER

Library of Congress Catalog Card Number: 76-81913

FIRST EDITION 38780

TO FÉLICITÉ

for the years bound here among these pages

Contents

Preface   xi

Chronology   xiii

PART I: COLLISION COURSES
(2100 B.C. to July 1956)

Prologue   1
1 The Gaza Raid (28 February 1955)   5
2 Isaac and Ishmael (2100 B.C. to 1948 A.D.)   23
3 Foremath (1948 to 28 February 1955)   47
4 The Turning Point (28 February 1955 to 19 July 1956)   83
5 A Common Enemy (1830 to 19 July 1956)   129
6 The Lion and the Sphinx (1798 to 19 October 1954)   167
7 Eden For and Against Nasser (1954 to 20 July 1956)   193
8 Enter, The Bear (1237 A.D. to 19 July 1956)   225
9 The Pistol (1820 to 16 May 1956)   265
10 Renege on the Dam (3400 B.C. to 19 July 1956)   297

PART II: PRETEXTS
(20 July 1956 to 29 October 1956)

11 "This Canal Belongs to Egypt" (20 July 1956 to 26 July 1956)   333
12 Call to Arms (27 July 1956 to 2 August 1956)   361

13 Palaver (3 August 1956 to 15 September 1956)   391
14 Collusion (15 September 1956 to 9 October 1956)   433

PART III: WAR

(Evening of 29 October 1956 to 2 A.M., Cairo Time, 7 November 1956)

15 War in the Sinai (Evening, 29 October 1956 to Evening,
       31 October 1956)   481
16 Retreat (Evening, 31 October 1956 to Midday, 2 November 1956)   525
17 Lull (1 November 1956 to Dawn, 5 November 1956)   557
18 Port Said (Before Dawn, 5 November 1956 to 2 A.M.,
       7 November, 1956)   589

PART IV: REPRISE
(7 November 1956 to the Future)

19 Disgorging (7 November 1956 and after)   633
20 Reprise (1967–)   675

    Notes   703
    Bibliography   737
    Index   745

Maps

The Mediterranean World, October 1956	xxiv
The 1956 War as it unfolded	485
Mitla Pass	499
Abu Aoueigila	537
Rafah, al-Arish, and the Gaza Strip	547
Sharm al-Sheikh	593
Port Said	597
Israel's expansion, 1947 to 1967	693

Preface

Retracing the history of Suez has led me some 50,000 miles during the last five years. I sojourned in Cairo, Gettysburg, Jerusalem, London, New York, Paris, Tel Aviv, and Washington and I reconnoitered other places like Abu Aoueigila, Amman, Aswan, Ismailiya, Jericho, Port Said, Sèvres, and "Terrapin." I had been over the terrain before, historically and geographically, as a *New York Times* correspondent during the central years of the story. I went back to it for mixed reasons: first, sheer journalistic dissatisfaction that too much that was too important remained unrevealed or told only in prejudice or in part; second, because there at the world's oldest crossroads the fates of East and West have stumbled together twice in half a generation and the pitfalls need marking lest a third jostling wholly unbalance the nuclear giants and they pull each other down in the last fall of civilization; third, Suez is an intricate drama of great men, bold action, pride, prejudice, and guile that is worth retelling for the pleasure of it, quite aside from its grave lessons for the immediate future.

Suez is tragedy, not melodrama, for it has no villains. There are only heroes, some of them with tragic flaws, and millions of innocent victims. The most tragic figure is Eden, the hero in search of a role, whose flaws of temperament, enlarged by illness, cast him down from the summit of the Western world. The curtain of final triumph or tragedy has not yet rung down on Nasser, who long ago answered the summons of a role in search of a hero. The incredibly durable central figure in the twice-fought war, many times marked for destruction, is no more a villain than his chief antagonists, Ben-Gurion and Dayan. Yet part of the thrust of events derives from the false image of Nasser as villain in Israel and the West. This is one of the pitfalls into which judgment has twice stumbled when statesmen decided for peace or war. It can happen again.

One general lesson of Suez is that democratic leaders can be as dangerously wrong as dictators when they act in secret upon secret information. An ignorant or prejudiced public offers no protection. As Eden maneuvered toward war many a worried Englishman surrendered his critical faculty on the assumption that "the Government must know what they are doing"—that official actions which seem irrational on the basis of public knowledge will prove rational in the light of secret information available only to the decision makers. Now we know what half of Britain and most of the world suspected at the time—that Eden had no privileged information significantly different from public knowledge. Seen in hindsight with all its secrets bare, Suez turns out to have been as foolish and self-destructive for Britain as its more confident contemporary critics said it was. The Lavon Affair, Kennedy's Bay of Pigs, Khrushchev's Cuban missiles, Johnson's Dominican invasion and Vietnam are similar examples of secret policy and public acquiescence. The world has become too dangerous for this lesson to remain unlearned. A people should never surrender its right to know and to criticize. As for journalists, if they are unable to penetrate the secrecy with which officialdom seeks to cloak its enterprises, basically for self-protection, they should go back again as historians to make the record whole and clear.

It is this that I have tried to do, going back over the printed record and such unpublished documents as I could obtain and above all questioning as many as possible of the persons in the story. I have done research and interviewed major figures in all the countries importantly involved except Russia. Some I had interviewed as a correspondent, some later as a historian, and some at both stages. Some were evasive, some were misleading, but most were forthright and candid. Among those who accorded me especially long and penetrating interviews were five leading members of Eden's cabinet, including Eden himself, President Eisenhower, Nasser, Pineau, Abba Eban, Generals Stockwell and Beaufre, but I talked to scores upon scores more of the multitudinous dramatis personae of this narrative.

The cooperation of the actors in this historical drama would have been to no avail if I had not been helped by many other generous souls, only a few of whom can be thanked here by name. My greatest debt is to the Cranshaw Foundation of New York, to its gentle benefactress, Mrs. Frank K. Sanders Jr., and its trustees, particularly Frederick B. Payne, a shrewd risker of capital. Cranshaw gave me the freedom from other commitments without which this work could not have been undertaken. The venerable American Philosophical

Society of Philadelphia and its executive officer, George W. Corner, were my first institutional backers, providing a generous travel grant and, implicit therein, the credentials of respectability so helpful to a newspaperman seeking his way in groves of academe. The Carnegie Endowment for International Peace and its president, Dr. Joseph E. Johnson, not only greatly enhanced my funds and credentials but also introduced me to Mr. Payne just when I had begun to fear I would have to return my two grants for lack of funds to ensure finishing the work. Professor Morroe Berger, then director of the Program in Near Eastern Studies at Princeton University, opened the door to an academic home for me there. It was all such a home should be. Princeton's great library possesses the private papers of John Foster Dulles, through which I was shepherded by Alexander P. Clark, Curator of Manuscripts. To the late President Eisenhower I am indebted for an illuminating interview and also for giving me access to his papers, then housed at his office in Gettysburg. For help in mining another rich trove of unpublished documents in the Egyptian Military Archives in Cairo I am especially grateful to Brigadier General Hassan al-Badri and Lieutenant-Colonel Mohammed Zohdy, who literally spent weeks ferreting out documents for me and helping me translate them. The Israeli Defense establishment in Tel Aviv, which had already completed an official war history, gave me equal help but without having to dig so hard. I thank Jacques Chaban-Delmas both for his own ministerial insights into Suez and for opening to me the library of the Assemblée Nationale, of which he had become President. With ungrudging courtesy and candor both the former and the present owners of the Suez Canal helped me study their historic quarrel. The Suez Financial Company's Raymond Didier in Paris and Claude Boillot in New York gave generously of documentation and time, as did Aatah Mahmoud Mohammed and Asad Moussallem of the Suez Canal Authority's Cairo and Ismailiya offices. Miss Elizabeth Campbell of the incomparable Press Library at Chatham House, London, and John Sheringham of the BBC Monitoring Service welcomed me into those unique repositories of the contemporary human record. My days of research in the clipping morgues of the *Jerusalem Post*, the *Egyptian Gazette*, and *al-Ahram* were made both possible and pleasant by their editors, Ted Lurie, Dr. Ameen Abu al-Enein, and Mohammed Hassanein Heikal, respectively. Mr. Heikal, in addition, showed me some of the Nasser holographs and other Suez documents in his custody. The Library of Congress, the British Museum, and the Zionist Archives and the library of the Council on Foreign Relations in New York kindly accommodated my many requests for special facilities and help.

To Professor J. C. Hurewitz of Columbia University, who read all of my manuscript, and Eugene Black, who read part of it, I am grateful in equal measure for both approval and criticism, although I did not accept all of the latter. For devoted labors on this work exceeded only by my own I give particular thanks to Lemma Endersby, who typed and typed and typed—notes, letters, manuscript, and revisions—and corrected lapses of grammar and spelling. I owe thanks to my publishers for patience and to my past and present editors —Edward Kuhn Jr., Frank Taylor, Larry Grow, and Tony Velie—for tender loving care. I am beholden to Harry Carter for maps that reveal the grand simplicity hidden among the chaotic details of war. My gratitude to Roberta Blaché will be shared by all who use her index.

Princeton, N.J.
June 1969

Chronology

Napoleon conquers Egypt	1798
British drive French from Egypt	1801
Mohammed Aly repulses second British invasion of Egypt	1807
French begin conquest of Algeria	May 1830
De Lesseps obtains Suez Canal concession	Nov. 1854
Grand opening of Suez Canal	17 Nov. 1869
Britain buys out Egyptian Suez Canal shares	Nov. 1875
Britain and France take control of bankrupt Egypt's finances	1876
Britain invades Egypt, beginning 74-year occupation	**19 Aug. 1882**
Ben-Gurion is born in Plonsk, Poland	16 Oct. 1886
Dulles is born in Washington	25 Feb. 1888
Constantinople Convention on Suez Canal signed (Britain adheres in 1904)	29 Oct. 1888
Eisenhower is born in Denison, Texas	14 Oct. 1890
Khrushchev is born in Kalinovka, Ukraine	17 Apr. 1894
Eden is born at Windlestone, Durham, England	12 June 1897
Political Zionism is born at Basel conference	**29 Aug. 1897**
British build Aswan Dam	1898–1902
Pineau is born near Le Mans	14 Oct. 1904
Mollet is born in Normandy	31 Dec. 1905
Zionists reject British offer of Kenya as Jewish national home	30 July 1905
Egyptian Premier assassinated to stop extension of Suez concession	Feb. 1910
World War I begins	28 July 1914

Dayan is born at Degania, Palestine	20 May 1915
McMahon promises Arabs independence if they revolt against Turkey	**24 Oct. 1915**
Sykes–Picot agreement secretly negates McMahon promise	**16 May 1916**
Arabs revolt against Turkey on strength of McMahon promise	**June 1916**
Balfour Declaration promises Jewish home in Arab Palestine	**2 Nov. 1917**
Nasser is born in Alexandria	15 Jan. 1918
World War I ends with Britain ruling Egypt, Palestine, Jordan, Iraq	11 Nov. 1918
Decade of Palestine Arab protest against Jewish influx erupts in bloody riots	Aug. 1929
Hitler becomes Chancellor of Germany	**30 Jan. 1933**
Eden becomes Foreign Secretary	Dec. 1935
Hitler reoccupies Rhineland	Mar. 1936
Three-year Arab rebellion begins in Palestine	Apr. 1936
Anglo-Egyptian treaty; Nasser leads student demonstrations	26 Aug. 1936
Hitler launches World War II	1 Sep. 1939
Nazis secretly adopt "final solution" for Europe's Jews and Gypsies	**Jan. 1942**
British tanks force King Farouk to change premiers	4 Feb. 1942
World War II ends in Europe; Jewish survivors begin exodus to Palestine	8 May 1945
UN votes Palestine partition after US lobbying; Arabs vow resistance	29 Nov. 1947
Ben-Gurion proclaims establishment of Israel; US grants recognition	**14 May 1948**
Arab armies join Palestine Arab resistance; Egypt bars Israeli shipping in Suez Canal	15 May 1948
Egypt signs armistice with Israel	24 Feb. 1949
Israeli force takes Um Rashrash, future site of Elath	11 Mar. 1949
Egypt fortifies entrance to Gulf of Aqaba	1949
US, Britain, France issue Tripartite Declaration guaranteeing Middle East borders and barring arms race	25 May 1950
Korean War begins	25 June 1950
Egypt blockades Gulf of Aqaba	1 July 1951
Security Council calls on Egypt to end Suez restrictions on Israel	1 Sep. 1951
Egypt abrogates treaty with Britain, claims sovereignty in Sudan	15 Oct. 1951
Black Saturday; mobs sack and burn downtown Cairo, kill Europeans	26 Jan. 1952
Nasser's revolutionary junta seizes power in Egypt, exiles King	**23–26 July 1952**
Eisenhower inaugurated; Dulles is Secretary of State	20 Jan. 1953
Stalin dies	5 Mar. 1953
Dulles makes Middle East tour	11–29 May 1953

Korean armistice signed	27 July 1953
Russia announces successful H-bomb test	20 Aug. 1953
Israeli raiders kill 20, wound 62 at al-Bureig refugee camp in Gaza Strip	28 Aug. 1953
Israel begins diversion of Jordan River	2 Sep. 1953
Israeli raiders kill 66 villagers at Qibya, Jordan	14 Oct. 1953
US sends Eric Johnston to seek Arab–Israeli development of Jordan River	—
Israel halts Jordan diversion project; US resumes suspended aid	28 Oct. 1953
Ben-Gurion announces his retirement; Sharett succeeds him	**2 Nov. 1953**
Vyshinsky veto signals Russian shift toward Arabs	29 Mar. 1954
Iraq accepts US arms with strings	21 Apr. 1954
Israeli agents launch incendiary campaign against British evacuation of Suez base	2 July 1954
Israel begins secret arms purchases from France	**1 Aug. 1954**
Israel attempts to send *Bat Galim* through Suez Canal	28 Sep. 1954
British sign Suez base evacuation agreement with Nasser	**19 Oct. 1954**
Moslem Brotherhood tries to kill Nasser for Suez accord with Britain	26 Oct. 1954
Algerian rebellion against French rule begins	**1 Nov. 1954**
Nasser tells Burns he wants continued quiet on Israeli border	15 Nov. 1954
Six Moslem Brotherhood leaders hanged for assassination plot	7 Dec. 1954
Egypt returns *Bat Galim* crew to Israel	1 Jan. 1955
Arab League premiers try to heal Egypt–Iraq rift over pacts	22 Jan. 1955
Egypt hangs two Israeli spy-saboteurs for 1954 arson campaign	31 Jan. 1955
Lavon resigns as Israeli Defense Minister	2 Feb. 1955
Khrushchev comes to power in the Kremlin	8 Feb. 1955
Ben-Gurion named Defense Minister; Lavon resignation announced	**17 Feb. 1955**
Eden meets Nasser at British Embassy in Cairo	20 Feb. 1955
Iraq and Turkey sign Baghdad Pact	24 Feb. 1955
Gaza Raid	**28 Feb. 1955**
Eden promises Nasser in secret moratorium to freeze Arab membership in Baghdad Pact if Egypt stops propaganda; Britain joins pact	**5 Apr. 1955**
Eden becomes Prime Minister	6 Apr. 1955
Nasser in Bandung for Afro-Asian conference	18–24 Apr. 1955
Big Three end occupation and bring West Germany into NATO	5–9 May 1955
Warsaw Pact formed	14 May 1955
Nasser asks Russia if she would sell Egypt arms; Russia says Yes	**18–21 May 1955**
Paris shifts NATO troops to Algeria	19 May 1955

Tories increase Commons majority in general election	26 May 1955
Nasser offers to demilitarize Israeli frontier (distorted publication portrays him as warmonger)	1 June 1955
Nasser tells Byroade US may force him to buy Russian arms	9 June 1955
Ben-Gurion and Sharett say Israel will fight to open Aqaba Gulf	8 July 1955
Summit Conference in Geneva	18–23 July 1955
Shepilov begins 9-day visit to Egypt, discusses arms	21 July 1955
Activists gain in Israeli general election	26 July 1955
Israeli purchase of Mystère IV jets disclosed	1 Aug. 1955
Israeli unit storms Egyptian position in Gaza Strip	22 Aug. 1955
Nasser launches first *Fedayeen* reprisal raids, decides on Russian arms	**25 Aug. 1955**
Israeli raiders kill 39 at Khan Yunis in Gaza Strip	31 Aug. 1955
France halts delivery of arms purchased by Egypt	2 Sep. 1955
Nasser unilaterally demilitarizes Egypt's side of border	20 Sep. 1955
Eisenhower suffers heart attack	24 Sep. 1955
Nasser announces Russian arms deal after Britain discloses it	**27 Sep. 1955**
Russia offers Egypt aid for High Dam	12 Oct. 1955
Egypt and Syria sign defense pact as rival to Baghdad Pact	20 Oct. 1955
Ben-Gurion summons Dayan from Paris vacation to plan Sinai war	**22 Oct. 1955**
Israel storms Jebel al-Sabha, consolidates grip on al-Auja invasion gateway	2 Nov. 1955
Eden, in Guildhall speech, launches peace effort; Nasser is responsive	9 Nov. 1955
Egypt, US, Britain begin talks in Washington on High Dam financing	21 Nov. 1955
Templer mission to Jordan violates secret Eden–Nasser moratorium on Baghdad Pact	**6 Dec. 1955**
Anderson mission to "buy" Palestine settlement with High Dam aid is initiated in Eisenhower-Dulles conversation	**8 Dec. 1955**
Israeli raid on Syria wrecks Eden's peace effort and Johnston mission on Arab–Israeli Jordan River development	11 Dec. 1955
US and Britain promise Egypt aid for High Dam	**16 Dec. 1955**
Riots abort Templer effort to bring Jordan into Baghdad Pact	—
Tory press attacks Eden for dithering	3 Jan. 1956
Mollet confirmed as French Premier	1 Feb. 1956
European colonists bully Mollet into harsher Algerian policy	6 Feb. 1956
Nasser and Black of World Bank agree on High Dam financing but, secret Anderson mission having failed, US has lost interest	9 Feb. 1956
Khrushchev launches de-Stalinization at Communist Party Congress	**14 Feb. 1956**

US approves French arms shipment to Israel — 24 Feb. 1956

Lloyd persuades Nasser to renew secret Baghdad Pact moratorium — **1 Mar. 1956**

King Hussein of Jordan ousts General Glubb; Eden vows to destroy Nasser — —

Pineau meets Nasser, who launches Algerian peace effort — 14 Mar. 1956

Nasser's abatement of propaganda (in renewed secret Baghdad Pact moratorium) is remarked by Foreign Office — 4 Apr. 1956

Israeli bombardment kills 63, wounds 102 in Gaza on eve of Hammarskjold peace mission — 5 Apr. 1956

Egypt launches second *Fedayeen* reprisal campaign, killing 14 Israelis in five days — 7 Apr. 1956

Russia dissolves Cominform, supports UN Palestine peace effort — 17 Apr. 1956

Khrushchev in Britain proposes UN arms embargo on Middle East — **27 Apr. 1956**

France reports Big Three agreement to "ration" arms to Middle East — 6 May 1956

Nasser recognizes Red China to avert danger of UN arms embargo — **16 May 1956**

Egypt and Suez Canal Company reach new accord — 30 May 1956

Ileitis renders Eisenhower inactive for nearly six weeks — 8 June 1956

Britain completes Suez base evacuation five days early — 13 June 1956

Ben-Gurion forces Sharett from Cabinet, resumes war planning — **18 June 1956**

Poles riot in Poznan, climaxing months of East European dissidence — 28 June 1956

Nasser begins eight-day visit to Yugoslavia for Brioni conference — 12 July 1956

Dulles reneges on High Dam — **19 July 1956**

Nasser nationalizes Suez Canal; Eden and French decide on war — **26 July 1956**

Eisenhower sends Murphy to London to prevent war — 28 July 1956

Eden, Macmillan tell Eisenhower they plan immediate attack — 31 July 1956

Eisenhower sends Dulles to London to prevent war — —

British begin to mobilize, order Stockwell to plan Anglo-French invasion of Egypt — 2 Aug. 1956

Dulles pressures British into holding international conference first — —

Egypt withdraws Sinai troops to defend Delta against Anglo-French invasion — 6 Aug. 1956

France gets assurance Israel will cooperate in war on Egypt — 7 Aug. 1956

Stockwell completes plan for 15 September invasion at Alexandria — **8 Aug. 1956**

Eden names Nasser in world telecast as sole enemy, insults him — —

Eden personally approves Stockwell's war plan	10 Aug. 1956
Nasser rejects London conference invitation, citing Eden's insults	12 Aug. 1956
London Conference ends in split; East denounces West's demand for internationalization of Canal	23 Aug. 1956
Canal traffic above normal in first month of nationalization	27 Aug. 1956
Britain announces French troop movement to Cyprus	29 Aug. 1956
France briefs Israel on Anglo-French war plans	1 Sep. 1956
Eisenhower chides Eden for spiking peace moves, warns against war	**2 Sep. 1956**
Menzies presents West's internationalization plan to Nasser	3 Sep. 1956
Dulles invents Suez Canal Users Association (SCUA) to stall war	4 Sep. 1956
Eden postpones invasion, shifts attack from Alexandria to Port Said	—
Nasser tells Menzies he rejects internationalization of Canal	5 Sep. 1956
Anglo-French invasion is ready, awaiting new date	**8 Sep. 1956**
Menzies announces failure of his mission	9 Sep. 1956
Nasser proposes large conference of all Suez Canal users	10 Sep. 1956
Bulganin warns Eden and Mollet against attacking Egypt	11 Sep. 1956
Eden presents a provocative SCUA to Commons	12 Sep. 1956
Dulles pulls SCUA's teeth—won't "shoot our way through" Canal	13 Sep. 1956
European pilots leave Canal *en masse*; Egypt maintains traffic	**15 Sep. 1956**
Ben-Gurion assures France of cooperation; tells Mapai of "true ally"	23 Sep. 1956
Dayan and French arrange arms shipments for Sinai campaign	1 Oct. 1956
Dulles states US aloofness in "colonial" disputes; Eden furious	2 Oct. 1956
Dayan briefs his generals for 20 October attack after feint at Jordan	—
Dayan and Air Force plan to destroy Egyptian Air Force on ground	3 Oct. 1956
Meinertzhagen records seeing Egyptian document which Israel supposedly didn't capture until 2 November	4 Oct. 1956
Monckton resigns as Defense Minister over Eden's war plans	11 Oct. 1956
Basis for Suez settlement adopted at UN; Eden plans to evade it	**13 Oct. 1956**
Eden discusses collusion plan with French secret emissaries	**14 Oct. 1956**
Eisenhower learns of Israeli mobilization preparations	15 Oct. 1956
Eden and Mollet adopt collusion plan at sudden Paris meeting	16 Oct. 1956
Poles defy Khrushchev threat to "crush" their new leadership	19 Oct. 1956
Anglo-French commanders get final invasion decision and date	—
Nationalists win election in Jordan	21 Oct. 1956

Lloyd, Ben-Gurion, Pineau open secret conclave at Sèvres on Ben-Gurion's demand for written collusion guarantees	22 Oct. 1956
French kidnap five Algerian rebel leaders	—
New Hungarian leaders follow Polish example toward autonomy	—
Pineau flies to London to get Eden commitment for Ben-Gurion	23 Oct. 1956
Britain, France, Israel sign secret collusion accord at Sèvres; war to be staged as Anglo-French police action between Egypt and Israel; British to destroy Egyptian Air Force for Israel; ultimatum is drafted for use on 30 October	**24 Oct. 1956**
Invasion orders issued to Anglo-French command	—
Jordan, battered by Israeli raids, joins Egypt–Syria defense pact	—
Russian forces invade Budapest	—
British invasion fleet starts loading in Malta	27 Oct. 1956
Ben-Gurion orders UN observers ousted from al-Auja	—
Eisenhower warns Ben-Gurion against war	—
Lloyd lies to US Ambassador Aldrich about British plans	28 Oct. 1956
State Department advises Americans to leave Middle East	—
Israeli paratroopers drop near Mitla Pass to "create a military threat to the Suez Canal" as required by collusion accord	**29 Oct. 1956**
Britain tells US the Tripartite Declaration is a dead letter	—
Nasser orders army back into Sinai under restrictions against interfering with Canal shipping	—
Anglo-French ultimatum issued to Egypt and Israel	30 Oct. 1956
Russians withdraw from Budapest, promise non-interference to satellites	—
First vetoes by Britain and France paralyze Security Council	—
British begin bombing Egypt; Nasser orders retreat from Sinai, tells Arab allies to stay out of fight, plans guerrilla resistance if Egypt is occupied	31 Oct. 1956
Nasser asks help from Eisenhower, who promises non-military help	**1 Nov. 1956**
Premier Nagy withdraws Hungary from Communist bloc	—
Canal is blocked	—
Egypt completes withdrawal from Sinai	2 Nov. 1956
US spearheads UN General Assembly effort to stop the war	—
Syria blows up oil pipelines	—
Israel mops up Sinai and Gaza Strip; fighting at lull for two days	3 Nov. 1956
Israel reneges on cease-fire at Anglo-French request	—

Red Army reenters Budapest, crushes Hungarian rebellion	4 Nov. 1956
UN General Assembly adopts plan for Emergency Force	—
Israel takes Aqaba straits, ending her war	5 Nov. 1956
Anglo-French "police action" begins with airborne assault	—
Kremlin tells Nasser military help is impossible, then it sends rocket-rattling threats to Eden, Mollet, Ben-Gurion	—
Anglo-French seaborne force invades Port Said	6 Nov. 1956
Eden, Mollet agree to cease fire	—
Eisenhower wins reelection in landslide	—
Anglo-French invaders cease fire after 23-mile advance down Canal	7 Nov. 1956
Ben-Gurion gives Knesset to believe Israel will keep conquests	—
Eisenhower cables Ben-Gurion that Israel must withdraw	—
Ben-Gurion tells Eisenhower Israel will withdraw, then he broadcasts to nation that withdrawal is not certain	8 Nov. 1956
Moscow warns that "volunteers" may help Egypt end occupation	10 Nov. 1956
Hammarskjold arrives in Egypt with first UNEF contingents	16 Nov. 1956
US says emergency oil shipments await "definitive" Anglo-French promise to withdraw	29 Nov. 1956
Lloyd announces British and French will withdraw from Egypt	3 Dec. 1956
Israel begins pull-back in Sinai	—
British and French complete withdrawal from Egypt	22 Dec. 1956
Eisenhower Doctrine is presented to Congress	5 Jan. 1957
Eden resigns; Macmillan is to succeed him	9 Jan. 1957
US *aide mémoire* supports Israeli right of "innocent passage" in Gulf of Aqaba	11 Feb. 1957
Israel ends struggle to retain "liberated" Sinai and Gaza Strip, withdraws last forces	**7 Mar. 1957**
Jordan terminates 1948 Treaty of Alliance with Britain	13 Mar. 1957
At Bermuda Conference with US, Macmillan and Lloyd still press for destruction of Nasser	21 Mar. 1957
Suez Canal is reopened	8 Apr. 1957
Egyptian declaration on Suez Canal reaffirms 1888 Convention and accepts compulsory jurisdiction of World Court	24 Apr. 1957
Suez Canal Company begins study of tunnel under English Channel	July 1957
Egypt and Syria merge as United Arab Republic	1 Feb. 1958
French Fourth Republic overthrown; De Gaulle comes to power	13 May 1958
Egypt and Suez Canal Company reach compensation agreement	13 July 1958
Revolution in Iraq overthrows monarchy	**14 July 1958**
US Marines land in Lebanon to protect pro-Western regime	15 July 1958

US withdraws from Lebanon	25 Oct. 1958
Egypt and Russia sign aid agreement for High Dam	**27 Dec. 1958**
Nasser denounces Khrushchev for supporting Middle East communism	17 Mar. 1959
Britain and Egypt reestablish diplomatic relations	1 Dec. 1959
Construction of High Dam begins	9 Jan. 1960
Kennedy is inaugurated	20 Jan. 1960
Syrian army coup ends union with Egypt	28 Sep. 1961
Algeria wins independence from France	July 1962
Egyptian expeditionary force supports republican regime in Yemen civil war; Saudi Arabia backs Royalists	1963–1967
Kennedy assassinated; Johnson becomes President	22 Nov. 1963
Israel completes Jordan River diversion project	1964
Egypt and Syria sign new defense alliance	4 Nov. 1966
Israeli raiders demolish al-Samu, Jordan, with tanks and planes	13 Nov. 1966
As *Fedayeen* raids increase, Israeli jets down six Syrian planes	7 Apr. 1967
As Israeli leaders threaten Syria, Nasser reinforces Sinai	**14 May 1967**
Nasser requests UNEF to withdraw; it complies	16 May 1967
Nasser reimposes Aqaba blockade	22 May 1967
Nasser promises Egypt will not attack Israel but will fight to destroy Israel if Israel attacks	26 May 1967
Nasser says he won't ask Russian intervention even if US helps Israel	29 May 1967
Jordan joins Egypt–Syria defense pact	30 May 1967
Dayan becomes Israeli Defense Minister	1 June 1967
Nasser accepts Johnson invitation to send Mohyeddeen to US	3 June 1967
Israeli air strikes wipe out Arab air forces; Israel invades Egypt and Jordan	5 June 1967
Israel accepts cease-fire after completing conquests of Sinai, Western Jordan, and southwestern Syria	**10 June 1967**
Robert F. Kennedy assassinated by a Palestinian Arab	5 June 1968
High Dam at Aswan is completed	1969

Military incidents, *Fedayeen* raids, and Israeli reprisals continue to escalate on land, in the air, and at sea; peace efforts slowly revolve around impasses

Map Number 1

1. British Reinforcements:
   3rd Infantry Division from England
2. Anglo-French Invasion Fleet from Malta
3. Bombers from Malta to Alexandria,
   Cairo and Port Said.
4. Bombers from Cyprus to Alexandria,
   Port Said, Cairo and Luxor.
5. Paratroopers from Cyprus to Port Said.
6. Bombers from Israel to Luxor.
7. Iraq Petroleum Company Pipeline
   from Kirkuk, Iraq to Banias, Syria
   and Tripoli, Lebanon.
8. Trans Arabian Pipeline (TAP)
   from Bahrein to Sidon Lebanon.

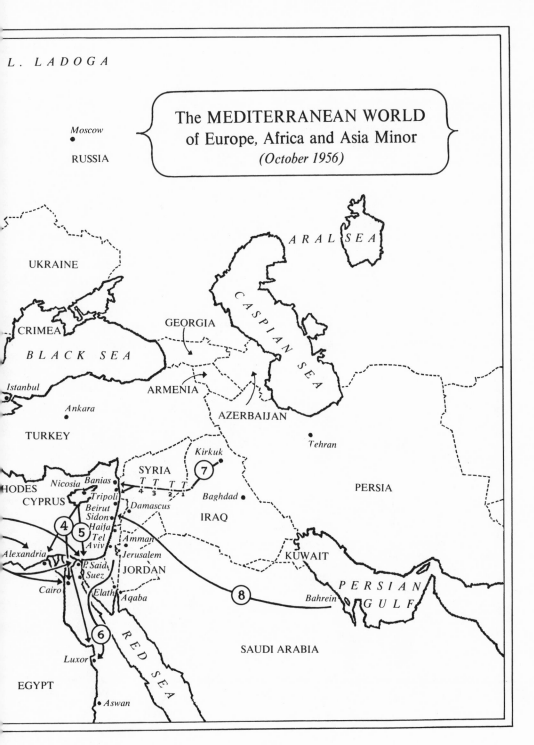

L . LADOGA

The MEDITERRANEAN WORLD
of Europe, Africa and Asia Minor
(October 1956)

Moscow

RUSSIA

UKRAINE

ARAL SEA

CRIMEA

CASPIAN SEA

GEORGIA

BLACK SEA

Istanbul

ARMENIA

Ankara

AZERBAIJAN

TURKEY

Tehran

Kirkuk

SYRIA

⑦

RHODES
Nicosia   Banias
CYPRUS   Tripoli
        Beirut
        Sidon
        Haifa
        Tel
        Aviv

T T T T
4 3 2 1

Damascus

Baghdad

PERSIA

IRAQ

④
⑤

Amman

Alexandria

Jerusalem

KUWAIT

P.Said
Suez

JORDAN

Cairo

Elath
Aqaba

PERSIAN

⑧

Bahrein

GULF

⑥

RED SEA

SAUDI ARABIA

Luxor

EGYPT

• Aswan

Part

COLLISION COURSES

(2100 B.C. TO 20 JULY 1956)

Prologue

At Gaza between supper and bedtime on Monday, 28 February 1955, two platoons of paratroopers on a night raid out of Israel stormed an Egyptian encampment, ambushed its reinforcements, and thereby gave history a rowdy shove that sent it reeling across the intervening months into the Suez Crisis. There, for one climactic week, it tottered on the brink of World War III. The attacking Israelis lost eight killed and thirteen wounded, all of whom they carried back to their base in keeping with their superb military tradition. They left dead or dying in the terrified darkness behind them thirty-seven men, a seven-year-old boy, and all hope for peace in their time with the Arabs.

The Gaza Raid started a chain of reactions between Gamal Abdel Nasser of Egypt and David Ben-Gurion of Israel—raids, counter-raids, an arms race, and new alignments with the Great Powers—which developed a drift toward war that neither human will nor political ingenuity was able to deflect. The raid transformed a stable level of minor incidents between the two countries into a dialogue of mounting fear and violence in which the distinction between measures of defense and acts of aggression faded and became invisible to the world at large. The flow of events from Gaza toward war at the crossroads of the world affected faraway currents of national assertiveness and personal antagonism. These currents swept the leaders of Britain and France into a collusive alliance with Ben-Gurion; brought Russian influence into the Middle East on behalf of Egypt and the Arabs, and drove Dwight D. Eisenhower and his

Secretary of State, John Foster Dulles, onto a chartless course of stubborn pacifism and neutralism.

Like a wave started by the shock of the Gaza Raid, the crisis gathered momentum until it crested on 29 October 1956 in the ten-day Suez-Sinai War. Then it scattered its fury in ever-widening consequences over the years that followed.

Men bulk larger in the story than governments or impersonal societal forces. Democratic ideals, the complexity of modern politics, lightning communications, and the interdependence of nations are often thought to have reduced the personal influence of individual leaders on events. But Suez was like the wars of old-time kings in the degree to which nations and armies were set in motion by the personal philosophies, ambitions, and animosities of such men as Ben-Gurion, Nasser, Sir Anthony Eden, Premier Guy Mollet of France, Nikita S. Khrushchev, Eisenhower, and Dulles. Paradoxically, the democratic leaders acted with no less secrecy and no more restraint than the dictators.

At the peak of the crisis the American leaders stopped the dangerous little war without firing a shot or rattling a saber. Immediately afterward the increased dependence of Britain, France, and Israel on American money and oil —a direct result of their invasion of Egypt—enabled Eisenhower to force the conquering armies back from their territorial spoils. The Americans succeeded in restoring the frontiers in the war theater for a decade.

But Suez, like the fall of Christian Constantinople to the Moslem Turks in 1453, had shaken and transformed the world in ways that would alter the map time and again in many regions. Suez was a catalyst in the emergence of backward, weak, and dependent peoples into nations that now assert themselves against Great Powers as stridently as against one another. Suez permanently lamed the North Atlantic alliance and imposed new caution and new methods on the Cold War. For the Israelis, the modern world's most purposeful adepts at improving upon their own history, Suez served as a rehearsal for a reprise nearly eleven years later in which they won larger and more enduring conquests.

What is commonly thought of as the Suez Crisis was in fact a confluence of four contributory crises, each of them affected by events resulting from the Gaza Raid. The complexity of the story can be baffling unless we—reader and narrator—have the total pattern in mind in advance. The crisis was like a river system in which the contributory streams of events converged to form the main stream. The Gaza Raid was like the seeding of a cloud to produce a rainstorm. The storm burst over the course of relations between Israel and Egypt, but its precipitation fell also upon the separate streams of political dialogue between Britain and Egypt, France and Egypt, and the United States and Egypt, augmenting their pace and turbulence. And it started a freshet in the dry bed of relations between Russia and Egypt, which also joined the main stream. When Nasser nationalized the Suez Canal in July 1956 all these contributories combined in the main sweep of events known as the Suez Crisis.

Language being linear, the prenationalization crises, moving together toward their point of confluence while interacting laterally upon one another, cannot be narrated in all their simultaneity. Words, strung one after another like beads, can recreate the details only one at a time, although in any order. It seemed to me confusing to shift laterally back and forth from one line of events to another in order to keep the telling of the whole concatenation of stories as nearly as possible in chronological order. Instead I have followed the course of each tributary crisis without interruption, taking one after another. The pattern of this book, therefore, hews to the river-system pattern of the Suez Crisis itself. Part I, which comprises the first half of the book, traces first the relations between Israel and Egypt, which constituted the chief tributary crisis; then the closely linked Franco-Egyptian crisis; following this, the long, bitter dialogue between Britain and Egypt; then the profoundly important opening of normal communications between Russia and Egypt; and finally, the short, unhappy affair between the Eisenhower administration and Nasser's Egypt.

Although simultaneity cannot itself be recreated in narrative, it can be simulated by signaling attention in the midst of one episode to a historically simultaneous happening already or soon to be recounted in fuller detail in the narrative line where it best belongs. I have scattered such signals or cross references wherever they were relevant. Some events, of course, belong in more than one line, just as a mountain can influence the courses of rivers on either side, or an escarpment can be a spectacular feature across a whole watershed. The Baghdad Pact and the Russian-Egyptian arms deal are among the historical features that influenced the courses of more than one of the contributory crises. I have divided my descriptions of these major landmarks, allotting to each narrative line the aspect most relevant to it. I ask the indulgence of the reader for the repetitions intrinsic to this method of telling a history.

The second half of the book, in three parts, describes the main stream of the crisis from the nationalization of the Canal, through the war and the restoration of the *status quo ante*, to the remarkable refighting of the war in 1967. Even after the tributaries joined in the main stream, the crisis remained bewildering to contemporary observers because the surface dispute over the Canal was not the real issue. The real issue was the private determination of Eden, Mollet, and Ben-Gurion to destroy Nasser, a determination which antedated the Suez nationalization in the minds of all three men. Knowledge of this underlying current, hidden but strongly influencing the surface of events, is essential to understanding the crisis. Otherwise, many of the curious twists and turns of the Canal dispute are inexplicable.

Why did the Gaza Raid rather than some of its own antecedents mark the beginning of the Suez-Sinai wars? Because it was the last free action in the dialogue between the two nationalist premiers, Ben-Gurion and Nasser. What followed was not freely chosen action but rather reaction and counterreaction. These consequences stirred up strong feelings among Egyptians and Israelis which affected every decision of their leaders in the international field. And every decision then furthered the inexorable march of events toward war. Ben-Gurion's personal decision to strike at Gaza—to seed the storm cloud—begins the story.

CHAPTER

1

The Gaza Raid

(28 FEBRUARY 1955)

Now Joshua was old and stricken in years; and the Lord said unto him, . . . there remaineth yet very much land to be possessed. . . . All the inhabitants . . . will I drive out from before the children of Israel: only divide thou it by lot unto the Israelites for an inheritance. . . .

(JOSHUA 13)

This is the inheritance of the tribe of the children of Judah according to their families . . . Gaza with her towns and villages, unto the river of Egypt, and the great sea.

(JOSHUA 15)

I will send a fire on the wall of Gaza, which shall devour the palaces thereof: . . . and the remnant of the Philistines shall perish.

(AMOS 1)

THE LAST night of February, 1955, was ideal for the Raid and, because of an Egyptian blunder, the Israelis were to succeed beyond their expectations. The weather was fine under scattered clouds. Sunset was at 5:40 P.M. Full night would have fallen by 7:00. A crescent moon, one day short of the first quarter, would silhouette for the raiders the minaret, water tower, and other landmarks before setting just after midnight. Its dim light would give advantage in a fight to swift movement and initiative.

The torpid old Arab town of Gaza lies nestled in rolling hills between the beach and the Negev plain. As the sun slipped down a broken yellow sky into the Mediterranean, the inhabitants began their preparations for supper unaware of the crisp activity at the headquarters of Israel's Southern Army Command in Beersheba, 27 miles to the southeast. There Ben-Gurion's orders, in operational form, were given to the troops selected for the night's mission —two platoons of husky, eager young paratroopers comprising the striking force—and to the units posted in alert reserve in case anything went wrong.

Peace still reigned as the last light of day sparkled on the darkening sea. A feeble surf whispered along the golden sands that slope up toward the dunes and hills. Chickens clucked and fluffed as they settled to roost beside the lichened plaster dome over what local tradition holds to be Samson's tomb. The hiss of Coleman lamps, the indistinct murmur of Arab male conversation across rickety wooden tables, and the clear rhythmic wail of radio music in the open-front coffee shops wrapped the warm evening in familiar sound. Out of the east, the raiders drove through the twilight to their jumping-off place, a line of newly fortified Israeli settlements facing the armistice demarcation line.

The point of no return came shortly after dark when the raiders split into two parties. The larger, about fifty men, was to strike through an orange grove and a cemetery at a small army camp and railroad station on the northern outskirts of Gaza. The smaller force, some fifteen men, went to where the main road from Egypt forked four miles south of town. There they set an ambush. Their job was to prevent Egyptian reinforcements from either reaching the scene of the main assault or taking the fork to the right to cut off the raiders' line of retreat. After the two parties separated, there was no longer any possibility of calling off the attack, whose repercussions were to be felt around the world.

An Egyptian corporal described the first casualties of what eventually came to be called the Suez Crisis. He was at an outpost halfway between the Gaza army camp and the armistice demarcation line in fields of knee-high grain that sloped gradually down to the east. He told a UN military observer the following day:

"Last night about 8 o'clock one of our sentry trenches was attacked by the

5

Israelis. They killed two men, one in the trench itself, the other just outside the trench. . . . We fired on them from our position. They fled away in several directions."

The Israelis did not flee. They advanced rapidly after this first brush, trampling a yard-wide swathe through the new grain, undeterred at having alerted the enemy. They covered the remaining mile between the outpost and the camp, divided into three attack parties, and went into action at 8:30. They savaged the Egyptians for three hours, raking and blasting their positions with machine guns and bazooka rockets, burning tents and trucks, shooting animals, and demolishing stone and sheet-iron buildings with TNT charges.

"At about a quarter past eight I heard some shooting far from here in the direction of east," said Sergeant Major Abdel Baseet Ismail the next day. "I prepared myself and ordered my soldiers to occupy the trenches. After half an hour an attack started from the northern direction by submachine guns. . . . The firing continued for about three hours. They forced our camp in spite of our resistance and they blew it up. . . . Seven soldiers of my unit were killed along with the captain in command."

"We were sleeping in our tents," said Private Ahmed Shabar. "We all woke up and started to fire upon the attackers. We had our ammunition in the middle tent. During the firing the ammunition exploded and the tent caught fire. I have four soldiers killed."

UN observers estimated that seventy-five to one hundred pounds of TNT were used to blow up a stone building in the camp and fifteen pounds each for four Nissen-roofed brick huts. Some 150 pounds of TNT were used to disintegrate a concrete pumphouse that supplied one-third of the water used by Gaza's hundred-thousand inhabitants. The pump's civilian guard was killed. Robert Doty of *The New York Times* described the pumping station the following day as "a blackened ruin" and the army camp as "a mass of shattered concrete and twisted metal roofing."

The raiders tossed hand grenades into the railroad stationmaster's bedroom, wounding his nine-year-old son. They killed a seven-year-old boy and wounded his father in a grenade-and-demolition attack on another house. UN observers later cited such details as "three bloody Egyptian caps with pieces of brain substance" at a burnt tent near the railroad station; a dead camel; Israeli field dressings and an E. R. Squibb & Sons morphine needle; Israeli toffee from Ramat Gan; abandoned sacks of TNT; pools and trails of blood all over the field of battle and along the tracks of the withdrawal.

During the fighting the observers noted the sounds that reached them at their quarters across town nearly three miles away. First they heard machine-gun and rifle fire and the thump of bazooka rockets to the northeast in the direction of the camp and railroad station. Later, between 10:30 and 11:00, heavy explosions, ten in all, punctuated the chatter of battle. Then they watched the orange glare of fires rise above the rooftops and trees. In the distance, beyond the armistice line, searchlights played into the sky during the entire engagement, boldly marking the rendezvous point for the raiders.

The firing at the camp died away at 11:00. At 11:15 the observers heard automatic fire to the south. The ambush had been sprung and executed with simple ferocity, visiting the implacable punishment of war upon soldiers who blunder.

A three-ton Egyptian truck crammed with 35 soldiers and a lieutenant had come careering up the main Gaza-Rafah road from Deir al-Balah, headlights blazing and with no scout car as vanguard. As it hurtled over a ditch culvert it struck a wire stretched over the road and yanked Molotov cocktails against its sides. An explosion of flame enveloped the truck while Israeli paratroopers crouching on either side of the road directed a hailstorm of machine gun bullets into it. The blazing truck lurched off the road to the left and came to a stop with three flat tires.

Salim Abd Rabbo, guard at the military checkpost at the road fork 150 yards further on, reported what happened next:

I lay down immediately and heard somebody shouting "*Kadima!*" [Hebrew for "Forward"]. Then I saw some soldiers advancing toward the truck and throwing hand grenades in it. I went back to the checkpost; there everybody jumped in the trenches and started to fire against the attackers.... After one hour I saw the attackers crossing the road from west to east. I came near the truck but could not approach it as ammunition was exploding inside. After the ammunition stopped bursting, we reached the car and started to drag the living soldiers out. The dead were left inside till the fire was extinguished.

Lieutenant Hassan Abdullah, wounded in the left foot, and the driver, unscathed, escaped from the cab. Twenty-two of the ambushed soldiers were burned or shot to death and twelve were wounded. The raiders withdrew single file through fields of green corn across the armistice line three miles away to their searchlighted rendezvous.

The carnage was over. The next day UN observer Captain Huc of Belgium counted 105 bullet holes in the metal and glass parts of the truck; innumerable holes riddling the unburned parts of the canvas cover; 13 perforated, blood-drenched helmets on the ground; and a litter of hundreds of exploded cartridges, grenade splinters, and bloody equipment inside the truck. He also counted the impacts on the checkpost wall of the bullet and rocket fire that had pinned down Abd Rabbo and the defenders there.

7

To the overwhelming evidence amassed by the UN Military Observers Israel offered the perfunctory excuse that the Raid had been a running battle which developed after an Egyptian force ambushed an Israeli patrol inside Israeli territory. UN adjudicators rejected this story. Instead, the entire body of evidence led the UN's Mixed Armistice Commission and the Security Council itself to condemn Israel for a "prearranged and planned attack ordered by Israeli authorities" which was "committed by Israeli regular army forces against the Egyptian regular army force."

Assessing the guilt was a formality without practical consequences since Israel had been prepared for an adverse judgment. Far more important was the effect on Nasser and his revolutionary government of young officers who had seized power from the cynical and corrupt monarchy only two and a half years before.

Three circumstances combined to heighten its impact on Egypt's nervous new rulers. First, the border itself had been sufficiently quiet over the preceding months and years to lull the Egyptians into a sense of security. Second, Nasser himself had taken a pacifist line in opposing military expenditures, prevailing over his junta colleagues with the argument that the border was not only quiet but safe. Third, the regime was struggling to keep its footing in the face of murderous opposition within the country and a shifting pattern of diplomatic pressures from abroad.

In order to appreciate the impact of the Raid it is necessary to have at least a summary understanding of the circumstances that lent it its catalytic qualities.

The period of relative tranquillity on the Egyptian-Israeli border which the Gaza Raid shattered had endured either for six years or for eighteen months, depending on what is understood by the word *relative*. General E. L. M. Burns, who took over as Chief of Staff of the UN Truce Supervision Organization on 2 September 1954, told the Security Council in his report that the raid was "the most serious clash between the two parties since the signing of the General Armistice Agreement."

The size and historical significance of the Raid give a peculiar cast to the omission of any reference to it in the memoirs covering that period by Israeli leaders, including the two who were chiefly responsible for mounting it, Ben-Gurion and General Moshe Dayan, the Chief of Staff of the Israeli Defense Forces. There is no mention of the Raid in Ben-Gurion's *Years of Challenge* or in Dayan's *Diary of the Sinai Campaign*, both of which cover the years and events leading up to the 1956 invasion of Egypt. Walter Eytan, long-time Director-General of Israel's Foreign Ministry, utterly ignores the Gaza Raid in his book, *The First Ten Years*, although he refers to other major incidents including the Qibya raid in October 1953. Abba Eban, Israel's top diplomat, does not even list it in the chronology at the back of his *Voice of Israel*.

Egypt had been the first Arab country to sign an armistice with the victorious Israelis after the Palestine War. The war began officially on 15 May 1948 immediately after the embattled Jewish minority in Palestine proclaimed the State of Israel a successor to British rule over the territory. The Moslem and Christian Arab majority in Palestine, preferring an Arab government as successor to the British and opposing the UN partition compromise, welcomed the intervention of the armies of Egypt, Trans-Jordan, Syria, Lebanon, and Iraq.

Israel's unexpected skill and vigor in war, together with the rivalries and the diplomatic and martial ineptitude of the Arabs, decided the issue after nine months of intermittent fighting and broken truces. Israel expanded and integrated her conquests with the territory allotted her by the UN, drove back the Arab armies, and goaded nearly one million Palestinian Arabs to flee into exile. Egypt signed an armistice on 24 February 1949 after six weeks of negotiations on the Greek Isle of Rhodes. By the end of July 1949 Lebanon, Trans-Jordan, and Syria had also signed.

Iraq, the only belligerent Arab state not possessing a common border with Israel, never concluded an armistice, a circumstance that was to figure importantly in the secret preparations for the Suez War. Lack of physical contact, however, kept Israeli-Iraqi friction to a minimum, in contrast to the endemic disturbances along the trucial borders. The armistices between Israel and the four contiguous Arab states have not evolved into peace treaties. On the contrary, they have been used to cover what the Arabs call a technical state of war, a situation in which both sides pursue conflicting objectives with as much violence as they can get away with.

Violence was infrequent on the Egyptian-Israeli frontier before Gaza. Nearly all of the Egyptian officers who took part in the revolutionary *coup d'état* of 23 July 1952 and the exiling of King Farouk three days later were veterans of the Palestine War. But they declared publicly after taking power that they had opposed Egyptian intervention in Palestine. Ben-Gurion welcomed the Egyptian statements and shrewdly suggested to the Knesset (Israeli Parliament) on 18 August 1952 that the new Egyptian junta would be too preoccupied with consolidating its authority at home to indulge in military excursions abroad. There were no grounds for quarrels with Egypt, he said, and added a characteristic Biblical allusion:

"We have no enmity against Egypt for what was done to our ancestors in the time of Pharaoh and not even for what was done four years ago."

Israel's practice of mounting reprisal raids against Arab villages suspected of harboring marauders dates back to the 1920s. Zionist colonists responded to theft, harassment, and violence by taking justice into their own hands when they considered the British administration too lax. In the 1930s Orde Wingate, the British guerrilla-warfare genius who was to find glory and death in World War II, trained Jewish squads of night raiders. Their punitive retaliations inflicted more casualties and damage on the Palestinian Arab community than Arab terrorists inflicted on the Jews. Independent Israel continued the pattern, striking with gunfire and explosives at Arab villages beyond her borders in raids designed to punish past incursions and deter future ones.

On the Egyptian frontier the only incident in any way comparable in scope to the Gaza Raid had occurred precisely eighteen months earlier, on 28 August 1953. On that night Israeli raiders attacked the Arab refugee camp of al-Bureig, which was organized and administered by the UN Relief and Works Agency (UNRWA) near the town of Gaza. Major General Vagn Bennike, General Burns's predecessor as UN truce chief, described the raid to the Security Council as follows:

Bombs were thrown through the windows of huts in which the refugees were sleeping and, as they fled, they were attacked by small arms and automatic weapons. The casualties were 20 killed, 27 seriously wounded, and 35 less seriously wounded. ...A likely explanation is that it was a ruthless reprisal raid. This seems probable in view of the fact that a quarter of the Israeli complaints during the preceding four weeks referred to infiltration in this area. The Egyptian authorities have taken measures to cope with the problem of infiltration. The presence of 200,000 Palestine refugees in the Gaza Strip, however, renders their task particularly difficult.

The hot brutality of the attack, in which two-thirds of the casualties were women and children, brought an outraged condemnation from the UN truce keepers. The Egyptians, however, then entering the second year of their revolution, were so anxious to keep the border quiet that they all but hushed up the incident.

Significantly, the ensuing year and a half of what General Burns called "comparative tranquillity" on the Egyptian-Israeli truce line coincided roughly with the period of Ben-Gurion's temporary retirement from national leadership. Quiet prevailed despite the fact that during all this period touchy young Israeli veterans were building and settling a chain of military-agricultural communities within sight and earshot of the Gaza Strip. Their armed tractor drivers plowed the fields between the truce line and the settlement perimeters of barbed wire and earthworks under the protective guns of the watchtower guards.

Al-Bureig was the last raid on Egypt before Gaza. The last comparable raid on any Arab frontier before Gaza was the destruction of the Jordanian village of Qibya on the night of 14/15 October 1953. Sixty-six Jordanian villagers, nearly three-quarters of them women and children, were killed in the raid, which Ben-Gurion ordered shortly before his fourteen-month retirement, overriding the opposition of Moshe Sharett, then Foreign Minister.

During Ben-Gurion's retirement the most troubled frontier was that between Israel and Jordan. The worst incidents there were a Bedouin massacre of nine men and two women passengers on a Negev bus on 17 March 1954, and an Israeli retaliation on the Jordanian village of Nahhaleen eleven days later in which eight men and a woman were killed.

There were occasional minor clashes along the Gaza Strip during the period of "comparative tranquillity." Some grew out of the silent war that continues between hostile intelligence organizations once their governments have suspended full-scale war. The machine-gunning of an Israeli cyclist near a railroad crossing 17 miles from the border three days before the Gaza Raid, for example, was done by Palestinian members of an espionage mission sent into Israel from Gaza. It is among the justifications sometimes cited for the Gaza Raid by persons who forget Israel's official contention that the raid was nothing more than the outgrowth of a running battle. Moreover, even the flexible Israelis cannot mount a raid like Gaza on three days' notice and, as will be made clear in Chapter Three, they did not.

Aside from such occasional eruptions of the silent war of espionage, UN truce records list firefights between Israeli motorized patrols and Egyptian positions; mortar exchanges between the Egyptians and the hardening line of fortified Israeli frontier settlements; and a great deal of stealing, mostly by Arab refugees. The last seek to justify their depredations by saying they are only taking their own back even when their loot includes hundreds of yards of irrigation pipes and sprinklers such as they never had.

Less publicized at the time but subsequently of great strategic significance was the maneuvering for control of the demilitarized zone around the old Turkish garrison at al-Auja, now renamed Nitzana by the Israelis. It lies a quarter of the way down the Sinai frontier from the Mediterranean to the Gulf of Aqaba. Control of the strategically important road junction there is essential for an invasion in either direction across the border between Egypt and Israel. Israeli forces had based their brief invasion of Egypt in December 1948 on al-Auja. Two months later it was demilitarized by the Armistice Agreement in order to render impossible any future offensive.

In 1950 Israel expelled 3,500 Azazme Bedouins from the zone with air and ground attacks. Israeli patrols burned the Bedouins' tents and shot the thirsty tribesmen and their camels and goats when they came to the wells to drink and fill their water skins. On 28 September 1953 an Israeli force established the fortified settlement of Ketziot on a low hill dominating the road junction. The

11

Israeli Army, insisting despite contrary UN findings that Ketziot was merely a pioneering farm settlement, improved its grip on the zone in a period of diplomatic and military maneuvering in the summer, fall, and winter of 1954. Even so, al-Auja was not an exception to the "comparative tranquillity" between Egypt and Israel.

Nor was the celebrated incident of the *Bat Galim*, a small freighter flying the Israeli flag which presented itself at Suez on 28 September 1954 for northward passage through the Suez Canal, although it was the first Israeli ship to request a canal transit. Egypt, which had maintained restrictions against Israeli shipping since 15 May 1948, seized the vessel and its crew of ten on the trumped-up charge that the crew had shot at Egyptian fishing boats off Suez. Egypt released the captain and crew on 1 January 1955 on the truce line near Gaza.

The border was so quiet, in fact, that Sir Anthony Eden, then the British Foreign Secretary, congratulated Israel on 19 October 1954 in a note to Ambassador Eliahu Elath reassuring him that the British evacuation of the Suez base, under the agreement signed that day, would not shift the balance of power against Israel but would lessen tension. Secretary of State John Foster Dulles, on 11 January 1955, called the Suez evacuation agreement an "act of peace."

Behind the tranquillity on the borders were the personal pacifism of Nasser and the restraint exercised by Moshe Sharett, who was both Premier and Foreign Minister of Israel during Ben-Gurion's fourteen-month withdrawal into the Negev desert settlement of Sde Boker.

During Sharett's premiership, Egypt had taken the lead in persuading the Arabs to accept the principle of sharing international control of the Jordan River waters with Israel despite menacing overt opposition both within Egypt and in the Arab Levant. Eric Johnston had been sent by President Eisenhower in October 1953 as his personal ambassador to bring the Jordan waters proposal to the Middle East as a first step toward an Arab-Israeli peace.

Johnston's mission ultimately failed in the fall of 1955 when cabinet crises in Syria and Lebanon frightened their respective governments into retreat. An Israeli raid on Syria in December 1955 killed all hope of reviving the Johnston Plan, as it had come to be called. During the negotiations Johnston spoke often about the help the Egyptian delegates gave him in overcoming the resistance of the Jordanians and Syrians. The delicacy of the negotiations, in which Johnston shuttled between Israel and the Arab countries, prevented public declarations of gratitude to the Egyptians but Johnston was unstinting in private praise for Egypt's constructive role.

Despite the shock of the Gaza Raid, Nasser continued his efforts on behalf of the Johnston Plan for the better part of a year after it. He took other pacific initiatives too in 1955, offering to demilitarize the frontier in June and endorsing a British mediation overture in November.

Unfortunately, although Nasser achieved mastery of his political house, Sharett did not. There is tragic irony in the fact that Sharett was not able to exert control long enough to see where the drift toward peace would lead.

Nasser himself thought peace was merely a question of time if the border remained quiet. Eventually, passions would subside and a strong Arab government could conclude peace without fear of assassinations. During the negotiations leading to Britain's agreement in 1954 to evacuate the Suez Canal base he spoke optimistically to the British of his hopes of giving a lead toward an Arab-Israeli settlement. At a press conference after signing the agreement on 19 October, when a euphoric Egyptian journalist asked if Egypt would now create a powerful army in the Suez base, Nasser wearily passed the question to his Army chief, General Amer, who replied that the needs of economic and social development must limit the strengthening of the Army. Nasser told a visiting group of American editors on 15 March 1956, more than a year after Gaza, that the Egyptian revolution had opened the way to eventual peace. In a statement distributed widely by Egyptian embassies abroad, he said:

"Peace could have been achieved with the passage of time. In fact, peace reigned on the borders, except for a few minor incidents which took place. . . . But on 28 February 1955 [the date of the Gaza Raid] we were not merely threatened but nightmared."

Nasser had said much the same thing before Gaza to General Burns. At their first meeting, in Cairo on 15 November 1954, Burns reports, Nasser said he wanted no disturbance of the six years of quiescent armistice, no military adventures. Nasser told me in June 1955 that he had clearly implied the possibility of peace to Burns at that Cairo meeting.

> I told Burns, "We want peace in order to spend money that is now being devoted to defense on our economic and social projects." We felt that our eastern frontier was quiet. I told Burns that good conditions lead to better conditions and that better conditions might lead to the best condition.

He assumed that Burns would pass the word on to the Israelis.

In January 1955, the month before the Gaza Raid, Nasser elaborated his development-versus-defense plans in an interview with Richard H. S. Crossman, M.P., one of Britain's most prominent Zionist sympathizers. Nasser received Crossman at his austere married officer's bungalow in the garrison suburb of Manshiet al-Bakry. "The Israelis will destroy themselves if they go on spending 60 per cent of their budget on armaments," he said. "We are not going to make that mistake here."

Nasser went on to say that he did not think Israel constituted a military menace and that he intended to hold Egypt's arms purchases to the minimum commensurate with keeping his army efficient and contented. He said he was devoting the bulk of his budget to industrialization, agricultural improvement, schools, hospitals, and housing. Crossman, recalling the recent attempt on Nasser's life by a Moslem Brotherhood fanatic, ended his dispatch on the interview for the *New Statesman* as follows:

> Driving back to Cairo that night, I could not help thinking that not only Egypt, but the whole Middle East, must pray that Nasser survives the assassin's bullet. I am certain that he is a man who means what he says; and that so long as he is in power directing his middle-class revolution, Egypt will remain a factor for peace and social development.

The endorsement of Nasser's pacifism could not be more authoritative. When Crossman spoke of the whole Middle East praying for Nasser's survival, he was thinking primarily of Israel, then still under the moderating influence of Premier Moshe Sharett. In that same month, January 1955, the prestigious American quarterly, *Foreign Affairs*, published an article by Nasser saying: "War has no place in the constructive policy which we have designed to improve the lot of our people. We have much to do in Egypt and the rest of the Arab world has much to do. A war would cause us to lose, rather than gain, much of what we seek to achieve."

Nasser was not speaking merely for foreign consumption. Egyptian pacifism was proclaimed in the Arabic press and in Cairo broadcasts after Britain agreed in October 1954 to end her 72-year occupation of Egypt by withdrawing the 80,000 British troops in the Suez Canal Zone bases. "Neither Egypt nor any Arab country bordering on Israel would attack anyone," said the Government newspaper *al-Gamhouriya*. Cairo broadcasts emphasized a British minister's statement that Whitehall was "interested in the maintenance of peace in the Middle East and in the ending of the state of war between the Arab states and Israel."

Cairo's Radio "Voice of the Arabs" quoted Nasser as saying that the evacuation of the last British troops from Egyptian soil would enable the country "to play an important role in maintaining peace in the Middle East" and that Egypt's attitude toward Israel would continue to depend on Israel's behavior.

Tom Little, the British journalist and historian who since 1943 has been one of the most respected chroniclers of Egyptian affairs, writes of Nasser:

Underlying his military character there is a deep-seated pacifism which is truly Egyptian. In his younger days he rationalized his emotional repugnance to assassination; as a dictator he explains his reluctance to execute political enemies on the grounds of expediency. In his explanation of political situations he constantly refers to the futility of military solutions.

Some of Nasser's pre-Gaza manifestations of pacifism were difficult for him to live with after the Raid. Nasser has recalled that it occurred shortly after he visited the Gaza Strip and personally reassured the troops that there was no threat of battle there. These were bitter words to have to swallow. Similar statements to his military chiefs and the officers of the junta became a political embarrassment after the Raid. As Nasser recalls it, "In the Army they were asking for arms. I made a big effort before Gaza to convince them to be patient. There were assurances from the United States and the United Kingdom that everything would continue quiet. After Gaza the position changed because reason was on the side of the Army."

For a year before the Gaza Raid, the debate within the junta over armaments versus development had taken place against the background of a power struggle between factions headed by Nasser and by Major General Mohammed Naguib, who had been selected shortly before the *coup d'état* of 1952 as the revolutionary regime's figurehead. Naguib was fifty-one, a hero of the Palestine fighting, and a senior officer whose leadership was more likely to be accepted by the army and the country in the first dangerous days of power than that of a young lieutenant colonel like Nasser, who was only thirty-four at the time.

On 22 February, 1954, Naguib split the junta by resigning after a vain demand for powers commensurate with his responsibilities as President and Premier. Two months of internal convulsions, which Nasser has called "the work of the devil," followed before the revolutionary regime recovered temporary stability with Naguib as President and Nasser as Premier. "It looked as if the regime was about to end," Nasser said later. "The alternative was a government formed by the Communists, the Moslem Brotherhood, and members of the old political parties."

It was during this period of temporary stability that Nasser staked his political future on the concessions that won Britain's agreement to evacuate the Suez Canal base. They almost cost him his life. The Supreme Guide of the Moslem Brotherhood, Hassan al-Hodeiby, denounced the evacuation agreement as treasonable. On 26 October 1954, a week after the agreement was signed, a member of the Brotherhood fired eight wild shots from close range at Nasser as he was giving a speech in Alexandria.

Shaken but unscathed, Nasser seized the microphone and shouted again and again to the crowd: "If Gamal Abdel Nasser dies, every one of you will be

15

another Gamal Abdel Nasser." The Revolution Command Council, as the junta styled itself, outlawed the Moslem Brotherhood and unleashed a vast manhunt for its leaders and the members of its secret terrorist wing. The police said the Brotherhood had planned to wipe out the entire regime with the notable exception of President Naguib.

Some two weeks later Naguib was relieved of his official duties and placed under house arrest. The pipe-smoking, fatherly general, who had been immensely popular from the outset of the revolution, was never brought to trial.

Seven leaders of the Moslem Brotherhood and its secret terrorist corps were condemned after an extraordinary propaganda trial that established their guilt and fanaticism. Six of them, showing astonishing spiriutal strength and defying the revolution to the end, were hanged on 7 December 1954.

The junta broke the formidable power of the Brotherhood in Egypt for more than a decade without seriously compromising its reputation for bloodless politics. It was a remarkable achievement since the Moslem Brotherhood, claiming divine sanction for its xenophobic program of religious orthodoxy and social-welfare, had achieved semi-underground political power on a national scale in the generation since its founding.

At its peak in the last years of the monarchy, its claim of a million members was accepted as a realistic figure. This means that approximately one out of every five adult males in Egypt's mid-century population of 20 million was a Moslem Brother. The Brotherhood's increasing resort to political murder in the postwar years provoked the monarchy in 1949 to engineer the assassination of the founder and first Supreme Guide, Hassan al-Banna.

The destruction of an organization of true believers like the Moslem Brotherhood can seldom be considered final. This was demonstrated by the nick-of-time discovery in July 1965 that the Brotherhood had secretly reorganized and was ready to wreak vengeance on Nasser with three efficient assassination plans, each designed either for independent execution or as a back-up plan for the others.

Past links between several junta members and the Moslem Brotherhood contributed to the atmosphere of political uneasiness in the winter following the hanging of the six leaders. The Government's policy of repression tempered by clemency disclosed its anxiety.

In the season of discontent before Gaza, foreign pressures also crisscrossed the domestic crises through which Nasser's regime was struggling, and the foreign and domestic problems interacted. Altogether, they constituted a critical mass of problems difficult merely to describe, let alone cope with. Each separate element will be considered more fully later. Here it suffices to show how the

Gaza thunderbolt imposed a heavy new strain upon men already fighting for the life of their revolution and, occasionally, their own lives as well.

Opposition to the Anglo-Egyptian Suez evacuation treaty provided the impulse for the Moslem Brotherhood's abortive assault on Nasser's regime. It also provoked Israel's Defense Ministry to mount a clumsy, violent, and equally abortive effort in Egypt to wreck the treaty negotiations. The Moslem Brotherhood terrorist cadres and the Israeli espionage and *agent provocateur* ring operating in Egypt in 1954 were surely among the strangest bedfellows ever made by politics.

Israeli Defense Ministry agents in July 1954 placed fire bombs that damaged British movie theaters and US Information Service libraries in Cairo and Alexandria. The object was to persuade London and Washington that Egyptian instability and anti-Westernism would render the impending treaty worthless and that Britain would be well advised to keep strong military forces in Egypt. One of the agents caught fire from a bomb he was carrying in Alexandria on 14 July. Egyptian authorities learned of the plot from him and began to round up the Israeli agents, but not in time to prevent further arson.

The Israeli agents were awaiting trial when the Moslem Brotherhood's death struggle with the revolutionary regime played itself out. Eleven of the agents went before a military tribunal on 11 December, four days after the six Moslem Brotherhood leaders were hanged. The prisoners were not tried in civil courts because Egypt and the other Arab states regarded themselves under the armistice as legally still at war with Israel. The trial itself was open and fair. International observers confirmed the statements of the accused and their families denying foreign allegations of Egyptian brutality.

After being found guilty of spying in time of war, two of the agents were condemned to death on 27 January 1955 and hanged four days later, after appeals for clemency had been turned down. Although international law and custom accept the death penalty for wartime espionage, and although the guilt of the condemned men was not in question, the execution of such inept and amateurish agents was criticized as harsh. Nasser himself is believed to have opposed the executions but to have acquiesced in the majority view within the junta that convicted enemy spies could not be shown greater clemency than the six Egyptian Moslem Brothers who were hanged less than two months before.

Far more serious for the Egyptians than the plots of the Israelis or the Moslem Brotherhood was the formation during this same period of the Baghdad Pact by Iraq and Turkey with the blessing and speedy adherence of Britain. Nasser, having staked his own and his government's life on the evacuation treaty with Britain, would not risk further commitments to Western pacts. The would-be assassin had indicated the limit beyond which neither the people nor a faction within the junta would allow Nasser to lead Egypt. But Britain, following Western failures to bring Egypt into a pact, was now building up the Iraqi regime as a counterweight to Egypt, stirring into new life the centuries-old rivalry between Baghdad and Cairo.

Arab League ministers and premiers held emergency meetings to prevent an open break over the Baghdad Pact issue between factions headed by Nasser and Premier Nuri al-Said of Iraq. Sir Anthony Eden, then British Foreign Secretary under Winston Churchill, conferred with Nasser in Cairo on 20 February 1955. Ten months later the Baghdad Pact was to become the cause of historic personal hostility between Nasser and Eden. But for a few days after their meeting, the formation of the proposed pact seemed to have been deferred until a more propitious time. Only Britain, Iraq, and Turkey knew better.

The news on 24 February 1955 that the Iraqi and Turkish premiers had signed the pact fell like a bombshell not only on Cairo but on Washington. After his trip to the Middle East in May 1953, John Foster Dulles had conceived the idea of extending the containment of Russia by sponsoring a pact in the non-Arab Northern Tier of the Middle East. But he abandoned the effort by the US, Britain, France, and Turkey to bring the Arabs into a pact as among "concepts that have no reality."

Washington privately swallowed its irritation, publicly issued a perfunctory and pious statement welcoming the pact, and quietly adopted a policy of amiable aloofness toward it. The world at large was unaware of Washington's private thinking about the pact. The impression got about that the pact was a State Department coup, ill-advised perhaps, but Washington's work all the same. This impression persisted for years as one of the many irritants in American-Egyptian relations. It was a relatively minor matter to the Americans.

To Nasser it looked like a menacing Great Power attempt to isolate Egypt and weaken his regime by building up Nuri al-Said of Iraq as leader of the Arab world. Egypt hastily organized a counter-campaign to isolate Nuri instead, using both propaganda and diplomacy. Under the circumstances, many Egyptians thought they saw a sinister connection between the Baghdad Pact "conspiracy" and the Gaza Raid four days later; imperialism's lackeys seemed to be in league against emergent Egypt.

It was no comfort to Nasser that both France and Israel were, like him, opponents of the Baghdad Pact—yet another example of the strange bedfellows politics can create. Egypt regarded Israel's stand as a sly piece of hypocrisy. As for France, no hope of support from that quarter could be expected in the face of Egypt's commitment to the cause of Algerian independence. Algerian nationalist leaders had taken refuge in Cairo. Nasser had personally ordered shipments of arms sent to the nationalist guerrilla forces before they raised the flag of open revolt on Halloween, 1954.

It was small wonder that the quiet border with Israel looked to Nasser like one of the brighter spots on his stormy horizons. Only recently he had won a shaky victory in his desperate struggles with the Naguib faction inside the regime and, outside it, the terroristic Moslem Brotherhood—both far more popular than he himself was at that time. Now he found himself plunged into a rivalry with Nuri al-Said of Iraq over the Baghdad Pact. The conflict with Nuri immediately damaged the good relations Nasser had cautiously built with the British and Americans in ratifying the Suez evacuation treaty with the British. Within the Arab world the Egyptian-Iraqi quarrel could not help endangering Nasser's prestige. Nasser's dispute with the third Western Great Power, France, had already started down the long road from the mountains of Algeria to the beachhead on the Suez Canal.

At odds with the West, Nasser had not yet dreamed of seeking support from the Communits of the East. Anti-Communism was and is one of the basic tenets of his intensely nationalistic revolution. Any significant degree of cooperation between Egypt and Communist governments abroad seemed at the time impossible.

New policies, however, are the result of political pressures. By the beginning of February 1955 Nasser was the focus of a fearsome accumulation of political pressures, all unrelated to Israel. They were so evident that Sharett publicly acknowledged them in a statement of anger over the hanging of the two spies. In the preceding months Nasser had: Pushed through the controversial Suez base evacuation agreement with Britain in the face of opposition by men who preferred to murder him rather than tolerate his concession to the British; challenged the powerful Moslem Brotherhood and hanged six of its leaders for their conspiracy against the regime; dismissed the disruptive but wildly popular General Mohammed Naguib from the presidency; fallen into a bitter and enduring quarrel with Iraq over the nascent Baghdad Pact, which split the Arab world and led the West to take sides against him; and reassured his troops in Gaza that Israel had no desire for border strife and that they were therefore secure despite the military vulnerability of the Gaza Strip.

In such circumstances renewed pressure from Israel was sure to be not so much a final straw as a bale of explosives on the camel's back. Sharett's statement showed that the Israelis were fully aware of the effect of a raid on the drift toward peace. And the first dispatches reaching Cairo that night made it look like the opening assault of full-scale war. It was inevitable that such news of an unprovoked attack would prompt Nasser and his cabinet to make drastic changes in Egypt's defense and foreign policies.

Nasser's decision to rearm his military forces was made during the confused and sleepless night of the Raid. If any doubts lingered about the urgent political necessity of rearming, they were swept away within hours after the last shots and explosions died away.

There was hardly a lull before mobs of Palestinian Arab refugees surged out of their tents and huts in the Gaza Strip camps to vent their anger against Egypt and the UN for failing to protect Arabs in Arab territory from Israeli attack. Soon after the sun rose on the battered town of Gaza, 200 youths braved Egyptian police in the first of two days of attacks on Egyptian and UN installations, smashing windows, burning vehicles and trampling on flags. The chain of reactions had begun. The Suez Crisis, although long to remain unnamed, was born.

CHAPTER

2

Isaac and Ishmael

(2100 B.C. TO 1948 A.D.)

What men believe to have happened in the Middle East has been no less formative in world history than that which is known to have occurred.

(ABBA EBAN, My People, Random House, 1968)

It is natural that the Arabs should view us as expansionists...

(MOSHE DAYAN)

We made the Palestinian Arabs homeless to make a home for our own people. This is the simple truth as history will see it...

(I. F. STONE, 1969)

ECOGNIZING THE Gaza Raid as the starting point of the Suez Crisis does not mean that the raid had no antecedents. Nor does recognizing its distinction as the last free act in the dialogue between Nasser and Ben-Gurion mean that Ben-Gurion did not have reasons that seemed good to him and to some of his colleagues.

But the grounds on which Ben-Gurion based his decision were not directly related to the border situation. Some of his motives appear to have had nothing at all to do with Egypt, but to have derived from purely internal political considerations. Even the factors relating to Egypt were far from compelling. Other minds in Israel, including the then Premier Moshe Sharett's, reached other conclusions from exactly the same premises. In significant contrast to these deliberate analyses, no subsequent line adopted by either Nasser or Ben-Gurion was free from the pressures created by the Raid.

For an outsider to understand Ben-Gurion's motives for the Raid and Nasser's reactions to it (which will be discussed in Chapters Three and Four), it is necessary to recognize the Raid's place in the Palestine Dispute between the Arabs and Israel, which reaches back across two generations to the Balfour Declaration. The Balfour Declaration was Britain's promise in World War I to sponsor a national home for the Jewish people in the ethnically Arab province of Palestine after severing it from the defeated Ottoman Turkish Empire.

There would, of course, have been no Palestine Dispute if the Jewish movement to return there after a 2,000-year absence had not been opposed by the Arabs' insistence on remaining in their homeland.

To understand the stubborn intensity of these rival claims, particularly the attachment of the Jews to a land that only a few thousand of them had ever seen, it is necessary to look back to the legendary time when two of the sons of Abraham became the progenitors of the Arabs and the Jews respectively. The division has never troubled the Semites more than it does in this generation. Ishmael, Abraham's son by Hagar, the handmaid his wife had brought from Egypt, is the Biblical ancestor of the Arabs. Isaac, born to Abraham's wife Sarah, is the father of Israel and the Jews. Thus Egypt and Israel figure in the rivalry from the beginnings of the Old Testament.

Abraham himself, whose name was at first Abram, was a nomad from Ur of the Chaldees, a native of what is now southern Iraq. The modern Zionist claim to Palestine and other territories comprising the Land of Israel (*Eretz Israel*) goes back to the Biblical account of God's Covenant with Abraham. In the Book of Genesis, chapters 15 to 17, God is quoted as defining the promised land as follows:

I am the Lord that brought thee out of Ur of the Chaldees, to give thee this land to inherit it.... Unto thy seed have I given this land, from the river of Egypt unto the great river, the river Euphrates...the land wherein thou art a stranger, all the land of Canaan, for an everlasting possession...

Abram had gone down into Egypt to sojourn there after passing through the land of Canaan and finding it stricken with a grievous famine. Abram and his wife returned out of Egypt to Canaan laden with Pharaoh's gifts of cattle, silver, and gold. In return for the Promised Land Abraham and his descendants were to acknowledge God and God alone and to be circumcised as a token of the Covenant.

Ishmael was excluded from the Covenant when he was thirteen, the Bible says, on the same day that he and his ninety-nine-year-old father Abraham were circumcised. God limited the promise to the lineage of Isaac, whose birth, He foretold, would be "at this set time in the next year."

Neither Isaac nor his seed have ever made good their claim to the entire tract stipulated in the Covenant. Joshua, who destroyed or expelled the people of thirty-one kingdoms, failed to take Gaza. This prompted God to say to him that "there remaineth yet very much land to be possessed." The chief obstacle, then as now, was that the non-Jewish indigenous peoples of the Promised Land refused to recognize the claim of the Jews. Canaanite, Amorite, Jebusite, or Arab, they bitterly resisted implementation of the Jewish claim no matter whether God, Lord Balfour, or the United Nations upheld it. The Arabs hold that the Covenant has no civil standing and was never endorsed by nor made binding upon third parties. Many Zionists, both Jewish and Christian, maintain that divine sanction overrides civil legal considerations. They contend further that the covenanted territory is a sounder geopolitical entity than any national unit ever created in the region by men.

As the result of a factional quarrel among the Jews during the post-Abrahamic wanderings, one of their outstanding leaders, Abraham's great-grandson Joseph, was sold to nomads who took him to Egypt. He became the Pharaoh's Prime Minister. Providentially situated and of a forgiving nature, Joseph arranged for his father and brethren to come to Egypt, as Abraham had done, when famine threatened them with extinction. There the Jews lived until Moses, a princely leader in the time of a later Pharaoh, persuaded them that they could not live a free and dignified life on Egyptian sufferance. He and his successor Joshua led them out of Egypt toward statehood of their own in the Promised Land, as related in the books of Exodus, Deuteronomy, and Joshua.

Despite the popular impression, the Bible makes clear that life in Egypt under the Pharaohs was not one of unmitigated oppression. There was much good will between the Jews and the Egyptians. The Jewish account in the Book of Exodus charitably ascribes Pharaoh's cruelty to God's having hardened his heart in order to create conditions suitable for dramatic demonstrations of His favor for the Jews. Pharaoh asked the Jews' blessing when he released them. Just before they departed the Jews borrowed raiment and jewels of silver and gold from the easygoing Egyptians and took it all with them when they left.

The long struggle for the Promised Land was forecast in terms strikingly relevant to modern times. "I will not drive them out from before thee in one year lest the land become desolate and the beast of the field multiply against thee," said God to Moses after handing down the Law. "By little and little I will drive them out from before thee until thou be increased and inherit the land."

Later Moses laid down the harsh policy of conquest followed by Joshua:

When the Lord thy God shall bring thee into the land whither thou goest to possess it, and hath cast out many nations before thee ... seven nations greater and mightier than thou; and when the Lord thy God shall deliver them before thee, thou shalt smite them and utterly destroy them; thou shalt make no covenant with them nor show mercy unto them ... thine eye shall have no pity upon them.

The Book of Joshua records the first Hebrew conquest of the land of the Canaanites. Joshua's military campaigns and the Hebrew deployment of settlements to occupy the land were remarkably paralleled by the modern Zionist establishment of Israel.

As a reminder of the Divine favor that made possible the first Jewish conquest of Palestine, Joshua quoted the Lord God of Israel as commenting:

I have given you a land for which ye did not labor, and cities which ye built not, and ye dwell in them; of the vineyards and oliveyards which ye planted not to do ye eat.

Exile in Babylon and dispersion under Roman rule limited the physical tenure of the Jews in the Holy Land to broken periods totaling roughly a thousand years between the conquests of Joshua at the end of the thirteenth century B.C. and the destruction in 70 A.D. of the Second Temple, together with the last vestiges of Jewish statehood, by the Roman legions of Titus. For much of those thousand years the Jews of Palestine were not independent but were ruled by emperors in Babylon, Persia, Egypt, Macedonia, or Rome. The periods of independence were troubled by tribal and national splits and secessions. Jewish territory was sometimes no larger than a county. But the spiritual attachment confirmed by Moses has endured strong and unbroken for more than three thousand years.

Martin Buber expressed the mystical depth and strength of the Jewish yearning for Palestine in an open letter to Mahatma Gandhi in 1939:

> The question of our Jewish destiny is indissolubly bound up with the possibility of ingathering, and that is bound up with Palestine. . . .
> But you say that Palestine belongs to the Arabs and that it is therefore "wrong and inhuman to impose the Jews on the Arabs." . . . Two vital claims are opposed to each other, two claims of a different nature and a different origin . . . between which no objective decision can be made as to which is just, [and] which is unjust. We . . . consider it our duty . . . to endeavor to reconcile both claims. We could not and cannot renounce the Jewish claim. . . .
> By what means did the Arabs attain to the right of ownership in Palestine? Surely by conquest and in fact a conquest with intent to settle. . . . The conquered land is, in my opinion, only lent even to the conqueror who has settled on it—and God waits to see what he will make of it . . .

The history of Arab Palestine does not begin until six centuries after Rome stamped out Jewish nationhood in Palestine, when the Arab Caliph Omar carried the sword of Islam into the Eastern Roman Empire of Christian Byzantium. In 638 A.D. Omar placed the Crescent among the Crosses on the towers of Jerusalem.

The conquering Arabs converted only a part of the Palestinians to Islam. The others remain Christian to this day, whether in Israel or as refugees in the adjacent Arab countries. Some of them claim direct descent from the original Canaanites. Although only partly converted to Islam, Palestine was culturally Arabized along with the rest of that part of the Arab Empire lying between the Atlantic Ocean and the Persian Gulf. The Palestinians were not driven out to make way for Arab colonists. They adopted Arabic speech and manners and intermarried with the Arab rulers until there was no longer any distinction between the conquerors and the natives.

The Moslems, like the Christians before them, added new elements of sanctity to the Holy City of Solomon and Jesus. They built the Dome of the Rock on the vacant foundations of the vanished Jewish temple and made it the third holiest site in Islam after Mecca and Medina. The Rock, they believe, is where God stopped Abraham from sacrificing, not Isaac the ancestor of the Jews, but Ishmael the father of the Arabs. From that same rock, in Moslem lore, Mohammed bounded toward Heaven upon the steed Burak.

Moslems believe that the Koran was dictated by the Archangel Gabriel to Mohammed and that it is the final word in a series of divine revelations issued through Jewish and Christian prophets, among them Ibrahim (Abraham), Musa (Moses), and Issa (Jesus). Moslem theology therefore regards Jews and

Christians as People of the Book, people possessed of incomplete religious truth but whose errors were to be tolerated in contrast with the pagans, whom early Moslem militants forced to choose between conversion and the sword.

To Christian Jerusalem Omar brought a tradition of religious toleration that has often been violated but which is still a living part of the city's legend. When the Christian Patriarch invited Omar to enter the Church of the Holy Sepulcher and pray at the site of Christ's crucifixion, the great Moslem conqueror demurred and prayed instead outside the church's forecourt. If he prayed inside the church, he warned, his zealous warriors or their descendants would probably commemorate the event by converting the church into a mosque. As he predicted, the Mosque of Omar was built over the spot where he prayed and stands to this day immediately south of the great domed Christian shrine. The ferocious incursion of Christian European Crusaders into Palestine and Egypt in the eleventh and twelfth centuries did not destroy the fabric of toleration. But since the Crusades the keys to the Holy Sepulcher have been entrusted to a Moslem family of Jerusalem.

Through the centuries of the Arab Golden Age, which faded as Europe entered the Renaissance, and the long night of stagnation under the Ottoman Turkish Empire, Palestine remained ethnically Arab but host to small communities of devout Jews in the four Jewish holy cities of Safad, Hebron, Tiberias, and Jerusalem. Arab and Jewish nationalism alike slept the sleep of the unborn, antique seeds from the flowering of Semitic civilizations under vanished caliphs and prophet-kings.

It was the struggle of the Great Powers of Europe for the moribund Ottoman Empire that broke and fertilized the ground where the two modern nationalist movements would strike root. First came Napoleon at the turn of the nineteenth century, conquering Egypt and then relinquishing it in the space of three years. The British came to speed his departure but, that time, did not stay either.

France then turned her attention toward developing links with the Maronite and Catholic Arabs of Syria, Lebanon, and Palestine. Russia arrogated to herself guardianship over the Orthodox Church, its shrines, and its mostly Greek and Arab membership in Palestine. For lack of Protestant Arabs to cultivate, Lord Palmerston directed British interest from the 1830s to the 1850s toward the claims of the Druzes, a break-away sect from Islam, in Syria and Lebanon and toward the Jewish communities in Palestine. Palmerston, a hundred years ahead of history, sought to encourage a vast return of European Jews to Palestine as a vehicle for British imperial influence.

Ironically, Egypt itself, having conquered Palestine and most of Syria under Mohammed Aly, promised to sponsor the agricultural Zionism of Sir Moses

27

Montefiore in the 1830s if Palestine remained under Egyptian suzerainty. Mohammed Aly, aspiring to Great Power status, was bidding against Palmerston for Jewish support. The beguiling prospect of Egypt becoming the patron of Zionism evaporated when the Powers of Europe decided for the time being to prop up the ailing Ottoman Empire against Mohammed Aly. They forced him back into Egypt in the early 1840s.

After Palmerston's death in 1865 British interest in Zionism faded. Finding the Druzes and Jews too small a constituency, Britain turned away from them to the Arab Moslems and away from the Levantine coasts toward the desert hinterland and the Persian Gulf.

It was France which transmitted European concepts of nationalism to the Arab and Egyptian provinces of the Turkish Empire. Arab nationalism first found voice among the Christian Arabs of Syria and Lebanon, graduates of French and American missionary schools and colleges.

Germany came late into the arena and reached for Middle Eastern hegemony, not through the Arab provinces, but with an all-or-nothing campaign for influence at Constantinople, the imperial capital of the Turkish Sultan. Germany's success with the Sublime Porte culminated in a formidable German-Turkish alliance in World War I. Britain and France countered German influence at the capital by encouraging Arab nationalist movements aimed at separating ethnically Arab lands from Turkey. This policy reached fruition in World War I in the Arab Revolt against Turkey and an Anglo-Arab alliance based on Britain's promise to support the emergence of the Arab provinces of the Ottoman Empire as a single independent Arab state.

Thus, on the coming field of battle itself in the Arab Middle East, Arab nationalism came into being while the Jews of the region remained politically dormant except for the few who threw themselves into furthering the cause of Arab nationalism.

It was among the Jews of Europe that political Zionism, the nationalism of the Jewish people, germinated. Like Arab nationalism, it arose among people with no political voice in the counsels that governed them. It was inspired and led by politicians with no outlet or scope for their ambitions in the establishments of their native lands. Just as Arab nationalism was born among a subject people of the Turkish Empire, so Zionism developed among the despised and threatened Jews in the Polish and Russian ghettos of the Tsarist Empire.

Zionism matured more rapidly than Arab nationalism as an organized political program and it maintained a singleness of purpose which continues to elude the Arabs to this day. In the mid-nineteenth century, while excited circles of Christian Arab intelligentsia in Beirut were discussing vague concepts of Arab statehood, Sir Moses Montefiore was promoting the migration of unhappy

Eastern European Jews to farming colonies in Palestine without a thought of political nationhood. But in 1896 Theodore Herzl, the Viennese journalist who is the founding philosopher and theoretician of political Zionism, published *The Jewish State.* The following year Herzl organized the First Zionist Congress in Basel and inspired it to form the Zionist Organization and to work out a practical program "to create for the Jewish people a home in Palestine secured by public law." Zionism had become a full-fledged political movement with the definite objective of statehood although, for diplomatic reasons, the objective was long obscured in public statements.

Herzl was shouldered aside six years later when he urged acceptance of a British offer of land in Kenya for Jewish colonization. The leadership of Zionism passed on to such forceful personalities as Chaim Weizmann, David Ben-Gurion, and Vladimir Jabotinsky. For all of these men normal political careers were unthinkable in their anti-Semitic native lands. As Zionists they quarrelled bitterly over means but never over the ultimate objective.

By contrast Arab nationalism never united under a single leadership and never developed a single organization to articulate a common objective and a common program. It lost even the unifying influence of the revolt against the Turks when suzerainty over the Arabs was divided after the Allied victory in World War I among British and French Mandatory regimes, which provided neither clear-cut colonial status nor clear-cut independence.

Separate independence movements developed in each of the political divisions of the Mandatory system, which eventually led to the creation of independent states after World War II. These remain a barrier today to the Arab dream of unity. In the frustratingly ill-defined Mandatory system the subjects had nominal but false independence while, for their part, the French and British overlords lacked the creative and affectionate concern of good colonial masters. The Mandatory system stunted the growth of Arab political maturity. Responsibility was weak on both sides of the struggle between the Arab nationalists and their self-appointed European guardians.

Jewish colonization in Palestine, first inspired by the agricultural Zionism of Montefiore in the middle third of the nineteenth century, assumed small but significant proportions in the 1870s and 1880s with the munificent financial help of Baron Edmond de Rothschild of the Paris branch of the famous banking family. Herzl and his successors drew on the momentum generated by this agricultural movement as well as upon the millennial Jewish vision of a return to Jerusalem for the ideological bases of political Zionism.

Foreseeing the need of a common national language for the returning Jews, they eschewed all the languages of the Diaspora including the beloved Yiddish and revived the majestic Hebrew of Moses and Solomon, which had become a liturgical tongue as fossilized as Latin. It lent dignity and cohesion to polyglot Jewish nationalism and provided a living link with the Palestine of a glorious past. This was an important step, for unlike Arab nationalists, Zionism's constituents were Europeans and Americans living far away from their envisioned territorial basis in Palestine. Palestine was, in fact, as overwhelmingly Arab as Poland was Polish or Russia Russian. Against this fact the Zionist dream, as Weizmann stated it, was to make Palestine as Jewish as England is English.

This presented a unique problem which required unique solutions. A new kind of diplomacy was needed for representatives of a political movement that lacked such fundamental apparatus of statecraft as a state and an army. The first requirement was to obtain the endorsement and protection of states that could exert decisive military power in Palestine while the Zionists acquired national territory there and created a military force of their own.

Covering all actual and possible masters of Palestine, the Zionist leaders sought German, British, and French protection for the Jewish colonies in Palestine while bargaining for concessions from the Turkish Sultan—all to no avail; the Sultan refused Herzl's suggestion that Jewish resources and influence might help him out of his financial straits. At the same time, the Zionist leaders showed remarkable political acumen by cultivating influence in President Wilson's America through the increasingly numerous and rich Jewish communities there.

Understandably, the Arabs of Palestine did not regard the prospect of Zionist rule as the kind of liberation from the Turks that they sought. In the last two decades of the nineteenth century the Jewish proportion of the population of Palestine was increased by early pioneers from 1 or 2 per cent to nearly 5 per cent. At the outset of World War I there were 80,000 Jews in Palestine, among them Ben-Gurion and Sharett. By 1917, the year of the Balfour Declaration, the number dropped to 65,000, less than 10 per cent of the population. Only a fraction of this minority were political Zionists. Nevertheless, Zionism already had begun to make thoughtful Arabs uneasy, belying Herzl's forecast that they would cooperate enthusiastically in the rebuilding of Zion.

Britain became a directly interested party to the Palestine question in World War I, first by promising it to the Arabs; then by promising it to the Zionists; and finally by taking it for herself. The slithery cynicism that allowed this tissue of contradictions to be woven provoked the bitter saying among both Jews and Arabs that Palestine was the Twice-promised Land.

The promise made to the Arabs was embodied in an exchange of ten letters between Sir Henry McMahon, British High Commissioner in Egypt, and the Sherif Hussein, ruler of Mecca, who was presumed competent to speak for the Arabs. In all, the preliminary negotiations and the letters spanned the period from February 1915 to January 1916. The bargain struck was that if the Arabs helped the British war effort by revolting against the Ottoman Turkish Empire, which was allied to Germany, Britain would "recognize and support" the independence of all ethnically Arab territory freed from the Turks.

Fulfilling their side of the bargain, the Sherifian family launched the Arab revolt in June 1916, coordinating their operations east of Palestine with the British Army based in Egypt to the west of Palestine. Accompanied and advised by the romantic British agent, T. E. Lawrence, the Arabs harried Turkish communications and fought, raided, and besieged Turkish units. Their main strategic contribution was to divert some 30,000 Turkish soldiers from the main front on the west. The Turkish western front crumbled under a British offensive in November 1917—the very week that the Balfour Declaration was given to the Zionists.

Publication of the Balfour Declaration on Friday, 9 November 1917, a week after it was given to the Zionists, was overshadowed in most newspapers by headlines on the Bolshevik seizure of power in Petrograd and the British breakthrough in Palestine.

The revolutionary Soviet Government in Russia lost little time in publishing the secret diplomatic correspondence of its Tsarist predecessors with their wartime allies in the West. These documents included an Anglo-French-Russian agreement to carve up among themselves the prospective territorial spoils in the Arab part of the Ottoman Empire lying between Turkey and the Arabian Peninsula, where the ambitious Sherif Hussein's little domain was actually situated. It became known as the Sykes-Picot Agreement.

This was the accord by which Britain, soon after secretly pledging Palestine to the Arabs and more than a year before she promised it to the Zionists, ensured that she would take control of it herself at the end of the war. Between the Sykes-Picot Agreement and the Balfour Declaration there was no conflict since the transformation of Arab Palestine into a Jewish state was predicated on sympathetic British rule during the Zionists' build-up of a Jewish majority. The Sykes-Picot Agreement was irreconcilable, however, with the Hussein-McMahon Agreement. And it was made in full awareness of the contradiction.

The British Foreign Secretary told the French ambassador about the Hussein-McMahon exchanges in October 1915. Their meeting initiated talks on breaking up the Arab lands into separate entities as zones of influence and buffer zones. The negotiations overlapped the last four months of the Hussein-McMahon correspondence. The Sykes-Picot Agreement, which secretly voided the promise to Hussein, was concluded on 16 May 1916, the month before the Arabs launched their revolt by capturing the Turkish garrison at Mecca and besieging other Turkish garrisons throughout the Meccan hinterland.

Serious negotiations culminating in the Balfour Declaration did not begin until 7 February 1917, two months after the expansionist David Lloyd George succeeded Asquith as Prime Minister of wartime England. Sir Mark Sykes, having successfully negotiated the Sykes-Picot Agreement, was assigned by the new British Government to treat with the Zionist leaders. Although the Declaration was cautiously to limit its commitment to the vague concept of "a national home," Jewish statehood in Palestine was mentioned in the Zionists' first conference with Sykes.

Arthur James Balfour, Foreign Secretary in Lloyd George's cabinet, had been Prime Minister from 1902 to 1905, years in which the British Government first considered encouraging Zionist colonization in British-controlled territory. In 1902 the Sinai Peninsula was seriously discussed and in 1903 Britain proposed Jewish settlement in the White Highlands of Kenya, where Mau Mau terrorism was to draw world attention in the 1950s. These suggestions came to naught. The Zionists deemed only Palestine capable of attracting Jewish mass immigration. Furthermore, neither the Egyptian Government nor the earlier white settlers in Kenya welcomed the prospect of Jewish immigration.

During the spring of 1917, while the Foreign Office was negotiating with the Zionists in London, Lawrence and Auda Abu Taya were leading the Huweitat warriors on their famous three-month raid which culminated in the capture of Aqaba, the first morsel of Palestine to be liberated from the Turks by Arabs in fulfillment of the Arab side of the Hussein-McMahon pact.

In July the Zionists suggested a draft declaration. Its key phrase, "that Palestine should be reconstituted as the national home of the Jewish people," was incorporated in Lord Balfour's own first draft the following month. The more cautious final version was approved by the British War Cabinet on 31 October and communicated officially to the Zionists on 2 November 1917.

This was the decisive breakthrough, only twenty years after the birth of political Zionism. It was a remarkable achievement, due mainly to the dedication and skill of Chaim Weizmann, then forty-three, the Russian-born chemist who spent most of his life in England working for Zionism and who lived to become Israel's first president.

There were mixed reasons for what Sir Mark's son Christopher Sykes calls "the most surprising act of state in the history of modern England." Lloyd George said he was prompted by gratitude for Weizmann's wartime chemical inventions; Balfour had a simple, lofty belief in the rightness of Zionism; other members of the British War Cabinet were moved by a variety of political, strategic, propagandistic, and diplomatic considerations.

The eventful Declaration was embodied in a three-paragraph typewritten letter from Balfour to the second Lord Rothschild, Zionist-philanthropist member of the great banking family's English branch. The central paragraph contained the cabinet's considered declaration of sympathy with Zionist aspirations:

His Majesty's Government view with favour the establishment in Palestine of a national home for the Jewish people, and will use their best endeavours to facilitate the achievement of this object, it being clearly understood that nothing shall be done which may prejudice the civil and religious rights of existing non-Jewish communities in Palestine, or the rights and political status enjoyed by Jews in any other country.

Lord Balfour, like God, promised to one people the country of another. The concept of "a national home" was, in effect, immediately equated with Herzl's concept of a Jewish State although many Englishmen and a number of Zionists themselves were sincere in making a distinction between the two. Balfour himself said he personally hoped the Declaration would lead to the founding of a Jewish state in Palestine but he wrote to a Foreign Office expert in 1918 that "it is not likely to become more possible if it is prematurely discussed."

When the "existing non-Jewish communities" learned of the Declaration, they and their fellow Arabs throughout the Middle East discerned in its cloudy language a clear and menacing prejudice to their civil and religious rights.

Arab resentment prompted British efforts to reconcile the Balfour Declaration with the assurances which McMahon had been "empowered in the name of the Government of Great Britain to give." On 4 January 1918 Britain told Hussein that "since the Jewish opinion of the world is in favor of a return of Jews to Palestine . . . His Majesty's Government are determined that in so far as is compatible with the freedom of the existing population both economic and political, no obstacle should be put in the way of the realization of this ideal." The letter warned that "the leaders of the movement are determined to bring about the success of Zionism by friendship and cooperation with the Arabs, and such an offer is not one to be lightly thrown aside."

Later, arguments were put forward that the Hussein-McMahon letters had no treaty status and that, in any case, Palestine was excluded from the area of the promised Arab state.

If the Balfour Declaration, made through an unofficial intermediary to an unprecedented non-governmental organization has treaty status, then governmental promises to a king must surely have at least equal validity. Furthermore, British undertakings to the Arabs were solemnized by the Arab revolt and by the subsequent Arab rejection of a German-Turkish offer for a separate peace.

The contention that Palestine was excluded from the promise to Hussein is based on a tortured construction of Arabic territorial definitions and on Mc-Mahon's lame but loyal claim afterward that Palestine had been excluded in his mind. Not only did McMahon omit to inform Hussein of any such mental reservation, but the name *Palestine* does not appear once in the letters. Nearly fifty years afterward Christopher Sykes examined the evidence and concluded that "anyone reading (or writing) McMahon's definition could not but suppose otherwise than that Palestine was part of it."

Lord Balfour himself wrote in 1919 that "so far as Palestine is concerned, the Powers have made no statement of fact which is not admittedly wrong, and no declaration of policy which, at least in the letter, they have not always intended to violate." In that same memorandum on the future status of Syria, Palestine, and Mesopotamia (now Iraq) he wrote:

"And Zionism, be it right or wrong, good or bad, is rooted in age-long traditions, in present needs, in future hopes, of far profounder import than the desires and prejudices of the 700,000 Arabs who now inhabit that ancient land."

It was in this spirit that the League of Nations Mandate for Britain to rule Palestine was formulated. The Zionist organization was officially recognized as Britain's partner in creating the Jewish national home. No single Arab agency was recognized as representing the interests of the overwhelming (nine-tenths of the population) Arab majority. Nor was there an international Arab organization to focus Arabdom's attention and political and financial resources on retaining Palestine.

There has been wishful talk through the years about a *modus vivendi* between the Zionists and the Arabs, about missed opportunities and reneges on one side or the other. Most of this speculation is as pedantic as it is academic, for there was no reconciliation possible between the claims of two peoples for nationhood on the selfsame territory. It was as impossible as having two majorities, one Arab and one Jewish, within a single state. Until the Gaza Raid, Israel might have made peace with Egypt, with the likelihood that Lebanon and Jordan would follow suit, which would have left Syria and the other Arab countries with little alternative but eventually to make peace too. But peace with the Palestinian Arabs was never possible on the only terms acceptable to the Zionist movement and Israel, namely the permanent subordination of the Arabs within the Jewish State—numerically, politically, and culturally. Peace offers nothing to the Palestinian Arabs, whether in exile or under Israeli control, except acquiescence in the loss of their national identity.

Zionists have often accused Arabs of going back on an agreement signed in January 1919 between Weizmann and the Emir Faisal on cooperation between the projected Arab State and Palestine, particularly regarding Jewish immigration into Palestine. But Faisal included a paragraph making the agreement conditional on the Arab State's achievement of the promised independence, stipulating that "if the slightest modification or departure were to be made [in regard to Arab independence], I shall not then be bound by a single word of the present agreement which shall be deemed void and of no account or validity."

Furthermore, as George Antonius reported in *The Arab Awakening*, Faisal made the agreement only after Weizmann assured him in June 1918, at a meeting at Faisal's camp near Aqaba, that the Zionists had no intention of working for the establishment of a Jewish government in Palestine. The assurance was false because political Zionism was predicated on Jewish statehood in Palestine and had been declared frankly to be so in previous negotiations with the British government.

The very extent of Israeli expansion in the creation and enlargement of the state was always limited by what Israelis call "ethnic considerations," by which is meant the exclusion of any possibility that Arab citizens should ever become a majority in Israel. The territory conquered in 1948 and 1949, for example, was promptly annexed because the Arab inhabitants had fled and could be prevented from returning to their homes. By contrast, formal annexation of most of the territorial conquests of 1967 was delayed because most of the Arab inhabitants resisted Israel's vigorous encouragements to depart. Israel feared that if these Arabs were annexed along with their land, within a generation or so they might become a majority. Expressed in simplest terms, the watchword governing Israel's birth and growth thus far has been: Territory, Yes; Arabs, No. This is as true in our own time as it was in Joshua's day.

The Arab World emerged from World War I with neither the independence nor the unity promised, not once but several times, by Britain and endorsed by France. The Sykes-Picot Agreement was reflected in the League of Nations awards of tutelary authority called Mandates in the Middle East. France got Syria and Lebanon in the north and east, which was the general region of her nineteenth century interests. Britain got Iraq, Trans-Jordan, and Palestine. Trans-Jordan was originally intended to be part of the area available for the Jewish national home and was incorporated in the early drafts of the Palestine Mandate. It was separated from Palestine in 1921 as a consolation prize for the royal family of King Hussein. The old King himself died in exile ten years later, after the warriors of his rival, Ibn Saud, chased him out of the Kingdom of the Hedjaz, as he had styled his little domain.

The Palestine Mandate differed from the others chiefly in its lack of provisions "to facilitate the progressive development" of the other mandated territories "as independent states." In Palestine Britain retained "full powers of legislation and administration." The Jewish national home would have been stillborn if the Palestine Mandate had implemented the final Anglo-French wartime promise to the Arabs, made on 7 November 1918, that they would have "governments and administrations freely chosen by the populations themselves."

In Egypt, where Britain had been in control since 1882, the only question after World War I was what form that control should take. British paramountcy in Egypt was acknowledged by France in 1904 and Britain regularized it by making Egypt a protectorate in 1914. Despite a postwar upsurge of nationalist agitation, there was no question in British minds of abandoning control of Egypt. Military occupation continued until 1936. Then an Anglo-Egyptian treaty provided Egypt with sufficient independence to join the League of Nations and stipulated that British occupation be restricted to the Suez Canal Zone.

Thus, at the war's end, the Zionist leaders had achieved an incredible equalization of the odds against them. The promise of a national home from the fortuitously sympathetic government of David Lloyd George was made binding on subsequent British Governments and given international sanction by the League of Nations Mandate for Palestine. Not only was Britain the protecting power in Palestine but she was in a position to curb Arab opposition to Zionism in the flanking territories of Egypt and Trans-Jordan. Moreover, France, which remained in control of Syria and Lebanon until the end of World War II, had issued a formal expression of sympathy for the Zionist cause in 1917. Thus, during the critical first generation of nation-building in Palestine, the surrounding Arab countries, all more or less hostile to Zionism, were held in check by the two European powers committed to the support of Zionism.

The ultimate consequences to Britain of the Mandatory system, which balked Arab unity and protected the infancy of Israel, fulfilled the reproachful prophecy made by old King Hussein's son, Prince Faisal, to Lloyd George in 1919:

The future Government of the Arab provinces will be the last lesson to be given by Europe to the East. If it does not turn out to be in accordance with the wishes of the people, confidence will be lost in every future official treatment, and a wide channel opened for intrigues and troubles.... Will there be any means left to convince the Moslems... that they have not been the object of a special scheme aimed against them...?

Faisal, with fading confidence in British promises, based his case on President Wilson's famous stipulation that the peoples liberated by the war should be allowed to choose their own form of government for themselves.

The three peoples most closely concerned with Palestine had conflicting intentions regarding the implementation there of Wilson's stipulation on popular national self-determination. The Arabs, forming 90 per cent of the population, naturally wanted an immediate plebiscite in fulfillment of the promises Britain had made to the Meccan rulers in the Hussein-McMahon correspondence. The Zionists wanted it deferred until the number of Jews could be increased by immigration to an effective majority. As for the British, until the Arab-Zionist conflict got out of hand, they would have been content to rule indefinitely.

In the countries whose support was essential to their success, particularly Britain and America, the Zionists skillfully made their cause an issue of rivalry between major political parties, each bidding for the Jewish vote. A party in opposition would attack the party in power for failing to do enough for Zionism and then, upon coming into power, would find itself under attack for failing to honor the pledges it made while out of office.

On British governments during the Mandate, as Michael Ionides pointed out, the Zionists used three avenues of influence while the Arabs had only a single channel. First, the Jewish Agency in Jerusalem exerted pressure through Colonial Office channels on the Colonial Secretary. Second, Zionist organizations in England used propaganda, public relations, and lobby pressure on Members of Parliament and cabinet ministers. Third, Zionists abroad, particularly in the United States, applied propaganda, public relations, and lobby pressure on legislators and government officials so that they would in turn bring pressure on the British government. The Palestinians could compete with the Zionists only in the first avenue, by bringing pressure to bear in Palestine.

After the demise of Palestine in 1948 the UN became a channel for both sides to influence public opinion. But by the time the pro-Arab nations of Africa and Asia were numerous enough to offset the pro-Zionist Western powers, Israel proved strong enough to ignore the UN, provided the US and Russia did not combine against her.

Paradoxically, it was the Arabs, with a futile policy of boycott, who from the beginning of the Mandate to its bitter end prevented the establishment of any kind of representative government rather than accept proposals that fell short of giving them full majority rule. British administrators, as faithful to democratic principles as they were to the interests of Empire, made several attempts during the Mandate to establish a legislative assembly. But, conscientiously honoring the Balfour Declaration, they always incorporated reservations protecting not only the Jewish minority but Zionist objectives as well. The Zionists in Palestine also were dedicated to democratic principles, sometimes even when their interests were opposed to them. To their credit, they were officially willing to consider some of the earlier British constitutional proposals, but Arab opposition saved them from the risks of having representative government become a reality until the state of Israel had replaced the mandate.

The British were content to defer self-government and self-determination indefinitely and retain control of Palestine as an appanage of empire, guarding the Asian approaches to the Suez Canal and offering a potential alternative land base if Egypt should ever become independent enough to winkle the British out of the Suez base itself.

The Zionists, too, welcomed delay so long as they commanded less than an electoral majority in Palestine. They were preoccupied with trying to persuade the British administrators to permit an immigration rate sufficient to achieve a Jewish majority and to persuade Jews to emigrate to Palestine. Until well into the 1930s their most exasperating problem was the apathy of much of world Jewry.

Arab incredulity at the Balfour Declaration had turned to uneasiness over immigration in the 1920s and finally, in the 1929 riots, to violence at a cost of 133 Jewish and 116 Arab lives. Otherwise, Arab resistance remained manageable until the mid-1930s when the Zionists stepped up their immigration activities in response to the desperate need to save Jews from Hitler.

The Zionists were to prove themselves descendants worthy of Joshua in making good their claim to the disputed Holy Land. The fire that tempered their resolve was the holocaust in Nazi-dominated Europe. Unimaginably dreadful as this persecution was, it did furnish Zionism with elements essential to success.

Every revolutionary nationalist movement needs both an external enemy, whose defeat provides a unifying objective, and an internal enemy to serve as a foil for disciplining the revolution's mass constituency. If these enemies do not exist in reality, they are always invented. The American revolutionaries had the British externally and the Tories within as enemies. The Bolsheviks had capitalist-imperialist powers without and bourgeois counter-revolutionaries within. Zionism, which is nothing if not revolutionary, had external enemies in the Europe of its birth and in the Middle East of its maturity. The internal enemy was assimilationism, that school of Jewish thought which favors the integration of Jews into the national communities where they live. Assimilationists regard Zionism as retrograde in that it seeks the same separation of the Jews from other peoples that anti-Semites seek.

The external enemy in Europe was anti-Semitism, first in Tsarist Russia and Poland, where pogroms fostered the birth and nourished the infancy of political Zionism. Later in Nazi-occupied Europe, production-line slaughter in concentration-camp gas chambers and crematoria drove Zionism into becoming a mass movement among the Jews of the world. Hitler's hideous "final solution" narrowed the alternatives for European Jews to escape or death.

It remained for the Zionists to direct as much of the desperate emigration as possible to Palestine on the grounds that only by the creation of an independent

Jewish State there could Jews anywhere hope for a defense against anti-Semitism. The Zionists organized a vast network to assist both legal and illegal immigration to Palestine. They violently opposed emigration to any other country, taking a stand that was morally heroic regardless of whether it was right or wrong.

Nazi terror served other functions too for revolutionary Zionism. Most nationalist revolutionaries have resorted to terrorizing their own people in order to weed out collaborators from the apathetic majority and to ensure the passive if not enthusiastic support of the masses. Terror also enlarges the gap between the revolution's own potential constitutents and the external enemy, the alien oppressor, thus deepening the commitment to battle on both sides. The Mau Mau in Kenya, the National Liberation Front (FLN) in Algeria, the EOKA in Cyprus, the Viet Cong, all have employed what might be called self-terrorism. Hitler's savagery obviated any need for such measures among Jews. Nazism provided so persuasive an argument against the assimilationists in Europe and Palestine that self-terrorism was unthinkable, and Zionist terrorism was employed against non-Jews, mainly against the British in Palestine and Egypt and against the Arabs in and around Palestine.

After Germany's surrender, Zionism's external enemies became the British who ruled Palestine and the Arabs who populated it. Both were obstacles. They occupied the land that was to be, in Zionist terminology, liberated. Terrorism, like the dynamite it frequently employs, is a device for removing obstacles.

It is interesting to note in passing that both Arab and Jewish nationalism turned to Britain for help in World War I and away from Britain in the time of fulfillment after World War II. Although some Arabs regarded Nazi Germany with favor ("the enemy of my enemy is my friend," as their proverb has it), others were sympathetic to the plight of European Jewry. But they felt that the whole world should share in offering the Jews a haven, not just the area of Palestine where the Jews had not been singled out for mistreatment since Roman times.

Under Palmerston, British interest in promoting Zionism as a vehicle for imperial influence antedated political Zionism itself. Under the aegis of Englishmen like Montefiore and Frenchmen like Rothschild, Zionism began as an agricultural colonizing movement reaching out from countries with vigorous colonial traditions. At that time Nationalism was associated only with the Western world.

Colonizing Zionism took on the impetus and ideology of political nationalism among the Jews of Russia, a country that used strategic military and agricultural colonization in its 19th-century empire-building drive into Central Asia and Siberia.

From Russia and her Cossack frontier settlements came the concept of situating Jewish colonies according to the strategic needs of the whole Jewish community of Palestine rather than according to the economic convenience of the individual colonies themselves. The objective, as in Joshua's time, was the occupation, close settlement, and defense of the land to be obtained for the Jewish State by diplomacy, purchase and conquest. The Cossack concept is most fully manifest in the *Nahals*, which are fortified agricultural settlements established by young military veterans on the frontiers they won by arms in 1948 and 1967.

From another aspect, the Russian custom of deporting undesirables to penal or political colonies was so deeply ingrained that Herzl counted on it plus traditional Russian anti-Semitism to favor Jewish emigration to the State he envisioned, be it in Palestine, Sinai, or Uganda.

The Arabs have never been anti-Jewish. Traditionally, their folk-enemy has been Western Christendom, first in the early Moslem conquests of Europe, again at the time of the Crusades, and most recently in the 19th-century empire-building outburst of Europeans into Africa and Asia, which lasted through World War I, and which the Suez War of 1956 did much not only to end but to reverse.

The Arabs tend to view Zionism less as a nationalist movement than as the latest phase of Europe's colonizing impulse. Did not Zionism find its most emphatic support among the colonialist powers of Western Europe? Was Zionism not, in fact, a front for the perpetuation of British influence in the Middle East? When the Arabs ask themselves these questions, inevitably the answer they come up with is *Yes*.

The Arab view of Zionism as a new form of European imperialism was articulated in 1945 by Abdur Rahman Azzam, Secretary General of the Arab League:

> Our brother has gone to Europe and the West and come back something else. He has come back a Russified Jew, a Polish Jew, a German Jew, an English Jew ... with imperialistic ideas, with materialistic ideas, with reactionary or revolutionary ideas, trying to implement them first by British pressure, then by American pressure, and then by terrorism. ... He pretends that he has a particular civilizing mission with which he returns to a backward, degenerate race in order to put elements of progress into an area which has no progress. Well, that has been the pretension of every power that wanted to colonize and that aimed at domination. ... The Arabs simply say "No"—we are not going to allow ourselves to be controlled either by great nations or small nations or dispersed nations.

In Arab eyes, Jewish colonizing in Palestine was more unwelcome than the post-World War I European imperialism in the other Arabic-speaking countries around it. Jewish colonies meant the displacement of the Arabs, even on a local scale. Weizmann and Ben-Gurion, years before Israel's independence, had frankly stated that the creation of the Jewish State would necessitate large-scale transfers of the Arab population. By contrast, the British and French proconsuls of empire in the Arab World did not displace the native people. Except in Algeria, where a million stubborn Frenchmen struck colonial roots in the course of 130 years, the agents of European power were transients who were induced to pack up and leave without prolonged fighting. The *colons* of Algeria fought bitterly before leaving. In Palestine the Jews, mostly from Europe, fought and stayed.

The intrinsic expansionism of the Zionist movement was, of course, another danger in Arab eyes. The Zionist policy of unlimited Jewish immigration unto a Land of Israel defined as the immense tract named in the Covenant appeared to threaten the Arab inhabitants of the tract from Egypt to Iraq. Ben-Gurion told a British Royal Commission of Inquiry in 1936: "The Bible is our mandate." Of the partition proposal of the commission, often called the Peel Commission after its chairman, William Robert Wellesley, Earl Peel, Ben-Gurion wrote: "I did not consider a Jewish State within the area proposed by Peel as capable of fulfilling Zionism, but in my eyes the proposal could have been a decisive stage on the road toward 'greater Zionism' because within the briefest possible time it would have established an effective Jewish force."

When he proclaimed Israel a state, Ben-Gurion was careful not to limit its size in advance. "A few days before our Declaration of Independence," he wrote, "there arose the question whether we should define the State's borders. Two lawyers in the provisional government claimed that the law obliged it. I was opposed to this. I claimed that no such law existed, that the American people when it declared its independence did not define its borders." Ben-Gurion's taking the American precedent—vast expansion in fulfillment of "manifest destiny"—certainly would not have allayed Arab fears. Ben-Gurion held that the Arab war against the UN partition freed Israel's hands. "If we could expand our borders and liberate Jerusalem in the war that the Arab peoples were launching against us," he wrote, "we would liberate Jerusalem and Western Galilee; they would become part of the State."

Ironically, Egypt, the chief external enemy and villain in Ben-Gurion's Biblical vision, did not take an enthusiastic role in the forefront of Arab opposition to Zionism until long after the establishment of the State of Israel. Egypt did not officially classify herself as Arab until 1945. In that year Nuri al-Said of Iraq made it clear that he was as ready (with British backing) to help organize the Arab League without Egypt as with her participation. Nuri's rough-and-ready initiative goaded Egypt into joining the League and offering Cairo as its headquarters. The obligations of Arab League membership induced Egypt to accept a more active role in the Arab cause, including belligerency in the 1948 war—that abortive, mismanaged, uncoordinated, last-ditch effort of the Arabs to prevent the establishment of Israel in their midst.

Participation in the Arab League and in the Palestine War drew Egypt officially closer to the Arabs of Asia Minor although more vital concerns continue to direct her most constant attention up the Nile into Africa. Nevertheless, the Palestine War provided several new bonds with the Arabs which were eventually to work themselves into the consciousness of the Egyptian people.

The Palestine War stopped with Arab grievances unredressed and Israeli geographical objectives unfulfilled. Thus there were motives on both sides for the renewals of the war that came in 1956 and 1967. One of the bones of contention in all three rounds of the war was the Gulf of Aqaba. Israel, in fact, did not acquire her foothold there, which later became the port of Elath, until after the end of the first round. Israel and Egypt accepted a cease-fire on 7 January 1949. They began armistice talks on the Island of Rhodes on 12 January but did not conclude the armistice until 24 February, by which time Israel still had not reached Elath.

"After fighting had ceased," Ben-Gurion reminded the Knesset in 1957, "our forces were unable to reach Elath because this was a death trap, being a narrow triangle whose sides were occupied by enemies. Only after we signed an armistice with Egypt and ensured ourselves of one free flank were we able to send the Israel Defense Forces to occupy the Gulf of Elath without shedding one drop of blood."

Actually, it was not until after the Jordanian delegation had also come to Rhodes for the next set of truce parleys that Israel was able to dispatch two columns southward with tongue-in-cheek orders to "defend yourselves all the way to Elath." David Kimche, an Israel officer-scholar, and his brother Jon, a journalist-historian, described this first postwar coup of Israel's "manifest destiny" in their book, *Clash of Destinies*. They said the column started on 9 March 1949, thirteen days after the Egyptian armistice and more than two months after the cease-fire. It reached Um Rashrash, the Arab settlement on the site of what is now Elath, on the 11th. Elath might thus be called the last conquest of the first round of the Palestine War. It was to become the first official cause of the second and third.

Egypt emerged from the war with responsibility for the Gaza Strip, where more than 200,000 Arabs fleeing from the Israelis crowded in upon the original inhabitants and swelled the population of the five-by-twenty-five-mile strip to nearly 300,000. Egypt and the United Nations Relief and Works Agency share the burden of feeding and housing the Gaza refugees. Egypt, herself increasing every year by more than 300,000 and already overpopulated, could not absorb the people of Gaza. In any case, the Arabs of Gaza do not wish to be absorbed by either Egypt or Israel. For the most part, Arab refugees in Gaza and elsewhere are grimly determined to wait in their camps for the implementation of the UN resolutions, revalidated every year by the General Assembly, which prescribe for them the right to choose either repatriation to their lost homes in what is now part of Israel or compensation for their lost property. Many refugees live along the truce and cease-fire lines in plain view of the farms and orchards from which they were driven by fear or by fighting. The bitterness emanating from these refugee communities is a fearsome factor in Arab politics.

The experience of war, siege, and parleying in 1948 and 1949 deeply influenced the young Egyptian officers who, four years later, took the reins of government in their bloodless "khaki revolution" from King Farouk and his ministers. However, they regarded Egyptian participation in the war as a diversionary tactic by King Farouk and the British and declared after the revolution that they had opposed it.

Nasser, who won Israeli admiration for his "distinguished part" in the 1948 fighting, was ever afterward haunted by the plight of the refugees. Their humiliation and defeat were for him a prevision of the pitiful fate in store for a people who remain powerless in a world where strength and dignity—*"ezza wa karama"* in one of Nasser's favorite Arabic phrases—were inseparable. In his experience imperialism, particularly British imperialism, was the primary cause of weakness among the peoples of the Middle East.

Consequently, removing the last vestiges of British power over Egypt and the Arabs is an older and stouter plank in Nasser's foreign policy than hostility toward Israel. Even in the heat of battle, Nasser and his fellow officers determined that their real enemy lay not in the Israeli trenches but in London and Cairo. Captain Yeruham Cohen of Israel's elite Palmach force wrote in 1953 of his meetings with Nasser during truces in the Palestine fighting:

> Gamal blamed the British for having caused Egypt to enter the war. He believed that this had been a British device whereby rising Egyptian nationalism was diverted from the British to Israel.... And though he fought well, he treated the campaign more as a sporting encounter. His true hatred was reserved for the British.... We parted with the hope that the day would not be far off when we could be friends without barbed wire coming between us.

CHAPTER
3

Foremath
(1948 TO 28 FEBRUARY 1955)

A national polity always remains an organization based upon force.

(HERBERT CROLY)

History itself is nothing but the activity of men pursuing their purposes.

(KARL MARX)

OHEN'S AND Nasser's wartime hope for peace came closest to fulfillment during the first fourteen months of the premiership of Moshe Sharett, from November 1953 to February 1955, when Ben-Gurion was officially in retirement. Sharett and Nasser went so far as to begin cautious contacts with each other through intermediaries who included among others the United Nations truce chief, General Burns, and a British Laborite member of Parliament. These were the months when Sharett's policy of moderation was given its run.

Sharett was on a short leash, however, and Ben-Gurion never really let go of it. On the contrary, unbeknown to Sharett, Ben-Gurion actually stimulated undertakings that ran directly counter to the pacific policies of the Premier. General Burns wrote of Ben-Gurion in this period:

Even during his self-imposed exile in the Negev, when he had been living in the desert settlement of Sde Boker, practicing the avocation of a shepherd, it had seemed that the center of power was in that remote spot. After his return to the Government rumors began to spread that as a result of his meditations in the wilderness, he had developed new ideas of the direction Israeli policy should take—that he had in mind adventurous and potentially dangerous lines of action.

The Gaza Raid was the first manifestation of the shift in Israeli policy brought back by Ben-Gurion from the Negev. His prestige and personal force gave his views the ascendancy in the Government as soon as he returned even though, as Defense Minister, he remained officially subordinate to Premier Sharett until he resumed the premiership from him on 2 November 1955. In truth, Gaza represented not so much an implementation of "new ideas" as a resumption of the old militant activist policy which had created the State of Israel and which continued to dominate Israel's Arab policies under Ben-Gurion's leadership until his withdrawal into the wilderness in November 1953.

By February 1955 Ben-Gurion clearly had decided that Sharett's moderate and gradualist policies must be abandoned. There is abundant evidence that he had found them wanting at the outset and was reluctant to give Sharett a trial as Premier. After only a few months sojourning in the Negev Ben-Gurion began launching independent policies of his own through his Defense Ministry henchmen, which often left Sharett and his Foreign Ministry floundering in bewilderment. Sharett was forced off balance so often by Defense Ministry initiatives that he was hard put to maintain even the appearance of leading the Government and country, much less develop and implement his own policies, which were both more complex and less popular than the satisfyingly simple activism of Ben-Gurion.

At the time, the United States under Eisenhower and Dulles was shifting from Truman's open partisanship for Israel toward impartiality between Israel and the Arabs. Britain was approaching agreement with Egypt on evacuation of the seventy-two-year-old British base on the Suez Canal. Both Britain and the US were groping for a formula to bring the Arabs into a regional defense pact that would fill the gap between the North Atlantic Treaty Organization and the Southeast Asia Treaty Organization.

Sharett and Ben-Gurion alike felt that Israel would be hurt by these developments. But while Sharett, in Jerusalem, employed open diplomacy, making protests and seeking guarantees, Ben-Gurion, in the desert and out of office, acted more vigorously and in secret to counter these international developments with Israel's own resources. At Ben-Gurion's reported instigation, a ring of Israeli agents in Egypt turned from espionage to sabotage in July 1954, using fire bombs on British and American property in an attempt to wreck the Anglo-American rapprochement with Egypt. This was the beginning of the Lavon Affair. And Ben-Gurion's chief lieutenants in the Defense Ministry, Director General Shimon Peres and Chief of Staff Moshe Dayan, were in Paris in August to begin the secret arms purchases that started an arms race with Egypt and led to the Suez-Sinai war.

A third Defense Ministry activity that ran counter to the drift toward peace of Sharett's premiership was the continued tightening of the Army's grip on the strategic demilitarized zone around al-Auja, the key to invasion in either direction across the central Sinai frontier.

Sharett, repeatedly confronted with *faits accomplis* by the Defense Ministry, struggled vainly to hold the initiative for his policy of moderation. In the continued troubles on the Jordanian truce line Sharett often went along with army activists to keep them from pulling him entirely off balance.

After eleven months as Premier, Sharett turned in desperation to General Burns to help him in his struggle, which he was losing even though the activists were a minority in his government and their chief, Ben-Gurion, was out of office. Urgently summoning Burns to his office to discuss a minor sheep-stealing incident, Sharett said he needed diplomatic help from the UN to win against the Arabs on the small issues in order to prevail on the major issues against people of great influence in Israel in the Government and elsewhere who always advocated retaliation against the Arabs by force.

"Unhappily," Burns wrote later, "during the two years from September 1954 to September 1956 the pacifists fought a losing battle and the militarists more and more imposed their point of view and policies. The turning point was when Mr. Ben-Gurion came back to active politics as Minister of Defense late in February 1955."

Sharett's major move *vis-à-vis* Egypt, aside from his discreet communications with Nasser, was to send an Israeli ship, the *Bat Galim*, to demand transit through the Suez Canal, hoping that the inevitable resulting fracas would stimulate effective Great Power support for Israel's claim to use the canal on an equal footing with the other nations of the world. But the *Bat Galim* incident merely provoked the contempt of the Defense Ministry militants.

"It was difficult to be Prime Minister with Ben-Gurion in the wings," Sharett said later. The conflict between activism and moderation that ended in the gunfire at Gaza was fundamentally a conflict between the personalities and political philosophies of Ben-Gurion and Sharett. The differences began far back in careers that were intertwined in lifelong service to Zionism.

Ben-Gurion was born on 16 October 1886 in Plonsk, a town 36 miles northwest of Warsaw in what was then the Tsarist Russian empire's Pale of Settlement, a kind of ghetto on a regional scale. He was the sixth child of Avigdor Green, a self-made court pleader and a member of a pre-political Zionist organization called the Lovers of Zion. David Green founded a Zionist youth society in Plonsk when he was fourteen. He went to Palestine in 1906, tried his hand at agricultural labor and political journalism, and took the Hebrew name *Ben-Gurion*, which means *Son of Gurion*. *Gurion* is a Hebrew modification of *Green* that echoes the names of Jewish heroes of the revolt against the Romans and is related to *gur*, the Hebrew word for lion.

Sharett's name means *servant* in Hebrew. He was born on 15 October 1894 in Kherson, the Ukraine, the son of Yaakov Shertok. Like Avigdor Green, the elder Shertok was a pre-political Zionist, being a member of the agricultural colonization organization, Bilu. The family moved to Palestine in 1906, the same year that Ben-Gurion went there. Sharett did not take his Hebrew name until the establishment of Israel in 1948.

Ben-Gurion and Sharett attended law school together in pre-World War I Istanbul, the Ottoman Turkish capital. The war itself found the two young men on opposite sides. Ben-Gurion went to Britain and the United States as a Zionist organizer and ended the war as a noncommissioned officer in the British Army's Jewish Legion. Sharett, faced with the prospect of detention in Ottoman Palestine as an enemy alien, took Ottoman citizenship and became an officer in the Turkish Army. His extraordinary linguistic facility led to service as an interpreter for a German officer commanding a Turkish unit.

After the war Sharett continued his studies at the London School of Economics. Ben-Gurion plunged into Zionist politics and the Zionist labor movement in Palestine. He merged two Zionist groups to form the still-dominant Mapai party in 1930. A firm believer in Jewish self-reliance and a disbeliever in the efficacy of British protection against hostile Arabs, Ben-Gurion was a major political voice in the counsels of Haganah, the semiclandestine Zionist army, from its beginnings in the 1920s to its triumphs in 1948 and 1956 as the Israel Defense Forces.

Sharett returned to Palestine in 1925 to join the editorial staff of *Davar*, the newspaper of the monolithic Zionist labor federation, Histadrut. His work brought him an offer from Chaim Arlosoroff, gradualist head of the Political Department of the Zionist Executive, which was the Zionist equivalent of a Foreign Ministry. Sharett, who had acquired fluency in Arabic, Turkish, Yiddish, Hebrew, French, German, and English, became the Political Department's specialist in Arab-Jewish relations. When Arlosoroff was murdered by Zionist Revisionists in 1933 Sharett was elected by the Zionist Congress to succeed him.

At thirty-nine he was, in effect, Zionism's Foreign Minister. It was inevitable that he become Israel's Foreign Minister in 1948. He held the post until June 1956, when he was forced out of the Government for opposing Ben-Gurion's plans for war against Egypt. It was a bitter ending to more than forty years of association between the two men.

The decisive disagreement between the two Israeli leaders on the issue of war against Egypt will be narrated in the next chapter. It was a natural outgrowth of their long-standing divergences on activism versus gradualism and moderation. These divergences reflect Ben-Gurion's reliance on the armed forces to implement policies as against Sharett's reliance on diplomacy and the Foreign Ministry.

For Ben-Gurion, the Army was always far more than the war-making and war-deterring implement of traditional theory. At the seventeenth Zionist Congress in 1931 he spoke of "the Army of fulfillment, linked in destiny for life or death with the realization of Zionism." A decade earlier the tiny units of *shomrim*, the heroic watchmen of the early isolated Jewish colonies, had evolved into Haganah, the Zionist military force whose name means *The Defense*.

Haganah defended the Jews in Palestine during the Arab rebellion in the late 1930s and organized the illegal immigration of Jews into Palestine from the rise of Hitler in 1933 until the end of the British Mandate in 1948.

World War II provided Haganah men with opportunities not only to join the fight against Nazism but also to obtain training and arms for the foreseen prospect of having to achieve statehood in Palestine by force. Pursuing these objectives, the Jewish Agency sought incessantly to obtain the formation of a Jewish Army, with only partial and belated success. Most young Jews joined the British Army as individuals. They numbered over 14,000 by the end of the war. Regarding themselves as servants of two masters, the Haganah command as well as the British, they seized wartime opportunities to steal vast quantities of weapons and ammunition for Haganah's secret arsenals. The arms and training were significant factors in the Arab-Israeli war in 1948.

Under Ben-Gurion's first premiership, from 1948 to 1953, the Army was not only the guardian of Israel but an active force in the education and unification of immigrating Jews from the ends of the earth and the lands between. Its universal conscription and programs for education in Hebrew were the flame under the melting pot. Armed-forces publications are among the most influential in Israel. Along the borders, the Army sponsored and Army veterans established the front-line chain of military-agricultural communes called Nahals. Israel is not a militarist society, but there is scarcely an aspect of that society that is not touched by the Army's influence. In 1954, when Ben-Gurion no longer exercised supreme authority over the Foreign Ministry, Defense Ministry men under Ben-Gurion's influence added clandestine diplomacy to the Army's functions.

For the first fifteen years of Israel's statehood, the Army's influence on Israel was fundamentally a product of Ben-Gurion's influence on the Army. Just as Sharett retained the Foreign Minister's portfolio during his term as Premier, so Ben-Gurion always held the portfolio of Defense, his pet ministry, during his terms as Premier. The armed forces were almost as essential an element in Ben-Gurion's constituency as they were and are in Nasser's.

Ben-Gurion's activism, it should be noted, was not extremism. In Mandatory days Ben-Gurion took middle ground between the fiery aggressiveness of Vladimir Jabotinsky's Revisionist Party and the pacifist views of Dr. Judah Magnes. In Mandatory days as today, the contest between activists and moderates or gradualists was for control of the middle ground in Zionism's internal politics.

Ben-Gurion made activism the dominant mode when he challenged the gradualism of Dr. Weizmann at the Zionist conference in 1942 at the Biltmore Hotel in New York. Within two years he had taken the substance of Zionist leadership from the urbane scientist-diplomat who, twenty-five years earlier, had talked Britain into giving Zionism the Balfour Declaration. Talk was never enough for Ben-Gurion.

Ben-Gurion's activist foresight in building Haganah ensured victory in Israel's final struggle to birth. Ben-Gurion sometimes winked at and certainly profited by the terrorism of Jabotinsky's political heirs, the Irgun Zvai Leumi and the Stern Gang. Terrorist raiders and assassins helped break Britain's will to stay in Palestine and galvanized nearly a million Arabs into flight across the borders in fear, leaving their homes empty for the coming of Jewish immigrants. But Ben-Gurion never condoned the extremists. Occasionally he fought them openly and bitterly at considerable political hazard to himself. An act that can still raise hackles in Israel today was Ben-Gurion's order in 1948 for shore batteries to sink the *Altalena*, which was laden with smuggled arms for the Irgun.

The political heirs of Jabotinsky on the one hand and of Dr. Magnes on the other continue to represent the extremes of aggressiveness and conciliation in Israeli political attitudes toward Arabs. Jabotinsky's disciple, the former terrorist Menachem Beigin, transformed the Irgun into the *Herut* (Freedom) party, the second strongest in Israel. The *Ihud* (Unity) party, on the pacifist extreme, is far less significant. The *Mapai* (Socialist) party, which has dominated every Israeli government, was itself the middle-ground prize for which the activists and gradualists strove. Although Sharett abandoned the spokesmanship of the gradualists after he left the Government, the party eventually wearied of the demanding leadership of the man who had founded it in 1930. In 1965, following a recrudescence of the Lavon Affair, Ben-Gurion took his Young Turks out of *Mapai* into an activist break-away party called *Rafi*.

The difference between the gradualists and the activists was largely a difference between watching for opportunities and creating them. Sharett believed Israel's best prospects for peace with the Arabs and acceptance in the Middle East lay in responding quietly to any softening in Arab attitudes while making clear to the Arabs that Israel could not be whittled down or eliminated. Aside from an irreducible territorial position, Sharett took a flexible view of other concessions that could lead to a compromise peace.

Ben-Gurion believed in forcing the Arabs to a direct confrontation, with no Great Power or UN intermediation, as the best road to peace on Israel's terms. For Ben-Gurion Israel's total position was not only irreducible but insufficient. Ben-Gurion wanted to finish the war against the Arabs which had been interrupted by the Great Powers and the UN in 1948 and 1949, leaving an inconclusive armistice. A renewed war could achieve political and territorial objectives for Israel while forcing the Arabs to sue for formal peace on Israel's terms.

Dr. Arieh Loya, Israeli diplomat and scholar, said of that period:

Although we always offered peace to our Arab neighbors, there was an element of fate in their intransigence. For example, King Hussein's last-minute entry into the June 1967 war despite our entreaties resulted in the restoration of Jerusalem to us. Seen in retrospect, peace with the Arabs in the early stages of the State could have had disastrous effects. The half-million Jews from the Arab countries would not have been forced to immigrate to Israel. Had peace come, say in 1952 or 1953, these immigrants, having arrived impoverished and despoiled in an unfamiliar, even hostile culture and facing hard social, economic, and dietary adjustments, would in all probability either have gone back to their former homes or, under the impact of free and peaceful association with the Arabs, maintained their old culture, which is incompatible with a modern, strong, and homogeneous Israeli nation capable of survival. There might be no one speaking Hebrew today in Beersheba—perhaps not even in Jerusalem. The people would have lost their sense of crisis and purpose. We were fighting in those days, as we still are, for survival and the creation of one homogenous nation—one culture, one language. Everything was subordinated to this.

Contemporary Israeli protestations to the contrary, peace was chief among the things subordinated to Ben-Gurion's grand vision of Jewish statehood. "Ben-Gurion never intended peace," Allen Dulles told me afterward in an interview on American intelligence in the Middle East during the pre-Suez period. Many Israelis and Zionists acknowledged this with increasing candor even before their second winning of the Suez-Sinai War, although Ben-Gurion has not.

Ben-Gurion's view is implicit in his actions as well as in his statements in later stages of the Suez Crisis. He warned several times in 1955 that he would go to war for such an objective as freedom of passage through the Straits of Aqaba. After Suez, when he was losing the diplomatic struggle to hold Israel's Sinai conquests, he summed up his views at a Defense Loan rally in Tel Aviv on a bitter note:

Military success today means even less than in former times. A battle is only a means for attaining political aims. Force, of course, should not be underrated. The Armenians, for instance, who were given a promise about the time we received the Balfour Declaration that their country would be restored to them, are still a dispersed people because they failed to build an organization to secure implementation of the promise.

Long before they split in June 1956 on the issue of war with Egypt, Sharett and Ben-Gurion had disagreed over the role of the Army in the formulation and execution of policy toward the Arabs. In the years before Suez the issue was not war but the practice of reprisal raids, which underwent several stages of escalation before reaching the stage of war.

Retaliation raids or reprisals were the most controversial of the Army's activities. They were first done in 1937 by a small section of Haganah assigned to defend outlying Jewish farms and settlements during the Arab Rebellion. In the first year of the rebellion, 1936, Haganah accepted a policy of *Havlagah* (Self-restraint). *Havlagah* had antecedents in the early settlements and in an ancient Jewish belief that in the Promised Land their weapons must remain pure (*tahor*) of the blood of any but proven enemies. In effect, this limited Haganah to static defense and left the initiative to Arab attackers.

53

The policy was so unpopular that even the prestige of Weizmann could not sustain it for long. Activism won out. Patrols organized by Isaac Sadeh in the FOSH section of Haganah began in 1937 to pursue Arab guerrillas and attack them on their home grounds. (Like many modern Hebrew terms, FOSH is composed of initial letters, those of the Hebrew words for *Field Troops*.) In 1938 a young Scottish intelligence officer named Orde Wingate, who had become an ardent Zionist after his assignment to Palestine, recruited men from FOSH and created a force of Special Night Squads. They became specialists in commando-style night raids and reprisals against Arab strongholds. One of Wingate's best men was a twenty-three-year-old *sabra* (Palestine-born Jew) named Moshe Dayan.

The Arab Rebellion was suppressed by the time World War II broke out in September 1939. Serious strife between the Jews and Arabs in Palestine did not revive until March 1947, the month following Britain's announcement that she intended to turn the League of Nations Mandate for Palestine back to the United Nations, the League's successor. The policy of reprisal was revived at the same time by Zionist forces.

Like other societies in which tribe and clan and family are strong social units, Arab culture has an ancient tradition of revenge and blood feud. Similar violent traditions have bloodied the histories of Scottish clans, Kentucky mountaineers, and the vendettists of Corsica. The Israeli policy of reprisal differs from revenge in having wider objectives than simply paying off scores. It is a political implement more akin to terrorism than to the custom of revenge.

In the last fifteen months of the Mandate, as the Great Powers, the UN, and a succession of commissions wrestled with it, the Palestine problem moved inexorably toward its own solution on a rising tide of terrorism and reprisal, atrocity and counter-atrocity. It was every bit as vicious on the Arab side as on the Jewish, although the Arabs were uncoordinated and less skillful. For much of that time Zionist terror was directed more against British rule than against the Arabs.

The most grisly exchange in the Arab-Jewish conflict began on 8 April 1948 when patrols of the Irgun Zvai Leumi and the Stern Gang massacred at least 254 men, women, and children in the village of Deir Yasseen near Jerusalem. Jacques de Reynier, the Red Cross representative who investigated the massacre in the face of death threats by the Irgun, estimates the total slaughter at nearly 350 persons of Deir Yasseen's population of 400. Reynier found only three persons alive in the village, two old women and a little girl, amid corpses stacked by the killers. Young men and women of the Irgun brandished still-bloody knives and submachine guns at Reynier as he went about his grim inspection. A final victim was a little boy who escaped the massacre but died of a heart attack after screaming "She is one of them" when he was approached by an American missionary woman.

Four days later Arab terrorists ambushed a convoy in Jerusalem carrying supplies to the Haganah garrison in the Hadassah Hospital on Mount Scopus, killing 77 doctors, nurses, teachers, and students in addition to Haganah men in the escort.

The political effect of Deir Yassen was to impel the Arabs, already fleeing in large numbers from Jewish-controlled areas, into a panicky mass emigration. The Arab exodus was deliberately and implacably spurred on in later stages of the war by Jewish threats and aggressions.

Arab publicity given to the Deir Yasseen massacre added immensely to the impetus of fear, but there is no evidence to support the Zionist allegations that the Arab leadership planned and deliberately encouraged the flight of the refugees. Arab propagandists sought only to incite hatred of the Jews with the Deir Yasseen story but they instilled terror more strongly than hatred. There were nearly a million Arab refugees when the fighting ended. They assumed they would return home, as had those who fled violence during the Arab Rebellion ten years before.

Zionist propagandists made no such play with the convoy massacre. Instead they emphasized morale-building news. The convoy massacre remains to this day almost unknown by comparison with Deir Yasseen.

Deir Yasseen, like the later massacre at Qibya, has often been compared to the Nazi massacre of the Czechoslovak villagers of Lidice on 10 June 1942 in reprisal for the assassination of the chief of the SS, the Nazi Elite Guard, in the country. The Nazis shot all 185 men of the village, which had a total population of 500. They sent the women to concentration camps and most of the children to gas chambers. The village was razed and barely planted on the site. The name of Lidice became a byword for atrocious reprisals. After the war 160 surviving women and children returned and Lidice was rebuilt. About 450 people live there now. Deir Yasseen has disappeared from the map.

Although the two massacres were comparable in savagery, they differ in that Deir Yasseen was not an act of policy by the official Zionist agency while Lidice was ordered by the Nazi German authorities. Nevertheless, the Zionist and Israeli officials, however much they may have deplored atrocities like Deir Yasseen and the assassination of Count Folke Bernadotte a few months later, made no effective effort to apprehend and punish the killers. Furthermore, after the Deir Yasseen massacre the Zionist authorities ratified an agreement for cooperation between the Haganah and the Irgun which had been concluded before the massacre.

Reprisals were continued after the Palestine War as a deterrent to Arab infiltration. The hastily drawn armistice lines were a stimulus rather than a barrier to infiltration, especially on the westward bulges of Jordanian territory north and south of Jerusalem and along the Gaza Strip. There were several reasons for this. Chief among them was the fact that in both areas the lines agreed upon by the armistice negotiators and their governments worked severe economic injustice on the Arabs living along the lines by severing the villages in which they lived from the fields on which they grew their crops and which constituted the economic basis of village life.

The hardship was worst on the Jordanian frontier, where the villages typically are located on the rocky lower slopes of the Judean Hills with their fields adjacent to them in the fertile plains extending from the western edge of the hills to the Mediterranean Sea. Unfortunately, this geography influenced the positions of the opposing armies when the fighting ended. The Arab Legion of Jordan was left holding the hills while the Israeli forces occupied the plains. The armistice lines were drawn roughly along the center of the space between the opposing forces. The unfortunate villagers along the truce line, thus cut off from their livelihood, did not qualify for UN refugee aid because a refugee was defined as one who had lost both his lands and his house.

It can easily be imagined what rage and frustration these people felt at seeing Israeli tractors turning the earth that had been plowed for centuries by the yoked oxen and asses of their forebears. Hunger and destitution and the ragged plight of their wives and children drove village men to harvest for their families what they could of the Israeli crops and to forage and steal in areas they still regard as their own property. Full-fledged refugees in camps near the truce lines often sneaked back under cover of night to their former houses to fetch abandoned possessions and dig up buried caches of money or jewelry. It was a short step from this to stealing from the Israelis, who consolidated their conquests as rapidly as possible by establishing settlements all along the line.

Larcenous infiltration was transformed into murderous infiltration in instances when Israelis shot a border crosser and his relatives returned for vengeance. When this happened the cycle would worsen as Israel struck back in punitive raids against houses and villages. Sometimes the Israeli forces would hit communities suspected of harboring the marauders. Sometimes they would strike at villages not necessarily suspected of complicity but sited across the truce line near enough to the scene of the marauder outrage to drive home the lesson of reprisal, as at Qibya. Sometimes retaliation was wreaked on villages utterly unconnected with the marauder's crime. Sometimes, according to expert opinion, the raids were planned long in advance to be unleashed whenever an incident occurred that could be considered a pretext for retaliation.

Both Qibya and Gaza are believed to have been planned and rehearsed before their alleged pretexts occurred. The Gaza pretext remains a blurred issue but the Qibya raid on the night of 14/15 October 1953 was officially linked to the murder two nights earlier of two children and their mother in Tirat Yehuda by means of a hand grenade thrown into the window of their house.

Glubb Pasha, then the British commander of the Jordanian Army, believes it extremely unlikely that Qibya was planned and executed in less than 48 hours. Noting the Haganah tradition of careful rehearsals of raids, the specially prepared back packs for the demolition charges used at Qibya, the necessity for careful reconnoitering of the target terrain for such a raid, and the drills needed for soldiers to place and detonate explosives under covering fire in the dark without injuring one another, Glubb estimates "that this massacre was prepared several months before, in April or May, when there were many incidents and acute tension." He adds:

"Then the energetic measures taken by Jordan put a temporary end to infiltration, and there was no excuse for the proposed operation. When the woman was murdered in Tirat Yehuda, the Israeli Army jumped at the chance." It so happened that the Israeli Army had been in the area since 22 September on the largest war games maneuvers since statehood and on the eve of Qibya, Israeli military correspondents reported rumors of an impending "attack" on the Israeli Blue Army by the Greens.

For several years Israeli authorities vaguely attributed reprisal raids to irate settlers who were said to have taken the law into their own hands. The fact that the Government itself was conducting a policy of reprisals and that they were carried out by Israel's regular armed forces was a stubbornly held secret, although the international officer corps of UN military observers found the Israeli Army responsible in most instances.

After Qibya, for example, despite a UN truce commission determination on 15 October 1953 that the previous night's raid was carried out "by a force approximating one half of a battalion from the Israeli regular army," Premier Ben-Gurion made a surprise broadcast on 19 October to insist that the raid was carried out by frontier settlers, "mostly Jewish refugees from Arab countries or survivors of Nazi concentration camps," whose patience had been exhausted two days earlier by the hand-grenade murder of the Israeli mother and two children. Ben-Gurion said "the Government of Israel rejects with all vigor the absurd and fantastic allegation that the men of the Israel Defense Forces took part in the action."

The effort damaged Ben-Gurion's credibility. And the Government's disavowals combined with the repugnance expressed by the world, including many Jews, must have depressed the morale of the raiders, who acted and sometimes died on Defense Ministry orders. In any case, the policy of disavowing the raids was dropped within a year.

Israeli military censors cleared an article for the March 1955 issue of *Harper's Magazine* saying that the Qibya raid had been carried out by Israeli commandos. The article, entitled "Israel's Policy of Reprisals," was written by Moshe Brilliant, an American resident of Israel and a respected correspondent for both *The New York Times* and the *Jerusalem Post*, the English-language organ of Ben-Gurion's Mapai party.

"There has been nothing reckless or impulsive about the lethal raids across the borders," Brilliant wrote. "On the contrary, the policy of reprisals is the fruit of cold, unemotional political and psychological reasoning."

Expressing the activist approach to policy, Brilliant wrote that back in the days of British Mandatory rule restraint won praise for the Jews but opened the door to disaster. Then they turned to "gun powder and dynamite" and found that although it brought down on them international condemnation it "earned them . . . ultimately the coveted prize" of statehood. Israelis never forgot that lesson, Brilliant wrote, explaining that border raids were not merely retaliations but also part of a deliberate plan to force the Arabs to the peace table. Ever since the Palestine War, he said, "each reluctant step the Arabs took from hot war toward peace was taken when they were held by the throat."

The article was published two weeks or so before the Gaza Raid, plenty of time in advance to have influenced the reaction of Nasser, who is a voracious reader of the English and American press. Significantly, it was prepared and cleared by the Defense Department censors some six weeks before publication at a time when Ben-Gurion, the chief proponent of the policy it expressed, was still officially in retirement.

As for Gaza, Sharett told me that it was ordered by Ben-Gurion upon his return to office and that he couldn't say what pretext Ben-Gurion had selected as providing the propitious moment for the raid.

Sharett's concept of reprisals was far more limited than Ben-Gurion's. Sharett admitted their role in deterring Arab infiltration but he did not endorse Ben-Gurion's larger concept of reprisals as a means to force the Arabs to sue for peace.

The first admission by the Israeli Government that it had a policy of reprisals at all came during a foreign policy debate in the Knesset that began on 30 August 1954. The official disclosure of the obvious fact that Israel was employing reprisals against infiltration followed a three-week re-evaluation of

Israeli foreign policy by Sharett and his top foreign ministry officials together with the Israeli ambassadors to Washington and London, Abba Eban and Eliahu Elath.

At the same time, according to leaks to the press from Government circles, the Government directed the Army to shift its attacks from Arab civilian villagers to Arab soldiers. Although Gaza was the first major raid on an Arab military installation, there had been skirmishes in the summer of 1954 that involved patrols and outposts rather than civilians. These were later listed among admitted reprisals.

The policy of reprisals against civilian villagers had been badly tarnished by the Qibya raid. Even such sympathetic newspapers as the *New York Post* and the *National Jewish Post* of Indianapolis were moved to compare it with Lidice.

Israeli commandos, their faces smeared with soot, occupied Qibya from 9:30 P.M. to 4:30 A.M. on the night of 14/15 October 1953. UN military observers reached the village two hours later. Their description, reported to the Security Council, read:

Bullet-riddled bodies near the doorways and multiple bullet hits on the doors of the demolished houses indicated that the inhabitants had been forced to remain inside until their homes were blown up over them. . . . Witnesses were uniform in describing their experience as a night of horror, during which Israeli soldiers moved about in their village blowing up buildings, firing into doorways and windows with automatic weapons and throwing hand grenades.

When the UN truce commission condemned Israel and demanded that Israel take "vigorous measures to prevent the recurrence of such aggression," the *Jerusalem Post* commented coldly that "it would be no cynicism to say that . . . Israel has in fact already taken the vigorous measures required. . . . It is a great pity, but it is an unhappy fact that when there is no law in high places, rough justice may come into its own." The newspaper's political correspondent wrote two days afterward that "while the Qibya incident is being exploited outside the Middle East for an anti-Israel campaign, the attack is apparently taken for what it is worth by the inhabitants of the border area."

The impenitent attitude of Ben-Gurion and his party press shocked many Israelis, just as the reports of the raid filled many of them with shame.

Sharett recorded in his diary at the time that Ben-Gurion had ordered the Qibya raid over his, Sharett's, opposition. In its aftermath it was he and Israel's diplomats who had to repair the national image, which the Defense Ministry's action had shattered along with the dwellings of Qibya. If the sixty-six persons slain had all been soldiers instead of village men, women, and children, the job would have been easier. And Israel's image was not the only Foreign Ministry concern damaged by the raid.

By a mischance of fate, the raid occurred almost at the very hour that President Eisenhower in Washington announced the mission of Eric Johnston as his personal ambassador to seek Arab-Israeli agreement on a unified Jordan Valley plan for irrigation, power, and development similar to the Tennessee Valley Authority. Israel had already begun her own project to divert the Jordan to the Negev through vast canals, tunnels, and pipelines, declaredly unaware of the American intentions. Major General Vagn Bennike of Denmark, General Burns's predecessor as UN truce chief, acting on the complaint of Arab states sharing the Jordan Valley, had ordered Israel to stop work on the Jordan diversion project. After Qibya the US forced Israel to suspend work by suspending US aid.

Israel nevertheless put on a bold front in the face of world disapproval and tried to use the impact of Qibya to bring Jordan into direct negotiations, a thing which all the Arab governments dogmatically avoided except through the UN truce commissions. Israel's brilliant Ambassador to the UN and US, Abba Eban, actually succeeded in having the demand appended to the Security Council's resolution of censure for Qibya. Secretary General Dag Hammarskjold, to the disquiet of the Arabs, worked hard to achieve high-level face-to-face talks between Israel and Jordan. But the effort ultimately proved to be one more example of the failure of reprisals to achieve any significant objective beyond the immediate killing of hapless Arabs.

The only possible justification for reprisals would be that they worked. For gradualists the aim was limited to deterring border incursions. For activists it encompassed larger political objectives. A third function was to satisfy Israeli public opinion in times of tension, whether the tension had to do with border incidents or more remote issues such as the fate of Israeli saboteurs in Egypt or, still more remote, the attitude of the Western Powers toward Israel's security.

There is no doubt, as Ben-Gurion well knew, that the third function was valid. I have myself been in Israel when border troubles charged the public temper with a kind of emotional electricity that made faces taut and set nerves on edge. The tension would grow until news of a reprisal raid released it in a current of jubilant satisfaction that spread immediately throughout the population.

But the first two aims, deterrence and peace on Israel's terms, were illserved by reprisals despite arguments to the contrary by their proponents. General Bennike reported back to the Security Council, at its request, on the border situation four months after Qibya. He said:

"Acts of violence, apparently committed in some cases by groups bent on retaliatory action, have . . . not only maintained tension along the Demarcation Line, but actually increased it."

Nonviolent infiltration, it is true, usually fell off when the two sides cooperated in police measures to curb it. It is also true that Arab authorities found it politically difficult to curb and punish infiltration and that Israeli reprisals occasionally served to persuade Arab governments that it might be politically more difficult not to do so. This was certainly true of Jordan while Glubb was there because reprisals made him a target for Arab resentment and for charges that British favor for Israel was behind any failure of the Arab Legion to repel Israeli raiders. Glubb went so far in "straining every nerve to prevent infiltration" as to order village National Guardsmen to shoot Arab infiltrators if necessary to stop them. Half the men in west Jordan prisons in 1954 were there for infiltration.

The Gaza situation was different. The people there were not linked by kinship and citizenship to the protecting country, Egypt. And the Gaza Strip was separated from the bulk of the Egyptian population by 120 miles of Sinai Desert. It is a cold fact that Egyptian public opinion was less affected by raids on the distant aliens in Gaza than Jordanian public opinion was by raids on west Jordanian villages that were once part of Palestine.

The killing of Egyptian troops in Gaza is naturally a more vital matter to Egyptians than the killing of Palestinians, just as American deaths in Vietnam are of more consequence to Americans than the deaths of our allies there. This difference may account in part for the difference in the Egyptian reactions to the al-Bureig raid in August 1953 and the Gaza Raid of February 1955, although to an outsider the toll of women and children at al-Bureig makes it the more outrageous of the two.

The worst single Arab reprisal committed in Israel was the ambush-massacre at noon on 17 March 1954 of eleven Israelis on a bus laboring up Scorpions' Pass in the eastern Negev. Efforts to identify the killers were overtaken and overshadowed by subsequent events but the incident provided a curious link between the Egyptian and Jordanian frontier situations. Following leads that began turning up the next day, UN, Jordanian, and Egyptian investigators determined after a month of cooperative detective work that the killers were members of the Azzazma tribe of Bedouins whom Israeli troops had driven, with casualties, into the Egyptian Sinai Desert from their traditional grazing and watering grounds southwest of Beersheba.

UN records show that more than 7,000 Bedouins were forced out of Israel in the first five years of the Armistices. The majority were rendered destitute when Israel sealed off their annual migration routes across the Negev, which

61

followed a seasonal grazing pattern. The killers of Scorpions' Pass belonged to the Bedouin Black Hand gang, formed for purposes of robbery and revenge after the Azzazma expulsion from Israel. It operated out of an encampment at Qussaima, seven miles southwest of the al-Auja demilitarized zone. General Bennike forwarded the results of the investigation, with the identities of the killers, to the Security Council. But by then Israel had retaliated against the Jordanian village of Nahhaleen and General Bennike's report went quietly into the files.

Israelis were shocked by the ruthlessness of the bus massacre and the public mood was such that Army and Government leaders evidently felt that a reprisal was a political imperative. Despite preliminary evidence to the contrary, Israeli army men insisted on Jordan's guilt and unleashed a propaganda barrage that UN truce officials characterized as both inflammatory and mendacious. When, after six days, the truce commission refused to incriminate Jordan for lack of evidence, the Israeli delegates stalked out with harrowing threats against the American chairman, Commander Elmo H. Hutchison. The boycott persisted until Hutchison was replaced seven months later at the end of his tour of duty. The day after the walkout Premier Sharett told the Knesset that "it was the patent truth that the perpetrators of the crime had come from Jordan. No amount of quibbling could cover it up."

Dag Hammarskjold responded to the threat to Hutchison and to Sharett's prejudgment by notifying Israel of his "full endorsement" of Hutchison and stressing "the vital importance of a most complete appraisal of any evidence which may be made available to the Mixed Armistice Commission on the basis of strict judicial standards." Dulles warned Israel the same day to avoid both inflammatory statements and reprisals.

Sharett's reaction was uncharacteristic. Perhaps, since the Army and the public were bent on having a reprisal, he decided to acquiesce in the Army's determination to hit Jordan rather than Egypt. World reaction to Qibya had left a residual desire in Israel to demonstrate that Qibya was not so unjustified as its critics claimed. Activist spokesmen harbored an old grudge against Nahhaleen, terming it a base for brigands as they said Qibya had been. Nahhaleen's inhabitants, according to Israeli rumor, helped wipe out the Jewish settlement of Kfar Etzion in the first Palestine War and also participated in a massacre of 35 Hebrew University students trapped in the Hebron hills.

Still, lack of evidence seems to have stayed the Army's hand until a watchman was killed at Kesalon in the Jerusalem corridor on 26 March. On the 28th Israeli night raiders struck at Nahhaleen, nine miles southwest of Jerusalem and nine miles southeast of Kesalon. Unlike Qibya, houses were not wholly demolished but doors were blown in to enable the raiders to toss in hand grenades and spray the interiors with submachine guns. Nine persons, including the village chief and a young father and mother of seven children, were killed and nineteen persons wounded in the raid.

Five days before the Nahhaleen reprisal the *Jerusalem Post*, in an editorial fulmination against the weakness of the UN and the unreliability of the Great Powers, wrote: "If a situation is not sufficiently serious, Mister Dulles cannot receive Ambassador Abba Eban: this is the way of the world and no amount of holy wrath and righteous indignation will change it. Only a more serious situation will." As noted above, Dulles did in fact see Eban on 25 March in an unsuccessful effort to prevent Israel from creating "a more serious situation."

On 1 May Assistant Secretary of State Henry A. Byroade, in a speech to the American Council for Judaism, the major anti-Zionist Jewish organization in the US, warned Israel: "The world will carefully watch for any indication of an adoption of a philosophy, known to be held by a few, that the only way to make things better is to first make them worse."

The *Jerusalem Post* editorial and Byroade's carefully considered comment were part of a dialogue that began with the advent of the Eisenhower administration in 1953. The US opened with an effort to move from Truman's avowed pro-Zionism toward impartiality and even-handed friendship as regards both Israel and the Arabs. Israel's response was best described by Abba Eban more than a decade later:

It gave the Israeli public the impression that American friendship for Israel had been a fleeting and accidental circumstance of history, linked organically with the Truman administration.... Therefore a greater policy of militance should develop in Israel for two reasons: both as a compensation for American friendship and, perhaps, as a way of forcing the US to recoil from any change adverse to Israel.... The response in Israel was one toward greater self-reliance, a very active policy of retaliation on the frontiers.

Israeli militancy, in turn, fed its own stimulus by further antagonizing the Great Powers, particularly the US and Britain. Later in 1954 France replaced the US as Israel's chief patron among the Great Powers. Qibya seemed to have prompted Washington to take a harder line against Israel's unilateral diversion of the Jordan River. Nahhaleen brought a warning from Britain that Israel would have to fight both Britain and Jordan, allied under a 1948 treaty, if she tried to seize any Jordanian territory. Byroade, speaking *ex cathedra* for the State Department, told Israel bluntly after Nahhaleen to "drop the attitude of the conqueror and the conviction that force and a policy of retaliatory killings are the only policy your neighbors will understand." He added: "Make your deeds correspond to your frequent utterances of the desire for peace."

These scoldings did not worry Israel so much as tangible developments of policy, such as the progress Egypt and Britain were making toward an agreement on Britain's final evacuation of her vast military base on the Suez Canal, and the Anglo-American moves to furnish arms to the Arabs. The arms were offered as inducements in connection with both the Anglo-Egyptian Suez evacuation treaty and the proposals for a Middle East Defense pact, whose Arab members would certainly insist on excluding Israel.

Dulles noted some of the Israeli fears in a secret memorandum on his trip to the Middle East in May 1953. The Israelis were "jittery," he wrote, because of uncertainty over the intentions of the new Eisenhower administration, fearing it might try to impose a peace settlement involving a reduction in the territory Israel had controlled since the Palestine war. The Israelis were also worried that the US might proceed with water-development schemes that would conflict with their plans to bring Jordan River water to the Negev.

Ben-Gurion told Dulles that he saw nothing inconsistent with Israel's interests in Dulles's effort to recover Arab-American friendship. Dulles recorded that Ben-Gurion seemed inclined to relax his "total-peace-or-nothing" attitude in favor of a policy of seeking ultimate peace through a step-by-step reduction of tensions.

Presumably Dulles, who had just spent two days in Egypt, passed on to Ben-Gurion the pacific intentions of the ten-month-old revolutionary regime in Egypt, still a closely knit junta under Nasser and Naguib. Dulles recorded in his summary of the trip's important points: "Naguib feels moving forward on arrangement with Israel not too difficult once he solves his problems with the British.... He will insist on corridor arrangement linking Egypt with other Arab states."

"David Courtney" (Roy Elston) of the *Jerusalem Post* expressed Israel's persistent anxieties on 15 May 1953, the morrow of Dulles's departure:

...from all accounts [Dulles] has made no attempt to lay his hands on Israel's rights, in order to carry some part of them to this country's neighbors.... The Secretary of State remains for most of us the stranger he was before he came. But he did not seize Haifa or cut away Elath or hold open the Mandelbaum Gate to the influx of the Arab refugees...

The anxieties seemed justified when Dulles, in his broadcast on the trip on 1 June, said peace "will require concessions on the part of both sides." Israel immediately asked for clarification but what was forthcoming was not clear enough to end anxiety.

The al-Bureig and Qibya reprisals in August and October showed that Ben-

Gurion no longer inclined toward gradualism. Activism was also manifest in the Jordan River diversion project, where construction began 2 September 1953 on a round-the-clock work schedule in order to forestall the US effort to bring about joint Arab-Israeli development of the hallowed river.

As noted previously, Ben-Gurion's retirement in November 1953 did not mean a wholehearted experiment in gradualism under Sharett. Ben-Gurion preferred Levi Eshkol to Sharett as Premier and tried hard to persuade the Mapai to nominate him, but the party insisted on giving gradualism a try under Sharett. Ben-Gurion nevertheless succeeded in having his personal nominee, Pinhas Lavon, take over the Defense Ministry in his absence. Another Ben-Gurion man, Shimon Peres, remained as Director General of the Defense Ministry, ensuring "the Old Man's" control of the political and civilian side of the ministry. Continuation of Ben-Gurion's dominance in the ministry was completed and consolidated by the appointment of the thirty-eight-year-old Major General Moshe Dayan as Chief of Staff in December 1953. Dayan was personally devoted to Ben-Gurion. Identity of viewpoint, mutual trust, and deep affection were the ties of a relationship that remains close and unbroken, in office or out, regardless of the vicissitudes of politics.

Thus Ben-Gurion was able, in effect, to conduct policies of his own when he felt that Sharett was proving ineffectual against the Arabs, the Great Powers, or the UN.

The United Nations and its Truce Supervision Organization (UNTSO) in the Middle East constitute a factor so central to the whole history of the Palestine problem that the reader should have a clear idea of UNTSO's role and place in events.

International endorsement of a Jewish State in Israel was expressed by the UN General Assembly in the Partition Resolution of 29 November 1947. The Arabs contested the right of the UN to establish a separate state in Palestine for the Jewish minority, then numbering one-third of Palestine's total population of 1,800,000. After failing to abort Israel by diplomacy, they went to war against implementation of the Partition Resolution. Because the Great Powers were in agreement at that time on handling the Palestine problem through the UN, the Security Council was given the task of restoring peace.

The Truce Supervision Organization evolved out of the Security Council resolutions passed in response to the on-again off-again fighting in 1948. It kept its name although the truces became formal armistices in the first half of 1949. The position of Chief of Staff was created in 1948 when the Truce Supervision Organization was made responsible to the UN Mediator, Count Folke Bernadotte of Sweden. Bernadotte's Chief of Staff, the Swedish General Aage Lundstrom, was ordered to withdraw when Israeli terrorists assassinated Bernadotte on 17 September 1948, the day after he recommended allotting the Negev to the Arabs. Brigadier General William E. Riley of the US Marine Corps was then appointed Chief of Staff. The title has remained unchanged although the UNTSO became a full-fledged subsidiary organ of the UN in August 1949 and its chief became, in effect, a commanding officer rather than a chief of staff.

Riley remained as Chief of Staff of UNTSO until 1953. He favored Israel in his handling of armistice disputes, a judgment on which both Israelis and Arabs concur whatever they think Riley's motives may have been. His successor, General Bennike of Denmark, by contrast, soon won the antipathy of Israel as the reprisal policy led her into deliberate collision with the Truce Supervision Organization. General Burns, the third head of UNTSO, took over on 2 September 1954. Despite increasingly overt Israeli defiance of UNTSO, culminating in the Suez-Sinai war, General Burns succeeded in maintaining a reputation for impartiality with both sides.

Subordinate to UNTSO are four Mixed Armistice Commissions (MACs). They were established by the Armistice Agreements signed in the first seven months of 1949 on the Greek island of Rhodes. The armistices were concluded separately between Israel and each of the belligerent Arab states except Iraq in negotiations assisted by Dr. Ralph Bunche of the United States, who was appointed Acting Mediator by the UN after Bernadotte's assassination.

The first to be ratified was the armistice with Egypt, signed 24 February 1949 after six weeks of negotiations. It set the pattern for further Armistice Agreements between Israel and the three other Arab states on her immediate frontiers, Lebanon, Jordan, and Syria.

By August 1949, when UNTSO was made directly responsible to the UN Secretary General, and until 1967, each international segment of the armistice demarcation lines around Israel had its own Mixed Armistice Commission. Following the frontier clockwise from the Mediterranean shore, there was a Lebanese-Israeli MAC, a Syrian-Israeli MAC, a Jordanian-Israeli MAC, and an Egyptian-Israeli MAC. The chairman of each was a senior military observer attached to UNTSO and appointed by the Chief of Staff after consultation with the parties to the Armistice Agreement. Each mixed commission included an Israeli delegation and an Arab delegation. The chairman's vote was decisive in assessing blame for an incident because the Israeli and Arab delegates were almost invariably paired for and against every censure vote. The Chief of Staff himself could take the chair of any of the Mixed Armistice Commissions, although this seldom happened.

UNTSO's headquarters and communications center were in Government House, the fortress-like seat of the departed British Mandatory government. Built of the tawny stone of Judea, it broods over the domes and turrets of

Jerusalem from an adjacent mountain top. Until the 1967 war it was insulated from both Jordan and Israel by a broad stretch of the trucial No Man's Land, wherein anyone who strayed was fair game for the touchy sharpshooters of either side. The mountain beneath it is called the Mountain of Graves by the Arabs and the Hill of Evil Counsel by the Israelis.

Until Israel repudiated the Armistices—that with Egypt in 1956 and those with Jordan and Syria in 1967—the MAC's met in neutral shelters along the several borders. The Egyptian-Israeli MAC met in a shack of wood and corrugated iron on the truce line east of Gaza at a location called Kilo 95, 95 kilometers from Jerusalem on the road to Cairo. The road was barred by antitank dragon's teeth and the shack was marked by the bullets of more than one incident. The Jordanians met the Israelis in a fine stone house, ruined and abandoned in the 1948 fighting, in the narrow stretch of No Man's Land at Jerusalem's Mandelbaum Gate, the only place on all the frontiers where diplomats, pilgrims, and tourists could cross, under strict controls, between Israeli and Arab territory. The Syrian-Israeli MAC met in a stucco farmhouse with a red tile roof overlooking the Bridge of Jacob's Daughters on the Jordan River north of the Sea of Galilee. The Lebanese-Israeli MAC rarely had much to do and when it did it met in the old Palestine Frontier posts at Metulla in the east and Ras Naqura in the west.

This then was the organization—UNTSO and its four ancillary MACs—responsible for maintaining and repairing the Armistices, which were explicitly designed as steps toward formal Arab-Israeli peace treaties. When no further progress toward peace treaties occurred, the armistice machinery began to suffer breakdowns, having been designed for a short run rather than a long one. Antagonisms hardened. The spirit of conciliation evaporated. On 1 April 1950 the Arab League resolved unanimously that no member state could negotiate or conclude a separate peace treaty or any other political, military, or economic agreement with Israel on pain of expulsion, ostracism, and sanctions.

Arab-Israeli relations settled into a state of warfare by means short of war. In the MACs, both sides often ignored the practical object of trying to keep the border tranquil. "Delegates were apt to wrangle like shyster lawyers," General Burns wrote, "with the object of securing a condemnation of the other party in the strongest terms for subsequent political and propaganda use."

The reason for this indecisive condition is that the Great Powers, acting through the UN, prevented the Arab-Israeli war from reaching the usual conclusion of wars. Wars end in peace in the following circumstances: after one side has defeated its opponent, occupied his territory, and imposed a government ready to make peace; or when the prospective loser and the prospective victor both decide that continued fighting will be more unprofitable than agreement on terms favoring the prospective victor. The three rounds of the Arab-Israeli war to date, in 1948, in 1956, and in 1967, were stopped by the Great Powers, acting through the UN, short of a complete military decision. The UN cannot oblige the parties to make peace.

Warfare by means short of war continued after all three rounds. Between the rounds, the MACs did the day-to-day work of investigating incidents and accusations of truce violations. These ranged from stone-throwing, sheep-stealing, and aerial overflights to artillery and mortar shelling, murder, and organized attacks. So overloaded did the MAC dockets become that by tacit consent only complaints accompanied by requests for emergency meetings were investigated and acted upon. Even the emergency dockets often had large backlogs, which required that extra priority be given to incidents resulting in dangerous situations.

Although the MACs assessed blame by the vote of their UN chairmen in most cases, keeping score was avoided because of the assumption that the most injured side might feel justified in attempting to even it up. However, records were kept and figures were added up from time to time in an effort to find a pattern that might help show the causes, and thus indicate a cure for serious incidents.

The usual pattern was that in which Israeli troops or, rarely, posses of irate settlers struck in an organized assault against an Arab village or military position following a period of individual incursions into Israel. It was politically difficult for Arab authorities to punish marauders who, in the eyes of the Arab public, were merely stealing their own back from those who had robbed them. Arab police forces and frontier guards were inadequate to apprehend more than a fraction of the infiltrators. When Arabs clashed with Israeli police, casualties were heavier among the infiltrators. Israeli civilian casualties naturally tended to provoke reprisal raids more quickly than mere thieving, especially when they resulted from deliberate murder. Then, agitation in Israel would increase rapidly for several days until news of a reprisal raid brought a relaxation of public emotion.

Thus the basic pattern of violence along the frontiers was one of recurrent forays by individuals or small groups of individuals from the Arab side and, from the Israeli side, punitive attacks by military units aimed at deterring individual Arab marauders or forcing their governments to deter them by inflicting casualties and damage sufficient to provide a warning example of the consequences of marauding.

Although the death toll ran five to one against the Arabs on all four frontiers, reprisals seemed no more successful in discouraging individual Arabs from marauding than hanging deterred pickpockets in 18th-century England, who boldly plied their trade in the crowds that came to watch the executions of their confreres at Tyburn Oak.

The pattern of border violence influenced the relations of each side with UNTSO. Until Nasser organized reprisal squads of his own after the Gaza Raid, Arab governments always disclaimed responsibility for marauding. UN military observers never discerned any link between the marauders and the Arab governments. Consequently they were obliged to accept the disclaimers while urging the Arab governments to intensify police efforts against marauders, no matter how difficult this was politically.

Conversely, although Israelis also disclaimed responsibility for reprisal raids up to and including Gaza, UNTSO never believed the disclaimers because the military observers always found massive circumstantial evidence, such as army equipment and ammunition, of official endorsement of the raids. Thus Israel's frontier violations represented official defiance of UNTSO while Arab violations were carried out in apparent defiance, not of UNTSO, but of Arab governments that supported UNTSO.

General Burns attributed part of the Israeli Army's aggressiveness to the personality of its Chief of Staff, General Dayan. "With such a man at its head," Burns wrote, "offensive spirit was rife in the Israeli Army. The emphasis was on maintaining moral ascendancy over the Arab enemy. Every act of violence had to be repaid—with heavy interest. The result, it must be admitted, was that the Israeli Defense Forces were a very fine fighting organization, but one which was always looking for trouble, from the viewpoint of the UNTSO."

Israel regarded UNTSO as a barrier to the direct confrontation, either at the conference table or on the battlefield, which Israel was always seeking and the Arabs were always avoiding. UNTSO prevented Israel from bringing to bear on the refractory Arabs her chief bargaining asset, which was her superior armed strength.

In February 1955, when activists resumed control of Israel's policy, they did so with the conviction that UNTSO had outlived its usefulness as far as Israel was concerned. Its chief function seemed to them to be to protect the Arabs from the consequences of their nibbling belligerency in the "technical state of war" they claimed under their interpretation of the Armistices.

Unfortunately for the gradualists, Israel's relations with UNTSO were channeled through the Army, with the Foreign Ministry playing a secondary role both in framing policy toward UNTSO and in actual contacts with it. As a result, Israel's desire to bypass UNTSO in order to deal directly with the Arabs sometimes led to inventive efforts to cripple UNTSO and MAC functions. One of these functions, for example, was to provide a channel for essential communications across the gap of Arab nonrecognition of Israel. On several occasions, for periods of weeks and months, Israel blocked the channel by boy-cotting one or another of the MACs in the hope that the very essentiality and urgency of some communications would induce the Arab government in question to contact Israel through third-country consuls or any other non-UN channel. To no avail.

The only sanction enabling UNTSO to preserve both itself and the Armistices against an Israel that was chafing under them was the assumption of ultimate support from the three Great Powers of the West: Britain, France, and the United States. Any Israeli move to destroy the armistice system in order to visit the consequences of real war on the Arab governments shielded by it, it was presumed, would be reversed and punished by the Big Three, by force if need be. The three Western Powers had made their determination explicit in the Tripartite Declaration of 25 May 1950, in which they stated their unalterable opposition to the use or threat of force by the Middle Eastern states and their intention to act immediately, within and outside the UN, to prevent any violation of the armistice lines.

In effect, if Israeli military power was holding the Arabs to an armistice system, the military power of the Big Three was forcing Israel to observe it. All the while both sides engaged in as much warfare as they were able to get away with: the Arabs chiefly by blockades and the boycott, to which neither the Armistice Agreements nor the Tripartite Declaration make any reference; the Israelis by means of raids from which the raiders usually returned to base before news of the raid reached the outside world and long before either the UN or the Big Three could intervene.

Except for the Egyptian *Fedayeen* operations from August 1955 until the Suez War, the Arabs violated the spirit of the Armistice Agreements while Israel violated the letter. But despite her irritation with and contempt for the Armistice Agreements, Israel did not denounce any of them until the early hours of her assault in Sinai in October 1956, when Ben-Gurion declared the Egyptian-Israeli Armistice Agreement to be null and void. Until her "second round" against Egypt, Israel's official view of the Armistice Agreements was that she would observe them provided the Arabs did—always reserving the right of reprisal.

When Ben-Gurion withdrew into the Negev in December 1953, the month after his resignation, two international developments that were causing Israel intense anxiety seemed to have fallen into abeyance. The Anglo-Egyptian negotiations on British evacuation of the Suez Canal Base had been deadlocked since October. And the joint Western and Turkish effort to bring the Arabs into a defense pact armed by the West had been declared by Dulles in June to be "a future rather than an immediate possibility."

Early in 1954 the two issues revived. In January authoritative reports were published that the US was negotiating an agreement to supply arms to Iraq, the only Arab belligerent of 1948 that had never signed an armistice with Israel. Baghdad announced the agreement on 25 April. In February Turkey and Pakistan announced preliminary steps toward what eventually became the Baghdad Pact. Early in March the Premier of the newly restored civilian regime in Syria expressed his government's willingness to go along with such a pact. It was a remarkable departure—and a brief one—from Syria's stubborn resistance to any kind of aid or alliance agreement with the West.

Intense diplomatic activity in February and March presaged a resumption of the Anglo-Egyptian Suez evacuation talks. They were in fact resumed in Cairo in July, and on the 27th of that month the British and Egyptians reached and published their formal *Heads of Agreement* on all the major points that were embodied in the final Suez evacuation treaty signed on 19 October.

Since both the Suez agreement and the formation of a Middle East defense pact with Arab members would satisfy Western conditions for supplying arms to Arab governments, Israel saw both developments as tilting the balance of power dangerously against herself. Sharett began warning the West in March 1954 against arming the Arabs. In July he called the Anglo-Egyptian *Heads of Agreement* on the Suez base evacuation a "most important change in the balance of power" and in August he complained that it had been drafted as if Israel did not exist.

A third disturbing trend appeared in April and May, after the Nahhaleen reprisal had revived Western criticism of Israel. US Assistant Secretary of State Byroade told Israel in carefully considered policy speeches on 9 April and 1 May that she should, in effect, de-Zionize herself and abandon the policy of unlimited Jewish immigration that had been from the very beginning the chief cause of Arab hostility.

After noting the pressure of "special groups" and declaring that there was no place in American thinking for either a pro-Israel or a pro-Arab policy, Byroade recommended to the disputants:

To the Israelis I say that you should come to truly look upon yourselves as a Middle Eastern State and see your own future in that context rather than as a headquarters, or nucleus so to speak, of world-wide groupings of peoples of a particular religious faith who must have special rights within and obligations to the Israeli State.

Byroade added his warning to Israel to "drop the attitude of the conqueror" and then turned to the other side: "To the Arabs I say you should accept this

State of Israel as an accomplished fact." He warned the Arabs against the "dangerous policy" of "deliberately attempting to maintain a state of affairs delicately suspended between peace and war."

On 1 May he stated as "the first fundamental" of the Palestine problem that "the possibility of an early and formal peace-treaty type of settlement between Israel and the Arab States just does not exist." He elaborated his advice to Israel to break with the Zionist dogma of total Jewish immigration, saying the Arabs

should have the right to know, with far greater assurances than have ever been given them, the magnitude of this new State.... Their fears are enhanced by the knowledge that the only limitation imposed by statute on immigration into Israel is, in fact, the total number of those of the Jewish faith in the entire world.... They see only one result—future attempt at territorial expansion—and hence warfare of serious proportions.

He observed pointedly that Israel was using German reparations "while doing nothing toward compensation of Arab refugees."

Israel and American Zionists reacted in fear and anger against what seemed to them an assault on the vital and sacred purpose of Israel and Zionism. There were flickerings of an ugly whispering campaign that Byroade was an anti-Semite, a tactic to stifle criticism of Zionism and Israel initiated by Ben-Gurion in 1943. In July Israel and the World Zionist Organization retorted to Byroade by adopting a charter, signed by Premier Sharett and two WZO officers, giving the Zionists special status in Israel with prescribed duties and privileges. The chairman of the Zionist organization was accorded an official rank beside Israeli cabinet members and the members of the Zionist executive were ranked with members of the Knesset.

Israelis felt their sovereignty threatened by a Big Three memorandum delivered on 19 July proposing a great increase in the authority, powers, size, and independence of the Mixed Armistice Commissions. The Israeli Defense Ministry saw this as tantamount to making the MACs into Security Council custodians of Israel's frontier defense policies. The memorandum was rejected, Dayan said later, on the grounds that it "would have strengthened the authority of the UN at the expense of Israel's sovereignty." Solutions were not to be found through the offices of a third party, Israel insisted, be it the UN or a foreign power, but only through direct confrontation of Israel and the Arabs.

Paradoxically, the Mapai platform at the time declared its foreign policy to be "based on the strengthening of the political and moral authority of the United Nations Organization."

The Soviet Union's new espousal of the Arab cause in 1954 was a fourth source of anxiety for Israel, although at the same time the Kremlin abandoned the anti-Semitism of Stalin's last days and restored full diplomatic representation. Russia had broken off relations following an explosion in the Soviet Legation in Tel Aviv in February 1953, a month before Stalin's death.

Andrei Y. Vyshinsky, Soviet delegate to the UN, once supported Israel's position on many issues, including right of passage through the Suez Canal and direct negotiations with the Arabs. In the spring of 1954 he supported the Arab cause in the Security Council so vigorously that he won an unprecedented vote of thanks from the Parliament of Jordan, although the country still had no diplomatic relations with Russia.

Sharett took Russia to task in the Knesset foreign policy debate on 1 September for courting Israel's enemies with the veto. In keeping with Mapai's policy of "nonidentification with any bloc," he added that Israel would welcome Russian friendship in addition to, but not instead of, American friendship.

While Sharett and the Foreign Ministry made protests, the Ben-Gurion stalwarts in the Defense Ministry planned in May and acted in July. The Intelligence Department ordered its ring of agents in Egypt, headed since 1951 by Colonel Avraham Dar of Yemenite Jewish origin, to sabotage American and British cultural centers, British-owned movie theaters, and Egyptian post offices. The intention was to wreck the Anglo-American rapprochement with the Egyptians by creating the impression that violent elements opposed the rapprochement and that the two-year-old Nasser-Naguib regime was too weak and inefficient to control them.

The fanatical Moslem Brotherhood was at that time openly opposing any concessions to Britain in the Suez base evacuation talks. And the world had not forgotten Black Saturday, 28 January 1952, in the last year of King Farouk's reign, when mobs burned foreign-owned hotels and shops in downtown Cairo in an orgy of violence that cost scores of lives including those of thirteen Britons. Mysterious violence in the summer of 1954 might persuade both Washington and London that British troops should remain astride the canal.

It was an amateurish and abortive campaign that did not outlast the month of July 1954. The first fire bomb went off in the Alexandria post office on 2 July. Nine days later the Anglo-Egyptian Suez negotiations resumed after a nine-month deadlock, Britain released £10 million ($28 million) of blocked Egyptian sterling and Egypt removed nearly all restrictions on sterling imports.

On 12 July the Israeli embassy in London got an assurance from the Foreign Office that the British evacuation of the Suez base would not result in the stores of arms there being handed over to Egypt. But the Israeli Defense Ministry activists remained unconvinced. Their agents in Egypt, in clandestine radio contact with Tel Aviv, severely damaged United States Information Service libraries in Cairo and Alexandria on 14 July with fire bombs. On that same day the failure of the "security operation," as it was called in Israel, was ensured when a 21-year-old agent named Philip Natanson was nearly burned alive in front of the Rio Cinema in Alexandria as a result of premature ignition of a phosphorus bomb he was carrying in a spectacles case. His arrest and subsequent confession enabled the Egyptian police to crack the ring.

But not until the sabotage campaign had progressed through several more alternations of clandestine action and diplomatic failure. On 15 July President Eisenhower wrote President Naguib that "simultaneously" with the signing of a Suez agreement the US would enter into "firm commitments" for economic aid to strengthen Egypt's armed forces. On 23 July the Israeli agents still at large had a final fling at arson in the Cairo central post office and two movie theaters. London announced that same day that War Secretary Antony Head was going to Cairo. On the 27th, Head and the Egyptians initialed the *Heads of Agreement* on the terms of Britain's evacuation.

The "security operation" in the Israeli Intelligence Department had failed disastrously on all counts but the episode remained obscure until October. In the interval, apparently unaware of the activists' sabotage effort to spike the Suez evacuation agreement, Sharett made a dramatic bid to have safeguards and benefits for Israel written into the final evacuation treaty that was being drafted in detail on the basis of the *Heads of Agreement*. He tried to send an Israeli ship, the *Bat Galim*, through the Suez Canal for the first time since Egypt had imposed blockade regulations in May 1948.

The *Bat Galim* was a small freighter of Israeli registry with a crew of ten. It presented itself at the southern end of the canal on 28 September 1954, the same day that British Minister of State Anthony Nutting arrived in Cairo to participate in drafting the final evacuation treaty. Dayan wrote later that the *Bat Galim* incident was a diplomatic attempt "to break . . . the natural stranglehold," done "in the knowledge that the Egyptians would not allow her to pass, but with the aim of bringing the matter to the Security Council." Israel's hope was to make Britain insist that Egypt end the blockade as part of the final agreement on British evacuation of the Suez Canal base. Instead, Dayan wrote bitterly, "only the weakness of Israel and the readiness of the UN institutions to swallow affronts to Israel were demonstrated."

The Egyptians seized the *Bat Galim* outside the canal on a charge that the Israelis, while waiting to enter the canal, had shot and killed two crew members of an Egyptian fishing boat. This diversionary maneuver was later dropped in lengthy MAC and UN proceedings but the Egyptians held to their refusal to let the ship through. They offered instead to deliver the cargo overland and to allow the ship to go to Israel around the Cape of Good Hope. Israel refused both offers. The captain and crew were released on the truce line near Gaza on 1 January 1955 but not the ship. The Egyptians maintained that the armistice had not ended the state of war and that the Constantinople Convention of 1888 obliged Egypt to protect the canal from possible sabotage by barring ships under enemy flags. A Security Council debate on the case ended inconclusively on 13 January 1955.

The activists too had launched a new effort after the failure of the Cairo saboteurs, although it had been planned earlier. Dayan and Peres, with Ben-Gurion's blessing and quite independently of the Foreign Ministry, initiated an unorthodox unwritten alliance against Nasser between the French and Israeli Defense Ministries. It was soon to make France replace Britain and the US as Israel's main source of armaments.

In Paris on 31 July 1954, four days after the *Heads of Agreement* on Suez were signed in Cairo, Shimon Peres telephoned the French Defense Minister, General of the Army Marie-Pierre Koenig. Koenig received him the next day, Sunday, and Peres gave him a list of arms he wanted for Israel. Dayan arrived a week later after a disappointing visit to the US. Within five days agreements were reached under which France began secret arms shipments to Israel in the fall. The arms included Ouragan jet fighter planes, which were better than anything the Arabs had at that time.

Israel's guardians could breathe easier despite Eisenhower's promise to help strengthen Egypt's army and Britain's lifting of its arms embargo as rewards for the Suez agreement.

The Defense Ministry's new mood of quiet confidence was reflected in the lack of tension along the borders, where the main activity, aside from the never-ending gathering of intelligence, was at al-Auja. On 6 October an Israeli deserter drove a water truck across the frontier and surrendered to the Egyptians. Questioned in the presence of a UN observer, he said he was a private in an Israeli Army unit which constituted the "settlers" in the zone. Commanded by a captain, the unit had 4 noncommissioned officers, 65 men and 15 women soldiers, and the usual armament of an infantry company. Egypt won a debater's point on the deserter's evidence but limited her reaction to official complaints.

By coincidence, it was the same day that Ambassador Eban at the UN proposed an Arab-Israeli nonaggression pact as a step toward peace.

Although the border was quiet, General Burns reports, by mid-November "there had been a good deal in the Israel press to the effect that the infiltration and the resultant crimes were getting worse, and that if they continued Israel could not remain passive.... The facts did not indicate that the frequency and severity of the incidents really amounted to a critical situation." On the advice of old trucial hands, however, Burns drew up proposals for joint action to prevent border crossings. Israel rejected them in January on the grounds that Egypt alone was responsible for stopping infiltration.

Tranquillity, relative tranquillity that is, continued. On 8 February Burns made a speech on the danger and futility of reprisals at the Rotary Club in Haifa. "At that time I felt that the Israel Government was turning away from the retaliation policy," he recalled. "The Gaza raid, twenty days later, showed how mistaken I was."

By that time the Israeli censors had long since approved Moshe Brilliant's authoritative exposition of the Ben-Gurion-Dayan faction's reprisal policy and it was on the verge of delivery to *Harper's* subscribers and news dealers. More relevant still, the failure of the Cairo sabotage operation had already led to the removal of Pinhas Lavon from the Defense Ministry on 2 February, although his resignation was still secret, thus setting the stage for the return of Ben-Gurion.

Nasser disclosed the breakup of the Israeli sabotage ring to me in an interview on 19 August 1954. Interior Minister Zakaria Mohyeddin gave a detailed description of its activities at a press conference on 5 October. Its equipment included secret transmitters, invisible ink, codes, microfilming cameras, darkrooms, incendiary chemicals, and explosives. The thirteen members of the ring included a core of professionals like Colonel Dar, who escaped and eventually settled in a kibbutz, and Max Bennett, of Hungarian origin, whom Mohyeddin described as a former career spy in Germany. In Cairo, where he was employed by Anglo-Egyptian Motors, Ltd., Bennett was an affluent man-about-town. His Chevrolet, imported from France, was equipped with three secret transmitters. He hanged himself in his prison cell during the trial, which lasted from 11 December 1954 to 5 January 1955.

Some of the spy-saboteurs were trained in France, Mohyeddin said, others in Israel. Some of the members were Egyptian Jews coerced into joining the ring. Some held foreign passports. Among these was Dr. Moussa Lieto Marzouk, a twenty-eight-year-old surgeon at the Jewish Hospital in Cairo, a Tunisian-born citizen of France who, according to Mohyeddin, received his intelligence training in Haifa. Marzouk and Samuel Azar, a twenty-six-year-old Alexandria engineering professor, were convicted and condemned by a military tribunal. Despite representations from France, Britain, and the US State Department, the two men were hanged in the Cairo prison on Monday morning, 31 January 1955.

The guilt of the executed men and six others sentenced to long prison terms was not protested so much as the severity of the sentences. The reaction of Israelis and Jewish groups in the West was charged with grief and anger. Marzouk and Azar "died the death of martyrs," said Sharett on the same day to the Knesset, whose members stood in silent tribute. Israel went into unofficial mourning the following day. Beersheba and Ramat Gan announced the naming of streets after the executed men. Israeli delegates to the Egyptian-Israeli MAC refused to attend its meeting, saying they could not sit with representatives of the Cairo junta. In New York there were bomb threats against the Egyptian consulate at 900 Park Avenue and at midday on 5 February a sniper fired four shots into its fourth floor windows. Israel remembered the imprisoned as well as the condemned. After the 1967 Suez War she held 4,481 Egyptian prisoners for seven months in the hope of obtaining the release of the Lavon Affair convicts as part of the prisoner-of-war exchange.

Sharett told me later that Nasser had "half promised" him, through the intermediation of an Anglo-Jewish Member of Parliament, that there would be no executions. This must have been a misunderstanding at best, prompted by wishful thinking. There was no inducement for Nasser to give such an assurance, least of all to Israel, and there were many political deterrents to clemency.

In Sharett's own interpretation before the Knesset, Marzouk and Azar were made scapegoats to offset public reaction in Egypt to the hanging on 7 December of the six Moslem Brethren condemned for complicity in the attempt on Nasser's life. Could Zionist spies be spared after devout Moslem terrorists had been hanged? Sharett noted with equal perceptiveness that the sentencing and execution of the spies occurred during an emergency conclave of Arab premiers in Cairo trying to prevent the impending Egyptian-Iraqi rift over the Baghdad Pact. It is noteworthy that Sharett publicly recognized the fearsome political pressures on Nasser even as he denounced the executions.

The story persists that Nasser broke his word in allowing the death sentences to be carried out, that the defendants were maltreated, and that the trial was unfair. Roger N. Baldwin, a New York lawyer specializing in civil liberties cases and Chairman of the International League for the Rights of Man, was sent to Cairo in January 1955 by private Americans with official Israeli backing to try to prevent death penalties and to investigate the human rights aspects of the trial.

In his published account of the mission, Baldwin wrote:

The trial appeared to have been fairly conducted. Press coverage was adequate, and the public had been admitted. Charges had been made to me that confessions were extorted and that brutalities had been practiced on the defendants. These

77

could not be substantiated by the records or by persons close to the defendants, with whom I talked. . . . The defendants' chief counsel, Dr. A. Rouchdy, was considered one of the ablest lawyers in Cairo and he made no complaint to me about any abuse of the lawyer's right to consult with client.

Baldwin conferred with Nasser for nearly thirty minutes on 15 January. "I cannot say I got any assurances," Baldwin wrote me later, "but he indicated that personally he appreciated my point [regarding] unfavorable world reaction to death verdicts for political purposes. In the course of our half-hour talk he emphasized the fact that he was one of eleven in the Revolutionary Command Council and that his views were personal. The Council had recently approved death sentences for members of the Moslem Brotherhood. . . . It was a difficult case for clemency because it was so political."

Baldwin said the other intermediaries, the British MP and a French lawyer, fared no better in getting assurances of anything other than Nasser's personal dislike of death penalties, which had been repeatedly manifested ever since he prevailed on the Revolutionary Command Council to spare King Farouk. Nasser had been overridden by the RCC on several occasions and presumably it happened once more in regard to the Zionist saboteurs.

Baldwin's published report said the announcement of the death sentences, after he left Egypt, prompted him to cable Nasser for clemency, saying "all assurances given me recently in Egypt expressed moderation and humanity of your regime." He called the executions, carried out three days later, "a shocking reversal." However, he acknowledged the political circumstances and said his main concern was with the political effects, including Israeli treatment of captured infiltrators. Israel had already been accused by Egypt of unjustly sentencing some Palestinian Arab students to five-year prison terms as spies in order to create a bargaining counter for the release of the Egyptian-held saboteurs.

The executions brought the originating episode of the Lavon Affair to its sorry end. Lavon quietly resigned on 2 February, when unwitting disclosure of his removal could no longer affect the fate of Marzouk and Azar. The resignation was kept secret until 17 February, when it was announced that Ben-Gurion would return to take Lavon's place as Defense Minister.

The other career victim of the abortive "security operation" was Colonel Benyamin Givli, head of Intelligence, and so ardent a supporter of Ben-Gurion that he was known as "Little B-G." He was replaced as head of Intelligence by Yehoshafat ("Faty") Harkavi a short while after Lavon's ouster. Ben-Gurion's favor saved Givli from suffering severe consequences, although he was directly in charge of the "security operation." Givli was appointed commander of the Northern Command and served with distinction in the 1956 Sinai invasion. Eventually he resigned from the Army in honorable circumstances and became an industrial executive.

The lucky, likable Colonel Dar stayed on in the Army for several years after making good his escape from Egypt. He returned there briefly during the Sinai invasion.

The Lavon Affair is still kept under wraps of military censorship by Israel, but the story is well known to the public. In December 1954, when the Cairo trial disclosed details of the July "security operation," Sharett ordered a secret inquiry into the matter at Lavon's request. Until the Cairo disclosures, no member of the Israeli cabinet knew about the adventure. Givli submitted papers indicating that Lavon had ordered it. Dayan and Peres also gave evidence against their minister. Lavon, who had been increasingly at odds with the Ben-Gurion salwarts under him, chiefly Dayan and Peres, denounced Givli's papers as forgeries. He demanded the resignations of Dayan, Peres, and Givli. Sharett insisted that Lavon resign instead. He told me later that the Cairo operation was "a very irresponsible thing to do" and that "no matter whether Lavon gave the orders or not, he was Defense Minister and therefore had ministerial responsibility for the 'security operation.' "

Lavon was appointed Secretary General of Histadrut, a powerful position from which he struck back at Ben-Gurion after a 1960 court martial accidentally brought to light evidence of forgeries against him. The Lavon Affair exploded into public. Lavon alleged that Ben-Gurion himself, who remained in close contact with Dayan and Peres during his ostensible retirement, had either initiated or connived at both the Cairo operation and the frame-up afterward.

In any case, when Lavon resigned the Defense Ministry, the circumstances were such that no one but Ben-Gurion could take control of the office. Ben-Gurion's protégés had triumphed over Lavon and were unlikely to submit to anyone other than "the Old Man" himself. Furthermore, general elections were only five months away and the Mapai party's appeal was sagging badly among the electorate. Israel's problems were many: adverse trade balance, too little foreign aid, unassimilated immigrants, raucously divisive Jewish sectarian controversies, too little water, uneven economic development. The list is long and no premier would have been able to do much better than Sharett in solving the problems. Mapai's program was unlikely to be bettered by any other party. But the public was restive and potentially in a mood for change. The return of the flamboyant old hero Ben-Gurion would surely brighten Mapai's chances.

So Sharett, who in 1953 had urged Ben-Gurion to remain as Premier, sent Mrs. Golda Myerson, Labor Minister, down to Sde Boker to deliver his formal invitation to Ben-Gurion to return to his old post as Defense Minister. It was as a Mapai politician, subject to party pressures and versed in electoral tactics and psychology, that Sharett recalled Ben-Gurion. The diplomat in him, although anxious about what new adventures Ben-Gurion might embark on, gave way to the politician.

Ben-Gurion went to the Knesset on 21 February in his shepherd's khaki shorts and heard Sharett tell the legislators, with great economy of truth, that Lavon had resigned when "his proposals for organizational changes in the direction of Defense affairs [i.e., the dismissal of Dayan and Peres] had not proved acceptable to the Prime Minister." The Knesset endorsed Ben-Gurion's return by 74 votes to 22.

Nine years later I asked Sharett if there had been any connection between the Lavon Affair and the Gaza Raid. He answered: "The connection is this, that when Ben-Gurion returned as Defense Minister he decided on the Gaza Raid. The Gaza Raid would not have been mounted if Ben-Gurion had not returned to the Cabinet."

CHAPTER
4

The Turning Point
(28 FEBRUARY 1955 TO 19 JULY 1956)

The defensive form in War is therefore no mere shield but a shield formed of blows delivered with skill.

(CLAUSEWITZ, *On War*, Book VI, Ch. 1) [Vol. II, p. 134]

A war is never merely an intention; a war is an intention and a date.

(SHIMON PERES, 1964)

"**G**AZA WAS revenge for nothing," says Nasser. "Everything was quiet there." Therefore, he recalls having reasoned at the time, it must have some other cause. Since it could not be a reprisal for things past, it must have some connection in Ben-Gurion's mind with the future. It must be the beginning of a new aggressive policy by Israel, full of dangers for Egypt.

Nasser calls the Gaza Raid of 28 February 1955 the "turning point" in relations between Egypt and Israel. No longer was there a drift toward peace. On the contrary, the danger of war became a daily preoccupation. Border incidents turned explosive in response to the elemental need to save face as well as to defend national territories. No longer could Nasser tell visiting Members of Parliament and soldiers at the frontier that Israel was no menace and that he, Nasser, did not intend to make Israel's mistake of spending 60 per cent of the national budget on arms. On the contrary, the Egyptian revolution's development and welfare programs surrendered their primacy in the national budget published four months after Gaza. Military appropriations were half again as big as the year before.

"That aggression was an alarm bell," said Nasser to Egyptian military academy graduates seven months later, on 2 October 1955. "It was a calamity for which I thank God because it enabled us to avert greater calamities."

The immediate reverberations kept the Gaza Strip in turmoil for three days and the alarms they signaled were not only of dangers to Egypt's national security but to the stability of the revolutionary regime and to the personal safety of Nasser. On 2 March mob action spread from Gaza down the Strip to Khan Yunis and Rafah. Crowds of Palestinian Arab refugees burned stores of UN rations sufficient to feed 50,000 of their fellows for a month. Groups of Arabs, howling insults at the Army for its failure to protect itself and the Gaza Strip against the Israeli attack, stoned trucks carrying Egyptian soldiers to trouble spots. A menacing assembly of five hundred demonstrators besieged Egyptian officers and foreign correspondents at a hospital where they were visiting wounded victims of the raid. Troops, unable to budge the mob by firing submachine guns overhead, ultimately fired into the crowd to rescue the officers and correspondents. Refugees marked the visit of General Burns to Gaza on 3 March by besieging MAC headquarters and burning two of its jeeps and by sacking the homes of two UN officials and one Egyptian.

"Arms," was the refugee demand at every encounter with Egyptians, whether by pillagers and demonstrators in the streets or between refugee spokesmen and Egyptian authorities in offices. "Give us arms," they said. "We will defend ourselves."

Nasser had already decided to give his forces new arms. That was the first major Egyptian policy change wrought by the Israeli raid. The second was Nasser's personal decision to organize retaliatory units of Palestinian Arabs under the ancient and honorable Moslem name of *Fedayeen*. The word designates those among the faithful who are willing to sacrifice everything, including their lives, for their cause. A third policy decision was to intensify, as much as political circumstances would permit, Egyptian support for UN endeavors to prevent border clashes.

Nasser made his decision to re-equip his armed forces late on the night of the raid. When reports of the Israeli withdrawal indicated that it was not, after all, the first onslaught of war, Nasser and the anxious men around him could look up from the dispatches and think beyond the immediate military situation at the front. Nasser decided to buy arms from the West if possible. He gave an account of the decision in an interview with me nearly eleven years later. He said:

This was the first raid. It was a surprise to us. Our casualties were high. And there had been a debate in the Army about arms. We had sent Aly Sabry to the United States at the end of 1952, when Mr. William C. Foster was Undersecretary of War. And we were not able to get arms from the United States.

At the beginning they agreed. But because of the pressure from the United Kingdom they refused. We learned after that that there was pressure from Britain not to give us arms because at that time there were negotiations about the future of the Suez base. But in the Army they were asking for arms. I made a big effort before Gaza to convince them to be patient.

There were assurances from the United States and the United Kingdom that everything would continue quiet. After Gaza the position changed because reason was on the side of the Army. That's why we agreed to have new arms.

Nasser's own revolution in July 1952 had been greatly aided by Army discontent over having been ordered to war against Israel in 1948 with inadequate and faulty arms, including hand grenades that exploded immediately when the pin was pulled. The revolutionaries saw the arms scandals as symptoms of deeper maladies in the monarchial government which could only be cured by overthrowing it. With this in mind, I asked Nasser if he had considered that history might repeat itself and that a persistent refusal to rearm might turn the Army against him in a new revolutionary cycle. Was there any truth to stories widely current in 1955 to the effect that the commander in chief, General Abdel Hakim Amer, and other officers had threatened to resign if they didn't receive arms?

Nasser laughed and said: "You know, there are many stories about that but it did not happen. We don't deal with each other like that. You know, we sit together and talk—discuss any question."

What if he had told them that Gaza was just a single raid and not a sufficient cause to divert money from social and economic projects into rearmament?

"Really, I was not in a position to say that," Nasser said, "because I had told them that I had assurances from the United Kingdom and the United States, and they had been convinced. Then the raid proved that there were no assurances. So I myself decided on that night that we must have arms."

From the Gaza Raid until he nationalized the Suez Canal on 26 July 1956, Nasser was in constant anxiety lest Israel launch a full-scale war, as indeed both Ben-Gurion and Sharett threatened in the summer of 1955. Nasser voiced his anxiety in public speeches and in private interviews with correspondents, including myself. Later he reanalyzed Israeli policy as follows:

You know, it was not easy for Ben-Gurion to begin war against us. It is easier for him to have raids. And you know the philosophy or the idea of Ben-Gurion was to force a settlement. To force a settlement doesn't mean peace. This, to us, means war. He was always following this strategy, forcing a settlement. And he was waiting for the opportunity. And they got the opportunity after the nationalization, when they cooperated with Britain and France.

The belief that the Gaza Raid was intended to force the Arabs toward peace was expressed by most members of the Security Council when they took up the raid on 4 March. US delegate James J. Wadsworth called the raid "indefensible from any standpoint" and added that it was the more deplorable because it broke upon a relatively peaceful and stable period.

As for the second major policy decision prompted by the Gaza Raid, Nasser said in an authoritative interview published in the Egyptian magazine, *Akher Saa*, on 29 May 1956, that the formation of the *Fedayeen* was also personally initiated by him. He summarized his reasoning to me in 1966:

The *Fedayeen* was an old organization from the War of 1948, but they were not *Fedayeen* then. They were Palestinians organized to get information; not to fight, just to get information. And they were small in number.

After Gaza we had a meeting and we decided to increase the number because, according to the circumstances of raids, Israel was always in the better position. They were able to make a raid against us and return. But in front of us there were no targets for raids. And their settlements there are defended well with barbed wire and so on, which is completely different from Gaza and the sector of Gaza. So we thought that the best way is to have commandos. And after Gaza we decided to have this organization of commandos based on the small organizations which were only for information.

Nasser does not recall the date of the decision. Dayan, presumably on the basis of Israeli intelligence reports, places the decision in April 1955, more than a month after Gaza, and he says the original strength of the *Fedayeen* was 700 men. The *Fedayeen* did not go into action until 25 August 1955, by which time the Egyptian public was wondering ominously why the Government and Army were not giving as good as they were getting from the Israeli soldiery. Immediately after Gaza, before any thought of the *Fedayeen,* Egyptian troops were ordered to be quicker on the trigger in encounters with Israeli patrols. The results were reflected in Ambassador Eban's complaint at the UN on 6 April that there had been a significant shift in emphasis from infiltration to "overt acts" by Egyptian troops. Eban said it added up to a "new and purposeful military design." He warned that if the Egyptians continued to lay mines along the border and to fire on patrols and frontier settlements, "then the situation may well arise in which the Armistice Agreement will, in effect, have cease to exist."

This was good enough, perhaps, to keep troop morale on the frontier from flagging but it was not enough to counteract the impression Gaza had left on the public mind. A Gaza-type raid into Israel by the Army might have satisfied the public but Nasser believed Ben-Gurion was spoiling for war and that such a raid might give him the necessary pretext. Nasser had predicated his policy before Gaza on the assumption that the drift toward peace would continue. After Gaza, he persisted in angling to restore the pre-Gaza conditions along the frontier but at the same time he felt obliged both to prepare for the war he believed Ben-Gurion was seeking and to raise public confidence in the military vigor of the Army.

There is contemporary support for the belief that Ben-Gurion, if not actually seeking war, was ready to welcome it from the time he ordered the Gaza Raid. The raid seemed to clarify an article by Dayan in the January 1955 issue of *Foreign Affairs.* Dayan insisted despite all evidence to the contrary that tension had lately become acute. He concluded:

"The Israel Government and its Defense Forces will not neglect any idea or opportunity which seems likely to offer hope of a remedy.... Does there exist any international influence which can overcome the comprehensive negation which the Arab Governments have chosen to adopt...?"

In a speech given wide publicity on 4 September 1955 Dayan disclosed that Israel had contemplated war as Egypt's reaction to Gaza. Israel made ready for war before every raid. The major border operations against Egypt in 1955 were preceded by partial mobilization of reserves and their deployment as a mass of maneuver ready for any escalation of the fighting.

Officially, Israel's motives for Gaza have never been made clear. No reference to the raid appears in memoirs written about the period. Dayan's memoirs in 1965 merely reasserted his unsupported contention that "in the second half of 1954, ... the anti-Israel terrorism was intensified." This was not the case, nor did any other discernible provocation exist. Nasser had to draw his conclusions from circumstances and from conflicting Israeli statements at the time.

For example, ninety minutes before the raid an Israeli intelligence officer at headquarters in Tel Aviv briefed newspapermen to the effect that infiltration from Egypt in the preceding six months had cost 7 Israelis killed and 24 wounded. He said footprints showed that three infiltrators who stole a telephone book from a government office in Rishon Le-Zion on 23 February had shot an Israeli bicyclist near Yad Mordecai on 25 February and had returned to the Gaza Strip on 26 February after one of their number was killed by an Israeli patrol. The obvious inference that the raid was a reprisal for this kind of thing was officially negated, however, by Israel's argument that the raid was an escalation of a clash between patrols.

Sharett, speaking in the Knesset on 2 March, gave a wider political implication to reprisals than he ever had before, saying:

> If Egypt, in contravention of its international obligations, declares again and again that it maintains and has a right to maintain a state of war against Israel ... then Egypt bears responsibility for the results. ... Egypt must choose between the existing situation, with all its losses and dangers, or absolute abstention from hostile actions, strict observance of the Armistice Agreement and progress toward peace. It is for Egypt to decide.

But the Premier-Foreign Minister was outlining a policy that his Defense Minister had aleady left behind. Ben-Gurion was doing the deciding, not Egypt.

The following day in New York Eban presented to the Security Council what he described as the "context" of the raid, complaining not only of border skirmishes and infiltration, but also of Egyptian propaganda, the Arab failure to make peace with Israel, and the barring of the Suez Canal to Israeli shipping.

In Egypt Nasser broadcast his retort to Sharett. Gone were the "hopes" and "lively sympathy for Mr. Sharett" which he had expressed in January to an Israel-bound British Member of Parliament, Maurice Orbach. Nasser said:

> I heard a threat from Israel yesterday. ... Today in 1955, our situation is quite different from that in 1948 ... We shall rely on our own strength, not on the Security Council or its resolutions. ... The commander in chief of the Armed Forces has been instructed to answer aggression with aggression.

The words were bold but Nasser felt dangerously weak. He turned first to Washington in his quest for arms, fully aware of President Eisenhower's declared policy "that if our aid to any country . . . is misused and directed against another in aggression, I will undertake immediately, in accordance with my constitutional authority, appropriate action both within and without the United Nations to thwart such aggression." On 10 March Nasser called in US Ambassador Byroade, who relayed Nasser's arms request to Washington. When President Eisenhower saw the Egyptian list of desired arms he exclaimed: "Why this is peanuts!" There was no doubt in Washington that Nasser was preoccupied with defense, not aggression. Nevertheless, as Eisenhower candidly described it in *Waging Peace*, the US stalled.

Nasser gave a careful statement of his position on 28 March in a speech which he delivered at the Officers Club but which he addressed by radio and wide publicity to the world at large. The West was trying to contain Russia, he said, while Russia seeks to extend its domination by subversion. Nasser said he considered communism a menace, but not so serious a menace as imperialist domination.

"We are prepared to organize the defense of the Middle East, but this defense should be the responsibility of its people," he said.

We are prepared to strengthen the Arab Collective Security Pact [of 1950] if we are supplied with arms. In the event of aggression, we undertake to defend this area without any link or partnership with the West. Thus we will be secure from the menace of imperialism. . . . The West offered us military aid. Two years ago I told you that arms and aid were expected to arrive on payment. A mission was sent to the USA, but negotiations failed because of Jewish and Zionist influence. I think it would be a miracle if we ever obtained any arms from this direction.

Nasser said in his nationalization speech sixteen months later that he had asked Britain also for arms. But the British, he said, told an Egyptian arms-purchasing mission that the price would include the cessation of Egyptian propaganda against Western efforts to make defense alliances with the Arabs.

Do we want arms to dictate our policy . . . ? Do we want arms to lead us and guide us as these arms wish or as the sellers wish . . . ? Of course not. There is no reason at all for us to buy arms and pay for them with our personality and principles. Therefore we could not secure arms. We asked and asked for arms without result. We asked for arms at a price and not free of payment or as aid or in the form of alms.

But his most persistent effort, before contracting to buy Communist-bloc arms, was with the US. The effort became more urgent when news agencies disclosed on 29 March some of the secret Israeli arms orders from France which were made by Dayan and Peres in Paris in August 1954. That same day, as the Security Council unanimously condemned Israel for the Gaza Raid, the French delegate said that as a friendly ally of Israel he had cast his vote with difficulty.

On 31 March Ben-Gurion, counter-reacting to the Egyptian Army's "get-tough" reaction to the Gaza Raid, warned:

The enemies to the south and the east should know that their vile and nefarious conspiracy ... will encounter a Jewish force capable of ... striking any aggressor or enemy so that they shall not rise again, as in "Operation Joab" [against Egypt] in 1948 and the Gaza operation a month ago.

Nasser returned to Cairo that day from a secret visit to Gaza, during which he warned the troops that Israel was working to enlarge her territory. He urged the Palestinians and Egyptians to "persevere, unite, work, and be patient and learn a lesson from the Jews: to work so that we repel aggression and defend our homeland."

After further dickering with the US and Britain over arms and the Baghdad Pact, Nasser left Cairo on 9 April for the conference of twenty-nine independent African and Asian countries at Bandung, Indonesia. It was his first major trip abroad, although he had made the Moslem pilgrimage to Mecca in Saudi Arabia in August 1954. He scored a notable diplomatic triumph at Bandung, unexpected even by the Arab delegations, by persuading the conference to endorse the Arab position on Palestine. The Arabs had earlier obtained the exclusion of Israel from the conference although Israel was fully qualified by the conference's own criteria to attend. Of the Palestine dispute, which was originally excluded from the conference agenda, the final communiqué on 24 April said:

In view of the existing tension in the Middle East, caused by the situation in Palestine and of the danger of that tension to world peace, the Asian-African Conference declared its support of the rights of the Arab people of Palestine and called for the implementation of the United Nations Resolutions on Palestine and the achievement of the peaceful settlement of the Palestine question.

Nasser returned to Cairo with vastly increased prestige as an Arab spokesman and as a major figure among the leaders of emergent nations. But his quest for arms remained at an impasse. Washington was refusing credit or barter and demanding cash payment of an amount that would have emptied Egypt's reserves of foreign exchange. Selling Nasser arms would have caused a vigorous outcry among American Zionists and it was impossible to predict what reaction it might provoke Ben-Gurion to make. So the Eisenhower administration did not say no but it continued to set financial and political terms that were unacceptable to Egypt, hoping perhaps that the problem would fade in time.

Nasser did not believe he had much time to spare. He discussed with the members of the Revolution Command Council the idea of turning to Russia. They approved. Nasser approached the Soviet Ambassador, Daniel Solod, on 18 May 1955 at a reception at the Sudan Agency. As he described it to me later:

I took the responsibility for the whole question. There was a reception for [Ismail] al-Azhary, Prime Minister of the Sudan, in the Sudan Embassy. And at this reception I met Solod, the Soviet Ambassador. It was very brief. I asked him: "We want to have arms from you; what will be your answer?" And after a few days, [on 21 May] he came to me and he said that they were willing. It went on very simply.

Then I sent to Byroade [on 9 June]. I told him that we had asked the Soviets and the Soviets had agreed. There was no reaction from Byroade. The reaction came next day from the British Ambassador [Sir Ralph Skrine Stevenson]. He came to me and said that they had information—he got the information from Byroade—that we will take arms from the Soviet Union. If we do so, [Stevenson said] they [the British] will not supply us with arms, ammunition, or spare parts.

I told him: "I said that to Byroade for understanding, not to have people give me ultimatums. You are a free country; you can do what you like. We are a free country; we can do what we like." And the meeting ended. They thought that I was bluffing.

Nasser wasn't bluffing but he still hoped to deal with the West. On 16 June he told Byroade he had postponed his military mission to Moscow. He formally asked for US arms. Washington replied on 22 June that it would consider specific requests. On 28 June the Egyptian national budget showed a 50 per cent increase in appropriations for arms.

Egypt made a final try in Washington on 30 June, submitting a reduced list of requested arms worth less than $10,000,000, according to a State Department disclosure three months later. The effort came to naught. Nasser's account of negotiations with the Russians continued:

We sent a delegation to Prague. The Soviets said that they agreed but they preferred that we deal with the Czechs. I don't know what were the reasons. Of course, in July there was the visit of Mr. [Dmitri] Shepilov [editor of *Pravda* and later Foreign Minister of the Soviet Union]. I discussed with him—we were at Alexandria at that time—about the delivery, about quantities, whether they would give us facilities in paying. And they agreed.

Shepilov was in Egypt as the guest of the government from 21 July to 29 July. In Geneva, while Shepilov was in Egypt, the Russian and Western leaders held their Summit Conference. Failing to take Nasser's plea at face value, Eisenhower and Dulles did not bother to raise with the Kremlin leaders the issue of Communist-bloc arms sales to Egypt.

I asked Nasser why it had taken two months more to complete the arms agreement with Czechoslovakia and Russia. Did the Egyptians hesitate over possible diplomatic repercussions? There was no hesitation, Nasser said:

"You know, we were all completely ignorant about the Soviet arms. We had to prepare our requirements. And the discussions, of course, were not brief. But there was no particular reason [for the delay]. We had taken the decision."

Events between Nasser's first approach to the Russian Ambassador on 18 May 1955 and the public announcement of the Czech arms agreement on 27 September gave no cause for Nasser to change his mind. In the week before Nasser spoke to Solod, three Egyptian soldiers were killed by Israeli raiders and three Israeli officers were killed when their patrol car went up on an Egyptian mine. On 18 May itself an Israeli Army spokesman announced that reprisal raiders had stormed and destroyed an Egyptian position at Deir al-Balah deep inside the Gaza Strip. General Burns warned the Israelis that the situation would deteriorate if they persisted in a boycott they were conducting against the Mixed Armistice Commission.

On 31 May, Walter Eytan, director general of Israel's Foreign Ministry, summoned General Burns and read to him a statement in *Newsweek* by Sharett to the effect that Egypt had forfeited her right to control the Gaza Strip. Israeli broadcasts in Arabic to Gaza the next day told the inhabitants to keep their sets tuned for an important message at 6:30 P.M., at which hour the announcer said Egypt did not want peace and that Egypt would be responsible for anything that might happen to Gaza.

Eytan urged Burns to fly to Cairo and impress upon Nasser the dangers of the situation. *Newsweek*'s interview with Sharett was published tandem with a Nasser interview denying aggressive intent, saying Egypt needed peace on the terms set by the UN in order to press on with economic development. Nasser also stated his fears of Israeli expansionism.

The day after meeting Eytan, Burns flew to Cairo and told Nasser that the Israelis seemed to be in a dangerous mood. Nasser said he could not issue drastic orders imposing a strictly passive attitude on the troops in Gaza after the shock of the Gaza Raid. Toward the end of their 70-minute talk, Nasser said experience had taught him that it was inherent in a soldier's psychology that if hostile troops were close enough to see each other, there would always be incidents of

91

firing. He proposed that each side withdraw all posts and patrols one kilometer from the Demarcation Line, thus interposing nearly a mile of separation between them. Israel never accepted the proposal, contending it was a restriction on her sovereignty. Nasser, however, unilaterally ordered his troops back half a kilometer on 20 September after the Security Council had endorsed his proposal.

Nasser's proposal was part of an effort that lasted until the Suez-Sinai War to steer Egyptian-Israeli relations back into the drift toward peace that had prevailed before the Gaza Raid. At the same time he continued to prepare for possible war and maintained a bold face for the benefit of his Arab critics. He disclosed his offer to demilitarize the frontier to me in an interview on 2 June.

For reasons never satisfactorily explained, *The New York Times*, for which I was then the Middle East correspondent, failed to publish the interview. Instead, in a chain of events not wholly the fault of the *Times*, distorted versions of Nasser's effort to pacify the frontier were splashed across New York's front pages under headlines representing him as a warmonger. The incident merits retelling in some detail because of the permanent danger it did, not only to the Western image of Nasser, but to Nasser's confidence in the fairness of the West's most respected newspaper.

Unknown to me at the time, Nasser was still hoping for arms from the US and he was concerned to counteract Zionist propaganda, which had intensified its efforts after the Gaza Raid to portray him as bellicose and irresponsible and obsessed with a desire to wipe out Israel.

After outlining to me his proposal to demilitarize the frontier he discoursed at some length on his fading hopes for the repacification of the border. Before Gaza, he said, he had felt that the trend on the border was toward peace. His pacific proposal and his comments were politically courageous in that they were vulnerable to criticism by Arab extremists. Toward the end of the interview I returned to his pull-back proposal, suggesting that it looked like bad tactics. It would crowd his front line of defense back upon the roads that served as its lateral line of communications, I said, making it difficult to shift troops along the front to strengthen sectors under attack.

Nasser explained that this was a minor consideration because the Gaza Strip was so narrow and exposed that the Israelis could pinch it off within two hours any time they wanted to, no matter what disposition of forces he maintained there. He said the only deterrent to Israel's seizure of the Strip was the knowledge that it would mean war. This was a commonplace. Any nation's seizure of territory controlled by another is grounds for war. His comment was significant chiefly in the light of Sharett's recent statement that Egypt had forfeited her right to retain Gaza.

In my dispatch I put Nasser's supplementary explanation on the vulnerability of Gaza near the end, quoting him as having said:

"If they try to take the Gaza Strip it will mean war. They are capable of taking it, but it will mean war. They will not be able again to keep gains won by defying the United Nations Security Council [cease-fire orders, as they did in 1948]."

After radioing the dispatch to New York and sending Nasser's staff a complimentary copy, I departed early the following morning for a long-scheduled trip to Gaza, which I had delayed for the interview at Nasser's request. I was out of direct touch with New York for several days because of the limited communications between Cairo and Gaza.

Nasser cabled on 3 June for a report from the Egyptian Ambassador in Washington on American reaction to his undeniably pacific overture in *The New York Times* interview. The Ambassador replied, in effect: "What interview?" Nasser's office, indignant, issued a statement to the local press in Cairo based on the final paragraphs of the complimentary copy of my dispatch, which quoted the warning that an Israeli attempt on Gaza would mean war. The United Press picked up the report from the Cairo newspapers on 4 June and sent it worldwide.

"Nasser Rattles Sabre at Israel," headlined the *Journal-American* in New York. The *World-Telegram and Sun* carried the story under a headline four columns wide proclaiming: "Egypt Warns Israel of War Over Gaza." The bitterest mockery of all was *The New York Times* front-page headline, "Gaza War Threat Voiced by Egypt." The editors had used the second-hand, truncated, and inverted news agency version of the statement two days after failing to print our exclusive firsthand version.

The Egyptians, aghast at the distortion of the original pacific statement, issued to foreign correspondents in Cairo on 5 June a statement redisclosing Nasser's offer to demilitarize the border. *The New York Times* of 6 June gave it two paragraphs on page 5 in a "shirt-tail" appended to a front page report that UN Secretary General Dag Hammarskjold had appealed to Nasser and Sharett to exercise restraint. Still in Gaza, I was unaware that the interview remained unused while excerpts from it had got into print in such a way as to falsify Nasser's import. More damage was still to be done.

On 8 June *The New York Times* printed a report from the UN that "Many neutrals say Premier Nasser's statement [on Gaza] was bellicose and is certain to increase tension." On 9 June it printed a letter on the "war threat issued by Premier Nasser" contending that it proved that "Israel wants peace; the Arabs want war."

Thus was Nasser's attempt to restore tranquillity to the border portrayed as bellicosity. Nasser told Ambassador Byroade that he was bitterly disillusioned by *The New York Times*. Ten weeks later Nasser took the matter up with Cyrus Sulzberger, the paper's chief foreign correspondent. From time to time over the decade that followed he made bitter or derisive references to the *Times*'s failure to print the interview.

The slight did not stop Nasser's efforts to pacify the border. He confirmed the good faith of his offer to demilitarize the border by unilaterally, with no reciprocal concession from Israel, withdrawing his own positions half a kilometer on 20 September, after repeated maulings of his troops by Israelis made it more politically embarrassing to pull back than it had been in June. Meanwhile, Israeli officials said at the time, he must have issued orders to the frontier commands to impose restraint because, until late August, incidents abated. Later in June Nasser agreed to negotiations on proposed permanent improvements in the trucial arrangements and Egyptian and Israeli delegates, under the chairmanship of General Burns, wrangled through the midsummer weeks in the broiling tin hut at Kilo 95.

In a surprising concession, contravening Arab League policy and Egyptian regulations on travel between Israel and the Arab countries, Nasser acceded to my request that he authorize an exchange of posts for two months between me and Harry Gilroy, then *The New York Times* correspondent in Israel. Throughout August and September, I reported from Israel and Gilroy from Cairo; then we switched back again.

In Israel the election campaign brought forth real threats of war as Ben-Gurion and Sharett campaigned to stave off extremist inroads into the Mapai's parliamentary strength. Although they were concrete warnings, they were overshadowed by the sensational distortion of Nasser's pacification offer into a war threat. On 8 July, Sharett in Rehovot and Ben-Gurion in Beersheba made campaign promises to use armed force if necessary to obtain free passage for Israel through the Gulf of Aqaba. Menachem Beigin, the former Irgun terrorist and leader of the Herut party, Israel's second largest, said he had proposed months earlier that Israeli forces destroy the Egyptian batteries guarding the mouth of the gulf. These statements were reported by *The New York Times* three days later on page 6.

In the voting on 26 July, the Mapai lost five of its 45 seats in the Knesset while the Herut representation jumped to 15 seats from eight. The election was taken as an increased mandate for activism. But Ben-Gurion continued to exclude the extremist Herut from any part in his plans for the next coalition government, which he did not succeed in completing until 2 November. Israel has always been governed by Mapai-dominated coalitions. Coalitions need the support of a majority of the Knesset's 120 members.

At the beginning of August the British leaked to the press that Israel was secretly getting arms from France and that new consignments included not the Ouragan jets of the 1954 contracts, but Mystère IVs, which would give Israel air superiority throughout the Middle East. This was just eleven days after Israel asked France to cancel an order for a squadron of Mystère IIs and to send instead two squadrons of Mystère IVs. British intelligence kept admirably close to the secret contracts between France and Israel. The British said that the secret Franco-Israeli arms agreements had been a bone of contention between London and Paris for more than a year. The British dismissed categorical denials by France and Israel by leaking further details.

The British seem to have been acting in the interests of their Arab protégés in Iraq and Jordan. Whitehall expressed fears that the Israeli elections had given a mandate for activism and that Israel's aggressive nationalist leadership might attempt what they diplomatically called a "dynamic solution" to territorial problems. Israel's order for Mystère IVs even before she was aware of Nasser's efforts to match her Ouragans and Mystère IIs fitted better into a pattern of offensive intentions than into one of simple defensive concerns, particularly since there had been no aerial encounters between Arabs and Israelis after the Palestine Armistice Agreements.

The difference in degree between Egyptian and Israeli dynamism impressed itself on both Harry Gilroy and me. He reported from Cairo on 14 August that, in sharp contrast to Israel, he had not heard anyone in Egypt express any interest in the border situation. "To the correspondent who has shifted his base of operations," he wrote, "this remoteness from the 'Palestine question' seems significant."

Egyptian passivity was swept away on 22 August when an Israeli motorized patrol stormed and occupied Egyptian positions in the Gaza Strip near the UN truce hut at Kilo 95, killing an officer and two soldiers and ending the period of tranquillity that began on 1 June. Two days later Nasser summoned General Burns and learned from him that no progress had been made toward Israeli acceptance of his proposal to demilitarize the frontier. He then told the truce chief that Egypt could no longer continue the midsummer border negotiations with Israel.

The following day, 25 August, the *Fedayeen* were ordered into Israel. That night they launched a week-long series of ambushes, mine-layings, and attacks on persons, vehicles, and buildings in which they killed 5 Israeli soldiers and 10 civilians and wounded 9. Three days later, after a wounded member of the *Fedayeen* had been captured and interrogated, the Israeli Army spokesman said Egypt's tactics were "something entirely new." He said the Egyptian radio and press had never before "boasted of attacks against Israel but, on

95

the contrary, suppressed information concerning them." Radio Israel warned Gaza in Arabic that it was courting disaster.

Concerned over what seemed to be a rapid slide toward war, I cabled a lengthy military analysis emphasizing Israel's overwhelming superiority. Israel could mobilize 250,000 men and 100,000 women soldiers in forty-eight hours, I wrote, while the total strength of all the Arab League armies was only 205,000 men of mixed quality, of which 100,000 were in the Egyptian Army. Israeli troops had rehearsed every military contingency they could imagine while the Arabs had neither a unified command nor even a code signal to alert their several armies. I said that despite Egyptian assertions of confidence, any friend of the Arabs would advise them to avoid hostilities with Israel. My concern was not made less by the fact that my wife and four small children were at home in the "enemy" city of Cairo. The Israeli military censors approved the dispatch, which Nasser later cited as a justification of his Russian arms deal.

Fedayeen operations reached a peak of activity on the 29th and 30th of August, when the paramilitary bands penetrated 27 miles into Israel, hunting their victims from the thicket-like cover of the fragrant orange groves around Rehovot. They killed seven Israelis and blasted down a Radio Israel transmitter mast. Israeli Army trackers with hounds combed the groves, fields, and hedgerows. From daybreak to dusk, low-flying aircraft swept the broad coastal dunes north of Gaza. "There has never been anything like it on any of the armistice lines," said Lieutenant Colonel Jacob Nursella, Israel's senior armistice commission delegate.

Israel, having already prepared the revenge for which the public was clamoring, gave an evasive answer to General Burns's request on 31 August for a cease-fire. Arthur Lourie, Acting Director General of the Foreign Ministry, told me that evening:

Terrorist operations have bitten deep into the public mind and emotions, as you can see in every newspaper headline. In all my experience, there has never been anything like it. Just because Egypt has now decided to turn it off . . . it does not mean that the situation has changed. They can't get away with hitting us like this and then crossing their fingers.

In the afternoon Israeli military authorities detained six UN military observers in Beersheba, which infuriated General Burns. When night fell an Israeli light-armored half-battalion struck four miles deep into the southern part of the Gaza Strip in a two-pronged attack that converged on Khan Yunis. There, while machine gunners pinned an Egyptian police detachment inside the British-built Teggart fortress, sappers worked under a full moon piling dynamite against the walls. The raiders blew the fortress down on the heads of the men inside, shot their way back out of the Gaza Strip, and returned to base before midnight, carrying with them their casualties of one killed and eight slightly wounded. The Egyptians lost 39 killed, four of them soldiers and the rest policemen, Palestinian guards, and villagers. "The Israeli Armored Corps unit had carried out the attack with skill and daring," General Burns wrote afterward. "Conversely, the inertness of the defense reflected little credit on the Egyptian military forces in the Strip."

Crossing their own fingers as soon as possible after the raid, the Israeli Army and Foreign Ministry summoned correspondents to a press conference at 1:30 A.M. to tell the world they had struck and withdrawn. Any Egyptian reaction, which might lead to war, would thus be an action distinct from immediate defense against the raiders.

At 7 A.M. Israel's new jet fighters shot down two Egyptian British-made Vampire jets that ventured northward of Gaza. They were the first aerial kills since the Armistice. The settlers of the region, armed to the teeth against *Fedayeen*, turned out in a holiday mood of exultation over the Khan Yunis raid and the aerial victory. An Army spokesman said the raiders could have taken the whole Gaza Strip from Egypt, as Nasser had admitted three months before.

"After our forces took and destroyed the police fortress," the officer said, "they encountered no further resistance and could have advanced in any direction." This prompted the Herut party to castigate the government because it didn't "liberate the whole Gaza Strip from the Egyptian invaders" when the troops had it in their hands for several hours.

But Egypt was in no mood for war, although she feared one. Women and children were evacuated from the Strip on 3 September and did not return until it was clear that the danger was over for the time being.

Israeli statements following the raid were not reassuring. Dayan said in a lecture published on 3 September that reprisal raids not only "set a high price for our blood" but that they could make the Arabs accept Israel rather than continually lose face by opposing her. The Mapai's English-language newspaper, the *Jerusalem Post*, said the following day: "The world would not, perhaps, greatly blame Israel, for example, if she were to shorten the life of the present Cairo junta by a year or two..."

Egypt kept up a bold face by tightening controls over shipping in the Gulf of Aqaba on 11 September while seeking to avoid further border clashes by pulling troops back half a kilometer from the Gaza border on 20 September.

On 21 September an Israeli force occupied the strategic demilitarized zone at al-Auja in a pre-dawn swoop that provoked a strong protest from General Burns. The Israelis coolly told the UN truce officer in al-Auja to stay in his quarters for his own safety. The next day Israeli drillers struck oil in commercial quantities at Huleikat, increasing the country's military power by providing internal petroleum supplies.

On 25 September, Ben-Gurion told me in an interview in Sde Boker that his Government would open the Gulf of Aqaba within one year, adding that if force was necessary, "we can do it by air, by land, or by sea." He said Israel would not take the dispute to the Security Council or the World Court. It was not an idle threat, as his Sinai campaign was to prove just over a year later.

During these events the Egyptian-Czechoslovak arms deal moved toward its conclusion. On the evening of 23 August, the day after the humiliating temporary loss of the Egyptian position at Kilo 95 had set the border ablaze, US Ambassador Byroade told General Burns that Nasser was under much political pressure to accept Russian offers of arms at advantageous economic terms. On the 25th Nasser made absolute his decision to buy from the Russians. This was the same day he decided at last to unleash the *Fedayeen*. There was still a month to go, however, before Nasser told Marshal Amer to cable the Egyptian mission in Prague to sign the agreement to buy arms in exchange for cotton.

"I cannot remember the date," he told me in 1966. "There was Khan Yunis and some other raids from Israel. There were continuous clashes.... There were too many raids and clashes.... It was a few days before my declaration [on 27 September]."

The Khan Yunis raid raised tempers within the Army just as the Gaza Raid had done. General Amer, who was both War Minister and Commander in Chief, wanted to launch a counteroffensive when the first dispatches from Khan Yunis reached him. Nasser withheld approval until the picture became clearer. He rejected the idea of a counteroffensive when word came that the raiders had withdrawn. Egypt's weakness made the very idea of war with Israel foolhardy but the Army's twice-wounded pride made inaction increasingly dangerous. Negotiations with the Czechs and Russians pressed on toward a conclusion.

"No Israeli," General Burns wrote later, "ever so much as suggested that it was the tough Ben-Gurion–Dayan policy that had practically forced Nasser to accept the Russo-Czech arms proposals. What other enemy threatened Egypt?"

On 2 September, the day after the news of the Khan Yunis raid, France stopped delivery to Egypt of 100 fast light AMX tanks armed with high-velocity 75 mm. guns and added the consignment to a similar one on its way to Israel. France acted in retaliation for Egyptian propaganda broadcasts on the 20 August massacres of Frenchmen in Morocco and Algeria.

Israel, no doubt delighted by the windfall but concerned about reports of the Russian arms offer to Egypt, made inquiries in Moscow and received a painstaking denial on 12 September.

The date that Nasser told General Amer to cable Egypt's negotiators in Prague to sign the deal lies buried in the files of the parties involved. Nasser's memory, only approximate, is that it was "a few days"—less than a week—before his announcement on 27 September. The recollections of Ambassador Byroade indicate that it was on Saturday the 24th. Other evidence, valid but less precise, supports Byroade's memory by placing it between 21 and 24 September. But the date of the signing is less important than the date Nasser made his final decision—25 August—because from that time onward the arms deal was a certainty and beyond the influence of events either on the border or in the great capitals of the West.

Israel's forcible seizure of al-Auja, the strategic key to both the Sinai and the Negev, on 21 September, an action in crude contrast with Nasser's pull-back of troops from his side of the Gaza truce line the previous day, can have had no influence other than to increase Nasser's confidence in the necessity of the arms purchase he was about to make.

Nasser broadcast his announcement of the deal in an unscheduled speech on the evening of the 27th. Two themes in his impromptu speech were that Egypt wanted the arms only for peace and security against Israeli aggression and that the West had stalled endlessly and tried to exploit Egypt's need by attaching unacceptable conditions to sales of arms.

Nasser attributed the deal to Czechoslovakia in order to soften the shock he knew it would give to the West. The Czechs, he explained afterward, had acted as intermediaries in the final contractual formalities, thus making it technically a Czech deal although it was the Russians who made the decisions. The heavy weapons delivered to Egypt—tanks, planes, artillery, and eventually ships and submarines—were Russian.

Angry as they were at the march that Russia had stolen on them, the Western capitals seemed to accept the truth of Nasser's statement that he wanted the arms for peace and safety, not for aggression. Israel's conduct since Ben-Gurion's return as Defense Minister in February had already convinced the foreign ministries and intelligence departments of the Great Powers that Israel was distinctly the more aggressive of the two antagonists, a conclusion upon which the French were busily capitalizing in their own quarrel with Egypt. By the same reasoning, the arms deal was expected to make Israel, not Egypt, more dangerous to peace. The analysis was correct. High Israeli officials began immediately to talk of a preëmptive or preventive war and within a month Ben-Gurion secretly ordered Dayan to draft operational plans for war against Egypt.

Washington officials candidly speculated on the chances of an Israeli attempt to destroy the Egyptian army in a Sinai campaign. By contrast, Egypt would not attack Israel with its new arms even if convinced of a certain and easy victory, according to the view accepted by the State Department. The chief of the Middle East division said a week after the announcement of the arms deal that the US did not regard the possibility of an Arab attack on Israel as "great enough to affect our thinking."

Dulles himself told a news conference on 4 October 1955 that while "it is not easy or pleasant to speculate on the probable motives of the Soviet bloc leaders" in furnishing arms to Egypt, it was "difficult to be critical of countries which, feeling themselves endangered, seek the arms which they sincerely need for defense."

Policy is a complex matter, however, and is rarely based entirely on the merits of the immediate situation. The Russian arms would not—and did not —overcome Israel's military lead over the Arabs, according to statements from governments outside the Middle East at the time and for years afterward. But political considerations deriving not only from the Cold War, but also from Zionist lobbying in the US and Britain, and, in the case of France, from the struggle for Algeria, influenced Great Power policies toward the Middle Eastern arms race as much or more than did the circumstances in the Middle East itself. The first reactions by the US and Britain were to try to undo the Russian-Egyptian arms deal or at least to hold down the new prestige it gave both Nasser and the Russians in the Arab world.

The day after the arms deal was announced Whitehall ordered Trevelyan to express its "grave view" of the matter to the Egyptian Government. Secretary of State Dulles ordered George V. Allen, Assistant Secretary of State for Near Eastern, South Asian, and African Affairs, to fly to Cairo with a warning letter from Dulles to Nasser. Relations appeared near the breaking point. But Allen, caught between an irate Dulles and a defiant Nasser, skillfully calmed explosive tempers and wisely obtained Dulles's permission not to deliver the letter.

On 2 October, while Allen was still in Cairo, Nasser linked the arms deal to the Gaza Raid, which he called a "turning point" in Egypt's modern history, "the danger gong . . . that enabled us to avert greater misfortunes."

Addressing newly commissioned graduates of the military academy, he read a British War Office intelligence report to show that the West regarded Israel as not only stronger but more aggressive than Egypt. He read from a French list of US and British arms sales to Israel. He quoted reports of French sales of tanks and Mystère jets from the authoritative Israeli newspaper, *Davar*. It was a deception, he said, to claim that the Czech deal had upset the balance of power. He asserted that Israel had planned to follow the Gaza Raid with further aggressions until she learned that Syria had prepared its Army to attack in the event of Israeli-Egyptian hostilities.

Three days later Nasser told me the West had left him no alternative but to rearm Egypt from the East. "I know what Israel has contracted to receive in the next ten months," he said, citing the fast AMX tanks and first-line Mystère jet fighters from France. "I am thinking of Israel's Army not as it is today but what it will be tomorrow.... Now we will be meeting Mystères with MIGs. This is better than meeting Mystères with nothing." He reiterated Egypt's desire for peace with justice for the Palestinian Arab refugees and regretted having to give priority to defense over development. "I cannot defend Egypt with schools and hospitals and factories, and what will be the use of them if they are destroyed?" He said he had been expecting an Israeli attack ever since 28 February. Now, he hoped, the Czech deal would make Israel think twice about aggressive actions, including preventive war.

Israel was taken by surprise by the Czech deal, although the Government knew about the Egyptian-Russian contacts. Confused reactions within the government led to contradictory statements on 3 October by Premier Sharett's office, which was not fully informed on the Defense Ministry's secret purchases in France, and Shimon Peres, Director General of the Defense Ministry, who had made the secret purchases.

"The reports published in Cairo about Israel's alleged superiority in arms are absolutely unfounded," said a communiqué from Sharett's office in Jerusalem.

"With regard to the acquisition of arms," said Peres to Defense Ministry employees in Tel Aviv, "we have provided Israel with superiority over the Arab States."

Peres disclosed that Ben-Gurion had drawn up a rearmament program two years earlier, just before his temporary retirement as Premier and Defense Minister. Peres said the program had been more than two-thirds completed, "thanks to the generous attitude of the French Government" and the efforts of Dayan. "Although we still need several types of heavy guns, with regard to other sorts of guns we have approached the saturation point.... We purchased modern aircraft, which gave us a new air superiority.... The real advantage which the Arabs cannot imitate is the Jewish ability to invent new arms.... In the field of electronics, rockets, and many other things, we have achieved concrete results." Nevertheless, Peres said, Israel's superiority could not last forever; Israel would have to counteract the strengthening of the Arabs because it gives their rulers "a false feeling of self-confidence ... and drives them to the perpetration of acts of aggression against Israel."

Ben-Gurion, still technically subordinate to Sharett as Defense Minister, was with Peres at the ministry meeting in Tel Aviv. He modified Peres's confident appraisal to the extent of saying the Arab countries had a larger quantity of arms than Israel but that Israel's superiority was maintained by superior quality in manpower.

If Gaza was the turning point for Nasser, the Czech arms deal was the turning point for Ben-Gurion. He expressed his view in the Knesset on 2 November a few hours before the Israeli strike at Jebel al-Sabha broke Egypt's last remaining toehold in the heights around al-Auja.

I cannot pass over in silence the grave and dangerous issue which the government of Czechoslovakia calls a "commercial transaction." Formally, of course, the sale of poison to a known murderer, even when the vendor is aware of the use to which the poison will be put, can also be called a commercial transaction. ... The Czechoslovak government knows that the Egyptian rulers are buying these arms for one reason and one reason only—to destroy the State of Israel and the people of Israel. ... The UN does not absolve its members from the duty of looking after themselves.

The arms deal divides the twenty months between the Gaza Raid and the Sinai invasion into two distinct parts. The first seven months saw the fruition of Nasser's double reaction to the Gaza Raid: retaliation with the *Fedayeen* and the conclusion of his quest for modern arms. The remaining thirteen months were significant chiefly for Ben-Gurion's counter-reaction: acceleration of the arms race; stepped-up frontier activity, including the seizure of full control over the strategic central Sinai invasion springboard in the al-Auja demilitarized zone; and, most important of all, the formulation of concrete operational plans for war against Egypt.

These latter thirteen months fall again into two periods, nine months in which Ben-Gurion's war policy was balked by a cabinet faction led by Sharett until his ouster, and four months in which Ben-Gurion and his activist stalwarts skillfully implemented their war plans to take advantage both of Egypt's critical estrangement from the Western Big Three and Russia's troubles with Poland and Hungary.

Ben-Gurion did not delight in war but he regarded it as an extension of diplomacy, a political method that had served Israel well at crucial moments of history. "A battle is only a means for attaining political aims," he said.

Peace as an end in itself was never at the top of Ben-Gurion's list of political aims, unless one accepts his concept of peace at no price, or rather a peace for which the Arabs will pay Israel. The birth of Israel was, naturally, more important in 1948 than peace. After 1948, equally naturally, growth in its broadest sense was more important than peace; growth by Jewish immigration, economic and commercial growth, growth in prestige and international influence, growth in military power.

Territorial growth, which has continued ever since the first Jewish colonies were established in Palestine, remains an objective concomitant with other forms of growth, perhaps the most important of all in the long run. It was a primary objective for the Israeli Army in 1948 and 1949, when the state grew by conquest one-third larger than its allotment under the UN partition plan. Military and agricultural encroachments into demilitarized zones on the Syrian, Jordanian, and Egyptian frontiers brought important additions between wars to the territory under Israel's control. In 1956, claiming in familiar 20th-century style to be reacting against aggression, Ben-Gurion took the Gaza Strip and the Sinai Peninsula, constituting all of Egypt east of Suez, and sought international recognition of his claim to keep it by right of conquest.

Ben-Gurion was remarkably candid in 1956 about his aim to annex the territory taken from Egypt. In general, however, Israeli expansionists are as discreet and contradictory about their intentions as the Zionist movement was about using Balfour's promise of a "national home" to prepare for the conquest of a national state. In truth, growth to a viable and secure size is an impulse naturally consequent upon birth. Whatever the immediate international reaction at the moment of expansion, in the long view of history growth is considered no more immoral than birth. That Israel, if she were not to abandon the mission of Zionism, had to expand or eventually perish is self-evident. That Israel intended to expand is amply shown by actions and statements. Even formal peace with the Arabs, in the long view, need not mean putting a permanent limit to expansion.

In 1955 and 1956, Ben-Gurion's attitude toward peace negotiations comprehended no thought of compromise, least of all territorial compromise. Both he and Sharett and every other responsible Israeli angrily repudiated every suggestion of territorial compromise by Eden or Dulles or anyone else. Ben-Gurion's approach to negotiation was always to regard Israel's *de facto* position as an irreducible point of departure.

The Arab stand on negotiations for peace is that Israel must agree beforehand to implement outstanding and annually revalidated UN resolutions giving the Palestine refugees the choice of repatriation to their former homes or compensation for their losses. The number of refugees has grown to 1,500,000 from the 904,000 registered in June 1951 at the first accurate count by the UN. The Arabs also demand that Israel return to the boundaries set by the 1947 UN partition resolution.

Israel says the Arabs forfeited any claims under the partition resolution by fighting to prevent its implementation and the establishment of Israel. Israel brought in 684,000 Jewish immigrants between 1948 and the end of 1951, and they quickly put abandoned Arab homes and farms and other enterprises to use. Israel has now settled more than a million Jewish immigrants and asserts that repatriation is a practical impossibility, not to speak of the threat to national security that returned refugees would constitute.

The Arabs reply that Israel's Law of Return accords to every Jew in the world the right to settle in Israel and that if Israel has room for them she must certainly have room for the return of the rightful inhabitants who fled.

Peace may be somewhere in the No Man's Land between these two positions. It was there once. Sharett and Nasser, if they had had time, might have ventured out to get it. But no Arab could venture all the way to the lines held by Ben-Gurion without being shot down from his own camp.

For Ben-Gurion peace had to incorporate other objectives. Otherwise he saw these objectives as problems to be solved only by war. Freedom for Israeli shipping through the Gulf of Aqaba was one problem which he frankly promised to solve by war. The *Fedayeen* became another in August 1955. The barring of the Suez Canal to Israeli commerce was a long-standing problem likely to be solved only by finishing the war that was suspended in 1949 by the Armistice Agreements. The Arabs claimed limited belligerent rights such as the economic boycott under the armistices. And there was Israel's need for more territory.

The elimination of Nasser's leadership in Egypt was a hope of Ben-Gurion's even before he learned of the Czech arms deal. In his interview with me on 25 September he insisted that Naguib could have brought Egypt to the peace table with Israel but that Nasser's "overthrow" of Naguib in November 1954 had ruined Israel's hopes for an acceptable peace with Egypt. That Ben-Gurion should stubbornly have held such erroneous ideas about matters vital to Israel's security seemed hardly credible to me. All reporting from Egypt had long since made clear that Nasser was the key figure in the Egyptian revolution from its very conception and that Naguib was dismissed only after he tried to transform his popularity as a figurehead into real power.

Furthermore, it was well known that Naguib's bid for power in 1954 was based largely on the support of the fanatical Moslem Brotherhood. Perhaps Ben-Gurion felt that the kind of extremist anarchy Naguib's ascendancy would have created in Egypt was safer in the long run for Israel than the soberly constructive government of Nasser. Rampant extremism in Egypt might have been more troublesome for Israel in the short run, but Ben-Gurion always maintained confident mastery over the short run. War itself was always a short-run concept in Ben-Gurion's thinking.

War would have to be a lightning war in which Israel would beat the Arabs into suing for peace on Israel's terms before the Great Powers could step in and impose another armistice. If the Great Powers could be trusted to come in on Israel's side, so much the better, but that was not a practical prospect until after the nationalization of the Suez Canal.

Peace was not really a practical prospect for Israel in 1955, certainly not in the thinking of Ben-Gurion and his activists. The Director General of Israel's foreign service, Walter Eytan, wrote that the "incidental advantages for Israel" of non-peace were "cold comfort" but he said Israel had "welded a million new immigrants into a united people much faster than she could have done but for their consciousness of a common danger."

All of the motives which in 1954 had prompted the activists to seek a revival of their policy with the return of Ben-Gurion became stronger in 1955. Israel's anxieties that the British and Americans were moving closer to the Arabs assumed more substance when Sir Anthony Eden, active sponsor of the Baghdad Pact, succeeded Sir Winston Churchill as Prime Minister on 6 April 1955. Sir Winston had often said: "I am a Zionist." Eden was an Arabist.

On 4 April, Eden had urged a settlement of the refugee problem, the frontiers, and the use of the Jordan River waters. On 26 August, Dulles, speaking carefully with Eisenhower's specific approval, listed the "tragic plight of the 900,000 refugees," mutual fear of attack, and "the lack of fixed permanent boundaries" as the main barriers to peace. Both Eden and Dulles offered to assist and guarantee a settlement. Israeli sensitivity over the mildest hint of suggested compromise on the refugee and boundary problems revealed itself in sharply hostile reactions. The most ominous proposal of all, from Israel's point of view, was Eden's speech on 9 November recommending that Israel and the Arabs "make some compromise" between the armistice boundaries won by Israel and the UN partition plan boundaries demanded by the Arabs.

Ben-Gurion, again Premier as well as Defense Minister, lashed back on 15 November that Eden's proposals tended to "truncate the territory of Israel for the benefit" of the Arabs and that they had "no legal, moral, or logical basis and cannot be considered." Ben-Gurion had already determined his policy, although it was to take him nine months to get rid of Sharett and bring the cabinet effectively into line with his own thinking.

On 22 October Ben-Gurion summoned Dayan back from a vacation in France and on the following day instructed the Army chief to make preparations to capture the Straits of Tiran at the far end of the Egyptian Sinai Peninsula. On 2 November, presenting his new government and program to the Knesset, Ben-Gurion cited marauding, the barring of the Suez Canal, and the blockade of the Gulf of Aqaba as among Egyptian violations of the armistice. He warned: "This one-sided war will have to stop, for it cannot remain one-sided for ever."

Dayan wrote later that "there could have been no clearer statement from the Prime Minister before the Knesset forum on his intention to instruct the Army to cross the border if the anarchic situation continued." But the cabinet, Dayan added, "despite his [Ben-Gurion's] plea and his explanations...decided that the moment was not propitious." The decision was transmitted to Dayan. He responded on 5 December with an eloquent plea to the cabinet for action within one month.

Dayan's view was that the use of force was necessary because the Arabs refused the alternative, which was to settle controversial problems by negotiation. He argued against submitting to Egypt's interpretation of the armistice. He warned that Russian planes would make Egypt harder to beat.

"It may be, of course, that one of these days a situation will be created which makes military action possible," Dayan wrote the cabinet, "but this will be the fruit of chance and not the planned result of postponing it to a specific 'time' and 'place.'" But Sharett's gradualist faction remained adamantly opposed to war.

The Israeli war faction was aided by the fact that anti-Arab propaganda had intoxicated nearly all Israelis and prevented their recognizing and capitalizing on Nasser's pacifism. By contrast, Washington's view at the time was that Egypt had no intention of attacking Israel even if the Egyptian leaders were convinced of certain and easy victory. The State Department conceded that the Czech arms deal would go far toward eliminating Israel's lead in weapons. But the US worried chiefly about the possibility that Israel's fears might lead her to launch a preventive war. Washington did not believe at that time that Israel had territorial ambitions.

Israel's anti-Arab intoxication was manifested in repeated expressions of anxiety about the 60,000 Jews in Egypt despite the fact that the Egyptian Jewish community was both secure and outstandingly affluent. After the Suez-Sinai war the situation deteriorated and most Egyptian Jews left the country. But in 1955 there were twenty-three active synagogues and a full range of Jewish welfare, medical, educational, and philanthropic institutions in Cairo. The Grand Rabbi of Egypt, Chaim Nahum, who had officiated at the marriage in Cairo of Abba Eban, intervened without hesitation in instances when security measures seemed to violate the Government's policy against discrimination. He said that the distinction between Jews and Zionism was accepted as a matter of course by the Government, the press, and the Jewish community itself.

Roger Baldwin reported during the trial of the Israeli agents early in 1955 that the position of the Jewish minority was "reasonably good for a Moslem land—perhaps as good as that of the Christian Copts." Harry Gilroy, reporting on the Rosh HaShanah celebrations in Cairo in September 1955 after nearly a month of savage border clashes, said Egyptian Jews were concerned that a full-scale war might affect the Government's policy of toleration.

Anti-Arab feeling has a unifying and invigorating effect on Israelis. Israelis are fond of saying that enmity to Israel is the only constant element in Arab unity and that, therefore, the Arabs would have had to invent Israel if it didn't exist. Conversely, Israel too needs an external enemy and Ben-Gurion would have had to invent Nasser if he had not existed. In a sense, Ben-Gurion did invent Nasser, or rather a new Nasser, as a remedy for Israel's period of dispiritedness. He used the Gaza Raid to create the new bogeyman Nasser. Israel's border harassment of Egypt and her skillful propaganda fixed the image of a menacing enemy and prevented Nasser's pacific actions from restoring the image of the old pre-Gaza Nasser.

Nasser's pacifism endured until the Suez-Sinai war itself. It might even be said to have survived it in view of the fact that Egypt accepted, while Israel opposed, the interposition of the United Nations Emergency Force along the border between the two armies, which prevented clashes for ten years. It was, of course, a relative pacifism aimed at the recovery of peaceful conditions. After Gaza it no longer envisioned formal peace. Nevertheless, it was far enough in advance of other Arab leaders to bring criticism and risks. Nasser's pacific actions in the fall of 1955 included the following: In September 1955, after the border flare-up, Nasser unilaterally pulled his troops back. He told the Arabs that his Czech arms were for peace and security and not for aggression. He responded warmly to Eden's peace proposals of 9 November, calling them a "positive constructive step" and "a handsome action." Egyptian and British diplomats, despite Ben-Gurion's harsh rejection of Eden's proposals, worked intensively together for a month to develop Eden's initiative. Then the combination of an Israeli raid on Syria and Britain's effort to get Jordan into the Baghdad Pact wrecked further progress.

Curiously, these developments got much less publicity than Ben-Gurion's offer in his 2 November address to the Knesset "to meet with the Prime Minister of Egypt and with every other Arab ruler as soon as possible in order to achieve a mutual settlement." *The New York Times* published Ben-Gurion's offer on the front page. On the very night of Ben-Gurion's offer the Israeli army, after restricting UN military observers in al-Auja, attacked Egyptian positions at al-Sabha ten miles to the southwest, killing 70 of the defenders and taking 40 prisoners. The paper reported the attack on page 3 of the same issue.

The *Times* was not necessarily guilty of bad or biased editorial judgment.

The famous Ben-Gurion's return to the premiership with a warning and a peace offer had a higher rating in news value than conflicting reports of obscure soldiers clashing in a seemingly isolated incident at a place no editor had ever heard of.

Only later did it become clear that the al-Sabha attack was not an isolated reprisal but an episode in Israel's campaign to dislodge Egyptian forces from the al-Auja area and secure it for Israel. It was not until the Sinai invasion that the significance of Israel's tenacious and successful campaign for control of the strategic military gateway became clear. It became even clearer a decade later when Dayan disclosed that Ben-Gurion had ordered him on 23 October 1955 to prepare for a Sinai operation. Control of al-Auja was a prerequisite for exploiting the opportunity foreseen when, as Dayan phrased it to the cabinet, "one of these days a situation will be created which makes military action possible."

Actually, the struggle for al-Auja began in 1948. Ben-Gurion's order in 1955 merely increased its urgency.

The Israeli General Yigal Alon first captured al-Auja from the Egyptians in a fierce 24-hour battle on 27 December 1948. It was the fourth day of Operation Horeb, the largest and most important of the Palestine war. As Jon and David Kimche reported in their history of the war, "the road into Sinai lay open before the victorious Israelis, who hastened to exploit this opportunity. Alon had already decided that if political circumstances were favorable he would continue the advance and capture the entire Sinai peninsula."

On 31 December Ben-Gurion, succumbing to an ultimatum from Britain and the US, ordered Alon to withdraw just as he was preparing to capture the main Egyptian base at al-Arish. Ben-Gurion gave up his prize "with a heavy heart" to avoid war with Britain. But Alon's invasion forced Egypt on 6 January 1949 to agree to armistice talks. The conquest of Sinai had to be shelved until the Suez crisis in 1956 created a situation which made military action possible once again.

But al-Auja remained the key to Ben-Gurion's hopes. Walter Eytan, chief of the Israeli armistice delegation, says Israel accepted Dr. Bunche's recommendation to demilitarize the al-Auja zone in 1949 only "when it became clear that the successful conclusion of the armistice depended on it." In addition, there were to be no Egyptian defensive forces closer to the al-Auja zone than Qussaima and Abu Aoueigila. And the Egyptian-Israeli Mixed Armistice Commission was to have its headquarters and its meetings in the stone buildings of the old Turkish garrison at al-Auja.

Israel began the long effort to recover al-Auja in 1950 by expelling 3,500 Bedouins of the Azzazma tribe. Some of them later formed the outlaw Black

Hand gang, whose members perpetrated the March 1954 massacre of eleven Israeli bus passengers at Scorpion's Pass. The remaining Bedouins and their herds were periodically harassed by aerial strafing while Israeli patrols shot at tribesmen approaching the zone's two main wells and burned the tents at their encampments. General Bennike, then the UN truce chief, reported to the Security Council in the fall of 1953 that the operations against the Bedouins appeared to have been a preparation for the establishment in September 1953 of an armed settlement.

A year of wrangling in the MAC established the fact that the settlement, named Ketziot, was an organized unit of the Israeli armed forces. But the settlement remained and the young soldiers in civilian disguise sometimes clashed with Egyptian checkpost personnel. Once they took away the jeep of an Egyptian MAC delegate in spite of protests from a UN truce observer who was present.

On 21 September 1955 Israeli forces occupied the whole demilitarized zone. Israel was aware of the seriousness of the action and had deployed mobile forces under camouflage nets in virtually every wadi in the Negev hinterland in case Egypt should decide to fight. The move marked a significant shift of the focus of border conflict from the Gaza Strip.

The international furor over the Egyptian-Czech arms deal drew attention away from the maneuvering around al-Auja. On 27 September, the day Nasser disclosed the arms deal, there was announced an agreement by both sides that Israel would withdraw forces from the demilitarized zone while Egypt would withdraw its defensive positions beyond the rectangle formed by the Sinai edge of the zone and the desert villages of Qussaima and Abu Aoueigila. The withdrawal was accomplished 2 October under UN supervision.

Two weeks later Egypt accused the Israeli Army of having re-entered the zone. On 20 October, General Burns was summoned to UN headquarters in New York for consultations on the al-Auja struggle. On the 26th, the Egyptians proved their point by taking two prisoners from the Israeli post at Bir Ain near the southern end of the zone and confirming, through interrogation, that they were regular soldiers disguised in civil police uniforms. General Burns, disillusioned, said he had agreed to Israel stationing civil police in the zone because he "was still sufficiently naive to believe that statements of senior officials of the Ministry of Foreign Affairs could be relied upon to represent the intentions of the real directors of Israel's foreign and defense policies." Burns had agreed to accept civil police as a means of getting the two Israeli infantry companies out.

Israel exacted swift retribution for the Egyptian raid on Bir Ain, which the Israelis call Beerotayim. Israeli raiders swooped far to the south upon the Egyptian post at Kuntilla and took 30 prisoners after killing 5 of the defenders. The intention was to exchange the 30 for the 2 Israelis captured at Bir Ain, but this was not to be accomplished until the general prisoner exchange following the Suez-Sinai war.

On 29 October, Israel accused Egypt of advancing positions into the demilitarized zone. In Cairo the Defense Ministry announced that forward observers reported large Israeli troop movements in the Gaza and al-Auja areas. Six teams of UN military observers in radio jeeps shuttled across the zone trying to avert a battle. General Burns in New York warned both governments to cease forthwith "all aggressive activities" in the al-Auja area. It was to no avail. Gilroy of *The New York Times* reported on 30 October that Israel seemed ready for anything. Burns's deputy, Colonel R. Hommel of the US Marine Corps, cabled him on 31 October that "tension is such that it only seems a question of which party will attack first." In New York Burns pleaded in vain with Big Three representatives to take forceful action to prevent an outbreak of fighting. On 2 November 1955, after shooing away the UN observers, Israeli troops smashed the Egyptian position at al-Sabha facing the demilitarized zone.

Israel was now unchallenged master of the al-Auja zone, which she transformed into a stronghold and an invasion base in anticipation of a situation being created which would make military action possible. In the year that was to elapse before the war there was much talk and diplomatic activity but no change in the military situation at al-Auja. Israel remained in full possession, excluding the UN Emergency Force from the trucial zone after the first Suez war as she had excluded the UNTSO observers before it. She mounted her central invasion of the Sinai from al-Auja in 1967 as she did in 1956.

On his way back to Cairo Burns stopped in London to confer with Eden and Foreign Office officials. He suggested the interposition of UN troops along the border, emphasizing that this would require Big Three backing. A year later to the day, at the height of the Suez-Sinai war, the UN adopted a renewal of the suggestion by the Canadian Foreign Minister, Lester Pearson, and the United Nations Emergency Force was born.

History more than bore out General Burns's observations at the time. Of al-Sabha, he wrote, "the siting of the defenses said very little for Egyptian tactical training, as there was no depth nor defense against an attack coming from the right flank, as the Israeli night assault did." Burns estimated that it would take the Egyptians two years to learn to handle the Russian and Czech arms and improve training enough for offensive operations. "What the Egyptian Army needed more than modern arms," he believed, "was better morale, better discipline, better training. The defects in these respects were plain to be seen whenever one met any Egyptian troops, even the small posts near the borders, and when one considered their performance in the face of the Israeli reprisals. This really meant that their officer corps needed improvement . . ." It took two defeats in war to bring Nasser to give the officer corps its much-needed shaking up.

Great Power concern over al-Auja seems to have overcome Ben-Gurion's resistance to meeting Burns, who had sought several times to see the Israeli leader. Burns had first met Nasser a year previous, in November 1954. The difference in the readiness of the two leaders to meet the truce chief reflected their differing attitudes toward the UN. Nasser regarded the UN as a buffer, both diplomatic and military, against Israel while Ben-Gurion regarded the UN as an obstacle to the direct confrontation, either diplomatic or military, which he sought.

Ben-Gurion received Burns on 9 November and told him that Israel had been obliged to drive the Egyptians away from al-Auja, which he claimed was Israeli territory, because the UN had proved unable to do it. "The flaw in this argument," Burns wrote later, "lay in the fact that there was a special status, internationally recognized, for the al-Auja demilitarized zone, which admittedly the Egyptians had been violating, but because the Israelis had previously violated it also."

On 12 November Burns discussed al-Auja with Nasser and Amer. The Egyptian problem, Amer said, was that the defense of the Gaza Strip was open to an Israeli thrust from al-Auja. If Israelis were in the demilitarized zone, Egypt had to guard against them with defensive positions inside the prohibited rectangle facing the zone. Thus Egypt could comply with the prohibitions in the Armistice Agreement only if Israel complied with the prohibition against deploying offensive forces west of Beersheba. Nasser confirmed Amer's position. "He reiterated that Egypt wanted peace," Burns wrote, and said he had ordered forward troops not to open fire.

Dag Hammarskjold offered a solution looking toward a restoration of the situation that obtained in mid-October. Both sides had declared their acceptance by the end of January 1956, the month in which Hammarskjold made his first visit to the Middle East, but Israel withdrew her acceptance in February. After a second, month-long peace mission in the spring, Hammarskjold reported to the Security Council on 9 May 1956 that both sides were presumed to be violating the armistice provisions concerning al-Auja. Ben-Gurion said he would refuse to comply while Egypt barred Suez and the Gulf of Aqaba to Israeli commerce. Egypt said she would not relax restrictions on Israeli shipping so long as Israel refused any concessions on the refugees.

On 19 June 1956, in the same speech in which he gave his version of the removal of Sharett from the cabinet three days earlier, Ben-Gurion told the

111

Knesset that Israel would not budge from al-Auja so long as Egypt maintained an aggressive policy. On 20 July, Ben-Gurion refused a request by Hammarskjold, then on his third Middle East mission, to remove restrictions on UN military observers in the al-Auja zone.

By then Dulles's withdrawal of Western aid for the Aswan High Dam had both increased and obscured the importance of the struggle for al-Auja. Nasser and Hammarskjold discussed it on 22 July, but Nasser was already preoccupied with weighing the risks and gains of nationalizing the Suez Canal Company. An Israeli attack was one of the possible risks Nasser considered and rejected. If he had predicted more accurately, Israel's possession of al-Auja would have weighed heavier among the risks.

"If, indeed, the zone had remained demilitarized," Burns wrote later, "that is to say, if it could not have been traversed or occupied by the armed forces of either side, it would have been almost impossible for either to have carried out an offensive successfully, the balance of forces being as they were."

Closely related to the struggle for al-Auja but ranging far and wide around the world was the Egyptian-Israeli arms race. It began quietly in the fall of 1953 with Ben-Gurion's five-year rearmament program. Although Egypt was unaware of and had not joined the race, it became more urgent in Israel's opinion when Britain agreed in July 1954 to cede her great Suez Canal base to Egypt. Dayan and Peres initiated Israel's secret purchases from France within a month of the Anglo-Egyptian agreement. Egypt entered the race in earnest after the Gaza Raid, turning first to the US and Britain for modern arms and finally to the Russians. Israel stepped up her pace again when Nasser announced the deal with the Czechs and Russians in September 1955.

Sharett launched a world-wide appeal to Jews for arms on 18 October, three days after the Egyptian army had launched a public fund drive to pay for its new arms. Sharett said later that the idea came from a shoemaker in Ness-Ziona, who wrote him that he would contribute a week's wages. Sharett echoed Nasser also in declaring that Israel would not hesitate to obtain arms "from every possible source."

Although Israel came nowhere near approaching the Soviet bloc for arms, there was a curious and insistent effort by Washington to hurt Russia's new prestige with the Arabs by official assertions that Russia was willing to arm Israel too. The US statements were denied by Israel and labeled by the Russians as a "complete invention," which seems to have been just what they were.

On 23 October, the day Defense Minister Ben-Gurion ordered General Dayan to prepare an invasion plan for Sinai, Sharett flew to Paris to seek arms from the Big Three foreign ministers before their meeting in Geneva with the Russian Foreign Minister, Vyachislav Molotov. Sharett was still Premier and

Foreign Minister but he knew that his Defense Minister was, in fact, the real master of his cabinet. Sharett later recalled with a bitter laugh that Dulles had offered to come to his, Sharett's, hotel in Paris on the protocolary grounds that Sharett was still a premier while Dulles was only a foreign minister. Sharett insisted on going to the US Embassy to see Dulles on the grounds that it reflected reality regardless of protocol.

The first four shiploads of Russian arms were reported to have arrived in Alexandria several days before. The reports were unverified. They may have been inspired by the Egyptians for propaganda reasons. Nasser says now that no Soviet bloc arms reached Egypt until early in 1956.

Also in late October 1955, Egypt announced military alliances with Syria and Saudi Arabia. These had been foreshadowed more than six months earlier and were primarily designed to stiffen Arab resistance against Western recruitment for the Baghdad Pact. Nevertheless, Sharett cited them in appeals to the Big Three for alliances as well as arms. How much he knew about the working alliance between the French and Israeli military establishments remains obscure. It is unlikely that either the French or the Israeli Foreign Ministries knew much about them.

Sharett told me later, for example, that he had got arms on his trip from the French government of Edgar Faure. He recalled it as a "good start" but added that "the big supplies came after I left the government" in June 1956.

In Geneva, where the Big Four foreign ministers met in a sequel to the July Summit Conference, Sharett continued his appeals to the Western representatives. He completed his mission on 1 November with a warning to Molotov that Russian arms had raised the danger of a new Arab-Israeli war, which, he added, would inevitably draw the Great Powers into a World War. Molotov told him he did not think Israel had any cause for worry. Sharett flew back to Israel to relinquish the premiership on the next day to Ben-Gurion who, paradoxically, not only had decided upon the war Sharett feared but had already ordred an operational plan for it to present to his new cabinet.

Although Sharett's only solid success was with the French, who were already secretly shipping arms to his country, he won sympathetic consideration from Dulles and British Foreign Secretary Macmillan. The fighting in and around the al-Auja zone did not erase Sharett's gains. In the first two weeks of November, the State Department and the White House several times declared the Administration's willingness to consider Israeli requests for arms. Nasser's reactions were a measure of Sharett's success.

Nasser said in a speech on 8 November that Washington's policy of "promise and postponement" had forced him to turn to the Russians. On the 16th, when Israel made a formal request for US arms, Nasser accused Washington of a "deliberate attempt to maintain the military superiority of Israel over the Arabs." He warned that he would not shrink from an arms race, saying Egypt was determined to avoid "the fate that befell Palestine . . . mutilated by the UN with the consent of certain of the Great Powers for no other reason than to satisfy the Zionist Organization."

Undeterred by Nasser's warnings, US officials conferred on arms with Sharett, now Foreign Minister but no longer Premier, during an extended transcontinental tour he made for the United Jewish Appeal and the Israel Bond drive. Sharett arrived in New York on 10 November, the day after Eden had made his proposal for a compromise peace between Israel and the Arabs. The ensuing Anglo-American pressure for a compromise peace worried Israelis, especially Ben-Gurion. So did the Anglo-American offer to help Egypt build the High Dam at Aswan, which was announced on 17 December after nearly a month of talks in Washington with an Egyptian delegation.

Other developments favored Israel. Secret arms deliveries from France increased to the extent that they were difficult to conceal. Both France and Israel hastily denied authoritative reports on 25 November that the latest model Mystère jets were refueling at Rome's Ciampino Airport on their way to Israel. Heavy bribes and a shift of refueling stops to Brindisi helped keep subsequent deliveries more secret. Best of all, as far as Sharett was concerned, the US seemed on the verge of furnishing Israel with F-86 jets equal to both the Israeli Mystères and the Egyptian MIGs.

Ben-Gurion wrecked Sharett's mission at the last minute with a ferocious raid into Syria on the night of 11/12 December. As Abba Eban, a member of Sharett's mission, recalled it:

We were going to get a reply to our request for four squadrons of jet aircraft and other equipment on a certain date in December, and Mr. Sharett was with me in Washington for that purpose. The next day there was an outbreak in Kinneret [Galilee] in which our forces killed 73 [Syrian] Arabs in retaliation for an Arab attack on our fishing vessels which had caused slight damage and had not caused any casualties. This was, of course, an appalling international situation, because the gulf between the effects of the retaliation and the thing which had brought it about was greater than any engagement before or since. It is no secret that Mr. Sharett finally protested Mr. Ben-Gurion's decision. . . . Although Mr. Sharett and I disagreed with this action, we had to defend it. We later heard that we would have received a conditionally positive answer to our arms request. As it happened, we got a conditionally positive reply only in May.

Characteristically, the news of the raid shared front-page space with a Ben-Gurion peace offer. The Israeli Premier had told William Longgood of the

World-Telegram and Sun that he would like to meet Nasser on Christmas Day at Kilo 95 or Geneva or anywhere Nasser wanted. He said he believed Egypt would attack Israel within five or six months unless a peace settlement was reached before then.

The obvious effect of the raid, however, was to kill the peace prospects that had been the subject of intense diplomatic activity since Eden's compromise proposal of 9 November. In addition to talking with Nasser, Britain and other Western governments had been urging Israel to negotiate a settlement soon, arguing that she would get a better deal from the Arabs then than she could get ten years later. The British urged indirect talks on the pattern that had solved the Yugoslav-Italian dispute over Trieste in October 1954.

Burns, who had been "urgently" summoned from his Sunday leisures by Ben-Gurion some four hours before the raid, dismisses the official Israeli claim that the raid was provoked by Syrian shots at an Israeli patrol boat in the Sea of Galilee. Burns said Ben-Gurion was "vaguely threatening" on the topic of Egypt at their meeting. He said the casualties were 56 Syrians killed, including 5 men and 3 women civilians, and 6 Israelis killed. Nine Syrians were wounded and 32 were missing, of which 30 turned up as prisoners of the Israelis. The extraordinarily high proportion of killed to wounded was strong evidence of willful savagery on the part of the attackers.

"No one with any knowledge of military affairs would believe that such an elaborate, coordinated attack had not been planned well before, and probably rehearsed," Burns wrote. "Certainly it was not improvised in a few hours. When he was talking to me Mr. Ben-Gurion must have been well aware that the attack was mounted, and what the zero hour was."

Some Israelis were as outraged by Ben-Gurion's highhandedness as General Burns was. The respected Hebrew newspaper, *Haaretz*, said the raid had "brought Israel dangerously close to dictatorship by the chief of government." Ben-Gurion had consulted no other cabinet minister about the raid, said *Haaretz*, which was a violation of the constitution. Critics within Ben-Gurion's own Mapai party forced a three-day hearing on Ben-Gurion's reprisal policy at the end of December. Ben-Gurion and Sharett clashed in the secret party conclave but Ben-Gurion emerged strengthened by a vote of confidence in his conduct of Israel's security.

The raid ruined Israel's immediate hopes of getting arms from the US, just as the Gaza Raid had made Dulles drop consideration of military guarantees for Israel. But it caused no interruption in the secret flow of French arms to Israel. Furthermore, it spiked Anglo-American endeavors toward a compromise peace, which Ben-Gurion feared. And it ensured once and for all the failure of the two-year effort by Eric Johnston, President Eisenhower's personal ambassador, to construct a supranational Jordan Valley Authority to oversee the sharing and use of the Jordan River by Israel and the riparian Arab states. Israel, suspicious of any supranational limitation on her sovereignty, had disliked the Johnston Plan at the beginning. The wrecking of Johnston's work meant that Israel would recover her freedom, albeit at the risk of war, to pursue her interrupted project to divert the entire river to the Negev through a series of canals and giant pipes beginning within gunshot of the scene of the raid on Syria.

The raid prompted Nasser to write Hammarskjold on 15 December that Egypt "could not continue her peaceful attitude if Israel continued aggressive actions against Arab countries." He listed six major Israeli aggressions, beginning with the Gaza Raid of 28 February 1955. The others were: the Khan Yunis raid on 31 August; the temporary first occupation of the al-Auja zone on 21 September; the Kuntilla raid on 27 October; the al-Sabha attack on 2 November; and the 11 December assault on Syrian farms and military positions on the slopes overlooking the Sea of Galilee.

Nasser said Egyptian and Syrian forces would be used jointly against any further Israeli aggressions. He added that the Security Council had shown itself unable to restrain Israel from repeated aggressions. His actions were less bold than his words. Osgood Caruthers, who had newly succeeded me as *The New York Times* correspondent in Cairo, cabled a report that Nasser had issued strict orders to the troops to avoid border clashes during the delicate period following the raid on Syria.

The next day Nasser got the heartening assurance from Washington of the Western offer to finance the High Dam. But it was counter-balanced the same day, 16 December, by wild rioting in Jordan, which signaled the beginning of the final quarrel between Nasser and Eden over the Baghdad Pact (whose details will be examined in Chapter Seven).

The arms race continued unabated through the winter and spring. Both Egypt and Israel bought reconditioned British tanks from Belgian middlemen. The tacit military alliance between Israel and France moved up from the shadowy clandestinity of the Defense Ministry level at the end of January 1956 when French elections brought the Socialist Guy Mollet to power as Premier. From that time on, the French-Israeli alliance was at the premiers' level.

Alfred Robens, shadow Foreign Secretary, recalled a decade later: "It was very well known to those who were close enough to the situation that the Israelis were contemplating a defensive war. I was made aware of this in January of that year, and conveyed this information to the appropriate quarters, which included Selwyn Lloyd and Anthony Eden."

Although there were lively rumors of an impending Israeli spring offensive, the border itself remained quiet for nearly four months after the raid on Syria. Intelligence reports that an Israeli offensive was planned between March and November caused the Jordanian army, still under the British General, Glubb Pasha, to issue a warning order to all units as early as mid-January 1956. "The irony of the situation," Glubb wrote later, "was that we could not discuss these possibilities with the Egyptian army, because the Egyptian government had embarked on a full-scale propaganda attack on the Arab Legion [Jordan's army]."

The Egyptian propaganda campaign, touched off by Britain's attempt in December to force Jordan into the Baghdad Pact, lasted until King Hussein of Jordan dismissed Glubb Pasha on 1 March. But the Egyptians had their own intelligence of an Israeli spring offensive. Nasser spoke of it to newly commissioned pilots on 19 February. He discussed it with British Foreign Secretary Selwyn Lloyd on 2 March.

Reports from Israel of continuing shipments of French arms prompted Nasser to begin negotiations with the Russians for a second major arms agreement, equal in cash value to the September 1955 agreement and providing Egypt with the more advanced MIG 17s to replace the MIG 15s in her first line of aerial defense. The second agreement, also allowing Egypt to pay with cotton and rice, brought the value of Russian arms purchases to $336 million, Nasser told me ten years later. He said the Russians gave Egypt twelve years to pay for the first two agreements, adding that a third agreement was concluded immediately after the Suez-Sinai war to make good Egyptian material losses. Again in 1967 the Russians immediately made good Egypt's losses. Syria now joined Egypt in turning to the Soviet bloc for arms after failing to get them on satisfactory terms from the West. Syria confirmed the fact on 4 May 1956. British sources said Syria had contracted with Czechoslovakia six weeks before to buy $30 million worth of tanks, planes, armored cars, and small arms and ammunition. The Middle Eastern arms market, at one time an exclusive Western preserve, had become highly competitive in response to the Israel-Arab arms race.

Every Western move seemed to make the situation worse. In January, the Foreign Office and the State Department summoned their diplomats home from the Middle East for conferences. Eden went to Washington at the end of January to talk with Eisenhower about the Middle East. On 24 February, Washington officials disclosed that the US had informed France that it would not object to the shipment of twelve Mystère IV jet fighters ordered by Israel.

"Later these 'twelve' Mystère fighters would display a rabbit-like capacity for multiplication," wrote Eisenhower. He should have been aware that they had already done so. France was merely going through the motions of obtaining US approval for the release to Israel of the planes which she was manufac-turing for NATO forces. Approval was technically necessary because the planes were paid for by funds from the US offshore procurement program. Sometimes France covered her secret shipments to Israel by the device of re-cycling documents embodying US approval through the weapons bureaucracy, using them again and again to engender a "multiplication" of the shipments. Sometimes the French made their secret shipments without the bother of such bureaucratic folderol.

In mid-April 1956, as one squadron of 15 Mystère IVs was being delivered, Israel let it be known that she would need 60 more. By mid-October France had slipped the additional 60 into Israeli airfields for use in the secretly im-pending war.

In any case, the growing US readiness to approve French and Canadian arms shipments to Israel was what persuaded Nasser to make his second arms agreement with the Russians. No sooner had he made it than, to his great alarm, Khrushchev, on a visit to England, publicly approved of a UN arms embargo on the Middle East.

It was on 27 April that Khrushchev spoke. Since Russia was a member of the UN, she would be bound by such an embargo to shut off arms deliveries to Egypt while Israel would no doubt continue to get secret supplies from France, which was acting independently of Britain and the US already. Moreover, France had shown herself quite capable of walking right out of the UN Gen-eral Assembly over the Algerian question, which in French minds was closely related to Egypt.

Nasser cast about for a major arms supplier outside the UN. His anxiety was increased when he received intelligence reports that the Big Three had agreed at the NATO foreign ministers' meeting in Paris early in May that Israel should be given arms sufficient to counter all the Arabs. Communist China was the only major power outside the UN capable of meeting Egypt's arms needs in the event of a UN embargo.

Nasser exchanged full diplomatic recognition with the Peking government on 16 May 1956. Israel had recognized Red China on 6 January 1950 and had sent a month-long good-will mission there in 1955 without incurring US ire. But Egypt was the first Arab country to recognize Red China. Dulles was outraged.

Ben-Gurion was delighted. France had long since taken sides with Israel against Egypt because of the Algerian question. Britain had openly turned against Egypt in a growing contest over whose influence should prevail in the rest of the Arab world. Now the US estrangement from Egypt meant that the Big Three, who for six years had maintained a promise embodied in the

Tripartite Declaration to prevent any forcible change in the Arab-Israeli *status quo*, were solidly hostile to Israel's major Arab opponent.

Russia, Egypt's only Great Power friend, was facing unrest in her East European satellites, Poland and Hungary. At best, from Ben-Gurion's point of view, the new conjunction of stars in the Great Power constellation portended favorable circumstances for Dayan's and Ben-Gurion's desire to create a situation "which makes military action possible." At the very least it reduced the danger of concessions inherent in the latest UN peace campaign.

That Nasser considered a compromise peace to be at least potentially in Egypt's national interest was made explicit in his favorable reaction to Eden's 9 November proposal. On 12 January, upon his return from a visit to Egypt, Marshal Tito of Yugoslavia said in a speech: "Egypt does not arm for revenge." On 25 January 1956, during Hammarskjold's first mission to the Middle East, the major Cairo newspaper, *Al-Akhbar*, went so far as to say: "In the presence of good will, a settlement of the outstanding dispute between Israel and the Arabs is not at all impossible." On 22 February, before the breach between Eden and Nasser had hardened, Selwyn Lloyd told the House of Commons that Britain had endorsed to Hammarskjold Nasser's proposal that both Israel and Egypt pull their troops back one kilometer from the border.

On 15 March Nasser told a visiting group of 43 American journalists that, "in fact, peace reigned on the borders" before the Gaza Raid, that Egypt still wanted to give priority to economic and political advancement and that "we have, therefore, no intention to solve this problem by war or attack Israel." Egyptian embassies abroad gave the statement international circulation. On 31 March, Nasser told Osgood Caruthers of *The New York Times* in an interview published on 2 April:

"We have no intention of attacking Israel. Our whole thought is on preparedness against an attack from the Israelis. We are putting strong forces in the Sinai Desert, but I would not be so foolish as to put them near the Gaza Strip, where I could easily lose them."

Nasser's forces in the Sinai, as Marshal Amer had explained to Burns in November, were admittedly in violation of the Armistice Agreement, but Egypt was forced to this by the Israeli buildup in the Negev focused on the al-Auja zone.

The continuing dangers in the al-Auja dispute and renewed talk in Israel of completing the suspended Jordan River diversion project prompted consideration by an anxious Security Council. The Council passed a resolution on 4 April 1956 requesting Hammarskjold to visit the Middle East again and report on the situation, paying particular attention to the degree of Israeli and Egyptian compliance with the resolutions it had passed following the Gaza, Khan

Yunis, and Syria raids. The resolution endorsed Nasser's proposal that both armies withdraw one kilometer from the border.

To Ben-Gurion, the references to Israeli raids and the endorsement of Nasser's demilitarization proposal were repugnant if not ominous.

The following morning, 5 April, Israeli mortars began a day-long bombardment of downtown Gaza, where the weekly market had filled the streets with shoppers. The shelling killed 63 persons and wounded 102. Among the dead were 28 civilian men, 27 women, 4 children, and 4 soldiers. Ninety-three of the wounded were civilians, including 53 men, 32 women, and 8 children. UN military observers on the spot verified that the mean point of impact of the mortar bombs was in the principal square, nearly a mile from any conceivable military target. They reported also that nine of the women were killed by direct hits on the Gaza Emergency Hospital. The American Baptist Hospital was struck by fragments.

Hammarskjold did not leave New York until 6 April. The "unjustifiable savagery" of the mortaring of Gaza may have "shocked the Israeli authorities," as Burns wrote later. There is no doubt about its impact on Hammarskjold's mission. It increased its urgency in the same measure that it damaged its chances of success. More damage was to come.

Egypt retaliated with a second major wave of *Fedayeen* terrorism. By ten o'clock on the night of 7 April messages began to reach Burns's truce headquarters in Jerusalem of attacks during the day on vehicles in the Negev, grenade-throwings, and demolitions. In five days the *Fedayeen* killed 14 Israelis. "A particularly repulsive act of one of the *Fedayeen* gangs," Burns wrote later, "had been to attack a group of schoolchildren... not far from Ramle, when they were at their prayers." Six children were killed and two wounded by shots fired into the school. Israeli police and soldiers killed 10 *Fedayeen* and captured 7.

The Egyptian press, hailing the *Fedayeen* as heroes, said 300 had participated in some fifty reprisal raids. Cairo newspapers claimed on 12 April that the *Fedayeen* had killed 31 Israelis and wounded 123. A month later the Egyptian claim was raised to 400 Israelis killed and wounded during the five-day guerrilla rampage. It helped assuage public opinion.

For several days during the *Fedayeen* operations it seemed inevitable that Israel would mount a counterreprisal, which could lead to war. Burns worked desperately to prevent it. On 8 April he got an assurance of two days grace from Ben-Gurion and Sharett. At the same time, he urged the Big Three, through their consuls in Jerusalem, to restrain Cairo and Tel Aviv. The next day, Eisenhower and Dulles warned grimly that the US would "support and assist" either side which might be subject to aggression. The warning, backed by the presence of the powerful US Sixth Fleet in the East Mediterranean, evidently was sufficient to extend Ben-Gurion's two days of grace until after the *Fedayeen* had withdrawn and the shooting died away.

Ben-Gurion held his peace and asked France for still more arms. Nasser had not yet antagonized Washington by recognizing Red China. At midnight on 12 April, Ben-Gurion and Peres conferred with the General Staff at Ben-Gurion's house and decided to send Peres on an urgent mission to Paris. Peres flew to Paris the next day with a letter from Ben-Gurion to Mollet. The reply was an additional twelve Mystères and a veiled televised assurance from Mollet that "France will continue to fulfill her obligations to Israel."

French war shipments for an Israeli "separate front" against Nasser were so well advanced before the Suez nationalization that the British no longer feigned ignorance of them. "We believe that Israel is in a position at the present time to defend herself successfully," Lloyd told the House of Commons 48 hours before nationalization. As for Egypt's Russian bombers, he added, "one has to take into account the current availability of the bombers and the fighter resources which may be available to Israel." Psychological preparation and public relations kept pace with the military preparations.

Ben-Gurion broadcast a warning to his countrymen on 15 April that "the hosts of Amalek" were rearming in Egypt and that Israel faced in the coming year "a supreme test graver and more difficult than that which we faced successfully eight years ago." A week later he told the Knesset that "Israel should not be deceived by signs of decreased tension along the Egyptian border." He said that "on the one hand, the danger of war has increased as never before since the war of independence, and on the other, opportunities have recently arisen for reducing tension which never before existed." He specified Egypt's Suez and Aqaba blockades as causes of tension. His meaning became clear in the afterlight of the Sinai campaign. French weapons and suport were his opportunities and war his method for reducing tension by eliminating Arab practices injurious to Israel.

Although tension remained abated on the Egyptian border and Nasser and the controlled Egyptian news media continued to hazard pacific statements Ben-Gurion wrote later that by the middle of May, "defense had now become our chief preoccupation." Ben-Gurion was not the only historical figure to hold that the best defense is offense. His security policy had been based specifically since October 1955 on plans for offensive action against Egypt. First he had to remove Sharett.

The Egyptians, understandably, maintained a feeling of favor for Sharett. The basis for this sympathy was summed up in an interview Sharett accorded to Ibrahim Ezzat, a nervy Egyptian journalist for whom I had arranged, in cooperation with the Israeli Embassy in London, a daring eleven-day tour of Israel. Ezzat's courage in braving his government's certain wrath was matched by the candor of his reporting in a four-part series on his trip in the Cairo weekly magazine, *Rose al-Youssef*. The series was reprinted in other Egyptian papers. In his second article, on 28 May, Ezzat quoted Sharett as having told him, with remarkable prescience:

A war between Israel and Egypt would only mean Britain's return once more to the Middle East after we fought her here and the Egyptians fought her in Egypt and forced her to evacuate the Suez Canal Zone. We do not want—and we know very well that Premier Gamal Abdel Nasser does not want—a British comeback in the Middle East. The only guarantee against this is a peace settlement between Egypt and Israel.

On 12 June 1956, nine days after Sharett had learned in a frank conversation with Ben-Gurion that it would be impossible for him to remain in the government, Cairo Radio's regular broadcast to Israel in Hebrew urged Israelis to support Sharett and oppose his removal from office. "The Arab countries and the nations of the world are interested in seeing that the person responsible for Israel's foreign policy is moderate, quiet, normal—a person who tackles matters with wisdom," said Cairo Radio. It added that Ben-Gurion "believes that what happened in 1948 is also possible today."

But Ben-Gurion, after a flurry of hesitation, had decided to oust Sharett and replace him at the Foreign Ministry with Mrs. Golda Myerson, the Minister of Labor, who Hebraized her last name to Meir a few weeks later.

On 16 June, Sharett submitted his resignation to Ben-Gurion. It was accepted at a cabinet meeting two days later. Sharett walked bitterly out of the meeting, waved away his official car, and strode home to prepare to speak later in the day at a Knesset session summoned to debate his resignation. He disclosed that he had asked Ben-Gurion after the July 1955 elections not to include him in the new cabinet. "I had well-founded reasons," Sharett said, "for fearing that this time cooperation between my comrade David Ben-Gurion as Premier and myself as Foreign Minister would not be successful."

Meir Argov, chairman of the Knesset Foreign Affairs and Security Committee, told the house:

From the international point of view, Sharett's resignation is to be regarded as a demonstration against the Great Powers' disregard of Israel's security needs. A dictate by a third party will not decide between us and the Arabs. There are only two alternatives: either direct negotiations or a direct clash.

Replying to the debate the following day, Ben-Gurion said:

Recently the State's security situation became unusually grave . . . I reached the conclusion that in these circumstances the interests of the State required, as far as humanly possible, full coordination between the Foreign Ministry and the Ministry of Defense and that a different direction of the Foreign Ministry was now necessary. . . . This explains what Sharett told you yesterday—that he is compelled to resign from the government.

Some years later, Sharett told me the story in plainer language:

The reason B-G forced my resignation was because he felt that I was an impediment to his policy in a situation in which he had decided there was going to be a war with Egypt within a very short time. Whether it was Egypt that was going to attack Israel or Israel that was going to attack Egypt or whether the situation was just so intolerable that Israel had to break out of the suffocation, it doesn't matter. War was coming and B-G wanted me out of the way.

I don't say that I would have opposed war under all circumstances. I was raised in the Haganah tradition. But my wisdom was different from his. He insisted I had to go and threatened to resign. My colleagues said they couldn't permit this because we needed him. Which meant they didn't need me. I submitted my resignation on the 16th of June. I forget when it was announced.

Sharett had good reason to recall the circumstances in bitter detail. It meant the end, at the age of sixty-one, of a political career in which he had been Zionism's and Israel's Foreign Minister without a break since 1933. It meant the defeat of moderate gradualism, which he saw as the only hope for Israel in the long run.

Although the Suez Crisis, out of which grew the collusive alliance that attacked Egypt, was still in the future and Ben-Gurion could not have known the exact circumstances that would make military action possible, the remainder of his speech on Sharett's resignation contains uncanny relevancies to the Suez-Sinai war and its immediate aftermath.

"We shall not start a war in which it would be certain or even probable that we would have to fight British, Soviet, or US forces," he said. ". . . On every front where we are the attackers we may also encounter forces which do not belong to our neighbors. . . . I shall not support anything which, on our own initiative, would involve the Israeli armed forces in a war against any European, American, or Asian forces. Like all of you, I assisted in the establishment of Israel. I shall not assist in its destruction. . . . On the other hand, I shall not hesitate for a moment . . . to mobilize the full strength of Israel's armed forces

123

against every attacker, whether from Egypt, Jordan, Syria, Saudi Arabia, or all these countries together, without being afraid of the outcome of this contest. . . . The Armistice Agreements are not an ideal solution and cannot last forever. . . . We are willing to implement the entire agreement on condition that the other side does the same. Otherwise the agreement does not exist and is not binding for us. This is not an easy matter and may lead us into a difficult position. . . . We must be prepared for attempts by Great Powers to dictate a settlement. We must muster all our strength so that we can say *No* to the greatest powers in the world. . . ."

In the arrangements for war which Ben-Gurion deftly selected from among the opportunities offered by the Suez Crisis, he fulfilled every condition he outlined in his speech on 19 June except for a near miss on the last one quoted above. He was not able to say *No* quite forcefully enough to Eisenhower to keep his Sinai conquest.

Ben-Gurion still had to plot a difficult course to take his ship of state into battle and to work out a rendezvous for attack with other captains. But by forcing Sharett to resign he had cleared his own decks for action.

General Burns called on him on 28 June in a follow-up to Hammarskjold's month-long peace mission in April and May 1956. It had turned out to be nothing more than a cease-fire mission and the results already were eroding. "Mr. Ben-Gurion's demeanor throughout the interview had made me very uneasy," Burns wrote later. "I felt that he was in a dangerous mood."

The first targets in Ben-Gurion's move against Nasser were the Egyptian intelligence officers in Gaza and Amman. The Israeli Intelligence Department, headed since March 1955 by Yehoshafat ("Faty") Harkavi, addressed a package to an Egyptian officer in Gaza who was regarded as the rival of Lieutenant Colonel Mustafa Hafez, chief of Egyptian intelligence in the Gaza Strip and director of the *Fedayeen*. The package was sent by a double-agent in the hope that the agent would take it to Hafez instead. He did. Hafez opened the package on 11 July and was killed instantly by the explosion of the bomb it contained. On 14 July, Colonel Salah Mustafa, the Egyptian military attaché in Amman, received a registered parcel through the Jordanian mail which revealed through its thin paper wrapping that it contained a book, *The Leader and the Man*, by the Nazi wartime general, von Runstedt. He incautiously opened the package and was terribly mutilated by the explosion of a bomb inside the book. He died a week later. Israeli authorities in Tel Aviv recalled pointedly on the 15th that Harkavi had named both men as *Fedayeen* organizers.

Burns reported his anxiety about Ben-Gurion's mood to Hammarskjold, who was sufficiently alarmed to return unexpectedly to the Middle East. He spent five hours alone with Ben-Gurion on 19 July, vainly trying to persuade him that implementation of the cease-fire agreements was an essential first step toward peace.

Homer Bigart, reporting the meeting for *The New York Times,* wrote:

"Mr. Ben-Gurion sharply disagrees. He regards the cease-fire clause in the General Armistice Agreements as secondary to 'broader issues,' such as the free passage of Israeli shipping through the Suez Canal . . . "

Bigart reported that "the main reason for Mr. Hammarskjold's unexpectedly early return to the Middle East was his anxiety over what Israel might do."

Whatever Ben-Gurion's plans were for concerted action with France against Nasser, he was compelled by a distant event that night to embark on a three-and-a-half-month period of elaboration and adaptation before he could put them into action. For on that night in Washington Dulles bluntly canceled Western aid for Egypt's High Dam.

CHAPTER

5

A Common Enemy

(1830 TO 19 JULY 1956)

Egypt is the most important country in the world.

(NAPOLEON)

The Suez Canal . . . will be a gateway to the oceans. . . . Everybody will compete for its possession. You have thus marked the site of a great future battlefield.

(President of the French Academy to de Lesseps upon his election in 1884)

"I N ACTING at last against Nasser, France is hitting the head on the octopus whose tentacles have for so many months been strangling
French North Africa," wrote Jacques Soustelle during the week in
November 1956 when French, British, and Israeli invasion forces
shot their way into Egypt. "The dirty offices from which orders
for bloodshed were issued, the quays from which weapons for killing in Algeria
were loaded, the camps and barracks where commandos were trained, have all
come within our reach.... Everyone understands that the future of French
North Africa hangs on what is happening and will happen in Egypt."

Soustelle's exultant pen expressed precisely the illusion and the emotion
which, after two years of frustration, vented the armed fury of Frenchmen
upon Egypt. It was immediately republished in Israel, which was appropriate
because it explained the motives that had led France into a tacit military alliance
with Israel against Egypt long before the Suez Canal became a factor and a
pretext for action.

Soustelle was a distinguished anthropologist who in World War II began a
brilliant political career as a left-wing member of the Gaullist movement.
Before Suez he had served for a year, from January 1955 to February 1956, as
Governor General of Algeria. The Algerian rebellion against French rule was
three months old, still small and localized, when Soustelle arrived. The predominantly right-wing French *colons* in Algeria were hostile to him and his
reform program to integrate the Moslem and European communities. Within
his year, however, Soustelle became the darling of the *colons*. Refusing, like
most Frenchmen, to see that the Algerian problem was insoluble on any terms
other than independence, Soustelle fell into the error of looking outside Algeria
for a solution. Egypt was supporting the Algerian rebels materially as well as
morally. Like many Frenchmen, Soustelle fabricated upon the foundation of
this very secondary fact the chimerical theory that stopping aid from Egypt
would cause the rebellion in Algeria to collapse. This illusion led likeminded
Frenchmen to respond to the overtures of Israelis seeking arms against Nasser.
Was not Nasser, after all, the common enemy of both Israel and France?

This school of thought failed to see that Egypt's support of fellow nationalists in Algeria was a political imperative as well as a result of the natural
sympathy among Asian, African, and even Latin American leaders. In the
1950s it was as unthinkable for an Arab not to support Arab nationalism as for
an American politician not to be anti-Communist. But men like Soustelle
insisted on seeing dark religious or racial hostility to the West as Nasser's chief
motive. Algeria, Soustelle said, is part of the Egyptian dream of an Arab Empire
uniting the Orient with the Atlantic, "a perspective that fatally excludes the
Occident, and France in particular." Even so respected a savant as André Sieg-

fried attributed the "acceleration of history" in 1955 to an Islamic "counter-crusade ... a rising tide, coming from the East, that threatens the whole of Western civilization, which only yesterday was mistress of those regions." Siegfried saw Nasser as a Moslem dictator who was "above all an anticolonialist sentimentally hostile to the Occident" and he saw the Arab-Israeli conflict as "merely a particular aspect of this countercrusade."

Immense frustrations predisposed France toward such illusions as André Siegfried's goggle-eyed magnification of Nasser into a threat to Western civilization. French frustrations were the inescapable result of reasserting and trying to maintain imperial status and commitments against the surge of nationalism after World War II had crippled her ability to do so. Defeat and occupation had so reduced France's military, economic, and political resources that she no longer had the material strength of a Great Power. It was De Gaulle's force of personality that made the Allies accept France as a Great Power participant in the rewards and responsibilities of victory in World War II, including permanent membership on the UN Security Council. But France no longer had the resources to meet such commitments. Ceaselessly fighting in one colony after another, France had to relinquish her empire bit by bit like a debt-ridden nobleman who cannot meet the mortgages on his estates. Britain, in the person of General Spears, foreclosed Syria and Lebanon. Then the nationalists began to do it themselves; Ho Chih Minh and General Giap in Indochina, Habib Bourguiba in Tunisia, the Sultan Mohammed in Morocco. Tough Israel could hardly help France in Algeria itself, but she could hurt Egypt, and this enhanced the lure of seeing the Algerian revolt as an octopus with its head on Nasser's shoulders.

The Israeli motives for seeking the alliance were far more realistic than the French motives for accepting it. Ben-Gurion and his men wanted specific things for Israel which Egypt stood in the way of their getting. They knew they would have to obtain their objectives by force and they wanted not only weapons to facilitate beating Egypt but also a Great Power patron to delay international intervention. France offered both. Ben-Gurion's objectives, described in the preceding chapter, included freedom of passage through Egyptian-controlled waterways, freedom from Arab economic and political discrimination, freedom from harassment by Arab infiltrators, and, last but not least, more territory.

North Africa itself was a minor factor in Israeli thinking. Encouraging immigration by Jews from the ancient North African communities had actually led Israel into friction with France. Zionist propaganda dwelt on the theme that Jewish communities would be unsafe in independent Moslem states and that North African Jews would be well advised to emigrate to Israel while there was still time.

A paradox in the alliance was that anti-Semitism in Algeria was strongest among the French, who were both anti-Jewish and anti-Arab. The *colons* showed their initial dislike of the Gentile Soustelle by denouncing him as a Jew. Their embarrassment when France and Israel joined forces against Nasser provoked a celebrated right-wing lawyer to exclaim: *"Nous voici donc You-pinophiles!"* ("So now we're kike-lovers!"), an epithet which rapidly circulated in Paris and Algiers.

Zionist propaganda in North Africa was self-fulfilling to a certain extent in that it exacerbated relations between the Moslem and Jewish communities. These had been far better for centuries than Christian-Jewish relations in Europe. Most North African Jews were descendants of Jews who fled with the Moors nearly five hundred years ago from the persecutions of Catholic Spain. French officials resented the Zionists first for stirring up trouble for North African Jews and then for exaggerating it to the world at large. They also disliked the emigration of the Jews because the Jews were more tolerant than the Moslems of continued French rule. Franco-Zionist friction, however, proved ephemeral.

France began her conquest of Algeria in May 1830 with a flamboyant expeditionary force of 35,000 men and 600 ships. The pretext was an ill-tempered slap with a flywhisk given three years earlier by the Dey of Algiers to the French consul. The real motives of the expedition were a mixture of strong-arm mercantilism and the desire of King Charles X to divert his critical and unruly subjects with an easy and profitable foreign adventure. But Charles was overthrown two months after the force set sail and the Algerian adventure proved neither easy nor profitable.

It took the French more than 17 years of ferocious warfare to crush Arab and Berber resistance in Algeria. They were years in which Marshal Thomas-Robert Bugeaud transformed the policy of scorched earth from a defensive tactic of last resort into a standard concept of offensive warfare. In reprisal for the burning of their villages and crops, the Arabs mutilated French prisoners. The French, in turn, once suffocated 2,000 Algerian men, women, and children in caves. The same quality of merciless violence was to characterize the eight-year war that led Algeria to independence in 1962.

From Algeria the French moved into Tunisia on the east in 1881 and Morocco on the west in 1911, establishing protectorates over both countries. Algeria, far more heavily colonized than either Morocco or Tunisia, was ruled under the constitutional fiction that it was an integral part of metropolitan France. The Arabs and Berbers of Algeria, however, were treated as inferiors.

Nationalist violence came earlier to Morocco and Tunisia than to Algeria. By 1951 it was significant and sustained in the two protectorates, with the Egypt of King Farouk offering diplomatic support at the UN and a haven for political outlaws in Cairo. But it was briefer and milder than in Algeria because France, locked until 1954 in a distant war against nationalist forces in Indochina, did not sustain the repressive measures initiated by her administrators in Morocco and Tunisia. The French authorities in Rabat deposed and exiled the Moroccan sultan on 20 August 1953. A little more than two years later Paris restored him and in March 1956 recognized him as King Mohammed V of an independent Morocco. France recognized Tunisian independence that same month.

The presence of more than a million European colonists in Algeria, where many of them had been established for generations, occasioned far greater resistance by France to the nationalist agitation there among the 9 million Arabs and Berbers. The European *colons* possessed and enjoyed French citizenship, regardless of their countries of origin, and they supported a powerful lobby that no French government of the Fourth Republic dared to ignore.

The *NorAfs*, Arab and Berber, also possessed French citizenship but they did not enjoy the same political and civil rights as "French" Frenchmen, including the *colons* in Algeria. The *NorAfs* had no lobby and their nationalist political movements exerted no significant pressure on Paris until after the outbreak of armed insurrection on Halloween night 1954. By then Cairo had already assumed a major supporting role.

Egypt has been a haven for exiles and refugees since Joseph arrived there after escaping assassination by his brothers. The Holy Family fled into Egypt from Herod's baby-killers. Jews from the Spain of the Inquisition, an Albanian king, and a Czechoslovakian tennis champion are among the exiles who have sought and found shelter in Cairo over the centuries. North African rebels have lived in Cairo for decades. The Moroccan chieftain, Abdel Krim, eventually made his way there in 1946 after years as a French prisoner following the suppression of his revolt in the Riff mountains in the 1920s. Britain was the power in Egypt then. Cairo remained a traditional haven as power passed from the British into the hands of Egyptian kings and finally colonels.

The particular Algerians who broke off from older and milder nationalist parties to organize the long, decisive rebellion began appearing in Cairo in the early 1950s. They were members of the *Organisation Secrète*, also called the *Organisation Spéciale*, but better known as the OS, which they had formed in 1947. It was the grandparent organization of the *Front de Libération Nationale*, the famous FLN of the headlines of rebellion. Its strongest personality was

Ahmed Ben Bella, then 31, a former top sergeant in the French Army who was decorated four times for valor in the World War II fighting in Italy. In 1949 the OS mounted a daring fund-raising holdup of the Central Post Office in Oran. Ben Bella led the masked raiders, who made off with $9,000 for their cause.

The French police in Algeria discovered the existence of the OS and destroyed it in the spring of 1950. They arrested Ben Bella, among others, and seized OS arms caches all over Algeria. Mohamed Khider, who was not only an OS member but also one of the Algerian deputies in the French National Assembly, escaped to Cairo together with Belkacem Krim, Hocine Ait Ahmed, Lakhdar Ben Tobbal, and Omar Ouamrane. All five were to play prominent roles in the rebellion. Ben Bella joined the group in Cairo after escaping from prison in Algeria in March 1952.

By then a Maghrib Office was operating in Cairo under the auspices of the Arab League. Its aim was to further the independence of the three French territories in North Africa, which is known in Arabic as the *maghrib* (the place of sunset). Morocco and Tunisia were of greater concern than Algeria in 1952 to both the Egyptian government and the Arab League. But over the next two years Ben Bella and Khider and seven young Algerian colleagues, meeting with other nationalists in Switzerland, France, and Algeria as well as at their Cairo headquarters, built the nucleus of a revolutionary organization and made plans for action that soon dwarfed the Tunisian and Moroccan struggles for independence.

The nine Algerians, known informally in those days as the *club des neuf* and later as The Nine Historic Leaders, founded a successor organization to the OS in March 1954 under the name *Comité Révolutionnaire pour l'Unité et l'Action*. It was the parent of the FLN. By July 1954 the nine leaders had sent word through the lower levels of the CRUA organization that a revolt was in preparation. By September CRUA leadership had divided Algeria into six war zones, called *wilayas*, and had selected guerrilla commanders for each.

Six of the nine top leaders went to Algeria, which led to their being called the "interior" chiefs. Ben Bella, Khider, and Ait Ahmed remained in Cairo with responsibility for obtaining Egyptian arms and other support. The three in Cairo worked closely with a special section of the Egyptian Army headed by Major Fat'hy Deeb and Major Ezzat Suleiman. Ben Bella enjoyed the particular favor of Nasser. Both men had won honors in war before going on to plan revolutions; the bonds of sympathy between them were spontaneous.

Nasser told me in 1966 how his regime became involved in the Algerian revolt:

Our object from the beginning of the [Egyptian] Revolution towards Algeria was: Algeria must be an Arab country. Then we got in touch with Shaikh al-Ibrahim of Algeria. His efforts were mainly directed to building schools, teaching the Arab language and the Koran. But there were no political questions.

Then came Ben Bella. He came to me. He said that the only way is armed revolution. After this meeting we discussed the question in the Revolution Command Council. And there were question marks. But we concluded that we had to believe him. He said that on the 31st of October the revolution will begin in Algeria. We sent him arms.

My first shipment was with my yacht, the *Intisar*. It had been Farouk's yacht—not the *Mahroussa* but the other, smaller one called *Fakhr al-Bihar*. This shipment helped them to begin the revolution. [Houari] Boumedienne [who replaced Ben Bella as Algerian Premier in a *coup d'état* in 1965] went with the ship. He was in Al-Azhar [University, as a student].

He went with the ship and the first shipment was successful. There was a plan for the Algerians to bring boats to the ship and get the arms in these boats and return by night. And signals—there were details about the operation which I don't remember. The one who was responsible [on the Egyptian side] is now in the Socialist Union. Fat'hy Deeb. He is a specialist now on Arab affairs.

Nasser said that Egypt had previously sent arms and other aid to Moroccan and Tunisian nationalists and that his regime sent great quantities of weapons and supplies to the Algerian rebels from the outset of the insurrection until its bloody conclusion.

In the summer before the Algerian revolt two events occurred, an ending and a beginning, which were to affect the course of it. In Geneva in July French negotiators agreed upon ending eight years of war in Indochina and withdrawing French forces. In August Peres and Dayan came to Paris and persuaded the French Defense Minister, General Koenig, to sell Israel modern arms, beginning an agreement that soon developed into a tacit alliance against Egypt.

The Geneva accords on Indochina, concluded on 21 July 1954, were shaped by Britain's opposition to widening the war, which prevailed over Washington's desire for intervention by France's Western allies. The friction between Eden and Dulles during the nearly three months of intermittent negotiations was to recur in the Suez Crisis. A more important consequence linking the Indo-Chinese armistices with Suez was the return home of the French Army, full of mutinous bitterness over what many of its officers regarded as a humiliating betrayal by the politicians.

The first clandestine officers' oaths began to circulate after the fall of the French stronghold at Dienbienphu on 7 May 1954, which many blamed on the failure of the French government to throw in more reinforcements and air support. "Never, never will we accept such shame a second time," muttered the officers. With an unbroken record of defeats since the fall of France to the Nazis in 1940, the Army saw every one of them as the fault of the politicians.

The soldiers in Indochina were professionals and volunteers, not conscripts. They lacked a conscript army's ties with the civilians back home. In isolation from civilian life in France, they developed an exaggerated *esprit de corps* and militaristic modes of thought. When they began arriving in Algeria to suppress the rebels they developed sympathies with the political and civic leaders of the European *colons*, who tended toward arch-conservatism in contrast to the general left-wing flavor of political life in France itself.

The inability of a succession of postwar French governments to impose firm political authority on Algeria encouraged the Army to begin doing its own political thinking. It went to Algeria as the servant of civilian government in Paris but it progressively shifted its allegiance to the remarkably independent French administrators in Algeria, whose autonomy had the backing of the *colon* lobby. The frustrations of the Algerian war affected the Army at least as strongly as they affected the *colons* and administrators. So it was not surprising that the Army adopted such appealingly simplistic concepts as that the rebellion was the creature of a militant pan-Islamic movement directed from Cairo, which could be destroyed more easily in Cairo than in Algeria.

France had 50,000 troops in Algeria when the revolt broke out at 1 A.M. on 1 November 1954 with the first of some seventy guerrilla attacks that day at points scattered throughout the country. Within hours of the first raid, in which two French sentries were killed at Batna in the Aurès mountains, Cairo Radio was broadcasting: "At one o'clock this morning Algeria began to live a worthy and honorable life."

Six months later French forces in Algeria had been doubled. By May 1956, after French countermeasures had provoked the Arab and Berber masses into widespread support for the armed rebels, Paris had 250,000 soldiers in Algeria. By then the war was growing in scope and ferocity by the day. The illusion that a quick solution could be obtained by striking at Cairo spread from Europeans in Algeria upward through the Army and Defense Ministry until it captivated Premier Guy Mollet himself. By June 1956 the flow of French arms to Israel was increasing and both allies were impatient for a pretext to destroy Nasser.

Until the summer of 1954 Israel's thoughts of Great Power friendships had been directed almost entirely to Britain and the US, the two countries that had made possible Israel's birth and survival. The idea of giving greater importance to Franco-Israeli relations was pressed on influential Israelis in and out of office by Pierre-Eugène Gilbert, a tall urbane career diplomat of compelling charm and high-spirited enthusiasm for Israel. He had been appointed at his own request in April 1953 as France's Ambassador to Israel. Like most of the Frenchmen who helped create the alliance with Israel he had been a hero of the French underground resistance in World War II.

Hitler's Germany was then the common enemy of the thousands of Frenchmen and Israelis-to-be who found camaraderie in the resistance movements, in military service, and in the Nazi concentration camps. Again, in the postwar years, Frenchmen and Zionists found that they had a common enmity toward Britain in the Middle East.

A British army under General Sir Edward Spears occupied Damascus in May 1945. That and an ultimatum from General Spears was sufficient to evict French forces from Syria and Lebanon, where France was seeking to reconstitute her prewar paramountcy. France never forgot or forgave this humiliation.

The Zionists, in their final postwar drive for an independent Jewish state in Palestine, were already fighting bitterly against British rule in Palestine, especially its restrictions on immigration. France helped the Zionists in many ways. The Haganah operated secret training camps on French soil. Its espionage and intelligence networks had offices and radio transmitters in France. Smuggled arms, volunteers, and illegal immigrants moved through France to embattled Palestine along Zionist underground routes. French governments refused to cooperate with British efforts to stop the rusting, leaky ships, including the famous *Exodus 1947*, carrying Jews from the concentration camps to Palestine. French help to the Zionists severely strained relations between London and Paris in the postwar years.

Israel repaid the favors with diplomatic support after the founding of the state. Israel sided with France to block a special UN session on Tunisia in 1952 and voted with France to keep Algeria off the UN agenda in 1955. Yet the Foreign Ministries of the two countries remained fundamentally antipathetic or indifferent to a *rapprochement*.

The Quai d'Orsay wanted to preserve French influence in the former mandated territories of Syria and Lebanon although "the Spears affair" had rooted out the last vestiges of direct French control in those two countries. Practical French diplomats perceived that the Arabs were far more numerous than the Israelis both in numbers of people and in numbers of states. This made the Arab countries appear more important than Israel, both commercially and diplomatically, in a world of expanding foreign trade and in a United Nations organization whose ideal was: one nation, one vote.

Furthermore, there were the Arab and Moslem territories in the French

Empire to consider. Until nationalist movements in North Africa turned to overt resistance against French rule, it seemed wise to avoid provoking any part of the Arab and Moslem world inside or outside the French Empire. Finally, there was a long tradition of Arabic scholarship in the French military and civil services which had enjoyed international renown since Napoleon's occupation of Egypt at the end of the 18th century. There was no Hebraist tradition in the French services.

The reciprocal indifference to France of the Israeli Foreign Ministry arose from habit rather than practical considerations. The Foreign Ministry was a continuation of the Political Department of the Jewish Agency, which had dealt chiefly with the British during the Mandate and whose members were predominantly British-trained. The French mandates over Syria and Lebanon reflected a rivalry with the British in the Levant that lasted from the 18th century through World War II. France had hoped to get the Palestine mandate for herself too and she looked with ill favor on the British Mandate there and the growth of the Jewish National Home under the British aegis. In the face of French standoffishness, the secondary thrust of Zionist diplomacy, outside London, was directed toward the United States before, during, and immediately after the period of the Mandate.

Under these influences the Israeli Foreign Ministry remained sluggishly unresponsive to Ambassador Gilbert's ideas so long as Sharett, with his gradualist views and purely defensive military outlook, remained at the helm.

The tough young career men in the Defense Ministry were more imaginative and flexible than the diplomats and more indifferent to tradition and protocol. By the middle of 1954 they were impatient with Sharett and their own minister, Pinhas Lavon, for not showing enough vigor in implementing the rearmament program that Ben-Gurion had ordered before his temporary retirement in November 1953. And they felt that rearmament had been made more urgent since Ben-Gurion's retirement by developments in Anglo-American policy, particularly Britain's agreement on 27 July 1954 to withdraw from the Suez base.

Until then even Ben-Gurion, with whom Gilbert maintained a close friendship during his retirement to Sde Boker, would dismiss Gilbert's arguments for joint economic enterprises or new cultural links with his characteristic and peremptory "*Lo ha-shuv*" ("Not important") and change the subject to Greek philosophy. The idea of French arms, however, became "*Ha-shuv*" ("Important") when Britain agreed to remove her army from Egypt.

Israeli activists were worried also by the eleven-point memorandum submitted on 19 July by the US Embassy in Tel Aviv on behalf of the Tripartite Powers. It proposed to strengthen both the UN Truce Supervision Organization's manpower and its authority to deal with border incidents. The activists viewed the memorandum, in Dayan's words, as a "paternalistic" move that would in effect "turn Israel into a puppet state forced to take orders from outside in matters of its own security." They wanted arms, not paternalistic protection.

Shimon Peres, Director General of the Israeli Defense Ministry, had always dismissed the US as unlikely to furnish arms to Israel. He recalls having recommended an approach to France on the basis of five factors:

1. a general hostility among Frenchmen toward dictators like Nasser, deriving from the experience of Nazi wartime occupation,

2. the friendship of certain influential Frenchmen for Israel, particularly in the Radical and Socialist parties,

3. the belief in French military circles that Nasser had a hand in North African nationalist violence,

4. growing pro-Israel sentiment in the French press and,

5. the fact that French coalition cabinets were not closely united by party discipline but contained ministers of a variety of political and personal opinions, thus permitting an approach to the French government through whichever ministry looked most susceptible.

Peres, a bold practitioner of literal shirt-sleeve diplomacy, was not deterred by the fact that normal diplomatic channels were clogged at one end by the habitual Anglo-Americanism of the Israeli Foreign Ministry and at the other by the residual Arabism of the Quai d'Orsay. He recalls that he dispensed with formal approaches to the Quai d'Orsay because: "When you are struggling for your life it's not necessary to stick to formal diplomacy. Every foreign office represents the prudence of its nation and prudence doesn't necessarily promote aid to Israel." Military men, he felt, might be more easily persuaded than diplomats that Israel offered France the prospect of a voice in Middle Eastern affairs that would compensate for the loss of Syria and Lebanon.

So in Paris on Saturday, 31 July 1954, Peres telephoned the French Defense Minister, General Pierre-Marie Koenig, whose Zionist sympathies dated from his wartime meetings with Palestinian Jewish troops when he was commanding a Free French division in the Western Desert. To Peres's surprise Koenig told him to come at 11 o'clock the next morning, although it was a Sunday.

When Peres arrived Koenig asked if he had brought a list. Peres pulled one from his pocket. Koenig looked at it carefully and told Peres to return the following day and submit it to an aide. Peres did so. The aide referred back to Koenig for confirmation and the negotiations were under way. They were continued by Dayan, who arrived on 8 August on his way home from a disappointing tour of the United States. After conferences with Koenig and his sub-

ordinates Dayan left Peres to sign a formal but secret agreement with Diomède
Catroux, Secretary of State for Air. It provided for French delivery of Ouragan
jets, fast AMX-13 tanks, 75 mm. guns, and radar equipment. Several knowledg-
able officials say Mystère II jets were also included. The agreement had the
approval of Premier Pierre Mendès-France. Deliveries began in the fall.

The agreement broke the solidarity of the Tripartite Powers, swinging
France toward Israel as a counterbalance to Washington's drift toward neutrality in the Palestine dispute and Britain's alarming Suez base concessions to
Nasser. It alleviated the anxieties aroused in Israel by the eleven-point Tripartite proposal of 19 July as well as by the Anglo-Egyptian Heads of Agreement on the Suez base, which was initialed on 27 July. As Dayan wrote later:

> The French were fully aware from the first that we did not seek arms solely in
> order that they should serve as a deterrent but that we contemplated the possibility
> of war on Arab terrorism. . . . General Koenig, the French Defense Minister at the
> time, expressed the opinion that "Israel should be given more arms in order that its
> excellent soldiers can make use of them."

At that time France did not yet contemplate the evacuation of Algeria and Nasser's
dream of an All-Arab Middle East cleared of all strangers was diametrically opposed
to French policy. They had a clear interest in reducing his stature and opposing his
policies. This created an identity of interests between France and Israel and the
French Army could look upon *Zahal* [the Israeli Defense Force] as a force fighting
a common enemy on a separate front.

The eruption of the Algerian rebellion on 1 November, as these first secret
deliveries were being incorporated into the Israeli forces, encouraged still further the community of interest between the French and Israeli Defense Ministries. Premier Pierre Mendès-France had withdrawn France from her colonial
war in Indo-China and made constitutional concessions to Tunisia during the
summer. But he resolved to use force to put down the Algerian uprising.

Mendès-France and Edgar Faure, who succeeded him as Premier in February 1955, attempted a two-pronged policy aimed on the one hand at suppress-
ing the armed insurrection and on the other at wooing the Arab and Berber
masses with widespread reforms. They sought to implement constitutional reforms that had remained dormant in the face of *colon* opposition since 1947.

Thus, in January 1955 Mendès-France authorized a major operation by
5,000 troops with air and armored support against rebel strongholds in the
Aurès mountains. Meanwhile, to carry through the reforms, he appointed
Soustelle as Governor General of Algeria. Faure reappointed Soustelle after a
two-week cabinet crisis brought him to the premiership.

Soustelle presented his program in the Algerian Assembly on 23 February, saying: "Algeria and all its people are an integral part of France, one and indivisible ... and France will no more quit Algeria than Provence or Brittany. ... France has made a choice; this choice is called 'Integration.' " The *colons* found his liberalism offensive and they set their faces doggedly against such distasteful integration measures as a single electoral roll giving each *NorAf* the same vote as a European.

Five days later Ben-Gurion, newly returned from retirement to his old cabinet post as Defense Minister, launched the Gaza Raid. Even before the French offensive in the Aurès had come to its end, with insignificant results, Dayan's excellent soldiers showed their mettle in Gaza as "a force fighting a common enemy on a separate front."

Ben-Gurion believed Israel deserved still more French arms to support his new hard line. He had already sent Peres back to Paris with a personal letter to the new government of Edgar Faure saying that Israel had decided to re-equip her army entirely with French arms, beginning with French planes. Peres again saw Koenig, who had returned as Defense Minister in the Faure cabinet. Koenig had resigned from the Mendès-France government on 14 August 1954, a few days after initiating the first secret arms agreement with Peres and Dayan.

The second secret Franco-Israeli agreement included more planes and tanks, howitzers, rockets, antiaircraft guns, and ammunition. Koenig went so far as to promise Vautour jet bombers. Four Israeli purchasing missions came to Paris. They were followed shortly by Dayan and his air force commander, General Tolkovski. According to Michel Bar-Zohar, who wrote a history of the Franco-Israeli alliance with the encouragement and help of Peres, Generals Dayan and Tolkovski signed "certain accords for military cooperation" with the French.

Straws in the wind appeared on 29 March when the French ambassador at the UN, although joining the unanimous Security Council censure of Israel for the Gaza Raid, stated that as a friendly ally of Israel he had cast his condemnation vote with difficulty. The same day news agencies reported from Paris that Israel had "ordered 15 Mystère II jet fighters." But Israel kept her new arms out of sight during the annual Independence Day military display in May. Fuller word of the first Franco-Israeli arms agreement leaked into print that same month in the bulletin of Edouard Sablier's *Centre d'Information du Proche-Orient*. Nasser mentioned it on 2 October among the intelligence reports he cited as justifying his arms deal with Czechoslovakia. It was available by 18 May, the day Nasser approached the Russian Ambassador for arms after failing to obtain them from the US and Britain.

The idea of war with Egypt seems to have been in Ben-Gurion's mind from the time he decided to return to the Defense Ministry. Bar-Zohar, Ben-Gurion's authorized biographer, says it was first discussed with the French in June 1955, the month that began with Nasser's luckless offer to demilitarize the Egyptian-Israeli frontier. The subject came up in a conversation between Peres and Maurice Bourgès-Maunoury, then Interior Minister in the Faure cabinet. Josef Nahmias, by then a more or less permanent representative of the Israeli Defense Ministry in Paris, had begun to broaden his ministry's contacts with the French Government. Relations between the two defense ministries having been established firmly with Koenig, Nahmias opened a channel to the Interior Ministry through Abel Thomas, the minister's right-hand man. This was a logical second channel because Algeria was at that time in the bailiwick of the Interior Ministry.

On 19 May 1955 France announced the transfer to Algeria of 20,000 troops from her NATO contingent in Germany. A few days later Soustelle, already turning away from his optimistic liberalism, publicly fell back on a policy of "pitiless severity" in an all-out war against the nationalist rebellion. A second major French offensive in the Aurès mountains was in preparation. With the elusive Algerian *fellaghas* defying French troop commitments in proportions as high as two hundred to one, the will-o'-the-wisp of a solution by war in Egypt had begun to take shape.

In July 1955, although joint French-Israeli war plans were still more than a year in the future, Israel asked that her orders for Mystère II jet fighters be canceled and two squadrons of first-line Mystère IVs, each of twelve planes plus three spares, be delivered instead. Israel had no inkling at this time of the Egyptian arms negotiations with Russia and Czechoslovakia. Reports of the negotiations first reached Israel late in August.

The very inner differences within the French cabinets which Peres exploited to Israel's advantage sometimes worked to impede the realization of the benefits after Israel had obtained them. The Quai d'Orsay, with its Arab concerns, was always uneasy about the Defense Ministry's arms contracts with Israel and tended to delay or balk delivery by a variety of means. Sometimes it alerted the Near East Arms Committee, which the Tripartite Powers established to control supplies of arms in accordance with their Declaration of 25 May 1950. But the Defense Ministry developed bookkeeping devices that circumvented the NEAC. The French had no compunction about such evasions. As Pineau said later of the vast secret shipments to Israel during the build-up for the Suez War: "The US didn't consult France about sending arms to Iran and Pakistan and Iraq; why should France ask about sending arms to Israel?"

In the summer of 1955 the Defense Ministry contracted to sell 100 fast

AMX-13 tanks each to Israel and Egypt. Foreign Minister Antoine Pinay, however, approved delivery to Egypt but delayed the shipment to Israel. Israeli agents alerted Koenig and Bourgès-Maunoury, recalling recent news reports that Egyptian-trained Algerian rebels were killing French troops with Egyptian mortars. Koenig immediately blocked the shipment of tanks to Egypt until Pinay gave in on the shipment to Israel.

Ultimately both shipments went to Israel as a result of new violence in North Africa that broke out on 20 August, the second anniversary of the forcible exile of the nationalist Sultan of Morocco. In Oued Zem, Morocco, Berber tribesmen came down from the hills for a hideous massacre of at least 51 Europeans, slashing open the stomachs of pregnant women, cutting out men's tongues, smashing infants' heads, and burning people alive in gasoline-soaked mattresses. The Foreign Legion and vigilante groups retaliated equally hideously, killing 300 Berbers and Arabs before they were satisfied.

Simultaneously, in and around Philippeville, Algeria, disciplined rebels of the *Armée de Libération Nationale* in league with sympathetic local peasants armed with knives and clubs killed 71 Europeans and 52 *Beni Oui Oui* ("Sons of Yes-Yes," a contemptuous designation for Arabs and Berbers who cooperated with the French). The massacre and retaliation were worse than in Morocco. The French listed 1273 rebels killed, but most of them were local peasants and not trained guerrillas of the ALN, which was the military arm of the FLN.

The terrible weekend of 20/21 August opened a chasm between the European and Moslem communities of Algeria that was never bridged again. Bands of Europeans, sickening for revenge, hunted Moslem villagers into the hills and sacked their dwellings while grim rebel partisans struck at isolated European farms and made the bodies of hapless *Beni Oui Oui* into dreadful warnings against collaboration with the colonial rulers. With Philippeville communal civil war began in Algeria.

Cairo Radio's exultation over the massacres provoked the anguished French into suspending all arms deliveries to Egypt on 2 September, including consignments already paid for. The 100 AMX-13s consigned to Egypt went to Israel instead. The ban on arms for Egypt was revoked in November in exchange for an abatement of Cairo's devilish anti-French propaganda. No significant amount of French arms went to Cairo again, however, and nothing light enough to be transported from Cairo to the mountain lairs of the Algerian guerrillas.

The Israeli-Egyptian arms race, forced upon a reluctant Egypt both by Ben-Gurion's raids and by intelligence of his secret rearmament by France, entered a new phase as a result of Nasser's announcement on 27 September 1955 of the Czech arms agreement. The announcement took the Israelis completely by surprise and gave them an additional war aim.

Ben-Gurion and Sharett had threatened war over Aqaba in campaign speeches in July. In August, coincidentally with the far greater bloodletting in North Africa, shooting on the "separate front" of Israel had opened up again when an Israeli patrol stormed an Egyptian position on the 22nd. This was followed by the first *Fedayeen* campaign on the 25th and the major Israeli reprisal against Khan Yunis on the 31st. The *Fedayeen* too gave Ben-Gurion a new cause for war. As for Suez, Ambassador Gilbert urged Ben-Gurion to develop Israel's exclusion as a pretext for war, counsel which he was to renew after Nasser nationalized the Canal. Two days before Nasser announced the Czech arms deal Ben-Gurion set a time limit of one year for Egypt to unblock the Aqaba Gulf to Israeli shipping or face an attack. The emergence of Russia as a Great Power friend and arms supplier to the Egyptians made Ben-Gurion's war plans still more urgent as well as more dangerous. The alliance with France became more important, more *Ha-shuv* than ever.

Preventive war, or more accurately, pre-emptive war became a lively consideration for Israel's military planners from the moment they learned of the Egyptian-Czech arms contract. An Egypt armed and protected by a Great Power would be more able than ever to balk Ben-Gurion's war aims and, worse yet, might become bold enough to attack Israel. It was now that Ben-Gurion swiftly consolidated his hold on al-Auja, ordered Dayan to prepare an operational plan for the invasion of the Sinai Peninsula, opened a new arms drive in Washington and Paris, and settled down to the long struggle either to bend Sharett to accept pre-emptive war or remove him from the cabinet.

The sense of urgency among French activists grew apace with that in Israel. On 2 December, after his government crumbled under the impact of the Algerian war, Premier Faure ordered the first dissolution of a National Assembly in 76 years and scheduled a general election on 2 January 1956. Ever-rising violence and a wave of Moslem resignations from local and municipal councils made elections unthinkable in Algeria. Therefore, despite the juridical fiction that Algeria was part of metropolitan France, Soustelle postponed the elections there. As it turned out, the postponement was permanent.

At the beginning of November 1955, while Sharett, in Paris and Geneva, was persuading Premier Faure to increase arms deliveries to Israel, Peres had conferred with General Pierre Billotte, Koenig's successor as Defense Minister. Peres received extraordinary courtesies. A member of Faure's staff installed Peres in his office in the Hôtel Matignon during the election campaign to facilitate his work on arms contracts. The tireless Peres went out into the constituencies and contacted virtually all the candidates who were potentially useful to Israel. During one rally Peres conferred unseen with Billotte inside his campaign sound truck. Peres constantly urged France not to consult Washington about arms sales to Israel—"Above all, not Dulles."

The French parliamentary election on 2 January strengthened the extremes of Left and Right at the expense of the Center, from which the coalition governments of the Fourth Republic were formed. Consequently the new National Assembly was more ungovernable than the old. It was nearly a month before a new government could be put together with enough parties supporting it to stand independently of the Communists on the Left, who constituted the largest single party in the Chamber of Deputies, and the Poujadists on the Right, the extremist party of small businessmen which made the greatest gains of any party in the election. Although the 30 seats representing Algerian constituencies remained vacant because the rebellion had prevented elections there, the inherent instability of the new Assembly ensured more influence than ever for the lobbyists of *l'Algérie Française*.

As a result, no new government could resist the momentum of the hopeless but ever-growing war in Algeria. The Socialist Party had campaigned under the slogans: "Peace in Algeria" and "Not a Penny, Not a Soldier for the War in Algeria." But the government of Socialist leader Guy Mollet, which took office on 1 February 1956, swiftly succumbed to the Algerian emotion and stepped up the war effort in July with immense new tax levies and the call-up of tens of thousands of French conscripts to join the professional soldiers fighting in Algeria.

With Mollet, the informal alliance between Israel and France entered its most fruitful phase, culminating just nine months later in the collusive attack with Britain on Egypt. Indeed, cooperation between the Mollet and Ben-Gurion governments was closer than that between most formal allies.

Even before the election Mollet had promised Peres that he would prove a good friend to Israel. Peres replied:

Fine, but I'm afraid you might be like Bevin [the Laborite British Foreign Secretary during the last, postwar years of the Palestine Mandate], like all the other Socialists. When they're in opposition, they're always on our side, full of promises and sympathy; but as soon as they're in office they turn against us.

The day after he took office Mollet again saw Peres, who had brought him a letter from Ben-Gurion. Said Mollet: "Now you are going to see that I am no Bevin."

Mollet was the twenty-second French premier since the liberation of France from the Nazis, which he had fought for as a leader in the underground resistance. He was a teacher of English before the war. He first fought the Germans as a uniformed soldier of France until he was wounded and captured. He entered the underground after his release in 1941. This led him into politics. When he became Premier at the age of 50 he had served ten years as Secretary General of the French Socialist Party.

Like many Frenchmen of his age, he had what he called an "anti-Munich complex." By the time he became Premier he had already begun to equate Nasser with Hitler. He kept Nasser's slim book, *The Philosophy of the Revolution*, in his desk, likening it to *Mein Kampf* and construing quotations out of it to allege that Nasser lusted for empire over the Arab world as well as for vengeance against the West. He warned callers, including US Ambassador Douglas Dillon, that Nasser wanted to fasten his own control upon Middle Eastern oil in order to force his will on Europe.

Nasser was an obsession with Mollet from the start of his premiership. For Israel, Mollet's obsession served as one of the pillars of the alliance; Ben-Gurion too likened Nasser both to Hitler and to Pharaoh as a historic enemy of the Jews. The bond of Socialism between the two premiers was another pillar of the Franco-Israeli alliance. A third pillar was the French illusion that the Algerian rebellion could be paralyzed by striking at Egypt.

Christian Pineau, Mollet's Foreign Minister, says the forced parallel with Hitler led Mollet to overestimate Nasser's strength. Pineau is a more complex man than Mollet. Born in 1904, a year before Mollet, he also was named Premier a year earlier, in February 1955, but he failed to form a cabinet. In contrast to Mollet's rather typical career as a Socialist, Pineau's was oddly paradoxical. Before entering politics on the Left, he was a banker and businessman and he returned to business after serving as Foreign Minister under three premiers. He is also a talented writer, having published more than a dozen books of fiction and nonfiction. They include a sensitive biography of Khrushchev and a series of beguiling children's books with such titles as *The Bear with Green Paws, The Planet of Lost Children*, and *Stories of I Don't Know When*. Behind Pineau's impassive, somewhat Oriental visage is a contradictory mixture of capitalist hardheadedness, socialist idealism, and the enchanted imagination of a modern fabulist and fairy-tale spinner. There is also self-criticism and a Gallic skepticism. Where Mollet insists that if he had Suez to do over again he would do precisely as before, Pineau makes no secret of his own changes of mind. His candor about the collusive alliance with Israel haunts his British partners like a bad conscience.

Mollet raised the level of the alliance from ministerial channels to the premier's office itself. He also multiplied the ministerial links by including in his cabinet men who were not only partisans of Israel against the Arabs but who shared the illusion that the vital source of the Algerian rebellion lay in Egypt. The key men for Israel in Mollet's cabinet, in addition to Mollet himself, were Foreign Minister Pineau, also a Socialist; Defense Minister Maurice Bourgès-Maunoury, a Radical Republican-Socialist who had furthered the alliance as Interior Minister in 1955; and Robert Lacoste, a Socialist stalwart who espoused the reactionary cause of the *colons* as Minister Resident for Algeria, the cabinet post created by Mollet to replace the office of Governor General.

Equally important to Israel were men in subministerial posts, especially the directors of ministerial cabinets. The minister's cabinet is a staff institution peculiar to France and is not to be confused with the cabinet itself, which is known in France as the Council of Ministers. The *directeur de cabinet* is the personal appointee of the minister and is a political rather than a civil service office. Activities entrusted to the *directeur de cabinet* are extraordinarily varied and can be handled with remarkable flexibility because they do not necessarily involve or commit the government. These *directeurs de cabinet* were among the first functionaries to be approached by the perceptive Israeli representatives; and when contact had been established with a minister, the day-to-day contacts were usually maintained by his *directeur de cabinet*. Such a man was Abel Thomas, director of Bourgès-Maunoury's cabinet at both the Interior and Defense ministries. Thomas, as loyal and immodest an aide as a politician could ask for, claims for Bourgès-Maunoury and himself the credit for rearming Israel. He belittles Koenig's role as an accidental preliminary.

Mollet's liberal intentions toward Algeria lasted less than a week. His first appointee as Minister Resident was the seventy-nine-year-old General Georges Catroux, whose name was anathema to the *colons* because of his key role in 1955 in negotiating the restoration of the exiled Sultan Mohammed of Morocco. The *colons* were afraid Mollet would surrender their privileged dominance in Algeria by giving each *NorAf* a vote equal to a European's and then negotiating peace with elected *NorAf* representatives. Their fears were sharpened by Mollet's inclusion in his cabinet of Mendès-France, who had surrendered Indo-China and Tunisia. The *colons* feared their options would soon be narrowed to "the suitcase or the shroud," departure or death. Catroux abandoned in advance Soustelle's policy of full Moslem and European integration and stated that "there is no historical basis for the recognition of a national Algerian state" but he failed to abate the rising temper of the suspicious *colons*. Tens of thousands of Europeans crowded the docks of Algiers on 2 February to cheer Soustelle as a hero and demonstrate against his departure. They paraded him through the throng on their shoulders and let him embark, dizzy with their acclaim, only after he vowed to defend *l'Algérie Française* in Paris.

The tumultuous farewell was a mere foretaste of the epic bullying that shook Mollet into line when he arrived in Algiers on Monday, 6 February, for a five-day visit that was scheduled to be climaxed by Mollet's personal installation of Catroux as Minister Resident. "Death to Mollet," "Catroux to the gallows," roared the mob as it pelted the Premier with mud and tomatoes at a wreath-laying ceremony at the municipal war memorial. Bodyguards frantically caught garbage, mud, and stones in the air as Mollet stood at attention for the *Marsèillaise*. White-faced and shaken, the Premier returned to the Moorish palace of the French Governors with the rabble hard on the heels of his motorcade. Five thousand demonstrators rushed the palace, lowered the Tricolor to half-mast, and tore up the garden with little hindrance from the complaisant European police.

Mollet got Catroux's resignation by telephoning Paris that same evening. On the 8th he agreed to let Alain de Sérigny, the doughty *colon* publisher of *L'Echo d'Alger*, print in Mollet's name the statement: "France is at home in Algeria, and she will remain there." On the 9th Mollet named Robert Lacoste as the Minister Resident. Like his predecessor, Soustelle, Lacoste quickly espoused the *colon* cause. The real measure of what had happened inside Mollet during the ordeal of 6 February showed itself on the 9th in a broadcast which the journalist-historian Edward Behr described as "an orgy of self-abasement."

"You have been depicted as colonialists," said the Socialist Premier to his racist and reactionary radio audience. "I do not share this view.... Farmers, workers, tradespeople, teachers, doctors, who have been established in Algeria for several generations and have their homes, their families and their dead in Algeria. Since my arrival, I have heard the voice of all of them and have been greatly moved by it.... I understand their despair.... That is why I say to you in all sincerity that, even though for me the experience was painful, the unfortunate demonstration on Monday had a wholesome aspect. It provided many with an opportunity to express their attachment to France and their fear of being abandoned.... I assure them that they have been heard. France will remain present in Algeria."

The voice of the nationalist Moslem majority, however, was given no hearing and the insistent language of knife, gun, and bomb was nowhere near being understood.

The *colons* never forgot the apparent lesson of 6 February 1956, which was that street violence could bend and even break the will of French governments in Paris. The overthrow of the Fourth Republic following demonstrations that erupted on 13 May 1958 seemed to be added proof. But the real key was the complaisance of the military toward the *colons* and its contempt for the Fourth Republic. The inevitable solution in Algeria had to wait for General de Gaulle to resubordinate the Army to civilian government and make it stop fighting the terrible, unwinnable, unlosable, guerrilla war. As Vietnam was to demonstrate again, the professional soldier is content to fight such wars indefinitely. War is his trade. Only politicians can make him forego the experience of it.

Conversely, when politicians succumb to military thinking, war proliferates. "One French division in Egypt is worth four divisions in North Africa," said Lacoste when France took the nationalization of the Suez Canal as a pretext for shifting troops from Algerian operations to build up an invasion force for Egypt. It was a natural sequel to his statement months earlier that "the rebels are carried on the wave of pan-Arabism inspired by the Egyptian Army." On Ambassador Gilbert's advice, the Israeli war party promptly sent Yehoshafat Harkavi, the chief of military intelligence, to recruit Lacoste into its circle of key ministerial contacts.

Far-flung events soon added to the impetus which Mollet's encounter with the *colons* gave to the Franco-Israeli alliance against Nasser. When King Hussein of Jordan rudely fired his British army chief, Glubb Pasha, on 1 March 1956 and the Tories sneered anew at Eden's "dithering," the British Prime Minister decided upon Nasser as the enemy who had to be cut down to restore his political prestige and safeguard British influence in the Middle East. Eden accordingly made overtures of friendship toward Britain's erstwhile antagonists in the Middle East, Israel and France. He abated Britain's objections to France's secret arms supplies to Israel, came out strongly in support of French policy in Algeria, and hastily arranged an "intimate" talk on the Middle East with Mollet. The US followed Britain with official support for France on the question of Algeria. In Algeria itself the French lost control of mountainous Kabylia to the rebels, who set up an independent government there. At the end of March the FLN announced that since France had abandoned civilized rules of warfare in trying to suppress the rebellion, the Algerian army could no longer be bound by humane considerations and would fight back with the same methods. Simultaneously with the Anglo-American shift against Nasser, there were defiant stirrings in Russia's East European satellites. These developments doubly weakened the major deterrents to Israeli action on the "separate front" against Nasser at the same time that aggravation of the Algerian fighting made it more attractive to the French activists.

Meanwhile Foreign Minister Pineau made an impromptu visit to Nasser in Cairo on 14 March 1956 on his way home from a conference in Karachi of the foreign ministers of the Southeast Asia Treaty Organization. So as not to offend neutralist India, Pineau had gone from Karachi to New Delhi to meet Prime Minister Jawaharlal Nehru. It was Nehru who suggested to Pineau that he break his return journey in Cairo for a talk with Nasser. Nehru said Mollet had a false image of Nasser and he urged Pineau to obtain a true impression at first hand. The hastily prepared conversation between Pineau and Nasser lasted more than three hours, most of it devoted to the topic of Algeria.

The meeting had two interesting consequences. First, Pineau made no secret of his favorable impression of Nasser, an indiscretion that was to goad him with political embarrassment after Nasser nationalized the Suez Canal. Second, at Nasser's prompting, French representatives began a series of secret negotiations with Algerian rebels in Cairo, Belgrade, and Rome.

Nasser, who speaks good English but almost no French, brought the aristocratic Aly Sabry, his chief aide and later a premier of the United Arab Republic, into the meeting to translate between French and Arabic. On the French side, in addition to Pineau, were the courtly Ambassador Armand du Chayla and Georges Gorse, a young career diplomat who came a day in advance as Mollet's personal emissary.

Eleven months before, at the Bandung Conference, Nasser had introduced the resolution in which 29 Asian and African nations declared their "support of the rights of the people of Algeria, Morocco, and Tunisia to self-determination and independence" and urged the French Government to "bring about a peaceful settlement of the issue without delay." With Moroccan and Tunisian independence assured, Nasser told Pineau that Egypt did not insist on independence for Algeria but that Egypt could approve only a negotiated solution, not an imposed solution, and that the Algerians should by right determine for themselves whether they wanted independence or some kind of association with France.

Nasser questioned Pineau about a newly disclosed shipment of Mystère IVs to Israel. Pineau told him that it was in fulfillment of an old contract made by a previous government. He assured the Egyptians with cheery hypocrisy that the sales to Israel were less than reported and that the Arabs would have every right to protest any new Franco-Israeli arms contracts. Pineau made clear, however, that France was of no mind to abandon her Israeli friends. Pineau said Nasser replied: "I can give you the promise that Egypt will never attack Israel. I favor peaceful relations with that country, although I cannot put this into effect because of public opinion in Egypt and the Arab World." The two men agreed in their opposition to the Baghdad Pact, which Pineau said should be transformed from a military into an economic accord.

Pineau's frenetic day in Cairo included: meetings with King Saud and President Shukry al-Kuwwatly of Syria, who had come to confer with Nasser on the consequences of Glubb Pasha's summary expulsion from Jordan; a luncheon with Foreign Minister Mahmoud Fawzi of Egypt, at which François Charles-Roux, chairman of the Suez Canal Company board, was also a guest; and a lightning sightseeing tour of the Citadel, the Mohammed Aly Mosque, the Pyramids, and the Sphinx. The visit ended with an evening press conference at the airport. Pineau, in high spirits, said Nasser impressed him as unlikely to start a war because he was channeling his main efforts into economic and social development. He said Nasser had given his word of honor that no Algerian guerrillas were being trained in Egypt. Pineau treated the visit when he got home as a personal diplomatic triumph.

He repeated to the National Assembly the following week Nasser's pledge that no North African commandos were training in Egyptian camps. Nasser did not give any such assurance about shipping arms to Algeria, Pineau said, adding with incautious wisdom:

"But according to the information we have, these supplies do not have the importance that certain people allege. I believe one must avoid, in diplomatic affairs, the process that consists of reconstructing the diplodocus on the basis of a single vertebra." French agents promptly placed Egyptian military camps under surveillance.

After the Suez nationalization, Pineau used curiously discrete phraseology when he said, the surveillance "has led us to aver that several Algerians and Tunisians were getting military training there." Apparently Nasser had broken his word of honor on this point, he added. Pineau's tiptoe semantics became more comprehensible in the light of French Ambassador Armand du Chayla's low regard for French intelligence in Egypt at the time. He appraised the reports as "unverified, exaggerated, and ultimately irrelevant because the Egyptian contribution in Algeria was small." Whenever guerrillas receive adequate help, he said, they become a regular army. Guerrilla warfare is crueler than conventional war because it cannot be decisively won by either side, with the consequence that each vies in increasing the viciousness in the hope of making the opponent quit. A guerrilla war is a contest not of strength but of will.

Despite the cordiality of the meeting between Pineau and Nasser the visible policy of the Mollet government toward the Algerian rebels continued to harden and individual ministers continued with Mollet to construct their diplodocus—the illusion that Egypt's defeat would end the rebellion.

Behind the scenes, however, Mollet commissioned Georges Gorse and Joseph Bégarra to meet secretly in Cairo with Mohammed Khider and another FLN representative in negotiations arranged by Nasser as a result of his meeting with Pineau. There were five meetings between 12 April and 1 May 1956. "But suddenly," Nasser recalled later, "there was something about that in the French newspapers. And then, without any warning, the French people left Cairo and returned very quickly to France and Pineau denied what was in the newspapers about this meeting. . . . They were afraid to discuss the question in the Assembly."

A colleague of Gorse's says it was Gorse who deliberately brought the negotiations to nought after perceiving that the political mood in Paris would not only preclude any useful result of the talks but would probably damage his career for having participated in them. Gorse took no part in the second series of talks, which began in July. His shrewdness served him well; he later became Ambassador to Algeria.

While Gorse's mission to the FLN was in preparation, the Arab League offered full support to the Algerian rebels and accused France of atrocities. Pineau angrily protested and canceled a visit to Syria and Lebanon. The French gave the Israelis to understand that henceforth they regarded force as the only means of stopping Egyptian aid to the FLN and that they would therefore step up the arming of Israel.

By coincidence or design, the bombardment of Gaza by Israeli mortar crews on 5 April not only crippled Dag Hammarskjold's impending armistice mission to the Middle East but also brought home to the French Government the prospect of an Israeli-Egyptian war, with all that this might mean for France.

On 12 April, as France issued the biggest draft call since World War II to 75,000 young men for service in Algeria, Ben-Gurion sent Peres to Paris with an urgent reminder of Israel's arms needs on the "separate front." The first squadron of Mystères had begun to arrive that day. The immediate result of Peres's visit was another squadron and a televised declaration by Mollet of French support for Israel.

By mid-April the lines of Franco-Israeli cooperation against Egypt were fixed. The influence of events in the months to come merely speeded the development of the alliance. Pineau disclosed to the National Assembly on 3 August that, while making repeated protests to Egypt in April and May over her aid to the Algerian rebels, the French leaders had already countenanced the idea of "an eventual conflict" and were trying to avoid responsibility for it. The concept of France and Israel each fighting Nasser on a "separate front" was giving way to the prospect of both allies striking directly at Egypt. While Ben-Gurion prepared for war by forcing the moderate Sharett out of his cabinet and attaching all manner of loophole conditions to the armistice undertakings sought by Hammarskjold, Pineau conferred in Washington on those same mid-June days trying to persuade Dulles to step into line for Big Three action against Nasser. Pineau's proposals were not so sharply defined as

Ben-Gurion's war plans but the American Government, he informed the Assembly, "showed itself at the time to be rather hesitant." He added wishfully: "It has subsequently progressed."

The struggle for Algeria turned ever worse for the French, who resorted to more and more desperate measures. French authorities in Algeria executed two rebels on 19 June for bearing arms against France. The FLN published leaflets vowing to kill 100 European civilians for every patriot executed by France and they followed suit by extending their violent operations from the countryside into the cities. They achieved an ominous success with a general strike on 5 July. Vigilante societies of die-hard Europeans, hardly bothering to keep their societies secret, embarked that month on six years of counterterrorism in the *casbahs* (Moslem quarters) of the cities. They began by blowing up an entire tenement building in Algiers, killing 53 Moslem tenants and rendering 280 homeless.

Mollet had forgotten his campaign promises but his Socialist Party had not. At its annual congress on 1 July at Lille it voted a recommendation to the government to seek a cease-fire. Mollet could not ignore this, but neither could he survive public knowledge of overtures to the rebels. So in uneasy secrecy he appointed Pierre Commin, a senator and his Socialist Party second-in-command, to meet the FLN chiefs. This second series of talks began on 25 July in Yugoslavia. Nasser, Tito, and Nehru had refused a week earlier to receive the FLN chiefs at their neutralists' summit conference on the Yugoslav island of Brioni and they devoted a paragraph to Algeria in their communiqué, urging "cease-fire and negotiation."

Thus Nasser urged upon the FLN exactly what the Socialists had obliged Mollet to seek for France. These convergent promptings gave the secret negotiations enough impetus to continue into the fall in Belgrade and Rome despite the fact that Mollet had selected party men rather than diplomats for the talks in order to avoid directly engaging his government. The failure of the talks did not come until Mollet, with the kind of bad faith that is born of political weakness, sanctioned the 22 October 1956 aerial kidnapping of the five FLN leaders, including the chief representative at the secret negotiations, Mohammed Khider.

The only hopeful current in the darkening waters around Algeria, France, Egypt, and Israel showed in the relations between Egypt and the *Compagnie Universelle du Canal Maritime de Suez*, the famous Suez Canal Company founded by the genius of Ferdinand de Lesseps.

The low-lying desert isthmus joining Africa to Asia, only 105 miles wide between the Bay of Pelusium and the Gulf of Suez, was not so much a link between continents as a barrier, tantalizingly slight, between the great oceans of the world. The convenience of a canal across it has been obvious since the building of the pyramids. When de Lesseps, bettering the half measures of ancient pharaohs and caliphs, built the canal, it became obvious that it was not a convenience but a new necessity.

In 1870, the Suez Canal's first full year of operations, 486 ships went through carrying 436,609 tons of cargo and 26,758 passengers. In 1955, the last full year before nationalization, 14,666 ships traversed the canal carrying 115,756,398 tons of cargo, three times the tonnage handled by the Panama Canal, and 520,774 passengers. The troopship year of 1945 set the record for passenger transits with 983,937. Revenue from tolls rose from 4,345,758 francs in 1870 to 32,371,728,846 in 1955. Egypt had got very little of the profits and was demanding more, plus a larger role in management and operations. The company, feeling tremors of vulnerability because of the contrast between Egyptian poverty and its own power and riches, was giving way a little in order not to lose all.

As it turned out, the company had become so rich and powerful that the amputation of the canal itself would seem not so much to have injured it as to have freed its energies for another project of equally grand scope, the cutting of a tunnel under the English Channel between England and France. The channel tunnel, or "Chunnel," as the project has come to be called, was, like the Suez Canal, seriously considered by Napoleon. It is an eighteenth-century European concept which may yet become an indirect result of de Lesseps' enterprise.

The concept of the Suez Canal had its origins before European history began; the fabulous profits gained by de Lesseps' company were a natural consequence of so many people having wanted it for so long a time. The first canal linking the Red Sea to the Nile, and thus incidentally to the Mediterranean, of which there are fully verified historical records was begun by the Pharaoh Nechos between 609 and 593 B.C. and completed a century later by the Persian conquerors of Egypt. It tapped the Nile at Bubastis, near present-day Zagazig, on the easternmost of the seven ancient branches, which entered the Mediterranean at Pelusium, near present-day Port Said. The Pelusiac branch silted up centuries ago. Nechos's canal ran due east to the Bitter Lakes along a shallow wadi where the Sweetwater Canal runs today and thence south to the head of the Red Sea near present-day Suez. Being dependent on the level of the Nile, it was navigable only during the seasons of high water.

The ancient canals lapsed into long periods of disuse alternating with periods of renewal and improvement. The last restoration before modern times was by the Arab conqueror Amr Ibn al-Aas in 641 to transport Egyptian grain to famine-ridden Mecca. It remained in use nearly 150 years until a Moslem caliph in distant Baghdad ordered it blocked to shut off supplies to rebels in Medina.

Not only the water route but also the overland route through Egypt to the Indies fell into disuse after Vasco da Gama in 1497 opened the way around Africa and, twenty years later, the Ottoman Turks extended their mighty empire across Egypt into North Africa. Nearly a hundred years later an Italian admiral in the Sultan's service urged the reconstruction of a canal between the Mediterranean and Red Seas. Such a project was urged on the kings of France in the 17th century by a number of eminent men, including the mathematician Leibnitz.

But it was not until Napoleon, carrying instructions from the Directory to chase the British out of the East and "cut a canal through the Isthmus of Suez," conquered Egypt in 1798 that a serious study was made of the project. Napoleon himself explored at first hand the traces of the ancient canals, nearly drowning himself and his horse in a bed of quaking ooze near Suez. But the idea fell foul of a miscalculation by his chief engineer, Jacques-Marie Le Père, who reported that the levels of the Red Sea and the Mediterranean differed by nearly 10 metres, an error which was supported by antique tradition.

The French withdrew from Egypt in 1801. Frenchmen and Englishmen continued, nevertheless, to promote canal projects. One of the most famous, sustained, and eccentric canal promotions was conducted by the disciples of the soldier, scientist, and mystic Henri de Saint-Simon. They saw the piercing of the isthmus in sexual imagery as a consummation of marriage between the male civilization of the West and the female Orient.

Neither mystical appeal nor practical arguments persuaded Mohammed Aly, the Albanian soldier of fortune who ruled Egypt under the nominal suzerainty of the Turkish Sultan from 1805 until 1849 and who founded the dynasty that was expelled with Farouk in 1952. Mohammed Aly came to Egypt in 1801 with the Anglo-Turkish force that forced the withdrawal of Napoleon's army. He secured his power by an old-fashioned massacre of his Mameluke rivals, whom he trapped *en masse* by inviting them to a ceremony, and went on to achieve vast modernizing reforms inspired by Napoleon. Shrewdly foreseeing that a Suez Canal would attract Great Power interference in Egypt, he decided instead in 1834 to build the first great Barrage across the Nile below Cairo to dam the waters for irrigation in the Delta.

While Mohammed Aly was bringing Egypt out of her long night of stagnation under Turkish rule, the evolution of steam navigation from paddle-

154

wheels to screw propellers increased the potential economic rewards of a Suez Canal that would cut in half the sea journey from Europe to India. The distance from Marseilles to Bombay is 10,400 miles by way of the Cape of Good Hope, Vasco de Gama's route, against 4,600 miles by way of Suez. From Liverpool to Calcutta it is 11,600 miles by the Cape against 7,900 miles through the canal. The saving was well worth it, even for sailing vessels that would have to be towed through the canal. Paddle steamers, well adapted for narrow waters like rivers and canals, were clumsier than sail on the high seas outside. Propeller-driven ships, which began to replace sidewheelers around 1850, could carry heavy cargoes as well on the oceans as through the canal.

Mathieu de Lesseps, Ferdinand's father, had gained the favor of Mohammed Aly during four years of diplomatic service in Egypt following Napoleon's withdrawal. Ferdinand was born in 1805, shortly after the family returned to France. He too embarked on a diplomatic career and was posted as vice-consul in 1832 to Alexandria, then Egypt's capital. He renewed family acquaintance with Mohammed Aly and befriended his teenage son, Mohammed Said, during a five-year tour of duty. He also developed an interest in the possibilities of a Suez Canal.

De Lesseps pursued this interest after his retirement from diplomacy in 1849. He returned to Egypt in November 1854, two months after the accession of Mohammed Said. By the end of the month he obtained the first of a series of Suez Canal concessions from the ruler he had befriended as a boy. De Lesseps then had to raise the money, fend off interference by both the Powers of Europe and commercial rivals, and organize the immense and complex construction of the canal. Fifteen fevered years were to pass before a triumphal procession of ships marked its opening on 17 November 1869.

They were hard years for Egypt and its rulers, Mohammed Said and Ismail, whose easygoing friendship and extravagance made them vulnerable marks for de Lesseps' ruthless exploitation, particularly in those periods when financial ruin faced him. The Egyptian Treasury itself was insufficient for the insatiable needs of de Lesseps' great work, even in the fat years of the American Civil War when the Northern blockade of the Confederacy forced cotton-starved British and European textile mills to bid up Egyptian prices to record levels. So the Egyptian rulers borrowed vast sums in Europe for capital finance, public works, and ceremonial connected with the canal. Egypt spent additional millions building the Sweetwater Canal, which brings drinking water from the Nile to the Suez Canal and the three cities based on it. Millions more went into the opening ceremonies and the building of an opera house and palaces for a brilliant assembly of guests, including the Empress Eugénie

155

of Frances. Giuseppe Verdi was commissioned to compose the opera *Aïda*, which he did not finish in time.

In all, the building of the Suez Canal led Egypt to borrow some 400,000,000 francs (about $80 million in those days), a sizable share of the debt that brought bankruptcy in 1876. All Egypt had to show for it in 1869 was a 44 per cent capital-share holding and the right to a perpetual 15 per cent royalty on the company's net profits. In an effort to stave off bankruptcy in 1875 Ismail sold his 44 per cent holding to the British Government for 100,000,000 francs. The perpetual right to a 15 per cent royalty went to a French investment syndicate in 1880 for 22,000,000 francs. Eleven years after the canal opened for commerce Egypt had no equity left in it at all. There remained only the concession agreement by which, 99 years after its opening, the canal was to revert to Egypt upon payment for the company's assets.

Egyptians say that their country paid 40 per cent of the total cost of the canal after all the transactions have been set against one another. Not only did Egypt have nothing to show for this investment, which helped ruin the country and invite foreign occupation, but Egyptian ships had to pay regular tolls for transit through the canal. There is no question but what the major burden of both the cost and construction of the canal fell upon the Egyptian peasant, in grinding taxes to pay the national debt and in forced labor by thousands of *fellahin* during the early years of construction. Ottoman law and European criticism eventually induced the Egyptian ruler and de Lesseps to stop forced labor on payment of an indemnity of 84,000,000 francs to the company.

This selling back to Egypt rights and real estate that had been conceded to the company was a favorite device of de Lesseps for extracting money. After the canal was opened he cynically stripped the Khedive Ismail of his power as the largest single stockholder by getting a majority to suspend the voting privileges of shares during periods for which they lacked interest-bearing coupons. Ismail had disposed of his coupons for the 25 years ending in 1894 in order to raise 30,000,000 francs to pay one of the indemnities obtained by de Lesseps.

These successes encouraged a peremptory, bullying attitude toward Egypt and Egyptians on the part of the company. This became so marked that the French consul-general in Egypt wrote months before the canal opened that company administrators seemed "to regard the Company as a State within a State." The phrase was echoed bitterly by Egyptians ever afterward.

The sense of grievance and humiliation felt by Egyptians of all classes and political persuasions was expressed by the young anti-Nasser novelist, Waguih Ghali, writing nearly a decade after the nationalization:

It is a very good thing this canal was nationalized, particularly to those who knew the French club in Port Fuad and saw the French having cushy jobs and being arrogant to everyone. . . . The Suez Canal Company was a haven for the very worst type of French string-pulling good-for-nothings.

Long before there was any serious thought of cutting short the concession there were lively anxieties in Egypt lest it be prolonged. Any proposals or suspected maneuvers to obtain an extension of the concession invariably brought Egyptian tempers to the threshold of violence. In 1909 the Company asked for a 40-year extension of the concession in return for immediate payment of £4,000,000 plus 4 per cent of the profits after 1921, 12 per cent of the profits after 1961, and a fifty-fifty sharing of the profits after the original terminal date of the concession in 1968. In February 1910 a young nationalist assassinated Premier Boutros Ghali with a revolver, declaring he had done so to save the country from the danger of extending the canal concession, on these terms or any others. The Egyptian consultative assembly voted against the proposal two months later with a unanimity broken by only one vote. The assassin, a young chemist named Wardani, was hanged in June. His act, the first important political assassination in Egypt since the bloody climb to power of Mohammed Aly, was celebrated by nationalists high and low. Wardini became a national hero.

The issue of extending the concession was often raised by stockholders. The company took the position, soothing to stockholders, that it was best to let Egyptian opinion evolve as the end neared and the practical problems of taking over from the company became clearer. The company did not leave the evolution of Egyptian opinion entirely to chance. Right up to the end, the company sought to heighten the obstacles in the way of Egyptian management by such devices as slowing down the recruitment and training of Egyptian pilots in unacknowledged violation of the spirit and letter of agreements with Egypt.

For Egyptians, however, the issue remained psychological rather than practical, regardless of economic inducements. They wanted to recover full sovereignty over every inch of Egypt and to eliminate foreign influence over their economy. Sixteen months before Nasser's revolution, Foreign Minister Mohammed Salaheddeen wrote:

Egypt is striving to put an end to this wrong, which gravely infringes her sovereignty. She is devoting herself all the more wholeheartedly to this task because she is determined to see the canal belong to Egypt and not Egypt to the canal. . . . Such are the convictions and the goals of every Egyptian.

The truth of the conservative Salaheddeen's statement of Egyptian feelings is underlined by the fact that his very phrases were echoed by Nasser, whose revolutionaries eventually imprisoned Salaheddeen along with other politicians of the old regime.

Within three months after the revolution rumors that the government would nationalize the canal company prompted foreign demands for clarification. An Egyptian cabinet statement denied the rumors but disclosed that the government had created a department in the Commerce Ministry to prepare for Egyptian administration of the canal at the termination date of the concession. The company was perturbed a year after the revolution when *Al-Tahreer*, an official revolutionary journal, called the company officials a band of robbers, declared that the canal belonged to the Egyptian people and not to the company or England or France, and demanded that the government not bother to nationalize the company but merely annul its concession without compensation on the grounds that it had repeatedly violated the concession. The company demanded a retraction. There followed a cycle of propaganda skirmishes that eventually numbed company officials into disbelief of any warnings of nationalization, even the final and true rumors that circulated on the day itself.

For years, Egyptians had regarded the termination of the canal concession together with the removal of British forces from the Suez Canal base as complementary requirements in the recovery of full territorial sovereignty. Officially, Egypt's attitude remained to the end as Nasser stated it in a broadcast on 17 November 1954, the eighty-fifth anniversary of the opening of the canal and, more importantly, less than a month after Britain signed the agreement to evacuate the canal base and turn it over to Egypt.

Nasser spoke of the canal historically as having been "among the principal causes that impelled Imperialism to the occupation of our country." This era, he said, would end with Britain's withdrawal. He announced "the beginning of the period which will facilitate Egypt's taking over the ... canal upon the expiry of the term of the concession," explaining that Egypt was beginning 14 years in advance in order "to beware of falling anew into the mistakes of the past, when problems caught us unawares and weak." But he commended the "friendly good relations existing" between the Egyptian Government and the company and expressed his belief that the company "will continue to give its true help in order that the remaining period will be brought to an end in the best manner and with the best of results."

The date Nasser first considered nationalizing the company before the end of the concession probably cannot be precisely fixed, even by Nasser himself. He does not keep a diary. And the idea of nationalization seems to have developed originally as a remote contingency to be negotiated, like the British evacuation of the canal base, on an assumption of good relations. It was not until Egypt's relations with the West deteriorated in 1956 that the idea developed of making it a defiant assertion of sovereignty as well as a source of revenue. In the early summer of that year, after Washington and London had relegated their offer to help finance the High Dam to a state of withering neglect, Nasser began to foresee the definite withdrawal of that aid as the contingency in which he would nationalize the canal. But his first generalized thoughts came long before that.

Nasser's first recorded comment on the prospect of nationalization seems to have been made privately to President Tito of Yugoslavia as they cruised up the canal aboard the Egyptian training ship *Ghaleb* on 5 February 1955. They talked for six and a half hours at this meeting, their first, for which Tito had interrupted his return home from a visit to India and Burma. Tito disclosed Nasser's private remarks a few days after the Suez War:

> Even at the time of our first meeting Nasser told us that he would have to nationalize the Suez Canal one day because Egypt, as an independent country, could not tolerate foreigners exercising authority on her territory. It is obvious that they were fully entitled to this nationalization, for which only the right time had to be chosen.

Nasser says Tito must have misunderstood him, that he had no such definite ideas at that time. Other Egyptians had. Late the following month 5,000 canal workers marched from the Cairo railroad station to Nasser's office to present him with a huge gilded "key to the canal" signifying, according to the controlled Cairo press, that the hero who liberated Egypt from British occupation "will assure the liberation of the Suez Canal itself so that it will belong to Egypt." Nasser told the crowd: "If we want to win, we have to will it and to know how to act in order to achieve what we wish."

Shortly after the nationalization Nasser told Edward R. Murrow that Egypt had been studying for two years the rights of the company, of Egypt, and of the users of the canal and had concluded that the company was "a State inside the State." After learning that the company was seeking powerful support for prolonging the concession and that certain governments were hoping to "internationalize" the canal, Nasser said: "Now we came to the decision that this concession must come to an end and must not be prolonged. We haven't really fixed the time at all but we thought, that will be within one year or two years or three years."

Dulles insisted afterward that Nasser provoked the withdrawal of Western aid for the High Dam in order to obtain a pretext for long-prepared plans to seize the canal. This contention is ill-supported by known circumstances and it is contrary to the opinions of the Big Three ambassadors in Egypt at the time. They believe that Nasser wanted Western aid for the High Dam much more than he wanted the canal.

The question bears on the good faith or lack of it on the part of Egypt in negotiating new agreements with the company in the winter and spring before nationalization. These accords committed the company to hire more Egyptian pilots and to invest in Egypt by the end of 1963 about £16,000,000 ($44,800,-000 of the foreign currencies it had traditionally held outside Egypt. In return, Egypt passed a law confirming the company's exemption from certain foreign exchange controls and taxes by allowing canal tolls to be paid in Paris and London as well as in Egypt, thus by-passing Egyptian fiscal controls.

Egypt acted in bad faith if Nasser's intention to nationalize the canal became firm before 30 May 1956, the date of the agreement, or even before 10 June 1956, the effective date of the law implementing Egypt's part of the bargain. The Director-General of the company, Jacques Georges-Picot, believes Egypt signed the agreements "just to chloroform us."

Even if Nasser contemplated subsequent nationalization by negotiation "within one year or two years or three years," such an intention would dictate seeking the propitious moment in a period of good relations. If only an off chance remained of obtaining Western aid for the High Dam it was mere common sense to keep good relations with the company until the last minute.

If Nasser wanted to "chloroform" Georges-Picot, it was not to cloak a prior decision to nationalize, but to anesthetize the company's alertness to the contingency in which an Anglo-American renege on the High Dam would make nationalization the least evil of the alternatives that would confront Nasser. Nasser was so anxious to prevent a Western renege, in fact, that he accepted politically dangerous conditions attached to the Western offer, as will be described in Chapter 10. What is relevant to note here is that the event that prompted the nationalization, Dulles's brusque renege, had nothing to do with the canal company. Although Nasser foresaw it as a probability, it did not occur until a month and a half after the agreement between Egypt and the canal company. And there is no evidence that I am aware of that Nasser made his mind up about nationalization before 22 July, three days after Dulles's renege and the day before he got the assent of his old junta colleagues.

The legal background of the 1956 agreements includes not only the original concession granted to the company but two laws promulgated in the name of King Farouk in 1947. One required every corporation in Egypt to be at least 51 per cent Egyptian owned, to have at least 40 per cent Egyptian membership on the board of directors, and to have at least 75 per cent of the personnel be Egyptians. The other law separated the Egyptian pound from the pound sterling, established currency-exchange controls, and required all companies to submit their entire earnings to Egyptian exchange controls and taxes.

On 7 March 1949 the company obtained a *modus vivendi* with Egypt in the form of an exchange of letters exempting the company from full application of the laws. In return, the company raised its payments to Egypt from a flat $1,440,000, begun in 1937, to 7 per cent of the gross profits, guaranteeing an increase of at least $240,000 a year. The company also agreed to increase Egyptian participation throughout the company from the board of directors down to unskilled laborers. The most important increases were in the 32-member board of directors and in the roster of pilots. Two of the 18 French directorships and one of the 10 British seats were given to Egypt, raising Egyptian membership to five. Two additional seats were promised by 1964.

As for pilots, the company promised to hire 20 new Egyptian pilots and thenceforth to hire Egyptians for half of all future vacancies. This promise carried the reservation that if the company could not find qualified Egyptians for new vacancies within a reasonable time it had the right to recruit non-Egyptians. The reservation proved stronger than the promise, being deliberately overexploited by the company in order to limit Egypt's ability to take over from the company at the end of the concession in 1968. Egypt tried to force the company to live up to the 1949 convention by refusing to issue entry visas for foreign pilots.

In October 1955 the exasperated Egyptians declared that the 1949 *modus vivendi* was illegal. Egypt demanded full application to the company of the fiscal controls and taxes enacted both before and after the 1949 convention. Negotiations began in Paris in December, the month in which the US and Britain offered large initial grants for the Aswan High Dam and the assurance of vast additional aid to follow.

Georges-Picot, who took personal charge of the negotiations, did not expect the new accords to last out the life of the concession. He expected them to last two or three years and to be superseded by new accords negotiated one after another in an accelerating rhythm. He had been working quietly for three years urging American oil companies and the US Government to use their influence to obtain a successor arrangement to the concession after 1968 in which the company would play an important role.

On half-a-dozen missions to the US he conceded that Egypt's share of the profits would have to be raised in a proposed new agreement between Egypt and the canal users in which the company would remain as the technician running the canal. Georges-Picot said user interests, which preponderated on the company's board, had traditionally shared in the profits through the lowering of tolls, but that this had left Egypt out. The company lowered its tolls twenty-seven times during its eighty-seven years on the canal.

Georges-Picot urged both Britain and the US not to wait until 1968 or a nationalization crisis. But the British told him: "Don't worry; when the time comes we'll be there." And the Americans said that if the British were not worried, they were not going to intervene. When a demand was made in the House of Commons on 15 May 1956 for "effective international control of the waterway of the Suez Canal," a Foreign Office undersecretary stated with bland confidence that "questions affecting the administration of the canal are best left to them [the company and Egypt] to settle on the basis of cooperation and mutual interest."

Georges-Picot felt Nasser's invisible presence at the talks. Foreign Minister Mahmoud Fawzi and Finance Minister Abdel Moneim Kaissouny were agreeable opponents, he recalls, "but you always had the impression you didn't have anybody in front of you who could speak with authority." Georges-Picot got the impression from Fawzi that Egypt might agree to a new contractual relationship with the company after 1968. The company was still self-confident enough to take the attitude: "They're hungry; let them come to us," which it had recommended to its stockholders.

In London *The Times* warned frostily on 20 February 1956 against giving way to pressure to employ more Egyptians in responsible posts, saying "the danger that a militantly nationalistic government would insist on managing the canal through its own nationals (whether they could do the work or not) ... is great." But the first fruits of the talks was a company agreement a month later to hire 32 Egyptian candidate pilots in return for Egyptian approval of visas for 26 foreign candidate pilots. The company felt obliged to justify this concession to its stockholders in June by reporting that the pilot shortage had caused delays to 130 ships averaging 12 hours each in the first four months of 1956, costing them anywhere from $1,000 for a tanker to $3,000 for other ships. None of the new pilots had entered service on the canal by the time of nationalization.

The company had 205 pilots at the time of nationalization; it needed 250. Its failure, despite its needs, to fulfil its 1949 promise to hire one Egyptian pilot for every foreign pilot is strikingly plain in the fact that only 40 of its 205 pilots were Egyptians. That Egyptians were available for qualification is shown by the fact that two years later the nationalized Egyptian canal authority had 99 Egyptian pilots in its roster of 216 and a year after that had raised the Egyptian proportion above half, with 124 out of a total of 233 pilots.

Under the financial accords, which took effect with the implementing Egyptian law on 10 June 1956, the company completed the transfer of £8,000,000 into Egypt by 10 July. The money, Georges-Picot exclaimed later, was "trapped" by nationalization. He had been effectively "chloroformed" and is free to admit that nationalization came as "a complete surprise."

The Israeli ambassador in France at the time, Jacob Tsur, was among the few who either foresaw or predicted the nationalization. With a combination of foresight and opportunism, he instructed his staff in March 1956 to spread the word that Nasser's next act would be to nationalize the Suez Canal. Tsur recalled later that he had learned how military dictators think from Juan Peron of Argentina, with whom he had been on close terms as Ambassador there. Tsur says he sat down in Paris one day and tried to imagine what the Egyptian dictator would do next, then he assembled his staff and told them: "Listen, my children, Nasser will nationalize the canal."

"They said 'Impossible!'" Tsur recalls. "I said it would do no harm to spread this around among the shareholders." This was done and some shareholders who sold their stock on Tsur's advice thanked him for it after the nationalization. The Persian ambassador reported Tsur's warning to the oil companies, he recalls, and they scoffed. "But Nasser followed the same line of reasoning I did."

Nationalization had no effect on the prohibitions against Israeli shipping in the canal, which were instituted by King Farouk on 15 May 1948, the day Israel declared herself an independent state and the Palestine War formally began. For its part, the company objected to government regulations that delayed shipping.

Nasser, who continued the old regime's blockade regulations as a political imperative, eventually became irritated by the company's uncooperative attitude. In 1955 he raised the subject with François Charles-Roux, chairman of the canal company's board, who habitually spent the latter months of every winter in Ismailiya and made an annual call on the chief of state, Farouk in his day, then Naguib, and, in 1955, Nasser. In 1956 Nasser ignored Charles-Roux's request for an audience, perhaps to increase pressure on the company during the negotiation of the new accords.

The blockade was merely an irritant in the relations between Egypt and the company, not a major issue. To Israel, balked of trade to the Orient and down the eastern coast of Africa, both the Suez and Aqaba blockades were important. Aqaba was the more important of the two, involving as it did the stifling of port development at Elath at the southernmost point of Israel, which in turn hampered the economy of the Negev.

It was Aqaba, not Suez, for which both Ben-Gurion and Sharett declared Israel would fight if necessary. And Ben-Gurion had put his cabinet on a war footing more than five weeks before nationalization gave the gathering crisis a public identity.

The accidental nature of the influence of the Suez Canal dispute on Israel's intentions was taken for granted by Michel Bar-Zohar, who reflects, with Peres's encouragement and help, the contemporary thinking in Ben-Gurion's official circle. After Ben-Gurion braced his cabinet for action by removing Sharett, the French leaders told Israel France would give military support against Nasser far beyond Israel's requirements for self-defense.

"At this moment," wrote Bar-Zohar, "the Suez Crisis occurred. It did not change in substance the plans of Israel, which would have attacked in any case, but it facilitated for her the so-difficult task of the quest for armaments and allies." Nationalization, in fact, suited Ben-Gurion's plans so well that it is surprising that the whole military-diplomatic apparatus of Israel did not join in Ambassador Tsur's agitation to invite it.

CHAPTER

6

The Lion and the Sphinx
(1798 TO 19 OCTOBER 1954)

The Englishman, straining far over to hold his beloved India, will plant a firm foot on the banks of the Nile and sit in the seats of the Faithful. . . .

(ALEXANDER KINGLAKE, 1884)

I T WAS the rivalry between England and France that engulfed Egypt in the mainsteam of modern history at the turn of the 19th century. Napoleon conquered Egypt in order to get at the British in India. The British had occupied the Cape of Good Hope, hampering French access to the Indies by the traditional ocean lanes. The Revolutionary Directory that then ruled France decided to seek another, shorter route to the rich prizes in the East. Inventing the pretext that the Egyptian beys had allied themselves with the British, the Directory instructed Napoleon to seize and colonize Egypt and "expel the British from all their possessions in the East, wherever they may be, and, in particular, to destroy all their trading stations on the Red Sea, to cut a canal through the Isthmus of Suez, and to take all necessary steps to ensure the free and exclusive use of the Red Sea by French vessels."

Reacting to French grand strategy, a British fleet under Nelson promptly marooned the French conquerors in Egypt by destroying nearly all of their ships in Abu Kir Bay on 1 August 1798, just one month after Napoleon landed with his army. A year later Napoleon eluded the British blockade and returned to France to make himself dictator. In March 1801 a joint Anglo-Turkish force under Sir Ralph Abercrombie compelled the French to abandon Egypt.

The British hardly endeared themselves to the Egyptians, however, for in the course of their campaign they let the sea into the ancient bed of Lake Mariotis, destroying 150 villages in a rush of water and turning rich farms into salt marshes that remain to this day. The British themselves withdrew in 1803, leaving Egypt to the harsh improvements of Mohammed Aly. They returned to try to overthrow him four years later with an ill-fated expeditionary force of 5,000 men under General A. Mackenzie Fraser. Mohammed Aly repulsed Fraser and subjected his British prisoners to the grisly humiliation of a parade between rows of the impaled heads of hundreds of their fallen comrades. Nasser, although he overthrew and dispossessed the Mohammed Aly dynasty nearly 150 years later, crowed over Fraser's defeat in his nationalization speech.

France and Britain returned to Egypt in the latter half of the 19th century by the roads of development and finance. Lord Palmerston, the dominant figure in British foreign policy in the middle third of the 19th century as Foreign Secretary and as Prime Minister, doggedly opposed projects for a Suez Canal. He did not want to weaken the ailing Ottoman Empire by strengthening Egyptian separatism. He let de Lesseps and the French win the struggle for a canal concession.

But by the time the canal was opened, four years after Palmerston's death, British thinking had begun to adapt itself to the practical realities of the canal's existence. The Canal shifted the focus of British interest in the Middle East from Constantinople to Egypt, to the detriment of Egyptian independence. On the morning of 17 November 1869, when de Lesseps and the Empress Eugénie aboard the paddle-wheeled French imperial yacht, *L'Aigle*, led the inaugural procession of fifty-one resplendent ships southward from Port Said, *The Times* in distant London bluntly declared Britain's interests in "this short cut from world's end to world's end" as follows:

> It will be found that the expense will wholly or mainly fall upon Egypt; that the glory may be ascribed to France, but the benefit must needs be reaped by England.... We are aware that in Paris, in Florence, and even in St. Petersburg, there is exultation at the notion that by the opening of the Suez Canal trade may be turned into new channels and a heavy blow dealt to the nation which made the best of the old ones. But we will not allow ourselves to be discomposed.... It was not we who first sailed around Africa.... We will ask no better favour at Port Said than the free competition which availed us so well at the Cape.

Seventy per cent of the ships that used the Canal in the succeeding years flew the Union Jack. The lack of a voice in the management of the Canal began to gall some Englishmen. Meanwhile, Ismail, who had succeeded Mohammed Said in 1863, unwittingly opened the door to eventual British influence in Egypt and in the Suez Canal Company in two ways. By expanding Mohammed Aly's vast program of public works as well as by personal extravagances, he raised the public debt more than thirty-fold, from £3,000,000 to nearly £100,000,000 ($500 million), most of it borrowed abroad. He also increased Egypt's autonomy within the Ottoman Empire, obtaining the right of hereditary succession for his own branch of the family in 1866 and obtaining the title of *Khedive* the following year, thereby raising his rank and powers from those of an important provincial governor to those of a viceroy. His financial vulnerability increased apace with his authority to treat directly with foreign powers without Ottoman hindrance.

The stage was set, just six years after the Canal opened, for the British Prime Minister Disraeli to buy out the Khedive's 44-per cent shareholding in the Canal company for £4,000,000. Ismail's 176,602 shares, in seven large cases, were turned over in November 1875 to the British agent and consul general in Cairo. The purchase eventually led to Britain's acquisition of 10 directorships on the company's 32-man board. The Conservative government of the day had progressed far beyond the vision of commercial interest declared by *The Times* on the Canal's opening morning. Disraeli, who added "Empress of India" to Queen Victoria's titles, told the House of Commons in February 1876 in defense of his financial coup:

I have never recommended ... this purchase as a financial investment ... although I believe that many of those who have looked upon it with little favour will probably be surprised with the pecuniary results of the purchase. I have always, and do now recommend it to the country as a political transaction, and one which I believe is calculated to strengthen the Empire. ... Because they think we are obtaining a great hold and interest in this important portion of Africa—because they believe that it secures to us a highway to our Indian Empire and our other dependencies, the people of England have from the first recognized the propriety and the wisdom of the step which we shall sanction tonight.

Ismail was only briefly reprieved by the sale. He went bankrupt in the spring of 1876 and accepted "Dual Control" over Egypt's finances by British and French commissioners. This surrender of sovereignty so aroused nationalist feeling that he tried to rescind it in 1879. The European powers balked Ismail's reversion to nationalism by inducing the Ottoman Sultan to depose him in favor of his eldest son, Tewfik. Egyptian nationalists then rallied to the standard of revolt raised in 1881 by Colonel Ahmed Arabi, the prototype of the nationalist *bikbashis* (colonels) who were to overthrow the dynasty under Nasser's leadership in 1952.

Disraeli had made the British fully conscious of the importance of the Suez Canal as the Imperial lifeline to India. The Foreign Secretary Lord Salisbury in 1879 told the British agent and consul general in Cairo:

The leading aim of our policy in Egypt is the maintenance of the neutrality of that country, that is to say, the maintenance of such a state of things that no Great Power shall be more powerful there than England. ... It should further be borne in mind that if the Ottoman Empire were to fall to pieces, and Egypt became independent, the part of Egypt which interests England is the seacoast, including the railway and other communications across the Isthmus.

Arabi's revolt, the British saw, might open the way for some other Great Power to gain ascendancy in Egypt.

Lord Salisbury had also written to his consul general:

It has been sufficiently proved that the Mussulmans [Moslems] will not willingly obey a Government which is nominally European, or of which the prevailing and most conspicuous elements are European. Their reluctance can only be overcome by force; and force the Europeans do not possess without military occupation.

Accordingly, three years later the British prepared to occupy Egypt with the ostensible object of restoring the Khedive Tewfik to his throne. Nationalist riots in Alexandria in June 1882 resulted in foreign deaths, including that of a Maltese subject of the British crown, and provided the initial prompting for British intervention. British warships bombarded Arabi's shore batteries in Alexandria in July.

On the night of 19 August a British expeditionary force under General Sir Garnet Wolseley steamed into the canal after sending a shore party into Port Said to seize the installations of the uncooperative Suez Canal Company. De Lesseps, then nearly 75, had warned the admiral of the British invasion fleet lying off Port Said that he would personally blow out the brains of the first British officer to set foot on shore. He did not carry out his threat. The British invasion interrupted canal traffic for the first time. Navigation resumed five days later, after the British force landed at Ismailiya. On 13 September Wolseley's force defeated Arabi's army at Tel al-Kebir, where the green Nile Delta meets the Eastern Desert, and the next day marched on to occupy Cairo. As Mohammed Aly foresaw, the Canal provided a side door for a Great Power invasion of his country.

The British entrenched themselves at the financial and political controls both of Egypt and the canal company, although technically their representatives were subordinate in the Government to the Egyptian ministers and in the canal company to the top French officials. In the 1870s Britain had taken a leading role in obtaining for maritime nations using the Canal a voice in the regulation of tolls and conditions of passage through the Canal and in making de Lesseps and the company adopt British-approved standards for measuring ship tonnage. In the 1880s she enshrined in international law the principle of the political neutralization of the Canal, but with reservations arrogating a specially privileged position to herself as the occupying power.

The neutralization of the Canal and its insulation from the rampant power politics of the 19th century was an ideal for which de Lesseps fought from the outset of his enterprise. General Wolseley's crude violation was the first breach of it. A few months later, with British forces in firm occupation, Whitehall was ready to restore the principle. On 3 January 1883 Foreign Secretary Lord Granville circulated to the powers a memorandum on British policy in Egypt, in effect proposing safeguards against a repetition of what Wolseley's force had done. He invited agreement by the Great Powers: "(1.) That the Canal should be free for the passage of all ships, in any circumstances. (2.) That...no troops or munitions of war should be disembarked in the Canal. (3.) That no hostilities should take place in the Canal or its approaches... (7.) That no fortifications should be erected on the Canal or in its vicinity." Granville also outlined reforms that Britain intended to accomplish in Egypt, including the suppression of slavery and the establishment of representative government, and he expressed Britain's desire to withdraw her troops "as soon as the state of the country, and the organization of proper means for the maintenance of the Khedive's authority, will admit of it." Egyptian nationalists spent the next 72 years trying to get the British to act on their expressed desire to withdraw.

France, hoping to weaken Britain's physical control of the canal, marshaled European opinion in favor of internationalizing it. Britain effectively blocked or ignored the work of international conferences toward this end in the mid-1880s. France then sought, as a second-best status, the neutralization of the Canal, a principle which Britain reluctantly accepted with paralyzing reservations. It was as a rear-guard action that British diplomacy led the major powers of Europe to join in the Constantinople Convention of 29 October 1888. Its first article declared:

"The Suez Maritime Canal shall always be free and open, in time of war as in time of peace, to every vessel of commerce or of war, without distinction of flag."

In a conflict of meaning that has not yet been settled judicially, Article X states that the provisions implementing the first article "shall not interfere with the measures which His Majesty the Sultan and His Highness the Khedive ... might find it necessary to take for securing by their own forces the defence of Egypt and the maintenance of public order." Egyptians today say Article X allows them to prohibit Israel, with whom they remain technically at war, from using the canal on the grounds that Israel might sabotage the canal or put spies ashore in a prelude to a new invasion.

Although Austria, Germany, Italy, the Netherlands, the Ottoman Empire, Russia, Spain, France, and Britain herself signed the Convention, it did not become operative for sixteen years. France and four other signatories balked at British reservations that the application of the Convention must "not be incompatible with the transitory and exceptional condition of Egypt nor fetter the British Government's liberty of action during the period of occupation."

Not until 1904, when Britain and France secretly agreed to give each other a free hand, France in Morocco and Britain in Egypt, not until then did Britain declare her adherence to the Convention she had sought and signed. In agreeing at last to the Convention being put in force, however, the British still required the other powers to hold "in abeyance" for the indefinite duration of the British occupation the functioning of the international supervisory commission provided for in the Constantinople Convention. The commission, in fact, never did function. And Britain, under the compulsion of world wars, continued to violate the Convention.

In December 1914, the fifth month of World War I, Britain declared a protectorate over Egypt. She announced Ottoman Turkish suzerainty to be terminated, deposed the Khedive Abbas Hilmi, named his uncle Hussein Kamel as the first Sultan of Egypt, dissolved Egypt's foreign Ministry and transferred its functions to Britain's chief representative, whose title was changed from Agent and Consul General to High Commissioner. British military authorities took over the installations, personnel, and direction of the Suez Canal for the duration, nullifying Suez Canal Company orders for strict compliance with the Constantinople Convention. In effect, Britain temporarily nationalized the canal and suspended the Convention.

As the self-declared protecting power, Britain arrogated to herself the rights reserved to Egyptian and Ottoman authorities by Article X of the Convention for the defense of the canal. The British built fortifications and earthworks, sited all manner of artillery, patrolled with armed boats and minesweepers, and billeted troops so that, in the words of a British canal-company director, "from end to end the banks of the canal resembled one long armed camp." The Constantinople Convention privileges of free passage and even of asylum were suspended for enemy shipping but the British kept the canal open for Allied and neutral vessels except for two brief interruptions. On the night of 2/3 February 1915 the vanguard of a Turkish invasion army forced a crossing to the west bank of the Canal before the British drove it back into the Sinai Desert; and on 21 July 1915 raiding German and Turkish planes dropped mines the length of the Canal.

Except for the big depot at Tel al-Kebir, the British did dismantle virtually all of their military installations in the Canal area after the war. But they did not come to terms with Egyptian nationalism because they would not evacuate their troops. The exasperated bearers of the White Man's Burden in Egypt explained to their wards in 1921:

The progress of Egypt towards her ideals will not only be retarded, but completely jeopardized, if her people are tempted to indulge their national aspirations, however sound and legitimate in themselves, without regard to the facts which govern international life.

Field Marshal Lord Allenby, the High Commissioner, warned Whitehall in January 1922 that "if the hopes of Egypt are once more disappointed...I despair of any future for the country, which will relapse into a state of alternating outbreaks and repressions..." The following month Britain took the peculiar step of unilaterally declaring Egyptian independence, but with characteristic reservations that kept Britain in control of:

(a.) The security of the communications of the British Empire in Egypt [i.e., the Suez Canal];

(b.) The defence of Egypt against all foreign aggression or interference, direct or indirect;

(c.) The protection of foreign interests in Egypt and the protection of the minorities;

(d.) The Soudan.

Egypt refused to associate herself with this foreign declaration of her independence. Her concept of complete independence was irreconcilable with Britain's concept of an independence limited by reservations protecting British interests. No Egyptian politician either wanted or dared to settle for merely conditional sovereignty. But all were forced to accept the fact that Egypt was not strong enough to assert her national interests against British imperial interests, even within Egyptian territory itself. Foreign Secretary Lord Curzon, two weeks after the declaration, bluntly warned the powers of the world against helping Egypt get any more independence than Britain had declared for her:

The welfare and integrity of Egypt are necessary to the peace and safety of the British Empire, which will therefore always maintain as an essential British interest the special relations between itself and Egypt . . . defined in the Declaration. . . . His Majesty's Government have laid them down as matters in which the rights and interests of the British Empire are vitally involved, and will not admit them to be questioned or discussed by any other Power. In pursuance of this principle, they will regard as an unfriendly act any attempt at interference in the affairs of Egypt by another Power . . .

Allenby's prediction was borne out by outbreaks of political terrorism, the weapon of the weak, which culminated in November 1924 in the assassination on a Cairo street of Sir Lee Stack, Governor General of the Sudan and *Sirdar* (Commander in Chief) of the Egyptian Army. British repression was swift. While British cavalry sealed off approaches to the Parliament building, Allenby read out an ultimatum to the Premier which required Egypt to: apologize, find and punish the killers, suppress all popular political demonstrations, pay a £500,-000 fine, order Egyptian units and officers out of the Sudan immediately, and drop all opposition to Britain's wishes concerning the protection of foreign interests in Egypt. Allenby said the murder "holds up Egypt as at present governed to the contempt of civilized peoples" and that Egyptian hostility to Britain was "founded upon a heedless ingratitude for the benefits conferred by Great Britain."

Most ominous of all, Britain notified Egypt that henceforth the Sudan would have unlimited irrigation rights to the Nile waters. In effect, Britain ended Egypt's partnership in the condominium the two governments had exercised over the Sudan since the destruction in 1899 of the Dervish Empire in the Sudan by a joint Anglo-Egyptian force under Lord Kitchener. Egypt's utter dependence upon the Nile for her very life had underlain her interest in her upstream neighbor for 5,000 years. Mohammed Aly conquered the Sudan in the 1820s and Egyptians ruled it as a nominally Ottoman province until the mid-1880s. By that time Egypt herself was under British occupation. Egyptian authority under Turkish suzerainty remained as a legal fiction and British power placed the romantic general, Charles George ("Chinese") Gordon in the governorship of the Sudan. Gordon was killed in 1885, with a British-led relief force literally in sight of besieged Khartoum, when the city fell to the Mahdi's Dervishes. These religious warriors ruled in independence until Kitchener came with his cannon and Nordlinger guns against their spears and swords. Gordon's drama had so gripped the hearts of Queen Victoria and her subjects that Kitchener's reconquest, thirteen years later, had a strong flavor of revenge. Kitchener disinterred and dismembered the Mahdi's body.

The practical motive of the Kitchener expedition was to turn back a French imperial penetration from the heart of Africa and to make sure permanently that no European power could hurt the British position in Egypt by interfering with the Nile as it passed through the Sudan. Kitchener's expedition was mounted when Britain determined that it could be financed out of the increased tax revenues that would result from the original Aswan Dam, on which construction was beginning when Kitchener marched up the Nile in 1898.

The Anglo-Egyptian Condominium was Consul General Lord Cromer's "creation of some hybrid form of Government, hitherto unknown to international jurisprudence," designed to soothe Egyptian and French feelings while establishing British power in the Sudan. The condominium remained in name only after the murder of Sir Lee Stack but the name lent legality to Egypt's persistent claims of sovereignty over the Sudan.

Suez and the Sudan, British evacuation and the unity of the Nile Valley, these two cardinal nationalist demands hardened and fused, so that fragile agreements on one repeatedly crumbled at the impact of disagreement on the other. Britain held sway in Egypt without any formal instrument of consent until 1936. British policy hewed to the line laid down by Prime Minister Ramsay MacDonald in 1924, that the security of the Suez Canal was "the foundation on which the entire defensive strategy of the British Empire rests."

The Fascist power of Italy, already in neighboring Libya and newly carried into Ethiopia by Mussolini, was what persuaded Egyptians in the mid-1930s

174

to consent to keeping British troops in their midst. It was at this juncture that Eden entered the Egyptian picture. Eden became Foreign Secretary for the first time in December 1935 and one of his first major actions was to negotiate the Anglo-Egyptian Treaty of Preferential Alliance of 1936. He later recalled it as "the only event which had given me any satisfaction during these dismal months."

Eden's interest in the Middle East dates back to World War I, when he accompanied Sir Mark Sykes on a mission to Mesopotamia, as present-day Iraq was then called. Eden also served with distinction in the trenches, winning the Military Cross for bravery as well as promotions from lieutenant to major. Demobilized in 1919 after four years of active duty, he embarked on a course of Oriental Studies at Christ Church, Oxford, with an eye to a diplomatic career. His main language was Persian but he also studied Arabic and read the Koran "and an agreeable Arab historian of the early caliphs." By the time he took his degree in 1922, at the age of 25, he recalls:

"It seemed to me, in my impatience, that responsibility in one of our embassies would be long in coming. I should be for-ever handing round teacups in Teheran. Parliament was an alternative approach to foreign affairs." So he turned to politics, taking Lord Curzon's early career as his model. After one unsuccessful campaign in 1922, he won a by-election in December 1923 at Warwick and Leamington, the constituency he was to represent until the end of his career 33 years later. His career in foreign affairs began in July 1926 when he was named Parliamentary Private Secretary to Foreign Secretary Sir Austen Chamberlain.

At Oxford Eden had preferred the early Arabic of the Koran and of the caliphs of Damascus and Baghdad to that of the medieval caliphs of Egypt. The preference was a forerunner of his relatively low esteem for Egyptians as compared with the Arabs of the Levant and the Arabian Peninsula, especially the Iraqis and Jordanians. But his most significant successes, like his ultimate failure, were with the Egyptians.

In January 1936, foreseeing "all the problems common to powers who have military bases on unfriendly soil," Eden made proposals "having regard to legitimate Egyptian aspirations and to vital Imperial interests." His instructions to the British High Commissioner, Sir Miles Lampson, added: "but if the Egyptians prove unreasonable, His Majesty's Government will be compelled to abandon the first and rely on the fairness of their offer to justify the consequences." In relation to the British Suez Canal base, Eden thought of the Cairo government as an "outside power" upon which "our imperial communications could not be dependent."

Eden shrewdly insisted that the negotiations take place in Cairo, "for there was always the danger that any Minister who came to London would be overthrown on his return." And he insisted that the chiefs of all Egyptian political parties sign the treaty, the opposition as well as the ministers in office, so none could denounce it later. Eden and thirteen Egyptian representatives signed the treaty in London on 26 August 1936 after successful negotiations in Cairo. A formal photograph of the signing was reproduced on a commemorative series of Egyptian postage stamps four months later. Under a magnifying glass, Eden is recognizable at the head of a long table flanked by Egyptians wearing tarbooshes, the only European ever to appear on an Egyptian stamp. Eden later called the treaty "an unusual but invaluable arrangement by which an Egypt, nominally neutral, afforded us every facility to meet our wartime needs."

The treaty made Egypt only nominally independent as well as only nominally neutral. It declared the British military occupation to be "terminated" but provided for the maintenance of 10,000 soldiers, 400 pilots, and all necessary support personnel in the Suez Canal base. It declared Egypt to be "a sovereign independent State" and ensured Egypt's admission to the League of Nations. Sir Miles Lampson was transformed from a High Commissioner into an Ambassador.

Of the four British reservations embodied in the 1922 declaration of Egypt's "independence," only one could be said to have been eliminated by the treaty. Responsibility for the protection of the lives and property of foreigners was returned to the Egyptians and the "capitulations," which for a hundred years had given extraordinary immunities to foreigners in Egypt, were consigned to extinction. The defense of Egypt ostensibly was shared under a clause committing each party to come immediately to the aid of the other in the event of war, but this was plainly a one-way arrangement for Britain to defend Egypt against threats to her own Imperial interests. The British reservations on the security of the canal and the administration of the Sudan remained virtually unaltered by the treaty. The treaty was to last twenty years but the alliance was to be permanent and embodied in any revision or extension.

Although the party leaders had all joined Premier Mustafa Nahhas in signing the treaty, countless thousands of Egyptians saw it as a sham. They felt humiliated that their politicians had thereby given consent to British domination. Among them was Nasser, then an 18-year-old student deeply imbued with the nationalism that Napoleon had awakened in Egypt.

"I once tried to understand an expression I often shouted as a child when I saw planes flying in the sky," Nasser recalled in his slim, impressionistic memoir, *The Philosophy of the Revolution.* "I used to say: 'O God Almighty!

Calamity betake the English!' I found out later that we inherited the expression from our forefathers who said in the days of the Mamelukes ... 'O God Almighty! Destroy the Ottomans!' "

During the 1936 treaty negotiations, Nasser wrote:

I led demonstrations at *al-Nahda* (The Awakening) School. From the bottom of my heart I clamored for complete independence ... for all leaders of Egypt to unite on that one thing. Our rebellious, cheering crowds went to their homes, one by one, demanding in the name of the youth of Egypt that they should unite on that one thing. It was a calamity to my faith that the one thing they united on was the Treaty of 1936.

Three years later, as a newly commissioned lieutenant in the Egyptian army garrison at Mankabad, 200 miles up the Nile from Cairo, Nasser formed a secret revolutionary society dedicated to Egypt's liberation. In June 1940, when the British forced the dismissal of the pro-Axis Premier Aly Maher in favor of the pro-British Hassan Sabry, Egyptian nationalists became more conscious than ever of the incompleteness of their independence. Worse was to come.

On 4 February 1942, as student demonstrators hailed the approach of Rommel's *Afrika Korps* toward Egypt, Sir Miles Lampson transmitted an ultimatum to King Farouk to appoint Mustafa Nahhas as Premier. Nahhas was the leader of the Wafd party, Egypt's largest, which had been formed by a nationalist delegation in the early 1920s and had developed grass-roots mass support in the 1930s. The King hesitated. Not only was Nahhas too strong for the King's liking but Aly Maher would give Egypt a freer hand to treat with the Axis if Rommel drove the British out. Lampson's patience ran out. At 9 P.M. he smashed through the palace gates with three tanks while British troops deployed in the surrounding streets. He strode into the King's study flanked by officers with drawn pistols and told Farouk to appoint Nahhas forthwith or be thrown out. Farouk submitted within the hour. Nahhas gave full Egyptian cooperation to the British in the desperate months that followed when Rommel hammered at the gates of Alexandria and Allied fortunes reached their nadir in theaters of war around the world.

As the tide of war turned, Lampson's peremptory shake-up of the Egyptian government seemed amply justified in Allied minds. In Egyptian minds the date marks the worst humiliation they had ever been forced to swallow. "Hearts were full of fire and sorrow," Nasser recalled.

Colonel Anwar Sadat, one of Nasser's closest revolutionary colleagues, described the junta's reaction in *Revolt on the Nile:*

Up till now the King had been synonymous with the patriotic idea, and the violation of the Royal Palace was regarded by all patriotic Egyptians as an outrage against Egypt herself. But from now on Farouk changed utterly, and Egypt began to despair of him. . . . This latest affront to our country gave a new stimulus to the revolutionary movement. Abdel Nasser and Abdel Hakim Amer determined that Egypt must never again suffer such a humiliation. The real revolutionary conspiracy dates back to this time. . . . We would carry out a military *coup d'état* in Cairo, . . . join up with the Axis troops, and the fate of the British Empire would be sealed.

Arab sympathies with the Axis grew out of the same desire for independence that led them to welcome British help in World War I to remove the imperial presence of the Turks. In World War II it was the imperial presence of perfidious Albion that needed expelling, and the Germans were trying to do it. The unspeakable character of Hitler and the urgency of war made the Allies regard the Arab overtures toward the Nazis as immoral and they have criticized the Arabs for it ever since. But the Allies themselves joined forces with Stalin, a tyrant of Hitler's ilk, and Winston Churchill said he would shake hands with the Devil if it would help win the war. The Arabs often quote Churchill to explain their policies to Westerners.

Sadat himself was assigned to make liaison with both the Moslem Brotherhood and two agents sent into Cairo by Rommel. But the conspiracy was balked by British agents, Sadat was jailed, and the Axis pincer movement on the Middle East was broken by Allied victories at Alamein and Stalingrad. Nasser reorganized his secret society of officers into sections, each composed of separate cells, and patiently worked and watched for the opportunity that came ten years later.

"I really believe that Imperialism is playing with only one card in its hand and is merely bluffing," Nasser wrote a friend from Alamein. "If it ever knew that there were Egyptians ready to shed their blood and meet force with force it would recoil like a harlot."

British official quarters remain notably silent about Lampson's coup of 4 February 1942. Eden, who was Foreign Secretary again at the time, makes no reference to it in his three volumes of detailed memoirs.

Eden was to work against Arab unity at the end of his career, but he pledged Britain to support it in the dark days of 1941. "It seems to me both natural and right that the cultural and economic ties between the Arab countries, and the political ties too, should be strengthened," Eden said. "His Majesty's Government for their part will give their full support to any scheme that commands general approval." Churchill's wartime government went on to bless the formation of the League of Arab States in March 1945 "for reasons," as Tom

Little acidly says, "which have been explained but remain incomprehensible."

The divisions upon which Eden was to play ten years later were a crippling weakness to the Arab League from its inception. Nuri wanted Egypt and Iraq to defer their claims against the British in order to encourage the West to favor the Arab cause in Palestine. The Egyptians refused and eventually went so far as to take their demand for British evacuation to the Security Council in 1947 at the time when the General Assembly was deliberating on the Palestine question.

The Egyptians renewed their demands for British evacuation immediately after the war, arguing that the 1936 treaty was no longer suitable. The Egyptian Premier wrote the British Foreign Secretary in December 1945:

> The presence of foreign forces on our soil in peacetime, even if stationed in distant areas, is still wounding to national dignity and can only be interpreted by Egyptian public opinion as the tangible sign of a mistrust which the British Government themselves, we believe, must regard as unjustified.

Britain had made an agreement with the Ottoman Sultan in 1887 to withdraw her troops from Egypt in three years, conditional upon retaining the right to return "if there are reasons to fear an invasion from without, or if order and security in the interior were disturbed." But France and Russia did not like the precedent implied in the right of return and they prevailed on the Sultan not to ratify the agreement. The 1887 agreement bears striking parallels with the final British agreement in 1954 to withdraw subject to the right to return in the event of an outside power attacking any Arab League State or Turkey.

In the intervening seven decades the Middle East became a major theater in two world wars. This enhanced the value to Britain of a great base on the Suez Canal, to which the Mediterranean and Red Sea provided both a front and a back door. The global strategy of the early years of the Cold War between North Atlantic and Asiatic superpowers did nothing to abate Britain's reluctance to give up the base. Although India gained independence in 1947, Suez became more important than ever as a lifeline because of British and European dependence on ever-increasing supplies of Middle Eastern oil.

Egypt's position on Suez had hardened too. It became increasingly dangerous for any politician to accept any conditions whatsoever as the price of British evacuation. And anxieties over ensuring adequate water from the Nile for Egypt's bursting population gave urgency to the claim of sovereignty over the Sudan.

These unfavorable trends were briefly overcome, however, by the flush of liberalism in Britain and hope in Egypt that followed the landslide Laborite victory in the British elections in the last months of World War II. In October 1946 Egyptian Premier Ismail Sidky and British Foreign Secretary Ernest Bevin initialed a draft agreement for British evacuation within three years, not conditional upon any automatic right of re-entry, but merely prescribing consultative cooperation in the event of "armed aggression against countries adjacent to Egypt." British troops actually began moving the base to Palestine. But the agreement collapsed under Egyptian opposition to a protocol allowing the Sudanese "active preparation for self-government and consequently the exercise of the right to choose the future status of the Sudan." Egypt then tried and failed to get the UN to take up the issue.

The triumphant establishment of Israel in Palestine and the deterioration of the Cold War distracted both sides from their long quarrel for the next few years. It revived in October 1951 when Britain's wartime friend, Mustafa Nahhas, once again Premier of Egypt, retorted to new Western proposals to base a Middle East Defense Organization on Egypt by abrogating the 1936 treaty and proclaiming Egyptian sovereignty over the Sudan. Egypt could not, of course, implement these gestures in the face of British power on the Suez Canal and in the Sudan. But once they were made, it became impossible for any Egyptian politician to accept less without running the immediate risk of assassination. Only new regimes on both sides could hope to work a way out of the dangerous impasse. They were not long in coming.

A Conservative electoral victory in England brought Eden back as Foreign Secretary at the end of that month. He found two major Middle Eastern crises on his hands; one in Iran, where Premier Mohammed Mossadegh had nationalized the Anglo-Iranian Oil Company, and the other in Egypt, where guerrilla fighting in the Suez Canal zone broke out upon Britain's refusal to accept Egypt's unilateral abrogation of the 1936 treaty. The Egyptian crisis culminated in Cairo's Black Saturday on 26 January 1952, when underworld mobs with the connivance of the Palace burned, sacked, and killed until downtown Cairo was a smoking shambles and dozens of Europeans lay dead. Among them were nine Englishmen and a Canadian slaughtered by the rabble as fire forced them out of the Turf Club.

Concerning Iran, Eden wrote later, "I thought we should be better occupied looking for alternatives to Mussadiq rather than trying to buy him off." His approach to the Egyptian crisis was similar. On Black Saturday Eden was Acting Prime Minister as well as Foreign Secretary, Sir Winston Churchill being absent from England. "A plan had been worked out under which our forces would intervene in Cairo and Alexandria to protect the lives and property of British subjects, including Maltese," Eden records in his memoirs. "However, during this Saturday a message arrived from the British command in Egypt expressing concern at the resistance shown [by Egyptians] in the recent fighting. . . . Serious doubts were expressed as to whether the forces available from the canal zone would be enough for the tasks allotted them under the plan." Eden told the commander to be prepared to intervene, whatever the risks. "The belief that we had the forces and the conviction that we were prepared to use them," he wrote, prodded Egyptian authorities to quell the riots. Furthermore, Eden supposed, Britain's firmness influenced the Palace to dismiss Nahhas and make Aly Maher the new Premier—a reversal of Lampson's 1942 shake-up.

Although the 1936 treaty allowed only 10,000 British troops in the Canal base, there were still 60,000 there in October 1951, more than six years after V-J Day. After Black Saturday the garrison was increased to 88,000. King Farouk, Eden says, was confident that "if a revolution occurred, British forces would in the last resort come to his rescue. In this he was mistaken. . . . I had frequently indicated to our Embassy that British forces would not intervene to keep King Farouk on his throne." When Nasser's *coup d'état* came, on the night of 22/23 July 1952, Farouk appealed through US Ambassador Jefferson Caffery for intervention. London turned a deaf ear. Farouk was deposed and sent into exile on the 26th. It was the first crucial encounter between the careers of Eden and Nasser. Like most of those that followed in the four and a half years of political life remaining to Eden, this first encounter redounded to Nasser's benefit.

The next was a kind of exchange of favors on the Sudan question. Nasser's junta succeeded, where Old Regime politicians had failed, in disentangling the Sudan question from Suez. In what Eden acknowledged as "an act of statesmanship," Egypt dropped her claim to sovereignty over the Sudan in the fall of 1952 in order to open the way for negotiations. An agreement signed on 12 February 1953 provided early self-government for the Sudan and the right within three years to choose either full independence or some kind of association with Egypt. Nasser had prevailed over the die-hards among his colleagues and disarmed hostile critics by sugar-coating the agreement with a prospect of Sudanese-Egyptian unity and by persuading the British to forego including an explicit option of Sudanese membership in the British Commonwealth. Upon independence, of course, the Sudan could have applied for it. The agreement was implemented with a modicum of friction and Egypt eventually had to swallow her disappointment at seeing the Sudanese eschew union in favor of sovereign independence.

It had been no easier for Eden than for Nasser to persuade his party and government to accept the Sudan Agreement. Eden found himself in one of his rare disagreements with Churchill. Churchill had won early fame in the Sudan

as a brash young war correspondent and cavalry officer, galloping with the
21st Lancers against the Dervish army at Omdurman in 1898 and writing a
classic description of the charge. Churchill's respectful liking for the soldierly
Sudanese added to his reluctance to lower the Union Jack over Khartoum. "I
should have had to resign," Eden recalled, "if I had not got my way."

Agreement on Suez, unexpectedly, proved far more difficult. Egypt asked
for negotiations on Suez at the same time as on the Sudan, having approached
Britain as soon as the junta could devote attention to these problems after securing control of the government and charting domestic reforms. But where
the Sudan dispute was settled in little more than three months, the Suez negotiations dragged on through rupture and renewal, terror and reprisal, and what
Churchill called "wordy warfare," for nearly two years.

On Suez, even more than on the Sudan, Nasser and Eden alike had each to
overcome among his own constituents formidable resistance to any compromise. The carping of the Laborite Opposition was a minor impediment to Eden
compared with the die-hard imperialists in the right wing of the Tory Party
who later became known as the Suez Rebels. Eden had also to change the
mind once again of his long-time chief, Churchill. Nasser's foremost opponents
were more deadly—the Moslem Brotherhood and its secret brigade of terrorists
and assassins. Like Eden, Nasser was only Number Two in his government
during the Suez talks and he too had to prevail over a reluctant superior,
President Mohammed Naguib. The balkiness among Eden's cabinet colleagues
was more than matched by the resistance to compromise among Nasser's junta
members.

Full liberation from British occupation had been Nasser's primary objective
in forming his secret society of young officers back in 1939. Lampson's peremptory intervention at the Palace in 1942 merely strengthened his conviction that
full independence was essential to Egyptian betterment. And the postwar
emergence of Israel convinced him that Egypt's liberation would not be secure
until British influence was eliminated throughout the Middle East. "After the
siege and the battles in Palestine I came home with the whole region in my
mind one complete whole," he wrote late in 1953. "One region, the same factors and circumstances, even the same forces opposing them all. It was clear that
imperialism was the most prominent of these forces; Israel itself was but one
of the outcomes of imperialism. If Palestine had not fallen under the British
Mandate, Zionism could not have found the necessary support to realize the
idea of a national home there." Ever since then Nasser's foreign policy has
been constant and openly publicized.

Overthrowing the Egyptian monarchy did not become an objective of
Nasser's group until it decided that the Palace was an obstacle to getting the

British out of Egypt. Revolution itself was essentially subservient to nationalism. Getting rid of the British was the psychological *raison d'être* of the revolution. After the *coup d'état* the junta felt that its survival depended on how it honored its commitment to restore Egyptian sovereignty over the Suez base, the last part of Egypt where the British still held sway.

The base sprawled over an area measuring 90 miles from north to south by 60 miles from east to west, with the canal itself as its eastern boundary. It comprised dozens of individual installations—camps, supply depots, Royal Air Force stations—the biggest of which was the 15-square-mile ordinance depot at Tel al-Kebir, built where Wolseley defeated Arabi in 1882. The stores and equipment were worth £200,000,000 and the base itself had a replacement value of £300,000,000. In World War II, it is said, it was the largest military staging base in history, supporting at its peak of operations some 15 divisions simultaneously with 65 air squadrons and the Royal Navy fleet in the Eastern Mediterranean. It employed 300,000 Egyptians during the war; 80,000 in 1951.

When Egyptian labor was withdrawn at the end of 1951 and guerrilla attacks began to flicker throughout the zone, housekeeping and self-defense crippled the garrison's military effectiveness. Reinforcements merely meant that more and more of Britain's over-extended army was tied down. Eventually, the British had to bring in all food and supplies by sea as Egypt progressively isolated the base. The threat of increased terrorism was always in the air and as a last resort Egypt could have cut off all fresh water from the canal zone, although this would have afflicted Egyptians in the cities and farms as well as the British in the base.

Suez was an emotional issue in both Britain and Egypt at the end of 1952 when the first preliminary contacts were made. Accordingly, these contacts were kept secret. The British still hoped to tie a Suez arrangement to a regional defense pact along lines that had already been rejected by Egyptian governments before the revolution. For this they sought US support.

The prospects of US support looked good. President Truman in 1947 had broken the 150-year-old isolationist spell of George Washington's warning against "entangling alliances" by launching the Marshall Plan for Western Europe and the Truman Doctrine for Greece and Turkey. Both Eisenhower and Dulles had been prominently associated with the Truman Administration in creating NATO in 1949 and they were known to favor extending the NATO precedent to other regional collective security pacts.

Therefore, although Eden's prejudice against Jefferson Caffery, the US Ambassador in Cairo, was as great as his distrust of Dulles, both he and Churchill personally urged Eisenhower to bring the US into the talks as the prospective mainstay of a defense pact. In January 1952 Churchill had outraged

Egyptian sensibilities by asking the US, France, and Turkey to station token forces in the British base. Prerevolutionary Egypt balked then at internationalizing the base and revolutionary Egypt equally stubbornly resisted internationalizing the subsequent negotiations over it. The US refused to join the talks without Egypt's consent and the negotiations remained bilateral between Egypt and Britain.

In compensation, Churchill asked Eisenhower to avoid giving any appearance of support to Egypt, writing that he felt like the American frontiersman who prayed when treed by a grizzly: "O Lord, if You can't help me, please don't help that bear." The US accordingly let Egypt know it could expect no American military or economic help until after settling the Suez question with the British. Unofficially, Washington allowed Caffery to facilitate the talks in Cairo as an intermediary. Eden complained with bad grace in his memoirs about Caffery, about US "pressure" on Britain in place of the "wholehearted support which their partner in NATO had the right to expect," and about alleged US anticolonialism. Caffery deserved better thanks for it was he who wheedled the Egyptians into virtually every concession they made. He said after his retirement that the negotiations were the most complicated in his 44 years of diplomatic experience.

The areas of disagreement were numerous and stubborn. Britain cleared away the first major stumbling block—insistence on a defense pact—when Washington refused to back it. The duration of the agreement and the time to be allowed for evacuation were much wrangled over. Eden at first wanted a new 20-year treaty in place of the one he obtained in 1936 but he settled for seven years. Nasser had been hard put in 1953 to persuade the junta to allow 15 months for evacuation but he persuaded it in 1954 to allow 20 months. The knottiest issues proved to be whether uniformed British troops or civilian contractors should maintain the base after evacuation and whether any non-Arab countries should be in the defense area where outside aggression would automatically permit British reactivation of the base. Britain wanted both Iran and Turkey in the area. Nasser disliked admitting Turkey, which had recognized Israel, and he feared that a Communist coup in northern Iran was too real a possibility to risk including it among the automatic causes for British re-entry. The visible presence of uniformed troops to maintain the base, Nasser foresaw, would allow his extremist opposition to claim that British occupation had not really ended. Eventually Nasser gave way on Turkey and Britain gave way on maintenance by civilian technicians.

The first formal negotiations began on 27 April 1953 only to break down on 6 May after six meetings. Dulles arrived a few days later on a major tour of the Middle East. He was unable to cool tempers although he spent five hours with

Naguib on 11 May and also conferred with Nasser, the leader of the Egyptian negotiating team. Egypt sealed off the base from all commercial transactions. Terrorist attacks, sabotage, and pilfering increased. Egyptians demonstrated in the streets shouting: "We are the Mau Mau of the Canal."

Barricaded behind barbed wire and earthworks, guarded by spotter planes overhead and hundreds of motorized patrols on the ground, always moving in pairs, the British garrison grimly stood its ground. But the officers and men alike chafed at the siege combination of boredom and danger. Lieutenant General Sir Francis Festing, the Irish-born commander of the British forces in Egypt, made contingency plans and waited for orders from London. "No problem to reoccupy Cairo and the Delta," he told me when I visited the base after the talks broke off, "but the aftermath—horrible problem." Three years later and against far greater difficulties Eden was reckless enough to court the "horrible problem."

A second round of talks in August, September, and October, informal and largely secret, came so near to success that Nasser said after one meeting that an agreement "is as good as signed." The prospect of an early agreement worried the Israelis. Israeli diplomats in all countries interested in the Suez problem were instructed to warn the governments that British evacuation of the Suez base would upset the Arab-Israeli balance of power and nullify the value of the 1950 Tripartite Declaration underwriting the military *status quo*.

Despite substantial compromises on both sides, full accord proved to be a mirage when the negotiators put their positions in writing and found unreconciled issues. Lord Salisbury, Eden's deputy, said in England that the government was prepared for "a permanent continuation of the present situation" and that Britain would make her own decisions on Suez. Nasser retorted in Cairo that talks were not the only way for Egypt to achieve her objective and that "the period when the British treated Egypt's governments as mere playthings has entirely passed." He said the British kept backtracking from previously agreed positions.

The long hiatus in negotiations after October 1953 was chiefly due, as Britons candidly acknowledged, to London's belief that Nasser would not last long. British doubts hardened in February 1954 when the revolution's figurehead president, General Naguib, nearly shattered the regime with a try for real power with the incongruously assorted backing of the Moslem Brotherhood, the outlawed Old Regime political parties, and the Communists. Nasser admitted afterward that "it looked as though this regime was about to end." He regained his footing and the premiership in mid-April.

While London watched and waited, violence ebbed and flowed along with the "wordy warfare" between the British and the Egyptians. Both sides committed murders in the canal zone. The strategic uselessness of a base in hostile territory became ever more apparent. War Secretary Antony Head frankly told the House of Commons in March 1954 that the Government's military advisers could see no point in sitting it out indefinitely in Egypt. Churchill himself conceded later that the successful testing of the hydrogen bomb, disclosed by Eisenhower in February 1954, had made bases like Suez obsolete even in friendly territory. "Not a single soldier is in favor of staying there," Churchill said in July. "Why don't Waterhouse and the [Suez] rebels see that?"

Toward the end of spring, the British were ready for a new effort. They recognized that Nasser was strong enough to be worth talking to. But Eden was preoccupied with the Geneva conference on Indo-China and negotiations were not resumed until Britain submitted a new offer on 10 July. Progress then was rapid. The final issues were settled when War Secretary Head flew to Cairo on 24 July. Head and Nasser initialed the agreement-in-principle, called *Heads of Agreement*, in Nasser's office at 9:20 P.M. on 27 July 1954.

Head, who as Defense Minister at the height of the Suez Crisis was to accept a large share of the responsibility for the invasion of Egypt, recalled more than ten years later that Nasser had impressed him favorably as being a responsible, reasonable, capable man. After initialing the agreement, Nasser asked him to tell the British government that Egypt's major needs, now that the end of the British occupation was in sight, were arms for its soldiers and the High Dam at Aswan for the people as a whole. Head remembered Nasser telling him, not as a threat but as a matter of fact, that the Army was insistently demanding improved weapons and that Nasser would prefer to get them from the West, especially from Britain, but that if the West would not supply him he would turn to Czechoslovakia. Head said he gave the message to the cabinet upon his return to London. Nasser forgot the idea of turning to the Soviet bloc for arms until further refusals from the West in the spring of 1955, after the Gaza Raid, drove him to it.

The *Heads of Agreement* provided for complete British evacuation within 20 months of the signature of the formal agreement that was to follow. For seven years from the date of the formal agreement Britain would have the right to reactivate and return to the base in the event of an attack by an outside power on any of the Arab League States or Turkey. The base installations were to be maintained by commercial firms with civilian technicians, not by uniformed British military personnel.

Three days later Washington assured Egypt that aid and arms would begin flowing as soon as the formal agreement was signed. The US did grant $40,-000,000 in economic aid in November, as it promised, but Nasser was never to get any American arms.

Dangerous opposition among Egyptians to the *Heads of Agreement* was not long in showing itself. On 2 August the Supreme Guide of the Moslem Brotherhood distributed a pamphlet warning Nasser to renounce the "treasonable agreement." Brotherhood terrorists and Egyptian Communists took up where the "Lavon Affair" saboteurs left off, hurling homemade bombs into British camps and dynamiting bridges in the canal zone.

Nasser's enemies in exile raised powerful voices of guidance for the voiceless opposition within Egypt. Mahmoud Abul Fath, former publisher of the Wafdist newspaper, *Al-Misri*, declared in *The Times's* letters columns on 4 August that the *Heads of Agreement* "contain conditions and obligations which can hardly prove acceptable to the Egyptian people as a whole" because they bound Egypt in new "strategic entanglements for several years beyond the term of the 1936 treaty." "Mr. Eden himself stated that after 1956 Britain could not have sustained her claims to keep forces on Egyptian soil," Abul Fath wrote. He predicted ominously that Britain would have "further difficulties in Egypt, for the nation will not give up its opposition to imposed instruments or arrangements to which it has never given free consent."

Egyptian Communists learned from *Pravda* on 8 August that the Suez agreement was "a dangerous step in the direction of . . . American plans for a Middle East Command" and that it "threatens the peaceful coexistence of Egypt with other countries."

Eden too ran into persistent criticism. Even neutral observers pointed out with a certain relish the contradictions between Britain's claim that the hydrogen bomb had made the base obsolete and her insistence on the right of re-entry in the event of war. They noted that if the hydrogen bomb made the Suez base obsolete it made a new base on the island of Cyprus even more obsolete. A month before the *Heads of Agreement*, the military correspondent of *The Times* wrote: "Cyprus has no particular merit, military or political, as a site for the new joint headquarters, but no better alternative is to hand."

The Tory die-hards of the Suez Rebels had registered their protest even before the Russians or the anti-Nasser Egyptians. Theirs were the only negative votes when the House of Commons approved the *Heads of Agreement* on 29 July by 257 to 26. One Tory peer had already gone so far as to quit the party. He returned when Eden went to war against Nasser in 1956.

The final agreement was signed in Cairo on 19 October 1954 by Nasser and Anthony Nutting of the Foreign Office. Its thirteen articles, filling two-and-a-half pages, followed closely the lines of the *Heads of Agreement*. There were 52 additional pages of elaboration in the form of annexes, appendices, exchanges of letters, lists, and an "Agreed Minute." The emotional compulsion of nationalist commitments inherited from the Old Regime was evident in two subtle touches. The instrument called itself an "agreement," eschewing the term "treaty" with its—to Egyptians—humiliating connotations of subservience. And in Article II Britain alone declared the 1936 treaty to be terminated because Nasser would not risk seeming to admit that Nahhas's unilateral abrogation—ten months before the revolution—was in any way invalid.

In the *Agreed Minute* Egypt cannily excluded Israel from the expression "outside power" so that an Israeli attack could not be taken as a pretext for the British to return to the base. The *Agreed Minute* was the only appended item to receive the same full roster of signatures as the *Agreement* itself. But Nasser's precaution was to prove as vain as it was shrewd when Britain invaded two years later on the pretext of taking police action against an Israeli invasion.

Eden himself, who called the agreement "a declaration of convenience" in his memoirs, said its "most serious weakness" resulted from the technical state of war existing between Egypt and Israel. Eden also said that under the 1936 treaty "no British troops could have been on the canal in the autumn of 1956, for by then it would have expired." The new agreement was not to expire until 19 October 1961, more than five years later than the terminal date of the 1936 treaty.

The extent of the risks Nasser ran in signing the evacuation agreement had been signaled by the criticism directed against the preliminary *Heads of Agreement* in July. Nasser expressed his awareness of the dangers in an interview with me on 19 August 1954, stressing particularly the inadvisability of pressing a Western defense pact on the Arabs. "It is a matter of group psychology with deep roots," he said, "and until the Arabs realize that there's no longer any hidden domination or control in pacts of that sort, any pressure to obtain them will be dangerously premature." He said his regime would hold the Moslem Brothers collectively responsible for any acts of violence committed by its individual members, adding: "I was a member of the Moslem Brotherhood and I know them well."

The Brotherhood regarded the Evacuation Agreement itself as a pact perpetuating British control and hidden domination in Egypt. It accused Nasser of having sold out to imperialism. It was on 26 October 1954, just one week after the final agreement was signed, that a Brotherhood assassin fired eight pistol shots at Nasser as he addressed a nighttime rally from a balcony overlooking the newly renamed Liberation Square in Alexandria. The attempt was as clumsy as it was dramatic.

Nasser had been recalling to the audience that as a student demonstrator in 1932 in that same square, then called Mohammed Aly Square, he had first heard shots fired in anger. He had escaped unscathed, he said. "I am still alive and am participating in the freeing of my country," he added just as the first wild shots rang out from the front row seat of the assassin fifteen yards away.

Once more Nasser escaped unscathed. Pieces of glass from a lamp shattered by the bullets injured a Sudanese minister and an Alexandria lawyer seated near Nasser. Nasser shook off the security agents that rushed to shield him and took up the phrase: "I am still alive." He shouted into the microphone over the hubbub below where the assassin, a Cairo tinsmith named Mohammed Abdel Latif, and a handful of suspected accomplices were wrestled into submission by military policemen. In a voice breathless and high-pitched with emotion, Nasser reassured the crowd and the radio audience that he was unhurt but that even if the attempt had succeeded the revolution would have continued because "You are all Gamal Abdel Nassers."

The live drama had been recorded on the tape machines set up for the speech. It was rebroadcast three times the following day as Nasser returned to Cairo through tumultuous demonstrations. The demonstrations indicated that the attempt had brought him, for the first time, real personal popularity. When he finally reached his office Nasser found hundreds of messages from well-wishers in Egypt and abroad, including one from Prime Minister Churchill saying: "I congratulate you on your escape from the dastardly attack made on your life yesterday evening." One crowd of Egyptian supporters sacked and burned the seedy Cairo mansion where the Moslem Brotherhood had its headquarters while the police busied themselves with mass arrests of Brotherhood leaders and suspected terrorists.

The assassination attempt made it easier for Nasser to secure the regime against the Brotherhood. Popular repugnance for its violent ways made Egyptians more tolerant of repressive police action against the Brotherhood. A show trial exposed the Brotherhood to contempt and ridicule before six prominent members were hanged on 7 December. By commuting the death sentence of the Supreme Guide, Hassan al-Hodeiby, the junta mitigated the severity of the punishments in the public eye. More than a thousand Brotherhood members were arrested and tried and hundreds were sent to prison.

The troublesome figurehead, President Naguib, was swept out of office and into harmless obscurity in the immediate aftermath of the assassination attempt. He was placed under house arrest at midday on 14 November after Brotherhood leaders implicated him in their conspiracy. Naguib went quietly into permanent retirement and the Egyptians, with scarcely a shrug, removed his picture from millions of household, shop, and office walls. Only nine months before, the awesome enthusiasm of the Egyptian masses had looked like a force strong enough to sustain Naguib against any adversary, Nasser in particular. But the very Moslem Brotherhood leaders with whom Naguib had appeared on balconies to hear the intoxicating thunder of the people's cheers were those who dragged him down in their own discredit after the assassination attempt.

It was the day after Naguib's removal that Nasser met General Burns for the first time and told him he hoped the drift toward peace would continue. It was part of the risky personal effort to reassure Israel that he had begun during the evacuation negotiations with the British. In his 19 August interview with me, for example, he emphasized that the Arabs had no intention of attacking Israel. Israel's sabotage campaign in July had not changed that policy nor had it affected the good relations between non-Jewish Egyptians and the large, predominantly non-Zionist Jewish community in Egypt of about 65,000 persons. But it had made Nasser anxious to prevent Israelis from transforming their fears about the British evacuation of the Suez base into any further violent actions.

Thus Cairo Radio repeatedly broadcast statements by Nasser and other Egyptian spokesmen and commentators that the continuation of tranquillity was up to Israel, that the evacuation agreement was no threat to Israel but, on the contrary, would enable Egypt "to play an important role in maintaining peace in the Middle East."

Cairo Radio also broadcast British reassurances to Israel, including Anthony Nutting's statement that Britain sought "the ending of the state of war between the Arab states and Israel." Selwyn Lloyd had assured Israel on 12 July that Egypt would not get the British arms in the base. On 28 July, the day after the *Heads of Agreement* were initialed, Eden reaffirmed the Tripartite Declaration "relating to peace and stability between the Arab States and Israel" and said the agreement itself should "contribute to a reduction of tension." On 19 October, when the final agreement was signed, Eden again reaffirmed the Tripartite Declaration and said the British were "glad to note the absence of serious incidents in the last few weeks and trust that this will continue."

The relative tranquillity on the Sinai border continued four more months. It ended when Ben-Gurion returned from the wilderness to launch the series of great raids that began at Gaza and ended at Suez.

The "honeymoon" between Egypt and Britain that began with the Suez agreement proved strong enough to withstand the border strife which it inadvertently helped engender by way of Ben-Gurion's reaction. "Honeymoon" was Nasser's term for the "new basis of mutual understanding and firm friendship" which the Suez agreement sought and, for a time, achieved. What strained the "honeymoon" almost from the beginning and wrecked it in little more than a year was Britain's Baghdad Pact policy.

CHAPTER

7

Eden For and Against Nasser

(1954 TO 20 JULY 1956)

A British Prime Minister appears to be in the position of the steersman of a surf-boat lying outside the mouth of an African river. He has to wait for a high wave to carry him over the bar.

(CROMER, 1908)

He was one of the martyrs to that terrible delusion, which should teach us, among its other morals, that the influential classes, and those who take upon themselves to be leaders of the people, are fully liable to all the passionate error that has ever characterized the maddest mob.

(HAWTHORNE, *The House of Seven Gables*)

I have seen the moment of my greatness flicker,
And I have seen the eternal footman hold my coat, and snicker...

(T. S. ELIOT, "The Love Song of J. Alfred Prufrock")

HAVING GIVEN up Palestine and agreed to leave Egypt, Britain promoted the Baghdad Pact as a device to secure a strong, permanent lodgment for British authority in the former British mandate of Iraq, from which she could extend her influence into the rest of the Arab Middle East. Iraq was linked to Britain by a 25-year treaty of preferential alliance valid until October 1957. After a stormy 14 years of rule in Iraq, Britain had surrendered the mandate in 1932 in exchange for the preferential alliance, which recognized Iraqi independence but attached conditions safeguarding British imperial interests. The treaty was, in fact, patterned after a draft treaty rejected by Egypt in 1930. Nevertheless, it served in turn as a guide for the 1936 Anglo-Egyptian treaty.

Iraqi and Egyptian nationalists alike saw their treaties as unpalatable limitations of sovereignty. The treaties endured as long as they did only through the endeavors of pro-British rulers and politicians in both countries who owed their power in great part to British support. The pillars of the pro-British leadership in Iraq, which was murderously overthrown in July 1958, were the royal family and Nuri Pasha al-Said, a comrade of Lawrence in the Arab Revolt against Turkey in World War I. Nuri served as Premier fourteen times before he was hunted down and killed by revolutionaries for having, in their eyes, held Iraq out of the mainstream of Arabism in humiliating deference to Britain.

Iraqi nationalists had made two major demonstrations of their dissatisfaction with the British alliance. In 1941 British military action was required to throw out a nationalist *coup d'état* regime that looked to the Axis to help it end British hegemony. In 1948 savage rioting aborted the British Labor Government's effort to adjust the alliance to postwar realities. As a result the frightened Prince Regent of Iraq and an assembly of political notables repudiated the new treaty of alliance, which had been signed at Portsmouth, England, and they assured the Iraqi people "that this treaty will not be concluded, nor, indeed, any other treaty which may ignore the full rights of the country."

As the original 25-year alliance approached its appointed end both Britain and the pro-British regime in Iraq felt an urgent need for some kind of extension. Both feared that the lack of a legal instrument for the continuation of the British presence and British influence would allow the nationalists to insist on the withdrawal of British troops and that this would open the way for the overthrow of Nuri and perhaps the Hashemite monarchy itself. The British had installed Faisal I as King in Baghdad, far from his Meccan home, after World War I. British power had proven necessary to restore Nuri and shore up the monarchy after the nationalist coup in 1941 and the nationalists, despite Nuri's repressions, were stronger in the 1950s than ever before. The Baghdad Pact, in the new style of regional defense treaties, seemed to offer a solution that would join American power to British to sustain the *status quo* in Iraq.

Dulles encouraged the concept of a defense barrier against Russian communist penetration into the Middle East after his tour of the region in May 1953, the first visit to the area by an American Secretary of State. In a broadcast on 1 June he acknowledged that the Arabs were more concerned with their disputes with Israel, Britain, and France than with the "menace of Soviet communism," but, he said, "the northern tier of nations shows awareness of the danger." He endorsed a collective security system but noted that none could be imposed from without. "It should be designed to grow from within," he said, "out of a sense of common destiny and common danger." It was a conscious, if tacit, suggestion to the British to leave the initiative for defense alliances to the Arabs.

Dulles expressed himself more plainly in an unpublished memorandum of conclusions on his trip. "We must also accept the fact," he said, "that the political situation is such that Arab States will not, at this time, openly join defensive arrangements with a combination of Western powers.... We must therefore avoid becoming fascinated with concepts that have no reality."

His reasons were summarized bluntly:

> British position rapidly deteriorating, probably to the point of nonrepair.... Such British troops as are left in the area are more a factor of instability rather than stability.... There is no respect for the French as a political force.... The Israeli factor, and the association of the US in the minds of the people of the area with French and British colonial and imperialistic policies, are millstones around our neck.

Nevertheless, Dulles concluded, the US had to undertake the delicate task of increasing its influence in the Middle East as rapidly and as widely as possible. In the memorandum, which informally charted the broad lines US Middle East policy would follow during the Eisenhower administration, Dulles identified one dilemma that hampered his freedom of action. "We must attempt solutions of local problems in the Near East," he wrote, "without so worsening our relations with Britain as to unduly weaken or wreck the NATO alliance. Our efforts with the British must be such as will avoid being placed in a position where we must choose between maintenance of the NATO alliance and action to keep a large portion of the world that is still free from drifting into Soviet hands."

Nasser, like the monarchial regime he overthrew, had consistently opposed the idea of an Arab pact with the West, although he was willing to accept defensive arrangements between non-Arab Middle Eastern states and the West. On 13 April 1954, shortly after the announcement of the Turkey-Pakistan pact (which was the forerunner of the Baghdad Pact), Nasser declared that Egypt would oppose any attempt to bring Iraq into it on the grounds that this would deliberately weaken Arab support for Egypt in her struggle against the British occupation of the Suez Canal zone.

Dulles hoped for a pact in the Middle East that would complete the missing link between NATO in the West and SEATO in the Far East in the strategy of containment against the spread of communist influence. His practical intentions were far more modest than his hopes. Eden and Nuri, however, based their plans on Washington's hopes rather than on its more solidly based doubts. Nuri knew he needed British support to survive and the British knew they needed Nuri for the survival of their influence in the Arab world. Their awareness that each was lost without the other overrode the obvious fact that Arabs were easily stirred to violence against Western alliances, especially in Iraq.

Nuri was confident, in any case, that with British support he could control his opponents. Behind a façade of constitutional democracy he built a dictatorial power structure in 1954 by abolishing party politics, muzzling the press, and staging two elections. Dissatisfied with the first, he left nothing at all to chance in the second and obtained the largest parliamentary majority in the modern history of Iraq. By the end of 1954 Nuri possessed enough police power to commit Iraq to the Baghdad Pact in the face of overwhelming, albeit silenced and shackled, popular opposition.

Nuri had already made his first overt new commitment to the West in the spring by concluding an arms agreement with the US on Washington's terms. Nasser felt that Nuri had thereby weakened Egypt's bargaining power in the still unresolved Suez dispute with Britain as well as in the Palestine dispute. Like the majority of Arabs everywhere, Nasser wanted the Arabs to maintain a united front, refusing alliances until the West, in exchange, induced Israel to conclude a Palestine settlement the Arabs could consider reasonable: Collective aloofness was one of the better bargaining counters among the skimpy resources the Arabs had for dealing with the rest of the world. Nuri had broken the Arab front and seemed determined to move still further out of line. Nasser, although critical of Nuri and what he stood for, nevertheless hoped to heal the divisions between Egypt and Iraq. The rivalry between Cairo and Baghdad had kept the Arab League ineffectual since its birth and had made a mockery of all the bombast about Arab unity. "Nuri is in power in Iraq; this is the time to reach an understanding with him," Nasser told a friend in August 1954. Under Nasser, Egypt was ready for the kind of cooperation Nuri had asked in 1945. A compromise was needed on the issue of defense pacts with the West.

In September, after his rigged electoral triumph at home, Nuri went to Cairo for three days of talks, mollifying Nasser with a public assurance that, while Iraq would continue to accept Western help against the Soviet menace, it would join no formal Western defense pacts because of its commitments to the Arab League's Collective Security Pact. Then he blandly went on to London and Ankara in secret pursuit of his plans for the Baghdad Pact. He ignored mutterings throughout the Arab world that the rumored pact would split the Arabs, dissipate their bargaining power, and make them vulnerable to Israeli initiatives. Nuri sincerely believed that safety for his regime and for all the Arabs lay in close ties with the West, and the sooner the better.

Nasser described the meeting to me some years later, saying:

I tried to convince him about the idea of the Arab defense organization without the participation of any other country. But he told me: "What are the Arabs? They have nothing. What do we gain from that? We can gain from the Turks and Iran." I told him: "From the military point of view, this is nonsense, because they will be the front line and you will be their depth. So they can gain from Iraq and Iraq can't gain at all from them. On the other hand, with the Arab organization, you will have the Arab depth. You can gain from the Arabs if any attack reaches your country." But he was not at all convinced with the idea. He said: "Now it is the time of [multilateral] pacts, the period of [bilateral] alliances has passed and now it is the time of pacts." And he left.

Nuri also saw in the Baghdad Pact a framework for his old ambition to unite Iraq, Syria, Lebanon, and Jordan. This dream aroused intense anxiety in Syria, which would be subordinated to Iraq in such a union. Nuri's scheme was named after the region called the Fertile Crescent, which encompasses the four states in a broad sweep from the Mediterranean down the Tigris and Euphrates valleys to the Persian Gulf. Israel too saw a threat in such a union. These factors were secondary, however, to the disagreement between Nasser and Nuri over the Western links with a pact.

Nasser's dispute with him was on the matter of timing rather than on the principle of alliances with the West. "It is clear that any aggressor will come from the other side—the Communist world," he told me in August, after the *Heads of Agreement* on Suez. The West was already present in the Middle East and possessed of vast oil and other interests, he said, and only the Russians had anything to gain by aggression there. "The next step," he continued, "will be when the people understand that they cannot stand alone against an attack by a major power. Then it will be the time for pacts because they will seek help of those major powers they recognize as friends.... But this hammering, hammering, hammering for pacts [now] will only keep alive the old suspicions in the minds of the people—and the Communists know well how to exploit these suspicions."

Egypt's anxieties about Nuri's intentions were lulled again at an Arab League foreign ministers' meeting in Cairo in December 1954. The Iraqi Foreign Minister, Musa Shabandar, apparently unaware of Nuri's continuing preparations and Eden's encouragement of them, announced that Iraq would conclude a new agreement with Britain along the lines of Egypt's Suez evacuation agreement; Britain would evacuate her air bases in Iraq with the right of re-entry in the event of outside aggression against any of the Arab States and, instead of Turkey, Persia. Tom Little, the best-informed correspondent in Egypt in those years, says it was Nasser who made the suggestion to Shabandar. But Nasser now says: "Shabandar? I don't even remember his face.' Shabandar said at the time that his talks with Nasser had achieved full agreement between Iraq and Egypt on strengthening the Arab collective security pact.

So effectively had Nuri lulled the Arab world that the arrival of Premier Adnan Menderes of Turkey in Baghdad on 6 January 1955 stirred only mild and inaccurate speculation. The mood of the Iraqi public, however, was expressed in the sullen silence of the crowds that watched Nuri and Menderes drive through the flag-decked streets of the city.

When Nuri and Menderes announced on 12 January that they had "decided to conclude a treaty as soon as possible," Egypt's reaction, echoed throughout the Arab world, was one of outraged astonishment. Nasser asked all the Arab premiers to meet in Cairo to try to avert a critical split among them. At the same time he explicitly assured the US and the British that Egypt stood with the West despite her opposition to the gestating Baghdad Pact.

A virulent propaganda war flared between Cairo and Baghdad, reviving the millennial rivalry between the two cities. Cairo's fire was aimed at Nuri personally, in keeping with Nasser's perception that Nuri was the key to British success in Iraq just as like-minded politicians had been the key to British influence in prerevolutionary Egypt. But the Egyptian radio exhortations to Iraqis to overthrow Nuri eventually became so scurrilous that they provoked a reaction in Nuri's favor.

Nuri refused to come to the Cairo meeting and remained in Baghdad with a clear case of diplomatic illness. All of the other Arab League premiers and foreign ministers assembled in Cairo on 22 January for more than two weeks of urgent discussion during which a high-level mission of Egyptian, Syrian, Lebanese, and Jordanian ministers went to Baghdad for a futile final appeal to Nuri. Nasser threatened to pull Egypt out of the Arab Collective Security Pact itself if the Baghdad Pact materialized.

The Arab pact, signed in 1950, was, and still is, a paper organization of symbolic rather than military significance. Nasser never did withdraw from it although the Cairo conference ended in failure on 6 February. Arab dissensions hardened as Syria, the Yemen, and Saudi Arabia gave Egypt unqualified support for an additional, purely Arab defense and economic pact to rival the Baghdad Pact. This proposal did not achieve even a paper existence for nearly a year.

Nehru, the most powerful nonwhite leader in the British Commonwealth, came to Cairo on 16 February and joined Nasser in a formal condemnation of "military alliances and power entanglements which increase tension and rivalry in armaments." Nehru's support, designed mainly to rally African and Asian neutralism against Pakistan's alignment with the West, was inadequate consolation for the reverses the emergency conference had inflicted on Nasser's Arab policy. The very intensity of his effort to block the Baghdad Pact made him look more than a little foolish when it failed. It increased his vulnerability in those chancy first months after he had come forward to take from President Naguib the titular leadership of Egypt. Every move he made, or hoped to make, was rendered riskier. Nasser had to calculate to a nicety the degree to which every conciliatory soft gesture toward watchful foreign and domestic opponents needed to be balanced by a hard gesture.

It was during the tense days of the emergency Arab conference that Egypt hanged the two convicted Zionist saboteurs, an action which more than offset in Israeli eyes the freeing of the crew of the captured Israeli ship, *Bat Galim*, and the public and private avowals of a peace policy which Nasser was making to men like General Burns, R. H. S. Crossman, and Eric Johnston.

On 20 February 1955, four days after meeting Nehru, Nasser was visited by Eden, who paused in Cairo on his way to the first SEATO conference in Bangkok. It was the only meeting between the two men, whose pervasive influence on one another's fortunes was to reach its climax in a very personal war. Nasser went to the British Embassy for the meeting, the first such visit by an Egyptian Premier in eleven years. The honeymoon was strained but it still had ten months to run.

Eden described in his memoirs the meeting, in which the other participants included Field Marshal Sir John Harding, Chief of the Imperial General Staff. He wrote:

Sir John gave an excellent strategic appraisal, with which Nasser entirely agreed. Nasser declared that his interest and sympathy were with the West, but he argued that the Turco-Iraqi pact, by its bad timing and unfortunate content, had seriously set back the development of effective collaboration with the West by the Arab states.

I was familiar with this plea: it is never the right time for some. We used every argument we could to persuade Nasser at least to restrain his criticisms and, if the agreement were reasonable in terms, to cease his opposition. I do not think, however, that we made much impression. Colonel Nasser, whom I thought a fine man physically, was friendly throughout our talks. He referred repeatedly to the great improvement in Anglo-Egyptian relations, to the importance which his Government attached to this improvement and to his hopes for its continuance in the future. Nasser was not, however, open to conviction on the Turco-Iraqi enterprise. I commented on this in my report to London at the time, adding: "No doubt jealousy plays a part in this and a frustrated desire to lead the Arab world." Before our talks began we were photographed together. As the flashlights went off, he seized my hand and held it.

Nasser recalled it somewhat differently:

I began to express our point of view about the Baghdad Pact and the results of the pact—the splits in the Arab country. And Mr. Eden was just listening. I was not, of course, pleased with that—just listening without any comments. Then I talked from the military point of view about the defense of this area. I said to Mr. Eden that we can have an Arab Defense Organization—united—and this can represent a defense in depth if there is any aggression from the Soviet Union. But we don't want any other country to be a partner because if you participate in this agreement, this would mean to our people that we are working as agents for your interests, not for the interests of the Arabs.

"We want you to help us with the infrastructure. Then, if the Soviet Union attacks us, we will ask you to help us. And if you attack us, we will ask the Soviet Union to help us." Yes, that's what I told him. And, of course, the answer was that there was no possibility of attacking us from the United Kingdom.

Then we talked about the Soviet units facing Europe and facing the Middle East. General Harding was convinced by the idea of the defense in depth. There was no comment at all from Mr. Eden. And I learned after that he went to Baghdad and told Nuri al-Said: "Go on with the Baghdad Pact"—right after our meeting.

Lulled again into thinking the pact had at least been deferred for a while, Nasser was again surprised and outraged when Menderes returned to Baghdad and signed the pact with Nuri on 24 February 1955, four days after Nasser and Eden had talked. Eden stopped in Baghdad on 4 March on his return from the SEATO conference to congratulate Nuri and discuss with him Britain's accession to the pact and the new Anglo-Iraqi agreement that would then come into force.

Dulles was taken as much by surprise as Nasser was. When Byroade, then Assistant Secretary of State for Near Eastern affairs, brought in the cable with the news of the pact on 24 February, Dulles asked him if he had known about it in advance. Byroade replied that if anybody had asked about it five minutes earlier he would have said they were crazy. Byroade said it was an unfortunate development but that the US would have to express approval, which was cautiously done the following day.

From the standpoint of regional defense, the Baghdad Pact was certain to be a net loss if it destroyed the harmonious relations between Britain and Egypt which were essential to preserve British access to the Suez Base as granted in the Anglo-Egyptian evacuation agreement just four months earlier. In view of Nasser's outspoken opposition to the pact and the sympathy accorded to his stand by Arab nationalists, who were in overwhelming majority throughout the region including countries like Iraq where they had no voice in government, it is inescapable that Eden deliberately sacrificed the larger interests of Western defense in favor of preserving a British foothold, which proved to be a will-o'-the-wisp.

Israel reacted officially against the pact almost immediately, particularly against a letter annexed to it by Nuri stating that Iraq and Turkey would collaborate closely, not only to repulse any aggression against either country, but also for the implementation of the UN resolutions on Palestine, which are the basis of the Arab position vis-à-vis Israel. The Israeli Foreign Ministry stated on 26 February that the annex's hostility toward Israel was "obvious to anybody" and that "this new alliance must encourage aggressive ideas and tendencies of hostility to Israel . . ." Ben-Gurion had returned as Defense Minister five days before with forceful plans full-fledged to discourage aggressive ideas and tendencies of hostility to Israel.

The Gaza Raid on 28 February cut violently across whatever reply Nasser was planning to make to the Baghdad Pact. It came so suddenly that many Egyptians saw the pact and the raid as a deliberately coordinated double blow designed to humble Egypt and force peace on Israel's terms. Egyptian cabinet ministers went so far as to allege that Iraq had incited the Israeli attack. Yet with commendable fairness, Cairo newspapers reported that Washington deplored the raid as certain to confirm the Arab belief that Israel was a greater threat than Russia.

The raid magnified in Nasser's eyes the gravity of Nuri's having defected from the Arab ranks by accepting US arms on conditions Nasser himself would not risk accepting. Most unpalatable to Nasser was the condition that Iraq accept US officers to advise and supervise Iraq in using the arms. Nuri's internal security problems were enough to induce him to accept US arms, regardless of the strings attached. Iraq's lack of a common frontier with Israel made it easier for Eisenhower to woo Iraq with arms in the face of Zionist opposition to arming any of the Arab states. By accepting the terms of the US Mutual Security Act, Nuri had all but eliminated the possibility of any other Arab country getting US arms without accepting those conditions.

The conditions were no more onerous than those attached to US military aid to Western European countries. But the Arabs had different preoccupations from Europeans and felt threatened by different dangers. Above all, they were still working their precarious way to real independence and were much more sensitive to limitations on their sovereignty than Europeans. Acceptance of arms with strings that included uniformed American military advisers reminded Egyptians that European financial advisers were the precursors of the British occupation in 1882. In Iraq itself, the only Arab country ever to join the Baghdad Pact, support for the pact rested essentially on one man, Nuri al-Said. The hand-picked Iraqi parliament, when Nuri presented the pact, applauded loudly only the provision establishing Iraqi sovereignty over the RAF bases at Habbaniya and Shuaiba.

Nasser's opposition to the Baghdad Pact narrowed still further his slim chances of modernizing Egyptian armaments from the West. The US and Britain, having endorsed the Iraqi-Turkish alliance and supplied arms to both partners, would find it embarrassing to arm simultaneously an Egyptian-led coalition of Arab States hostile to the Baghdad Pact. France was already arming Israel. If additional Arab States acceded to the Baghdad Pact Egypt's isolation would be worsened. The text of the Baghdad treaty was not reassuring because it envisioned the accession of additional Arab and Western members, stating: "This pact shall be open for accession to any member of the Arab League or any other state actively concerned with the security and peace in this region and which is fully recognized by both of the High Contracting Parties." The last phrase excluded Israel because of Iraq's nonrecognition.

Yet the Gaza Raid, by giving a sudden urgency to Egypt's quest for arms, gave new importance to restoring Egypt's friendship with Western sources of arms. Nasser and his vigorously anti-Communist regime had not yet even considered the possibility of seeking arms from the Communist bloc. Therefore Nasser decided to pare the horns of his dilemma by accepting the Baghdad Pact and Iraq's membership in it without further protest provided no additional Arab countries were recruited for the pact. While making urgent new efforts to persuade the US and Britain to sell him arms, Nasser offered Eden a compromise to suspend their dispute over the Baghdad Pact: if Eden would freeze the Arab membership of the pact Nasser would halt his propaganda and diplomatic campaign against it.

"This was in April 1955, before my departure to Bandung," Nasser told me. "There were discussions with the British Ambassador here, Stevenson... because I told them that now, by trying to join the Arab countries to the Baghdad Pact you create a dispute in the Arab countries, which is not at all for the benefit of the Arab countries. If you stop that, everything will go easy. And they agreed. They answered that they agreed in an oral message, an answer from Mr. Eden through the Ambassador to me ... in which he said that they will freeze the Baghdad Pact and make no efforts to join the Arab countries to it."

Stevenson spent an hour and a quarter with Nasser on 5 April. It was the very day Britain formally joined the Baghdad Pact and put into effect the new *Special Agreement* with Iraq. In keeping with the new understanding, held secret because it would embarrass both Nasser and Eden, Egypt muted her propaganda. In the months that followed, despite newspaper reports that the British or the Turks were trying to recruit now Jordan, now Lebanon, into the pact, Cairo Radio remained bland while two more non-Arab Moslem countries joined, Pakistan in September and Persia in November. Nor did Cairo raise an outcry when the foreign ministers of the five member countries assembled in Baghdad from the 20th to the 22nd of November for the inaugural meeting of the pact council. Eden seemed to be keeping his part of the secret bargain when Amman, during the pact's inaugural meeting, issued a declaration of neutrality between the Baghdad Pact and the rival pact Egypt had formed with Syria and Saudi Arabia.

Three seasons of violence along the Israeli frontier had made it difficult for Egypt to refrain from diatribes against the Baghdad Pact but Nasser had held firm to his understanding with Eden. Eden explicitly repudiated on 30 March 1955 any anti-Israeli aspect of the pact and asserted that, on the contrary, it was a "truly desirable development" for Israel. These words may have disarmed Labor Party opposition to the pact but it had the reverse effect in the Arab world, including Iraq. Even so, Egypt kept quiet, as Nasser had promised.

Eden, after half a generation as "crown prince," succeeded Winston Churchill as Prime Minister on 6 April 1955, the day after Sir Ralph Stevenson's long meeting with Nasser. The moratorium agreement on the Baghdad Pact was thus perhaps Eden's last important action as a successful Foreign Secretary. His violation of the moratorium in December was his first important step toward disaster as Prime Minister.

Jordan's declaration of neutrality between the Baghdad and Egyptian pacts on 21 November 1955 was soon revealed as wholly false. It was issued to cover secret preparations already under way for Jordan to join the Baghdad Pact the following month. Jordan had begun definite steps toward accession by 2 November, when President Celal Bayar of Turkey arrived in Amman on a state visit. By the kind of unfortunate coincidence that had dogged the Baghdad Pact since the Gaza Raid, that was the date Ben-Gurion's troops attacked the Egyptians at al-Sabha and secured permanently Israel's grip on the strategic al-Auja demilitarized zone.

The Turks, having nothing to fear from Nasser or their own nationalists, were less discreet than the Jordanians in their broadcasts about Bayar's visit.

Bayar told Jordanian troops that they might have Turkish allies if they were ever victims of aggression. Radio Ankara explained that what Bayar meant was that Jordan would soon join the Baghdad Pact. Cairo Radio, still under the impression that Eden was keeping his promise to Nasser, retorted on 7 November that Bayar's efforts to recruit Jordan into the pact were in vain.

That same evening, however, King Hussein and Glubb Pasha conferred with the Turks on arrangements by which Jordan would join the pact in return for increased British military aid. On 16 November the British Ambassador in Amman received Jordan's memorandum outlining her military needs. The Ambassador had already discussed the matter with King Hussein. The British prepared shipments of planes, armor, and guns for Jordan and drafted an agreement to be substituted for the Anglo-Jordanian Treaty upon Jordan's accession to the pact, as had been done with Iraq.

Egypt being still in ignorance, Cairo Radio remained quiet. But Baghdad knew that Egypt would react violently when she learned what was afoot and that Saudi Arabia and Syria would sympathize with her. Cairo Radio would inevitably incite Arab nationalists against the pact while Saudi money would finance demonstrations. Accordingly, during the inaugural meeting in Baghdad, Nuri, with Britain's blessing, urged the US observer to find means of stopping, even for six months, American oil payments to the Saudi Government. In Eden's opinion, cutting off Saudi revenues would not only permit Jordan safely to enter the pact but would also make possible other seemingly impossible objectives, including an Arab-Israeli settlement. The irrationality of Eden's hopes was never proven because Washington had no intention of forcing such a violation of American oil company agreements with Saudi Arabia.

The final steps toward bringing Jordan into the pact began on 6 December 1955 when General Templer, who had accompanied Foreign Secretary Harold Macmillan to the inaugural meeting, led a British military mission to Amman. Egypt still refused to believe what obviously was happening, although Israel broadcast it plainly on 7 December. In Cairo the British ambassador was holding almost daily meetings with Egyptian leaders and diplomat, discussing the approach to an Arab-Israeli settlement which Eden had proposed on 9 November and which Nasser had publicly welcomed. In Washington the British were working out Western aid for the Aswan High Dam with American and Egyptian negotiators. As late as 10 December, when the Jordanian Government began to crack under pressure from the King and the British, Cairo's censored press stubbornly attributed the crisis to a Jordanian refusal to join the pact. But suspicion and tension increased apace.

Again Ben-Gurion dogged the ill-starred pact with a border raid that set Arab nerves on edge—the wholly unprovoked assault on the night of 11 December that took nearly 60 Syrian lives, a third of them civilians. The raid wrecked the promising British-Egyptian efforts in Cairo toward a Palestine settlement, as Ben-Gurion evidently intended. Cairo broadcasters coupled it with Templer's Baghdad Pact recruitment mission to Jordan as a two-pronged effort to force the Arabs to make peace with Israel.

From 12 December onward Cairo Radio began expressing concern about the Templer mission. Two days later, as the Jordanian cabinet fell apart, Egyptian propaganda opened up full blast against the Templer mission, calling it a Zionist-Imperialist plot to drag Jordan into the network of foreign alliances. On 15 December Cairo said that if Jordan joined the Baghdad Pact, Arab military secrets would thereby become available to Israel and Israel would be able to dictate terms to the Arabs.

On 16 December, while Britons and Americans were agreeing with Egyptians in Washington to help build the High Dam, desperate rioting against the Baghdad Pact broke out in Jordanian cities. During six days of disturbances 41 persons were killed, 150 were injured, and two more cabinets formed and fell. The King held out for the pact until the 18th in stubborn resistance to nationalist sentiment fanned by Cairo broadcasts and Saudi money. Cairo, doubtless informed by dissident Jordanian cabinet ministers, broadcast in detail the terms reportedly agreed on between the Jordanian and British negotiators. These terms were to have been kept secret until both countries had ratified them and Jordan's membership in the pact was a *fait accompli*. There was renewed rioting on 8 January 1956 and a fourth new Jordanian premier named before the immediate turmoil over the Templer mission subsided. Jordan had learned such a costly lesson that, more than two years later when she joined in a short-lived federation with Iraq, she insisted on an escape clause exempting her from any link with the Baghdad Pact.

The Egyptians, together with Saudi Arabia and Syria, tried to use the crisis to end British influence in Jordan by offering to substitute in full their own aid for that of Britain. The Jordanian government refused to respond.

The Egyptian press was kind enough to report on Christmas Day that Washington had warned Britain against trying to inveigle Jordan into the pact. Eisenhower gave the reason some years later, saying he had always felt that there should be no pact member possessing a common border with Israel, thus reassuring Israel that she had nothing to fear from it.

Nasser, who had praised Eden for "constructive thinking" in mid-November, was bitterly disillusioned by the Templer mission. He regards it as a gross breach of the 5 April 1955 moratorium in which he agreed to stop campaigning against the pact in return for Eden's promise to recruit no additional Arab Governments into it. The honeymoon that began with the Suez evacuation agreement on 19 October 1954 was over.

Nasser drew the conclusion from the Templer mission that Eden was not to be trusted. Eden seemed to have learned no lessons at all, although he made an abortive effort through Selwyn Lloyd to revive the Baghdad Pact moratorium on 1 March 1956. The near destruction of the regime in Jordan did convince Eden "that we should not continue to press Jordan to enter the Baghdad Pact at this time," but he and King Hussein agreed that they might try again one day.

At the turn of the year, before all the debris of the Templer mission disaster had yet fallen back to earth, an eruption of disaffection within his own Conservative Party arose to plague Eden and to limit still further his freedom of action in the crises to come. For some months murmurs of discontent with Eden had been spreading through the moderate majority of the party, a development far more dangerous to Eden and his moderately progressive foreign policy than the dissent of the die-hard Suez Rebels. As early as the Conservative Party Conference at Bournemouth in October 1955, Eden's friend, Drew Middleton, reported in *The New York Times* that Conservatives, especially in the business community, were increasingly critical of Eden's delays in reorganizing the government and acting against inflation. Little more than four months after leading his party to a decisive victory in the May 1955 general election, Eden was being impatiently derided as indecisive. Randolph Churchill wrote that the Tories began calling Eden "a fidget, a fusspot . . . slow to make up his mind and quick to change it."

Eden finally reorganized his cabinet on 20 December, while Western consulates in Jerusalem and other Jordanian municipalities were still fending off mobs inflamed by the Templer mission. Macmillan, whose advice prompted the Templer mission, was shifted from the Foreign Office to the Exchequer. With his eye already on Eden's chair, Macmillan made sure the move was no punishment but rather a promotion. He was already nearly sixty-two. Lengthening service under the fifty-eight-year-old Eden chafed his ambition. As Lord Kilmuir wrote, Macmillan accepted the Treasury "on the strict understanding that this was to be regarded as a step towards, and not away from, the Premiership." He was succeeded at the Foreign Office by the more docile Selwyn Lloyd. Lloyd was little more than an implement for Eden's reassertion of control over foreign affairs, often against Lloyd's easily silenced better judgment.

The reshuffle failed to satisfy the Tories. Conservative dissatisfaction burst into the open on 3 January 1956 with a cruel editorial in the *Daily Telegraph* by its deputy editor Donald McLachlan.

"Why are Conservatives around the country restive, and Ministers and backbenchers unenraptured with their leader?" asked the *Telegraph*, which traditionally expresses the consensus viewpoint of the party and which had said of Eden after his elevation to the Premiership: "He incarnates as well as any man the new Conservatism." Answering its own question, the editorial said: "There is a favorite gesture of the Prime Minister's which is sometimes recalled to illustrate this sense of disappointment. To emphasize a point he will clench one fist to smack the open palm of the other hand—but the smack is seldom heard. Most Conservatives, and almost certainly some of the wiser trade union leaders, are waiting to feel the smack of firm government." The editorial went on to complain of Eden's "half measures" and "clumsy courtship of unfriendly and fickle Arab statesmen" and to snort that "collies cannot growl like the bulldog." It blamed Eden for being too concerned with his own personal popularity and for looking too much over the Foreign Secretary's shoulder.

Conservative readers added to the outcry against Eden in the *Telegraph's* letter columns. The Opposition followed suit. The Laborite *Daily Herald* labeled Eden "The Ditherer" and said "he dithers about Cyprus, he dithers about the whole of Middle East policy." The Laborite *Daily Mirror* reprinted pungent Conservative editorial epithets under the banner headline, "EDEN IS A FLOP." Rumors that Eden was about to resign became so strong during the week that they provoked an unprecedented "emphatic denial" from 10 Downing Street on the night of 7 January. But the criticism continued until July when the Tories rallied behind Eden's fateful decision to break Nasser.

By then Eden had suffered two additional reverses, the dismissal of Glubb Pasha from Jordan and a parliamentary fiasco over ending the death penalty. The abolition of capital punishment had been a perennial issue, coming ever nearer to enactment. In March it was brought up again by Sidney Silverman, a Laborite and long-time advocate. The Government sought to please everyone by allowing a free vote not subject to party discipline but it foolishly engaged its prestige by advising against abolition in order to placate the Tory right wing. The Government got the worst of both worlds when the abolitionists won in the Commons only to see the measure defeated once again in the House of Lords in mid-July. Eden's shilly-shallying left the right-wing Tories disgusted and the Tory abolitionists feeling betrayed.

Eden was indeed in a bad way, physically as well as politically. His system and his judgment were suffering from the toxic effects of a faulty bile duct which had been only imperfectly repaired by three operations in 1953, two in England and one in Boston. Eden's own words about Ernest Bevin were equally applicable to himself: "the man was very ill, past bearing the burdens of his office yet bravely not wishing to admit it." Eden's physical and political mala-

dies had begun to inter-react with great damage, his weakened judgment leading him into political ordeals that in turn added to his physical strain.

It was the dismissal of Glubb Pasha by King Hussein of Jordan on 1 March
1956 that unhinged Eden's judgment. He jumped to the emotional and inaccurate conclusion that Nasser was behind all his troubles in the Middle East. He
made a fateful decision that Nasser must be destroyed in order to restore
Britain's international prestige and his own political leadership. The misguided
pursuit of Nasser's destruction hurried Eden down the blind road to Suez,
where British prestige, and Eden's career and health all collapsed together.

If the Templer Mission was the turning point for Nasser in his relations with
Eden, the dismissal of Glubb three months later was the turning point for Eden.
The story is full of anti-coincidences, missed connections, lost opportunities,
and misunderstandings, some of them comical. The effects of its consequences
on the Suez crisis require its retelling in considerable detail.

Nasser had unleashed Egypt's propagandists against Britain and the Baghdad
Pact when Eden broke the moratorium by trying to haul Jordan into the pact.
Glubb, the right hand of Britain's hold on Jordan, was a natural target of
Egyptian propaganda. He was, equally understandably, a major force in Jordan's counterpropaganda, which she launched in January 1956 by jamming
Egyptian broadcasts with new British equipment and by opening a pan-Arab
transmission in Amman to rival Cairo's "Voice of the Arabs." The actual
removal of Glubb, however, was so far beyond Egypt's wildest hopes that it was
never considered among the objectives of the propaganda campaign even
though the campaign included exhortations for Glubb's expulsion. Paradoxically, if the Egyptian campaign had any influence at all on Glubb's position, it
tended to strengthen it, and the Egyptians were aware of this. Nasser's real aim
was to isolate the Hashemite Kingdoms of Jordan and Iraq and their British ally
within the Arab world in order to prevent them from isolating Egypt. King
Hussein was as much a target as Glubb was.

The Hashemite-British front was actually solidified when Egyptian propaganda and Saudi money caused renewed rioting by Jordanian nationalists early
in January. King Hussein asked the British to relay an appeal to Baghdad for
Iraqi troops to be flown into Jordan. Nuri agreed to send enough troops to
ensure success. In addition, he told the British that Nasser was the root of the
trouble in Jordan and urged them to request Washington to put pressure on
Egypt. Eden quotes Nuri as suggesting that Egypt be warned that, "if she
persisted, we would no longer consider the protection afforded by the Tripartite Declaration as applying to Egypt." The following day, 10 January 1956,
Britain announced an airlift to Cyprus of 2,000 paratroopers, the same unit that
later spearheaded the invasion of Egypt. British forces stationed in Iraq were

alerted to move into Jordan. "Britain's national interest," as Eden saw it, "was to maintain the independence of Jordan, which was an outpost of Iraq."

Eden at that time—before Glubb's ouster—was still toying with the idea of restoring the "honeymoon" with Nasser. He thought to do it by renewing the secret moratorium on the Baghdad Pact, which he had broken by endorsing the Templer Mission. The idea was discussed and approved at a conference of British Middle East diplomats in London on 4 and 5 January 1956. Foreign Secretary Lloyd was instructed to offer to renew the moratorium when he called on Nasser in Cairo on 1 March 1956.

The dismissal of Glubb, which was to turn Eden against Nasser on the very day Lloyd delivered Eden's offer, had been under consideration by King Hussein for a year. "What most people did not realize," King Hussein wrote in his memoirs, "is that the dismissal of General Glubb was a strictly Jordanian affair.... My main motive in dismissing him was because we were in disagreement on two issues: the role of Arab officers in our Army, and defence strategy."

On the issue of Arab officers, Hussein wrote:

I was gravely informed that the Royal Engineers of the Arab Legion would have an Arab Commander by 1985! Was it possible that any outside government could be so unrealistic? It was. The British Government at that time was incapable of realising that one cannot brush aside a nation's aspirations with the words: "We will talk about it in thirty years."

On strategy, Hussein wrote:

To my way of thinking a purely defensive strategy was to invite disaster .... I also felt strongly that we should answer with force the Israeli commando attacks against Arab villages.... The UN condemned the Israelis, but that did not stop them. Our soldiers were ridiculed and a great gulf grew between the Army and the people. In vain I pointed all this out to Glubb. To all my pleas he advised cautious patience. He advocated at first a withdrawal in the event of attack to the East Bank [of the Jordan River], pending the arrival of reinforcements to counterattack.... It was unthinkable.... Indeed, I would say that if Glubb had been in command of the Army a year longer it would have been the end of Jordan.

Of Glubb's power in Jordan, Hussein wrote:

Glubb ... despite his love for Jordan and his loyalty to my country, was essentially an outsider whose attitude did not fit into the picture I visualised.... To be blunt about it, he was serving as my Commander in Chief yet could not ignore his loyalty to Britain. . . . He operated from a position of such strength that our political leaders tended to turn to him or the British Embassy before taking the slightest decisions. A classic example of this occurred when the Soviet Union, wishing to establish diplomatic relations with Jordan, approached our Chargé d'Affaires in Cairo and requested him to transmit a message to me. This message . . . came into the hands of the Prime Minister. When he received it, the Prime Minister did not consult me but took the message, without informing me, straight to the British Embassy!

"Although I felt Glubb must go, I had not yet fixed the exact time," Hussein says, recalling that two events decided him. The first was Prime Minister Samir Rifai's refusal of the King's request on 28 February 1956 to shift the control of the police from Glubb to the Interior Ministry—for fear of British opposition. The second, on 29 February, was the presentation for the King's signature of a list of officers to be dismissed. "Their only fault, as far as I could see," wrote the King, "was that they were nationalists and ambitious. . . . That night I decided Glubb Pasha would have to go immediately. . . . Glubb . . . efficient, energetic, good-mannered, unchanging . . . largely isolated from the outside world . . . too much of the Victorian . . . a fine soldier . . . the last thing I desired was to hurt his feelings, nor was it a pleasant task to dismiss a man who had served our country so faithfully for twenty-six years."

Hussein says he considered allowing Glubb to resign gracefully with a little extended leave but he decided that a leisurely change-over was too hazardous in view of the Israeli threat. Glubb himself believes the King feared an Army *coup d'état* on Glubb's behalf, noting that telephone lines to the houses of British officers were cut the night before his dismissal. He adds: "In practice, one or two units did contemplate action when they heard of my dismissal. In every case it was the British officers who prevented incidents."

Glubb believes the King was influenced by intriguers in Jordan and by British newspaper articles saying Glubb was "the real ruler of Jordan." Glubb took a nobly forgiving view of his dismissal and effectively moderated Eden's reaction against Hussein. "We nearly all act from mixed motives," he wrote. "The King was probably influenced partly by the illusion that I had neglected to provide ammunition [for Army stockpiles], partly by a desire himself to exercise authority unfettered by a middle-aged and cautious adviser. He also believed that to defy Britain would restore his popularity [after the Templer fiasco] and, finally, his imagination was fired by the idea of being the hero of his country."

King Hussein wrote out the order for Glubb's immediate dismissal on the morning of 1 March, took it to his Prime Minister at 10 A.M., and told him: "These are my wishes; I want them executed at once." Rifai summoned Glubb and informed him of his dismissal at 2 P.M., suggesting that Glubb leave the country in two hours.

"No, sir!" Glubb recalls saying. "I cannot! I have lived here for twenty-six years. Almost all my worldly possessions are here, to say nothing of my wife and children." It was agreed that Glubb's departure would be deferred until 7 A.M. the next day. Returning home to tell his wife the stunning news, Glubb sadly looked out at the cemetery where his second son had been buried nine years before. "I had thought that perhaps I should be buried there too," he wrote, "amongst the simple Jordan folk whom I loved."

Hussein later justified Glubb's hasty expulsion, writing: "How right I was. All that night, while Glubb and his wife were packing, I faced an unremitting barrage from the British to make me change my mind." Cables, including one from Eden, piled up on the King's desk and the British Ambassador came to the palace an hour after midnight with a cable from London to warn that "the consequences could be very serious as far as you yourself, the monarchy, and the whole future of Jordan is concerned." After further consultation with London, the Ambassador tried to obtain another audience at 3 A.M. but was refused.

Glubb's ouster was not disclosed to the public until 7:30 A.M. on 2 March, a half hour after he, his wife, his son Godfrey, and his adopted Arab daughter Naomi, had been flown out of Amman for Cyprus and London. It was truly the end of an era. Glubb had first arrived in Amman on a camel in 1924 after riding 500 miles across the desert from Baghdad.

The news of his dismissal reached the British Embassy in Cairo that same night of 1 March while Selwyn Lloyd and Nasser were dining amicably together at a formal banquet given by Egyptian Foreign Minister Mahmoud Fawzi at the Tahra Palace. Lloyd had arrived in midafternoon with Sir Harold Caccia, who had worked closely with Eden at the Foreign Office for twenty years and who was soon to be named Ambassador to the United States.

Nasser had complained to Lloyd that the British were stirring up the Sudanese Government against the Aswan High Dam, which could not be built without Sudanese agreement. Lloyd had denied it. Nasser was unconvinced but he did not say so and the talks progressed cordially. Their high point was a renewed understanding on the Baghdad Pact moratorium.

Lloyd broached the issue, telling Nasser that Eden and the Foreign Office had decided after the Templer mission "to have a real go" at freezing the Baghdad Pact in return for Egypt's calling off her propaganda against the pact.

Nasser felt that any renewal of the moratorium would have to have some kind of public commitment by Britain in order to avoid another breakdown. He proposed that the pact be "frozen" by an announcement that it would not be extended to any Arab country other than Iraq. This would constitute a public assurance to the Arabs that they would no longer be under pressure to join the pact, which would eliminate the threat of dissension among them. Egypt could then stop her propaganda against the pact and begin once more to cooperate with Iraq.

Lloyd, who was on his way to a SEATO conference in Karachi, said it would take about a fortnight to get the approval of his cabinet colleagues for such an arrangement but he obtained Nasser's agreement to a preliminary moratorium pending cabinet approval. The "honeymoon" that Eden had wrecked by his breach of promise seemed to have been restored. British and Egyptian spirits alike warmed in the accord reached among Dr. Fawzi's guests. For the British, however, it seemed as evanescent as the wisps of steam from their after-dinner coffee.

At the end of dinner a message was brought in to Sir Humphrey Trevelyan, the British Ambassador. He looked at it and then said to Lloyd: "I think we had better be going home." In the Rolls-Royce on the way back to the British Embassy Trevelyan told Lloyd the news that Glubb had been dismissed. They stayed up all night trying to decide whether Lloyd should go to Jordan.

Nasser was not informed of Glubb's dismissal until he returned to his own house. His information was much sketchier than Lloyd's. He did not even consider it as a possibility that King Hussein had acted in defiance of the British. After all, Jordan was heavily dependent on Britain both for military assistance and a budget subsidy. Nasser recalled the story a decade later with many a rueful laugh.

Mr. Selwyn Lloyd got the information during dinner because someone came from the Embassy. We realized later that he had informed him about the dismissal of Glubb. But I was not able to have information until I returned here [to my house]. In fact, I got information only about the dismissal of Glubb; but there was no information about the whole story. I thought that it was the British [who had themselves removed Glubb].

Nasser chuckled at his mistake and went on with his account:

And there was a meeting with Mr. Selwyn Lloyd next day in the morning on his way to the aerodrome. And when I received him, I told him: "Congratulations! This was a very good move from your side."—Glubb, of course, was a symbol of colonialism in Jordan—"And you are taking a very reasonable step by getting rid of him."

Mr. Selwyn Lloyd was shocked because he thought that I was sarcastic about him and making jokes. He was angry—nervous. He thought that I misled him, which was completely untrue. And they said [afterwards that] I planned the dismissal of Glubb

211

to take place while I was having dinner with Selwyn Lloyd. I wonder how one can plan something like that.

Then he [Lloyd] went to Bahrein and was stoned there by the people. And the responsible people told him that Nasser organized that. [But]it was completely outside of our imagination. So when he returned back [to London] he was—because of Glubb and because of what happened in Bahrein—he was completely hostile to us.

Nasser later told Trevelyan in jest that he sometimes didn't remember what he actually did but only what he was accused of doing.

Lloyd was unaware of the misunderstanding, which strongly colored his own attitude toward Nasser, until he learned of Nasser's account ten years later. Otherwise, his recollection of the meeting on the morning of 2 March, when he paused at Nasser's house on the road to the airport, was in accord with Nasser's:

Nasser said he supposed Britain had removed Glubb in order to make our agreement a bit easier. I thought he was pulling my leg in rather bad taste—I having been up all night trying to decide whether to go to Jordan.

Of the Bahrein demonstration later that day, Lloyd recalls:

One man threw one handful of sand against my car, which hit Sir Harold Caccia, not me. I asked what they were shouting. They were shouting "Belgrave must go." [Sir Charles Belgrave was the chief British political representative in Bahrein.] I decided to wait to leave until six hours later than scheduled to ensure no one would be killed by soldiers clearing the way [to the airport]. I left at night and the streets were empty.

Lloyd was indignant at the newspapers for treating the incident as a British humiliation.

Eden admits that it was Glubb's dismissal that turned him against Nasser, although he ignores this misjudgment in his memoirs. He wrote that "there was no excuse for dismissing him suddenly like a pilfering servant," but he added: "I thought at the time, and I am convinced now, that part of the King's sentiment towards Glubb was based on jealousy of a younger man for an older one long established in a position of authority . . . the result of a personal dislike which had grown to something of a phobia. . . . The coup against Glubb was no sudden brainstorm; it was planned carefully for weeks beforehand. It was extraordinary that the General failed to hear about it at any time before its execution."

Anthony Nutting, at the time Minister of State for Foreign Affairs, disputes Eden's published version and supports his private admission. Nutting says the

Suez drama actually began when Eden, upon learning of Glubb's dismissal, "declared a personal war on the man whom he held responsible . . . Gamal Abdel Nasser." Nutting, in his own memoir of Suez, goes on:

> As one who spent the evening and half of the night after Glubb's dismissal arguing with Eden, I can testify that, at the time, he put all the blame on Nasser . . . and on that fatal day he decided that the world was not big enough to hold both him and Nasser. . . . From now on Eden completely lost his touch.

Eden immediately conferred with his Defense Minister and military chiefs. Word quickly reached Eisenhower that officials in Whitehall were talking of "when war comes" rather than "if war comes." Nevertheless, Washington agreed immediately to let France ship to Israel a squadron of 15 Mystère IV jet warplanes which the French had built for NATO under an offshore procurement contract. In Paris French Foreign Minister Christian Pineau, in an I-told-you-so speech, said that if the British had paid more attention to French warnings against promoting the Baghdad Pact they might have been spared "the gestures of which you measure the consequences today."

Glubb arrived in England on 3 March and persuaded Eden over lunch at Checquers the following day not to take a punitive line toward Jordan. Although Eden saw Glubb's removal as "damaging to British authority" he agreed that "it was not to our advantage to drive King Hussein to extreme courses." Eden bolstered the spirit of the alliance with Jordan and promoted closer relations between the young first cousins on the thrones of Jordan and Iraq. They met in the desert with Eden's blessing on 14 March. Eden was rewarded three days later with the satisfaction of seeing Hussein reject an offer by Nasser, Syria, and Saudi Arabia to replace the British subsidy to Jordan with an Arab subsidy.

Eden compensated for his moderation toward Jordan by his hostility toward Nasser. His first overt reaction was to swing closer to France, where the Mollet government blamed Nasser for the Algerian rebellion and was busily arming Israel for war against the Egyptians. Eden invited Mollet to Checquers for a weekend talk and instructed the British Ambassador in Paris to salute in public France's conduct in her Algerian struggle. Eden's second reaction was to turn pro-Israel himself after a generally pro-Arab diplomatic career. His third anti-Nasser reaction to Glubb's dismissal was to reverse his support for the High Dam at Aswan and to begin lobbying against it in Washington.

Before he had time to translate resolve into action, however, Eden had to face a troubled House of Commons, whose members, for the most part, had not adjusted their outlook to the winds of change already moving on the face of Africa and Asia, especially in Egypt where the two continents met. Eden staved off the debate for nearly a week, during which he made a new effort to persuade Eisenhower to join the Baghdad Pact. It was in vain. When Eden rose to wind up the debate on the night of 7 March, he had nothing to tell the House, neither good news nor mitigating circumstances. All he could muster was a sterile warning to Nasser that Egypt could not combine professions of friendship with incitements to hostility and still maintain friendly relations with the West.

"I had no time to prepare the speech I must make," Eden recalled in his memoirs, "and it is always difficult to say nothing convincingly.... The speech which I made in the debate was regarded as one of the worst in my career. ... My friends were embarrassed and my critics exultant.... But as diplomacy, the speech served its purpose. It broke no bridges with Jordan.... It was an occasion for doing nothing."

The reality was worse than Eden's description. His friend Drew Middleton reported in *The New York Times* that Eden "was subjected to a storm of vituperation and abuse beyond anything heard in the Commons since the last days of Neville Chamberlain's Prime Ministership." Randolph Churchill wrote: "The debate marked the beginning of the disintegration of the personality and character that the public thought him to possess." A British columnist, Ian Waller, reported that Eden "met an outburst of barracking and contemptuous roars of disapproval [from which he] had to be rescued at one stage by the Speaker restoring order ... a shocking scene ... Sir Anthony suffered a blow to his prestige that was clearly reflected in the silent, devastated ranks on the Conservative benches behind him.... If the year goes on as it has begun, it will not be Sir Anthony but Mr. Harold Macmillan who reigns in Downing Street in 1957."

Nutting described how, "to the horrified amazement of his supporters, he [Eden] finally lost his temper." Nutting added: "What I did not know was how much of this metamorphosis was due to sickness and to the poison from a damaged bile-duct, which was eating away at his whole system." Contemporary medical articles on cases similar to Eden's say that the endemic effect of the body poisons on the judgment is literally intoxicating.

In the debate itself Hugh Gaitskell, Leader of the Opposition, gave the cold appraisal that Eden's policy in the Middle East was "ill-formed, ill-prepared and has managed, rather remarkably, to be both weak and provocative at the same time."

Eden won his vote of confidence on straight party lines, 312 to 252. Two days later he raised his standing with the Tory right wing by deporting the

Cypriote nationalist leader, Archbishop Makarios, to the Seychelles. But his obsession with Nasser had hardened. When Nutting and a group of Foreign Office experts sent him a memorandum on 12 March containing suggestions on how to neutralize Nasser and isolate Egypt from Britain's Arab allies, Eden telephoned Nutting at the Savoy Hotel, where he was giving a dinner for Harold Stassen. Nutting reports that Eden shouted at him:

What's all this nonsense about isolating Nasser or neutralizing him, as you call it? I want him destroyed, can't you understand? I want him removed, and if you and the Foreign Office don't agree, then you'd better come to the Cabinet and explain why.

Nutting, trying to calm Eden, suggested that before deciding to destroy Nasser, some less hostile leader should be found to put in his place. Otherwise Nasser's fall would lead to anarchy. In reply, Nutting recalled, Eden shouted at him:

But I don't want an alternative; and I don't give a damn if there's anarchy and chaos in Egypt.

Eden's reported reference to the Cabinet indicates that his colleagues, who moved in full accord with him from the Suez nationalization in July into the collusive invasion of Egypt in November, had already endorsed his determination to "break Nasser" nearly five months before nationalization provided the pretext for it.

Lloyd says he turned against Nasser long before Eden did. He told the House of Commons on 3 December 1956 that the situation after the Russian arms deal "was one which sooner or later was likely to lead to war. The only doubtful question was the scope or extent of that war." Thus at least one member of the Cabinet says he was contemplating war against Nasser as much as five months earlier than Eden and ten months before the canal crisis. Lord Birdwood, in his biography of Nuri, disclosed that an anti-Nasser group in the Foreign Office showed Lloyd the way. "Within the Foreign Office," Birdwood wrote, "there had been a growing recognition that somehow and at some time Nasser would have to be restricted, isolated, and brought down, perhaps by his own people through his own follies. More particularly after his personal reaction to the Baghdad Pact did a mere understanding become a set policy." But it was Eden's conversion to anti-Nasserism that gave the policy both its impetus and its vendetta quality.

Eden's own justification of his policy as a national rather than a personal one figures blandly in his memoirs: "Our general policy in the Middle East was founded on the need to protect British interests in Iraq and the Persian Gulf. The main threat to these interests was the growing influence of Nasser with his anti-Western ideology and collusion with Soviet Russia."

On 13 March 1956 Lloyd, on his way home from the SEATO conference, stopped in Israel for a day of talks with Ben-Gurion and his colleagues. But Israel was still so far from regarding Britain as a possible ally against Arabs that Dayan snorted at Lloyd's visit and commented bluntly: "What Israelis are doing on the spot to fortify their country counts for more than all the visits of this country's ambassadors to the State Department and the Foreign Office." Dayan did not mention what France was doing to help Israel fortify itself. Nasser discussed it the following day, however, with Pineau, who had been at the Karachi conference with Lloyd. As related in a previous chapter, the Pineau-Nasser meeting, despite its initial success, was to prove as negative in its results as Nasser's meeting with Lloyd.

On 24 March Eden and Lloyd tried again to bring Washington into line against Nasser with letters to Eisenhower and Dulles reportedly proposing these alternatives: Either (1) establish a *modus vivendi* with Egypt, going ahead with economic aid and suspending arms deliveries to Israel, or (2) ignore Egypt and attempt to stabilize the Middle East by isolating Nasser. Eden's preference for the second alternative, despite its political foolishness, was emphasized at the Paris meeting of the NATO foreign ministers early in May when Lloyd urged the abandonment of the undertaking to help Egypt with the Aswan High Dam. Eden's and Lloyd's opposition to the High Dam was in flat contradiction to the advice of the British Ambassador in Cairo, who actively sought to bring Egypt and the West together for a conclusive agreement on the project.

Eden tried to obtain Dulles's collaboration in engineering a coup against Nasser. The effort probably began after Nasser recognized Red China on 16 May. This action infuriated Dulles against Nasser, in contrast to his unruffled attitude toward the dismissal of Glubb. The first meetings to consider a coup were held at Eden's initiative between Foreign Office and State Department men. When Dulles showed interest, the matter was transferred to specialists in clandestine operations from Britain's MI-6 and the CIA. There was a clear precedent in the CIA-directed overthrow of Premier Mossadegh in Persia in 1953, which aimed at preventing Persia from falling under Communist influence. But there had been an effective body of opposition in Persia ready to rally to the Shah against Mossadegh while in Egypt there was neither an armed and organized opposition nor a rival leader. Dulles's recurrent reservations eventually wearied the British and Eden abandoned planning for a coup and pinned his hopes on war.

Nasser remained unaware of the extent of Eden's new hostility, which did not come into the open until late July when the US and Britain withdrew their offer of aid for the High Dam. So far as Nasser was concerned, his renewal with Lloyd of the moratorium on the Baghdad Pact was valid. On 4 April 1956, having waited in vain for a British announcement freezing the Arab membership of the Baghdad Pact, Egypt nevertheless went ahead with the agreed abatement of anti-British propaganda.

British radio monitors reported that attacks on Britain were virtually abandoned. Foreign Office officials noted late in April that there had been a marked change in Cairo's Swahili broadcasts to British East African territories as well as in the "Voice of the Arabs." In previous months Egyptian broadcasters had flavored their attacks on Britain with phrases like "colonialist bloodsuckers." As in the eight months before the Templer mission wrecked the first moratorium, Cairo's restraint extended to the Baghdad Pact meeting in Teheran in April at which the US joined the pact's Economic and Countersubversion committees. As late as 24 July, several days after the Anglo-American renege on the High Dam, Lloyd told the House of Commons that Britain welcomed the improved tone toward Britain adopted by the Egyptian press and radio and blandly observed that if it continued it should be possible to recreate better relations.

British troops completed their orderly withdrawal from the Suez base according to the terms of the 1954 agreement. War Minister Antony Head paid a courtesy call on Nasser on 17 March and two weeks later the last British fighting units embarked for home. The special correspondent of *The Times* (London) sent a nostalgic dispatch: "Fittingly, the last on board the white-painted ship were the Grenadier Guards, for the Grenadiers fought at the battle of Tel el Kebir in 1882, when Arabi Pasha's army was defeated and the way opened to Cairo." "It seems regrettable that such an era in British military annals should have been concluded so unobtrusively," *The Times*' man wrote, but he noted that British civilian contractors maintaining the base "enthusiastically affirm that their relations with the local Egyptian authorities are 'really excellent.' "

The withdrawal of the "administrative tail" of 500 officers and men was completed on 13 June, five days ahead of schedule. Brigadier John H. S. Lacey, unaware that he was soon to return in the British invasion force in November, handed over the keys of his headquarters at Navy House and stepped aboard the launch to his ship at 6:25 A.M. A crowd of Egyptians cheered as their flag was hauled to the headquarters masthead. A British colonel explained the lack of ceremony characteristic of the whole withdrawal by saying: "We feel we should go quietly like good friends."

Selwyn Lloyd, in an interview published in Cairo on 18 June, the original date scheduled for the final British departure, expressed disappointment that the Evacuation Agreement had not improved Anglo-Egyptian friendship as much as had been hoped. "There are no actual disputes or conflicts between Great Britain and Egypt which justify the present lack of confidence between the two countries," Lloyd said.

Nasser replied a week later with a friendly "message to the British people" given in an interview with W. N. Ewer of the *Daily Herald* (London). "I have told my own people that in thinking of Britain they should no longer think about the past," Nasser said. "A new chapter has begun. . . . I agree with Mr. Selwyn Lloyd, in the statement he gave to our newspaper *al-Akhbar*, that there are now no reasons for any conflict between us. . . . But allow me to say that it takes two to make a friendship; and that there are some newspapers and some politicians in Britain who are anything but helpful." At the end of his dispatch Ewer said there was no doubt about Nasser's sincerity in wanting friendship with England.

Meanwhile Eden was finding encouragement for his own hostility to Nasser, not only in the Cabinet but in Parliament, in the press, and the country at large. As the Anglo-Arab scholar, Albert Hourani, put it:

> While Egyptians liked and respected Englishmen even when they opposed them, most Englishmen did not much like Egyptians even when they agreed with them. The contempt which power breeds had been directed above all onto the Egyptians, just as in France it had been directed onto the Algerians. It is doubtful whether an attack on any other people in the world would have aroused so much enthusiasm in England as an attack on the Egyptians.

In the middle of May an adjournment debate in the House of Commons had already singled out the Suez Canal as a likely bone of contention with Egypt. Discussing Egypt's prohibition against Israeli shipping in the canal, initiated under King Farouk four years before Nasser's revolution, a Tory MP said:

> I do not wish to waste my time on abusing somebody who may, after all, be only a very temporary leader of his country. . . . It may well be that someone else far worse will shortly follow Colonel Nasser, but even as things are at present we have little justification for relying on the word of the Egyptian Government. It is an intolerable situation that either now or in the future the body in control of the Suez Canal should fall entirely under the hand of Egypt. . . . There was a time when this country was not afraid to enunciate policies. . . . There is an increasing demand in this country for a clear formulation of policy on behalf of our people.

Eden had displayed an undiplomatic and uncharacteristic belligerence on the Middle East in April to his Russian visitors, Khrushchev and Bulganin. "I said I thought I must be absolutely blunt about the oil, because we would fight for it," Eden recalled in his memoirs. "Mr. Khrushchev replied that I would hardly find sympathy with the Soviet Government if I said I was prepared to start a war." Eden had not yet perceived how the Suez Canal might become an issue but he reiterated in public his determination to fight for oil (without saying how it was threatened, if at all).

Oil was always a good issue with which to keep British emotions high. Eden was to use it to good effect to intensify alarm over the Suez nationalization. Only a few voices raised the question why oil should be fought for instead of simply bought. As Hugh Thomas, who left the Foreign Office after Suez for a career as a historian, wrote: "Ever since Churchill converted the Navy to the use of oil in 1911, British politicians have seemed to have had a feeling about oil supplies comparable to the fear of castration."

One of the topics Eden discussed with the Russians had the unexpected and indirect effect of turning Dulles against Nasser, which was vastly encouraging to Eden. This was the question of a Middle East arms embargo. Khrushchev's public proposal of a UN embargo prompted Nasser to recognize Red China in order to have an arms source outside the UN. Eden at first endorsed the Khrushchev proposal. By 10 May he had reversed himself on the grounds that Britain had arms commitments to Iraq and Jordan and therefore could not join an international embargo. But Nasser had already committed Egypt to recognizing Peking. He announced it on 16 May. This action, probably more than any other single factor, decided Dulles to withdraw the US offer of aid for the High Dam, which provoked Nasser to nationalize the canal, which gave Eden his pretext for a campaign—by all means including war—to destroy Nasser.

The pretext was timely. Eden needed a popular foreign adventure more by the middle of the year than at its beginning, when the press of his own party had labeled him a ditherer. On 7 June the party had been severely jolted by a massive desertion of voters in a by-election at Tonbridge. The party professionals were still reevaluating Eden's leadership when Suez opened a familiar field for him to exercise it in.

Eden's problem, as he saw it throughout, was to break Nasser without estranging Britain from her Arab allies and clients, particularly Nuri's Iraq and Hussein's Jordan. This made oil itself an awkward issue to pick a quarrel over because it involved other Arabs more than it involved Egypt. The Suez Canal, being entirely within Egypt and carrying most of the Arab oil shipments destined for Britain, was to fulfill perfectly Eden's requirements for a pretext.

It should be borne in mind that France and Israel were on a course toward war invisibly convergent with Eden's, moving ever closer to a rendezvous in history as the months of spring and early summer rolled by while Eden, who had yet to find his pretext against Nasser, continued the withdrawal of British troops from Egypt under the agreement he had made with Nasser in better days. As described in earlier chapters, France was shipping more and more war materiel to Israel. Mollet hurled insults like "megalomaniac" at Nasser on public occasions while secretly sending emissaries to meet Algerians in talks begun under Nasser's aegis.,

It was a confusing time. The policies of both great and small nations seemed full of contradictions. But it was a time full of opportunity for resolute men with clear, if secret, intentions—men who were single-mindedly initiating action rather than men who were merely reacting to the confused surface of events. It was a time when the determined leader of a small nation could use to his own advantage the power of greater nations by playing on the prejudices and emotions of their leaders. Ben-Gurion had created Israel by seizing such opportunity out of such confusion. The anti-Nasser obsessions of Eden and Mollet, the anti-Communist preoccupation of Dulles, and the satellite revolts facing Khrushchev were creating the kind of situation in which men like Ben-Gurion calculate and run great risks for the sake of great gains. By summer it was evident that Eden was, like Mollet, ready to approve any enterprise that would hurt Nasser.

Eden was as pleased as he was surprised when Dulles announced on 19 July 1956 the cancellation of the American offer of aid for the High Dam at Aswan. Late in April the British Government was still defending aid for the High Dam as reasonable and worthwhile. But by mid-July, Eden wrote, his cabinet had decided not to go through with Britain's commitment on the High Dam. Eden had adopted the second of the two alternative policies he and Lloyd had proposed to Washington on 24 March. As *The Times* (London) put it on 14 July: "The attempt to stabilize the Middle East in cooperation with Egypt is now over."

World Bank findings to the contrary, Eden alleged that Egypt's financial position had deteriorated as a result of allotting more and more money toward paying for Russian arms and thereby mortgaging the economy. He accused Nasser of anti-Western subversion throughout the Middle East and, British radio monitors to the contrary, said Egypt was "blaring out hostility to the West and ... in the same breath more money was being demanded for the scheme to build the dam."

He described how Lloyd "set to work to exchange views on this state of affairs" with Washington. Whatever the effect of British lobbying, Dulles fulfilled Eden's hopes with disturbing suddenness—"like a bolt from the blue," says Eden. He attributed the American renege, however, not to the merits or demerits of the High Dam project or to a faltering of the Egyptian economy or to any other specifically Middle Eastern consideration. Dulles acted, Eden wrote, "for reasons connected with the Senate's attitude toward foreign aid and the critical climate towards neutralism then prevalent in Washington."

The French, who had tried unsuccessfully to join in Western financing of the High Dam, were, as Eden put it, "hopping mad" over Dulles's unilateral cancellation. As for the British, Eden complained: "We were informed but not consulted and so had no prior opportunity for criticism or comment. . . . We were sorry that the matter was carried through so abruptly, because it gave our two countries no chance to concert either timing or methods, though these were quite as important as the substance."

Consultation between Eden and his own Cabinet colleagues seems to have been little better than that between London and Washington. Lord Kilmuir, Eden's Lord Chancellor, writes that although "the withdrawal of Western aid in this peremptory manner was a stinging personal rebuff" to Nasser, "the immense political implications of the step seem not to have been apparent to the Americans or to the Foreign Office. I, certainly, have no recollection of this crucial aspect of the situation being brought home to Ministers."

The Foreign Office was caught so completely off guard that, only a few hours before Dulles withdrew it, the Foreign Office spokesman reaffirmed Britain's share of the aid offer, although in a wary statement that emphasized possible obstacles. The next day the Foreign Office covered its embarrassment by claiming falsely that there had been "continuous consultation" with Washington. In a studied insult to the Egyptian Ambassador, the Foreign Office did not officially inform him until three and a half hours after it told the press that Britain too had cancelled her offer of aid for the High Dam. He could have learned it from Cairo Radio an hour before he was summoned to the Foreign Office.

Most British Foreign Service men disliked this kind of peremptory, rude, and makeshift diplomacy, in which emotion overrode calculations of true national interest. But some of the men in the Foreign Office relished the mood across Downing Street in the Prime Minister's quarters. Sir George Young, chief spokesman at the Foreign Office, invited correspondents of the leading foreign news bureaus into his inner office and told them in exultant understatement that "the elimination of Colonel Nasser certainly could not make the situation any worse." Such was the frame of mind of those who, like Eden, saw the Suez nationalization a week later as the sought-for opportunity to go over onto the offensive against Nasser. Such was the mood of the men who led Britain down the short road to the most humiliating little war in her history.

CHAPTER

8

Enter, The Bear

(1237 A. D. to 19 JULY 1956)

Russia had no local interests to serve, and stood aloof. Possibly, however, as events developed, something might occur which could be turned to the advantage of Muscovite interests.

(CROMER, 1908)

I T WAS Nasser who spoke first, not the Russian ambassador, on the evening of 18 May 1955 at a reception at the old Sudan Agency in Cairo. "We want to have arms from you; what will be your answer?" Nasser asked in a low voice after taking the ambassador aside. Their brief, unscheduled, unreported encounter broke open the West's traditional preserve in the Middle East and made Russia a power to be reckoned with there.

The Russian ambassador, Daniel Semenovitch Solod, had to inquire of the Kremlin and wait three days before he was able to call on Nasser and tell him Moscow was willing. The Russian arms deal stunned the world when the news came out four months later. It was a major shift in the balance of forces that determine the course of history. The weight of its consequences was in dramatic contrast with the casual low key of its beginning.

Four days in February had set the stage for it by creating separate problems for Russia and Egypt which led their leaders toward the arms deal as a common solution. On 24 February the signing of the Baghdad Pact by Turkey and Iraq materialized Russian fears of a Western-dominated defense pact in the Middle East. And on 28 February the Israeli raid on Gaza frightened Nasser into shifting his economic priority from development to rearmament. For Egypt the deal gave Nasser the arms which his Army and his junta colleagues insisted on and which he could no longer get from the West. For Russia it outflanked the "Northern Tier" siege line of the Baghdad Pact and established Russian influence in the heart of the Middle East. It was a diplomatic triumph for the Kremlin on the scale, not of ephemeral months or years, but of centuries.

The assertion of Russian power and interest in the Middle East was blocked for hundreds of years by the Mongol empire. Genghis Khan's cavalry rode across Asia into Eastern Europe while the Crusaders of Western Europe were crashing into Egypt and the Arab world like waves of the distant future. The Mongols crossed the Volga on the ice in December 1237 and sacked Moscow, then a place of minor importance. They conquered the Russian Northern Provinces by the end of the winter, and turned south to establish the long-lived domain of the Golden Horde.

For three hundred years the Grand Duchy of Muscovy lay under Mongol suzerainty and tribute. Russian expansion, which has yet to ebb, began under Ivan the Terrible in the 16th century. It took two hundred years to reach the shores of the Black Sea. Under Catherine the Great a six-year war established Russian power on the Black Sea, until then an Ottoman lake, in 1774. The achievement opened the prospect of Russian control of the Turkish straits—the Bosporus and the Dardanelles—leading out to the Mediterranean. That ambition is still strong and unsatisfied.

The main thrust of Russia's imperial expansion in the 19th century, however, was across Siberia and into Central Asia. It reached eastward until it disturbed the sleeping giant China and spread southward as far as British India would allow. Unlike the crowded maritime powers of Western Europe, which built their empires far overseas from home, Russia expanded on the Eurasian land mass, always into borderlands contiguous with Mother Russia herself. The empire was extended both officially and unofficially—both by government military expeditions and by popular migrations away from Tsarist tyranny into territories at the frontiers and beyond.

The trauma of the Mongol conquest instilled into Russian rulers a persistent sensitivity about frontiers and a desire for buffer areas. Anxiety as much as ambition prompted the imperial government to protect and incorporate pioneer colonies. As each buffer area became incorporated into the Russian Empire, the next layer of outlying lands became buffer territory in Russian eyes and the process began again.

Cossack rebels were famous among the early frontiersmen. Eventually they were incorporated into the imperial army and dispatched officially to the frontiers to establish military-agricultural settlements at the farthest reaches of Russian power. These Cossack settlements, incidentally, were prototypes of the Israeli *nahals*, military-agricultural settlements established on the frontiers whenever new territory was conquered.

Access to year-round ports on warm seas was not a primary motive in Russia's expansion either under the tsars or the Soviet rulers. The main impulse was a possessive sensitivity over frontiers which led to their progressive advancement across the interior of the Asian and European land masses rather than outward toward warm seas.

But Constantinople and the Straits to the Mediterranean were not forgotten, nor were the Persian approaches to the Indian Ocean. Russian frontiers moved toward these positions too, reaching halfway down the Black Sea shores of the Ottoman Empire and much more than halfway down the Caspian shores of the weaker Persian Empire. Like the Western European powers in the nineteenth century, Russia too took an interest in the fortunes of the Ottoman Empire and its Arab provinces, arrogating to herself the protection of the Orthodox Christian minorities there. Official atheism did not prevent the Soviets from maintaining these Christian sectarian connections after the revolution.

In the century between Napoleon and World War I each of the Great Powers kept a jealous eye on the territorial prizes that might be seized in the event of the breakup of the vast, moribund Ottoman Empire. Each knew, however, that an attempt on the Ottoman territories would mean war with the others. To avoid war the powers repeatedly chose to prop up the Ottoman imperial edifice rather than dismember it. At the same time they maneuvered for advantage in case Ottoman rule should collapse in spite of their efforts. Each sought clients and influence, not only in the Sultan's capital but also among the Arabs and minority peoples of the empire, particularly the Christian sects.

This policy of stalemate did not wholly prevent wars. But it preserved the Ottoman Empire until it went down to defeat with its ally, Germany, in World War I, at which time victorious Britain and France each took as much as she could of the Ottoman Arab domains and held them until after World War II by the device of the League of Nations mandates.

While outwardly accepting the principle of preserving the Ottoman Empire, Tsar Nicholas I secretly sought a gentlemen's agreement with Britain in 1853 to settle in advance a division of the Ottoman inheritance if the empire should collapse. He warned the British ambassador he would not allow British control of the Straits and said that lack of a prior agreement "might place me in the position of occupying Constantinople." Britain coolly rejected the Tsar's overtures and warned that neither England nor France would tolerate Russian possession of Constantinople. The British reply contained a heavily ironical reference to the Tsar's claim to protect the Greek Orthodox subjects of the Sultan.

Within weeks the British ambassador went further and encouraged the Sultan to deny the Tsar's right to protect Christians. Russian troops occupied Ottoman provinces on the Danube to enforce the Tsar's claim and the Crimean War was on. Britain and France sent land and naval forces against the Russians in 1854 under a treaty of alliance with the Sultan. Their deeds included the mindless gallantry of the Light Brigade. Their wounded, in the foul hospital at Scutari, gave rise to the nursing reforms of Florence Nightingale. And their blundering war achieved its purpose. The Treaty of Paris, which terminated the Crimean War in 1856, formally committed the European powers to respect and guarantee the territorial integrity and independence of the Ottoman Empire.

The Sultan turned Cyprus over to Britain in 1878 as a base for British power to help him repel any further Russian incursions. As late as 1956 it proved inadequate as a base for invading Egypt. Around the shores of the Caspian, too, Russia continued from decade to decade to nibble away at Persian authority. The Turks and the Persians, as a consequence of Tsarist expansionism, developed a permanent defensive anxiety toward Russia. But the Arab world, slumbering still under Ottoman rule, was unaffected by Russian aggressions against their alien Moslem overlords. These contrasting reactions persisted into the latter half of the 20th century.

Russia was among the eight Great Power signatories of the Suez Canal Convention in 1888. Thereafter, in the twilight of the Tsars, her prestige

227

among the colonial empires dwindled. In the Russo-Japanese War of 1904–1905 she became the first Western power in modern history to suffer a major defeat at the hands of an Asian government. Africans and mainland Asians, if they thought about Russia at all, began to regard her as the enemy of their enemies, who were the colonial empires of Western Europe. This regard strengthened after the Bolshevik Revolution in 1917.

The new Communist masters of Russia made impassioned, if sterile, efforts to export revolution into Asia and the Middle East, a reversal of the old Tsarist fears of importing revolution from the East. On 3 December 1917, scarcely a month after seizing power themselves, the Soviets appealed to the Moslem workers of the world:

The ground is slipping from under the feet of the imperialist pillagers. . . . It is not from Russia and its revolutionary government that you have to fear enslavement, but from the robbers of European imperialism, from those who have laid waste your native lands and converted them into their colonies. Overthrow these robbers and enslavers of your lands.

The Bolsheviks had already begun their gleeful publication of the secret treaties between the Tsar and his wartime Western allies, declaring their own denunciation of them. Among them were the Sykes-Picot agreement to partition the Ottoman Arab provinces among Russia, France, and Britain and the Allied endorsement of Russian annexation of Constantinople and the Straits.

In 1920 the Soviets convened the First Congress of the Peoples of the East in Baku, newly conquered by the Red Army. The chairman, Gregory Zinoviev, President of the Comintern, told nearly 2,000 delegates from countries as distant as Morocco and China: "You who have met for the first time in a Congress of the Peoples of the East must here and now declare a true Holy War against the English and French robber-capitalist."

Stalin, the proponent of consolidating "revolution in one country," namely Russia, before exporting it to others, dampened the Trotskyite fervor for Russian involvement in "permanent revolution" around the world. He made do with diplomacy instead of revolution. But Russian relations with most of the Arab world in the 1920s and 1930s were nonexistent. Egypt, before World War II, went so far as to deprive of his nationality any Egyptian who visited Russia. The Kremlin gave little thought to the small beleaguered Communist organizations in the Arab world, treating them with almost as much indifference as it treated the governments that outlawed and harassed them.

Stalin's secret talks with the Nazis in 1940, however, revealed the enduring nature of Russian imperial policy. A draft protocol declared that Soviet "territorial ambitions center south of the national territory of the Soviet Union in the direction of the Indian Ocean." Thus, in World War II, Stalin raised again the bugbear of Russian expansionism that had haunted England in Curzon's day.

Regarding the Turkish Straits, Stalin's demands, first on the Nazis and later on his allies, echoed the very Tsarist treaties that the early Bolsheviks had published and denounced. Stalin wanted an end of the 1936 Montreaux Convention, which gave Turkey considerable sovereign control over foreign rights of passage. In its place he demanded from the Nazis in 1940 "the right of unrestricted passage of the Soviet Navy through the Straits at any time" and the renunciation of naval rights of passage by all other powers except Germany and Italy. The documents were cited by the US in 1951 to prove Russian designs on the Middle East and justify the proposed Middle East Command.

Anti-British considerations, which later prompted Stalin's uncharacteristic espousal of Zionist statehood in Palestine, moved the Kremlin in May 1941 to the sterile and foolish act of recognizing the abortive Rashid Aly regime in Iraq. Just a month before the Nazi armies thundered into Russia, Stalin established diplomatic relations with the pro-Nazi Rashid Aly government. Three years later, as a wartime ally of Britain, Soviet Russia opened her first legations in Cairo, Damascus, and Beirut and re-established diplomatic relations with Baghdad. In the same way that they had earlier looked toward Hitler's Berlin, Arab politicians now looked on Moscow as an anti-Zionist power that might counteract Zionist influence in Britain and the US and oppose Jewish colonization in Palestine. Their expectations from the Kremlin proved as false as their hopes from the Nazis.

Russian designs on the Middle East were pressed more directly at the end of World War II. At the eastern end of a wide pincer movement, Russia prolonged her wartime occupation of northern Iran, hatched a short-lived secessionist movement there, and demanded from Turkey the adjacent provinces of Kars and Ardahan. At the western end she fomented Communist rebellion in Greece and made ugly demands concerning the Straits. These Russian efforts faded rapidly but not before they had drawn US power and interest into the Middle East.

The Truman Doctrine, announced before a joint session of Congress on 12 March 1947, was a historic reversal of the American isolationist tradition. Truman's commitment to contain Communism in Greece and Turkey became a precedent for commitments along the entire Eurasian rim of the Communist bloc: NATO, SEATO, and, far less successfully, the Baghdad Pact. The failure of the Baghdad Pact was due partly to the fact that, unlike its more successful precursors, it sought to pre-empt an area where no threat existed while the earlier pacts on either side were reactive to dynamic situations and therefore were clearly justified in the eyes of the weaker members.

The pacts were designed for the three regional groups of relatively small countries clustered along the periphery of the Communist camp. NATO was a response to the immediate postwar intrusion of Russian authority into Europe. This was first manifested in the transformation of the East European buffer states into satellite puppets and Soviet dependencies in the imperial nineteenth century manner. Then came the 1948 Communist coup in Czechoslovakia and the Berlin Blockade. NATO was formed in 1949 at the height of the blockade. It was reconciled with the UN Charter's provisions for regional collective defense arrangements by stretching the meaning of "region" a first time to span the North Atlantic and once again to include Greece and Turkey, so that the NATO "region" encompassed 230 meridians from the Aleutians to Kars and Ardahan.

The formation of SEATO in 1954 was a response to events that included the Communist victory in the Chinese civil war in 1949, Communist rebellions in Malaya and the Philippines, Communist China's conquest of Tibet, and the Korean and Indo-Chinese wars.

In the Middle East, by contrast, the Communists took no serious expansionist initiatives after Stalin's abortive adventures against Persia, Turkey, and Greece. Commercially and diplomatically as well, Moscow's attitude was one of indifference, stirred occasionally into passive protest over Western efforts to form a Middle East pact as a link between the containment pacts to the West and to the East.

In the Arab world especially, Russia could have seen little opportunity for immediate gains throughout most of the first postwar decade. The Arab countries, for the most part, were still governed by Western client-regimes, usually under the framework of tutelary arrangements that dated, despite treaty modifications, from World War I and before, ranging from treaty-bound Iraq and the Persian Gulf protectorates in the British-dominated East to the areas of direct French metropolitan rule in North Africa in the West.

Palestine was a major exception to Russian aloofness from Middle Eastern affairs in the late 1940s. It was an exception also to thirty years of ceaseless Soviet opposition to Zionism. Here Russia was motivated by a desire to oust Britain from one of her Middle East strongholds.

Tsarist Russia's ancient and virulent anti-Semitism had been a major impulse behind Herzl's and Weizmann's transformation of agricultural Zionism into political Zionism with the objective of achieving Jewish statehood. Russia had the largest Jewish population in the world. There were 5,215,000 Jews in the Russian Empire in 1909, nearly half of the 11,500,000 Jews in the world. Emigration and the loss of Western territories to Poland after World War I reduced the total to 2,600,000. New annexations of Western territories early in World War II brought the total back to more than 5,000,000, at that time slightly above the US figure. The Nazi invasion brought death to 17,000,000 Soviet soldiers and civilians, among them 3,000,000 of Russia's Jews.

Until the last years of Stalin's rule, anti-Semitism was not condoned under the Soviets as it had been under the Tsars. As a community, the Jews were, if anything, even less a political factor in the years of Communist toleration than they had been under Tsarist persecution. Individual Jews became outstanding leaders in Communist party and governmental machinery but not one of them is known to have regarded himself as part of a distinct Jewish community. All seem to have taken for granted the desirability of assimilation.

Zionism, however, was officially opposed as being a bourgeois nationalist movement running counter to the Communist vision of the future. The creation of the autonomous province of Birobidzhan on the Chinese border in Eastern Siberia in 1934, however, was predicated on recognition of the Jews as one of the nationalities of the Soviet Union. The prime mover of the Birobidzhan experiment was Mikhail Kalinin, then president of the USSR. Not a Jew himself, he was the only Soviet leader to take a practical interest in the Jewish question. Not only did he urge Soviet Jews to build a Jewish state in Birobidzhan, but he encouraged the immigration there of Jews from abroad. For the most part, however, Soviet leaders regarded Birobidzhan as a counterattraction to Zionism and Jewish statehood in Palestine. The Kalinin Declaration establishing the province was regarded as a Russian Balfour Declaration. Russian propaganda denounced Zionism as a cloak for British imperialism and, in the latter 1930s, Moscow gave verbal support to the Palestine Arab rebellion.

Soviet anti-Zionism itself was abated during the Nazi onslaught in order to eliminate resentments that could hurt the war effort. For the same reason militant official atheism was relaxed toward Jews as well as Christians and Moslems. For a time, emigration of Soviet Jews to Palestine was permitted, although this was probably motivated as much by a desire to strengthen the Jewish resistance to British authority in Palestine as by a concern to conciliate Jews in Russia.

At the United Nations Soviet-bloc delegations campaigned against any prolongation of British rule in Palestine. The Russians, to the bitter disappointment of the Arabs, played an important role in obtaining the necessary votes near the end of 1947 for the partition of Palestine. Partition cleared away the last outside political and diplomatic restraints in the way of Jewish statehood. Moscow was among the first powers to recognize the State of Israel in 1948. Arms from Czechoslovakia, then newly taken over by the Soviet block, helped Israel defeat the Arab armies in the first Palestine war.

At about this same time the Kremlin began showing hostility to Jews at home. But, aside from halting emigration, Russia did not begin to side with the Arabs against Israel until 1954. At home, Jews were accused of "cosmopolitanism" and, one after another, the wartime concessions were rescinded. The Jewish Theatre in Moscow was closed. Yiddish publications were forbidden. A recrudescence of Tsarist-style anti-Semitism appeared in Russia and the satellites in the last winter of Stalin's life. Rudolph Slansky and other Jewish Communist leaders in Czechoslovakia were tried and executed on charges that included Zionism, espionage, and conspiracy to kill President Gottwald. Soon afterward, in January 1953, a group of Jewish doctors was arrested in Moscow and accused of terrorist conspiracy and assassinations dating back to the war. This eerie prosecution came to an end with Stalin's death on 5 March 1953. Stalin's successors declared the "doctors' plot" to have been a fabrication.

The establishment of Israel served two purposes for the Kremlin in the Cold War. First, it ended thirty years of rule in Palestine by the British, whose imperial power had contained Tsarist Russia for a hundred years along the marches of the Ottoman and Persian empires and in the approaches to India through Central Asia. Second, it split the Middle East into two vastly unequal populations, the hardy band of Jewish newcomers on one side and the entire indigenous Arab world on the other. This enabled Russia to weaken Western— especially American—influence in the Arab world as a consequence of Washington's susceptibility to Zionist influence in American domestic politics. America had taken over from Britain the containment of Russia but Russian politics could work as well against the one as against the other. With Vatican-like patience, the Kremlin waited six years before moving to cash in on the situation thus created.

The Kremlin's last important diplomatic favor for Israel at the expense of the Arabs was to acquiesce (by abstention) in the Security Council resolution of 1 September 1951 calling on Egypt to end its restrictions on Israeli shipping in the Suez Canal. Nationalist China and India joined Russia in abstaining, allowing the council to pass the resolution 8 to 0. Although never enforced, it still stands on the books, with Israel arguing its validity on political grounds while Egypt rejects it on legal grounds.

A diplomatic rupture between Russia and Israel of no enduring significance began shortly before Stalin's death when, as the "doctors' plot" thickened, a bomb exploded at the Soviet Legation in Tel Aviv. Stalin's successors restored normal diplomatic relations in July following Israel's promise that she "would not be a party to any alliance or pact aiming at aggression against the Soviet Union." Yet within less than two years Israel was offering military bases to the

US in return for a treaty guarantee. The proposed alliance with the US came to naught partly because sections of the Israeli Left violently opposed formal adherence to the anti-Soviet camp.

It was not until a year after Stalin's death that the Russians initiated a positive policy favoring the Arabs. In the meantime, on 24 November 1953, Russia abstained from the Security Council vote of censure against Israel for the Qibya raid, an empty favor that allowed the resolution to pass 7 to 0. A hint of change came on 22 January 1954 with the first Soviet veto on an immediate Palestine question, applied in this case to a Western effort toward settling a Syrian-Israeli dispute over Israel's diversion of the Jordan River.

Serious Russian wooing of the Arabs began with another veto, on 29 March 1954, on the selfsame Suez Canal issue from which the Russians had abstained in 1951. Russia proved a rather inept suitor at first as a result of several years of inattention to the Arab position in the dispute with Israel. Andrei Vyshinsky cast the Russian veto with the cynical explanation that, since Egypt had not complied with the 1951 resolution supporting Israeli claims to equal rights in the Suez Canal, there was no use in reaffirming it. Instead, he advised, the Security Council should work for a general settlement through direct negotiations between the Arabs and Israel. He was apparently unaware that Israel had always sought direct negotiations but that the idea was anathema to the Arabs, absolutely incompatible with their nonrecognition of the new state in their midst.

Nonetheless, the Arabs were grateful for all favors. In April, in the diplomatic aftermath of another stunning Israeli raid, this time on the Jordanian village of Nahhaleen, Vyshinsky supported the Arab demand for a resolution of censure while the Western Big Three, with Israel's approbation, held out for a Security Council debate on the border situation as a whole. The Jordanian parliament, in a turbulent session on 20 April, voted by acclamation to cable their thanks to Vyshinsky. Jordan and Russia had no diplomatic relations until 1963.

The United Nations Truce Supervision Organization, with its quasi-judicial border role, would have been a useful vehicle for Russia's new pro-Arab policy. But the resolution originating the truce commission on 23 April 1948 limited its composition to representatives of Security Council member-nations which had career consular officers in Jerusalem—"a neat way of keeping out the Soviet Union," wrote Walter Eytan, director general of Israel's Foreign Ministry.

For a time Russia balanced its shift toward the Arabs by signs of favor toward Israel. In June 1954 diplomatic representation between Moscow and Tel

Aviv was raised to the ambassadorial level and the first Russian ambassador affronted the Arabs and departed from the practice of other Great Powers by presenting his credentials in the Israeli sector of Jerusalem. The refusal of the US and many other governments to recognize western Jerusalem as Israel's capital derives from UN resolutions in 1947, 1948, and 1949 calling for the internationalization of Jerusalem.

Even after the Russian shift to the Egyptian side of the Suez question another year elapsed before Russia's pro-Arab policy developed a broad consistency. Paradoxically, Egypt, which was to be the first of the Arab countries to give the Russians a firm helping hand into the region, was late in receiving Russian approbation. Although it was the pactomania inspired by Dulles and exploited by the British that revived Russia's active interest in the Middle East, the Kremlin long remained blind to its obvious identity of interest with the Arab antipactomania emanating from Egypt.

The Arabs were overwhelmingly opposed to pacts of any kind with the West, although Nasser himself was not until the heady experience of Bandung in April 1955 led him into the neutralist camp of Tito and Nehru. For nearly three years after seizing power Nasser's revolutionary regime was more pro-Western in thought and action than the civilian governments of the old regime. Nasser had, in fact, turned his back on an Egyptian tradition of neutralism. Mohammed Salaheddeen, an eminent foreign minister of the monarchy's last years, sought in the early 1950s to find in neutralism an escape from Egypt's 150 years of exposure to Great Power rivalries. Even Nahhas, whom Britain forced on Egypt as Premier in 1942, welcomed the wartime establishment of a Russian legation in Cairo in the hope that Russia might someday strengthen Egypt's hand against the British occupation.

The common opposition of Moscow and Cairo to Western pacts with Arabs long antedated Nasser's revolution. Yet the Kremlin long remained obtuse enough to suspect the sincerity of Egypt's opposition. On 21 November 1951, more than a month after the Nahhas government had peremptorily rejected Western proposals for a Middle East Defense Organization (MEDO) based on the Suez Canal, the Kremlin gratuitously warned Egypt that its participation "would cause serious damage" to Russian-Egyptian relations. In one of a flurry of angry notes, the Russians warned Washington three days later that "it cannot pass by these new aggressive plans."

Although MEDO was dead by then and the leadership in Moscow, Washington, and Cairo had changed, the Russian Minister in Egypt called on Foreign Minister Mahmoud Fawzi in April 1953 to protest any possible Egyptian participation in a Middle East pact. The Kremlin was anticipating Dulles's visit the following month. Again, in 1954, the Kremlin issued a barrage of notes against the Turkey-Pakistan pact but took virtually no cognizance of Nasser's rejection of it.

On the contrary, Russia treated Egypt's reluctant concessions to obtain Britain's evacuation of the Suez base as harbingers of accession to a Western pact. On 8 August 1954 the Moscow press attacked the Anglo-Egyptian *Heads of Agreement* on evacuation as "a dangerous step" which "threatens the peaceful coexistence of Egypt with other countries." That was not all. Russian propagandists persisted in libeling Nasser as a Fascist lackey of the West and went on not only to accuse him of treason but to urge Egyptians to revolt. Into the early months of 1955, the Soviets supported the Naguib faction and castigated Nasser not only for his suppression of Egyptian Communists but also for the trials of the old regime politicians and the Moslem Brotherhood terrorists who had tried to kill Nasser. The leading Soviet expert on Egypt, L. N. Vatolina, characterized the Cairo revolutionaries as "madly reactionary, terroristic, antidemocratic, demagogic . . . "

In the winter of 1954–55 the Kremlin ordained a reinvigoration of Soviet Middle Eastern studies after eighteen years of de-emphasis, prompting new books and monographs and authorizing the revival of specialized periodicals. In the meantime, Soviet policy in the Middle East remained essentially passive, ignoring for the time being the opportunities discernible in revisions of policy toward the Soviet Union which were initiated in 1954 by Egypt and Iraq. Egypt was opening doors and Iraq was shutting them in a new phase of the age-old dichotomy between Cairo and Baghdad. Egypt, seeking new markets for cotton, took the lead in the first Russian-Egyptian trade agreement, signed in March 1954. Iraq, secretly preparing the Baghdad Pact, announced on 6 November 1954 that it was "suspending diplomatic relations with the Soviet Union for reasons of economy."

The real reasons behind this bizarre and disingenuous excuse emerged with the announcement and signing of the Baghdad Pact in January and February 1955. Moscow then said it could not "remain indifferent to the intrigues of aggressive circles in the United States and their associates close to the borders of the USSR" but it made no immediate move to exploit the inviting rift among the Arabs which the pact made manifest.

There were several explanations for Russia's continued passivity. On the Russian side, Khrushchev had only just emerged on top in a renewed struggle for power within the Kremlin and he was not ready for serious new initiatives in foreign policy. He gave little study to foreign affairs until after 8 February 1955, the day he displaced Premier Malenkov and put his own nominee, Marshal

Bulganin, in the premiership while retaining his own control of the Communist Party as its First Secretary. On the Egyptian side, Nasser was still as fundamentally pro-Western as Nuri, the core of their disagreement being whether to enter immediately into a formal alliance with the West or to wait until the Arab masses were ready to accept such an alliance.

Aside from the unreadiness of both Cairo and Moscow for dramatic new policies, wholly external factors tended to deter the Kremlin from meddling in what was accepted as a traditional Western sphere of influence. After Stalin's death in March 1953, the Kremlin worked toward a relaxation of Stalin's petrifying tyranny at home and his brutish power politics abroad. Within the year of 1953 the tentacular power and autonomy of the secret police were broken and its chief, Lavrenty Beria, was tried and shot, or, as some authorities say, shot and then tried. At the same time, the Malenkov regime made halting steps toward a *detente* with the West.

The mood of Russian policymakers in the post-Stalin period was set forth in Malenkov's long speech to the Supreme Soviet on 8 August 1953. Although he warned the US against falling into any illusions "about the weakness of the Soviet Union" and disclosed that the US no longer had a "monopoly of the hydrogen bomb," Malenkov said that "one feels for the first time since the war a certain easing of the international situation." He made the Kremlin's first friendly references in years to established governments outside the Soviet bloc in Asia and the Middle East.

Regarding Israel, Malenkov said: "We believe that resumption of diplomatic relations will facilitate cooperation." Promising Russian cooperation with the Arabs too, he added: "The assertion made by certain foreign newspapers that resumption of diplomatic relations with Israel will tend to weaken the Soviet Union's relations with the Arab states is devoid of foundation."

Moscow had already, on 30 May 1953, renounced on behalf of Georgia and Armenia and itself all territorial claims on Turkey together with claims for special privileges in the Straits.

Malenkov also reversed Stalin's five years of implacable hostility to Tito, who had long since found survival in an accommodation with the West. Tito coldly accepted a renewal of diplomatic relations with the comment that even "the worst enemies exchange diplomats" and he went ahead with Greece and Turkey to conclude the Western-sponsored Balkan Pact. Tito's surly independence in profiting from both sides of the Cold War was to make Nasser turn to him two years later as an example, mentor, and friend.

In the Malenkov era, from Stalin's death until February 1955, the Kremlin itself remained passive toward the Middle East in general and grumpily suspicious of Nasser in particular, but events related to Russian power affected Egyptian fortunes indirectly. Russia's successful explosion of a hydrogen bomb in August 1953 all but closed the weapons gap between the two Super-Powers and brought the Cold War into the phase of nuclear stalemate. Egypt benefited when Churchill concluded in the following spring that it made the British military concentration in the Suez Canal base obsolete for strategic purposes. Churchill accepted the prospect of evacuation but he bargained to extract as many concessions as possible from the Egyptians in return for agreeing to return their territory to them.

The Korean Armistice in July 1953 also had side effects upon Egypt, ending the wartime cotton boom and inducing Nasser to find new markets in the Soviet bloc for Egypt's chief commodity. Russia responded as part of the new emphasis on peaceful coexistence and commerce, a policy which had lain in abeyance under Stalin since Mikhail Suslov, a man of Khrushchev's faction, formulated it in 1948.

Far greater changes came when the ebullient Khrushchev himself took over the Kremlin's "collective leadership" on 8 February 1955. The Baghdad Pact and the admission of West Germany to NATO were the first major Cold War measures by the West that confronted Khrushchev after he displaced Malenkov. The West, insisting that its pacts were clearly defensive, discounted the sincerity of Russian protests that they were aggressive in intent and potentially threatening. The Russians were in fact worried enough to maintain two contradictory policies, one of *detente* and the other of power politics against the Western pacts. Having failed to prevent the Paris accords on NATO and the Baghdad Pact under Malenkov, Moscow under Khrushchev felt it had to exert equal and opposite pressures against the two pacts.

Russia responded to the admission of West Germany to NATO by constructing the Warsaw Pact, a Soviet-bloc counterpart of NATO, just five days later, on 14 May 1955. It was a formality which added little to the Russian scale in the balance of power because the Eastern European satellites had little to add to the Red Army. The Red Army was the main support of most of the satellite governments. National armies were not encouraged for fear that they might serve nationalist rather than Soviet Russian interests. For example, the Warsaw Pact joint command deferred any East German participation comparable to NATO's admission of West German forces for fear that armed German nationalism might prove stronger than the East-West division of Germany.

The chief practical effect of the Warsaw Pact was to give a new treaty basis to the permanent stationing of Russian troops in Rumania and Hungary. Under the previous bilateral treaties the presence of the Red Army in these two countries was not to last more than ninety days after an Austrian peace treaty was signed. The Austrian peace treaty, Khrushchev's first major step toward peaceful coexistence, was signed on 15 May, the day after the Warsaw Treaty.

Unlike NATO and SEATO, the Baghdad Pact was created in an area that had been free of Cold War pressures for nearly a decade. Not only had the Russians shown a reluctance to risk adventuring in this traditional Western sphere of influence but, after Stalin's death, they had sought to remove old traces of pressure against Turkey and Persia. The sudden creation of the Baghdad Pact seems to have taken the Kremlin unawares as much as it did Cairo and Washington.

For a time Moscow's propaganda against it added little to the diatribes that had been delivered against the earlier efforts to create a Middle East defense pact linked to the West. Then on 16 April 1955 the Soviet Foreign Ministry issued a major statement. Echoing earlier protests, it said:

> Of course the Soviet Union cannot remain indifferent to the situation arising in the region of the Near and Middle East, since the formation of these blocs and the establishment of foreign military bases on the territory of the countries of the Near and Middle East have a direct bearing on the security of the USSR.

It added a pledge that rang with a new note of menace, portending action as well as words:

> Upholding the cause of peace, the Soviet Government will defend the freedom and independence of the countries of the Near and Middle East and will oppose interference in their domestic affairs.

Just how the Russians would offset Western "interference" had not yet become clear. Nasser, who arrived that day in Bandung for the great gathering of African and Asian national leaders, had still not abandoned his importunate quest for arms from Washington and London. True, he had told his officers on 28 March: "I think it would be a miracle if we ever obtained any arms from this direction." But he did not utterly abandon hope until July or August, weeks after he first approached the Russians on 18 May.

Eden's promise early in April to freeze the Baghdad Pact's Arab membership and his succession to the premiership upon Churchill's long-awaited retirement made it worthwhile for Cairo to re-explore the possibilities of arming from Britain. If the Baghdad Pact were truly frozen for the Arab world, then Egypt's refusal to join it need not be a barrier to arms purchases. And as for the change at No. 10 Downing Street, the Arabs saw it as a general improvement.

On the specific question of arms, Churchill had set forth his policy less than two years before, saying:

> Ever since the Balfour Declaration of 1917 I have been a faithful supporter of the Zionist cause. . . . Fortunately for them [the Israelis] they have formed the best army in the Levant. . . . Nothing that we shall do in the supply of aircraft to this part of the world will be allowed to place Israel at an unfair disadvantage.

It had been left to Eden to brave both Zionist and Tory hostility in negotiating an end to Britain's long occupation of the Suez Canal zone. Beginning with his first term of office as Foreign Secretary Eden's diplomatic record had been one of realistic accommodation with the Arabs. In World War II he had promised Britain's support for Arab efforts to fulfill their yearning for unity. As Foreign Secretary again in the 1950s he had been cautiously pro-Arab on the question of arms, repeatedly turning aside Israeli protests with the reply that the military balance of power was already weighted in Israel's favor. Britain continued her traditional limited sales of weapons to the Arabs, including Egypt.

But, according to Nasser, the arms-purchasing mission he sent to London in his hour of need after the Gaza Raid was no more successful than the missions sent to Washington. Despite the Eden-Nasser moratorium agreement, the British officials approached by the Egyptian mission sought to make additional sales contingent on a softening of Egypt's attitude toward Western alliances and they wanted to see evidence of it in Nasser's conduct at Bandung. This seemed to violate the spirit if not the letter of the moratorium agreement and in any case Nasser was neither willing nor able to chaffer on this basis.

Nevertheless, Nasser did in fact side with the friends of the West on two major issues at Bandung. He backed the condemnation of "colonialism in all its manifestations"—Communist as well as the traditional kind—and he supported the conference's adoption of the Western thesis linking the prohibition of nuclear weapons with effective international control and a general reduction of conventional armaments and armies. In addition, he told Chou en-Lai that he was unwilling to discuss political matters such as Egyptian recognition of Red China or its admission to the UN.

But Nasser's speech at the Officers' Club on 28 March had already disclosed a change in his thinking about neutralism. A year earlier he had said publicly that neutrality was a policy that could be maintained only by the strong and that Egypt was not strong enough for it. When the Baghdad Pact raised the prospect of Western bases in Arab countries, Nasser's anxieties went beyond the political dangers to his regime. He feared that such bases might make the region a target for nuclear bombs in a war between the Super-Powers over issues that had nothing to do with the interests of the Arab world itself. "If the West uses atomic bombs in this area," he said to the officers, "how shall we defend ourselves?"

Both by inclination and as a matter of political necessity, Nasser wanted arms without any strings attached to bases or alliances. He was fully aware of the dangers of turning to the Russians. It would worsen his already troubled relations with Western powers that were within striking distance of Egypt. And Russian military supplies would have to come by Western-controlled sea lanes through NATO and Baghdad Pact territory. These supplies could be cut off if Israel or Britain attacked. Furthermore, Russia had been as hostile to Nasser as to King Farouk and might not prove to be a durable friend. Only the greater urgency of the dangers from neighboring Israel made him willing to risk the dramatic diplomatic shift inherent in seeking arms from the major rival of his traditional suppliers.

The Russians too were aware of the dangers of such a shift, of intruding themselves as a sudden new factor in a relatively stable Western preserve. But Khrushchev was of a more active temperament than either Malenkov or Stalin, capable, as he proved later, of running even such risks as placing missiles in Cuba. Moscow was not laboring under any sense of urgency comparable to Cairo's. The considerations that made the risks of the arms deal worthwhile were more complex, being concerned both with counteracting the Baghdad Pact, which was itself a sudden new factor, and, in a more positive vein, extending Russian contacts and influence into a new and hitherto closed area.

As for the Baghdad Pact, however innocent of aggressive intent it may have seemed to its members and their allies, no Russian strategist worth his keep could fail to interpret it as, at worst, a political framework for potentially offensive missile bases. At best it was a definite Western defense commitment that sharply restricted Russia's freedom of action in dealing with small neighbors and near-neighbors just as Russia's commitment to Cuba a few years later sharply restricted American freedom of action in dealing with Castro.

When in February, at the height of Nasser's public struggle to prevent Nuri of Iraq from going ahead with the Baghdad Pact, Nehru and Nasser had condemned military alliances, their communiqué was a diplomatic tactic—by Nehru against Pakistan's policy and by Nasser against Nuri's—rather than a considered policy statement of neutralism. Nasser was still as pro-Western in outlook as Nuri, however much they differed over methods and timing. Indeed, Nasser told Eden a few days after seeing Nehru that he personally had no doubts that any outside attack on the Arab world would come from Russia but that the Arab peoples could not be hurried into pacts. The Gaza Raid and the signing of the Baghdad Pact splintered old policies into wreckage by the end of the month, presenting the choice of reconstructing them or building new ones.

Nasser's initial effort was to reconstruct old policies, contingent on the West acknowledging and fulfilling Egypt's need for arms. In this he was hampered by economic as well as political considerations. Egypt's cotton exports had fallen 26 per cent below the previous year and Washington was talking about subsidizing American cotton exports, a move that could shoulder Egyptian cotton out of Western markets entirely. Russia and Red China had begun to buy small quantities of Egypt's growing surplus but Egypt's imports were still based on traditional Western supplies.

Arms, Egypt's major new need, would be a logical import to take in trade for unsold cotton. On the other hand, Egypt's army had always been equipped with Western matériel and rearming would not have to be so thorough if it could be done from Western sources. Spare parts and retraining would be simpler problems if the new arms came from the West. But the West was reluctant to rearm Egypt on any basis and Western cotton markets were glutted with the surplus created by production geared to the now-ended Korean War. The logic of turning eastward for arms was plain but logic runs uphill against custom.

It was not until Nasser returned from Bandung at the end of April 1955 that his earnest three-year endeavor to base Egyptian policy on friendship with America began to fade into history's limbo of lost opportunities. Bandung was Nasser's first appearance in a major world forum. It became Egypt's door out of the parochialism of the Arab world into the new horizons of awakening Africa and Asia. There the Egyptians met the men of new China, a giant no longer sleeping. China's 100 tireless delegates at Bandung broke the ostracism that had isolated mainland China since the Communists seized power in Peking in 1949.

Nasser's "diplomatic reconnaissance," as he called his Bandung trip, discovered to his bold and restless imagination the respectable numerical strength of neutralism, a dogma long since expounded to him by the great spokesman of Asia, Pandit Jawaharlal Nehru. The reconnaissance, in view of Egypt's circumstances after the Gaza Raid and the Baghdad Pact, could not help drawing Nasser's attention to possibilities hitherto obscured by Egypt's quasi-colonial traditions.

Wednesday, 18 May 1955, fell in the lunar month of Ramadan in which, throughout the Moslem world, absolute fasting from daybreak to sunset creates a hungry lassitude among the faithful and shortens both tempers and efficiency. It is neither a good month for getting things done nor for making major decisions. But time and the non-Moslem world wait for no man and, in any case, Nasser, a Moslem of exemplary devotion, never allowed the rigors of the fast to interfere with duty or decisions. May 18th was as busy as any other day for Nasser, and its tasks were uncommonly important.

He had already discussed with the Revolution Command Council the idea of buying arms from Russia. The junta had given him full authority to explore the question. But it was not the only item on his docket for the day. The High Dam project took the lion's share of his time, largely in meetings with Ismail al-Azhary, Premier of the Sudan, whose agreement on a new partition of the Nile waters was a prerequisite for building the new dam. Nasser spent an hour with Azhary at the Semiramis Hotel in the morning. He gave an *Iftar* banquet for Azhary at dusk to break the fast. Both men then attended the reception at the Sudan Agency where Nasser discreetly broached the purchase of arms to the Russian ambassador. Finally, after a midnight meeting of the Egyptian cabinet, Nasser and Azhary met again in conference with their ministerial aides.

In the afternoon, in an interview with Robert Doty of *The New York Times*, Nasser gave a reassuring explanation of the new Egyptian foreign policy which he was then in the early stages of formulating and which he was to follow with dogged consistency through years of vicissitudes that included the two Suez-Sinai wars and estrangements, at one time or another, from both Russia and America. The new, more independent policy, he said, meant only that Egypt would reject dictation "from London, Washington, or Moscow." (On 12 July, at the end of a second visit from Nehru, a further policy definition emphasized a more positive note, that of liberation. In a joint statement, Nasser and Nehru declared their mutual interest in "the preservation of peace and in the extension of freedom to such areas as are still under Colonial rule." They also declared "their conviction that involvement in military pacts or alignments with Great Powers does not serve the cause of peace, and indeed, often has the opposite effect." Early the next year the policy became known as "positive neutralism," creating a fashion among neutralist Third World governments each to give a highly specific sobriquet to its own policy of nonalignment with any of the Super-Powers.) Nasser did not succeed in reassuring the West either in the interview with Doty or in countless other statements in the ensuing years but neither Western rebuffs nor Russian and Chinese blandishments ever succeeded in winkling him out of the middle of the neutralist road, along which he made his first steps when he took the Russian ambassador aside for a private inquiry on this Wednesday evening.

An unscheduled item in that long, crowded Ramadan day made those first steps a little easier to take. Israeli troops stormed an Egyptian position near

Gaza in a demolition raid, retaliating for a retaliation in a sequence that cost three lives on each side. And Israeli representatives began a boycott of the Mixed Armistice Commission, drawing a warning from General Burns that unless both sides tried sincerely to improve the situation it would surely deteriorate. The deterioration that began with the Gaza Raid had already given the severely anti-Communist Egyptian junta such lively anxieties about Ben-Gurion's warlike intentions that they were risking rearmament from the USSR itself.

Two members of the junta accompanied Nasser to the Sudanese reception, Major General Abdel Hakim Amer, the Minister of War, and Major Salah Salem, who held the portfolios of National Guidance and Sudan Affairs. At this reception, Nasser says, he broached to Solod, the Soviet Ambassador, Egypt's desire to buy Russian arms.

The springtime request must have been a surprise to the Kremlin in view of the fact that its wintertime propaganda had urged Egyptians to overthrow Nasser and had treated him and his colleagues like a common banana-republic variety of junta with fascist leanings. Here, out of the blue, was a reasonably safe way to outflank the Baghdad Pact and honor the vague but ominous pledge of 16 April to "defend the freedom and independence" of a Middle Eastern country against Western "interference." On 21 May Solod called on Nasser at the Presidency with an affirmative answer from the Kremlin and spent two hours closeted with him. Nasser later told Keith Wheeler of *Time* magazine: "Really, I was surprised when he accepted."

The Baghdad Pact, in the words of the British historians Geoffrey Barraclough and Rachel Wall, now began "to call up the very devil it was seeking to exorcise." Eden had secretly cleared the Baghdad Pact and Britain's accession to it with Nasser but he had not cleared it with Khrushchev. Nasser's top priority need for arms after the Gaza Raid dovetailed with Khrushchev's need to undermine the Baghdad Pact even in the form that Nasser was willing to accept. It was the perfectly carpentered logic of this set of independent circumstances, created in the last four days of February, that drew Nasser and the Russian ambassador together in those days in May to the surprise of both.

Ironically, Dulles and Eisenhower, who were later to call the arms deal a violation of the "spirit of Geneva," appeared on television to voice high hopes for the forthcoming "Summit Conference" on the very day that Nasser approached the Russian ambassador. Citing the Austrian peace treaty among recent events that may have "turned the tide of history," Dulles said: "We find for the first time a softening of the Soviet attitude." Eisenhower spoke of a "new dawn" of peace. Dulles interpreted the change as symptomatic of Soviet weakness rather than to any sincere esteem for a *detente* as a good in itself.

His presumption that it vindicated Washington's tough policy of pactomania provoked Khrushchev to say shortly before the Summit meeting: "We are not going to Geneva with broken legs."

While *detente* was in the air, Russian-Egyptian arms negotiations ticked away through the spring and summer. The arms deal was like a time bomb with a two-month clock but only two-week works, which might never have detonated if it had not been rewound at intervals by Israeli raids and Western rebuffs. Washington and London heard the ticking in plenty of time to stop it. Nasser, who still would have preferred arms from the West, frankly told US Ambassador Byroade on 9 June that he was negotiating with the Russians and would have no alternative but to buy arms from them if the West would not meet his needs. Byroade informed Washington and also the British ambassador, who had his heated discussion with Nasser on the subject three days later. In mid-June Nasser told Byroade that he had delayed the dispatch of a military mission to Moscow. Washington responded by saying it would consider specific Egyptian requests. At the end of the month Nasser sent a list of his needs to Washington. Attesting the seriousness of his request, the newly published Egyptian national budget increased military appropriations by $53 million over the previous year's $109 million.

"We were desperately weak," Salah Salem disclosed five years later to Patrick Seale, a British journalist-historian. "Our armed forces were short of everything. At the time of the Gaza Raid, Egypt had six serviceable planes. About thirty others were grounded for lack of spare parts; Britain had stopped deliveries. We estimated that our tank ammunition would last for a one-hour battle. Nearly sixty per cent of our tanks were in need of major repairs. Our artillery was in the same deplorable state. We were even short of small arms. We had tried to buy arms from Britain and America—but in vain."

Neither Washington nor London took Nasser's problem at face value. Egyptian rearmament was not mentioned at the Summit Conference in Geneva, where the leaders of the US, Russia, Britain, and France met from 18 to 23 July. The conference did not even have a Middle East item on the agenda. In an ironical coincidence, at the very time that the Big Four leaders were meeting and ignoring the Middle East, Nasser resumed his Russian arms negotiations with Dmitri Shepilov, editor of *Pravda* and a prominent Khrushchev protégé who visited Egypt for the third anniversary celebrations of the Egyptian revolution. Nasser correctly suspected that his latest request for US arms, like the previous ones, had been placed in a contrived maze of red tape and procrastination. He and Shepilov reached agreement, he says, about delivery dates, types, and quantities of armaments, and payment terms. They also agreed to bring Czechoslovakia in as a front for the Russians.

There was a third arm to the ironical coincidence that found Nasser and Shepilov talking of arms while the Summit statesmen were forging the "spirit of Geneva." In Paris on 20 July, Israeli emissaries asked their friends in power to send them two squadrons of Mystère IV's in place of the single squadron of Mystère II-Cs on order. Ben-Gurion was thus rounding into the second lap of the arms race before Nasser, so far as the Israelis were aware, had even started running. While Nasser, unknown to the Israelis, was seeking MIG-15s to match Israel's Mystère II-Cs, Israel, unknown to Nasser, was already moving to obtain Mystère IVs. It was a major step for Israel, far beyond her ordinary defense justifications at the time. Had Nasser known of it, it would have sharpened the fears of an Israeli offensive that had obsessed him since the Gaza Raid.

The mutual secrecy, so long as it lasted, of these developments in the aerial armaments race kept them from interacting upon one another. Lesser developments were sufficient to rewind the springs of Nasser's negotiations with the Russians and the Czechs. They included Israel's intransigence on the border, news that the US was considering Israel's request for a security treaty, activist gains in the Israeli elections, the unfortunate results of *The New York Times'* failure to publish Nasser's interview disclosing his offer to demilitarize the frontier, and the long slow silence in Washington on Nasser's request to buy US arms.

President Tito of Yugoslavia gave the key a turn with a speech on 28 July, while Shepilov was still in Egypt. He had recently won new importance in Europe and had become a hero in the uncommitted world as a result of a visit from Khrushchev at the end of May. Khrushchev accepted in full Tito's conditions for future Yugoslav-Soviet relations, including Belgrade's freedom to maintain profitable connections with the West and to remain in the Western-sponsored Balkan Pact with two NATO members, Greece and Turkey. It was a triumph for Tito's Communist brand of neutralism which eased his dependence on American arms. He declared in his speech on 28 July that Yugoslavia "cannot accept more arms if an attempt is made to impose new conditions in conformity with some United States law. It is the laws of Yugoslavia and not those of the United States which hold good in this country."

The sentiment was identical with Nasser's. Nevertheless, he inquired of Washington on 31 July about what had happened to the list of arms he had submitted, at US suggestion, on 30 June. Washington remained silent until 25 September when the State Department, too late, sought to disrupt the Russian-Egyptian arms contract that had been signed in Prague a day or so before.

Nasser had balked at having strings attached to arms from the West, being all too aware that extremists might hang him with them. But he did make other concessions, particularly in fulfilling his end of the Nasser-Eden moratorium on the Baghdad Pact. Cairo curtailed propaganda against Iraq as well as against Britain. The "clandestine" Radio Free Iraq, which had waged a virulent war of words with Nuri's slanderous Radio Free Egypt, announced its own shut-down on 13 June. Britain's retiring Ambassador Stevenson, after a farewell call on Nasser that day, said "Anglo-Egyptian relations are on a normal, healthy basis for the first time since we had anything to do with Egypt."

The abatement of propaganda was not without risks, for less than a week later a Government spokesman was impelled to state that "Egypt's agreement with Iraq to stop cruel attacks on responsible individuals does not mean at all that Egypt has changed her policy toward Iraq's joining this pact" which had "seriously shattered Arab unity." In return, London announced on 25 July that it would sell two old destroyers to Egypt "to preserve a balance" with two it had already sold to Israel.

But the balance that the West was preserving was, to Nasser's mind, intolerably weighted in favor of Israel. Border eruptions in August deepened his conviction and gave a final rewinding to the clock of the Russian-Egyptian arms deal. On 22 August Israeli troops, after recklessly drawing Egyptian fire by straight-on rushes to within yards of Egyptian earthworks on the Gaza truce line, stormed an Egyptian position with humiliating ease, killing three of its defenders and wounding five without loss to themselves. They occupied the position during a two-hour fire fight with other Egyptian positions and contemptuously released their prisoners when they withdrew, under a UN-arranged ceasefire, to continue their patrol.

The following evening US Ambassador Byroade was sufficiently alarmed to tell General Burns, who could relay the warning to the Israelis, "that the Russians were offering Egypt arms and many economic advantages and the Prime Minister [Nasser] was under much political pressure to accept the Russian offers." Burns evidently relayed Byroade's report promptly to the Israelis for it was circulating in diplomatic and journalistic circles in Jerusalem, from where, within four days, I reported it to *The New York Times*. The stout-hearted Israelis were not much dismayed and not at all deterred by the prospect of facing Russian arms in Arab hands.

Sharett told me in an interview published on 25 August that Israel was prepared "to leave the Gaza Strip as it is provided it is not used as a springboard for continued attacks against and incursions into Israeli territory." Against the background of Sharett's statement three months earlier that "the Egyptians have forfeited their title to this Gaza Strip," and Nasser's warning that an Israeli seizure of Gaza would mean war, Sharett's new reference seemed once again to place Gaza's status on Israeli sufferance.

It was later on that same day, Thursday, 25 August 1955, that Nasser finally committed to action both of the policies he had evolved under the impact of the Gaza Raid of 28 February. That night the *Fedayeen* crossed into Israel to begin a week of unprecedented terrorist reprisals and Nasser made his conclusive decision to abandon his futile efforts in the West and re-equip his army from Russia. As he told Slade-Baker of the *Sunday Times* (London) a few weeks later:

The final decision to accept Russian arms was postponed for nearly three months, in the hope of obtaining what we required from the United Kingdom and America. It was only when it became clear that we should receive nothing, and the situation on the Gaza front had deteriorated to a dangerous extent, that I finally decided to accept Russian help. This was on August 25th.

General Burns described the pressures on Nasser to make his final decision:

Israeli forces flouted their patrols along the demarcation line, as if to challenge the garrison of the Strip to interfere with them. . . . Something had to be done to restore the Army's self-esteem. Nasser cannot have forgotten how the revolution which placed him in power had begun. . . . Nasser could not have wanted history—or, at any rate, revolution—to repeat itself.

As Nasser himself put it to Cyrus Sulzberger of *The New York Times* in those troubled August days: "Our revolution was stimulated in the Army by a lack of equipment. If our officers feel we still have no equipment, they will lose faith in the Government."

During the nearly four weeks that remained before the arms agreement could be worked out in sufficient detail to be signed, Israel mounted a major raid against Khan Yunis in the Gaza Strip, shot down two Egyptian planes between Gaza and Migdal-Ashkelon, and in general worried the Egyptians to such an extent that they evacuated their wives and children from the Gaza Strip. It was at this time, too, that the French, while extending a state of emergency throughout all Algeria, halted delivery of tanks and other weapons they had sold to Egypt.

Word of the Russian-Egyptian negotiations, meanwhile, began to emerge in public. *Les Echos de Paris* reported the Russian offer on 27 August, the same day that I cabled from Israel the gist of what Byroade had told General Burns on 23 August. Israeli officials speculated that Dulles's major peace proposals delivered in a speech on 26 August, proposals which they did not like, were prompted by concern over Byroade's reports to Washington on the Russian offer. On 30 August Dulles confirmed at a Washington press conference that he had received indications that Russia had offered military equipment to

Egypt. He evinced concern over the reports, which he said were unofficial but which bore the mark of reliability. Cairo Radio retorted that night that the US, having furnished arms to Israel but not to Egypt, should not be surprised if Egypt accepts arms from Russia. The Government newspaper, *al-Gamhouriya*, called Dulles's statement "glaring interference" and said Egypt would neither deny nor confirm it.

The first public official confirmation of the offer came on 4 September 1955 from Deputy Premier Gamal Salem of Egypt, who was in Calcutta on a good-will tour. On 12 September the Russian Foreign Ministry denied the reports when the Israeli ambassador inquired about them, saying that Russia had not sold any arms to Arab states, was not conducting any negotiations for arms with these states, and was unaware of any similar negotiations "by any of the peoples' democracies."

The clumsiness of the falsehood is hard to account for. The negotiations were nearing their conclusion with the Russians making all the decisions for the Czechs who were going through the motions. Since 25 August the talks had been beyond the influence of day-to-day events either on the border or in distant capitals.

The precise date of the signing of the arms deal has not been publicly verified but it was probably between 21 and 24 September. Dulles warned Molotov on 20 September that such a deal would violate the "spirit of Geneva." He borrowed Central Intelligence Agency men from his brother Allen Dulles for missions of dissuasion to Nasser. But neither the Russians nor the Egyptians could or would back out at that late stage. It was probably on Saturday, 24 September, that Byroade relayed to Washington the information given him by an Egyptian diplomat that the deal was signed "today."

The next day the State Department, in a thirteenth-hour attempt to spike the Russian-Egyptian contract, inspired unattributed but authoritative news reports that the US would sell arms to Egypt on credit if Egypt would not buy from Russia. Whitehall reacted sharply against this apparent invasion of a traditional British market in which Britain had sacrificed her own interests by restricting sales in keeping with Western policies.

With a diplomatic kick the British detonated the bombshell disclosure of the arms deal before it was quite ready to go off. The Foreign Office had Ambassador Sir Humphrey Trevelyan verify the arms deal by a telephone call to Nasser and then published the news from London early on the 27th, calling it a Russian-Egyptian deal. Nasser, angered by the discourtesy of the British, announced the arms deal himself that evening, attributing the contract entirely to the Czechs and omitting mention of the Russian role in order to soften the impact of the news on the West.

Nasser recalls that he got the approval of the Revolution Command Council for the announcement at 4 P.M., overriding General Amer, who wanted to postpone the announcement until the arms were safely delivered. The best available forum that day was the opening of an exhibit sponsored by Armed Forces public relations officers. A hasty summons brought a crew from the Egyptian State Broadcasting Company. They were bewildered as to why they were to dignify so inconsequential an event with broadcast coverage. Their bewilderment deepened when Nasser appeared. The Egyptian press and radio had not been allowed to report Britain's disclosure of the arms deal. Nasser's live audience totaled no more than 100 persons, most of them technicians, newsmen, and anxious officials.

Characteristically, Nasser led up to the point of his speech, the disclosure of the Russian-Czech arms deal, with an off-the-cuff history of "the long and bitter story" of his efforts and failures to get arms from the West. He said:

We never intended to strengthen the Army for wars. . . . We want arms so that we can be tranquil, so that we feel at peace and not threatened. . . . We humiliated ourselves . . . we begged for arms, but at the same time were determined to hold to our principles . . . and what was the result. . . .

France always haggled with us, telling us that they would give us weapons on the condition that we . . . ignore the butchery that was going on in North Africa. We asked them in reply how we could abandon our Arab nature or give up our humanitarianism. The supply to us of French arms was always like a sword dangling over our heads; France continually threatened to cut us off from the supply of arms and to provide them for Israel. . . .

I shall now tell you about America. From the start of the revolution, we kept on asking her for arms. . . . We received promises with conditions attached. . . . We re-refused to sign any mutual security pact, any form of alliance; and so, my brothers, we were unable to obtain arms from America.

Now, what was the tale of Britain? . . . It was that Britain supplied us with quantities of arms that did not accord with our revolution's objectives. . . . The Israeli Army was receiving weapons from Britain, France, Belgium, Canada, and several other countries. . . . We had to read in foreign newspapers . . . that the Israeli Army could defeat all the Arab armies combined . . . and that the Israeli Army was our superior in arms and equipment. . . . I have asked them, "If you feel like this, why do you withhold weapons from us?"

We decided to ask every nation in the world to supply us with arms unconditionally . . . and in doing so emphasized that the weapons would not be used for aggression, but for defense. We harbor no aggressive intentions. Our aims are only peaceful.

Last week Egypt signed a commercial agreement with Czechoslovakia for a supply of weapons to her. This agreement stipulates that Egypt shall pay for these weapons with products such as cotton and rice. . . .

As I talk to you today, my brothers, I hear an uproar in Washington and London which is composed of calls for the continuation of arbitary control and influence. We shall struggle to eliminate this arbitrary control and influence;... we shall struggle to create a strong national army, which shall be capable of realizing the revolution's great goals and achieving peace for Egypt. Yes, brothers, Peace—the peace we have preached at Bandung and on many other occasions.

If we are building up this army, it is for the sake of peace.... We are building it up so that Egypt will not be a State of refugees. We are building it up against aggression and we are building it up against any ambitions over the territory of this homeland.

Ten months after announcing it as a Czech deal, Nasser disclosed in his Suez nationalization speech on 26 July 1956 that the arms had come from Russia— "I say from Russia and not from Czechoslovakia." The crowd applauded. In 1966 he told me that the Russians had chosen the Czechs as middle men and that the negotiations had taken place in Prague with the Czechs. "The Soviets said that they agreed but they preferred that we deal with the Czechs," he said. I asked if this had been because the Russians themselves had been apprehensive about the Western reaction. Nasser laughed and said he did not know their reasons. From the beginning Egyptians, including Nasser, loosely attributed the deal as often to the Russians as to the Czechs.

The Russians themselves feigned ignorance of the origins of the deal until 24 hours after Nasser's nationalization speech, when TASS, the Russian news agency, distributed a text of Nasser's speech that included his attribution of the arms deal to the Russians while deleting another Nasser statement that the Russian ambassador had offered aid for the High Dam. The Moscow newspapers then linked the arms deal to Shepilov's visit to Egypt in July 1955. Until then the Russians called it a Czech arms deal. On 3 October 1955, when Western agitation was at a fever pitch, a TASS statement on "reports" of a Czech-Egyptian barter agreement to exchange arms for cotton and rice said that "in this connection groundless claims have been made on the USSR."

Overnight, the deal made Nasser the darling of the Arab world. Messages of congratulations poured in, not only from the Arab countries but from far and wide in Africa and Asia. "I have also received messages applauding my decision from people I know who have frequently opposed our policy in the past," Nasser told Slade-Baker.

The all-but-unanimous approval of Nasser's step among the Arabs and in the wider world of Islam surprised and disappointed Westerners who, despite the strength of Communism in Roman Catholic France and Italy (not to mention Catholic Poland and Holy Russia herself), believed that Islam was an insurmountable barrier to Communism. The belief was widely held. It played a role in Western policy-making in spite of the evidence in the Moslem republics of Soviet Central Asia that Communism is no more incompatible with Islam than with Roman Catholicism. History was more important than religious dogma in determining the Arab reaction to Nasser's arms coup.

The Arabs to this day have no historical experience of Russia's iron fist. On the contrary, so far as they are concerned, it has beat, not upon the Arab but upon the Turk, the Frank, the Persian, and the Englishman, all alien imperial oppressors of the Arabs. For a century and a half the Arabs had lost repeated encounters with the West, culminating in the loss of Palestine to Western Zionism. Zionism's colonizing conquests, ironically, derived their impetus from Western man's inhumanity to Western man and not from any racial crimes by the Arabs. Consequently, the Arabs by and large had no fear that Russian influence would come with Russian arms. Nasser had, in fact, consulted several other Arab governments, not including Iraq, about the arms deal in advance.

Nasser himself was aware of the dangers of dependence on Russia. If his own anti-Communist wariness needed any stimulus he had always the example and advice of his friend Tito on this as on other matters. The chief risk, of course, was that once the Egyptian Army was relying entirely on Russian arms the Kremlin might use Egypt's need for ammunition and spare parts to impose its will on Egypt. But the Russians proved themselves to be the most bountiful and dependable of suppliers, not only in the original sales of arms but in the replacement of war booty captured by Israel in the two Suez wars.

Another danger, smaller perhaps but more immediate, was that the Russian arms deal might be seized upon by Nasser's enemies as a pretext for violence against him—a pre-emptive war by Israel, perhaps, or a *coup d'état* or assassination instigated by Western agents. Or perhaps the West would be sufficiently alienated to make Nasser's new neutralism meaningless. Therefore, in his speech announcing the arms deal and in interview after interview with Western correspondents in the following months Nasser emphasized that the arms were solely for security against attack by Israel and that he would not allow Russian arms to become a vehicle for Communist influence.

He told James Morris of *The Times* of London that he would have preferred British arms but that Britain would not supply nearly enough for his needs. "I do not want to spend money on war," he said, "I want to build our High Dam at Aswan—our new pyramid. But I want to sleep easily at night, and so I must strengthen our Army how[ever] I can." He told me a few days after my return from two months in Israel: "... it was not a matter of bluffing. I needed the arms and I had no alternative but to supply myself from the East. ... I do not think there will be any need for foreign technicians to look

251

after the Czech arms." Egyptian technicians, he said, had assembled and maintained British jets with nothing but factory manuals in English to guide them. To Slade-Baker of the *Sunday Times* of London, he said: "Communism is illegal in Egypt. Two years ago it was active but today it has been completely neutralized.... I have the leadership of the country. Communism could increase only if I lost it, and if people began to think that I was a foreign agent." Nasser conceded that the arms deal had given the Russians £100 million worth of favorable propaganda in the Arab world, but he added that he did not think they would want to negate it by subversive activities.

The Russians coolly commented, in the TASS statement of 3 October on "reports" of the Czech deal, that "every state has the lawful right... to buy arms for its defence needs from other states on the usual commercial terms, and no foreign state has the right to interfere in this. ..." Czechoslovakia too called it an ordinary commercial transaction. But Ben-Gurion said on 2 November a few hours before permanently smashing Egypt's remaining toehold near al-Auja: "The character of this 'transaction' is not affected by the name given to it."

By strengthening the nascent neutralism of Nasser in providing arms free of any limitations on their use, the Kremlin promoted an alternative to the Baghdad Pact and undercut the bargaining value of Western arms. Nasser's popularity among the Arab masses came earlier outside Egypt than inside. It was already discernible in the cities of the Levant in 1954 during his struggle with Naguib. After a century and a half of European "divide and dispose," the Arabs yearned for unity and neutrality as an escape from further misfortunes incidental to Great Power rivalries. Nasser's recourse to Pan-Arabism and neutralism after the Gaza Raid responded to Arab yearnings. The dramatic neutralist success of the arms deal brought him his first personal triumph among the cynical worldlings of old Egypt and enhanced his appeal among Arabs abroad, where Jordanians, Iraqis, and Lebanese were already comparing Nasser favorably with their own Western-client leaders.

The resulting disharmony between the pro-Western leaders and their people limited the freedom of action of men like President Camille Chamoun of Lebanon and King Hussein of Jordan. It ensured that no Arab government would join Nuri's in the Baghdad Pact, whether or not Eden honored the moratorium. Within three years, even Nuri's options were pared down to escaping or being killed—and he failed to escape. In the meantime, the arms deal transformed the possibility that Nuri and the Baghdad Pact would isolate Nasser into the reality of Nuri finding that he himself was isolated within the Arab world by the Baghdad Pact and alienated from his own people.

Within a month of announcing the arms deal, Nasser brought to a successful conclusion the negotiations he had begun with Syria and Saudi Arabia in March for military alliances intended to rival the Baghdad Pact. The treaties gave a kind of paper substance to the "Southern Tier," as the Nasserist fraternity was called for a time in contrast to the Baghdad Pact's "Northern Tier" alliance. Ben-Gurion's raids on al-Sabha in November and Syria in December showed up the ineffectiveness of Egypt's October treaties just as, on a grander scale, the Suez wars of 1956 and 1967 were to show up the ineffectiveness of the successors to those treaties. But the violence of Israel, whom the Arabs regard as America's protégé, strengthened the sentiment of Arab neutralism even as it revealed Arab military weakness.

Military weakness in the face of Israel, in fact, became more than ever an argument for obtaining arms from Russia, particularly when France, ever more beset by the spreading Algerian rebellion, began to multiply her secret shipments of first-line planes and tanks to her anti-Egyptian ally on the "separate front" in the Sinai. The French-Israeli acceleration of the Middle East arms race led Nasser to negotiate a second arms contract with the Russians in the early months of 1956. In the spring of 1956 Syria followed suit and became the second Arab country to buy Russian weapons.

The first arms deal brought Egypt MIG-15 fighters, capable of meeting Mystère IIs on equal terms, Ilyushin IL-28 bombers, and a few submarines. The second deal brought MIG-17s, Russia's counterpart to the West's best jet fighters, among which were the Mystère IVs that France was supplying to NATO and also shipping secretly to Israel. The second arms deal was a closely held secret. Rumors of it did not reach Washington until July 1956. The State Department speculated that Nasser would conclude the deal on his scheduled official visit to Moscow the following month, a visit that was postponed as a result of the Suez Crisis until April 1958. Nasser confirmed that there had been a second deal in an interview with me ten years later.

"Yes, there was a second agreement about MIG-17s," he said. "The first agreement was about MIG-15s." When I asked the date of the second agreement he replied: "I don't know exactly. Of course, we have all of that in our files. I think it was mainly an agreement about the MIG-17s and about the submarines. Maybe we increased the number of submarines." Reflecting further, he said the second agreement was concluded before May 1956. That was the month in which he recognized Red China in order to secure an arms source outside the compass of a UN embargo such as Khrushchev proposed on a visit to England in April.

Nasser demurred at giving the numbers of the weapons received from Russia, figures which have been the subject of widely varying estimates by Western authorities ever since. Ben-Gurion estimated in his memoirs of Suez that

Egypt had "more than one hundred MIG-15s, fifty Ilyushin fighter bombers," and a number of older British jet fighters. Dayan wrote in his *Sinai Diary* that Egypt had received "about two hundred MIG-15 fighters and some fifty Ilyushin-29 bombers" but in the appendix on the Egyptian air force he said that only two MIG-15 squadrons, comprising thirty planes, were operational on the eve of the war, and only a single squadron of twelve IL-28 bombers. Neither Ben-Gurion nor Dayan mentions the MIG-17s.

Nasser did give the cash value of the two agreements, a figure that also had been the subject of wide speculation in the West. "The second agreement was not bigger than the first agreement," he said, adding that together they totaled £120 million ($336 million). "There was no effect on our economy because we agreed to pay in installments for twelve years. They said that we mortgaged our cotton and so on. Nonsense!" He said that the Russians had replaced Egyptian matériel losses immediately after the Suez War with a third agreement. In 1967 they again immediately replaced far greater war losses.

The open-handed dependability of the Russians in furnishing arms without strings and on easy terms looked like irresponsible trouble-making to Westerners but it was deeply appreciated by the Arabs. Their weakness in the face of Zionism had been demonstrated since World War I with a regularity made all the more humiliating by their own rodomontade. Those Arabs who continued to depend on Western, particularly American, sources of arms continued to get with them not only foreign supervision and conditions limiting their use, but also much public rudeness and uncertainty over deliveries. Those slights were occasioned by purely domestic political pressures on US administrations from a variety of highly vocal interests such as the Zionist movement, the cotton lobby, and liberal groups sympathetic to Jews but ignorant of Arabs. It seemed to Arabs as if the Russians dealt with the Arabs on a dignified assumption that they had neither the right nor the need to impose conditions in order to ensure responsible behavior by the Arabs. By contrast, it seemed that the West would never get over the condescending tutelary attitude of the colonial era, an attitude that seemed to have been transmitted full-strength to anti-colonial America. The conditions attached to US economic and military aid appeared to presume an innate irresponsibility in the Arab character. US editorial writers, in any case, took this patronizing view.

Deliveries under the first Russian arms contract did not begin until the end of the year. Shipment schedules were arranged by General Hassan Raghab, who went to Prague on 29 September while the State Department's George V. Allen was on his way to Cairo on a futile mission to nullify the deal. The Egyptians did not deny premature reports of the arrival of Russian arms at the time Nasser announced the deal. They wanted to preclude US interference and also to deter any spoiling attack by Israel. Nasser told me the early reports were wrong, adding: "We began to have Russian arms by the beginning of '56."

The Russian arms were first reported in use on Egyptian maneuvers in February 1956, the month the first photographs of them were published. They were not displayed at an Egyptian military parade until late in June 1956.

The Russians were as open-minded and as open-handed with economic aid as they were with armaments. On 10 October 1955, Ambassador Solod announced in Cairo that his government had decided to offer industrial and agricultural equipment and technical assistance to all underdeveloped Arab and Asian countries that wanted it. Laughing and joking after a meeting at the Egyptian Foreign Ministry, Solod told reporters: "We will send economic missions, scientific missions, agricultural missions, meteorological missions, and any other kind of mission you can imagine that will help these countries."

Solod's exuberant announcement signaled the beginning of a race for influence in the underdeveloped nations in Africa and Asia that is still going on. Eric Johnston was then in Cairo, still trying with Egyptian help to formulate an integrated Arab and Israeli project to develop the Jordan River Valley with US financial backing. When he heard of Solod's statement he said the big danger was that the Russians would steal a march on the US in helping Egypt build the High Dam at Aswan. Within 24 hours Solod made an offer to Nasser to help build the dam with equipment, technical assistance, and cash with repayment in Egyptian commodities over 25 years.

But Nasser, now dependent on Russia for arms, was fearful of placing Egypt's economy at the mercy of Moscow. The project would absorb so large a proportion of Egypt's economic resources for so many years that dependence on a single foreign government for necessary assistance, even in the absence of onerous economic or political conditions, seemed to him more threatening to Egypt's independence than the more costly and complicated Western aid already under consideration. Western proposals provided that more than one government would participate and the equipment and technical services would be supplied by private contractors. Also, it made for wiser neutralism to offset the Russian arms deal by preferring Western help on the dam.

Serious negotiations with the West did not begin, however, until mid-November, when the Egyptian Finance Minister, Abdel Moneim Kaissouny, went to Washington for a month of talks with representatives of the US, Britain, and the World Bank. The discussions resulted in a joint undertaking to finance the first stage of the dam with grants and loans. Nasser recalls the offer as the high point in his government's relations with the US. Not with the British. On the very day the Anglo-American assurance was given to Kaissouny, 16 December 1955, the rioting broke out in the cities of Jordan which aborted within a week Macmillan's ham-handed attempt to bring Jordan into the Baghdad Pact in violation of Eden's moratorium.

Tito is believed to have advised Nasser for the sake of neutralism and safety to prefer Western aid for the dam. He made his second visit to Egypt at the turn of the year, having conferred with Dulles in advance of the visit on the Adriatic island of Brioni. In February Eugene Black, president of the World Bank, went to Egypt to negotiate an agreement on the Western offer. Although Black did not eliminate all of Nasser's doubts about conditions attached to the financing, the talks made substantial progress. It was at this time that Nasser's policy got the name "positive neutralism." The journalist Mohammed Hassanein Heikal wrote in *Akhbar al-Yom* that the combination of arms from Russia and aid for the dam from the West was a victory for "positive neutralism."

In Moscow, later in February, the momentous "de-Stalinization" of the Communist world began. Its consequences nearly shook that world to pieces even as they opened a new era of liberalization within the Russian empire and led to easier and fuller relations with the world outside. De-Stalinization was the link, aside from coincidence, between the Suez War and the Hungarian revolt, those two abortive crises in the rival camps of East and West that brought them shudderingly close to World War III in the first week of November. The Kremlin's disavowal of Stalin's legend and methods let loose a wave of discontent and nationalism in the satellite countries that culminated in the Budapest uprising. Nasser's enemies perceived in Russia's troubles that they were entering a period when they could strike at Egypt with minimum risk of a confrontation with Russia.

The Kremlin had begun to abandon Stalin's methods soon after his death on 5 March 1953. Lavrenty Beria, Stalin's sinister confidant and secret-police chief who was himself liquidated sometime between June and December, was made the scapegoat for the admissions of mistakes in the Stalin era by which Moscow opened the way toward renewed relations with Tito's Yugoslavia. It was not until the Twentieth Congress of the Communist Party of the Soviet Union, which met in Moscow from 14 to 25 February 1956, that Khrushchev made de-Stalinization an official policy. He carried it eventually to the point of renaming Stalingrad and removing Stalin's name from other places on the map. Khrushchev waited to make his move until he had been in power a year, summoning the first party congress since Stalin's death in order to provide a suitable forum.

Khrushchev set the themes for the congress on its first day in his lengthy "Report of the Central Committee" of the party. He declared the restoration of "the Leninist principle of collective leadership," which he said had "frequently been violated" in the past. Without naming Stalin, he condemned the "cult of the individual ... and making a particular leader a hero and miracle worker." He delivered his most shattering attack on Stalin in a long speech near the end of the congress, cataloguing the immense crimes of Stalin in graphic detail. The attack profoundly shocked the congress and the delegations of Communist Party leaders from satellite and non-Communist countries throughout the world. The speech has never officially been published. *The New York Times* printed a clandestine text on 5 June 1956 which is generally accepted as at least a generally accurate paraphrase. By that time the speech had been brought home and discussed at party meetings all over the Communist world. It launched a troubled transfer of power from the established Stalinist factions to more liberal leaders, many of whom had themselves been victims of the Stalinist hierarchies.

The Berlin riots of June 1953 had given a foretaste of what might happen when the iron hand of Stalinism was lifted, be it ever so slightly. Latent nationalism in the satellites, ready to burst out against the puppet leadership established in Stalin's day, made the pace and control of de-Stalinization critical problems for the Kremlin and its tutelary regimes in Eastern Europe. The Poznan riots in Poland in June and the sympathetic demonstrations in Hungary that culminated in the October revolt showed how dangerous it was to awaken nationalist hopes. The nationalist yearnings behind these spectacular events began to show even before the Moscow congress ended.

Imre Nagy, who was to lose control of the Hungarian revolt in November and lose his life as a consequence, had already started his comeback against the Stalinists in the party hierarchy. In Poland, Wladyslaw Gomulka was released after five years under detention for "nationalist deviationism." He won control of the new independence movement in the months that followed, obtaining a large measure of freedom from Russian control while preventing the complete break from the Soviet bloc that goaded the Kremlin to destroy Nagy.

A Polish party statement on 6 April attributed Gomulka's arrest in 1951 to "Beria-ism." It said "the revelation of the whole bitter truth about the terrible consequences of the cult of the individual was a profound shock to all Party members." But it warned against the reaction of "excitement or tendency to hysteria shown by some of our Comrades" in "an unhealthy, anarchistic tendency, the loss of the feeling of Party responsibility, and confusion of ideas."

The shock of de-Stalinization and the acknowledgement that different countries could take different roads toward socialism marked the transformation of Stalin's monolithic system of absolute control from Moscow over the whole Communist world into what the Italian Communist leader, Palmiro Togliatti, called a "polycentric" system, in which national Communist governments and parties gained considerable authority and independence but without being allowed to abandon either socialism or the Soviet bloc.

257

In accompaniment to de-Stalinization within the Soviet orbit, Khrushchev officially proclaimed "peaceful coexistence" as the central principle of Russia's relations with the non-Communist world. He declared it to be the only alternative to "the most destructive war in history." Other new principles of Russian foreign policy were the cultivation of links with "uncommitted" countries and recognition of the legitimacy of different forms of transition to socialism in different countries. The last principle, Khrushchev said, was a revival of a precept enunciated by Lenin before the Russian revolution and subsequently neglected. "It is not true that we regard violence and civil war as the only way to remake society," Khrushchev said, adding that since the Bolshevik Revolution "the historical situation has undergone radical changes which make possible a new approach to the question." He singled out for specific approval the different roads to socialism taken by Red China and Yugoslavia and conceded that even parliamentary means could bring socialism to "a number of capitalist and former colonial countries."

Under the new doctrinal aegis of "peaceful coexistence," the Russians pursued a policy of relaxing the tensions between East and West. In 1955 the policy brought the Austrian peace treaty in May, the Summit conference in July, and the return of the Porkkala naval base to Finland in September. In 1956 the Russians under Khrushchev seem to have tried to make coexistence more peaceful than before. In the Middle East itself, although they were now arming Egypt, the Russians went so far toward seeking peace that the Arabs became uneasy.

On 18 April, the day that Khrushchev and Bulganin arrived in England for a lively nine-day visit, the Cominform or Communist Information Bureau announced its own dissolution. The Cominform, successor to the Communist International or Comintern, was created in 1947 to reinforce Stalin's monolithic authority by coordinating and disciplining the Communist parties of the world, whether ruling in the satellite capitals or subserving the Kremlin's purposes in non-Communist countries. In 1948 it expelled Yugoslavia. The dissolution of the Cominform, like the dissolution of the Comintern in 1943, was a conciliatory gesture toward the Western powers, which were Russia's wartime allies against Hitler and her Cold War adversaries afterward. The dissolution of the Cominform was, in addition, an affirmation of the new polycentrism which looked toward "new and useful forms of establishing links and contacts" among the Communist parties commensurate with "the specific national features and conditions of their countries."

In England, where the Russian leaders arrived aboard the Soviet cruiser *Ordzhonikidze*, there were hostile demonstrations in London and other cities included in their tour and a disputatious evening with the leaders of the Laborite Opposition. But the talks that Khrushchev and Bulganin had with Eden and members of the governing Conservative Party were amiable almost to an extreme. When Khrushchev returned to Moscow he told the British Ambassador, Sir William Hayter: "Bulganin can vote Labor if he likes but I'm going to vote Conservative." Three months later, in July, Khrushchev said he felt relations with Britain had improved, adding: "I have great confidence in Eden, I have great confidence in Selwyn Lloyd, and I have great confidence in Butler; I am sure they are all anxious for peace and I think we are beginning to understand each other." Eden, for his part, told a television audience on the night the Russians departed that his talks with them had abated the danger of war and might turn out to be "the beginning of the beginning" toward lasting peace.

Middle Eastern topics struck the few grating notes in the Anglo-Russian talks. They also drew the most significant peace offering from the Russians. Eden and the Russians restated their disagreement over the Baghdad Pact. The most discordant exchange arose from Eden's gratuitously belligerent warning about oil. Khrushchev's annoyance did not prevent his making a peaceable proposal to curb the Arab-Israeli arms race. At a press conference before leaving London on 27 April Khrushchev went through the mendacious diplomatic formality of denying that Russia herself was shipping arms, still supporting the fiction that it was Czechoslovakia. Then he said:

> We would like it if there were no shipments to anybody. Shipments are taking place.... If it were possible to agree in the United Nations or otherwise that these should not take place we would only welcome that and would be prepared to take part in such an undertaking, which would help bring about peaceful conditions in the troubled areas of the world.

It was this statement, prominently featured in the Cairo press, that persuaded Nasser to recognize Red China. Nasser's reasoning was candidly summarized in the Egyptian newspapers on 17 May in the comments published with the news of the recognition. The papers noted that twenty-three governments, including Britain and Israel, had already recognized Red China. *Al-Akhbar* wrote:

> We did not recognize the People's Republic of China and did not vote for her admission to the United Nations and we received nothing in return for this courtesy to the West except conspiracies against the Middle East, meetings held without our presence at which decisions were issued without our knowledge about the future of our part of the world, attempts to convince Russia not to supply us with weapons, and maneuvers to have the UN ban the export of arms to us.... If the UN bans the shipment of arms to us, it will not apply to China unless the UN first recognizes the People's Republic of China.

Nasser told me ten years later that he had feared that Israel would succeed in getting arms despite a UN embargo, as she had done in 1948. "That's why we decided to recognize China," he said. "The only solution was to be in touch with China, which was not a member of the United Nations. This was for us the only source of arms if such an agreement had been made."

Khrushchev could not have foreseen the full chain of reactions to his proposal for a UN arms embargo, which led through Egypt's recognition of Red China to Dulles's renege on Aswan and Nasser's riposte by nationalizing the Canal. But he was undoubtedly aware that the offer would have serious consequences whether the West accepted it or not. The British ambassador in Moscow said of Khrushchev that "as soon as he applied his powerful intelligence and his encyclopedic memory to foreign affairs he mastered them completely." And Eden wrote: "I found Marshal Bulganin and Mr. Khrushchev perfectly capable of upholding their end of the discussion on any subject... without briefs or detailed guidance from any of their advisers....I viewed this performance with respect." Although the Western powers proved unwilling to test Russia's peace-seeking initiatives, the fact that they were made at the conscious risk of disturbing Russia's profitable new friendships with the Arabs is evidence of their sincerity.

Bulganin, at that same London press conference, aroused Arab apprehensions by emphasizing the phrase in the joint communiqué on the Eden-Bulganin-Khrushchev talks stating that both Governments "will support the United Nations in any initiative to secure a peaceful settlement on a mutually acceptable basis of the dispute between the Arab states and Israel." The Kremlin had endorsed the idea of a "mutually acceptable" solution of the Palestine dispute on 17 April in a major policy statement on the Middle East. The phrase re-appeared in the Security Council's draft resolution on the border fighting that flared up with Israel's mortar bombardment of Gaza on 5 April 1956. Arab delegates attacked it on the theory that it would allow Israel to veto any terms of settlement embodying previous UN resolutions on the partition of Palestine and the rights of the refugees. Russia finally reversed her stand and the phrase was deleted from the resolution as passed on 4 June in what Ben-Gurion contemptuously called an "emasculated version."

This concession to Arab sensitivity over Palestine was of small significance compared with the breadth of Russia's diplomatic campaign for peaceful coexistence, particularly in the two areas where Arabs were embroiled, Palestine and Algeria.

Pineau, in his biography of Khrushchev, reports that in 1956 the Russian leader undoubtedly hoped for a peaceful solution that would leave Algeria linked with France, if only to keep the US from replacing French influence there as it was already doing in Tunisia and Morocco. Mollet and Pineau discussed Algeria with the Russians when they visited Moscow in May. Pineau says Khrushchev went as far in expressing sympathy with France as he could without violating Communist dogma and thus risking dangerous criticism from Peking, which was already competing with Moscow for influence in the Third World.

Pineau was impressed both by Khrushchev's sincerity and by his capacity to hold liquor. Khrushchev's ability to drain his glass in toast after toast without apparent effect made Pineau suspect that his glass was not being filled with vodka like the others. Pineau's doubts were removed at a French Embassy reception, where he was able to ensure that Khrushchev got real vodka every time. One evening he tallied thirty-two toasts drunk by Khrushchev.

The visit by the French leaders to Moscow, like that of the Russian leaders to England, was part of an intensive round of traveling that brought the Russian policymakers into personal contact with other heads of state and government after the years of Stalinist isolation. The transition to warmer relations with the non-Communist world was marked on 2 June by the resignation of Foreign Minister Vyachislav Molotov, Stalin's famous spokesman who had stayed on through the post-Stalin changes in the Kremlin. Dmitri Shepilov, editor of *Pravda*, was appointed in his place.

Shepilov, who had talked with Nasser about Russian arms a year earlier, returned to Cairo for the ceremonies attending the completion of the British evacuation from the Suez base. The Russian ambassador had informed Nasser in May of his Government's "lively desire" for the re-establishment of peace in the Middle East through a UN settlement. Shepilov went further. He privately told the Egyptians that Russia would not underwrite a Palestine solution based on Arab demands. In a speech on Evacuation Day, 18 June, he said Russia had "no intention of encouraging the hostile agitation of the peoples of the Arab countries against any of the Western powers."

In Jerusalem, that was the day on which Foreign Minister Sharett walked out of his last cabinet meeting, leaving the field clear for Ben-Gurion and the war faction. War was now merely a matter of time; but this was not yet apparent to the world and the Russians continued to exert their influence, unfortunately on the wrong side of the armistice lines, toward restoring tranquillity. Khrushchev, in an interview published in *al-Ahram* on 1 July, warned the Egyptians that "war between the Arab states and Israel would mean World War III. . . . Be patient, strong, and united," he advised the Arabs, "make every effort to preserve peace in the Near East."

CHAPTER

9

The Pistol

(1820 TO 16 MAY 1956)

The nation which indulges toward another an habitual hatred or an habitual fondness is in some degree a slave.... Sympathy for the favorite nation, facilitating the illusion of an imaginary common interest in cases where no real common interest exists, and infusing into one the enmities of the other, betrays the former into a participation in the quarrels and wars of the latter without adequate inducement or justification.... As avenues to foreign influence in innumerable ways, such attachments are particularly alarming to the truly enlightened and independent patriot. How many opportunities do they afford to tamper with domestic factions, to practice the arts of seduction, to mislead public opinion, to influence or awe the public councils!... Real patriots who may resist the intrigues of the favorite are liable to become suspected and odious, while its tools and dupes usurp the applause and confidence of the people to surrender their interests.

(WASHINGTON, *Farewell Address*)

I know that the Americans are dreadful people to deal with. They cannot make firm promises, but they jolly you along with fair prospects and when you are committed they let you down.

(SIR RONALD LINDSAY, British Ambassador in Washington, 1932)

DULLES PLACED a .38 caliber pistol on the table between himself and Premier Mohammed Naguib when they sat down in Cairo on 11 May 1953 to talk of world affairs. Naguib betrayed momentary surprise until Dulles showed him the silver plate on the butt inscribed: "To General Mohammed Naguib from his friend Dwight D. Eisenhower." There were jokes afterward that this armament too had the strings attached which made the revolutionary junta so wary, for Dulles had said in serious pleasantry as he handed it to Naguib: "This is for keeping the peace, not for war." But it was an appropriate gift from one soldier-statesman to another and the Egyptians hoped it might be a portent of success in their attempts to buy modern military equipment from the US. They hoped in vain. The pistol is to this day the only weapon the US has supplied to Egypt.

To the British, with their garrison beleaguered in the base by guerrillas who called themselves the "Mau Mau of Suez," the pistol was an objectionable symbol of encouragement for Egyptian militancy, not at all in keeping with the loyalty that should prevail between the great English-speaking allies. "I had to ask our ambassador in London to assure Mr. Churchill," Eisenhower wrote in his memoirs, "that presenting one Colt .38 to General Naguib did not presage a flow of planes, tanks, and guns to arm that nation. Winston himself appeared quite relieved." It was the new Eisenhower administration's first contact with a dispute between a traditional European ally and a nation still in transition to full sovereign independence. It gave a foretaste of the awkward dilemmas they were to meet along the way to the terrible rift over Suez three and a half years later.

Dulles's twenty-day trip took him to twelve countries stretching from Libya to India. It was the first official visit to Middle Eastern leaders ever made by an American Secretary of State. At the wartime conferences, where allied leaders met for convenience in Teheran or Cairo to consider global issues, the local host governments were of tertiary importance or less. Dulles's trip signified belatedly the new postwar importance of the Middle East to the US and the reciprocal importance of the US in the Middle East. Oil, Zionism, and the strategic containment of Russia had brought US power into the Middle East in the fading footsteps of war-weakened Britain.

Early in the century of the Pax Britannica, which ended with World War I, the American presence in the Middle East was introduced on a small but durable footing by missionary-educators who established colleges and schools in Constantinople, Beirut, Aleppo, Cairo, and other cities. Many of the Westernizing nationalist leaders of the present generation began their careers in student organizations in these schools.

In World War I American interest in the Near East was not yet sufficient for Washington to declare war on Turkey although Lowell Thomas, on a romantic propaganda mission, drew popular attention to T. E. Lawrence and the Arab revolt in the desert. Nevertheless the twelfth of President Wilson's Fourteen Points, presented to Congress early in 1918 as the US peace program, stated that "the other nationalities which are now under Turkish rule should be assured an undoubted security of life and an absolutely unmolested opportunity of autonomous development."

Oil and Zionism expanded the American presence and American interest in the Arab world after the first World War as containment of Russia did after World War II. Official American support for Zionism eventually proved crucial to the creation of Israel, but it was slow in coming. Secretary of State Lansing, Dulles's uncle, warned President Wilson to resist Zionist pressure for US endorsement of the Balfour Declaration. Wilson's Twelfth Point aroused great hopes of self-determination among the Arabs and Kurds. Both were swiftly disappointed. Wilson's ideal was incompatible with the Balfour Declaration and with British interests in Iraq and Persia. Wilson was not much interested in Zionism but in March 1919, four months after the end of the war, he expressed absent-minded approval of laying "the foundations of a Jewish Commonwealth" in Palestine. In September 1922 President Harding signed a joint resolution of both Houses of Congress approving the Balfour Declaration. The resolution was a mark of Zionism's growing influence in domestic US politics.

That influence was to grow as Jewish immigrants from Central and Eastern Europe, where Zionism was born, entered the main stream of life in the big American cities that held the balance of power in national politics. As William Polk wrote after years of scholarship and reflection, "the Palestine problem has involved, more than any other of the overseas endeavors of the United States, an extension of domestic American politics." The State Department, whose cold counsels could not prevail against the heat of politics, remained convinced that support for Zionism did little good and much damage to larger national interests. In the US as in Britain, Zionism won its victories in political places like the White House and Number 10 Downing Street and not among career professionals in the civil and foreign services.

Oil seemed to professional diplomats to be an important national interest in contrast to Zionism, whose emotional, idealistic partisans were constantly at odds with the Arab-oriented oil men. The rich new fields in the Middle East looked particularly important in the years immediately after World War I, when US oil reserves were thought to be nearing exhaustion.

As the Ottoman provinces came under British and French rule, the State Department was quick to demand the same "open door" policy in the Near East that had become a tradition in the Far East. Early in 1920 US Ambassador John W. Davis took up with Lord Curzon, the Foreign Secretary, "matters that had created the unfortunate impression in the minds of the American public that the Authorities of His Majesty's Government in the occupied region had given advantage to British oil interests which were not accorded to American Companies." He said the US stood on the general principle that "any Alien territory which should be acquired . . . must be held and governed in such a way as to assure equal treatment in law and in fact to the commerce of all nations."

American diplomacy asserted equal rights for American commerce but it was content to leave the Middle East as a British sphere of influence, eschewing strategic and political responsibilities. This view persisted until well after World War II. For example, the US organized the immense wartime supply route to Russia known as the Persian Gulf Command, but shut it down after the war without keeping so much as a foothold there. Britain, exhausted and impoverished by the war, was soon obliged to plead that she did not have the military and economic resources to meet Cold War requirements in her sphere of influence. By 1947, British weakness in the face of Russian threats to Greece and Turkey obliged Washington to take over the British commitments there. The tradition of avoiding entangling alliances, handed down intact by President Washington's first thirty successors, was broken by the thirty-first.

On 12 March 1947 President Truman asked a joint session of Congress to provide $400 million to aid Greece and Turkey and to authorize sending military advisers to both countries. Enunciating the new doctrine that self-interest required the US to defend freedom everywhere, he said: "This is no more than a frank recognition that totalitarian regimes imposed upon free peoples, by direct or indirect aggression, undermine the foundations of international peace and hence the security of the United States." Isolationism was dead. A new era of global responsibilities, soon to be embodied in the NATO and SEATO pacts, made obsolete Washington's farewell advice: "It is our true policy to steer clear of permanent alliances with any portion of the foreign world . . . "

Truman had already played a leading role a year earlier in forcing Russia to withdraw from Northern Iran, but he made no continuing commitment there. The Truman Doctrine was promulgated when Russia's postwar expansionism continued to threaten the Middle East with the fate of Eastern Europe. Moscow supported a Communist rebellion in Greece and pressed Turkey to give up both territory and control of the Black Sea straits. Russian pressure brought about the very US intervention in the Middle East that it had hoped to preclude. In like manner Western pressure for a Middle East defense organization brought about, eight years later, the very Russian intrusion that it had sought to preclude.

By the end of World War II Zionism's center of gravity had shifted from London to New York. This was due to a combination of factors: the deepening estrangement between Zionist leadership and successive British governments over Jewish immigration into Palestine; Ben-Gurion's displacement of the Anglophile Weizmann at the summit of Zionist leadership; the growth of the US Jewish community in numbers, wealth, and organizational activity; the relative freedom of New York as a Zionist meeting place from the inconveniences of war; the emergence of the United States as the leader of the Western world; and the location in the New York area of UN headquarters, where vital diplomatic victories had to be won in the Zionist struggle for statehood.

The Nazi holocaust had by this time given Zionism a galvanic sense of urgency complemented by guilt-stricken sympathy among non-Jews. It was an accident of history, albeit a convenient one, that the demands of the Zionists would be satisfied only at the direct expense of the Palestinians. The US was by no means anti-Arab but Zionism and the plight of the surviving Jewish displaced persons in Europe took precedence in American postwar Middle East policy over all other interests in the Arab world whether they were Palestinian, British, or even American national interests. They took precedence also over simple justice.

In broad terms, US policy toward Zionism followed the recommendations brought back to President Truman in August 1945 by Earl G. Harrison from a mission to investigate the problem of displaced persons in Europe, particularly the Jews still confined in camps in Germany and Austria. Harrison noted that his report was made "on a purely humanitarian basis with no reference to ideological or political considerations so far as Palestine is concerned." Nor, one might add, humanitarian considerations for the Arab majority there. He concluded that "the main solution, in many ways the only real solution, of the problem lies in the quick evacuation of all nonrepatriable Jews in Germany and Austria, who wish it, to Palestine.... The civilized world owes it to this handful of survivors to provide them with a home where they can again settle down and begin to live as human beings." Harrison gave a twist to the knife in the conscience of Western Christendom by suggesting that the Germans, seeing the Jews remain in camps under Allied instead of SS guards, might suppose "that we are following or at least condoning Nazi policy."

The Palestine Arabs were rendered desperate by the tide of Jewish immigrants, themselves desperate, which was swamping them toward minority status in their own native land. They violently denied any right of God, Lord Balfour, or the UN to give their home or any part of it to strangers. Realizing that the forces carrying the tide of Jews into Palestine were beyond their strength, the Palestine Arabs welcomed the help of armies from the surrounding Arab states. They lost their battle and in defeat they watched the creation of a Jewish State incorporating Arab cities and farms and embodying theocratic laws that gave the newest Jewish immigrants a status more privileged than Arabs who traced their local lineage back for thousands of years.

The world's recompense for the sufferings of the Jews was rank injustice to the Palestinians. A million of them were made displaced persons by and for the benefit of the displaced Jews of Europe. Humiliation was added to injustice when Arab armies were beaten back by the soldiers of Zion. The bitterness of the defeat was turned in many directions, inwardly against Arab leaders by revolution and assassination and outwardly in resentment and suspicion against the powers that supported Zionism, including Russia as well as the West. The greatest resentment was directed against Britain and America. Britain, whose presence remained in many Arab countries, had admitted the Jews to Palestine in the first place. And America had eventually outdone even Britain in giving massive and ardent support to Zionism.

President Truman accorded diplomatic recognition to the intrinsically expansionist State of Israel within hours of its proclamation by Ben-Gurion on 14 May 1948. "The State of Israel will be open for Jewish immigration and for the ingathering of the exiles . . . and will take steps to bring about the economic union of the whole of Eretz Israel," Ben-Gurion proclaimed. Within seven months his soldiers had enlarged Israel's territorial allotment by one-third. Truman's recognition and support of such a government were regarded as a calculated bid for the Jewish vote in the presidential election that year. The first US ambassador to Israel, James G. McDonald, was a passionate Zionist who relished the Israelis' fond joke of calling him their ambassador to the US. Extraordinary tax allowances were given to Zionist fund-raising. Private and government financial aid flowed to Israel from the US, largely to finance Jewish immigration and settlement, while no comparable effort was made to induce Israel to let the Palestinian refugees return to their homes. America's humanitarianism seemed not to encompass Arabs.

On 24 April 1950, nearly two years after Israel was established, Jordan, with Britain's blessing, annexed the part of Palestine remaining in Arab hands along the West Bank of the Jordan River. The US took the lead in guaranteeing the new *status quo* by issuing with Britain and France the Tripartite Declaration of 25 May 1950. The three powers "declared their opposition to the development of an arms race between the Arab states and Israel" but they acknowledged the need of "a certain level of armed forces for the purposes of assuring their internal security and their legitimate self-defense and to permit them to play their part in the defense of the area as a whole." They said that arms requests would be considered in the light of those principles and that they would permit arms shipments from their countries only to those Middle Eastern countries giving assurances that they intended no act of aggression against any other state.

Having dealt with the arms issue, the three powers declared "their unalterable opposition to the use of force or threat of force in that area" and added: "The three Governments, should they find that any of these states was preparing to violate frontiers or armistice lines, would, consistently with their obligations as members of the United Nations, immediately take action, both within and outside the United Nations, to prevent such violation."

Rarely has so solemn a pledge by great powers been so thoroughly dishonored. Britain and France dismissed it as a dead letter in 1956, which was not surprising because they themselves, in collusion with Israel, were at the time carefully and secretly "preparing to violate frontiers or armistice lines." The US alone constantly maintained the Declaration as a basic factor in its Middle East policy but took no action to honor it in the Suez War of 1967 when Israel violated all her Arab frontiers except Lebanon's.

Such subsequent history makes Israeli and Arab reservations about the Declaration appear more realistic than the Declaration itself. They did not actually reject it. Small and weak powers do not lightly offend great powers.

Ben-Gurion told the Knesset on 31 May 1950 that the sentiments of the Declaration were all very laudable but that Israel "views its existence, security, and future as dependent primarily on its own efforts"; that "the policy of Israel is formulated only by the government of Israel"; that any Arab assurances of nonaggression were worthless, and that the three powers, to Israel's "astonishment and concern," had one-sidedly armed the Arabs. At this time Israel's military strength was responsibly estimated to equal, and her air strength to be double that of all the Arabs combined. Britain officially regarded Israel's armed preponderance as a major obstacle toward any peace settlement because it undergirded Israel's resistance to compromise.

The Arabs were slower to reply and less blunt. They discussed the Declaration at an Arab League meeting and issued a joint statement on 21 June 1950. Like Ben-Gurion's statement, it lauded the motives of the three powers but served notice that the Declaration was not acceptable as a basis for infringements on their sovereignty. "It goes without saying," they said, "that the level of armed forces maintained by every state . . . is a matter that can only be estimated by the state concerned. . . . The Arab states can only affirm once again that, despite their anxiety for peace, they cannot approve any action that would harm their sovereignty and their independence."

The next major US initiative in the Middle East, the proposal for a Middle East Defense Organization in the fall of 1951, was less successful than the Tripartite Declaration and a good deal more unwelcome to the Arabs. The Korean War had raised Western anxieties about the defense of the Middle East and the proposal was aimed chiefly at keeping the British Suez base, which had been so important in World War II, available to the allies. The US obtained the association of Turkey in its proposal as well as Britain and France. Britain presented the proposal to Egypt. Egypt rudely rejected it amid a series of anti-British actions in that last disordered autumn of the monarchy. Nasser, although originally more cooperative with the West than the postwar governments of the monarchy, ultimately rejected the concept when it reappeared in the form of the Baghdad Pact.

When the Republican Administration under Eisenhower took office in January 1953, the US was well on its way to displacing Britain as the paramount foreign influence in the Middle East, albeit unwillingly. Truman and the Democrats had bequeathed a legacy of Arab resentment over the fate of Palestine but this handicap was partly offset by the Arab hope for better treatment at the hands of the new administration.

In Egypt, where the revolution was still in its first year, Palestine did not become a major preoccupation of either the Government or the public until after the Gaza Raid, although the Egyptians went through the motions of Arab solidarity on the issue. Egypt's major objective was to rid itself of the British occupation. It hoped the US would use its influence toward this end without participating directly in the Anglo-Egyptian quarrel.

Israel was as suspicious of the new administration as the Arabs were hopeful. All of the countries of the region, Israel even more so than the Arabs, put on an assertively nationalistic face for Dulles's visit. They were instinctively fearful that their recently won sovereignty might be bruised by contact with the new colossus of the West, whose own assumption of world-wide responsibilities had somewhat diluted its traditional anticolonialism.

Dulles began formulating an improved US policy on the Middle East as soon as he took office in January 1953. Byroade, then the Assistant Secretary in charge of the Middle East, gave Dulles a memorandum outlining a proposed new US policy at the end of Dulles's first week as Secretary. Byroade, a Democrat brought into the State Department from the Army by Truman, stayed on in the new administration in the hope that it would rectify the Truman Administration's errors in the Middle East. Dulles took Byroade's memorandum with him at the end of January on a ten-day tour of European capitals.

The Cold War confrontation with Stalinism in Europe and the shooting war with Stalinism in Korea limited Middle Eastern affairs to small consequence in the public mind. Few Americans in 1953 could have told the difference between the Arab League and the Arab Legion, or whether Iraq was a misprint for Iran or what. Most people were ignorant of the distinction between Palestine and Israel and they vaguely assumed that it had always been ethnically Jewish in any case.

Dulles's inclusion of Middle Eastern questions on his European tour signified not only his determination to give the Middle East greater attention in US policy but also his realization that taking an active hand there would strain US relations with traditional European allies, particularly Britain, whose paramountcy in the Middle East was regrettably waning.

Dulles's private memorandum of conclusions on the trip he made to the Middle East three months later shows shrewd perceptiveness, blunt logic, good intentions, and cautious hope. The memorandum illuminates Dulles's approach to the crises that were soon to shift the attention of the world from Europe and the Far East to the Middle East.

Dulles was himself laggard in responding to the changed circumstances brought about by the de-Stalinization of Russia. Nevertheless, he recognized that Middle Easterners did not share his Cold War preoccupations. He noted that "almost the entire area is caught in a fanatical revolutionary spirit that causes countries to magnify their immediate problems and depreciate the Soviet threat." He attributed this to political disputes, such as those between Egypt and Britain and between the Arabs and Israel, which "serve to produce situations of intense Xenophobia and distrust of the West," and to the inability of Middle Eastern governments to fulfill the rising economic and social demands of the "awakening" masses.

"In this situation," he continued, "the position of the Western powers has deteriorated to the point where they are not at present serving as factors of stability.... The United States position also is not good, and the loss of respect for the United States varies almost directly with the nearness of the respective Arab states to Israel. The Israeli factor, and the association of the US in the minds of the people of the area with French and British colonial and imperialistic policies, are millstones around our neck."

Dulles said the US must convince the Arabs of its independent approach to problems of colonialism. That meant pressing the French and British toward relinquishing their tutelary powers while warning the Arabs of the need for orderly evolution to avoid allowing the Kremlin to use their nationalism for its own purposes. Dulles envisioned a "delicate" middle role for the US in Britain's Middle Eastern dilemmas. The application of this precept in the Suez crisis three years later accounted for a caginess on the part of Dulles that frequently baffled not only the British and the Egyptians but his own countrymen. As he said in 1953: "Efforts by the US, which by natural inclination and self-interest finds itself somewhat in the middle between the British and Near Eastern positions, are increasingly resented by the British." Dulles echoed this observation in a press conference a month before the Suez war. Eden remembered the echo years later as "savage."

Dulles perceived that "the Near East wavers between outright neutralism in the East-West struggle and the desire (but also the fear) of being protected by the West." Regional defense of the Middle East, he noted, consisted of nothing more than a relatively strong Turkish flank. But he recognized that the Arabs would not join Western defensive arrangements, which he sensibly dismissed for the time being as "concepts that have no reality."

This realization was why the US stubbornly resisted British pressure to join the Baghdad Pact. Eden concocted the pact with Nuri behind Dulles's back and against American warnings that were transmitted privately whenever preparations for the pact came to Washington's attention. Britain's main objective was to lay a foundation in Iraq to which she could shift her military and political footing in the Middle East after giving up the Suez base in Egypt. By encouraging Nuri and the Turks to take the lead, Britain could claim that the pact fitted the prescription Dulles gave in his 1 June 1953 broadcast—that any such collective security system "should be designed and grow from within out of a sense of common destiny and common danger."

This was not an absolute prohibition of a British initiative in Iraq any more than US statements in 1956 opposing the use of force over Suez were an absolute prohibition. But in both cases the US served notice that its allies would be proceeding at their own risk. In both cases Eden took his chance, like a quail dog who runs a rabbit in the hope that his master, however much angered, will assent when presented with a *fait accompli*. In both cases he was wrong. The fact that he was let off lightly on the Baghdad Pact, however, may have encouraged his second and greater violation at Suez of the restraints that should bind the weaker member of an alliance to refrain from independent actions that compromise the stronger member.

When Byroade and Dulles got the news that Iraq and Turkey had formed the nucleus of the pact they suspected that Britain was behind it. They agreed that it was not a good thing but decided that the US, which already had bilateral military aid agreements with both Iraq and Turkey, should not oppose it.

273

Little more than a month later, on 3 April, the day before the House of Commons approved Britain's adherence to the pact, the Americans told the British that the US would not join the pact until the inter-Arab and Arab-Israeli conflicts in the Middle East had cooled off. The US sent observers to pact meetings but in 1968, ten years after Iraq itself had abandoned the pact in the wake of revolution, the US association was still limited to representation on its military and political committees.

Eden, as unrepentant over the Baghdad Pact as he was over Suez, wrote more in anger than in truth in his memoirs:

Having played a leading part to inspire the project, the United States Government held back while Britain alone of the Western powers joined it. Worse still, they tried to take credit for this attitude in capitals like Cairo, which were hostile to the Pact. . . . Nobody credited the involved pretexts produced by the United States Government for not joining . . .

In fact, far from trying "to inspire the project," Dulles's broadcast on his Middle East trip was intended to allay the Arab and Israeli fears that had been aroused by the abortive effort in 1951 to create a Middle East Defense Organization on the NATO pattern. Byroade had begun drafting the speech even before the trip, on which he accompanied Dulles, and they discussed it during the trip on the Greek island of Prinkypo. Despite their contrary intentions, both Dulles and Byroade were blamed by the Arabs for what was Eden's pact-making, not their own. The timing of the pact was particularly embarrassing for Byroade, whom the Arabs regarded as its architect, for it was launched three days before he arrived in Cairo on 27 February 1955 to take up his new assignment as US Ambassador. The shock of the Gaza Raid the next day, linked as it was in Egyptian suspicions to the Baghdad Pact, worsened Byroade's predicament and prolonged his embarrassment.

Nasser had emphasized and re-emphasized, both in public statements and in private discussions, that the concessions he had made in the Anglo-Egyptian Suez evacuation agreement were as far as he could go for the time being in coordinating regional defense with the West. He said he believed as the West did that the only external threat was from Russia but that it would be suicidal for his government to flout the people's hatred of pacts with foreigners. The attempt on his life showed what he was talking about. These dangers give a cynical cast to Eden's use of Nuri, whose acquiescence in return for British aid led him and his king to the fate Nasser had narrowly avoided. The end of Nuri in July 1958 spelled the end of the Baghdad Pact because Iraq withdrew, the staff had to leave Baghdad, and the Baghdad-less pact changed its name to the Central Treaty Organization, CENTO for short. It cost the West more good will in Egypt, where it counted most, than it could possibly have gained in the client-states, Iraq and Jordan. But in fact, it also lost good will there. The cost in good will may be measured by the fact that the effort to bring Jordan in nearly cost King Hussein his throne just as Iraq's membership cost his cousin, King Faisal, both his throne and his life.

Eventually the pact lost significance even for the non-Arab client-states that remained in it. Pakistan made friends with Red China in the 1960s and Iran bought arms from Russia. The pact was a failure from the beginning but it was Eden's failure, not Dulles's. Dulles, thinking in wide terms of Western advantage, foresaw it as a net loss but had to compromise when it came into being. Eden took the narrow view, seeking British rather than Western advantage. He used the pact to strengthen British influence where he thought he could, in Iraq and Jordan, regardless of the consequences in Egypt, where he had to write off British influence in any case. Glubb in Jordan and Nuri and Faisal in Iraq paid for Eden's failure.

Dulles's conclusions concerning aid following his Middle East trip were that economic aid should be increased and given a sharper political application by focusing, for example, on "water development which will alleviate certain specific problems such as resettlement of refugees." In the same vein, he concluded, "It is also in our interest to provide a small amount of military equipment to certain selected states. Such military assistance would be utilized for purposes of internal security, of strengthening defense of the area and obtaining political advantage." The Eisenhower administration, however much it denied that there were political strings attached to US aid, regarded such strings as an essential justification of it. In this respect Dulles and Eisenhower added an element of national self-interest to the concept of Truman's Point Four. Point Four aid commenced in 1949 as "a bold new program for making the benefits of our scientific advances and industrial progress available for the improvement and growth of underdeveloped areas."

From the beginning of his secretaryship, peace between Israel and the Arabs was a major political objective for Dulles as well as a personal ambition. As a first step he tried on his trip to establish a position of impartiality, privately in his talks with leaders and publicly in his broadcast report to the nation on 1 June 1953. "The United States should seek to allay the deep resentment against it that has resulted from the creation of Israel," he said. "In the past we had good relations with the Arab peoples. . . . Today the Arab peoples . . . are more fearful of Zionism than of communism, and they fear lest the United States become the backer of expansionist Zionism. . . . The leaders in Israel themselves agreed with us that United States policies should be impartial so as to win not only the respect and regard of the Israeli but also the Arab peoples. . . . Israel should become part of the Near East community and cease to look upon itself, or be looked upon by others, as alien to this community. This is possible. To achieve it will require concessions on the part of both sides."

Israel, certain that any change from Truman's policies would be for the worse, vehemently opposed any concessions, particularly of conquered territory. She demanded an explanation. Whatever lip service Israel's leaders had paid to US impartiality in their talks with Dulles, they didn't like it because it was a loss for themselves and a gain for the Arabs in Washington's scale of priorities.

Israel's mood was well expressed immediately after Dulles's visit by the front-page columnist of the *Jerusalem Post*, the governing Mapai party's English-language newspaper. With surly sarcasm he expressed relief that Israel was still intact after Dulles's visit. Although it was Dulles who wrote the paragraph in the 1952 platform committing the Republican Administration to support Israel's independence, Dulles was tainted with anti-Semitism in the minds of many Zionists as a result of campaign smears from partisans of Herbert H. Lehmann, who won a New York Senate seat from Dulles in 1949.

The US shift toward impartiality on Palestine provoked increasing militancy in Israel, manifested partly in a stepped-up policy of retaliation on the frontiers. The first Israeli raid to inflict a death toll running into two figures was 28 August 1953, on the refugee camp at al-Bureig in the Gaza Strip, leaving 20 dead and 62 wounded. In the eighteen months between the Bureig and Gaza raids, the Israelis concentrated their strikes mainly against Jordan, beginning with the grisly all-night foray into Qibya on 14 October 1953, when 66 Arabs were killed by gunfire and dynamite, three–quarters of them women and children.

The Qibya raid not only shocked the world into awareness of Israel's reprisal policy but it also ensured a bad beginning for the first major peace effort of the Eisenhower Administration. At about the hour of Qibya's destruction the White House announced that Eric Johnston would go to the Middle East as President Eisenhower's personal ambassador to discuss the regional development of the Jordan River. The announcement emphasized that the project would employ many Arab refugees and contribute toward stability.

Israel had already begun excavations on 2 September on her own project to divert the Jordan River for the benefit of future agriculture and industry in the Negev. She was not sorry to have hurt Johnston's chances of obtaining Arab cooperation with the US plan, which would set international controls over Israel's use of the river.

The far-seeing Zionist leader Chaim Weizmann had tried in 1920 to bring the entire Jordan and Litani river systems within reach of the future Jewish State. "Your Lordship, I am sure, realises the enormous importance of the Litani to Palestine," he wrote to the Foreign Secretary. "Even if the whole of the Jordan and the Yarmuk are included in Palestine, it has insufficient water for its needs." The Litani remains in Lebanon, so far, and the Yarmuk in Jordan, but Weizmann did persuade the British to include most of the Jordan river system in Palestine by such curious devices as drawing the border of Syria ten yards back from the shore of the Sea of Galilee. The usual practice is to draw frontier lines down the center of inland watercourses that serve as natural boundaries.

Control of the Jordan's water was one of Israel's war aims in 1948. The following year she drew up her own plan to utilize the river. She completed the project in 1964 after the US forced a long suspension of work. The Arabs then threatened to divert the Syrian headwaters of the Jordan. Israel precluded this possibility in 1967 with the conquest of southwestern Syria. In 1953, as in 1948 and 1967, Israel's attachment to her own plans for the development of the Jordan River was strong enough, not only to make her willing to fight the Arabs for it but also to lead her to defy the UN and the US.

Washington had pinned great hopes on the Johnston plan as the beginning of a quest for ultimate peace through "a step by step reduction of tension." The UN, on both trucial and legal grounds, had ordered Israel to halt its unilateral diversion of the river, to which both Syria and Jordan had riparian rights. Despite armed clashes with the Syrians at the diversion site in the Israeli-Syrian demilitarized zone, Israeli earth movers worked around the clock, using floodlights at night.

Israel ignored US requests to stop the work until Dulles announced on 20 October 1953 that the administration had suspended economic aid to Israel. When Israel announced an indefinite cessation of the project on 28 October and promised to cooperate with the Security Council, Dulles immediately allocated $26 million in resumed aid to Israel.

Johnston pursued his mission for two years, until the Israeli raid on Syria in December 1955 annihilated the very wreckage of his work. The mission was hopeless from the outset. Israel wanted Johnston to fail so she would have a free hand on the Jordan but she did not dare boycott Johnston for fear of US anger. The Arabs wanted the mission to go on and on but they did not dare reach agreement for fear of refugee reaction. The realistic Egyptians, despite the resumption of Israeli raids in 1955, repeatedly earned Johnston's frank gratitude by persuading the Syrians and Jordanians to remain at the negotiating table. But with one side opposed to agreement and the other afraid of it, Johnston's mission was foredoomed to futility. The wonder is that it lasted so long.

Byroade reasserted the Eisenhower administration's policy of impartiality between Israel and the Arabs in his two speeches in the spring of 1954, a period of obsessive Israeli violence against Jordan. On 9 April he identified the three pillars of US policy as: 1) the people, no longer primarily the Israelis but all of the region's "65 million souls"; 2) strategy, quoting President Eisenhower as saying "there is no more strategically important area in the world"; and 3) oil, without which "the industries of our allies would be paralyzed and our own would be overworked." In an allusion to Zionist "special groups," he said the US would shape and conduct its policy "to represent the interests of the majority of our people where vital issues affecting our own security are concerned." It was in this speech that he advised Israel to "drop the attitude of the conqueror and ... make your deeds correspond to your frequent utterance of the desire for peace."

Israel's reaction prompted him to say on 1 May:

We see no basis in our acts to justify her fear that her legitimate interests are placed in jeopardy by United States concern over the area as a whole.... When we ask the Arab States to accept the existence of the State of Israel and refrain from hostile acts toward her, it seems only fair to me that they should have the right to know, with far greater assurances than have ever been given them, the magnitude of this new State. They look upon it as a product of expansionist Zionism.... I believe the Arab world today believes that the United States would not allow an attack by them upon Israel with the purpose of driving her into the sea. I also believe, however, that in general the Arab people are not convinced that the opposite is true—and that they question our ability to fulfill our obligations in opposing aggression under the Tripartite Declarations of 1950.

US connivance at Israel's conquests in 1967 justified the Arab doubts.

Egypt was not worried about Israel expansionism at the time Byroade spoke. It was not until after the Gaza Raid and Ben-Gurion's return to relentless activism that Egypt began to fear for her own safety. Nasser felt impelled by a new sense of danger to commit Egypt more earnestly to the Arab cause against Israel and to seek safety in promoting Arab unity. Previously he had paid lip service to these policies. He continued the monarchy's policy of participation in such Arab League activities as the boycott and partial blockade against Israel, but with little vigor. The Egyptian junta was much more lax than the monarchy in these measures although it could not actually drop any existing anti-Israel policy. Palestine and pan-Arabism became pillars of Egyptian policy, along with positive neutralism, only in reaction to Ben-Gurion's militant pressure. Until the Gaza Raid, Nasser had been content to leave the Palestine issue aside in his relations with the US, refusing to allow Washington's special favors to Israel to become a bone of contention.

"After the Suez settlement, there is nothing standing in the way of our good relations with the West," Nasser told me after initialing the *Heads of Agreement*. "But this hammering, hammering, hammering for pacts will only keep alive the old suspicions in the minds of the people—and the Communists know well how to exploit these suspicions. It is a matter of group psychology with deep roots and until the Arabs realize that there is no longer any hidden domination or control in pacts of that sort, any pressure to obtain them will be dangerously premature.

"Where the history of relations between two groups [the Arabs and the West] has been notable for deceit and lack of confidence, suspicion dies hard on the weaker side. You Americans do not realize this feeling because you have been independent throughout modern history.

"With the passage of time, people will learn to think strategically and distinguish clearly between their friends and their enemies. They will learn to ask the question: 'If there is to be aggression, will it be the West or the Communist powers who will attack us and occupy our land?' It is clear that any aggressor will come from the other side—the Communist world. Western interests—Arab oil and friendship—are intact now and only the Russians stand to gain by aggression in the Middle East.

"The next step will be when the people understand that they cannot stand alone against an attack by a major power. Then it will be the time for pacts because they will seek the help of those major powers they recognize as friends."

The next step was never made. Nasser tried to base his international policy on solidarity with the US but found that he could not. As Senator Fulbright said after an exhaustive study in 1957:

I have been impressed with the difficulty of determining what our policy was in the Middle East during these last three or four years. I am unable to find any consistent theme or principle involved in our attitude toward Egypt. At one moment we seemed to encourage Nasser and at another to thwart him without any compelling reason for such shifts being evident, at least to me. Such rapid changes of attitudes were, I am sure, confusing to our allies and friends as well as to our enemies.

One of the persistent blind spots in Washington's view of Egypt was its inability to take into account the limitations which Nasser's extremist opposition imposed on his freedom of action. Ironically, the State Department and the

White House, having been bullied into semiparalysis by Senator Joe McCarthy from 1951 to 1954, should have understood only too well the effects of an extremist opposition.

In the first two years of the revolution Egypt's main demand on Washington was for sympathy in the struggle to end Britain's occupation of the Suez base. Egypt wanted the sympathy to be expressed in influence on the British but strictly without direct US participation in any Suez negotiations. The junta also sought arms from the US, beginning in the last six months of the Truman Administration, and economic aid for internal development projects, chiefly the High Dam at Aswan. US Ambassador Jefferson Caffery satisfied Egypt's hopes in those years by playing a vital sidelines role in the Anglo-Egyptian dispute. While influencing Britain toward a Suez settlement, the US applied inducements to Egypt too by making arms and economic aid contingent on an Anglo-Egyptian agreement.

It was not the Arab-Israeli dispute that first made arms a bone of contention between Cairo and Washington but the disputatious rivalry between Nasser's Egypt and Nuri's Iraq. When Nuri, seeking wider Western backing for his regime, accepted US conditions for obtaining arms in April 1954, Nasser was angered because he felt that Nuri had all but ruined the chance of any other Arab country getting US arms without accepting the same conditions.

Nasser objected to the conditions, required by the US Mutual Security Act, on the grounds that they would look to extremists like subservience to the West. Nasser's fears were allayed when Eisenhower promised on 15 July 1954 that "simultaneously" with the signing of an Anglo-Egyptian agreement on Suez the US would enter into "firm commitments" with Egypt to strengthen the Egyptian armed forces. But no US arms were ever supplied. The recollections of both Nasser and Eisenhower form complementary parts of a picture of US conduct that was far from straightforward.

US-Egyptian arms negotiations began shortly after the overthrow of the monarchy in July 1952. William C. Foster, then Deputy Secretary of Defense, went to Cairo in the fall. "We had lunch together," Nasser recalls, "and I talked with him about the question of arms. And I told him that this was a military revolution, that the first need for military people will be to have arms, and that we were willing to get arms from the United States. I talked with him and we reached agreement. Then we sent a mission [to Washington] with Aly Sabry.

"They asked us to accept the Mutual Security Pact. We refused. Then they raised the question of American officers, a Military Advisory Group. Again we refused. Then they said that if we don't agree to the Mutual Security Pact, we must pay. We said we were ready to pay in Egyptian money in installments and they agreed. Then suddenly they changed their mind and they refused. And Aly Sabry returned. This was the first story."

The end of the first story has been told in detail by Brigadier General Abdel Hamid Ghaleb, Egyptian military attaché in Washington at the time and a member of Sabry's mission. Agreement in principle was reached on a list of arms worth $10 million. Before signing, an American official asked for time to prepare a fresh true copy of the list, which contained so many deletions and additions as to be almost illegible. It was to be ready for signing at 4 P.M. the next day. But shortly before the appointed hour a State Department official telephoned Ghaleb that complications had arisen. "Is the list ready?" Ghaleb asked. "Shall I come for it?" But the State Department man blandly put him off, saying, "We are always glad to see you any time you call on us here. And we hope we can always maintain the good relations we have enjoyed in the past."

Egypt and the US did conclude a cash-reimbursable agreement on 10 December 1952 under which the Egyptians bought about $1 million worth of army supplies, excluding weapons and ammunition, in three years. Israel made similar purchases under a similar agreement signed on 27 February 1952.

But as for weapons that would augment Egyptian firepower, the Anglo-Egyptian Suez evacuation dispute shut off virtually all Egyptian purchases from 1951 until Britain lifted her own embargo on 30 August 1954, a month after initialing the preliminary *Heads of Agreement* on evacuating the Suez base. Egypt resumed limited purchases from her traditional British suppliers. She looked forward to additional purchases from the US, in fulfillment of Eisenhower's promise, after the final signing of the Suez Evacuation agreement on 19 October 1954. But Egypt felt no sense of urgency and did not press the matter in Washington until after the Gaza Raid.

"The second story was in '55 . . . shortly after Gaza," Nasser says. "I asked Mr. Byroade about arms. We asked him about tanks, and we asked him about some bombers. They agreed to give us some tanks, [and] some B-17s, old bombers. But there was an obstacle—paying cash—$29 million. . . . We said we cannot pay $29 million in cash. And everything stopped. Then we discussed the idea of asking the Soviets."

These were the arms that Eisenhower described at the time as "peanuts." In his memoirs, nearly a decade later, he wrote: "Apparently alarmed over the ferocity of an Israeli reprisal raid in the Gaza Strip Nasser requested $27 million worth of arms. Our State Department, confident that he was short of money, informed him that payment would be expected in cash rather than barter. . . ." Nasser's "threats" in June to turn to the Russians "sounded suspiciously like blackmail," Eisenhower wrote, but he conceded that hindsight may show this interpretation to have been "unrealistic."

In June Britain delivered a consignment of arms, including several Centurion tanks, which had been ordered two years before the revolution. It was far short of what Nasser considered Egypt's minimum requirements.

As the summer passed, the US not only ignored Nasser's communications on arms but planned to dump surplus American cotton on the world markets. This would cripple Nasser's hope of selling Egypt's own growing surplus in the West and weaken its value in barter with the East. But Agriculture Secretary Ezra Taft Benson wanted to discourage foreign cotton growing at the same time as reducing the American surplus. Egypt was particularly vulnerable. The junta inherited a cotton stockpile swollen by almost the entire 1951/52 crop, which remained unsold because King Farouk sustained artificially high prices to save two favored cotton brokers who had tried, with palace support, to corner the cotton market during the Korean War. Benson dumped a million bales of US Government-owned cotton on the world market at cut rates after winning Eisenhower's support against Dulles's objections that the move would accelerate Middle Eastern neutralism and jeopardize US oil interests.

Nevertheless, Nasser clung for several months to the hope that Washington would relent. He did not sign his arms agreement with the Russians until after repeated additional humiliations at the hands of Israeli raiders made his officers restive. By then he had lost hope not only of getting arms from the US but also of getting a conclusive straightforward answer from Washington. "We have had nothing from the United States except discussions and promises," Nasser told Tom Little of the British-owned Arab News Agency. "They never refuse us arms but we never get them." Nasser's preference for Western arms was such that he would have settled for less and paid more until the day he abandoned hope of getting even so much as a straight answer.

Dulles had spoken publicly of the Egyptian-Russian arms negotiations a month before the deal was announced, but he did not take the talks as seriously as his Central Intelligence Agency advisers thought he should. At one point he insisted to them that Russia didn't have surplus arms to sell to Egypt. In addition to Byroade's report to the State Department on 9 June, Dulles received a two-page memorandum from the CIA early in August reporting somewhat prematurely that the arms deal was a solid fact. He dismissed it as impossible, declaring abruptly that it was "contrary to the Spirit of Geneva," a reference to the Summit Conference the previous month.

The fact that Dulles's brother, Allen Welsh Dulles, was head of the Central Intelligence Agency during Dulles's Secretaryship of State contributed to particularly close cooperation between the two organizations. John Foster Dulles often relied on CIA men for diplomatic missions as well as for intelligence, notably in the Middle East. In the middle of September 1955, having been persuaded at last to take the Russian-Egyptian arms talks seriously, the Secretary of State summoned from a Nantucket vacation Kermit Roosevelt, one of the CIA's Middle East hands and a personal friend of Nasser's. "I want you to go to Cairo, Kim," said Dulles, "and tell your friend Nasser that this would be a foolish thing to do." Roosevelt recalls that he agreed to make the trip after telling Dulles, still prematurely perhaps, that Nasser had already made the deal, and asking how he was to convince him that it was foolish. Allen Dulles told his brother that Roosevelt would have to travel at State Department expense because the CIA would not send a man out to check intelligence that was already confirmed.

As Roosevelt recalls it, it was he who gave Nasser the idea of softening the impact of his announcement by attributing the deal to one of the satellites rather than to Russia. Roosevelt says he was with Nasser on the evening of 26 September when Trevelyan, the British ambassador, telephoned to verify the deal. "Shall I say it's Czechoslovakia?" Nasser asked, pursuant to Roosevelt's suggestion. "Sure," said Roosevelt. But Whitehall's disclosure that night called it a Soviet-Egyptian deal.

"This was discourteous," Nasser told Slade-Baker six weeks later. "I should have been consulted before the statement was made, and I therefore decided to make my broadcast announcing the agreement to purchase Czechoslovak arms."

Another reason, Nasser said afterward, was to forestall further interference by the US. "We decided not to leave any opportunity for discussions.... That's why I went and gave my speech; because I learned that the American ambassador might come to me and say: 'We are ready to give you arms.'"

The CIA channels to Nasser were particularly important at this time because Nasser had quarreled with Byroade a few days earlier and refused to see him. The quarrel arose over the beating of a US Embassy Labor attaché in Ismailiya. There were suspicions that the attaché, who was a friend of Byroades's, was beaten up for trying to promote stronger trade unionism among Egyptian workers than the authoritarian regime was willing to tolerate. Byroade made a strong personal protest to Nasser in the presence of Amer and Fawzi at an evening meeting at Nasser's house. When Byroade suggested that the Government had connived at the beating, Nasser stalked out in anger saying, "You deal with Fawzi from now on." The breach lasted about ten days and was repaired during the visit to Cairo of George V. Allen, Assistant Secretary of State for Middle Eastern Affairs.

Allen's trip was an exercise in futility. He made it reluctantly, foreseeing that it would balk its own objective by making it virtually impossible for Nasser to give way on the Russian arms even if he were amenable to persuasion, which he was not. When Allen arrived at his office the day after Nasser's announcement he found that Herbert Hoover, Jr., Undersecretary of State, was trying to reach him. Hoover had learned from the CIA about the breach between Byroade and Nasser and had decided that Allen ought to go to Cairo immediately with a direct remonstrance from Washington. He had already arranged Allen's transportation through the Pentagon.

Allen protested that the trip would "make a lot of noise." Hoover replied that he could say it was just a routine swing around the area. A "routine swing around the area" had, in fact, been mooted publicly some time before but the foolishness of clutching at this coincidence was typical of the fluttery crisis thinking that became a kind of hallmark of the Eisenhower Administration's Middle East policy. Washington was particularly rattled at this time because Eisenhower had had a heart attack on 24 September and was lying in an oxygen tent in a Denver hospital.

Hoover put Allen on the telephone to Dulles, who was in New York attending the UN General Assembly meeting. Hoover had convinced Dulles that Allen should depart for Cairo that very day. Allen said he ought to have a clear message to take to Nasser. Dulles asked him to draft a letter and bring it to New York. Allen drafted a message to the effect that the US recognized Egypt's sovereign right to use its funds as it thought best but that the US had a responsibility of its own to understand as clearly as it could the intentions of other countries. To this end, the letter said, the US would like as much information as Nasser might care to give about his intentions in buying arms so that both the US and Egypt would be in a better position to make wise decisions. Dulles read the letter and signed it, making no changes. Allen caught an overnight plane to Paris.

Dulles, on his return to Washington from the UN that day, said Allen's trip was "only a more or less routine visit" of an assistant secretary to the region he was responsible for. Dulles failed to make Hoover's cover story credible and he gave Nasser the option of treating the trip at its official face value. Dulles thereby made it easier and safer for Nasser to reject US pressure to cancel the Russian arms deal, which was the obvious and true purpose of the trip. Allen himself, loyally supporting the official cover story, fended off reporters' questions as he departed, falsely listing Beirut and Athens in his itinerary in an effort to blur the obvious focus of the mission on Cairo. He did chance to spend a day in Beirut on the way home but did not bother with Athens, deciding that it would look even sillier to go on clutching the cloak of fiction around the trip than to let it fall.

Allen whiled away the 29th in Paris in conferences at the Quai d'Orsay until he boarded a US Air Force transport for a second overnight flight. He was the only passenger.

When he arrived in Cairo at 9:40 on Friday morning, 30 September, he saw from the window a crowd of newsmen waiting for him. Ambassador Byroade bounded out of the crowd and up the steps to tell Allen that the Cairo newspapers had splashed across their front pages an Associated Press dispatch by John Hightower saying that Allen was bringing an ultimatum to Nasser. This had created a hell of a situation, Byroade said, and he urged Allen to be very cautious because the tension had pushed the Egyptians to the verge of breaking relations. As Allen started to follow Byroade down the boarding ramp an Egyptian messenger dashed up to the plane with an envelope marked "personal. To be opened on the plane." It was from Kermit Roosevelt. The two men went back inside the plane and read: "Advise extreme caution in whatever you say. (signed) Kim."

Allen and Byroade then descended to face the sweating jostle of reporters and cameramen. Looking owlish in the flickering barrage of light flashes from the photographers, Allen answered questions in his courtly North Carolina accents. No, he was not bringing an ultimatum and, in fact, had no appointment fixed with Premier Nasser. What had he come for then? Well, the trip had been decided upon very early in the year. He had come to try to understand Egyptian policy and clarify United States policy. He declined to answer further questions, saying he might meet the press again before he left.

At the Embassy when Allen and Byroade drove in from the airport were Eric Johnston, Roosevelt, and Miles Copeland, the resident CIA man in Egypt. Allen showed the group the letter he had drafted for Dulles's signature. Johnston said: "I don't suppose it would do any good to tell you just to tear it up and throw it away." Another suggestion was for Allen to mumble when he read it. In the end, they all agreed that it would be best not to leave anything in writing with Nasser but to present the message orally. Allen reported this consensus to Dulles in a telegram asking permission to make his presentation orally. Use your own judgment, Dulles replied the next day.

Byroade, whose own "plenipotentiary" standing had been compromised by Allen's arrival, to say nothing of his personal embarrassment, waited until evening, after the others had left, before asking Allen: "Why did you come?" Allen told how Hoover had insisted on the trip because of Nasser's quarrel with Byroade. At Allen's request, Byroade gave him full details on the incident, ending by asking Allen if he wanted him to go with him when he went to see Nasser. Allen said he did, both on the principle that "visiting firemen" should not undercut an ambassador's authority and also to test the chances of ending the quarrel.

The embassy translator was asked to telephone Nasser's office for an appointment. He returned with the reply that the Premier was not available. The next morning, however, Nasser sent word that he would see them at noon.

Nasser had been so upset by reports that Allen was bringing an ultimatum that he might have refused to meet Allen at all if it had not been for the intervention of Kermit Roosevelt. Identifying Roosevelt only as "an American official," Nasser related the story accurately, except for a dash or two of humorous exaggeration, in his Suez nationalization speech. Nasser told how Roosevelt had urged him to accept Dulles's message from Allen by admitting that it was "strongly worded" but arguing that its bark was worse than its bite. Nasser continued:

I told him: How can I accept a message which contains a threat or injury to Egyptian dignity? ...I told him: Look, I am not a professional premier. I am a premier of a revolution. ... If your representative comes to the office and says something unpleasant, I shall throw him out. (Applause) ...

He then came again and told me that he had told this to Mr. Allen and that Mr. Allen was wondering whether he would be thrown out when he came to convey his message to me and also whether Mr. Dulles would throw him out if he went back without conveying this message. (Applause and laughter) What would happen? I told him: I do not know. I only know one thing, if he comes to convey this message to me, I will throw him out. Whether Dulles throws him out or not is no concern of mine. Then Mr. Allen came and did not open his mouth at all. He sat and listened to the Egyptian point of view and briefly advanced the American point of view.

Nasser received Allen and Byroade in his office at the ornate old Presidency of the Council of Ministers on Kasr al-Ainy Avenue. It was built in the heyday of empire when Egyptian premiers might be kept waiting in the anterooms of the British High Commissioner. Nasser had scheduled meetings requested by the French and British ambassadors at 10 and 11 o'clock and had requested the Russian ambassador to call at 1 o'clock. All of them, as it happened, were kept waiting except the British ambassador. He, following his instructions, expressed London's "grave view" of the arms deal.

When the two Americans, after cooling their heels for nearly two hours, were ushered into Nasser's office at 1:45 Nasser gave a friendly grin to Byroade. The quarrel that had impelled Hoover to send Allen so hastily to Cairo was no more. Allen said immediately that there was no sense pretending that the arms deal was not the purpose of his visit. Speaking in generalities about the US desire to prevent an arms race, he said the US was against the introduction of more modern weapons into the area because they increased the danger of war and diverted resources from economic development. Then he read from Dulles's letter, changing the pronoun "I" to "we" throughout and covering Dulles's signature with his hand so that Nasser would not perceive that it was a personal letter. He was determined not to leave the letter even if Nasser asked for it. Nasser did not ask for it.

Allen went on to emphasize that the US needed to know whether Egypt was a friend or a nonfriend in formulating its own policy toward Egypt. He said the US could understand a policy of neutrality, having itself been a neutral until World War II, but that it was not neutrality to depend exclusively on one source for arms. He asked if Nasser would like to say anything about the matter of Russian advisers and technicians and the training of the Egyptian forces to use the new Russian weapons. Nasser's own anti-Communism was not in doubt, but behind Allen's question lay Western fears that Russian influence would pervade Egypt along with Russian technicians and advisers.

Nasser replied pleasantly enough that future relations depended on the US. He had been unable to get clear answers from the US, particularly in his quest for arms. His responsibilities as Premier of Egypt required him to ensure the nation's defense. Whether the Russian deal was a "one-shot" affair or not, he said, depended on the West. If the West reacted by trying to restore Israel's military advantage, Egypt would have to continue arming from the East.

Throughout the meeting Nasser referred repeatedly to the dispatch I had filed from Israel on 28 August, a month before Nasser announced the Russian arms deal, analyzing Israel's military superiority over all the Arabs together and her determination to maintain this advantage. Nasser told Allen that the article gave proof that Egypt needed arms to redress the imbalance.

Allen and Byroade said the article had done a favor to Nasser and that it had made the State Department think more seriously about helping him as well as providing intelligence about Israel's strength. Allen said the US would pay a million dollars for an article like that about the Red Army. But Nasser replied that the US obviously wanted Israel to be preponderant or there would not have been such a hullabaloo about the Russian arms deal. He patted a pile of US newspaper clippings about the arms deal and said: "This is what is wrong with your policy."

As for the danger of Egypt being overrun by Russian Communist technicians, Nasser said, he had not got rid of the British and refused a US military mission only to let the Communists in. That would be dangerously unpopular, he added.

Egypt's project for the High Dam at Aswan came casually into the conversation when Allen cited it as an example of Egypt's great need for foreign assistance in economic development. As on the arms topic, the discussion was amicable but inconclusive.

At 3:15 Allen looked at his watch and remarked that the Russian ambassador was waiting and that perhaps he and Byroade should take their leave. Nasser asked Allen what his further plans were. Allen said they were indefinite and that he would be glad to see Nasser again. Good, said Nasser. He asked Allen to come again two days later, on Monday, 3 October. At their second meeting Nasser did not keep Allen waiting.

In the interim, on 2 October, Nasser made a speech to cadets graduating from the Military Academy in which he accused the Western Big Three of paying lip service to peace and a balance of power in the Middle East while actually arming Israel and denying arms to Egypt. This was the speech in which Nasser displayed and quoted from two documents obtained by Egyptian intelligence services, a French report of US and British arms shipments to Israel and a British intelligence analysis contrasting Egypt's pacific intentions with Israel's warlike policy. The purpose of keeping Israel stronger, he said, was to force Egypt to submit to Western protection under the Tripartite Declaration at the price of continued Western domination and influence in Egypt.

"You know as well as I do," Nasser told the cadets, "that this piece of deception which they call 'balance of power' is in truth nothing but a bid for domination. . . . They know that, without arms, we cannot but stay under their influence. They know also that if we find arms, regardless of where we get them from, we will be really liberated in the fullest and truest sense. And now that we have been able to get arms—unconditionally—we have become truly liberated."

After describing the Gaza Raid of 28 February as "the turning point" and "the alarm bell" that alerted Egypt to avoid bigger calamities in the future, Nasser said: "Since then we have begun to examine what is really meant by peace and balance of power in this region and what we have found was that they only meant partiality to Israel."

Allen took issue with Nasser over the speech at their ninety-minute meeting the following night. He said afterward that he told Nasser he was surprised at his lambasting the West as liars and intriguers, at his pumping steam into the crisis while we were trying to let it out. He said Nasser replied that the speech was his reaction to US press treatment of the arms deal and that it was the only way he could get his side of the story across. Byroade did not think the speech great cause for worry but Allen professed to be shocked by what he considered to be an attempt by Nasser to win popular acclaim at the expense of Western good will.

In talks with American correspondents in Cairo Allen said the Russian arms deal would go far toward overcoming Israel's lead but that the State Department did not think Egypt would attack Israel even if convinced of certain victory. Washington's real concern, he said, was about the possibility of a preemptive war by Israel, a suspicion that Ben-Gurion and Dayan began fulfilling later in the month.

Allen referred to Eric Johnston's mission in an illustration of Egypt's desire to avoid hostilities with Israel. Egypt was encouraging the Arabs to accept Johnston's plan for Arab and Israeli development of the Jordan River, Allen said, because the Egyptians knew that, "sure as shooting, if they don't accept it, Israel will take the Jordan."

In Washington, Dulles was kept closely informed of Allen's mission. His reactions show that Allen was remarkably successful in cooling tempers in both angry capitals. Dulles told a news conference on 4 October 1955, the day Allen left Cairo, that there had been a reciprocal gaining of "insight" in the two "rather full" talks between Allen and Nasser. Dulles remained as dogmatically suspicious as ever of Russian motives, but of Egypt he said it was "difficult to be critical of countries which, feeling themselves endangered, seek the arms which they sincerely need for defense."

Dulles said the US and Britain still hoped to avoid participating in "what might become an arms race." But Israel had begun the arms race more than a year earlier when Peres and Dayan visited Paris and initiated with the French Defense Minister the first major purchases. And Israel was now running harder than ever. The day after Dulles's news conference, Dana Adams Schmidt of *The New York Times* reported: "Authoritative estimates are that Israeli military strength is at present superior to Egypt's in every respect except the number of jet aircraft. An Israeli deal with France for Mystère jet fighters will probably soon overcome the Egyptians' lead." He added that pressure was increasing in Israel for expansionist and adventurous policies.

The US and Britain still held themselves bound by the Tripartite Declaration opposing an arms race in the Middle East and committing the signatories to "take action" against any violation of the Palestine armistice lines. But France, the third signatory, had become unstable and reckless in her vain obsession with the rebellions in her North African territories. She was not merely backing an arms race but trying to give Israel enough superiority to make war on Egypt.

Washington itself contributed indirectly to the development of the Franco-

Israeli partnership. Byroade's two speeches in the spring of 1954 re-emphasized the Eisenhower Administration's shift toward impartiality between Israel and the Arabs just when Russian diplomacy returned to the Arab camp. It looked to Israelis as if both Super-Powers were abandoning them to the Arab wolves. Then, in the summer, Britain agreed to return its great Suez base to Egypt, transforming what had been a barrier into a potential springboard. Not surprisingly, Israeli activists began to think about showing up the Arabs, to themselves as well as to the West, as merely sheep in wolves' clothing. Numbers might make the West believe the Arabs were to be preferred as potential allies and customers but a demonstration of Israel's qualitative superiority might reverse the logic of numbers. The readiest forum for such a demonstration was the field of battle.

Israel's fears of abandonment by the US paralleled France's estrangement from Washington over the National Assembly's final rejection on 30 August 1954 of the European Defense Community. Dulles warned of an "agonizing reappraisal" of US defense commitments in Europe. American opinion makers were plunged into a mood of disillusionment tinged with isolationism. France was already antagonized and worried by the Eisenhower Administration's revival of American anticolonialism. This trend was set out by Byroade in a major speech toward the end of 1953. Asserting Washington's "direct interest in North Africa," Byroade said the US had "important security interests in the strength of the French nation" but that "we also have a firm policy of supporting the right of dependent peoples to self-determination." In this "dilemma," he said, the US would follow a "middle-of-the-road policy." French resentment ran high as this policy developed, erupting from time to time in major incidents like the sacking of the US consulate in Tunis on 9 March 1956 by a French mob which burned the American flag.

Washington thus moved away from both Israel and France toward a stance of impartiality in their disputes with Arabs. A year before Egypt and Russia did so, France and Israel found a common solution in arms agreements, beginning with the unscheduled, unreported meetings in August 1954 between Peres and Koenig. Israel began getting arms without strings from France a year before Egypt began getting them from Russia.

The final seal of futility on the Eisenhower Administration's ever-tottering policy of impartiality in the Israeli-Arab arms race was what Eisenhower called "arms in escrow." His account cannot be improved upon. He wrote:

The plan was to store appreciable quantities of military equipment aboard a United States vessel located in the Mediterranean, ready for instant dispatch to any nation in the Middle East which might be a victim of aggression. The Department of Defense was doubtful about the value of the project, but I thought it would have important advantages in its demonstration of complete impartiality between the Arabs (primarily Egypt) and the Israeli. We pushed the plan through, and by the middle of July 1956, a vessel, so supplied, was on station in the Mediterranean. It remained there only a short time. Aggressive acts by Nasser a few days later [presumably the Suez nationalization] minimized the likelihood that we would be supplying him with any arms for some time. The scheme serves, however, as an example of the lengths we were prepared to go to show impartiality and to deter aggression.

The US remained impartially restrictive in its own arms supplies to Israel and her Arab neighbors but took an increasingly tolerant attitude toward France's secret supplies to Israel. Since arms cannot ever be sterilized of political influence, the consequence was that Israel slipped away from the moderating influence of Washington and came willingly under the more sympathetic and reckless influence of France.

The Franco-Israeli preparations for war were, in fact, the steadiest political development in the confused evolution of the crisis that came to be named for Suez. The Paris-Tel Aviv military axis grew steadily in strength and purposefulness with every cabinet shuffle in either capital from August 1954 until the collusive attack on Egypt in the fall of 1956. The French response to the Russian-Egyptian arms deal was simple and direct: ship more and better weapons to Israel. At the same time, Israel completed her seizure of the central military gateway to Sinai at al-Auja. And she continued the border attacks against Egypt, Jordan, and Syria which had the effect of aborting every international peace initiative that might have slowed the momentum of approaching war. Not surprisingly, the logic that brought Nasser to his first arms deal with the Russians dictated a second one.

The publicity attendant on the first deal had been largely created by the West, to whose diplomats Nasser had disclosed his negotiations in the hope that the West itself would see the urgency of his needs and help him to fulfill them. Nasser made use of the publicity touched off by Whitehall. He said he believed the deal would make Israel think twice about further aggressions rather than attempt a preventive war. (Israel began demonstrating the error of this belief with the raid on al-Sabha on 2 November.) Nasser also used the deal to stimulate national consciousness among the people, launching a popular fund drive to pay for the Russian arms by contributing a month's salary of his own as an example.

By contrast, the second deal remained a closely held secret, partly in the futile hope of avoiding a further stimulation of the arms race. As Nasser told the London *Times*'s James Morris after announcing the first deal: "I do not want to spend money on war. I want to build our High Dam at Aswan—our new pyramid. But I want to sleep easily at night."

Nasser emphasized the purely defensive nature of his arms purchases in a marathon series of interviews with foreign correspondents that continued throughout the ten months between the first Russian deal and the nationalization of the Suez Canal. He also emphasized that the arms, wherever he got them, were to ensure Egypt's independence by freeing her from reliance on the West for defense against Israel. "Our foreign policy has two objectives," he said over and over, "to be completely independent ourselves, and to help others to self-determination." This was the philosophy underlying Egyptian neutralism. "It is not like the Monroe Doctrine," he says, "because that was isolation. This is independence. There is a difference between independence and not to commit ourselves in other problems. Of course, we were for the independence of the Arab countries and we were always against the idea of spheres of influence."

These ideas were anathema to Empire-minded Britons who, absentmindedly forgetting that the sun had already set on the Empire east of Suez, still thought of the Canal as the "life-line of Empire." These men thought romantically of the Arabs as gentlemen of the desert among whom nationalism could only be an urban corruption emanating from the Gyppos. They forgot that they had controlled the Arab Middle East for little more than a generation—not long enough for the Arabs to forget that they had entered it across a threshold of broken promises. Their romantic attachments were shared by few Arabs but to Britons they gave a proprietary feeling that was outraged by Nasser's growing influence. This possessiveness was particularly strong toward Middle Eastern oil, upon which Britain was increasingly dependent, and toward the Suez Canal, through which much of their oil reached them. They ignored the fact that, except for those rulers who were the instruments of British control, the Arabs had always resented British patronage and had often revolted against it.

"The British, with the longest experience in the area, have a keen, indeed, a nostalgic appreciation for the desert poetry of the Bedouin Arabs," concluded a US Senate study in 1960, "but they have clearly lacked an understanding of either the scope or nature of Arab nationalism."

The postwar emergence of the US and Russia as the deciding powers of the world had ended Britain's unchallenged preëminence in the Arab world concurrently with two other developments there: the spread of modern communications, which gave new scope and coordination to nationalist movements; and the establishment of Israel, which fulfilled the worst Arab fears about British mastery in their lands. These changes manifested themselves in piecemeal

erosions of British authority. This resulted in an accumulation of emotional resentment among Britons which found its outlet when Eden turned against
Nasser. As the Anglo-Arab historian Albert Hourani wrote: "The dismissal of
Glubb Pasha was the symbol of these changes, and from this moment Nasser
came to embody, in the political imagination of half England, all those forces
which were weakening the British position in a region where it had for so long
been unchallenged."

Britain went over to Nasser's enemies at the beginning of March 1956.
Within two months Whitehall was making important arms shipments to Israel
while lobbying against Nasser in Washington. But Britain's residual colonialist
motivations, although cloaked as anti-Communism, carried little weight among
the anti-imperialist Americans, whose Secretary of State regarded his own
articulate anticolonialism as good national policy. Anticolonialism was a factor
in the uneven development of his tolerance for neutralism.

Dulles told a news conference on 3 April 1956, after a month of British
warnings that Nasser had become an enemy of the West, that Nasser was
"actuated primarily by a desire to maintain the genuine independence of the
area." Dulles said that Egypt had taken no irrevocable decision "to repudiate
ties with the West or to accept anything like vassalage to the Soviet Union."

The British, like the French and the Israelis, knew that anti-Communism
was the vulnerable area in the Eisenhower Administration's thinking. Despite
Nasser's own militant anti-Communism within Egypt, they kept harping on
Nasser's diplomatic and economic shift toward the Communist bloc. They
ignored the fact that the West's restrictive arms policies and France's evasions
in favor of Israel had made Nasser turn with reluctance to Russia for arms as
a matter of practical necessity. They ignored the fact that American cotton-
dumping crowded Egyptian cotton out of Western markets so that Nasser had
to barter it eastward to prevent its piling up and rotting on Egyptian docks.
They characterized these moves, together with Nasser's anticolonialism, as a
kind of neurotic xenophobia against the West which had pro-Communism as
an inevitable concomitant.

Nasser's recognition of Red China on 16 May 1956 was what finally set
Dulles against him, thus completing the alienation of the Western powers and
setting the stage for serious war thinking by the Franco-Israeli axis and, separately, Eden. The Western leaders ignored Egypt's explanation that the recognition of Red China was part and parcel of her policy of ensuring an
independent arms supply. In vain, Egyptian diplomats and the Egyptian press
repeatedly emphasized that the move was prompted by Khrushchev's proposal
in England on 27 April for a UN arms embargo on the Middle East, which
would close off the supplies that Nasser regarded as essential to Egypt's safety.

Egyptian Ambassador Ahmed Hussein, leaving Washington on 18 May for nearly two months of consultations at home, said that the recognition of China had no implications beyond Egypt's desire to maintain an independent policy. He noted that Britain and Israel were among the countries that had recognized Red China years previously.

But the State Department admitted the following day that US-Egyptian relations were under review. Dulles's first public comment, at a news conference on 22 May, was: "It was an action that we regret." He added ominously that the US was not likely to find it "practical or desirable" to help Egypt build the High Dam if Russia had a share in the project. Eisenhower said bluntly that Egypt's recognition of Red China had been a mistake. He added the thinly veiled warning that a single such act did not necessarily destroy US friendship. The clear implication was that it might.

Part and parcel of Nasser's arms policy though it was, his recognition of Red China, or rather Washington's reaction to it, gave the death blow to Western cooperation with Egypt in building the High Dam, one of the greatest irrigation and power projects in history, which meant the difference for Egypt between catching up with the modern world or starving within a generation.

Egypt's arms purchases took priority over development plans after the Gaza Raid for the simple reason that survival is prerequisite to progress. The recognition of Red China placed Egypt's development at the hazards of the Cold War. Nasser's own action inadvertently misled Dulles, as Eden and Nuri and Mollet and Ben-Gurion had tried vainly to do, into thinking that he was a willing tool of International Communism.

There were other factors in turning Dulles and Eisenhower against the High Dam, but it was the recognition of Red China that set them on the new tack in their thinking about Nasser. Dulles's ultimate reaction two months later in rudely canceling Western cooperation on the High Dam was what provoked Nasser to nationalize the Suez Canal, which in turn offered a pretext to those seeking to destroy him by war. The story of Dulles's renege on the High Dam merits a chapter of its own.

CHAPTER

10

Renege on the Dam

(3400 B.C. TO 19 JULY 1956)

The higher Nilus swells,
The more it promises.

(SHAKESPEARE, *Anthony and Cleopatra*)

Every time Egypt has turned to the Nile, she has never been disappointed.

(SIR WILLIAM WILLCOCKS, 1919)

Which of you, intending to build a tower, sitteth not down first, and counteth the cost, whether he have sufficient to finish it? Lest haply, after he hath laid the foundation, and is not able to finish it, all that behold it begin to mock him, saying,
   "This man began to build, and was not able to finish."

(LUKE 14.28)

So they built as men must build
With the sword in one hand and the trowel in the other.

(T. S. ELIOT, *Choruses from the Rock*)

It was the greatest disappointment of my professional life when the United States Government saw fit to back out of that agreement in the heat of the moment. It was a classic case where long-term policy was sacrificed because of short-term problems and irritations. And war came shortly after.

(EUGENE BLACK, 1968)

THE HIGH DAM is a monument of humane endeavor. It will transform on a millennial scale the life of the oldest nation in the world. By its historical impact, by its sheer mass and durability, it must inevitably dwarf the Suez Crisis through which it emerged so that men may one day look back on all the folly and turmoil and see it as a mere rivulet of history running off the back of a broaching whale. Who remembers the politics of the Great Pyramid? The dam, seventeen times greater than the pyramid, will shelter, not a solitary dead soul, but endless millions of living souls until its story is as shrouded in legend as the pyramid's. It will be a legend of Nasser and the Russians in which any mention of the United States, which was otherwise the richest and most generous of nations, will be a footnote of irritability and meanness. Of all the interacting chains of events that ran through the Suez Crisis, the one that led to the building of the dam will be the longest and the most important.

The needs to which the High Dam is the latest response are the same that mothered Egypt's emergence as a nation at the dawn of civilization. Central government itself arose out of the need of the primitive dwellers along the banks of the Nile for an authority that could build and protect irrigation works and allocate water among the disputatious cultivators. Their descendants to this day will cleave a neighbor's skull with a mattock in fights at the ditch gates over water shares. The need to predict the arrival of the annual flood led the ancient Egyptians to devise a solar calendar of 365 days and to develop a practical astronomy. The necessity to measure the river levels was mother to the invention of mathematics. The need to keep river records fostered the development of writing.

The advantages of unity for the Nile Valley, which underlie Egyptian policy to this day, led to the creation of the first federal governments when the prehistoric principalities or "nomes" were subordinated to two kingdoms, Upper Egypt in the narrow valley and Lower Egypt in the delta. These in turn were united by Menes in 3400 B.C. but their distinct identities were symbolized for thousands of years in the double tiara of the pharaohs, the white crown of the South and the red crown of the North. The river was the ligament that bound the two together.

"Egypt is the gift of the Nile," wrote Herodotus in the fifth century before Christ. Without the river there would be no nation. No other people in history has depended so wholly on a single resource for its survival.

From a satellite high above the earth the Nile might resemble an immense attenuated plant with its tributary roots deep in the mountains and swampy forests of tropical Africa, rearing a slender green stem through the desert latitudes to branch at the top, palmlike, in the heavy crown of the delta. "In

Egypt," the British hydrologist, H. E. Hurst, wrote of the Nile, "it is the whole life of the country, and away from the river only a few nomads exist." Except for isolated oases and sparse intermittent pastures along the Mediterranean coast, Egypt is green only where the Nile waters reach,—the narrow valley, the delta, and, since de Lesseps, along the Sweetwater Canal to the west bank of the Suez Canal. The rest is shimmering sand and stone, part of the great desert that stretches from the Red Sea to the Atlantic. Of Egypt's 386,000 square miles, only 15,000 are green and habitable. Upon them live Egypt's millions—7 million in the 1870s, 21 million when Nasser's revolutionaries took power in 1952, 28 million a decade later, and a predicted 40 million by the mid-1980s.

Modern health services, breaking the dreary stability imposed on the population by infant mortality and disease, gave a desperate urgency to Napoleon's prophetic dream of controlling the Nile so that "not a drop of water would be lost in the sea." The mighty fluctuations of the Nile, not only from season to season but from one year and one decade to the next, made taming it a project of international scope.

The problem was to store all the flood waters of the fat years for distribution in the lean years. Ancient records and modern observations, culminating in a monumental survey of the entire Nile basin, led Hurst to the conclusion that "any periodic variation in Nile floods is negligible compared with the irregular changes, and is of no use as a means of forecasting." Hurst developed the concept of "Century storage" as a measure of the capacity of river works needed to ensure the total utilization of the river. This does not mean a capacity to hold the Nile's total discharge of a century. It means taking one hundred years as the base period for calculations needed to take account of long successions of good years and bad years.

The extraordinary variability of the Nile and its tributaries is described in Hurst's book, *The Nile*, published in 1952. The Blue Nile at its maximum flood in late August averages forty times the flow of its low water time in April before the rains begin in Ethiopia. The White Nile's maximum is only two and a half times its minimum. Hurst provides figures in cubic meters (a cubic meter is 1.31 cubic yards) for the effect of the tributaries on the main stream as measured at Aswan. At maximum flood in a typical year, on or about 8 September, the flow is 712 cubic meters a day, of which the Blue Nile and Atbara contribute 90 per cent. The flow at low water, on or about 10 May, falls to 45 million cubic meters, of which the Blue Nile's contribution is 17 per cent and the Atbara's is nothing. The daily discharge at the peak of the 1878 flood, the highest on record, was 1,140 cubic meters a day. In a typical year the flow is sufficient for the country's needs only from August to February, when there is nearly always more than enough water and sometimes a disastrous surplus. The dearth of water from February to August can be made up by seasonal storage in typical years, but over-year storage is needed to provide for lean years, as the following figures from Hurst's book show.

Egypt's overall annual need, even after the High Dam has added more than a million acres to the 6 million now under cultivation, will be 58 billion cubic meters. In 1878 the flow was 148 billion cubic meters, most of it wasted in the sea after devastating the countryside by flood. In the low year of 1913 the annual flow was only 41 billion cubic meters. These are extremes. Long-term variations are not so great but they show even more graphically the need for "century storage" calculations. From 1870 to 1900 the average annual flow was 109 billion cubic meters; from 1900 to 1950 it was 83 billion.

Lean years began to recur in the Nineties, withering the additional summer crops on which the country came to depend in the fat years. Bad years brought poverty, even starvation. Better irrigation became a vital need. British engineers from India built the Aswan Dam between 1898 and 1902, inaugurating seasonal storage. The original Aswan Dam stored one billion cubic meters. Two heightenings, in 1912 and 1933, raised its capacity to five billion. The second heightening of the dam enabled it in 1946 to check the crest of the first twentieth century flood comparable to those of the nineteenth century. It was a calculated risk for if the dam had broken the unpent deluge would have flushed man and his works out of the valley.

The High Dam is sometimes called the Aswan High Dam or, simply and erroneously, the Aswan Dam, which leads to confusion. The High Dam is built athwart the old reservoir four miles south (upstream) of the Aswan Dam. The old Aswan Dam served Egypt well, especially the rich landowners. The total rentable value of land increased sixfold in its first two decades. The Aswan Dam will continue to serve as the nerve center controlling the distribution of irrigation water released to it by the High Dam, which has no sluice gates. But the old dam, too small for over-year storage, was swiftly overtaken by Egypt's population. It's inadequacy was recognized at the outset by the engineers who built it. The young lancer Winston Churchill, who saw it under construction as he marched up the Nile with Kitchener's army on its way to conquer the Sudan, wrote prophetically in 1899 that "these gigantic enterprises may in their turn prove but the preliminaries of even mightier schemes, until at last ... the Nile itself, flowing for three thousand miles through smiling countries, shall perish gloriously and never reach the sea."

There were two approaches to century storage. One was by way of a number of dams throughout the river system based on Lake Victoria as a control reservoir that could shut off the White Nile when the Blue was in spate. The other was the High Dam scheme, worked out by Adrian Daninos, an Egyptian engineer of Greek origins, after a survey of the Aswan region in 1947. Daninos, born in Alexandria in 1887, proposed as early as 1912 to build a hydroelectric station at the original Aswan Dam. Built a half century later by the revolutionary government for a fertilizer plant, it was to prove an essential source of power for the building of the High Dam.

Daninos presented his plan at the Institut d'Egypte on 12 January 1948. It was pushed into the background by the Palestine war, the clashes with Britain over the Suez base and the Sudan, and by the civil disorders that marked the declining years of the monarchy. On 30 July 1952, four days after King Farouk was sent into exile, Daninos submitted his project to Wing Commander Aly Sabry, one of Nasser's revolutionaries and a left-wing aristocrat who later became Premier.

Within three months Nasser's regime adopted the plan and accepted a German offer to submit tenders. The junta had by then promulgated land reform as the first major step toward their aspiration to raise Egyptians out of their millennial poverty. Moved by the natural sensitivity of Egyptians to potential upstream interference with the Nile, upon whose flood their very lives depend, the junta rejected the alternative century storage proposals for dams throughout the Nile basin because most of the system would be beyond Egyptian control.

Sir William Willcocks, the British engineer who planned the first Aswan Dam and gave Egypt year-round perennial irrigation, once said that Lake Victoria was the key to the Nile "and whoever holds it has the destinies of Egypt in the hollow of his hand." The complete blocking of the great lake, he said, was a feasible undertaking that would raise its level only 20 inches a year and make it easy to deprive Egypt of summer water for ten or fifteen years in succession. The High Dam, under Egyptian control, would enable the country to survive such a hostile maneuver, which was seriously proposed by a Member of Parliament as a means of crushing Nasser in the spring of 1956, when Lake Victoria was still in British imperial territory. Egypt's destinies are too beset by dangers for Nasser to wish them in the hollow of someone else's hand.

In 1897, the year before the British began building the Aswan Dam, Egypt had 5.1 million acres under cultivation. Taking into calculation the two harvests a year in some areas of the delta, the crop acreage figure was 6.7 million. The crop acreage per capita was .70. When the revolution came in 1952 the irrigated area had grown to 5.8 million acres and the crop acreage had risen to 9.2 million but population growth had cut the crop acres per capita to .42. Modern medical science was saving Egyptians from disease so that they could starve to death. The High Dam was essential for Egypt to feed itself until it could turn its power into the industrialization essential to economic security.

The West German combine of Hochtief and Dortmund, after two years of surveys and study, presented designs for a rockfill dam larger than any in the world to be built across the reservoir four miles above the old Aswan Dam. The Dam actually built by the Egyptians and Russians followed the Hochtief design with only minor modifications. Daninos's figures, based on his own relatively rudimentary survey, were remarkably accurate. The High Dam will store 130 billion cubic meters of water, twenty-six times the old Aswan reservoir's capacity, with an allowance for flood surpluses up to 157 billion cubic meters. Its massive turbines will generate 10 billion kilowatt hours per year themselves and the constancy of the Nile's flow will enable additional hydroelectric plants to be built at a number of the dams and barrages downstream.

The dam cost £60 million ($170 million), about double Daninos's twenty-year-old estimates. Irrigation, land reclamation, power lines, compensation for the Nubians displaced by the High Dam's reservoir, and other related costs brought the total for the project to about £415 million ($1.16 billion). Egypt required foreign aid, in equipment and technical help, for between a quarter and a third of the total.

The dam is 365 feet high, two-thirds of a mile thick at the base, two and a quarter miles long, and seventeen times greater in volume than the Great Pyramid of Cheops. In somewhat oversimplified terms, its construction is that of a mountain of rocks piled over an impermeable clay core overlying a thick curtain of cement grouted 600 feet into the sand and silt of the riverbed to the granite floor beneath.

Leaving aside the industrialization that will spring from it, its benefits to agriculture, river navigation, and electrification will raise the national income by an estimated £255 million ($700 million), nearly 20 per cent of the 1960 figure and more in a single year than half the total cost of the project. But financing had to come first and in spite of its extraordinary profitability the size of the project made financing a problem for a country so poor in money and in international esteem.

Nasser won world confidence by his Suez evacuation agreement with Britain in October 1954. The Hochtief design was completed that month. It was endorsed by a board of American and European experts. The World Bank then began a determination of whether the Egyptian economy could stand the strain of the project and whether the benefits would be worth the cost. Egypt announced an allocation of $8 million on 25 June 1955 for preliminary work at the dam site. Construction began immediately on access roads, railroad tracks, and workers' housing. Wing Commander Hassan Ibrahim, Minister of National Production, said there was no difficulty about obtaining the needed foreign financing.

When the World Bank delivered a favorable preliminary report on 30 August, Nasser ordered white lines painted on the rocky banks of the river to show where the dam would rise. The turbaned captains of the paddlewheelers on the run from Aswan to Wadi Halfa in the Sudan took to saluting the brave lines with their ship's horns. West German, British, and French companies formed a consortium in September 1955 to bid for the construction contract.

At the end of that month Nasser announced his arms deal with Russia. After their initial shock and anger, Western leaders realized that turning their backs on Nasser would force him more and more toward the Russians. Nasser was particularly averse to turning to the Russians for the foreign help he needed to build the High Dam because it would place not only Egypt's Army but her entire economy at their mercy. In any case, he had predicated his plans for the dam from the beginning—two years before the arms deal—on partnership with the West.

Eisenhower's heart attack on 24 September 1955 slowed down Washington's responses in foreign affairs for the better part of two months. As a consequence the Russians were the first of the two Super-Powers to offer help to Nasser for the dam. Ambassador Solod launched the Kremlin's race for influence in Africa and Asia in Cairo on 10 October with a free-wheeling offer of all kinds of aid to any Arab and Asian country that wanted it. In Denver on that day, Eisenhower was wheeled out of his hospital room for the first time since his heart attack, but only as far as the sundeck outside his room. Within two days Solod had delivered a Russian offer on the High Dam directly to Nasser. It was to be a barter arrangement like the arms deal but on much easier terms. Nasser replied that he was already discussing aid with the World Bank and therefore could not engage in any talks with Russia about the dam.

The Egyptian ambassador in Washington, Ahmed Hussein, called on Dulles on 17 October to tell him that Egypt would prefer US to Soviet aid in spite of the easier Russian terms. On the 20th the State Department let it be known that the US was ready to help with the High Dam in Egypt as well as with the Johnston Plan for the Jordan River in a Middle Eastern version of the Marshall Plan aimed at blunting the Soviet aid drive. The US overtook the Russians on 21 November when the Egyptian Finance Minister, Abdel Moneim Kaissouny, sat down with World Bank officials in Washington for talks that were soon joined by US and British diplomats. The outcome was a joint offer on 16 December by the US and Britain of $70 million for the first stage of the dam. Fifty-six million dollars would be a grant from the US and $14 million would come from Britain in the form of a special release of blocked Egyptian sterling which Britain had owed Egypt since World War II. The announcement of the offer said that the two countries would "be prepared to consider sympathetically, in the light of then existing circumstances, further support towards financing the later stages to supplement World Bank financing."

The first stage of the work comprised upstream and downstream coffer dams, the diversion of the river through artificial gorges and huge tunnels, and irrigation works using the water surplus held by the upstream coffer dam to create new crop acreage. The first stage was to be done within five years. The final stages, to take ten more years, included completion of the immense rock-fill dam, incorporating both coffer dams into itself, construction of the hydro-electric plant and power lines to the Delta, and completion of a new irrigation system for full utilization of the waters in reclaiming and improving farmland.

Nasser, in retrospect, calls the joint offer the high point in his relations with the US. He said of the British that they went back on an offer by the Chancellor of the Exchequer to Kaissouny in London before the Washington talks of a loan nine times larger than the sterling release offered on 16 December.

The World's Bank share was to be a loan of $200 million, contingent on the Anglo-American grant for the first stage and carrying the understanding that the US and Britain would raise their contributions for the later stages to $200 million, bringing the total Western aid to $400 million, half from the World Bank and half from the US and Britain.

Fulfillment of the Western promise, however, was doomed almost from the start by the failure of a US peace-making mission which is shrouded to this day in such secrecy that I have been able to learn only the bare outlines of it. These I gathered piecemeal.

The story begins with Dulles's ambitious hope of becoming the man to bring peace to the Holy Land. In October 1954 Dulles appointed Francis H. Russell, a foreign service officer with experience in the Middle East, as his special assistant on the Palestine problem and put him in charge of an exhaustive study of the possibilities of a peaceful settlement. In 1955 the need for peace took on new urgency as the Israeli Army, once again controlled by Ben-Gurion and the activists, hammered at the Egyptian border, provoking Egyptian counter-raids and bringing Russia into the arms race. The tension jeopardized the first major peace effort of Dulles and Eisenhower, which was the Johnston Plan for integrated Arab and Israeli development of the Jordan River.

On 26 August 1955, during the bloodiest series of clashes thus far between Israel and Egypt, Dulles made a major speech based on Russell's study and endorsed by Eisenhower. It offered US help in overcoming what Dulles listed

303

as the three main obstacles to peace. They were: "the tragic plight of the 900,000 refugees," "the pall of fear" of Israeli expansion on one side and of eventual Arab revenge on the other, and "the lack of fixed permanent boundaries." Ben-Gurion promptly and flatly rejected any thought of territorial compromise. Arab leaders maintained a gingerly silence.

The Russian arms deal the following month had a double effect on the prospects of a settlement; it increased the urgency and it brought Nasser to new prominence as a pan-Arab hero who might be strong enough to achieve and survive a peace settlement. A third consequence of the arms deal was to bring sharply to Washington's attention the fact that whoever helped Egypt build the High Dam would hold Egypt's economy in thrall for ten or twenty years. Nasser was also thoroughly aware of this and he much preferred multisided Western help to assistance from the Russian monolith. Western financing would come mainly from the nonpolitical World Bank and only partly from governments subject to political and diplomatic considerations. Western technical aid and equipment would come under contract from private enterprise. The combination was far less fearsome than the prospect of having undivided control by a foreign government over the financing and construction contracts alike. With Communist-style monolithic aid Russia would be in a position to exert whatever pressure she wanted when the project was under way and Egypt could no longer back out.

Egypt's urgent need for the dam and Nasser's preference for Western help in building it enticed the mind of Herbert Hoover, Jr., Undersecretary of State, to the tactic of offering help for the dam in return for a peace settlement with Israel. Although Hoover denies that any decision was reached to offer aid on the dam as a *quid pro quo* for a settlement with Israel, other parties affirm that the effort was made. Their independent accounts conform with one another and with known events in such circumstantial detail as virtually to eliminate doubts about either their honesty or accuracy.

Hoover, the son of the late President Hoover, followed his father into an engineering career. He joined the State Department in 1953 at the age of fifty as an adviser on petroleum questions, notably in negotiations with Iran after Premier Mossadegh was overthrown in a coup aided and financed by the CIA. The following year he was named Undersecretary of State, the number two position in the department. His background in the oil business led Dulles to accord him considerable influence in the formulation of Middle East policy although his tendency to approach problems in terms of barrels of oil per day aroused distrust and dislike among Israelis, Arab nationalists, and a number of Middle East hands in the department itself. He was hard of hearing, a handicap to which some of his colleagues attributed his suspicious, peremptory manner.

As an engineer, Hoover was naturally attracted toward big projects like the High Dam. And he knew of Dulles's deep personal interest in a Palestine settlement. When Dulles decided that the US should make a positive reaction to offset the arms deal rather than a negative one, Hoover became the chief proponent of the High Dam in Dulles's inner circle.

The US has consistently worked against Arab unity, whether to prevent a threat to American oil interests or a threat to Israel, and has always encouraged rivals to offset the claim of any leader to speak for all the Arabs, most notably in the case of Nasser. But Hoover was willing to make an exception to obtain a Palestine settlement and to tell Nasser, in effect: We will treat you as the leader of the Arabs on this issue and no other but we will strengthen you with aid for the High Dam so that you can safely conclude peace with Israel.

The professionals in the department had long been wary of the dam because it was the kind of long-term financial commitment that Congress has never authorized in advance. They foresaw an annual abrasion of US-Egyptian relations when Congress debated the annual appropriations. The Zionist and cotton lobbies, both firmly opposed to the High Dam, would be certain to make the annual appropriations struggle an ordeal humiliating to the State Department as well as to the nationalist sensibilities of the Egyptians. As for Hoover's plan to barter the dam for a peace treaty, one prominent diplomat warned Dulles that in the likely event of the plan's failure Washington's wrath would be turned inevitably against Nasser, regardless of what caused the failure. Dulles assured him it would not. Hoover's enthusiasm and influence carried the day.

The most ardent champion of the dam on its own merits, quite apart from its value as bait for a peace treaty, was Eugene Black, president of the World Bank. Black became interested in the dam in 1953, when he discussed it on a visit to Egypt with General Naguib, who was then the figurehead leader of the revolution. Black recalls telling Eisenhower on his return that the most important thing the US could do at that time was something big in Egypt and that the thing to do in Egypt was the High Dam. He told Eisenhower that the dam was a larger project than the World Bank could handle alone and that when the plans were ready he would come back to him to get US backing for the bank's participation. Black remained in close touch with the technical studies and launched the bank's economic study as soon as the technical studies were completed in October 1954. The bank made a preliminary report to Egypt on 30 August 1955 that the project was not only technically sound but, on the basis of the anticipated increase in perennial irrigation, economically sound also.

"The only effect of the arms deal on World Bank thinking," Black said afterward, "was that it made it easier to get the US and Britain to go along. The possibility that the deal would affect Egypt's economic capacity to sustain the project was proved not to exist." On 24 October, nearly a month after Nasser announced the arms deal, the bank sent its dam construction expert and a staff engineer to Cairo to help work out the technical and economic details that would have to be covered in an aid agreement with the West.

It was at this point that Hoover espoused the project and obtained Dulles's support for it. As Hoover was preparing his delicate bargain, Nasser, still unaware of it, showed that he was willing to try for peace the better to be able to build the dam. The first indication was Nasser's praise for Eden's peace proposal on 9 November 1955 in the Prime Minister's annual speech at the London Guildhall. Eden suggested that Israel and the Arabs seek peace in a compromise between the "1947 and other United Nations resolutions" on Palestine, on which the Arabs stood fast, and the 1949 Armistice Agreements, on which Israel stood fast. A week before, Ben-Gurion had talked peace in the Knesset in the morning and in the night had smashed Egypt's last military toehold in the vicinity of al-Auja, thus not only ensuring Israel's control of the invasion route but driving the Egyptians out of observation range even within their own territory. It should be recalled here that on 22 October Ben-Gurion had summoned Dayan home from France to plan a Sinai invasion.

Israel immediately responded to Eden by rejecting any idea of territorial compromise, as it had done with Dulles's proposal of 26 August. Sharett deplored Eden's speech, saying it "encourages ... illusions and excites appetites which can never be satisfied." But Nasser, in an interview with Stephen Barber of the *News Chronicle* (London) which was prominently reprinted in Cairo, praised Eden's "constructive attitude."

Nasser thus became the first Arab leader to accept publicly the idea of a compromise retreat from the UN resolutions on the partition of Palestine and the rights of the refugees. Previously the Arabs had insisted adamantly that Israel implement those resolutions as a precondition for any settlement negotiations. Nasser then engaged in intensive discussions with the British ambassador, Sir Humphrey Trevelyan, fully aware that the British ambassador in Tel Aviv was conducting parallel talks with Israeli leaders. Both sets of talks aimed at arranging peace negotiations unimpeded by the Arab demand that Israel accept the UN resolutions in advance. At the UN on 25 November the Egyptian Undersecretary for Foreign Affairs said that Egypt would accept negotiations conducted through an intermediary. The talks in Cairo made such progress that Haikal, Nasser's unofficial spokesman, said privately that there was "a strong possibility of a settlement" in the near future. A Senate Foreign Relations Committee staff study, published in 1960, found Nasser's peace effort to be of more than transient importance, stating that "there is significance in the mere fact that Nasser in 1955, when his power and prestige were less than they are now, showed willingness to lead the Arabs into a Palestine compromise."

But the Israelis, already planning for war, stubbornly rejected any compromise. By the end of November the Egyptians had become exasperated and worried by Israel's refusal to match their own risky flexibility. An official Egyptian spokesman said that Israel was looking toward a preventive war, not to forestall an Arab attack but to forestall a just peace.

Nasser wanted peace in order to build the dam but he did not want to bargain one for the other. In mid-November, shortly before the start of the negotiations in Washington that led to the Western offer, he disclosed to his friend Tom Little, correspondent for *The Economist* (London) as well as head of the Arab News Agency, his suspicion that his need for a loan for the High Dam was being used as a form of pressure for peace with Israel. Much as he wanted both peace and the dam, he wanted them separately and regarded with repugnance any effort to tie the two together. He seems to have decided to treat them separately when he received the US peace emissary.

Hoover himself joined the negotiations that began on 21 November between Kaissouny and Black. Ambassador Sir Roger Makins represented Britain. On 8 December Dulles went to see Eisenhower at Camp David. They spent a half hour walking in the woods while Dulles told Eisenhower of his hope that the US might help Nasser build the High Dam, thereby improving American-Arab relations. It was evidently at this meeting that Dulles disclosed Hoover's hope that aid for the dam would, in effect, buy a Palestine peace treaty. Eisenhower's assent raised the problem of whom to entrust with this extraordinarily bold and delicate mission to Nasser and Ben-Gurion.

Eisenhower selected Robert B. Anderson, a forty-five-year-old Texas oil man and financier who had held high posts in the Eisenhower Administration and who was a close friend of Hoover's. Anderson served as Secretary of the Navy in 1953 and 1954 and as Deputy Secretary of Defense until July 1955. He succeeded George Humphrey as Secretary of the Treasury in 1957 and Eisenhower considered him as an alternative to Nixon for the vice-presidential candidacy in 1956. At the time of his secret Palestine peace mission he was in private business.

On 12 December *The New York Times* reported: "The US Government is tying its proposals for a ten-year aid program to build the High Aswan Dam in Egypt to a settlement of the Egyptian-Israeli disputes. The hope here is that the negotiations for economic aid to Egypt can lead to a general settlement of the disturbing Near East situation." This was the only breach in the secrecy surrounding the effort.

Peace hopes appeared to have been swept out of reach by the headlines the following day on Israel's overnight raid into Syria on 11/12 December in which fifty-six Syrian soldiers and civilians were killed and thirty prisoners were taken. Nasser wrote Hammarskjold on 15 December that "Egypt has tolerated these continual acts of hostility [since the Gaza Raid] in order to affirm clearly to the world its policy of peace" but that henceforth Egypt would have to reply in kind to such attacks on Syria as well as upon Egypt under the terms of the recent Syrian-Egyptian alliance. Osgood Caruthers of *The New York Times* reported that Nasser was "virtually forced by political circumstances, both internally and in the rest of the Arab world, to issue the warning that the Egyptian-Syrian pact was not a mere piece of paper." The raid wrecked the promising peace effort then in progress by the British. Any hope of reviving it was stifled within the next few days by Britain's attempt to bring Jordan into the Baghdad Pact in violation of the Eden-Nasser moratorium.

Nevertheless, Anderson went forward with his mission, having the burnt-over peace field very much to himself. Secrecy was maintained within the State Department, not only by entrusting the mission to an outsider, but by informing no one except the men directly involved at ambassadorial level or above. The desk chiefs were not told. Even the Senate Foreign Relations Committee was and still is excluded from the secret.

Anderson, like Hoover, denies that the High Dam offer was specifically linked to a Palestine settlement or that Nasser was presented with the two issues in such a way as to make clear that US aid for the dam was contingent on peace with Israel. Eugene Black too saw the two issues as entirely distinct from one another. It is not necessary to doubt the truth of these denials in order to accept authoritative testimony that the two issues were, nevertheless, associated together in State Department policy deliberations and that Nasser was given to understand that, from the US lender's point of view, peace would significantly enhance the appeal of the High Dam as a political and financial investment. Without in any way impugning the veracity and sincerity of the denials, which can arise as well from incomplete knowledge as from diplomatic discretion, I am myself persuaded by the evidence that peace and the dam were tied together in Washington and that Nasser was so informed. The precise nature of the link and the manner in which Nasser was informed of it may lie whole among the secret documents. It exists in fragments, too substantial to ignore, in the minds of the handful of men involved and in the circumstances and chronology of events.

Anderson went out to the Middle East directly at the orders of President Eisenhower. As he shuttled between Ben-Gurion and Nasser he kept up a continuous exchange of telegrams with Washington, all of which remain under secret classification.

The upshot was that Ben-Gurion said he would negotiate with Nasser directly but not through the US or any other intermediary. He also rejected the idea of secret negotiations. He said he must meet Nasser personally and that it must be done publicly.

Nasser told Anderson that he was willing to work out a framework for peace in the area but that he could not yet speak for the other Arabs. He said that he could not begin by direct talks with Ben-Gurion nor could he negotiate publicly. Nasser was willing to seek peace but not even getting the High Dam as a reward would induce the Egyptians or any other Arabs to tolerate public direct talks between Nasser and Ben-Gurion.

Anderson's mission failed because Ben-Gurion deliberately set impossible conditions. Unknown to Anderson, Ben-Gurion was even then pressing his cabinet to accept Dayan's first war plan, presented on 5 December, to seize the eastern Sinai.

Nasser's cooperative willingness to compromise on Palestine certainly gave no grounds for rescinding the US offer of aid for the High Dam. Even if Nasser had accepted Ben-Gurion's conditions, Egyptian and Arab reaction would immediately have aborted the peace effort and endangered the lives of Nasser and his regime. It was Ben-Gurion's secret war policy that wrecked Anderson's mission. Nevertheless, Anderson's failure doomed Western aid for the High Dam. Major policies and costly projects need active sponsorship within a government if they are ever to emerge as practical realities. It was Hoover's sponsorship that had brought about the Western offer on 16 December but when it failed to bring about a Palestine peace settlement Hoover decided that the costly, long-term project was no longer worthwhile for the Administration. "Pressure for the High Dam practically disappeared after Anderson's failure," said one party to the secret; "only Black and Byroade kept it alive." "Hoover wanted out of Aswan the moment he couldn't buy Egyptian-Israeli peace with it," said another. "This was the real reason we backed out. Hoover was responsible for the Aswan offer in the first place as a *quid pro quo* to buy Arab-Israeli peace and it was he who dumped it when the deal failed."

Neither the documents on the Anderson mission nor the fact that such a mission was undertaken were disclosed to the Senate Subcommittee of the Committees on Armed Services and Foreign Relations which, after the Suez war of 1956, investigated US policy in the Middle East. On the basis of other documents and testimony, however, the chairman of the subcommittee, Senator J. William Fulbright, reported after months of exhaustive study of the High Dam case: "The evidence is that the Administration itself began to reconsider the offer only a few weeks after it was made."

Personal antipathy for Nasser's neutralist nationalism contributed to Hoover's shift against the dam. As one former colleague put it: "He didn't think Arabs should be allowed to shove us around. Hoover was a nationalist who couldn't tolerate nationalism in others." Before the winter was over, Hoover was bringing directly to Eisenhower a request that the US agree to France's sending Mystère IV jets to Israel instead of delivering them to NATO. Eisenhower replied that the US position should be "no objection."

Anderson himself lost no face either in Cairo or at the White House. Eisenhower entrusted him with a second private mission during the Suez Crisis and President Johnson sent him on another peaceseeking mission to Nasser after the 1967 Suez war.

Ironically, Anderson's failure ended Hoover's vital support for the dam at the very time that Eugene Black, on a mission of his own to Cairo, was achieving "substantial agreement" with Nasser on the World Bank's role. Black left Washington on 24 January 1956 with an enthusiastic personal promise from Dulles of US backing. He paused for two days of talks in London, during which Eden, too, personally assured Black of Britain's support. "What Mr. Dulles and Mr. Eden were really saying to me was that this was a very important thing and that they hoped I wouldn't act like a banker ... and would not be too inflexible in working this out," Black recalled. Black flew on to Cairo on the 27th. In Washington on that day Senators Morse and Neuberger of Oregon berated the Administration for granting money for the High Dam while refusing it for the proposed Hell's Canyon Dam in their state.

The Egyptians, meanwhile, had themselves berated the Administration for the conditions attached to the $70 million, which they saw as slurs on Egyptian sovereignty. The US and British *aides mémoires* transmitting the 16 December offer and setting out the conditions have never been published but the gist of the conditions have been disclosed. They required guarantees that Egypt would concentrate her development program on the High Dam and not disperse her resources on other projects and that she impose controls to prevent the immense expenditures on the dam from inflating her currency. The World Bank loan hinged on an additional guarantee that Egypt incur no other foreign loans nor any payments agreements without World Bank assent. This looked to Cairo like a sly maneuver to block any further arms purchases from Russia.

Nasser regarded these demands as prejudicial to Egypt's sovereignty and dignity. They seemed ominously reminiscent of the Anglo-French "Dual Control" of Egyptian finances in the 1870s, which led to the British occupation. Nasser was particularly uneasy about the reluctance of the US and Britain to more than "consider sympathetically, in the light of then existing circumstances," the financing of the later stages of the dam. The confusing maze of interlocking clauses binding the Western offers together did nothing to abate Nasser's sense of hidden dangers. He voiced the suspicions that beset him in his Suez nationalization speech six months later:

Thus the trap in the operation appeared. It appeared that we were to take the $70 million and begin building the projected dam.... And then we should be stopped halfway through the project after having spent $300 million [of our own] in vain—thrown down the drain. Or we would be compelled to yield and accept the World Bank's terms—the sending of someone to occupy the Finance Minister's seat, another to occupy the seat of the Minister of Trade, and yet another to occupy my post—while we sat in this country unable to make a move without their instructions and orders.

Although foreign controls were anathema to Egyptians and consequently full of political risks for Nasser, the Government showed itself willing to impose its own controls by asking all ministries and departments in January to cut expenditures by at least 10 per cent and to abolish all duplication of duties. Egypt also yielded quietly to an Anglo-American requirement that the construction contracts be awarded by competitive bidding in order to minimize costs. Egypt wanted to assign the contracts on a cost-plus basis directly to the Western consortium, saying that it would save time, and arguing further that she could not exclude Soviet-bloc bids if the contracts were to be competitive. And Egypt took for granted the prerequisite of a new Nile waters agreement with the Sudan, whose major northern city, Wadi Halfa, would be submerged in the 300-mile-long lake created by the High Dam.

But Nasser and the controlled press vented angry criticisms of the conditions that seemed to seek for foreigners a voice in Egyptian policy. As a consequence, Nasser had to change publicly stated positions in reaching his agreement with Black in negotiations that continued from 28 January to 9 February. On Nasser's desk when Black made his first call were the *aides mémoires* in which the US and Britain had transmitted their offers. Nasser had marked the conditions he did not like.

Their first meeting lasted an hour and a quarter and was so stormy that it seemed the negotiations might end right there. Dulles cabled Kermit Roosevelt in Athens to go to Cairo and try to bring Black and Nasser together again, an assignment which Roosevelt said "put quite a strain on my persuasive powers." In the end, Nasser and Black developed a friendship which survived severe strains over the years.

Black was not flustered by Nasser's stubborn suspicions. He was used to explaining to leaders in underdeveloped countries obtaining their first World Bank loans that the conditions they found objectionable were standard international banking practice and, in addition, were often in the recipient country's own interest. He told Nasser that the US and British offers were generous and he advised him to accept them and get started. The effects of the first stage being entirely confined to Egyptian territory, the US was willing to go ahead in advance of a new Sudanese-Egyptian Nile waters agreement. Black allayed Nasser's suspicions sufficiently to reach an accord on the World Bank loan, subject to ratification by both the Egyptian cabinet and the bank's board of directors, which represented the high water mark in Western-Egyptian cooperation. But the tide had already turned in Washington.

The Egyptian-World Bank communiqué on 9 February said that the talks between Nasser and Black had "led to mutual understanding and substantial agreement on the basis of which the bank will, when requested, take part in financing of the High Dam project with an amount equivalent to $200 million. ..." Black told reporters that the project would cost $1.3 billion, comprising $400 million in foreign exchange and $900 million in Egyptian expenditures. He said the agreement meant in general that Egypt had accepted strict guarantees that her economy could sustain the burden.

Black told a BBC interviewer before his departure the following day that the dam was "the largest single structure ever undertaken in the history of the world" and that the World Bank was "very happy to have the opportunity of participating in such a dramatic undertaking."

Quite by accident, during a brief stopover at the airport in Rome on his trip home, Black met Byroade, who was returning to Cairo from a month of consultations at the State Department. Byroade told Black that US interest in the High Dam had lost its steam and he urged Black to try and build a fire under it again. Byroade had originally cautioned against US Government involvement in the project but once the offer had been made he vigorously opposed withdrawing it. Black did his best. Upon his arrival in New York on the 12th he had "high praise" for Nasser and when asked if Nasser were leaning toward the Soviets he replied: "Not the slightest. As far as I can see, he is friendly toward the United States." Nevertheless, he recalled subsequently, "When I got back thinking I had done one hell of a good job, I found things had changed."

The virtual abandonment of the High Dam project made it desirable to shift Byroade out of Egypt. Dulles and Hoover told him before he returned to Cairo in February to anticipate a transfer. Some months later, as the Administration adopted a hard anti-Nasser line, and in some apprehension lest Byroade resign in protest, Dulles persuaded him to accept the Ambassadorship to South Africa, arguing that it would be good for his career to get away from Zionist criticism. The transfer was announced on 15 July 1956, four days before the renege on the dam. It was regarded as a mark of Washington's new coolness toward Nasser.

If Eden's memoirs are correct on this point, the ebb tide had set by the time he and Lloyd sat down with Eisenhower and Dulles in Washington on 30 January to discuss the Middle East. "We agreed that the future of our policy in the Middle East depended to a considerable extent on Nasser," Eden wrote. "The Americans thought that the present talks about the Aswan Dam with Mr. Black might indicate his state of mind. If his attitude on this and other matters was that he would not cooperate, we would both have to reconsider our policy towards him."

As Eden presents it, it was a cold change from the warm endorsements he and Dulles had given the project in their meetings with Black less than a week before. And Nasser was cooperative on the dam and "other matters," including the Anderson mission. It would have been more accurate for Eden to use the verb "submit."

Washington began to treat Nasser's need for the dam as it had treated his need for arms, leaving his messages unanswered and its own promises unhonored. Nasser agreed to give the West the economic guarantees it demanded but he wanted to be able to deny to critics at home that they would subject Egypt to the humiliation of foreign controls. It was mainly a question of wording. In the 9 February accord he had, in effect, accepted a World Bank voice in Egyptian economic policy, including foreign loans, in the following phraseology:

The Government's own contribution to the project will be provided in such a way as to avoid inflation and impairment of Egypt's credit worthiness. To this end, the Government and the Bank will reach an understanding on, and will periodically review, an investment program which will recognize the priority of the High Dam project and the need for adjusting total public expenditures to the financial resources which can be mobilized.

Although the accord was a large step forward, Nasser still had to reach a new agreement on the Nile with the Sudan as well as to iron out the language of the US and British offers. He abandoned his hopes of beginning construction

313

in June and ordered a suspension of the preparatory works at the dam site pending agreement with the Sudan and completion of the financing.

Before the end of February, after talks with the US and British ambassadors, Nasser sent inquiries to Washington and London about the conditions attached to their offers together with suggestions for altering the *aides mémoires* so that they would be, as he put it in his nationalization speech, "free of any passage indicating that they would dominate our policy or sovereignty or economy and any passages representing domination over Egypt's independence." He never got an answer. The High Dam project was moribund, as far as Hoover was concerned, and that meant there wasn't enough backing for it in the State Department even to answer mail from a Prime Minister.

Britain's silence is explained by Eden's personal declaration of war on Nasser in reaction to King Hussein's expulsion of Glubb Pasha from Jordan. On 12 March Eden had shouted at Nutting over the telephone: "I want him destroyed, don't you understand?" In such a mood he was hardly likely to answer letters from Nasser. Mollet, sinking ever deeper into the Algerian bloodbath, also wanted Nasser destroyed and was working with Ben-Gurion to accomplish it. Like Eden and Lloyd, they too were lobbying against the High Dam in Washington, with the support of the powerful US Zionist movement. Sherman Adams, Eisenhower's chief aide, wrote of the High Dam project that "any attempt to give aid to the Arabs always met with opposition behind the scenes in Washington, where . . . alert representatives of the many well-organized pro-Israel lobbies. . were always effective and influential in the Capitol. Consideration for the great body of private opinion in the United States favoring Israel was a large factor in every government decision on the Middle East."

Nasser had no friend in court except Black. On 8 May, in a speech that was printed in the *Congressional Record* on 9 July, Black told the Connecticut Chamber of Commerce that the dam was "entirely feasible" and that "the value of new agricultural and industrial production and other benefits will within a short span of years be more than equal to the investment required." He said the aid offered by the US and Britain was "contingent on lending by the [World] Bank" and that he and Nasser had "reached an understanding which was satisfactory to me" regarding the bank's loan.

Despite his influence in both places, Black did not get either the State Department or the White House moving again on the project. And as the weeks and months rolled by forces and events adverse to Nasser and the dam came crowding upon the scene, making it ever more unlikely that anyone could break the inertia into which the Anglo-American offer had settled. By July, when Nasser himself tried to break the inertia by accepting the Anglo-American *aides mémoires* as they were, conditions, phraseology, and all, the array of adverse forces had become so formidable that the Western offer itself broke apart rather than move forward.

The renege was as abrupt as a punch in the stomach and as humiliating as spit in the face. Egypt's ambassador, Ahmed Hussein, had hurried home on 21 May to tell Nasser of the hostility he had provoked by recognizing Red China and to urge him to accept the US and British *aides mémoires* without further ado. He reported to Nasser on 23 May and conferred with him again about a week before returning to Washington, obtaining Nasser's acceptance of the *aides mémoires* at the second meeting. Hussein arrived back in Washington on 17 July. He made his fateful call on Dulles at the Secretary of State's office on 19 July.

In the office with Dulles were Hoover and George V. Allen. As Allen recalls it:

> Only Hussein and Dulles spoke substantially. Hussein was always very pro-American. He used to wear Nasser out by telephoning him, pushing pro-Americanism very emotionally. He is an ebullient man, but serious. There was some preliminary chit-chat. Then Hussein began by saying he was greatly concerned by the Russian offers and the expectations they raised. He eulogized the High Dam, emphasized Nasser's strength of vision, and said how much he, Hussein, wanted the US to do it. He showed that he realized we had problems. But he touched his pocket and said "We've got the Soviet offers right in our pocket." This gave Dulles his cue. Eisenhower had said often that the first person to say such a thing, he'd tell him to go to Moscow.
>
> Dulles didn't read the statement [which was released to the press immediately afterward] but more or less paraphrased it. Dulles's reply was kindly in tone. He said we had seriously considered it and realized how important it was. But frankly, he said, the economic situation makes it not feasible for the US to take part. We have to withdraw our offer.

Allen does not recall what discussion there was of Nasser's acceptance of the conditions in the Western *aides mémoires*. The meeting lasted 50 minutes. Hussein was glum when he emerged and declined to comment to reporters but other Egyptian officials were bitter. Dulles's kindly tone during the meeting was a mark of personal friendship for Hussein. He was under no illusions about the impact of the renege on Nasser. State Department officials told newsmen that Dulles had acted in full anticipation of angry reactions against the US and Britain in Egypt and throughout the Arab world.

There was no simple reason for Dulles's renege. Many of the reasons alleged by Dulles and others prove groundless upon examination. They must be examined because they may falsify or distort the historical record if accepted uncritically and also because their very confusion illuminates the state of mind—the thinking and the nonthinking—of Dulles as he made his momentous decision.

The official explanation given in the State Department press release announcing the renege on 19 July was that because of "developments" in the intervening seven months "the ability of Egypt to devote adequate resources to assure the project's success has become more uncertain than at the time the offer was made." This was regarded from the outset as a deliberately transparent cover story, designed to satisfy diplomatic niceties and at the same time shake or topple Nasser to drive home a warning to neutralists. Murphy called it "that uninformative statement."

Nasser was acutely offended by the slur on Egypt's credit. Black was scarcely less so and he regards the official statement as both cruel and mendacious. "Imagine going to the Chase Bank and asking to borrow $10,000," he exclaimed, "and then reading in the newspapers that you were turned down on the grounds that your credit was no good!"

Senator Fulbright said thirteen months later that, "contrary to the statement of the Department of State," his subcommittee had found "no substantial evidence of a radical worsening in Egypt's economic condition at the time of the withdrawal of the offer." He said bluntly that "the reasons given to the public . . . were not, in my opinion, valid reasons."

Chief among the "developments" cited in background information given out to supplement the press release were the Russian arms deals. Eisenhower writes in his memoirs that the second arms deal "mortgaged" Egypt's cotton stockpile and "made it obvious that Egypt could never fulfill her part of the financing on terms we could accept." Dulles, Murphy, and Eden, among others, echo the theme. Black says tartly that this excuse for the renege is not good enough because it was the World Bank's responsibility to answer for the soundness of both the project and the Egyptian economy and it was satisfied on both counts.

Black, who was not consulted about the renege, had said in Cairo on 21 June after a meeting with Nasser that the World Bank loan awaited only the implementation of the Anglo-American offer and that he hoped the agreement on it would be concluded. When he returned to Washington he told Dulles, Murphy, and Hoover in specific refutation of their doubts about Egypt's economy that there had been no deterioration and no diminution of Egypt's ability to sustain the project. He reaffirmed the World Bank's favor for the project again in a letter to Kaissouny on 9 July, just ten days before the renege.

The US Embassy in Cairo said some years after the third Russian arms deal, which replaced Egypt's losses in the 1956 war, that servicing the Russian loans for arms was "no strain on the Egyptian economy at all," that they were costing

Egypt $25 million a year in commodities that were surplus in Western markets, and that the Egyptians had got the Russians to take yarn instead of raw cotton, thus raising the value in-put by Egyptians.

The fact that Egypt actually built the dam while continuing to buy large quantities of Russian arms seems to be a conclusive refutation of the charge that she had already mortgaged her economy for arms by July 1956. The Egyptian share of the construction costs in building the dam with the Russians was between $800 and $900 million, the same amount that was called for in the Western proposals, while the Russian contribution was equivalent to $310 million, more than 20 per cent less than the West offered.

Nevertheless, the idea that the US reneged because Nasser mortgaged his economy for arms is so strong that some of the Western leaders of the time, in memoirs and in conversation, say or imply that the arms deal came after the Western offer, a reversal of true chronology that gives a more logical appearance to the renege. "As a matter of fact," said Senator Fulbright after his investigation of the Suez crisis, "the arms deal was . . . the principal reason for the offer being made. So to argue that the arms deal was both the reason for making the offer and also the reason for withdrawing the offer is wholly illogical."

Another accusation often used to justify the renege is that Nasser was using Russian offers of aid for the dam to "blackmail" the West into meeting Nasser's terms. Eisenhower says in his memoirs that Nasser "gave the impression of a man who was convinced that he could play off East against West by blackmailing both." Dulles told a luncheon meeting of Latin American ambassadors in Washington on 7 August: "We have indicated that we would not go ahead with the Aswan Dam project because we felt that, in effect, the Egyptian Government was trying to blackmail us into carrying out that operation, and we are not willing to be blackmailed." Robert Murphy, the third-ranking diplomat in the State Department at the time, also uses the word in his memoirs, attributing it to Dulles.

The truth is that Nasser repeatedly emphasized his preference for Western aid both in public and in private, and not only for the dam but also for arms. In speeches and interviews after announcing the Russian arms deal he told how he had besought the West and stated, with ungrateful candor that might well have provoked Moscow, that he would have bought Western arms instead if only he had been allowed. He persistently declined to discuss the dam with the Russians, although they often reiterated their offer in public, and he made no secret of the fact that Egypt had not even studied the Russian offer. Far from "blackmailing" the West to accept his terms, he accepted the West's terms at some personal risk in his 9 February accord with the World Bank. By the end of June he had gone so far as to drop his request for mere changes in the phraseology of the Western conditions and said he would accept the West's terms in the West's words. Nasser was not even shopping between East and West to obtain the best bargain.

Russia was, in fact, the first government to offer help for the dam, in October 1955. This, added to the fright occasioned by the arms deal, was what stimulated Washington and London into action on the dam and made possible Hoover's abortive peace effort. On 18 December 1955, when news of the Anglo-American offer on the dam reached the front pages in Cairo, Ambassador Solod said: "We still intend to take part in its building, unless there is something in the agreement with the West which specifically excludes us." Washington commented tartly that exclusion of the Russians was "implicit" in the Western offer.

The evidence most often cited for the accusation that Nasser was dangling the Russian offer before the West was his interview with Osgood Caruthers of *The New York Times*, printed on the front page on 2 April 1956. As Caruthers paraphrased it in his lead paragraph, Nasser "declared that he still holds in his pocket a Soviet offer to help finance the construction of the proposed High Dam" which he would consider accepting if negotiations with the West broke down. Caruthers quoted Nasser as saying: "I do not mention the Soviet offer of aid as a threat or as bluff. The Soviet offer was very general and, really, we have not studied it." Nasser told Caruthers, with more hope than truth, that negotiations on the Anglo-American offer had not faltered and that he had every hope a successful agreement would be reached. He said he was worried by recent demands in Parliament for the withdrawal of Britain's offer.

The *Times* printed a profile accompanying the interview calling Nasser a "tiger" and a "fox" and attributing to him "a taste for power." A very foxy picture of Nasser illustrated it. But Dulles, a careful daily reader of The *Times*, could still see the interview for what it was, a candid discussion of the whole range of Egyptian policy in which the Soviet offer was merely one of a number of important facts. The following day, with the interview fresh in his mind, Dulles described Nasser as a patriot seeking "the genuine independence of the area" who was nowhere near "vassalage" to the Russians. Nasser's desire for the liberation of the Arab world from the remnants of British and French domination was apparently as acceptable to Dulles as his own desire for the liberation of Eastern Europe from the Russians.

Eisenhower, however, cited the interview in his memoirs as "this threat of blackmail." The Administration seems to have adopted this view when Nasser recognized Red China, an act which Eisenhower says "added to our annoyance." Explaining his renege at a press conference on 2 April 1957, Dulles said:

Only a few days [It was two months.] before I was asked for a definitive answer by the Egyptians they had recognized Communist China—being the first Arab nation to do so. . . . And in that way the Egyptians, in a sense, forced upon us an issue to which I think there was only one proper response: That issue was, do nations which play both sides get better treatment than nations which are stalwart and work with us? . . . and stalwart allies were watching very carefully to see what the answer would be; stalwart allies which included some in the same area.

Nasser's neutralism was equated with blackmail, but Dulles had a double standard. Neutralism in the West's sphere of influence, he told an audience in Iowa on 9 June, "is an immoral and shortsighted conception." But four days later he urged the Senate Appropriations Committee not to restrict aid to neutralist Yugoslavia, saying that it was in the US interest to support Tito's "passionate dedication" to Yugoslav independence even though Tito was "willing to take help wherever he can get it so long as he does not jeopardize that [independence]." He also told the committee that tying the Administration's hands would "force irrevocably into the Soviet camp a nation which is still trying to keep in both camps." It is ironical to reflect that Nasser, although taking Tito as an example for his neutralism, was trying to achieve independence without leaving the Western camp.

Another allegation by Americans who defend the renege is that Nasser had neglected the Anglo-American offer so thoroughly that Washington thought he had lost interest in it. This allegation appears in the memoirs of Eisenhower and Murphy and is attributed to Dulles in a book of his quotations by his press secretary, Andrew H. Berding. "Nasser, despite our urging for six months," wrote Murphy, "had chosen not to discuss these important details." Eisenhower speaks of "Egyptian silence." Berding says Dulles said: "The matter had been on the shelf for six months and no effort had been made by Egypt to push it."

In fact, Nasser had conferred twice with Black, sent diplomatic messages to Washington, sought to keep the issue alive in the press, and finally yielded on all points. Dulles himself, denying a suggestion by Eisenhower that he had been "abrupt" and undiplomatic in his renege, wrote the President on 15 September 1956:

For several months we had left unanswered an Egyptian memorandum on this subject, and the Egyptians knew full well the reasons why. Telephone conversations of which we learned indicated that the Egyptian Government knew that when they came, as they did, to get a definitive reply it would be negative. . . .

If I had not announced our withdrawal when I did, the Congress would certainly have imposed it on us, almost unanimously. As it was, we retained some flexibility.

Of course Egypt, in its flirtations with the Soviet Union, had itself consciously jeopardized our sharing in this project, and then had tried to bluff us by pretending to [accept] Soviet "offers."

Dulles here refutes the thesis, elsewhere attributed to him, that it was Egypt and not the US that neglected the question of Western aid. But, in addition to the incidental disclosure of electronic espionage by the US, he adds two more to the multifarious reasons he gave from time to time for the renege. The first has some validity: that Congress would try to block the aid anyway.

The second, that Nasser had "consciously jeopardized" Western aid, is developed in subsequent statements by Dulles into a thesis that Nasser deliberately courted the renege on the dam to obtain a pretext for nationalizing the canal. Dulles remained extremely sensitive to the doubts he knew Eisenhower harbored about his handling of the renege and, after another critical Presidential comment, wrote him again on 30 October 1957:

President Nasser has since said that he planned for nearly two years to seize the Suez Canal Company, but was waiting for a good occasion. He knew that if he pressed for a decision from us when he did the result would be negative because the Congressional action had been announced. Nevertheless, he pressed for a definitive answer, and I suspect he did so in order to create the "occasion" for which he said he was looking.

It was no longer a mere suspicion in the words Berding attributes to Dulles: "Nasser therefore deliberately created a situation which would enable him to seize the canal."

Black calls this thesis "impossible—completely ridiculous." The Big Three ambassadors in Cairo at the time agree. Dulles's information came from a speech made by Tito in November 1956; perhaps also from a rather braggadocious magazine article by Nasser's friend Haikal in August 1956, although neither these nor any other sources I am aware of adequately justify Dulles's positiveness. I know of no statement by Nasser that he planned for two years to seize the canal and merely awaited a good occasion to do it. He did not "know" Dulles would renege, he merely suspected it. And Dulles's contention that Nasser sacrificed the dam in order to have a pretext to seize the canal is a reversal of logic that would not be worth disposing of if it had not been endorsed by Eisenhower and accepted by others. Dulles said, in effect, that Nasser had deliberately thrown away the end to excuse seizing the means.

Nasser's actual sequence of cause and effect was more logical. When Dulles

slammed the gate on the Western financial avenue to the dam, Nasser opened a
new one by taking over the canal for its lucrative foreign currency earnings
twelve years before it was to revert automatically to Egypt. If the West would
not lend him the money for the dam, he would buy it himself with the income
from the Canal. The dam, not the canal, was what Nasser had set his heart
on. The Canal was de Lesseps' monument; the High Dam would be Nasser's.
Egypt's "new pyramid" would be the greatest milestone on the journey through
history of the world's oldest nation. It was the rock on which a pauperized folk
would build a dignified and prosperous future.

Nasser announced in November 1954 that he had ordered studies looking
toward the end of the canal company's concession. He concedes that the prospect of nationalizing the canal before the end of the concession came under
consideration early in 1956 as a means to preclude foreign efforts to extend
the concession or "internationalize" the canal, but there was no target date,
not even a target year. He disclosed to me in 1966 that he thought of nationalizing the canal to finance the dam when he realized, shortly before the event,
that the West's offer was probably dead.

Nasser said he mentioned his thoughts to Ambassador Hussein who came
home in May for nearly two months of consultations. They met in Alexandria,
where Nasser spent the five days from the 5th to the 10th of July.

"I told him, from our appreciation [of the circumstances] we feel that the
United States will not finance the High Dam," Nasser said. "He denied that and
he said that they will, if we agree about some conditions. I told him: Well, go
ahead. We agree to all the conditions but I am 100 per cent sure that there will
be no financing. And he was astonished. And I mentioned the idea about the
Suez Canal—that we would nationalize the Suez Canal to finance the dam if
necessary." Nasser laughed heartily as he recalled the ambassador's reaction.
"He didn't believe that. He looked at me strangely. You know, such people
don't imagine such things."

(Nasser's scoffing to the contrary, it was a bureaucrat, and an Englishman
at that, who first thought of using the Canal revenues to build a great dam
at Aswan. Lord Milner, who controlled Egyptian finances under Cromer, wrote
in 1893, when plans for the Aswan Dam were in abeyance for lack of money,
that England had profited greatly from her Suez Canal shares and might well
grant Egypt enough of the earnings to build the dam.)

Nasser flew to Yugoslavia on 12 July for a week of conferences in Belgrade
and on the island of Brioni with Marshal Tito and Pandit Jawaharlal Nehru.
Hussein departed for Washington on 15 July with the news that Egypt had
accepted the Western terms. When he arrived, on the 17th, he telephoned

Black, who was vacationing at Winthrop Aldrich's island house in Dark Harbor, Maine. He wanted to come up and tell Black the good news. "Don't tell me," said Black. "Tell Dulles."

The Egyptians had in fact already informed Dulles that Nasser had withdrawn his unanswered request for changes in the US *aide mémoire* and would accept it as it was. Dulles reported this to Eisenhower at his Gettysburg farm on 13 July. He told the President he suspected Nasser had made an unsuccessful request for Russian aid to Shepilov, the Foreign Minister, who was in Cairo from 16 to 22 June to attend the celebrations of Britain's evacuation of the Suez base. Dulles suggested that this was what made Nasser agree to the West's conditions. He told the President he had warned the Egyptians that the Administration was no longer in a position to proceed with the matter because of Senate opposition and because of changes in the Administration's own views. He told the Egyptians he would consider the matter and consult with them the next week. Just six days later he announced his renege to Hussein.

I know of no hard evidence contrary to Nasser's assertion that he neither decided nor acted on nationalization until after Dulles's renege. He merely conceived of it as a contingency plan in the event the US did renege. It was an unwelcome contingency even though he expected it. Black and the Big Three ambassadors, Byroade, Trevelyan, and du Chayla, all believe that if the West's offer had been made good instead of cancelled, Nasser would never have jeopardized the building of the High Dam by cutting short the canal concession.

Dulles's imaginings about Shepilov having withdrawn Russian aid apparently arose from speeches Shepilov made in Damascus and Beirut on his way home from Cairo in which he spoke of aid for industries but did not mention the dam. While Shepilov was in Cairo the Western press reported rumors of a renewed Russian offer to finance the dam on better terms than ever. When Shepilov left, *The Times* (London) reported that "a sigh of relief swept through the Western chancelleries" at the omission of any mention of the dam in Nasser's and Shepilov's joint communiqué. If Dulles interpreted these things as evidence of a Russian rebuff he was wrong. They meant only that Nasser, punctilious to the end, continued to avoid the subject so long as the Western offer stood.

Egyptians closely informed on Moscow politics have told me that if anyone was rebuffed it was Shepilov, whose reputation was said to have suffered from Egypt's refusal to discuss the standing Russian offer. The Kremlin hoped Washington's procrastination would provide Shepilov the opportunity to move in on the dam just as Washington's procrastination a year previous enabled Shepilov to get on with substantive negotiations on arms. The Americans had, in effect, opened the door so wide to the Russians that it was embarrassing to them when the Egyptians did not let them in. Khrushchev said hopefully at the US Embassy reception in Moscow on the Fourth of July that Egypt alone had the right to decide who would help her build the dam.

Shepilov admitted in Moscow on 21 July, two days after the renege, that no one had raised the subject of the High Dam with him in Cairo. He said the question was not "in such an acute form as the United States thinks." Nasser had, in fact, suspended in February the preliminary work such as building access roads to the site which had been begun optimistically in 1955. The work was suspended pending both the financing and a new Nile agreement with the Sudan. Shepilov said he got the impression that industrialization was more important but he did not minimize the High Dam. Russia would consider favorably "any Egyptian requests," he said. *The New York Times* copy editor must have been thinking like Dulles and drawing conclusions larger than the facts supported because he headlined the dispatch on Shepilov's comments: "Moscow Asserts It Does Not Plan Aswan Dam Aid." There must have been many who did not read the entire dispatch for the impression spread that Dulles had called a Russian—or perhaps an Egyptian—bluff and won.

In London, the *Observer* said that the Western representatives who in December had been "tumbling over themselves in trying to entice the contract away from Russia" had now revealed the Western offer as nothing but "a quick spoiling operation against Russian promises." Apparently, it said, "in its approach to economic aid, the West is as politically motivated as Russia."

Aly Sabry, Nasser's chief aide, told me in London exactly one month later that Shepilov's statements about giving financial assistance for factories were made to save Shepilov's own face after Egypt demurred at discussing the dam with him. "We can't understand why the West based a policy on Shepilov's statement without checking its real reason," Sabry said. "Nasser chose nationalization to keep free of Russia. Russian aid would have been the simple solution and it would have been cheered. Nationalization was dangerous." At the time Sabry made these candid comments he was in daily consultation with Shepilov, who was upholding Egypt's cause at the London Conference on Suez.

Congressional opposition to the dam could have been a serious problem. "We had little zest for an all-out legislative fight," wrote Eisenhower, "in behalf of a nation that thought it could do as well by dealing with the Soviets." But Dulles was zestfully conducting an all-out fight for aid to Tito, who was doing as well by dealing with the Soviets. In Nasser's case, after his recognition of Red China, the Administration seems to have forgotten that the primary purpose of the Anglo-American offer in everybody's mind but Hoover's was to dissuade Nasser from dealing with the Soviets. When Dulles first urged the project on Congressional leaders at a meeting on 13 December 1955 he told Senator Lyndon B. Johnson, an opponent of aiding Egypt, that Western financing would make any change in Egypt's affiliation with the US improbable for ten years.

The career men in the State Department say that Dulles could have explained his legislative problems to Nasser and persuaded him to lie quiet while a new effort was made to get the aid through Congress. The original allocation of $56 million was transferred to other projects at the end of the fiscal year on 30 June, at which time it would otherwise have lapsed by law. Cairo was officially informed of this, as *al-Ahram* reported on its front page, on 7 July.

By then Dulles and Eisenhower were as unwilling to seek a new appropriation for the High Dam as the Senate Appropriations Committee was to approve one. Dulles appeared before the committee on 19 June and a week later he wrote the chairman a promise that "none of the funds which may be appropriated for the fiscal year 1957 will be committed to finance the Aswan [High] Dam without specific prior consultation with the committee." Just to make sure, the committee appended a directive to its report on the foreign aid bill on 16 July saying:

The committee directs that none of the funds provided in this act shall be used for assistance in connection with the construction of the Aswan [High] Dam, nor shall any of the funds heretofore provided under the Mutual Security Act, as amended, be used for this dam without the prior approval of the Committee on Appropriations.

Eisenhower privately rejected the legal force of the directive, fearing it would paralyze the conduct of foreign relations, but as William S. White of *The New York Times* reported, "few believed the Administration would want to challenge it." Dulles said on 2 April 1957 that the directive was "perhaps first of all and most imperative" among "a number of reasons which dictated our declining to go ahead with the Aswan proposal." Senator Fulbright said four months later, after his exhaustive subcommittee study, that Congressional opposition was confined to the Appropriations Committee and that "there is no evidence . . . that the Administration ever made any serious effort to persuade the few members of Congress who had expressed opposition."

So the cotton men and the Zionists prevailed in Congress, apparently by default. Perhaps even a zestful fight might not have been able to get money out of Congress for the dam. But instead of quietly explaining this to the Egyptians, Dulles chose, in the words of one diplomat, to "kick Nasser in the teeth with a missionary twist."

"Those of us who worked with Dulles were never told explicitly why he acted so abruptly," wrote Murphy. He adds that the effects of the renege had not been weighed carefully in advance. Dulles summoned no staff meeting and did not mention the High Dam matter to Murphy, who was working with him on Middle Eastern problems at the time. "Even President Eisenhower was not consulted until the morning of [Ambassador] Hussein's visit," says Murphy.

Eisenhower's intestinal operation for ileitis had kept him away from the White House from 8 June until 15 July. The ailment prevented the full consultations on the High Dam that Dulles had with the President on all his other important foreign policy acts. On the morning of the renege Dulles, accompanied by Hoover, spent only twelve minutes with Eisenhower. He showed Eisenhower the press release that would be issued after his meeting with the Egyptian ambassador. Eisenhower approved it.

Nevertheless, the renege on the High Dam was more purely Dulles's action than any other major foreign policy decision during the Eisenhower Administration. Afterward, members of Eisenhower's old White House staff blamed Dulles for detonating the Suez Crisis on his own by gratuitously slapping Nasser down in a way that was bound to provoke a reaction. They felt that Eisenhower would not have approved if he had known how Dulles was going to do it. Eisenhower's requests for explanations from Dulles show that he was not happy at the time about it and he does not seem to have been fully satisfied with the explanations.

Eisenhower's memory, instinctively seeking to justify US conduct, played him false on a number of important points. In his memoirs, Eisenhower attributes to Dulles an account of Black's meeting with Nasser on 20 June that is the opposite of the truth. "At this meeting," Eisenhower writes, "Nasser gave Black a series of counterproposals, some of which would be totally unacceptable to all three of the financing authorities. . . . When Foster described the extraordinary counterproposals . . . the two of us concluded that Nasser was not really interested in serious negotiation on the project, and we considered the matter dead for all practical purposes."

Perhaps, in their sketchy consultations, Eisenhower misunderstood Dulles, for both Nasser and Black deny this version. Black is emphatic. He says:

There was no new list of conditions. Quite the contrary. It was a question of Nasser giving up the still unanswered queries on the US and British conditions he had sent long before. Nasser couldn't understand why he hadn't gotten an answer. I explained Dulles's difficulties, including the Senate Appropriations Committee. There was no question at all of new Egyptian conditions. My understanding was that Nasser would accept the US and British *aides mémoires* as they were, which he had not yet done.

Eisenhower treats the Nasser-Black meeting as the point at which the alleged Egyptian "counterproposals" killed the Western offer. But on 19 June, the day before Black called on Nasser and several days before Dulles could have learned of these "counterproposals," Dulles told the Senate Appropriations Committee that he saw no likelihood of US aid for the project in the foreseeable future, adding casually that the Soviets might furnish the aid instead.

If Dulles's consultations with Eisenhower on the renege were minimal, they were nonexistent with the other parties to the offer, the World Bank and the British. Dulles played a lone hand. Amid the welter of explanations and apologetics that followed the renege, his own are various and contradictory. At one time or another, he cited the Senate prohibition, the dubious state of Egypt's economy, the "mortgaging" of Egypt's cotton for Russian arms, Nasser's "flirtations" with Russia, the mood of our "stalwart allies," the recognition of Red China, and, finally, the thesis that Nasser had tricked him into the renege to get an excuse to seize the canal.

He eventually adopted also the argument which men like Byroade and Allen had used against making an offer on the dam in the first place. It appears among reasons he gave for the renege at his press conference on 2 April 1957. "The Egyptian component of that [project], in terms of domestic currency and effort, would involve a gigantic effort and call for an austerity program over a period of twelve to fifteen years," he said. "Undoubtedly, that would be a burden and cause of complaint on the part of the Egyptian people, and probably the responsibility for that would be placed upon the foreign lenders, and they would end up by being disliked instead of liked."

In hindsight, Dulles sought to make it look as if he knew what he was doing to a far greater extent than he did know, that he had calculated in advance and calculated well. Dulles's explanations all must be interpreted among other circumstances to arrive closer to the truth than Dulles's own words. It is hard to find evidence supporting the claim that Dulles's renege was consistent with any logic, even the logic of "brinkmanship." On the contrary, as Fulbright said, "to summarize, there is much evidence in the Aswan Dam papers that our policy was influenced too much by emotion and not enough by hard-headed realities."

Dulles's emotion was readily stimulated by what he and Eisenhower constantly referred to as "International Communism," an imprecise concept which frequently disabled his thinking. Pineau, a Socialist, said Dulles was unable to distinguish between communism and socialism. Fulbright said he believed Dulles confused Egyptian nationalism and neutralism with communism. All the available evidence points to Nasser's recognition of Red China as the event that beclouded Dulles's thinking about Nasser. His references to Nasser in public statements changed in tone from sympathy to antipathy. He seemed to adopt the view that Nasser was a kind of traitor in the Cold War and he lost his perception of the well-grounded Egyptian fears—fear of Israel, fear of starvation—that forced Nasser to turn to the East for arms and development when help failed in the West.

After all the testimony and explanations have been weighed, it seems that circumstantial evidence provides the truest insight as to why Dulles rebuffed Nasser in so injurious a fashion. Circumstantial evidence indicates that Nasser's recognition of Red China convinced Dulles that Nasser ought to be eliminated. At Eden's behest, he approved joint Anglo-American planning for a coup to overthrow Nasser. Although Dulles's reservations eventually smothered the undercover enterprise, the manner of his renege on the High Dam bore all the earmarks of a design to shake Nasser's position. The State Department communiqué on the renege bears many similarities to the letter Eisenhower wrote Mossadegh in 1953 refusing US aid to Iran which, when leaked to the Iranian public, loosened the aging Premier's position preparatory to the Palace-CIA coup against him. Nasser read between the lines and said in his nationalization speech a week later:

> There was another queer thing in this US communiqué. The US Secretary of State addressed himself to the Egyptian people, saying that this American attitude has nothing to do with the ties between the American people and the Egyptian people. This means that it is directed against Gamal Abdel Nasser alone. This method was quite obvious. We have had many years of experience with it.

Nasser believed the renege was designed to undermine the stability of the regime and to overthrow him. Some of Dulles's friends read the same message between the lines. "It was not only a mistake in turning the project down and the way he turned it down," said Eugene Black of Dulles's action, "but in his guess that by turning it down this would be the death knell of Nasser."

Part

II

PRETEXTS

(20 JULY 1956 TO 29 OCTOBER 1956)

11

"This Canal Belongs to Egypt"

(20 JULY 1956 TO 26 JULY 1956)

I tell you, when that canal was nationalized, Font and I could have kissed the Colonel's feet in admiration.

(WAGUIH GHALI, *Beer in the Snooker Club*, 1964)

"We dug the Canal with our lives, our skulls, our bones, our blood."

(NASSER, 26 July 1956)

WHILE DULLES was making his Cold War gambit in Washington, Nasser and Nehru lingered with Tito at Brioni, his Adriatic island retreat, drafting a communiqué on their week of deliberations on how to end the Cold War. The neutralist triumvirate urged a reconciliation between the power blocs through continued summit contacts, disarmament, and free trade. They recommended the admission of Red China to the UN. On Algeria they were as moderate as Washington and London, saying they "recognize that there are considerable numbers of people in Algeria of European descent whose interests should be protected, but this should not obstruct the recognition of the legitimate rights of the Algerians."

"In the Middle East," they said, "the conflicting interests of the Great Powers have added to the difficulties of the situation. These problems should be considered on their merits, safeguarding legitimate economic interests, but basing the solution on the freedom of the people concerned." It was a far cry from seeking to use the Cold War to blackmail the Super-Powers.

Nasser and Nehru delayed their departure from Brioni more than five hours while the communiqué was drafted, taking off at 8:20 P.M. in Nasser's British turboprop plane. They were airborne when the news of Dulles's renege flashed round the world.

In Jerusalem Dag Hammarskjold and Ben-Gurion too spent five hours that day closeted in a discussion of peace, which Hammarskjold feared Ben-Gurion was planning to break. Not surprisingly, he got little reassurance from Ben-Gurion, who was in fact planning war against Nasser. Ben-Gurion told Hammarskjold that as far as he was concerned the cease-fire clause in the armistice, that is to say, *de facto* peace, was secondary to "broader issues" such as free passage through the Suez Canal, free access to the Holy Places in Jordan, and the cessation of hostile Arab propaganda. Ben-Gurion rejected Hammarskjold's request that he allow UN truce observers to return to the demilitarized zone at al-Auja. He was unmoved by Hammarskjold's warning that if the restrictions were not lifted in ten days he would take the matter to the Security Council.

When Nasser and Nehru landed at Cairo at 2 A.M. on 20 July, Interior Minister Zakaria Mohyeddin was waiting at the airport to break the grim news of Dulles's renege. Nehru went to the Indian Embassy and Nasser went to his home with Mohyeddin and three other members of the old junta. Not only the dam but also the survival of the regime were suddenly at stake.

"You know, I was ready for it because this was my anticipation," Nasser recalls. "But what hurt me was the part in the statement about our economy. I regarded that as a slap in the face. Of course, they are at liberty to say Yes or No, but it must be said politely. It was [done that way], of course, to undermine the stability of the regime here. . . . To give us a lesson. There was some talk about that [getting rid of Nasser] in the American press and in the British press at that time."

Less than a month before, on 23 June, Nasser had been elected President of Egypt on a single-slate ballot that won 99.84 per cent of the votes in a turn-out of 97.6 per cent of the registered voters. The revolutionary junta was formally transformed into a civilian cabinet. Egypt was pursuing new courses with new freedom. Since the arms deal with Russia in September 1955 the regime, despite its vigorous internal anti-Communism, had taken an increasingly neutralist line in foreign affairs. The departure of the last British troops on 13 June 1956 had ended three generations of foreign occupation.

Nasser was riding high. The regime's enemies, both in Egypt and in the Arab world, were watching for it to stumble. Dulles's brusque slap looked like just what they were waiting for. Representatives of the monarchies in Iraq, Jordan, and Saudi Arabia were too delighted to be discreet.

The wider international situation looked equally bleak for Nasser. The Western Big Three, who had declared themselves in 1950 to be the guarantors of the Arab-Israeli armistice, were lined up solidly against Nasser. France wanted to eliminate Nasser because of his aid to the Algerian nationalist rebellion. Britain wanted to eliminate Nasser's support for independence movements in her Middle Eastern sphere of influence. And now Washington had struck hard against Nasser's neutralism. Across the Sinai Desert in Israel, Premier David Ben-Gurion had ousted Foreign Minister Moshe Sharett to obtain a free hand for war against Nasser.

Russia, Nasser's only Great Power sympathizer, was increasingly preoccupied with upsurging independence movements in Poland and Hungary that had already erupted in riots in Poland and were headed toward full-scale revolt in Hungary. Nasser's opponents were active; his friends were busy elsewhere.

Egyptians, privately stunned by Dulles's rebuff, were slow to react publicly. For one thing, Government offices and the newspapers were closed for the Bairam holidays that end the month-long fast of Ramadan. Cairo Radio limited itself to reporting the news from Washington and London without comment.

Nasser is not averse to taking spectacular risks but he likes to calculate them in advance if he has time. The first requirement was information, the fullest possible, from abroad. Diplomatic communications hummed on Friday, 20 July 1956, but outwardly official Cairo remained as quiet as it did on any other summer Sabbath. Egyptian liaison officers on Cyprus obtained reports from the outlawed nationalists of EOKA on British military strength on the island: two infantry brigades and three paratroop battalions, all tied down in anti-EOKA operations, and two air squadrons, one of fighters and one of transports. Egyptian agents in Malta and Aden reported on British naval and troop strengths. The Tenth Armored Division was divided between Libya and Jordan, whose Arab governments would perforce prevent its use against Egypt. No other significant British forces were nearer than England itself.

On Saturday, 21 July, Wing Commander Aly Sabry, Nasser's top political aide, interrupted his Bairam holiday to tell newsmen: "Naturally it upsets our plans, but the High Dam will be built." Cairo Radio uncoiled in the afternoon to denounce "the stupid mentality of Imperialism" for having "given birth to action oozing with evil, hatred, and malice . . . prompted by nothing but the selfish desire to retard the efforts of President Nasser to raise the living standards of Egypt's millions."

In Moscow, at a Belgian embassy reception, Shepilov made the comments to newsmen on Russian aid to Egypt that were so wishfully misinterpreted in Washington as signifying that Russia had backed down on the High Dam and that Dulles had successfully called bluffs by both Cairo and Moscow. Washington clung to this error even though Ambassador Kiselev said in Cairo the following day that he felt sure Russia would keep her promise to finance the High Dam if Egypt should request it. Two days later, after querying Moscow about what Shepilov actually did say, Kiselev stated: "I reiterate what the Soviet Foreign Minister, Mr. Shepilov, has already said: that the Soviet Government is prepared to finance the High Dam scheme if Egypt requests such financing." Years later, after Egypt had completed the dam with Russian help, there were members of the Dulles entourage who still clung to the illusion that the Russian offers in 1955 and 1956 were bluffs, cleverly designed to force the US to bleed itself economically in foreign aid projects.

Eugene Black's 9 July letter to Kaissouny was reported in the Egyptian newspapers as a refutation of Dulles's statement that the Egyptian economy had deteriorated in the past seven months. Editorials said that, on the contrary, Black had confirmed the strength of the Egyptian economy four times in those seven months, first in the Western offer of 16 December, next in the accord of 9 February, a third time after his meeting with Nasser and Kaissouny on 20 June, and finally in the letter to Kaissouny.

By Sunday afternoon, 22 July, Nasser's thinking about how to retort to the West had reached the writing stage. He wrote out longhand what he called "an appreciation," covering eleven pages. This is a military term for the analysis of a situation on which an operational plan is based. In it Nasser calculated the risks of nationalizing the Suez Canal Company. Regarding Britain as the chief danger, he tried to put himself in Sir Anthony Eden's shoes and to predict British reaction.

"I [wrote]: 'Appreciation from the point of view of Mr. Anthony Eden,'" he recalled. "Then I discussed the question of the use of force, including its use in cooperation with Israel. I said, [from Eden's point of view] it is impossible. Because if the British cooperate with Israel, this would affect all their positions in the Middle East and all their interests. And they have great interests in the Middle East.

"Then I studied the distribution of the British armed forces, and I came to the conclusion that they would need two months to mobilize a force against us. We came to the conclusion that in these two months, through diplomacy, we can reach a settlement. This was the deduction.

"Our appreciation was: the reaction will come from Britain, not from France. France was against the Baghdad Pact. There were other contradictions in this area between France and Britain. We were not completely aware of the French bitterness over Algeria. On the other hand, I thought France was occupied in Algeria to the extent that she would not be able to participate in armed action against us. That's why we excluded France and we concentrated on Britain.

"As for the United States, we were under the impression that the United States would not participate in any action of force.

"This was the appreciation. We excluded Israel. We excluded France. We excluded the United States. And about the possibility of British armed action against us—not before two months."

Nasser laughed at the recollection of his miscalculations on the roles of France and Israel and the possibility of Britain cooperating with Israel. But he feels that on the latter point, although his prediction was wrong, his analysis was correct. Britain's collusion with Israel in the November war against Egypt, he says, resulted directly in the destruction of Britain's traditional influence and power in the Middle East.

A part of Nasser's appreciation was economic, strongly influenced by a speech of Harold Macmillan, then Chancellor of the Exchequer.

There was a statement by Mr. Macmillan just one or two days before this appreciation. I studied this statement and he was worried about the position of sterling. We considered this as a factor also, that if they use force, this will affect sterling. And [there was] the factor of their need of petrol—that if we closed the canal [in the event of war] this will affect the United Kingdom.

Even after the two months required for mobilizing a force, Nasser thought, the risk to sterling and oil supplies might continue to deter the British from attacking. By that time, even if a settlement had not been concluded, world opinion would be so alerted as to make war virtually unthinkable. It looked safe enough, not only to nationalize the canal company and apply the profits toward building the dam, but to make a dramatic political coup out of it to redress the injury done by Dulles and the British Foreign Office.

Dag Hammarskjold, Secretary General of the United Nations, who had been shuttling between Cairo and Israel in an urgent effort to shore up the battered Armistice Agreement, conferred with Nasser at noon. It is curious that their discussion did not stimulate Nasser to give greater weight to Israel in his appreciation. One of the topics he and Hammarskjold discussed was Israel's entrenchment in al-Auja.

The Israeli danger had been brought to Nasser's mind in the morning too. At 10 o'clock he attended the funeral of Colonel Salah Mustafa, the Egyptian military attaché in Amman who had been mortally wounded by an Israeli parcel bomb on 14 July. Nasser and Mustafa's father walked together ahead of the horse-drawn gun carriage that bore the coffin through streets lined with silent spectators. Mustafa was the second victim of underground warfare within three days. Colonel Yehoshafat Harkavi, who was put in charge of Israeli intelligence after the bungled Lavon Affair operation, artfully contrived the delivery of the first parcel bomb to Colonel Mustafa Hafez in Gaza on 11 July. It killed him instantly. Harkavi had publicly named Hafez in October 1955 as director of the *Fedayeen*.

Although as President, Nasser did not legally require cabinet approval for decisions, he says he did not commit himself to nationalization of the Suez Canal Company until after he had discussed the idea and his appreciation of the prospects with the officers of the original revolutionary junta, the Revolution Command Council, which had been merged into the cabinet after the Presidential election. Nasser met with them on Monday, 23 July. At the meeting, he said, "there were three ideas: to nationalize the canal, or to nationalize fifty per cent of the canal, or to give an ultimatum that if they don't finance the High Dam we will nationalize the canal.

"Then we reached the decision to nationalize," he said. "We said: If we give an ultimatum, the answer will be another ultimatum. They will say: If you nationalize, we will use force. They would put us in a corner. Then we decided that, rather than nationalize fifty per cent, it is better to nationalize completely.

"This was the year in which there were no celebrations on the 23rd [the anniversary of the revolutionary coup]. And Marshal [Abdel Hakim] Amer, [Defense Minister, Commander in Chief, and Nasser's closest friend] left on the 23d at night for Alexandria. So we reached agreement on the 23. I told Mahmoud Yunes on the 24th."

It was on the morning of the 24th, a Tuesday, that Nasser made his first public comment on Dulles's renege. After five days of brooding over the slap-in-the-face manner in which Dulles had done it, Nasser was in a black rage when he appeared at the sun-baked village of Mostarod, five miles north of Cairo, to open an oil pipeline from Suez and the new refinery it fed.

"Drop dead of your fury," Nasser shouted at Washington. He abandoned classical Arabic for the kind of rough-and-ready speech that brought explosions of applause from the working-class Egyptians in his audience. "When Washington sheds every decent principle on which foreign relations are based and broadcasts the lie, snare, and delusion that Egypt's economy is unsound," President Nasser roared, "then I look them in the face and say: Drop dead of your fury for you will never be able to dictate to Egypt."

In London that day Foreign Secretary Selwyn Lloyd defended the renege in the House of Commons, saying Egyptian military spending made the High Dam of doubtful feasibility. He conceded that the Egyptian press and radio had adopted a friendlier tone toward Britain but he said a restoration of good relations would "depend upon the facts and upon the willingness of Egypt not to undermine the legitimate British interests in the Middle East." He had evidently not seen the news flashes on Nasser's speech at Mostarod, which created an atmosphere of defiant hostility that made the world see violence two days later in what was actually a wholly legal act. Never before had the head of a small, backward country used such language toward a great power. Much more was to come.

"Our reply today," Nasser said, "is that we will not allow the domination of force and the dollar. I will tell you on Thursday, God willing, how Egypt has acted so that all its projects—such as this project—may be projects of sovereignty, dignity, and not those of humiliation, slavery, domination, rule, and exploitation. The projects which we draw up will build our national economy and at the same time build our sovereignty, dignity, and independence."

A few minutes earlier President Nasser had leaned toward Colonel Yunis, the efficient chief of the Egyptian Petroleum Authority and whispered that he wanted to see him back at the Presidency in Cairo after the ceremony.

"I went into his office at 12:35 P.M.," Yunis recalled in an interview. "He told me: 'I am going to nationalize the Suez Canal Company.' I was stunned. Then I kissed him on both cheeks. I was unable to speak. Then he said to me: 'You are going to do that job. Make an outline plan and come tomorrow at 9 o'clock.' Then he gave me the Army Mobilization Department's book of statistics and I left."

Yunis was then forty-four, six years older than Nasser. He had been one of Nasser's instructors at the staff college and later they had been instructors together.

"You know, I trust Yunis," Nasser said. "I know that he is an able man. He doesn't raise problems for anybody. And I was sure that he would do it. He told me: I can run this whole thing completely; don't worry about me. This was the answer of Yunis to me.

"I told him that he can take officers from the Navy, as he likes, for pilots or for any support. And on the other hand he could take officers from the Army for the whole management. We used to study such questions in the staff college, about canals and so on. Any staff officer would be able to run something like that. I left it completely for Yunis."

The legal and financial arrangements were already assigned to Dr. Mustafa Hefnaoui and Dr. Mohammed Abu Nossair. Abu Nossair was Minister of Commerce. Hefnaoui was a young lawyer whose advocacy of nationalization had made him the *bête noire* of the Suez Canal Company from the day he earned his doctorate in law at the University of Paris in 1951 with a thesis on the Canal. Hefnaoui is now a member of the Suez Canal Authority's board of directors. He and Abu Nossair were told to draft within four days nationalization and organizational decrees based on the studies Nasser had ordered in November 1954 to avoid being caught "unawares and weak." Nasser conferred with Hefnaoui on the 22d in the garden of his house in the garrison suburb of Manshiet al-Bakry. It was the same modest married officer's villa he had lived in before the revolution. He still lives there today, although it has been considerably enlarged since Suez.

Hefnaoui and Abu Nossair were able to get to work right away on familiar material, preparing the legal and financial basis for the main job, the take-over, which was Yunis's. They also had a two-day head start over Yunis, having got their orders before the nationalization decision was final.

"That day [the 24th] I was giving a big party at the Semiramis Hotel for oil men and contractors," Yunis recalled. "Secrecy had to be kept at a maximum. If I didn't appear at the party or if I left early it might have caused suspicion. So I was unable to begin my study of the situation until after midnight when I returned home to Heliopolis. I read the statistical book and Hefnaoui's thesis to get an idea of the organization of the company. I learned that the operating organization was divided in three parts along the Canal, one in Port Said, one in Ismailiya, and one in Suez. And there was an office in Cairo."

The pressure on Yunis would have shattered anyone less phlegmatic. The deadline had been announced by Nasser in his speech at Mostarod. Yunis and the diplomats, oil men, and workers in the audience heard Nasser promise to give his real answer to Washington two days later.

After his post-midnight study Yunis went to Nasser at 9 A.M. on the 25th and told him he had not been able to begin drafting a plan. They agreed that

339

Yunis would return with a plan at 9 P.M. While Yunis worked on his plan Nasser began making notes for his nationalization speech. He ordered a cabinet meeting the following afternoon at his official residence in Alexandria in order to tell the members in advance what was going to happen.

This is not a plan, Nasser said when Yunis took his first draft to him at 9 P.M. Tomorrow it will be complete, Yunis replied. He emphasized the importance of absolute secrecy and obtained from Nasser the handful of names of persons to whom Nasser had disclosed his decision. Nasser promised to inform Yunis of any additional persons who might have to be brought into the secret. Yunis settled down to work through the night, redrafting and refining both an "appreciation" and an operational plan. Despite the military approach to planning and the availability of officers as technicians and administrators, the take-over was to be a purely civilian affair.

The big question confronting Yunis was whether the Suez Canal Company employees would try to obstruct or sabotage the orderly movement of shipping through the Canal. A second question was the attitude of the 400 maintenance personnel, many of them soldiers in civilian dress, which the British were allowed by the 1954 evacuation agreement to keep in the Suez Canal base. After the take-over it was of paramount importance to keep canal traffic moving without interruption in order to avoid adding material cause for Great Power intervention on top of the calculated but carefully legal affront of the nationalization itself. The two local "powers" in the Canal area, the French company's non-Egyptian employees and the British maintenance personnel in the base, constituted a potential threat to canal traffic. Yunis would need to have forces in reserve to protect canal operations from these local powers.

These questions had troubled Yunis during the day. Before completing his plan during the night of 24/25 July Yunis had obtained from Nasser the authority to call in the Army if necessary to prevent interference from the French and British "powers" in the Canal area. The colonel was thus given authority by the President to order major generals into action if he felt it necessary to override the President's own prohibition against using force. Nasser did indeed trust Yunis. The 2d Armored Group, which had been withdrawn from Sinai in June for training on new Soviet weapons at Fayid on the west bank of the Great Bitter Lake, was alerted to protect Canal installations against demolitions and to protect the major airfields at Abu Suwweir, Fayid, and Kabrit against paratroop drops. The 1st Armored Group, in the northeastern Sinai, was alerted against any sudden Israeli attempt to capitalize on the situation.

In the event, force proved unnecessary. Yunis had measured the strength of the potential opposition by obtaining such informative details from Army Intelligence as the small arms, including sporting shotguns, in the possession of every member of the Suez Canal Company personnel. As an additional precaution he decided to move at an unexpected time, when immediate resistance would be least and when company authorities would be least ready to spread the alert.

Nasser and Yunis agreed that the Egyptians designated to seize control of the company would take ready positions during Nasser's scheduled speech in Alexandria on the evening of the 26th.

When you hear me say the name *Ferdinand de Lesseps*, Nasser told Yunis, move in and take over.

At 9 A.M. on Thursday, 26 July, Yunis brought his finished plan to Nasser at the Presidency on Kasr al-Ainy Street, less than four blocks from the stately compounds of the British Embassy and the Suez Canal Company. Nasser read it and asked Yunis if he needed anything more. "No," said Yunis.

Yunis had made a plan full of melodramatic precautions to ensure absolute secrecy without hampering efficient execution. He began contacting the thirty men he had selected to take over operating control of the company. They were not to learn of their mission until they had all but completed it. Yunis summoned them individually to meet him at an office of the recently dissolved Revolution Command Council in the Kubri al-Kubba quarter on the edge of Cairo.

"I told each one of them that I was going to carry out a secret business in the Western desert and that he was to come with me," Yunis recalled. "I told them: Pack your kit for three nights. We will leave at 3 P.M. by car for Alexandria. We will go to hear the President's speech in Alexandria and will spend the night there. Then on Friday we will begin the mission in the Western desert."

Yunis insisted on the attendance of all thirty bewildered men, some of whom had planned family or other activities over the Moslem weekend. All of them were acquaintances of long standing. Yunis knew their characters and their abilities. Most were civilians: Government refinery men, professors, accountants, an undersecretary of state at the Ministry of Works, businessmen, and a few Army engineers. The promise of drama in Yunis's summons appealed to their spirit of adventure and the official invitation to attend the President's speech appealed to their vanity. In reserve, Yunis had authority to draft their cooperation in the higher interests of state.

At Kubri al-Kubba Yunis had assembled six assorted civilian cars, each with a driver. Five men were assigned to each car, one in each group being named leader. To each "car commander" Yunis handed a fat sealed envelope bearing instructions to go to a designated place and open the envelope.

Each of the envolepes, whose contents were still unknown to the men, contained a series of smaller envelopes nested one inside another, each bearing instructions to drive on to another place before opening. Inside the last envelope were instructions to go to the outskirts of Ismailiya to the barracks office of Brigadier General Mohammed Fuad al-Toudy. Al-Toudy was one of the thirty men and he was as uninformed as the others, even of the fact that the last instruction would be to go to his own office. Yunis had timed the itineraries so that the groups would assemble at about 6 P.M. at Ismailiya, seventy miles by road from Cairo. He dispatched the cars at ten minute intervals from Kubri al-Kubba to avoid any suspicions that might be aroused by the departure of all of them as a group and also to avoid the possibility of their meeting along the route.

Meanwhile, Nasser finished a morning's work at the Presidency and departed by train for Alexandria shortly after noon. He reached the Mediterranean port and resort city, which had been a summer capital for the monarchy, at 4 P.M. and went to his official residence there. The cabinet was awaiting him. The former junta officers had already endorsed Nasser's nationalization plan. The civilians were now brought into the secret. Several were frightened, Nasser recalls, but all of them assented after a discussion. Then they all went together to the building on the old Mohammed Aly Square, newly renamed Liberation Square, where Nasser was to speak from the same balcony on which, in October 1954, he had narrowly escaped an assassin's fusillade. If any member of the cabinet thought of disclosing the secret he had no opportunity to do so.

In London at about this hour, US Ambassador Winthrop Aldrich was boarding a plane for a summer holiday at Dark Harbor, on an island in Maine's Penobscot Bay, where he had a house. At Number 10 Downing Street Eden's staff was preparing a dinner party honoring King Faisal and Premier Nuri al-Said of Iraq, Britain's Baghdad Pact ally. In Paris shares of the Suez Canal Company closed on the Bourse at $260. Across the Seine the deputies in the National Assembly headed for an all-night debate on raising the military budget for the war in Algeria against Arab nationalist rebels. In Washington virtually everybody had forgotten French Ambassador Maurice Couve de Murville's week-old warning that Nasser would retort to Dulles by nationalizing the Suez Canal. Dulles was on a tour of Latin America.

In Cairo itself speculation had touched on nationalization, but very lightly. At the tennis club a friend asked the French Ambassador, Count Armand du Chayla, if he knew what Nasser was going to announce. *"On dit que c'est la nationalisation du canal,"* the friend said. Du Chayla didn't think it was important enough to telephone Count Jean de Grailly, the Suez company's chief executive in Egypt. De Grailly himself says he had long since stopped paying much attention to nationalization rumors. On the evening of the 26th he sought relief from a torrid week-old heat wave with an iced whisky at his residence in the company's walled and landscaped compound. Across the lawn, which Egyptian gardeners clipped with hand shears, was the office where he would resume after dinner his perusal of what was to be the last report of Alphonse Grange, the company's chief engineer.

At the Kubri al-Kubba meeting, Yunis had been grave in response to the good-humored mystification of the men he had summoned there on one pretext only to send them paper-chasing off in a different direction with no explanation at all. When they assembled at the barracks on the edge of Ismailiya he put a cold stop to any further banter or speculation.

Two more men were waiting with Yunis in al-Toudy's office as the cars drove up through shadowy streets where the lowering sun still lighted the tops of the buildings. They were Major General Aly Aly Amer, Eastern commander of the Egyptian Army, who had orders to move if Yunis asked him, and Mohammed Riad, Governor of the Canal Zone, whose assignment was to bring the chiefs of the company's three operating divisions to Yunis after the take-over. Amer and Riad remained silent spectators at Yunis's second meeting with the thirty, their high rank adding to the gravity and mystery of the occasion.

Yunis redivided the thirty into three teams, one to go to Port Said at the north end of the Canal, another to go to Suez at the south end, and the third to remain under Yunis's leadership in Ismailiya. To the Port Said and Suez teams Yunis gave a second series of nested envelopes. The outer one bore instructions to open when the team reached its assigned city. The second was inscribed with orders to go to certain streets and to wait, listening to the radio, until Nasser began to speak before opening it. The third envelope was to be opened when Nasser spoke the name *Ferdinand de Lesseps*. It contained orders to go to designated key installations of the Suez Canal Company, to establish control of operations, and to report by telephone to Yunis at company headquarters in Ismailiya.

"In order to ensure absolute secrecy and obedience," Yunis related, "I told them that one man in each group, unknown to the others, had instructions to shoot on the spot anyone who violated secrecy or failed to carry out the orders. This made a hard impression. Some of them sweated. I remember one man twisting his handkerchief nervously. There was no more joking and there were no more questions except about the orders, such as when they should start, and so on."

Yunis had arranged for each group to have working radios. He timed the departures so that neither the Port Said nor the Suez team would have more than thirty minutes waiting before Nasser began speaking, in order to keep speculation at a minimum. Suez was approximately ninety minutes to the south. Port Said was an hour's drive to the north.

Back in Cairo a fourth team composed of aides from Yunis's staff waited in his office with an envelope to be opened when Nasser began to speak. The second envelope instructed the team to reconnoiter Lazoghly, Rustum, and Ibrahimi streets, within which the company compound was situated, and then to open the envelope. The third envelope, to be opened at the name of Ferdinand de Lesseps, contained orders to enter the company offices, de Grailly's residence, and the company guest house, to establish control and take possession of all files, and to report by telephone to Yunis in Ismailiya.

In Alexandria as the sun went down at their backs the throng packed tighter and tighter into the stately square that owed its origin to the British naval guns of 1882, when the area was pounded into rubble. There were Asian and African faces among the notables. Foreign dignitaries occupied the folding chairs in the front ranks. Laborers in long *galabiyas* perched on the lamp-posts. The entire square and its tributary streets were an agitated sea of expectant faces, white-capped here and there with turbans. Their numbers were estimated at 250,000. As the brief twilight gave way to darkness, the catenary curves of lights festooning the surrounding building facades took on a hard brilliance. On the north side of the square lights framed a big sign proclaiming "99.9%", a slight inflation of the 99.84 per cent presidential vote Nasser had received a month before.

The members of the cabinet took their seats on the balcony of the Bourse, where Nasser was to speak. Foreign Minister Mahmoud Fawzi, impassive, bland, knowing, stared obliquely downward. Salah Salem, wearing his dark glasses as always, smoked and rested an elbow on crossed knees. A hard-eyed unknown with a black mustache stood at the balustrade beside the microphones scrutinizing the crowd, presumably a secet service man on guard against another assassination attempt.

Nasser looked happy and preoccupied as he strode through the French doors to the microphones, smiling vaguely at his colleagues. De-emphasizing militarism, he wore a dark business suit with a handkerchief in the breastpocket. He carried a sheaf of notes in his left hand.

Nasser began speaking at 7:41. The tense groups of men in Cairo and in parked cars in Port Said and Suez tore open their envelopes to learn their next orders. In Ismailiya no envelope was opened because Yunes had the night's great adventure lodged in his brain like an orrery ticking away toward predicted times and positions.

Sir Humphrey Trevelyan, the British ambassador, listened in Cairo to a running English translation of the speech, broadcast on one of Cairo's frequencies simultaneously with the live transmission of Nasser's Arabic on another.

The translation could not put across the distinction between the classical Arabic of customary speeches and the vernacular that Nasser had first tried at Mostarod and was now using again. Nor could it put across Nasser's gestures, sometimes jabbing, sometimes rhythmically pounding his open right hand on the clutch of notes in his left. His mood varied from expansive good humor to dark bitterness against the injustices of the past to emotional assertions that reached a crescendo in the declaration nationalizing the Canal.

Nasser played the throng like an immense organ, touching a key of laughter here, one of anger there, bringing forth responding thunder like a virtuoso. "*Ezza wa karama*"—"Strength and dignity"—the two words recurred thematically throughout the two-hour-and-forty-minute speech. Both have the wide range of meanings characteristic of abstract words. *Ezza* can be translated also as might, honor, glory, or renown. *Karama* also means nobility, generosity, prestige, favor. But Nasser, the first ruler of purely Egyptian origins since the Persian invasion 2,500 years ago, was addressing a nation all too aware that the world had held it in contempt for centuries as weak, corrupt, easily bought, diseased, ignorant—at worst a nation of sinister intriguers, at best a nation of clowns. To some translators, including those of the Western monitoring stations who relayed the first texts to Washington, London, and Paris, Nasser seemed to be harping on "grandeur." But to Egyptians the words meant that Nasser was asserting a restoration of independence and dignity.

"In the past we were kept waiting at their offices—the offices of the High Commissioner and the British Ambassador," he said, launching a long history that ranged from foreign domination to the dangers expected from Israel to the negotiations for aid for the High Dam. "Today . . . they take us into account."

Nasser began with a lengthy tribute to Colonels Hafez and Mustafa, who were killed by Harkavi's letter bombs. He called them victims in the battle against Imperialism, which he said had created Israel "to annihilate our nationalism in the same way as it annihilated Palestine." He declared that Arab safety lay in Arab unity, adding a word of welcome for Syria's request a few days before for union with Egypt. Bursts of applause and shouts of "Long live Gamal" came from the crowd.

He placed the rising international importance of Egypt as a truly independent and neutralist nation in the context of the Bandung and Brioni conferences. He summarized Egypt's battles against the British, beginning with the rout of Fraser's Anglo-Turkish force in 1807 and said: "On 18 June we were able to raise in the sky of Egypt the flag of Egypt alone." America, the leader

345

of the free world, he said, was now in league with British and French imperialism. He criticized the political conditions attached to Western aid, saying: "Not everyone will sell his country for money."

Reviewing Egypt's efforts to obtain arms after the Gaza Raid, he confirmed that the new arms were coming from Russia, not Czechoslovakia. "Do we want arms to dictate our policy or our policy to dictate arms?" he asked, answering himself with: "I do not know whether they are 'Communist arms' or 'non-Communist arms.' In Egypt these arms are Egyptian arms." As for the West, "when they give the 70 million Arabs one rifle, they give the million Zionists two rifles, so that the Zionists can always maintain supremacy."

Nasser accused the British of having fostered Jewish immigration to Palestine, of having connived at the arming of the Zionist settlers, and of having deliberately abandoned the Arabs to the Zionists in 1948, all in order to annihilate Arab nationalism. After other wars, he said, people went back to their countries and their nationalism remained intact. Israel's refusal to let the Arab refugees return to their homes, he said, was "a process of annihilation." He warned that Israelis referred to the Palestine war as a war of liberation and that they had spoken of resuming the war of liberation "to liberate Sinai from Egypt, and liberate Jordan from the Arabs, and also liberate a part of Iraq." (In 1967, Israelis and Zionists elsewhere spoke of the new conquests of Sinai, western Jordan, and southern Syria as "liberated" parts of Eretz Israel.)

"We needed arms to defend ourselves so that we would not become refugees like the Palestinians, who became refugees although they were under Britain's protection and under a mandate," Nasser said. The audience laughed and applauded Nasser's account of George V. Allen's hasty visit after the Russian arms deal. Then he turned to the story of the High Dam, having already spoken for an hour and a quarter.

Characterizing the High Dam negotiations as "long and bitter," Nasser said the West's terms constituted "Imperialism without soldiers." He said that when Egypt first contacted the World Bank in 1953 it had said Egypt would have first to settle her disputes with Britain and Israel and that, since there was no parliament to give a broad national endorsement to the project, Egypt would have to submit it to a plebiscite before the Bank would loan money. Although Egypt was a member of the Bank and had paid $10 million into its working capital, Nasser said, it was evident that no help could be expected from that quarter. The Egyptians then decided to deal directly with private German, British, and French firms for financing and engineering help.

After describing in detail the conditions set by the Bank in the renewed round of negotiations that led to the Western offer, Nasser compared the West's attitude toward aiding the Arabs with its attitude toward aiding Israel.

He told about US Government aid to Israel of $30 to $50 million a year, about Israel bond sales and other American capital investment totaling nearly $500 million, about tax-exempt gifts from American Jews that then totaled $3 billion, part of it to settle Jewish immigrants in the homes of Arab refugees. "The matter depends on desire," he said ruefully, "if one wants to help somebody, he does it."

Nasser told how he had declined Russia's offer pending the outcome of the talks with the West. He told how he had sought modifications of the US and British grant offers in line with the agreement he had reached with the World Bank. He told how he waited in vain for an answer while Britain lobbied against the High Dam in Washington and in the Sudan and British lords and MPs attacked Egypt in Parliament and the British press turned hostile. Egypt had not asked for the £5 million ($14 million) offered by Britain, he said and added scornfully, "we accepted it only in order that our rejection might not be considered an insult."

Analyzing the State Department press release, Nasser said it was obviously intended to poison relations between Egypt and the other riparian states along the Nile. He countered its economic insinuations with statistics on Egypt's economic growth since the revolution and particularly in the seven months mentioned in the press release as a period of economic deterioration.

"They are punishing Egypt," he said, "because she refused to side with military blocs. Egypt calls for peace and the realization of human rights. Egypt calls for principles which they wrote into the UN Charter but which they have forgotten. . . . For this they punish us by withholding the $70 million which they were going to advance at the rate of $12 million a year. . . . They also declare in their papers that they are doing this so that the Egyptian people will know that Gamal Abdel Nasser has harmed them. . . . They do not know that I am refusing because the Egyptian people do not approve what they are asking."

Nasser made the transition from the story of the High Dam negotiations to the history of the Suez Canal by saying:

"I began to look at Mr. Black sitting in his chair and I imagined that I was sitting in front of Ferdinand de Lesseps."

A fat moon had risen over the Canal and the clocks of Egypt were closing the circle on the hour of 10 when this secret signal went out on the air waves. It was unrecognized by all but an infinitesmal fraction of the millions listening to the speech in Egypt, the Arab world, and at the monitoring stations of the intelligence services of the Great Powers. The full meaning of the signal was known only to the cabinet members seated on the balcony behind Nasser and to Yunis in Ismailiya, who had already begun to move.

To the picked teams of men waiting in cars parked in dark side streets in Port Said, Suez, and Cairo the signal meant only that they could tear open another envelope and hope that they would find out just what they were doing. Seconds later they knew it all. By flashlight, with trembling hands and pounding hearts, they read the final orders of the most extraordinary day of their lives, orders to take over and run the Suez Canal Company.

Just in case the original signal might have been blotted out by a moment of inattention or a rasp of static, Nasser worked the name *de Lesseps* into virtually every other sentence for a while. "De Lesseps arrived in Egypt. . . . " "We have a complex as a result of de Lesseps, Cromer, and political occupation by way of economic occupation." "De Lesseps secured the Canal concession . . . " "De Lesseps told the Khedive . . ."

The British ambassador, the translator who was ordered to follow the speech for the French ambassador, and the man making the tape recording at the American Embassy, if they had been aware of what was being unleashed by the name Nasser kept repeating in his seemingly endless speech, could have counted it fourteen times in the ten minutes before they were galvanized by Nasser's reading of the nationalization decree.

Nobody could have known all of what was being unleashed. It was beyond calculation. Dulles had miscalculated Nasser's reaction. Nasser, in reacting, miscalculated the West's counter-reaction. These were but the first of a chain of miscalculations that were to bring the world fourteen weeks later to the brink of disaster as the giant Powers, stamping out the Israeli, British, and French invasion of Egypt, threatened to stamp on each other's toes. In the years beyond the ten-day war itself (29 October to 7 November), the consequences were to eradicate Britain's influence in the Middle East, split the NATO alliance, and accelerate the expulsion of foreign white power from Africa.

Curiously, the world was to be distracted both from the christening of the Suez Crisis and from its climax by the coincidence of other great events. The Hungarian revolution was to double the world's agony in October and November. On that July night it was disaster at sea.

The passenger liners *Andrea Doria* and *Stockholm* had collided in a midnight fog near the Nantucket Lightship. Rescue ships, including the great liner *Ile de France*, put down boats that searched for survivors until the abandoned hulk of the *Andrea Doria* sank in a sparkling geyser of spray at 10:09 A.M., Eastern Daylight Saving Time. At that hour in Alexandria, 4:09 P.M., Nasser was confiding his plans to an anxious cabinet. The world at large was hanging on the radio bulletins from the rescue ships that began arriving at New York in the evening with the survivors, the injured, and the dead. *The New York*

Times, which lost a distinguished correspondent in the disaster, allotted three quarters of its front page the following morning to reports and photographs of the sea tragedy. The Suez nationalization, which detonated one of history's great chain reactions, got a small second place and lacked even the dignity of a byline.

But these things were far away in space or time as Nasser worked up to the announcement of the nationalization. He repeated several times an out-raged assertion that 120,000 Egyptians had died in forced labor on the Canal. Whether Nasser believed this exaggeration or not, he was unable ten years later to remember where he got the figure. It was probably a folkloric echo of Herodotus, who tells in Book II of his histories how Nechos, Pharaoh of Egypt from 609 to 593 B.C., "began the digging of the canal from the Nile to the Red Sea which Darius the Persian finished. . . . One hundred and twenty thousand Egyptians died whilst digging this canal in the reign of Nechos. And he, when the work was half done, put a stop to it, because an oracle restrained him . . ." The Suez Canal Company's contemporary medical records, which have not been refuted, say that during the entire construction of the Canal exactly 1,394 Egyptian workers died, including those who succumbed in the cholera epi-demic of 1865/1866. Nearly as many Europeans died on the project; exactly 1,314 according to company records.

"One hundred twenty thousand workers died digging the Canal gratis," Nasser said. "We dug the Canal with our lives, our skulls, our bones, our blood." He reviewed the complicated economic maneuvers which deprived Egypt of her share of the Canal's profits while making her pay a large part of the construction costs. "Instead of the Canal being dug for Egypt," he said, "Egypt became the property of the Canal. . . . The Suez Canal Company be-came a state within a state, one which humiliated ministers . . . It is no shame for one to be poor and to borrow in order to build up one's country; what is a shame is to suck the blood of a people and usurp their rights."

Nasser said that the Canal revenues in 1955 were $100 million—in five years, $500 million. He marked the contrast between this sum and the $70 mil-lion that had been offered over five years by the US and Britain, adding roundly that "it is they, of course, who take these $100 million." "We shall never repeat the past," Nasser said, "but we shall eliminate the past by regain-ing our rights in the Suez Canal. This money is ours and this canal belongs to Egypt because it is an Egyptian limited liability company."

"When he came here de Lesseps acted in the same manner as do certain people who come to hold talks with me," Nasser said, mentioning the canal builder's name for the fourteenth time. "Does history repeat itself? On the contrary! . . . We shall build the High Dam and we shall gain our usurped

349

rights. . . . The canal company annually takes £35 million ($100 million). Why shouldn't we take it ourselves? . . . Therefore I have signed today and the government has approved . . . a resolution . . . for the nationalization of the Universal Company of the Suez Maritime Canal." The fiction that Nasser nationalized the Canal with a burst of ugly laughter has gained wide currency but he did not laugh at all.

It was 10:10 P.M. when Nasser began reading the six-paragraph nationalization decree, which provided that shareholders would be compensated at the closing prices of the day on the Paris Bourse. Nasser did not make his stunning announcement until after the major stock exchanges of the Western world had closed for the day. The New York Stock Exchange had been closed for 40 minutes, since 3:30 P.M. Eastern Daylight Saving Time. There was thus a night's delay to dampen any panic financial reaction. Canal company shares had edged downward during the spring but—a measure of the unexpectedness of nationalization—had begun to climb again between 19 and 26 July. The day after nationalization they dropped 25 per cent in price before the exchanges closed for the weekend.

Where financial reaction, dampered by delays, was relatively mild, political reaction in Europe was as swift and instinctive as a snarl.

In Cairo, the "ambassador" of the "State within a State," the Count de Grailly, had been sitting for an hour in his lofty-ceilinged office across the garden compound from his house reading Chief Engineer Alphonse Grange's report on the planned program to enlarge the Canal. In common with most other Westerners, de Grailly had not learned Arabic although he had been in Egypt ten years as chief company representative. Nor is English easy for him. So he did not listen to the radio. He was content to wait for the morrow's French-language newspapers to find out what Nasser's speech was about.

De Grailly, now in retirement, does not fit the picture conjured up by Nasser of a company "staffed by French counts and English drones—agents of imperialism." He is a kindly family man, sympathetic to Egypt's struggle for social justice and national dignity. But Gallic realism was uppermost in his mind on the evening of nationalization. The company was a power on the world scene and whatever Nasser might do about his diplomatic dilemmas seemed less important to de Grailly than the company's plans for the Canal.

De Grailly learned that Nasser, too, had plans for the Canal when one of the telephones on his capacious desk began ringing and blinking. He picked it up. It was the Count Armand du Chayla, the French ambassador, calling from a friend's house, where he had gone for dinner and an evening of bridge. "Nasser is in the process of announcing the nationalization of the Canal in his speech," du Chayla said. "The Egyptian interpreter at the Embassy has just telephoned me."

De Grailly thanked him and hung up saying he heard the sound of truck motors. He stepped out into the garden and realized that they were outside the compound wall on all sides. "Well, that's it," de Grailly recalls having exclaimed to himself. "We're surrounded. Du Chayla's information, it is good." He re-entered his office just as a rather embarrassed group of five or six men in civilian clothes came in through the main door. From that moment it was no longer de Grailly's office.

"Excuse me," said the leader of the group. He introduced himself as Lieutenant al-Tunsi of Yunis's Petroleum Authority staff. De Grailly glimpsed a pistol in a holster on his belt. As the other members of the group fanned out into the adjoining offices and file rooms, al-Tunsi looked around hesitantly and cleared his throat.

"In the name of the Government of Egypt," he said in English, "I inform you that the Suez Canal Company is nationalized and I have come to take over the premises."

The telephone rang again as he finished. It was Gabriel Dardaud of the *Agence France Presse*. De Grailly told him about the intrusion of the men with revolvers at their belts and about al-Tunsi's statement. Al-Tunsi, under orders to prevent any communications that might jeopardize the take-over, kept signaling de Grailly to stop talking. Al-Tunsi understood no French. Dardaud, on the other end, pleaded with de Grailly to keep talking until he had finished.

Then du Chayla telephoned again to find out what was happening. He asked de Grailly to come to the Embassy at 9 o'clock the next morning. The uncertainty and anxiety of the moment were such that du Chayla added, "If you're not here by 9:15 I'll come find you."

In Ismailiya, Yunis moved simultaneously with al-Tunsi. "I started moving while President Nasser was talking about the High Dam and the World Bank," he recalls. "I was on my way to the company offices when I heard him say the name *de Lesseps*. I pushed open the door of Mennessier's office just as he was saying: 'Now your brothers are taking over.' I looked at my watch. It was 10:20."

That was the moment of nationalization. Yunis was in control at the company's main headquarters on the Canal. He hung a large photograph of Nasser on the wall and sat in the chair of Pierre Mennessier, the administrative chief. It remained to make Egyptian control stick and make it work.

In Alexandria the immense crowd was beside itself with jubilation. Strangers embraced one another and shouted *"Mabrouk!"*, an exclamation of delight and congratulation. Nasser's reading of the brief nationalization decree was interrupted five times by prolonged applause. The few paragraphs with which he wound up the speech were audible only in scattered breaks in what had become an almost unbroken din of clapping and cheering.

"Today, O citizens," Nasser shouted, "with the annual income of the Suez Canal amounting to . . . $100 million a year, $500 million in five years, we shall not look for the $70 million of American aid. . . . And whenever any talk comes from Washington I shall tell them: 'Drop dead of your fury.' We shall set up industries and compete with them. . . . In the same way as Farouk left on 26 July 1952, the old Suez Canal Company also leaves us on the same day." What Yunis heard as he brushed past the night watchmen into Mennessier's empty office and switched on the lights was the last paragraph of Nasser's speech.

"Now, while I am talking to you," Nasser shouted over the tumult, "brothers of yours, sons of Egypt, are rising up to direct the canal company and undertake its operation. Now, at this moment, they are taking over the canal company—the Egyptian canal company! not the foreign canal company! They have risen up to take over the canal company and its installations and direct ship traffic in the canal—the canal lying in the land of Egypt, which cuts through the earth of Egypt, and which is a part of Egypt and a property of Egypt's. We take this action now to make up for what has gone by and to compensate for the past and to build new edifices of strength and dignity. May God grant you success; peace be upon you and the mercy of God."

In Port Said the take-over team moved swiftly into the company building at the canal's edge from which, with the aid of the famous signal tower, southbound shipping is marshalled into the canal in convoys timed to cross the north-bound ships at by-passes along the 101 miles between the lighthouse, which dominates the Port Said waterfront, and Port Tewfik, the company's concessionary area facing the small city of Suez.

The building in Port Said is chalk-white and lapped round on three sides by the waters of the canal. It is roofed by three domes set upon two tiers of lofty arcades in an agreeable architectual concoction that might have been influenced by both the Taj Mahal and a wedding cake. Its nerve center is in the control cupola on top of the middle dome. When Yunis's men reached it, after climbing a final spiral staircase of cast iron, they announced their take-over in terms similar to Lieutenant al-Tunsi's in Cairo. The first orders of the new authority were for the company staff to go right on doing what it was doing and to avoid any hitch or break that might delay traffic.

At Suez, or rather Port Tewfik, Egyptian authority was clamped with equal smooth swiftness on the company transit service office, where a hexagonal tower on the roof looks over the fronds of palm trees to the bridges of passing ships. There was no break in convoy traffic. But the break in communications was abrupt and permanent between company installations in Egypt and its world headquarters in the sumptuous stone building at 1 Rue d'Astorg in Paris.

Within a half hour after settling himself in Mennessier's office Yunis received Mennessier, chief of Administration, and the deputy chiefs of the two other operating divisions, Transit and Works. Through the open windows came roars of cheers and chanting from a jubilant crowd that swarmed into the square in front of the company offices. The three men were brought in by Governor Riad, as Yunis had ordered.

"Now you will report to me, no more to Paris," Yunis remembers saying after explaining the new law to them. "You are to continue your duties as usual, but report to me. I hope everybody will be cooperative and follow my instructions. And rest assured nothing will happen to you or your families."

Articles IV and V of the new law took the most explaining. Article IV required all company personnel and staff to remain at their jobs. Article V prescribed imprisonment, fines, and loss of pension rights for violators of Article IV. In addition, the canal was placed under limited martial law. The military governor, Colonel Amin Hilmy, sent telegrams to all station chiefs at 10:25 to post notice that any canal pilot or other employee who stopped work would be liable to a court martial. These measures were far sterner than the long-standing statutory requirement that employees give a month's notice before resigning. They were seen in London and Paris as justifying military intervention, if only Britain and France had been ready, because they exercised coercion on British, French, and other non-Egyptian canal company employees. Otherwise the legality of nationalization was not officially questioned.

Eden reluctantly recognized the legality of nationalization itself but he determined to avoid what he called "legal quibbles." Here was his sought-for opportunity to take military action to "break Nasser," but he recognized that he would have to base such a policy on political and psychological grounds rather than legal grounds.

News of the nationalization was brought by a Foreign Office messenger across Downing Street to Number 10. A private secretary went upstairs to the late-Georgian room where the King of Iraq and his Prime Minister and other Iraqi and British leaders were dining with Eden. He gave Eden the message which was to lead him in a few fevered months to the ignominious end of an honorable career. Eden immediately told his guests the news. He wrote later: "Our party broke up early, its social purpose now out of joint."

The Iraqis, before departing, told Eden they hoped he would respond resolutely to Nasser's defiance. They were angered by Nasser's failure to consult any of the Arab states before taking an action that would affect all of them, particularly oil-producing states like Iraq. Nuri reportedly advised Eden: "Hit him [Nasser], hit him hard, and hit him now."

Foreign Secretary Selwyn Lloyd and two other cabinet ministers, Lord Salisbury and Lord Home, were among the guests. They went downstairs with Eden into the double-doored privacy of the Cabinet Room. Lord Kilmuir and the Chiefs of Staff joined the group. Eden then decided to invite the French ambassador and the US Chargé d'Affaires, Andrew Foster.

"The *mise-en-scène* of that meeting will always live in my mind," wrote Lord Kilmuir. "Anthony Eden, Selwyn Lloyd, Salisbury, and I were, of course, in full evening dress and decorations for the Royal Dinner—Anthony and Bobbety [Salisbury] with the sash and kneebreeches of the Garter. Then M. Chauvel, the able and acute French ambassador, came in a lounge suit. He was followed by Mr. Foster from the American Embassy, similarly clad.... Then Gerald Templer, the CIGS [Chief of the Imperial General Staff], and Dickie Mountbatten, obviously prised from private dinner parties, came in dinner jackets. It was a remarkable gathering to discuss one of the most serious questions since World War II. We had a long discussion, and I got home some time after 2 A.M."

The French ambassador telephoned the Ritz Hotel and asked Jacques Georges-Picot, director general of the Suez Canal Company, who was in London on business, to come to Downing Street. Georges-Picot was not admitted into the meeting, however, but was kept waiting in a small room. After the meeting Eden silently shook his hand and he departed with the French ambassador. That was all. It was to prove symbolic of a curious official indifference to the company that lasted throughout the crisis.

As the London meeting got under way, Yunis's meeting in Ismailya with the canal company's operating chiefs was breaking up. Yunis bedded down in his underwear on the carpet in the office from which he had just dismissed Mennessier.

At the company headquarters in Cairo, Etienne Minost and another aide joined de Grailly. De Grailly gave Minost a key and asked him to get from a strongbox in an adjoining office some company records and some jewelry left in de Grailly's safekeeping by a vacationing friend. Minost found that sentries had already sealed all files and desk drawers. Neither the jewels nor the papers were ever recovered. Even de Grailly's private office in his house had been placed under seals and a sentry.

"All personal and official papers were seized," de Grailly recalled. "This happened only in Cairo. They evidently hoped to find evidence of fraud or corruption or espionnage or smuggling of money." Unlike Yunis, de Grailly did not sleep at all that night. But he was spared worry about his family for it had been in France on leave for several weeks.

The immediate question, in Cairo as in London, was whether the company would order its canal pilots and other personnel to walk out or to cooperate with the Egyptian authorities. The question was settled in London. After several days of indecision the employees were ordered to remain at their jobs for the time being. They were not withdrawn until mid-September, by which time the Egyptians, using their own navy officers and newly hired pilots including Russians and Americans, were able to do without the company technicians. "The Egyptian pilots worked wonderfully," a top company officer said afterward.

Andrew Foster cabled the State Department at 5 A.M. a report on the meeting at No. 10 Downing Street. It is probably the most authoritative and succinct account of the meeting in existence. Furthermore, it shows that the motives that led Eden to war had hardened within hours of the nationalization. Foster drafted his cable for relay to Dulles in Lima, Peru, after making a preliminary report by telephone to Hoover. Foster wrote:

Eden sent for me at 11 o'clock tonight, within a few minutes after the news from Cairo reached here, and I found myself attending a two-hour emergency meeting of the Cabinet attended also by the British chiefs of staff and the French Ambassador to discuss Nasser's action in nationalizing the Suez Canal.

Cabinet takes an extremely grave view of situation and very strong feelings were expressed, especially by Eden, to the effect that Nasser must not be allowed to get away with it.

As to legal aspect, consensus of Cabinet discussion was that although Nasser had certainly breached the Canal Company's concession it was not clear that his act of expropriation itself violated the Convention of 1888. Such violation would presumably occur, however, if practical effect of expropriation impaired maintenance and operation of Canal.

Cabinet agreed that recourse to UN Security Council ran too great risk of matter becoming "hopelessly bogged down." Regardless of international legal aspects, interested western governments must consider possible economic, political, and military measures against Egypt to ensure maintenance canal, freedom of transit through it, and reasonable tolls. The question confronting Cabinet tonight was of course extent to which US would go in supporting and participating in firm position vis-à-vis Nasser in terms of economic sanctions and, beyond that if necessary, military action. I said that the US would certainly also consider the situation a most serious one and that I would try to obtain on the most urgent basis at least a preliminary indication of our position. It is arranged that I shall see Eden and Lloyd at 5 o'clock this

355

(Friday) afternoon by which time they hope department will have given me some word for them.

Tentatively I expressed that US, France and United Kingdom should continue discussions for the moment and that other interested friendly governments, e.g., the Commonwealth members and such leading users of the canal as Norway, should join in later and broader consultations. List of signatories of 1888 Convention not considered much use in this connection. Eden said Washington, London, or Paris equally agreeable to him. He evidently has in mind that a US-United Kingdom-French meeting at the ministerial level may be called for in the very near future.

Cabinet had before it a telegram from British Ambassador at Cairo asking what to tell Canal Company which had asked his advice concerning Nasser's decree that company personnel would not be allowed to resign and would be punished if they failed to continue work. Eden strongly of view that HMG [Her Majesty's Government] should not advise personnel to continue work under expropriation, even though this meant they might go to prison and canal might have to close down. To advise them to continue to work meant conceding Nasser's position and giving in to his blackmail. Decision on this held over, however, until today.

Cabinet decided to have Chiefs alert British commanders in Mediterranean to situation. Chiefs were instructed to produce soonest a study of what forces would be required to seize canal and how they would be disposed if military action became necessary.

Cabinet decided upon statement to be issued by HMG at 11 o'clock this morning, London time, along following lines:

"The unilateral decision of the Egyptian government to expropriate the Suez Canal Company, without notice and in breach of the concessions, affects the rights and interests of many nations. HMG are consulting other governments immediately concerned with regard to the serious situation created; both in respect of the effect of the decision upon the operation of the Suez Canal and also of the wider questions raised by this arbitrary action."

Eden expressed the strong hope that US and French governments would issue similar statements today. French Ambassador left meeting and returned to say he had phoned Paris which agreed issue comparable statement.

As meeting broke up Lloyd told me he himself was moving toward conclusion that only solution lay in a western consortium taking over and operating the canal, establishing itself if need be by military force.

Please telegraph soonest concerning possible public statement by US as well as what I can tell Eden and Lloyd today concerning US position.

It is noteworthy that Eden was prepared to disrupt Canal traffic immediately by calling away the pilots, which would create a practical violation of the Convention of 1888, thereby inflating the *casus belli* which Eden already eagerly perceived in the nationalization. Ready as he was to use the 1888 Convention as a legal basis for war, Eden dismissed the idea of being bound by its consultative provisions. Eden's cavalier attitude toward the UN comes strongly through Foster's sober prose.

Eden, writing in his memoirs of that night, shows that Foster's report of his reaction was, if anything, an understatement. He saw nationalization as a challenge, the outcome of which would decide whether British or Egyptian influence would prevail in the Middle East. "From the start we had to prepare to back our remonstrances with military action," he wrote. "If assistance were not forthcoming from our friends, we had to be in a position to take action alone." Eden saw the dispute as essentially a personal contest between himself and Nasser, one which, if he played his cards right, would be decided by guns.

"This was the challenge for which Eden had been waiting," wrote Anthony Nutting. "Now at last he had found a pretext to launch an all-out campaign of political, economic and military pressures on Egypt and to destroy for ever Nasser's image as the leader of Arab nationalism."

The first need of the engines of war is petroleum. De Grailly says that the first concern of the British and French governments, transmitted to him through diplomatic channels, was to get tankers through the Canal. Eden told Eisenhower later on the morrow of nationalization that Britain had a six-week reserve. But, de Grailly points out, that allowed for only a few days of wartime operations.

At 4 A.M. in Ismailiya, at the time when Foster was drafting his cable in London, an excited swarm of reporters broke in upon Yunis's sleep. They had driven through the night from Cairo after filing their first dispatches on the nationalization.

"I told them everything was normal," Yunis recalls. "I said the ships are moving. But I did not feel that my mission was complete. I was at the control post and I would be very difficult to dislodge. But the question remained whether it would go smoothly when the employees came to work in the morning."

At the start of the working day on 27 July Yunis posted his own liaison officers in every department of the nationalized company. Through them Yunis imposed his own fully centralized control. At first, senior French officials delayed and obstructed Yunis's orders but he by-passed them and dealt directly with the junior staff. After some icy reminders, of which Yunis is a master, the French staff fell into line.

Yunis took financial control as well as operating control by transferring more than £8 million (nearly $25 million) in company accounts from foreign-owned banks in Egypt to the National Bank. Most of the money was newly deposited in Egypt under the agreement concluded in May between Egypt and the company.

At 8 A.M. Yunis's secretary summoned de Grailly to come to Ismailiya. De Grailly replied that he had a 9 A.M. appointment with the French ambassador and would not be able to come to Ismailiya until after it.

In Paris at this hour the Chamber of Deputies, after an all-night debate on the military budget for Algeria, was giving Premier Guy Mollet a large vote of confidence. Pineau had come out of the chamber for repeated visits to the news ticker in the *Salle des Pas Perdus* (the Hall of Wasted Steps), as the entrance hall is known. He was badgered so severely by deputies for his previous manifestations of sympathy for Nasser that he debated seriously with himself over whether to resign.

De Grailly found the British ambassador awaiting him with the Count du Chayla at the French Embassy, one of a row of mansions on the bank of the Nile in Giza. They gave him their governments' instructions to cooperate with the Egyptians for the time being. Du Chayla provided him an office in the French Embassy, from which he was able to maintain communications with Paris although he was cut off from Ismailiya. In fact, the company had been using diplomatic channels illegally for four years, sending its archives home periodically by pouch and sending telegrams in cipher, which was prohibited in ordinary commercial cables.

When de Grailly reached Ismailiya at 10:30 he assured Yunis of his cooperation. Yunis was coldly angry about de Grailly's visit to the French Embassy. Then, turning amiable, he expressed his hope of cooperation from the company.

"I know how to obey," de Grailly said.

"It is not a question of obeying but of collaborating," Yunis replied.

De Grailly, whose position had evaporated with nationalization, said he did not know what his function would be.

"Don't worry," Yunis said, "we will find work for you."

In the event, de Grailly had little to do until, in mid-September, the company used the inducement of pension settlements to withdraw its pilots and other employees. De Grailly had to help arrange their departure. He recalls the intervening six weeks as a "nightmare," at the end of which those who left, including the majority of the non-Egyptian employees, were blacklisted from ever returning again to Egypt.

"When I walked out of Colonel Yunis's office on the 27th of July," de Grailly recalls, "I saw an Arab woman sitting with her children on the portico around the courtyard. I realized that the Egyptians were truly in possession. That was the signature."

CHAPTER

12

Call to Arms

(27 JULY 1956 TO 2 AUGUST 1956)

... an act of international brigandage ...

(*The Times*, London, 28 July 1956)

... a piece of political violence and poetic justice, when the Ruler of Egypt took possession of the Canal over which European statesmen had wrangled and for which Egyptian peasants had paid.

(JOHN MARLOWE, *The Making of the Suez Canal*, London, Cresset Press Ltd., 1964)

THE SUEZ CRISIS had a name at last. The name tended, and still tends, to conceal the true character and shape of the crisis—its origins, its age, its complexity. Nationalization drew together the several strands of conflict that were to fuse in the November war. It tended thereby to make the world think about the crisis as if it began when Nasser took over the canal company. Within a few days most people had forgotten even Dulles's provocative renege on the High Dam. The few who thought of it as having prompted the nationalization of the Canal considered themselves very perspicacious. But, as Chapter 10 shows, Dulles's renege had been brewing since February and simmering since Nasser recognized Red China in May. On Nasser's side, nationalization had been evolving, at least as a contingency plan, for months, perhaps years. The consequences of nationalization, full of excitement and danger, were so absorbing that they tend to be regarded as entire unto themselves. But our backward look has revealed nationalization to be part of a web of reactions and counterreactions that began with the Gaza Raid of 28 February 1955.

Duplicity, propaganda, and side issues continued to obscure the crisis. The debate over the legality of nationalization, for example, took on the appearance of a real issue. But it was never more than froth on the surface of events, utterly without effect on the events themselves. Beneath the legal quibbling the maneuvering among the Western leaders over the use of force against Nasser was only partly visible, as beneath murky water. It gave an illusion on the surface that there were real doubts about the use of force in the minds of those who eventually used it. The illusion persists to this day. In fact, for the three who made war on Nasser, using force was not a solution to the Suez dispute; the Suez dispute was a solution to using force.

The three wars that had been waiting to happen found their cause, their pretext, in nationalization. Although Britain, France, and Israel ultimately were obliged to collude on a new pretext for invading Egypt, nationalization gave them the opportunity to prepare for war. Had Britain and France been ready to attack Egypt, they would have done so on the morrow of nationalization. They regretted later that they had not been ready. But the preparations they made would have been impossible to justify to their own taxpayers and to the world before nationalization.

The world had been watching Moscow for the next move in the High Dam drama. It was flabbergasted when, instead, Nasser took over the Canal and said its earnings would pay for the dam. There was hardly a capital in which anxiety did not underlie astonishment because nearly every country in the world trades through the Canal in its own or in other countries' ships. Bismark once called the Canal "the world's neck." The image appeared again and again in

Western comment. Eden wrote on the 27th that he could not tolerate Nasser's "thumb on our windpipe" and Dulles spoke offhandedly to Eden a few days later about making Nasser "disgorge."

Nasser had so effectively presented nationalization as a blow against Western imperialism that he had only himself to blame for the real fears that his act provoked. Whether or not the West itself had provoked Nasser's hostility, it added an element of fear to the grudges they bore him for other real or imagined injuries. Britain and France had shifted from coal to oil since World War II to fuel most of their industries and heat most of their homes. The bulk of their oil came from the Middle East through the Suez Canal. "The continuing supply of fuel," Eden wrote in his memoirs, "was now subject to Colonel Nasser's whim."

In fact, neither Britain's oil nor any other traffic through the Canal was any more subject to Nasser's whim than it had been before nationalization. Egypt had had physical control of the Canal's entrances since World War II and had effectively barred Israeli shipping since 1948. The British Suez garrison might conceivably have challenged Egypt's control before its withdrawal under the 1954 agreement, but it never did so. In the exercise of her control, Egypt continued to acknowledge the restraints embodied in the Suez Canal Convention of 1888, which she claimed as legal sanction for her discrimination against Israel.

Nationalization changed nothing of this. As with Dulles's renege on the High Dam, it was the manner of it which caused worry. Most of Africa and Asia, although they supported Nasser's right to nationalize the Canal, did not like the way he did it. Nehru, who had shared with Nasser the news of Dulles's renege, was offended by Nasser's failure to confide his nationalization plans. Nehru said frostily in the Indian parliament on 31 July that he learned of the nationalization from press reports after his return to New Delhi.

Egypt took immediate pains to assure the world that the efficiency and freedom of the Canal were unchanged by nationalization and that nationalization was within Egypt's sovereign rights and entirely in accordance with international law. "It is very important," said the government newspaper, *al-Gamhouriya*, on 29 July, "to distinguish between nationalization, which is an internal right of the Egyptian Government, and violation of international agreements." The new Suez Canal Authority announced at the end of its first day that 49 ships had made the transit, four ships better than average. On 1 August, the authority gave comparative statistics for its first five days: 237 ships with a total tonnage of 1,946,638 passed through the Canal compared with 213 ships totaling 1,573,795 tons in the same final five days of July in 1955. It was as good an answer as any to the Blimpish sneer of *The Times* (London) on 28 July that "an international waterway of this kind cannot be worked by a nation with low technical and managerial skills such as the Egyptians."

The Egyptians were aided by the canal company's message the day after nationalization which, while repudiating Egyptian authority, advised its employees in Egypt that until the situation was clarified they should "carry out duties strictly necessary for the operation of the Transit Department." The company's foreign employees included 350 Frenchmen, 135 Britons, some 900 other Europeans, and 2 Americans. On 6 August the company told its non-Egyptian employees to choose, before 15 August 1956, between loyalty to the company and service under the "*de facto* authority which has seized the management." It added that those who chose loyalty to the company "should postpone their departure from Egypt and continue their work . . . until a date which will be communicated to them later." The departure of the foreign employees was deferred until mid-September.

Technically and juridically, the nationalization was impeccable. One of the British officials I spoke to in London on the night of nationalization said there might be nothing to do in riposte "except twiddle our thumbs." The following day government officials speculated ruefully that blocking Egyptian sterling would hurt Britain more than Egypt by appearing to serve notice that the use of sterling balances was conditional on British favor. They were unaware that the Cabinet was already deciding to do it. Persuading the US to dump more cotton, they said, would hurt British Commonwealth and colonial territories as much as Egypt.

"We would like to be beastly to Nasser," one official told me, "but we haven't figured out a sensible way to do it." The British never did.

On 28 July Britain blocked all Egyptian sterling. This was a unilateral violation of the Anglo-Egyptian currency agreement concluded in 1955. "It is an ordinary action of sovereignty," an official said defensively, unconsciously echoing Egypt's defense of nationalization. He added that the Government expected Egypt to challenge it in the World Court at the Hague but without success. Egypt did not.

Egypt's sterling balances were the remainder of a World War II debt owed by Britain for cotton and military goods and services obtained against credits. Egypt's sterling credits stood at £400 million at the war's end, having accumulated on the understanding that they would then be placed at Egypt's disposal. The balances were blocked in 1947, however, to protect the British pound. Along with other holders of sterling, Egypt incurred a 30 per cent loss when Britain devalued the pound in September 1949. The Anglo-Egyptian currency releases agreement of August 1955, the latest of a series, provided for the transfer of £20 million ($56 million) in January of every year from the blocked balances into a current account. About £110 million ($308 million) remained in the blocked balance on 28 July 1956 and there was about £20 million unblocked. The latter included: the unspent part of the current account, British payments for imports from Egypt, and the bank accounts of private individuals. All was frozen.

Kaissouny said on 30 July that Egypt would not retaliate against Britain's economic measures, observing that they hurt Britain more than Egypt because the sterling balances were used for purchases in Britain.

From the night of nationalization until he saw the British Canberras drop their bombs over Cairo at nightfall on 31 October, Nasser went to what might be called extremes of moderation to avoid provoking Eden further or offering the slightest pretext for military action. Egyptian restraint went so far as to allow Britain to take ammunition and bombs from the Suez base stores, as allowed under the 1954 agreement, knowing they were being stockpiled in Cyprus for possible use against Egypt. In the first two days of the war, when Israel was still the only enemy belligerent, Egyptian reinforcements across the Canal were repeatedly delayed so as not to interfere with ship convoys passing through.

There was no need to exacerbate the situation further. Nasser had more than offset the damage of Dulles's renege. Long files of delighted Egyptian motorists drove down from Cairo and the cities of the delta and valley to park alongside "their" Canal and wave handkerchiefs at passing ships. Overnight the Canal became a tourist attraction for Egyptians and a place of patriotic pilgrimage. For Arabs everywhere, and for some of their rulers, it was the same. King Hussein of Jordan cabled Nasser his "hearty congratulations" and said "the shadow of financial exploitation is disappearing from the Arab lands and the voice of wrong has vanished in the face of truth." In Iraq, Nuri's men bowed to popular feeling by stating that nationalization was within Egypt's rights but it was left to an Opposition leader, Mohammed Mahdi Kubba, to say that Nasser's action had "deeply moved the Arabs' hearts." Nehru told a Bombay audience on 1 August that the nationalization was "a sign of the weakening of European domination of Asia and the Middle East which has lasted more than 100 years."

This was Eden's first thought too, immediately after hearing the news of nationalization. "I had no doubt how Nasser's deed would be read, from Agadir to Karachi," he wrote. "On its outcome would depend whose authority would prevail." For Eden, even in his first reflex to nationalization, the issue was never the Suez Canal; it was how to break Nasser. Although Dulles had not allowed plans for an undercover plot against Nasser to reach fruition, Eden still hoped to associate the US with his campaign against the Egyptian. His first act toward this end was his invitation of Andrew Foster to the midnight meeting of cabinet ministers and military chiefs on 26 July.

The next day he cabled Eisenhower urging "a firm stand" or else "our influence and yours throughout the Middle East will, we are convinced, be irretrievably undermined." He insisted that there was an immediate threat to oil which might require supplies from America. As for the Canal, he said: "Apart from the Egyptians' complete lack of technical qualifications, their past behaviour gives no confidence that they can be trusted to manage it with any sense of international obligation." Urging Eisenhower to "take issue with Nasser on the broader international grounds," Eden wrote:

"We should not allow ourselves to become involved in legal quibbles about the rights of the Egyptian Government to nationalise what is technically an Egyptian company, or in financial arguments about their capacity to pay the compensation which they have offered."

Eden went on to dismiss economic pressures as insufficient and to urge immediate maximum political pressure. "My colleagues and I are convinced that we must be ready, in the last resort, to use force to bring Nasser to his senses," Eden said. "For our part we are prepared to do so. I have this morning instructed our Chiefs of Staff to prepare a military plan accordingly." Eden said the first step should be for Britain, France, and the US to meet and concert together.

Eden's airy dismissal of "legal quibbles" and "financial arguments" showed his perception that Egypt was on solid legal and financial ground. If Eden wanted to fight Nasser over Suez he would have to avoid the actual merits of the case. Only a political approach would serve. And the more emotional it could be made the better it would serve. In setting himself above the law, Eden crossed Eisenhower's and Dulles's attachment to the ideal of a rule of law in international affairs.

The basic text in international law covering the nationalization of foreign property treats "legal quibbles" and "financial arguments" as interdependent. It is Secretary of State Cordell Hull's statement to the Mexican Government on 3 April 1940 concerning Mexico's nationalization of US oil enterprises: "The right to expropriate property is coupled with and conditioned on the obligation to make adequate, effective and prompt compensation. The legality of an expropriation is in fact dependent upon the observance of this requirement."

Eden preferred to evade the issue by deriding Nasser's promise of compensation instead of giving it practical consideration, which would risk an implied recognition of the legal validity of nationalization In order to deride, Eden had to ignore or distort the facts, which he did.

The prestigious *Financial Times* published an analysis two days after nationalization which showed, perhaps without intending to, that Egypt would be more than able both to meet her promise to compensate the Suez Canal Company stockholders and to finance the High Dam. The company shares were worth a total of £65 million ($182 million) at the closing prices on 26 July, the paper reported, a figure slightly higher than the company's net assets of £64 million shown on the balance sheet at the end of 1955. This was only half the amount of Egyptian sterling under the British control. Compensation was there for the taking.

As for the dam, the Canal's earnings in 1955 totaled £32.5 million ($91 million). Operating expenses were £15 million ($42 million), other expenses and interest were £3 million ($8.4 million), and another £3 million went into reserves for capital improvements. This left £11.5 million or more than $32 million a year for the dam even without allowing for a continuation of the upward trend in Canal revenues. $32 million a year is nearly $500 million in 15 years, the period estimated to complete the dam. It was double the amount needed to service a $400 million loan at 4 per cent even if Egypt were to borrow the entire sum at the beginning of the project.

Admittedly, Britain had a large stake in the Canal company. The shares which the British Government under Disraeli had purchased in 1875 for £4 million had a market value of nearly £24 million ($67 million) in 1956. The annual dividend had grown to more than £2.8 million (nearly $8 million). The British Government, with three eighths of the stock, was the largest single shareholder. Nine of the company's thirty-two directors were British. But Britain never made the slightest gesture toward restoring the company on the Canal. Nor was much attention paid to company interests.

The company apart, Britain had an immense economic stake in the Canal as well as a strategic interest, although the latter was shrinking along with the Empire. Two thirds of the ship tonnage that used the Canal in 1955 was accounted for by oil tankers. Northbound tankers carried 66.9 million tons of petroleum products that year, of which 20.5 million tons went to Britain, constituting two thirds of Britain's crude oil imports. British exports of refined oil accounted for a quarter of the southbound tanker traffic through the Canal. Of all Canal traffic, British tonnage comprised 28.3 per cent, making Britain by far the largest user of the Canal. With British and European oil consumption rising 7 per cent a year, the Canal's place in Britain's economy was increasing in importance.

By any measure of good sense, concern for the well-being of the Canal should have made Eden drop his belligerent designs against Nasser. On the contrary, he flaunted Britain's large dependence on the Canal emotionally, making a case for the war he wanted by playing on the fear and vanity of his countrymen. In addition, war could not help but would surely hurt the 16,400 British subjects in Egypt (5,700 Britons, 6,000 Maltese, and 4,200 Cypriotes among them), many of whom owned or were managing substantial British properties and investments such as banks, insurance companies, trading corporations, hotels, and countless other enterprises built up over three generations.

Eden could not have been indifferent to the human and commercial interests he was endangering. But his obsession to destroy Nasser made him irrational. When Anthony Nutting tried to point out that nationalization, far from making Nasser more dangerous, had given Egypt a larger incentive to promote traffic, Eden retorted that the capacity of the Arabs to cut off their nose to spite their face was infinite.

Eden and the French strove from the outset to blur the legal and financial verities and to keep the issue as political and as emotional as possible. French warnings to Washington the day after nationalization outdid the British in emotionalism. Pineau told US Ambassador Douglas Dillon that it was like Hitler's occupation of the Rhineland and that if the West did not react strongly the Middle Eastern oil pipelines would be nationalized within three months and Europe would be at the mercy of the Arabs. He demanded Washington's approval within twenty-four hours for the diversion from deliveries to NATO of two more squadrons of Mystère IVs for shipment to Israel. He said, erroneously, that the Canal company had ordered its employees to defy Egyptian work orders and that he expected the situation to worsen when Egypt jailed them. He said France and Britain were studying the reoccupation of the Canal zone, adding that they did not expect it to be difficult and that he doubted the Russians would be able to act to protect Egypt.

Eisenhower entered his office at 8:10 A.M. on the 27th for a long day's study of the messages from Andrew Foster, Eden, and Dillon and translations of Nasser's speeches at Mostarod and Alexandria. Allen Dulles, Hoover, and Colonel Andrew Goodpaster, his military aide, joined him. London, Paris, and Cairo were surcharged and super-heated with emotion, the group in the White House concluded, and the US should act both to abate the emotion and to prepare for the worst.

Eisenhower told Hoover to protest Nasser's rough talk about the US and to declare American interest in the efficient functioning of the Canal. He opposed, ineffectually as it turned out, the French shipment of more warplanes to Israel. He sent Eden a cautionary cable that an aide has well described as "the first 'Down, Boy!' ". The President added that he was sending Murphy to the Big Three meeting Eden requested. Murphy's mission was to discourage impulsive armed action. In case Murphy should fail, Eisenhower warned the Congressional leaders of both parties, there was a danger of war and he might have to recall Congress in a special session.

Eisenhower opposed the use of force from the beginning and emphasized this stand to Eden throughout. He told me later that he had felt all the way through the crisis "that they wanted to get rid of Nasser and they ought to have better grounds for it."

There was no legal justification for military action arising out of the nationalization, Eisenhower felt. Unjustified warfare would automatically weaken the UN, perhaps destroy it. As a young officer thirty years earlier, he had learned the complicated operations of the Panama Canal, which uses locks to lift ships over the spine of the isthmus. He was skeptical of Anglo-French claims that Egyptians could not manage the simpler operation of the Suez Canal, which is a lockless open cut between the seas. He believed that the only way to determine whether Nasser could and would keep the Canal operating efficiently and open to all nations under the Convention of 1888 was to wait and see. There were many ways to evade the letter and violate the spirit of the Convention. In addition to Britain's many violations during her occupation of Egypt, an American consul barred the Canal to the Spanish fleet in the Spanish-American War by cornering the supply of bunkering coal in the region and refusing to sell to the Spaniards.

In 1956 Britain and France did their best to rasp nationalist sensibilities, among their own people as well as Egyptians, in the hope of provoking a provocation for war. In a formal protest against the law "purporting to nationalize" the canal company, Britain said it threatened freedom of navigation, adding that she reserved the rights of British nationals as well as of the British Government and that "the responsibility for consequences must rest entirely upon the Egyptian Government." The Egyptians promptly returned the note.

In Paris Pineau summoned the Egyptian ambassador, Kamal Abdel Nabi, to the Quai D'Orsay and read him a protest denouncing the "spoliation" of the Canal by a dictator who broke his promise not to train Algerian rebels. Although Pineau and the aristocratic Abdel Nabi were friends, Pineau launched into the note without asking the ambassador to sit down. Abdel Nabi, a thin, elegant figure who speaks perfect French, leaned down to pound his delicate fist on a table as he exclaimed that the note was inadmissible to his government and personally offensive to himself. He brushed away Pineau's attempt to hand it to him and stalked out of the room trembling with rage. He never forgave Pineau's rudeness and saw him only once again, in November, when he called to break diplomatic relations.

(Abdel Nabi remained a friend of France, however. He called on de

Gaulle as the war approached to say he hoped the general would return to power without inheriting the enmity of the Arab world. "The true France and the true Egypt will always remain friends in spite of passing clouds," de Gaulle replied.)

The British and French press, with few exceptions, did their best to whip up national feeling against Nasser from the moment the news of nationalization came chattering over the wires. Editorialists demanded military action, if need be, to make Nasser back down promptly.

In the House of Commons on the 27th Eden got expressions of sympathy and support from speakers of all three parties together with advice on how to retaliate. At Westminster as in Fleet Street, Nasser was likened to Hitler. Eden assured the members that Britain was consulting with other interested governments on the fate of the Canal "and also the wider questions which it raises." Then he met with the Cabinet and Chiefs of Staff for two and a half hours. In addition to approving the protest note to Egypt, the Cabinet: ordered Egyptian sterling to be frozen as of the following day; blocked Egyptian access to canal company accounts in London; reimposed an arms embargo on Egypt; ordered bureaucratic harassment of four Egyptian destroyers in British and Maltese harbors; told the Foreign Office to warn British subjects in Egypt of "likely developments", and ordered a survey of shipping preparatory to requisitioning what might be needed for a military operation.

Eden also set up that day the inner committee of Cabinet ministers that was to master-mind the Suez crisis. Eden wrote four years later that its job was "to keep in contact with the situation on behalf of the Cabinet" and "to work out plans day by day to put our policy into effect." There were six members in addition to Eden out of the total Cabinet membership of eighteen. They were, in the order of their enthusiasm for war: Macmillan, Chancellor of the Exchequer; the Marquis of Salisbury, Lord President of the Privy Council; Alan Lennox-Boyd, Colonial Secretary; Viscount Kilmuir, the Lord Chancellor; Peter Thorneycroft, President of the Board of Trade; and Selwyn Lloyd, Foreign Secretary. Other ministers frequently sat in. The Chiefs of Staff attended when required. The group was informally known as the "Inner Cabinet" or the "Suez Committee". Although Lloyd had considered war against Nasser a likelihood since the Russian arms deal in September 1955, he was uneasy about the way Eden manufactured a war out of the Suez nationalization. Nevertheless, he remained compliant to the end.

Macmillan, later to be derided by Harold Wilson as "first in, first out at Suez," was the fire-eater of the group, goading Eden's desires and stiffening his resolve. Eden had shifted Macmillan from Defense to the Foreign Office in his first minor Cabinet reshuffle immediately after succeeding Churchill as Prime

Minister. It was strange for Eden to put the forceful and ambitious older man in charge of foreign affairs. In the end it proved disastrous, for it was Macmillan who led Eden to ride roughshod over his moratorium with Nasser on the Baghdad Pact. Having thus contributed so greatly to the destruction of Anglo-Egyptian amity as Foreign Secretary, Macmillan thrashed on into the bitter harvest at Suez with a recklessness unbecoming the keeper of the Treasury. His forceful personality and close friendship with Eisenhower and Murphy, dating from wartime missions in North Africa, gave Macmillan a particular authority within the Cabinet. His record enhanced it. Like Eden and Salisbury, he had been among the Tory minority that opposed appeasement in Hitler's day.

There were degrees of enthusiasm and ignorance in the Cabinet but no opposition to Eden's war policy. In the first reflex the Cabinet's enthusiasm for an immediate airborne attack on the canal zone grew so great that the three Chiefs of Staff threatened to resign before Eden could be persuaded to drop the idea. Of the three service chiefs, only Earl Mountbatten, the First Lord of the Admiralty, was opposed to war. The other two were Sir Gerald Templer, the army chief, who had been obliged by rioting to beat so ignominious a retreat from Jordan in December, and Sir Dermot Boyle, the air chief. All three refused to risk an air drop of troops without land and naval forces able to support them within twenty-four hours.

The service chiefs' canvass of resources for immediate attack quickly resulted in roughly the same conclusion Nasser had come to, namely that it would take two months or thereabouts to mount an invasion. But unlike Nasser, the British were aware of the French-Israeli concept of war against Nasser on two fronts and they weighed the utility of strengthening and using Israeli forces. As one Cabinet minister told me:

> The whole cabinet knew about Israel from the beginning. The Israel thing would have come to the top of the pile only after no other pretext remained. The funny thing was, the Cabinet preferred this [collusion] to a straight bash.

Eden's immense prestige in foreign affairs together with the boldness of Macmillan helped still any faint-hearted doubts that their Cabinet colleagues felt about embarking on the policy of duplicity and violence that soon disgraced Britain and speeded the end of the Empire. The duplicity, towards allies and Parliament as well as towards the enemy, developed after the Cabinet endorsed violence and had become at a loss as to how to commit it. There was more than a hint of duplicity among the members of the Cabinet itself. As the weeks passed, Macmillan, wishfully perhaps, succeeded in giving his colleagues the illusion that, contrary to appearances, the Eisenhower administration was sympathetic to Britain's determination to shoot Nasser down.

Nevertheless, the Cabinet was remarkably cohesive. Its solidarity rested on common upperclass backgrounds. Most of the members had gone to Oxford or Cambridge (half were Etonians), had seen military service in one or the other of the World Wars, and had behind them long Parliamentary careers as Tory regulars.

Outside the Government Conservatives in Parliament were less cohesive but their dominant mood was in harmony with Eden's temper. The die-hard "Suez Rebels," about three dozen MPs on the party's extreme right, saw nationalization as proof of its accusation in 1954 that the Suez evacuation agreement was a "scuttle" of imperial interests. They saw a connection between the departure of the last British soldiers from Egypt on 13 June and the nationalization six weeks later. The "Suez Rebels" were led by Captain Charles Waterhouse and Julian Amery, a son-in-law of Macmillan's. They showed their temper in March by heaping contempt upon Eden's failure to hit back for the dismissal of Glubb. Immediately upon nationalization they became the most vocal element in the party, quick to praise any promise of action against Nasser and quick to scorn hesitation.

The right wing of the party was disgusted with the Government's conduct of domestic as well as Middle Eastern affairs. An impassioned debate had developed during the spring and summer over abolishing capital punishment. The Government permitted a free vote in the Commons, allowing members to follow their consciences instead of party discipline, which pleased the Laborites and the liberal Tories. At the same time it sought to placate the right wing by advising against abolition, a posture that looked silly when free Tory votes enabled the Commons to approve abolition. The Lords blocked it in mid-July but the issue remained powerfully divisive at the Conservative Party conference in October, when the Suez crisis was approaching its climax. A dramatic drop in the Tory turnout at the Tonbridge by-election on 7 June, evidently a reaction to domestic rather than foreign policies, added to the incentives for Eden to brighten his image as a leader.

In embarking upon a foreign war to do so, Eden made mistakes from the outset that were bound to cripple such a policy even if it had been a wise one. The first was his failure to obtain bipartisan support, which is essential to a democratic government wishing to fight. Soon afterward he began his wishful evasion of the restraints imposed by his stronger ally, the United States. And he antagonized most of the Commonwealth, which nearly split apart over Suez.

Eden not only failed to obtain bipartisan support but he seemed indifferent to it. Hugh Gaitskell, the leader of the Labor Party, was among the dinner guests at No. 10 Downing Street when the news of nationalization arrived, as was Sir Hartley Shawcross, a prominent Laborite lawyer and diplomat. Eden did not bring Gaitskell into the deliberations that night on the presumed predicament of the nation, although he invited an American and a Frenchman to sit in. And he never afterward consulted Gaitskell, who was obliged to volunteer his advice and warnings throughout the remainder of the crisis. Personal dislike was part of the reason. Eden said in his memoirs of Gaitskell's victory over Herbert Morrison for the Laborite leadership: "I had no doubt that this was a national misfortune." He added disdainfully: "In all my years of political life I had not met anyone with his cast of mind and approach to problems. We never seemed to be able to get on terms."

Although Eden never tried to get on terms, Gaitskell did. He went to Eden on 30 July to warn him that the Labor Party was extremely unlikely to endorse a resort to arms unless there was some new and sufficient provocation by Nasser. Gaitskell did not think at that time that the Government was likely to seek a military solution. He changed his mind three days later when Eden issued a call to arms to 25,000 reservists.

As for his evasive conduct toward Washington, Eden admits that he was aware of differences between the two Governments within two days of nationalization. His remedy was to commit his Government time and again to objectives, like internationalizing the Canal or setting up a rival operating authority, that seemed certain to lead to war on the presumption that the US would have to accept the inevitable. He took loopholes in US prohibitions against war and magnified them into positive permission to wage war. Eisenhower's concession that force might be justified *in extremis,* for example if British lives were in danger, was taken by Eden to mean that war would be allowed if negotiation failed to satisfy British requirements. Eden's real requirement, of course, was to bring down Nasser, which was hardly a negotiable issue.

In private Eisenhower and Dulles made plain to Eden their adamant opposition to the use of force. But in public statements they sought to keep the threat of force alive as a tactic to help Eden push Nasser toward a settlement of the Canal dispute. Eden, who did not want any settlement which Nasser could survive, used their public hints in such a way that Dulles was repeatedly forced to negate them.

"It seemed impossible for Eden to keep in mind how much Britain's power had diminished in relation to the United States and Russia," Murphy wrote, "but Dulles never forgot this." Eden himself saw the same thing differently. Contrasting Dulles with his predecessor Dean Acheson, Eden wrote: "Mr.

Acheson . . . never forgot what was due to an ally and worked in the spirit of an equal partnership, even though the United States carried so much the heavier load."

The nations of the Commonwealth began to manifest doubt and disagreement as soon as the US did. Only Australia and New Zealand stood with Britain in the crunch—and New Zealand had doubters. The rest of the "Old" or "White" Commonwealth and all of the "New" Commonwealth of colored nations opposed Eden. Even so white a Premier as Johannes Strijdom of South Africa said on 27 July: "It is best to keep our heads out of the beehive."

Nasser returned by train to Cairo from Alexandria in triumph on Saturday, 28 July. He traveled behind a Diesel locomotive garlanded with flowers and ribbons and strings of lights. He was delayed in every town by frenzied throngs which swarmed along the route and surged onto the tracks. Men and boys scampered beside the train and leaped like hungry fish to touch the hand of the President, who leaned head and shoulders out of the open window of his carriage. Secret service men slapped angrily at the leapers but Nasser beamed with happy amazement and confidence. Men and women jammed the windows and balconies and rooftops along the way. Youths and boys perched on lamp standards, signal gantries, and overpasses. Confetti burst in little clouds from upper windows and colored paper tape looped and writhed in the air.

The sun blazed down from a cloudless sky. The waving arms and leaping bodies, the brandished victory streamers, two-handled banners, and placards lent the crowds the same fluttering animation as the confetti in the air. Nasser pulled his handkerchief from his breast pocket, fluttered it in response, and raised his arms in a victory gesture, Eisenhower-style. He spoke hoarsely into microphones at stations along the way and in Cairo, where the throngs in the streets forced Nasser's car to take an hour and a quarter to traverse the two and a half miles between the station and the Presidency.

Nasser came out onto the round balcony at the Presidency shortly before 3 P.M. Europe's angry uproar over the nationalization, he said, showed that the foreign concessionnaires had had no intention of returning the Canal to Egypt in 1968. "Why should Britain say that this nationalization will affect shipping in the Canal? Would it have affected shipping twelve years hence?"

Alternately high-spirited and darkly defiant, Nasser drew roars of applause when he said: "As for the impudence of France and the French Foreign Minister, I shall not reply to this. . . . The French Foreign Minister was rude to the Egyptian ambassador in Paris yesterday—I shall leave it to the struggling Algerians to teach France a lesson in behavior."

Anwar Sadat, a member of the original revolutionary junta who was in charge of Government-owned newspapers, referred to "conceited cowards like

Eden and Pineau and the rest of the felonious and stupid horde." But aside from a few such lapses into pungent invective, Nasser and all who spoke for Egypt kept to civil propriety and avoided inflammatory outbursts.

In Washington, Eisenhower delayed his weekend retreat to Gettysburg for a mid-Saturday-morning talk with Murphy. "The President was not greatly concerned," Murphy wrote later, "and there was no talk of recalling Dulles from Peru. 'Just go over and hold the fort,' the President told me."

Murphy reached London late Saturday night and began his talks with Lloyd and Pineau on Sunday morning, 29 July. They were less informative than an informal dinner reunion that night with Macmillan and Field Marshal Alexander. Both were wartime colleagues of Murphy's. Murphy recalls sensing that Macmillan had aspirations to move from the Chancellor's official residence to the adjoining house on Downing Street, Number 10. They talked of Suez over brandy.

"I was left in no doubt that the British Government believed that Suez was a test which could be met only by the use of force," Murphy recalled. "It was intimated that military moves might start in August and 'would not take much'—perhaps a division or at the most two. . . . The British did not like the risk and expense involved—the government had set aside five million pounds ($14 million) for the venture—but 'Nasser has to be chased out of Egypt.' It was believed that the British people were unanimously behind the government in its determination to defeat Nasser."

Murphy records that the Anglo-French military operation launched on 31 October turned out to be "strictly according to the staff plan which I had been told about in July." He wrote that the scheme provided for a strike at the Egyptian air force by bombers from Cyprus, Malta, Aden, and fleet carriers. The objective was to paralyze the Egyptians, knock out Cairo Radio, and "chase Nasser from Egypt" while preventing the blockage of the Canal. Murphy wrote that "nothing was changed in this plan, which had been carefully prepared for use in August." Israel's prospective role was not mentioned; it was still far from "the top of the pile."

Murphy says he shared British indignation and thought the presentation of Anglo-French plans by Macmillan and Alexander made good sense. "But I knew that United States policy opposed the type of eighteenth-century strategy which was in the minds of our friends," Murphy wrote. In spite of his sympathy with the British, Murphy was at odds with Pineau from the start. They accused each other over a leak to the press at the end of the first day. "Nobody can be more ruthless in playing power politics or more intellectually insolent than French Socialists," Murphy wrote afterward. He cabled Eisenhower at 2 A.M.

Monday (London time) a report on his talk with Macmillan and Alexander. Eisenhower replied that he was sending Dulles over.

Dulles had been away from Washington since he and Eisenhower went to Panama for a conference of American presidents on 21 July. Eisenhower returned on 24 July but Dulles went on to Lima for the inauguration of a new Peruvian President. He returned to Washington on the 29th. After they watched together the developments on Monday, the 30th, Dulles persuaded Eisenhower that the British were taking a calmer view and that Murphy could continue to "hold the fort" after all. Dulles felt that his own presence would increase the visible importance of the meeting and thereby increase international anxiety.

It is not clear why Dulles found the events of the 30th reassuring. In Paris Mollet denounced Nasser in a luncheon speech as an "apprentice dictator" of Hitler's ilk and he declared that France "has decided upon an energetic and severe riposte." *Le Monde* complained that "four days have passed . . . but no Western riposte has yet been made." In London Eden told the House of Commons that Britain would accept no arrangements for the Canal "which would leave it in the unfettered control of a single Power." When asked whether the renewed embargo on arms included the two destroyers recently sold to Egypt, Eden won boisterous applause from both sides of the house by replying: "I do not know where they are, but I think that we can leave it to the Royal Navy. It will take care of them wherever they are."

On Tuesday Britain rerouted troopships on the run to the Far East garrisons away from the Canal and around the Cape of Good Hope. The War Office announced that "certain precautionary measures of a military nature are being taken with the object of strengthening our position in the Eastern Mediterranean area and our general ability to deal with any situation that may arise." Eden and Macmillan sent Eisenhower messages through Murphy on a most secret basis informing him that Britain had decided to employ force without delay and without attempting any intermediate and less drastic steps.

Murphy lunched that day with Eden, Salisbury, Lloyd, and Macmillan and found a confident assumption that the US would go along with anything Britain and France did. Eden said there was no question of needing US help unless Russia intervened, in which case, he said, "we do hope you will take care of the Bear." It had suddenly become, in Murphy's words, "increasingly evident that there was serious and perhaps imminent prospect of Anglo-French military action." Eden's jingo cockiness in Parliament on Monday about the Royal Navy and the Egyptian destroyers was followed on Tuesday by private declarations of grim intent.

Early Tuesday morning Eisenhower received the messages from Eden and Macmillan, who stressed that the decision to invade Egypt had already been approved by the Government and was firm and irrevocable. Dulles brought in a confirmatory message from the US Embassy in London stating that the British had resolved to "break Nasser" and to start military operations at an early date for this purpose. Eisenhower writes in his memoirs: "I can scarcely describe the depth of the regret I felt in the need to take a view so diametrically opposed to that held by the British." His sympathy toward the British was warmed by wartime friendships but he felt that the US had to stand "firmly on principle and on the realities of the twentieth century." US and British policy in the Middle East remained diametrically opposed from that morning until 9 January 1957, when Eden, sick and defeated, resigned his office.

Eisenhower ordered Dulles to London after a ninety-minute discussion, from which Dulles emerged tight-lipped. "I left on two hours' notice," Dulles said a week later. "A somewhat humorous side light is the fact that I did not have time to supervise my own packing, and I called up my home and asked my butler-valet to pack a bag. He packed a bag with what he thought was suitable summer apparel. And when I arrived in London the temperature at the airport was 52 degrees, and there was a driving sleet and rain, and I had great trouble keeping warm during my two days in London."

Dulles took with him an English translation of the 1888 Convention and the CIA's translation of its monitored text of Nasser's nationalization speech. The CIA mimeograph had left blank *page four*, where Nasser: welcomed Syria's first demand for union, told how Egypt's leaders used to be kept waiting in the British ambassador's anterooms, and described the Brioni talks on easing world tensions. Dulles also took with him J. C. Hurewitz's excellent two-volume documentary collection, *Diplomacy in the Near and Middle East*.

Eisenhower sent a letter to Eden with Dulles saying that Dulles's mission was to persuade Eden to review "in its broadest aspects" the British decision to go to war against Nasser forthwith. Eisenhower did not countenance any objective other than assuring "the efficient operation of the Canal." Emphasizing "the unwisdom even of contemplating the use of military force at this moment," Eisenhower warned that "initial military successes might be easy, but the eventual price might become far too heavy."

In a tacit correction of Eden's assumption that the US would "take care of the Bear," Eisenhower said the employment of US forces would require reconvening Congress and that "there would have to be a showing that every peaceful means of resolving the difficulty had previously been exhausted" or else "there would be a reaction that could very seriously affect our peoples' feeling toward our Western allies." He added: "I do not want to exaggerate, but I assure you that this could grow to such an intensity as to have the most far-reaching consequences."

Eden wrote of the message in his memoirs: "The President did not rule out the use of force." This was the kind of thing that made Murphy write in his memoirs: "There were some in Washington who regarded Eden as 'slippery', and Eisenhower was determined not to have the United States used as a cat's paw to protect British oil interests.... Many Americans have found Eden uncongenial. Dulles disliked his attitude about Europe generally... Hoover 'couldn't stand him.' One State Department official asserted that he had never met a dumber man."

Eden's critics in his own party weighed heavier than those in America. The Conservative *Daily Telegraph*, which had turned the pack against Eden in January, spoke ominously in an editorial headed "Fifth Day on the Canal." It said Eden's statement on "unfettered control" of the Canal "was too vague to be impressive.... It reminded many members of the Government's well-known weakness for regarding the calling of a meeting as the substitute for policy." The paper warned: "If there is anywhere a lurking desire to appease Colonel Nasser, it should be brought out into the open."

In Washington, as Dulles left, the Treasury announced that it had frozen all assets in the US of both the Egyptian Government and the Suez Canal Company.

In Cairo Aly Sabry made public a statement by Nasser saying:

> The nationalization of this company in no way affects Egypt's international obligations.... The freedom of shipping in the Suez Canal will in no way be affected. Furthermore, there is no one more anxious than Egypt to safeguard freedom of passage and the flourishing of traffic in the Canal.

In response to a journalist's question, Sabry said that Egypt would fight if she were attacked. Sabry also dissolved the likeliest pretext for war by saying the Suez Canal Company employees were free to quit provided they gave the statutory month's notice.

In Moscow Khrushchev told workers at a stadium rally that the West had reacted with "too much excitement." Nationalization was a legal sovereign right, he said, and the dispute "can and must be settled by peaceful means." He warned that "war is more easily started than ended." Washington retorted that if the Russians moved in they would find the Americans alongside their allies.

Dulles arrived in London on Wednesday morning, 1 August. Among his handful of aides was Herman Phleger, the department's legal adviser. As they flew through the night across the Atlantic Dulles drafted a final communiqué for the two-day meeting he was about to join. Copies quickly reached Lloyd and Pineau. It was issued almost without change on Thursday night, a testimony to Dulles's hard homework as well as to US power.

The Times (London) continued its almost daily barrage of editorials on Suez during Dulles's visit. In language too similar to Eden's first cable to Eisenhower for coincidence, it said: "Quibbling over whether or not he [Nasser] was 'legally entitled' to make the grab will delight the finicky and comfort the faint-hearted, but entirely misses the real issues."

Since US and British policies had become diametrically opposed, it was not surprising that the two lawyers, Dulles and Phleger, resorted to just the kind of legal quibbles Eden and *The Times* sought scornfully to avoid. "The two lawyers," wrote Murphy, who remained at the talks, "had devised various delaying tactics designed to support Eisenhower's policy of avoiding military intervention. It was philosophically assumed that the danger of bellicose action would disappear if negotiations were prolonged, and that delays would reduce the heat and make possible some kind of nonviolent settlement in Egypt." Dulles's stalling tactics remained as constant as the Anglo-French determination to go to war and they were just as skillfully cloaked in ambiguous language.

All the wordy activity of the ensuing three months, all the conferences, decisions, diplomatic missions, and negotiations which seemed to the public and to many of the participants to be aimed honestly at settling a dispute over a canal were really a veiled struggle over whether Eden could make war against Nasser in spite of US opposition. Suspenseful diplomatic advances and retreats seemed often to be divorced from reality because the intentions of the contestants were not what they declared them to be. Outsiders were like myopic spectators watching their first basketball game. Unable to see the goals, they were bewildered by the twists and turns, dodges and stratagems of the star antagonists, one trying to shoot and the other blocking, both pursuing constant and irreconcilable but invisible objectives.

Soon after Dulles began his talks he cabled Eisenhower that Britain and France were still determined to take the Canal by force unless Nasser backed down but that he was persuading them to try first to engage world opinion behind an international solution. But Nasser, not the Canal, was the real issue. Macmillan told Dulles that Britain would be finished as a world power if it let Nasser get away with it, exclaiming: "This is Munich all over again!" Pineau emphasized from the first that France's position in North Africa hung on the issue, for if Nasser succeeded, the Algerians would take fresh heart and would, furthermore, get more arms and diplomatic support from Egypt.

Dulles had to cement his obstacles with sympathy if they were to stand up against the Anglo-French rush to war. He said on the first day: "A way must be found to make Nasser disgorge." Eden was moved to recall in his memoirs: "These were forthright words. They rang in my ears for months." Murphy says Dulles made that type of statement in private as a relief from pressures and that it was never intended to be given literal importance. It was an impulsive expression of the sympathy he felt for our Allies' anger at Nasser, Murphy suggested. By way of illustration, he said Dulles was entirely capable of exclaiming in a critical situation: "It's about time we started throwing bombs in the market place!"

Nevertheless, Dulles gave Eden what seems to have been an accurate impression that he was both anti-Nasser and anti-Egyptian. "He agreed emphatically that the seizure of a great international waterway was intolerable," Eden wrote. "This was still more so when the single nation that set out to dominate the Canal was Egypt." Since the Canal is an artificial piece of geography lying entirely within Egypt, to regard Egypt as the single nation least qualified to dominate the Canal presupposes an extraordinary anti-Egyptian bias.

Personal sympathy between Eden and Dulles was impossible. Eden believed Dulles had been guilty of bad faith toward the British in the Japanese Peace Treaty negotiations in 1951. In 1952 he told Eisenhower he hoped that if he were elected President he would appoint someone other than Dulles as Secretary of State. Eden said he had enjoyed cordial and intimate relations with Dulles's four predecessors. "My difficulty in working with Mr. Dulles was to determine what he really meant and in consequence the significance to be attached to his words and actions," Eden wrote. "A preacher in a world of politics, Mr. Dulles seemed sometimes to have little regard for the consequences of his words . . ."

Eden's difficulties derived chiefly from his own practice of acting on the one odd word or gesture out of a thousand that seemed to encourage his belligerent desires and ignoring the 999 contrary words. One subtle device for shutting off the restrictive words was to claim that the US deliberately turned a blind eye to Britain's warlike moves. Eden says he told Dulles at this first Suez meeting that before acceding to a request from the US Naval Attaché for information about British military preparations he wanted to make sure the Government really wanted the information. "Mr. Dulles replied that the United States Government perfectly well understood the purpose of our preparations and he thought that they had had a good effect," Eden wrote. "It was preferable that the United States Government should not seek detailed information." Under strained constructions of such isolated comments Eden took leave to make war.

He made free use of strained interpretations and downright distortions in the House of Commons debate on 2 August in order to build up his case against Nasser. And he was not above a legal quibble or two himself. His skill at creating a false impression through allusions and juxtapositions without technically lying was marvelously displayed in this debate. It was one of the things that made reporting British policy so exasperating for correspondents in London at that time. Our problem was to present within the limited space of a news dispatch not only what Eden said but also what he implied and at the same time attempt to make clear where he departed from the truth. The latter obligation to accuracy was handicapped by the fact that most Western copy editors assumed as a matter of course that Englishmen were truthful and Egyptians were liars, that British lies were forgivable mistakes and that Egyptian mistakes were unforgivable lies. In Eden's war with Nasser, truth, as in all modern wars, was the first victim long before a single shot was fired.

Eden fabricated the impression for a sympathetic and grimly demonstrative House of Commons that Nasser had not merely abrogated a commercial concession but violated innumerable treaties and promises. I asked the Foreign Office the following day for a list of the "broken promises...solemn undertakings, many of them recently given" which Eden attributed to Nasser, including indications of how each was broken. The spokesman was unable to specify any, other than the Canal concession, and asked for time to prepare a list. He never produced a single item. I stopped asking a week or so later when it became clear that my request could obtain only embarrassment and irritation. It was Britain, in fact, which broke a list of promises and agreements, among them Eden's moratorium on the Baghdad Pact, the offer of aid for the High Dam, and the sterling releases agreement, not to speak of the planned violations by war of the Tripartite Declaration, the 1954 evacuation agreement, and the UN Charter.

As for the concession, its ending was provocative but it broke no law or treaty. The Suez Canal Company's president told stockholders at the ninety-eighth annual meeting on 12 June 1956 that while the company "played an undoubted international role, it did not, for all that, enjoy an international status." He said the company was doubtless well armed with arguments but that the outcome of any juridical controversy on the issue was uncertain. Britain never challenged the legality of the nationalization, although Eden spun the issue into the fabric he stuffed to make his straw bogey man of Nasser.

Eden revealed his technique when he asked the House "to note, what is not generally known, that there is a link between the Convention of 1888 and the concession of the Canal Company...in Articles 2 and 14 of the 1888 Convention." He said Article 2 "deals with the engagements of Egypt toward the Suez Canal Company as regards the freshwater canal." In fact, the article states that the Convention signatories merely "take note" of the Egyptian khedive's engagements; it is the signatories themselves who are bound by the article "not

380

to interfere" with the Sweetwater Canal. A fine distinction, perhaps, but made more significant by Eden's glide into other topics without ever reverting to Article 14 after having cited it to create the impression of multiple links between the international Convention and the commercial concession. This was more clever than ethical because Article 14 mentions the concession only to repudiate any link with it—"the engagements resulting from the present Treaty shall not be limited by the duration of the Acts of Concession . . . "

The purpose of fabricating a link between the concession and the Convention was to create the false illusion that by breaking the concession Nasser was violating the Convention. Eden recalled that the Anglo-Egyptian evacuation agreement of 1954 reaffirmed the determination of both parties to uphold the 1888 Convention. "Now, Sir, I ask," said Eden, hammering home the imaginary connecting nail, "how can this be reconciled with the Egyptian Government's action against the Suez Canal Company?"

Eden falsely accused Nasser of having announced in his nationalization speech that he would divert to the High Dam the very revenues the company would earmark for improving the Canal. Eden and Mollet rarely argued against what Nasser actually said or did; they always argued against what they said Nasser said and few bothered to consult the record. The Egyptians, to whom the West seldom listened and then rarely with the modicum of sympathy and attention required to hear truly, found it a great handicap to counter arguments that required them first to correct the false quotations upon which the arguments were premised.

Eden went on into specious economics purporting to prove that it was impossible for Egypt to compensate the shareholders, build the dam, and develop the Canal. He ignored Aly Sabry's statement that company employees were free to quit and insisted that Egypt was holding them at their posts in violation of human rights.

Having skillfully created an impressionistic portrait of Nasser as a knavish bankrupt and bully, unable to rise to Western standards of competence or ethics in operating the Canal upon which "the industrial life of Western Europe literally depends," Eden made two commitments to war. Neither was fully appreciated at the time by an unwilling world. He announced a partial mobilization and he committed his government hard and fast to force upon Nasser "an international authority" over the Canal.

The call-up proclamation was approved by the Cabinet, evidently without much discussion, early that afternoon and rushed to the Queen at Goodwood, where she was attending the races. She signed it, they say, against the rump of a racehorse. It recalled to the colors about 25,000 men and it prolonged service for conscripts due for discharge. With the call-up Eden deliberately tied himself to the mast after setting his course for war. From this moment onward, either Nasser had to back down into his own destruction or Eden had to make war against him. Releasing the reservists otherwise would have been a victory for Nasser that Eden could not accept. Navy, Army, and Air Force units were already moving from England, Eden said—"precautionary measures...to strengthen our position in the Eastern Mediterranean and our ability to deal with any situation that may arise."

As for the Canal, Eden gravely repeated his vow not to leave the Canal in Egypt's "unfettered control." Its free use and efficiency, he said in conclusion, "can be effectively ensured only by an international authority. It is upon this that we must insist. . . . Nothing less than this can be acceptable to us."

There was the mast to which Eden tied himself. He had committed himself to internationalize the Canal or fight while Nasser had committed himself to fight internationalization. All the forthcoming palaver over the use of force as a last resort missed the point that in the minds of Eden, Mollet, and Ben-Gurion "peaceful means" were mere formalities which would have to be got through in order to get down to the last resort.

Antony Head, then Minister of War, told the Commons that the proclamation was "equivalent to general mobilization" but that the Government was "really using very large powers to obtain a very small complement which we consider essential." A War Office spokesman said that in addition to regular Army, Navy, and Royal Air Force reservists, mobilization notices were going to specialists and technicians such as crane drivers, heavy construction and dock workers, postal and transport specialists. He conceded that the preparations looked like those for an assault, invasion, and occupation force. Officials in Whitehall spoke unofficially but pointedly of the Canal as the primary target and of contingency plans for the occupation of Cairo and Alexandria and the seizure of Egyptian Government leaders.

The Foreign Office disclosed that it had warned British nationals in Egypt that if they had no compelling reasons to stay, they should consider "whether it would not be wiser and in their own interests to leave while the situation was still quiet." The warning was described as directed primarily at women and children.

In his memoirs Eden said one reason for the military measures was to be able to protect British subjects in Egypt. He also claimed that the military threats deterred Nasser from interfering with British ships and from trying to compel payment of tolls to the new Egyptian canal authority. Eden's real intention, however, was war, to the inevitable and foreseeable detriment of British lives and property in Egypt as well as of British shipping in the Canal.

Eden's failure to obtain a national consensus for his war was not apparent on this last day of the Parliamentary session. Gaitskell jumped on the band-wagon of jingo distortions, declaring: "We cannot forget that Colonel Nasser [Many Britons refuse to this day to promote him from Colonel to President] has repeatedly boasted of his intention to create an Arab empire from the Atlantic to the Persian Gulf." Since Nasser has never once, either before or after Suez, either boasted or hinted at any intention to create an Arab empire anywhere, Gaitskell could hardly forget what he could never have learned. But he was careless that day of his own decent and truthful nature.

Gaitskell endorsed Mollet's comparison of Nasser with Hitler. "It is all very familiar," he said. "It is exactly the same that we encountered from Mussolini and Hitler in those years before the war." Gaitskell disclosed imperial anxie-ties identical with Eden's as he warned: "The fact is that this episode must be recognized as part of the struggle for the mastery of the Middle East." Both sides of the house cheered. When Herbert Morrison, the former Laborite For-eign Secretary, said of the Cabinet's weighing of the use of force, "let them not be too much afraid," it looked indeed as if Eden had bipartisan support.

But Gaitskell's peroration, drafted by Kenneth Younger, kept a leg on the other side of the fence in a straddle that was little noticed at the time but which Gaitskell was to make much of subsequently when he led his party against the use of force. "We are members of the United Nations," Gaitskell reminded the House. "We must not, therefore, allow ourselves to get into a position where we might be denounced in the Security Council as aggressors, or where the majority of the Assembly were against us." Gaitskell said Britain had long acquiesced in the only thing Nasser had done to justify using force, namely the stopping of Israeli ships from using the Canal. "It would, I think, be difficult to find in anything else he had done," Gaitskell said, "any legal justification for the use of force."

Eden had already privately considered making an issue of the Israeli case. "Forgetting the view he had expressed to me in Berlin two years before that Egypt had a case under the Constantinople Convention for refusing passage through the Canal to ships of a nation with whom she was in a state of war," Anthony Nutting wrote, "he now contended that Israeli shipping had been unjustly barred from using an international waterway and that Britain and France must help to restore to Israel her rights of passage."

In Paris the National Assembly, "cognizant of the situation created brutally and unilaterally by Colonel Nasser, . . . [who] constitutes by his behavior a permanent menace to peace," declared its determination not to accept the nationalization and demanded that the French Government and its allies take "the most energetic measures" for redress.

While the parliaments in London and Paris fulminated against Nasser and the ministries of War and Foreign Affairs issued belligerent disclosures and warnings, the Allied foreign ministers in London thrashed out compromises in which Dulles restrained the Anglo-French lunge toward war, but not too much. Dulles's main accomplishments were to obtain British and French agreement to an international conference and a draft plan for international control of the Canal.

Ten days later Dulles told Congressmen assembled to meet Eisenhower that he had been forced to rush to London because the British and French were preparing to attack and it had been difficult to persuade them to agree to a conference at all.

Very little had to be done to Dulles's advance draft of the communiqué. He was proud of the prescience and power thus disclosed and his copy of the draft in his papers at Princeton carries an aide's penciled notation: "I think the Secretary would like this copy preserved to show that actually the final statement was very little changed from the one he drafted going over [to] London on the plane."

The main change between the draft and the communiqué was in having Britain issue the invitations for a conference in London in place of Dulles's proposal for a conference in Geneva under the sponsorship of the signatories to the 1888 Convention. Eden, true to Britain's traditional treatment of the Convention, flouted it even while trying to prop it under his case against Nasser. "The Convention was an important element in our case," Eden wrote later, "but it was by no means the whole story. . . . Russia had signed it, but the United States had not. This was likely to land us in vexing problems . . ."

Eden wanted neither Russia nor Egypt at the conference, according to authoritative reports, and proposed that it be comprised of the sixteen states belonging to the International Chamber of Shipping, of which neither Russia nor Egypt was a member. Dulles said that if the conference had a spurious foundation its results would not win the world's endorsement. Eden and Pineau wanted an immediate conference weighted in favor of the West. The problem was to find a formula that could appear objective and yet assure an overwhelming majority for the North Atlantic nations and their client states in Africa and Asia.

The formula ultimately arrived at was to invite eight signatories of the 1888 Convention, eight nations whose citizens owned two million tons or more of the shipping that used the Canal in 1955, and eight nations exclusive of those previously named whose trade patterns showed the largest use of the Canal, including seven whose export-import totals passed at least 50 per cent through the Canal, plus Indonesia, whose trade was 43 per cent through the Canal.

The signatories to the 1888 Convention who were invited were Egypt,

France, Italy, the Netherlands, Spain, Turkey, Russia, and Britain. Neutral Austria and Communist Hungary, heirs to the Hapsburg empire, were excluded for unexplained reasons. Germany was also excluded from among the group of Convention signatories but West Germany appeared in the list of shipowning nations. Panama and Liberia were excluded from among the shipowning nations on the ground that most of the vast tonnage sailing under their flags of convenience was owned by citizens of other nations. The sixteen shipowning and canal-using nations were: Australia, Ceylon, Denmark, Ethiopia, West Germany, Greece, India, Indonesia, Iran, Japan, New Zealand, Norway, Pakistan, Portugal, Sweden, and the United States.

British officials said hopefully that evening that they frankly expected Egypt to refuse to come and that Russia too might stay away. In the event, only Egypt and Greece refused to join the twenty-two nations who attended. The conference was scheduled to open in London on 16 August.

At their final session, from 4:15 to 8 P.M., the Big Three foreign ministers drafted a plan for submission to the forthcoming conference that would create an "International Authority" to: run the Canal, enforce freedom of passage under the 1888 Convention, arrange compensation for the Suez Canal Company, fix tolls, and carry out improvements. In return for displacing Egyptian authority, it would "ensure to Egypt an equitable return which will take into account all legitimate rights and interests." If Egypt did not accept the International Authority's view of her rights and interests, the World Court would arbitrate. The governing board of the International Authority "would be nominated by the powers chiefly interested in navigation and seaborne trade through the canal."

Eden, who knew his Egyptian history, could rest assured that Nasser would never survive anything but a flat rejection of such a plan. A flat rejection, Eden assumed, would justify war. Egyptians had agitated against the Suez Canal Company concession for fifty years, sometimes violently, and this plan was a worse infringement on Egyptian sovereignty and dignity than the concession. It looked as if Dulles, wittingly or not, had endorsed a first draft on war. The plan was circulated to the invited governments on 6 August. Egypt published it on 9 August, prompting a lame justification from the State Department the following day.

The final communiqué of the tripartite meeting contained striking similarities to Eden's statement a few hours earlier in the House of Commons. Eden had, of course, obtained Dulles's draft the day before. In both there was the same slithery treatment of the legal status of the Suez Canal Company. As laid down in the de Lesseps' 1866 concession, the company, "being Egyptian, is governed by the laws and customs of the country." But the communiqué said that the company "has always had an international character in terms of its shareholders, Directors, and operating personnel..." When a lawyer like Dulles takes the happenstance citizenship of personnel as the determinant of a company's nationality or lack of nationality, in contradiction to general concessionary law and the nationality defined in the company's own charters, it is clear that he knows he has got a weak case.

In a sly elision, the communiqué went on to say that the 1888 Convention was created so that the "international character of the Canal would be perpetuated for all time, irrespective of the expiration of the Concession." Dulles here slipped the company's "international character" upon the Canal itself, which, however useful to the world, was a purely Egyptian piece of geography.

Turning tougher, the communiqué said Egypt had the sovereign right "to nationalize assets not impressed with an international interest" but that this was no simple act of nationalization. "It involves the arbitrary and unilateral seizure by one nation of an international agency" responsible to all the beneficiaries of the 1888 Convention. Ignoring Egypt's rescission of the order forbidding the company employees to quit, the communiqué repeated the accusation that Egypt violated fundamental human rights. Ignoring Egypt's assurances that the 1888 Convention was unaffected, the communiqué said Egypt's action, "threatens the freedom and security of the Canal." It concluded by announcing the convening of the conference "to establish arrangements under an international system designed to assure the continuity of operation of the Canal as guaranteed by the Convention."

The communiqué itself, or rather its Big Three authors, rode roughshod over the Convention in the way they convened the London conference. Article 8 of the Convention provides:

> In case of any event threatening the security or the free passage of the Canal, they [the agents in Egypt of the signatory powers] shall meet on the summons of three of their number under the presidency of their Doyen, in order to proceed with the necessary verifications. They shall inform the Khedivial [Egyptian] Government of the danger which they may have perceived, in order that that Government may take proper steps to insure the protection and free use of the Canal.

Nothing of the sort was done.

Dulles and Pineau flew home to their respective capitals that night. Another phase of the crisis had ended without war, but as Dulles told a closed meeting of Latin American ambassadors on 7 August, "hostilities are not remote, and if they once start, it is hard to see surely whether they would be limited or they might expand."

The main reason hostilities had not begun was that neither Britain nor France was ready when nationalization gave them their pretext. "Had they done it quickly," Eisenhower said later, "we would have accepted it." Eden answered critics of his delay by saying, "We had nothing like enough air-borne troops for an operation of this kind." Without enough paratroopers, the invasion had to be launched from Malta, a thousand miles east of Egypt, and the service chiefs had told Eden that they would not be ready before six weeks. As Dulles told the Latin American ambassadors: "It is the present feeling, I know, of the British and French Governments that there aren't any pressures other than military pressures which would suffice to assure what they regard as their rights and vital interests in the event there is no voluntary agreement."

Dulles had internationalized the dispute by making the British and French accept a relatively broad-based conference and he had thereby slowed down their haste to exhaust peaceful means of redress. "I think the more time that there is," he said, "the more people will be thinking of alternatives." Of Dulles's declared intention to bring the moral pressure of world opinion to bear on Nasser, Eden wrote bitterly: "In practice it was to mean conferences and resolutions, but no action. The result was words."

It was undoubtedly one of the wordiest of crises, but words did not prevent Eden from completing his war preparations. Following the adjournment of Parliament on that second day of August, Eden was free to complete his military build-up without having to answer embarrassing questions.

A shabby piece of vindictiveness marked the close of this phase of the crisis. Billy Butlin, the British holiday camp operator and impresario of the annual international swimming race across the English Channel, barred Egypt from the competition. An Egyptian held the Channel record at that time—10 hours and 49 minutes set in 1950—and the 1955 winner was a member of the Egyptian team. Egyptian swimmers were already in England training for the race, scheduled for 12 August, ten days hence. "This is definitely connected with the Suez situation," said a Butlin official. For months to come the traditional British sense of fair play and good sportsmanship seemed all but extinguished.

CHAPTER

13

Palaver

(3 AUGUST 1956 TO 15 SEPTEMBER 1956)

It is a dangerous thing for politicians ever to say in one word what they can say in two.

(SELWYN LLOYD, at London Conference II, 21 September 1956)

The British public have always had an instinctive dislike of these international gatherings.

(HAROLD NICOLSON, *Diplomacy*, 1939)

And how can we ever come to an understanding if I put in the words I utter the sense and value of things as I see them; while you who listen to me must inevitably translate them according to the conception of things each one of you has within himself. We think we understand each other, but we never really do.

(LUIGI PIRANDELLO, *Six Characters in Search of an Author*)

THE BREAKING of Nasser having been firmly resolved and war being the favored way to do it, Eden and the French focused their attention on creating a pretext for attacking Egypt timed to ripen by the date their invasion forces would achieve battle-readiness. They also had to go through the motions of exhausting every peaceful means toward a Canal settlement—a settlement which they did not want because it would render their planned invasion of Egypt virtually impossible to justify. In none of the diplomatic jockeying in August, September, and October is there persuasive evidence that Eden or the French seriously explored any alternative to using force. Instead they explored pretexts for war.

The contradictions involved in pretending to seek a settlement while actually preparing for war were formidable. Public gestures toward a settlement—conferences, diplomatic missions, parliamentary maneuvers, speeches—had to be conducted carefully in order to avoid success. Above all, Nasser had to be kept from the negotiating table, not only to avoid a reasonable settlement but also because his legal and diplomatic position was strong enough to withstand Britain and France in any unbiased international forum, court, or conference.

The logical way to break Nasser was to destroy the Egyptian armed forces, which were the power base on which his revolutionary regime rested. Accordingly, the destruction of the Egyptian Air Force and Army was the first objective in Anglo-French war plans from the beginning. A military build-up sufficient to invade Egypt and destroy its military establishment could not be concealed so it was cloaked under the cover of "precautions." To justify such precautions it was necessary to maintain an atmosphere of tension. Since Nasser was doing everything he could to mollify Britain and France, they had to build tension on their own recalcitrance, trumpeting nonexistent dangers, reacting to nonexistent provocations, claiming nonexistent rights, and ignoring reality as it was seen by the world at large.

When Dulles hastened to London to dissuade Britain and France from an immediate attack on Egypt, he found his work already done for him by the military chiefs, who had told Eden that they would need six weeks to make ready. But Dulles had no illusions that there had been a real Anglo-French change of heart. His insistence on a two-week delay for the London conference was part of a policy of procrastination and obstruction against the intention to use force which he believed remained in the minds of Eden and the French. His theory, like Nasser's, was that time would cool their warlike intentions and allow world opinion to create an atmosphere unconducive to war.

Eden and Mollet immediately began to make a virtue of necessity. They submitted to delays that would fill the six weeks needed by their fighting forces to make ready. At the same time, by means of insults to Nasser and saber-rattling, they strove to offset the calming effect of delay. They prepared airborne forces to be ready on short notice to jump into desperate action against any threat to European lives and property. But their main hope was to coordinate the achievement of battle-readiness with the walkout of the non-Egyptian Canal pilots and technicians. They believed the resulting shortage of skilled manpower would bog down Canal traffic and provide a pretext for moving in to run it themselves. The original target date was 15 September 1956. By that time, having reached the unpleasant realization that Egypt might be able to manage the Canal without the company personnel, they became receptive to the idea of using an attack on Egypt by Israel as an ironclad pretext to intervene.

Israel watched these developments, having herself looked toward an attack on Egypt since December 1955. Immediately after nationalization, as Britain and France began their war planning against Nasser, Israel asked France for a massive increase in arms supplies for her own assault. Israel said her operation would be as violent as circumstances might permit. Her tentative target period was the last week of the US electoral campaign, early in November. The French agreed at a meeting in Paris on 7 August to arm Israel for the attack. Bourgès-Maunoury asked Peres at that time if Israel would join France in a war on Egypt. Peres said Yes but collusion lay fallow for yet another month.

Meanwhile Anglo-French war planning was turned over to General Sir Hugh Stockwell, then commanding the 1st Corps of the British Army of the Rhine. Summoned from Germany on 3 August, he set up a secret planning headquarters in a long-deserted bombproof section of the War Office, a multi-level labyrinth of green-painted cinderblock corridors and rooms tunneled out in World II deep under the ground between Whitehall and the Thames. Stockwell gave the place the code name Terrapin.

The French accepted British overall command for the joint expedition, Pineau said afterward, because although France had larger land forces the British had troopships, heavy bombers, and the nearest invasion bases. De Gaulle, who was kept informed by the Mollet government, warned at the time against giving the command to the British. Many a French participant in the operation dreams to this day of what glory might have been won if de Gaulle's advice had been heeded. General André Beaufre, Stockwell's deputy and French counterpart, felt as de Gaulle did and tried to correct the handicap (as he saw it) of British leadership by creating a separate French task force rather than integrate French units into the British force. He built two staffs, an integrated planning staff with the British in London and a separate operational staff for his fighting units in Algeria.

Stockwell's directive from the British and French Chiefs of Staff was: "To be prepared to mount joint operations against Egypt to restore the Suez Canal to International Control." The military chiefs had already agreed to station French forces on Cyprus, although the move was not to be made until the end of August. They gave Stockwell the battle order or roster of units to be used in the invasion, which they directed should be made at Port Said.

The inclusion of the tenth Armored Division in the battle order showed a weakness in liaison between the Foreign Office and the War Office. The division was stationed in Libya under a treaty expressly prohibiting any conflict of purpose with the Covenant of the Arab League. In the context of Arab politics, it was impossible for Libya to permit Britain to attack a fellow member of the Arab League from her territory. That the division was still in the battle order when Britain went to war on 31 October indicates the degree to which the Foreign Office was kept in the dark about the military plans. Had Foreign Office men seen the military plans, they would have scratched the 10th Armored from the invasion force.

Eden's concern for British prestige was reflected in the first of the eight principles the invasion staff established in formulating their plans. It was: "We could not afford to lose. At no stage could we accept risks that might set us back."

In Paris on that 3d of August Mollet and Pineau spoke in the spirit of their mood and Eden's. "The three [Britain, France, and the US] have let Nasser know the rules he will have to bow to," Mollet said. "All steps ought to be taken to make him submit," said Pineau. "The Government will go all the way ... " Dulles, landing in Washington after his overnight return from the Tripartite meeting in London, revealed Washington's quite different concept of the weeks ahead, saying: "We do not want to meet violence with violence." Dulles, like his allies, always spoke of nationalization as an act of violence, although the canal company was taken over legally and by civilians without so much as a scuffle.

The fatal divergence from the US was beginning. Eden's split with the Labor Party, although it was to remain hidden for another ten days, also opened on 3 August. Gaitskell, alarmed by the mobilization proclamation, wrote Eden a "word of friendly warning" that the Opposition would not support the use of military force. Eden thus abandoned two essentials for a successful war policy, bipartisan support at home and the endorsement of his senior ally abroad.

Egypt was sufficiently alarmed by Eden's "precautions" to raise the military commands in northern Egypt on 4 August from an administrative to an operational footing. These were the Cairo, Alexandria, Delta, and Suez Canal commands. Previously only the Eastern Command in the Sinai had been operational. On 6 August Nasser began pulling back half of his 60,000 troops in the Sinai to defend the approaches to Cairo from Alexandria and the Canal.

Sir Frederick Leith-Ross, former Governor of the National Bank of Egypt, hit truer than he realized in a letter in *The Times* on 4 August saying that its editorial on "quibbling" was all right for an editor but "can scarcely be the attitude of a responsible Government." He said that nationalization had made no change in the physical control of the Canal and that Eden's "unfettered control" statement "appears somewhat unwise." Egypt's frozen sterling was more than enough for compensation. The "wild talk about the use of force" ignored the fact that Egyptian and Arab cooperation was the real essential for the security of the Canal. "Remember that once a country becomes independent," Leith-Ross admonished, "we must not be surprised if it acts independently." But not even after it ended in disaster could Eden be persuaded of the unwisdom of his Suez policy.

There was a reckless, heart-stirring gaiety in the troop movements toward the Middle East that began on the 4th. Pink-cheeked young paratroopers embarking at Portsmouth on the aircraft carrier *Theseus* grinned at Navy Day crowds on the dockside and gave Churchill's two-fingered V-for-Victory sign. Chalked boldly on an olive-drab lorry were the words: "Look out, Nasser. Here we come." It was all very familiar, almost exactly the same scenes encountered in those finest hours of war against Hitler and Mussolini.

Eden recalled those finest hours in the most revealing letter he wrote to Eisenhower during the crisis. Dated 5 August, it was a reply to Eisenhower's letter of 31 July. At the Tripartite meeting, Eden wrote, Britain had "gone to the very limit of the concessions which we can make." He continued:

I do not think that we disagree about our primary objective. . . . to undo what Nasser has done and to set up an International Regime for the Canal. . . . But this is not all. Nasser has embarked on a course which is unpleasantly familiar. . . .

I have never thought Nasser a Hitler. . . . But the parallel with Mussolini is close. Neither of us can forget the lives and treasure he cost us before he was finally dealt with.

The removal of Nasser, and the installation in Egypt of a regime less hostile to the West, must therefore also rank high among our objectives. We must hope, as you say in your message, that the forthcoming conference will bring such pressures upon Nasser that the efficient operation of the Canal can be assured for the future. If so, everyone will be relieved and there will be no need of force. Moreover, if Nasser is compelled to disgorge his spoils, it is improbable that he will be able to maintain his internal position. We should thus have achieved our secondary objective. . . .

Our people here are neither excited nor eager to use force. They are, however, grimly determined that Nasser shall not get away with it this time, because they are convinced that if he does their existence will be at his mercy. So am I.

In Eisenhower's circle of advisers only Admiral Arleigh Burke, Chief of Naval Operations, agreed with the British on the need to break Nasser. From the viewpoint of the man in charge of the world's greatest navy it was doubtless strategically desirable to acquire a share in the control of the world's most important waterway and therefore desirable to remove the chief obstacle to that, namely, Nasser. Dulles disliked Nasser but had reservations about breaking him, particularly in collaboration with two colonialist empires.

Eisenhower thought Eden was unwise to place so much stress on breaking Nasser. He felt that Nasser embodied the emotional aspirations of the Arabs for independence and that these aspirations would endure whether or not the Nasser symbol was broken. Moreover, Eisenhower felt a certain sympathy for Nasser, whom he continued to regard long after Suez as a dynamic, personable reformer whose vision unfortunately ranged too far beyond Egypt. Eisenhower wrote Eden bluntly on 2 September: "There must be no grounds for our several peoples to believe that anyone is using the Canal difficulty as an excuse to proceed forcibly against Nasser."

But Eden had long since brought the issue into the open as a personal contest between himself and Nasser, so much so that by the end of August the "Suez Rebels" in Parliament were circulating the slogan: "Either Nasser or Eden must go."

Eden drew the battle lines between himself and Nasser in a television and radio broadcast on 8 August. It is a masterpiece of provocation, surely an unprecedented example of personal vituperation by one national leader against another in time of peace. It is the single most revealing statement, public or private, of Eden's Suez policy.

In the letters columns of *The Times* that morning, Sir Ralph Stevenson, Britain's former ambassador to Egypt, warned that "in politics it is never wise to leave the other side with no loophole of escape from an untenable position." This is precisely what Eden aimed to do that night to both himself and Nasser. He said:

Why don't we trust him? The answer is simple. Look at his record. Our quarrel is not with Egypt, still less with the Arab world; it is with Colonel Nasser.

Colonel Nasser conducted a vicious propaganda campaign against our country. He has shown that he is not a man who can be trusted to keep an agreement. And now he has torn up all his country's promises towards the Suez Canal Company. . . . The pattern is familiar to many of us, my friends. We all know this is how fascist governments behave and we all remember, only too well, what the cost can be in giving in to fascism.

Ignoring all evidence to the contrary, including the letter to *The Times* four days earlier by Leith-Ross, which Ambassador Stevenson's letter endorsed, Eden derided the financial commitments by which Egypt legitimized nationalization. Scoffing at Nasser's plans for the High Dam, he said the only bills Egypt was paying were for arms. "See how the bills mount up. . . . The grand total is preposterous." Eden went on to give spurious proof that Egypt could not possibly afford to keep the Canal in good condition. And he warned:

> If Colonel Nasser's actions were to succeed, each one of us would be at the mercy of one man for the supplies on which we live. We could never accept that. With dictators you always have to pay a higher price later on, for their appetite grows with feeding.
>
> Just now Colonel Nasser is soft-pedaling; his threats are being modified. But how can we be sure that the next time he has a quarrel with any country he will not interfere with that nation's shipping, and how can we be sure that next time he is short of money he will not raise the dues on all the ships that pass through the Canal? If he is given the chance of course he will.
>
> If anyone is going to snatch and grab and try to pocket what really belongs to the world, the result will be improverishment for all. . . . We cannot agree that an act of plunder which threatens the livelihood of many nations shall be allowed to succeed. We must make sure that the life of the great trading nations of the world cannot in the future be strangled.

"Strangled," "plunder," "appetite," "dictators," "fascism," "vicious propaganda"; these emotive words shrewdly associated with the name "Colonel Nasser" can hardly be spoken without a snarl. Eden's press spokesman, William Clark, who eventually broke with Eden over Suez, disclosed to correspondents at a private briefing at No. 10 Downing Street the next day that Whitehall's experts had calculated the effects of the speech in advance, including the possibility that Egypt would break relations and stiffen her resistance to international control. Clark said the speech was intended at least to isolate and weaken Nasser and at best to provoke an act or a chain of actions that would turn world opinion against him and justify an attack. Eden's government believed that a Suez settlement was virtually impossible so long as Nasser was in power, Clark said, and it was therefore exerting military, economic, and diplomatic pressures toward his overthrow.

As Dulles said in the National Security Council meeting on the morrow of Eden's speech: "If only the issue were the Canal itself, there would probably be no problem."

Eden spoke for thirteen and a half minutes at prime evening time. The speech was the first to be carried on both of Britain's TV networks. The BBC broadcast it in forty-four languages and repeated it four times the next day. It was carried on four major US networks. An immense effort went into reaching the largest possible audience worldwide.

Egypt's reaction, in keeping with her remarkably self-disciplined policy of avoiding exacerbation, was mild and slow. The Egyptian Embassy in London remarked two days later on the "new tendency to differentiate between President Gamal Abdel Nasser and the Egyptian people" and stated that "such an action could never be deemed but incompatible with international courtesy and responsible relations between Governments." The statement noted that the company had distributed more than £50 million ($140 million) in profits to shareholders over the past five years and maintained cash reserves of more than £40 million ($112 million), while spending only £17 million ($48 million) on maintenance and improvement. An embassy spokesman offered to submit to an audit to prove that Egypt could compensate the shareholders, improve the Canal, and finance the High Dam at the then level of profits.

Eden's speech hardened the conflict but made few converts to his side, even in Britain. The *Manchester Guardian* said on 10 August: "The parallel between Nasser and Hitler is misleading. By 1938 Hitler had broken international treaties not once but four times. Colonel Nasser has not yet broken any treaty." The editorial said with mingled alarm and disgust that Eden's telecast was an attempt to "create an emotional readiness for war."

The parallels between Nasser and Hitler, as popular in the West as they are demonstrably false, were derided by Arabs as inept propaganda. The Moslem Brotherhood itself, surviving in Syria after Nasser smashed it in Egypt, said that Hitler had fought both the British and French, the traditional enemies of Arab nationalism, and therefore stood high in Arab admiration. "If such is our esteem for Hitler, with whom we had no bonds," said the Brotherhood, "imagine how much greater our esteem is for a brother Arab who inflicts defeat after defeat on our enemies." The statement ignored Hitler's Jewish policy, which was as repugnant to most Arabs as it was to most Westerners.

A few hours before Eden's telecast, General Stockwell and his planners emerged from their "troglodyte existence" in Terrapin to present the first fruits of their labors to the Chiefs of Staff at a large secret meeting in the lofty, paneled main conference room at the War Office overlooking Whitehall. There some 200 high officers of all three services assembled under the chairmanship of Lord Mountbatten. Stockwell had completed his military appreciation and strategic plan two days before, on 6 August. The major change from the preliminary plan drafted by the British and French Chiefs of Staff immediately after nationalization was the designation of Alexandria instead of Port Said as the point of invasion.

"Port Said is like a cork in a bottle with a very long neck," Stockwell wrote afterward. "We would have to extract the cork and squeeze down the neck before enjoying the rich juices in the bottle." The beaches at Port Said are shallow and shelving, the port facilities were poor, and the city is built on an artificial island surrounded by a vast marshy lake. The only exit to the Egyptian mainland is a vulnerable causeway along the Canal. The whole Canal zone could easily be deprived of fresh water by shutting off the Sweetwater Canal. The only airfield capable of handling military supplies was at Abu Suwweir, fifty miles to the south.

Alexandria had better beaches to assault, excellent port facilities, a major airfield convenient for immediate capture, and fine roads to the south down which the invaders could hurl themselves upon the Egyptian Army and destroy it before turning east toward the Canal zone. The Chiefs of Staff accepted Stockwell's plan, including the new code name, Operation Musketeer, which he gave it. The Chiefs originally had named the operation Hamilcar, after the great Carthaginian general. *H*'s were painted on the first vehicles assigned to the force. Then it was realized that the French called him Amilcar and were painting *A*'s on their vehicles.

Stockwell and the service chiefs presented the plan on 10 August to Eden and the Cabinet at No. 10 Downing Street. "Sir Anthony Eden gave us every encouragement, asking questions to clarify a point," Stockwell recalled. "He seemed confident and gay and with his natural charm thanked us and quickly gave his approval in principle to our ideas. . . . He instilled me with confidence and I left much encouraged that our efforts so far had borne fruit. We were now clear to go ahead and produce our operation order, which was ready by August 24." Throughout August and September, Stockwell wrote, British and French air-borne forces and commandos were prepared and trained for quick intervention if some crisis should require it.

General Sir Charles Keightley, commander of British land forces in the Middle East since 1953, was told on 11 August, the day after Eden approved Musketeer, that he would be Commander-in-chief of the Anglo-French invasion force. The appointment was not announced until 31 October.

Britain began airlifting 5,000 troops to Cyprus on 12 August. Libya and Jordan, both of them allied to Britain by treaty, had forced two delays of the airlift by refusing to cooperate in the build-up of forces in the Middle East.

Eden's calculated rudeness achieved its first concrete success on 12 August when Nasser announced that Egypt would not attend the London Conference. Before Eden's broadcast Nasser had planned to make an impromptu visit to England to discuss the Canal dispute personally with Eden. He also intended to accept a seat for Egypt at the conference. In a radio speech of his own on the night of the 12th Nasser spoke in the flavorful colloquial Arabic that had proven so effective in July. He told how he had intended to accept the conference. "Then Britain's prime minister spoke. He followed a queer style. 'We don't trust Nasser,' he said. 'It is Nasser we quarrel with.' Very well, if these people have no trust, there is no reason to go to London for talks."

Flashes of humor and defiance flickered through Nasser's speech. He challenged anyone to show one single international agreement violated by Egypt and he corrected the false economics Eden had used, adding: "They may insult the intelligence of their own people but can they insult our intelligence?"

Nasser had earlier read Egypt's formal rejection of the London Conference at a press conference of 300 correspondents in the domed Chamber of Deputies. It was conducted entirely in English. The Egyptian Government, Nasser said, "noticed to its complete surprise that the British Government extended an invitation to consider matters concerning the Suez Canal, which is an integral part of Egypt, without any consultation with Egypt." He said only twenty-four states were invited although ships of at least forty-five states used the Canal in 1955. Since the conference is incompetent to make decisions and has no right to discuss matters within Egypt's sovereign jurisdiction, he said, "the invitation to it cannot, therefore, be accepted by Egypt." But in the interests of peace, he added, Egypt would join the other signatories of the 1888 Convention in sponsoring a conference of all nations whose ships use the Canal to consider replacing the Convention with a new treaty to be registered with the United Nations.

The statement pointed out the unfairly selective quotations in the Big Three communiqué of 2 August which announced the London Conference. For example, it said, the Big Three communiqué quoted from Article 8 of the 1954 Anglo-Egyptian evacuation agreement that the Canal "is a waterway . . . of international importance" but ignored the immediately preceding phrase that the Canal "is an integral part of Egypt."

Accusing the Big Three of deliberately confusing the distinctions between the 1888 Convention and the company concession in order to find pretexts for interference in Egypt, the statement said: "The 1888 Convention stands intact whether the Canal is administered by the company or by the Egyptian Government. . . . It is the 1888 Convention which governs the freedom of navigation in the Suez Canal, and it is the Egyptian Government which supervises this freedom in its capacity as the country in whose territory the Canal lies and of whose territory it constitutes an integral part."

Nasser's statement was published by the Egyptian Government that same day in a seventy-two-page White Paper. Entirely in English, the White Paper set out the basic documentation showing: that Egypt had never relinquished sovereignty over the Canal, that Egypt herself had prescribed guarantees of equal transit rights and fees for all nations thirty-four years before they were embodied in the 1888 Convention, and that the Suez Canal Company was an Egyptian joint stock company subject to Egyptian laws.

On the last point, the White Paper included a British Government legal brief of 1939 stating that the title of the Universal Suez Maritime Canal Company no more made it international than did the title of the International Sleeping Car and European Express Train Company of Belgium. The British brief asserted the canal company's "binding submission to the laws and customs of Egypt." As usual, Western politicians and diplomats, including lawyer Dulles, ignored the telling legal arguments of Egypt and retorted only to such evidence of political defiance as they were able to pluck from Nasser's statement.

After reading his statement, Nasser answered questions for forty-five minutes. The press conference was broadcast live by Cairo Radio. When Nasser entered, wearing a blue-gray business suit, Asian, African, and many European correspondents applauded while British and French journalists ostentatiously refrained. American journalists, in a workmanlike tradition of objectivity, almost never applaud anyone and made no exception for Nasser. The British dispatches were contradictory. The staff correspondent of *The Times* (London) wrote that "the calm confidence with which he [Nasser] spoke was more eloquent of what Egypt conceives to be the strength of her position than any words of violence could have been." The *Daily Mail* (London) correspondent, dreaming of cheapjack glory, wrote: "I may be kicked out of Egypt tomorrow for saying it, but—mark my words—today I saw a close-up of an enemy of Britain who is desperately worried . . . the face of a man who is on the way out . . . drawn and at times almost a sickly yellow. . . . I am certain this is the psychological moment for us to counterattack."

The next day, 13 August, the seeming united front against Nasser in the British Parliament broke apart. The Labor Party's Parliamentary Committee, after a three-hour emergency meeting, issued a statement demanding the recall of Parliament immediately after the London Conference and asking assurances that the Anglo-French military measures were "not preparations for an armed intervention." Gaitskell and the Labor Party leaders had previously sought to dissuade Eden from his warlike course by private letters and meetings, to no avail.

The political split reflected deepening divisions in the population and the press. The tabloid *Daily Mirror* denounced *The Times*, the *Daily Mail*, and the *Daily Express* on 14 August as "cardboard heroes" that had all advocated appeasement of Hitler in the 1930s but now demanded "savage and instant revenge" against a minor adversary.

14 August was the fourth anniversary of Eden's second marriage, to Clarissa Churchill, a niece of Sir Winston's. They celebrated by attending a topical diplomatic comedy, *Romanoff and Juliet,* and returned home to find 500 demonstrators in Downing Street shouting "We want peace" and "Go to the United Nations." "We ate our supper to a noise like a palace revolution," Eden wrote. "Strange wedding bells, but it seemed a fitting epilogue to our play."

On the other side, driving the willing Eden ever farther away from a national consensus, were the "Suez Rebels" in the House of Commons. One of their spokesmen was Julian Amery, whose father-in-law was Macmillan. The original rebel group, formed in 1954 to protest the evacuation agreement, numbered no more than forty. After the nationalization it grew to perhaps one hundred of the most conservative Tories. The rebels had no official standing and little organization. Their main effect was to create the atmosphere of jingo Empire patriotism so well suited to Eden's Suez policy.

If Eden had chosen a policy of moderate realism instead of romantic belligerence the Suez Rebels would have been as ineffectual as they were in 1954, when Eden did in fact choose moderate realism. They could bluster but they knew that if they precipitated a general election by voting against the government they would lose the party's endorsement at the likely cost of their parliamentary seats and political careers. They could and did puff up the spirit of violence but they would have been weak against a spirit of peace.

Diplomats began to arrive in London on the 14th for the conference. Of the twenty-four countries invited, only Greece joined Egypt in refusing. Greece was estranged from Britain, her ally in NATO, over the nationalist rebellion on the island colony of Cyprus, which demanded union with Greece.

Shepilov, leading a fifty-man delegation from Moscow, was among the first to arrive. The Russians had embraced Egypt's cause as much as Nasser would let them ever since the arms deal. Radio Moscow continued hopefully to reiterate the Kremlin's readiness to consider any Egyptian request for aid to the High Dam project. Ambassador Kiselev conferred with Nasser at least every other day after nationalization as Nasser sought help against the militant array of Western powers ranged against him. Moscow called the nationalization "a correction of a historic error."

Moscow's acceptance statement on 9 August declared that the conference was convened in disregard of a number of relevant provisions of the 1888 Convention, that the list of nations invited was biased, and that acceptance "in no way commits" Russia to anything that might "harm Egypt's sovereign rights and dignity." The statement said the measures taken by Britain and France were "completely inadmissible" and could only hurt the interests of the Western powers themselves.

India voiced many of the same reservations. Nehru, announcing India's acceptance on 8 August, said: "In Asia as a whole, with its colonial memories, great resentment has been aroused [by the Anglo-French military movements] ... Force is the wrong way. It does not belong to this age and it is not dictated by reason." On the eve of the conference he warned again that "any effort, ... even by mistake, ... to settle the Suez issue by force or by threats ... will be disastrous ..."

Dulles arrived in London on 15 August. He cabled Eisenhower that day that the Allies were "quite sobered" by the "inadequacies of their military establishments to take on a real fighting job of this size." The British were so short of landing craft that they requisitioned garishly painted DUKWs from seaside resorts where, after surviving wartime amphibious assaults on Europe and North Africa, they had retired to civilian service as excursion boats.

Britain had confirmed two days earlier that she was withdrawing troops from her NATO force in Germany, as the French had done long since for their war in Algeria. While making ready to fight, the British kept up psychological and propaganda warfare. The first British women and children to be evacuated from Egypt in accordance with the Foreign Office warnings arrived by air on 9 August, grumbling bitterly. Mrs. Gladys Cotton, wife of one of the British technicians stationed in the Suez Canal base under the 1954 agreement, said: "I was very happy to stay on and I do not think there was any need for us to evacuate our homes."

Offsetting such homely common sense became a constant concern for Eden. He fought with the BBC to obtain broadcast time for Prime Minister Menzies of Australia. The BBC protested that the series of speeches in August by Eden himself, Menzies, and Selwyn Lloyd needed to be balanced by other views. The BBC later fought off Eden's attempt to transform it from an editorially independent public corporation into a government propaganda arm subject to wartime controls. But Eden won the battle over Menzies by saying the BBC's attitude was "insulting" to a Commonwealth Prime Minister.

Menzies, Eden's friend since 1935, went on the air August 13th to call nationalization an act of lawlessness that threatened Britain's standard of living. Sneering at the "disposition in some private quarters to find legal virtues in what Nasser has done," Menzies said roundly, "If such nonsense is the law, why have any international agreements at all?" Upon his arrival in London on 10 August Menzies had told reporters that Nasser was wrong from beginning to end and must be resisted. In his broadcast he said: "To leave our vital interests to the whim of one man would be suicidal. ... We cannot accept either the legality or the morality of what Nasser has done."

On 16 August, the day the conference opened, the Arab world conducted a general strike to demonstrate its solidarity with Egypt. The Arab League's Political Committee had declared its unanimous support for Egypt on 6 August, with even Iraq unwilling to stand aloof. The Syrians had already begun talk of cutting the great oil pipelines if Egypt were attacked, a promise they made good in November. On 16 August, as an earnest of their determination, they stopped the flow of oil for twenty-four hours. From midnight to midnight, planes were grounded at Arab airports, public transport was stopped, stores were closed, streets were empty. At 10 A.M. Greenwich Summer Time, the hour the London Conference opened, Arabs observed five minutes of silence for the "assassination of liberty."

It was a day of death on the Arab-Israeli borders. A rash of incidents broke the calm on the Egyptian and Jordanian truce lines and left 9 Egyptians dead and 4 Israelis.

In London, as the appointed hour approached, several hundred persons in raincoats and under umbrellas gathered outside Lancaster House to watch the statesmen arrive. A cold drizzle was falling, as it did on so many days that summer. Shepilov and the Russians arrived first, twenty minutes early.

The delegates sat at a huge semicircular table in the onetime concert room overlooking Green Park. Some took their places slightly winded from the ascent of the sweeping staircase with its marble balustrades, which continued along the galleries leading to the rooms of state. The places at the conference table were equipped with microphones and headsets for translations. Built for the Duke of York in 1830, Lancaster House was the most sumptuous private residence in London when it was given to the nation in 1912. On his visit to London in April Bulganin said of it, more prophetically than he knew:

"Lancaster House. This palace has seen a great deal. More than once the Ministers of the great powers have gathered in it, have reached agreement on some thing and, it has happened also, have gone their ways without anything being achieved."

Nasser's personal emissary, Aly Sabry, arrived in London on the 16th to observe from the sidelines and to meet with any delegates who wished to see him. All the delegates called on him at least once except those of Northern Europe, the United States, Australia, and New Zealand. The Western press like-wise ignored his presence although for a few he provided background information, comments, and news that balanced the anti-Nasser flavor of most conference sources. He conferred almost daily with Krishna Menon and Shepilov.

In the conference the Russians, on behalf of Egypt, took a position upon which the British themselves had stood fast in the 1880s, when they were the *de facto* sovereign power on the Canal. As Cromer reported of a somewhat similar conference in 1885:

> The British Government would have preferred "that all the Maritime Powers who applied should be permitted to send delegates," but to this proposal the French objected.... It will be sufficient to say that the object of the majority of the Powers was to internationalise rather than to neutralise the Canal, and that the British Government were opposed to the adoption of this course.

In 1956 it was Egypt which urged a conference of all the interested maritime powers. And it was Egypt which upheld the neutralization of the Canal but refused internationalization. The British, having relinquished their control of Egypt and the Canal, now objected to a wider conference and insisted on internationalization rather than the mere neutralization provided for in the 1888 Convention. Britain had also reversed herself on the nationality of the Suez Canal Company, as Egypt reminded her in the White Paper.

On 16 September, a month after the London Conference opening, Eden wrote Bulganin a defense of his Suez policy, closing tartly with: "I must remind you that in 1946 the Soviet Government proclaimed their support for the international control of the canal. That is what we seek..." He ignored the fact that in 1946, when Russia mentioned the issue in connection with a dispute over the Turkish Straits, Britain had vigorously opposed international control over the Canal. Such is the logic of proprietorship.

Selwyn Lloyd had called Nasser in a broadcast two days earlier an Axis-type dictator misusing Arab nationalism to further his own ambitions. His open bias did not prevent his being accepted as conference chairman. Dulles cabled Eisenhower on the eve of the conference that Lloyd "seems desperately to want it and... no one wants to seem discourteous in opposing it."

Lloyd proposed that the conference adopt the rules of the UN committees. But Krishna Menon of India, with Russia's and Indonesia's support, quickly rejected any such scheme for majority rule. UN membership was based on the principle of universality, he said, leaving the inference that the London Conference membership was not. Shepilov, after repeating with variations and elaborations the earlier Russian criticisms of the conference, said bluntly that it was "not sufficiently representative... to be able to provide a solution of substance..." The opposition to majority rule by the three, who represented a quarter of the world's population, was decisive. Lloyd's proposal was dropped. The conference became merely a forum for an exchange of views.

One of the curious developments at the conference was a brief friendship between Dulles and Shepilov. They met on the evening of the 15th and spent an hour and a quarter together. To their surprise, they liked each other. After a second and somewhat longer meeting on the 18th Dulles reported to Eisenhower:

I feel that the Soviets would be open to making some kind of an arrangement with us and perhaps join to impose it upon Egypt if, on the one hand, it were couched in a way which would not gravely prejudice the Soviet Union with the Arab world and if, on the other hand, we would more or less make it a two-party affair with some downgrading of the British and the French. I doubt whether Soviet agreement is worth having at that price but I shall do everything possible short of disloyalty to the British and the French to get Soviet agreement.

After the conference both men vented disillusionment. Shepilov said he had been mistaken in thinking Dulles truly sought a peaceful solution. Dulles accused Russia of transmitting "vicious" propaganda broadcasts in Arabic on the very morning he was explaining the US proposal on Suez to Shepilov.

The US, or Dulles, proposal was to turn the Canal over to an international board, on which Egypt would be among the members. The board would operate, maintain, and improve the Canal and fix tolls to cover costs and provide "a return to Egypt for the use of the Suez Canal . . ." A counterproposal by India recommended that, "without prejudice to Egyptian ownership and operation, . . . a consultative body of user interests be formed . . . with advisory, consultative and liaison functions."

After studying Dulles's draft proposal, Eisenhower cabled Dulles on 19 August: "Nasser may find it impossible to swallow the whole of this as now specified. . . . I see no objection to a board with supervisory rather than operating authority . . . with operating responsibility residing in someone appointed by Nasser, subject to board approval." In effect, Eisenhower preferred the Indian approach.

Dulles, in considerable agitation, replied early on the 20th that it might be impossible to get Britain and France to agree to Eisenhower's suggested modifications and that, furthermore, "I doubt whether we should make at this stage concessions which we might be willing to make as a matter of last resort in order to obtain Egypt's concurrence." Eisenhower promptly cabled back: "I understand the box you are in." He said he had suggested limiting the board to supervisory authority to avoid collapse over details. He added: "I will approve your decision and support you in whatever action you finally decide you must take."

Dulles went ahead with his proposal. With a great amount of pressure and a small amount of amendment he obtained the sponsorship of Ethiopia and three members of the Baghdad Pact. The Baghdad Pact members were Turkey, Iran, and Pakistan. They "betrayed us," said Egypt's government newspaper, *al-Gamhouriya*. The envoys of the three countries told me before they gave in to Dulles that they were in a painful dilemma; it seemed politically impossible for them to support the West's demand for internationalization of the Canal, they said, but their links with the West made it ill-advised for them to support India's counterplan. The envoys of small powers in London said internationalization was a far more dangerous principle to them than nationalization was to the Great Powers.

The conference ended on 23 August with eighteen nations lined up in the Big Three camp behind the US proposal and four supporting the Indian proposal, a division that was predictable when the invitation list was drawn up. The minority group, which exceeded the majority in combined population, included India, Russia, Indonesia, and Ceylon. It remained for each group to transmit its own proposal to Egypt. The only official act of the conference as a whole was to forward the verbatim record of its proceedings, some 800 foolscap pages, to the Egyptian Government. The end came on a desultory note. "I do not see what more we have to do, really," said Dulles. To which Chairman Lloyd replied: "I really think that we have gradually by a process of elimination got to that stage." He thanked the staff, made a little joke to the delegates about wishing he had the power of English judges to release them from further "jury service" for seven years, and thanked them for coming.

It was no better a finale than the conference deserved. More consequential events, some public and some secret, were going on elsewhere. Adlai Stevenson was renominated by the Democats on 17 August and President Eisenhower by the Republicans on the 23d. On the 20th some 200 military and political chieftains of the Algerian rebellion gathered in Algeria's Soummam Valley to plan for the bloody years ahead. On the 24th, the day Dulles departed London for home, General Stockwell completed his plan for Operation Musketeer, General André Beaufre was shifted from his Algerian command to become Stockwell's deputy, and Stockwell began a tour of units in Algeria, Cyprus, and Malta assigned to the invasion force. Anti-Russian pressure continued to build up in Poland and Hungary.

Eden had not changed his intentions. He prodded his fighting men to complete their preparations, complaining that they were overestimating the Egyptians, whom many of them had helped train, and that they were planning the invasion in terms of World War II. "Action against Egyptians is not militarily comparable with action against Germans, as I was constantly urging," he wrote in his memoirs. He refused to believe that he could not somehow bring Eisenhower around to his way of thinking, but he planned to go it alone if he had to. "We expected that the US would at least be neutral," he wrote afterward. "But if assistance were not forthcoming from our friends, we had to be in a position to take action."

When the London Conference ended he cabled Eisenhower:

The Bear is using Nasser, with or without his knowledge . . . first to dislodge the West from the Middle East, and second to get a foothold in Africa so as to dominate that continent in turn. . . . We have many friends in the Middle East and in Africa . . . but they will not be strong enough to stand against the power of the mobs if Nasser wins again. The firmer the front we show together, the greater the chance that Nasser will give way without the need for any resort to force.

Eden constantly tried to spook the US by conjuring up the Red menace. It had worked for others but it did not for Eden. Eisenhower preferred Gaitskell's approach and said as much to US Congressional leaders on 12 August. At the National Security Council meeting on 9 August Dulles reported that the British and French wanted: US moral support for any action they might take; economic support in the form of oil and dollar credits for oil imports; and an indication that the US would join its allies if Russia tried to intervene. Eisenhower told the meeting that "if Nasser were to prove (1) that Egypt could operate the Canal and (2) would indicate an intention to abide by the Treaty of 1888, then it would be nearly impossible for the United States ever to find real justification, legally or morally, for the use of force."

The US did, however, prepare for a massive oil-lift from the Western hemisphere in case Middle Eastern oil was blocked. Representatives of thirteen major oil companies were summoned to meet in New York on 8 August with US officials. Within two days they formed the Middle East Emergency Committee to pool oil production and shipping resources to meet Europe's needs in any emergency. The Justice Department cleared the committee of antitrust liability. Its formation was announced on the 14th.

While diverging at the summit from Britain on Egyptian policy the US was collaborating with Britain and Iraq at lower levels to overthrow the pro-Egyptian regime in Syria. The plan was to arm dissident Syrian groups for a revolt that would have the Iraqi Army standing by to intervene if needed. Details of the conspiracy came out in treason trials in Syria after the Suez war and in Iraq after the 1958 revolution. They have been assembled for English readers by Patrick Seale in his book, *The Struggle for Syria*. The British took a hand with the Iraqis shortly after the Glubb affair in March.

By July Americans had joined Iraqi and British agents in a joint committee

407

set up in Beirut to exchange intelligence, consider the international aspects of the plot, and work with the Syrian dissidents. Iraqi spokesmen in Beirut in August saw a pretext for invading Syria in the Syrian threats to blow up the oil pipelines if Egypt were attacked. Iraq's dependence on oil sales would justify such action, they said. The Iraqi Government continued into mid-October to emphasize that it could not let its oil remain at the mercy of nations that controlled the transit routes. The US supplied weapons to the Syrian conspirators but the plotters bungled. Syrian intelligence broke the ring in October and seized several hundred rifles which had been smuggled across the Iraqi border into the mountain fastness of the Druzes in southern Syria.

If the abortive Syrian adventure seemed like the work of juvenile romantics, a clandestine propaganda campaign against Nasser was yet sillier and more ineffectual. It began at 11 A.M. GMT on 27 July when an unidentified station transmitted an hour of music on the same frequency as Cairo's "Voice of the Arabs." It was apparently a test transmission. The next day at about the same hour the clandestine station broadcast an attack on Nasser's domestic record and assured Egyptians that they would soon be liberated by "the free sons of Egypt." The announcer asked his hearers to listen carefully to three messages:

"First message: Ali asks Salaheddeen to wake up the seven sleepers in the magic cave.

"Second message: There are forty camels in a caravan proceeding quietly towards the oasis.

"Third message: The moon shines on the Nile water."

The messages evidently were designed to give the impression that they had a cryptic significance for members of a presumed anti-Nasser Egyptian underground. That same day Britain began jamming Cairo's Greek-language broadcasts.

On its third day, 29 July, the clandestine radio called Iraq the "foundation stone of Arabism" and exhorted Egyptians to overthrow Nasser. It promised "a report about his removal." On subsequent days it made scurrilous allegations about Nasser's morals and parentage, saying his mother was a Greek prostitute. It accused him of selling out to the Zionists. It took to calling him Gamalov Abdel Fashil. In this clumsy blasphemous wordplay Nasser's Russian connections were mocked in the first name while the last name took a pattern typical of Moslem names in which Abdel, meaning "Slave of," is followed by one of the attribute-names of God such as Nasser ("the Victory-giver"), Rahman ("the Merciful"), Aziz ("the All-powerful"), etc. Fashil means "the Futile." Sometimes the clandestine station called him Chaim Gamalov, a Hebrew-Arabic-Russian anomaly. It urged Egyptians to hoard food and to help themselves from

Army stores. On 6 September a distinctly anti-American tone came into the broadcasts. The announcer said Americans were racists who could hardly be expected to have sincere friendship for colored peoples. He accused Nasser of conniving with the US against Britain and France. Ahmed Said, long-time director of Cairo's "Voice of the Arabs," told me that the clandestine transmitter, which called itself The Voice of Free Egypt, was located in southern France and was sponsored by the Abul Fath brothers, an old-regime newspaper dynasty broken up by the revolution. It was not the only secret anti-Nasser radio. A second clandestine transmitter, The Voice of Justice, added for a time to the diatribes against Nasser. The CIA admitted some years later that it had operated "black" radios against Nasser. Nasser told me afterward there were secret radios attacking him from Cyprus, Turkey, Aden, and Iraq in addition to the Abul Fath's in Marseilles.

In their open propaganda the French and British radios never descended to the scurrility of the clandestine stations but their program material was enough to induce a number of Arab employees to quit. The French expelled three Egyptians and a Lebanese on 8 August for refusing to broadcast anti-Nasser material and there were mass resignations later from the British station in Cyprus.

The British used clandestine printing presses too in their propaganda against Nasser. Early in August newspaper offices in London received a series of extracts taken out of context from Nasser's small book, *The Philosophy of the Revolution*, making it sound like a would-be world conqueror's daydream. Although the extracts were circulated anonymously, the oversized type used for the mimeograph stencil was the same that had been used on some Foreign Office material distributed previously. *Le Monde* had published similar extracts in Paris on 1 August, saying they "showed the broad lines" of Nasser's book, which Mollet the day before had called the Egyptian *Mein Kampf*. Two weeks later the *Daily Telegraph* (London) published extracts remarkably like those circulated anonymously in the oversized type used by the Foreign Office. The *Daily Telegraph*'s analysis, interspersed among the quoted extracts, said Nasser's failure to understand Britain's imperatives over the Suez Canal, like his failure to understand the imperatives of World War II for the British in Egypt, "can become calamitous." It ended by calling Nasser "the man with L-plates [learner license plates] on his juggernaut." The *Daily Telegraph* article was doubtless meant to expose Nasser for the edification of the London Conference. The *Sunday Times* printed lengthy extracts on 16 September, introducing them as Nasser's *Mein Kampf* and quoting Gaitskell's hasty remark immediately after nationalization: "It is exactly the same as we encountered from Hitler and Mussolini."

Englishmen who had read the serialization of *The Philosophy of the Revolution* in *The Observer* (London) two years before would have seen it clearly as the confessions of a young reformer, shocked by the cynical profiteering, place-seeking, and mutual intolerance among Egyptian politicians, explaining to his countrymen why the junta decided to retain power rather than return to barracks after removing the corrupt monarchy. It is a partly autobiographical cry from the heart of an idealist who sees a vast need for things to be done—in Egypt, the Arab world, Africa, Asia—and nobody willing to do them—"that wandering role in search of a hero to play it."

The late Dorothy Thompson, in her introduction to the American edition of the book, published early in 1955, said it showed Nasser as "pure, faithful, and brave." It was, she wrote, "remarkable for the absence of personal egotism and power-lust . . . for the painful, humble, self-searching and self-analysis of the author." This was a far cry from Eden's statement in his memoirs that it revealed Nasser's "prowl to conquest." Miss Thompson, incidentally, fought Hitler as a crusading journalist long before Eden or Mollet opposed him.

Nasser told me he once read *Mein Kampf* to see how true were the statements that his book resembled it. There is no resemblance at all. Nasser's book was actually compiled out of a series of interviews by Mohammed Hassanein Heikal, Egypt's leading journalist and a confidant of Nasser's since the revolution. It was first published in three installments in *Akher Saa*, the weekly magazine Heikal then edited. The first installment appeared 12 August 1953. It was broadcast in full by Radio Cairo that day. The monitored text was available in translation in the Great Power capitals the following day.

The *Jewish Observer* (London) delightedly pirated the article on 28 August 1953, pointing out an amiable citation by Nasser of an earlier *Jewish Observer* article by an Israeli officer describing his truce meetings with Nasser. *Akher Saa* published the second installment on 16 September 1953 and the third on 8 January 1954. The gaps were due to the pressure of Nasser's other business.

"Heikal used to come to me, as you have come now," Nasser told me, "and I used to speak—just giving these thoughts, thinking aloud—and then he brought me the articles to approve." The Egyptian Government published them as a booklet in English, French, and Arabic early in 1954, distributing it by the thousands in Egypt and abroad. It is less than fifteen thousand words long—seventy pocket-size pages—simple and easy to read.

Not for two years did anyone think to liken it to *Mein Kampf* although the Algerian war, the Baghdad Pact, the Gaza Raid, and the Russian arms deal all signaled Nasser's disputes with France, Britain, Israel, and America. Mollet was the first to claim to read danger in *The Philosophy of the Revolution*, quoting it out of context to visitors after he became Premier. After ten years of such distortions Nasser told me with a rueful chuckle: "I don't want to write another book. The first one caused me too much trouble." I asked him if he had actually read Luigi Pirandello's *Six Characters in Search of an Author*, which he mentioned in his book as the source of his concept of a role in search of a hero. Only the title, he admitted with a grin.

The part most often quoted by Nasser's enemies is his enumeration of the sources of strength that would make the Arabs a power to reckon with if only they would unite. These were: (1) the peoples of the Arab community, (2) the strategic location of their countries at the commercial and military cross-roads of the world, and (3) oil, without which the world's machines of peace and war "would become mere pieces of iron, rusty, motionless, lifeless." The last phrase is often taken as if it were the threat of a fanatic exhorting a warlike race of fanatics to a program of conquest and glory. But Nasser was speaking to a backward and defeated people, urging them to come out from centuries of subjugation and be "firm believers that they has a place in the sun which they should occupy for life." Rarely have a man or a book been so persistently and widely misunderstood by the Western world.

Toward the end of August a clever forgery of an Egyptian Information Department leaflet began to circulate. Imitating an authentic leaflet providing a compendium of facts about Egypt, the forgery described under the heading "OIL" a fictitious Egyptian-controlled pan-Arab marketing organization, saying: "While Egypt's enemies will thus be deprived of oil, Arab countries enjoying the goodwill of Egypt will have their supplies assured." The forgery was mailed to oil-company offices and the embassies of oil-producing Arab countries in the Middle East in August and to British Members of Parliament on 10 September, two days before they debated Suez in emergency session. It was clearly designed to convince Western readers that Nasser must be stopped and to raise doubts about Egypt's intentions among the Arab oil producers.

On 15 August Eden's candid press secretary, William Clark, said one of Eden's preoccupations was to maintain an acute national sense of crisis until Egypt's "thumb is off our jugular vein." The television speeches by Eden, Menzies, and Lloyd, he said, were largely intended to "keep the people worried." Eden was anxious lest the London Conference have a calming effect. The successive announcements of mobilization measures helped to keep the crisis feeling alive during that vacation month. So did Operation Nursery, a week-long evacuation of 872 British wives and children of the technicians maintaining equipment in the Suez Canal base which began on 22 August.

The London Conference was over the next day but, to the chagrin of Britain and France, an epilogue had been attached to it by the decision to send

411

a mission to Cairo to try to induce Nasser to negotiate on the basis of the US proposal for an international board to run the Canal. Eden wanted Dulles to lead the negotiating mission, if there had to be one, but Dulles refused. As he wrote Eisenhower on 20 August, he was too busy, and furthermore, he said, "I think it is preferable that we should become less conspicuous . . ."

Menzies, who plunged into the Suez Crisis and splashed about in it like a small boy in a swimming hole, got the job instead. His public statements against Nasser should have disqualified him. He was, in any case, the worst imaginable choice to head a successful mission but an excellent choice for a mission intended to fail. He told Nasser at the first meeting of his group with the Egyptian President that he was a born imperialist and would never try to deny it. Jowly and rugged, with white hair and thick black brows, Menzies, then sixty-one, was capable of a florid, rough-and-ready charm but he did not conceal his prejudices against the likes of Nasser. The Australians, who used to shoot their aborigines like varmints, now express their racism in immigration laws. Menzies was not ashamed of his prejudices. On the contrary, he once said of himself with jocular pride: "I am a reasonably bigoted descendant of the Scottish race."

He saw nothing amiss in asking Nasser to accept two premises for negotiations: (1) the incompetence of Egyptians and (2) the untrustworthiness of Nasser himself, these being the two tacit bases of the US—or as Dulles preferred to call it—the eighteen-power plan. He was so far from understanding the raw sensitivities of African and Asian nationalists that he thought it a reasonable inducement to assure Nasser that the proposed international board would do all the work on the Canal while Egypt would get all the profits. Menzies prepared for the mission by going to the BBC studios on 28 August to view a television interview with Nasser. He might have done better to give a careful and sympathetic reading to Nasser's nationalization speech.

But the mission was never intended to succeed. Eden and the French wanted Menzies to present the eighteen-power proposal on a peremptory take-or-leave-it basis to ensure that Nasser would reject it. For the Americans, it was another delaying device. "It was my own opinion that the Menzies committee never had a chance of success," wrote Murphy. "The proposed new treaty did not seem to me a practical device because there was no adequate reason why it should be accepted by the Egyptians." Menzies himself told Lord Kilmuir on the morning of the 23d: "The chances of failure are ninety-nine to one . . ."

Nasser reiterated his refusal to accept international control of the Canal in an interview published by the *News Chronicle* (London) on 24 August. That same day Shepilov denounced the Menzies mission as a violation of the rules of procedure adopted by the conference. He said it was "outside the framework of the conference" and that the proposed international board would be a "state within a state." The conference itself, he said, had been a "tendentious selection . . . and the majority of these are participants in aggressive military groupings—the North Atlantic Bloc, the Baghdad Pact, and SEATO." On the 25th Heikal, in *al-Akhbar*, Cairo's largest daily newspaper, mockingly proposed the internationalization of Australian sheep: "Those who use woolen clothes made of the wool of Australian sheep have the right to consider the future of this wool according to the principle of the London Conference, which says that the users, not the owners, have the primary rights. . . ." Nevertheless, Nasser agreed on the 27th to receive Menzies. The meeting was fixed for Monday, 3 September, in Cairo.

Eden and the French hastily enlarged the certainty of failure. On 28 August French forces began moving to Cyprus in accordance with the secret agreement made at the beginning of the month. "The question was," Eden wrote, "how long we could pursue diplomatic methods and economic sanctions, which very likely would not succeed, before the possibility of military action slipping from our grasp." The French move was announced the following day. "In a few weeks we should be poised to strike, if we had to strike," Eden added. "It would be very costly to keep up this position indefinitely."

On that same day the British Cabinet, in their methodical elimination of the barriers to using force, decided to exhaust the riskiest peaceful effort of all, that of recourse to the UN. The danger was that the UN might bring a settlement so close that Britain and France would be obliged to veto it. Nevertheless, the Cabinet decided that immediately after Menzies' failure, which was taken for granted, Britain would submit a resolution to the Security Council finding that a "threat to peace exists." This move, remaining undisclosed until after Menzies failed, could not contribute to his failure.

For this, in addition to choosing Menzies and posting French troops to Cyprus, the British and French issued new "amber light" warnings to their nationals on 30 August and 1 September to leave not only Egypt but also Syria and Lebanon. Eisenhower was angered by such overt jeopardizing of the Menzies mission. "By now," he recalled blandly in his memoirs, "I was wondering at times whether the British and French governments were really concerned over the success or failure of the Menzies mission."

Eisenhower himself seems to have taken the Menzies mission at face value. On 31 August he received Robert Anderson's report on a second secret mission to Nasser, this one to sound out the limits to which Nasser could or would go toward a compromise Suez settlement. Anderson reported that Egypt would agree to a new convention on freedom of navigation and might

413

give an international commission the prerogative of consulting on tolls and technical matters. Eisenhower regarded this as a ray of hope for Menzies. He said later: "It did seem to show evidence of flexibility, or at least willingness to discuss the matter in a sane and sensible manner."

In the interim between the conference and the Menzies mission the Egyptian police arrested three British subjects resident in Cairo on charges of military espionage. Two first secretaries at the British Embassy, J. G. Gove and J. B. Flux, were accused of directing the ring and were declared *personae non gratae*. The men subsequently tried and convicted as spies were James Swinburn, business manager of the British-owned Arab News Agency; Charles Pittuck, of the Marconi wireless company, who relayed intelligence reports to London in code on a special wave length; and a Maltese named James Zarb. Swinburn had come to Egypt as a schoolteacher twenty-five years before. His subsequent association with the Arab News Agency did not damage the agency nor hurt the high standing of Tom Little, its news chief. Nasser told a press conference on 2 September that Egyptian authorities had known of the spy ring for six months but that "only recently we learned it had become genuinely harmful to Egyptian security."

The British sniffed at the accusations and in reprisal expelled two Egyptian attachés, both young men studying for doctoral degrees at London universities. But Britain never seriously challenged the accusations nor sought to build a pretext on them. The Egyptians dealt firmly but leniently with the British spies and released them in subsequent years before their prison terms were completed.

The day Menzies arrived in Cairo, 2 September, was the day two emissaries from Mollet arrived in Rome for more secret talks with Algerian rebel leaders. The Rome meeting was the penultimate round in the negotiations that resulted from the good offices Nasser promised Pineau in March. Two high-ranking member of Mollet's Socialist party hierarchy, Pierre Herbaut and Senator Pierre Commin, spoke for France while Mohammed Khider, Abderrahmane Kiouane, and M'hammed Yazid represented the FLN. The FLN offered a cease-fire in return for recognition as a provisional government. The talks came to naught after a last meeting in Belgrade on 22 September.

Pineau, on 2 September, gave Menzies' mission another hopeful nudge toward failure by telling an audience that Nasser had played him false on Algeria. Although the secret talks in Rome were evidence of Nasser's good faith, Pineau ignored them and said: "It is no longer possible for us to go on trusting Colonel Nasser." *The Philosophy of the Revolution* shows Nasser's ambition to conquer the Arab world, Pineau continued, garnishing his distortion with the usual references to Hitler, *Mein Kampf,* and the Nazi reoccupation of the Rhineland. He said we cannot submit to the Egyptian dictator's *coup de force* even at the risk of war. He added that he doubted the solidarity of the Arabs, some of whom, he said, already thought Nasser had gone too far. All the Arab ambassadors in Paris protested the last remark.

Nasser ignored the whole speech. He told his press conference in Cairo that day that Egypt was willing to strengthen, expand, or renew the 1888 Convention. He said that the possibility of a British or French veto made him prefer to depend on world opinion rather than go to the Security Council for protection against British and French threats.

Britain's economic sanctions, he said, were an inconvenience rather than an injury because "85 per cent of our people live near the starvation level anyway" and did not miss British cars and cosmetics. Eden came to the same conclusion, namely that "Egypt was not seriously hit by the economic measures" and that any hardships they caused "were falling upon the opponents of the dictatorship." The previous British boycott, begun in 1951 over the Suez Canal base, had luckily forced Egypt to open trade channels to the East Bloc and these would be enlarged in the event of a renewed Western boycott. As for the talk of diverting shipping away from the Canal, Egypt had received so small a proportion of the Canal earnings before nationalization that being deprived of tolls, either by payment into blocked or company accounts or by boycotting of the Canal, had an insignificant effect on her economy.

Menzies' mission included the foreign ministers of Ethiopia, Iran, and Sweden and Loy Henderson of the US State Department, a tough old Middle East hand whose official designation was "Alternate" to Dulles. Dulles insisted that Henderson travel separately. Only the Swede, in fact, accepted whatever colonialist stigma was attached to riding to Cairo in the same plane as Menzies. Each group was cordially welcomed as it arrived. The mission came to grips with Nasser on schedule on Monday, 3 September. Menzies presented international control of the Canal in the homely analogy of tenant and landlord.

"I exhausted my energy and almost wore out my patience in explaining to him that . . . what we were seeking was *an agreement,*" Menzies reported to Eden afterward, "the kind of an arrangement which was an exercise of sovereignty and not a derogation from it, and could be described as 'domination' or 'seizure' only if he made his agreement under actual duress." Menzies evidently did not consider it duress to have told Nasser, as he did in a private evening talk on 5 September, that the British and French military preparations were deadly serious. As Menzies described the meeting:

"I explained to him the strength of opinion in both London and Paris, and added, in substance, 'I am not making any threats. . . . But frankness as between two Heads of Government requires me to offer my personal opinion that you are facing not a bluff but a stark condition of fact which your country should not ignore.' Nasser . . assured me that he did *not* treat the British action as a bluff."

As Nasser recalled the incident to me: "When Menzies began to threaten I closed the papers in front of me. I told him: 'We have nothing to discuss with you.' Then Loy Henderson intervened and others intervened to smooth it over."

Menzies' official report said: "It became clear by the end of the meeting . . . that the President was unwilling to accept the basic principles of the proposals" for international control. Menzies disclosed in private to Eden his exasperation with the "logical mess which exists in his [Nasser's] mind," adding that "with frightful reiteration he [Nasser] kept coming back to the slogans; our proposal was 'collective colonialism' . . ." Menzies concluded that the mission was at an impasse and spent the next two days drafting a letter reiterating the main explanations and illustrations he had used in presenting the proposals and in answering Nasser's objections.

Menzies' letter, dated 7 September, harped on, among other things, the danger that "the Canal dues, being within Egypt's sole control, . . . would be raised to the maximum that the traffic could bear; and that future development of the Canal might well be controlled by local budget considerations; a danger which independent financing by a special international body would entirely avert." Menzies seemed oblivious to the fact that the profit motive would operate on Egypt no differently than on the Suez Canal Company. The company had justified its last toll reduction, in 1954, to stockholders as a profit-seeking step to induce more and bigger ships to use the Canal.

The danger was, in any case, a small matter at worst. The 1956 Canal tolls of eighty-seven cents a ton represented 1 per cent of the wholesale cost of petroleum products in England. The route around the Cape of Good Hope would add $3.50 in shipping costs while avoiding the Canal tolls. The sum of $3.50 would amount to 4 per cent of the wholesale petroleum costs in England. This would be the maximum imaginable limit of tolls and Egypt would have to go daft to come anywhere near it because it would kill off Canal traffic in a very few weeks for economic reasons quite aside from whatever other measures it might provoke the world to take.

Menzies tripped heavily over chronology, common sense, and good manners when he blamed Eisenhower for wrecking the mission with a press conference statement in Washington on 5 September. Eisenhower said "the United States is committed to a peaceful solution of this problem." Forgetting his own official report that Nasser had given him a conclusive No on the evening of the 5th, Menzies wrote afterward:

By our conference session the following afternoon [6 September] his whole attitude had stiffened. He had, like the rest of us, read in the morning Egyptian newspapers a statement of USA policy which said, in headlines, that "there must be no use of force," and that if the 18-nation proposals were rejected others "must be considered." From that time on, Nasser felt he was through the period of danger.

There are at least as many errors as there are sentences in Menzies' version of events, which Eden accepted at the time and used in his own memoirs. First of all, according to his own official report as well as to Nasser, Menzies had no meetings with Nasser between the night of the 5th, when Nasser rejected the Western proposals, and the evening of 9 September, when the mission paid a farewell visit. Secondly, he mistook what Eisenhower said on 31 August for what he said on 5 September. Thirdly, Nasser did not, as Eden put it, begin "to feel it safe to say No" after Eisenhower's remarks. On the contrary, Nasser told Byroade and Tom Little separately that he expected an attack as soon as the British felt they had a satisfactory pretext. Nasser's junta colleague, Anwar Sadat, wrote similarly in *al-Gambouriya* on 8 September: "It has now become quite clear that Eden wants nothing but war.... He has no other course open to him than either to declare war or resign." Alfred Robens, the Laborite foreign affairs spokesman, spoke in the same vein in Caterham, England, the same day.

Menzies rudely expressed to correspondents in Cairo on 6 September his anger at Eisenhower's comments on the Suez crisis, saying they had cut the ground out from under his committee. He is said to have been equally rude to Eisenhower in person eight days later on his way back to Australia.

Most people who have met Nasser, including Eden, have acknowledged Nasser's charm even if they have not succumbed to it. Not Menzies. "So far from being charming," Menzies wrote Eden of Nasser, "he is rather gauche, with some irritating mannerisms, such as rolling his eyes up to the ceiling when he is talking to you and producing a quick, quite evanescent grin when he can think of nothing else to do."

The Egyptians, in turn, disliked Menzies. Kamel Georges, an Egyptian newspaperman, expressed the consensus: "Blunt, hostile, and arrogant, Menzies was like a bull in a china shop. He offended even England's best friends among the correspondents. He was often drunk and he sweated profusely. We began to refer to him as the Australian mule." When Menzies lashed out at Nasser in a speech to the Australian parliament in Canberra on 25 September, *al-Akhbar* retorted the next day:

> Menzies... spoke as an Australian mule... in fact, Mr. Menzies bucked, reared, plunged, and kicked up his hind legs.... The Australian Prime Minister kicked the UN Charter and trampled on all the principles by which the 20th century lives, threatening force, advocating economic sanctions against Egypt, and declaring that if the Security Council refuses to sanction the use of force against Egypt the Commonwealth has no alternative but to take the bull by the horns and use force anyway.

Menzies' futile dialogue with Nasser ended 9 September with Nasser's written reply to Menzies' letter of 7 September recapitulating the talks. Nasser began by calling the eighteen-power claim to represent 90 per cent of the Canal traffic "distinctly a statistical exaggeration." The "collective domination" of an international board, he wrote, "would plunge the Suez Canal into the turmoil of politics instead of... insulating it from politics." In his letter and again in a formal memorandum to all user nations on 10 September Nasser renewed his 12 August proposal for a conference of all user nations for the purpose of reviewing the 1888 Convention.

That night Byroade departed for his new post in South Africa after a farewell call on Nasser. "At our last meeting," Byroade recalled, "Nasser said the British and French are going to stay out there in the Mediterranean until they find a pretext to come in. He was sure of it." Byroade said he disagreed but he asked Nasser if he would guarantee the safety of Americans if the Anglo-French force did attack. Nasser replied: "Yes, so long as the regime remains in power." He was as good as his word, Byroade said, adding that if Nasser had fallen no American, British or French life in Egypt would have been worth a plugged nickel.

During the Menzies mission Eisenhower and Eden had a further exchange of letters on the use of force. Angered by the belligerent Anglo-French conduct immediately before the Menzies mission, Eisenhower expressed US concern to both London and Paris. He wrote Eden on 2 September: "I must tell you frankly that American public opinion flatly rejects the thought of using force." It happened that Nasser told his press conference that day that he received 20,000 letters a month from Americans, most of them friendly. A *Wall Street Journal* survey published on 18 September showed that 70 per cent of those interviewed opposed US military intervention in the Suez Crisis. Eisenhower's letter to Eden included the warning, mentioned earlier in this chapter, against using the Suez dispute as a pretext for attacking Nasser.

Eden said in his memoirs that he "found this most disturbing" and that he spent much care drafting his reply to Eisenhower, which was sent on 6 September. That same day Eden summoned Parliament to convene on 12 September in an emergency two-day session on Suez. Eden wrote Eisenhower that nationalization was "the opening gambit in a planned campaign designed by Nasser to expel all Western influence and interests from Arab countries" by defying Europe, raising his [Nasser's] prestige, mounting revolutions in the oil-producing countries, and making them Egypto-Russian satellites so that "we shall all be at his mercy." Eden said Nuri, the Shah of Iran, King Saud, and the Libyan ambassador had all warned him against Nasser.

Eden went on to say that the US divergence with Britain was over the assessment of Nasser's intentions and "the consequences in the Middle East of military action against him." Eden said he appreciated the risks of military intervention. "But if our assessment is correct," he wrote, "our duty is plain. We have many times led Europe in the fight for freedom. It would be an ignoble end to our long history if we accepted to perish by degrees."

Eisenhower thought this a "very emotional communication" and sat down with Dulles to draft a reply which he hoped would dampen Eden's ardor. He cabled Eden on the 8th that he drew "a picture too dark and ... severely distorted." He said tartly that "there is no evidence before the world that Nasser intends to do more than to nationalize the Canal Company." He warned Eden once more against using force and urged him to take the less dramatic approach embodied in an organization of Suez Canal users which Dulles had thought up over Labor Day weekend at his retreat on Duck Island in Lake Ontario.

Eden's apparently gratuitous reversion to gunboat diplomacy baffled many of us in the London press corps. I asked Clark the reason for it and he said ruefully: "Our policy is, perforce, to take the lesser of two evils. A condemned man approaching his hour of execution will turn the clock back if he can."

This sense of doom, of an Imperial *Götterdämmerung*, pervaded much of Tory England's reaction to Nasser. It seemed uncharacteristic in Eden in the light of his career before Suez. Perhaps it lay in the instincts of the man, beneath the disciplined intuition and forward-looking intelligence of the diplomat, and was brought to the surface like a mother-tongue by the double stress of illness and leadership. If Eden's fevered policies had not struck a responsive chord in the hearts of half his countrymen they would have been like a fuse without a bomb. These explosive emotions were best articulated in a famous *Times* first leader, Escapers' Club, published on 27 August. Urging resolute action in the face of national divisions, *The Times* said:

419

Nearly eighty years have gone by since Disraeli castigated "those cosmopolitan critics, men who are the friends of every country save their own." They are still with us ... The last strand of irresponsibility is that which is beginning to ask ... Does the Canal really matter? Cannot we believe either that this act of Nasser's portends nothing serious, or that if it does we can sidestep all the consequences? ... The sun of Venice set because of the double event of the Turkish blocking of the caravan routes and the discovery of the Cape route and America. A pleasure-loving people more interested in their revels than in their responsibilities did the rest.

One key member of the Government told me later that he thought the weakest part of Eden's policy of using the Suez crisis as a pretext to destroy Nasser was the lack of planning for a successor regime. "After we succeed, then what?" he asked. "What kind of new [Egyptian] government do we want? But the rest of the Cabinet thought it would be enough to knock over Nasser and that it was not important to worry specifically what to do afterward." Eden wrote vaguely to Eisenhower on 5 August about a successor regime, but he seems never to have progressed in practical planning beyond his shout over the telephone to Nutting in March: "I want him destroyed.... And I don't give a damn if there's anarchy and chaos in Egypt."

Menzies returned from Cairo on 10 September and told reporters at London Airport: "Egypt will have nothing to do with any peaceful solution of the Canal problem which does not leave Egypt sole master of the Canal." Mollet flew to London and he and Eden talked on that day and the next and then issued a grim communiqué saying they had "discussed the further measures to be taken and reached full agreement on them."

One of the measures they took was to tell the Suez Canal Company to go ahead and call its non-Egyptian personnel off the job. The company set the walkout for 14/15 September. Originally it was hoped that the paralysis of the Canal resulting from the walkout of the pilots would provide a usable pretext for Britain and France to seize the Canal and operate it, unseating Nasser as a consequence. The pilot walkout was set to coincide with the date the invasion force was ready.

The company had told its non-Egyptian employees on 5 August to stay at work and to register with their consuls within ten days their decision either to remain under the new Suez Canal Authority or seek repatriation. The director general of the Suez Canal Company, Jacques Georges-Picot, told a press conference in Paris on 14 August: "The near-totality of the company's non-Egyptian personnel have already signed at their embassies statements of loyalty to the company and asked for repatriation. I could tomorrow end all traffic on the Canal if I chose to give the order of repatriation."

There was a pilot shortage even before nationalization; the company needed 250 but had only 205 on its payroll. The shortage was a result of a struggle between Egypt and the company over increasing the proportion of Egyptians at all employee levels. Egypt resisted the company's preference for foreigners by delaying or refusing visas. A settlement was reached in the spring but the company was laggard in recruiting and training additional pilots.

Of the 205 pilots employed on 26 July, 61 were French, 54 were British, 40 were Egyptian, 14 Dutch, 11 Greek, 10 Norwegian, 4 Danish, and there were two each from Sweden, the US, Italy, and Belgium, and one each from Yugoslavia, Poland, and Spain. Of the total, 43 were on vacation, including five of the Egyptians, who broke off their leave and returned to work immediately. Mahmoud Yunis, head of the Egyptian Suez Canal Authority, accused Georges-Picot of writing pilots on leave, including the Egyptians, an offer of from one to three years' salary in advance if they would refuse to return to their jobs. Yunis produced one of the letters as evidence. Georges-Picot said it was a matter merely of informing them of their retirement benefits. Avoiding provocation, Yunis continued to authorize scheduled vacations abroad although many non-Egyptians were failing to return.

On 23 August Yunis announced that although 27 pilots had failed to return from leave, 21 pilots had been allowed to begin leaves after nationalization. He said 31 new pilots had been appointed, 26 of them Egyptians, mostly navy captains. Yunis reduced the work load on the pilots by combining the two daily northbound transit convoys into one. He also conducted an intensive recruitment campaign abroad. Most French and British newspapers refused the Egyptian advertisements for pilots. The *Manchester Guardian* was the only national British daily paper to accept the advertisement. At the end of August the company sheepishly admitted having sent large checks to French newspapers after *Libération* (Paris) printed on the front page a facsimile of its check for 100,000 francs ($285). Egypt charged that the British and French governments not only obstructed pilot recruitment but instructed their consuls in the Canal zone to encourage pilots to choose repatriation. The British Consul in Ismailiya threatened Maltese and Cypriote laborers that he would withdraw their British passports if they did not quit in September when the company so instructed them.

Britain's hopes to build a pretext for action on the Canal pilot situation focused at first on Egyptian orders at the time of nationalization prohibiting the company employees from quitting work on pain of imprisonment. Egypt quickly explained that it only meant to require a month's notice, according to a long-standing statute. On 22 August Sir George Young, the Foreign Office spokesman, interrupted a press briefing for correspondents covering the London

Conference to read a bulletin alleging an Egyptian threat to discriminate against British and French ships if British and French pilots quit. The next day, after Egypt said the report was false, the Foreign Office stubbornly insisted that the situation "is still regarded as grave and likely to become graver in spite of the denials." But no *casus belli* grew here.

Nasser's "soft-pedaling" had clearly become an increasing exasperation to Eden. On 4 August the new Suez Canal Authority had announced that shipowners could pay Canal tolls into frozen Egyptian accounts in Britain and France as well as to the old company. Three days later Yunis announced a five-year, £20 million ($56 million) program to widen and deepen the Canal to accommodate 55,000-ton ships, which was 10,000 tons larger than the maximum at the time. On 27 August Egypt announced that 1,311 ships transited the Canal in the first month of nationalized operations, raising the daily average to 44.2 ships from 42.3 for the same period in 1955.

The belief that the pilots' walkout would stop traffic began to fade as the secret invasion date approached. Georges-Picot recalls telling Pineau and Lloyd on the 7th and 8th of September respectively that he no longer believed the withdrawal of the foreign pilots would shut down the Canal. But Eden's and Mollet's decision to withdraw them anyway prompted a correspondent to ask Eisenhower at his press conference on 11 September if he thought Britain and France would be justified in using force if the walkout slowed or stopped traffic.

"I don't think that," Eisenhower said. "I think this: We established the United Nations to abolish aggression, and I am not going to be a party to aggression if it is humanly possible... to avoid or I can detect it before it occurs." The pilot walkout was not only no longer expected to create a pretext but Eisenhower was not going to tolerate using it in any case.

The remaining British, French, Dutch, and Italian pilots applied for their exit visas on 12 September, resigned from the new Suez Canal Authority, and departed Egypt on the 14th and 15th. They had been told by the company that they would forfeit their pensions if they stayed. They were told by the Egyptians that if they quit they would be blacklisted from ever returning again, even as tourists. Only the Greek Government refused permission to its nationals to leave Egyptian service, going so far as to withhold visas to enter Greece (which were needed even by Greeks), and finally instructing Greek consuls to call in the passports of Greek Canal workers. In all, some 600 foreign employees resigned on twenty-four hours' notice, according to the Count de Grailly, the company's chief representative in Egypt.

Yunis had hired German pilots from the Kiel Canal, Russian canal and river pilots, a handful of Americans, and a scattering of other nationalities. None of them had completed the qualification course on the Canal, which had been shortened from two years to four months for the emergency, when the departing foreign pilots began handing over the controls at 8:30 P.M. on the 14th. Most of the work in the next few weeks was done by seventy Egyptian pilots and the eleven Greeks. Cairo Radio reported jubilantly that fifty ships transited the Canal on the first day after the foreign pilots quit, calling it the highest figure in the history of the Canal. Nasser thought the sudden increase in ships was due to a plot to overstrain the Canal facilities simultaneously as the Egyptians were thrown on their own resources but Georges-Picot said it would be technically impossible for governments to control merchant shipping enough for such tactics.

How had the Egyptians done it? The world had been so certain they could not do it that Eden took their failure for granted as the automatic D-day for his planned invasion. For one thing, the European pilots of the old company had exaggerated the difficulties of the job in order to assert their own uniqueness and importance, as specialists are wont to do. And the world at large had for a century held the Egyptians in contempt, overlooking the fact that for 5,000 years they had been taking ships under sail up and down the shifting course of the Nile, which requires more technical virtuosity than piloting an engine-driven ship through a currentless canal.

The special problems of Suez Canal pilotage were explained to me by Fawzi Awad, harbormaster at Port Said. The fundamental requirement is to keep the ship dead center in the Canal. If it veers to one side in the narrow waterway the Bernoulli effect reduces the pressure between the hull and the near bank, sucking it still nearer as a spoon's bottom, in the classic general science grade-school experiment, is sucked inward by water from a faucet. An accelerating shear results. It can run the bow aground on one bank and the stern on the other with terrible suddenness. Variations in the banks of the Canal and its bypasses require detailed knowledge and constant attention from the pilot in order to keep to the central axis of the Canal. Desert cross winds can create formidable difficulty. The thirteen hours at the wheel required to transit the Canal is so severe a strain on a pilot taking the full trick that it is split except in emergencies.

Yunis eased the burden by cutting southbound convoys to one large one a day instead of two smaller ones, as he had done earlier with northbound shipping. New pilots were qualified on half the Canal at a time, enabling them to handle shipping sooner on the half they learned. And ship captains who transited the Canal regularly were able to take their ships through without a pilot, holding their position in convoys controlled by pilots on other ships, as was commonly done before nationalization.

423

Shipping continued without a break until the war. Georges-Picot was impressed by the Egyptian performance and later called Yunis a truly able man by any standards. Eden, ungraciously refusing credit to the Egyptians, wrote in his memoirs: "The replacements [for the pilots who quit], drawn from many lands, did their job much better than the company or we had been led to expect." Eisenhower, both more accurate and more generous on this point, wrote in his memoirs: "As it soon turned out, not only were the Egyptian officials and workmen competent to operate the Canal, but they soon proved that they could do so under conditions of increased traffic and with increased efficiency.... The assumption upon which the Users Association was largely based proved groundless. Furthermore, any thought of using force, under these circumstances, was almost ridiculous."

Not to Eden, although it obliged him to seek a new pretext. He had already begun the incessant modifications of Operation Musketeer that plagued and embittered his fighting men.

General Stockwell returned on 4 September from his tour of the invasion force units to find military preparations a week ahead of schedule but the invasion date doubtful. Later that day it was deferred from 15 September to 19 September. Two days later D-day was again postponed—to 26 September. "But we *were* ready by September 8th," Stockwell wrote later, "to do the job on the planned date of September 15th." The invasion point was shifted back from Alexandria to Port Said, entailing a sweeping revision of the battle order and ship loadings designed for an assault at Alexandria. "The planning dragged on through September," Stockwell wrote afterward, "and phrases such as 'police action' or an 'intervention' began creeping into our deliberations." Israel had been informed through Paris of Operation Musketeer on 1 September. Collusion now rose toward the top of the pile of potential pretexts as its phrases crept into the map rooms and offices of Terrapin, the underground planning headquarters across Whitehall from Downing Street.

Before making war, however, Britain had first to "go through the UN hoop," to use the phrase Nutting attributed to Lloyd. Nutting returned to the Foreign Office from sick leave late in August to warn Eden and Lloyd against warlike collaboration with the Franco-Israeli entente, France and Israel being the two nations most hated and suspected by Britain's Arab friends, and to urge going to the UN if Nasser rejected Menzies' persuasions. Going to the UN was essential to bipartisan support, Nutting said.

"Eden's reply to all this was blunt," Nutting wrote. "He did not care whether Gaitskell supported or opposed him. As for the UN, they had proved to be a dead loss ... Eden reverted to his theme that compromise with Nasser [through the UN] would only serve to whet his appetite and that I must get it into my head that this man must be destroyed before he destroyed all of us." Lloyd told Nutting that he would argue for UN action to "set the stage," whether for war or for negotiation. Lloyd prevailed with Eden but the French then balked, Nutting reported, because the US refused to guarantee that the Security Council would leave Britain and France free to use force. Dulles opposed taking the case to the UN, Nutting wrote, because the Big Three, lacking unity, would be vulnerable to Russia's divisive tactics in the Security Council.

Eden's cabinet, having decided on 28 August to "go through the UN hoop" after Menzies' foregone failure, sent Dulles for approval a draft resolution for the Security Council. Dulles replied on 30 August making plain his suspicion that it was "a device for obtaining cover" to use force. Dulles went to his Duck Island retreat for the Labor Day weekend with two problems on his mind: to prevent Britain and France from clearing the UN hurdle and to thwart their design to use the forthcoming pilot shortage on the Canal as a pretext to take it over by military force.

He devised what was later named the Suez Canal Users Association, SCUA for short, as a temporary answer to both problems, a stalling device if not a solution. Eden told in his memoirs how Dulles returned to Washington on 4 September with these "fresh thoughts" and passed them on to Ambassador Sir Roger Makins. "He now declared that we did not need a new convention with Egypt," Eden wrote, "though this was precisely what had been asked for by the eighteen powers in the London proposals, which he had himself put forward." Dulles told Makins the British position was "a weak one judicially." He said the threats of force implied that Britain needed to acquire more rights than the 1888 Convention provided, whereas, in fact, the 1888 Convention gave Britain all the rights she required. Dulles said the Convention gave Nasser no right to make a profit from the Canal. He suggested that the user nations could club together, hire the pilots, and themselves manage the Canal, requiring all ships to use their services.

Eden admitted afterward that SCUA did, indeed, "deflect the course of events." The British could see nothing in the 1888 Convention which gave the users anything like the rights Dulles claimed. Eden said he accepted SCUA for two reasons: as a means of withholding Canal tolls from Nasser and as something which Nasser would find still more unacceptable than the eighteen-power proposals. Eden said the French suspected on the contrary that it was a "device to prevent Britain and France from bringing matters to a head with Nasser." The decision to endorse SCUA, Eden wrote, "was one of the most crucial we had to face during the whole of the Suez crisis."

Eden and Mollet agreed to accept SCUA at their meeting on 10 September after a further elaboration of the scheme by Dulles was brought in to them. If Egypt refused to cooperate, Dulles wrote, the SCUA administrator would operate from ships stationed offshore at either end of the Canal. Full use would be made of the company pilots and technicians, Dulles said, and those still at their posts with the Egyptian canal authority should be encouraged to remain at their jobs. Mollet and Eden balked at the last idea but exchanged a basketful of cables with each other and with Dulles in the next 48 hours working out what Eden took to be full agreement on a most provocative and aggressive SCUA.

He outlined his conception of it on 12 September in the House of Commons, which was assembled for the third emergency session of Parliament since World War II. (The causes of the two previous emergency sessions were devaluation of the pound in 1949 and the Korean War in 1950.) As Eden worked over his speech that morning, Lloyd went to him after a sleepless night full of misgivings over SCUA. "I was naturally a good deal shaken," Eden recalled, but he and Lloyd resolved at last to go ahead with it. Eden revived Lloyd's spirits sufficiently for him to tell Ambassador Aldrich that Parliament was sure to be pleased with SCUA because it constituted a "slap in the face" for Nasser.

The Times that morning printed two columns of extracts from Nasser's seven-week-old nationalization speech, saying they "help to reveal the working of Colonel Nasser's mind—his pride, his ambitions, his sense of grievance, his abiding suspicions of the West ..." Eden referred to *The Times* extracts but otherwise they appeared to have no influence on the debate. Nor did the anti-Nasser forgery of the Egyptian leaflet which had reached the MPs by mail two days before.

Members were restive while Eden gave a detailed review of the crisis up through the Menzies mission. They subsided into intent silence when he began to describe the new plan. A roar of incredulous and derisive laughter burst from the Opposition benches when Eden said: "We also recognize that the attitude of the Egyptian Government will have an important bearing on the capacity of the association to fulfill its functions." The Tories tried to raise cheers in retort but from my seat in the press gallery I could see a number of them laughing too.

"Yes," Eden went on, "but I must make it clear that if the Egyptian Government should seek to interfere [Here a Laborite shouted: "Deliberate provocation!"] with the operations of the association, or refuse to extend to it the essential minimum of cooperation, then that Government will once more be in breach of the Convention of 1888. [Shouts of "Resign!" from the Opposition.]—I must remind the House that what I am saying [Scornful yell of

"What a peacemaker!"] is the result of exchanges of views between three governments—In that event, Her Majesty's Government and others concerned will be free to take such further steps ["What do you mean by that?"] as seem to be required ["You are talking about war!"] either through the United Nations, or by other means, for the assertion of their rights." [General tumult and hubbub.] Eden doggedly held the floor to insist that the situation paralleled the 1930s and to warn against "abject appeasement." He said that if negotiation failed "to secure our rights . . . the Government must be free to take whatever steps are open to them to restore the situation."

Gaitskell then rose to suggest that the Government itself had violated the 1888 Convention by withdrawing the pilots and that the world might well conclude that the Government was deliberately provoking an excuse for armed intervention against Egypt. "Our indictment against the government is that they have brought this country into . . . this dilemma," Gaitskell said, "either we carry out the threats of force or face the greatest diplomatic climb-down in our history."

At Dulles's behest, Eden presented SCUA as his own idea but Clark told correspondents in the lobby, with uneasy emphasis on an indiscreet pun, that it had "a *foster* father." Although the precise wording of Eden's announcement was agreed between Paris, Washington, and London, Dulles thought Eden's presentation was alarmingly warlike. Accordingly, he told a press conference the next day: "We do not intend to shoot our way through. . . . I do not recall . . . just exactly what Sir Anthony Eden said on this point. I did not get the impression that there was any undertaking or pledge given by him to shoot their way through the Canal."

Dulles's words were a bitter shock to Eden. "The words were an advertisement to Nasser that he could reject the project with impunity," Eden wrote in his memoirs. "Such cynicism towards allies destroys true partnership. It leaves only the choice of parting, or a master and vassal relationship in foreign policy." Dulles was even more cynical than Eden knew. According to Robert Murphy, who helped Dulles work out the SCUA idea: "If John Foster Dulles ever was actually convinced of the possibility of organizing a Canal Users Association to operate the Suez Canal, I was not aware of it."

Eden's grim conclusion was: "American torpedoing of their own plan on the first day of launching it left no alternative but to use force or acquiesce in Nasser's triumph." Eden had no intention either of acquiescing in Nasser's triumph or of accepting a vassal relationship in foreign policy. It was to be force against Nasser and a parting of the ways with America.

Dulles's phrase was taken up by Gaitskell toward the close of the two-day Suez debate. In a session as raucous and unruly as the first Gaitskell challenged

Eden across the well of the House: "Is he prepared to say on behalf of Her Majesty's Government that they will not shoot their way through the Canal?" Laborite members shouted "Answer!" as Eden went into a long-winded evasion. Insistent goading wrung from him, first the demurrer that no government could give an absolute pledge against force, and then: "Nevertheless, I will give this reply, which is as far as any government can go: It would certainly be our intention, if circumstances allowed, or in other words, except in an emergency, to refer a matter of that kind to the Security Council."

Many fell under the illusion that, despite his semantic obscurity, Eden had actually given the assurance Gaitskell demanded. Gaitskell was suspicious. In a letter published in *The Times* on 15 September Gaitskell said Eden left "grounds for uncertainty" and had not answered "that crucial question: . . . whether . . . the Government contemplate the use of force." The Eden Government's Solicitor General, Sir Harry Hylton-Foster, said at York that day that Eden definitely had not given an absolute pledge to avoid force in favor of UN action, an answer that showed indifference to, rather than concern over, Gaitskell's suspicions.

The Russians, the Egyptians, and Lloyd's of London were equally suspicious. On 11 September Bulganin wrote both Eden and Mollet. To Eden he said: "It is not Egypt who concentrates forces and threatens military action against anyone, but it is Britain and France . . . How, in such a situation, and guided by the noble principles of the United Nations, can one help standing on Egypt's side?" To Mollet he said: "We see that the war inciters have developed a new itch," and he warned of "severe consequences" if they gained the upper hand. Unreassured by the Suez debate in London and worried by what might follow the walkout of the pilots, the Kremlin issued a public statement on 15 September that the Soviet Union "cannot stand aloof from the Suez problem . . . as any infringement of peace in the Near and Middle East cannot but touch the interests and security of the Soviet state."

On 14 September General Burns cabled Dag Hammarskjold that UN military observers in Sinai reported that many of the Egyptian Army camps appeared vacant and that he believed the Egyptians had pulled two of the three divisions they had in the al-Arish–Qussaima–Rafah area back to the Delta "for defense against possible attempts to occupy key points on the Suez Canal." He added: "The Israelis, therefore, might find this a good opportunity to deal with the remainder of the al-Arish concentration, thus securing hostages to force a peace settlement . . . I don't think Israel will attack Jordan, except in the way of retaliatory raids." Israel had, in fact, raided Jordan on the previous two nights, killing 19 at Rahwa in the first raid and 11 at Gharandal in the second. Heavy raids on Jordan continued, part reprisal and part to decoy attention away from the planned invasion of Egypt.

As Burns reported, Nasser was more worried about an Anglo-French attack than an Israeli invasion, so much so, in fact, that he stripped his defenses on the Israeli frontier to cover the Canal and Delta. On the 15th Nasser addressed aviation cadets graduating from the air academy at Bilbeis, emphasizing the danger he saw in SCUA. Nasser said:

It is impossible to have two bodies to regulate navigation through the Canal.... By the same token we should be able to get together a number of countries and say we are forming an association of the users of the Port of London and all ships bound for London would pay to it. [Applause and laughter.] There will be international anarchy. [Applause.] ... This association cannot be one of Canal users. It is an association to usurp rights, to usurp sovereignty, to proclaim war.

Nasser told the West that he agreed with the aims of preserving free navigation and improving the Canal, "but if your aim is to steal and usurp the Canal from Egypt, this is a different thing and we cannot agree with you."

Lloyd's of London had already concluded that SCUA was an association "to proclaim war." War-risk insurance rates on cargoes to, from, or transiting Egypt were raised 250 per cent on 14 September.

14

Collusion

(15 SEPTEMBER 1956 TO 29 OCTOBER 1956)

In spite of all the books we had read demonstrating the slyness and cruelty of England's foreign policy, it took the Suez war to make us believe it.

(WAGUIH GHALI, *Beer in the Snooker Club*, 1964)

"Albion is sick!" said every Valley, every mournful Hill
And every River: "Our brother Albion is sick to death.
He hath leagued himself with robbers: he hath studied the arts
Of unbelief. Envy hovers over him: his Friends are his abhorrence: ... "

(WILLIAM BLAKE, *Jerusalem*)

COLLUSION WAS born of a marriage between Eden's anti-Nasser policy and the unwritten anti-Nasser alliance of France and Israel. The French-Israeli alliance began in August 1954 when influential men in the military establishments of the two countries concluded that they had a common enemy in Nasser whom they were fighting on separate fronts, Israel on the Sinai frontier and France in Algeria. In the beginning it was merely a matter of secret French arms deliveries to Israel. Then, in June 1955, there was talk of coordinated military action. This was shortly before Ben-Gurion warned Egypt he would fight if need be in order to open the Gulf of Aqaba.

The day after nationalization, when it was clear that the Western Big Three were all hostile to Nasser and that his Russian friends were likely to be preoccupied elsewhere, Israel requested a big increase in French arms shipments. On 7 August at a meeting in the graceful old Defense Ministry in Rue St. Dominique, not far from the Invalides, the French gave the Israelis their approval for massive deliveries. At the same time, they stopped giving the US and Britain the advices of such deliveries as required by the 1950 Tripartite Agreement. The Frenchmen present at the meeting included Bourgès-Maunoury; General Paul Ely, the French Chief of Staff; Admiral Pierre Barjot, who was to become Commander-in-chief of the French invasion forces; and Abel Thomas, Bourgès-Maunoury's chief aide and an ardent Zionist. Shimon Peres, Director General of the Defense Ministry, represented Israel.

At this meeting Defense Minister Bourgès-Maunoury invited Peres into the map room for a new discussion of joint action against Nasser. Michel Bar-Zohar, the young Israeli journalist adopted by both Peres and Ben-Gurion as their historian of Suez, described the meeting as follows:

Bourgès-Maunoury asked Peres how long it would take Israel's forces to reach the Suez Canal in an operation across the Sinai Peninsula. Peres replied: About one week. One of the high-ranking officers then asked Peres if Israel would be willing to attack Egypt in concert with France. Peres instantly answered Yes. There was no further discussion of joint action, Bar-Zohar reports, until September. The Israelis, however, began air and ground reconnaissance of Egyptian deployments in the Gaza Strip and along the Sinai frontier.

The French informed Israel of Operation Musketeer on 1 September, two weeks before the pilot walkout, which was then still expected to cause a breakdown of Canal operations and thus provide the pretext for an Anglo-French invasion. Dayan immediately ordered a staff study of a series of plans that had been prepared for military operations against Egypt, adding the new factor of Operation Musketeer into their thinking. Israel's own plans, which dated from 1955, had been a fringe factor in British political and military designs against Nasser. Britain's designs originated in Eden's mind in March, when they disclosed themselves in a new warmth toward Israel and support for France in Algeria. They had been elaborated on the tables of the war planners since July. The logic of collusion prompted the Spanish newspaper *Arriba* to state early in August that Britain planned to use Israel's forces as sepoys against Nasser. (Sepoys were Indian mercenaries of fame in colonialist days.)

The Foreign Office was indignant. Except for a few influential figures, chiefly Selwyn Lloyd, Sir Ivone Kirkpatrick, the Permanent Undersecretary, and Sir George Young, the official spokesman, the Foreign Office opposed the war. British embassies in the Middle East reported that popular nationalism was a greater force than the hostility to Nasser of a few of the Arab rulers. If fight you must, the Foreign Office experts advised the Government, make it an absolute principle to avoid any hint of association with Israel. This advice was abandoned when Egyptian capabilities frustrated Eden's hopes to obtain a pretext out of the pilots' walkout and when Dulles's deft stratagem pulled the teeth of SCUA.

By the time the Anglo-French invasion force was ready on 8 September to assault Alexandria, a week ahead of schedule, the Cabinet had shifted the invasion back to Port Said, which was more in keeping with the new factor in the revisions required of the planners in Terrapin. The operation was to be a "police action," an "intervention," rather than the "straight bash" which the military men and a minority in the Cabinet favored.

The idea of collusion with Israel as well as France was repugnant to many members of the Cabinet although ultimately it proved acceptable to all of them. This had an uncertain and disruptive effect on communications within the Cabinet, some members preferring to know as little about it as possible, as in a Victorian family having to arrange a shotgun wedding. As collusion rose to the top of the pile after other pretexts failed, this fastidious penchant for ignorance caused incidents of discoordination.

Collusion refers to the secret planned cooperation between Britain, France, and Israel against Nasser which was carried out under the guise of intervening in a fight between Egypt and Israel to save the Canal from war damage. Collusion was an answer to Eden's needs, not French or Israeli needs. Eden tried to reconcile two irreconcilable policies; one, Britain's traditional pro-Arab policy, and the other, the destruction of Nasser, who had become the hero of the Arab world regardless of the dim view of him privately held by some Arab leaders. These leaders, not their peoples, were the basis of Britain's influence in the Arab world. Their leadership and their very lives would be gravely endangered by a straightforward British war against Nasser's Egypt for it would force them to choose between Nasser and Britain. They would have either to renounce the British support that was the basis of their power or to renounce any semblance of popular support from their own countrymen. Neither Israel nor France was troubled by such considerations because both were openly hostile to the Arab world, to its leaders as much as to its people.

Eden's dilemma was still more complicated. He had not only to fool the Arabs about the purpose of his war against Nasser but also to fool the US and half of his own countrymen, at least until he could confront them with victory over Nasser as a *fait accompli*. For all this he needed pretexts to cover his real aims, pretexts to justify his military "precautions," and a pretext for war itself when his preparations were complete.

Recovery of the Canal faded as a pretext within days of nationalization as the world perceived that nobody had suffered material damage from the change of management. There had been no violation of anything but the feelings of Britain, France, and the US, which a good part of the world rather relished. Britain and France had been unready for the armed lunge back into the Canal that the world might have accepted as an immediate instinctive reaction. No danger to Europeans in Egypt ever arose to provide the still-valid, classic nineteenth-century pretext.

The pilot walkout itself, if it were to provide a pretext, had to be deferred until military preparations were complete. But Britain and France had to ensure that the pilots and other technical personnel would in fact walk out when instructed, and that the Egyptians would not succeed during the delay in persuading them to remain at their jobs. The Egyptians promised that life would be as good as ever for those who stayed, offering them new contracts precisely the same as their contracts with the company. To offset this, the British and French encouraged the company to all manner of chicanery, chiefly large financial inducements. The legal ground for the pilot walkout was to be the human right of the pilots to choose repatriation. The British and French also used direct persuasion through their consuls to develop and nourish antipathy among the pilots toward working for the Egyptians. In order to shut down the Canal as a pretext for war the British and French and the company did their best to prevent Egypt from recruiting replacements, persuading or bribing a majority of the press to refuse Egyptian recruiting advertisements.

The scope of Egypt's problem is measurable in the employment statistics. The company said that in July it had 910 staff members of whom 529 were foreigners, 311 of these French. Egyptianization over two decades, it said, "has taken place mainly in the lower ranks." When the pilots walked out, the Canal staff went down to 465, only 64 of them foreigners, mostly Greeks.

But the walkout failed to shut down the Canal. Within three days Yunis was telling a big press conference in Ismailiya that the pilot crisis was over. On 19 September, Tewfik al-Dib, chief of Canal operations, said: "Please tell the world to send us more ships; we can handle them. The more ships we have, the more money we earn." And on 25 September shippers removed the 15 per cent freight surcharge that was imposed on Suez cargoes in anticipation of delays when the pilots walked out. Eden and the French had by then abandoned any hope of a pretext for war here.

As an alternative they had snapped up Dulles's scheme for a Suez Canal Users Association, assuming that it could be made to jostle its own management onto the Canal and thus either administer a mortal humiliation to Nasser or provoke him to fight and thus allow the Anglo-French expeditionary force to destroy him. But Dulles began pulling SCUA's teeth the day after Eden announced it to the Commons. It had a brief, useless, and unhappy life.

Dulles and the British wheedled the eighteen powers that had endorsed the Menzies mission to reassemble in London for a second conference to make SCUA a reality. In order to persuade them to come, they were promised that their attendance in no way committed them to join SCUA. The agenda had three items: (1) Menzies' report on his mission, (2) Nasser's proposal for a universal conference on Canal guarantees, and (3) consideration of a plan for a Canal users' association.

The naming of SCUA provided a moment of comic relief at the closing session of the three-day conference on 21 September. The working title up to then was Cooperative Association of Suez Canal Users and the delegates used the acronym CASU, leaving out the second C for *Canal*. Foreign Minister Luns of the Netherlands objected:

"I, personally, do not like very much the word 'CASU.' It suggests an easy and not very funny joke—in *CASU belli*, and so on and so forth.... What about CASCU?"

Foreign Minister Cunha of Portugal: "... in Portuguese *CASCU* is something which really is not mentioned." (One possible meaning is *testicle*.)

Chairman Lloyd: "The representative of France will, I suspect, have something similar to say!"

Pineau: "... the term *CASCU* in French is extremely derogatory and I would ask you not to compel us to use it." (It sounds like *casse-cul* or arse-breaker.)

Lloyd: "It has been suggested that we should christen this organization

436

ASCU—Association of Suez Canal Users. . . . Does that translate satisfacto-rily?"

Cunha: "Mr. Chairman, I regret that in Portuguese and in Spanish the implications of *ASCU* are equally regrettable." (As pronounced in those languages it means *nauseating*.)

Foreign Minister Martino of Italy: "What about the Suez Canal Users' Association? I do not believe there is any objection on the part of my Portu-guese colleague."

Lloyd: "SCUA, Suez Canal Users' Association. Is that offensive in any language? SCUA—I hope it will never be used! . . . but still, SCUA, if it has to have initials."

The communiqué that day said Nasser's proposal "was placed before the conference but it was considered too imprecise to afford a useful basis for discussion." Here the communiqué exercised a great economy of truth for as Senhor Cunha and Foreign Minister Noon of Pakistan pointed out, the Egyp-tian proposal was not considered at all. Dulles himself conceded in the last few minutes of the conference that "we have not really ever discussed it," adding in justification that Egypt "didn't propose anything to have a discussion about."

Many other nations, including Russia, took a more positive view of Nasser's proposal. On 15 September, as the invitations went out for the second London Conference, Egypt disclosed that twenty governments had formally accepted her proposal for a conference of all nations interested in the Suez Canal. Representatives at the London Conference itself did not look kindly on the contemptuous dismissal of Nasser's proposal by the Big Three. Foreign Min-ister Halvard Lange of Norway told me on 20 September that Nasser was clearly "feeling for the middle ground" and that it was high time the whole dispute went before the UN. The conference was unable to adopt a "resolu-tion" establishing SCUA, merely a "declaration providing for a Suez Canal Users' Association."

Ever worried about International Communism boring from within, Dulles told correspondents he had set criteria for membership in SCUA at precisely the level that would keep Russia out. Member nations had to have either a mil-lion tons of shipping or 50 per cent of their trade pass through the Suez Canal. He added, by way of justification for SCUA's furnishing its own pilots for Canal transits: "I wouldn't think the US Navy would want Soviet pilots." There were then fifteen Russian pilots and five Americans training for Canal duty under the Egyptians.

In the end, only fifteen of the eighteen governments participated in SCUA. Japan, Ethiopia, and Pakistan stayed out. Pakistan planned to announce her refusal on the afternoon the conference ended and was deterred only by a grim note from Dulles saying: "It would be difficult for my Government to understand why your Government should decline even to study the Plan before taking an adverse decision. . . . I wonder whether your Government has had an adequate opportunity to weigh the pros and cons of precipitate negative action." For a fleeting twenty-four hours it looked as if France herself might stay out.

Pineau said afterward that nobody believed in SCUA, not even Dulles. He called it a device *"pour noyer le poisson"*—"to drown the fish." The *Daily Telegraph* (London) said in an apoplectic editorial on 2 October: "SCUA has become as harmless to him [Nasser] as a jester's bladder." The Egyptians, who were sufficiently worried by SCUA on 17 September to denounce it to the Security Council as a threat to peace, reported gleefully on 28 September that the lowest grade of hashish seized by the police in recent raids in Alexandria carried the brand name Users' Association.

The actual establishment of SCUA was completed by the ambassadors of the fifteen participating nations at a two-day meeting that opened on 2 October. Some of the fifteen joined only on the strength of Dulles's assurance that membership would entail absolutely no obligation; that SCUA would merely hope each government would act on an entirely voluntary basis to serve SCUA's purposes and build up its prestige and authority. Ambassador Aldrich said afterward of the organizational meeting: "It's a terrible thing to have to sit at these great conferences, setting up something that you don't think is going to work—can't possibly work."

Dulles made setting up SCUA more hopeless than ever at a Washington press conference on 2 October. Insisting that there was no difference between the original conception of SCUA and what the fifteen ambassadors were that day setting up in London, Dulles said: "There is talk about the 'teeth' being pulled out of it. There were never 'teeth' in it, if that means the use of force." That was bad enough in British eyes but what followed hurt far worse. Dulles said:

Now there has been some difference in our approach to this problem of the Suez Canal. This is not an area where we are bound together by treaty. . . . There are also other problems where our approach is not always identical. For example, there is in Asia and Africa the so-called problem of colonialism. Now there the United States plays a somewhat independent role. . . . I suspect that the United States will find that its role, not only today but in the coming years, will be to try to aid that process [of decolonization], without identifying itself 100 per cent either with the colonial powers or with the powers which are uniquely concerned with the problem of getting independence as rapidly, and as fully, as possible.

Nutting reported that Eden's private secretary brought in the news flash on Dulles's press conference at the very moment Nutting was pleading with Eden at No. 10 Downing Street not to get too far out of step with the US. Nutting wrote: "Eden read the Dulles statement quickly and then, with a contemptuous gesture, he flung the piece of paper at me across the table, hissing as he did so, 'And now what have you got to say for your American friends?' I had no answer. For I knew instinctively that this was for Eden the final letdown. We had reached the breaking point."

Eden retorted to Dulles in his memoirs four years later. In contrast to what he claimed was Britain's selfless and responsible elevation of her colonies toward self-government, he wrote, the US judged that there was nothing wrong in "deriving much gain" from capital expended in the development of a backward country while "accepting no responsibility for the administration of the country." He added: "It remains a fact that two of the more backward countries in the Middle East and in Africa, Saudi Arabia and Liberia, are also two where American interests play a conspicuously large part."

With so many Governments committed to it, it became impossible to abandon SCUA despite its lack of any admissible purpose. On 11 October, during the UN effort to settle the Suez dispute, Foreign Minister Fawzi reported to Nasser that Lloyd had inquired if Egypt would cooperate with SCUA. Fawzi described the exchange as follows: "I asked: 'Is this organization already born?' Selwyn Lloyd told me: 'It is born and it will live.' I said to him: 'The parents of this child have not disclosed yet whether it is a boy or girl.' It seemed to me Selwyn Lloyd did not like the joke."

SCUA was a classic example of the life force inherent in institutions no matter how young and useless they are. It survived for the better part of a year despite the fact that it had no more useful functions than the vermiform appendix. The concept was revived once more shortly before the second Suez-Sinai War in 1967 when the US proposed what was, in effect, a Gulf of Aqaba Users' Association. Not surprisingly, of the dozen and a half nations canvassed for it all were opposed except Israel, which had not been invited to join SCUA.

Cooperation between the French and Israelis intensified during September. On 7 September, midway through a two-week tour of Israel's fighting units, Dayan urged his air force to "hasten the pilot-producing process" to keep pace with the arrival of the new Mystère IVs. On the 17th he sat down with the full Operations Branch of the General Staff after a week-long study of the alternative operational plans against Egypt. In his diary he noted the difference between "international problems and our own special problems," adding: "The operation which is likely to be launched will have been prompted by the abrogation of the international status of the Suez Canal." Military action against the Gaza Strip or in the Straits of Tiran, he wrote, may be undertaken on Israel's "own initiative, either in association with the forces operating against Egypt or without any contact with them."

The first direct communications between Britons and Israelis now occurred. Robert Henriques, a member of an old Anglo-Jewish family, carried a message to Ben-Gurion from a British cabinet minister in mid-September. Henriques never publicly identified the cabinet minister but he reported three years later that the message was:

At all costs Israel must avoid war with Jordan. But if, when Britain went into Suez, Israel were to attack simultaneously, it would be very convenient for all concerned. Britain would denounce Israel's aggression in the strongest possible terms; but at the peace negotiations afterwards, Britain would help Israel to get the best possible treaty.

Ben-Gurion was skeptical, Henriques wrote, and he listened with a smile that seemed to say he had heard such promises before.

Israel had struck at Jordan on the 12th and 13th of September with major raids on Rahwa and Gharandal, killing thirty Jordanians. On 23 September a Jordanian soldier whose brother had been killed at Rahwa went berserk and opened fire with a Bren gun on one hundred members of an Israeli archaeological congress assembled 400 feet from the border at Ramat Rahel, where Hebrew-speaking guides with loudspeakers described new excavations. Four were killed and sixteen wounded. Israel retaliated at Husan two nights later, killing thirty-nine Jordanians including a captain and his jeep driver who were shot after capture.

When Henriques brought the British cabinet minister's proposal Ben-Gurion was already pondering a renewed suggestion by Bourgès-Maunoury for joint action with France, this time with Britain as well. Ben-Gurion hesitated over including Britain. But on 23 September he cabled Peres in Paris to give Bourgès-Maunoury an affirmative reply and he told the Mapai Central Committee publicly that Israel would soon have a "true ally." The French military establishment immediately relayed to the British Ben-Gurion's readiness to cooperate.

Pineau was able two days later to tell the Foreign Affairs Commission of the increasingly impatient National Assembly that France retained wide possibilities of action and that the trial of strength with Nasser was by no means over. Before Ben-Gurion's acceptance of joint action with Britain as well as France, Pineau had told Peres that he did not believe Britain would initiate action against Nasser because of the opposition Eden was encountering within his own party. Collusion solved this problem for Eden by arranging for Israel to start the war.

Although the prospect of carrying out Musketeer as a "police action" quickly filtered into the calculations of Stockwell's planners in their secret headquarters in Terrapin, it may not have reached Eden until some days later. Meanwhile, he and the French acted to clear the UN hurdle by placing the Suez situation on the Security Council's agenda. The move took Washington by surprise. Eisenhower called it evidence of a "growing rift" and wrote: "Was it, we wondered, a sincere desire to negotiate a satisfactory peaceful settlement (as the British insisted) or was this merely a setting of the stage for eventual use of force in Suez?"

Peres returned to Israel early on 25 September. He met Ben-Gurion and Dayan at the military airfield at Ramla and, as they drove up to Jerusalem, he reported on his talks with Pineau and Bourgès-Maunoury. French Defense Ministry circles, he said, were determined to attack Nasser even if they had to do it alone, but they were confident that the British would join in. The three men also selected Husan from among four possible sites for the reprisal to be launched that night for the incident at Ramat Rahel.

Eden and Lloyd flew to Paris on the 26th for overnight talks with Mollet and Pineau. Nutting said that the Englishmen found the French leaders "in great spirits and in a very belligerent mood." Nutting wrote that the French did not disclose to Eden the plans they were "concocting" with the Israelis but that they were so certain that Israel would soon provide a pretext for war that they no longer carped at going to the UN or setting up SCUA, regarding both as necessary to set the stage for attacking Nasser. Macmillan, incidentally, had candidly told an audience in Indianapolis, his mother's birthplace, on 22 September that stopping Nasser was the main issue in the Suez Crisis. "He must be stopped somehow," Macmillan said. "There is much more to this than a disagreement over the Suez Canal."

The French leaders received the Israelis again after Eden and Lloyd departed. Much of the shuttling back and forth between Paris and Tel Aviv in the forty days still to elapse before the war was done in a four-engined plane which President Truman had given to de Gaulle some years earlier. De Gaulle placed it at the disposal of the Defense Ministry after his return on 19 September from a tour of French possessions in the Pacific.

Dayan took off for Paris on the evening of 28 September with a final list of military equipment needed from France. With him went Peres and two Cabinet ministers, Mrs. Golda Meir, Minister of Foreign Affairs, and Moshe

Carmel, Minister of Transport. After pausing a few hours at Bizerte, the French base in Tunisia, the group arrived in Paris on the 29th for secret meetings that were scheduled when Peres and Bourgès-Maunoury met on the 23d.

On the morning of 1 October Dayan met General Ely, the French Chief of Staff at the flat of Louis Manjin on the Rue de Babylon. Manjin, the temperamental son of a famous, iron-willed general, made the arrangements for most of the collusion meetings. Accompanying General Ely were four other high-ranking officers including General Maurice Challe, his deputy for Air Force affairs. The French and the Israelis traded intelligence on Egyptian strength. Dayan handed Ely a request for 100 tanks, 300 half-track vehicles, 50 tank carriers, 300 trucks with four-wheel drive, 1,000 bazooka rocket launchers, and a squadron of transport planes. He told Ely that even without the additional weapons he believed Israel could defeat the Egyptian Army and capture the Sinai Peninsula within two weeks. Israel thought always in terms of short wars and kept only enough ammunition, spare parts, and fuel for twenty to thirty days of fighting. Ely promised to do his best to fulfill Dayan's request despite constant demands for more equipment from the French forces.

Dayan flew back to Israel after a rain-drenched evening on the town disguised in dark glasses. He wrote in his diary that as he left one café he heard a startled exclamation in Hebrew from one of the crowded tables: "Hey, fellows, did you see who just passed? Moshe Dayan and Shimon Peres. Must be something up, something secret, for Moshe Dayan was wearing dark glasses to avoid recognition!"

In London that day Eden tried again, in vain, to spook Eisenhower with a cable that said in part:

> There is no doubt in our minds that Nasser, whether he likes it or not, is now effectively in Russian hands, just as Mussolini was in Hitler's.... No doubt your people will have told you of the accumulating evidence of Egyptian plots in Libya, Saudi Arabia, and Iraq. At any moment any of these may be touched off unless we can prove to the Middle East that Nasser is losing.

On the evening of 2 October, the day Dulles made his comments in Washington about colonialism and the toothlessness of SCUA, Dayan called together the General Staff in Tel Aviv and electrified them with an Early Alert for the conquest of the Sinai. He ordered patrols and aerial reconnaissance of Egyptian positions. October 20th was the tentative date for the invasion. Dayan ordered the recall of all officers on training courses abroad. They would learn more by fighting, he wrote, and furthermore they would never forgive being left out of a war. Although mobilization was to be deferred until the last possible day as an aid to secrecy and surprise, Dayan ordered immediate preparation for it. "To avoid disclosure of our plans," he wrote in his journal, "such preparations should be explained in terms of the possible entry of Iraqi forces into Jordan, a move which would oblige the Israel Army to capture the west bank of the River Jordan."

The following day Dayan began operational planning with what he called his inner General Staff. The role of the Air Force was considered first. "If we do not succeed at the very outset in surprising the Egyptians and knocking out their planes while they are still on the ground," Dayan wrote, "our plan will fail." The shorter the war, he calculated, the less likelihood there would be of meeting Communist Bloc volunteers alongside of Egyptians. The whole Sinai Peninsula had to be conquered within two weeks, Dayan and his generals decided.

In the war that year the job of destroying the Egyptian Air Force was carried out mainly by British bombers. Dayan published his 1956 diary in Hebrew in 1965 and in English in 1966. The Egyptians failed to heed the warnings contained in it as the second Suez-Sinai war approached. At breakfast time on 5 June 1967, at the very outset of the war, the Israeli Air Force surprised the Egyptians and knocked out their planes while they were still on the ground.

Israel cultivated the crisis with Jordan as a cover simultaneously with her preparations for war against Nasser. She withdrew from the Jordan-Israel Mixed Armistice Commission on 3 October and two days later began to prohibit UN Military Observers from investigating incidents on Israeli territory. General Burns protested, to no avail. He reported to Hammarskjold, who endorsed Burns's view that "this is a dangerous negation of vital elements in the Armistice Agreement." Israel had more retaliation in store for Jordan; bloodshed proved effective in decoying the world's attention away from the ill-fated frontier of Egypt. And, as General Burns wrote later of the restrictions on the UN Military Observers: "The way was thus open for them [the Israelis] to elaborate or manufacture a *casus belli* against Egypt whenever they found the opportunity ripe, and it was not long before it ripened."

On that same 5th of October Dayan's men completed their first planning order for the invasion of Egypt and gave the operation the code name Kadesh, after a site near al-Auja where Moses and the Israelites paused on their way out of Egypt toward their first conquest of the Land of Canaan. The intention in this first version was to "capture Northern Sinai, establish a defense line on the east bank of the Suez Canal, and give protection to the State on its other sectors." The Canal itself was the objective at this stage as it was in 1967. Israeli aerial reconnaissance flights began photographing the approaches to the Canal, including Mitla Pass, within twenty-four hours.

As Israel was getting the UN out of her way in the Middle East, Britain and France were getting it out of their way in New York. Dulles, increasingly uneasy, asked Lloyd and Pineau on the morning of 5 October why they were bringing the Suez case to the UN at that time: "Was it for war or peace?" The three foreign ministers were preparing for the Security Council meeting on Suez. Pineau and Lloyd told Dulles they doubted that any peaceful way existed and that only a capitulation by Nasser could restore Western standing in Africa and the Middle East. Dulles disagreed vehemently, repeating the warnings in Eisenhower's recent letters to Eden.

Eden was felled that day, a Friday, by a chill, ague, and raging fever during a visit to his wife in the University College Hospital, where, it was authoritatively said, she was recuperating from a miscarriage. Eden lost consciousness in an elevator in a fit so severe that his aides thought he was going to die. His fever mounted to 106 degrees. He spent the weekend in the hospital instead of at Chequers but he returned to work on Monday. "This was mad," said an aide. Before collapsing, Eden had completed a letter to Bulganin justifying his "military precautions" as being compatible with UN principles in response to the "obvious danger that under the stimulus of Colonel Nasser's deliberate incitement the Egyptian mobs may once more resort to violence." Eden was to be proven wrong on this, as upon so many other things.

On that same 5 October, as the Security Council began three days of public debate on Suez, Nasser cabled Fawzi that he would accept an international advisory board, even one deriving from SCUA itself, and that Fawzi could disclose this concession or not as he saw fit. Nasser summarized a long talk he had with Kiselev that day, commenting that he was glad the Russians now saw the possibility of a compromise settlement and that they were going to make it as easy as possible for the West to back away from its demand for international control. Far from trying to exacerbate the crisis, Nasser told me afterward, the Russians tried to calm everybody down including himself. "They told us to be reasonable," he said. "It was contrary to what was published [in the West.]" Shepilov, at a luncheon with Pineau in Paris in mid-October, confirmed an earlier statement by Mikoyan that the Canal should be open to Israeli shipping.

Lloyd spoke more peaceably to Hammarskjold than he did to Dulles, according to one of Foreign Minister Fawzi's daily reports to Nasser on the UN meetings. Fawzi asked Hammarskjold what use there was in making the UN effort in the face of the British and French threats. Hammarskjold reassured him that he had known Lloyd for a long time and that he sincerely sought a peaceful agreement. Fawzi quoted Hammarskjold as adding: "I cannot conceive that Britain would resort to force. As for the French, they have their internal [Algerian] troubles and these are enough [to prevent their attacking Egypt.]."

Lloyd was given the last word in Edward R. Murrow's CBS television report on the Suez Crisis on Sunday, 7 October. The show was full of anachronisms and other errors that could not have been more damaging to Nasser if they had been deliberate, which is a reflection, not on Murrow's integrity, but upon the anti-Egyptian bias of the English-speaking world. An old film clip showed Nasser, in the colonel's uniform he had long since discarded in favor of civilian suits, criticizing the UN. Lloyd was allowed, not only to misinterpret *The Philosophy of the Revolution* in standard Western fashion but also to manufacture and falsely attribute to Nasser a boast that he would attack Israel if he won on the Canal.

On Tuesday, 9 October, Lloyd and Pineau met with Fawzi in private talks under Hammarskjold's aegis. Their ostensible purpose was to reach agreement in advance of formal Security Council action. It was the first direct negotiation of the ten-week-old crisis. A more obscure but more significant event that day was the departure of four French freighters from Marseilles laden with war materiel for Haifa. Two sailed under false names and flags; the *Sète* renamed *Setero* and flying the Finnish flag and the *Mortain* under the name *Moria* and the flag of Panama.

Early in the New York talks Lloyd dictated "off the cuff" what later were adopted as the "Six Principles" of a Suez settlement. "Dag wrote them down," Lloyd recalled, "and they suddenly became the word of God." The Egyptians proved surprisingly accommodating. Although Eden, in telegraphic communication with Lloyd, had the word "principles" changed to "requirements" in the introductory paragraphs, the Egyptians accepted them and the Security Council adopted them on 13 October. They were:

(1) There should be free and open transit through the Canal without discrimination, overt or covert—this covers both political and technical aspects;
(2) the sovereignty of Egypt should be respected;
(3) the operation of the Canal should be insulated from the politics of any country;
(4) the manner of fixing tolls and charges should be decided by agreement between Egypt and the users;
(5) a fair proportion of the dues should be allotted to development;
(6) in case of disputes, unresolved affairs between the Suez Canal Company and the Egyptian Government should be settled by arbitration with suitable terms of reference and suitable provisions for the payment of sums found to be due.

For Eden and Mollet, Egypt's acceptance of this came too near to opening the way for serious negotiations over the Canal. As Murphy put it, "they knew their military schedule would be disarranged if they became entangled in drawn-out procedures in New York." They brought what Murphy called their "courtesy gesture" toward the UN to an abrupt close by attaching a rider to the Six Principles so prejudicial to further negotiations that Egypt could not possibly accept it. Russia vetoed the Anglo-French rider, with Yugoslavia also voting against it, leaving the Six Principles to stand alone as a basis for negotiations.

The Russians seem to have concluded that the danger of war was over. Bulganin cabled Eden on 23 October his pleasure over the "agreed decision concerning the principles . . . for a final settlement," adding his hope that the accomplishment presaged an ever greater role for the UN in such matters. Lloyd's of London came to the same conclusion and dropped war-risk rates on Suez shipping back to normal on 12 October, when adoption of the Six Principles was seen as a certainty.

The rider, officially designated as Part Two of the resolution embodying the Six Principles, curtly insisted that Egypt had "not yet formulated sufficiently precise proposals to meet the requirements set out above," demanded that Egypt "promptly" submit proposals "not less effective" than those Nasser had already rejected to Menzies, and said that pending a definitive agreement Egypt should cooperate with SCUA, "which has been qualified to receive the dues payable by ships." Nasser was being told to work with what he had denounced as "an association to proclaim war." The rider was obviously contrived as a political affront, impossible for Nasser to accept.

Eden insisted that its defeat ended any prospect of a UN solution. "No method was left for harnessing the principles," he wrote later. "They just flapped in the air." One of Eden's senior cabinet colleagues told me that "Eden regarded this [the Six Principles] as too near a solution for comfort; he was determined on war from the beginning."

Lloyd and Pineau, in spite of their knowledge that Eden and Mollet wanted war, felt there was no way out of a peaceful settlement after Egypt accepted the Six Principles. They met all the West's demands, although in a way which Nasser could survive.

If Nasser could survive, Eden and Mollet believed, they themselves could not. Bourgès-Maunoury says a settlement could have brought Mollet's immediate downfall. Dulles reported to Eisenhower that Britain and France refused minor modifications that would have made their rider palatable. They felt they needed the Soviet-Yugoslav veto, Dulles said, for their political survival.

Nevertheless, Fawzi pressed forward in the hope that Egypt's proven readiness to make concessions would lead to fruitful talks. In any case, for Egypt it was a matter either of trying to make negotiations work or of waiting idly for the British and French to attack.

Further negotiations were planned for Geneva on 29 October. Hammarskjold prepared for them in private talks with the three foreign ministers involved. On 24 October he drafted a memorandum elaborating the points in agreement as he understood them from his talks as an intermediary. Dulles told the Senate Foreign Relations Committee early in 1957 that he was given to believe that direct negotiations would resume on 29 October but that he later realized Britain and France merely used this as a smoke screen. Nasser offered publicly on 19 October to negotiate personally with Eden and Mollet. It was a remarkable offer in view of their incessant personal insults. The following day Egypt disclosed the plans for a Geneva meeting on 29 October but Britain and France frostily and mendaciously disavowed knowledge of it. They were planning war instead, and Eden was by then deeply engaged in the collusive preparations.

Eden's Minister of Defense, Sir Walter Monckton, decided by 11 October that he was no longer willing to accept departmental responsibility for the coming war and he resigned. He remained in the Cabinet, as Paymaster General, feeling that to leave the government entirely might topple it. He confided to Nutting on 25 October that he intended to get out as soon as possible. Monckton's resignation and his replacement at Defense by Antony Head were not announced until 18 October. The announcement gave reasons of health but Ambassador Aldrich reported to Washington that Monckton had said at a small cocktail party on 23 October that the real reason he resigned was because he regarded the forthcoming war against Egypt as "a great blunder."

The red herring of Jordan was dragged about so vigorously to throw the world off the scent of the coming war with Egypt that it nearly caused a falling out between Britain and Israel. Israel's raids on Jordan also helped to set up her own pretext for the Sinai invasion by prodding Jordan into a defensive alliance with Syria and Egypt, a paper contraption which Ben-Gurion said was a "ring of steel" that had to be broken.

Feelings between Israel and Britain were ruffled on 8 October when Nuri proposed a Palestine settlement along the lines Eden had prescribed a year earlier in his Guildhall speech, implying the need for territorial concessions by Israel. The Foreign Office promptly endorsed Nuri's proposal. Walter Eytan, Director General of the Israeli Foreign Ministry, broadcast in retort that "Israel will defend her own territory and independence against any threat from any quarter, no matter whether it is directed against her with or without the connivance of one of the Great Powers."

Israel's raids in September set in train two rival Arab plans to defend Jordan, one by Egypt, Syria, and Saudi Arabia and the other by Iraq. The first originated at a conference in Saudi Arabia of Nasser, King Saud, and President Kuwatly from 22 to 24 September. The three leaders discussed Jordan's danger in addition to the Suez dispute. They agreed to offer Jordan financial aid and a link with the Egyptian-Syrian joint military command, which was still, after nearly a year, no more than a paper alliance. King Hussein, uneasy in such company, suggested to Iraq that the Hashemite armies be linked but the talks bogged down over who was to be commander.

On 10 October Israeli forces struck Qalqilya in reprisal for the daylight murder of two citrus laborers whose ears had been cut off. It was the largest-scale raid since the Palestine war. The objective was to blow up the police fortress in the town. Dayan personally took part. At least 48 Jordanians, including 5 civilians, were killed. The raiders encountered the fiercest resistance since the Palestine war, and suffered their largest casualties, losing 18 killed and at least 50 wounded.

Israeli planes took part to help extricate a unit cut off by the Jordanians. King Hussein personally asked General Keightley, the British Middle East commander, to honor the Anglo-Jordanian alliance by sending the RAF into action. "Our aircraft were on the point of going up," Eden wrote, "when a wise and rapid exchange of cautionary messages on the spot avoided catastrophe." The British chargé d'affaires in Amman, Peter Westlake, had told Burns after the Husan raid that one more reprisal would bring the Anglo-Jordan treaty into operation. But honoring the Jordan treaty would have hurt Eden's plans for war against Nasser, which accounted both for British anger at Israel and for British reluctance to help Jordan. "This was a nightmare," Eden wrote, "which could only too easily come true; Jordan calling for support from Nasser and ourselves, Nasser calling for support from Russia, France lined up with Israel on the other side."

King Hussein, disillusioned, sent his Foreign Minister to Cairo with an urgent appeal to Nasser to help relieve Israeli pressure on Jordan by sending forces back to the Sinai frontier. But Nasser replied that the threat of invasion by Britain and France made it impossible for him to return units from the Delta to Sinai. Eden, stung by the Jordanian Foreign Minister's visit to Cairo, cabled Nuri to send an Iraqi brigade to reinforce Jordan's Army and, incidentally, help prevent a pro-Nasser nationalist turnout in the elections coming up on 21 October.

Israel served notice that the entry into Jordan of troops from Iraq, which was the only Arab belligerent in the Palestine War that signed no Armistice Agreement, "would be a direct threat to the security of Israel and the validity of the Israel-Jordan Armistice Agreement." The *Jerusalem Post* had already called Jordan "the sick man of the Middle East" and warned: "If Jordan crumbles, Israel will not sit with folded hands, and Egypt will not inherit." Israel was quite prepared to forego or postpone the war against Nasser and, instead, take Western Jordan and Jerusalem if Iraqi troops entered the country. Eden backed down, first obliging Nuri to accept ever greater restrictions on the move to Jordan. Eden was embarrassed, having initiated the idea in the first place, but on 15 October Amman announced that Iraq would keep her troops out of Jordan, although poised near the desert border. Dayan, disbelieving the announcement, commented in his diary on 21 October:

I must confess to the feeling that, save for the Almighty, only the British are capable of complicating affairs to such a degree. At the very moment when they are preparing to topple Nasser, who is a common enemy of theirs and Israel's, they insist on getting the Iraqi Army into Jordan, even if such action leads to war between Israel and Jordan in which they, the British, will take part against Israel.... I doubt whether anyone can explain why Britain does not hold off her Iraqi plan until after the Suez campaign.

On that day the nationalists won a solid majority in Jordan's parliamentary elections. Suleiman Nabulsi was sworn in as Premier with a cabinet dominated by men who had campaigned for the termination of Jordan's alliance with Britain. The people clearly preferred Nasser to Eden and Nuri, suspecting that the Anglo-Iraqi axis was less interested in protecting Jordan against Israel than in trying to force Jordan into the Baghdad Pact. On 24 October Jordan's new pro-Egyptian Government concluded a defensive alliance with Egypt and Syria. It provided for a unified command that was to come into effect only in the event of an attack by Israel. Ben-Gurion, however, insisted that the clear purpose of the planned joint command was to destroy Israel, not to defend against Israel. Thus distorted, it was his final pretext for war.

The furor over Jordan erupted during the annual Conservative Party conference in Llandudno, Wales, where the prevailing mood was set by the Suez Rebels. Eden wound up the three-day conference on 13 October with a pugnacious speech that won cheers from the 5,000 Tories assembled there. Already informed of Egypt's acceptance of the Six Principles, which the Security Council approved that day, Eden made so bold as to counter the optimism expressed across the Atlantic by Eisenhower. Before speaking, Eden told Lloyd by transatlantic telephone he would "seize on the least optimistic of the President's phrases, underline it, and point out once again that force could not be excluded." He did so and he repeated his July vow never to accept Egypt's "unfettered control" of the Canal.

Mollet, who acted as an intermediary between Eden and the Israelis over Jordan, passing warnings back and forth, became acutely concerned lest the Anglo-Israeli dispute wreck their plans to destroy Nasser. He telephoned Whitehall on the morning of the 13th that he was sending two emissaries to deliver important information to Eden the following day in the utmost secrecy. Nutting relayed the news to Eden at Llandudno. Eden told Nutting to come to the meeting with the emissaries.

What Mollet was sending was an ingenious plan to provide a pretext for war, a pretext that would be invulnerable to circumstances beyond Anglo-French control, such as Egypt's unexpected ability to run the Canal. Israel would attack Egypt on pretexts of her own manufacture and this would be the pretext for the Anglo-French invasion. The Egyptian Army would be then destroyed between the Israeli force on its Eastern front and the Anglo-French force descending on the Canal at its back, while overwhelming allied air forces pounded it from overhead. Bourgès-Maunoury claims to have initiated the collusion plan, obtaining Mollet's approval at every stage.

The two emissaries were General Maurice Challe, who had already figured importantly in France's preliminary collusive planning with Israel, and Albert Gazier, Minister of Labor. Challe evidently acquired a taste for conspiracy; he ended his career in prison for his role in an abortive ultra-right-wing plot against President de Gaulle. For the sake of secrecy Eden received the two men at Chequers, the official country house of the Prime Minister in the Chiltern hills thirty miles northwest of London. They came by plane to the military side of Northolt Airport and drove straight to Chequers under a bright autumn sky, arriving at 3 P.M. Eden, Nutting, and Eden's private secretary were waiting for them in Eden's study. Nutting's report of the meeting is as follows:

Gazier first obtained Eden's promise to ask Nuri to call off the troop movement into Jordan. Eden silenced Nutting's protest at this reversal. Gazier then asked what Britain would do if Israel attacked Egypt. Eden mentioned the Tripartite Declaration of 1950 but he said with a half-laugh that he could hardly picture himself protecting Nasser. When Gazier observed that Egypt had denied the legitimacy of the Tripartite Declaration, Eden said excitedly (and erroneously) that that released Britain from its obligations under the declaration.

Nutting asked Gazier what information he had about any Israeli plans to attack Egypt. Gazier gave a meaningful nod toward the private secretary, who was immediately asked by Eden to stop taking notes. Gazier then asked

Challe to speak. Challe outlined a plan to invite Israel to attack Egypt across the Sinai Peninsula. When Israel had crossed Sinai, Britain and France would call on "both sides" to withdraw from the Canal area to permit an Anglo-French force to occupy the Canal on the pretext of preventing war damage to it. The two powers could claim to be "separating the combatants" while actually taking full control of the Canal. Challe did not go into operational detail other than to say that sea-borne forces could take Port Said while paratroops seized Ismailiya and Suez. He mentioned no timetable, although he spoke as if the thing should be done in the immediate future. Neither Challe nor Gazier said definitely that Israel had agreed to the plan but Challe made it clear that his mission to Eden was based on Israeli encouragement during recent contacts. Eden, unable to conceal his excitement, concluded the meeting by saying he would send Nutting to Paris in two days with his answer.

Challe reported back to Bourgès-Maunoury, who calls this meeting the most important contact in the series that led to the war against Nasser. Eden had already been alerted to the French-Israeli plans, Bourgès-Maunoury says, but Challe's meeting was the one that convinced him. Washington apparently received muddled intelligence of the contacts. William Rountree, Assistant Secretary of State for Middle Eastern Affairs, told Dulles and Eisenhower on 2 November that the Israelis had approached the British in Paris immediately after the Security Council meeting, adding: "That is when they were firmed up—and that is when we knew they were firmed up. The Baghdad thing was a complete smoke screen, just to divert attention."

Here in essence was the collusion plan that was carried out at the end of the month. Nutting wrote that Eden did not know of it until Challe's visit but Bourgès-Maunoury says Eden was informed before that. Furthermore, Stockwell's operational planners had been talking for two or three weeks about executing Musketeer as a police action. Lloyd was still in New York discussing with Hammarskjold the arrangements for the negotiations in Geneva on 29 October. Eden brushed aside Nutting's plea to "sleep on" the Challe plan and telephoned Lloyd within minutes, telling him to drop everything and fly home for consultations. Eden would not risk discussing the Challe plan by telephone or cable.

The Israelis were swiftly reassured by the French emissaries' report of Eden's reaction. Within two days members of the General Staff as well as political notables were letting it be known that they did not consider Britain's warnings over Jordan to be serious.

Nutting was appalled, not only by the immorality and illegality of the plan, which would violate the UN Charter and the 1954 evacuation agreement with Egypt, but also by its stupidity. He foresaw that it would divide the

Commonwealth, alienate the US, disrupt oil supplies, and provoke an anti-British and anti-Western reaction in the Arab World that would ruin British interests and destroy pro-Western Arab leaders like Nuri. Finally, Nutting believed, it would confirm Arab suspicions that Britain had created Israel, not as a haven for a long-suffering people, but as a colonialist base. He saw Selwyn Lloyd as the last hope of dissuading Eden from his obsession.

Lloyd caught an evening plane from New York on the 15th. Nutting spoke to him when he arrived on the 16th, telling him of the Challe plan and his own advice against it. Lloyd agreed, Nutting wrote afterward, saying: "You are right. We must have nothing to do with the French plan." Lloyd said later he had been dubious of the wisdom of invading Egypt from the beginning, and was always preoccupied with the question: "How the hell do we get out if we reconquer it?" But Eden's influence was stronger than Nutting's.

Eden persuaded Lloyd over lunch at No. 10 Downing Street that Nasser could not be trusted to honor the agreements Fawzi made at the UN and that the French plan offered the likeliest prospect of bringing Nasser to heel. Instead of sending Nutting secretly, Eden decided to go himself to Mollet that day with his answer to the Challe plan. Eden and Lloyd flew from Northolt to Paris at dusk on 16 October for a five-hour meeting with Mollet and Pineau at which no notes were taken and no other persons were present. The trip itself was not concealed but the extraordinary degree of secrecy at the meeting was widely remarked. The conference communiqué communicated little. On Suez it insinuated falsely that Egypt was already going back on the Six Principles and declared that Britain and France stood fast on the vetoed rider. There was also, it said, "a general exchange of views on the other problems of the Middle East." Eden cast a heavily shaded light on the "other problems" in his memoirs.

"If Israel were to act against one of her encircling enemies," he wrote, "the choice lay between Jordan and Egypt.... If there were to be a break-out it was better from our point of view that it should be against Egypt. On the other hand, if the break-out were against Egypt, then there would be other worries, for example the safety of the Canal. We discussed these matters in all their political and military aspects.... During recent months we had been mounting our military preparations to deal with any interference or other act by Nasser against our ships or our people. Now Nasser's policies were provoking Israel beyond endurance and this also we had to prepare for."

Nutting got plainer truth from Lloyd the day after. "He [Lloyd] admitted that Eden had confirmed his wholehearted endorsement of the French plan and that further consultations would take place in Paris between French and Israeli representatives," Nutting wrote. "He hoped that we would not have to be directly associated with these talks, at any rate at the political level; but he could not rule this out, as there were a number of crucial political as well as military problems involving us which would have to be settled in a very short space of time."

Nutting told Lloyd he would have to resign if "this sordid conspiracy" were carried through and he asked him to tell this to Eden.

In addition to the topics disclosed by Eden in his memoirs and by Lloyd to Nutting, Pineau told me, the four ministers also discussed the military preparations Israel was already making. And they examined in detail the problems posed by the UN and what might be done to forestall them. Of the problems, the most serious was the inevitable prospect of UN interference if the proposed war occurred; the most immediate was the evolution toward a Suez settlement in the preparations for continuing negotiations with Egypt at Geneva on 29 October which Dulles was actively promoting with Britain and France and among Egypt's neutralist associates.

The significance of the 16 October meeting had echoes, obscure at the time, in Ben-Gurion's speeches at the beginning and end of a Knesset debate on foreign affairs, which had been postponed for a week. Opening the debate on 15 October, Ben-Gurion complained that Egypt had illegal troops opposite al-Auja, ignoring the fact that his own illegal seizure of the demilitarized zone forced Egypt to guard that sector. Concerning the Canal dispute, he said the Six Principles "mean practically nothing." He directed his direst warnings against Jordan, saying, "Israel will reserve freedom of action if a foreign military force enters Jordan." His emphasis on Jordan clouded the real meaning of words which he reprinted, with his own italics, in his Suez memoirs:

"We are compelled to make a supreme effort for security. It is forced upon us by external factors and hostile forces. *We are perhaps facing momentous decisions and events."*

On the morning of 17 October he spoke of "positive developments" in the previous two days which, he said, may have been influenced by his previous speech. His emphasis shifted dramatically from Jordan to Egypt. "The fascist dictator of Egypt is our most dangerous enemy," he said. "If we are forced to defend ourselves, this will not be done at home. We shall carry the war to the other side with a lightning-like stroke." The "positive developments," he said, concerned Jordan and the freedom of the Suez Canal. Few people besides Ben-Gurion and his collusive allies were aware that the only development bearing on Israel's claim to freedom of the Canal was Eden's acceptance in Paris the night before of the Franco-Israeli plan to invade Egypt.

Ben-Gurion went on to make his customary rejection of the militant Herut party's demand for a preventive war, adding in gratuitous insult that Herut's

PRETEXTS

belligerency proved that its tears over Israeli losses on the Qalqilya raid were nothing but "crocodile tears." On 22 October Herut demanded that Ben-Gurion answer in person for the insult, but he was meeting in great secrecy that morning in the Paris suburb of Sèvres with Selwyn Lloyd and the French leaders. To silence the Herut demand the speaker of the Knesset read out a written apology that Ben-Gurion would never have made in person.

The day before Challe and Gazier went to Chequers, Ambassador Sir Gladwyn Jebb hastened home from Paris to report fresh intelligence that France had recently delivered seventy-five Mystère IVs to Israel, far in excess of the twelve that had been approved during the spring by the Tripartite Declaration signatories and NATO. Eden prevented Nutting from mentioning this violation of agreed procedures to Mollet's emissaries.

Washington learned of the multiplication of French warplanes in Israel from reconnaissance flights of the U-2, which had recently gone into aerial intelligence service. Seventy-five was a slight exaggeration; the U-2 flights showed sixty. Eisenhower was told about the Mystères on 15 October. He learned at the same time of Israel's mobilization, which was in a secret preparatory stage from 2 October until the call-up for reserves went out on 25 October.

The President dictated a "Memorandum for the Record" of the situation as he saw it that day. He conjectured that "Ben-Gurion's obviously aggressive attitude" was aimed at hastening the disintegration of Jordan so that Israel could "occupy and lay claim to a goodly portion of the area of that nation" while the Eisenhower Administration's hands were tied by the electoral campaign. As Murphy said in his memoirs, "the large and influential Jewish community could bring heavy pressure to bear on government officials, pressure which in the early days sometimes amounted to intimidation."

Eisenhower instructed Dulles to send Ben-Gurion a personal warning with Ambassador Eban, who had been called home for consultations. "There had been some speculative gossip that the United States will be very careful what we are doing now because of the great Jewish vote in New York," Eisenhower told me later. He recalled the message for Eban as: "You go out and tell Ben-Gurion if any of his moves are being made because he thinks we will in effect have to support him just because we're going to have an election, you tell him first, that I don't give a damn whether I'm re-elected, and secondly, that we're going to do exactly what we've been saying, [keep the peace] and that's that!" Eisenhower said he told Dulles: "Foster, you must not soften this thing and put it in diplomatic language. This has got to be absolutely my words."

Ironically, Eban's trip home, along with Israel's ambassadors to Britain,

454

France, and Russia, was for an assessment of Great Power attitudes and capabilities preparatory to the final decisions on war against Nasser. The ambassadors were forewarned that major developments should be expected but only Yacov Tsur, the ambassador to France, knew of the war plans in advance.

Eisenhower's warning to the contrary, Ben-Gurion did not believe the US would balk Israel. American pacifism was regarded as a campaign posture. The US seemed to be as strongly anti-Nasser in October as it had been in July. Whatever Eisenhower said, Ben-Gurion saw no reason to doubt that the Jewish vote had as much influence as ever on US policy in the Middle East and that it would be at its peak as the electoral campaign struggled through its anxious last days. Ben-Gurion rejected Eban's shrewd advice to defer until after the election whatever major development was planned. Furthermore, Russia's espousal of Egypt's cause could be expected to polarize Washington into alignment with Israel in the event of hostilities.

The reports of the four ambassadors strengthened the analysis of the international scene that had prompted Ben-Gurion in June to remove Sharett from his cabinet and begin preparations for war. (Sharett was removed still farther on 20 September, when he was sent on a two-month good will tour to the Orient.) Two of the Tripartite Powers, Britain and France, were about to join Israel in violating their own 1950 Tripartite Declaration while the third, the US, seemed to be in no position to honor the pledge alone. Equally important, Russia's de-Stalinization troubles with her East European satellites were getting worse every day.

On 19 October the Poles removed Marshal Rokossovsky, their Russian Defense Minister, and brought Gomulka to the threshold of the premiership after he had spent five years in prison as a Titoist. Khrushchev flew to Warsaw and threatened to crush the dissident movement with Red Army units that were even then moving toward the city. The Poles retorted that they would fight. Gomulka forced a halt to the Russian troop movements the next day and Khrushchev returned to Moscow.

On 22 October, as a consequence of Gomulka's success in Poland, demonstrations broke out in Budapest demanding the restoration to the premiership of Imre Nagy, who had been ousted in 1955 as a rightist-deviationist. Street-fighting broke out the next day and on the 24th the Red Army entered the city with 10,000 troops, eighty tanks, artillery, and armored cars. Jet fighters screamed out of the sky on strafing runs against the rebel barricades. Nagy was named Premier but he was unable to restrain the anti-Russian rage of the Hungarian revolutionaries. Any possibility of Russian intervention in the Middle East was now safely out of the way.

As soon as Eden became a full member of the collusive conspiracy to destroy Nasser, Mollet began to take bolder and wider actions in his war against Algerian nationalism. On the night of 17 October the French captured the Egyptian motor yacht *Athos* sailing under a British skipper off Morocco's Cap des Trois Fourches and found it loaded with enough arms for 1,500 men. The French alleged, probably correctly, that the arms were being smuggled from Alexandria to the Algerian rebels. Egypt offered to submit to an investigation, pointing out that the *Athos* had called at Sicilian and Spanish ports since leaving Alexandria on 5 October. But France wanted to create an atmosphere conducive to war.

Mollet ordered the French fleet to intercept and search any ship in the Mediterranean suspected of carrying arms. This kind of policy on the high seas has historically been a provocation to war. This time it covered the movement of French warships to the Eastern Mediterranean, where they later participated in a naval battle and a shore bombardment in support of Israeli forces.

On 22 October French officials highjacked an airliner in Moroccan service and kidnapped Ben Bella and four other Algerian nationalist leaders who were aboard. When President René Coty of France learned of the incident he exclaimed: "We are dishonored!" The plane, chartered by Morocco and under the protection of King Mohammed V, was carrying the FLN chiefs to a conference in Tunis with Moroccan and Tunisian leaders to consider a future federation of the three nations.

French officials learned of the trip early in the morning before it started, and when the plane was air-borne in the evening over Algeria they ordered its French pilot to circle in a turn too slight to be perceived by the passengers until the expected time of arrival in Tunis and then to land at Algiers. At 9:20 P.M. when the plane touched down at Algiers under a clear moonlit sky the cabin lights were suddenly extinguished, a French security officer aboard ordered all passengers, "Hands up!" and the plane braked to a stop in a ring of guards with submachine guns at the ready.

The Moroccan King, who had preceded the Algerians to Tunis for the conference, felt his sovereignty assailed by the operation and he considered expelling all French officials in Morocco. Alain Savary, the secretary for Moroccan and Tunisian affairs at the Quai d'Orsay, resigned in protest. European shops were sacked by enraged Tunisian mobs. Dozens of Frenchmen were massacred at Meknes in Morocco, some by being burnt alive in their automobiles. The Arab world called a general strike on 28 October, during which Jordanian demonstrators burned the French consulate in Jerusalem. Ben Bella and his colleagues remained in jail until he emerged in 1962 to take the premiership upon Algerian independence.

The day-long drama of the coup against Ben Bella, played out in radio dialogues between Rabat, Paris, Algiers, and the cockpit of the plane, occurred during the first of three days of meetings at Sèvres on the western outskirts of Paris where Selwyn Lloyd, Ben-Gurion, Dayan, Mollet, and Pineau hammered out in secret the details of the collusive war against Nasser.

Dulles had told Eisenhower the day before about a number of "weird schemes" he had heard the British and French were up to, including one to instigate anti-Western riots in Egypt to provide a pretext for invasion. He said he felt he had dissuaded them. But he had not. The scheme that Challe had brought to Eden at Chequers on the 14th and which Eden wholeheartedly accepted on the 16th at his secret conclave with Mollet and their two foreign ministers was much weirder than anything Dulles mentioned.

Eden's mixture of hesitation and ardor for war aroused doubts in Paris and Tel Aviv despite his commitment to collusion. Pineau said he asked Eden and Lloyd ten times in the latter part of October whether they would really see the plan through to the finish. Distrust of Britain was greater on the part of the Israelis. It derived originally from Britain's shifting policies during the Palestine Mandate and from the fundamental, if inept, pro-Arabism of the Foreign Office. The Israeli General Staff had lively suspicions for years that British officers relayed information on Israel to the Jordanians. In the months following nationalization Israeli agents made a game of feeding false information to British intelligence. For Ben-Gurion, Eden's word, given to the French on the 16th, was not good enough. He wanted the British committed directly to Israel as well as to France and he wanted the commitment on paper.

Ben-Gurion also was deeply concerned about the possibility that Egypt's fifty Ilyushin-28 bombers would destroy Israel's cities while Israeli land forces battled across Sinai. Israel had the Mystère IVs for air cover but there was no certainty that they could prevent all the bombers from reaching their targets. The only way to forestall Egyptian bombing raids, he felt, was for long-range bombers to destroy Egypt's Air Force on the ground. Only Britain, of the three colluders, possessed long-range jet bombers, Canberras and Valiants, and bases, on Cyprus and Malta, from which they could hit Egypt.

Ben-Gurion insisted on the Sèvres meetings in order to obtain a British commitment in writing to the collusion plan in general and, in particular, to the use of Canberras and Valiants to destroy Egypt's Air Force on the ground. His requirement fitted perfectly into British war plans, which provided for the destruction of Egypt's Air Force by air attacks as the first stage. Britain's problem was to find a pretext for such uncivilized conduct.

The war plan was Operation Musketeer Revise, which General Stockwell prepared after he returned on 4 September from his visits to the expeditionary force units to find that Eden had "kiboshed" the planned invasion at Alexandria and reverted to the original directive to assault at Port Said. As Stockwell said, "the restoration of international control of the Suez Canal didn't seem to read right if you landed at Alexandria."

Musketeer Revise was planned in three phases:

Phase I: The grounding and destruction of the Egyptian Air Force within thirty-six hours.

Phase II: A round-the-clock air offensive to disrupt Egypt's economy, communications, transport, and Armed Forces combined with a psychological warfare program to destroy Egyptian morale. The aerial operations of Phases I and II were allowed ten to fourteen days originally on the assurance of the air commanders that they would destroy Egypt's will and capacity to resist an invasion force.

Phase III: The domination and occupation of the Canal Zone with such land, sea, and air forces as might be necessary. Phase III was itself broken down into four stages:

Stage 1: A landing with amphibious and air-borne forces which would immediately strike south along the Canal if they met no resistance in Port Said. If the landing was opposed, the assault forces would subdue enemy resistance and a follow-up invasion force would pass through the lines of the first and move down the Canal.

Stage 2: The reinforcement of Port Said, the capture of Abu Suwweir airfield near Ismailiya, and the seizure of the Canal as far south as Ismailiya.

Stage 3: The occupation of the entire Canal.

Stage 4: An attack westward to the Delta and Cairo to complete the overthrow of Nasser and establish a successor regime. Stockwell did not discuss Stage 4 in his account of the Suez operation but Beaufre told me: "In the event, the plan was to turn right to Cairo after securing the Canal. We had no intention of staying in the Canal area." Pineau confirmed Beaufre's statement, adding:

This was not in the Sèvres accord but it was in the military plan and at the political level we all knew of it. It was the British who expected the Egyptian Army to resist and that the fight would have to be carried to the occupation of Cairo. It wasn't planned to stay there long after Nasser was ousted.

The invasion date was deferred from 15 September, the day of the pilots' walkout, to 19 September and then to 26 September. The reservists, who were called up on very short notice in August, turned restless. There were desertions, protests, and arrests among them. Vehicle batteries, after as much as three months waiting aboard invasion ships, began to weaken and corrode.

As the invasion hung fire for want of a pretext, some curious foreshadow-ings materialized. Colonel Richard Meinertzhagen, a British Gentile who be-came an ardent Zionist supporter during tours of Middle East service, recorded in his diary on 4 October that he saw on that day an order issued by the commander of Egypt's Third Infantry Division on 15 February 1956, which said in part: "Every commander must prepare himself and his soldiers... to overpower and destroy Israel in the shortest possible time and with the greatest brutality and bestiality in battle." This document, authentic or not, was the most publicized among the documents which Ambassador Eban produced at the UN on 15 November as having been captured in the Sinai fighting. How Meinertzhagen saw it in London a month before it was captured has not been explained. Israel treated it as showing that Egypt was planning war and added it, *ex post facto,* to the list of justifications for her own invasion of Egypt.

On 6 October the Anglo-French sea, land, and air task force commanders got word to prepare a winter plan for Musketeer Revise, which no longer had even a tentative D-day. The invasion force was to relax from its state of readiness, which had lasted since 8 September, but to be prepared to fight on ten days' notice. Headquarters issued the order for the winter plan on 12 October. It was canceled within three days by Eden and Mollet, who ordered the mili-tary chiefs to get ready to mount Musketeer Revise.

During those three days Challe and Gazier had persuaded Eden to collude with Israel and France in making war on Nasser. Then, the day after discarding the winter plan and ordering Musketeer Revise back to a state of readiness, Eden and Mollet held their famous 16 October meeting in Paris with only Lloyd and Pineau in attendance. The British Cabinet met on 18 October to hear Eden and Lloyd report on their Paris discussions. Their topics included, Eden said in his memoirs, "the growing danger that Israel, under provocation from Egypt, would make some military move." There had been no provoca-tion from Egypt for months; the tension at that time was all on the Jordan border. It was Eden's assurance of British collusion that made Israel's "military move" a certainty.

In Israel that day, the Foreign Ministry began its prewar assessment of the Great Power configuration in consultation with the ambassadors summoned home from the Big Four capitals. Out of New York and Cairo that day came the first disclosures of a new Indian proposal for a Canal settlement, prescrib-ing that the Egyptian Suez Canal Authority "recognize a Users' Association for the purpose of ... consultation and liaison." This was, in effect, the counter proposal which the West insisted must follow Egypt's rejection of the eigh-teen-power proposal presented to Nasser by Menzies. The eighteen-power proposal itself had no valid claim to Egypt's attention, being an unauthorized product of a conference that was itself of challengeable legality. Making a counterproposal to a technically nonexistent proposal, however expedient it was, raised difficult problems of protocol. Letting the Indians speak answered Egypt's problems of protocol. But the counterproposal, coupled with the thickening web of arrangements for more negotiations in Geneva on 29 October, made the Anglo-French problem of launching their war more urgent than ever.

On 19 October, Beaufre disclosed, the invasion commanders were told that their government leaders had decided to launch the operation in ten days. "By 20 October things began to happen rapidly," Stockwell wrote. The final touches were put to Musketeer Revise. The British were to assault Port Said on the west side of the Canal and the French were to assault Port Fuad, the twin city on the east bank. In the occupation of Egyptian territory the British were to have everything west of the Canal as far south as the Sweetwater Canal. The French were to occupy everything east of the Canal and everything west of it south of the Sweetwater.

At this point Ben-Gurion decided he had better get Eden's commitment in writing. He insisted on a cabinet-level meeting to seal the collusion compact with a written and signed accord. He told the French, who informed Eden that Ben-Gurion was coming and arranged for meetings in deep secrecy at the suburban villa of a prominent friend of Bourgès-Maunoury. Bourgès-Maunoury had hidden in the house during his wartime resistance days as a fugitive Nazi-killer and train dynamiter.

Before going to the extraordinary secret meeting in Paris, Ben-Gurion gave the Jordan red herring another flourish. He wrote Eisenhower on 20 October that "the entry of Iraqi forces into Jordan would be the first stage in the disruption of the *status quo.*" This was nearly a week after Eden promised no Iraqi troops would enter Jordan. Reiterating that Iraq had never signed an armistice with Israel, Ben-Gurion said Israel could not remain indifferent to the approach of Iraqi troops and he urged Eisenhower to approach the "appropriate capitals" to prevent it. He made his famous flight to Paris the next night.

Ben-Gurion, Dayan, and Peres landed, after circling in a thick fog, in the early morning on 22 October at Villacoublay, a military and ministerial airport less than ten miles southwest of Paris. Ben-Gurion carried with him, according to his biographer Bar-Zohar, a volume of Procopius, the Palestine-born Byzantine historian who wrote in the sixth century about an independent Jewish realm on the island of Tiran at the mouth of the Gulf of Aqaba. One of Ben-Gurion's chief war aims was to expel the Egyptians from Tiran, which is called Yotvat in Hebrew, and break the Aqaba blockade. Louis Manjin, the

Man Friday of collusion, whose duties were covered by the title of political adviser to the Defense Minister, was waiting for the Israelis. He chauffeured them to the villa in Sèvres, which is some five miles north of Villacoublay and midway on the main road from Paris to Versailles. Ben-Gurion took off the broad hat he had jammed over his springy white tonsure as a perfunctory disguise and promptly went to sleep upstairs to recover from the overnight flight and resist the onset of influenza.

Pineau spent most of the morning at the Quai d'Orsay, was driven home in his official car, and then drove in his own car to the Sèvres villa. The participants in the talks that day included, according to Pineau, the three Israelis, himself and Bourgès-Maunoury and Abel Thomas for France, and Selwyn Lloyd and Patrick Dean for England. Dean was chairman of the Joint Intelligence Committee at the Foreign Office, responsible for military-civilian intelligence liaison. He was later knighted and sent to Washington as ambassador.

The British were more anxious for secrecy than their partners. They had made it a condition of their participation. Lloyd and Dean avoided landing at Villacoublay, where ministries other than Defense might have informants. They probably used Persan-Beaumont near Pontoise, which the French journalist Jean-Raymond Tournoux called "that most discreet of airports . . . reserved for counterespionage missions." Lloyd covered his absence by leaving word at his office that he had a cold and should not be bothered even at home.

Pineau recalls Lloyd as having stayed two or three hours at the first day's talks at Sèvres, which were relatively brief and inconclusive. Lloyd's account of them, as reported by Nutting, is the fullest I have seen. Nutting got it from Lloyd the next morning after going to his office and asking "How's the cold?" Nutting gave this account:

For a moment he hesitated and then, looking like a schoolboy caught in some mischief, he said, "Oh! the cold! Yes. Well, I never had one. I went to see Ben-Gurion outside Paris."

Then before I [Nutting] could stutter out any comment, he added, "And you, my dear Anthony, will no doubt be delighted to hear that it doesn't now look as if the French plan will come off." He explained this by saying that Ben-Gurion had developed grave misgivings. In the first place, he and his military advisers did not like the military plans, which did not provide adequate air cover for the Israelis. He wanted to be assured that we would "take out" the Egyptian Air Force as soon as Israeli forces began their attack. If there were any delay in doing this, Tel Aviv and other Israeli cities might be obliterated by Nasser's Ilyushin bombers. But, since the essence of the Anglo-French role in the plan was to intervene only after Egypt had refused to withdraw her forces to the west bank of the Canal, we could not undertake to destroy Nasser's Air Force simultaneously with the Israeli invasion of Sinai.

There would have to be an interval to allow Egypt time to reject our ultimatum.

Secondly [Lloyd went on], Ben-Gurion was reluctant to become involved in the Suez dispute, although he was keen to take some action to crush once and for all the Egyptian *Fedayeen* threat to Israel and to remove the Egyptian blockade of the Gulf of Aqaba, which prevented Israel bringing supplies to her back door. Finally he was not convinced that Britain would give him real support and was therefore reluctant to become our stalking-horse. France might show willing, but Britain seemed to be too tied up with the Arab world—Jordan and Iraq especially. The French Ministers had pressed him very hard to fall into line, but he had refused to give any undertakings.

The ministerial talks were the most important but there were military and intelligence discussions as well, with small groups sitting now in the dining room, now in one of the ground floor reception rooms, and sometimes in the garden, which had a surrounding wall and dense screens of trees and shrubs. Pineau described the villa as "awfully common" *(d'une banalitè formidable)* and another minister said that, aside from its red tile roof, it was a house of "no color," indistinguishable from a thousand others in the suburb. The owners had turned it over to Bourgès-Maunoury for the meeting, complete with the regular staff of servants, who were accustomed to English and other foreign visitors and who knew how to keep their mouths shut.

Mollet joined the conversations on 23 October. He had been up late dealing with the kidnapping of the five Algerian leaders. Informed of the aerial coup at a farewell dinner for General Alfred Gruenther, the retiring Supreme Commander to NATO forces, he had held a cabinet meeting at 1 A.M. to consider the consequences. No Britons were present at Sèvres on this second day. The talks were chiefly concerned with reconciling Eden's and Ben-Gurion's requirements. Eden needed a seemly delay before bombing Egypt to give verisimilitude to the ultimatum while Ben-Gurion insisted on the destruction of Egypt's bomber force without any delay at all. Ben-Gurion said he had adequate land forces and fighter cover but that he did not dare to begin hostilities while Israel was vulnerable to Egypt's bombers. He insisted on a signed agreement with Britain.

Eden needed little encouragement. Lloyd told Nutting later on the 23d, in the evening, that Eden was "greatly put out" by Ben-Gurion's reluctance and had decided to press the French to try again to get the Israelis to commit themselves. He asked Mollet to send Pineau over that same evening to see him. Ben-Gurion, too, had asked Pineau to go to Eden on his behalf to get the necessary guarantee on the bombing. Ben-Gurion's desire to destroy Nasser by war was older than Eden's but as a matter of tactical psychology he wanted Eden to be the suppliant for cooperation, not himself.

Pineau arrived at London Airport just after 8 P.M. and went straight to Lloyd's official residence at 1 Carlton Gardens for dinner. Eden joined them at 10 P.M. for a little more than an hour. Pineau was on his way back to Paris by midnight with Eden's enthusiastic assurance that Israel could count on Britain's fullest support, to be put in writing on the morrow, if Israel launched the war by attacking toward the Canal. The only additional person present, Pineau told me, was Patrick Dean, who was there throughout the dinner and afterward. There were no other advisers and no official record was made of the talks.

Pineau's visit itself was not secret. *The Times* account noted "the suddenness that has become characteristic of the Suez affair" but its diplomatic correspondent swallowed the cover story—that the visit was prompted by new word from Hammarskjold and that direct negotiations with Egypt were now more likely than ever. Lloyd had told the Commons in the afternoon that Britain was doing her utmost for a peaceful settlement and was awaiting new proposals from Egypt. He questioned whether the new Indian proposals could be considered as Egyptian proposals. "For the British people," he promised, "force will always be the last recourse."

Eden had an audience with the Queen, as he often did on Tuesday evenings, before he went to join Pineau, Lloyd, and Dean. He is said to have told her about the collusive war plans and to have found her wholeheartedly opposed to them for fear that the operation would wreck the Commonwealth.

Pineau gave me the following account of his talk that night with Eden: Eden was chiefly concerned about the impact of the operation on Jordan and Iraq, where there could be extremely adverse reactions to destroying Egypt's air force with British bombers at the outset of Israeli-Egyptian hostilities. He talked about the general Arab reaction to the Canal dispute and questioned Pineau closely about Israel's land forces and equipment. Eden said he did not want Israel to beat Egypt singlehanded and he did not want Egypt beaten too badly. Pineau assumed that this was to preserve some balance between Egypt and Iraq after Nasser was overthrown in favor of a pro-British successor.

The ultimatums to Egypt and Israel, based on intervening to protect the Canal, were Eden's contribution to the collusion plan, Pineau said. Eden had put the idea forward at the 16 October meeting. At the 23 October meeting Pineau suggested letting Israel cross the Canal but Eden adamantly refused. Eden gave the necessary assurances on protecting Israel against Egypt's bombers. He arranged to send Dean to Sèvres the next day to participate in working out the ultimatums and drafting the written accord on collusion. Dean was empowered to sign the latter on behalf of the British Government.

Pineau spent the whole of 24 October at Sèvres. He and Ben-Gurion deliberated lengthily with Dean about how to word the ultimatum so as to avoid antagonizing Arab opinion in countries ruled by Britain's friends. Ben-Gurion was indifferent on this point, as were the French, but he accepted British requirements in return for the destruction of Egypt's air force by Britain's bombers. Ben-Gurion promised to accept the ultimatum and to refrain from crossing the Canal. He also promised not to attack Jordan. Pineau said the ultimatum was worked out in its final form at this meeting and issued unchanged six days later on 30 October. The text of the version issued to Egypt follows, with words addressed to Egypt alone distinguished by italics and the variants for the version issued to Israel in square brackets:

The Governments of the United Kingdom and France have taken note of the outbreak of hostilities between Israel and Egypt. This event threatens to disrupt the freedom of navigation through the Suez Canal, on which the economic life of many nations depends. The Governments of the United Kingdom and France are resolved to do all in their power to bring about the early cessation of hostilities and to safeguard the free passage of the Canal. They accordingly request the Government of *Egypt* [Israel]:

(a) to stop all warlike action on land, sea and air forthwith;

(b) to withdraw all *Egyptian* [Israel] military forces to a distance of ten miles *from* [east of] the Canal; *and*

(c) in order to guarantee freedom of transit through the Canal by the ships of all nations and in order to separate the belligerents, to accept the temporary occupation by the Anglo-French forces of key positions at Port Said, Ismailiya and Suez.

[A communication has been addressed to the Government of Egypt requesting them to cease hostilities and to withdraw their forces from the neighborhood of the Canal, and to accept the temporary occupation by Anglo-French forces of key positions at Port Said, Ismailiya and Suez.]

The United Kingdom and French Government request an answer to this communication within twelve hours. If at the expiration of that time one or both Governments have not undertaken to comply with the above requirements, United Kingdom and French forces will intervene in whatever strength may be necessary to secure compliance.

A similar communication has been sent to the Government of Israel.

In the event, Israel delayed accepting the ultimatum until after Cairo broadcast Nasser's rejection. Presumably the colluders at Sèvres agreed to follow this chronology to preclude the remote but possible embarrassment of having Egypt accept the ultimatum if Israel did so first. Requirement (c) in Egypt's version, the "temporary occupation" of the Canal zone, was made independent of either acceptance or rejection, which lent a certain transparency to the ultimatum.

In addition to the ultimatums, the colluders had to draft and sign the accord prescribing the role of each partner in the conspiracy. This was the "piece of paper" Ben-Gurion had come for and without which he would not act, for fear of being let down by the British. The Sèvres accord, Pineau told me, ran to three pages. At Eden's insistence, one of its provisions was that it was never to be made public. The three copies, one each for Eden, Mollet, and Ben-Gurion, were not to go into state archives that would one day be accessible to historians. Presumably Eden has destroyed his copy. Ben-Gurion's is among his personal papers, according to several of his aides and collaborators who told me they had seen it. Pineau indicated that the French copy, too, had been preserved but he told me sharply that I would not be able to see it.

The contents of the Sèvres accord were clearly manifested in the events of its implementation, according to Pineau and others who have seen it. The text is unlikely to be made public in Eden's lifetime. The accord specified the military and political timetables for the collusive invasion, which Israel was to initiate at dusk on 29 October. Israel was to create the illusion of an immediate threat to the Canal by a paratroop drop far in advance of the main force, at Mitla Pass, only twenty miles east of Suez and one hundred miles west of the Israeli border, where four hundred stout-hearted fighting men might hope to hold out until the main force reached them. When Britain and France feigned to learn of this "threat to the Suez Canal," after allowing it time to develop, they were to issue the ultimatum on the afternoon of the 30th. When Egypt rejected it, they would unleash Operation Musketeer Revise at dawn on the 31st by destroying Egypt's air force.

Ben-Gurion was assured of three additional squadrons of French Air Force fighters and pilots—forty-five planes—in addition to the sixty Mystère IVs newly incorporated into Israel's Air Force. He agreed, therefore, to let Britain defer the pulverization of Egypt's air force until Nasser rejected the ultimatum. Nasser, the colluders correctly assumed, was sure to find it politically imperative to issue a prompt rejection; in the brief interval before he did so the combined French and Israeli jet-fighter cover would provide a formidable defense against any Egyptian bombers that ventured to attack. Furthermore, as Dayan wrote in his diary the next day, "in the early phases we can give our operation the character of a reprisal action, and . . . the Egyptians are not likely to recognize it as the opening of a comprehensive campaign, and will not rush to bomb civilian targets in Israel."

The Israeli main force, striking along four lines of advance, would draw the Egyptian Army back into Sinai as the Anglo-French invasion force sailed from Malta to Port Said. From Port Said the Anglo-French force would lunge down the Canal and cut off the Sinai Peninsula with the Egyptian Army trapped in it. The Egyptian Army would then be destroyed between the Israeli hammer and the Anglo-French anvil.

Ben-Gurion promised that the Israelis, in compliance with the ultimatum, would stop ten miles short of the Canal. Britain and France would veto any attempt by the Security Council to act against Israel. While avoiding as much as possible any appearance of collaborating with Israel, Britain promised to help her win an advantageous peace. One prize Ben-Gurion hoped to keep, Pineau said, was the Sinai Peninsula.

France promised, in addition to air cover for Israel's cities and fighting men, to protect Israel's coast and shipping from Egyptian warships and submarines and to have the cruiser *Georges Leygues* soften up Egyptian defenses within reach of her guns. France also promised to parachute antitank guns, ammunition, water, and supplies to the men at Mitla Pass and other units that might need such help.

One item that was not covered in the accord, Pineau said, was any prohibition against a separate peace with Egypt. As a result, Israel accepted a cease-fire when she had eliminated all Egyptian resistance in Sinai two days before the scheduled Anglo-French invasion. At the urgent and secret insistence of Britain and France she reneged on the cease-fire by attaching conditions to it, although she had ceased firing because there was nothing more to shoot at.

The Sèvres accord was signed in triplicate on the evening of October 24th by Ben-Gurion, Pineau, and Dean in that order, as protocol required. Dean flew back to London to report to Eden and Lloyd. Ben-Gurion slept into the night at the now-historic but still anonymous villa and flew back to Israel with Dayan and Peres early on the 25th. Eden and his Cabinet had considered the reports from Sèvres on the 24th but they were unable to make their final decision until the Sèvres accord was complete and Ben-Gurion was firmly committed to start the war. The Cabinet meeting was adjourned, therefore, to the 25th.

Other events during the Sèvres talks fortuitously helped set the stage for Israel's attack. On 21 October, as the colluders prepared to converge at Sèvres, two Israeli military vehicles went up on Egyptian mines in the al-Auja demilitarized zone. Three soldiers were killed and twenty-seven wounded. The Israelis were in violation of the Armistice Agreement by being in the zone but they cited these casualties, making them appear as the result of many incidents, in their first communiqué justifying the attack on Egypt. Israeli newspapers, unaware that Ben-Gurion would exaggerate the incident as a pretext, called it "the end of the comparative lull at the Israel-Egyptian frontier." In the only other recent incident Israelis killed two Tarabin bedouin and captured two others on 14 October near Sde Boker. The four bedouin were on an intelligence mission for the Egyptians with orders not to fire on Israelis but to observe traffic in the area and report back to Abu Aoueigila. Ben-Gurion made this too look like a *Fedayeen* raid rather than a sign of Egyptian anxiety over Israel's intentions.

The Egyptian-Jordanian-Syrian defense agreement, the "ring of steel" which Israel listed with the *Fedayeen* "nests" as among its major war objectives, was not announced until the night of 24 October, after the Sèvres accord had, its signers hoped, sealed Nasser's fate. The Arab treaty, having been provoked by Israel's raids on Jordan, was conveniently added to Israel's pretexts for war. It fitted well with the use of Jordan as a red herring to draw attention away from Egypt.

In Hungary on the day the Sèvres accord was signed, Russian troops moved into Budapest to crush the burgeoning revolution. In Poland, Gomulka announced that the Russian troops in that country were returning to their barracks.

There was a poignant episode of Anglo-Egyptian camaraderie at Alamein the day before the Sèvres meetings. Egyptian buglers sounded Last Post for the British dead at the battlefield, where surviving veterans and officers held a commemoration on the fourteenth anniversary of the decisive World War II battle. Major General Ahmed Salem attended as Nasser's personal representative.

The Sèvres accord and the ultimatum were communicated to Eden by the morning of the 25th. The Cabinet resumed its session and gave its final approval that afternoon. Eden's account strikes a crafty balance between accuracy and vagueness. He wrote:

Ministers had already considered at several meetings the ways in which the situation might develop. These had also been canvassed with the French. On October 25 the Cabinet discussed the specific possibility of conflict between Israel and Egypt and decided in principle how it would react if this occurred. The Governments of France and the United Kingdom should, it considered, at once call on both parties to stop hostilities and withdraw their forces to a distance from either bank of the canal. If one or both failed to comply within a definite period, then British and French forces would intervene as a temporary measure to separate the combatants. To ensure this being effective, they would have to occupy key positions at Port Said, Ismailiya and Suez. Our purpose was to safeguard free passage through the Canal . . . To realize this we would put into operation the plan for occupation of the Suez Canal zone, prepared by the joint Anglo-French military staff . . . The same plan that had been intended to deal with Nasser's seizure of the Canal fitted equally well with our new objective.

Eden admitted in his memoirs that he had "for some time" been conducting aerial reconnaissance over Egypt by high-flying Canberras, which he believed had been unperceived because the Egyptians made no attempt to intercept them. The reconnaissance could have provided no grounds for the Cabinet to discuss "the specific possibility of conflict between Israel and Egypt" because Egypt had withdrawn most of her Sinai garrison west of the Canal and Israel had not yet begun to mobilize. Colonel Amin Hilmy, who handled liaison with the British, said the British carried out reconnaissance under privileges to fly over Egyptian territory granted in the 1954 evacuation agreement. The British requested permission for planes shuttling between Libya, Cyprus, and Jordan to overfly Egypt. Until the war, Hilmy said, he had to comply.

Immediately after the Cabinet meeting, Nutting reported, Lloyd, "grim-faced and tormented with doubts," gave him a full description of the Sèvres collusion plan as endorsed by the Cabinet. He included a complete outline of the Israeli invasion plan.

The Israelis expected to complete the occupation of Sinai within seven to ten days by means of a four-pronged attack. Three prongs, including a parachute drop near Suez itself, were to concentrate on seizing the Canal Zone between Suez and Ismailiya and sealing off the Gaza Strip, while the fourth prong plunged southwards to seize Sharm al-Sheikh, the Egyptian fortified position commanding the Tiran Straits at the entrance to the Gulf of Aqaba. These plans would give time for the British and French forces to move from their bases in Malta to the seizure of Port Said . . .

Eden said there were "no marked divergencies" in the Cabinet meetings on Suez. The several Cabinet members I have interviewed confirm this and deny the recurrent reports of dissenting factions. Eden attributed the consensus to "our having talked over the situation fully in its earliest phases. . . . Every senior member of the Government realized this and remembered the mood in which we had taken our first decisions. The others were their consequence."

Nutting wrote that he felt sick to the pit of his stomach after hearing Lloyd describe the Cabinet's decision to collude. He repeated his determination to resign if he failed to prevent "this crazy maneuver." Plunged into a feeling of helpless isolation and "torn between loyalty to principle and loyalty to friends," Nutting hurried across to the House of Commons to unburden his woes to Monckton. Monckton told him that he was right to resign unless he were willing to defend Eden's policy in the House of Commons and at the UN. On his way back to the Foreign Office, Nutting wrote, he was seized with a wild notion to tell the whole story to the US ambassador in order to bring

Eisenhower full tilt against the conspiracy. He suppressed the notion as "criminal folly" but he wrote later that he wished he had carried it through.

The final operational order for Musketeer Revise was issued to the Anglo-French commanders on 24 October as the collusion accord was completed. Ben-Gurion told Dayan to go ahead with Operation Kadesh as revised to meet the collusion requirements. Dayan issued his directive for the new Kadesh operational order to the senior officers of his Operations Branch at a meeting at 1:45 P.M. on 25 October, shortly after he and Ben-Gurion and Peres returned to Tel Aviv from Villacoublay. Ben-Gurion ordered the mobilization of 100,-000 reserves, about half the theoretical maximum. Call-up procedures maintained secrecy until the mobilization became physically obvious two days later as a result of the disappearance of waiters, taxi drivers, clerks, etc., and the appearance of military units and equipment in bivouac or moving on the roads.

Dayan described in his diary the changes made in Kadesh to suit collusion. "The first occurs in the paragraph on aims," he wrote. "Stress is now placed on the creation of a threat to the Suez Canal, and only after that come the basic purposes of the campaign—capture of the Straits of Tiran and defeat of the Egyptian forces." The territorial objective was no longer the east bank of the Canal but a "line parallel to, and at a distance of not less than fifteen kilometers [nine and one-half miles] east of, the Suez Canal." The first task of the Israeli Air Force was no longer the destruction of Egypt's Air Force on the ground in a surprise attack but "defense of Israel skies" and support of ground action. On the ground, instead of a broad advance across northern Sinai and into Gaza, the first phrase was limited to the drop of a paratroop battalion at Mitla Pass and an overland dash by the remainder of the 202nd Paratroop Brigade to link up with the battalion at Mitla.

By thus limiting the opening phase of ground and air action, Dayan hoped to persuade the Egyptian command that it was no more than an unusually daring reprisal raid and that the reinforcements rushing across the lightly defended desert track to Mitla Pass were intended to enable the presumed raiders to withdraw. He believed the Egyptians would limit their reaction to sending forces against the Israeli incursion but that they would not try to bomb Israel as they would do if they realized it was a full-scale war.

With the British and French committed to join the hostilities in thirty-six hours, Dayan wrote, "From the operational point of view we had to distinguish between the period up to the start of the Anglo-French action and the period after." When Britain and France launched their attack, he predicted, the Egyptian Air Force would cease activity against Israeli forces, Egyptian troops would be ordered to withdraw from Sinai, and the Israelis could "do after the

Anglo-French assault what we need not try to do before," namely launch their broad sweep of conquest across the peninsula.

Dayan hedged suspiciously against the possibility that even after Israel launched the war the British and French might renege on their part of the contract. The Air Force was to stand ready for instant attacks on Egyptian airfields, if need be. "If things go wrong and for some reason or other we have to halt the campaign," he wrote, "we shall evacuate our unit at Mitla . . . and claim that this was only a reprisal action." Dayan was hampered in briefing his commanders by Ben-Gurion's promise of secrecy to Eden. "Not all the information known to me was I able to transmit," Dayan wrote, "and not all I transmitted was I able to explain."

When someone asked if Israel intended to keep Sinai, Dayan wrote, "all I could say was that in any event our first job was to capture the whole of Sinai so that if we had to retire, we would have somewhere to retire from."

The red herring of Jordan was again dragged about on 26 October. "The Intelligence Branch is spreading the rumor that the Iraqi Army has entered Jordan," Dayan wrote. "This is part of the deception plan to produce the impression that our activity is aimed at Jordan and Iraq. In Operations they claim that Intelligence is so successful that they have begun to believe their own rumors." Most Israelis believed them, including the troops. So did General Burns. The units assigned to guard the eastern and northern frontiers moved up openly while the units sent south, down desert roads screened and beautified by triple rows of eucalyptus trees, moved later and more surreptitiously. Paris heightened the confusion with an official announcement: "We have learned that the King of Jordan has just been assassinated." Israel quickly broadcast the hoax as news. Radio Cairo replied with a reassuring interview with King Hussein, who denied that he was dead.

The assassination rumor was a major topic at the National Security Council meeting at the White House that morning. The question of Egypt does not seem to have come up. Hungary, where Premier Nagy was pleading with his rebel supporters to lay down their arms, was the most compelling topic for the President and his advisers.

The promised three squadrons of French jet fighters swept out of the setting sun over the Mediterranean that evening and landed at Lydda and Hatzor. The planes and their forty-five French pilots under the command of Brigadier General Maurice Perdrizet were to protect Israel from Egyptian bombers until the British bombers joined the battle. There were two squadrons of Mystère IVs and one of F-84 Sabrejets. An equally valuable shipment, 200 six-wheeled military trucks with direct drive on every wheel, arrived from

France the next day, 27 October, in renamed and repainted ships. Half were assigned to the 202nd Paratroop Brigade for its dash across Sinai to link up with its battalion dropped at Mitla Pass; half were assigned to the 9th Infantry Brigade for its march down the Gulf of Aqaba. "After the poor crop of Israeli vehicles mobilized from civilian owners," Dayan wrote, "I do not know what we would have done if these French trucks had not arrived."

The Israelis were not alone in worrying about the delays on Anglo-French action imposed by Eden's need for the "police action" fiction, which he hoped would preserve his Arab and American alliances while he destroyed Nasser. Stockwell and Beaufre were particularly worried about the ten-day lag—four days to load the ships in Malta and six days sailing time to Egypt—between the signal to launch the operation and the assault itself. Beaufre in particular feared that the world would not put up with ten days of bombing and would act to prevent the invasion. But Eden had given strict orders that no move to load or sail the invasion fleet be made before the expiry of the ultimatum.

Stockwell decided on a ruse of his own after a meeting with Beaufre on the 26th. Beaufre intimated much more about collusion than Stockwell officially knew. Impressed by Beaufre's sense of urgency, Stockwell flew on to Malta that evening and decided with Admiral Sir Guy Grantham to begin loading the next day. They would explain if asked that it was merely a naval and amphibious loading and communications exercise previously planned and named Exercise Boathook. Admiral Power agreed to sail with his three aircraft carriers, the *Albion*, *Bulwark*, and *Ark Royal*, to his operational area the next morning. The French expeditionary force, handicapped by at least two additional days sailing time from Algiers, was already embarking.

That same day Bourgès-Maunoury sent Abel Thomas to London to urge Eden to advance the sailing date of the invasion fleet at Malta, with no success. Thomas took the opportunity to call on Lloyd on behalf of the Israelis and press their claim to keep Sinai after they had conquered it, but this effort too was inconclusive.

By this time Washington realized that it had been cut off from the usual exchange of classified information from its two European allies. For nearly two weeks the routine flow of information given to military attachés, Foreign Service men, CIA liaison men, etc., had been curiously repetitious. The "clam-up," as Dillon called it, began when Challe visited Eden at Chequers on 14 October. It applied at all diplomatic levels. The retiring British ambassador, Sir Roger Makins, left Washington on 11 October and his successor, Sir Harold Caccia, did not arrive in Washington until 8 November, having taken the decision, strange under the circumstances, to travel by sea. Britain kept all her ambassadors everywhere in ignorance of her intentions and all of them were markedly embarrassed by the ultimatum. France did similarly but made some exceptions, notably Ambassador Gilbert in Israel.

"We felt the US did not want to be diplomatically informed or kept abreast of what we were doing," Pineau told me. "But we assumed that the secret services were in contact, especially the British and American. In any case, there were definite contacts with American admirals to keep the Sixth Fleet from running afoul of our movements." The contacts with the Sixth Fleet came later, after Pineau took it upon himself on 1 November to tell Dillon all about collusion.

The CIA had picked up a good deal of information. Its chief, Allen Dulles, told me afterward that its accurate forecasts of the collusive war were based largely on intelligence reports of the troops and equipment arriving in Cyprus, particularly the aircraft, which he said could have no other purpose than to attack. By 27 October it was common knowledge in CIA circles that Israel's mobilization was for war against Egypt. Eisenhower's warnings to Eden and Ben-Gurion were based on CIA reports. Eden's, Lloyd's and Ben-Gurion's evasions and denials placed Eisenhower in a delicate dilemma; either call his allies liars and conspirators before their actions revealed them to be so or defer effective counteraction until after they had showed their hands. Effective counteraction beforehand would have prevented proof of its own justification.

The only break in the clam-up, aside from what the CIA picked up, came when Jacques Chaban-Delmas, a Minister of State in Mollet's Cabinet, called on Dillon on 19 October. The Chaban-Delmas family seat is in Bordeaux where the Dillons have owned the superb Château Haut-Brion vineyards for three generations. The two men have been friends and mutual admirers for years. Chaban-Delmas told Dillon privately and informally that Britain and France were negotiating with Israel for "joint action" against Nasser and that they would not wait much longer. Dillon urged delay until after the Presidential election. Chaban-Delmas replied that the operation was scheduled immediately after the election. Dillon sent a detailed report of the talk, which he believes is now in the CIA files.

Ironically, Dillon believed that Chaban-Delmas was fully informed and that he knew more than he was telling. In fact, only Mollet, Pineau, and Bourgès-Maunoury among the Cabinet members were included in the collusion secret. Chaban-Delmas told me he knew of the Israeli solicitations but had no other solid information at the time, although he was convinced that a military operation was afoot. But he was aware of Dillon's uneasiness over the "clam-up" and he wanted to assure him that France was far from wanting to hurt Eisenhower during the election campaign.

Ben-Gurion was equally circumspect with his Cabinet colleagues. Only he himself, as Premier and Defense Minister, and Foreign Minister Golda Meir knew in advance of the collusion agreement and Operation Kadesh. On 27 October Ben-Gurion summoned the other ministers in his coalition Cabinet, one party at a time, and obtained the assent of all but two to the operation. On the 28th he assembled the whole Cabinet for further discussion, at which the two dissenters agreed to go along with the majority. Ben-Gurion distinguished between the Sinai Peninsula and what he called "the territory of Egypt proper" at these meetings. He told the Cabinet, "I do not know what will be the fate of Sinai" if Israel succeeded in conquering it. He avoided disclosing the Sèvres agreement or the Anglo-French role. Ben-Gurion held his meetings in his bedroom in Tel Aviv, where he was confined with influenza and a fever of 103 degrees. On the 29th, hours before the invasion began, he briefed the opposition parties except for the Communists.

Of the three colluding Governments, only the British Cabinet was kept informed of its leader's plans as they evolved. Paradoxically, the permanent and inflexible secrecy of collusion was desired by Eden alone of the three conspirators.

On the 27th, the invasion force in Malta pressed forward with the immensely complicated task of loading war materiel into transports in a manner that would allow each item to be unloaded and delivered to its designated unit in the anticipated order of need. When the loading continued unabated on Sunday, the 28th, and next-of-kin notification blanks were issued to certain officers, word began to spread that this was not "Exercise Boathook" but the real thing.

Dayan, with Ben-Gurion's agreement, ordered the removal of the UN military observers from al-Auja. "Better that they complain of being ordered to move," he wrote, "than that they should report the concentration of our forces preparing for action." But the mobilization could no longer be concealed.

Shortly after noon in Washington on the 27th (7 P.M. in Tel Aviv) Eisenhower cabled Ben-Gurion his concern over the mobilization and added, in ominous diplomatic phraseology, "I renew the plea ... that there be no forcible initiative on the part of your Government which would endanger the peace and the growing friendship between our two countries."

In Hungary, Premier Imre Nagy announced the formation of a new Government including non-Communist World War II leaders. Budapest radio announced that the revolution was over and Dulles promised in a campaign speech in Dallas to help Hungary rebuild. But the rebels kept on fighting, rejecting Nagy's restraints and forcing him toward extreme positions vis-à-vis Russia, which Gomulka and the Poles shrewdly avoided.

On the 28th, Sunday, Egypt nearly lost her Commander-in-chief, Major-General Amer, who was Nasser's closest friend. He had gone to Damascus after concluding the joint command agreement in Amman with Syria and Jordan. His party was scheduled to return in two transport planes. As Nasser described it, Amer ordered the plane carrying his aides to return to Cairo ahead of his own while he tarried in Damascus for an additional conference with the Syrians. "And this plane was shot down," Nasser said. "On that day it was easy to shoot down the plane because, as a result of the arrest of Ben Bella, there were demonstrations in all the Arab countries, and strikes. And there was a strike at the aerodromes, too. So there were no civil aeroplanes in the air at all. The only aeroplanes were General Amer's." Amer's own plane returned in the evening, unaware that the plane carrying his aides, presumably mistaken for his own, had gone down over the Mediterranean.

The Egyptians assume that French or British fighters from Cyprus destroyed the plane. The area was under surveillance by high-flying Canberras, which must have observed the flight and could easily have directed fighters to attack it. Amer's trip was not secret. The Egyptians doubt that Israelis shot down the plane.

Eisenhower, in mounting alarm over Israel's continued mobilization, cabled Ben-Gurion again, warning him to "do nothing which would endanger the peace." He told Ben-Gurion he had invoked the Tripartite Declaration in urging Britain and France "to exert all possible efforts to ameliorate the situation." Having addressed himself, wittingly or unwittingly, to the three partners in collusion, Eisenhower also cabled the Arab leaders to refrain from any action would could lead to hostilities. The State Department advised all Americans whose presence in the Middle East was not essential to leave the region.

A heavy increase in coded radio traffic between Paris and Tel Aviv added to Washington's alarm and suspicion. Ben-Gurion's Cabinet finally acknowledged the mobilization that Sunday night, calling it a "precautionary measure" and alleging that it was prompted by a variety of factors including: a renewal of *Fedayeen* raids, the Egypt-Syria-Jordan alliance, Jordanian threats to destroy Israel, and the marshaling of Iraqi forces on Jordan's border. Dayan described the Cabinet statement as "calculated to draw attention to the Jordan border as the source of tension and the likely scene of military conflict." The Red Mogen David (similar to the Red Cross) issued a call for blood donors "just in case."

In London, Lloyd dined with and lied to Ambassador Aldrich. On cabled instructions from Dulles, Aldrich asked him several times if he did not think Israel might be intending to attack Egypt, adding that Washington had received indications of this. Lloyd repeatedly said he had no knowledge of any such possibility and insisted that Britain was much more concerned over a possible attack on Jordan. Since an ambassador should not treat a foreign secretary as a liar, even when he knows he has lied, Aldrich punctiliously avoided candid comments on the matter. But in all his future dealings with Lloyd he made sure that Walworth Barbour, then US Minister in London, was present as he was at dinner that night.

Until a few days before the war the British continued to draw war materiel from the stores they maintained in the Canal zone bases by right of the 1954 evacuation agreement, Article 9 of which said: "The United Kingdom is accorded the right to move any British equipment into or out of the base at its discretion." The British always cited the article in ordering such items as concertina barbed wire, aerial bombs, and ammunition of all calibers from pistols to tank cannon. Colonel Amin Hilmy, chief of liaison with the British on the staff of Egypt's Eastern Command, transported the war goods in Egyptian trains and trucks to Port Said, where British ships bound for Malta and Cyprus loaded it aboard. Hilmy protested to the Foreign Ministry that the materiel was obviously being withdrawn for use against Egypt and he asked to be allowed to delay the shipments if he could not refuse them. "The Foreign Ministry always said, No, don't give them any pretext," Hilmy told me. "If they attack us, we will seize what is left in the base, but until then be scrupulous about complying with the agreement." Hilmy said he snorted in reply that the first paragraph of the agreement said it was for "firm friendship." But he obeyed.

Monday, 29 October 1956, was the seventy-eighth anniversary of the signing in Constantinople of the Convention Respecting the Free Navigation of the Suez Maritime Canal. It was an ill-omened day for two of the Convention signatories to launch a third partner in collusion on a war falsely aimed at protecting the Canal. The brief war and its equally brief rerun eleven years later created the only major blockages in the Canal's history.

At Malta British destroyers moved out of Sliema Creek to take up stations ahead of the invasion fleet. A thousand miles to the east three French destroyers, *Kersaint, Bouvet,* and *Surcouf,* began patrolling the sea approaches to Tel Aviv and Haifa.

As his troops made their final preparations for attack, Dayan committed to his diary some blunt thoughts about the US as well as his suspicions of the collusion arrangement. "The United States is adamantly opposed to any military action on the part of Israel, yet she does not—perhaps she cannot—prevent anti-Israel action on the part of the Arabs," he wrote, adding that Washington refused to arm Israel and thus exposed her to Arab aggression with Russian arms. He blamed the "sterility" of US policy on what he called the US habit of seeking to influence events in the Middle East by putting one-sided pressure on Israel. As for Eisenhower's two warnings, he wrote, he was struck by their "hollowness." They show, he added, that Eisenhower "thinks the imminent conflict is likely to erupt between Israel and Jordan and that Britain and France will cooperate with him in preventing this. How uninformed he is of the situation! In all its aspects, the reality is the reverse of his assumptions."

As for collusion, Dayan wrote: "Even now I am not certain that we shall not have to halt the action before its completion."

The first victims of the war were forty-seven civilians, men, women, and children of the Palestinian village of Kafr Kassem, which crowns a stony hill in Israel close to the then Jordanian armistice line east of Tel Aviv. Its 2,000 Palestinian Arab inhabitants were well known for their cooperation with the Israeli authorities. At 4:30 P.M. the Israeli Border Police told the village *mukhtar* (headman) that a curfew had been imposed from 5 P.M. until 6 A.M. and that anyone found out of doors after five would be shot. The *mukhtar* protested that it would be impossible to warn villagers in the fields or working in nearby towns. After a brief argument the police set up a roadblock on the only road into the village.

For an hour, between 5 and 6 o'clock, the police stopped men, women, and children returning home on bicycles, carts, automobiles, and trucks, made them dismount, and machine-gunned them in batches, occasionally conferring by radio with higher authorities. A 16-year-old girl was the only survivor of a truck carrying sixteen olive pickers, all but two of them women, one of whom was eight months pregnant. By 6 o'clock, sixty bodies lay in the road, thirteen of whom survived by feigning death as the police moved about finishing off those who stirred. The killing ended then with an order from battalion headquarters to shoot only persons who tried to escape or who forcibly rejected the curfew.

News of the massacre was suppressed by the Israeli censors for six weeks. On 12 December Ben-Gurion stated the facts in the Knesset and expressed the shock and regret felt by many Israelis over the senseless atrocity. Trials of the officers and men involved in the massacre, including a lieutenant, a major, and a lieutenant-colonel, continued for more than two years. The maximum penalty in Israel is life imprisonment (17 years), there being no death penalty. This sentence was imposed on the major.

There was speculation that the killings were intended to spur a stampede of more Arabs into exile in the event of hostilities with Jordan. General Burns said the case was "very sad proof . . . that the spirit that inspired the notorious Deir Yasseen massacre in 1948 is not dead among some of the Israeli armed forces." It may also have reflected what Dayan described as the feeling among the senior officers that the war was "an opportunity to settle accounts . . . when at last there can be release for the pent-up bitterness they have harbored for the eight years . . . of Arab threats to destroy Israel."

Part

III

WAR

(EVENING OF 29 OCTOBER 1956 TO 2 A.M.,
CAIRO TIME, 7 NOVEMBER 1956)

CHAPTER
15

War in the Sinai

(EVENING, 29 OCTOBER 1956 TO EVENING,
31 OCTOBER 1956)

Peace is the dream of the wise, war is the history of man.

(Arab proverb)

Love of their country, and more especially of *home*, is another predominant characteristic of the modern Egyptians. In general, they have a great dread of quitting their native land. ... Though very submissive to their governors, the fellaheen of Egypt are not deficient in courage when excited by feuds among each other; and they become excellent soldiers.

(EDWARD WILLIAM LANE, *Modern Egyptians*, 1835)

ASSER WAS watching over a birthday party for his five-year-old son, Abdul Hameed, when the first Israeli Army communiqué of the war reached him. General Amer, Egypt's Commander-in-chief and Nasser's closest friend, was there. Nasser's fifth child, still too young to join the party, was named for Amer. It was a small party and the children had been allowed to stay up late for it. "We were around the table with the children and Abdul Hameed was just preparing himself to blow out the candles," Nasser recalled. "And then I received the paper telling me that Israel had declared so and so and so and so."

The report concerned Israel's 9 P.M. announcement:

Units of the Israel Defense Forces have penetrated and attacked *Fedayeen* bases in the Kuntilla and Ras al-Naqb area, and have taken up positions to the west of the Nakhl road junction on the approaches to the Suez Canal. This operation was necessitated by the continuous Egyptian military attacks on citizens and on Israel land and sea communications, the purpose of which was to cause destruction and to deprive the people of Israel of the possibility of a peaceful existence.

News of the parachute drop near the eastern end of Mitla Pass, which began more than four hours earlier, had still not reached Nasser. The first report of the invasion recorded in the Egyptian command's message logs was at 7 P.M., two hours late, from an observation post code-named Hyena six miles north of Kuntilla. "Fifty lorries in Wadi Jirafi. Airplane engines heard overhead." Almost simultaneously Captain Wagdy Sharaf of the Frontier Force station at Nakhl reported by wireless: "Automatic fire opened from Mitla Pass on ration vehicle from Suez. Car accelerated and evaded fire. Road constructors report sixteen planes dropped about four hundred parachutists east of Mitla Pass. In four groups, each group four planes. About sixty kilometers west of Nakhl." Wagdy thought the firing was by smugglers. The road constructors' report was simply baffling to him.

By the time Nasser and Amer reached General Headquarters a few blocks from his house additional messages had come. One, from the Frontier Corps supply post at Shatt on the east bank of the Canal opposite Suez, reported that a second car, carrying personnel back from leave to Nakhl, had been forced to return to Suez by gunfire, which was now attributed to Israelis and not smugglers. Another contained an eyewitness account by a road construction worker to the effect that sixteen big planes and two small ones had dropped 800 parachutes (half of them presumably weapons and supplies containers) at Sudr al-Heitan, the slope that rises from the east toward the Mitla defiles.

Nasser and Amer presided at a General Staff appraisal of the situation as it

481

developed from those first reports of action at two widely separated localities in the midst of an uninhabited wasteland. "We made an appreciation that night," Nasser told me afterward. "We discussed the whole question and we came to the conclusion that it is the British plan to use Israel against us while they mobilize their troops in front of our country in Cyprus in order to let us have a cheap defeat by the Israelis alone."

"We realized immediately that we were facing a real military attack and that it was not merely one of those incidents which occurred often on the borders," Nasser said a month after the war. He reasoned that no attack in the empty part of the Sinai could be a reprisal raid because there were no Egyptian units there whose destruction would serve the purpose of a retaliation. Individual infantry and armored units were ordered eastward at once but not until 4:50 A.M. did the Egyptian command broadcast a general alert ordering all officers and men to report immediately to their units.

What Nasser was unable to believe was that Britain would hazard all her remaining interests in the Arab world by conniving with Israel. But he believed that the Anglo-French invasion force, having drawn the bulk of Egypt's army to the Delta and Canal, would now seek by its continued menace to hold Egypt's army west of the Canal while Israel beat the thinned-out forces in Gaza and the Sinai. He assumed that Britain hoped the defeat would break the revolution's prestige in Egypt and throughout the Arab world.

Nasser saw support for his forecast of British actions when he was informed that the Foreign Office spokesman in London had announced that Britain would not seek to exploit the opportunity offered by the outbreak of fighting in the Sinai.

Shortly after midnight the Egyptian military attaché in Amman reported:

Jordanian Undersecretary for Foreign Affairs has been informed by British ambassador in Amman that all the Israeli concentrations and preparations will not be directed against Jordan. It is understood that Egypt is the objective. A reliable source of the Jordan command emphasizes that the Israeli attack will develop within forty-eight hours. The command requests your orders.

The message was addressed to Hawk, the radio code name for the Egyptian-Syrian-Jordanian joint command at the Egyptian General Headquarters in Cairo.

"Then the Syrians got in touch with us," Nasser recalled. "By telephone. And they said that they were ready to go at once into the battle. We told them: 'Better not to involve yourselves; we are not clear about the whole plan.' And we told them we had information about a plot in Damascus by Syrian reactionary elements [the group with Anglo-American-Iraqi backing] which might take the opportunity of the engagement of the Army and create troubles in Syria in cooperation with Britain. And we insisted that they must not participate until we see everything clear."

Not for forty-eight hours did the Egyptians get a clear picture of what was happening. It was simply too difficult for them to believe that Britain had colluded with Israel. Nasser's intelligence from Cyprus was not as good as Allen Dulles's. "Although we had close contacts with the EOKA organization," he told me, "we were not able to have any information."

The simplest of wars are difficult to trace in comprehensible outlines, even afterward. The first Suez War was much compressed in time and space but its military actions were independent of one another to an unusual degree. Israel's four axes of advance were independent of one another rather than being mutually supporting and they were launched at different times determined by political rather than military factors. The Anglo-French invasion was militarily quite separate from the Israeli operations although foreknowledge of the Anglo-French aerial bombardment and amphibious assault enabled Dayan to take risks that otherwise would have been unacceptable. Instead of taking up the fragments of the war and then piecing them together, as Nasser was trying so desperately to do in the darkness of its first hours, it will be easier to look at it whole first, beginning with the terrain on which it was fought.

The Sinai Peninsula is a wedge of stony wilderness 125 miles across and 240 miles long which fits like a keystone where Asia and Africa lean together. Armies have crossed it from one continent to the other since the dawn of civilization. It rises in elevation from coastal flats and shifting sand dunes along the Mediterranean to peaks above 8,000 feet around Mount Sinai, which stands in a scorched and desolate range as jagged as the mountains of the moon in the broad point between the Gulfs of Suez and Aqaba. The mountains form a spine down the west side of the peninsula. This peninsular divide is about 15 miles wide where Mitla Pass cuts through it toward Suez. It becomes progressively wider and wilder and higher to the south.

Sinai is half as large as New York State, three times the size of Israel, and constitutes about one-sixteenth the territory of Egypt. Its area is 24,000 square miles, over which some 30,000 Bedouin still wandered in 1956. The only town of consequence in all that expanse is al-Arish, a market center of 15,000 on the Mediterranean near the northeast corner of the peninsula, where fishermen and nomads come to trade. Wadi al-Arish is the Brook of Egypt that marked the southwestern limit of Abraham's covenant. It drains all of Sinai east of the mountain ridge and debouches into the sea at al-Arish. Its bed is usually dry, like Sinai itself, but what water it brings makes al-Arish relatively green and

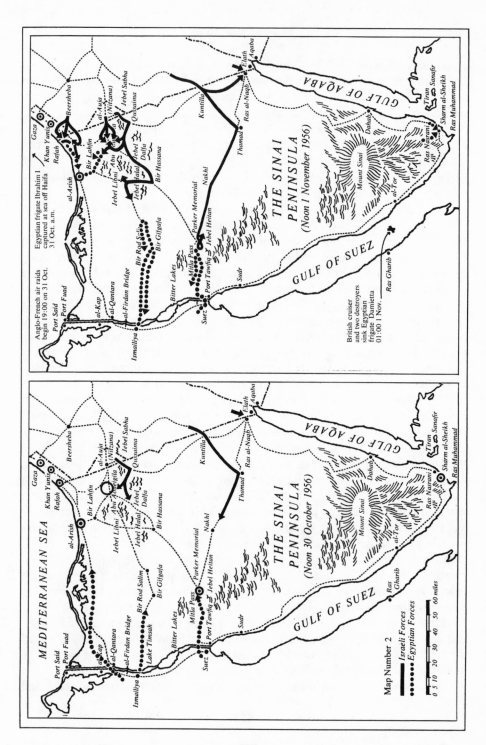

THE SINAI PENINSULA
(Noon 1 November 1956)

Anglo-French air raids begin 19:00 on 31 Oct.

Egyptian frigate Ibrahim I captured at sea off Haifa 31 Oct. a.m.

British cruiser and two destroyers sink Egyptian frigate Damietta 01:00 1 Nov.

GULF OF AQABA

GULF OF SUEZ

MEDITERRANEAN SEA

THE SINAI PENINSULA
(Noon 30 October 1956)

GULF OF AQABA

GULF OF SUEZ

Map Number 2

Israeli Forces
Egyptian Forces

0 5 10 20 30 40 50 60 miles

484

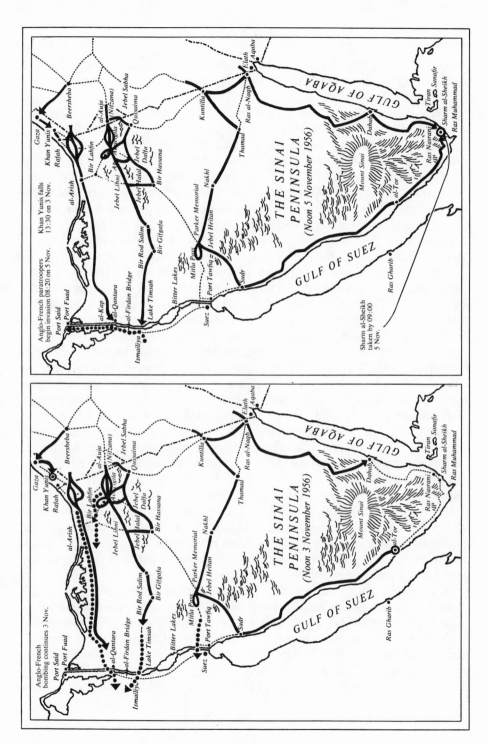

THE SINAI
PENINSULA
(Noon 5 November 1956)

Anglo-French paratroopers
begin invasion 08:20 on 5 Nov.

Khan Yunis falls
13:30 on 3 Nov.

Sharm al-Sheikh
taken by 09:00
5 Nov.

GULF OF AQABA

GULF OF SUEZ

Gaza
Beersheba
Khan Yunis
Rafah
al-Auja (Nitzana)
Abu Ageila
Jebel Dalfa
Quseima
Jebel Sabha
Elath
Aqaba
Kuntilla
Ras al-Naqb
Thamad
Tiran
Sanafir
Sharm al-Sheikh
Ras Muhammad
al-Arish
Bir Lahfan
Jebel Libni
Jebel Halal
Bir Hassana
Mount Sinai
Ras Nasrani
Dahab
Ras Muhammad
Bir Rod Salim
Bir Gifgafa
Parker Memorial
Nakhl
al-Tor
Port Said
Port Fuad
al-Kap
al-Qantara
al-Firdan Bridge
Lake Timsah
Ismailiya
Bitter Lakes
Mitla Pass
Jebel Heitan
Port Tawfiq
Sudr
Suez
Ras Gharib

THE SINAI
PENINSULA
(Noon 3 November 1956)

Anglo-French
bombing continues 3 Nov.

GULF OF AQABA

GULF OF SUEZ

Gaza
Beersheba
Khan Yunis
Rafah
al-Auja (Nitzana)
Abu Ageila
Jebel Dalfa
Quseima
Jebel Sabha
Elath
Aqaba
Kuntilla
Ras al-Naqb
Thamad
Tiran
Sanafir
Sharm al-Sheikh
Ras Muhammad
al-Arish
Bir Lahfan
Jebel Libni
Jebel Halal
Bir Hassana
Mount Sinai
Ras Nasrani
Dahab
al-Tor
Bir Rod Salim
Bir Gifgafa
Parker Memorial
Nakhl
Port Said
Port Fuad
al-Qantara
al-Firdan Bridge
Lake Timsah
Ismailiya
Bitter Lakes
Mitla Pass
Jebel Heitan
Port Tawfiq
Sudr
Suez
Ras Gharib

485

pleasant. For the rest, Sinai's settled population is concentrated at a few oil wells and mines along the Gulf of Suez and at isolated oases where there are villages and military posts.

The Gaza Strip is gentler terrain, twenty-five miles of broad Palestinian beaches backed by rolling fields and citrus groves. Along the line where vegetation meets the sand are the towns of Gaza and Khan Yunis and the frontier post of Rafah, all linked by the road and railroad from Cairo. The Strip is roughly five miles wide. Into its 125 square miles were crowded 300,000 Palestinian Arabs, more than two-thirds of them refugees from the hinterland occupied by Israel. The population density is 2,400 persons per square mile against Sinai's density of less than 2. Militarily, as Nasser told me in 1955, the Strip was Israel's for the taking, being vulnerable at any point and lacking depth in which to maneuver reserves.

Dayan's invasion used all of the major land routes in Sinai. Three roads cross the northern half of the peninsula, two run down the gulfs and converge at the southern end. The northernmost is a double route; side by side through the flat Mediterranean coastland run a road and a railway from Gaza to Qantara (which means bridge in Arabic) on the Canal. Before the creation of Israel they were the main links between Cairo and the cities of the Palestinian, Lebanese, and Syrian coasts. The central road in the north runs from al-Auja to Ismailiya between isolated ranges of thousand-foot hills that loom like islands in the desert. Inside Israel this road continued through Beersheba, headquarters of Israel's Southern Command, and beyond the Jordanian border to Hebron and Jerusalem. The third east-west route is the ancient Darb al-Haj, the Pilgrim Road from Cairo to Suez to Aqaba and thence southward to Mecca. Moving westward from Elath, the new Israeli port intervening between Aqaba and Sinai, the Darb al-Haj in 1956 was a rough but passable track as far as Nakhl, midway across the peninsula. It was graded from Nakhl to the Parker Memorial at the eastern end of the Mitla Pass, and an asphalted road from there to Suez. Of the roads down the coasts, the one down the Gulf of Suez offered no serious difficulties. The other, a tortuous track across the grain of the wadis on the Gulf of Aqaba side, was a formidable route for any vehicle at any time and fearfully vulnerable to air attack in time of war.

The pattern of the war was determined by the collusion agreement, which means that it was determined by Eden and his elaborately incongruous policy of trying to destroy Nasser in defiance of Washington and without hurting British interests in the Arab world. The destruction of Nasser was the common interest that brought the colluders together. The collusive alliance was based on political needs, not military needs. Any of the three partners alone was more than a match for Egypt on the battlefield. The problem for each was to insulate his war against Nasser from intervention by greater Powers, direct or through the UN, long enough to defeat the Egyptian Army and overthrow Nasser.

Israel needed a sure friend among the permanent members of the Security Council who would veto, if need be, any intervention by the council, which is ordinarily the only UN body capable of intervening. Israel also needed a dependable Great-Power source of weapons equal to the Russian arms which she herself had forced Nasser to buy. Ben-Gurion's anxiety over Nasser's Ilyushins seems to have been as much a diplomatic device as a bona-fide military consideration. In any case, he used it to obtain Britain's written commitment to collusion and then turned around and risked scheduling two days of war before the destruction of Egypt's Air Force.

France had the smallest stake in collusion and the greatest indifference to the secrecy surrounding it. It was not surprising that, after the war, it was always a Frenchman who led each new round of disclosures. De Gaulle had warned from the beginning against giving command of the invasion to the British, but the British had the shipping, particularly the landing craft, and the invasion bases. Unless the French were to attack side by side with the Israelis out of the Negev (which some of their pilots did), they had to accept British command as the price of using British facilities. Furthermore, without Britain as her partner, France could not have attacked Egypt in defiance of both the US and Russia.

Allied with eager Israelis on one side and subordinated to a hesitant British partner on the other, the French invented collusion as a diplomatic contraption to bridge the gap between Eden and Ben-Gurion and get the war started. Themselves indifferent to Arab opinion, the French leaders accepted Eden's insistence on secrecy as the price of bringing him in and committing him to act. But from the outset Pineau was contemptuous and ashamed of the hypocrisy of the scheme.

French contraption though it was, collusion was designed to Eden's specifications. He needed a pretext for war first of all, one that would allow him to fight in the guise of a peacemaker. Although the disguise was thin, victory would make it accepted. Nevertheless, in order to preserve appearances Eden insisted that the whole war must fit the fiction that he and his French partners were peacemakers. This meant avoiding any preparations that would show Eden's foreknowledge of the Israeli attack or Israel's foreknowledge of Anglo-French "intervention."

Circumstantial evidence showed Israel's foreknowledge, however, for it was implicit in the extraordinary risks Dayan took in his opening moves. These were: his failure to destroy Egypt's Air Force at the outset, his assault with a numerical advantage of little better than 3 to 2 where 3 to 1 is considered the essential minimum, and his commitment of paratroops deep in enemy territory. The last was something which Britain and France together did not dare to do, something which British generals and admirals threatened to resign over in July. The destruction of the Egyptian Air Force was the first stage in the ponderous Anglo-French invasion plan for two months before Israel entered into Stockwell's deliberations. As Dayan told a BBC interviewer in 1966, fore-knowledge of the Anglo-French air attack was "terribly important because otherwise I should say that *we* had to start that way. One can't in a desert warfare really commit infantry forces without . . . gaining a major amount of air superiority before." The same ineluctable logic made the destruction of the Arab Air Forces Israel's first move in the 1967 war.

Avoiding circumstantial evidence of Eden's foreknowledge of the Israeli attack, as well as of any sign of cooperation with Israel, prevented the speed necessary to present the world with the irreversible *fait accompli* of Nasser's destruction. The slight cheating in loading for invasion under the pretext of Exercise Boathook enabled the fleet to sail six hours before the expiry of the ultimatum. Eden undoubtedly knew about this evasion of his orders but he winked at it; it was covered by a pretext. But it did not enable the colluders to outrun the US and the UN in the race for a *fait accompli*, which Eden lost by two days. "As a result of previous preparedness and excellent work by all officers and men," Keightley wrote in his dispatch, the invasion force was loaded and making for Port Said at full speed on the night of 30 October. But the distance is 936 miles, he wrote, and "at the maximum speed of the landing craft this trip must take six days." Including the four days required for loading, this meant a ten-day lag between the time the invasion button was pushed and the time the troops hit the beaches.

Eden had been persuaded by the RAF that this time could be usefully spent, after destroying the Egyptian Air Force, in bombing to destroy both Egypt's war-making capacity and her will to resist, a combination of strategic and psychological warfare. Eden evidently never got over the psychological impact of aerial bombing as he experienced it in the last weeks of World War I. Recalling it in a speech in the Commons in 1931, he said thirty or forty bombs falling within ten or fifteen minutes had seemed like hundreds. He admitted feeling "personal terror, which was quite inexpressible, because bombing is more demoralizing in its effects than the worst shell-fire." Eden quoted the speech in his memoirs, which he wrote long after he should have learned from other wars, including World War II and Suez, that bombing tends to stiffen a nation's resistance rather than break it. This was particularly true of the Suez operation, in which the bombers skillfully minimized civilian casualties.

Not only did the peacemaking fiction, as defined in the collusion accord, create the fatal delay between the pretext and the invasion but it prevented improvised measures that would have overcome the delay—for example, by having the Israeli Army, triumphant and idle after conquering the Sinai, seize the southern reaches of the Canal and turn them over to the British and French. Eden refused to budge from his fictional stance of impartiality, insisting that the Israelis stay ten miles east of the Canal and warning that British forces would attack them if they approached closer. At Sèvres Lloyd is reported to have suggested bolstering the fiction at the beginning of intervention by dropping a few bombs on the Israeli forces.

The overwhelming military superiority of the colluding powers made it possible for them to schedule in advance the course of hostilities against Egypt. It provided a margin of strength great enough for Eden to practice politics as the art of the improbable rather than as the art of the possible. Eden's insistence on landing at Port Said, for example, was based on several improbable fictions. The first of them was that the Canal needed defending against its owners. The last of them was that, having focused his military preparations on the Canal, he found it the most convenient place to intervene between the Israeli and Egyptian armies, even though it was 125 miles behind the Egyptian lines. Militarily, of course, Alexandria was the logical place to invade Egypt from the sea. And Eden's real political objective, the destruction of Nasser, would have been served best by a swift strike at Cairo from Alexandria. But Eden allowed the cover story to dictate the shape of the real events it was to cover. The fictions embodied in collusion thus prescribed places of battle that made no sense militarily, as for example, Port Said and the Mitla Pass. Collusion also dictated the war's schedule. The schedule was in three stages, of which the third was interrupted prematurely.

In Stage I Israel struck at the thinnest part of the thinned-out Egyptian defenses in the Sinai, deferring the better defended objectives until the Anglo-French intervention forced Egypt to abandon the peninsula. In this stage Israel reduced the risk of an all-out Egyptian counteroffensive, which would include bombing Israel, by feigning to be making no more than a major hit-and-run raid rather than a territorial conquest. The destruction of the Egyptian Air Force, an essential prerequisite to full-scale war, was left by agreement to the Anglo-French. French pilots provided additional insurance against Egyptian bombing.

Stage I was to end with the expiry of the Anglo-French ultimatum at sunrise on 31 October, but the British sought to soften the impact on world opinion by delaying the start of the bombing until nightfall. Ben-Gurion was so angry and upset by the unscheduled delay of more than twelve hours that he suspected British treachery and demanded the immediate withdrawal of the paratroopers at Mitla Pass. Dayan, more confident than ever after the first encounters with Egyptian troops and the hostile Sinai terrain, persuaded Ben-Gurion to stay in the fight.

The Israeli attack, no more than a strong probe on the first night, caught Nasser offguard both militarily and psychologically. Never dreaming of collusion involving Britain and Israel, Nasser had braced his forces to resist an invasion at Alexandria. But after the apparent progress toward a Suez settlement at the UN on 13 October and the encouraging evolution toward further negotiations at Geneva, Nasser had relaxed his fears and now doubted the Anglo-French invasion that he had been so certain of only three weeks earlier. Dayan's extraordinary apparent risks in the early hours of the war raised questions in Nasser's mind but he did not believe collusion was diplomatically possible for Eden. He rejected the evidence of the ultimatum itself, particularly when Britain and France continued to refrain from hostile action for a whole day after it expired. Therefore, in Stage I of the war Egypt made great efforts to send men and armor eastward across the Canal to fight Israel.

Stage II began at nightfall on 31 October when the first British jet bombers began to pound Egyptian airfields. They were Canberra medium bombers from Cyprus and Malta and heavy Valiants from Malta. Nasser immediately halted the movement of troops into Sinai and ordered those there to withdraw immediately to avoid being cut off by the Anglo-French invasion along the Canal that was promised in the ultimatum. In this stage, as the Egyptians broke off all but rearguard actions and raced pell-mell for home, Israel stormed the Egyptian defenses and fastened a firm hold over the entire peninsula and the Gaza Strip. Israeli and French pilots strafed and bombed the retreating Egyptians at will, littering the desert with Egyptian dead, burned-out tanks, and personnel carriers. Nasser, still uncertain whether the main assault would be at Alexandria or Port Said, prepared to make Cairo a Stalingrad after a fighting retreat up the Delta. The Army, and finally the Government, were to go underground for guerrilla warfare wherever the British and French were in occupation. Nasser made a last-minute decision to send a token military force into Port Said for a battle in which civilians would join the troops in acts of desperate heroism that would inspire Egyptians in the guerrilla war to follow. Stage II lasted from nightfall on 31 October until the morning of 5 November, when Anglo-French paratroopers dropped at Port Said.

Stage III was the battle of Port Said, militarily worthless terrain which was a propaganda objective on both sides. Port Said is a handicap to any force that possesses it, being vulnerable in defense and so isolated by surrounding sea and marsh that it is a poor springboard for offensive action. Stage III was to have ended with the collapse of Nasser and his regime and the Anglo-French occupation of the entire Suez Canal, roughly the territory of the British base plus the three major cities on the Canal. If the occupation of the Canal failed to engender an Egyptian revolt against Nasser, the allied forces were prepared to go on to Cairo and overthrow him themselves.

Stage III came to a premature end in the middle of the night of 6/7 November after the British Cabinet agreed to a cease-fire as the price of emergency US action to save the pound sterling. Stage III lasted a little less than 48 hours and ended with the British and French in occupation of Port Said and the causeway down the Canal as far as al-Kap, a penetration of twenty-three miles into Egypt.

The armies involved in the opening stage of the Suez War, the Israeli and the Egyptian, were both developed under British tutelage in the days when Britain ruled in Palestine and Egypt, a rule which remained effective until the end of World War II, whatever constitutional disguises it wore. Dayan's early military experiences had been as one of Orde Wingate's Night Raiders. His Egyptian counterparts, Nasser and Amer, were also products of British military training, although of a more conventional order. Both the Israeli and Egyptian armies had been undergoing intensive improvements in training and equipment for two or three years before the Suez War. Their differences, however, were more fundamental than their similarities.

When an Egyptian thinks of himself and his country at war he thinks in terms of fighting on his own soil against an invader. Israelis, lacking ground to retreat into, think always of carrying the fight to the enemy on his territory by striking sooner and harder. This contrast between the defensive and offensive mentalities is reflected throughout the military establishments of the two countries.

Egypt maintains a standing army, a necessity for a nation which must be prepared for war whenever the enemy may choose to attack. Israel maintains only a professional cadre of officers and noncommissioned officers as the nucleus around which an army of reserves can be mobilized literally within hours. At the time of Suez the Israelis claimed to be able to mobilize twelve brigades—about 60,000 or 70,000 men—within twelve hours and to be able in forty-eight hours to mobilize a theoretical total of 250,000 men and 100,000 women. Such a total mobilization would bring the economy of the nation to a standstill and would be carried out only under the direst threat to national survival.

Egypt's standing army in 1956 numbered about 90,000 men organized in sixteen brigades which were grouped into five divisions. The brigades included ten of infantry, a coastal-defense brigade, a medium machine-gun brigade, an anti-aircraft brigade, and three armored brigades, of which one was only a skeleton cadre rather than a fighting unit. Egypt's total strength east of the Canal when Israel attacked was about 30,000 soldiers, half the normal garrison, deployed mainly in the northeast corner of Sinai in the areas of Qussaima, Abu Aoueigila, al-Arish, Rafah and the Gaza Strip. Only 10,000 of the 30,000 were front-line combat troops. An infantry battalion at Sharm al-Sheikh guarded the Straits of Tiran at the southern tip of the peninsula. The mountain solitudes in between were patrolled by 1,500 men of the Frontier Force, about half the force's total strength.

Israel's regular cadres in 1956 were organized in thirty to thirty-five skeletal brigades, each with its permanent staff and with a permanent supply clerk for each battalion. For the Sinai campaign Dayan mobilized nine brigades and part of a tenth for action against Egypt and about six infantry brigades which he held in reserve for defense against Jordan and Syria. The brigades that participated in the war included one air-borne, three armored, and five reinforced infantry brigades plus one battalion of a sixth, totaling 45,000 fighting men. The classical ratio of attacking forces to defending forces is three to one, which would have required double the number of Israeli troops on the Sinai front.

A characteristic of Israel's citizen army that has impressed professional soldiers all over the world is its high proportion of fighting troops to support personnel—of "teeth" to "tail." Most armies are 20 per cent "teeth" and 80 per cent "tail." Israel's Army is 50 per cent "teeth," a result of administrative economies and short supply lines.

Further to Israel's credit is the fact that her fighting is done mainly by reservists against Arab regulars. For regulars and their families, garrison duty and fighting are normal expectations in their careers. For reserves war duty is an extraordinary interruption of career and family routine, and the economic consequences of death and injury are far more uncertain than for regulars. Ordinarily such considerations tend to make reservists less stubborn in defense and less enthusiastic in offense than regulars. But Israeli reservists, partly as a result of their abundant training and partly because of the high stakes of victory and defeat, are as dependable as most regular troops.

In the air the Israelis were more fully operational than the Egyptians even though most of their Mystères arrived in August, less than three months before the war. Of Egypt's 100 Mig-15 jet fighters from Russia, only two squadrons of fifteen planes each were operational, according to General Dayan. Egypt had two additional squadrons of twenty-seven obsolescent British jet fighters and about sixty transport planes. Of the fifty dreaded Ilyushins only one squadron of twelve planes was operational, wrote Dayan, whose pilots had been tracking Egyptian flights for some time before the war. Of Israel's sixty Mystères, thirty-seven were operational. In addition, there were forty-five French pilots and planes, making a total of eighty-two first-line jet fighters for Israel against thirty Mig-15s for Egypt. Israel had forty-two second-line jets operational, compared with twenty-seven for Egypt. But to match Egypt's Ilyushins Israel had only two antiquated B-17 bombers until the British air armadas joined the war. Israel, like Egypt, was limited by pilot training from making full use of her war planes but she was able to turn out pilots faster than Egypt. And her pilots-in-training were at home while part of Egypt's were in Moscow, where they were cut off by the war.

Although Israel's new French weapons were generally less in quantity than Egypt's new Russian weapons the Israelis had more equipment operational than the Egyptians. The Israelis maintained their old equipment better than the Egyptians and trained faster on the new. Only about one in four of Egypt's two hundred new Russian tanks was operational when the Suez war began, a percentage nearly as small as that of the planes. General Burns had estimated that it would take the Egyptian Army two years to master and incorporate its Russian arms and he judged that his estimate was borne out by the Sinai fighting, which occurred less than a year after the arrival of most of the Russian weapons.

The contrasts between the two armies extended to their commanders. Amer was the most easygoing member of the Egyptian revolutionary junta. The rather affectionate disregard in which he was held by the Egyptian people and soldiery was reflected in the jokes that circulated about him. One joke told of an Egyptian police sergeant reporting to headquarters that he had arrested an officer intoxicated with hasheesh who claimed to be General Amer. "Impossible," said headquarters. The sergeant was ordered to check the officer's claim by asking him what was the strength of the Egyptian Navy, the Air Force, and finally the Army. The sergeant reported each time that his prisoner did not know. At last headquarters said: "He is telling the truth. He can't be anybody but General Amer. Please take him home."

Like Nasser, Amer was a Saidi, the ethnic term applied to Upper Egyptians from the narrow Nile Valley south of Cairo, who tend to be darker of skin and temperament than the Egyptians of Cairo and the Delta. He was born 11 December 1919, nearly two years after Nasser. The two young men met as cadets at the Royal Military Academy. They became fast friends and fellow conspirators on garrison duty and in the Palestine War. After the revolution Nasser put Amer in charge of the Armed Forces and eventually designated him as his political successor, apparently as much because of his devotion as his ability. The two men named sons after each other and took respite from the burdens of office by playing chess together. In 1967, after Amer lost the Sinai a second time to Dayan in very much the same way as in 1955, Nasser forced his resignation. Twenty years of close friendship notwithstanding, Amer fell in with plotters against Nasser. He committed suicide by taking poison, perhaps in remorse, when arresting officers came to his door three months after the defeat.

Dayan does not inspire jokes. Israelis gossip about his sexual prowess and his rough-and-ready philandering. But they regard him as the ablest and toughest soldier of them all. He was well known for his daring participation in reprisal raids, even when he was Chief of Staff. Ben-Gurion worried about losing him and chided him about his reckless forays. Dayan was born in 1915 at Dagania, a kibbutz south of the Sea of Galilee in what was then Turkish Palestine. He grew up bilingual in Hebrew and Arabic. He joined the Haganah at fourteen and at eighteen he was a veteran of gun battles with Arabs. The British sentenced Dayan to five years in prison in 1939 for training the illegal Haganah in the night-fighting tactics he had learned from Wingate. But he was released after two years to serve with the British as a scout against the Vichy French in Syria. He lost his left eye on one of these missions when a bullet rammed a telescope into it. As a colonel in the Palestine War he led jeeps mounted with machine guns into action, helped conquer the Negev, and later was a negotiator and signer of the Jordan-Israel armistice agreement.

When he took command of the Israeli Army in December 1953 he immediately instituted reforms to imbue it with his own aggressive spirit, initiative, pride, and confidence. He made it a requirement that all officers undergo paratrooper or commando training, himself choosing the former and breaking a leg on a jump. At the same time as increasing officers' training and reserve liabilities, he modified the pioneer egalitarianism of Haganah days and raised officers' pay and incentives. He reversed the tendency to assign the most intelligent and best educated conscripts to staff and clerical duties. He put them instead into fighting units. He made it a byword that Israeli officers give the command "Follow me!" instead of the command "Forward!" In the summer of 1954 he and Peres launched the major rearmament program with French weapons that led to the arms race with Egypt and the Suez war.

For two and three generations Jews had come from the ends of the earth to colonize and conquer Palestine. As Israelis, they were readier by temperament as well as necessity to sally forth from their hearths to make war on foreign soil than were the Egyptians, whose ancestors had lived and died in the same Nile Valley villages for thousands of years. But Dayan faced some handicaps in welding his people into a fighting force. Many of the Jews from African and Asian countries were as backward as the Egyptian *fellaheen* and they, like all the immigrants, faced a language barrier until they learned Hebrew.

There remains among Israelis of European origin a prejudice against the Oriental Jews, although it is not as strong as the class distinctions that Nasser tried to eliminate from Egypt. If the proportion of Oriental Jewish officers is less than the Oriental Jewish proportion of the population of Israel, whether because of cultural backwardness or prejudice, they are nevertheless fairly numerous, so that the distinction of rank is essentially a distinction of merit and is not augmented by race or class distinctions. Standards of discipline and dress are vigorously maintained in the Israeli Army but without creating the gap between officers and men that prevails in the Egyptian Army. Egyptian officers come mainly from the lower middle class, which tends to be more sensitive than the upper middle class or the old aristocracy to distinctions between itself and the peasantry. This militates against Nasser's revolutionary egalitarianism and against that mutual esteem and concern between officers and men which makes Israeli army units so cohesive.

Cohesiveness was a factor in the first major Israeli operation of the war, the paratroop drop at Mitla Pass of one battalion of the 202nd Paratroop Brigade and the overland dash to link up by the remainder of the brigade's four battalions. "In order to guarantee fully the junction with the paratroop battalion," an Israeli Army history said, "it was desirable that a special psychological link should exist between the brigade, which was to execute the mission, and the battalion, a link which would create a desire to surmount all obstacles, expected and unexpected; the link of a mother-formation to one of its units."

The military situation in Sinai was favorable to Israel, so much so that Israel had been confidently making war plans on her own for a year before Britain and France joined her in the Sèvres collusion agreement. Egypt's Eastern Command was itself largely inexperienced, having been formed after the Anglo-Egyptian evacuation agreement of October 1954. Headquartered in Ismailiya, it was intended primarily to deal with the take-over of the Suez base from the British. After the Gaza Raid in February 1955 the Egyptian High Command decided to raise it from an administrative status to an operational field command. The change-over was made, by coincidence, on 1 September 1955, the day after the Israeli raid on Khan Yunis. Headquarters moved to al-Arish.

In February 1956, when reports of a planned Israeli offensive reached Cairo at about the same time they reached Glubb, who was still commanding the Jordanian army), the Sinai garrison was strengthened to about 60,000 men. Eastern Command headquarters moved to Jebel Libni, a wilderness mountain overlooking the main road-junction in central northern Sinai. Its two armored brigades, the 1st and 2nd, were at Jebel Libni and Bir Gifgafa. In June the necessity of training troops on the newly arriving Russian equipment led to the withdrawal, among other units, of the 2nd Armored Brigade to Fayid on the west bank of the Canal.

A second and more drastic thinning out of the Sinai defenses began on 6 August, when Nasser concluded that Eden's extensive "military precautions" presaged an invasion and that he had better give priority to defending the Delta against Britain and France. The 2nd Armored Brigade, which carried a divisional headquarters, the 4th Armored, was shifted to the west bank of the Nile at Cairo. There it constituted Egypt's central strategic reserve at the disposal of the Supreme Command. It was strengthened by two tank regiments newly combined as a 3d Armored Brigade. The 1st Armored Brigade was pulled back across the Canal to defend the eastern approaches to Cairo from the sea. Eastern Command headquarters itself withdrew from Jebel Libni to Ismailiya on 2 September as the Canal pilot crisis approached and with it the threat of an Anglo-French invasion.

The whole of the Egyptian Army's striking force was thus camped west of the Canal, deployed in the main to meet an invasion by way of Alexandria. The only tanks left in Sinai were three squadrons of Shermans, one at Rafah and two in reserve at al-Arish. Regular army units east of the Canal were down to three thinned-out infantry brigades, one at Rafah, one at Abu Aoueigila, and one in reserve at al-Arish, all constituting a thinned-out 3d Infantry Division with headquarters at al-Arish. In the Gaza Strip was a National Guard brigade and two Palestinian brigades, all well below professional caliber. Preparing to take on a war with European Powers west of the Canal meant that Egypt could afford only the politically necessary minimum defense on the Israeli frontier, namely something to meet Israeli raids of the kind that Ben-Gurion began at Gaza and enough opposition to make an Israeli seizure of the Gaza Strip a clear-cut act of war. The Gaza Strip was legally the last remnant of Palestine, although under Egyptian protection. "The grouping of the Egyptian forces dictated by the necessity to defend the Gaza Strip, combined with the terrain and communications of the Sinai," wrote General Burns, "made their position inherently weak strategically."

By withdrawing her striking forces west of the Canal, Egypt gravely slowed down her capacity to react to any incursion from Israel larger than a reprisal raid. The handicap was the greater in that Israel, by gaining control of al-Auja, greatly increased her potential for speed and surprise in any invasion of the Sinai. There was only one bridge across the Canal in 1956, the combined railroad and automobile bridge at al-Ferdan. Road and rail traffic had to stop when it opened for the passage of ship convoys. It was the only place tanks could cross the Canal under their own power. There were ferries at Suez, Ismailiya, and Qantara. The Army engineers threw a pontoon bridge across the Canal at Ismailiya for the retreat from Sinai after Britain and France entered the war.

Although Egypt's strategic position was weak in Sinai and her forces greatly reduced, her positions were tactically sound and the troops manning them gave a good account of themselves. "Egypt had concentrated upon defense primarily and officers were well versed in the theory of this operation of war," wrote Major Edgar O'Ballance, a British historian of Israel's wars. "Defensive positions were always well sited, well concealed, had mutually interlocking fields of fire, good communication, were sited in depth and had protective wire and minefields. On the other hand, the attack and other aggressive operations of war had been neglected and practiced little."

Dayan ensured surprise by telling the reservists they had been called up for action against Jordan, by delaying the movement of the invasion forces to the Sinai frontier, and by going so far as to assemble his crack unit, the 202nd Paratroop Brigade, at Hatseva (Ain Hasb) on the Jordan border 17 miles south of the Dead Sea and 75 rugged miles from where they were to cross the Egyptian frontier. After crossing into Sinai the paratroopers had twice as much ground to cover as any other unit, first racing 125 miles to link up with the battalion dropped at Mitla Pass and then dashing more than 200 miles down the Gulf of Suez to complete a pincer attack at Sharm al-Sheikh.

Israel, like Egypt, had territorial commands: the Northern, the Central, and the Southern. The latter comprised the Negev, with headquarters in Beersheba. Colonel Asaf Simhoni, chief of the Southern Command, was in direct operational command of the Sinai invasion, although as Major O'Ballance reported, Dayan "exercised a much closer supervision and control of operations than might be considered either normal or desirable." Aside from Dayan's irksome but generally beneficial interference, Simhoni and the field commanders were allowed great latitude in fulfilling their assigned objectives.

The Israeli invasion units were grouped in four task forces that operated independent of one another along the axes of invasion, which followed the main roads described earlier. The 202nd Paratroop Brigade constituted the task force for the Southern Axis, Kuntilla-Thamad-Nakhl-Mitla Pass, and it was joined by a battalion of the 12th Infantry Brigade for the dash to Sharm al-Sheikh down the Western Axis. The Central Axis, al-Auja-Qussaima-Abu Aoueigila-Bir Rod Salem-Bir Gifgafa-Ismailiya, where the heaviest fighting occurred, as expected, was assigned to a task force designated as Group 38 and composed of the 7th and 37th Armored Brigades and the 4th and 10th Infantry Brigades. The Northern Axis, Rafah and the Gaza Strip-al-Arish-Qantara, was assigned to a task force called Group 77 and composed of the 1st and

11th Infantry Brigades and the 27th Armored Brigade. The Eastern Axis, down the Gulf of Aqaba to Sharm al-Sheikh, was assigned to the 9th Infantry Brigade. The task forces and their axes of advance have been listed in their scheduled order of movement.

In keeping with the opening pretense that the invasion was no more than a deep raid, the only major penetration in the first forty-eight hours was to be along the undefended Southern Axis to Mitla Pass. No armored forces were to be committed for forty-eight hours. Qussaima on the Central Axis and Ras al-Naqb on the Eastern Axis were to be taken by infantry units and held first to protect the flanks of the Southern Axis and then to provide forward jumping-off points for attacks along the Central and Western Axes that were scheduled to begin only after the Anglo-French air forces launched their destruction of Egyptian air power. Not until the night of 31 October were the revealing assaults with armored units to be launched on the Central and Northern Axes and not until 1 November was the 9th Brigade to begin its arduous march to Sharm al-Sheikh.

Simhoni, however, was mistrustful of Dayan's veiled explanation that "someone else," meaning the Anglo-French forces, would join the war on Israel's side. Dayan's orders were to halt movement on the Central Axis after taking Qussaima and to keep the 7th Armored Division for forty-eight hours "silent, motionless, unobtrusive" at Nahal Ruth on the hidden side of al-Auja. Simhoni disregarded these restraints. At dawn on the 30th he hurled the vanguard of 7th Armored into and beyond Qussaima and northward against the Egyptian positions around Abu Aoueigila. There it was brought to a bloody stop in the broad light of morning.

Dayan flew into a rage and stormed into Qussaima himself. His temper was not assuaged by the spectacle of soldiers chasing chickens through the brush, looting the village, and mowing down camels while squadrons of tanks churned across the desert trailing great plumes of dust. He was reminded, he wrote, of his childhood days "when a herd of cattle, stung to frenzy by summer flies, would go wild and bolt from my hands, while I, shamefacedly and utterly at a loss, would watch them disappear into the distant fields, their tails high as a final act of defiance." He decided, he wrote, that if the premature advance of the 7th Armored into Sinai was going to provoke increased Egyptian air activity "before the time expected on the basis of our original plans," the damage had been done and there was no help for it. Typically, he ordered the whole attack on the Central Axis speeded up. But this runs ahead of the story.

Four propeller-driven Israeli Mustangs tried with tow hooks to break the Egyptian telephone wires along the Southern Axis about 3 P.M. on 29 October, some two hours before the invasion began. When the hooks did not work they

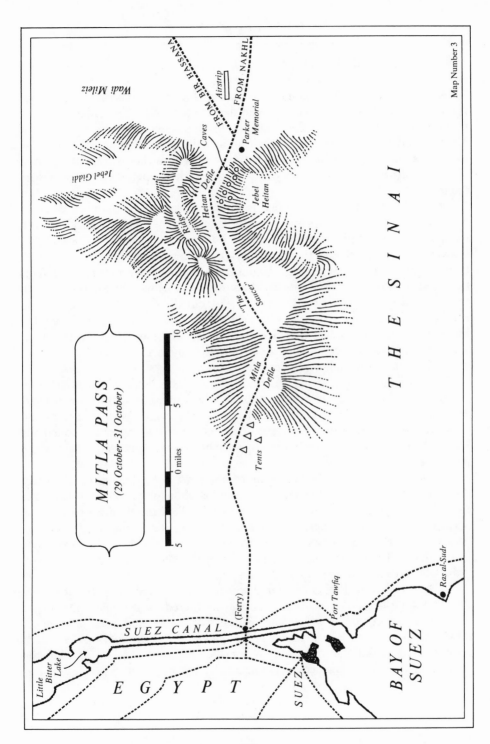

MITLA PASS
(29 October–31 October)

Map Number 3

Wadi Mileiz

FROM BIR HASSANA

FROM NAKHL

Airstrip

Parker Memorial

Caves

Heitan Defile

Jebel Giddi

Ridges

Jebel Heitan

The Saucer

Mitla Defile

Tents

THE SINAI

0 miles   5   10

5

Little Bitter Lake

SUEZ CANAL

(Ferry)

EGYPT

SUEZ

Port Tawfiq

BAY OF SUEZ

Ras al-Sudr

broke the wires with their propellers and wings in the kind of reckless innovation that made Dayan's army famous.

At 3:20 sixteen DC-3 Dakotas took off for Mitla, carrying 395 paratroopers. They flew at 500 feet to avoid detection by Egyptian radar, climbing to 1500 feet for the drop. Ten Meteor jets flew cover while a squadron of Mystères swept up and down the chain of airfields along the Suez Canal, ready to pounce on any Egyptian plane that tried to get into the air. Dayan reported that the only Egyptian reaction was to increase the dispersal of the planes on the ground.

Originally, the drop was planned for the western end of the pass, where it opens on to a desert plain sloping gently down to the Canal twenty miles to the west. But aerial photographs made on 6 October and again on 28 October showed tents and vehicles there, twenty-three tents at the latter count. Less than twenty-four hours before H-hour the Israelis, unaware that the tents belonged not to troops but to a road-construction camp, shifted the drop to the east end of the pass, nearly forty miles from the Canal. The world could still be told that Israeli troops were at Mitla Pass, which would not change the implied threat to the Canal that was so vital to collusion. Israeli Government sources, in fact, falsely announced during the night that Israeli forces had reached a point only eighteen miles east of Suez.

The configuration of Mitla Pass is that of a long defile divided into two sections by a broad "saucer" in the middle. The separation of the two narrow end-sections of the defile is so complete that the name Mitla is commonly applied to the western defile while the still narrower eastern end is called the Heitan Defile. It was on the eastern approaches to the Heitan Defile that the paratroopers were dropped.

The first parachutes billowed open at 4:59 P.M., according to Israeli Army dispatches. Because of faulty navigation the battalion was dropped three miles east of the intended drop zone, which was a knoll in the mouth of the Mitla defile with a limestone obelisk on it known as the Parker Memorial. It took the paratroopers, thirteen of whom were slightly injured on the drop, two and a half hours to regroup and march to the foot of the knoll, where they deployed in battalion defense formation.

What is called the Parker Memorial was actually erected to Professor Henry Palmer, a long-bearded Orientalist who was murdered by Bedouin on that spot while accompanying an intelligence survey of tribes and their allegiances shortly after the British occupation of Egypt in 1882. The chief of the killer's tribe offered to kill his own son to assuage British anger. As part of the traditional Bedouin atonement for a shameful act the tribe raised a cairn at the place of the murder, upon which custom required passersby to throw additional stones. Palmer's body was taken to England for burial in the floor of St. Paul's Cathedral but the British placed a stubby obelisk bearing a plaque inscribed in Arabic near the cairn at the site of his death. Years afterward, in 1912, the man to whom the memorial is commonly but erroneously attributed, Colonel A. C. Parker, became Governor of the Sinai Peninsula.

As they flew across the frontier, winding low through the mountain valleys, the men of the 202nd could see on the ground the motorized battalions of the brigade approaching Kuntilla after an all-day march from Hatseva. The difficulties of the road had already taken its toll of vehicles. Many of the trucks that lacked front-wheel drive had to be abandoned. Only seven of the thirteen French light tanks that left Hatseva reached Kuntilla on time. The Egyptians had five observation posts around Kuntilla armed only with rifles. They were under orders to avoid engagement with an enemy but to observe and report. Four of the posts succeeded in withdrawing to Thamad, leaving Kuntilla to the Israelis at 9 P.M. The men of the fifth post withdrew into the wilderness.

During the night, as the brigade moved toward the Frontier Forces post at Thamad, six French-piloted Nord-Atlas transports parachuted heavy support weapons, ammunition, water, food, and medicines to the battalion at the Parker Memorial. The Israelis had arranged in advance for these supply drops with General Beaufre. Beaufre was the most active and influential officer in the whole French expeditionary force although his actual command was only French land forces. The heavy equipment included eight jeeps, four 106 mm. recoilless antitank guns, and two 120 mm. mortars. The planes shuttled for two days bringing materiel from Cyprus to Ekron airfield near Tel Aviv and from there to Mitla Pass. They returned to Cyprus when Britain began bombing Egypt. Ekron was used, the French air commander told me, because it was difficult to coordinate supply drops direct from Cyprus.

At 8 P.M., more than an hour before Nasser learned of the still-obscure war, the Eastern Command alerted two infantry battalions at Fayid, the 5th and 6th, to prepare to advance against the Israelis at Mitla. An hour later the 5th Battalion began crossing the Canal on a chain ferry north of Suez under strict orders not to interfere with shipping in the Canal. The ferry, whose capacity was to move two automobiles across the Canal at half-hour intervals, got the first battalion across in eight hours. The 6th Battalion, with more shipping placidly enjoying its unprecedented priority over national defense, took twelve hours for the crossing.

By 11 P.M. Nasser and his generals had completed their appreciation and ordered the two full-strength brigades of the 4th Armored Division back across the Canal to assemble between Bir Gifgafa and Bir Rod Salem, midway on the Central Axis. From there the division was to send detachments southward through Wadi Mileiz to cut off the paratroopers at Mitla and to block any additional Israeli moves on the Central and Northern Axes. The first brigade rolled north from Fayid under its own power and was crossing the Ferdan bridge by midnight. The second group came on railroad flatcars from Cairo, dismounting its tanks on the east side of the Ferdan bridge. Like the infantry battalions crossing at Suez, the armored brigades were ordered to avoid interference with ship convoys, with the result that the first brigade did not reach Bir Gifgafa until 3 P.M. on 30 October and the second brigade did not complete its Canal crossing until dawn on the 31st. Each brigade had fifty-five Stalin T-34 tanks and twenty Russian SU-100 self-propelled guns. The 3d Armored Brigade remained in the desert west of Cairo.

"I do not know whether the Egyptians gathered the full import of our moves," Dayan conceded, "but it must be said that they lost no time in reacting to them." As the Egyptian infantry and armor began marching back into Sinai, the Israeli announcements of the attack flashed round the world. The first was the Army communiqué at 9 P.M. The second was a Foreign Ministry statement at 11 P.M., which was 9 P.M. in London and 4 P.M. Eastern Standard Time in the US. Said the Foreign Ministry:

Israel this evening took security measures to eliminate the Egyptian *Fedayeen* bases in the Sinai Peninsula.... With the conclusion of the Security Council deliberations, Colonel Nasser felt himself immediately free to authorize the *Fedayeen* units to renew their incursions into Israeli territory. Within the last week twenty-four Israeli casualties, dead and wounded, were caused by mines planted by the *Fedayeen* in the southern Negev.... It is not Israel which has sought to encompass Egypt with a ring of steel with the announced and flouted purpose of annihilating her at the appropriate moment. It is Egypt which has glorified in this effort, crowned a few days ago by the setting-up of a Syrian-Jordanian-Egyptian military command under the Egyptian military chief.... Israel has done everything in her power to achieve peace with Egypt.... The proffered hand of peace has always been brutally and even derisively rejected....

The twenty-four casualties, as General Burns noted, were from two vehicles blown up in al-Auja, where they had no right to be, in an incident which Israel refused to let UN military observers investigate. The statement reminded Burns of a widely-circulated concept of Ben-Gurion's, namely that it was the function of Israel's Foreign Ministry to justify the actions of the Israeli Armed Forces in the eyes of the world. Israel was launching the preventive war that Ben-Gurion had repeatedly foresworn, most recently in the Knesset debate on 15 and 17 October. Typically, Ben-Gurion's military action was accompanied by a peace offer couched, like its predecessors, in obviously unacceptable terms.

As for the "ring of steel," it did not exist until the night of the day Ben-Gurion, at Sèvres, committed Israel to war. Cairo's *al-Ahram* pointed out that the Arab alliance was formed as a consequence of "continuous Israeli acts of aggression against each of the three Arab states . . . but Israel wants to use it as a justification for its new acts of aggression." UNTSO tallies from 1 January 1955 to 30 September 1956, covering roughly the period since Ben-Gurion's return to militant leadership as Defense Minister, showed that border incidents had cost 121 Israeli lives against 496 Arabs. The cold statistics belie Ben-Gurion's insistence that it is the Arabs who bloody the border. Israel's two pre-emptive wars and her continued reprisal raids raised the proportion of Arab victims still higher.

Eisenhower learned of the Sinai invasion at 5:49 P.M., nearly eight hours after it began, when he landed in the *Columbine* at Richmond, Va., for a campaign speech. He had begun the day worrying about Hungary, authorizing Dulles to emphasize to the Kremlin that the US did not seek alliances with rebellious satellites but believed their independence would bring Europe closer to peace and unity. Then he and his wife had flown on a campaign sortie down the Atlantic seaboard for speeches at Miami, Jacksonville, and Richmond. Eisenhower went ahead with his Richmond speech and then hastened back to a meeting at the White House with his defense, intelligence, and diplomatic chiefs. Dulles voiced his suspicion that Britain and France would intervene "and may even have concerted their action with the Israelis." Eisenhower published a reaffirmation of the Tripartite Declaration and approved a demand for a Security Council meeting the first thing the next morning.

Already unofficially aware of the broad outline of collusion, although constrained by circumstance and diplomacy to feign official ignorance of it, Eisenhower ordered a strong warning sent to Israel. As he related it to me in an interview afterward:

> I said "All right, Foster, you tell 'em that, goddamn it, we're going to apply sanctions, we're going to the United Nations, we're going to do everything that there is so we can stop this thing." We just told them it was absolutely indefensible and that if they expect our support in the Mideast and in maintaining their position, they had to behave. . . . We went to town right away and began to give them hell. And, oh hell, I think we had plans that would allow no dollars to go into the thing. We had all sorts of economic sanctions that we were going to take against them . . .

At the UN that evening Sir Pierson Dixon, the British representative, told Henry Cabot Lodge, the US representative, that the Tripartite Declaration was "ancient history and without current validity" and that Britain "would not agree to any action whatsoever to be taken against Israel." Lodge was offended by the encounter and his mood showed it, the British, French, and Israelis said, in subsequent encounters for months afterward.

The Eisenhower Administration was far more offended by the three colluding Powers' secretive and mendacious conduct the next day, which culminated in the issuance of the ultimatums that had been written at Sèvres on the 24th. At 4:39 A.M. EST on the 30th, which was nearly noon in Tel Aviv, the White House received Ben-Gurion's evasive reply, dated the 29th, to Eisenhower's warnings. Ben-Gurion emphasized the "Iraqi troops poised on the Iraq-Jordan frontier" and closed with: "I feel confident that with your vast military experience you appreciate to the full the crucial danger in which we find ourselves." As Dayan put it, Israel was "in the difficult position of having to keep from her [the US]—and even be evasive about—her real intentions." Dayan had visited the sickbed where Ben-Gurion lay with a 103-degree fever preparing the reply to Eisenhower.

The British were a good deal more than evasive. As soon as US Ambassador Aldrich heard of the invasion, he asked Lloyd for an appointment. Their meeting was fixed at 9:30 on the morning of the 30th. Aldrich asked Lloyd what Britain intended to do. Lloyd replied that he thought Her Majesty's Government would immediately hale Israel before the Security Council as an aggressor against Egypt. Lloyd, of course, thought nothing of the kind, having told Nutting all about the ultimatum five days before. He fobbed Aldrich off by saying he would have nothing definite until after his and Eden's meeting with the French ministers, who were on their way to London at the time, but that he would give Aldrich their decision immediately after lunch. Aldrich was again fobbed off by Lloyd's plea at 1:30 P.M. that he had to go immediately from the meeting to the Commons but that Sir Ivone Kirkpatrick, Permanent Undersecretary at the Foreign Office, would receive Aldrich at 4:45 P.M. Kirkpatrick opened the interview by handing Aldrich the ultimatums. He replied with a shrug when Aldrich said Egypt could not possibly accept. He told Aldrich that Eden was announcing the ultimatums to the Commons at that very moment, which meant that Eisenhower learned of them on the news tickers before Aldrich could report. This was an offense to an ally and a humiliation to an allied ambassador. James Reston reported that when Eisenhower heard of the ultimatums "the White House crackled with barrack-room language the like of which had not been heard since the days of General Grant."

504

Pandemonium broke out in the House of Commons at Eden's announcement. It was the first of a week of scenes of parliamentary passion more characteristic of Mediterranean nations than of Britain. The Labor party, as Eisenhower put it, "went through the roof." Laborite spokesmen accused Eden of using the Sinai invasion as a pretext to attack the victim. They forced a vote of confidence. Tory discipline, as usual, proved stronger than dissident Tory consciences and the Government won the vote.

The ultimatum broke into what Eisenhower called "a sort of transatlantic essay contest" between himself and Eden. Eisenhower cabled Eden at 10:50 A.M. (3:50 P.M. London time) asking Eden's "help in clearing up my understanding as to exactly what is happening between us and our European allies." He said the US was "astonished" at Dixon's "completely unsympathetic" demeanor the previous night at the UN and noted that it was "only fair" for a signatory of a pact like the Tripartite Declaration to notify the others before renouncing it. He noted that he had publicly reaffirmed it as basic to US policy. He mentioned the prospect of Russia helping Egypt and warned: "We may shortly find ourselves not only at odds concerning what we should do, but confronted with a *de facto* situation that would make all our present troubles look puny indeed."

The message crossed with one from Eden, ostensibly drafted before his meeting with the French, saying Israel had guaranteed not to attack Jordan, that Egypt had brought war upon herself, and that "we feel under no obligation to come to the aid of Egypt.... Nasser and his press have relieved us of any such obligation by their attitude to the Tripartite Declaration." Eden claimed to "have a responsibility for the people in these ships" passing through the Canal and said "decisive action should be taken at once to stop hostilities." He said UN action was "unlikely to be either rapid or effective."

Eisenhower replied to this at 12:09 P.M. (5:09 P.M. London time), saying: "We find it difficult at this moment to see how we can violate our pledged word" in the Tripartite Declaration. The Tripartite Declaration was a commitment among the three signatories and its validity in that respect was invulnerable to the reservations expressed on several occasions by both Israel and the Arabs. Eden had said of it in the House of Commons less than two years before: "I know very few international instruments, if any, which carry as strong a commitment as that one does." Nigel Nicolson, MP, wrote that British Government spokesmen had reaffirmed the pledge no less than nine times in the first half of 1956. Eisenhower was on firm ground in disapproving Eden's cavalier dismissal of the pledge. He told Eden in his brief cable that he was awaiting Eden's promised further message. When Eden announced the ultimatums to the Commons he was hypocritical enough to say: "Certainly the spirit of the Tripartite Declaration—and more than the spirit—operates in our minds" but that Egypt's attitude to it had been "equivocal."

Within the hour Eisenhower learned of the ultimatum. He drafted a message to be telephoned to the US Embassies in Paris and London with instructions to telephone them to Eden and Mollet. Opening with the acid comment that he had learned of the ultimatums from the press, Eisenhower said: "I must urgently express to you my deep concern at the prospect of this drastic action even at the very time when the matter is under consideration as it is today by the United Nations Security Council. It is my sincere belief that peaceful processes can and should prevail..."

The message crossed cables, first from Mollet and then from Eden, notifying Eisenhower of the ultimatums. Eden, writing as if it were before his announcement in the Commons, said Israel might be accused of "technical aggression" but that she had a legitimate claim to be acting in self-defense. Referring to the ultimatum as a "declaration," Eden explained the Anglo-French determination to occupy the Canal zone regardless of whether Egypt submitted. "Knowing what these people are," he said, "we felt it essential to have some kind of physical guarantees in order to secure the safety of the Canal." As a justification for haste, Eden said "the Israelites appear to be very near to Suez." He said his knowledge of "the Constitutional and other difficulties in which you are placed" (presumably the elections) prevented him from inviting the US to associate itself with the ultimatum. He assured Eisenhower that the Anglo-French action was "not part of a harking back to the old Colonial and occupational concepts" and he closed with the pious sentiment that Britain and the US might work together "when the dust settles" to strengthen the weakest part in the line against Communism, namely the Middle East.

Eden feels that delaying the message long enough for Eisenhower to get the first word of the ultimatum from the press was a mistake; "but I didn't want to give time for Ike to ring up and say: 'Dulles is on his way again.'" At the time, upon learning that the White House had announced the gist of Eisenhower's messages to himself and Mollet, Eden sent a third cable that day saying that in view of the publicity he must be free to make public the gist of his own two previous cables "in order to justify British policy and action." Eisenhower penciled at the bottom of his copy one line for transmission to Eden: "By all means, use any part you see fit."

Neither at the time nor ever afterward did Eden succeed in justifying the ultimatum, least of all to the majority of British diplomats, nearly all of whom were stunned and made ashamed by it. A typical reaction was that of Sir William Hayter, the British ambassador in Moscow. At a Kremlin reception for the Afghan Prime Minister that evening Molotov told every ambassador he spoke to that Britain and France were behind the Israeli invasion. Hayter assured all who mentioned it to him that Molotov was wrong and that this would be revealed later that day by British and French votes against Israel in the Security Council. Hayter returned to the Embassy to find a cable with the text of the ultimatum. He wrote:

"As I read it I could not believe my eyes; I began to wonder if I had drunk too much at the Kremlin. I felt quite bewildered. The action we were taking seemed to me flatly contrary to all that I knew, or thought I knew, about British policy." Hayter lay awake most of the night pondering whether to resign. He drafted several letters of resignation during subsequent days but decided against giving the Russians an unmerited propaganda advantage since he himself received no orders to contribute to what he privately considered a detestable policy of banditry. If he had been in Dixon's shoes at the UN, he wrote, the difficulty would have been more crucial. Nevertheless, Suez helped impel Hayter's resignation eighteen months later in the heyday of Macmillan's unrepentant premiership.

At the Security Council on the 30th Dixon and the French ambassador to the UN, Cornut-Gentille, belied Hayter's predictions and cast the first British and French vetoes in the history of the UN. They vetoed first a US resolution which requested Israel to withdraw behind the armistice lines and called upon all UN members not only to refrain from using force or the threat of force in the area but also to withhold all aid to Israel until she withdrew. Then they vetoed a Russian resolution calling for an immediate cease-fire and an Israeli withdrawal. The Security Council was thus paralyzed by the vetoes.

The Russian draft resolution reflected the moderation that had characterized Russian policy in the Suez Crisis since the beginning. Eden acknowledged in his memoirs that it differed from the US resolution chiefly by omitting the latter's "most offensive paragraph directed at the French and ourselves," namely the appeal to UN members to eschew both force and aid to Israel. The British were willing to abstain on the Russian resolution rather than cast a second veto, Eden wrote, but Lodge's insistence on an immediate vote left no time for the necessary consultations.

Eden, in presenting the ultimatum to the Commons, conjured up visions of a threat to the Canal—"the Israeli spearhead was not far from the banks . . . air forces are in action in the neighborhood of the Canal." In fact, the only serious fighting up to the time the ultimatum was issued was in the extreme eastern part of Sinai where the Israeli 7th Armored Brigade made its costly premature assault on the Egyptian defenses at Abu Aoueigila, 120 miles from the Canal.

The Israeli paratroopers isolated at Mitla were digging in to fight for their lives against the Egyptians gathering on the heights flanking the long defiles, but at that time they had merely skirmished with the enemy. The main body of the 202nd was still four hours to the east when the ultimatum was issued. The Northern and Western Axes were quiet.

In Malta that morning, before many Londoners had learned of the Sinai war from their newspapers and radio, the invasion force officers attended a briefing at which they were given the Port Said assault schedule in detail. If Eden's cover story were true, the briefing would be a chronological impossibility. But as it was, it was one of the numberless items of circumstantial evidence of collusion that kept coming to the surface afterward and which would have given it away even if none of the colluders at Sèvres had broken their pledge of secrecy. Captain D. M. J. Clark, a gunnery control officer who was called up with the reserves in August, described the briefing in his memoir of Suez. There were wall maps of Operation Musketeer and blown-up aerial photographs of the Egyptian defenses. Four hours before the French ministers arrived in London to pretend to devise with Eden and Lloyd the six-day-old ultimatum text, more than eight hours before the ultimatum was announced, and more than twenty hours before it expired, the fiction of Exercise Boathook was discarded for the officers of the invasion force. Clark's LST sailed for Port Said that same morning, clearing the harbor breakwater as he and his fellow officers sat down to lunch in the wardroom.

Dayan's diary entries for the evening of the 30th state that he had ordered the paratroopers at Mitla not to advance further westward. "At this stage," he wrote, "we have no interest in further provoking the Egyptians and widening our military activity; we should try as far as possible to get through the next twenty-four hours without additional battles. ... At all events, tomorrow at dawn the Anglo-French forces will start bombing Egyptian airfields and, presumably, after that we should be able to gain our objectives with greater ease." Of the ultimatum Dayan wrote: "It is clear that the whole purpose ... is to give the British and French Governments a pretext ..."

The 202nd suffered its first battle casualties at Thamad at dawn on the 30th. Thamad was a Frontier Force post manned by a company of Sudanese armed with heavy machine guns, recoilless guns, and old Lee-Enfield rifles. It was the only defended locality on the southern axis, with earthworks and minefields on the perimeters. Its basic purpose was not defense against Israel but rather the endless war against Arab smugglers. The defenders had standing orders to withdraw before engaging superior enemy forces, but they defied them. In a brisk forty-minute battle, the Sudanese killed four Israelis and wounded six. Dayan estimated that more than fifty defenders were killed before they withdrew in jeeps to Nakhl. Three more Israelis were hit by four

Egyptian Vampires and four Mig-15s, whose early-morning strafing attacks were the first Egyptian air sorties of the war.

At Mitla itself, or rather at Jebel Heitan, the first clashes occurred at 8:30 A.M. when a morning fog burned away and revealed the opponents to one another. An Egyptian reconnaissance platoon of about thirty men was in possession of the Parker Memorial knoll and four companies of the Egyptian 5th Infantry Battalion, the first to cross the Canal, were astride the defile on the parapet of Jebel Heitan on the south side and the slopes of Jebel Giddi on the north. The Egyptian patrol opened fire from the memorial on the Israelis digging in below them. It seems that the Israeli battalion commander, in the darkness that came on as he marched west from the erroneous drop area, mistook two lesser hills for the sides of the Heitan defile and thereby found himself at daylight farther outside it than he intended. He tried three times during the morning to dislodge the Egyptians from the Parker Memorial and then decided to hold in defensive formation until the remainder of the brigade arrived at nightfall.

The quartets of Egyptian Vampires and Migs that had strafed the Israelis at Thamad also attacked the Israelis near the Parker Memorial. The Egyptian planes hit four men and a Piper Cub parked on an airstrip immediately east of the Israeli position. After the Egyptian air attacks the Israeli Air Force was given permission to strike at Egyptian ground targets and to attack planes rising from the Egyptian fields near Suez. The Israeli pilots remained under orders not to attack the Egyptian airfields themselves on the assumption that, as Dayan expressed it, "if we would not attack their airfields, they would not extend their activity beyond the borders of Sinai."

During the afternoon, as the Egyptians strengthened their grip on the sides of Mitla Pass, both west and east of the "saucer," invading jet fighters attacked the other infantry battalion, the 6th, as it advanced across the desert and moved into the Mitla defile from the west. The battalion, hampered by shipping, did not complete its crossing of the Canal until 3 P.M.

The invaders' planes came over in such numbers that the Egyptian high command concluded that some of them must be French. The French admit flying interdiction missions in the second phase of the war, as the Egyptians retreated to meet the Anglo-French invasion, but they deny that they attacked Egyptian units advancing into Sinai in the war's first phase. The presence of the French squadrons standing guard, however, freed more Israeli planes for close-support missions than would have been possible otherwise.

The Israelis, with their French backing, dominated the air over Sinai during the first two days of the war but they were by no means unchallenged masters of it, as they were after the British and French openly intervened. The Egyptians were desperately short of pilots, however. General Amer broadcast after the war that the pilots returning from missions would turn their planes over for refueling and servicing while they immediately climbed into the cockpits of combat-ready planes and took off without rest on further missions. On the Mitla axis alone the Egyptian Air Force logs record forty-nine missions on the first two days, only half of them by Migs.

The main body of the Israeli paratroop brigade reached the beleaguered battalion at 10:30 P.M. on the 30th, having chased Egyptian and Sudanese Frontier Forces from Nakhl in a brief and bloody assault just before sundown. Unlike Thamad, Nakhl had no tactical defenses, being merely an antismuggling station with no strategic function. The Sudanese company from Thamad and the Egyptian company quartered at Nakhl, knowing their withdrawal route was blocked at Mitla, lost fifty-six killed and a number of wounded as they escaped into the desert ravines. The action at Nakhl was an escape under fire rather than a fight. Two companies in an open post with neither tanks nor anti-tank guns could not hope even to delay an attack by three battalions with supporting artillery and tanks.

Meanwhile, Israeli aerial reconnaissance observed the marshaling of the Egyptian armor at Bir Gifgafa, from where it could strike southward to cut off the whole reunited 202nd Brigade at Mitla. The brigade commander, Colonel Ariel Sharon, viewed his situation as dangerously vulnerable, so much so that he determined to seize a more defensible position in the pass itself the next day even though that meant defying orders to stay outside the eastern end of the pass. "The brigade commander had good reason to be dissatisfied with his tactical position," wrote the author of an Israeli Army account of the war, "...chiefly because of the possibility of enemy armor penetrating from the Central Axis by way of Wadi Mileiz."

Headquarters ordered Sharon to refrain from further battles on the 31st for a number of reasons. The most compelling was the need to conserve Israeli air support for the major battle scheduled that day at Abu Aoueigila. Also Egypt's air strength remained an enigma and might yet be used against Israel's cities. Dayan presumed that it had been triply provoked on the 30th, first by the premature use of armor on the Central Axis, second by the Israeli air attacks against Egyptian troops moving to Mitla as well as against the Egyptian planes dispatched to protect them, and third by the Anglo-French ultimatum's transparent indication that Britain and France intended to intervene in support of Israel. The Israeli Government's anxiety disclosed itself in the promulgation of civil defense regulations, including the countrywide blackout that Dayan at first refused.

But Nasser, however much faith he had lost in Eden's word, still believed in his common sense. He summoned Ambassador Trevelyan at 10:30 P.M., the hour that Sharon completed his overland dash to Mitla, and warned him that Egypt could not possibly accept the ultimatum, which trespassed on Egypt's rights and dignity and violated the UN Charter. Cairo broadcast Nasser's rejection of the ultimatum a few minutes before midnight. An hour and a half later Foreign Minister Golda Meir broadcast Israel's acceptance, which Ben-Gurion had promised at Sèvres a week earlier. Nasser and his colleagues discussed the war situation in the light of the ultimatum but did not change their original appreciation. Nasser told me afterward:

We discussed this question of Mitla. And we said that this is a plot between the Israelis and the British in order to say that they are near the Suez Canal as a pretext for the British to declare their ultimatum. But we wondered about the movement of half-track vehicles and lorries in the direction of Mitla. And this also was an interrogation mark. But we thought that this was a move to reinforce these parachute troops. But we still didn't believe at all that Britain would participate with Israel. It was too much against their interests.

Nasser admitted his mistake a month after the war in a published analysis of the political and military events. The ultimatum, he said, led the Egyptians to revise upward the chances of British intervention from fifty-fifty to seventy-thirty. But after discussion, he said, "we excluded the possibility." Imagining himself in Eden's place, Nasser reasoned: "It was my conviction that any military operation against us, especially if taken in alliance with France and Israel, would inevitably result in a sure catastrophe . . . I imagined Britain's interests in the area: the oil, the pipelines, Britain's commerce, her cultural and political influence, and, at the end of the list, the Suez Canal, that vital artery for Britain, which would undoubtedly be closed as a result." Nasser stuck to his conclusion that "Britain wanted us to refrain from amassing all our forces against Israel in order that she might obtain a cheap victory while we hold our forces in reserve to face Britain."

Trevelyan had started the day by making arrangements with Foreign Minister Fawzi to evacuate the British civilian maintenance technicians in the Suez Canal base. When Trevelyan called again in the evening with the ultimatum, Fawzi told Nutting afterward, he appeared shocked and bewildered by his instructions. Fawzi said he would not ordinarily believe that Britain would keep her ambassador completely in the dark about such an obvious conspiracy. But Trevelyan's manner was unmistakably that of a man ignorant of the plot. The British ambassador in Tel Aviv knew more than Trevelyan but only through his own observations. He realized on the first day of mobilization that it was probably for action against Egypt, being far larger than needed for a Jordanian operation. He immediately reported his observations to Whitehall but was told nothing in return. Equal mystification prevailed at the charade in London where Gershon Avner, the Israeli chargé d'affaires, was summoned to the Foreign Office at 3:30 P.M. to have the ultimatum read to him. The realization of collusion dawned on Avner when he heard the requirement that Israel withdraw ten miles east of the Canal. The still-isolated battalion at Mitla was a full forty miles from the Canal.

There were no land encounters during the night of the 30th. In the air, the message log at Egyptian Air Force headquarters in Cairo records, Ilyushin bombers operating in pairs carried out six raids against Israeli airfields. Three raids were reported against Ekron, the relay base for French supply flights to Mitla, in the five hours from 7:45 P.M. to 12:45 A.M. The pilots reported extensive damage on the first two raids. One raid was reported on Qastina about 10 P.M. and two unsuccessful raids on Ramat David, on the second of which one of the raiding IL-28s was reported to have exploded in the air. Dayan says only a single IL-28 flew over Israel that night and dropped his bombs on a desolate hill south of Jerusalem. It was only by chance that a farmer of Ramat Rahel saw the bombing, Dayan wrote, and it was confirmed by the police in the morning when they found fragments of Russian bombs.

A sea action off Haifa, which has acquired a kind of slapstick fame in naval annals, was the major military event of the night in the Middle East. It was an abortive raid on Haifa by an antiquated Egyptian frigate, the *Ibrahim al-Awwal*, which ran afoul of the French destroyer *Kersaint* and ended up being towed into Haifa harbor as a war prize. The *Ibrahim* was commissioned in the British Navy in 1940 as the destroyer-escort *Mendip*. She served a year in the Chinese Navy as the *Lin Fu* before Britain sold her to Egypt in 1950. The Egyptians first named her after Mohammed Ali but soon renamed her after his son, Ibrahim the First. She had returned to Port Said just before the Sinai invasion after being overhauled, bureaucratically harassed, and delayed at the British naval shipyard in Malta.

At sundown on the 30th the *Ibrahim*'s captain, Lieutenant Commander Hassan Rushdy Tamazin, received orders by telephone to bombard Haifa. Egypt feared Israeli amphibious operations and wanted to cripple Israel's main naval base and destroy the tanks at the Haifa refinery which contained Israel's petroleum reserves, estimated by the Egyptians at no more than enough for six days of wartime consumption. The *Ibrahim* was the small Egyptian Navy's fastest fully-trained ship and it was hoped that she could complete her desperate mission and get back under Egyptian air protection by daylight.

At 3:35 A.M. on the 31st she opened fire on Haifa with her 4.4-inch guns at a range of five miles. Using her new English radar she fired 220 high-explosive shells in twenty-five minutes at Haifa's coastal guns, naval and harbor installations, and the tank farm. The captain reported starting big fires. "Some of the shots were quite accurate and shells fell on the quay, the navy compound, and the shipyard area," Dayan recorded, "but there were no casualties and not much damage was caused." Egyptian prisoners of war at Atleet, fourteen miles south, who were captured at al-Sabha a year earlier, reported when they were repatriated that they had heard the shelling. US Navy ships were lying off Haifa at the time, standing by to evacuate US citizens.

At 3:50, as the *Ibrahim* turned away at full speed, twenty-five knots, heavy shells began falling close to her. These were from the *Kersaint*, the first shots of the allied intervention, fired two and a half hours before the expiry of the ultimatum. One of the persistent myths of the war is that the French admiral, Barjot, had an anguished afterfear that the *Kersaint* had fired on an American ship and that he radioed Paris an apology for the US Sixth Fleet. The myth rests on the misapprehension that the *Ibrahim* was one of Egypt's Skory-class destroyers, recently acquired from Russia, whose silhouette is said to resemble that of a class of US destroyers. The *Kersaint* stopped firing at 4:25. The *Ibrahim*, still unhit in the darkness, radioed naval headquarters at Alexandria that the mission was successful. Alexandria ordered the *Ibrahim* to head due west and promised air cover at 5:15, about the hour of first light.

Instead of Egyptian planes two Israeli destroyers, the *Jaffa* and the *Elath*, both able to outrun and outgun the Egyptian frigate, showed up on the *Ibrahim*'s radar at 5:15. After querying the *Ibrahim*'s identity they opened fire. Alexandria ordered the hapless *Ibrahim* to head north for a Lebanese or Syrian port instead of continuing homeward. Alexandria again promised air cover. But Mystères showed up instead of Migs and began rocket runs on the *Ibrahim* as the two Israeli destroyers, now joined by two Israeli frigates, continued to shell the Egyptian ship. At 7 A.M. the *Ibrahim* reported that her ammunition was gone, her engine damaged, and that she was unable to maneuver. Four Israeli motor torpedo boats arrived and stood by as the destroyers closed in behind a curtain of 40-mm. cannon and machine-gun fire.

At 7:25 the *Ibrahim* radioed Alexandria that her log and papers were destroyed, that the sea cocks were open, and that she was sinking. An Israeli boarding party closed the sea cocks, seized the "destroyed" log, and summoned a harbor tug to tow their prize into Haifa. The *Ibrahim* was renamed for the fifth time when she was recommissioned in the Israeli Navy. Appropriately, her new name was the *Haifa*. Of the Egyptian crew of 153, two were killed, eight were wounded, and the rest joined the Sabha prisoners at Atleet. The *Ibrahim*'s mission, described by Commodore Shmuel Tankus of the Israeli Navy as "a very rash action which proved lack of planning," had been code-named Operation Amer, which some might think apt.

The collusive ultimatum made 30 October 1956 the most perfidious date in Albion's long history and it hastened the end of empire by bringing on all the certain disasters which Nasser erroneously regarded as a certain deterrent to British joint action with Israel.

By contrast, the day was the high point in the Hungarian revolution's short history. Budapest radio announced at 7:20 P.M. (London time) that the Red Army had agreed to withdraw immediately from the city. Moscow not only confirmed the agreement to withdraw from the capital but also announced that the question of stationing Soviet forces anywhere in Hungary was negotiable. The Moscow statements came in a declaration embodying the doctrine that "the countries of the great community of socialist nations can build their mutual relations only on the principles of complete equality, respect for each other's territorial integrity, state independence and sovereignty, and non inter-ference in each other's internal affairs." Allen Dulles told Eisenhower that the statement was "one of the most significant to come out of the Soviet Union since the end of World War II." Khrushchev and Mikoyan, the chief propo-nents of de-Stalinization, had prevailed in the Central Committee of the party over Zhukov, the Defense Minister and a proponent of force. The Polish mira-cle of nationalist self-assertion against Moscow seemed to have been repeated in Hungary. But Nagy was no Gomulka. Within a few days he had let the run-away Hungarian revolution provoke the Kremlin beyond endurance.

Other important developments in the Middle East on the 30th were: the departure of President Quwwatli of Syria late in the morning for a previously scheduled state visit to Moscow; and the British Government's take-over of the nominally independent Near East Arab Broadcasting Station on Cyprus at least an hour and a half before the ultimatums were announced. The station was renamed *Sawt al-Britannia* (The Voice of Britain) and it immediately launched a propaganda and psychological war against Cairo and Cairo Radio's *Sawt al-Arab* ("Voice of the Arabs") under the direction of Brigadier General Bernard Fergusson, who had come to Cyprus equipped with texts to broadcast and hundreds of thousands of leaflets to be dropped on Egypt along with the bombs.

Here it will be well to dispose of another of the myths of Suez, namely that Egypt broadcast piteous appeals for help which the other Arabs, particu-larly Egypt's allies, ignored. The reverse was true, as the monitoring records of the Arab stations show. Syria and Jordan led other Arab Governments in earnest and insistent offers to join battle with Israel. The Supreme Command in Cairo, code-named Hawk, ordered Amman and Damascus at 00:50 on the

30th to mobilize and to marshal armored and infantry groups near the Syrian-Jordanian border for an operation, code-named Beisan, to sever Israel. But Egypt then repeatedly deferred executing the operation until, at dawn on 1 November, she canceled it, fearing it would provide a pretext for an Anglo-French invasion of Syria. Egypt made no appeals for military help. On the last day of the war Cairo issued but did not broadcast a general appeal to the world at large for volunteers and arms. This was distinctly a psychological-warfare measure and was in no way a serious request for organized military assistance from other Arab Governments or anyone else.

As the ultimatum deadline—4:30 A.M. London time on 31 October—began receding into the past and no British bombers appeared over Egypt, Ben-Gurion's suspicion matched Nasser's hope, namely that the British were not going to intervene. Ben-Gurion's biographer, Bar-Zohar, said Mollet felt impelled personally to promise Ben-Gurion by telephone that the bombing would begin that evening.

Israel's feeling of reassurance was bolstered when the sandbags placed round the British Embassy on the Tel Aviv beachfront were rather ceremoniously removed. Also, not a single Briton accepted evacuation, in spite of the embassy's authorization of it. The Britons prided themselves on the impression this made on the Israelis in contrast to the hasty large-scale evacuation of American citizens, who left by special aircraft from Lydda and by ships of the Sixth Fleet at Haifa. The US ambassador took a large front-page advertisement in the *Jerusalem Post* of 30 October to urge Americans to leave the country, "without delay."

In Egypt Nasser continued to try to avoid allowing any possible pretext to the British by giving ship traffic along the Canal priority over military movements across it. At 9 A.M. Radio Cairo reported that shipping continued normally and that the northbound convoy of twenty ships had reached Port Said.

The 202nd Paratroop Brigade, which Ben-Gurion wanted withdrawn from Mitla when the British failed to begin bombing Egypt on schedule, fought a desperate battle on the 31st. The Israeli Army history called it "the big battle of the Sinai Campaign." Sharon had wanted to seize the pass before dawn but was specifically forbidden by General Headquarters. He then obtained permission to send forward a "patrol unit" on condition that it avoid battle. On the strength of this limited permission Sharon organized a full combat team consisting of two companies mounted on half-tracks, the brigade reconnaissance unit, three tanks and a troop of heavy mortars, all under a battalion commander.

Sharon thought that the two Egyptian infantry battalions from Suez had been all but destroyed by Israeli aircraft the day before and he believed he might find the defiles no longer defended. In fact, the 5th Egyptian Infantry

Battalion and one company of the 6th were strongly situated on both sides of the Heitan defile, in caves in the Jebel Heitan cliffs on the south side, where they were invisible from within the defile, and in sangars on the ridges to the north. The Egyptians had medium machine guns, 57-mm. antitank guns, and heavy mortars.

Sharon's underestimation of Egyptian resistance in the pass was a corollary to his overestimation of the threat of the Egyptian armor concentrating at Bir Gifgafa, thirty miles north of him, which he feared would come down Wadi Mileiz and cut him off. The fear was far from unreasonable. One of the contingency missions of the 7th Armored Brigade, supposedly held in reserve on the Central Axis, was to race down the diagonal valley road through Bir al-Hassana to the Parker Memorial to block any Egyptian armor coming down Wadi Mileiz. But the 7th Armored, having gone prematurely into action at Qussaima, was three times as far away as the Egyptians at Bir Gifgafa and it had moreover, hooked northward toward Abu Aoueigila instead of waiting to see whether the paratroopers would need its help on the Southern Axis.

Sharon sent the combat team into the defile at 12:30 P.M. and it immediately came under fire from both flanks. The first two half-tracks were hit. The troops scattered among the boulders on the floor of the defile where they were pinned down by Egyptian fire. The combat team commander, in the third half-track, unwilling to halt and thereby make his column a stationary target, drove on until he came to an Egyptian vehicle blocking the road where an Israeli air attack had disabled it the day before. His own half-track tumbled into the wadi when he used it to shove the Egyptian truck aside. The rest of the column raced on to the "saucer" between the Mitla and Heitan defiles.

The commander, still unaware of the Egyptians in the caves over his head, ordered the reconnaissance unit, which had not entered the defile, to clear the ridges to the north without entering the defile. When the unit moved onto the ridges from the east it came under fire from the caves and was driven back with heavy casualties. Egyptian Migs strafed the Israelis in the saucer and at the eastern end of the Heitan defile. Israeli planes were unable to give close support to their men on the ridges during a subsequent and successful combined attack from both the saucer and the east because the men were too closely engaged with the Egyptians. The caves were nearly invulnerable to air attack. But the Israeli planes did drive off Egyptian jets.

The Israelis were in possession of the ridges north of the defile by nightfall. Then they went after the Egyptians in the caves in savage isolated hand-to-hand combats in the dark. Night fighting had been a specialty of the Haganah since the days of Wingate and the paratroopers were superbly skilled at it. As the Army historian put it, "the caves which served him [the enemy] as excellent positions were also death-traps." Fierce fighting continued after dark for two and a half hours, during which the Egyptians began withdrawing in response to orders prompted from Cairo by the first British bombing raids. "This was a battle the like of which not even a veteran combat-hardened unit like this had ever experienced," Dayan wrote. The Israelis too abandoned the pass and withdrew to the brigade bivouac near the Parker Memorial, where they rested for nearly forty-eight hours. Evidently unaware that the Egyptians had withdrawn entirely, the paratroopers did not again attempt to go through the pass.

The paratroop brigade lost 38 killed and 120 wounded. Egyptian ground and air attacks destroyed or wrecked a fuel truck, an ammunition truck, four half-tracks, a tank, a jeep, an ambulance, and three other vehicles, according to Dayan. The Israeli Army history said over 200 Egyptian dead were counted after the battle.

"As to the comparatively high number of enemy dead and small number of prisoners in the battles along the Kuntilla-Mitla axis," Dayan wrote, "this is due to the way in which our paratroopers fight and not to tough resistance put up by the Egyptians holding the line." The paratroopers are conditioned to the point of reflex to attack sources of enemy fire directed at them rather than seek cover. Members of a platoon with whom I spent some days in the Negev the year before Suez told me that they were blooded in bayonet drill on sacks of live cats. Many were sickened at first by the screaming and writhing and bleeding of their targets but it paid off in hand-to-hand combat, they said, because it overcame their reluctance to spear a living creature and thus gave them a split-second advantage over a human enemy.

The beginning of the British bombing at nightfall and Nasser's order to the Egyptian Army to withdraw from Sinai eliminated not only Sharon's opposition in Mitla Pass but also the threat of the Egyptian armor at Bir Gifgafa. Dayan wrote that he was angered by Sharon's defiance of his order and saddened by the ruse Sharon used—obtaining permission for a patrol and then attacking with a combat team. "The valor, daring and fighting spirit of the paratroop commanders are qualities which should be applauded and encouraged," Dayan wrote, "but this battle was not essential."

The Egyptians had planned a paratroop drop of their own at last light on the 31st to cut off the Israelis there. But the unit was late in assembling and by the time they were ready to take off from Almaza Airport in Cairo Egyptian airfields were already under attack by Britain's bombers. Two companies of the Egyptian 6th Battalion at Mitla were ordered to hold the western end of the pass as a rear guard while the remainder of the two battalions there withdrew. These two companies recrossed the Canal in small boats on 2 November, the ferry crossing having been destroyed.

When the Israeli paratroopers resumed their advance on the evening of 2 November after two days of recuperation, the Israeli Army history recounted, they avoided the road through Mitla Pass and made their way directly southwest by night through a difficult mountain valley toward al-Sudr. There they rejoined the road they could have stayed comfortably on if they had gone through the pass.

On the Central Axis, where Dayan had moved his schedule ahead twenty-four hours as a result of Simhoni's premature use of an armored brigade, the Egyptian 1st and 2nd Armored Brigades completed their advance to their marshaling area along the middle section of the al-Auja–Ismailiya road after dark on the 31st. During the daylight hours the advance was subjected to severe strafing and napalm attacks by Mystère jets. The two armored brigades were to act as the hammer to crush the Israeli invasion against the anvil of the Abu Aoueigila defense positions. The battle for Abu Aoueigila will be more appropriately narrated in the next chapter; it will suffice here to give the general situation there at the time the Anglo-French aerial intervention began at nightfall on the 31st. The Israeli 7th Armored Brigade had hooked leftward around the Egyptian defense complex after its premature straight-in assault was repelled early on the 30th. By nightfall on the 31st the Israelis had battered their way into outlying Egyptian positions west of the main stronghold astride the roads to al-Arish and Ismailiya. The Egyptian armored brigades planned to break this encirclement on 1 November.

Although the British air raids did not begin until nightfall the Voice of Britain on Cyprus broadcast a warning in Arabic some two hours earlier, at 4:45 P.M.: "In order to protect their lives, all residents of Egypt are requested to stay away from all civil airports in Egypt from this moment until the Egyptian Government accepts the demand of the United Kingdom and France which was delivered on 30 October." The British clamped travel restrictions and wartime press censorship on Cyprus a few hours later.

At the UN Dag Hammarskjold threatened to resign in protest against the British and French ultimatum and their vetoes against Security Council action to halt Israel's invasion. He said he could not continue to serve as Secretary-General unless "all members honor their pledge to observe all articles of the Charter."

The Security Council, acting on a Yugoslav suggestion, invoked the procedure established by the Uniting for Peace resolution during the Korean War, according to which the vetoed issue was turned over to a special session of the General Assembly. As a procedural matter, this was not subject to veto, but it needed seven affirmative votes from the eleven Security Council members in order to pass. The US cast the seventh affirmative vote, joining Russia, Nationalist China, Cuba, Iran, Yugoslavia, and Peru. Britain and France voted against and Belgium and Australia abstained.

In Washington Eisenhower spent the day dealing with the Suez war, much of it drafting his major policy speech of the crisis, which he delivered on television that night. According to Dayan, Eisenhower also sent a third message to Ben-Gurion suggesting that since Israel had achieved her stated aim of destroying the *Fedayeen* bases she should withdraw from Sinai. If Ben-Gurion acquiesced, Eisenhower reportedly promised, he would immediately declare his deep appreciation of Israel.

Eisenhower's decision to make a major speech grew out of a morning conference. Dulles was assigned to write a first draft. By the time it reached speechwriter Emmet Hughes for polishing at 3:15 P.M. the British bombers were making their third raid of the evening on Cairo, where it was 10:15 P.M. A telecast to the nation from the White House Cabinet Room had already been scheduled for 7 P.M. Hughes sat down to rewrite the whole speech while Eisenhower relaxed by hitting golf balls on the lawn. Hughes, with a battery of stenographers, raced against the clock with Dulles standing by to review the pages as they were snatched from the typewriters. Eisenhower had told Hughes earlier in the day that the crisis was "the damnedest business I ever saw supposedly intelligent governments get themselves into." But during the hectic drafting of the speech he made only this request: "I want to be sure we show clearly in here how vital we think our alliances are. Those British—they're still my right arm!" When Hughes gave him the last page to scan at four minutes to seven Eisenhower chuckled: "Boy, this is taking it right off the stove, isn't it?"

The President's telecast told how, ever since the Suez nationalization, the US had opposed those "among our allies who urged an immediate reaction to this event by use of force." He said the US was neither consulted nor informed by its allies on the use of force and that the US therefore had full right to dissent from "these actions . . . taken in error," although it was determined to maintain its allied friendships. "There will be no United States involvement in these present hostilities," the President said. ". . . At the same time it is—and it will remain—the dedicated purpose of your government to do all in its power to localize the fighting and to end the conflict." He emphasized his intention to use the processes of the UN to the fullest possible extent and to work toward the further strengthening of the UN as "the soundest hope for peace in the world." . . . "There can be no peace without law," Eisenhower said. "And there can be no law if we were to invoke one code of international conduct for those who oppose us and another for our friends."

In London the Commons continued to debate amid divisive uproar. Booing and shouts of "Resign!" greeted Eden when he entered the House at the end of question time. He tried to justify the ultimatum and the vetoes. "We are not concerned to stop Egypt, but to stop war," Eden said over ironical Opposition cheers. "None the less, . . . there is no hope of a general settlement of the many outstanding problems in that area so long as Egyptian propaganda and policy continues its present line of violence." Gaitskell accused Eden of abandoning the three governing principles of British foreign policy—Commonwealth solidarity, the Anglo-American alliance, and the UN Charter—declaring that the Government had "committed an act of disastrous folly whose tragic consequences we shall regret for years." Eden insisted that he had consulted the Commonwealth, that the UN was too slow to wait for, and that "I do not think that we must in all circumstances secure agreement from our American ally before we can act ourselves in what we know to be our own vital interests."

Gaitskell raised the first public allegation of collusion in the debate. After saying the world regarded the ultimatum as a "transparent excuse to seize the Canal," Gaitskell added: "There is an even worse story going around. It is that the whole business was a matter of collusion between the British and French Governments and the Government of Israel." Lloyd, the senior British participant in the Sèvres talks, then told the first parliamentary lie about collusion. He began with the timeworn but effective device of answering a question that had not been asked, saying: "It is quite wrong to state that Israel was incited to this action by Her Majesty's Government." Then, in the clumsiness of exhaustion, he added the needless falsehood: "There was no prior agreement between us about it."

Lloyd announced the start of the bombing of Egyptian targets just before the session adjourned at 10:29 P.M. By that time the tumult in the Commons reached a new pitch of anger and the Labor party moved a vote of censure to be debated the following day.

Until Lloyd's announcement of the first raids, Gaitskell had been unable to worm out of Eden whether any military action actually had been taken or ordered. The final edition of *The Times* that morning had reported prominently that British and French forces were entering Egypt, taking as its source a 5 A.M. broadcast by the clandestine anti-Nasser radio. *The Times* writer assumed that the Anglo-French force had moved immediately upon the expiry of the ultimatum at 04:30, noting that Egypt had rejected and Israel accepted it. The false *Times* report contributed to the confusion and acrimony of a debate which *The Times* described the next day as "the worst possible setting for the launching of a great military adventure."

A spell of panic gripped Eden before he went to the Commons when word came by radio from the rooftop transmitter on the British Embassy in Cairo that some thirteen hundred US nationals in Cairo were being evacuated to Alexandria along the Desert Road adjacent to Cairo West airfield, a main base for the Ilyushin-28 bombers and a major target for the British medium and heavy bombers. The first waves of the big British jets were in the air.

Eden appealed desperately to Defense Minister Antony Head: "If you can stop those planes I'll make you a duke!" Head succeeded in reaching Keightley in Cyprus by telephone and Keightley succeeded in radioing the planes to scratch Cairo West from their list of targets. "We had an anxious moment," wrote Keightley in his dispatch. He added that Cairo West's "sudden reprieve was a matter of concern" because of the possibility that the IL-28s might strike back at Cyprus, perhaps with Russian pilots. But the planes at Cairo West were removed in the other direction, to Luxor, where most of them were burned out two days later by a French squadron of F-84s on French leave from their NATO command.

Nasser's information on the start of the bombing was direct. "I was here [at home] with the Indonesian ambassador," he told me. "Then there was an air raid alarm. Then I heard the aeroplanes and I said to the ambassador that these were bombers, so they were not Israelis because the Israelis don't have jet bombers. Then I went to the roof of the house. I saw the bombardment of the aerodrome.... I went to headquarters. The members of the Revolutionary Council came. There was a battle going on in front of Rafah—at Abu Aoueigila; all along the front there were engagements. And I said to General Amer: 'We have only one way open to us; the withdrawal of our troops completely from Sinai within two nights. We have to begin this very night."

CHAPTER
16

Retreat

(EVENING, 31 OCTOBER 1956 TO MIDDAY, 2 NOVEMBER 1956)

Or what king, going to make war against another king, sitteth not down first, and consulteth whether he be able with ten thousand to meet him that cometh against him with twenty thousand?

(LUKE 14)

The territory which an animal apparently possesses is thus only a matter of variations in readiness to fight, depending on the place and on various local factors inhibiting the fighting urge. In nearing the center of the territory the aggressive urge increases in geometrical ratio to the decrease in distance from this center.

(KONRAD LORENZ, On Aggression)

THE RHYTHM of the war reached its peak on 1 November as the Egyptian Army broke off desperate battles on the Central and Northern Axes and struggled back across the Sinai Desert under a pitiless storm of fire and steel from the skies, which the enemy now possessed unchallenged. By midday on 2 November, Nasser was able to broadcast to Egyptians that the bulk of the Army was safely west of the Canal, no longer in danger of being cut off and destroyed between the impending Anglo-French invasion and the Israeli Army.

Elsewhere in the world a vast symphony of events was taking its rhythm from the war. It too reached a peak of intensity on 1 November as the world expressed its will at the United Nations that Israel must end her aggression and withdraw. But while the Egyptians pulled back to defend their heartland, the colluders continued to advance in defiance of the UN. During the lull in the fighting between Egypt's retreat from Sinai and the Anglo-French invasion at Port Said, the war itself became less important than the events focused on it. Powers greater than the belligerents in the Middle East sought to forestall the final stage of the war, the Anglo-French invasion, fearing lest it draw the Super-Powers into a nuclear war that could bring the history of man to an end.

The second of the war's three stages began with the British bombing raid at dusk on 31 October. The bombs convinced Nasser at last that Britain and France were in collusion with Israel and that they intended to invade Egypt. The escape of the Egyptian Army from Sinai divides the second stage again into two parts. The first was the headlong retreat of the Egyptians to the west bank of the Canal with as much as they could save of their equipment while the British, French, and Israeli air forces tried to interdict their escape. This phase lasted from dusk on 31 October to the morning of 2 November. When it ended, most of the Egyptian Sinai force and its armor were out of the trap. The second phase, from 2 to 5 November, saw the Israelis mop up isolated pockets of resistance in the Sinai Peninsula and the Gaza Strip and occupy with relative ease and safety positions they would have had to fight for if Britain and France had not intervened.

The approach of an Anglo-French invasion force, heralded by the ultimatum and confirmed by the bombing, threatened the Egyptian Army with enemy attacks coming in at right angles—a textbook dream for attackers and a strategical and tactical nightmare for defenders. It forces defenders to face both attacks simultaneously to avoid presenting a vulnerable flank to either one. Instead of the hard front confronting an attack from a single direction, made possible at the expense of soft flanks, the defender against attacks coming in at right angles must present two diluted mixtures of front and flank.

Sinai, with its vulnerable communications across the Canal and the indefensible Port Said on the left flank, was the worst place to meet ninety-degree attacks. By withdrawing into the Delta, the Egyptians would convert the Canal as a military feature from a flank and communications weakness into a frontal obstacle on the east, thus allowing more strength to shift its face against the sea-borne attack from the north.

The ninety-degree principle figured tactically as well as strategically in the Sinai campaign, underlying much of the maneuvering on all three east-west invasion axes. Fear of right-angled Egyptian attacks at the Parker Memorial was what impelled Sharon to defy orders and fight Israel's bloodiest battle to gain the shelter of the Mitla Pass. Dayan took Rafah with three convergent attacks from a ninety-degree arc. The purpose of the stubborn Egyptian defense at Abu Aoueigila was to prevent him from blocking the Egyptian retreat through al-Arish with a right-angle attack against its southern flank.

General Keightley, Commander-in-chief of the Anglo-French forces, wrote in his official report of the Suez war that the bombing began at 18:15 with attacks on Almaza and Inshas airfields near Cairo and Abu Suwweir and Kabreet in the Canal Zone. It probably began somewhat later than Keightley said. Sunset was shortly after 5 P.M. and Cairo was in twilight at 6:15. An interview with a Canberra pilot, broadcast from Cyprus after the first raid, indicates that it was carried out in darkness. "The Egyptians were taken by surprise," the pilot said. "The target was excellently illuminated and the lights of Cairo could be seen clearly in the distance. The lights went out immediately after the first bombs were dropped. No Egyptian fighters were met, and anti-aircraft fire was completely off target." Radio Cairo reported that night that the raids, with high explosive and incendiary bombs, began at 19:00.

Not in this case but in others, British accounts appear to have discrepancies in chronology because the British forces kept their watches on Greenwich Mean Time, which is two hours earlier than local time in the eastern Mediterranean. In recalling the events, in interviews or in memoirs, Britons fall unawares into confusion between the Greenwich time they observed on their watches and the actual phases of day they observed without consulting their watches. Keightley used Greenwich times in his report and I have converted them to Middle East time, adding two hours.

Nasser, whose house is near Almaza, an air-force field, and who watched the bombardment from his roof, also placed the first attack at 19:00 and he insisted that Almaza was not hit. Heliopolis, Almaza, and Cairo International airports form a line on the northeastern outskirts of Cairo with no more than three miles separating one from another. "There was a mistake," Nasser told me. "They bombarded Cairo, not Almaza. And there were fires at Cairo Aerodrome, the civil aerodrome, but Almaza was not bombarded."

Three waves of British bombers had swept over Lower Egypt by midnight, attacking airports in the light of parachute flares released by pathfinder planes. Four-engine jet Valiants from Malta and twin-jet Canberras from Cyprus dropped contact and delayed-action bombs from high altitude to damage runways and discourage Egyptian planes from taking off. At daybreak on 1 November carrier-based planes and fighters from Cyprus began low-level attacks on the planes themselves with rockets, guns, and bombs. The three British aircraft carriers, *Albion, Bulwark,* and *Ark Royal,* had sailed from Malta early on 27 October and were on station in the eastern Mediterranean by the time the Israelis opened hostilities.

The British bombers over the Canal Zone endangered the 460 still-unevacuated British maintenance technicians. They also sank the first of the ships that blocked the Canal. Colonel Haney Amin Hilmy II, Chief of Staff of the Eastern Command, had brought the old US surplus LST *Akka* early in October from Alexandria to Lake Timsah, where he loaded her with cement and anchored her in the northwest shallows, handy for blocking the channel at the north end of the lake. Hilmy told me he was determined not to repeat the mistake of his grandfather and namesake, a major in Arabi's army, who waited too long to block the Canal against the British invaders under Sir Garnet Wolseley in 1882.

British intelligence had identified the *Akka* as a prepared blockship. She was 347 feet long, 55 feet in the beam, and displaced nearly 5,000 tons fully loaded. The surprises of the beginning of the war caught the *Akka* out of position. The Egyptian retreat from Sinai meant that the withdrawing armor needed a pontoon bridge across the Canal at Ismailiya in the spot where the *Akka* was to have been scuttled. Hilmy began a race with the British bombers to get the *Akka* into the Canal south of Lake Timsah. Two British aerial attacks on 1 November put the *Akka* in a sinking condition as she wallowed under tow down the lake but she made it into the Canal, where she settled diagonally athwart the waterway. Radio Cairo announced the sinking at 14:20.

Hilmy had not relied on the *Akka* alone. Captain Showqi Khallaf of the Army Engineers sank three belts of ships that day in Port Said harbor to hamper invaders. He was subsequently killed in an air raid and a sappers' camp at Ismailiya was named for him. On the morning of 2 November, after the Egyptian armor on the Central Axis had escaped across the pontoon bridge, the ocean-going tug *Edgar Bonnet* was sunk at the spot originally designated for the *Akka*. The rail and road bridge at Ferdan was dropped into

527

the Canal, Nasser said, by British bombers trying to prevent the withdrawal of the Egyptian Army. The frigate *Abu Kir* was scuttled in the Canal two miles north of Suez. She was raised and towed clear on 8 April 1957, the last to be removed of some fifty wrecks blocking the waterway.

The bombing was ostensibly the first part of Eden's plan to save the Canal from its owners and protect shipping from the Egyptian-Israeli war, which he helped contrive. In the event, it not only blocked the Canal but also caught fourteen ships in a southbound convoy between al-Kap and the Ballah station in the narrow northern cut of the Canal. Hilmy said Nasser telephoned him to ask about the convoy while the bombers were attacking the *Akka* and French and Israeli jets and British carrier planes were making rocket and bombing runs on the armor crossing the pontoon bridge. Hilmy replied that Canal traffic would have to stop and that the ships had better remain where they were. Hilmy sent presents aboard at Christmas, halfway through their enforced sojourn in the Canal.

By the end of 2 November, Keightley wrote, "the task of neutralizing the Egyptian Air Force was all but complete" and "the bulk of the air effort was switched from airfields to other military targets." That night British bombers from Cyprus and French F-84s from Lydda attacked Luxor airfield and the IL-28s assembled there on their way from Cairo West to safety in Saudi Arabia. Twelve escaped before the attack but a delay in refueling those remaining allowed the rocket-firing French jets to catch eighteen on the ground immediately after they had fueled. All eighteen were burned in their own gasoline.

Nasser conceded a month after the war, in an Egyptian magazine article, that the Egyptian Air Force was out of action from the morning of 1 November, twenty-four hours before Keightley claimed to have neutralized it. Egyptian fighters, however, continued to appear singly on occasional strafing missions over the battlefields until the end of the war.

Before the Anglo-French air intervention, the Egyptian fighter planes made a fair showing, according to Dayan, but not the bombers. Egyptian close support missions were "grave" only during the battle in the Heitan defile, he wrote; elsewhere they caused casualties but did not affect the course of battle. He said the Egyptian pilots "did not overwork" but that they flew about forty sorties on 30 October and ninety on the 31st. The Egyptians used their old Vampires and Meteors for attacks on Israeli ground targets with the Migs flying protective cover. Dayan said the Mig pilots did not avoid battle and at times set ambushes for Israeli planes returning from sorties but that they operated in comparatively large formations of four to eight planes and avoided prolonged combat. Dayan claimed that at least four Egyptian Migs and four

Vampires were shot down by Israelis in aerial combat but that the only Israeli losses were to Egyptian anti-aircraft gunners.

The relative losses on both sides were subject to widely conflicting claims between the Egyptians and the Israelis as well as between the Egyptians and the Anglo-French raiders. Nasser said on 1 November, for example, that before the Anglo-French bombing began the Israelis had lost eighteen planes and Egypt two. The Egyptians claimed to have knocked down many times more than the half-dozen planes the British and French admitted losing to Egyptian gunners. Egyptian civilians accepted the claims the more readily because many mistook jettisoned auxiliary wing-tip fuel tanks for falling enemy planes. Even with wing-tanks the Cyprus-based fighters averaged only fifteen minutes over their targets. Allied claims of Egyptian planes destroyed range from 100 to 260.

Cairo Radio and its "Voice of the Arabs" were silenced for several hours at 11 o'clock on the morning of 2 November when Canberras with French fighter cover bombed the short wave transmitters at Abu Zabel on the edge of the Delta twelve miles north of Cairo and knocked down the masts. The Voice of Britain immediately began broadcasting from Cyprus on the "Voice of the Arabs" frequency. One of the first transmissions, calling itself the Voice of the Allied Military Command, addressed Egyptians in Arabic at 14:45 in this wise:

O Egyptian people, your broadcasting station has been destroyed. From now on you will listen to the Voice of the Allied Military Command on this very frequency. . . . O people of Egypt, our fighter planes and bombers have been and are at this very moment flying over you . . . O Egyptians, this is the first blow which has befallen you. Why has this befallen you? First, because Abdel Nasser went mad and seized the Suez Canal which is of vital importance to the world . . . mad to an extent that he rejected all peaceful attempts leading to a fair solution . . . Abdel Nasser has exposed you to Israeli attacks . . . Abdel Nasser continued his threats to Israel at a time when he was aware that he could not defend Sinai. Now he bears the consequences. . . . Our warships will disembark tanks and guns on Egyptian soil. . . . Abdel Nasser . . . did not keep his promise[s] and betrayed Egypt. He thus brought war to the country. . . . He promised equality for the Egyptian people, but instead he adopted dictatorship. . . . O Egyptians, accept the proposal of the Allied states, for it will bring you peace and prosperity. Otherwise you will bear the consequences of Abdel Nasser's mad behavior, which will affect not only the guilty ones but many innocent persons.

The bombers attacked railroad marshaling yards, Egyptian armor and military vehicles, gun emplacements, and barracks areas in and around Cairo and the Canal Zone. The British took pains to avoid civilian casualties, both during the bombing and in the capture to Port Said. The Cabinet twice reduced the size of the bombs allowed to the air raiders—from 1,000 pounds to 500 pounds and again to 250 pounds. The ministers fretfully minimized the naval bombardment before the amphibious landings at Port Said. Their concern was not so much for Egyptians as for world reaction. After the war the British ungracefully wrangled with the Egyptians over how many Egyptians they had killed but General Burns gave them full marks for their bombing accuracy and the care they took to avoid casualties. "This wasn't so easy," General Stockwell grumbled in retrospect, "for if an enemy fights, you cannot be all that choosey when you have a job to do and your own neck is in danger."

The last bombers to fly over Egypt were those that carried out on the night of 3 November what Keightley described as "an attempted raid" at Alexandria "intended primarily to attract attention away from Port Said." Keightley wanted to induce Nasser to keep his armor reserves from sealing the vulnerable causeway exit from Port Said. "We hoped to do this by keeping them uncertain until the last moment whether our main attack was to be at Port Said or Alexandria," he wrote. "This, in fact, we succeeded in doing."

After concluding on the night of 29 October that Britain and France did not intend to intervene physically, Nasser and his generals had activated the plan prepared for a major Israeli invasion. "The defense of the frontiers was aimed at engaging the enemy and impeding his advance," Nasser said a month after the war, "while the movements at home were directed towards amassment centers from which our striking forces would move to face the enemy in the decisive battle at the most favorable time and place that would ensure to them the greatest elements of victory. Our appreciation at that time was that this would have to take place on the 5th or the 6th of November."

The 2nd Infantry Brigade was assigned to block the Southern Axis and two battalions were sent in the vanguard to the Heitan defile, as narrated in the previous chapter. The 1st Motorized Infantry Brigade was sent to reinforce the Northern Axis at al-Arish, where it arrived under day-long aerial attack on the 30th in what the Israeli Army historian described as "a bruised and battered condition but not yet destroyed." The main striking force, the 1st and 2nd Armored Brigades, was ordered across the Canal toward Bir Gifgafa and Bir Rod Salem, on the Central Axis, from where it could send elements slicing south to cut off the Israeli paratroopers, north against the flank of the Northern Axis by way of the Bir Hassana–al-Arish road, and east against the attackers at Abu Aoueigila. The two armored brigades were equipped with new Russian T-34 tanks and SU-100 self-propelled armored guns.

The ultimatum "came as a surprise to us," Nasser said mildly in his account a month after the war, but it took the start of actual bombing more than twenty-four hours later to make Nasser recast his defense plans. "I [then] saw the whole conspiracy," Nasser said. "The Israeli attack was intended only to drag our main forces to Sinai to be cut off there by the occupation of the Canal area. Thus the enemy would realise two objectives: first, to destroy our forces east of the Canal completely after depriving them of air support, and second, to occupy Egypt without meeting organized resistance once Egypt was deprived of the Army. It was obvious at this very moment that we had to revise all our plans."

When Nasser arrived at General Headquarters at 20:00 a meeting of his military commanders was already in progress. By 10 o'clock the group had adopted two major decisions: first, to pull the Army back across the Canal to fight Britons and Frenchmen in the Delta instead of Israelis in the Sinai, and second, to distribute arms to the people for permanent guerrilla warfare if the Armed Forces should be overwhelmed.

The order to reverse military movements into the Sinai was radioed at 20:40 from General Headquarters to all commands: "Halt all movements going east; these [units] will return to the west of the Canal." The reinforcements dispatched to the three invasion axes were ordered back first. The units stationed in the defensive positions on the Northern and Central Axes were given phased withdrawal orders later as were the two understrength battalions at Sharm al-Sheikh guarding the entrance to the Gulf of Aqaba. There were no defensive positions on the Southern Axis, only light lookout units.

The withdrawal was to be carried out on the nights of 31 October and 1 November, with the forces taking cover under camouflage from enemy air attacks during daylight on 1 November. The Rafah defenders were to withdraw the first night along with the 2nd Armored Brigade on the Central Axis. The men at Abu Aoueigila were to hold until the second night to shield the general withdrawal. On that night al-Arish and Abu Aoueigila were to be evacuated except for small rear-guard units, which were ordered to delay the Israelis until midday on 2 November. By then it was hoped that the main forces, including the 1st Armored Brigade on the Central Axis, would have reached the west bank of the Canal. "It was impossible for us to estimate a shorter period for the withdrawal," Nasser told Egyptians after the war. "Indeed, it was a miracle to complete the withdrawal in that short a time. We were racing against hours, minutes, and seconds." Conversely, he said, "had we delayed the withdrawal decision a mere twenty-four hours, the whole thing would have come to an end."

Orders to the commanders of the defensive positions began going out at

23:30. Jaafar al-Abd at Rafah messaged back that he was able to stand and fight but that he was too closely embattled to disengage except at grave risk. He was ordered to begin withdrawing by daybreak at any cost. The Supreme Command had sent specific commanders the new appreciation at 01:30 on 1 November, stating that the war was not merely with Israel and that the mission of the forces now was no longer merely to repel the Israeli invasion but to defend the national heartland itself.

Amer began signing and sending the withdrawal orders only after a protest, Nasser told me. "General Amer was following the battles at the front. He told me that we were successful in Rafah; we were causing casualties to the Israelis; we were beating them here and there, and so on. I told him: 'It is not a question of the Israelis now. It is a bigger question. . . . Our main object now is to save the Army.' And he agreed. And the others agreed." The Gaza Strip units, National Guards and Palestinians, were impossible to withdraw once Rafah was invested and they had to be left to their fate. They constituted the largest part of the nearly 6,000 prisoners taken by the Israelis.

Nasser admitted substantial losses in his postwar analysis of the Sinai fighting. "We lost, for example, thirty T-34 Czechoslovak tanks as a result of the air attacks," he said. "But I do not say that we had actually lost them. I should say rather that we won 170 tanks. We had 200 tanks at the Bir Rod Salem concentration area. Had the withdrawal been delayed, we would have lost them all. That is why I say we won 170 tanks." Similarly, he said that he felt Egypt had won 250 armored cars by withdrawing rather than having lost fifty. The trucks and command cars and other motor vehicles, he said, were replaced from British stores in the Suez base. "There were two thousand vehicles in the British Army depots," he said, "and we took them all."

As for his Arab allies, in the agonizing reappraisals of the night Nasser concluded that whatever help Syria and Jordan might give against Israel was outweighed by the risk that France and Britain would seize the pretext to reoccupy the Arab countries they had ruled between the two World Wars. The proclaimed intention of Britain and France to limit the war in Egypt indicated that they would be equally ready to stamp it out in Syria and Jordan, if it spread there. Nasser received ominous intelligence about French designs on Syria in addition to reports of the clumsy Anglo-Iraqi-US-supported *coup d'état* there. Therefore at 06:00 on 1 November the Supreme Joint Command in Cairo, code-named Hawk, signaled the military commands in Amman and Damascus:

Abu Nuwwar and Nizameddeen: Halt all offensive preparations. Postpone Operation Beisan [to sever Israel between Tel Aviv and Haifa] until further orders. Secure borders and prepare defenses against every possible invasion. We are furnishing detailed instructions. Coordinate operations with Hafez Ismail.

Major Generals Aly Abu Nuwwar and Tawfeeq Nizameddeen were the commanders of the Jordanian and Syrian armies. Brigadier General Hafez Ismail, Chief of Staff of the joint command in Cairo, had been caught in Damascus by the outbreak of war. The colonels of Syria protested bitterly to the Egyptian ambassador, Mahmoud Riad, complaining that honor required them to join the battle. The Syrians and Jordanians badgered Hawk with messages asking permission for "volunteer" operations against Israel.

When Cairo broadcast on 2 November the resolution of the Arab trade union confederation demanding the sabotage of Western-owned oil pipelines, the Syrian colonels hastened to tell Riad that the Syrian Army engineers would blow up the three big pumping stations on the Iraq Petroleum Company line to the Syrian port of Tripoli. When Riad reported the assurance, Cairo had sudden second thoughts that the promised sabotage might bring on a British, French, or even Turkish invasion. The Iraqis too had been muttering darkly about invading Syria to protect their oil outlets. Amer scribbled a message for Colonel Abdel Hameed Sarraj, the influential chief of Syrian intelligence:

"From Hawk to Military Damascus: Inform Sarraj not repeat not to destroy oil pipelines as this is injurious to the interests of other countries not implicated. . . . Acknowledge this message please." Sarraj replied on 3 November: "Sorry to report that [pumping stations] T-2, T-3, and T-4 already destroyed." The job was done on the night of 2 November. The Syrians refused to allow rebuilding of the big pumps to begin until after Israel completed her withdrawal from Sinai in March 1957.

By the time the news went out that the pipelines were blown up the colluders were in such a dither that none of them wanted a wider war than what they had scheduled, not even to restore the pipelines. Eden had begun casting about for a way to get out of the war and back into the good graces of America, Ben-Gurion had begun to suspect the British would sell out at Israel's expense, and the French were in between. Likewise, when Iraqi troops finally moved into Jordan at King Hussein's request on 3 November, Mrs. Meir quickly sent an assurance through the British ambassador that Israel would not attack Jordan. This red herring, having served its purpose, was tossed on the trash heap of history.

Zakaria Mohyeddin, Interior Minister and a member of the original revolutionary junta, was in charge of planning for guerrilla warfare by a Liberation Army of citizens if the British and French succeeded in occupying the country.

Planning for this contingency was well under way by 13 October, the date the talks at the UN resulted in an agreed basis for a Suez settlement and eliminated the Canal dispute as a pretext for war. The Egyptians, unaware that Eden had then accepted French and Israeli plans for Israel to provide a new pretext, believed that the war danger had passed. But they did not dismantle their preparations for repelling an Anglo-French invasion and, failing that, resisting occupation.

The plan was brought out at the meeting of Nasser and his aides on the night of 31 October during the first hours of the bombing. After Nasser's decision to withdraw the Army from Sinai the group decided to put the plan into effect and to distribute arms to the people. Recruitment for the Liberation Army began the next day at local National Guard headquarters. Hundreds of thousands of small arms were distributed in the remaining days of the war. In some areas lists were made of recipients but in others the weapons were distributed with no regulation at all by trucks traveling through the streets and giving guns and ammunition to whoever responded to the invitation to take them. Young women and small boys were not excluded. In some instances heaps of weapons and ammunition were reported to have been dumped on the pavement for passersby to help themselves. In Port Said, Keightley wrote, "on 8th November 45 Commando recovered fifty-seven 3-ton truck loads of arms and ammunition from the area around Arab Town... mainly surrendered by Egyptians in civilian clothes."

Mohyeddin, who was Premier when I interviewed him in 1966 about the war, said the country was divided into sectors and that leadership cadres for guerrilla warfare were assigned to each sector. "We knew we were making history at that time," he said, "and that if we prolonged the war we might get a chance in world opinion [to avoid recolonization]."

"We had made a plan for continuous war if they invade us," Nasser told me. "We distributed wireless sets, ammunition, arms, in different parts of the country.... Every one of us [of the old Revolution Command Council] was to be responsible for an area. Salah Salem was in Suez and Kamaleddeen Hussein was in Ismailiya and their orders were: If they [the British and French] occupy the area, they were to go underground, either in Sharqiya [the eastern province of the Delta] or in these areas."

I asked Nasser if he had ever contemplated taking his government into exile in the event of defeat and occupation in order to continue the fight from allied countries, as Churchill had said he would do in World War II if England fell. "No, no, no," he said. "We agreed completely to lie here. There was no idea of leaving the country. We agreed that we have to continue fighting underground." Nasser was to command the whole operation from underground in Cairo. "We had stored arms and ammunition and money in certain houses in order to follow up if the British occupy the country," he said. "I was going to one of these houses. Zakaria prepared that. They were equipped also with wireless contacts, not telephone contacts." Nasser never saw the house prepared for him. Only in occupied Port Said were guerrilla operations carried out. The British, with their curious double standards of sportsmanship, were outraged by the guerrilla attacks, having themselves, after their unprovoked invasion, treated the Egyptians with condescending decency.

Nasser's determination to remain in Egypt to lead the Egyptians in a people's war for mastery of their own land stemmed from the shock his home-loving Egyptian spirit experienced at the sight of Palestinian refugees during the first Israel-Arab war. "I said to myself: 'This might happen to my own daughter,'" he wrote in 1953 in *The Philosophy of the Revolution.* "I was convinced that what was happening in Palestine could have happened—and is still quite likely to happen—in any country in this region...." He was right. It happened in 1956 to Egypt and in 1967 it happened to Jordan, Egypt, and Syria.

Al-Auja is the gateway to the Central Axis of invasion across the Sinai, which is why it was demilitarized in the Egyptian-Israeli Armistice Agreement in 1949. It is also why Ben-Gurion persistently chipped away at the Arab presence there, first killing or expelling the hapless Bedouin, then building up Israeli positions disguised as agricultural settlements in prohibited areas east of the zone, and, finally, when he began preparing in the fall of 1955 to invade Egypt, seizing the zone itself in flagrant defiance of the UN and the armistice.

The Abu Aoueigila area is a kind of inner or secondary gateway, a vestibule door to this main invasion corridor. Control of the eastern half of the Central Axis is essential to any invasion of the Sinai because the roads and tracks running from it to the Northern and Southern Axes are perfect avenues for flanking attacks against these axes. This logic made it imperative for Egypt to hold the Abu Aoueigila area an additional twenty-four hours to protect the withdrawal along the Northern Axis. If Israel had broken through the Abu Aoueigila defenses, her fast French AMX tanks and motorized infantry would have outflanked the Egyptians at al-Arish within hours.

For simplicity's sake, the Abu Aoueigila defense area acquired the name of the tiny village at its northwest corner, where an important road branches northward to al-Arish. The defense area was a system of prepared positions centered on a hill stronghold called Um Qataf nine miles east of Abu Aoueigila. Um Qataf rises under the al-Auja–Ismailiya road immediately east of where that road is joined by the track from Qussaima. This track comes northwestering through a system of wadis that debouches into a valley floor two or three miles wide in the southern approach to Um Qataf. An old Turkish track from al-Auja joins the Qussaima track immediately south of Um Qataf. The stronghold thus dominates these three passageways, bestriding the main road and overlooking the tracks skirting it on the west and south. Northward from the Ismailiya–al-Auja road a sea of shifting sand dunes rolls twenty-five miles to the Rafah defenses. Impassable to vehicles, the dunes are called Mukassar al-Fanageel, which might be translated as A Breakage of Teacups. They were probably named, like most features in Arabian deserts, after some Bedouin incident shrouded in the poetical mists of tribal legend.

The broad valley looking down the track to Qussaima is flanked by mountain barriers, Jebel Wugeir on the east and Jebel Dalfa on the west. Between them three hills rise from the valley floor, the nearest called Jebel Nizaa, then a long north-south ridge called Red Mesa, and beyond them a little hill numbered 209. Forward defense positions were posted on them. There was a troop of self-propelled antitank guns on Jebel Nizaa, a company of infantry reservists on Red Mesa, and an outpost on Hill 209.

A narrow defile cut by the millennial rain freshets of Wadi Arish through the western mountain barrier proved to be the weak point in the Abu Aoueigila defenses. Through it came tank squadrons of the Israeli 7th Armored Brigade to attack from the rear while planes, armor, and infantry pounded the Egyptians from the south, east, and overhead. The defile is called al-Dayyiqa, the Strait, and it cleaves the mountain barrier six miles west of the Qussaima track, dividing it into Jebel Dalfa and Jebel Halal. The thinning out of the Sinai defenses before the war induced the Egyptians to relative neglect of this passage, where tanks would in any case be vulnerable to air attack.

Like all the Sinai defenses in the prewar months, when Egypt saw Britain and France as the main threat, Abu Aoueigila was assigned merely a contingency function. In the unexpected event of an Israeli invasion it was to bar the Central Axis and pose a threat to advances along the other axes while units of the central reserve came across the Canal and the desert to repel or destroy the invaders. It was fulfilling this function when the British bombers attacked, whereupon Abu Aoueigila's role was transformed from that of an advance guard to that of a rearguard covering the general Egyptian withdrawal.

The Abu Aoueigila sector was the responsibility of the 6th Infantry Brigade, which had been reduced from three to two battalions, the 17th and 18th, with supporting units consisting of the 3rd Field Artillery Regiment, the 78th and 94th Antitank Batteries, a jeep-mounted light reconnaissance company, and two companies of reservists. Brigadier General Sami Yassa was in command. He deployed the 18th Infantry Battalion and the 78th Antitank Battery in the Um Qataf position. He held the 17th Infantry and the 94th Antitank

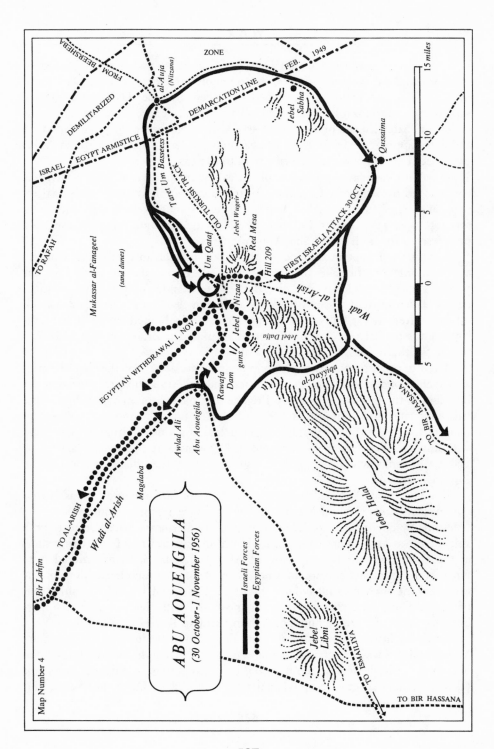

Map Number 4

ABU AOUEIGILA
(30 October-1 November 1956)

Israeli Forces
Egyptian Forces

ZONE

FEB. 1949

FROM BEERSHEBA

DEMILITARIZED

al-Auja
(Nitzana)

DEMARCATION LINE

Jebel
Sabha

ISRAEL EGYPT ARMISTICE

Tarat Um Basseess

OLD TURKISH TRACK

Quessaima

Jebel Wuqeir

TO RAFAH

Mukassar al-Fanageel

(sand dunes)

Um Qataf

Red Mesa

Hill 209

FIRST ISRAELI ATTACK 30 OCT

Jebel Nizaa

Wadi al-Arish

Jebel Dalfa

guns

EGYPTIAN WITHDRAWAL 1. NOV.

Rawafa Dam

al-Dayyiqa

TO BIR HASSANA

Awlad Ali

Abu Aoueigila

Magdaba

Jebel Halal

TO AL-ARISH

Wadi al-Arish

Bir Lahfn

Jebel
Libni

TO ISMAILIYA

TO BIR HASSANA

15 miles

10

5

0

5

537

Battery in reserve at the Ruwafa Dam in Wadi Arish two miles southeast of Abu Aoueigila. From there they were to counterattack toward the Dayyiqa if need be. The 3rd Field Artillery was emplaced on Jebel Dalfa, able to give supporting fire to both Rawafa Dam and Um Qataf. There were warning units at Jebel al-Sabha, scene of the Israeli attack on 2 November 1955, at Qussaima and in the approaches from the southeast, and at Auja al-Masri (Egyptian Auja) and Taret Um Basseess on the main road to the east.

Yassa's brigade at Abu Aoueigila was under the 3rd Infantry Division, commanded by Brigadier General Anwar al-Qadi, at al-Arish. In divisional reserve at al-Arish was the 4th Infantry Brigade, thinned out to two battalions, the 10th and 12th, under Colonel Saadeddeen Mutawally. It was the only near-reserve for both Rafah and Abu Aoueigila.

Against the Egyptian brigade at Abu Aoueigila Dayan threw two armored and two infantry brigades organized as Task Force 38. As related in the previous chapter, Colonel Simhoni, theater commander of the Sinai invasion, defied Dayan's orders to hold back his armor on the Central Axis and halt his infantry after taking Qussaima, the objective being limited in the first forty-eight hours of war to covering the right flank of the drive toward Mitla Pass on the Southern Axis.

The Egyptian reconnaissance troop at Jebel al-Sabha sent the first alarm of an Israeli probe at 02:30 on 30 October and fell back toward Qussaima. A battalion of the Israeli 4th Infantry Brigade occupied the empty al-Sabha post a half-hour later and continued toward Qussaima, now skirmishing with Egyptian units. The Egyptians fought a light delaying action, alternately firing and withdrawing. The Israeli infantry entered Qussaima at 07:00 with a support platoon of tanks which demolished a good part of the village in rooting out Egyptian snipers.

The Israeli battalion's advance was too slow for Simhoni and the task force commander, Colonel Yosef Harpaz. They feared the infantry would fail to take Qussaima by daybreak, as ordered, so they sent an armored battalion of the 7th Brigade toward Qussaima at 06:00. It arrived in time to fire a few parting shots at the Egyptians withdrawing toward Abu Aoueigila. Simhoni ordered it to pursue the Egyptians but not to attack Um Qataf. A misunderstanding of the order led the advance tank column to attack Um Qataf instead of halting out of range. The attack went in at 12:30 and failed with the loss of four Super-Sherman tanks after three hours of fighting around Red Hill and Hill 209.

Israeli shellfire, however, hurt the Egyptian brigade commander, Sami Yassa, while he was personally leading a company-strength counterattack from Um Qataf to Red Mesa at about 13:00. Pale, staggering, and dazed, Yassa was taken to a field surgery hospital and later removed to Cairo. His second-in-command was in Cairo when the Israelis attacked and had not yet been able to reach the front. Divisional headquarters at al-Arish ordered Colonel Mutawally to take over Yassa's command at Um Qataf. He arrived at 17:00 and was briefed by Colonel Mustafa Gamal of the artillery regiment in the midst of a bombardment.

The midday armored assault convinced al-Qadi at divisional headquarters that Israel had launched a full scale offensive, not a reprisal raid. Three of the 17th Infantry Battalion's four companies at Ruwafa Dam were drawn into the fighting at Um Qataf. Rafah was not yet under attack. So al-Qadi ordered half his divisional reserves, the 12th Infantry Battalion, plus an antitank troop of four self-propelled guns and a field artillery battery, to move into the Rawafa Dam camp vacated by the 17th Infantry. The 12th Infantry thus rejoined Mutawally in his new command at Abu Aoueigila.

In the morning, as the Israeli armored battalion swung north from Qussaima to attack Um Qataf, an armored reconnaissance team hooked westward to reconnoitre the Dayyiqa. As it arrived at 11:30 within 200 yards of a bridge at the entrance to the defile, the Egyptians blew up the bridge, exploded charges planted in the track and in the walls of the defile, and withdrew northward. Half of the Israeli reconnaissance team stayed to guard the southern entrance to the Dayyiqa. The other half bulled a path through the debris, emerged at the northern end at 16:15, reported by radio to the brigade commander, and dug in to hold the pass for the bulk of the brigade's tanks to come through from Qussaima during the night.

At 11:00, as these movements against Um Qataf and toward the Dayyiqa were under way, Dayan met with Simhoni and the commanders of Task Force 38 and the 7th Armored Brigade on the track between Qussaima and Um Qataf. After giving them a dressing down for defying his strictures on the use of armor, he made a virtue of necessity and ordered a speed-up of the whole schedule of the task force. In the evening, when he got word of the penetration of the Dayyiqa, he approved orders for two battalions of the 7th Armored to hook through the defile and attack Abu Aoueigila from the rear on the next day while the 10th Infantry stormed Um Qataf from the east. Another of the armored brigade's battalions headed southwest to take the Frontier Forces post at Bir al-Hassana, from where it could march to support the paratroopers at Parker Memorial or hook back north to the Central Axis at Jebel Libni.

Shortly after midnight, while the 7th Armored was grinding through the Dayyiqa, a plane equipped with loudspeakers circled over Um Qataf announcing somewhat prematurely: "You are cut off between tanks front and rear. Resistance is hopeless. Communications with al-Arish are cut. Surrender and save your lives. You will be sent home after the war." The plane dropped leaflets carrying the same message and promising the bearer safe conduct into the Israeli lines. The Egyptians fired machine guns at the plane, which shut off its running lights and loudspeaker and departed, only to return for a repeat performance shortly before dawn.

By this time, early on 31 October, the Israeli 10th Infantry Brigade was moving westward along the road from al-Auja with the Egyptian warning posts falling back before it and making their way to Um Qataf on foot through the Mukassar al-Fanageel. The brigade was under orders to attack Um Qataf from the east at 09:00 simultaneously with the 7th Armored's attack from the west on the crossroads village of Abu Aoueigila. The 7th Armored, although exhausted by an all-night march through the Dayyiqa, took the village at daybreak, after a short, fierce battle with Egyptian foot soldiers fighting with bazookas. When Dayan radioed to delay the attack to coincide with the eastern attack of the pincer, the Israeli commander was able to reply that he had already taken the village.

On the east, the Israeli 10th Infantry's part of the morning pincer attack failed east of Um Qataf after what Dayan irritably called "the first lukewarm attempt." The brigade commander got permission to withdraw and wait until nightfall before trying again.

Premature alarms of the approach of the Egyptian armored brigades from Cairo prompted some indecisive westward movements by detachments of the 7th Armored during the day. In the course of them, the Israelis dislodged the Frontier Force unit from Bir al-Hassana and took the undefended crossroads at Jebel Libni. Rocket-firing Mystères mauled the advancing Egyptian armor near Bir Rod Salem while Egyptian planes harassed the Israeli armor at Bir al-Hassana.

The fall of the village of Abu Aoueigila prompted al-Qadi to commit the rest of his reserves, Rafah still not having been attacked. Accordingly, the 10th Infantry Battalion advanced from al-Arish during the morning with two companies of Sherman tanks, about thirty in all, some of which had seen action at al-Alamein in World War II. Air attacks cost the Egyptian force heavy losses in fuel and ammunition lorries. The indefatigable Israeli tank men slammed four attacks against the Egyptian 10th Infantry at Awlad Aly, a place three miles north of Abu Aoueigila named for a well in Wadi Arish west of the road. All four attacks were beaten off but the battered Egyptians pulled back at dusk to Bir Lahfin at the northern apex of the Jebel Libni–Abu Aoueigila–Bir Lahfin triangle of roads. The Israeli tanks at Abu Aoueigila, approximately eighty in number by Egyptian estimate, were forced to move about constantly during the day to evade shellfire from the Egyptian 3rd Artillery Regiment on Jebel Dalfa.

A renewed pair of pincer attacks at night, at Rawafa Dam on the west and against Um Qataf on the east, were the major actions of the day in the Abu Aoueigila sector. At about the time these battles were joined, the British bombing attacks began and Dayan launched the assault upon Rafah. Fighting was still raging in the caves of Jebel Heitan on the Southern Axis.

At Ruwafa Dam, two miles southeast of Abu Aoueigila, an Egyptian lieutenant commanding a single infantry company supported by two troops of self-propelled antitank guns and a field artillery battery was ordered to hold until the pressure became unbearable and then to withdraw into the Um Qataf perimeter. "They fought like a brigade," said Mutawally. "They fired till their guns melted." Against this single company, the Israeli 7th Armored threw the better part of two battalions, leaving a detachment to watch for any renewed attack by Egyptian forces from al-Arish. In the course of probing attacks earlier in the day, Israeli soldiers captured two Egyptian lorry drivers, cut off their genitals, and released them to run back to the Egyptian lines, where they died soon after. The Egyptians assumed that this barbarity was intended to weaken their morale. The Israeli commander posted two troops of Super-Shermans on his right to the west of the dam to shell the Egyptians in the role of artillery and launched his main attack at sunset—delivering a straight punch at the center and a left hook with tanks and infantry in half-tracks against the Egyptian flank.

The Egyptians stood their ground, firing over open sights with their anti-tank guns trained flat as the Israelis closed. The Israelis broke through the wire and the battle fragmented all over the Egyptian position into scores of individual clashes. Every single Israeli vehicle was put out of action, at least temporarily. The fighting raged in the darkness. Tents, fuel drums, ammunition crates, and vehicles went up in flames. The Israelis were shelled by their own Super-Shermans on the rising ground to the west. The Egyptians gave ground, called in artillery fire on the Israelis in their erstwhile positions, and counter-attacked at 21:00. The Israelis gave ground in turn. An Israeli tank battalion commander tried to regroup at the "northernmost fire." But new fires kept breaking out and it was midnight before the Israeli attackers regrouped outside the Egyptian positions. The Egyptians "fought courageously and contested every inch of ground," the Israeli Army history said. "He [the enemy] did not cease his obstinate resistance until the whole area was in flames; tents, vehicles, and fuel and ammunition dumps. His losses were heavy and our forces took great quantities of spoils." The Ruwafa defenders withdrew to Um Qataf when the Israelis regrouped. The Israelis moved warily back into the empty position at 04:30 on 1 November.

The eastern pincer again won nothing but Dayan's angry contempt, failing to take Um Qataf on the night of 31 October as it had failed in the morning. The night attack was joined by elements of the 37th Armored Brigade, whom Dayan castigated for "over-eagerness" while he continued to heap scorn on the 10th Infantry for its "inability to execute a real assault." He also approved a change of commanders for the brigade. Dayan's blunt criticisms raised a national storm of criticism when he published his diary in 1965.

An important reason for breaking through from the east was to open the al-Auja road in order to feed fuel and ammunition to the 7th Armored, whose own route, by way of Qussaima and the Dayyiqa, was becoming increasingly difficult for wheeled supply vehicles as the roadways crumbled under the tread of war machines. The 10th Infantry was to hit Um Qataf from the north and south of the al-Auja road while the 37th Armored was to break through the Egyptian center along that road. Dayan ordered that Um Qataf be taken "as quickly as possible ... even if it meant a difficult frontal attack involving heavy casualties." The reason, he wrote in his diary, was that "time was fast running out.... From the political point of view, there is no doubt that time is working against us and the pressure on Britain and France—and certainly on us—to halt our military action will become more and more acute. Who knows how many more campaigning days are left to us?"

Israeli artillery had been shelling Um Qataf all day on the 31st. "Their artillery fire was no good," Lieutenant Colonel Mohammed Zohdy, an Egyptian gunner who was there, recalled. "But they were good with mortars from Jebel Dalfa, where they had a good O.P. [Observation Post]." The flanking forces of the 10th Infantry began moving forward at 20:00. Both lost their way in the night. Israeli artillery began a preparatory bombardment of Um Qataf shortly after midnight but there was no fighting until dawn, when a battalion of the 37th Armored dashed at Um Qataf across a minefield. The Egyptian antitank gunners opened up at 150 yards on an AMX tank, blew it into the air, and turned it about. But one half-track carrying the brigade commander, his deputy, and other officers broke into the Egyptian perimeter. An antitank gunner, thinking it was an Egyptian armored personnel carrier, shouted a protest at such reckless driving. Then he saw it was Israeli and started a fusillade of small arms fire which killed the Israeli brigade commander, his deputy, and most of the other men in the half-track before the driver was able to careen back out to his own lines. Thus two of the four attacking brigades—the 10th Infantry and the 37th Armored—as well as the Egyptian defending brigade underwent command changes in the heat of battle.

Air and ground attacks pounded at Um Qataf all morning. The Israeli 4th Infantry Brigade and a detachment of 7th Armored tanks that had remained in the southern approaches to Um Qataf since the first assault on 30 October launched assaults from the south while the 10th Infantry and 37th Armored continued hitting from the east. Scores of Israeli tanks and half-tracks coming into battle on the old Turkish track were put out of action in what became a tank grave in the open valley between Um Qataf and the antitank gunners on Jebel Nizaa. Hill 168, the anchor of Um Qataf's southeast perimeter, changed hands several times in hand-to-hand fighting with pistols, bayonets, hand-grenades, even stones. Some of the wrecked Israeli vehicles were so close that the Egyptians dashed forward during lulls in the fighting to get jerricans of water, orange juice, food, chocolates, cigarettes, trophies, and other loot. They also brought in a number of wounded Israelis. The Egyptians had received no food supplies and no addition to their meager water rations since the last ration convoy from Qussaima reached them at noon on 29 October.

At 09:40, the Egyptian officers recalled later, they had the curious experience of seeing strange planes, Mystère IVs with vertical yellow and black stripes on their tails, scream out of the sky pouring fire, not onto the Egyptian positions, but onto the disabled Israeli tanks and half-tracks. The markings were those of Operation Musketeer. The French pilots either mistook the armored vehicles for Egyptians or they had been asked to make sure the Egyptians, who had no armor, could not recover and use the Israeli tanks. At the time of this curious air attack, the Egyptians said, there were some forty Israeli tanks and seventy half-tracks on the battlefield.

At 10:00, Mutawally decided he had better bring the 3rd Artillery Regiment from Jebel Dalfa into the Um Qataf perimeter. As it was completing the move at 11:15 more striped-tailed Mystères roared in with rockets and napalm, the first napalm these Egyptians had seen, and destroyed five or six of the artillery regiment's ammunition lorries. For a time the Egyptians on the west side of Um Qataf were pinned down by chain-reaction explosions of their own artillery shells in the lorries. At noon Israeli mortar fire directed from the observation post on Jebel Dalfa intensified. The Egyptian artillery, newly arrived inside Um Qataf, was still not in position to shell the Israeli observation post, so an infantry platoon was ordered to destroy it. "We hated that O.P.—all the time firing upon us," Zohdy recalled. "A first lieutenant with a bushy mustache led the platoon. They approached up a two-hundred-yard slope—under fire. It was like watching a film. They went up in open order, stormed the post, and wiped it out."

By this time the Rafah garrison was in full retreat toward al-Arish, the 2nd Armored Brigade had turned back and recrossed the Canal on the platoon bridge at Ismailiya, and the 1st Armored Brigade was hiding under camouflage in the central Sinai desert, waiting to complete its withdrawal to the Delta under cover of darkness. At Um Qataf the surge and ebb of ground attacks abated at midday. The action thereafter consisted of artillery duels while air attacks pounded the Egyptians until nightfall.

At 17:00 Mutawally received Cairo's withdrawal order, which had been relayed by al-Qadi from al-Arish some hours earlier. The troops were to wait until dark and escape on foot with light arms through the Mukassar al-Fanageel to al-Arish, thirty-five miles to the northwest. Before leaving they were to destroy as much of their stores, heavy weapons, and vehicles as was possible without making any noise that would alert the besiegers that a withdrawal was afoot.

Mutawally, before disclosing the withdrawal order, called a conference of his commanders to discuss their plight. He told them there was only enough small arms ammunition left for an hour's fighting—not enough to repulse another attack—and no more than five or six rounds apiece for the artillery. Although rationing was so strict that cooking had been forbidden since the fall of Qussaima, only 200 gallons of water remained for some 4,000 men. Exhausted as they were by lack of hot food and sleepless nights under shell fire, not to speak of the strain of the fighting, some of the officers wanted to fight to the bitter end. Mutawally replied that if the ammunition ran out at the height of an attack, it would be difficult to transmit surrender signals. Many would be killed unnecessarily. It would be better to withdraw beforehand, he said. Some officers persisted in wanting to stay and fight.

"You can say it now," said Mutawally, "but you will never say it after two or three hours without water. Anyway, to make your spirits easier, I have in my pocket here the order to withdraw." He had conducted the conference, lightened with jokes and banter, as psychological preparation for the withdrawal order. He ordered the withdrawal in three groups, the first leaving in the dusk at 18:30, the second at 19:00, and the third at 19:30. A company of infantry was to remain until dawn to cover the withdrawal while a skeleton artillery crew continued firing the guns through the night. They successfully feigned preparations for a counterattack toward Abu Aoueigila.

The officers rapidly destroyed papers useful to Israeli intelligence without showing give-away fires. The drivers poured sand in vehicle crankcases, sugar in the gasoline tanks, machine-gunned the radiators during fire fights, and raced the engines. Gunners prepared charges to destroy muzzles with explosions set off under the covering roar of cannonades. The groups moved off on schedule. Mutawally, who had got a bullet in the knee during the morning fighting, left with the second group but soon ordered his companions to push on at their own speed and leave him behind. He took off his shoes, like thousands of others, for easier walking in the soft sand.

Mutawally's twenty-six day odyssey across the desert and Canal to Cairo became one of the folk-legends of the Sinai campaign. He escaped an Israeli patrol, was stung by a scorpion, and spent days with Bedouin who told him of the fall of al-Arish. He was amazed by their ability to hear approaching planes a full thirty seconds before he could. They also told him, inaccurately, that Cairo had fallen and that Nasser had gone to Assiut. Then on 17 November, still in the Mukassar al-Fanageel, he was taken to some Arabs who had a radio. He learned from a news broadcast that the bulk of the Um Qataf defenders had made their way back to the Delta and that the UN was in Port Said. The Bedouin killed a calf in celebration. Then they took him through the desert on camelback to the Canal at Qantara, sleeping by day and traveling by night.

So successfully did the Egyptians keep the secret of their withdrawal that the Israelis did not enter the Um Qataf positions for nearly twenty-four hours. Dayan relates that at midday on 2 November Simhoni's intelligence officer and an Israeli battalion commander of the 7th Armored near Abu Aoueigila sent a surrender ultimatum with a 2 P.M. deadline to the Egyptian commander at Um Qataf. They sent the note with two Egyptian prisoners driving a captured jeep flying a white flag. At about the same time Israeli pilots on bombing missions over Um Qataf signaled that they could detect no enemy movement and that the emplacements appeared empty. The Israeli 37th Brigade command at Qussaima sent a squadron of tanks to investigate the air force report. Finding the position vacant except for the two Egyptian ultimatum-bearers, the squadron commander sent them eastward to Southern Command headquarters, which had been moved forward from Beersheba to al-Auja at the beginning of the war. The squadron continued westward to rendezvous with the 7th Armored.

"It did indeed meet—with 7th Brigade's fire," Dayan related, "for the latter thought it must be an Egyptian unit who, instead of surrendering ... had no doubt decided with the power of its armor to break out of the ring. The only ones who realized immediately what was happening were our pilots, who knew that both armored columns were ours. They swooped low and with various signs got the unit to stop its fire. The firing stopped, but only one tank, the last in the column, had managed to retire behind the ridge and avoid being hit."

The Egyptian defenses at Rafah, gateway to the northern invasion route, had to make the best of a militarily weak locality. All of the Egyptian positions were in full view of the rising ground on the Israeli side of the frontier.

Although less vulnerable than the Gaza Strip, the Rafah topography lacked depth and was ill-secured against assault from the sea.

The Egyptian camps lay some four miles due south of the little border town of Rafah in an open area between the railroad and the main Qantara-Gaza road. The nearest point on the long curve of the seashore was five miles northwest. The camps were encircled by the lower loop of an angular figure 8 formed by the main roads, from which a network of minor roads and tracks branched off. For an invader seeking to cut off the Egyptian camps and the Gaza Strip, which extends twenty-five miles northeastward along the shore, the key objective was the crossroads of the Qantara-Gaza road and the old road from Rafah to al-Auja at the lower end of the figure 8.

Some twenty-six mutually supporting defense positions guarded the crossroads and camps. They were sited along both arms of the angle where the Gaza Strip truce line meets the Sinai frontier, extending four or five miles along each arm in a band two or three miles deep. Three minefields were laid southward along the Sinai frontier in parallel strips about three miles long. They spanned the area between the angle of the frontiers and the sand dunes impassable to tanks and trucks that extended to Abu Aoueigila. The minefields formed an artificial barrier across the natural line of advance for any flanking movement.

The Egyptian commander, Brigadier General Jaafar al-Abd, was left with half a brigade, the 5th Infantry, at his disposal after the Sinai forces were thinned out in August and September to guard Cairo and the Delta against the gathering Anglo-French force. He had as reserves some under-strength National Guard and Palestinian battalions. His heavy support weapons consisted of a company of sixteen old Sherman tanks whose gun muzzles had been shortened before they were sold to Egypt, a field artillery regiment of twenty-one British twenty-five pounders, and a dozen mobile antitank guns called Archers. He deployed a regular battalion along each arm of the frontier in company and platoon positions and held his tactical reserves in the camps, ready to sally forth in armored personnel carriers against enemy penetrations of the frontier defenses or against sea-borne or paratroop landings. He made the Rafah defenses self-contained, with ammunition, food, and water for seven days.

"We considered this to be a most difficult objective," wrote Dayan. He assigned two brigades of Task Force 77 to the attack, the 1st Infantry and the 27th Armored. The task force was under the command of Colonel Benjamin Givli of the 1st Infantry. Givli had been head of Israeli intelligence at the time of the disastrous spy-saboteur operation in Egypt in 1954, which led to his reassignment, started the Lavon Affair, and brought Ben-Gurion back into the Government. The task force also included the 11th Infantry Brigade, whose

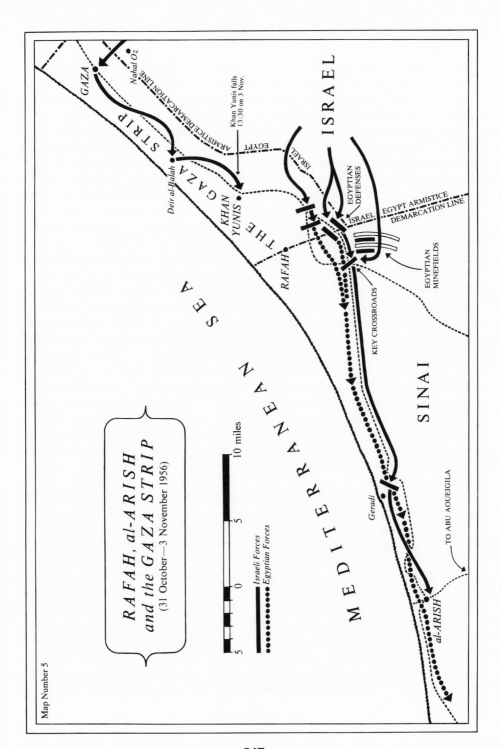

RAFAH, al-ARISH
and the GAZA STRIP
(31 October—3 November 1956)

10 miles

5

0

5

Israeli Forces
Egyptian Forces

MEDITERRANEAN SEA

ISRAEL

GAZA

GAZA STRIP

THE GAZA STRIP

Nahal Oz

Deir al-Balah

KHAN YUNIS

Khan Yunis falls
13:30 on 3 Nov.

ARMISTICE DEMARCATION LINE

EGYPT

ISRAEL

RAFAH

EGYPTIAN DEFENSES

ISRAEL

EGYPT ARMISTICE DEMARCATION LINE

EGYPTIAN MINEFIELDS

KEY CROSSROADS

SINAI

Geradi

TO ABU AOUEIGILA

al-ARISH

Map Number 5

547

main function was to stand by in reserve during the Rafah attack and, after Rafah fell, to subdue the defenders of the then isolated Gaza Strip. Dayan considered Rafah so important that he himself accompanied the 27th Armored Brigade during the attack.

Dayan planned a triple-pronged attack, a left hook by two battalions of the 1st Infantry against the crossroads through the minefield and up the al-Auja road, a straight punch through the central defenses by two more of the infantry battalions, and a right hook down the Gaza road by the 27th Armored, whose main mission was to race on toward al-Arish after a gap was forced at Rafah. The Israeli attackers outnumbered the Egyptian defenders by four to one in trained soldiery, and by nine to one in mechanized armor, having three battalions of Shermans, Super-Shermans, and French AMX fast tanks against Jaafar al-Abd's single company of lop-muzzled Shermans. As for artillery, the disproportion is hard to measure, for the Israelis firing from the east were supported by the French cruiser *Georges Leygues* and the French destroyers. The Israeli military attaché in Paris, Colonel Narkis, had arranged with General Beaufre days in advance for the French naval guns to soften up the Rafah defenses with a bombardment before the Israeli attack.

The attack was scheduled for the night of 31 October, when the Egyptian Air Force would be either destroyed by the Anglo-French pilots or would be wholly engaged in trying to stave off its destruction. Twenty-four hours before the attack, on the night of 30 October, Israeli engineers cleared three paths through the minefields for the 1st Infantry but left the paths unmarked in order to keep their preparations secret from the Egyptians. To save casualties, Dayan and Ben-Gurion had deferred the attack on Rafah until after the Anglo-French intervention. While they waited a storm of disapproval swept round the world. The mood at the UN, "and particularly the unexpected vigor of America's hostile stand," Dayan wrote, "made it essential to hasten the completion of the campaign."

At 8 P.M. on the 31st, an hour after British bombs began hitting the Egyptian airfields far to the west, Israeli engineers re-entered the minefields with covering forces to mark the lanes. They were driven back temporarily by Egyptian machine-gun fire. The battle for Rafah had begun. Nasser was over-hauling strategy in conference with his generals at Supreme Headquarters in Cairo at this hour. Sharon's paratroopers were grappling with Egyptians in the caves of Jebel Heitan for control of Mitla Pass. On the Central Axis the Israeli 10th Infantry Brigade was moving up for its floundering all-night assault on the main Egyptian strongpoint of Um Qataf, which was called off in the morning as a bloody failure.

Dayan was ungracious about the French naval bombardment. "The leviathan gave forth a sprat," he complained, adding that any self-respecting Israeli battery would have done better. The Israeli Air Force, called in to help soften up the Egyptian defenses, struck Israeli units instead, Dayan wrote, but was sent away before it did any damage.

The southern prong of the attack went in first, at 10 P.M. It had a grim time getting through the minefields. Israeli tanks and armored half-tracks supporting the infantry blew up on uncleared mines and blocked the paths while Egyptian guns poured concentrated fire on the blunted enemy spearhead. An Egyptian radio operator had the good luck to pick up the Israeli brigade commander's frequency. A translator was hastily summoned and the Egyptian fire developed what seemed to the Israelis an uncanny accuracy. The commander of the trapped battalion asked permission to withdraw but Givli told him the crossroads had to be taken by morning and to advance on foot if he could not get his vehicles through. Since the Egyptian fire could hardly be more punishing than it already was, the battalion commander ordered his lead half-track to turn on its headlights to help the engineers reclear the path. By such daring and luck, the southern prong broke through the minefield. It reached the al-Auja road at sunrise and turned north towards the crossroads.

The central prong fought a confusing action in citrus groves and cactus hedgerows where the Egyptian positions were so close and so interconnected with trenches that the attackers often mistook one for another. Artillery, small arms fire, tracer shells ripped through the darkness in all directions as the attackers forked first into two spearheads and then split into many smaller units and sub-units, breaking into the Egyptian positions with sub-machine guns and hand-grenades.

Jaafar al-Abd received the order to withdraw as the battle gathered full fury between midnight and dawn on 1 November. French naval gunners were shelling his northeastern defense positions to soften them up for the armored northern prong of the Israeli attack while tank-supported Israeli infantry battered at his southern and southeastern positions. He protested the order. "The brigade was in no position to carry it out," Dayan wrote later of his enemy's plight, "for, at the time, our attack on the Rafah defense area was at its height and the Egyptian troops could not break off to withdraw without turning retreat into panic flight."

The northern hook, carried out by the 27th Armored Brigade, cost the life of a battalion commander who, when his command tank's radio broke down, led his tanks standing in the open on a half-track giving visual signals. The armored attack broke through the outer Egyptian posts against heavy and accurate Egyptian artillery fire about 7 A.M. At that hour the southern prong was moving up the al-Auja road toward the defense positions at the crossroads, which were under attack by Israeli warplanes. The central prong was battering its way forward from one earthwork to another. Al-Abd was preparing a counterattack against the Israeli armor coming down from the northeast.

At this desperate moment, 7 A.M. on 1 November, al-Abd received a second —and absolute—order to withdraw. He protested bitterly then and afterward that a commander should never be ordered to withdraw when he is under attack. But he obeyed and succeeded in taking the bulk of his command back across the Canal, moving units at first along the main road and, after the Israelis got control of the road, along a track called the Darb al-Sultani (the Sultan's Way) between the road and the beach. Nasser said a month later that al-Abd "fulfilled the withdrawal order under the harshest possible conditions that could face a commander."

With all but a scattering of the Egyptian defenders on their way west, the southern and northern prongs of the Israeli attack closed on the crossroads at 9:30 A.M. Scattered shooting was still going on by rearguard troops and Egyptians who had failed to receive or were unable to implement the withdrawal order. But stray bullets could not restrain Israeli feelings, Dayan wrote, and they rushed forward to embrace their comrades, reckless of the shooting. Dayan said his "particular victim" was Givli's deputy . . . "we fell into each other's arms as in a classic Russian film."

The Israelis, having broken through the Rafah barrier, headed for al-Arish at 10:30. Dayan and his aides rode with the 27th Armored Brigade in two of the new French six-wheel-drive trucks. Despite Dayan's impelling presence, Egyptian rearguard posts at three points along the road delayed the Israeli entry into al-Arish until the following morning, 2 November.

The Egyptians had withdrawn overnight. When Dayan entered the town at 06:00 he found it empty of troops. Egyptian officers and men straggled into the Israeli net during the day after walking through the dunes from Um Qataf. They were unaware that al-Arish had fallen. One officer was captured as he walked into the 3rd Division Officers' Club. Dayan was nagged by the thought that if he had made a special effort to seal the western exit of al-Arish during the night he might have seized the vehicles and weapons of the 3rd Division. He wrote, however, that a huge quantity of military stores was left behind undestroyed. The Egyptians escaped so hastily, he wrote, that military surgeons abandoned an amputee to bleed to death on the operating table. Dayan does not explain why doctors should be so terrified at the approach of Israelis that they would violate their Hippocratic oath with such cowardly and flagrant totality as to defy credulity. His heavily edited diary is generally factual but he was not above making propaganda here and there.

Dayan reported being shown by an intelligence officer that morning a number of newly captured Egyptian documents. Among them, he wrote, was the Directive of the Commander of the 3rd Infantry Division. This was the curious document which Meinertzhagen recorded seeing on 4 October, nearly a month before its alleged capture at al-Arish—the document which Eban was to make famous by circulating it at UN headquarters on 15 November in justification of the war. It is one of only a handful of documents ever to be published out of the vast quantity Israel claimed to have captured. Dayan included in his diary the best known quotation from it—the introductory exhortation to prepare for "the destruction and annihilation of Israel in the shortest possible time and in the most brutal and cruel of battles."

The day after the capture of Rafah, fresh Israeli forces turned to the Gaza Strip with a certain relish in anticipation of settling scores with the *Fedayeen*. *Kol Yisroel* (the Voice of Israel) broadcasts had been assailing the morale of the defenders and inhabitants since the evening of 31 October with warnings, ultimatums, and political propaganda which treated the Strip as being legally a part of Israel.

"To the remaining *Fedayeen*," said one broadcast, "know that your names are well known to the Israel Defense Forces. When Gaza is cut off, severe penalties will be imposed on *Fedayeen* where it is proved that they have participated in activities of destruction and murder in Israel." The radio warned that all the Gaza Strip's inhabitants would be held responsible for any actions against Israeli civilians or property—"there will be no excuses."

On 1 November, after Rafah had fallen and the invading Israelis were approaching the gates of al-Arish, Israeli planes showered leaflets on the Strip that said:

> Egyptian rule in the Gaza Strip has come to an end. The Gaza Strip is cut off . . . The Egyptian Army is fleeing south. The soldiers of the Israel Defense Force will not harm you. We are driving the Egyptian Army from the soil of Israel, therefore we bring peace. . . . Do not keep or use any arms; do not leave your homes. Otherwise you may be killed on the roads or fields.

Along with the leaflets the Israelis began dropping bombs and mortar shells on the Strip, hitting the town of Gaza as well as the defense positions manned by the under-trained, under-equipped, and under-strength Palestinian and National Guard units. At 06:00 on 2 November the Israeli 11th Infantry Brigade, which had stood by in reserve during the Rafah battle, plus an armored combat team from the 37th Brigade, most of which was then watching the empty earthworks at Um Qataf, barged into Gaza from the southeast over the millennial route of the city's conquerors. They were hardly slowed down by

551

the stubborn but inept defenders on Ali Muntar, the hill where the British lost 10,000 men trying to drive the Turks out of Gaza in World War I. Dayan recalled the British losses and off-handedly recorded, for anyone who wished to make a comparison, that the 11th Brigade lost eleven killed and sixty-five wounded in the day and a half that it took them to subdue all organized resistance in the Strip.

The Israeli Army history of the campaign conceded that "the Gaza Strip is an area difficult to defend. . . . Its whole length must be defended for there are no key features. . . . The meaning of the capture of the Strip was the taking of fourteen big positions, each manned by a 'Battalion' of the National Guard, and another three real defended areas at Khan Yunis." The Army writer put the designations of the defending units in quotation marks because none had enough manpower or weapons seriously to merit the designations. Dayan, too, wrote: "The 'brigades,' 'battalions' and 'companies' were simply organizational frameworks and not operational formations, and they could not be used as military units." The defense positions were isolated and unable to give mutual support to one another. All suffered from a "paucity of support weapons."

The 11th Brigade received the surrender of the Egyptian Military Governor in Gaza, General Fuad Digwy, at 14:20 and fanned out into the rest of the Strip in what the Israeli Army historian called a "carpet-beater" operation. The Israelis regarded the capture of General Digwy with particular relish for he had been president of the military tribunal which tried the Israeli spies in the 1954 Lavon Affair operation in Egypt, two of whom were hanged in January 1955. The only real fight was at Khan Yunis, which refused to surrender. The last defense position there was subdued at 13:30 on 3 November, making complete the lull that fell over the fighting as the Egyptian main forces withdrew beyond the Canal.

The occupying troops thereupon went on a rampageous search for arms and *Fedayeen* from house to house and tent to tent, in the course of which hundreds of civilians were killed and wounded. In the UN investigation that followed, the Israelis said the casualties were a consequence of refugee resistance. But the inhabitants testified that there was no resistance, a version which seems to square with common sense and circumstantial evidence, including the lack of Israeli casualties during the operation. Henry Labouisse, the American Director of the United Nations Relief and Works Agency (UNRWA) for Palestinian refugees, in his official report, said that the total Palestinian casualties were unknown but that he had received "from sources he considers trustworthy" the names of 275 persons killed.

Dayan belied the Israeli excuse of refugee resistance with a diary entry the day after the massacre, stating: "So far there has been only one case where our troops were fired on from an Arab house—they were *Fedayeen* in hiding." Conversely, he wrote, "looting by our own men, both uniformed and civilian," caused much damage to Arab belongings "and much shame to ourselves." He said the looting began under the pretext of searches for armed enemy troops. Then Israeli soldiers, joined by settlers from across the border, pilfered property which the curfew prevented the Arabs from guarding.

On 12 November, during a roundup of refugees for intelligence screening at the large UNRWA camp at Rafah, at least 111 persons were killed when Israeli soldiers, for undetermined reasons, fired on the assembling crowd. Labouisse reported that the two incidents caused "anxiety and fear" among the refugees. General Burns cited Israel's "record of getting rid of Arabs whose lands they desired" and suggested that the killings, like Deir Yasseen in 1948, were preparatory to persuading the bulk of the inhabitants to settle elsewhere. "I have been credibly informed that what the Israeli authorities really had in mind, if they had been able to keep the Strip, was to absorb only about 80,000 of the Strip's population," Burns wrote. "That this is not a slander on the Israeli Defense Forces is, unfortunately, only too well attested by three separate incidents in which they took severe repressive measures against Arab civilians, killing large numbers of them." He mentioned the Kafr Kassim massacre in the last hour before the war as well as the two incidents after the Israelis occupied Gaza.

In an earlier incident immediately before the attack on Egypt the Israelis forced 700 Arabs to leave their village and nearly 1,000 acres of cultivated lands in the demilitarized zone on the Syrian frontier. After these Arabs had crossed into Syria over the Banat Yaqoub bridge, the *Jerusalem Post* reported, their village was demolished by bulldozers and ploughed under. The destruction of the village was carried out to prevent the Arabs from returning, as they had done through appeals to the UN after two previous evictions. "They have been a source of trouble and repeatedly asked to be issued with 'UN passports,'" the paper reported.

Although Ben-Gurion said afterward that he told his Cabinet on the eve of the war that the Gaza Strip was "an embarrassing objective and would be a burden for us," his Government tried hard to keep both it and the Sinai Peninsula. Walter Eytan wrote for world readership immediately after the war an article entitled "Background to Sinai" in which he said of the captured Gaza Strip: "No change has been made in its legal status. Where formerly there was Egyptian military occupation and administration, there is now the military occupation and administration of Israel. Gaza, a part of the former mandated territory of Palestine, never belonged to Egypt and Egypt never annexed it." He added that Israel had not annexed it either. Israel did not want to annex it so long as it contained 210,000 refugees demanding the right of return to their homes in Israel. Nevertheless, only dire pressure from Eisenhower eventually forced Israel to give up her *de facto* rule over the Strip.

With the fall of Khan Yunis, the only Israeli objective still to be taken was Sharm al-Sheikh at the entrance of the Gulf of Aqaba. With the Egyptian Air Force "neutralized" by the Anglo-French air war, Colonel Avraham Joffe's 9th Infantry Brigade was able to set forth at dawn on 2 November down the shore of the Gulf. The brigade was a day behind schedule because of the delayed start of the Anglo-French bombing. The Egyptian defenses were taken on 5 November, the day the Anglo-French paratroopers jumped into battle at Port Said. But the capture of Sharm al-Sheikh will be more conveniently narrated in the Port Said chapter, to which it is adjourned with this note on its timing. In the meantime a lull prevailed over the war theater and for nearly two days there was no fighting at all.

CHAPTER
17

Lull

(1 NOVEMBER 1956 TO DAWN, 5 NOVEMBER 1956)

Perhaps in our subsequent outcries against the English, there was the belief that if they *knew* that what they were doing wasn't fair play, they would stop it.

(WAGUIH GHALI, *Beer in the Snooker Club*, 1964)

In a democracy dissent is an act of faith.... The correction of errors in a nation's foreign policy is greatly assisted by the timely raising of voices of criticism within the nation....

Refusing to be deterred by calls for national unity in a crisis, Labour began the long, painful process of recovering Great Britain's good name at the very moment when the damage was still being done.

(SENATOR J. WILLIAM FULBRIGHT, 1966)

NASSER CALLED the withdrawal from Sinai, from the night of 31 October to the morning of 2 November, "the most crucial period in our history." His Army had obediently refused the purgatory of surrender to go through the hell of retreat across a merciless desert hounded by mortal enemies who were all but invulnerable and unchallengeable in their swift planes and tanks. It was Egypt's Dunkirk.

On the morning of 1 November Egypt was fearfully alone. Beset by the two strongest powers of Western Europe in league with the Sparta of the Middle East, Nasser's regime needed Great-Power support if it was to survive. Russia and the US were the only possibilities. Russia had proved a friend in need by supplying arms in 1955 when other sources were closed and by giving diplomatic support to Egypt's cause in the Suez Crisis. But Russia had grave troubles of her own in Poland and Hungary and her military power could not be applied in the Middle East except across neutral or pro-Western lands and waters. More important, Russian military intervention probably would have meant World War III. For this last reason chiefly, Nasser neither asked for nor wanted Russian help.

Instead, he turned to Eisenhower. He summoned US Ambassador Raymond A. Hare to meet him at General Headquarters about noon on 1 November. Nasser told me about it nearly a decade later when I asked him during a long interview about the Suez Crisis whether there was anything important I had failed to touch on. Nasser replied:

I think you are going on right. But there is one thing which happened and I promised the American Ambassador not to publish it. It was not published. I sent a message to President Eisenhower on the first of November, through his ambassador here, telling him that we were subjected to attack by Israel, France, and Britain and that we ask the help of the United States. Then they asked me: "Are you asking our help in order to ask the Russians if we refuse?" I told them: "I haven't asked the Russians."

Then the answer came to me, next day, that of course America cannot go to war against their allies but that they will do all they can to solve the problem in the United Nations—supporting the United Nations.

I asked him if he had suggested that the Sixth Fleet might intervene.

"No," Nasser said. "No, I said only: 'Help' . . . Then they asked me not to publish it. I said all right. I think it is all right to publish it now."

Hare told me that Nasser was disappointed at first that Eisenhower would work only through the UN. "At the time," Hare said, "Nasser could not imagine how the US would be able to stop the British and the French by acting only through the UN. But later he realized how effective our UN and diplomatic action had been. He has recalled the whole thing several times in talks with me." Hare pointed out that Eisenhower's answer to Nasser followed precisely the policy Eisenhower had outlined the night before in his television address to the nation.

I asked Nasser if he credited the Americans with the decisive role in stopping the war. "Of course their role was decisive," Nasser replied. "And of course this decision by President Eisenhower just before the elections was a very hard decision."

Nasser told Egyptians of their darkening situation in a broadcast at 15:10 on 1 November, by which time his secret request for American help was on its way to the White House. "Yesterday, 31 October, our forces were crushingly supreme," he said, adding wistfully: "I am certain that all the communiqués issued were reliable." Then came the British bombers from high over the twilit sea. "The plan was clear," Nasser said. "It was obvious that they intended to destroy our planes, to drag our forces into Sinai, to isolate them and destroy them and then to occupy Egypt without any resistance. A serious decision had to be taken. Should our forces be left on the borders without air protection?" The Egyptian Air Force was overwhelmed by the three enemy air forces, Nasser made clear, adding that a decision was made "to ensure that the greatest possible part of the Armed Forces join the people . . . The execution of this plan began yesterday."

"And now, O compatriots, that we are facing this situation, shall we fight or surrender?" Nasser asked. He went on to compare Egypt's situation with the national liberation struggles of Yugoslavia and Greece against the Nazis, Indonesia against the Dutch, Algeria against the French, and Cyprus against the British. Then, echoing Churchill after Dunkirk, Nasser answered his own question:

"We shall fight bitterly, O compatriots. We shall not surrender. We shall fight in defense of Egypt's honor, freedom, and dignity. Each one of you is a soldier in the National Liberation Army. Orders have been given for the issue of arms—and we have many arms. We shall fight a bitter war. We shall fight from village to village and from place to place. Let each one of you be a soldier in the Armed Forces so that we may defend our honor, dignity, and freedom. Let our motto be: 'We shall fight, not surrender. We shall fight, we shall fight; we shall never surrender.'"

The distribution of arms began forthwith to a populace whom the British, with psychological warfare and bombing, were encouraging to rise in revolt against Nasser. But the bombing rallied the people to Nasser, as the Nazi bombing rallied the British to Churchill in World War II and the American bombing rallied the North Vietnamese to Ho Chih Minh in the 1960s. Air force men the world over seem incapable of learning that conventional bombing is psychologically counterproductive. In Egypt the bombing evaporated what dissidence there was against the revolution. Expropriated landowners, nationalized businessmen, passed-over officers, all were transformed from grumblers into patriots.

The effect on Nasser was euphoric. "I have dedicated my life to this people," Nasser recalled in later years, "but they gave me something which is more valuable than any man's life; they trusted me . . ." Heedless of the dangers inherent in an armed citizenry under stress, Nasser drove openly through the city. Wherever he passed he was cheered by crowds shouting his own slogan: *"Hanhaarib, hanhaarib; lan nusallim abadan!"*—"We shall fight, we shall fight; we shall never surrender!"

Cairo Radio announced Egypt's intention to break off diplomatic relations with Britain and France at 10:10 on 1 November. Trevelyan, the British ambassador, was summoned to the Foreign Ministry at noon to receive formal notification of the break. He was surprised that the Egyptians had waited so long. Surprise was a familiar sensation to him by then. He was surprised by the ultimatum which he had delivered as instructed two days before. Then he was surprised by the lack of anti-British manifestations among Egyptians. Until the break in relations Trevelyan continued to drive around the city in the big embassy Rolls Royce with its Union Jack fluttering on a little chromium flagstaff. The Egyptians never cast so much as a resentful look at him, even during the bombing raids. After the break in relations the embassy staff was required to remain in the palatial embassy compound on the bank of the Nile until they were able to leave Egypt a few days after the cease-fire. There was only the usual single guard in the striped sentry box at the entrance gate.

Courtesy and civil discipline were the rule in Egypt during the war. Foreigners were profoundly impressed, particularly by the lack of violent xenophobia that commonly erupts against enemy nationals in countries at war. But the Egyptians were not all orderly. During the blackouts bands of self-styled vigilantes did some looting and settling of scores under the pretext of enforcing the blackout. These rabble would set up a shout of *"Noor! Noor!"* ("A light! A light!") outside the home of their intended victim whether a light was showing or not and then smash their way in through windows or doors. Rich Egyptians, mostly Copts but including a scattering of Moslems, were the main sufferers. A director of Barclay's Bank was taken to jail by the police to save him from a mob that accused him of signaling to enemy bombers.

Religious toleration, always weaker among the poor and ignorant in any society, was strained by the war. Father Henri Ayrout, the distinguished Egyptian Jesuit monk and sociologist, told me that after the cease-fire there were beatings, shootings, even lynch-mob hangings of persons accused as "collaborators" or "spies," as happened in France after the liberation. The victims were predominantly Christians, he said. The regime proclaimed several Christians as heroes, partly to dampen religious violence, and Nasser said that the bombs did not distinguish between Moslems and Christians. A cousin of Ayrout's, one Dr. Georges Naggar of Port Fuad, was at first acclaimed after the war for helping hundreds of Egyptian soldiers pass through the allied lines as they straggled back from Sinai. But when a French newspaper gave a passing compliment to Naggar for having helped keep order during the French occupation, the local police arrested him and beat him so severely during interrogation that he died a month after his release. Ayrout said this was done at a low level in the police hierarchy and in contravention of official policy and attitudes.

The Israelis, too, showed an impressive degree of civil discipline during the war, most notably in the swift and efficient response of reservists to the call to colors. The *Jerusalem Post* reported an increase in thievery during the blackouts but a British diplomat there said that among law-abiding Israelis there was no hoarding of scarce goods. "They behaved like Anglo-Saxons," he said.

The Egyptians issued an order on 1 November for all British and French nationals to register with local authorities within three days and in midafternoon that day the Government decreed the seizure of Anglo-Egyptian petroleum companies. All of these measures were carried out with "courtesy and helpfulness on all sides," the correspondent of *The Times* (London) reported a few days later. He said Europeans continued to move freely in the streets and that the Government Information Office gave ready cooperation to British correspondents comfortably interned at the Metropolitan and Semiramis hotels.

Eden got rougher treatment from Members of Parliament that day than any Englishman got in Egypt. As Lord Kilmuir, Eden's Lord Chancellor, described it in his memoirs: "A storm of booing would break out as soon as Anthony entered the Chamber, and would rise to a crescendo of hysteria when he actually rose to speak. At one point the chances of fighting actually breaking out between Members was very real, so intense were the passions on each side." On the afternoon of 1 November the Speaker, in an extraordinary action, suspended the sitting for a half hour to cool the passions aroused by the vain efforts of Gaitskell and other Laborites to make Eden and Defense Minister Antony Head say whether or not Britain was legally at war.

Head began by announcing the results of the overnight bombing raids and the sinking of the Egyptian frigate, *Damietta*, by the British cruiser *Newfoundland* in the Gulf of Suez. Labor members argued that without a British declaration of war the Egyptians could try any British prisoners for murder. Eden, who left the well of the House amid catcalls and shouts of "Resign!" when the session was suspended, said after it resumed that Britain was not at war with Egypt—"this is essentially a police operation"—but that the Geneva Conventions nevertheless applied, which would prohibit the prosecution of prisoners for civil crimes.

Aneurin Bevan accused Eden of using "the language of the bully" and said "We are dishonored." James Griffiths, the Deputy Opposition leader, then introduced a censure motion:

That this House deplores the action of Her Majesty's Government in resorting to armed force against Egypt in clear violation of the United Nations Charter, thereby affronting the convictions of a large section of the British people, dividing the Commonwealth, straining the Atlantic Alliance, and gravely damaging the foundations of international order.

Eden claimed credit for having originated in the ensuing debate the idea of a United Nations force. Insisting that Britain and France would go through with their intervention, Eden said: "If the United Nations were then willing to take over the physical task of maintaining peace in that area, no one would be better pleased than we. But police action there must be...' The censure was voted down along strict party lines.

"I have often known noisy interludes in the House, but never such a continuous abuse of the rules of order as during the Suez debates," Eden wrote. "It was impossible to respect or heed the House in such conditions."

In Washington, at the very time that the Commons were rudely displaying national disunity, an equally disastrous schism with Eden was hardening at the morning meet of the National Security Council at the White House. The meeting opened with Allen Dulles telling the group that the occurrences in Hungary, chiefly the formal Russian promise to withdraw the Red Army, were a "miracle" which "disproved that a popular revolt can't occur in the face of modern weapons." His brother, the Secretary of State, said that, the Security Council having been paralyzed by the Anglo-French vetoes, the General Assembly would take up the Suez war at 5 P.M. He added:

It is nothing less than tragic that at this very time, when we are on the point of winning an immense and long-hoped-for victory over Soviet colonialism in Eastern Europe, we should be forced to choose between following in the footsteps of Anglo-French colonialism in Asia and Africa, or splitting our course away from their course. Yet this decision must be made in a mere matter of hours—before five o'clock this afternoon.

Eisenhower had told Dulles on the telephone before the meeting that "we should not do anything that looks as though we had found an excuse to pick on Israel." At the NSC meeting he instructed Dulles to draft two statements: an announcement of US suspension of all military and some economic aid to Israel, and a moderate resolution for the General Assembly, designed to forestall a harsh Russian one.

Immediately after the meeting, at 11:10, Dulles telephoned the President a copy of a cable from Dillon reporting a full confession of collusion by Pineau, who admitted that the invasion was a result of plans long-contemplated. As Dillon reported the interview, Pineau said the bombing of Egyptian air bases was done to keep the Russians out. He said he fully expected a UN vote of condemnation but he appealed for a moderate US resolution. Pineau told me afterward that he had made a clean breast of things to Dillon, thus ending the colluders' "clam-up," in the hope it would be a "correction of the situation."

Eden's schism with the Commonwealth added a third major force that day to the surge of world opinion against him. Nehru cabled both Eisenhower and Dulles but he spoke most bluntly in public. "I cannot think of a grosser case of naked aggression than what England and France are attempting to do," Nehru said. "It is the most extraordinary argument that I have ever heard.... Israel is the invader and Egypt is made to suffer.... Our sympathies are entirely with Egypt."

Dulles led the case against the war in person at the UN that night. He expressed forcefully his own and Eisenhower's fear that the very existence of the UN was at stake. Speaking from hasty notes rather than from his usual prepared text, Dulles observed that it was the first emergency meeting of the General Assembly under the Uniting-for-Peace procedure, which he himself had shepherded to adoption early in the Korean War. He outlined the history of the Suez Crisis, emphasizing the efforts toward a peaceful solution. Referring to the agreement reached on 13 October for further negotiations based on six principles or requirements, Dulles said "it seemed as though a just and peaceful solution acceptable to all was near at hand."

"Under the circumstances which I described," Dulles continued, "the resort to force, the violent armed attack by three of our members upon a fourth, cannot be treated as other than a grave error, inconsistent with the principles and purposes of the charter, and one which if persisted in would gravely undermine our charter and undermine this organization." After introducing the US draft resolution, he urged its adoption with grim phrases: "I fear that if we do not act and act promptly, and if we do not act with sufficient unanimity of opinion so that our recommendations carry a real influence, there is great danger that what is started and what has been called a police action may develop into something which is far more grave. Even if that does not happen, the apparent impotence of this organization to deal with this situation may set a precedent which will lead other nations to attempt to take into their own hands the remedying of what they believe to be their injustices. If that happens, the future is dark indeed."

Dulles was proud of that speech. He told his special assistant, William B. Macomber, Jr., just before he underwent surgery for cancer on 3 November that if he died during the operation he would be content with the Suez speech as his last. Dulles remained at the UN after he spoke in order to maintain pressure for an Assembly vote that night. The following evening, while playing backgammon with his wife at home in Washington, Dulles began feeling the pains that were diagnosed at Walter Reed Hospital as cancer. He immediately assigned weekend tasks to his aides and turned over policy responsibilities for everything but Suez to Hoover, who became Acting Secretary of State. On the assurance from his doctor that he could begin doing ten minutes work a day on Monday, Dulles decided to retain responsibility for Suez policy. About 10 A.M. on Saturday, 3 November, Dulles underwent a two-and-a-half hour operation for intestinal cancer that kept him from returning to full active duty until January, although he attended a NATO Council meeting in Paris in mid-December.

Sir Pierson Dixon, in between constant transatlantic telephone talks with Eden, opposed Dulles's resolution in a speech as baldly cynical as any that could be asked of a hardened professional diplomat. He said the Korean War was "improperly invoked" as a precedent for summoning the General Assembly although he likened the Anglo-French attack on Israel's Egyptian victim to the US defense in 1950 of North Korea's South Korean victim. He had the gall to complain that the US was acting in the UN "without consultation" with Britain. Having himself just cast Britain's first two vetoes to balk the Security Council from blocking Britain's collusive aggression, he cynically blamed "the cynical misuse of their veto power by the Soviet Union" for the "unhappy limitation in the effective powers of the Security Council" which was, he said, precisely the reason Britain and France "were compelled to intervene at once." Using words Eden had spoken to the Commons in London that same night, Dixon made clear that Britain would ignore the resolution, arguing that the US would have ignored restraints if the UN had failed to endorse its Korean intervention. Said Dixon: "If the United Nations were willing to take over the physical task of maintaining peace in the area, no one would be better pleased than we. But police action there must be . . . "

Speaking for Israel, Eban had to make up his own list of war aims because there had not been sufficient time for full consultation with Jerusalem and Tel

Aviv. Eban had not been included in the small circle of persons privy to the collusion arrangement. But he was accustomed to the Foreign Ministry's task of justifying the Defense Ministry's actions to the world. His speech was eloquent, impassioned, and full of distortions against Egypt. When Eban asked Ben-Gurion in December 1955 the reason for the big raid against Syria, Ben-Gurion cabled back: "If you read your speech to the Security Council, you will find a brilliant and, to my mind, convincing explanation. I find nothing further to add." Substituting "General Assembly" for "Security Council," Ben-Gurion's cable would have been even more appropriate in November 1956.

The General Assembly adopted the US draft resolution at 2 A.M. on Friday, 2 November. Noting the Israeli violation of the armistice and the Anglo-French military operations against Egypt, resulting in the interruption of Canal traffic, the resolution:

1. urged an immediate cease-fire and a halt to the movement of military forces and arms into the area;

2. urged prompt withdrawal behind the armistice lines and scrupulous observance of the armistice, and

3. recommended that UN member states refrain from introducing military goods into the war area and eschew "any acts which would delay or prevent the implementation of the present resolution."

It went on to urge swift steps to reopen the Canal, to request Hammarskjold to report on compliance with an eye to supplementary enforcement action, and to resolve to remain in emergency session pending compliance.

The vote was 65 to 5, with only Australia and New Zealand joining the three colluders, Britain, France, and Israel, in voting against the resolution. Gaitskell later called it the largest majority in UN history. Canada was among six who abstained. The Canadian External Affairs Minister, Lester B. Pearson, explained the abstention by regretting the lack of time to consider the proposal for a United Nations force, with which proposal he loyally associated the British. Pearson, who won a Nobel peace prize for his part in instituting the United Nations Emergency Force, also complained that "we should have used this opportunity to link a cease-fire to the absolute necessity of a political settlement in Palestine and for the Suez." Premier St. Laurent of Canada praised Pearson but took a harsher line toward Eden, telling a television audience on 4 November that Britain's conduct had "strained both the Western alliance and the bonds of the Commonwealth more than any event since the Second World War."

Egypt promptly cabled Hammarskjold that she accepted the cease-fire urged by the General Assembly. Israel did likewise late the next day, 3 November, assuming that by the time it was arranged she would have possession of Sharm al-Sheikh. But Britain and France hastily begged Ben-Gurion for time to carry out their own invasion and Ben-Gurion accordingly negated his acceptance of the cease-fire by burying it under conditions. Egypt apparently had little confidence that her enemies would accept the cease-fire, cautioning Hammarskjold that she "could not implement the resolution in case attacking armies continue their aggression."

Nasser continued to encourage Egyptian resistance in a speech at the midday prayers that same day, Friday, 2 November, at al-Azhar mosque in Cairo. The custom of political leaders speaking in place of the sermon at Friday prayers dates back to the early days of Islam, when the caliph embodied both religious and political leadership. "Egypt has always been the graveyard of invaders," Nasser said. He told again how the first British bombers made clear the plot to cut off and destroy the Egyptian Army in the Sinai. He announced that the Army had withdrawn entirely from the Sinai except for rearguard "suicide" units. "I see a victory in the decision to withdraw and its successful implementation, which was more successful than I ever imagined, thank God," he said.

Nasser repeated his Churchillian vow to battle the invaders from village to village and house to house with a people's Liberation Army fighting alongside the regulars. He was repeatedly drowned out by the cheers of the worshippers in the ancient mosque as he said:

Along the Canal were the stores of the British, worth £300 million. We took them over so that we may compensate for [Cheers drown out end of sentence]. The English arms stores in the Canal have been taken over and distributed among the people. [Cheers] The ammunition dumps in the Canal have been taken over and distributed among the people. The English vehicles and tanks which they kept in the Canal have been taken over and assigned to the Armed Forces. . . . I am here in Cairo and I shall fight with you. I am here in Cairo. My children are here with you in Cairo. I have not sent them away and I shall not send them away. I also will stay with you in Cairo. . . . God will render us successful.

Egypt made provisions for guerrilla warfare that night. Eastern Command Headquarters was pulled back from Ismailiya in the Canal Zone to Zagazig in the Delta. Political commanders, essential to a national guerrilla movement, were placed over the military commanders in the Canal Zone. Kamaleddeen Hussein and Salah Salem, both officers in Nasser's original revolutionary junta with varied cabinet and diplomatic experience, received territorial commands with authority over career soldiers who had greater military experience and rank but less political experience. Hussein was given overall command of the Canal Zone. His Liberation Army headquarters moved in where the regular Eastern Command moved out. Salem was given the subordinate territorial command of Suez town.

Cairo Radio had been knocked off the air by British bombers an hour before Nasser spoke. Ahmed Said, the director and chief announcer of the Voice of the Arabs, remembered that a transmitter destined for the Algerian rebels was stored for shipment on the top floor of the Presidency. He taped Nasser's speech and began broadcasting it less than two hours after regular transmissions were interrupted by the bombing. Colonel Abdel Kader Hatem, Government Information Director, sent loudspeakers into the streets announcing the new frequencies of Cairo's broadcasts. The transmitter at the Presidency, while far weaker than the powerful shortwave equipment at Abu Zabel, was strong enough for British and US monitors in Cyprus to pick up Nasser's speech.

Phrases from Nasser's two wartime speeches were immediately transformed into songs to keep up the courage of Egyptians during the war. *"Hanhaarib!"* ("We shall fight!"), *"Allahu Akbar!"* ("God is Greatest!"), "I am the Nile, graveyard of invaders"—and dozens of other songs, some deriving from Nasser's words and others from folklore, history, and national themes, were written, scored, and broadcast by Egypt's top songwriters, composers, and singers. Office boys were brought in to strengthen the choruses of some of the songs. Some of the recordings were still popular more than a decade after Suez. From the 2nd of November until the 8th, when the cease-fire looked secure, the songmakers and the broadcasting staff remained day and night at the Egyptian State Broadcasting offices, churning out songs, news broadcasts, commentary, and retorts to foreign and clandestine broadcasts. The last were in a special program called Lies and Facts.

The shortwave transmitter of the "Voice of the Arabs" was off the air for five days, during which time the "Voice of Britain" from Cyprus occupied its frequency. It happened that a number of "Voice of the Arabs" broadcasters had been caught by the war in other Arab capitals, where they had gone to report on the general strike in sympathy with Algeria on 28 October. These men were given facilities for "Voice of the Arabs" programs. Their improvised programs gave an air of indomitability to the Egyptian image. At home, Cairo programs were broadcast from medium wave transmitters in Assiut and Minya. Because Arabs are more dependent than Westerners on radio for news and amusement, the Egyptians made extraordinary efforts to remain on the air. "People here felt there was something dead in their hearts when the radio was silent," Ahmed Said told me. His broadcasts in those days made him so famous throughout the Arab world that people would refer to their radio as *"sundouq Ahmed Said"*—"the Ahmed Said box."

Nasser's family did stay in Cairo throughout the war but they did not remain at their own house, which was in the target area of barracks and airfields in northeast Cairo. For all Nasser knew, it might be on the British target list itself. His wife and five children, aged from nine down to less than two years, moved on 2 November to a house in Zamálek, a residential district on al-Gezira (the Island) in the Nile after bombs hit close to their own house. Nasser himself had set up his personal headquarters on 1 November at the old Revolution Command Council building at the other end of al-Gezira.

"Then one of my assistants tried to convince my wife to leave," Nasser recalled. "She refused until she got it clear from me. She got in touch with me at Army Headquarters. I told her to stay here [at home]. This continued until the 2nd of November, when they informed me that the bombardment was very near to the house. And so I told them to take my family to a house in Zamálek. They went there. I didn't see them from the 1st until the 15th of November."

Nasser was constantly on the move, driving from the RCC building to General Headquarters, then back to the Presidency, to al-Azhar, to meetings at government buildings, waving to the Egyptian rabble in arms as he went. Ambassador Hare said he appeared cool-headed and calm throughout the war. "You know, I was very busy at that time," Nasser recalled. "I used to work until 2 o'clock or 3 o'clock after midnight, reading every statement, every scrap of information, following the whole situation." One of the ten thousand matters great and small brought to his attention was the acute interest of British embassy personnel at the outset of the war in signs of dissidence. "They had got their previous information from the old politicians and reactionary elements—that the country is against the regime, and so on," Nasser said. "So they thought that if they attacked us, there would be some who would rise in the country against the revolution, which was completely false."

There was one exception, Nasser recalled: "There was a meeting of some of the old politicians. And they agreed about that [the necessity for a new regime]. 'We must save the country,' [they said]. Old politicians. There was one called Hafez, Suleiman Hafez [a distinguished lawyer and former Councilor of State], and some others. And I received from the Intelligence a report about that meeting. And I said to my assistant, 'If they come here, I will shoot them in the garden of the Presidency.' But they disagreed about who would bring the note to me. And there was nothing further."

The British had wired their ammunition and weapons dumps in the Canal zone for demolition before the war, Hilmy told me, but his men cut most of the wires before demolition. Otherwise there would have been fewer British guns and ammunition for the Egyptian people and Army.

Arabs everywhere declared their sympathy with Egypt and their anger against Britain and France. Jordan announced her decision to break relations with France four hours after the Egyptian announcement of 1 November. But even the nationalist government of Suleiman Nabulsy hesitated to break with Britain at the risk of an invasion by Israel or Britain or both. Syria broke with both Britain and France on 2 November and during the night cut the pipeline of the Iraq Petroleum Company, which is owned by Britain, France, and the US. Egypt tried at the last minute to prevent the destruction of the oil pipelines. The entirely US-owned Trans-Arabian Pipeline, called TAPline, was not harmed. Iraq broke only with France but Nuri agreed to a Baghdad Pact meeting from which Britain was barred. The Arab people everywhere raged against Britain and France. British dwellings and business property were pillaged and burned in the quasi-colony of Bahrein, necessitating an airlift of British troops. So intense was the Asian and African reaction that Nehru felt impelled to caution Indians against attacks on Britons or British property.

The General Assembly's demand for a cease-fire and withdrawal rasped at the weakest link in collusion, which was the ailing Eden's will to see the invasion through to the end. Within two or three hours of the UN vote, which came at 7 A.M. London time, Lloyd was working on a plan for a UN force to take over from the British and French after their invasion, which was still at sea scarcely more than halfway from Malta to Port Said. In Commons, convened in special session that day, Gaitskell pressed Eden to accept the cease-fire resolution but Eden insisted on studying it further. Dennis Healey, noting that every Commonwealth capital and Washington had contradicted Eden's statement that he had consulted them all, asked the Speaker of the House: "What parliamentary expression comes closest to expressing the meaning of the word 'liar'?"

In mid-afternoon Eden left the Commons to receive Pineau, who flew from Paris to discuss the joint Anglo-French reply to the UN. Pineau learned that Eden, the senior partner in collusion, no longer dreamed of achieving a triumphant new dispensation for the Middle East with Nasser gone or broken. Eden was now ready to cut his losses and retreat as best he could. Pineau spent nearly five hours trying to brace Eden's resolve, with only moderate success, before flying back to report to Mollet.

Eden was nearing exhaustion as a result of having to meet his public and secret responsibilities in England during the day and remain available during London's nighttime for consultation with Dixon at the UN. He was in poor physical condition to brave the opposition and opprobrium rising on all sides—from his giant Western ally, from a vociferous half of his own countrymen, from most of the British Commonwealth, and from an overwhelming majority of the other Governments of the world. The UN provided a forum where every nation could stand and be counted, which gave a graphic quantitative impact to the vast international rally against him.

The real purpose of the war, which was the destruction of Nasser, was a swiftly fading hope. Instead of rising up against Nasser to escape the calamity of invasion, Egyptians were rallying to Nasser in his hour of adversity. In defiance of military defeat, Nasser was growing stronger by the hour as Egyptians, Arabs, and the world at large rallied to his side. Eden's support at home was ignorant of what he was really doing. His international support rested on the triangular collusive alliance whose existence and purpose he did not dare admit outside of his Cabinet circle. Indeed, he denied one leg of the alliance, Israel, to the point of offending it.

Nasser's strength was bewildering to Eden's cast of mind. As Michael Ionides wrote in *Divide and Lose*: "The English language is deficient in that words like 'courage' and 'competence' are associated with what is good in men. We have no words to denote these same qualities while associating them with evil." Nasser, whom the British press and politicians insistently depicted as evil, was therefore incomprehensible to Eden, the Tories, and most of the British public.

By the time Eden announced the Anglo-French reply to the General Assembly's cease-fire resolution to the Commons at noon on Saturday, 3 November, the pretext for the war as defined in the ultimatum, namely the "cessation of hostilities," was disappearing. Khan Yunis had surrendered a half hour earlier, bringing all fighting between Egypt and Israel to a cessation for some thirty-six hours. True, Israeli forces were hastening through the empty desert toward the isolated Egyptian garrison at Sharm al-Sheikh. But this was not public knowledge and the attack there would not go in until early on 5 November, the morning Britain and France were to begin their invasion at Port Said.

At 01:00 on 2 November the Eastern Command reported completion of the withdrawal across the Canal of all the Sinai troops that could have hoped to make it. The Palestinian and National Guard troops in the Gaza Strip and the thousand men at Sharm al-Sheikh were cut off and would be taken prisoner. Most of the other units escaped with light losses except for Mutawally's 6th Infantry Brigade at Abu Aoueigila, remnants of which continued crossing the Canal for weeks. A number were caught at Bir Lahfin. The Egyptian general, Hassan al-Badry, told me that he and a UN man named McCarthy found a mass grave at Bir Lahfin full of partly burned bodies of Egyptian soldiers who had been tied up and shot.

On 2 November, recovered from his bout with influenza, Ben-Gurion gave full rein to his optimism about the war and his contemptuous disregard of the restraining efforts of the UN. He personally banned the UN military observers from the Gaza Strip, telling Dayan, who had just come from al-Arish, that there was no more armistice "so what will the observers supervise?" Before leaving, Dayan wrote, "I heard Ben-Gurion amiably chiding officials who had come to him with Job-like tales of what was happening at the UN Assembly. 'Why are you so worried?' he asked. 'So long as they are sitting in New York, and we in Sinai, the situation is not bad!' "

The next day, Dayan reported, Ben-Gurion was full of grave doubts about whether Britain and France would carry through their part of the collusion bargain. He feared that Israel would be left alone to face the combined pressure of the US and Russia for withdrawal. Overnight Ben-Gurion and Dayan had approved a French proposal for Israel to capture Qantara on the Canal in order to protect a French paratroop drop south of Port Said early on 4 November, two days in advance of the amphibious assault scheduled for 6 November and deep behind Egyptian lines. Dayan offered in addition to let the French and the British land behind Israeli lines anywhere in Sinai and use the Israeli invasion axes. But these proposals would not square with the ultimatum. Therefore, the Israelis were not surprised when the disappointed French representatives relayed Eden's refusal early on 3 November.

Britain's anxiety to avoid contact with the Israelis in order to maintain the fiction of a "police action" led to a near clash east of Qantara that same morning when a British pilot parachuted from his damaged plane between the Israeli ultimatum line and the Canal. The Israelis rushed to his assistance, Dayan wrote, but were driven back when British fighters raked the intervening ground with warning gunfire. A British helicopter came and picked up the pilot.

The Anglo-French reply to the UN did nothing to assuage Ben-Gurion's doubts, primarily because of its attachment to the prospect of a UN force to take over the war area. This provided the basis for still another spurious excuse for the impending invasion, the claim that the Anglo-French expeditionary force was actually serving the UN by paving the way for the UN force. Eden seemed to assume that normal, intelligent adults would accept anything he said. For a long time many of them did because of the high esteem which his honorable career had brought him.

Buoyed up by Tory cheers, Eden read to the Commons the British reply to the General Assembly, to wit, that the British and French "maintain their

view that police action must be carried through urgently to stop the hostilities,"
and that:

They would most willingly stop military action as soon as the following conditions could be satisfied:
(a) Both the Egyptian and the Israeli Governments agree to accept a United
Nations Force to keep the peace;
(b) The United Nations decides to constitute and maintain such a Force until an
Arab-Israel peace settlement is reached and until satisfactory arrangements have been
agreed in regard to the Suez Canal, both agreements to be guaranteed by the United
Nations;
(c) In the meantime, until the United Nations Force is constituted, both combatants agree to accept forthwith limited detachments of Anglo-French troops to be
stationed between the combatants.

Gaitskell protested that this was defiance of the General Assembly resolution and unnecessary because the fighting had virtually ended. Eden replied
that a General Assembly resolution, unlike a Security Council resolution, was
not binding. Of the UN force he said: "We would naturally not expect to be
excluded from it. . . . We are not burglars." Gaitskell silenced his party's cries
of "You are burglars!" by saying: "The Prime Minister is perfectly right. What
we did was to go in to help the burglar and shoot the householder." Gaitskell
issued an impolitic invitation to the Tories to disavow Eden:

If the country is to be rescued from the predicament into which the Government
have brought it, there is only one way—a change in the leadership of the Government. Only this can save our reputation and reopen the possibility of maintaining the
United Nations as a force for peace. We must have a new Government and a new
Prime Minister. The immediate responsibility in this matter rests on the only people
who can affect the situation—members opposite.

Nutting's absence from the House during the Suez furor was widely
remarked. Having resigned on 31 October on the grounds that he could not
defend the Government's conduct either in the Commons or at the UN, Nutting absented himself from the House but, in order to fend off speculation until
after Eden's parliamentary ordeal, he continued to come to the Foreign Office.
His absence from the censure vote on 1 November was attributed to asthma.
On the 2nd the Foreign Office stated that there was no truth in the rumor
that he was about to resign, which was technically true because he had
already resigned.
When Eden clutched at Canada's face-saving proposal for a UN force,
Lloyd asked Nutting to help him draft a plan for it, Butler urged Nutting to

571

withdraw his resignation, and Eden offered to shift him to the Colonial Office. Nutting's mentor in the Cabinet, Sir Walter Monckton, after all, not only had switched ministries—from Defense to Paymaster General—instead of resigning but had accepted the directorship of wartime propaganda on 1 November. But Nutting still felt unable to defend the collusive war. His resignation was announced at midnight on Saturday, 3 November. I was in a coffee house in Jerusalem when the news came over the radio. The Arabs, who tend to pay more attention to first names than last names and who exaggerated the importance of Gaitskell's afternoon demand for a new prime minister, thought it was Anthony Eden who had resigned. Their pandemonious celebration drowned out the rest of that newscast and prolonged their illusion of triumph.

If anything, Gaitskell's appeal had a contrary effect, like Eden's encouragement to Egyptians to disavow Nasser. But he carried it to the nation on television the following night, 4 November, pledging to support a new Tory prime minister who would stop the war and comply with the UN. From a practical point of view, Gaitskell's appeal to the two dozen or so Tories who were deeply opposed to Eden's policy made it more difficult for them to come out openly against Eden. And it infuriated the men of the invasion force steaming eastward from Malta. "The temper of the troops rose," wrote D. M. J. Clark " . . . and the men vowed they'd never again cast a vote for those who couldn't sink their political differences once our forces had been committed to action."

Gaitskell had obtained equal television time to reply to a television address by Eden on 3 November which the BBC judged to be partisan and controversial rather than national in character, as Eden claimed. A few days earlier, the BBC had successfully resisted Eden's attempt to take it over and make it a propaganda arm of the Government instead of an independent journalistic and cultural agency.

Eden's television speech was an emotional apologia, mostly a rehash of earlier justifications based on lurid hypotheses about "the horror and devastation of a larger war" which Eden claimed to be preventing. He added the new claim which must have confirmed Ben-Gurion's worst fears, that the Anglo-French invasion of Egypt would ensure Israel's withdrawal. "A dishonest but able performance," was Harold Nicolson's diary judgment on the speech.

Ben-Gurion had already determined the drift of Eden's spirit. His punishment was on its way Saturday night, 3 November, even as Eden was speaking. It was an Israeli Cabinet declaration to Hammarskjold: "Israel agrees to an immediate cease-fire provided a similar answer is forthcoming from Egypt." Although Egypt had already sent her "similar answer" the day before, the Israelis expected that by the time a cease-fire was actually arranged they would have reached and taken Sharm al-Sheikh. In any case, Israel had taken the site of Elath after the armistice in 1949 and could easily take Sharm al-Sheikh, which was far more isolated, after a cease-fire in 1956.

Britain and France, as Dayan put it, "almost jumped out of their skins" when they got word of the Israeli cease-fire. Britain asked France to throw all her influence into making Israel retract the cease-fire. Eden threatened to call off the invasion if Israel did not renege. Ben-Gurion finally agreed, Dayan wrote, on the "cold calculation that it is better for Israel not to appear alone as an aggressor who disturbs the peace and ignores UN resolutions; it is better that Britain and France should be with her on this front." More than twenty-four hours after accepting the cease-fire Ben-Gurion, angry and reluctant, approved instructions to nullify it by insisting that "Egyptian troops are continuing to fire and *Fedayeen* attacks continue" and by demanding clarification of Cairo's attitudes on five issues long in dispute with Israel. Golda Meir sent the nullification from Jerusalem shortly after midnight on 5 November, about the time that the 9th Infantry Brigade made its unsuccessful first attack on Sharm al-Sheikh and about the time the British and French paratroopers were tumbling out of their bunks on Cyprus for the air-borne invasion of Port Said.

By now Eden, spurred on by the more belligerent French, was trying to disconnect the invasion from the shut-off switch of a cease-fire. Between midnight and dawn on 4 November the General Assembly had stepped up its pressure on Eden with two more resolutions. The first was the Canadian resolution instituting what later came to be called the United Nations Emergency Force. "The General Assembly," it said, "bearing in mind the urgent necessity of facilitating compliance with its resolution 997 (ES-I) of 2 November 1956 [for cease-fire, withdrawal, and military quarantine of the area], requests, as a matter of priority, the Secretary-General to submit to it within forty-eight hours a plan for the setting up, with the consent of the nations concerned, of an emergency international United Nations force to secure and supervise the cessation of hostilities in accordance with all the terms of the aforementioned resolution." The second resolution, sponsored by India and eighteen other Asian and African nations, reaffirmed the cease-fire resolution of 2 November and requested Hammarskjold to report within twelve hours on compliance.

That Sunday morning Chalmers Roberts of the *Washington Post* published a 3,000-word revelation of the British, French, and Israeli collusion arrangements on the basis of secret and still incomplete information garnered by the State Department and CIA. He reported not only secret French shipments of tanks and planes to Israel but also Selwyn Lloyd's "deliberate deception" of Ambassador Aldrich on the eve of the war. He added up the evidence of "the grand design of Britain, France, and Israel" and asked: "But at what cost to the world's opinion of [them]?" Fifteen years of Anglo-American alliance, he wrote, "has ended with deliberate British deceit of the United States." He likened Nutting's resignation to Eden's own resignation nearly twenty years earlier in protest against appeasing the dictators. Roberts ended by saying Eden and Mollet had gambled the future of their nations on a false analogy between Nasser and Hitler.

Hammarskjold began immediate efforts to obtain a cease-fire by 8 P.M. London time, a deadline he agreed to delay because of "certain practical difficulties" until 5 A.M. London time the next day, 5 November. He reported back to the General Assembly before midnight on the 4th on his efforts to implement both resolutions. He said that offers of military contingents for the UN force had begun coming in and he recommended that the Assembly immediately resolve the establishment of a UN command for the force and appoint General Burns to head it. The Assembly did so forthwith, by 57 votes to 0, with 19 abstentions.

Ben-Gurion's antipathy to the UN agencies dealing with Palestine, particularly the UN Truce Supervision Organization, made him view with disgust and apprehension the birth of the Emergency Force. Before the day was out, word came through the Foreign Ministry that Israel would not tolerate the presence of any UN agency to police the Sinai and that Israel had no intention of accepting any settlement permitting Egypt to have military bases anywhere east of Suez.

As the UN increased its pressure on Eden to halt action, the French increased their pressure on him to speed it up. Pineau and Bourgès-Maunoury flew to London for another in what had become a series of daily French ministerial visits across the Channel. The outcome was a reply to Hammarskjold's cease-fire efforts stating that the UN force had not yet been legitimatized and that Anglo-French operations were therefore continuing. They argued for the problem to be returned to the Security Council, presumably to recover their veto power. They added Eden's extraordinary new pretext to the justifications for their impending invasion of Egypt. It was "to secure the speedy withdrawal of Israeli forces."

It was now Ben-Gurion's turn to jump out of his skin. Dayan said Ben-Gurion "cannot be surprised by any new expression of British hypocrisy" but that he was astonished at the French. He cabled instructions to Paris to tell the French: "They have no authority to make such announcement and am amazed that our friends in France are party to such a proposal. It will be an act of unfriendliness against us if they base their entry into Suez as protection from Israel and no declaration on their part will be binding on us." The French explained that they had acquiesced in the treacherous phrase as the price of getting the British to speed up the landings. At the UN, to make amends, the

574

French lamely interpreted the phrase as meaning only Israeli withdrawal from the Canal Zone.

That was not good enough for Ben-Gurion, who promptly reneged on the renege of Israel's original agreement to cease fire. As the British and French paratroopers were making their assault on Port Said, an Israeli letter to Hammarskjold clarified the request for clarification that nullified the cease-fire acceptance, saying: "I wish to make it clear that this request does not affect the cease-fire undertaking which I gave to the General Assembly on 3 November.... (Signed) Abba Eban." The capture of Sharm al-Sheikh was accomplished that morning. That night, while the Anglo-French armada carrying the main invasion force was wallowing off Port Said preparatory to the dawn amphibious assault, Israel cabled Iban: "Inform Secretary General immediately that Israel agrees unconditionally to cease-fire. Since this morning 5 November all fighting has ceased between Israel and Egyptian forces on land, sea, and air and full quiet prevails."

But the invasion had been disconnected by then from the cease-fire shut-off switch, which had been only a mock-up anyway, by the Anglo-French assertion that they would, in any case, station their troops "between the combatants" pending the arrival of the UN Emergency Force.

Anxiety about the time lag between the start of the Anglo-French air offensive and the assault on Port Said had haunted the soldiers of Operation Musketeer from the beginning. It had prompted Stockwell and Beaufre to start loading the expeditionary "police-action" force at Malta nearly three days before there was any Israeli-Egyptian war to police. It had contributed to the twelve-hour delay in starting the bombing on 31 October. It led, during the war, to repeated French visits to London to prod Eden into approving more speed while the generals on Cyprus worked out plan after plan for advancing the date and hour of the touch-down of troops on Egyptian soil.

The early loading in Malta advanced the date of the amphibious landing from 10 November to 7 November. An additional day was cut from this by adoption of a plan, code-named Penelope, to sail the invasion fleet somewhat faster by running the slowest ships at better than normal speed. To advance the amphibious assault more than that would require abandoning the collusive device of having Israel provide the pretext for police action. Given good weather, 6 November at dawn was therefore the earliest that the seaborne assault could be launched.

All subsequent efforts to accelerate the landing of allied troops on Egyptian soil concerned the paratroopers, who were originally scheduled to jump and take key points behind Egyptian lines while the amphibious troops were hitting the beaches and not before. The efforts led to a series of operational plans

575

supplementary to Operation Musketeer—Omelette, Omelette II, Simplex, Tele-scope, and Telescope Modified. Much of the impetus for these plans and much of the work on them came from General Beaufre, whose sensitivity to the psychology of war made him more pessimistic than most about the long period of bombing before the invasion.

Beaufre flew from Algiers with an airlift of three French paratroop regi-ments to Cyprus on 29 October and set up his headquarters at Tymbou airfield, which was allotted to the French forces. Stockwell arrived the next day and established himself at the British base of Akrotiri. Operation Omelette had already been prepared. It was for an unopposed landing by an occupation force in the event that Nasser's regime collapsed during the days of aerial bombing. The unexpected vigor of American opposition to the war and the crescendo of world criticism impelled Beaufre and those who thought like him to seek ways to get troops into Egypt before international politics made it impossible. He reworked Omelette into Omelette II, for an emergency landing against opposition. On 2 November, Beaufre told me, he wanted to unleash Omelette II but was turned down. That night he drafted the plan for Operation Simplex and reworked it the next day into Operation Telescope.

It was on the night of 2 November that the French military attaché in Tel Aviv contacted Dayan to propose direct Israeli cooperation along the Canal to facilitate a speed-up of the air-borne landings. When the British rejected the plan and the French showed signs of thinking about launching a paratroop operation independent of the British, the Israelis offered to cooperate across the Canal, seizing it and the ports on the west side. French Ambassador Gilbert, in direct radio-code contact with the Defense Ministry in Paris, relayed Israeli offers of a "Red Plan," in which the Israeli soldiers would put on French uni-forms and repaint their vehicles in French colors before seizing the Canal, and a "Black Plan," under which they would take the Canal and its ports in their own uniforms and surrender them to the French as soon as they could get there. These plans too, according to Gilbert, were passed all the way up to Eden before being finally rejected.

French-Israeli contacts were maintained through several channels during the fighting. Beaufre told me he had an Israeli liaison officer at Tymbou and three or four French liaison officers in Israel. He said he had to keep the Israeli at Tymbou hidden from the British. In the Defense Ministry's commu-nications room in Paris there were Israeli translators and cryptographers handling direct traffic with Tel Aviv. Gilbert, who was out of sympathy with the pro-Arab tendencies at the Quai d'Orsay, communicated directly with Pineau over the Defense Ministry's Paris-Tel Aviv radio link.

Beaufre had liaison problems with the British. Tymbou airfield is nine miles east of Nicosia. Akrotiri, where Stockwell was headquartered, was in the southernmost peninsula of Cyprus, forty-five miles southwest of Nicosia and fifty miles from Tymbou as the crow flies. By road it was a good two hours between the French and British headquarters; by plane, about half an hour door to door. When war planning was ordered, Akrotiri was still under construction for the RAF and Tymbou, long neglected, had to be almost entirely renovated. The bases did not become fully operational until a couple of weeks before the war. The main British airbase was five miles west of Nicosia. The headquarters to which the British Middle East Command had moved after leaving the Suez base was at Episkopi, seven miles northwest of Akrotiri. All in all, it was a confusing and hampering dispersion.

The wall of secrecy concerning political objectives between the Cabinet and the military command caused serious internal liaison problems for the British. These augmented the inconveniences attendant on pretending that Britain's relations with her Israeli ally were no different from her relations with her Egyptian enemy, namely that both were being "policed" alike. An example of the lack of political communication between Downing Street and Episkopi was Keightley's belief, uncorrected until 4 November, the eve of invasion, that he could count on the 10th Armored Division in Libya, which was the most powerful British force in the Middle East and the only armored unit in his order of battle.

On 3 November, the cautious British generals were persuaded to advance the air-borne assault twenty-four hours. Eden, anxious to get the war over with if he could not call it off, also approved. Beaufre swiftly prepared Operation Telescope, providing for British paratroopers to drop at Gameel Airfield three miles west of Port Said and advance on the city from there while French paratroopers captured the twin city of Port Fuad on the east bank of the Canal. The waterworks and the two bridges over the Raswa Canal at the southern entrance to Port Said were to be taken by British troops landed in helicopters. The paratroopers in Cyprus were alerted that evening that they would go into action twenty-four hours early.

In London the Cabinet anguished over Keightley's requirement for a naval bombardment of Port Said before the amphibious landings. A naval bombardment to soften up shore defenses for an amphibious landing is a fearsome thing, commonly resulting in the utter devastation of the target area. The target area of Operation Musketeer was, unlike most beachheads, a densely populated city upon which the world's attention was focused. The Cabinet was in a dilemma. If it curtailed the bombardment, as it had curtailed the size of the aerial bombs, the likely cost in British lives during the assault would have ugly political repercussions at home. If the bombardment was given free rein, the destruction of Egyptian lives and property would have ugly political repercussions abroad, particularly in the United States.

The Cabinet decided to send its Defense Minister, Antony Head, to Cyprus for a first-hand assessment of military thinking. Head hurried home to pack and found Randolph Churchill among half a dozen dinner guests there. Churchill, a correspondent for the *Evening Standard*, was inconveniently nosy about the trip but Head departed without disclosing his mission, flying from the RAF station at Biggin Hill with General Templer, Chief of the Imperial General Staff. Stockwell said they brought "clear instructions to keep damage in Port Said to a minimum . . . we had to be careful over casualties, particularly to the civilian population."

Stockwell grumbled over the restrictions. So did Sandy Cavanagh, a young paratroop medical officer, who wrote in a memoir of the operation that "the dubious political object of conserving our enemies' lives was being achieved by imperiling our own. . . . Most incredible of all was the [radio] warning to civilians to keep clear of the beach area in Port Said. . . . Had we known about this we would have laughed at our efforts to maintain security."

Head conferred with Keightley, Stockwell, and Beaufre and returned to Biggin Hill on Sunday morning, 4 November, in time to attend an 11 o'clock Cabinet meeting. He reported that headquarters in Cyprus had not really wanted a full-scale bombardment and had accepted the limitations as an endurable handicap. In addition to limiting the preinvasion bombardment and confirming London's agreement to a paratroop drop on the 5th, Beaufre wrote afterward, Head canceled the military plans for a move on Cairo, insisting that the operation be limited to the Canal Zone. "This robbed it of all its political purpose," Beaufre wrote.

Eden sent a cable to Eisenhower insisting that "now that police action has been started it must be carried through . . . we cannot have a military vacuum while a UN force is being constituted." But he did not disclose that paratroopers would begin the invasion of Egypt in the morning. Touching matters nearer the heart of truth, Eden said: "I have always felt, as I made very clear to Mr. Khrushchev, that the Middle East was an issue over which, in the last resort, we would have to fight. . . . If we had allowed things to drift, . . . Nasser would have become a kind of Moslem Mussolini . . . taking the tricks all round the Middle East. . . . I am sure that this is the moment to curb Nasser's ambitions. . . . By this means, we shall have taken the first step towards re-establishing authority in this area for our generation." He went on to speak of his grief at having to breach the Anglo-American alliance. He threw himself on Eisenhower's mercy—"If you cannot approve, I would like you at least to understand . . . "

Eden had got Churchill the day before to spend some of his immense prestige on Eden's behalf by publishing a letter to his constituency slandering Egypt and saying: "I am confident that our American friends will come to realize that, not for the first time, we have acted independently for the common good." Churchill urged support for Eden.

Not even Churchill was able to abate the rage of Eden's domestic opposition. Thousands upon thousands turned out with "Law, not War" placards and shouts of "Eden must go!" at a mass rally in Trafalgar Square on Sunday afternoon, 4 November. Five hundred extra police deployed in Whitehall when thousands streamed down from the rally to attempt to demonstrate in Downing Street. Aneurin Bevan told the crowd: "We are stronger than Egypt but there are other countries stronger than us. Are we prepared to accept for ourselves the logic we are applying to Egypt? If nations more powerful than ourselves accept this anarchistic attitude and launch bombs on London, what answer have we got?" Eight policemen were injured resisting the demonstrators. Eden dismissed the event in his memoirs by quoting with approval a letter from a London bus driver: "Eighty per cent of the crowd were of foreign extraction so that was no true census of opinion and can be ignored."

In a final flurry of hesitation that evening, Eden asked Keightley at 8:15 to state the last minute to which a decision could be delayed on whether to postpone the air-borne assault the next morning. Keightley replied: 11 P.M. London time. That was only fifteen minutes before reveille for the attack units (1:15 A.M. Cyprus time). Keightley added that a postponement would be a very serious matter and should be avoided at all costs. Eden dropped the idea of a postponement and told Keightley to go ahead.

By then Beaufre had converted Operation Telescope into Operation Telescope Modified by shifting the job of taking the waterworks and the Raswa bridges from a British helicopter force to French paratroopers. The only available drop zone near the waterworks was the triangular head of the causeway with no more than a few hundred yards of open space in any direction. In the cellars of Terrapin it had been thought that only helicopters could put air-borne troops into so small an area but Beaufre said the French paratroopers could and would take the isolated Raswa area in addition to Port Fuad.

The relationship of the air-borne operations to the amphibious assault seems to have confused most writers on the war. It is not surprising. The French say that Admiral Barjot himself never understood the connection between Telescope Modified (the air-borne assault on 5 November) and Musketeer Revise (the sea-borne invasion on 6 November), not to speak of the discarded versions of both. In essence, the relationship as explained to me by Beaufre and

579

Stockwell was this: originally the air-borne operation was to have been a simultaneous part and parcel of the amphibious invasion but the race to get men into Egypt in the face of international opposition induced Britain and France to advance the air-borne assault by twenty-four hours, thereby giving it far more independence and importance than before in relation to the main sea-borne invasion.

Operation Telescope Modified would have occurred still earlier, perhaps as early as 2 November, if the British had been willing to risk paratroopers in enemy territory for longer than twenty-four hours without follow-up support or if they had been willing to let Israeli forces support paratroop units. In the latter case the whole Canal could have been seized at once.

In the hour before Eden queried Keightley about postponing the airborne assault, Moscow broadcast the text of a protest the Kremlin had delivered to the British and French embassies against the closing of the eastern Mediterranean and the northern Red Sea by the Anglo-French command. "The establishment of zones closed to shipping in the Mediterranean and the Red Sea makes the use of the Suez Canal impossible and thus amounts to an obvious violation by the UK and France of the Constantinople Convention of 1888," the note said. "The Soviet Government regards the aforesaid actions by the UK and France as an act of aggression affecting the interests not only of Egypt but of other states as well. The Soviet Government cannot disregard these unlawful actions . . . and declares that the responsibility for all the possible consequences of such actions rests with the British and French Governments."

The Russians were turning their attention again to the Middle East after having crushed the Hungarian revolt earlier that day, Sunday, 4 November. What had happened in Hungary was that Imre Nagy, although nominally restored to power as Premier, never achieved control over the revolutionaries, particularly the militantly anti-Communist and anti-Russian elements among them. On the contrary, they effectively steered Nagy into extreme policies, apparently on the assumption that whatever reaction the Kremlin made, the West would step in and protect the Hungarian revolution. But the West was no more willing to risk a world war over Hungary than Russia was over the Middle East.

For a year and a half before the revolution Hungary had endured the Stalinist regimes of Matyas Rakosi and Erno Gero. These men stood against the tide of de-Stalinization and liberalization which had been emanating from the Kremlin, tacitly since Stalin's death in March 1953 and explicitly since Khrushchev's famous denunciation of Stalin's crimes at the Twentieth Communist Party Congress in February 1956. Both Nagy, a former premier, and Janos Kadar were popular leaders in the de-Stalinizing wing of the Hungarian

Communist party. Because they had been under the shadow of revisionism charges during the Rakosi and Gero premierships, they were acceptable as new leaders when Hungarian dissidents began on 22 October to demand nationalist reforms like those newly won by the Poles.

The crumbling Stalinists sought to associate Nagy with their regime, naming him as a figurehead premier on 24 October. They did associate his name with the appeal for Russian help that brought Red Army tanks into Budapest on 24 October, the day of the Sèvres accord. Nagy never erased that taint although he denounced it as a lie after he assumed the actual powers of the premiership. He formed a new Government on 27 October, a day after the Stalinist leaders took flight. The killing of Hungarians by Russian tanks had stimulated local and provincial revolts all over Hungary, some by Communists and some by anti-Communists, with nationalism as their only common denominator.

This had convinced the Kremlin that it would be better to engineer a change of leadership in Hungary than to resort to stronger repression. Mikoyan and Suslov were sent to Budapest to transform Nagy from a figurehead into a real premier. Kadar became First Secretary of the Hungarian Communist party. On the 28th, the eve of the Israeli Sinai invasion, Nagy announced Russian agreement to an immediate cease-fire and withdrawal from Budapest. On the 30th, the day of the Anglo-French ultimatum, came the momentous Soviet statement offering to negotiate complete withdrawal of the Red Army from Hungary and declaring a new basis for relationships between Russia and her satellites—"noninterference in each other's internal affairs." Nagy announced the restoration of multi-party democracy. De-Stalinization had won the day, it seemed, in Budapest as in Warsaw and the Kremlin. It was this that Allen Dulles called a "miracle."

But the revolutionary factions in Hungary, dizzy with success, began to compete with one another in demanding that Nagy obtain still more concessions. And the killing that first began between the revolutionaries and the Stalinist Hungarian security forces now began to break out between Communist and non-Communist revolutionary factions, some of it merely a settling of personal feuds. One revolutionary faction headed by Colonel Pal Maleter, who was shortly to become a byword in the West for hopeless heroism, broadcast a demand on 31 October that Nagy repudiate the Warsaw Treaty, the Eastern Bloc's answer to NATO. Provincial councils demanded Hungarian neutrality and threatened to secede if Budapest refused their demands.

Nagy did broadcast a declaration of neutrality on 1 November. When Red Army reinforcements began entering Hungary that same day he immediately informed the Russian ambassador that Hungary repudiated the Warsaw Treaty and was asking the help of the UN and the great powers to defend Hungarian neutrality. Even the sympathetic Poles were shocked. The Central Committee of the Polish Communist party issued a statement on 2 November that denounced Nagy's predecessors for having called in Russian troops but also condemned the new "forces of reaction pushing Hungary to disaster." The Polish Central Committee said Hungary was falling into "chaos and anarchy" and that "reactionary bands are committing lynchings and are bestially murdering Communists."

While the Red Army built up its strength within reach of Budapest but outside of the city, there were three days of vigorous debate within the Kremlin over whether to send the Red Army back in. Khrushchev and Mikoyan had favored the original withdrawal that began on 28 October, hoping Nagy and the Hungarians would follow Gomulka's pattern for Poland. Marshal Zhukov, Defense Minister and World War II friend of Eisenhower's, led the hard-line faction. Hayter, the British ambassador at the time, believed that Nagy's endorsement of the extreme nationalist revolutionary policy made it impossible for Khrushchev to stand aside from Hungarian developments. Hayter conjectures that Suez gave the hard-liners in the Kremlin three good arguments: first, it would divert African and Asian criticism away from Russia; second, Russia could take the law into her own hands more freely after Britain and France did so; and third, "the Soviet Government could not do much for Egypt and could not take two simultaneous defeats, Egypt and Hungary."

Murphy, who was working day and night on the Suez and Hungarian crises as the third ranking man in the State Department, said Russia had to intervene in Hungary "because its entire Eastern European security system was at stake." He said the decision to intervene apparently was taken with the greatest reluctance but that when it was taken Zhukov was authorized to use all the force necessary for total suppression of the revolt. "From the Russian point of view," Murphy wrote, "this was an absolute political and military necessity, and once the offensive was launched, they followed through. Putting ethnics and the humanities aside, their judgment was sound."

Hayter and American Ambassador Charles Bohlen, both anti-Suez men, believed that Nagy's policies forced Russia to intervene. There was no causal relationship between Suez and Hungary, they say, but Suez was a heaven-sent coincidence for the Kremlin, putting the West on weak moral ground while diverting attention from the blood-letting in Budapest. Murphy too said the Suez War "could not have been timed more advantageously for the Russians."

By dawn on 4 November some 200,000 Russian troops and 4,000 tanks, by Eisenhower's count, moved into Budapest. The re-entry was heralded by a Moscow broadcast analyzing the revolution as the "fruit of subversion by the imperialist powers." Radio Moscow said Hungary was in a reign of terror and that "Imre Nagy is unable and unwilling to fight the black forces of reaction; the Nagy Government has virtually disintegrated." Budapest radio reported the new Russian attack at 6:19 A.M. Budapest time. At 8:12 A.M. it appealed to the Russians not to shoot. At 10:13 A.M. (3:13 A.M. New York time) the Russians cast their seventy-ninth veto against a US resolution calling for a Red Army withdrawal from Hungary. At 2:05 P.M. Budapest time, Moscow broadcast that the "reactionary conspiracy" against the Hungarians had been crushed and that a new government had been formed under Janos Kadar as Premier.

Kadar had parted company with Nagy on 1 November, the day Nagy declared Hungary's neutrality and repudiated the Warsaw Pact. The day before, Kadar had participated with Nagy and non-Communist leaders in a final round of talks with Mikoyan and Mikhail Suslov. Nagy and Zoltan Tildy, a leader of the former Smallholders Party, reportedly told the Russians that any Hungarian government would be thrown out if it did not accede to the demand for formal neutrality, which was coming from both Communist and non-Communist factions in the revolution. The Kremlin apparently hoped that the reinforcement of Red Army units outside Budapest would exercise a steadying influence. On the contrary, it provoked Nagy and the revolutionary rank and file. Kadar quietly left Budapest for the Russian headquarters at Szolnok and set up a rival government, which issued statements urging Russian intervention. Kadar was reviled in Hungary and in the world at large as a Quisling. But a decade later he seemed to have won acceptance as a practical liberal, courageous enough to stand by Khrushchev after he was deposed.

As Eisenhower wrote in his memoirs, the Russian move into Hungary "almost automatically" raised the question of US intervention. But he concluded that it was "out of the question" for US and NATO forces to cross the intervening Communist Bloc countries or Austria, which was formally neutralized by treaty. Although the General Assembly took up the Hungarian case following the Soviet veto, as it did with Suez after the Anglo-French vetoes, and passed a resolution calling for Russian withdrawal, Eisenhower realized that "it was obvious that no mandate for military action could or would be forthcoming." So the idea of helping Hungary was dropped and the talk about liberating the captive peoples of Eastern Europe disappeared from the speeches of Dulles and other members of the Eisenhower Administration. The US also toned down the inflammatory broadcasts of the American propaganda stations, Radio Liberation and Radio Free Europe, which were blamed for irresponsibly encouraging impossible hopes among the Hungarian revolutionaries. There was an unanswerable reproach in the desperate appeal of the Hungarian rebel radio

583

at Gyor for the civilized people of the world to come, not with declarations but with arms, to save Hungary. Moscow had already crushed the heart of the revolt in Budapest.

Andrew H. Berding quotes Dulles as follows on the issue of helping Hungary:

> This would be madness. The only way we can save Hungary at this time would be through all-out nuclear war. Does anyone in his senses want to start a nuclear war over Hungary? As for simply sending American divisions into Hungary, they would be wiped out by the superior Soviet ground forces. Geography is against us. And in either event . . . the Hungarians would be the greatest sufferers.

Although the Red Army overwhelmed the Hungarian revolution on 4 November it was days, and in some places weeks, before armed resistance was stamped out. Passive resistance, in the form of strikes, endured longer. Kadar was nominally in power soon after Nagy took refuge in the Yugoslav Embassy toward noon on the 4th. But Red Army unit commanders exercised actual power in the first days and Kadar did not appear in public until 9 November. Nagy was treacherously kidnapped by the Russians on 23 November when he ventured out of the Yugoslav Embassy on a safe-conduct pass. He was later executed. Rebel radios in the provinces continued to broadcast for some days and tens of thousands of Hungarians streamed across the Austrian border into exile. These were the dying consequences of the mortal blow which the Red Army delivered to the Hungarian revolution on that Sunday.

As the decisive battle of Budapest began to subside, the indecisive battle of Port Said began to take shape. At 4 o'clock that Sunday afternoon General Stockwell sailed from Limassol on his headquarters ship, the *Tyne*, with a small convoy carrying the follow-up battalions of paratroopers scheduled to go ashore after the first assault. The men of the battalions assigned to jump in the first assault were not roused from sleep for their air journey to Port Said until 01:15 on Monday, 5 November. At that time Nasser too was on his way to Port Said.

"I left here at 1 o'clock—at 1 o'clock after midnight," he told me in Cairo nearly ten years later. "And my destination was Port Said. And when I reached Ismailiya, there was Kamaleddeen Hussein, the leader of Ismailiya. I went to him and he said: 'You spend tonight with us and then tomorrow night go to Port Said.' I had intended to see Ismailiya and Port Said, but to begin with Port Said. But I agreed and I went to bed about 4 o'clock in the morning at Ismailiya, in the house of Kamal Hussein. He had taken over the house of the British consul. And then Kamal Hussein came to me in the morning. I was in bed. He told me they had landed paratroops in Port Said. So I returned to Cairo."

Nasser laughed deep and loud at the thought that if it had not been for Kamaleddeen Hussein's importunity he would have waked up in a city whose exits were sealed by enemy paratroopers. "It was [almost] a good opportunity," he said, shaking with laughter, "for Mister Eden to catch me there."

CHAPTER
18

Port Said

(BEFORE DAWN, 5 NOVEMBER 1956,
TO 2 A.M., 7 NOVEMBER 1956)

The next British lion is Malta, four days further on in the Midland Sea, and ready to spring upon Egypt or pounce upon Syria, or roar so as to be heard at Marseilles in case of need.

(WILLIAM THACKERAY, *Eastern Sketches*, 1845)

A man is the slave of what he says and the master of what he does not say.

(Turkish proverb)

In time of war belligerent powers shall not disembark nor embark within the Canal and its ports of access either troops, munitions, or materials of war.

(Article V, Constantinople Convention of 1888)

B Y THE time the Anglo-French invasion of Egypt began at Port Said—
"to separate the belligerents" as Eden put it—the belligerents were
firing the last shots of their war at Sharm al-Sheikh, some two
hundred sixty-five miles away at the other end of the Sinai Peninsula.
At 8:20 Monday morning, 5 November, the first planeload of British
paratroopers stepped into the warm slipstream of their Valetta transport six
hundred feet over Port Said's Gameel airfield. By 9 o'clock, at Sharm al-
Sheikh, the last battle of the war they were supposed to be stopping had come
to an end of its own accord.

"You have brought to a successful conclusion the greatest and most glorious military project in the history of our people," Ben-Gurion told the victors
at Sharm al-Sheikh in an emotional message on the morrow. "With a mighty
sweep of all the combined arms of the Israel Defense Forces, you have
stretched out your hand to King Solomon. . . . Elath will again be the leading
Hebrew port in the south, the straits of Suez will be opened to Israel shipping,
and Yotvat, hitherto called Tiran, which was an independent Hebrew state until 1,400 years ago, will return as an integral part of the Third Israel Commonwealth."

The Third Israeli Commonwealth's interest in the Gulf of Aqaba sea
lanes dates from far back in Mandate days when leaders like Weizmann and
Ben-Gurion began thinking in geopolitical terms of the future state of Israel.
Israeli forces quietly occupied the head of the gulf after signing the armistice
in 1949, thereby acquiring the site of the future port of Elath and making Israel
a two-ocean state, potentially able to offer competition to the Suez Canal. It
was the first step toward making the Arab gulf into an Arab-Israeli gulf. The
next step was to open the gulf to Israeli shipping in the face of Arab claims
that Israel's occupation of Elath was illegal and that the Straits of Tiran at the
entrance of the gulf were entirely overlapped by Arab territorial waters. In
1949 King Farouk's Egypt placed platoons on Tiran and Sanafir, the islands in
the mouth of the straits, to forestall the possibility of Israel occupying them.
Two six-inch British coastal guns made in 1907 were placed at Ras Nasrani
(Cape Christian) on the Egyptian shore of the strait.

Israel's interest in the strait remained constant and practical. An Italian
frogman hired by Egypt in 1949 to train Egyptian frogmen chose the remote
bay, Sharm al-Sheikh, as his training site. In 1953 he was discovered to be an
Israeli spy. Sharm al-Sheikh is ten miles south of Ras Nasrani. It is the administrative center and main defense position for the Egyptian forces at the
southern end of the Sinai Peninsula. It possesses a small harbor and airfield.
Road connections go up the west shore of the peninsula to Suez and up the

east shore as far as Dahab, a warning post thirty-five miles north of Ras Nasrani.

Ben-Gurion and Sharett in the summer of 1955 proclaimed the opening of the Gulf of Aqaba to Israeli shipping to be an aim for which Israel would go to war—within a year, Ben-Gurion added early in the fall. Egypt reaffirmed the prohibition against Israeli shipping and air traffic on 11 September 1955 and issued regulations requiring three days' advance notice from shipping bound for the Jordanian port of Aqaba. Israeli airline flights to South Africa ended in late October 1955. Dayan, in the introductory background to his Sinai diary, said the widening of the blockade was "the last straw" that prompted Ben-Gurion to summon him home from a vacation in France to plan the Sinai invasion. Ben-Gurion was making plans for the straits on the night of 21 October 1956 as he flew toward his secret conference with Lloyd and the French at Sèvres, reading Procopius's history of the ancient Jewish colony on Tiran.

Nasser stated that Egypt's obligations as a member of the League of Arab States required her to maintain the blockade wherever it was legally possible. Nasser, Aly Sabry, and other Egyptian leaders as well as Eisenhower, Dulles, and US Senator Fulbright have suggested that the World Court was the place to settle this legal question. But Israel ignored these suggestions and twice preferred the arbitrament of war—in 1956 and 1967.

Egyptian defenses at the straits were based on Sharm al-Sheikh with a strongpoint at Ras Nasrani. A mobile reserve company was posted on Jebel Aida, which forms a triangle with the two shore positions. It was capable of moving to the support of either shore position in tracked vehicles. Each corner of the triangle was prepared to fight independently, carrying a two-week stockpile of ammunition and supplies. This flexibility was designed to cope with a parachute drop, which was considered to be the likeliest form of attack. The frigate *Rasheed* stood by against the remote possibility of a sea-borne attack. Warning posts of Frontier Forces extended as far north as Dahab, a third of the way up the gulf, but the terrain and track between there and the Israeli frontier were so bad that an overland attack was considered almost out of the question. The Egyptians had a battalion of regular infantry minus two companies—about 400 men—at Ras Nasrani with a troop of four 3-inch dual purpose anti-aircraft and antitank guns and a troop of three 30-mm. anti-aircraft guns as support weapons. The two 6-inch coast guns could not swing round against land targets. At Sharm al-Sheikh was an undermanned National Guard battalion—about 200 men—plus one of the regular infantry companies of the battalion at Ras Nasrani, and a troop of three 30-mm. anti-aircraft guns. The other regular infantry company was on Jebel Aida. On Tiran and

Sanafir were observation posts of twelve men and two Oerlikon 20-mm. guns each.

The Egyptian commander at Sharm al-Sheikh was Colonel Raouf Mahfouz Zaki, newly transferred from Abu Aoueigila. His reply to the withdrawal order on 1 November was that it was simply impossible to obey and that he might as well stay and fight it out as long as he could. This was accepted at headquarters. Zaki had neither vehicles nor shipping to transport his men and equipment out. And if he had, the Israelis barred the land route home while the British cruiser *Newfoundland* and a flotilla of destroyers barred the sea lanes.

The first casualties of the battle for Sharm al-Sheikh were the men of the Egyptian frigate *Damietta*. She was sunk by the British on the night of 31 October as she headed down the Gulf of Suez to the relief of Sharm al-Sheikh. The *Damietta* carried no radar. Shortly after midnight she was running with her navigation lights on near Ras Gharib on the African shore. The watch sighted three lightless warships standing abreast 400 yards ahead. The darkened ships were the *Newfoundland*, flanked by two destroyers. The *Newfoundland* signaled "Halt!", to which the *Damietta* replied "What ship are you?" Repeating the order to halt, the *Newfoundland* turned her searchlights on the *Damietta*, which replied this time with her single 4-inch gun, aimed at the light. She missed. The *Newfoundland* answered with a salvo from her three 6-inch guns, hitting the *Damietta* forward. The Egyptian commander, Shakr Hussein, replied with two more wild shots. A second salvo from the *Newfoundland* knocked out his gun. He was trying to ram the *Newfoundland* when a third salvo smashed his engines and rudder. The sinking *Damietta's* 40-mm. guns blazed away at the *Newfoundland* until Hussein ordered "Abandon ship." He was last seen making his way forward to investigate a cry for help. The British picked up sixty-eight survivors. The entire action was over in fifteen minutes. Twelve hours later the British flotilla was patrolling off Sharm al-Sheikh. The *Rasheed* had escaped to the Saudi Arabian port of Wejh.

Sharm al-Sheikh, although first in importance among Israel's war objectives, was the last on the schedule of operations, being the most distant and the most difficult to approach. It was assigned to Colonel Avraham Yoffe's 9th Infantry Brigade. As related in Chapter 15, the vanguard company of the brigade took the Egyptian frontier post at Ras al-Naqb on the night of 29 October in the third hour of the war. At Ras al-Naqb, five miles northwest of Elath, converge the Egyptian tracks from Kuntilla in the north, Thamad and Mitla in the west, and Dahab and Sharm al-Sheikh to the south. The track to the south, invisible at places as it threads among rocky clefts and blind ravines, had been marked with wooden signs embedded in cement by an Egyptian officer, Hassan al-Badry. "I thought of this when the Israelis came down my trail," Badry told me afterward with a regretful laugh.

The remainder of Yoffe's brigade, two battalions plus a reconnaisance unit, artillery, and mortar support units—1,800 men in all—had assembled far to the northeast as part of the feint against Jordan. It moved to Ras al-Naqb on 1 November, the day Rafah fell while Abu Aoueigila stood fast on the Central Axis. Yoffe was scheduled to begin his march to Sharm al-Sheikh immediately. But the Anglo-French air attacks had not finished eliminating the Egyptian Air Force so Dayan ordered Yoffe to wait another day at Ras al-Naqb. He set out at 05:00 on 2 November in one hundred of the French six-wheel-drive trucks that had arrived in Israel only a week before and one hundred half-tracked personnel carriers, self-propelled guns, command cars, and jeeps. Landing craft from Elath supplied Yoffe's column at rendezvous points on the shore. The land route was a punishing ordeal for men and machines. The troops had to manhandle the trucks through passages of engulfing sand. The half-tracks needed constant applications of grease which was dropped by air.

On the other side of Sinai a battalion of the paratroopers recuperating at the Parker Memorial headed through the mountains on the evening of 2 November in a southwesterly direction toward Ras al-Sudr while a combined parachute and infantry force was dropped to occupy Tor, an oil town far down the Gulf of Suez shore. Both arms of the pincer envelopment of Sharm al-Sheikh were now in motion.

On the morning of 3 November Dayan flew over Dahab, where the 9th Brigade was waiting for landing craft bringing fuel. Circling overhead, he contacted Yoffe by radio and urged him to finish the campaign the next day if he possibly could. Yoffe had just lost three killed and five wounded when ten camel-mounted Egyptian soldiers at Dahab shot it out with the advancing Israelis. The Israelis, who had expected no resistance there, machine-gunned all the Egyptians. Dayan flew across to Tor to order the western arm of the pincer to close on Sharm al-Sheikh as rapidly as possible before international opposition forced Israel to stop advancing. Part of the force dropped at Tor had been on its way to a drop at Sharm al-Sheikh itself, Dayan recorded, when the transport planes were overtaken at the last minute by an Israeli fighter plane which signaled that anti-aircraft fire from Sharm al-Sheikh indicated that a paratroop drop there would be too risky.

Israeli air raids began inflicting heavy casualties and damage on Sharm al-Sheikh at 9 A.M. on 2 November. They kept up the pounding, with bombs, rockets, and napalm, and the strafing for three days. Shortly after dark on the

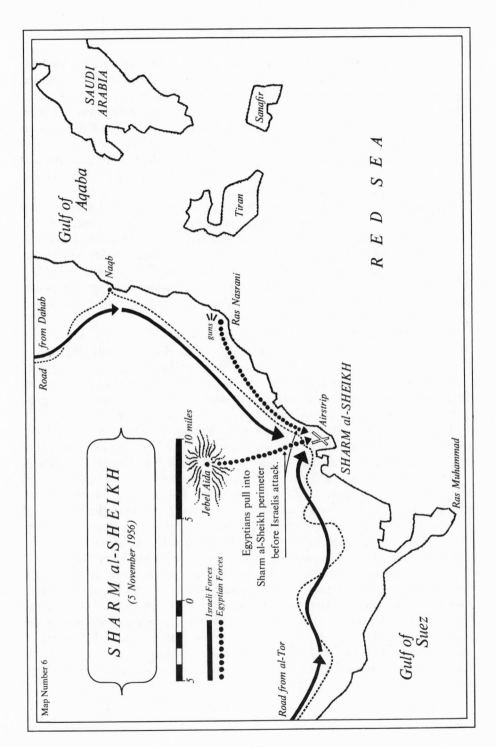

Map Number 6

SHARM al-SHEIKH
(5 November 1956)

—— Israeli Forces
•••• Egyptian Forces

5   0   5   10 miles

SAUDI ARABIA

Sanafir

Gulf of Aqaba

Tiran

R E D   S E A

Road from Dahab

Naqb

guns

Ras Nasrani

Jebel Aida

Airstrip

SHARM al-SHEIKH

Egyptians pull into
Sharm al-Sheikh perimeter
before Israelis attack.

Ras Muhammad

Road from al-Tor

Gulf of Suez

2nd a loudspeaker plane like the one used at Um Qataf circled for an hour telling the Egyptians they were surrounded and could honorably surrender. Egyptian anti-aircraft gunners shot down two Israeli Mystères on the 2nd. The Egyptians captured the pilot of one of them when a patrol sent out from Ras Nasrani after dark found him wounded in the leg and brought him in at 21:00. He was brought to Sharm al-Sheikh the next morning and sent to Cairo in a sailboat carrying civilian laborers and wounded soldiers. He was returned to Israel in the prisoner exchange after the war. The other pilot was rescued by an Israeli Piper plane just before dark.

By midday on 3 November the Israeli fighter-bombers had knocked out two of the four 3-inch AA guns at Ras Nasrani and wrecked workshops, the water filtration plant, and water tanks at Sharm al-Sheikh. When Colonel Zaki learned from the captured pilot that the advancing Israeli brigade had armor, and that a second Israeli force was coming down the Gulf of Suez in landing craft, he decided that he should abandon Ras Nasrani and regroup in the Sharm al-Sheikh perimeter. The coastal guns at Ras Nasrani were spiked and the withdrawal was carried out after dark.

Just before dark four Israeli Mystères mistakenly attacked the British destroyer *Crane*, which was patrolling off Sharm al-Sheikh with the cruiser *Newfoundland*. Each of the four planes in turn hit the ship with a full salvo of thirty-eight high-explosive rockets, setting her afire but neither piercing her armor nor causing severe damage. Zaki, thinking the planes must be Egyptian, signaled headquarters in Cairo: "Aqaba troops thank you."

Dayan concedes that Zaki's decision to abandon Ras Nasrani and concentrate his forces at Sharm al-Sheikh was justifiable. The Egyptian battalions were below strength and could not expect to hold both Ras Nasrani and Sharm al-Sheikh against two Israeli forces attacking simultaneously. It was logical to choose Sharm al-Sheikh. If Zaki had selected Ras Nasrani because of its stronger emplacements, the Israelis would have been able to use the harbor and airfield at Sharm al-Sheikh to rush additional forces in. The trenches, minefields, wire barriers, and outposts at Sharm al-Sheikh, however, "were not sufficiently powerful to withstand a determined attack," Dayan wrote.

By the end of 4 November, Dayan was out of patience with the 9th Brigade for not having taken the Egyptian positions. The brigade was two days behind schedule, having lost one day because of the delayed start of the Anglo-French destruction of the Egyptian air force and a second because the route down the Gulf of Aqaba was even worse than anticipated. Control of the Straits of Tiran was "the primary aim of the campaign," Dayan wrote. "If the fighting had stopped when we had in our possession the whole of the Sinai

Peninsula but not Sharm al-Sheikh . . . this would have meant that we had lost the campaign. The time element was crucial." Dayan flew to Tor early on 5 November and dashed after the paratroopers in a command car with his escort following in two buses.

The paratroopers reached the southern perimeter of Sharm al-Sheikh just as Yoffe's men were subduing the last Egyptian resistance. Dayan arrived shortly after the paratroopers. He described the scene as one of the most spectacular he had ever laid eyes on—deep blue waters framed by hills of crimson rock, a white mosque with a tall minaret—"the picture of a wonderland hidden among lofty mountains"—but with the smoke and wreckage of battle fresh upon it.

Israeli planes had kept up constant punishment against Sharm al-Sheikh all day on 4 November while the 9th Brigade literally dynamited its way through some of the narrow defiles and passed through the empty defenses at Ras Nasrani. Yoffe's first attack on Sharm al-Sheikh went in shortly after midnight. In spite of the Israeli advantage in possessing armor for their spearhead, the Egyptians beat off the attack. Yoffe withdrew at 04:30.

Yoffe attacked again at first light, about 05:30, this time with air support and aerial observation for pinpoint fire by his heavy mortars and artillery. Planes had not been feasible at night. The Israeli armor steamrollered into the Egyptian positions at 08:00 behind waves of diving planes hurling a fiery deluge of bombs, rockets, and napalm on the defenders. "The decisive element which brought about the speedy collapse of the enemy was the Air Force," Dayan wrote. The emplacements were captured one by one in an hour of stubborn fighting. The battle was over by 09:00. A half hour later the surrender was formalized and the roundup of prisoners began.

The 9th Brigade lost 10 killed and 32 wounded in its campaign, which Dayan called "the most ambitious mission in Operation Kadesh." The Israelis counted 864 prisoners caught as the arms of the pincer swept shut on Sharm al-Sheikh. The stubbornness of the Egyptian resistance is attested by the ratio of killed to wounded—about 100 killed and only 31 wounded by Dayan's count. Ordinarily the ratio is five, even ten wounded for each man killed.

After congratulating the troops and hearing hasty accounts of the end of the Sinai campaign, Dayan hurried back to Tel Aviv. "This new 'empire' of ours," he wrote in his diary, "raises problems that need urgent attention." The most urgent, as he saw it, was the pressure building up abroad for Israel's unconditional withdrawal from her new empire.

Two old empires, at that hour, were about to spend their vital force in a mean little victory over a country each had invaded, conquered, and exploited more than once in the past. What was to hurt Britain and France most of all was the inadmissible connection between the two-day war they were beginning and the seven-day war Israel had just ended.

Port Said's remoteness from the fighting which the invaders were supposed to be policing was part of the unrealism that plagued the whole operation and tore holes in the disguises thrown over it. The battle of Port Said was conceived in terms of public relations, for Eden had sought to make the recovery of the Canal a seemly pretext for his unseemly attempt to destroy Nasser. The battle was planned in terms of public relations, for an assault at Alexandria was strategically preferable, even if mastery of the Canal had truly been the objective, but Port Said was easier to explain to the laymen of the world. And the battle was fought in terms of public relations—by both sides. The assaulting forces went into action under extraordinary restrictions against killing the enemy for fear of outraging world opinion. Conversely, the defenders accepted battle in the city precisely in order that the assault should outrage world opinion and also to set the pattern for the guerrilla war planned afterward. Port Said, commanders on both sides told me time and time again, is militarily worse than useless.

Stockwell's two essential requirements for success were to (1) ground the Egyptian Air Force, and (2) bring the Egyptian Army to battle. He called the hinterland of Alexandria the only sensible place to bring the Egyptian Army to battle. "Port Said you couldn't get out of," he said. "A good mining of the causeway would have created another Arnheim. Militarily the Canal was irrelevant. Once you had done the two requirements you could do what you liked. And the place for that was Alexandria. On the Canal, whether we were at al-Kap, Ismailiya, or at Suez was irrelevant [to forcing battle on the Egyptians]."

The Egyptians agreed. "The British allowed their strategy to depend on a bad tactical situation," said Brigadier General Abdel Rahman Fahmy. "Their annihilating, overwhelming strategical power was absorbed in solving a tactical problem. They were using a sledgehammer to crack a peanut." With restrictions, it might be added, against hurting the peanut too much. The firepower assembled by the British and French at sea and in the air needed only a simple mathematical application to obliterate Port Said. The British used great care to avoid any such thing.

From the Egyptian military point of view, Port Said was a symbol rather than an objective. Nasser made detailed military analyses of the Sinai campaign but he discussed Port Said always in mythic terms. There was plenty of bloodshed and heroism in the city but the real battle of Port Said was fought at the UN and at the White House and in Eden's Cabinet Room. "The discus-

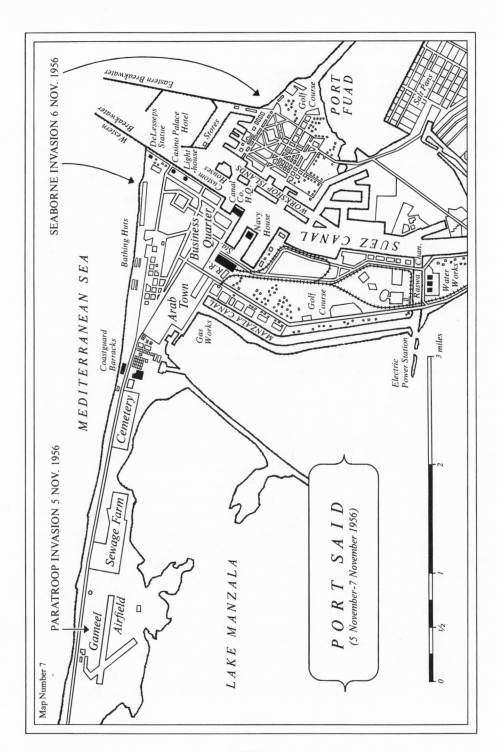

Map Number 7

PARATROOP INVASION 5 NOV. 1956

SEABORNE INVASION 6 NOV. 1956

MEDITERRANEAN SEA

Gameel
Airfield

Sewage Farm

Cemetery

Coastguard Barracks

Bathing Huts

Western Breakwater

Eastern Breakwater

DeLesseps Statue

Casino Palace Hotel

Light-house

Stores

Custom Houses

Canal Co. H.Q.

Business Quarter

Arab Town

Gas Works

Golf Course

MANZALA CANAL

LAKE MANZALA

PORT FUAD

Golf Course

WORKSHOP ISLANDS

Navy House

SUEZ CANAL

Salt Pans

Raswa Chan.

Water Works

Electric Power Station

PORT SAID
(5 November–7 November 1956)

0   ½   1   2   3 miles

597

sion cannot be of a military battle professionally," Fahmy said. The defenses were centered on the native quarter, al-Manakh, which the English called Wog Town, because it was considered more secure against spying and sabotage than the business and international residential areas, where many Britons, Frenchmen, and Jews lived. Even the people of Wog Town, or Arab Town, as it was called in politer usage, were considered relatively rootless by Egyptian standards, no family having lived there for so much as a century.

De Lesseps created Port Said by dumping earth dug out of the Canal to make an artificial island in a marshy inland sealet, Lake Manzala. It is nourished from the mainland through an artificial neck comprising a road, a railroad, and the Sweetwater and Suez canals. This neck is easily cut, particularly at the road and rail bridges over the Raswa channel, which runs between the Suez Canal and Lake Manzala south of the city. On the south bank of the Raswa channel, between the two bridges, are the waterworks that pump the fresh water of the Sweetwater Canal, which ends there, into Port Said. The vulnerability of the fresh water supply was to be a factor in the battle.

Until the first week in September, the Egyptian high command planned to evacuate Port Said rather than try to defend it against an invasion. It was never fortified and the only major weapons emplaced there, aside from anti-aircraft batteries, were some coastal guns left behind by the British. The standing garrison consisted of two battalions of infantry reservists. The Egyptian Army planned to meet the Anglo-French forces, if they landed on that side of the Delta instead of at Alexandria, as they emerged off the causeway onto the high ground west of Qantara, some twenty-five miles south of the city. There, the Egyptians reasoned, they could mass their armor effectively and hit the invaders coming off the causeway like rats coming out of a pipe.

But as Nasser and Mohyeddeen developed their guerrilla-war plan, they envisioned for an armed populace in Port Said the role of harassing the invasion supply lines. To give more bite to the guerrilla force, first one, then two companies of a regular infantry battalion, the 4th, were designated to offer initial resistance to the invaders and then to discard their uniforms and merge into the population as the nucleus of a partisan force. On the night of 31 October, when the British bombers persuaded Nasser that there would be an Anglo-French invasion after all, he decided to stiffen the organized element of military resistance in Port Said in order to put the invaders in the ugliest possible light, to gain a little more time for world opinion to act, and to set a heroic example for guerrilla war in the Delta.

Three National Guard "battalions" totaling 600 men with rifles were added to Port Said's motley fighting force. A third battalion of reservists was ordered in. On the evening of 4 November four Russian self-propelled guns arrived.

Toward dawn, shortly before the bombing preliminary to the air-borne assault, a train bringing arms for distribution to the people pulled into the station. The city was unfamiliar to most of the troops in it, including the crews of the four Russian SU-100s, which are turretless 100 mm. cannon mounted on chassis of Stalin tanks. Even the general who ended up in command of the hodge-podge Egyptian forces had seen the city only twice before.

He was Brigadier General Salaheddeen Moguy, Chief of Staff of the Eastern Command. He was in Ismailiya at 8 P.M. on the 4th, about to follow the headquarters to Zagazig, when he heard the 2nd Infantry Division commander tell Amer on the telephone that he could not spare anyone to make a tour of inspection of the Port Said defenses. Moguy volunteered to go. He drove immediately to Port Said, where he found the SU-100s near the railroad station, not knowing where to go. Command had already passed a few days earlier to Colonel Abdel Raheem Qadry of the reservist brigade from Colonel Ibrahim Anwar, who was military governor (but not administrative governor) of the city as well as commander of the coast artillery and the senior officer present on 29 October. Moguy alerted Qadry and Anwar to the presence of the SU-100s, toured the units and defenses, and finally went to bed at Anwar's headquarters. He was awakened by the report of the paratroop drops, which sealed off the city and automatically placed him in command as senior officer present.

Many of the British officers knew Port Said better than the Egyptian commander did. Stockwell had served in the Canal Zone in command of an infantry division before the evacuation agreement. The 16th Independent Parachute Brigade Group, whose 3d Battalion was the first unit of invaders to land in Egypt, had been the first unit to leave the Suez base after the evacuation agreement. The brigade, nicknamed the Red Devils, was commanded by a wiry Irish brigadier general, M. A. H. Butler, who was incongruously nicknamed Tubby. Butler and the brigade were airlifted to Cyprus in January after the Templer riots in Jordan led to savage Tory criticism of Eden. They constituted the first saber to be rattled by Sir Anthony in his own right. "The problem then was if Israel went into Jordan," Butler told me. "Our task was to assist, if necessary, King Hussein and Jordan." It was also to quiet nationalists not only in Jordan but also in England's Tory party. Now, in striking at Nasser, its task was to quiet Arab nationalism everywhere.

Keightley's original schedule called for a combined sea-borne and air-borne invasion to begin at dawn on 6 November. The invaders were to take Ismailiya by 8 November and Suez by 11 November. On the 3d he approved Beaufre's plan, Operation Telescope, to advance the air assault twenty-four hours to 5 November. Weather conditions, always uncertain at that time of year, proved excellent for the jump, clear and with almost no wind. Aerial attacks, beginning at daylight, struck at defense positions, particularly the anti-aircraft batteries. A "cab rank" of fighter planes was assigned to stand by in relays over the assault area to give close support whenever requested by the invaders on the ground.

The planes carrying the first waves of paratroops—600 British from Nicosia and 500 French from Tymbou—signaled "Good morning" as they flew in the early sunlight of 5 November over the ships from Limassol carrying Stockwell and the follow-up battalions of paratroopers. A pathfinder plane marked the drop zones with smoke grenades. The British planes swung west as they approached the barrier beach that separates the sea from Lake Manzala. Then the pilots turned into the dazzling eye of the rising sun as the sticks of paratroopers stood to and told off over the roar of the engines and the rush of air in the open hatchway. "Twenty Okay." "Nineteen Okay." "Eighteen Okay." ... The red light over the door switched to green—the order to jump—and the men shuffled rapidly forward and out into the air over Gameel Airfield.

General Keightley recorded the time of the jump as 08:20 Greenwich Mean Time, or 10:20 Port Said time, but this is one of a number of slipshod errors that appear in his much-revised and heavily edited dispatch. The errors are unfortunate because his dispatch is the basic official narrative of the Anglo-French operation. Shadows in photographs made immediately after the jump show the sun to be no more than two and a half hours above the horizon. Sunrise at Port Said that day was at 06:08. Assuming that General Keightley got the figure right and stumbled only over the time zone, the jump began at 08:20 Port Said time (06:20 GMT). It was very close to that time in any case.

Fifteen minutes later 500 men of the French 2d Colonial Parachute Regiment jumped south of the Raswa bridges. Because of the small size of their drop zone they jumped from only 450 feet. Paratrooper Pierre Leulliette gave striking vignettes of the assault in his book, *Saint Michael and the Dragon:*

> Sergeant B's body hanging by the ropes of his parachute from the top of a palm tree and slowly dripping blood into the sand. ... The moment we are in possession of the reservoirs, we cut off the water. In an hour, all the inhabitants of Port Said will be thirsty. ... One Egyptian remains alone at the entrance to the bridge and, with nothing but a rifle, furiously defends it against our whole company.

The French paratroopers had far more combat experience than the British and had developed more flexible equipment and techniques. Their Nord-Atlas transport planes had two jump ports, allowing twice the concentration of men the British were able to achieve in a given target area. The French jumped with their submachine guns or carbines ready for instant use. The British weapons were strapped in containers that took "thirty long seconds" to unpack, a harrowing delay for men landing under fire.

For whatever it was worth, the French also had an advantage in brutality, brought from the vicious antiguerrilla war they had been fighting in Algeria. Leulliette describes shooting Lake Manzala fishermen on the faint suspicion that they were partisans:

They have their hands up and are trying to convince us that they are noncombatants, which is quite likely.... But: "No useless prisoners!" ... We empty our magazines. And one after another the prisoners fall into the water. There are only two left and they jump overboard in a desperate effort to hide along the hulls. Private L... leans over the gunwale and kneels, waiting... A face emerges. Ta ta ta tatata tata... and the head disappears, mangled, blasted, at point-blank range.... A large round pink spot slowly widens on the surface.... The second head comes out of the water a little further off, with close-cropped hair like the first and the same wide open, terror-stricken eyes, and it shares the same fate.

A French captain had an Egyptian officer machine-gunned for haughtily refusing a French sentinel's order to sweep the floor. Leulliette, who watched the execution, quoted the captain as saying: "Good job. A prisoner is sacred but so's a sentinel. Get him buried in a hurry after the last bullet [the *coup de grâce*]."

Leulliette paid tribute to the reckless bravery of many Egyptian defenders while giving unsentimental accounts of how they were exterminated.

A French error, the Egyptians said, drew them out of position at Raswa. The French dropped man-size containers with machine guns, ammunition, mortars and mortar bombs, and other equipment before they dropped the *paras* themselves. With the sun behind the drop, the Egyptians mistook the containers for men and were moving to attack when the real paratroop drop caught them in the open.

Gameel Airfield was defended by a company of reservists which had been formed by merging the remnants of two companies that were decimated by strafing on 1 November as they moved up the causeway to Port Said. There was also a light battalion of National Guards. Four concrete pillboxes with machine guns on the rim of the airfield offered the main resistance at first. The Egyptians had placed oil drums filled with sand on the landing strips at Gameel to prevent enemy planes landing there. These drums served to shield individual Red Devils against Egyptian fire from the edges of the field. The sight of General Butler and the battalion commander, Lieutenant Colonel Paul Crook, walking coolly through the shooting, had an electric effect on the attackers, wrote Sandy Cavanagh, the battalion medical officer, in his *Airborne to Suez*.

So thoroughly had the Egyptian Air Force been eliminated that the senior staff officer of the French air-borne forces, Brigadier General Jean Gilles, was able to maintain an aerial observation and communications post in a Nord-Atlas that circled a thousand feet over the city. Stockwell and Beaufre, in their headquarters ships offshore, kept in close touch with the fighting units.

By 9 o'clock the British were in firm control of Gameel and the French had taken the main Raswa bridge and the vital waterworks. The Egyptians had destroyed the less important pontoon bridge at Raswa. The city was cut off from reinforcements and from water. The British pushed toward the city past its sewage farm, whose foul troughs were the scene of some particularly unpleasant skirmishes. Carrier planes demolished the Egyptian Coastguard barracks when defenders there delayed the advance.

"Egyptian resistance was very stubborn throughout the morning," Keightley wrote. "It centered mainly round the SU-100s, which were being used as mobile centers of resistance.... These guns were most skillfully handled and caused us considerable trouble. The fighting here was hard." The four SU-100s were moved about and used to such good effect that some British accounts stated that there were thirty or forty of them in the city.

In the afternoon a second battalion of French paratroopers jumped on the golf course on the southeastern outskirts of Port Fuad, the twin-city to Port Said. The Egyptians developed stubborn resistance there too, Keightley reported, but the French *paras* broke the defense so thoroughly that the sea-borne landing on the Port Fuad side of the Canal the next day was unopposed. Simultaneously with the French drop on Port Fuad, a second drop of 100 British paratroopers with heavy equipment and new supplies reinforced the battalion at Gameel.

Nine troop-carrying planes were hit by ground fire during the day but all returned safely to Cyprus, testimony not only to the virtual totality of the destruction of the Egyptian Air Force but also to the effectiveness of Anglo-French air strikes against anti-aircraft guns. "The showpiece of their performance was an anti-aircraft gun mounted on the quay just outside the Canal company's office," General Fergusson wrote. "It received a direct hit from a rocket, as neat as you could wish, and was much admired by visitors. When the salvage people took it away, Stockwell made them put it back again."

At times the Egyptian war communiqués were more blatantly erroneous than any put out by the invaders, although when it came to official lying there is no doubt that the colluders, individually as well as collectively, scored far higher totals than the Egyptians. The evidence pervades this history. But November 5th was one of the days when the optimism typical of war communiqués reached a peak of falsity on the part of the Egyptians. At 10:50 A.M. the Assiut transmitter broadcast: "Our forces are in complete control of the situation. The first paratroops who were dropped have been exterminated in the Port Said area. The entire population is taking part in the resistance." The announcer said seven enemy planes had crashed in the sea. The Egyptian radio announced the second paratroop jumps at Port Fuad and Gameel at 2:36 P.M., adding that they too were being annihilated and that fifteen planes had been shot down during the day. This brought the total of claimed kills of enemy planes to 102. Eighty-seven Israeli, British, and French planes were claimed by Cairo to have been shot down by the night of 4 November.

By mid-afternoon Port Said was suffering from thirst. Fires were raging out of control. The hospitals were running short of water. After touring the city and its defenses, Moguy told the Governor, Mohammed Riad, that the civilians were bearing the brunt of the war and that the military ought to parley with the enemy to alleviate civilian suffering and gain time for newly arrived troops to get oriented. Moguy had refused a French offer to parley about noon but shortly after 4 o'clock, at the behest of the civilian authorities, Moguy got in touch with the French at the waterworks through Colonel Hassan Rushdy, a police officer assigned to Port Said as a kind of political commissar. Rushdy was only nominally under the authority of the police chief, Major General Hassan al-Banna.

Rushdy telephoned the waterworks from Moguy's headquarters in Beit Hadeedy (the Castiron Building). Before heading for the truce rendezvous, Moguy and Rushdy tried for nearly an hour to get through by telephone to Cairo. Leaving an aide behind to complete the report to Cairo, Moguy and Rushdy departed with Police Chief al-Banna and Military Governor Anwar. The aide got through to Amer at General Headquarters a few minutes after they left. He evidently failed to get it across to Amer that the parleys were more ruse than surrender. Amer's false first impression that Moguy was too ready to yield contributed to a prejudice against Moguy that later cost him his career.

The French paratroop colonel, Pierre Chateau-Jobert, a diminutive figure with a pointed beard who fought under the *nom de guerre* "Conan," asked Butler to come to the waterworks to receive the Egyptian truce mission. The British and French forces had not yet linked up. Butler flew over in a Navy helicopter that had been shuttling casualties to the ships lying offshore. Moguy and Rushdy and the two city officials came just at dusk—sunset was at 5 P.M. —in a command car under a white flag.

The waterworks engineer was brought in by the French, who had captured him in the morning. He said he could repair the broken main if he had twenty-two men and the proper equipment. Rushdy took notes, the laborers were rounded up, and the pipe was quickly repaired. Moguy assumed a harsh, even rude demeanor to avoid seeming too much a suppliant. When a photographer entered, he said: "Get that dirty dog out of here or I'll break his neck." Moguy spoke impeccable English. With his clipped accents, trim gray mustache, and military bearing, he could have been type-cast as a peppery British general. He had, in fact, been classmate to many of the invading British officers during the total of five years he had spent on training courses in England.

Habit, struggling against circumstance, made Moguy start to introduce himself as Chief of Staff, Eastern Command, and then to hesitate over his hours-old new title. Butler came to his aid by suggesting: "Commander, Port Said?" Moguy said Yes and opened the parleys by stating firmly: "Make no mistake about it; I am here for two reasons only: One, to stop your troops from killing civilians trying to leave the city by boat across Lake Manzala and, Two, to restore the city water supply." Moguy said 600 civilians had been killed and that both that and the interruption of the water supply were violations of civilized behavior, even in war. Butler was "very much a gentleman," Moguy told me, and so was Chateau-Jobert, who evidently did not understand English. Moguy kept him abreast of the talks with asides in French.

Butler told me that Rushdy, "a very nasty chap," clearly interfered with Moguy's efforts, asking in Arabic what was being said in English and giving advice. Butler promised to investigate the reported killing of civilians. He wrote out six conditions under the heading, *Surrender Terms*, and handed it to Moguy. Moguy looked at the heading and tossed it back. Butler crossed out the heading and wrote in: *Cease-Fire Terms*. The main condition was for the Egyptian troops to march to surrender points and deposit their arms. Moguy said he could not accept the terms on his own initiative. Butler and Moguy agreed to maintain a *de facto* cease-fire as from about 5:30.

Having obtained relief for the civilian population, Moguy was now playing for time. In discussion of the time limit to be set for his answer he asked for twenty-four hours. Butler refused to allow a mere *de facto* cease-fire to run so long. It was finally agreed that Moguy must reply by 9:30 P.M. Butler urged him to persuade headquarters to accept the terms, suggesting that the Egyptians propose any amendments they saw fit. Moguy said he would relay the suggestion but that, if headquarters didn't accept, "why, we will fight again." Taking Butler and Chateau-Jobert into another room, Moguy said that if they didn't hear from him by 9:30, firing would resume. The Egyptian delegation departed as it had come. The parleys lasted some forty-five minutes with such concentration from both sides on the business at hand that no one thought to sit down, although there were chairs in the room.

Moguy went to civil defense headquarters, which had direct underwater telephone lines to Cairo and Ismailiya. The invaders failed to locate the lines in their efforts to isolate Port Said. In an account published in Cairo in September 1957 in answer to Keightley's dispatch, Moguy presented the parleys, after city water was restored, as nothing more than a ruse to gain time for guerrilla preparations and a respite for his hard-pressed troops. He said he never relayed the cease-fire terms to Cairo. Instead, he prepared for street fighting on the morrow, when the invaders would try to break into and through the city. Moguy told me that his only report was to Kamaleddeen Hussein in Ismailiya, the Liberation Army leader in the Canal Zone, at 9:15, describing the situation in Port Said. When Butler telephoned a few minutes later asking for an hour's extension of the *de facto* cease-fire, to allow helicopter evacuation of casualties, Moguy gladly granted it. Meanwhile he instructed the Information Department to prepare its loudspeaker trucks to circulate through the streets to raise the morale of the people. Moguy told me his protest over the killing of civilians was partly designed to deter the British and French from killing fighting troops after they discarded their uniforms and turned partisan.

Whatever the military effect of the cease-fire—and it was much debated both in England and Egypt—its effect on Nasser's global propaganda battle was disturbing. Nasser was angry and in no mood to make allowances for the fact that Moguy's battle was hopeless and that there were good military and humane grounds for the cease-fire. Nor did he allow for Moguy's soldierly insensitivity to propaganda values. Nasser dealt out peremptory punishment. "You know, they agreed about a cease-fire—to talk—on the 5th," Nasser told me. "I was in the Revolutionary Council and they got in touch with me. I dismissed the commander, General Moguy, and appointed another commander and ordered him to continue fighting.... Not Hassan Rushdy, Fuad Naguib, the commander of the infantry battalion there." Nasser's order does not appear to have become effective until after the end of the war and certainly not until after Moguy's capture the following morning. But in mid-January Moguy and sixteen other high-ranking officers were suddenly placed on the retired list.

Unlike Moguy, Butler used the cease-fire to report to his superiors. He talked to General Gilles, still circling overhead, on a radio relay through a Forward Air Controller. Gilles asked what the chances were of the Egyptians quitting. Butler told me he replied: "Reasonable, but I'm not too enthusiastic. I think if they were going to quit they'd have done it right away."

Butler's report of the parleys had its strongest impact in the House of

Commons, where Eden announced the cease-fire within an hour. The news had gone from Butler to Gilles to Stockwell aboard the *Tyne* to Keightley on Cyprus and from there to Whitehall and Downing Street.

Eden hurried into the House at 4:30 P.M. (6:30 Port Said time) flushed with excitement. He broke into the debate just as Gaitskell rose to speak.

I think that the House would wish to know that I have had a flash signal from the Commander-in-chief in the Eastern Mediterranean which affects even the discussion which is now taking place. That is why I intervened, as I know the right honorable Gentleman the Leader of the Opposition will understand. This is the flash signal, which is, of course, subject to confirmation:

"Governor and Military Commander, Port Said, now discussing surrender terms with Brigadier Butler. Cease-fire ordered."

Wild and noisy were the Tory benches as they erupted in celebration when Eden sat down. They cheered and waved their order papers and made gestures of derision across the well of the House. When Gaitskell rose again they yelled "Resign!" at him, as the Laborites had yelled so often at Eden. Gaitskell showed uncommon shrewdness in his reply to Eden's stunning surprise.

"If the Prime Minister's statement means that there has been a general cease-fire in Egypt and that all military operations have ceased, then, for my part, I am only too delighted," Gaitskell said. "But in that case I want to ask the Prime Minister whether, in his announcement, he meant that it was a local cease-fire or a general cease-fire... If, indeed, this cease-fire is general, will he undertake to carry out the rest of the United Nations Assembly resolution and withdraw our troops from the area?"

Eden came back with a smug slur at Gaitskell's patriotism, saying: "Quite clearly I cannot possibly know how wide or narrow is the area covered by the cease-fire; but I should have thought every one of our fellow countrymen would have been delighted it has taken place."

Within the hour, at 5:21 P.M. London time (7:21 in Egypt), Cairo Radio's transmitter at Assiut went on the air to say: "There is no truth to reports, attributed to Eden's statement in the House of Commons today, that Port Said has offered to surrender. On the contrary, the Armed Forces and the people are fighting with great determination despite the heavy air raids to which they have been subjected throughout the day."

The formal prorogation of the parliamentary session at 5 P.M. saved Eden from further questioning until the new session of Parliament convened the next day.

The Government had already had a punishing time. Before Eden's intervention Laborites produced the text of a broadcast and leaflet addressed to the Egyptian forces by the Allied Command in Cyprus the previous evening. Demanding to know whether the Government accepted responsibility for its generals' utterances, members quoted passages including the following:

We have the might and we shall use it to the limit if you do not give in.... It means that we are obliged to bomb you, wherever you are. Imagine your villages being bombed.... This will happen to you if you hide behind your women in the villages.... One thing you can do is to wear civilian clothes and go back home to see if any soldiers or tanks are concealed in your villages.... If they do not evacuate there is no doubt your villages and homes will be destroyed. You have committed a sin. You placed confidence in Abdel Nasser and believed his lies. Now you are hearing the truth.

There was laughter from the Laborite benches and cries of "Shame!" when Aneurin Bevan read the last line. He went on to say:

"This is not a military action to separate the Israel and Egyptian troops. This is a declaration of war against the Egyptian Government in the most brutal terms. It is hard to use moderate language to describe behavior of that sort. Will the Government stop lying to the House?" (Loud Opposition cheers.)

Lloyd had denied knowledge of the message but Geoffrey de Freitas brought out that *The Times* that morning reported a UN protest to the Government against the message's threat to bomb civilian areas. The controversial broadcast was part of General Fergusson's psychological warfare and propaganda campaign. The Suez chapter in his book on combined operations, *The Watery Maze*, tacitly explained his reasoning. When radio warnings of target areas made clear that the British bombers would avoid civilian targets, he wrote, "as an immediate result military vehicles at once, and naturally, mingled with civilian traffic, while tanks nudged their way cozily into villages." Except for the incitement against Nasser, Fergusson's threat seems to have been a bluff. But half the Commons was incensed that such brutish bluffing should be done, as they asserted, in their name.

Debate had opened with a statement by Lloyd on the reply sent "very early this morning" to Hammarskjold's intensive cease-fire effort based on the UN resolutions of 4 November, which reaffirmed the cease-fire demand and directed Hammarskjold to plan a UN force. The British reply was obviously a stalling device, pleading that neither Egypt nor Israel had accepted a UN force and that the UN itself had not yet established one. It was in this reply that Britain formally included the withdrawal of Israel among her objectives. Lloyd elaborated on this point:

It is the policy of Her Majesty's Government to ensure that the Israel forces withdraw from Egyptian territory. We have also told the United Nations that we believe it is necessary to secure the speedy withdrawal of Israel forces. But we cannot ensure that the Israelis withdraw from Egyptian territory until we are physically in the area to keep the peace. . . .

To such depths had honor among the colluders sunk under pressure. Even as the British message was being written, the UN passed a resolution establishing the United Nations Emergency Force. The British abstained. Lloyd explained that it was because the resolution did not guarantee that the war would stop and not resume. For that, he said, an Anglo-French armed presence in Egypt was needed. The Laborites declared their suspicion that Lloyd and Eden had deliberately delayed the reply to Hammarskjold until after the parachute landings began.

Burns replied early that day to Hammarskjold's request for an estimate of what was required for a UN force and why. Among other things, Burns recommended that UNEF should be strong enough so that it could not be treated as cavalierly as Israel treated the UN Truce Supervision Organization. He suggested that it should be a division organized as an independent fighting force, with a tank brigade and reconnaissance and fighter planes. Burns said his estimate was based on the following premises: (a) that Egypt would accept the force, (b) that sanctions would be used if needed to make Israel withdraw, (c) that Israel could be left with responsibility for the Gaza Strip and its refugees, and (d) that Sinai could be an empty buffer zone until peace. These premises were not all realized but they looked as valid as ever after the 1967 war.

Shooting resumed around Port Said at 10:30 P.M. (8:30 P.M. in London and 3:30 P.M. at UN headquarters). Neither the British nor the French forces had entered the city but patrols skirmished on the outskirts, particularly in the slum area at the west end of Arab Town. Distribution of the arms brought in by train had begun in the morning on a haphazard basis. A more systematic distribution got under way in the evening, after the parleys. The distribution was carried out entirely by Egyptians, Moguy said, and the Russian consul, Anatoly Tchikov, had absolutely nothing to do with it.

British and French officers who arrived later in Port Said and a number of journalists who spoke to them have conjured up a sinister image of Tchikov as the driving force behind the Egyptian resistance at Port Said, evidently in the belief that Egyptians never do much of anything unless led, as the phrase used to go, "by white officers." One foolish story, popular in the West, blames Tchikov for prolonging the war, saying that he telephoned Cairo and told his ambassador, Kiselev, to prevent Nasser from giving up. Another legend, accepted by more than one soldier-memoirist of Suez, is that a mysterious Russian Canal pilot known as "the Admiral" was responsible for the sinking of blockships in the Canal. Butler, who was on the spot, does not attribute any activities at all to Tchikov. None of the numerous accounts of Tchikov's alleged activities, so far as I know, emanate from anything solider than unverified statements based on hearsay and conjecture by one or two high-level allied officers. The cumulative array of these accounts, commonly plagiarized from one book to another, evidently persuades some writers that if so many people say it, it must be true, and if not, it is at least safe to use. Thus do popular fictions enter written history.

Tchikov is also falsely credited with having arranged for the loudspeaker trucks to tour the city announcing that Russian help was on the way and that Paris and London had been bombed by Russian missiles. Moguy himself ordered the loudspeaker trucks into the streets with instructions to: "Say whatever you like, but raise morale." The idea of announcing Russian aid came from the loudspeaker truck crews, he told me.

Butler's critics say the *de facto* cease-fire broke the momentum of the assault and cost the invaders precious time which they could have have used to push farther down the Canal before world pressure stopped the war the next night. "Butler made a mess of it by asking too much," Beaufre said. "He wanted a kind of parade. His demands made the Egyptian call Cairo." In the military message logs I was given access to in Cairo there were action messages to and from Moguy but I saw no record of any consultation on the cease-fire. Butler told me the cease-fire did not affect operations for two reasons: first, he could not occupy and control Port Said with 600 men, and second, even if he had entered the city he would have had to pull back for the amphibious assault in order to avoid having his men killed by the preparatory naval fire.

Dayan's acerbic comment in his diary indicated that he didn't think the separate air-borne operation had much military value at all. "After the lengthy incubation," he wrote, "two chicks finally burst through. A French paratroop battalion . . . and a British paratroop battalion . . ."

The Russian role in the Suez War, particularly on 5 November, consisted in making offstage thunder that terrified the world audience. But no lightning struck in Egypt. Quite the contrary. Khrushchev told the Egyptians that day that it was impossible to give them material help. At 16:30, an hour before the *de facto* cease-fire in Port Said went into effect, Supreme Headquarters in Cairo received from the Egyptian military attaché in Moscow the following message:

Khrushchev told the ambassador [Mohammed al-Kony] that Russia cannot offer material help because of geographical obstacles. He said [for us] to strengthen our will to resist.

The Russians were in the same difficulty in respect to Egypt as the US was in respect to Hungary. The White House knew it. Sherman Adams reported that Eisenhower and his Cabinet and military advisers were agreed that "if Russia came openly to Nasser's assistance, a war was inevitable." But Eisenhower did not rate the risk very high, according to Robert Murphy. "Look at the map," Murphy quoted the President as saying. "Geography makes effective Soviet intervention in Egypt difficult, if not impossible."

When I asked Nasser whether the Russians had offered help, he said: "President Quwwatly [of Syria] was in Moscow at that time [from 31 October to 3 November]. So the contacts were with President Quwwatly, not with Kiselev [the Russian ambassador in Cairo]. And President Quwwatly sent to me and said he had asked for a meeting with Bulganin, Khrushchev, and Zhukov. He discussed the question with them. And they said that they were ready to send us arms and technicians. [Not volunteers.] And we were not in need of arms because by that time we had 150 aeroplanes, for instance, fighters, but only forty trained pilots. And some of our pilots were in Moscow. So we were not in need of aeroplanes at all."

The Russian thunder offstage came in a series of messages from Bulganin on the night of the 5th to Eden, Mollet, and Ben-Gurion which were hastily taken by many people to be thinly veiled threats of ballistic missile attack. Hayter and the French and Israeli ambassadors were summoned from bed in the middle of the night to receive the messages, which were broadcast by Radio Moscow at 1 A.M. on the 6th (10 P.M. on the 5th, London time, and 5 P.M. in Washington). To Eden Bulganin wrote:

The Suez Canal issue was only a pretext for . . . aggressive predatory war against the Arab people, aiming at the liquidation of the national independence of these states . . . In what situation would Britain find herself if she were attacked by stronger states possessing all types of modern weapons of destruction? Indeed, such countries, instead of sending to the shores of Britain their naval or air forces, could use other means, for instance rocket equipment. If rocket weapons were used against Britain and France, you would certainly call it a barbaric action. Yet, what is the diference . . .

To Mollet he included a demand to explain how the ideas of socialism could be reconciled with "open colonial war." He told Mollet, as he had told Eden, that Suez could expand into a third world war and that "the Soviet

Government has already addressed to the United Nations and to the President of the United States of America a proposal to use, jointly with other members of the United Nations, naval and air forces to end the war in Egypt and to curb aggression. The Soviet Government is fully determined to use force in order to smash the aggressors and restore peace in the East."

To Ben-Gurion Bulganin accused Israel of "acting as an instrument of outside imperialist forces." He said:

Such actions by the Government of Israel graphically show the worth of all the false assurances about Israel's love for peace and her desire for peaceful coexistence with the neighboring Arab states. With these assurances the Israeli Government has in fact only tried to blunt the vigilance of the other peoples while preparing a traitorous attack against her neighbors. Fulfilling the will of others, acting on instructions from abroad, the Israeli Government is criminally and irresponsibly playing with the fate of peace, with the fate of its own people. It is sowing a hatred for the State of Israel among the peoples of the East such as cannot but make itself felt with regard to the future of Israel and which puts in jeopardy the very existence to Israel as a state.

Bulganin informed Ben-Gurion that he was immediately recalling the Russian ambassador from Tel Aviv and said he hoped Israel would "properly understand and assess this warning of ours." It was unquestionably the most menacing of the three messages.

The messages were the basis for Russia's claim to credit for stopping the war and saving Egypt. Many Arabs accept the claim, the more readily in periods of bitterness against American bias towards Israel. Nasser made his most vehement denial of the Russian claim in a speech in Damascus on 22 March 1959 in a period of angry Egyptian protest against Russian subversion in Arab countries, especially Iraq. Khrushchev had chided Nasser from Moscow a few days before for youthful passion and hot-headedness. Radio Moscow commentators were telling Egypt that the triple aggression had failed in 1956 because of Russian action, while in 1882, without Russian intervention, Britain alone was able to beat Egypt.

"We fought Israel, Britain, and France, the three aggressors, singlehanded, relying on nobody but God and ourselves," Nasser retorted. "No country stood by us and we had no agreement with the Soviet Union. . . . We fought the battle singlehanded with passion and hot-headedness. Had it not been for this passion and hot-headedness, our country would have been turned into rocket bases against the Soviet Union. . . ." In addition to claiming that the debt of gratitude should be acknowledged from Russia to Egypt rather than vice versa, Nasser insisted that the Russian warning messages came after other factors had already ensured a cease-fire. His statement to me that Eisenhower deserves full credit for stopping the war and his disclosure of his appeal to Eisenhower for help appear to be his first such acknowledgement of the American role.

The Egyptians did not think much of the Russian messages, even at first sight. Amer telephoned Moguy at 2 A.M. on 6 November. As Moguy recalled the conversation, it went as follows:

Amer: "What did you do, Moguy, about the talks [with Butler]?"

Moguy: "I did what was right!"

Amer: "Okay, okay. Have you heard about the Bulganin ultimatums?"

Moguy: "No."

Amer: "Don't you listen to the radio?"

Moguy: "I have no wireless."

Amer then read news dispatches reporting Bulganin's messages and said: "Even this ultimatum does not please us and we have asked them to issue a severer one."

Moguy: "M-m-m."

Amer: "We want you to hold on another twenty-four hours. Two thousand National Guards are on their way via [the barrier beach track and bridge that passes] Gameel. They should arrive in a half hour."

Moguy said the National Guards never appeared. Butler said no Egyptians even tried to come by way of Gameel.

Eden is not known to have been rattled by Bulganin's rough message. He wrote in his memoirs that he did not think it needed to be taken literally. "Only some days after it became clear that the United States was in the lead against us at the United Nations," he wrote, "... the Russians felt they could snarl with the pack." Hayter's informed suspicion afterward was that the Russians knew the invasion of Egypt was about to collapse and they hoped to cash in on the Anglo-French failure by posing as saviors of the Arabs without risk to themselves. But at the time, he wrote, he thought the Russians might take "some violent action ... against our sea communication in the Mediterranean by submarines or aircraft which might well be unidentifiable." He therefore cabled Whitehall his belief that only an immediate realignment with the US would forestall the Russian threat.

Bulganin's impact on Mollet was stronger. Mollet woke Dillon about 1:30 A.M. on the 6th, some two and a half hours after news of the Bulganin messages had flashed round the world. Dillon reached the Matignon, the French Premier's official residence, at 2 o'clock and found most of the Cabinet there. Dillon told me that Mollet took him into his first floor office and showed him news ticker dispatches containing the text of the message. Dillon assured

Mollet that the US would respond with full vigor to a Russian missile attack on Britain or France. But Mollet wanted an assurance about what the US would do if Russia attacked British and French forces in the Middle East, which was outside the area covered by the NATO treaty. Mollet said he needed the assurance right away from the highest possible level as an argument against Eden's growing desire to cease fire. Eden had already telephoned Mollet about Bulganin's message.

Dillon told me that Eden telephoned Mollet again while he was still in the room. After talking with Eden, Mollet hung up the receiver and told Dillon the British were definitely going to stop and he, Mollet, felt the French had to stop too, although he disliked it. Mollet pointed to a map and told Dillon that the advance troops were already in Ismailiya and might reach Suez within twelve hours. In fact, the French paratroopers at that hour were still squatting astride the Raswa channel and no advance south of Port Said developed until the following evening.

Jacques Chaban-Delmas, Mollet's Minister of State, told me that Mollet spoke more boldly to his Cabinet members at that post-midnight gathering than he did to Dillon, telling them that Eden and he were both uninfluenced by the threat but that he, Mollet, was less ready to dismiss it than Eden. He wanted Cabinet support for his decision to act without regard to the threat. Both Eden and Mollet, in their replies to Bulganin, threw the Hungarian bloodshed in his teeth.

Ben-Gurion was infuriated by the difference between Bulganin's letters to Eden and Mollet and the message to himself, Dayan wrote. The letter to Ben-Gurion not only questioned the future of Israel as a state, Dayan said, but contained "terms of contempt and scorn" and "coarse mockery" that did not appear in the other two letters. Ben-Gurion too refused to be influenced by the letter, but Dayan said it was a good thing that it was not sent until twelve hours after the last Israeli shots of the war. "Who knows whether this Sinai Campaign would have been launched," Dayan wondered, "if the Russian messages had been sent to Britain, France, and Israel before the 29th of October?"

Ben-Gurion, in his reply to Bulganin on 8 November, quoted the prize paragraph from the interesting document alleged to be the Egyptian 3d Infantry Division commander's directive to the troops to prepare to destroy Israel "in the most brutal and cruel battles." As mentioned previously, this is the document which Meinertzhagen said he saw in London on 4 October and which Dayan said he was shown immediately after the capture of the 3d Infantry Division headquarters at al-Arish on 2 November. Ben-Gurion sent Bulganin a photocopy of the whole document, which fills two foolscap pages.

At least five hours before Bulganin issued his rocket-rattling messages to the three colluders he proposed to Eisenhower a cooperative effort to stop the Suez War by the "joint and immediate use" of their naval and air forces under a United Nations directive. At the same time, Shepilov cabled the Security Council president a draft resolution giving Britain, France, and Israel twelve hours to cease fire and three days to withdraw from Egypt, failing which the Council would find it "necessary that all the United Nations member states, and primarily the United States and the USSR, as permanent members of the Security Council which have powerful air and naval forces, render armed and other assistance to the victim of aggression, the Egyptian Republic, by dispatching naval and air forces, military units, volunteers, instructors, materiel, and other aid ..."

Shepilov summoned Ambassador Bohlen to receive the message to Eisenhower. "I couldn't believe my eyes," Bohlen told me. "I looked at Shepilov and said: 'Are you kidding?' He said: 'No. This is a serious proposal.' I said I'd send it but that the answer would surely be No."

Moscow broadcast the message to Eisenhower at noon, Washington time. Bohlen's cable containing the message arrived about 5 P.M. Within twenty minutes Eisenhower, Hoover, Phleger, Sherman Adams and other aides had drafted a warning that any Russian military intervention in the Middle East would bring the US in immediately against it. The White House statement called the Bulganin letter "an obvious attempt to divert world opinion from the Hungarian tragedy." It described his invitation for military cooperation to stop the Suez War as an "unthinkable suggestion." Pointing out that UN resolutions opposed the movement of outside military forces to the Middle East and that Russia herself had failed to vote for the UN Emergency Force, the White House said any introduction of new forces would violate the UN Charter and that "it would be the duty of all United Nations members, including the United States, to oppose any such effort." Eisenhower replied formally to Bulganin along those same lines, but not until 11 November.

Eisenhower's personal reaction to the rocket-rattling messages, he told me some years later, was that:

As usual, the Russian, when he threatens, he is trying to bulldoze you a little bit. And we would not let our friends or the Free World believe two weeks too late that the Russian could expect us to be on his neck because we knew, or we felt certain, that just a complete defiance of this threat would stop him, and it did.... Because long ago Foster and I had come to the conviction that the last thing that the Russians wanted was a war, a global war. They'd shown this way back in '47 when they occupied that province in Iran, Azerbaijan.... Now when they went into Korea—

it was always through some other troops, satellites. Every place they were threatening and the Communists were making noises, the Russians were always very careful not to use their own troops. So we were just perfectly certain that they didn't want to go to war. Of course, neither did we. But we were not the ones making threats around the world and so we just told them that this would be, well, we just told them, really, it would be global war if they started it, that's all. . . . We didn't even, as I remember it, consult with Defense or anything else.

Eisenhower evidently was not averse, however, to letting the Russian threat add to the pressures pushing Eden and Mollet toward a cease-fire. Mollet's urgent inquiry through Dillon for a top-level assurance covering the Middle East as well as NATO territory seems to have been neglected in Washington. On the morning of 6 November Eisenhower ordered high-altitude reconnaissance flights over Syria by the newly operational U-2s to keep surveillance over any movement of Russian planes toward Egypt. Eisenhower received "intelligence reports" later in the day of unidentified jet aircraft overflying Turkey, which he said were not confirmed. But they were flashed throughout the NATO command by the US. Other frightening flashes were listed by Jean-Raymond Tournoux in his *Secrets d'Etat*. Tournoux's military and political sources are acknowledged to be excellent. There were flashes of a Russian request to send five warships through the Turkish straits, of an Anglo-French air alert against Russian planes and submarines, of a report of Russian frogmen at Alexandria. Tournoux, reflecting official French suspicions, said these reports seemed to be part of a campaign of systematic intoxication designed to frighten the British and French into a cease-fire.

One report imparted a flavor of truth to the mixture. A Canberra was truly shot down by Syrian jets on the afternoon of 6 November. But the Syrian jets were old Meteors, not Migs, as reported, and they attacked the Canberra, not at 45,000 feet, but beneath a 5,000-foot cloud layer. The Canberra crashed in Lebanon and its crew of two parachuted into Lebanon too. It was one of a relay of Canberras that had been keeping Syria under surveillance since before the Israeli attack. The report that Migs had downed the Canberra from high altitude was later attributed, rightly or wrongly, to what was called a CIA "rumor-factory" in Turkey. The rumors, contrary to popular history, had no influence on the British cease-fire decision because they came after it.

Eisenhower saved his strongest reply to Bulganin until after the war, when Russia was talking of sending volunteers to the Middle East. It was delivered in a speech by General Alfred M. Gruenther, the Supreme Allied Commander in Europe, on 13 November. "Whether or not such [Russian] rockets exist, they will not destroy the capacity of NATO to retaliate," he said. "No nation is going to push that button if it means national suicide. That is just what it would mean." If Russia attacked the West with missiles, he said, the Soviet Union and the Soviet Bloc would be "destroyed . . . as sure as day follows night."

The extraordinary ambivalence of Eden's policies pursued the Suez adventure to the bitter end. As Dillon disclosed, he told Mollet between midnight and dawn on 6 November that he intended to quit, but he allowed the seaborne assault to go ahead that morning, still with its curious limitations on hurting the enemy. It was of a piece with Eden's other strange contradictions —his hope to fight the hero of the Arab world without antagonizing the Arabs, his charade of negotiating publicly for a Canal agreement while secretly thwarting it, his collusion device of contriving a war in order to rush in as a policeman to club the victim, his blocking the Canal in the name of saving it, his mortal injury to what was left of the British Empire by a blow aimed at its enemy. It was the kind of conduct that Gaitskell had characterized in March as being, at one and the same time, both provocative and weak.

One anxiety departed as the 270 French and British ships from the Western Mediterranean closed in on Port Said; it was the US Sixth Fleet. "Anxiety was caused by the activities of the US Sixth Fleet which, since 31st October, had been moved to and stationed in the same operating areas as our own carriers, in order to provide protection for the evacuation of US nationals from Alexandria and the Levant," Keightley wrote. "Despite the very real difficulties created by this situation and the great inconvenience experienced by our forces, thanks to the good sense of the two naval commanders both were able to carry out their functions efficiently and without incident. The US fleet withdrew from the area during the night 4/5 November."

Stories of deliberate Sixth Fleet interference with the Anglo-French invasion fleets are as many and as varied as the stories of Russian Consul Tchikov's activities in Port Said. A month after the war, the Sixth Fleet Commander, Vice-Admiral Charles R. Brown, categorically denied that any of his fifty ships were "deliberately maneuvered in any fashion to embarrass those British and French units." He specifically denied reports that US submarines maneuvered under the Anglo-French ships, stating that Sixth Fleet submarines were under orders throughout to remain on the surface, to be lit up at night, and to display under floodlights the largest US flag available. "I've never seen a shred of evidence that the Sixth Fleet interfered," Eden told me. "I've heard it said," he added, "but I know of no evidence."

All of the American evacuees from Egypt were taken by sea from Alexandria because the Egyptian airports were closed when Israel attacked. They sailed at sunset on 3 November. The Sixth Fleet also evacuated UN personnel and dependents from the Gaza Strip as well as Americans and UN people in Israel and Jordan. The UN evacuations followed plans first worked out during the December 1955 Templer riots in Jordan. Some 1300 people were evacuated from Egypt and nearly 900 from the Levant. Most of the Americans who lived in the Middle East or were members of families assigned there spent two or three months in Rome before returning.

Egypt's main naval effort of the war began the night the Sixth Fleet withdrew with the evacuees from Alexandria. Admiral Mahmoud Nasheet, before dawn on 4 November, ordered a good part of Egypt's new Russian war craft to run along the coast from Alexandria to Port Said to reconnoiter enemy fleet movements and then return between midnight and dawn on 5 November. Egypt was no longer capable of aerial reconnaissance. The flotilla included the two five-year-old Skory-class destroyers delivered at Alexandria in June and renamed the *Zafir* and the *Nasir*, and three of the twelve motor-torpedo boats Russia had delivered in April. Part of the mission of the torpedo boats was to attempt to sink enemy aircraft carriers whose location was roughly estimated by calculating the convergence of the flight tracks of carrier-based enemy planes.

The Egyptian radio transmitter at Minya reported on the night of the 4th that Egyptian naval units had sunk a French cruiser at 10 A.M., claiming that this brought the bag of enemy ships to one cruiser, two destroyers sunk and three destroyers badly damaged. Allied records show no ship losses. But both sides agree that two Egyptian motor torpedo boats were sunk off Burullus, the northernmost point of the Delta, during an attack by allied carrier planes, with a third escaping into Lake Burullus.

Within a few days the Arab world was mourning as heroes the young captains of the lost torpedo boats, Ibrahim Dessouqi of Egypt and Jules Jamal, a Christian from Latakia in Syria, and crediting them with having sunk the French battleship *Jean Bart*. I was in Latakia later in November on a day when the whole town had turned out for a holiday parade and ceremony at which the school was renamed for Jules Jamal. A street in Damascus was also renamed for him. About sixty Egyptian officers were flown from the Israeli prisoner-of-war camp to visit aboard the *Jean Bart* in Toulon, so anxious were the French to quash the legend. But the Arab leaders, although they know the story is unfounded, have allowed it to flourish as part of the folklore of Suez. When I asked President Quwwatly about it he loyally refused to concede the error of the new legend but he was equally careful to avoid adding credence to it.

The *Zafir* and *Nasir* were more fortunate, although they had to play a grim game of tag with allied war planes for six hours on 5 November when they were caught in the open off Alexandria. The two destroyers zig-zagged between five and ten miles offshore from mid-morning to mid-afternoon, dodging rockets and bombs, with never enough respite between attacks to risk entering the narrow pass into the harbor, where there was no room to dodge. General Badry, who watched the whole engagement, said large crowds of spectators assembled in the sunshine on the Corniche as if it were a sporting event out there on the sparkling blue sea.

Eden's dithering about the preparatory naval bombardment plagued the gunners aboard the invasion ships until just before the assault. They prepared their bombardment task-tables on the basis of aerial reconnaissance photos of Port Said, which were flown daily to the approaching invasion fleet. Douglas Clark, a gunnery officer attached to the commando brigade, wrote that on Monday night, as they waited to make the final changes in the morrow's bombardment plan, Whitehall radioed the order: "No gun of a greater caliber than 4.5 inches will be fired."

This order prohibited the participation of the main guns of the cruisers in the fleet and of the French battleship, *Jean Bart*. The *Jean Bart* was doubling as a transport and carrying the bulk of the two French divisions, the 10th Air-borne and 7th Mechanized, from the Algerian to the Egyptian front. Then a revised target list came, shortly followed by an order to cancel the bombardment entirely. The order plunged the assault commanders into consternation. Clark quoted a commando colonel as exclaiming: "I can't allow my men to move against a defended beach without support." The paratroopers already in Port Said had informed the fleet that it would meet Egyptian resistance in Port Said.

The fleet requested an explanation from Whitehall, Clark wrote, but none came. He and the commando colonel decided to evade the prohibition from London by agreeing that "in our trade we differentiate between Naval Bombardment and Naval Gunfire Support . . . a nice distinction, but it's valid. . . . The pre–H-hour bombardment may be canceled, but the gunfire support goes on, unaffected by the order from London."

Eden and Head, perhaps making the same nice distinction, both told the Commons the next day that the assault had taken place with "no preliminary bombardment of any kind." Clark, who heard this news on the radio, called it a half-truth from which most people would gather that no guns had been fired. Keightley, in his dispatch published ten months later, said he had ordered that "supporting fire was to be confined strictly to known enemy defenses and to those which engaged our assault." He added that "air bombing was prohibited and heavy naval guns were banned." Keightley said destroyers laid down "extremely accurate" and "comparatively light" covering fire against known enemy positions among the bathing huts on some two miles of beachfront for forty-five minutes before the troops landed. A ten-minute air strike preceded the shelling, he wrote, and planes raked the beaches with low-level attacks just before the troops reached the shore. A lone Egyptian Mig strafed the British at Gameel just before the ten-minute air strike and once again later in the morning. Keightley said that reports of heavier gunnery and aerial support than he described were "distorted and exaggerated."

Stockwell, however, who was on the scene, said the destroyers put down "saturation fire on the beaches to soften up any defenses that might hinder" the landing. Clark, who watched the gunfire and aerial attacks from the open bow doors of a landing ship half a mile offshore—"far too close for an invading convoy"—called the scene an "inferno." The beach was obscured by billowing smoke, he wrote. "As the shells landed, the smoke was pin-pricked with flashes, while here and there, fierce red flames showed where the lines of wooden beach huts were on fire. The thud of guns added to the confusion, and screaming aircraft plummeted earthward, their guns and rockets blasting." The Egyptians said napalm was used against them.

The leading waves of the 3d Royal Marine Commando Brigade hit the beaches in tracked and armor-plated amphibious "Buffaloes" at 6:50 A.M. The Egyptians in weapons pits under the beach huts had been killed or forced out of them by their own ammunition exploding in the flames as much as by enemy fire. The teeming slums on the west end of Wog Town were set ablaze during a gun duel between a British destroyer and an Egyptian gunner in a self-propelled SU-100. "Fanned by a stiff breeze," Keightley reported, "a large area of this collection of shacks was burnt out."

Air strikes were called down in the morning on the Governorate in the center of the city and on the prison near Wog Town in order to break Egyptian resistance at these strongpoints. A final air strike was called down at dusk on Navy House, which had to be demolished to subdue the Egyptian cadets there. Organized resistance ended with the fall of Navy House but street fighting and sniping continued.

Moguy told me he was captured in the lighthouse at 10 A.M. By that time fighting was raging throughout the city and Egyptian regular troops had begun discarding their uniforms and merging into the population, which was itself armed to the teeth. Every Egyptian mortar and bazooka, not to speak of the self-propelled guns, formed a nucleus of resistance. Little boys hurled grenades from upper windows at British troops. Any civilian was as likely as not to whip a gun out from under his *gallabiya* and open fire. "Streets had to be cleared house by house and sometimes room by room," Keightley wrote. British troops incurred avoidable casualties in their haste to get through the city, he said, and added: "It is a tribute to their patience and forbearance that so little damage was done to Port Said."

Clark was outraged at the fighting style of the armed rabble. He was angrier still at any acceptance of reports of British brutality. "The Egyptians knew no code of war," he wrote. "It was immaterial to them whether a commando was helping one of their own people or not. Just as long as he wore a green beret, he was fair game." Clark described "the downright decency of men who, while being shot at, walked from cover to help old women to safety, to carry babies out of harm's way, to quieten hysterical women and to help wounded enemies who, a moment before, had been yelling and firing with all the abandon of drunks at a shooting gallery."

Young Dr. Cavanagh too gave evidence of British decency but he filled in the shadows of the picture as seen by himself and his fellow paratroopers after the final cease-fire. "However much damage the 'children's war' and the callous, cynical distribution of Russian arms had caused, there was no doubt [among the paratroopers] that much of what had occurred in their own area was their own doing," Cavanagh wrote. "The number of dead appalled them. ... They arrived in trucks, hearses, ambulances and even a Coca-Cola lorry. Loads and loads of bodies, of all ages, and both sexes. They were buried in roughly bulldozed mass graves. The actual number of corpses created a great argument in Parliament, with the result that a Commission of Inquiry was sent out to verify the facts. ... The soldiers on the spot were in no doubt that a larger number of Egyptians had been killed than was estimated in the Report."

Leulliette reported no acts of decency by the French, unless one counts the contemptuous sparing of Egyptian partisans captured after the fighting, in order to make servants of them instead of shooting them "for sport." Leulliette made clear why there was no resistance left in Port Fuad when the French seaborne force landed there on 6 November. Leulliette and his fellow *paras* had so thoroughly savaged the resistance on the 5th that the only fighting left on the 6th was in Port Said, the British invasion allotment. "Port Fuad is a pretty town, mostly European," Leulliette wrote. "But the destruction is so complete that everything has taken on a tragic mask. ... Palm trees are blazing like torches. The whole city reeks of fire, grease, metal, gasoline, powder, and carrion. ... The huge American warehouses along the wharf had been broken into, first by the Egyptians, and then by us. ... For several weeks, whisky and turkey are the staples of our diet. ... The looting of the warehouses goes on for days, despite the sentinels. We find all sorts of strange objects, from Swiss cuckoo clocks to American ashtrays. ... Tremendous all-day drinking parties. ... There is talk that a few Egyptian soldiers who didn't have time to get away may still be hiding in [the Suez Canal Company villas]. Any private investigating is about to be forbidden, because there were quite a few women raped in the city, and even some very young girls, also a number of shops were looted and some European apartments wrecked."

The only event of military significance in the battle of Port Said began an hour after the first commandos went ashore. It was the use of helicopters to transport troops into battle. The helicopter pilot carrying the colonel of the follow-up commando unit lost his bearings in the smoke of battle while reconnoitering the landing zone for the unit. He put down in a sports stadium. As the commando, Lieutenant Colonel N. H. Tailyour, got out to look around, a hail of Egyptian small-arms fire poured down from the stands. The helicopter lofted without the colonel, dropped down again to take him aboard, and flew away with twenty-two holes in the fuselage and one in each rotor. Within the next hour and a half twenty-two helicopters from the aircraft carriers *Ocean* and *Theseus* shuttled 400 fighting men and twenty-three tons of supplies to the Casino Pier. A new war technique was born. It was to be developed into a full fighting arm by the US in Vietnam, where helicopters were used not only to carry troops and supplies into battle and casualties out but also as offensive hovering gun platforms. The twenty-two holes in Colonel Tailyour's craft showed it could take more shooting up than military men had thought.

At 11 A.M., an hour after Moguy was captured, Stockwell and Beaufre went ashore to try to negotiate the unconditional surrender of the city, where, Keightley said, "a tough battle was taking place." As the launch carrying his truce party of invasion task force commanders approached dockside, Stockwell recalled, "we were smartened up by an Egyptian light machine gun, which put a series of bursts round us, one hitting the wooden bridge where we were standing."

The Italian Consul, Count Vicente Mareri, seeking on his own initiative to bring the fighting to a stop, had invited negotiations at his consulate. Mareri entered into popular history in the first hasty books about Suez as the good angel of Port Said in melodramatic opposition to bad angel Tchikov. There is authentic evidence of Mareri's beneficent errands but dubious hearsay constitutes all the knowledge there is about Tchikov's malefic enterprises. Mareri's cease-fire initiatives came to naught because Moguy, although already a British prisoner, had no intention of surrendering the city. As Keightley vaguely put it, he "failed to come to the rendezvous and as a result fighting continued throughout the day." British courtesy did not flag. Brigadier General R. W. Madoc, commanding officer of the commando brigade, assigned to Moguy as his escort Major David Graham, a gunnery officer who had been a classmate of Moguy's ten years earlier at a long gunnery staff course

621

at the Royal Citadel, Plymouth. The British did not make Moguy come to the rendezvous.

Stockwell had to get on with the war. He was unaware that Eden, having already decided to stop, was merely awaiting the formality of agreement by the French Cabinet before issuing the order. At 4 P.M. Stockwell called a conference of commanders and issued his orders for the next day's fighting: Butler was to break out south from the causeway with his paratroopers and seize Abu Suwweir airfield, the French paratroopers under General Massu were to capture Ismailiya, and Madoc's commando brigade was to mop up guerrilla resistance in Port Said.

It was time for Stockwell to get back to his headquarters ship, the *Tyne*. The helicopters had all returned to their carriers and dusk was falling. Stockwell and a party of aides went down to the jetty and found a landing craft with an amiable Marine coxwain who said he could find the *Tyne* for them in the gathering darkness. Outside the breakwater they ran into howling wind, rain, and big waves. The craft's pump quit. Then the steering gear broke. It was after 7:30 P.M. and pitch dark when the assault boat, steering by its twin propellers, wallowed into the lee of a ship which turned out to be the *Tyne*.

"I thought this was the end of an exhausting day of adventure and drama," Stockwell wrote. "But the real shock was now to come. All I wanted at that moment was a whisky and soda. But my chief of staff ... appeared holding an urgent signal. ... It read: 'Cease-fire at midnight.' It was difficult at that moment for me to take in the words, let alone grasp the full impact of that brief signal." Stockwell believed that Ismailiya would have fallen the next day and Suez the day after. Now he was thwarted in the midst of success. "So we made the best of it," he wrote, "by urging Brigadier Butler to get as far down the Canal as he could by midnight. He didn't need much urging ... " The midnight they spoke of was London time, to which their watches were set. That was 2 A.M. in Port Said.

It was not in Mareri's hospitable consulate but in dialogues across the Atlantic and the English Channel that the cease-fire was decided. There were many pressures upon Eden to stop the war. His own conduct and his own words following the dismissal of Glubb bear convincing evidence that he would have braved them all if there had been a fighting chance that continuing the war would destroy Nasser. That was the objective that had made him seize upon the Suez Canal dispute as a pretext for war. When that objective faded, the ordeals brought on by the war were no longer worthwhile bearing. So Eden allowed his Cabinet to press upon him the handiest pretext available to stop the war, regardless of its transparency.

Eisenhower was fully aware of Eden's real objective, that it was not the

Canal so much as Nasser. He told me a few years afterward: "Now there never was any intimation given to me that they had [merely] the intention of going on down the Canal. Not at all. What they were doing, as we understood it at least, as I understood it at that moment, was to get control of northern Egypt, including the Government, and really compel them to do something."

Eisenhower said US pressure for a cease-fire "was completely consistent with what we'd been doing up till this moment, that is: Stop it! We said: You made a mistake and don't make it worse. . . . And then . . . we objected to the actual movement and said we would just be against them in the United Nations and that sort of thing . . . " [As he had promised Nasser]. In addition to making it clear that the US had no intention of using force to stop its allies, Eisenhower said, he warned the Russians to keep their military power out too in retorting to Bulganin's messages. "So to that extent we did show that with somebody else getting into it, why, we would still stand with our friends."

American pressure for a cease-fire emanated directly from Eisenhower, who was more directly in command of foreign policy during Dulles's operation and convalescence than at any other time. Instead of confining himself to diplomatic channels, Eisenhower exerted his pressure in ways that would press the hardest, for example, through the Secretary of the Treasury. Murphy, who was working day and night on the Suez and Hungarian crises, evidently was by-passed for he wrote that he was amazed when Eden quit short of his objective.

Although Eden had already telephoned Mollet that he intended to stop, he might not have given up if he had felt he could carry the Cabinet with him. Until then, one leading member of the Cabinet told me, "Eden's ministry was a dictatorship; nothing Churchill did in five years of war was as dictatorial as Eden's conduct of Suez." The minister continued: "Eden was dead set on war from the beginning. He used to see Keightley without even telling us. He was determined to fight the dictator, Nasser, before nationalization. Glubb was an important factor. You must realize in writing about Suez that Eden was reliving 1938; he saw England as being slack in the face of a dictator. And he was sick. Remember that."

Not even Bulganin's letter nor the "more formidable threat" to the British pound nor the dissidence in the Tory party, Eden wrote, determined the decision of his Cabinet colleagues when they met at 9:45 A.M. on Tuesday, 6 November, to consider ceasing fire. These factors were in their minds, Eden wrote, but what "weighed even more" in their minds was that Egypt and Israel had stopped fighting. "We had intervened to divide and, above all, to contain the conflict," he continued. "The occasion for our intervention was over, the fire was out. Once the fighting had ceased, justification for further intervention ceased with it."

The patent transparency of this face-saving pretext is evident in the fact that Israeli-Egyptian fighting had ended more than twenty-four hours before that Cabinet meeting. It ended with the surrender of the Egyptian garrison at Sharm al-Sheikh in the same hour that the speeded-up air-borne assault on Port Said began. Dayan illuminates the transparency by his disclosure that Britain used extreme pressure to annul Israel's agreement to cease fire on 3 November, when Eden still wanted a pretext to continue the war rather than a pretext to stop it.

In contradiction to the overwhelming consensus of the most competent political observers on the spot, including Britain's diplomats, Eden insisted in his memoirs four years after Suez that Nasser's position was "badly shaken." Clinging to this thesis, he tacitly admitted his prime objective. "Nasser's position in Egypt was by this time threatened," he wrote. "Our patrols reported growing panic on the roads back from the Sinai peninsula to Cairo, but the fighting had stopped and we had no justification for going on." Still dreaming his dreams, he went on to say:

> The factor which must now always remain unknown is the effect of a rapid advance down the Canal, and its clearance, upon Nasser's position in Cairo. Militant dictators have more enemies at home than the foreigner ever dreams. It may be that even the Soviet entry into the lists would not have sufficed to save the regime in Cairo, humiliated by defeat and lacking the Voice of Egypt [sic] to call disaster victory.

The Cabinet insisted to an amenable Eden that, to quote one member, "the Government had to abide by the ultimatum—to accept the limitations of its own statement." Another minister put it to me this way: "To go on would have made it look as if the—what you call the—ostensible reason wasn't the real reason. We felt we had set out objectives in the ultimatum and had to abide by their limitations."

Several members, however, were chiefly influenced by the plight of the pound. Eden conceded in his memoirs that the run on the pound early in November developed "a speed which threatened disaster to our whole economic position." Allowance had been made for seasonal pressure against sterling in the fall. Britain's dollar reserves fell by $57 million in September and $84 million in October. The rush in November drained off $279 million, 15 per cent of Britain's total dollar reserves, as the Bank of England bought sterling offered on the world market in order to hold up its price in relation to the dollar.

Although Chinese and Indian sterling balances were offered on the currency exchanges, Eden blames speculation against sterling "in the American market on American account" for a weakening of the pound which "could have been decisive within the next few days."

It was decisive in turning Harold Macmillan, Chancellor of the Exchequer and strong man of the Eden cabinet, against the Suez War. Just before the decisive Cabinet meeting, Macmillan lobbied against the war with Lloyd, telling him Britain's financial predicament was grim. One minister later told the historian Hugh Thomas that Macmillan announced to the Cabinet that he could "not any more be responsible for Her Majesty's Exchequer" unless there was a cease-fire. It was this turnabout that led Harold Wilson to mock Macmillan as "first in, first out at Suez." The belief endured for years in England that the US Federal Reserve Bank increased pressures on Britain by dumping large holdings of sterling. In fact, neither the Federal Reserve Bank nor the US Treasury had held foreign currencies since they sold the last of their pesetas in the 1930s. The US did not begin operating in foreign exchange markets again until 1961, when Douglas Dillon, by then Secretary of the Treasury, resumed the practice to dampen fluctuations in the price of the dollar.

US fiscal pressure for a cease-fire was exerted on that desperate 6th of November when Britain begged for US approval to withdraw a vast sum of dollars from the International Monetary Fund in order to continue buying sterling to hold it above the official minimum level of $2.78 per pound. R. A. Butler, Leader of the House of Commons, addressed Britain's plea by transatlantic telephone directly to US Treasury Secretary George Humphrey, with whom he had developed a close friendship when he had been Chancellor of the Exchequer from 1951 to 1955. US approval was necessary for Britain to withdraw capital from the IMF because the US stake in the fund gave it the most heavily weighted directorial vote. Humphrey said on the telephone, in effect: We'll give you all the financial help you need provided you guarantee to comply with the UN cease-fire resolution right away, say by midnight tonight.

Upon getting Britain's promise to accept the cease-fire, Humphrey agreed to endorse dollar credits of about $1.5 billion, comprising over $500 million from the IMF, a billion-dollar loan against Britain's dollar securities, and deferment of interest payments. The pound was saved, for a decade, partly by the mere news of the credit. "It was not exactly blackmail," one of Eden's ministers told me elegantly, "but compliance with the UN was a postulate of American help."

Eden said he was uninfluenced by Tory opponents of his policies, dismissing them as a minority of "weak sisters." Among the many important omissions from his memoirs, however, are any references to three damaging resignations

625

from his official circle: Anthony Nutting's from the Number Two post at the Foreign Office, Sir Edward Boyle's from the Treasury, and William Clark's from the prestigious press secretaryship at Number 10 Downing Street. Nutting's resignation nearly touched off a much larger exodus from the Foreign Office, which Nutting dissuaded by saying that it might irreparably damage the Government at a time of national crisis. Nutting said that Macmillan, when he took over the premiership, "churlishly rewarded" the loyalty of three foreign office men who agreed not to resign, dismissing two and demoting the third.

After his Cabinet had decided in favor of halting the war—unanimously, according to all five of the ministers with whom I have discussed it—there remained the problem of coordinating with the French. Eden telephoned Mollet of his Cabinet's decision about 11 A.M. Paris time (10 A.M. London time), Pineau told me, which would confirm a swiftness of decision possible only through unanimity. Konrad Adenauer and Foreign Minister von Brentano of West Germany, who had arrived that morning on an official visit, were with Mollet and Pineau when Eden telephoned. Mollet was embarrassed by Adenauer's presence. He asked Eden for more time. Eden said he could not withstand American pressure in view of the threat to sterling. Pineau said he particularly remembered Eden's emphasis on the threat to sterling.

Adenauer advised Mollet to accept a cease-fire. Paradoxically, it was Adenauer's presence that then delayed Mollet from giving Eden the reply of the French Cabinet until about 6 P.M. (5 P.M. London time). Protocol and the customary schedule of ceremonies prevented Mollet from calling a Cabinet meeting until evening, or so he claimed.

Unlike the British Cabinet, the French Cabinet held divided opinions. Both Pineau and Bourgès-Maunoury wanted to go on without the British. Pineau said he argued that once Britain quit, Israel was released from her pledge not to cross the Canal and could finish the job in cooperation with the French. But Chaban-Delmas said that "the British are in front of us and going on alone would mean shooting at them first." Pineau conceded that it would be difficult to disentangle the French command, which was closely enmeshed with the British, and reconstruct it as an independent command. Pineau said he had always thought that the British fixation on the Canal was stupid and that the attack should have gone straight to Cairo. He was never enthusiastic for intervention but felt that France, having begun it, should go through with it. It took nearly an hour to reconcile Pineau and Bourgès-Maunoury to the necessity of accepting a cease-fire if the British did.

Although the protection of British and French lives and property had been one of the main pretexts for the military measures that were begun immediately after nationalization, no one in the British or French cabinets thought of attaching stipulations to the cease-fire to protect their nationals against punitive action, including seizure of property. "The question never came up," a British minister told me. "I wish it had. I had to spend a lot of time afterwards trying to get compensation for them."

Instantly upon receiving the assent of Mollet at 5 P.M. Eden signaled Keightley to order a cease-fire at midnight London time (2 A.M., 7 November, in Port Said). Stockwell was floundering in the dark, stormy sea toward the *Tyne* when the signal went out. Eisenhower had just returned by helicopter from a morning automobile trip to Gettysburg with his wife to cast their ballots in the US election. He got word of the cease-fire about the same time Stockwell did and promptly telephoned Eden at 12:55 (5:55 P.M. London time) from a noon meeting at the White House with the US Joint Chiefs of Staff. It was their first conversation on the new transatlantic cable. Eisenhower reached Eden at his House of Commons office just as he was about to go into the chamber to announce the cease-fire. Eisenhower expressed great gratification over the cease-fire but he cautioned Eden against trying to attach any conditions to it and also against seeking Anglo-French inclusion in the UN Emergency Force. Excerpts from their talk, taken from the White House transcript, follow:

Eisenhower: "This is a very clear connection."

Eden: "I can just hear you."

Eisenhower: "First of all, I can't tell you how pleased we are that you found it possible to accept the cease-fire, having landed."

Eden: "We have taken a certain risk, but I think it is justified."

Eisenhower: "Anthony, this is the way I feel about it. . . . I would go ahead with the ceasefire, not putting any conditions into the acceptance of the resolution—and after the cease-fire talking about the clearing of the Canal and so on. . . ."

Eden: "I have to go to my Parliament."

Eisenhower: "Oh, all right."

Eden: "In five minutes. Would you authorize me to say that you think this is helpful outside—

Eisenhower: "You can say that I called to say how delighted I was you found it possible to cease fire tonight so that negotiations could start."

Eden: "I am just getting it down. . . . Proceed."

Eisenhower: "Yes. Wait a minute. Well, I will tell you what I am trying to get at. I don't want to give Egypt an opportunity to begin to quibble so that this thing can be drawn out for a week. . . . I would like to see none of the great nations in it. I am afraid the Red boy is going to demand the lion's share. I would rather make it no troops from the Big Five. I would say: 'Mr. Hammarskjold, we trust you. When we see you coming in with enough troops to take over, we go out....'"

Eden: "If I survive here tonight, I will call you tomorrow. How are things going with you?"

Eisenhower: "We have given our whole thought to Hungary and the Middle East. I don't give a damn how the election goes. I guess it will be all right...."

Eden then entered the House at 6:04 P.M. Designed to seat considerably fewer than the 630 members, it was jammed with standees. Word had gone round that Eden would make an important announcement at 6 P.M. "Remembering the 'siege of battering days' he has endured," wrote the *Manchester Guardian's* parliamentary correspondent, "he seemed astonishingly fresh and vigorous. He was as self-confident as he has been through the whole affair." The members listened in attentive silence, rare in those Suez days, as Eden told of hearing from Hammarskjold during the night that Egypt and Israel had [for the second or third time each] stated their acceptance of a cease-fire and of receiving Hammarskjold's second and final report on what UNEF would be and do. Eden then read Britain's reply that, assuming confirmation of the Israeli-Egyptian cease-fire and the formation of a competent UN force, and proposing that Anglo-French salvage technicians begin clearing the Canal at once, "Her Majesty's Government are ordering their forces to cease fire at midnight GMT unless they are attacked."

The Laborite benches erupted in unconfined jubilation, cheering and waving order papers, celebrating what they regarded as a political victory for themselves as well as a diplomatic victory for the UN. Although most of the Tories stood and cheered Eden when he defended the war as having achieved its aims, a number of backbenchers, ostentatiously glum, refused to budge.

Eden's announcement climaxed a day of high pageantry and drama. The Queen had driven in state in a gilded carriage and six horses from Buckingham Palace to open the new session of Parliament. In the House of Lords, where the Commons joined the brilliant array of peers in robes and trappings, the Queen read the Address from the Throne, which is written by the Government of the day setting out its program for the coming session. Back in their own House, the Commons broke long tradition by debating the Middle East situation instead of confining themselves to noncontroversial replies to the Royal Address.

Gaitskell pilloried the government, itemizing its ever-growing list of war aims and pointing out their contradictions and failures. "There is not a shred of evidence that there was any really serious danger [to the Canal] until we intervened," Gaitskell said. He linked Suez with Hungary and quoted a letter in *The Times* that morning from Lady Violet Bonham-Carter: "Like us she [Russia] claims to be conducting a 'police action.' We have coined a phrase which has already become part of the currency of aggression." Gaitskell added his own comment: "The truth of the matter is that the law of the jungle has been invoked by the British Government and the Russians are following suit."

Eden declared that no action short of what the British and French did would have induced the UN to act. "Surely everybody has learned that moral force in support of the United Nations alone is not effective to meet the challenges of this world," Eden said. "If as a result of the actions we have taken, the United Nations is more ready to employ force adequate to the duties it has to discharge the better it will be for the peace and the future of the world." He ignored Gaitskell's parting question: "May we now take it that the objective set out in the leaflets dropped over Cairo, which was clearly to destroy the Egyptian Government, is now also abandoned by Her Majesty's Government?"

An hour after he spoke to the Commons Eden received a cable from Eisenhower putting in writing for greater emphasis the main points he had made on the telephone. They were: (1) that Britain accept the cease-fire unconditionally and only afterward raise the issue of Anglo-French salvage men clearing the Canal, (2) that all the Great Powers be excluded from UNEF, and (3) that compliance with the UN resolutions be "immediate" in order to forestall menacing developments of the utmost gravity, by which Eisenhower evidently meant the dispatch of Communist-bloc volunteers to the Middle East. Eisenhower said he sincerely hoped Eden would affirm to Hammarskjold his acceptance of these points before the evening UN session.

General Butler recalled that the cease-fire order reached him about 10:30 P.M. along with Stockwell's encouragement to see how much of the Canal he could capture before the cease-fire went into effect. Butler took his 2d Paratroop Battalion, which had come ashore earlier in the evening, and a squadron of tanks and headed south with himself aboard one of the landing tanks. They made it to al-Kap, a station twenty-three miles down the Canal, just short of where the causeway reaches the southern shore of Lake Manzala. "It was damned silly," he recalled, "not a military exercise. I should have gone to wider and higher ground a thousand yards beyond al-Kap." But it was 2 o'clock. The music had stopped. The players had to freeze where they were, although Butler was in an extremely dangerous spot, cramped on a vulnerable causeway where he could be cut off and destroyed by a resolute enemy raid.

Twenty-eight minutes after the cease-fire the Voice of Britain broadcast in Arabic: "Britain and France have saved Egypt from being occupied by the Israelis. . . . If Britain and France had not put a shield between the two fighting armies, the Israeli forces would have undoubtedly entered the Canal and penetrated into Egypt and probably occupied most of the country."

Stockwell's bitterly sarcastic cable to the War Office shortly after the cease-fire, when some military units were being withdrawn to Cyprus while others were being landed to replace them, summed up the whole Suez adventure in all its aspects. Said Stockwell: "We've now achieved the impossible. We're going both ways at once."

Part IV

REPRISE

(7 NOVEMBER 1956 TO THE FUTURE)

CHAPTER
19

Disgorging
(7 NOVEMBER 1956 AND AFTER)

The problem after a war is with the victor. He thinks he has just proved that war and violence pay. Who will now teach him a lesson?

(A. J. MUSTE)

Israel came also into Egypt, and Jacob was a stranger in the land of Ham. And he increased his people exceedingly, and made them stronger than their enemies...

Egypt was glad at their departing; for they were afraid of them.

(Psalm 105)

THE WAR was over, the war that Ben-Gurion had long planned as the way to win sea lanes and more land, the war that Mollet dreamed would be the key to victory in Algeria, the war that was Eden's personal duel with Nasser—ostensibly to make Nasser "disgorge" the Canal but actually to destroy him. Ben-Gurion had taken all his objectives. The French, on balance, had won nothing and lost nothing. Eden, in terms of Dulles's graphic metaphor, had wrestled one end of the Canal out of Nasser's throat but the piece now stuck in his own and Eisenhower was pounding on his back to get it loose. Eden would now have to disgorge and Ben-Gurion along with him.

It was Eisenhower who stopped the war and it was Eisenhower who made the victors disgorge in the conviction that unless war, like crime, could be shown not to pay, the UN would be gravely weakened and man would move closer to destruction by his own terrible new devices. "We not only had a little difficulty in getting Britain and France to come out," Eisenhower told me in an interview on Suez, "but later we had much more difficulty in getting the Israeli to come out. Finally we had to be very tough with them, really, but finally they agreed."

Nasser clearly lost the war but it was equally clear before it ended that his conduct of the war had strengthened him in Egypt, in the Arab world, and as a spokesman for Africa and Asia. The overwhelming superiority of the forces and equipment against him ensured not only Egypt's military defeat but, equally, that the defeat would be no disgrace. This disparity of forces made it difficult to assess the quality of the Egyptian Army. The outcome would have been the same whether the Army was good or bad, just as the performance of a swimmer being swept over Niagara Falls would be the same whether he were an Olympic champion or a dogpaddler.

The strain of racism in the attitudes of the three victors came out in a tendency to sneer at the fighting qualities of the Egyptians. They derided the Wogs or Gyppos, as the British commonly called them, for supposed irrational cowardice and clownishness on the part of the men. They attributed to Egyptian officers not only cowardice and clownishness but also selfishness, foppishness, snobbery, and callousness. Napoleon's dictum that there are no bad soldiers, only bad officers, was trotted out with a scornful laugh as a kind of epigraph for many a war story about Egyptian officers. The Israelis, in particular, loved to say they collected thousands of shoes which the Egyptians had discarded in order to run away faster. There were numberless Israeli tales of Egyptians who threw away their guns and took to their heels without firing a single shot. Many of these were belied by other Israeli accounts. In fact,

Egyptians who withdrew without firing were generally observation squads under orders to do just that.

Colonel Mutawally, who took off his shoes to walk more easily through the dunes from Um Qataf, told me: "There is no war in the world where one side does nothing. If only through fear and a desire to stay alive, soldiers will shoot. If I am not brave maybe I shoot two or three shots and run away. But to leave my gun and run away without shooting it at all? Why?"

It is a matter of record that the only real defended position taken in battle by Israelis from Egyptian regulars was Sharm al-Sheikh. At Rafah the commander performed the difficult and dangerous feat of disengaging and withdrawing under attack. The Israelis failed to catch the withdrawing Egyptians on the Northern Axis. They merely trailed them through abandoned positions. On the Central and Southern Axes the defenders bloodied the attackers so severely that they did not venture into Um Qataf or the Mitla Pass until a day or more after the Egyptians had obeyed Nasser's withdrawal order. Even at Sharm al-Sheikh, Dayan wrote, what was decisive were the air attacks, against which the Egyptians had nothing but guns on the ground. The elimination of the Egyptian Air Force by the British and French, as Dayan readily acknowledged, was sufficient to decide the whole desert campaign. "It is no exaggeration," he wrote in his diary after twenty-four hours of Anglo-French bombing, "to say that our aircraft have accounted for at least half of the enemy casualties in men and equipment." The enemy's total control of the skies made the Egyptian withdrawal with the bulk of their equipment a military feat comparable perhaps to some of the celebrated Israeli accomplishments in the Sinai but it has been little appreciated in the West.

There is no doubt that the Israeli fighting man is more than a match for the Egyptian. He is, on the average, better trained and better led. He has the initial advantage of having grown up with an understanding of modern machinery—tractors, irrigation pumps, automobiles—which the Egyptian *fellah* lacks. The Israeli has a high minimum standard of schooling while Egypt has not yet eliminated illiteracy. The Israeli is more flexible and opportunistic. He lives in an innovating society while Egypt is still emerging from hidebinding custom and tradition. The Israelis still have the dash of conquerors sallying forth to win an empire promised by God while the Egyptian has a purely defensive image of war. In the two Suez-Sinai wars Israel had the undeniable advantage of striking first. Even more of an advantage in desert fighting was the obliteration of the Egyptian Air Force in both wars, which transformed the sky into a wholly hostile element for the Egyptians. Having and exploiting these advantages to the full does not detract from the soldierly caliber of the Israelis. But scoffing at a handicapped victim is a bully's game and it ill suits Israel's claim to want peace.

The casualties reflected the course and character of the war. The Israeli Army announced on 19 November that it lost 171 killed and one prisoner, the pilot shot down at Sharm al-Sheikh. The list included thirty officers, a high percentage that bore witness to the high standards of Israeli combat leadership. To lose no prisoners was to be expected in a lightning advance across mostly undefended desert. The few prisoners that the Egyptians did take they left behind with their own wounded and rear guards at places like Um Qataf.

The last Israeli casualties of the war were Colonel Simhoni, theatre commander of the whole Sinai campaign, and his aide, Lieutenant Colonel Asher Drome, who were shot down in a light plane by Jordanian anti-aircraft gunners near Ajlun in the mountains east of the Jordan River at 3:30 A.M. on 7 November, an hour and a half after the cease-fire. They apparently lost their way on a flight from Elath to Tel Aviv. The papers and notebooks found in the wreckage contained the Israeli order of battle together with candid criticisms of Dayan and the Israeli operations. The papers were circulated in the Arab world with as much publicity as the West gave to the documents Israel claimed to have captured in Gaza and al-Arish.

Nasser published facsimile copies of Simhoni's notes with his own analysis of the Sinai campaign in the magazine *Akher Saa* on 5 December. Simhoni told of Egyptian air attacks on the Southern Axis so severe that the Israeli wounded could not be evacuated. Simhoni was evidently writing down his complaints of confused orders and discoordination on the Central Axis when he was shot down, for the last page is blank after eleven numbered complaints followed by the numeral 12. He complained of Dayan's absences from headquarters and his issuance of commands independently of the coordination of activities by the operations branch.

The British casualties, Keightley reported, were 16 killed and 96 wounded while the French lost 10 killed and 33 wounded. Although the British and French eventually put 22,000 men—13,500 British and 8,500 French—and 4,400 vehicles into Port Said and Port Fuad, only a fraction of that number were in combat during the two days of their war. Counting the fleet and the follow-up units dispatched from England, more than one hundred thousand men were set in motion against Egypt. The low allied casualties testified to the huge advantage in firepower of the invaders, which enabled them to pulverize defended positions with naval guns and air strikes rather than having to storm them.

Egyptian casualties were not officially disclosed, aside from the tallies of prisoners taken by the Israelis and the Anglo-French forces. The Israelis, in a week-long exchange that began under UN supervision on 21 January 1957, returned nearly 6,000 prisoners to the Egyptians, most of them the National Guards and Palestinians that were cut off in the Gaza Strip. In addition to the Israeli pilot, the Egyptians returned three prisoners taken in border clashes in 1955.

Dayan wrote that the Israelis generally did not bother to count the Egyptian dead. He also said the Israelis were encouraged, and at times ordered, not to take prisoners, which led sometimes to driving disarmed prisoners into the desert. It also led to unnecessary killing, such as that described on the radio by Uri Dan, an Israeli war correspondent who entered al-Sudr with the paratroopers from Parker Memorial. They killed a lone Egyptian soldier on the way in, Dan reported, and then stopped an Egyptian truck by shooting the driver. "Sixty Egyptian soldiers traveling in it were eliminated by a hail of bullets," he went on, as matter-of-factly as if they had been rats in a barn, adding that virtually all the rest of the Egyptian soldiers in the town were eliminated shortly thereafter, many "in various vehicles they had stolen from the oil fields."

By compiling such fragmentary Israeli reports Erskine Childers, in a brilliant early history of the Suez War, estimated that 1,000 Egyptians were killed by Israelis in the Sinai and another 1,000 died during the withdrawal—from aerial attacks, thirst, and hunger. The Israelis estimated on 10 November that 3,000 Egyptians died in battle or in the desert.

The Egyptians recorded many Israeli atrocities. They included aerial attacks on hospitals, hospital trains, and ambulances by rocket and napalm, particularly on the Northern Axis. In addition to the live mutilations at Rawafa Dam and the large-scale shootings verified by the UN in the Gaza Strip, the Egyptians reported that the Israelis threw a hand grenade into a room full of prisoners in al-Arish on 2 November, killing several, and that another batch of prisoners was shot in the legs and left in the desert near al-Arish. Egyptian workers were found hanging from telegraph poles between Qantara and al-Arish when the Egyptians returned there in the winter. Many bodies lay unburied along the roads, the Egyptians said, while graves were found containing victims of strangulation and close-range shots in the head, some with their eyes gouged out. In view of the atrocities exchanged across the truce lines over the years, there is no reason to doubt the Egyptian evidence and no reason to think the Egyptians would not have replied in kind if they had been advancing instead of retreating.

In Port Said, General Burns reported, about 185 Egyptian prisoners were taken by the British and French. They were exchanged on 21 December for the 460 British maintenance technicians from the Suez Canal base.

The total of Egyptians killed in Port Said was the subject of squalid and unworthy bickering which culminated in the British Government appointing Sir Edwin Herbert, president of the Law Society, to make an investigation. No one questioned Sir Edwin's integrity but not even the British troops believed his report on 2 December that only 650 Egyptians had been killed and 900 wounded. General Burns estimated that "nearly a thousand Egyptians—soldiers, police and civilians of all sexes and ages—had been killed in the fighting."

Some of the saddest casualties were not physically injured. These were the *magnoon al-ma'raka*, the "battle loonies," who were a familiar sight in the streets of Port Said for years: the woman who nursed and petted a pillow in lieu of the baby killed in her arms by strafing, the man who kept trying to wipe blood off himself, the mad commander who directed invisible legions in an endless battle.

In memory of the killed, the Egyptians erected the Tomb of the Martyrs in the municipal square of Port Said over an underground museum of the battle and its heroes and victims. Visiting the tomb became a fixed ritual for foreign dignitaries, like laying wreaths at the Cenotaph in Whitehall or at the Tomb of the Unknown Soldier in Arlington Cemetery and in Paris. Port Said immediately acquired a prominent place in Arab folk history somewhat like the Alamo in American folk history. December 23d, the date Egypt recovered control of the city, became Victory Day, second only in importance to the anniversary of the Revolution on 26 July.

On the day the war ended, however, there was no certainty that the invaders could not turn a profit by diplomacy out of what they had won by war. Long before the casualties and costs of the war were tallied Ben-Gurion, Eden, and Nasser staked out their claims in the struggle to keep their winnings or recoup their losses. The French, having lost nothing and gained nothing, merely shrugged and turned back to Algeria.

Ben-Gurion was the first of the collusive allies to shift from guns to diplomacy and defend with words what he had taken by storm. Without pausing to rest or count his gains, Ben-Gurion plunged into the political battle to hold the new empire won by Israeli arms in what was, in fact if not in name, the Second Round of the Palestine War. His opening tactic was to deny that Israel's gain had been Egypt's loss. He treated Sinai as historically part of Israel and asserted Israel's every intention of staying there. "Our forces did not infringe upon the territory of the land of Egypt and did not even attempt to do so," Ben-Gurion told the Knesset the morning the war ended. "Our operations were restricted to the area of the Sinai Peninsula alone."

In a declaration of intentions toward the end of his long victory speech, the Israeli leader said: "The Armistice Agreement with Egypt is dead and buried and will never be resurrected. . . . Together with the Armistice Agreement, the armistice lines between us and Egypt are vanished and dead." His determination to hold fast to Israel's territorial gains was endorsed by an overwhelming majority of his countrymen and their representatives in the Knesset. He directed the Israeli representative at the UN to cast what turned out to be the sole negative vote against a new General Assembly resolution that day which "call[ed] once again upon Israel immediately to withdraw all its forces behind the armistice lines." Britain and France, who were likewise called upon to withdraw, merely abstained rather than set themselves once more against world opinion.

As for the UN Emergency Force, Ben-Gurion laid down a permanent policy a good deal harder than Israel's antagonistic policy toward the UN Truce Supervision Organization. "Israel does not accept under any circumstances that a foreign force, whatever its name may be, shall be stationed in its territory or one of those territories which Israel now occupies." The UNEF was never allowed on Israeli soil, not even to facilitate its withdrawal from positions in Egypt before the Third Round of the Palestine War in June 1967.

Ben-Gurion rewrote the map in his victory speech. He referred to "the Bay of Shlomo, hitherto called Sharm al-Sheikh." He called Tiran "Yotvat" and said it had been "liberated" by the Israeli Army. He spoke of the Sinai as a "foreign desert" to the Egyptians.

Ben-Gurion made veiled references to the background of the war. "We did not win through chance," he said, "the operation was planned in advance." Only those privy to collusion knew what he meant by the "unique measures" he said had protected Israel against Egyptian bombers. "It was not the Suez Crisis, which broke out a few months ago and caused a storm throughout the world that dragged us into this storm," he said. "We took action . . . because several years ago our right to freedom of shipping had been violated in a rude and arbitrary manner by the Egyptian rulers. . . . For Israel's economy and future, freedom of shipping in the Red Sea, to Elath and from Elath, is not less and is perhaps far more important than freedom of shipping in the Suez."

Ben-Gurion took the opportunity to reiterate his false accusation that "Abdel Nasser declared day after day that Egypt was at war with Israel and he did not conceal his principal aim which was to attack Israel and wipe it off the face of the earth at the first opportunity." Through repetition Israel maintained the currency of such charges in the West, although they have never been substantiated by a single documented quotation from Nasser. It is a clever tactic since it is impolitic for an Arab to deny making hostile statements about Israel.

Being therefore unchallenged, such Israeli accusations tend, through incessant repetition, to become accepted.

The *Jerusalem Post*, which serves as the international organ of Ben-Gurion's Mapai party, published a history of the Sinai Peninsula on 7 November designed to impugn Egyptian sovereignty there. Mohammed Aly obtained part of the peninsula from Turkey as a buffer zone in the 1840s in exchange for Egyptian withdrawal from Palestine and Syria, the *Post* reported. The boundary was undemarcated but was understood to run from al-Arish to Suez, which "left most of the territory in Palestine, with only a small triangle in the northwest portion belonging to Egypt." The Anglo-Turkish boundary agreement of 1906, which remains accepted by all nations except Israel despite the 1956 and 1967 wars, was "purely tentative," the *Post* said, adding that "it is questionable how much validity it really possesses." The *Post* recalled Britain's offer of al-Arish to Herzl in 1902 as a site for Zionist settlement. It went on to describe the "acquisitive Arishis" of 1956 as a mongrelized and lazy population that was degrading the "nobility and purity" of the Sinai Arabs. "If Israel is given the opportunity to bring to this neglected peninsula . . . the passion and skill for development she has brought to the land of her fathers," the *Post* concluded, "there is little doubt that a new era of prosperity and plenty will dawn for the hungry and emaciated tribes who now inhabit it."

Reports of Ben-Gurion's defiant speech reached Eisenhower in the midst of a painful series of transatlantic telephone talks with Eden, who was himself hoping, if not to keep Port Said, at least to use it as a bargaining gage, which he would trade back to Egypt in return for such concessions as he could get. Eisenhower immediately cabled Ben-Gurion that the United States viewed his stand "with deep concern." He told Ben-Gurion that Israel would "seriously undermine" United Nations peace efforts with such a policy, which, moreover, "could not but bring about the condemnation of Israel as a violator of the principles as well as the directives of the United Nations."

The sternness of Eisenhower's message, which went on to suggest that Israeli intransigence might "impair the friendly cooperation between our two countries," disturbed Ben-Gurion. But that was not all. Ben-Gurion's biographer and confidant, Michel Bar-Zohar, said a simultaneous message from Hoover to Golda Meir raised the prospect of economic sanctions against Israel and of a broad-based movement in the UN to expel Israel. Oral messages from Washington were said to have warned that Israeli recalcitrance would prevent the West from opposing a possible Russian intervention with volunteers.

Ben-Gurion convened his Cabinet twice to work out a formula that might placate Eisenhower without surrendering. He replied to Eisenhower the following afternoon, 8 November, that "we have never planned to annex the Sinai Desert" and that "we will, upon conclusion of satisfactory arrangements with the United Nations in connection with this international force entering the Suez Canal area, willingly withdraw our forces."

It was not by accident that Ben-Gurion said less than he appeared to be saying, that he contemplated the entry of UNEF only into the Canal area, which was occupied by Britain and France, and that he was vague about the withdrawal of forces, not saying where they would be withdrawn from or how far and without mentioning any withdrawal of police or other elements of occupation and control. A somewhat similar formula had cloaked the extension of Israeli control into the al-Auja demilitarized zone. As Bar-Zohar phrased it: "He had given in, but neither definitely nor completely. The veiled terms of his reply to Eisenhower were in fact the prelude to a hard diplomatic struggle that lasted four months, during which Ben-Gurion had but one aim—to preserve a few of the fruits of his victory."

That night, a few hours after his ostensible assurance to Eisenhower, Ben-Gurion gave a conflicting assurance to his people in a radio broadcast: "None of us knows what the future of the Sinai Desert will be." Ben-Gurion said Israel had three principal aims in the Sinai operation:

1. The destruction of forces that all the time attempted to subdue us.
2. Liberation of that part of the homeland which was occupied by the invader.
3. Insuring freedom of shipping in the Straits of Elath and also in the Suez Canal.

Although for the time being, only the first and principal aim has been attained, we are certain that the other two aims as well will be attained in full.... In the Liberation War [of 1948] we did not attain all that we desired.... Only a short-sighted people would not use the great things which we attained this time, although the struggle is not yet ended.

Ben-Gurion told Bar-Zohar and many other writers that the withdrawal decision was the most painful decision in his life. It was politically unpopular. In debate on 23 January 1957 Menahem Beigin said that not even the Knesset Foreign Affairs and Security Committee knew what happened between 7 November and 8 November that led the Government to agree to withdraw.

Israel cabled Hammarskjold that 8th of November that she would withdraw her forces "from Egypt" once she had concluded satisfactory arrangements concerning UNEF with the UN. But in view of the limited meaning Ben-Gurion allowed to "Egypt," excluding the Sinai from it, one must measure the worth of this assurance by Israel's own conduct, which was to resist and delay withdrawal at every stage in 1956 and 1957 and then to reconquer the whole peninsula in 1967 and stay there. In 1957 it was not until 16 March that the last Israeli soldier marched back into his pre-Suez territory. Attempting to stave off US pressure, Ben-Gurion had vainly warned Dulles that the withdrawal was opposed by "our entire people," which could be taken to include the Jewish voters in the US.

Eisenhower had a frosty dislike of that kind of pressure. "During the campaign," he wrote later, "some political figures kept talking of our failure to 'back Israel.' If the Administration had been incapable of withstanding that kind of advice in an election year, could the United Nations thereafter have retained any influence whatsoever? This, I definitely doubt."

The polls began closing in the US as the allied invasion of Egypt braked to a halt. At 1:30 A.M. in Washington Eisenhower appeared at the Sheraton-Park Hotel to join Republicans in celebrating his second landslide victory over Adlai Stevenson. The voting patterns indicated that Eisenhower's personal popularity prevailed over Zionist sympathies and other factors among the electorate.

He told me that when his threat of sanctions against Israel leaked into the news, "I got calls from New York City and some of my friends [said]: 'Well, you've lost New York.' And I said I don't give a goddamn. . . . We said, well, we thought the American Jew was probably an American before he was a Jew so we'll just take the salt thataway. . . . Anyway, it had no effect on our politics. . . . And we went along, the whole damn—I mean the Cabinet—no one kicked. They said that's exactly what you've got to do if you're going to go by a principle. . . . So, hell, it turned out just fine. We carried [New York by] a million six hundred thousand. Nobody'd ever carried the state that heavily."

Other Republicans fared worse and the party failed to win control of either house of Congress. Jewish candidates like Senator Jacob K. Javits of New York lost Jewish votes because of their support of Eisenhower's Middle East policy. After Javits's re-election in 1962 *The New York Times* reported that its special computer analysis "showed that Mr. Javits did almost twice as well among Jewish voters as he had in 1956 when President Eisenhower's stand on the Suez crisis hurt the Republican ticket in Jewish communities."

In contrast to their generally up-to-the-minute reporting on the war, the Russians delayed broadcasting the news of the cease-fire more than eleven hours, until 1:20 P.M. Cairo time, when Valentin Zorin announced it in a commentary claiming it was Russia who forced an end to the fighting. Only Damascus, among the Arab capitals, allowed Russia the full credit she claimed.

The cease-fire was precarious. The British and French commanders were itching to renew the fighting. The Egyptians were provoking them by running guns across Lake Manzala for a simmering guerrilla operation that subsequently underlay Egypt's claims to have forced the allied withdrawal. "My immediate preoccupation after the cease-fire," wrote Stockwell, "was to redeploy my troops so that, if authorized, we could make a break-out south from al-Kap to complete our original task..." Leulliette wrote of constant alerts by hopeful allied generals. One night his unit prepared to march on Qantara and was stopped by a telephoned order at the last minute. Keightley kept his full force ready for a renewal of hostilities until the UN contingents began taking up their posts in Port Said in late November.

Wives of career soldiers were as upset as their husbands over the cease-fire. The beautiful Madame Beaufre said the emotional shock gave her weeping fits for six months, which upset the children. She had expected to celebrate Christmas in Ismailiya, where she had often paused on trips to and from Indo-China.

Eden's first preoccupation after the cease-fire was to recover his and Britain's standing in the Western alliance. He telephoned Eisenhower at 8:43 A.M., Washington time, on 7 November, and suggested that he and Mollet should fly across the ocean for a full discussion with Eisenhower, departing that very evening. Eisenhower responded with instinctive warmth to his friend's overture. He said the allied disagreement over the attack on Egypt was no more than "a family spat" and he said he would be delighted for Eden and Mollet to fly over that night. Eden relayed the invitation to Mollet. A couple of additional calls settled with the White House that the visit would be announced at 11 A.M. Washington time (4 P.M. in London and 5 P.M. in Paris) so that Eden and Mollet could give the good news to their parliaments before departing.

Meanwhile, Eisenhower told Acting Secretary of State Hoover of the impending visit. The State Department people immediately and, Eisenhower wrote, almost unanimously decided that it was premature for Eisenhower to welcome the allies in aggression of Ben-Gurion, who had just publicly vowed neither to withdraw nor accept a UN peace force. Ben-Gurion's continued defiance of the UN would share the headlines with the news that those who had broken the peace with him in defiance of the UN and the US were now to visit the US as honored guests. It would look as if the Presidential election was the hinge of US policy, not moral principles, and that the US was far from disapproving the attack on Egypt. The US would be compromised in its support of the UN peacemaking mission in the Middle East and that mission might well fail in consequence.

At 9:55 Eisenhower telephoned Eden the doubts that had been implanted. "I don't want to put us in a false position," he said. "... I was afraid we would get to talking about certain features and you would feel that you couldn't go along with the UN plan.... Then we would be in a bad spot if we had to have a divided communiqué." Eden reassured him: "As long as it works, I don't care what kind of international force we have." But the State Department was not reassured, least of all Hoover, who felt, Eisenhower wrote, as if the Arab world might turn wholly against the US. The meeting would have to be postponed until after Britain and France complied with the UN resolutions.

Eisenhower accepted the State Department recommendation "with reluctance and impatience," according to Sherman Adams, who brought it to the President. Adams said Eisenhower disliked so much fuss over appearances when he thought it would be good for the world to see that US friendship for Britain was unaffected. Nevertheless, Eisenhower telephoned Eden again at 10:27 to say: "I have just had a partial cabinet meeting on this thing, and they think our timing is very, very bad. . . . The boys at the UN they are trying to put the pressure on now are Egypt and Israel. They are trying to put the squeeze on them. The general opinion is that any meeting until that gets done would exacerbate the situation . . . We will have to postpone it a little bit. I am sorry."

Eden had to tell the Commons a half hour later that the information he had hoped to give the House must await further consultations with the Commonwealth, the US, and France. Gaitskell extracted a promise that the British and French would not advance from the cease-fire line nor build up forces in the Port Said beachhead "in order to enable anything further to be attempted later on." The Government had earlier announced a 10 per cent cut in oil consumption, which elicited caustic sarcasm from the Opposition benches and a derisive suggestion that if ration coupons were issued each one should have a portrait of Eden on it.

Islands of resistance continued to hold out in Hungary as the dust of battle settled over Port Said. A few rebel radios still issued appeals for help. But refugees were now streaming across the bridge at Andau. Suslov, in a speech on the anniversary of the Bolshevik Revolution, admitted that the former Stalinist leadership in Hungary had made mistakes. But an extremely dangerous situation for the Socialist camp arose, he said, when Nagy made concession after concession to the reactionary elements among the rebels while arms entered the country from the West. So a new Hungarian Government was formed, he said, and it asked Russian help. The Poles, whose careful bid for limited freedom had touched off the wild Hungarian uprising, broadcast a cold farewell to the Hungarian revolt on 7 November. "We are realists," said Radio Warsaw. "We do not renounce heroism, but we do not intend to become heroes with the poor reward of the ephemeral sympathy of the world."

Nasser had two definitions to make after the war: He had to state his policy for the recovery of the Egyptian territory taken by Israel and he had to make clear to the Communism-obsessed Americans that he was not and never had been a Russian puppet.

US Ambassador Hare on 8 November discussed with Nasser the Russian moves to capitalize on the Suez War. "You need not worry about that," Nasser told him. He said Egypt had struggled many years to expel foreign domination and did not intend to repeat that experience. "I don't trust any Big Power," he said. He laughed when Hare mentioned Bulganin's proposal to Eisenhower to join forces against the Anglo-French invasion. In his report on the talk, Hare said Nasser also made the following points:

Although Egypt's Air Force was severely crippled her Army was still in good fighting trim. More important, Egyptian morale was higher than ever before and so was the sense of unity among the Arabs. Britain and France had lost prestige and gained nothing but Arab hatred which would make it impossible for them to maintain their positions in the Arab world. Furthermore, they faced economic hardship when the closure of the Canal made itself felt. Nasser professed to be unable to fathom why Britain and France undertook such a senseless adventure. Nasser reiterated his conclusion that the collapse of British and French positions meant that ties with the West could be maintained only with the United States. These would be hampered to the degree to which the US might be bound by links with Britain, France, and Israel. However, by pursuing an independent policy, the US should have no trouble reaching an understanding with Egypt and the other Arab states.

The next day Nasser told Egyptians in a broadcast speech at the midday prayers at al-Azhar mosque that both Russia and the US had acted to stop the war. "Today there are two Big Powers on our side," he said, "Russia, which denounced the threat, and America, which informed me it opposes this aggression."

Nasser gave full credit to the leaders of Syria, Jordan, and Saudi Arabia for their demands to be allowed to enter the war. They would have opened new war fronts with full vigor, Nasser said, if the Egyptian Supreme Command had not ordered them to stay out of the war and take defensive positions. He said he was speaking in answer to the jibes of foreigners who interpreted the inaction of the other Arabs to be desertion of Egypt's cause. As for the Egyptians, he declared: "Abroad they said that the Egyptian people could not possibly oppose or fight anyone. I used to say to them that I was one of these people and that I knew what they were and their qualities. . . . Egypt, brethren, has always been the burial place of greedy aggressors. . . . We emerge from the crisis . . . more resolute and steadfast, and much stronger."

Egypt's advocacy of peace did not mean readiness to surrender, Nasser said. "Peace, my brothers, means that we should live a free and honorable life in which we enjoy our freedom, independence, integrity, and prestige, as well as enjoy our land and the privilege of governing ourselves." War was forced upon Egypt, he said, because "Imperialism wanted me and you to be their lackeys." Nasser was talking here about precisely the same thing Eden meant when he said in his 4 November cable to Eisenhower that he was taking the "first step towards re-establishing authority in this area for our generation." There was no lack of authority in Egypt; what Eden objected to was that it was no longer British authority but Egyptian authority.

Those days were gone, Nasser made clear. "So long as there is a foreign force, one single foreign soldier in Egypt, we shall not begin repairing the Canal, and we shall not begin running the Canal because this affects our plan for defense against aggression."

On 21 November Nasser issued a foreign policy manifesto in reply to persistent accusations, chiefly by Britain and Israel, that Egypt and Russia had plotted to take over the Middle East for Communism, with Egypt serving as the front. In a statement distributed worldwide through diplomatic and press channels, Nasser said:

I vow I will not become the stooge or satellite or pawn or hireling of anybody. Just as Egypt is determined to have political independence, so also Egypt is determined to have and maintain ideological independence from all foreign ideologies such as Marxism, racism, colonialism, imperialism, and atheism, all of which incidentally are European in origin.

Nasser said Egypt was, by her geographical situation, "profoundly aware" of the need for international cooperation. "I pledge myself to the strict observance of all the international law that now exists," he said. "More than that, I desire the expansion of international law to meet the needs of the complex modern world." He said that the movement toward inter-Arab cooperation was no different from the European efforts toward unity or the movement toward a Pan-American union. "Egypt, like all other nations, has a special fellow feeling for those nations which share its cultural traditions and for those ex-colonial nations which are in a similar phase of transition to independent democracy and economic progress. But the idea of trying to create an Arab empire or of attempting to dominate such an empire is repugnant to Egypt and to me. . . . The concept of Arab imperialism is a foreign fiction or foreign propaganda based on ignorance or worse."

The nationalism, neutralism, and Arabism expressed by Nasser were themes rooted in Egyptian political thought long before the revolution. Nasser himself did not adopt neutralism until 1955, nearly three years after the revolution, when his need for arms and markets overwhelmed his fundamental sense of affinity with the West, particularly the US, which still remains. With this exception, his policy has been stubbornly consistent. Unfortunately for Nasser, Washington was always turned aside by other pressures and concerns from developing a practical policy toward the Arab world in general and Egypt in particular. Chief among these pressures and concerns were domestic Zionism and the Cold War, with the British and French alliances ranking far behind.

Egyptian and Middle Eastern realities affected Eisenhower's policies after the cease-fire as little as they affected British and French policies before it. The day after the cease-fire, while Ben-Gurion was parrying against withdrawal and Eden was nursing his snubbed hope to visit Washington and Nasser was analyzing Middle Eastern prospects with Hare, Eisenhower dictated a memorandum of ideas for the Middle East which he later included in full in his memoirs as having been the precursor of the Eisenhower Doctrine. That policy was patently inappropriate and ineffectual in its first applications and it looks more misguided in hindsight with every year that passes. The memorandum, like the subsequent Doctrine, perceived only one reality, that the British and French had forfeited any future they might have had in the Middle East. But this perception was turned to no avail by Washington's conclusion that it should step into the shoes of its ousted allies and throw its weight around in the Middle East with all and more of the arrogance, riches, and power its allies had displayed in the century that died in the Suez war.

The overriding objective of Eisenhower's memorandum was to "exclude from the area Soviet influence." This goal was a year and a half too late, 6,000 miles too far away, out of kilter with the global balance of military power and other geopolitical realities, and against the revolutionary spirit of the times. The specter of Communism now haunted Eisenhower more than the Zeitgeist. In a region still shaken by the invasion which Israel and the old arch-colonial powers had launched against an Egypt armed, not quite in the nick of time, by Russia, Eisenhower proposed to "make certain that every weak country understands what can be in store for it once it falls under the domination of the Soviets." To an Egypt which had bought Russian arms in desperation after years of US stalling and had used them to repel an invasion whose senior partner, perfidious Albion, had ended three generations of military occupation only three months before, Eisenhower proposed to "provide ... an agreed-upon amount of arms—sufficient to maintain internal order and a reasonable defense of its borders, in return for an agreement that it will never accept any Soviet offer."

The most constructive and humane idea listed by Eisenhower was to "provide to the area, wherever necessary, surplus foods, and so on, to prevent

646

suffering." The Administration promptly and persistently did the opposite, particularly in respect to Egypt, where war injuries, devastated housing and communications, and the scarcity of supplies after three months of western economic warfare threatened that overpopulated country with hunger and epidemics. Washington not only refused Egypt's first request for emergency food, fuel, and medicine but turned down a second appeal to release some of Egypt's blocked $27 million so that she could buy the desperately needed supplies. As she had for arms, Egypt again turned to Russia. Bulganin had admonished Eden and Ben-Gurion on 15 November that Britain, France, and Israel should compensate Egypt for the damage they had wreaked. Now the Russians immediately airlifted drugs and medical equipment to Egypt and shipped 600,000 tons of wheat. On 30 March Nasser accused the US of having tried to starve the Egyptian people by refusing to sell them wheat.

It seemed as if Eisenhower fell heir, immediately after the cease-fire, to the lurid anxieties about the Red Menace which Eden had tried to stir up over the months in which his vendetta with Nasser marched toward its climax. But virtually every action—or inaction, as in the case of Egypt's emergency postwar needs—which Eisenhower took to counter the Red Bugbear either helped Russia or hurt the US. For example, the Eisenhower Administration, particularly after Suez, seemed unable to keep in mind the distinction between nationalism and International Communism. Equating these two antagonistic forces was clearly a service to the Russians, who had been trying with little success for forty years to persuade African and Asian nationalists that Communism was in harmony, not in rivalry, with them. Unlike Eisenhower and Dulles, Nasser never confused nationalism with Communism. His policies in Iraq and Syria as well as at home, in fact, did far more to curb Communist influence in the Middle East than all the comings and goings of the Sixth Fleet and all the outpouring of millions of dollars of aid with anti-Communist strings.

The only other item in Eisenhower's two-page memorandum that bore a practical relation to the realities of the war just ended was his thought of translating the Tripartite Declaration of 1950 into bilateral treaties with the countries of the Middle East. In view of the six-year-old distrust of the Declaration by Arabs and Israelis alike, it was not surprising that nothing came of this idea. Instead, the US left the Tripartite Declaration intact for future dishonor and promulgated unilaterally the Eisenhower Doctrine, by which the US arrogated to itself the Western influence forfeited by Britain and France.

Before the Doctrine was signed into law on 9 March 1957, Eisenhower and Dulles had winkled Egypt's invaders out of their conquests, not out of friendship for Egypt nor even in the interest of justice for Egypt, but in order to enhance the prestige and effectiveness of the UN. Eisenhower believed that US support was vital to the UN and that the UN was vital to the safety of the world in the nuclear age. Eisenhower was wholly free of cynicism but it is not without significance that the US had sufficient influence in the UN in those days to use it as a major arm of national policy.

The United Nations Emergency Force and American pressure were the fulcrum and the lever that pried first the Anglo-French troops and then the Israelis out of Egyptian territory. An international police force had been a recurrent dream of twentieth-century seekers after a peaceful and democratic world order. There had been a good deal of philosophizing and speculative planning but no real precedents when the General Assembly resolved on 4 November that the force should be created.

Israel's occupation of al-Auja in the fall of 1955 had led to a serious UN military study of such a force early in 1956. The proposal was raised by Foreign Office people when Burns conferred there with Nutting on 4 November 1955 after Israel attacked al-Sabha opposite the demilitarized zone. The idea was to interpose UN troops between Israeli and Egyptian forces so that no incident could escalate into an invasion without the invaders first clashing with the UN force and thus automatically calling down upon themselves international retribution and deterrent measures. Hammarskjold asked General Burns in the spring of 1956 to recommend what military dispositions and arrangements would be required.

Burns recommended stationing an independent combat brigade at Rafah and a reinforced battalion at al-Auja. But, Burns wrote in his memoir of UN service, "I never thought there was a possibility of putting it into effect." The US would have had to exert extreme pressure on Israel, he thought at the time. And he noted that even after the Suez War Israel adamantly refused to allow UNEF troops anywhere on territory she controlled, particularly in al-Auja. Egypt, too, was wary of any intrusion of foreign troops because she was only then seeing the last of the British occupation of 1882. Burns believed there was no hope of obtaining agreement among the permanent, that is, Great Power, members of the Security Council on measures sufficient to overcome Israeli resistance and Egyptian doubts.

It was logical that Burns's country, Canada, should take the lead in transforming the idea of a peace force into reality. It was Canada's Foreign Minister, Lester Pearson, who introduced the one-sentence resolution between midnight and dawn on 4 November requesting Hammarskjold to submit within forty-eight hours a plan for the force. And it was Pearson, in company with the Colombian and Norwegian representatives, who introduced what was adopted twenty-four hours later as Resolution 1000 of the General Assembly. In accordance with Hammarskjold's recommendations, which drew heavily on Burns's advice, the resolution established a UN Command for an emergency international force "to secure and supervise the cessation of hostilities," appointed Burns as commander, and authorized him to recruit officers "who shall be nationals of countries other than those having permanent membership in the Security Council." The last provision was designed to exclude not only Britain and France, who were committing the aggression that occasioned the resolution, but more especially Russia, who was unacceptable to the United States.

The next day Hammarskjold presented a second and final report defining UNEF as "more than an observer corps, but in no way a military force temporarily controlling the territory in which it is stationed." Hammarskjold said the force was not intended "to influence the military balance in the present conflict and, thereby, the political balance affecting efforts to settle the conflict." And he said the General Assembly "could not request the force to be stationed or operate on the territory of a given country without the consent of the Government of that country." This too was approved by the General Assembly the next day in a resolution that further established an Advisory Committee of seven minor and middling powers to carry out any further planning that might be needed and to request the convening of the General Assembly in the event of a major emergency or matter affecting the force.

Burns arrived at Cairo International Airport early on the afternoon of 8 November to settle the terms for Egyptian acceptance of UNEF. His white-painted UN plane, a DC-3 Dakota, was the first to land there since the Israeli invasion. He observed, incidentally, that the airport had been raided, as Nasser affirmed and the British denied. He also observed, as he drove through the streets of Cairo, much movement of armor, which he presumed was there for two reasons: to escape aerial attack and to show the people the Government still possessed armed strength. A prior reason was Nasser's decision to make Cairo into another Stalingrad should the invasion reach that far.

Burns was shocked to learn from Fawzi, the Foreign Minister, that the Canadian contingent that had been offered, called the Queen's Own Rifles, might not be acceptable. Nasser and Fawzi thought that the name of the regiment coupled with the generally British appearance of Canadian troops might lead Egyptians to suspect that they were in fact British troops. In the end, Egypt accepted Canadian air transport and administrative units and, eventually, an armored reconnaissance squadron, but not the Queen's Own Rifles.

The next day Burns met Nasser and got the impression that Nasser feared UNEF might be used to internationalize the Canal if it remained in the Canal Zone after the British and French departed. In the event, UNEF units were stationed in Port Said between Egyptian and allied positions from 21 November to 22 December, when the last Briton departed. UNEF had sole control of the city overnight, handing it over to the returning Egyptians on 23 December. After that UNEF moved across the Sinai as the Israelis slowly and reluctantly withdrew.

The first UNEF detachments, from Colombia and Norway, arrived from Naples at Abu Suwweir airfield near Ismailiya early on 16 November. The same plane brought Hammarskjold on a mission to complete arrangements with Egypt covering the functions of the force. Within three days Hammarskjold and Nasser and Fawzi had approved a formal understanding that UNEF's presence in Egypt was conditional upon Egypt's consent but that Egypt, "when exercising its sovereign rights on any matter concerning the presence and functioning of UNEF ... will be guided, in good faith, by its acceptance of the General Assembly Resolution" that established the UN Command. Hammarskjold promised on behalf of the UN to be guided in good faith by the relevant resolutions and he reaffirmed the UN's "willingness to maintain the UNEF until its task is completed."

Hammarskjold's agreement with the Egyptians cleared the way for the first UNEF contingent, a company of Norwegians, to enter Port Said on 21 November. Stockwell wrote that the "vociferous and spirited welcome" accorded to them by Egyptians "mad with excitement" became so tumultuous that the Norwegians had to be guarded by the British. "A somewhat incongruous situation," wrote Stockwell with evident relish.

A uniform to distinguish the UNEF men from the erstwhile combatants was one of the problems Burns had to work out as the peace force began its work. The first distinguishing items were US helmet liners painted UN blue. Then came blue berets and blue ski-troop caps. Burns wrote that in designing his own uniform he sought to avoid the criticism aimed at, certain famous generals who designed special uniforms for themselves. He said he did not entirely escape ribbing in the press. Two French journalists, Merry and Serge Bromberger, for example, who shared the general ironic hostility of the French troops toward the UNEF, called it a *"uniforme de music-hall,"* in their book *Les Secrets de l'Expédition d'Egypte.*

As UNEF took positions around the perimeter of the Port Said beachhead, Eden continued to try to retain the captive city as a "gage" to be ransomed to Egypt for a price that would make Nasser a political bankrupt, namely, "a lasting settlement for the Arab-Israeli conflict and for the future of the Canal." Eden complained bitterly that the US insisted that "all the advantages gained must be thrown away." Eden's mind was still in the 1930s. His arguments echoed his memorandum on the Rhineland twenty years before: "It would be preferable for Great Britain and France to enter ... into negotiations ... for the surrender on conditions of our rights in the zone while such surrender still has a bargaining value."

Washington made clear that the Middle East Emergency Committee would do nothing until Britain and France agreed to a rapid withdrawal schedule. The US government had brought together thirteen American oil companies operating abroad to form the committee on 10 August to plan emergency oil supplies for Western Europe if Middle Eastern oil sources were stopped. By November the committee included fifteen companies.

Just as Britain's desperate need for dollars had broken the Cabinet's resistance to a cease-fire in Port Said, so her need for oil would make her submit to Washington's insistence that the British and French forces must withdraw from Egypt without obtaining anything from Egypt in return. The French had not needed dollars but they were in the same predicament as the British with regard to oil. They too could see hardship in the winter months ahead if the US did not help replace the interrupted supplies from the Middle East. *Le Monde* disclosed French fears the day the war ended, 7 November, by publishing a special four-page supplement explaining to Frenchmen with text and diagrams how to get the most out of their house-heating fuel.

Before Suez about three-quarters of Western Europe's oil came from the Middle East by way of the Canal (49 per cent of the total) and the pipelines (24 per cent) and about one-quarter came from other sources. If no remedial action had been taken, Europe's oil supplies would have been cut to little more than one-third, the 27 per cent from non-Middle Eastern production and the 9 per cent of the total that normally flowed through the American-owned Trans-Arabian Pipeline, which the Syrians did not sabotage. It was a grim prospect. It was grim too for Eden's only Arab ally, Iraq, whose oil output was cut 75 per cent by the sabotage of the pipelines across Syria. By the time the pipelines were repaired in the spring of 1957 Iraq had lost $180 million in oil revenues.

The Syrians, despite losses in transit fees which they could ill afford, vowed that they would allow no repairs on the pipelines until all the invaders, including Israel, withdrew from Egypt. Despite his similar pledge on 9 November, Nasser allowed a UN salvage organization under Lieutenant General Raymond A. Wheeler of the US to begin clearing the Canal in January, after the British and French departed. But he did not allow the last blockships to be removed until the Israelis too had withdrawn.

Eden sought in vain for UN permission to let the Anglo-French salvage crews and equipment, which had come with the invasion fleet, clear the whole waterway. They did clear Port Said harbor and the Canal as far south as al-Kap, but that was all. Some of the Anglo-French salvage units were later incorporated into the UN operation under humiliating strictures concerning authority and dress. Eden wrote that the UN refusal to allow clearance of the Canal and the US refusal to set in motion the emergency oil lift to Europe gave Egypt an undeserved position of bargaining strength. "The United States Administration seemed to be dominated at this time by one thought only, to harry their allies," Eden wrote.

There were many flickers of sympathy, however. Ambassador Bohlen, in spite of his personal disgust with Eden's Suez policy, led two walkouts by NATO ambassadors in Moscow on the 17th and 18th of November when Khrushchev loudly abused Britain and France at diplomatic receptions. Khrushchev said at the Kremlin on the first occasion that Britain and France were bandits who had "cut the throat" of Egypt while pretending it was a police action. The next night, at the Polish Embassy, Bohlen led the NATO ambassadors into another room when Khrushchev said the Suez War was launched by "imperialists and their puppet" and that "Fascist gangs" formed part of the Hungarian revolt. Seeing the walkout, Khrushchev turned red and said: "If you don't like us, don't accept our invitations and don't invite us to come to see you. Whether you like it or not, history is on our side. We will bury you."

The last remark was a vernacular phrase meaning merely that Russian Communism would outlive Western Capitalism. It was akin to the American expression: "I'll dance at your funeral." But it sent a tremor of fear and rage throughout the Western world, where it was quoted for years and hampered rational appraisals of Khrushchev. More significant but less noticed was his statement, in the presence of Gomulka and his Polish hosts: "We had Hungary thrust upon us. We are very sorry that such a situation exists there. . . . But the most important thing is that the counterrevolution must be shattered."

In Washington on the day of Bohlen's first walkout Dulles gave another flicker of sympathy which has bemused the British ever since. Lloyd and Sir Harold Caccia, the new British ambassador, visited Dulles at the hospital. Both Lloyd and Caccia, separately, described the meeting to me as follows: As Dulles came forward to shake Lloyd's hand he said: "Why on earth did you stop?" Lloyd replied, in effect: "I wish you had asked that earlier." As Lloyd reported the incident to Eden, Dulles went on to deplore the fact that the operation had stopped short of achieving Nasser's downfall. Later on, Dulles confided to Lloyd that US policy would have been easier on Britain if he, Dulles, had been on duty. Most of the Suez decisions during Dulles's operation and convalescence were made by Eisenhower in consultation with Hoover.

Lloyd was in the US on what Eden described as a futile ten-day mission, "struggling to inject some sense of values." The real issue was whether Lloyd could talk the US out of exerting pressure, directly and through the UN, to force Britain and France to quit Port Said. There was a painful incident when Lodge at the UN supported an Afro-Asian resolution on 24 November demanding that the invaders leave Egypt "forthwith." This was regarded as a mean humiliation and was said to have been perpetrated in spite of State Department assurances that the US would vote to delete the offending word.

Eden, meanwhile, was arguing that the Russian penetration of the Middle East, particularly Syria and Iraq, had gone farther than the US knew and that the best antidote to this was the Anglo-French presence in their bottle-neck beachhead. The US Embassy in Syria connived at false reports issued in Washington and London through diplomatic and press channels to the effect that Russian arms were pouring into the Syrian port of Latakia, that "not more than 123 Migs" had arrived in Syria, and that Lieutenant Colonel Abdel Hameed Serraj, head of Syrian intelligence, had taken over control in a Communist-inspired coup. I traveled all over Syria without hindrance in November and December and found there were indeed "not more than 123 Migs." There were none. And no Russian arms had arrived for months. And there had been no coup, although some correspondents in Beirut, just a two-hour drive from Damascus, were dispatching without attribution false reports fed to them by embassy visitors from Damascus and a roving CIA man who worked in the guise of a US Treasury agent. Serraj, who was anti-Communist, had just broken the clumsy British-US-Iraqi-supported plot. Syria was quiet but worried lest the propaganda presage a new *coup d'état* or a Western-backed invasion.

I went to Iraq in December and found Nuri's regime in a somber contest with nationalists infuriated by his failure to support Nasser even by so much as breaking diplomatic relations with Britain. Frustrated resentment against Nuri for steering Iraq against the Nasserist mainstream of Arab nationalism erupted in spontaneous demonstrations scattered all over the country. They were put down with no little bloodshed. Nuri's police then arrested and tried to courtmartial in secret a number of respected leaders of the outlawed nationalist opposition parties. It is difficult to determine the precise Communist quotient in any nationalist movement but it was certainly no more than a very minor factor in the post-Suez nationalism of Syria and Iraq. The reports published by myself and the few other correspondents who made firsthand investigations in Syria and Iraq were voices blown away in the wind of propaganda. Our dispatches were not entirely ignored, however, for I was denounced by the US Embassy in Damascus and roughed up and threatened by Iraqi officers in Baghdad while the US Embassy turned its back.

As for the allegations of Nasser's subservience to Communism, Khrushchev gave expert testimony about them on the night he said Communism would bury Capitalism. "The Western powers are trying to denigrate Nasser," he said, "although Nasser is not a Communist. Politically he is closer to those who are waging war on him and he has even put Communists in jail. . . . But he, Nasser, is fighting for independence. He is the hero of his nation and our sympathies are on his side."

The US by then was both concocting and swallowing the anti-Communist alarmism prescribed by Eden, but Washington would not relent on Suez. Britain had to submit. R. A. Butler, as Acting Prime Minister, had to bear the political onus of submission. Eden, on his doctors' advice, departed on 23 November for a three-week rest at the Jamaica retreat of Ian Fleming, creator of James Bond. On 30 November, Eisenhower wrote, he was satisfied that Britain and France would rapidly and unconditionally withdraw their troops from Egypt and that, accordingly, he ordered the emergency oil shipments to begin.

As promised, Lloyd announced in the House of Commons on 3 December that the allied forces would soon withdraw from the Port Said area. He said Lodge had defined the word "forthwith" in the 24 November resolution to mean a phased withdrawal and that Keightley had been instructed to work out a timetable with General Burns. In the course of a dutifully hypocritical defense of the war, during which the Opposition jeered at every repetition of the now worn and familiar excuses, Lloyd repeated Eden's dishonorable tenet that Israel too must withdraw from the Sinai and from Gaza. Ben-Gurion, with the Sèvres accord in his files at Sde Boker, kept his silence because it was the US, not Britain, that would determine whether Israel had to withdraw. The question of who was responsible for Britain's withdrawal was more immediate.

Tory resentment over this "scuttle" fell full upon Butler. Together with his record of impish and equivocal remarks like "Anthony Eden is the best Prime Minister we have," it cost him the support of the party's unrepentant right wing in the rivalry with Macmillan for the succession which was soon to come.

As Harold Nicolson wrote in his diary: "For the moment, all Tory opinion, bemused though it be, is in favour of Eden. Simple minds work simply. The ladies of Bournemouth do not like the Russians, the Americans or Nasser: Eden has dealt a blow to these three enemies: therefore Eden must be right. It is as simple as that."

It was indeed. My small children at the French Lycée in London found themselves called "dirty Americans" by British schoolmates who brought the phrase from home. They thought it was an obscure joke and they laughed. It was more difficult for Americans who had reached the age of political understanding and much, much worse for Englishmen in disagreement with their friends and relatives. There were quarrels which never healed.

Oil already on the way kept November shipments from falling more than 20 per cent below normal. In December the emergency reallocation of world oil resources carried out under US sponsorship went immediately into full operation. The flow of Saudi Arabian oil through the Trans-Arabian Pipeline was increased. Oil production in the Western Hemisphere was increased. Augmented tanker fleets were pressed into service to carry Persian Gulf oil around the Cape of Good Hope and others were shifted to the North Atlantic run. Europe was blessed with a mild winter. Moderate rationing and price increases, including the "Suez sixpence" that was added to London taxicab fares, helped reduce consumption. All in all, there was no hardship and little inconvenience. The temporary abatement of London traffic, due chiefly to voluntary restraint in motoring, was accepted by many as a blessing. During the five months that elapsed before the Canal was reopened Europe's oil consumption fell only 8 per cent, an average of monthly reductions ranging from 20 per cent in November to 4 per cent in March.

The bitterness of the French troops over withdrawal became a factor in the overthrow of the Fourth Republic in May 1958. As Leulliette expressed it: "... it did fall to us to stomach the shame, the ridicule, the ignominy of retreating as if disgracefully beaten, after we had won ... though conquerors, we are also vanquished." Cavanagh said his comrades "all realized that what had occurred so far had been a futile and expensive waste of time." He added: "We did not yet know the worst; did not know that a lukewarm homecoming awaited us in a country impatiently suffering from petrol rationing; did not know that two years later we would be ridiculed in Jordan." The French paratroopers who departed by way of Cyprus, made cynical by what they regarded as another in an unbroken series of sell-outs by politicians since 1940, sold their booty of Czech and Soviet small arms to the EOKA terrorists in the black market. These were again swiftly turned against the British, by Cypriotes instead of Egyptians.

Terrorism increased in Port Said in December, reaching a peak on the 15th with seventeen separate incidents. The Egyptians ambushed patrols, threw bombs at military vehicles, threatened shopkeepers to stay closed while the British threatened them to open, papered the streets with anti-British posters, and maintained a general atmosphere of defiance and mockery. British accounts all say the British conducted themselves with restraint. And UN investigators reported no evidence of outrageous repressive measures by the British aside from using tanks in one bloody battle with Egyptians in a group of buildings. But the Egyptian Government accused Britain of "indiscriminate shooting of the population." And Leulliette said the British were "not content to return tit for tat like bored players, the way we do. They raise the ante every time, and with a vengeance." He went on to describe a big fire one night in the British sector which began "amid a pandemonium of gunfire," probably the battle in which the British used tanks. Thirty-three dead civilians were picked up the next morning, Leulliette said, adding that the Egyptians hated the British "with an incredible hatred."

Early in December a young British lieutenant, Anthony Moorhouse, was kidnapped while pulling down posters of Nasser. When British search parties approached the house where he was held, his captors bound and gagged him and hid him in a cupboard before going out to merge into the crowd in the street. The Egyptians said the two British search parties working their way from both ends of the street met in front of that house and each thought the other had searched it. Moorhouse suffocated before his captors could return. A cruel hoax, in which a UN investigator was shown a man in British uniform at a distance at a night rendezvous, led to an official report on 22 December that Moorhouse was alive and well. His body was handed over to UNEF on 2 January and returned to England for burial. The incident figured in John Osborne's play, *The Entertainer*, which opened in London in April. The story also figured among the many tales of Port Said in a fifth-grade reader I saw that has been in use in Egyptian schools since 1959. It is presumably in other schoolbooks too.

Like the war, Port Said's resistance movement had its songs, written, scored, and recorded at white heat in Cairo's equivalent of Tin Pan Alley. The resistance songs had a rollicking confidence in place of the intense heroics of the war songs, a difference reflected in their titles. *Etla'! Barra!*, roughly translatable as "Git up! Git out!," and *Idrub! Idrub! Idrub!* (Hit 'em! Hit 'em! Hit 'em!) joined *Hanhaarib!* (We shall fight!) and *Allahu Akbar* (God is Greatest) on the Arabic hit parades. One song was known by its chorus, "*Tak, tak, tak*," the lyric imitation of a resistance machine gun. Some of the titles seem unbearably mawkish in English (*I am eager to embrace you, my rifle*) but they evidently went over well in Arabic because they traveled as swiftly as the other songs throughout the Arab world. I heard them sung in the streets of Baghdad, which was even then doing its best to jam Cairo Radio.

On 22 December, the day the last of the allied invasion forces withdrew under allied jets shrieking overhead, some French soldiers wired the Tricolor to the hand of the huge statue of de Lesseps at the entrance to the Canal. Burns, who took over from Stockwell on behalf of UNEF a few hundred yards from the statue, called it "a forlorn gesture." The next day, after Burns had handed control of the city over to Governor Mohammed Riad, crowds of celebrating Egyptians climaxed hours of parades and speeches by dynamiting the statue off its pedestal.

Eden came back from Jamaica on 14 December. When he reappeared in the House of Commons, Lord Kilmuir wrote, he was greeted "with a stony silence from the Opposition and the feeblest of cheers from the Government benches. One loyal Conservative, Mr. Lagden of Hornchurch, rose to cheer and wave his order paper, to find himself alone and unsupported. It was a grim and revealing episode." Soon afterward Eden's doctors told him to resign, which he did after a final Cabinet meeting on 9 January. He was the first of the Suez leaders to go. Kilmuir and Salisbury polled the Cabinet members one by one in the Privy Council offices for their recommendations on Eden's successor. Kilmuir recorded that Salisbury, who has a pronounced lisp, asked each one: "Well, which is it, Wab or Hawold?" An overwhelming majority favored Harold Macmillan over Richard Austen ("Rab") Butler.

Macmillan's seniority (he was nearly nine years older than Butler), his acceptability to the party's fractious right wing, and his personal friendship with Eisenhower dating from wartime service in North Africa all weighed in his favor as the candidate most likely to maintain Tory unity and resolder the Anglo-American alliance. Furthermore, his leadership would seem less like a repudiation of Eden's Suez policy, which the public opinion polls showed to be popular not only with Conservatives but also with a good proportion of Laborites.

Without repudiating Eden's policy, Macmillan achieved the remarkable feat of turning his back on Suez as a political issue and making it go away. He led the Tories to an electoral triumph in 1959 and remained at Number 10 Downing Street for nearly seven years, the longest premiership since World War I. He restored the Anglo-American alliance at the Bermuda Conference with Eisenhower in the first days of spring. The chief result of the conference was an American undertaking to station intermediate-range ballistic missiles in Britain for the purpose, Dulles told correspondents, of giving Whitehall a deterrent capacity in the face of any future Russian rocket threats. Eisenhower called it "by far the most successful international conference that I had attended since World War II." The chief reason for its success, he wrote, was "the fact that Harold and I were old comrades."

Suez was still a sore spot, however. As Eisenhower described it:

Foster and I at first found it difficult to talk constructively with our British colleagues about Suez because of the blinding bitterness they felt toward Nasser. Prime Minister Harold Macmillan and Foreign Minister Selwyn Lloyd were so obsessed with the possibilities of getting rid of Nasser that they were handicapped in searching, objectively, for a realistic method of operating the Canal.

Eisenhower told them that they could not at the same time seek Nasser's cooperation and combat him. Even then, it wasn't the Canal but Nasser the British wanted to control.

The truth about collusion began to come out soon after the shooting ceased. When Gaitskell raised the charge in Commons on 31 October and Lloyd categorically denied it, six Laborite MPs known for their Zionist sympathies cabled Ben-Gurion for an assurance that there had been no collusion. Ben-Gurion's reply, broadcast by Israel on 6 November, denied that Israel had worked as the agent of any foreign power. The State Department, however, continued piecemeal disclosures of the kind that formed the substance of Chalmers Roberts's broad summary of the evidence in the *Washington Post* on 4 November. The *Observer* (London) noted on 11 November that many persons, regardless of their views on Eden's Suez policy, found it hard to believe the accusations of collusion. The paper adduced additional evidence to make the accusations easier to believe. A *New York Times* snippet attributed to the State Department on 19 November provided the point of departure for an extensive compilation of collusion evidence in *The Times* (London) the next day.

James Morris, a special correspondent for the *Manchester Guardian*, published on 20 and 21 November the first direct admissions of collusive warfare —interviews with French pilots who described flying for Israel before the Anglo-French bombing began. Morris went to Cyprus to evade Israeli military censorship and dispatched French pilots' accounts of attacking Egyptians in the Sinai, of flying cover over Israeli territory, and of dropping supplies to Israeli paratroopers at Mitla Pass. Morris attributed to French flyers a "ghastly accuracy" in napalm attacks on Egyptian war vehicles he saw burnt out in the desert. He said the French role was possibly decisive in Israel's Sinai victory. Against all this he reported Dayan's official—and false—denial of French participation. The French and Israeli Defense and Foreign Ministries, too, promptly denied Morris's dispatches.

British Cabinet ministers, in general, evaded parliamentary questions about collusion by answering questions that were not asked instead of giving concrete replies to questions that actually were asked, a tactic which the *Manchester Guardian* characterized as "deft." Antony Head, however, early in December stumbled into a disclosure that "our first true knowledge that it [Israel's attack on Egypt] was going to take place was when we were informed about the mobilization [on 26 October]." His admission of three days' foreknowledge was not pursued in that debate. But Eden was cornered on 20 December into giving the House the false statement: "There was not foreknowledge that Israel would attack Egypt." In his memoirs Eden utterly ignored the accusations of collusion.

Merry and Serge Bromberger published the first thorough account of collusion in March 1957 in their book, *Les Secrets de l'Expédition d'Egypte*. They did not disclose their sources and, in their haste, they made many minor errors in chronology and terminology. But their story proved to be broadly accurate.

Pineau, in interviews published in 1964 and after, was the first participant in the collusion negotiations to make firsthand disclosures. These led Laborite MPs to demand an inquiry but Sir Alec Douglas-Home, who had by then succeeded Macmillan as Prime Minister, refused to open one. Lord Kilmuir, in his memoirs published that year, still loyally insisted that the "wild accusations of collusion...have absolutely no foundation in fact." But Dayan's *Diary of the Sinai Campaign*, published in Hebrew in 1965, confirmed much of the collusion story as it was then known and added new facts, although about 100 pages were deleted at Ben-Gurion's request in conformity with the pledge of secrecy given at Sèvres. Incomplete though it was, Dayan's book contained the first evidence published by a participant in the collusion arrangements.

Nutting's memoir of Suez, *No End of a Lesson*, which appeared in serial form in *The Times* (London) in April and May 1967, was the first full account to be published by an official involved, albeit unwillingly and only in part, in collusion. It is conclusive and comprehensive proof, although not so complete in detail as participants at Sèvres, such as Pineau, have furnished in interviews. Nutting waited to tell his story until the ministers involved had left office and there was no danger of injuring their value to the nation. He had sacrificed his own political career by refusing to explain his resignation at the time to the enraged Tories of his constituency. Macmillan had promised him on 13 November 1956: "If you keep silent now, you will be revered and rewarded; you will lead the party one day." But Macmillan rewarded Nutting churlishly, as he rewarded most men who made political sacrifices for him.

After Ben-Gurion lost his telegraphic skirmish with Eisenhower immediately after the cease-fire, Israel sought to develop public pressure on the White House to let her keep her winnings. Emissaries like Teddy Kolleck and Avraham Harman hastened to the US to lobby and lecture and enlist the help of Zionist groups.

On 15 November at the United Nations Eban unveiled the documents he said were captured at Egyptian Army Headquarters in the Sinai. The most quotable was the alleged directive of the Third Division commander dated 15 February 1956, telling each unit commander to "prepare himself and his subordinates for the inevitable annihilation of Israel and her destruction in the shortest possible time in the most brutal and cruel of battles." This was the directive Dayan reported seeing at al-Arish on 2 November among the newly captured documents. How it reached the British Zionist sympathizer, Colonel Meinertzhagen, on 4 October has never been explained. Eban said it was proof of an Egyptian intention to annihilate Israel.

Egyptians at the UN noted that Eban's document was full of grammatical errors and contained seventeen words not in Arabic usage. Furthermore, they said, it lacked the superscription of the War Ministry which would be on a genuine document. They noted that the alleged date of the directive, 15 February 1956, coincided with a period in which Ben-Gurion was making extensive propaganda for a preventive war. Eban passed off with a joke the doubts raised by the Egyptians as to the authenticity of the document. He asked for a diagnosis of the grammatical errors and said: "If the officers responsible for the documents are under our control, we shall reprimand them for their faulty usage."

I was given a photocopy of the document, among others, at Israeli Army Headquarters in Tel Aviv in 1964. Quite apart from its grammatical lapses, Arab officers have told me, it is not conceivable that a division commander would issue such vague and wordy trash. In truth, it reads more like the directive of a lunatic fringe paramilitary society. It is doubtless a fake but it continues to be quoted as authentic in books and articles.

None of the documents provided any evidence of an Egyptian plan to attack Israel, either sooner or later. As the military correspondent of the *Jerusalem Post* reported on 21 November, "there is little hope of finding a definite plan of attack among the items captured in the Gaza Strip." On the contrary, circumstantial evidence such as the thinning out of Egyptian forces in Sinai before the war indicates not only that Egypt planned no attack but also that she did not think Israel was then planning one. But as Dayan confirmed, Israeli forces had been developing offensive positions for a year along the frontier while the Egyptians remained on the defensive.

Another funny coincidence involving Meinertzhagen was his diary entry for 20 July 1956 stating, in terms precisely like those circulated by the British and Israelis after the war, that Sinai contained vast stores of blankets and other equipment in stockpiles that were so far in excess of Egyptian needs that they could only be for future use by a Russian army. Meinertzhagen says this would mean the destruction of Israel, "who surely should attack before an Arab offensive develops."

The actual list of Russian equipment captured by the Israelis was only a fraction of what the impressionistic Israeli statements at the time indicated. Dayan listed only twenty-seven Russian tanks and six SU-100 self-propelled guns in his register of captured booty. There were seventy British and American tanks in his list and sixteen dummy tanks. The quantities of light arms listed in Israel's war booty were about what would have served to equip the number of prisoners Israel captured. Mostly from the Gaza Strip, Sharm al-Sheikh, and the *Ibrahim al-Awwal*, there were nearly 6,000 prisoners. The personal weapons captured included 4,300 rifles, 1,170 sub-machine guns, and 300 revolvers. The portable infantry support weapons included 840 light and medium machine guns, 780 bazookas, antitank rifles, and recoilless guns, and 220 light mortars. The equation between captured weapons and prisoners is circumstantial evidence against two Israeli allegations; that the Egyptians threw their weapons away and ran, and that there were vast surplus stores for a Russian Middle East force.

When Eban called on Dulles after the war Dulles asked: "Now tell me, what did you find there? You have been telling me all year how much stronger the Egyptians were than the Israelis and I was telling you it was not so. Who is right?" Eban conceded that Israel did overestimate Egyptian strength.

The Israelis also contributed mightily to the wave of rumors after the war about *coup d'états* and Russian arms and influence in Syria. Israeli broadcasts to this effect were cited fully by Western news agencies. The point Israel was promoting was that Washington should keep Israel stronger than the undependable Communist-leaning Arabs around her and let her keep her Egyptian conquests.

I went to Israel in November and found the people so exhilarated by victory and determined to keep their gains that I doubted anything would budge them. Gaza in particular had been incorporated into Israel's postal, banking, and communications systems. Tourists flocked there in a steady stream of buses and cars to see that part of their new empire and to buy such exotic items as matches made in the USSR and boxes labeled "Toffee Gamal" which had a few pieces of candy rattling around inside and a chromo of Nasser on the cover. The Americans at the Baptist Hospital in Gaza, whose wards were full of children wounded during the quick-triggered Israeli search for arms and *Fedayeen*, roundly condemned the Israelis for careless or deliberate brutality. The Israelis said the children were regrettable but normal accidents of war. My Egyptian and Palestinian acquaintances in Gaza were wholly opposed to Israeli rule but felt no certainty that it would be removed.

Gaza and Aqaba were the areas to which Ben-Gurion was most stubbornly attached. He resigned himself fairly early to relinquishing the Sinai but Gaza, part of the inheritance of the tribe of Judah, and Tiran, where Jews of old maintained the tiny state of Yotvat, were more clearly associated with Israel's stated war aims, which included the elimination of the *Fedayeen* and the opening of the Gulf of Aqaba. If Ben-Gurion could have fulfilled his dream of restoring Yotvat to the Third Israeli Empire it would have brought the straits within Israel's territorial waters and freed Israel's shipping there from dependence on the presence of UNEF.

On 3 December, the day Lloyd announced the Anglo-French withdrawal, Israel drew back thirty miles from the Canal. By 7 January she had withdrawn from half the Sinai, systematically destroying telephone and telegraph lines and breaking up the railroad and asphalted roads behind her with an ingenious giant plow-like device. In despite of protests by Hammarskjold that this devastation violated Israel's promise to help UNEF maintain the peace, the Israelis destroyed the many military buildings in al-Arish and razed to the ground every single building in the hapless villages of Qussaima and Abu Aoueigila. It took Egypt and the UNEF several years to restore the roads. By 22 January Israel had withdrawn to the frontier except before Rafah and along the coast of the Gulf of Aqaba.

Ben-Gurion then set his heels to resist further withdrawal. On 23 January he declared his resistance to an applauding Knesset and a disapproving UN. He told both that Israel must remain in the Gaza Strip and that she would hold the Aqaba coast until her freedom in the gulf received ironclad guarantees.

"The Israel administration in Gaza will be a pilot plant of Israel-Arab cooperation in contact with the United Nations," Ben-Gurion said to the Knesset. An Israeli *aide mémoire* to Hammarskjold paralleling his speech said "the entry of UNEF into the Gaza area is not envisaged" in Israel's plans but that Israel was ready to negotiate a "suitable relationship" with the UN on Gaza. Israel did not want to accept all the Gaza Strip refugees, however, and the Knesset resolved that, while "Israel shall keep the Gaza Strip," the UN would make a plan for the refugees, including those in Gaza. The resolution also: vowed to hold the Aqaba straits until free navigation was assured "by real guarantees made with Israel's consent," demanded the demilitarization of the Sinai, and stipulated that any Suez Canal solution must guarantee freedom of transit for Israel.

Ben-Gurion said Gaza had never belonged to Egypt but that Egypt had "held it for eight years as a reward for her invasion of this country" without ever doing a thing to develop it. The promise of more efficient exploitation always buttressed Israel's territorial claims. Ben-Gurion denounced the UN for a softness toward the Arabs and a toughness toward Israel over Sinai that was "nothing but a caricature" of justice. He quoted from a letter he wrote to

Supreme Court Justice Louis D. Brandeis on 4 June 1935 predicting that Britain would leave Egypt and that Haifa-Elath would be the only alternative to the inadequate and easily-blocked Suez route to India.

Ben-Gurion said Israel was ready to sign a non-belligerency and non-aggression pact with Egypt but that the Armistice Agreement, "violated and broken, is beyond repair." Israel's *aide mémoire* said in effect that the Security Council resolution of 1 September 1951 on freedom of transit through the Suez "has legal and chronological precedence" over the withdrawal resolutions.

Hammarskjold embodied his reply in a report to the General Assembly the next day, saying that the Armistice Agreement was tantamount to a non-aggression pact and needed only full compliance in order to be effective. The 1951 Suez resolution, he said, was based upon and drew its validity from an intact Armistice Agreement. He emphasized the importance of implementing the Armistice Agreement's provision for the demilitarization of al-Auja and suggested that at least there the UNEF should be stationed on Israel's as well as Egypt's side of the truce line. Regarding Israel's assertion of intent to keep Gaza, Hammarskjold said the UN "cannot condone a change in the *status juris* resulting from military action contrary to the provisions of the Charter," that UNEF must not influence political conflicts, that the Armistice provisions could be changed only by agreement, and that "these considerations exclude the United Nations from accepting Israel control over the area."

Ben-Gurion wrote in his memoirs that "the controversy in which Israel was engaged at that time was not only with the Soviet Union but with the entire United Nations Organization, and in the first place with the Government of the United States." It was true, for behind the complex and tedious wrangling that was visible to the public, the Eisenhower Administration was trying to screw its courage up to use sanctions or the threat of them to compel Israel's compliance with the UN resolutions.

On 2 February the General Assembly passed its sixth resolution demanding Israel's immediate withdrawal and another resolution calling for restoration of the Armistice and the stationing of UNEF troops on the armistice line. Despite a cable from Eisenhower warning that continued defiance of the UN "could seriously disturb the relations between Israel and other member nations including the United States," Ben-Gurion and his Cabinet rejected the Assembly's demands the next day. As if to register the stubbornness of Israel's resistance, the Foreign Ministry disclosed that week that the anticipated losses in US aid had led to a projected reduction in Israel's budget from £I 850 million to £I 750 million to be accompanied by economy layoffs of 2,500 civil servants. The Israel pound was valued at £I 1.80 to the dollar. The ministry said Israel would lose an expected grant-in-aid of $25 million, agricultural surpluses worth $30 million, and an Export-Import Bank loan of $75 million. Israel's standard of living would be reduced but she seemed prepared to accept this.

Ben-Gurion was trying to stir up sympathetic lobbying and aid from the American Jewish community as well as to disarm in advance any threat of sanctions. Mass meetings all over Israel were called on 9 February to demonstrate the nation's refusal to relinquish its demands even under duress. The demonstrators pilloried Hammarskjold as an Arab-lover, an epithet in Zionist circles which came to bear an ugly kinship to the American racist's "Nigger-lover."

On 11 February Dulles handed Eban an *aide mémoire* which Israel later accepted as the basic document assuring her requirements for withdrawal. Regarding Gaza, the *aide mémoire* said the UN had no authority to require of either Egypt or Israel a substantial modification of the Armistice Agreement and that: "Accordingly, we believe that Israeli withdrawal from Gaza should be prompt and unconditional . . . " It continued:

With respect to the Gulf of Aqaba and access thereto—the United States believes that the Gulf comprehends international waters and that no nation has the right to prevent free and innocent passage in the Gulf and through the Straits giving access thereto. . . . In the absence of some overriding decision to the contrary, as by the International Court of Justice, the United States, on behalf of vessels of United States registry, is prepared to exercise the right of free and innocent passage and to join with others to secure general recognition of this right.

Ben-Gurion was not yet ready to give in. In a very long secret *aide mémoire* on 15 February Israel retorted bluntly that "there is no basis for the restoration of the *status quo ante* in Gaza . . . " Stating that Israel's stand was influenced by her own security, by the economic welfare of the regular residents of the Strip, and by the problem of the refugees, the *aide mémoire* said Israel was prepared to make a "supreme effort" to alleviate Gaza's poverty and to contribute to a UN program for settling the refugees "both in the payment of compensation and in the settlement of a part of the refugee population of Gaza." Without stating numbers or suggesting where the compensated refugees were to go, Israel invited the US to join her in working out a plan for submission to the UN.

As for Aqaba, Israel supported the replacement of her troops by UNEF provided the UNEF troops would stay there until a peace treaty was agreed with Egypt or permanent arrangements for free navigation were secured. Israel went so far as to envisage settling for "a precise guarantee . . . for the specific protection of Israel-bound shipping" through the straits. Admitting that "no context of withdrawal arises in the case of the Suez Canal," the *aide mémoire* said nevertheless that "it is inconceivable that the Suez Canal can be opened by the United Nations and remain closed to any of its member states."

By now Eisenhower and Dulles were being forced toward taking a stand on sanctions whether they wanted to or not. Majority sentiment for sanctions to compel Israel to withdraw was developing in the UN with the support of the Arabs and the rest of the Afro-Asian Bloc together with the Communist Bloc. If it came to a vote the US would have to make the public choice of whether or not to join the majority or stand out against it as the special champion of Israel right or wrong. Upon receipt of Israel's *aide mémoire*, Dulles and Lodge flew to confer with Eisenhower at the Thomasville, Georgia, plantation of Treasury Secretary Humphrey.

They debated the issue for an hour and a half on Saturday morning, 16 February. As Eisenhower described the talk: Lodge said the issue of sanctions was sure to reach the debating floor at the UN in the coming week. Dulles said the US had reached the limit in efforts to make it easy for Israel to withdraw. Anything more, he said, would endanger Western influence by convincing Middle Easterners that "United States policy toward the area was, in the last analysis, controlled by Jewish influence in the United States." This would drive the Arabs to see Russia as their only hope. And it would wreck the Eisenhower Doctrine before it started. Lodge said the result might well be renewed war.

Eisenhower rejected the idea of a resolution merely suspending governmental aid. US governmental aid to both Israel and Egypt was already suspended. "I preferred a resolution which would call on all United Nations members to suspend not just governmental but *private* assistance to Israel," Eisenhower wrote. Humphrey called the Treasury and got an estimate that American private gifts to Israel totaled $40 million annually and sales of Israel bonds totaled $50 to $60 million. The unique income tax deductibility accorded to Zionist fund raising in the US had enabled the Treasury to compile the figures from tax return statistics.

As Sherman Adams phrased it in his memoirs, the three cabinet ministers "decided with the President that the White House had to make a stand against Congress and against Israel." Lyndon Johnson led the pro-Israel bloc among Democratic senators, Adams wrote, while William F. Knowland, the Senate Republican leader, threatened to resign from the US delegation to the UN General Assembly if sanctions were applied to Israel. Eisenhower cut short his quail-shooting vacation and invited Congressional leaders to discuss the issue with him early on 20 February. Some of them were "more than a little nervous," he wrote. Adams said the meeting was "tense and strained." Toleration of Israel's defiance of the UN, Eisenhower said, would not only raise Russian influence among the Arabs but also, by preventing a restoration of Middle East oil production, would further hurt Britain and Western Europe. He reminded the legislators that the US had applied sanctions against Britain and France by withholding oil from them for the very same purpose of obtaining their withdrawal from Egypt. Dulles added that the US was not adopting an anti-Israel policy but that it was determined to oppose Israel's defiance of the UN.

Johnson had already written Dulles a letter opposing sanctions which had leaked to a New York newspaper. Both he and Knowland argued that since there was no talk of sanctions against Russia over Hungary, the application of sanctions to Israel would mean adopting one standard for the weak and another for the strong. Lodge explained as a diplomatic fact of life that the UN would never try to impose sanctions on either Russia or the US. "It became obvious that the Congressional leaders were too conscious of the unpopularity of the stand that the President was being forced to take against Israel to be willing to share with him the responsibility for it," Adams wrote. Senator Russell ended the discussion, Adams said, "by saying . . . the President should simply shoulder the burden alone." Lyndon Johnson hastened to tell the reporters outside that his views were unchanged.

Eisenhower sent a cable of courteous warning to Ben-Gurion and prepared to make a television speech on the issue that night. In his text he avoided the word "sanctions" in favor of the word "pressure." In his television broadcast Eisenhower said:

> Should a nation which attacks and occupies foreign territory in the face of United Nations disapproval be allowed to impose conditions on its own withdrawal? If we agree that armed attack can properly achieve the purpose of the assailant, then I fear we will have turned back the clock of international order. . . .
>
> If the United Nations once admits that international disputes can be settled by using force, then we will have destroyed the very foundation of the organization and our best hope of establishing a world order. That would be a disaster for us all. . . . The United Nations must not fail. I believe that in the interests of peace the United Nations has no choice but to exert pressure upon Israel to comply with the withdrawal resolutions.

Ben-Gurion's retort in the Knesset the following day was like a squeal of rage. "Every attempt to impose on us perverted justice and a regime of discrimination will encounter unshrinking opposition from the Israeli people," he said. "It is well known that the Gaza Strip has never been Egyptian territory.

Its life and economy will always be bound to Israel. . . . No matter what may happen, Israel will not submit to the restoration of the *status quo* in the Strip. . . . [In the Gulf of Aqaba] Egypt will again interfere with Israel's navigation as she openly proclaims her intention to do. The fact that American and other ships will be passing through the straits does not in the slightest degree detract from this danger." Appealing over the heads of the Eisenhower Administration, Ben-Gurion said "our opposition to any injurious proposals by the American Government cannot weaken in any manner our feelings of appreciation of and friendship for the American people." Ben-Gurion did not mention this violent diatribe in his memoirs of Suez. He was shortly obliged to accept what he vowed to refuse.

The day after Ben-Gurion spoke Lebanon, Iraq, the Sudan, Pakistan, Afghanistan, and Indonesia introduced a resolution demanding an end to all aid to Israel if she did not comply with the withdrawal resolutions. As it moved day by day toward a vote, there were intensive negotiations and much writing of memorandums and *aides mémoires*. Hammarskjold assured Israel in a memorandum on 26 February that the Advisory Committee on UNEF would be informed before any withdrawal of UNEF from the Strait of Tiran. But he refused to countenance Israel's insistence that Egypt be kept out of the Gaza Strip.

With the threat of sanctions becoming ever harder, Ben-Gurion gave in in time to prevent the sanctions resolution from being brought to a vote. He ordered Golda Meir to announce in the UN on 1 March Israel's "plans for full and prompt withdrawal from the Sharm al-Sheikh area and the Gaza Strip." She was to add certain face-saving interpretations. One was that "the takeover of Gaza from the military and civilian control of Israel will be exclusively by the United Nations Emergency Force" and that "if conditions are created in the Gaza Strip which indicate a return to the conditions of deterioration which existed previously, Israel would reserve its freedom to act to defend its rights."

Ben-Gurion balked one last time over Lodge's comments on Mrs. Meir's statement. Lodge said the US did "not consider that [Mrs. Meir's] declarations make Israel's withdrawal 'conditional'." He said the future of Gaza remained to be "worked out within the framework of the Armistice Agreement," which contravened Ben-Gurion's denunciation of the Armistice Agreement. Lodge paid tribute to Egypt's "commendable forbearance . . . during these trying weeks."

Lodge also stipulated that UNEF's function in the Aqaba straits "would, of course, be without prejudice to any ultimate determination which may be made of any legal questions concerning the Gulf of Aqaba." Lodge emphasized the Administration's often-repeated suggestion that the status of rival claims in the Gulf of Aqaba should be determined by the World Court. He said "these views are to be understood in the sense of the relevant portions of the report" of the UN International Law Commission's formulations on the law of the sea in the spring and summer of 1956. It was a particularly interesting remark because those formulations consciously avoided encompassing the Strait of Tiran. And Israel persistently avoided submitting to the World Court the legalities of her cases in both the Gulf of Aqaba and the Suez Canal.

Ben-Gurion called his Cabinet into emergency session the next day and ordered Dayan to break an appointment with Burns on the final withdrawal arrangements. Eisenhower's cable of gratification over the withdrawal, expressing the US belief that "Israel will have no cause to regret having thus conformed to the strong sentiment of the world," was somewhat of an embarrassment under the circumstances. Ben-Gurion said in his memoirs that he delayed the withdrawal pending clarification of Lodge's remark about the return to the Armistice Agreement in the Gaza Strip. But he did not tell whether it was some unpublished clarification or a grim warning to keep his word that induced him to set Dayan urgently in motion on the afternoon of 4 March to find Burns, make final arrangements, and get the troops home with all possible haste.

Israeli troops moved out of the Gaza Strip and UNEF moved in on the night of 6 March. A strict curfew was imposed to prevent the inhabitants of Gaza from fetching guns out of hiding to take potshots at the departing Israelis. Some made the attempt, Burns wrote, but were "vigorously repressed." The Israelis were gone by 6 A.M. on 7 March except for a rear guard at Rafah, which departed with its vehicles later in the day.

Wild demonstrations for Nasser broke out in the Strip the next day. By the 10th, when UNEF moved its headquarters to Gaza, the demonstrators had become riotous. Danish and Norwegian UN troops used tear gas and shots in the air to disperse them. A ricochet caused one Arab death. On the 11th, Burns and Ralph Bunche concluded that the popular agitation, under stimulation from Cairo, could get out of hand if Egypt were not restored to at least nominal authority in the Strip. Quite separately, the Egyptian Government in Cairo announced that it had appointed an administrative governor for Gaza and that he would take up his functions immediately. Burns wrote that the announcement came as a shock to himself and most of the United Nations. Munir al-Rais, the former Mayor of Gaza who was imprisoned by the Israelis and released by UNEF, told Burns that day that the people feared the UNEF had come to internationalize the Strip. Burns reassured him that it was not so.

Nasser told me he was impelled to restore Egyptian authority in the Strip in order to discountenance Israeli statements that it would be internationalized and that Egypt would not return. Nasser said there had been no agreement with Hammarskjold to delay Egypt's return and certainly no agreement not to return at all. Eisenhower and others have treated the Egyptian return to Gaza as a violation of an understanding between Nasser and Hammarskjold, but I have found no evidence of such an understanding nor any substantial basis for doubting Nasser's account. Nasser sent no troops back into Gaza until the eve of the 1967 war, only administrators. Nevertheless, Israel raised fears that she regarded the Egyptian re-entry as grounds for reoccupying the Strip. The fears did not die down until after Hammarskjold completed a scheduled visit to Cairo on 21 March to work out detailed terms for the relationship between UNEF and the Egyptian Government and people.

The last Israeli soldiers to leave Egypt were men who had struggled back up the coast with vehicles from Sharm al-Sheikh. They crossed the frontier back into Israel at Ras al-Naqb on 16 March. An Indonesian UNEF contingent, which had been waiting 20 kilometers west of Ras al-Naqb, moved up to the frontier and a decade of peace between wars began. UNEF troops had already taken up their stations at Sharm al-Sheikh, Ras Nasrani, and the island of Tiran. On 18 March they watched the Israeli freighter, *Queen of Sheba*, which had gone up the gulf under Israeli protection, sail out again under their own. Egypt had not renounced her right of blockade; she had simply agreed not to be in position to enforce it for the time being.

Hammarskjold and Nasser worked out an agreement on the main principles and more important controversial points covering UNEF's functions. Further details were elaborated by Burns and the Egyptians in the ensuing weeks. The main problem was how much authority and force the UNEF required to be effective. The provisions were drafted on paper but were adopted merely by oral agreement between Nasser and Hammarskjold. Egypt agreed to prevent border crossing, to reinstate the prewar penalties, and to inform the people that UNEF was empowered to arrest suspected infiltrators within 750 meters (nearly half a mile) of the truce line. Israel adamantly refused UN requests to mark the truce line in keeping with her contention that it, like the Armistice, was "vanished and dead."

The Egyptians disliked allowing the UNEF to shoot at infiltrators but agreed to make it known that the UNEF could fire in self-defense. Although there was no publication of actual incidents, word spread among the people when Danes, Norwegians, and Indonesians shot infiltrators who were trying to rush them. Burns found the restrictions on UNEF's use of arms frustrating. He feared that if the prohibitions against UNEF's using force except in self-defense became known, Israeli troops might assume "they could walk past our posts without interference, [and] in the mood they were in, attempt to do so and re-establish their position in the Gaza Strip." Burns said the Israelis "had been accustomed to pushing UN Military Observers around, and an Emergency Force which couldn't use its weapons would be little more than a corps of observers." But his anxieties never materialized and Israeli patrols that crossed the line, sometimes firing at Arabs from within the Strip, always withdrew when requested by the UNEF troops on the spot. Incidents were fairly frequent until June 1957, Burns recalled, but they "declined to a very low figure thereafter." The *Fedayeen* were reorganized as special police and they continued intelligence work but no violent operations between the wars.

As soon as the last Israeli was back across the border the Egyptian Navy began removing explosives from the frigate *Abu Kir*, which was lying on the bottom of the Canal two miles north of Suez. These explosives were officially cited as the reason for preventing the UN salvage crews from moving the ship out of the channel until the Israelis left. The first convoy to make the Canal passage since 31 October comprised nine freighters small enough to bypass the *Abu Kir*. It made a northbound passage on 29 March.

The *Abu Kir* was removed on 8 April. Two huge submersible lifts sank into the water on either side of the frigate at 1 P.M. When they pumped themselves out and rose up again, the *Abu Kir*, gray-green with slime and barnacles, was cradled between them in a web of steel cables. The ships and small craft in Suez harbor applauded with whistles and horns. The *Abu Kir* was carried to a ship graveyard in the Great Bitter Lake. The Canal was open again to full-sized shipping. The clearing cost $8.4 million. It was financed by a voluntary 3 per cent UN surcharge on shipping paid by the governments of the shipowners.

Egypt issued on 18 March a preliminary statement of policy to the effect that she would continue to respect the letter and spirit of the Convention of 1888 and abide by the same limitations on raising tolls that the Suez Canal Company had agreed upon with Egypt. The statement neither mentioned the Six Principles which Egypt had accepted before the war in October nor made any other reference to a formal relationship with Canal users. In a fuller declaration on 24 April, Egypt again reaffirmed her adherence to the Convention of 1888 and promised to accept the compulsory jurisdiction of the International Court of Justice in questions of interpretation or applicability of the Convention. Egypt completed the legal formalities of accepting the compulsory jurisdiction of the World Court with a declaration to that effect on 18 July. These instruments were deposited and registered with the UN Secretariat.

Egypt let it be known that her prohibitions against Israeli shipping in the

Canal remained in force but that Israel was free to take the case to the International Court. Israel has consistently refused every suggestion that she take her Suez or Gulf of Aqaba complaints to the World Court. She feels that her claims in those two waterways, like her title to Palestine, rest more securely on politics than upon law. Politics is a matter of force and influence. Law depends on precedent, analogy, and logic.

Egypt's asserted right to curb Israeli shipping through the Canal derives from Article X of the 1888 Convention which says that the guarantees of free and open passage provided in earlier articles "shall not interfere with the measures which His Majesty the Sultan and His Highness the Khedive... might find it necessary to take for securing by their own forces the defense of Egypt and the maintenance of public order." Apparent contradictions within the Convention, the effect of the Armistice Agreement, and the validity of the 1 September 1951 Security Council resolution add to the complexity of the legal issues, which are given a fascinating analysis in R. R. Baxter's *The Law of International Waterways*.

The disgorging was complete when the Canal was reopened. It was not Nasser but his assailants who were made to disgorge. A tedious period of settling accounts followed. The settlement between the Suez Canal Company and Egypt was the first to be concluded. On 13 July 1958 Egypt agreed to pay the company, which had by then changed its name to the Suez Financial Company, £E 28.3 million ($81 million) for its assets inside Egypt and to leave all the external assets to the stockholders. The company was greatly relieved by Egypt's abandonment of the claim, asserted in the nationalization decree, to all the company's assets in Egypt and abroad. The claim to the assets abroad could have led to years of legal battles with no certain outcome.

The settlement of claims and counterclaims with Britain and France took longer. Egypt made claims for war damages countering British and French claims on behalf of their nationals for Egyptianized commercial property, sequestrated private property, and pensions for British and French persons retired from Egyptian service. Egypt concluded an agreement with France on 22 August 1958 providing for individual settlement of each claim. These settlements were still being negotiated a decade later. The settlement with Britain, dated 28 February 1959, provided for Egypt to pay a lump sum of £27,500,000 ($77 million) within one year to the British Government, which would distribute settlement payments to individuals. The lump sum had to be spread thin. The assets lost outright by Britons dispossessed or expelled from Egypt were valued by them at £45 million ($126 million) plus an unknown amount of depreciation on assets worth £130 million ($365 million) placed under Egyptian custodianship. Britain had to swallow the loss of her assets in the Suez Canal base and accept Egypt's wartime abrogation of the evacuation treaty, which had given Britain rights in the base for seven more years.

The settlements fell far short of erasing the cruel hardship the war caused to individual Britons and Frenchmen who had made their careers in Egypt and had lost everything. For hundreds of Jews with foreign passports who were roughly expelled there was no compensation at all. Some Jewish families had lived in Egypt with foreign passports for generations and knew no other home, although they had cherished a foreign nationality. No Egyptian citizen was expelled but several thousand Egyptian Jews too felt that the time had come to leave. Israel and Zionism had made their circumstances precarious, as had happened earlier to Jewish communities in other Arab countries. Eden's estimate of the cash cost to Britain of the military preparations and operation was £115 million ($320 million). There were almost incalculable extras such as the higher cost of some imports, the carrying charges on the dollar loans to save sterling, the loss of exports, the cost of oil from the dollar area. A Labor party handbook in 1959 estimated the total at £328 million ($920 million).

For Britain and France, the "vital interests" they had lost by fighting for them turned out to be not so vital after all. When the oil was shut off and the Canal was closed they did not suffer. Although the Russian presence was firmly established on the Middle Eastern scene, the area remained as open as ever to the West. If the savings and careers of many hapless nationals were destroyed by the war, others returned to revive profitable commerce after the restoration, first of trade, and then of diplomatic relations. The Suez Canal Company, far from being mortally wounded by the amputation of the Canal, remained rich and powerful and took a leading role in reviving another Napoleonic dream, the carving out of a tunnel under the English Channel. Nasser survived, which the Eden and Mollet governments feared would shorten their tenures, but the Tories and Mollet stayed on to succumb to other causes. Britain's clients either abandoned her, like King Hussein's Jordan, or were destroyed, like Nuri and the King of Iraq, but Britons hardly noticed. The Baghdad Pact lost not only Baghdad but its vitality without causing visible damage to Britain. Indeed, Suez marked the end of the British Empire without hurting the British.

For the sun did finally set on the British Empire at Suez. Sunset would have come anyway. The dust kicked up by Eden's last imperial fling with Ben-Gurion and Mollet merely made it more lurid than it might have been.

CHAPTER

20

Reprise

(1967–)

What's past is prologue.

(SHAKESPEARE, *The Tempest*)

Those who do not remember the past are condemned to relive it.

(GEORGE SANTAYANA)

It is not absurd to imagine Arab leaders ardently urging a return to the frontier of 1966 or 1967, just as they now urge a return to the frontier of 1947 which they once set aside by force.

(ABBA EBAN 1965)

JERUSALEM, Nov. 11—Premier Levi Eshkol said in Parliament today that the factors that led to the six-day war last year were present in the Middle East again.

(*The New York Times*, 12 November 1968)

And I don't have to tell you that war in the Middle East, far more than war in Vietnam, carries with it the horrible promise of World War III.

(EUGENE BLACK 1968)

WHEN THE disgorging was over in 1957 Ben-Gurion and Nasser both had emerged with clear gains. Nasser had won a respite, which was to last a decade, from the dangerous obligations of Arab policy toward Israel. His acceptance of the shield of UNEF on his territory while Ben-Gurion adamantly refused it is *prima facie* evidence that Egypt was the country more threatened, if any such evidence were needed after the Sinai campaigns of 1948 and 1956 and the years of border raids between. The presence of UNEF excused Nasser from his Arab League obligation to blockade the Aqaba Gulf without his having formally to renounce the blockade. Nasser used his decade of tranquility on the Israeli frontier to carry forward the sweeping development programs based on the High Dam at Aswan.

Military recuperation from Suez and the new political bearings it required Nasser to take delayed the dam. Not for nearly two years did he send General Amer to Moscow to accept Russia's offer to contribute the foreign equipment and technical personnel needed for the project. Khrushchev announced on 23 October 1958 that Russia would loan Egypt 400 million rubles (about $110 million) for the first stage of the dam, repayable in Egyptian products at 2½ per cent interest over twelve years beginning a year after completion of the first stage. The formal agreement was signed 27 December that year, conditional upon Egypt's reaching a new accord with the Sudan on the distribution of the Nile waters. Egypt settled with the Sudan on 8 November 1959.

On 9 January 1960 Nasser detonated a charge of dynamite that blasted 20,000 tons of rock out of what became the new channel of the ancient river, leading it under a mountain wall through six gigantic tunnels where turbines would convert the power of the river into electricity. Khrushchev came to Egypt for the spectacular diversion of the Nile into its new bed on 14 May 1964. The first of the twelve great turbines went into operation on 9 January 1968. The immense rock-fill barrier of the dam was raised to its final height a year later.

Aswan itself grew apace from a sleepy, old-fashioned resort town of about 15,000 souls into a city of 120,000 with a promising industrial future and the tall white and pastel blocks of flats and office buildings that give twentieth-century towns a brash sameness wherever they spring up.

Ben-Gurion admitted that Israel had not attained everything she wanted in the Suez War and her four-month political struggle afterward with the US and the UN. Nor had she in 1948 and 1949. "I do not know of many instances in history when a nation, even a bigger nation, attained everything it wanted through war or political struggle," Ben-Gurion said on 2 April 1957 to a Knesset still grumbling like right-wing British Tories about the surrender of empire. He listed two major gains, one tangible, the other intangible and, as it turned out, erroneously claimed.

The freedom of the Gulf of Aqaba was the tangible gain. The war had served as a matchless publicity campaign for Israel's claim, Ben-Gurion said, for "without the Sinai Campaign . . . a thousand Ebans would not be able to enlighten the world on this subject." In citing the intangible gain, Ben-Gurion revealed that his verbal caricatures of Nasser as Hitler and Pharaoh did not emanate from emotional hostility but rather served a practical aim. He said:

> This campaign diminished the stature of the Egyptian dictator and I do not want you or the entire people to underestimate the importance of this fact. As one of those persons who receive their salaries for looking after our security . . . I always feared that a personality might rise such as arose among the Arab rulers in the seventh century or like him [Kemal Ataturk] who arose in Turkey after its defeat in the first World War. He raised their spirits, changed their character, and turned them into a fighting nation. There was and still is a danger that Nasser is this man.

Ben-Gurion greatly overestimated the effect of the Suez-Sinai defeat on Nasser's stature. Nasser proved to be by far the most durable of all the major figures in the Suez War. Of the others, Eden was the first to fall, on 9 January 1957, and Mollet the second, in June of that year. Pineau went permanently out of office in April 1958. Dulles died in May 1959. Eisenhower came to the end of his term in January 1961. Ben-Gurion himself retired from office, although not from politics, in 1963. The following year saw both Selwyn Lloyd and Khrushchev unhorsed by political turnovers in the fall.

Nasser endured. He accepted the merger of Syria and Egypt into the United Arab Republic in 1958 and survived the breakup of that union in 1961. He moved skillfully through the besetting complications that flowed from the Eisenhower Doctrine, including the US landing of Marines in Lebanon in 1958. He fought openly with Khrushchev in 1959 over Communist subversion in the Arab world without losing the Russian aid on which the High Dam then depended. He became drawn into a bitter war in the Yemen, which Egyptians referred to as "our Vietnam." There were victories as well as defeats. The demise of the Baghdad Pact as a result of the Iraqi revolution of 14 July 1958 was a victory, although Nasser's relations with Nuri's successors were never smooth.

Nasser's greatest achievement in political survival came when, having failed to learn the lessons of the first Suez War, he was forced to relive the defeat on a far greater scale in 1967. It is said that soldiers learn from defeat, not victory. But Nasser and his generals learned less from defeat in 1956 than the Israelis learned from victory. In 1967 the Israelis reused to great effect the successful techniques and tactics of 1956 while discarding and replacing the less successful ones.

From the beginning the Israelis have studied the battles of their ancestors for lessons to be applied today. Among Israel's greatest military leaders are archeologists, notably Yigal Yadin and Moshe Dayan, with a particular interest in the ancient battlefields that may become battlefields tomorrow. Yadin's archeological knowledge enabled him to use an ancient road for a surprise march in Israel's first Sinai campaign in 1948/49. The commanders in 1967 were men who had fought victoriously over that same terrain and marched along those same invasion axes in 1956. Dayan in 1967 knew first-hand what his new generation of soldiers could expect, having marched with their older brothers in 1956, when he used to pause after the battles to pick up potsherds and arrowheads of wars fought before men were able to record them. From the moment Israel realized she would have to withdraw, Sinai was recognized as a campaign that would sooner or later be refought. Plans for the new war were drawn immediately after the old. They were kept up to date by constant improvement.

Brigadier General Mordecai Hod, who directed the aerial assault that broke the Egyptian Air Force in the first three hours of the June 1967 war, was reported by Randolph Churchill and his son Winston to have said that not ten but sixteen years of planning went into that assault. "We lived with the plan, we slept on the plan, we are the plan," Hod said. "Constantly we perfected it." Brigadier General Peter Young, another British historian of the war, discussed the war plan with Brigadier General Ezer Weizman, the Israeli Deputy Chief of Staff, in October 1966. The Israelis had every last detail worked out, Young wrote. Early in the 1967 war he said in a BBC commentary that it looked to him as if "the pattern of 1956 is being followed with an unhistorical repetitiousness."

From Israel's point of view, the 1956 war served as a rehearsal for 1967. The plans for the earlier war were only a year old when they were tested in action. Long before 1967 they had matured to near perfection and, as in 1956, required only favorable circumstances and a political decision to be put into action.

In 1966 as in 1955, Israel was beset by economic troubles. The dominant party in the governing coalition was still the Mapai. But it was torn by factions. Ben-Gurion himself, the party's founder, had broken with Eshkol in 1965 and formed the splinter party, Rafi, taking with him popular figures like Dayan and threatening Mapai's electoral prospects. By the spring of 1967 immigration had fallen to zero net. As a result of a planned economic slowdown aimed at curbing inflation, more than 10 per cent of the labor force was unemployed by the end of 1966. In March 1967 job seekers rioted in Tel Aviv and stoned City Hall.

Such circumstances tend to encourage diversionary adventures on the part of governments. These are not necessarily cynical. Policies are made by men, and when tempers are shortened risks are lengthened. Part of Ben-Gurion's political legacy was his belief that any attention-getting activity, even if it put Israel in a bad light, was preferable to being ignored. Violence served to bring Israel's problems to world attention and to stimulate Jewish support for Israel's needs and aims even when Jews criticized Israel's conduct.

Just as the Suez War of 1956 had its origins in the Gaza Raid of 1955, so the Suez War of 1967 resulted from a chain of reactions and counterreactions that began with an Israeli raid on 13 November 1966, which demolished the Jordanian village of al-Samu. Eighteen Jordanians died at al-Samu and 134 were wounded. Like the Gaza Raid, al-Samu had no convincing justification. The Israelis said it was a reprisal for acts not by Jordanian but by Syrian marauders on the grounds that al-Samu had harbored them. Like Gaza, the al-Samu raid escalated the vigor of such attacks to a new level, being the first reprisal carried out in full daylight and the first in which tanks and aircraft took part throughout.

The Security Council censured Israel on 25 November in the strongest language it had used in ten years, saying such reprisals "cannot be tolerated" and warning of "further and more effective steps." It had no more effect on events than the series of similar Security Council censures in 1955 and 1956.

At the time, it appeared that Israel had retaliated against Jordan instead of the real offender because of the risk that an attack on Syria might activate the new Egyptian-Syrian defense alliance and thereby start a war which might bring the Russians in. The Egyptian-Syrian alliance, signed on 4 November, provided that an attack upon either state would be regarded as an attack on the other. Later the Arabs speculated that Israel actually intended to drive Jordan into the Syrian-Egyptian alliance in order to recreate one of the major pretexts used for the 1956 war, the "ring of steel."

Israel had always based her arms policy on maintaining the capability of defeating all the Arab armies at the same time, being ever haunted by the possibility that the evolutions of inter-Arab politics might suddenly coalesce in real unity. Ben-Gurion told the Knesset after the first Suez War:

> Since I became responsible for security, I adopted two rules . . . one of these rules is positive and the other negative. The positive rule is that the Israel Defense Forces must be strong enough to win even if we have to fight all the Arab armies. The

negative rule is never to involve the Israel Defense Forces in a war against European, American, British, or Russian forces.

Ben-Gurion had been responsible for security since he ran the Haganah in Mandate days. When Israel proclaimed her existence in 1948 he became Defense Minister as well as Prime Minister. The two portfolios went together until the eve of the 1967 war except during Sharett's premiership, when first Lavon and then Ben-Gurion was Defense Minister.

Israel never lost military superiority over the Arabs, although she often claimed to have lost it in arguments supporting her recurrent quests for arms. Washington and London repeatedly stated during the whole period between the Gaza Raid and the first Suez War that Israel was more than a match for the Arabs militarily. Likewise, on 24 May 1967, less than two weeks before the second Suez War, *The New York Times* said: "Western intelligence estimates are that Israel's armed forces hold military superiority over Egypt and are the equal of any conceivable combination of Arab armies."

Israel demonstrated her contempt for the Egyptian-Syrian defense alliance on 7 April 1967 when Israeli jets chased Syrian Migs all the way to Damascus, shooting down six of them on the way. The Israeli Air Force commander, Colonel Mordecai Hod, was promoted to Brigadier General as a "mark of esteem." There was no lack of provocation for these reprisals. Arab guerrilla organizations were becoming bolder, particularly those based in Syria, and Arab governments were finding it increasingly unpopular to restrain them.

Nevertheless, Ambassador Charles W. Yost of the American UN delegation raised the suggestion in the January 1968 issue of *Foreign Affairs* that Israel had artfully contrived the crisis that gave grounds for her attack on Egypt. "It is difficult to see," he wrote, "how any Israeli leader could have failed to foresee that such repeated massive reprisals must eventually place the leader of the Arab coalition in a position where he would have to respond." There is circumstantial evidence that Israel did seek, in 1967 as she had done in 1956, to create a situation favorable for war, particularly in the chronology of Israeli actions which provoked foreseeable Arab reactions. Certainly her territorial objectives, as part and parcel of her war plans, were adopted long before the crisis.

At the same time there were apparently genuine Israeli endeavors to arrest the march of events toward war, among them her efforts in mid-May to reassure Russia and Egypt that she had not mobilized forces on her Syrian frontier. It is a matter of record that Israel did not begin mobilizing overtly in 1967 until several days after Egypt had done so. It is equally verifiable that Arab threats against Israel, although emptier than Israeli threats against Arabs, became more offensively extravagant as the month of May passed. Newspaper pictures of Arab leaders confidently laughing and smiling added to the impression that they were gleefully ganging up for the kill. The pictures did not reveal that Nasser, for one, was merely putting a bold face over his fears in the vain hope of scaring Israel off.

Once Israel mobilized war became virtually certain unless the Arabs could manage to demobilize and eliminate the war provocations arising from their reactions to the Israeli reprisals and threats. Israel's economy cannot support a protracted state of mobilization but the Government could not risk demobilization until the Arab threat was ended, even if this had to be done by war. By the time this dilemma materialized Israel was as much a prisoner of events as Egypt. The question is: Did her leaders or a faction within the Government or Army consciously maneuver her into this dilemma?

Unlike the secrets shared in collusion in 1956, the secrets of the second Suez-Sinai war are Israel's alone, it seems, and it may never be proven to the world's satisfaction whether she did or did not contrive the second war in order to secure the prizes of which she had been balked after the first. Yost himself took the position that no one really wanted war in 1967 but that leaders on both sides blundered into it under the pressure of political imperatives.

Nasser, in particular, was taunted by Syria and Jordan for hiding behind the skirts of the UNEF. UNEF had kept the Egyptian-Israeli border quiet for ten years by virtually eliminating Arab infiltration and barring Israeli reactions to what little occurred. No *Fedayeen* nor any members of the Palestinian guerrilla groups on the far side of Israel operated through UNEF lines from Egyptian-controlled territory.

Nasser extended Egyptian hospitality, however, to Ahmed Shuqairy, an orotund Palestinian refugee who had made his living as a kind of itinerant diplomat for several Arab governments as well as for the Arab League and who had got himself recognized as chairman of the Palestine Liberation Organization. Shuqairy's pronunciamentos about what the Palestine Liberation Army would do to Israel and to King Hussein, whom he accused of being soft on Israel, and about how he was arming his "troops" from Red China were merely a continuation of a twenty-year career of big talk whose greatest effect was to intoxicate Shuqairy himself. The result was to conjure up a mirage of ferocity over the tranquillity on the Israeli-Egyptian border and to create a fearsome public image of Shuqairy, who is really a family man as kindly and avuncular as he is wordy.

By mid-May Israel's threats and raids against Syria and Jordan had alarmed the Middle East and the world at large as much as the "red herring" campaign against Jordan in 1956 had done. It had focused attention again on that part of Israel's frontier and it was creating the same kind of pressure for an Egyptian-Syrian-Jordanian alliance that the attacks on Jordan achieved in September and October 1956. Premier Levi Eshkol, Foreign Minister Eban, and Major General Itzhak Rabin, the Israeli Chief of Staff, made extraordinary public threats. General Rabin threatened to send a force to Damascus to overthrow the Syrian Government. Premier Eshkol stated in interviews that Israel was prepared to use force against Syria. Eban warned that the Syrians had "filled their quota" of violence and that retribution was at hand.

Then on 13 May Nasser received what he called "accurate information," which he later attributed to aerial photographs, that Israel was concentrating eleven to thirteen brigades opposite the Syrian frontier. The Knesset Foreign Affairs and Security Committee was reported to have endorsed on 9 May armed action against Syria. Thoroughly alarmed, Nasser ordered reinforcements into the Sinai on 14 May. He was bound by treaty to attack Israel if Israel attacked Syria.

UNEF still stood along Egypt's eastern frontier. If Egypt should have to help Syria, Nasser would have to ask the UNEF to stand aside if he were not to attack through and over them. In order to avoid the risk of either impediment to Egyptian troops or injury to the UNEF in a war emergency, Nasser requested their withdrawal on 16 May, the day his reinforcements reached the frontier. He praised UNEF for having "honorably and faithfully carried out its duties," but he insisted on its rapid withdrawal and sent Egyptian units into some frontier posts before the UNEF troops had withdrawn. Israel, having refused for ten years to allow UNEF forces on her side of the line, refused once again to allow any of them to shift their buffer function to the Israeli side. She refused even to let them withdraw through her territory.

The prompt withdrawal of UNEF brought down a storm of criticism on the head of U Thant, Dag Hammarskjold's successor as Secretary General of the UN. Most of the criticism was ignorant; much of it was intemperate; some of it was cynical propaganda. UNEF entered Egypt in November 1956 on the explicit condition, approved by the UN General Assembly and accepted by agreement between Hammarskjold and Nasser, that the force could not "be stationed or operate on the territory of a given country without the consent of the Government of that country." The interlocking resolutions, reports, and *aide-mémoires* governing UNEF nowhere abridged the stipulation that it was in Egypt by Egypt's consent and that it would have to withdraw when Egypt's consent was withdrawn.

Even if it had not been solemnized in international instruments, Egypt's consent would have been decisive for more elemental reasons. UNEF had only

1,800 men available to police nearly three hundred r.iles of land and sea frontier. They had only light arms and were under orders to fire only as a last resort in self-defense. They could not dream of staying in the face of Egyptian displeasure. The clamorous Western opposition to their withdrawal, moreover, touched Egyptian sensitivities about foreign occupation. "We felt," Nasser said on 22 May, "that there were attempts to turn UNEF into a force serving neo-imperialism." If the UN had tried to keep UNEF in Sinai it would have seen participating Governments such as India and Yugoslavia withdraw their contingents.

Israel denounced the hastiness of the withdrawal but she herself soon showed that it had not been hasty enough. Israeli gunners shelled UN headquarters in the attack on Gaza, killing 14 and wounding 24 Indian UNEF troops. Israeli soldiers had three UNEF Swedes in front of a firing squad when an officer stopped the execution. After the fighting, Israeli troops persistently looted UNEF stores and property.

There was controversy too over whether Nasser wanted UNEF to remain in the Strait of Tiran while withdrawing from the Gaza Strip and the Sinai frontier. Anthony Nutting says Nasser told him in Cairo on 3 June 1967 that he had requested UNEF to withdraw in order to make effective his deterrent threat against an Israeli attack on Syria but that he had not expected UNEF to pull out of Sharm al-Sheikh and the islands guarding the straits. He told Nutting he did not want them to leave the straits but that he could not insist that they remain there while pulling out elsewhere to suit his convenience.

With UNEF gone, Nasser was once again face to face with his obligation, never renounced, to blockade the Gulf of Aqaba against Israel. His excuse for inaction departed with the UNEF forces from Sharm al-Sheikh. And their departure opened the possibility that Israel might occupy the vacant islands of Tiran and Sanafir in the throat of the straits if Egypt did not get there first. Egyptian troops took up the positions they had manned in October 1956. Nasser, emphasizing the legal basis of Egypt's action, announced on 22 May 1967 the reimposition of the Aqaba blockade. This had been for Israel the key issue in the first Suez War and she warned in 1967 that it was still an automatic *casus belli*.

James Reston reported from Cairo to *The New York Times* on the eve of Israel's attack: "Cairo does not want war and it is certainly not ready for war." Nasser had been led willy-nilly into his predicament by a concatenation of political imperatives that could not have been set in train by anything other than Israel's extraordinary public threats against Syria. A direct threat to Egypt would have required Nasser only to strengthen his positions behind the line of UNEF troops on the frontier and wait to see if Israel would dare so great an affront to world opinion as an attack on that blue line would mean. But the explicit Israeli threat to Syria forced Nasser either to respond with a counterthreat to Israel or to admit that his alliances were worthless scraps of paper. A military threat to Israel required removal of the interposed UN Emergency Force. And the removal of the UN Emergency Force forced Nasser to reoccupy the Strait of Tiran or risk letting Israel take the islands. Occupying the Strait forced Nasser to reimpose the blockade or admit, as Syria and Jordan mockingly charged, that he was too much afraid of Israel to fulfill his Arab responsibilities.

If Israel had intended to maneuver Egypt into position to be attacked she could not have done it more effectively. Regardless of the legalisms at issue in the Gulf of Aqaba—and Egypt has a strong juridical position—Israel had put Egypt in the position of having revived what the Western maritime nations had conceded for ten years to be a *casus belli*. Surely Israel's skilled diplomatists saw in advance the virtually automatic path Nasser would have to follow to that politically vulnerable position once he was set in motion by their threat to Syria. The threat to Syria following an Egyptian-Syrian alliance had to be taken seriously because there had been a clear precedent in Ben-Gurion's raid into Syria on the night of 11 December 1955 following the Egyptian-Syrian alliance of that year. Another old source of Syrian-Israeli friction that was revived in 1967 was the unflagging Israeli encroachment into the demilitarized zones and Israel's harassment and expulsion of the Arab villagers in the zones.

The Aqaba dispute in 1967 evoked a curious echo of 1956 when Washington sought to organize a Gulf of Aqaba users association to exercise the right of innocent passage through the straits. The effort was less successful than Dulles's Suez Canal Users Association. In 1967 it was the US that was prepared to shoot its way through. Britain, France, and at least a dozen other maritime nations that were invited to join begged off with polite excuses. Eshkol said the US had told Israel that forty or fifty nations would join.

Washington's attitude in 1967 was markedly different from 1956 not only on Aqaba but in every respect. Instead of sailing to Alexandria to evacuate Americans, the Sixth Fleet moved to within striking distance of Egypt as the war approached to ensure the preservation of Israel whatever happened. US intelligence was satisfied that Israel would quickly defeat the Arabs in any conflict. But Washington ensured that no Russians would intervene to tilt the balance the other way. Even without Russian intervention, Richard Rovere reported in the *New Yorker* after the war, the US would have intervened on behalf of Israel if the war had dragged on to a point where the outcome was in doubt.

Early in the crisis, on 23 May, the Kremlin stated that any aggression in the Middle East "would be met not only with the united strength of the Arab countries but also with strong opposition to aggression from the Soviet Union." But four days later the Russians were worried enough to have their ambassador wake Nasser at 3:30 A.M. to urge Egypt not to be the first to open fire. A message of similar import but different manner came from President Johnson, who warned Nasser that if Egypt was the first to open fire she would face serious consequences. Nasser, increasingly fearful of an Israeli attack, promised Washington in reply that Egypt would make no move against Israel if Israel refrained from attacking. He gave a similar assurance that Egypt "would not initiate offensive action against Israel" to U Thant, who visited Cairo from 23 to 25 May.

On 26 May Nasser disclosed his promise to Egyptians in a speech. Egypt would not start a war, he said, but if Israel began hostilities, "the battle against Israel will be a general one and our aim will be the destruction of the State of Israel." Western and Israeli newspapers bannered Nasser's statement about the elimination of the State of Israel but they scanted the essential fact that Nasser's deterrent warning was predicated on Israel starting the war, not Egypt. By contrast, a deterrent statement by the US State Department of graver import to the world—that the US would "retaliate with everything it has" if Red China intervened in Vietnam—was given less prominence on 24 May and was promptly forgotten. The sensational half of Nasser's statement became a permanent part of the standard propaganda against him. Even in its full context it was by far the strongest statement Nasser had ever made against Israel.

The Israeli reaction was conditioned by years of Arab propaganda and their own, which had long since put Nasser and the Arabs in the place of Hitler and the Nazis as the folk-enemies of the Jews. "It is no wonder that the first part of the phrase was overlooked, or that it seemed an irrelevant decoration," wrote Uri Avnery, an Israeli journalist and Member of the Knesset, in his book, *Israel Without Zionists*. "What came through was a direct threat to destroy the State of Israel, the annihilation of every single man, woman, and child."

Avnery too believes that both Nasser and the Israeli Government blundered into a war neither of them wanted. A sharp critic of Zionist dynamism and racism and an advocate of compromise and reconciliation with the Arabs, Avnery says Israel was indeed preparing in May to attack Syria, but with the sole motive of putting an end to terrorist incursions. He believes Nasser tried to deter Israel from war but says his every step alarmed Israelis and, far from deterring them, made them readier to fight. If Israel had submitted to the Aqaba blockade, he wrote, "the credibility of the Israeli military deterrent would be shattered—quite apart from the economic consequences of the blockade." Nasser's false announcement that Egypt had mined the straits, Avnery says, was aimed at averting war by deterring Israeli ships from forcing a passage. On the contrary, it helped persuade all Israelis that the sooner they went to war the better. The same was true of the alliances concluded among Egypt, Jordan, and Iraq in the week before the war and also of the propaganda that the Palestinian refugees would soon be able to go home.

Nasser told Egyptians the month after the war that Egypt had never considered attacking Israel because of fears of American intervention. He said Washington knew in advance of Israel's plans and had deceived Egypt until the war began into believing a non-military solution was in prospect. On 3 June, at Johnson's invitation, Nasser agreed to send one of his vice presidents to Washington to discuss the crisis. Nasser named Zakaria Mohyeddeen, known for his moderation and Western affinities. Mohyeddeen was scheduled to reach Washington on 7 June. He never made the trip because Israel attacked on the 5th.

On 29 May Nasser reaffirmed for 1967 a crucial policy of 1956. To correspondents at a nighttime news conference he promised that even if the US Sixth Fleet came to Israel's aid in her present confrontation with the Arabs he would not request intervention by the Soviet Union. He explained painstakingly the "legality and legitimacy" of his request for UNEF to withdraw and of his Aqaba blockade. He welcomed U Thant's proposal to revive the Mixed Armistice Commission with Israel, which Israel refused, and he asked: "What have we done to provoke the United States to take sides with Israel?"

Johnson had been firmly in Israel's camp since his days in Congress and had opposed Eisenhower during the 1956 Suez War. In 1967 he directed US policy to be unabashedly pro-Israel. The difference in policy reflected the difference in the political philosophies of the two presidents. Eisenhower, who was fundamentally a nonpolitician, preferred the upholding of principle to the exercise of power. Johnson, like Kennedy before him, brought to the White House a professional's delight in the exercise of power, sometimes at the expense of such cardinal principles as truth, justice, and peace. The urban Jewish vote meant power in America and Israel's fighting forces meant power in the Middle East.

With regard to the Aqaba question, for example, Eisenhower and Dulles repeatedly said they would support any move to take the issue to the World

Court. It was in keeping with the endeavors of both men to promote world law. When the Aqaba issue revived in 1967, Senator Fulbright was the only prominent figure in Washington to advocate placing it before the World Court. By contrast, Johnson bluntly warned Nasser that he considered the blockade an act of aggression against which the US might ultimately use force. He disclosed the warning to the press during the urgent peace-seeking visit to Cairo by UN Secretary General U Thant, a reckless act of diplomatic discourtesy that could only make it more difficult for Nasser to crawl back off the limb he had got himself out on.

During the war, Johnson deliberately delayed applying effective US pressure for a cease-fire until Israel had completed her conquests on all three Arab fronts. After the war the US canceled aid agreements with the defeated Egyptians while favoring a massive private aid campaign to help victorious Israel's economy recover from the war and, in consequence, finance the occupation of Arab land. The US encouraged as well a movement of nonmilitary US volunteers to fill the gaps in the home front caused by Israel's mobilization. As for the Tripartite Declaration, Johnson paid lip service to the American commitment to the territorial integrity of all Middle Eastern nations but he took no effective action before or after the war to implement the pledge. When, a year after the war, there seemed to be a possibility that Russia's rearming of the Arabs might bring them to a par with Israel in equipment, the US joined the arms race on Israel's side.

Between 1956 and 1967 the US had shifted from impartiality to support for Israel. France had shifted from support for Israel to impartiality. This led Zionists to accuse General de Gaulle of anti-Semitism and Nasser to hail him as "one of the greatest men of our century." Britain was not a factor in the 1967 war, having hardly an outpost left anywhere in the Arab world. Russia was the only great power to remain constant in both Suez wars but she was more reserved and cautious in her support of Egypt the second time despite her freedom from such problems as Hungary. The configuration of Great Power attitudes was more favorable for Israel in 1967 than in 1956, however, because the might of the US was standing by to underwrite her new gamble against Nasser. And if Egypt was not again handicapped by having to guard against an Anglo-French invasion, Nasser's forces were nevertheless spread thin by the demands of the war he was fighting in the Yemen.

Another of the 1956 factors fell into place on 30 May when Nasser and King Hussein signed a five-year defense alliance which, like the alliance of 24 October 1956, placed Jordanian forces under Egyptian command. The pact was a surprise, in view of recent hostility between the two leaders that had descended into personal vituperation on both sides, with Hussein accusing Nasser of cowardice and Nasser accusing Hussein of having prostituted his country to the US. Ben-Gurion's "ring of steel" was forged again around Israel, a little bit stronger than paper this time. Shimon Peres used the same homely image to describe it to the Churchills that he had used some years before to describe to me the earlier Arab treaty: "We were surrounded like a banana in an empty stomach—lined with Russian guns." There was an important difference; in 1967 Jordan had no alliance with Britain to deter Israel.

The aging Eden, like a ghost of Suez, now reappeared as Lord Avon at the edge of events to speak again the delusion which had decoyed him to his own defeat. "I do not feel myself back ten years ago," he told the House of Lords on 1 June, "I feel myself very much in the nineteen-thirties at the present time." For Eden, Nasser would always be reoccupying the Rhineland.

Dayan, who had been out of office after siding with Ben-Gurion in his break with Eshkol, returned to the center of the stage as Defense Minister on that same 1st of June. The appointment responded to obvious popular demand, particularly in the Armed Forces, which had become restive over what seemed to be Eshkol's indecisiveness. Indeed, there were rumors that the Army might be planning a *putsch* to replace Eshkol with a more militant leader. These rumors apparently were what prompted Ben-Gurion to warn on 29 May against any abandonment of democratic principles under the stress of the crisis. "An army in a democratic republic does not act on its own," he said, "but rather on the orders of a civilian government and according to its instructions." The rumors evaporated with Dayan's appointment. The change in the mood of Israel was electric. Israelis showed no doubts about their ability to defeat all comers in the Arab world. A bold, offensive spirit was rife.

The Arabs, as they had been in 1956, were deployed defensively although they were now more numerous and better armed than before. This defensive disposition was to prevent them from going over to the offensive on short notice. As a consequence, despite the Arab alliances and the presence of an Egyptian commander in Jordan, Egypt's allies were unable to hit effectively at Israel when she attacked Egypt. Their military responses were just sufficient to allow Israel to claim that they struck first. Then she dealt with them at her convenience, one by one, delaying her conquests in Syria, for example, until after she had completed the destruction of the Egyptian forces in the Sinai.

In 1956 Dayan had omitted the classic opening of modern warfare—the massive air assault. As described in Chapter 15, he feigned for two days to be conducting a limited operation. His mission in the first forty-eight hours, as agreed among the colluders, was merely to draw Egyptian forces into the Sinai and set the scene for Eden and the French to join the attack from the rear in the guise of policemen. He kept his air arm cocked, however, for an instant all-out strike if Egypt put her bombers to effective use and he stood ready to evacuate his paratroopers and call the operation a reprisal raid should Eden fail to intervene. He unleashed the full weight of the invasion only after the Anglo-French bombers and fighters destroyed the Egyptian Air Force. If the collusive arrangements had not dictated these unorthodox preliminaries, Dayan said afterward, Israel would have had to mount the opening air strike herself. Dayan believed she was capable of it. The participation of Israel-based Mystères in the raid on the Egyptian Ilyushins at Luxor, over 400 miles away, confirmed his belief.

With no collusive partners to complicate his strategy in 1967, Dayan sprang to war with a first strike by air of such destructive efficiency that it not only decided the outcome of the war but ensured that Israel's victory would be of stunning swiftness. A classic among classics, Dayan's opening blow outdid the Japanese at Pearl Harbor for daring and despatch.

At 7:45 A.M. on 5 June 1967 Israeli fighter-bombers—Mystère Vs and supersonic Mirages—attacked ten Egyptian air bases at the same instant. Some had hooked far out over the Mediterranean and streaked in to their targets from the Western Desert. They had flown at ground level to elude the radar on the Egyptian mainland and aboard the Russian ships that were shadowing the Sixth Fleet beyond the horizon. They timed their departures perfectly so as to arrive over their targets simultaneously. Ten minutes later the second wave hit the nine remaining Egyptian air bases. Ten minutes later a third wave struck. Ten minutes after that, a fourth. The blows continued at ten-minute intervals for two hours and fifty minutes, at the end of which the new Egyptian Air Force was broken and the outcome of the war was a scheduled certainty.

The Israelis told the Churchills they had picked 07:45, which is about three hours and fifteen minutes after sunrise, for four reasons: (1) the Egyptian dawn alert, on aerial guard at the likeliest time for an attack, would be relaxing; the Egyptian planes, timed in the air by Israeli radar, would be returning to refuel and would have too little gasoline left for combat; (2) the Israeli pilots would be fresher and quicker-witted—after three hours more sleep— than they could have been before a dawn strike; (3) the morning mist would have burned off and the sun would be higher, thus doubly improving the visibility so vital to the accuracy of such a vast split-second operation; (4) the Egyptian High Command and Government leaders begin their working day at 08:00 and at a quarter before the hour they would be in their cars between their homes and their offices and their reaction would be delayed until after they reached their desks and found out what was happening.

Of her 400 war planes, Israel threw into that first assault all but twelve, keeping eight always in the air and four on the ground to guard against Arab air attacks. The Israelis estimated that their opening air attack destroyed more than 300 of about 340 operational Egyptian warplanes. Nearly all of the 300 were destroyed on the ground, many of them as they were taxiing to take-off, so that the pilots too were destroyed. The Israeli planes went in to the attacks four at a time, first bombing the runways, then wheeling back for cannon and rocket runs to destroy the planes. The bombs were mostly "dibber" bombs, devised by the Israelis for attacks on airfields at rooftop level. The "dibber" is slowed by retro-rockets to avoid blasting its own release-plane and then is slammed deep into the runway surface by a booster rocket. Its delayed-action detonators make repair of the runways dangerous and impermanent.

The Syrian Air Force was broken later in the morning after it raided Haifa. The Jordanian Air Force was destroyed at midday. The Iraqi Air Force was decimated the following morning after Iraqi planes attacked Natanya. In those two days the Israelis flew a thousand sorties and destroyed 416 Arab planes, all but two dozen of them on the ground.

At 8:15 A.M. on 5 June, a half hour after the air attacks began, Israeli infantry and armor marched onto the Sinai invasion routes that they had followed a decade before. Yoffe, Sharon, Bar-Lev were again among the commanders, unrestrained this time by collusive allies. New techniques and new weapons played a part in the retaking of the Sinai. At Abu Aoueigila, instead of depending on the luck of slipping armor through the Dayyiqa to encircle the Egyptians, Sharon, now commanding on the Central Axis, used helicopters to land his paratroopers on the road junction west of Um Qataf in the dark of night. He had familiarized his men with the terrain by using a sand table to rehearse the night attack in miniature scale. The Egyptian stronghold, which had broken every enemy attack in 1956 and blocked the Central Axis for four days, was in Israeli hands by 6 A.M. on the second day of the 1967 war after a night of fighting climaxed by a ferocious tank battle at dawn.

On every axis it was the same story of grim zeal, efficient execution, and disregard of casualties as the Israelis broke through the Egyptian forward positions and raced westward to entrap the Egyptian Army and stop its exits from the peninsula. The Israelis were bent on killing as many Egyptians as possible and destroying or capturing their equipment. The Israeli Air Force, again unchallenged over Sinai, strafed and burned with grisly effect. When the fighting was done Israel coldly blocked a Red Cross effort to rescue the human ruins staggering and dying in the desert under the pitiless midsummer sun. By 19 June, when the daily count of cracked and blistered survivors of Egypt's Sinai forces struggling toward the Canal had fallen to near zero, the

Israeli Army estimated that 20,000 Egyptians had died, seven to ten times the number of dead in 1956. Nasser estimated Egypt had lost 80 per cent of her fighting strength. Israel listed 679 dead in her own forces, four times the toll in 1956.

On the first day of the war Eshkol and Dayan forswore territorial conquest. Two days later, after the fall of Jerusalem, Dayan went to the Wailing Wall and proclaimed: "We have returned to this most sacred of our shrines never to part from it again." Israel marched swiftly to the Jordan River, completing her conquest of Palestine. By sundown on 10 June Israel had stormed the bunkered Syrian highlands containing the eastern part of the watershed sources of the Jordan, an area that Weizmann had urged Curzon to incorporate into Palestine for the Jewish national home. The third round of the Palestine War was over. And there would be no disgorging.

On the morrow of the war the Israeli leaders, replete with territorial conquests, declared one after another that there would be no return to the old frontiers. Eshkol denounced all the Israeli-Arab Armistice Agreements and vowed to his exultant nation that "the position that existed until now shall never again return." Even before the war ended, when Egypt and Syria were begging for a cease-fire and Washington was stalling in order to let Israel encompass her objectives in Syria, Dayan said Israel would now deal face to face with the Arabs without the intermediation of the UN. If the Arabs ignored Israel's invitation to negotiate peace directly, Dayan said, "then there will be a new map . . . of Israel; . . . we shall stay where we are."

Whether or not there was any collusion in 1967, the Arabs believe that Israel obtained by gift or theft American satellite photographs of their air bases. Major General Carl von Horn of Sweden, writing in 1966 of his experiences as United Nations truce chief from 1958 to 1960, said that, "unsurpassed in the Middle East for gathering information and mounting special operations, . . . Israeli Intelligence was aided by . . . [among other things] the benefits accruing from its penetration of almost every other important intelligence agency in the world." At first Nasser accused the US and Britain of participating in the opening air strike. It was incredible to him that Israel could have done it without help. The planes that came from the west could not have been Israel's, he thought. Nasser later conceded that he had been wrong. But many Arabs disbelieve American denials as much as they disbelieve the stubborn British denials of collusion in 1956.

Nasser was so stricken with remorse for having been forced to relive defeat in the Sinai that he felt neither Egypt nor history would forgive him. He tried to resign in favor of Zakaria Mohyeddin on 9 June, telling his people in a broadcast that he accepted the "entire responsibility" for the disaster. Cairenes wept openly in the streets and a soldier guarding one of the Nile bridges was seen to throw himself on the ground and howl with grief, then jump up and empty his submachine gun, burst after burst, into the river. At least two suicides were attributed to despair over Nasser's announcement.

But Egypt did not hold him accountable. The Cabinet rejected his resignation. The next day Nasser told a relieved nation that he would remain at the head of the Government. The incident reaffirmed one of the lessons of 1956, namely that Nasser's position did not depend on ephemeral effects of victory or defeat on his prestige but on the solid achievements and fundamental decency of the man himself and his revolutionary colleagues. This was true as well of Nasser's standing in the Arab world. Even his old enemy Ben-Gurion said, a week after the 1967 war: "I have a great respect for Nasser. Nasser is a patriot who wants to do something for Egypt."

Parallels with 1956 did not end with the cease-fire. In 1967 Israel again published captured documents purporting to prove that she had preempted an Egyptian attack in the nick of time. The new documents were described as Egyptian Air Force orders, but they lacked dated execution clauses. Like the 1956 documents, they required a good deal of interpreting in order to make Israel's point that her shattering victory had really been a lucky forestalling of destruction.

The role of geography in shaping the policy of its possessor was demonstrated in 1967 when Israel acquired a veto position on the Canal by taking the east bank and making the waterway her new boundary with Egypt. In 1956 the possessor of the Canal, which was Egypt alone, made the world ransom its reopening by forcing Britain, France, and Israel to withdraw their invasion forces. After 1967, it was Israel, now a co-possessor, which held the Canal closed in order to obtain passage for her shipping and other items of political ransom.

The real lesson of the 1967 war was that the Palestine War, of which it was the third round, will never end so long as Israel remains as the focus of a worldwide Zionist movement. Israel, having been born by the sword and having lived for a generation by the sword, cannot any longer hope for peace on terms compatible with Zionism. She will have to go on living by the sword, ever on guard lest she perish by the sword. Ben-Gurion perceived this truth in 1957, when he told the Knesset:

Every victory might be followed by another round. Only naive and treacherous persons will tell us that once we deal a blow peace will come thereafter. In theory, final victory can only be against us since if the Israel Defense Force is defeated, God forbid, this nation may be destroyed. We should entertain no illusions in this regard.

691

Suez-Sinai was a war fought twice by the same men on the same ground. This extraordinary reprise of history occurred because the circumstances that caused the first Suez War were recreated when the *status quo ante* was finally restored by the departure of UNEF and the reimposition of the Aqaba blockade. This particular war will not be fought a third time unless the *status quo ante* is restored again. But the Palestine War, of which the Suez wars were the second and third grounds, will go on. The danger that it constitutes for the world is many times greater than that presented by Southeast Asia. The Middle East, because of its resources, its communications, its centrality among the continents, is more permanently important to outside powers than Southeast Asia. Unlike Southeast Asia, the Middle East has always been a focus of Great Power rivalry since the days when Egypt and Persia fought over the lands between, including Palestine.

The achievement by the Zionist movement of statehood for Israel in Palestine at the expense of the original people there has resulted in Palestine becoming the territorial prize for two Irredentist movements, Zionist and Palestinian, both claiming the right of return to statehood on the same land. Both movements have allies abroad who could be drawn into any renewal of the Palestine War. The Powers of the world halted the fighting in the first two Palestine Wars, in 1948 and 1956. Their failure to impose peace led to the theory that peace might be achieved by the parties themselves provided they were left to themselves to fight a war to its military conclusion. That happened in 1967 but peace came no closer than before, even though the 1967 war satisfied most of the Israeli geographical demands that were among the goals of the first two rounds.

In 1948 Israel had to fight for territory upon which to be born. It was not sufficient to grow on, being difficult to defend, short of water and resources, and unable to use the potential trade lanes of the Gulf of Aqaba. It also lacked the spiritual magnet of the Zionist movement, old Jerusalem, where the Wailing Wall was quarantined against Jews. In 1956 Israel took some of these geographical objectives but succeeded in keeping only the freedom of the Gulf of Aqaba. In 1967, when she lost even that, she fought again and recovered all she had won in 1956 and much more.

Israel's western border is now far beyond Wadi Arish, the Brook of Egypt promised in the Covenant, although her northeastern border is far short of the promised River Euphrates. The most likely area for further expansion is the Litani River basin just beyond the border in Lebanon. This was the river which Weizmann, foreseeing that the Promised Land would thirst for more water than it possessed, so earnestly begged of Lord Curzon, to no avail. Israel has now reached 90 per cent utilization of her known water resources. She

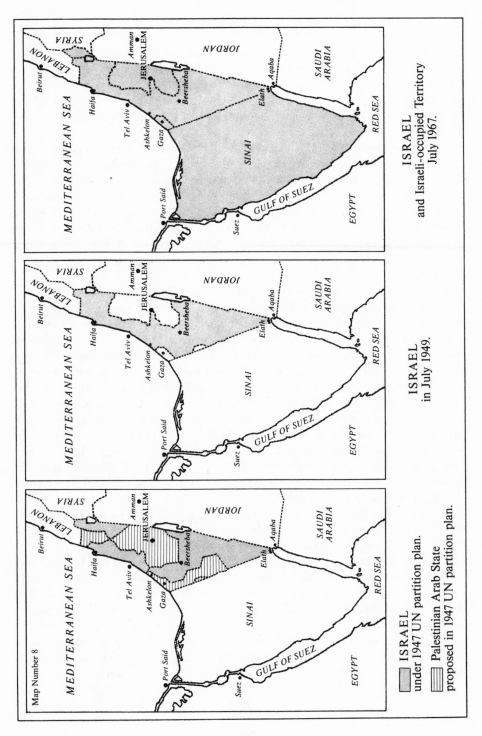

Map Number 8

ISRAEL
under 1947 UN partition plan.

Palestinian Arab State
proposed in 1947 UN partition plan.

ISRAEL
and Israeli-occupied Territory
July 1967.

ISRAEL
in July 1949.

693

expects to be using 100 per cent in a few years, which will make the Litani more desirable than ever. But if the United States helps Israel de-salt the sea for additional water, as President Johnson promised in parting, even the most ardent expansionist may not soon again raise the cry of Joshua to the children of Israel: "How long are ye slack to go to possess the land which the Lord God of your fathers hath given you?"

But the Palestinians, all of them now exiles abroad or strangers in their own land, raise that cry among the children of Ishmael. The Arabs are listening the more readily as a result of the second Suez-Sinai War, which convinced them that Israel was too dangerous a neighbor to be accepted. More and more the Arab governments are tolerating and encouraging violence as the way to re-cover the Palestinian birthright. Having lost a third war in 1967, the Arabs nourish the dream of a guerrilla war patterned after the Viet Cong's or the Algerian guerrilla and terrorist rebellion that won independence from France in 1962.

The danger of this mood to people far from the Middle East was symbol-ized by the assassination of Senator Robert Kennedy by a young Palestinian on the first anniversary of the second Suez-Sinai war. It was not a manifestation of a streak of violence in America but of the violence of Palestine Irredentists on both sides, a violence that has made assassination a tradition among Zionists and Arabs for half a century. Kennedy had vied on television with his rival, Senator Eugene McCarthy, in expressions of favor for Israel, which has be-come standard practice among political candidates seeking the urban Jewish vote. He did not appreciably outdo McCarthy but his being the brightest star in the 1968 constellation of Presidential hopefuls probably made him the assassin's choice. Kennedy was the victim of an implacable struggle between two foreign peoples to secure their mutually exclusive national identities upon the same land, called Palestine by the one and Israel by the other. The admitted killer, Sirhan Sirhan, is a hero to many Arabs who sincerely deplore his act and who mourn the death of his victim. To them Sirhan is one of the *Fedayeen*, the Self-sacrificers, Palestinian Arabs who are seeking by violence to wreck the State of Israel and recover Palestine for their own people.

Israel's answer to the violence of the *Fedayeen* has always been greater violence. The steady growth of the *Fedayeen* organizations in numbers, weap-onry, sophistication, efficiency, daring, and political power in the face of ever-larger and swifter Israeli reprisals is good evidence that the reprisal policy, leaving aside its morality, is a failure. When Glubb was commander of the Arab Legion, retaliation raids spurred him to try harder to prevent infiltration from Jordan into Israel but Arab opinion limited the severity of his efforts. He always maintained that reprisals, whose victims were nearly always innocent, merely made matters worse. Last year *Fatah*, the best known of the *Fedayeen* organizations, had achieved such popular support in Jordan that its leaders there concluded a concordat with King Hussein in November under which they obtained extraordinary indulgences and immunities from the Government.

As Eric Pace of *The New York Times* wrote from Jordan at the end of 1968: "The country is already so buffeted by past Israeli attacks that new ones do not radically alter the nature of things.... The raids also deepen the black mood that some diplomats call 'Palestinian nihilism', the feeling of desperation that has spurred the commando movement to its present fevered pitch." The late Dr. Hussein Fakhry al-Khalidy, then Foreign Minister of Jordan and one of dozens of Palestinian refugees who have achieved cabinet rank in one or another of the Arab countries, told me fifteen years ago that he would gladly bring down calamity on himself if it would hurt Israel—"Like Sampson, I say: On me and on my enemies!" The present leaders of the *Fedayeen*, who regard themselves as revolutionaries as well as liberators, say that their aim is to eliminate the State of Israel as a political entity but "not to throw the Jews into the sea." But they denounce any Arab who would settle for less than the elimination of Israel. King Abdullah of Jordan was assassinated by Palestinians in 1951 on suspicion of contemplating a settlement with Israel and the memory of it makes every Arab leader reckon today with the views of the *Fedayeen*.

Since the 1967 Suez-Sinai war the *Fedayeen* have gained more adherents and support than ever. They are recognized throughout the Arab world and beyond as the vanguard in a war of national liberation to recover their home-land from the Israelis. In many parts of Africa, Asia, the Communist Bloc, and Latin America and among United States black people the *Fedayeen* are re-garded as modern counterparts of the underground resistance fighters in Nazi-occupied Europe. Just as the French Maquis and the Yugoslav Partisans received arms as well as sympathy from the Allies, so the *Fedayeen* receive the recognition implicit in supplies of weapons and training from Russia and China. Reprisals help them. An Israeli raid on Beirut International Airport which destroyed thirteen planes at the end of 1968 in reprisal for a *Fedayeen* machine gun attack on an Israeli airliner in Athens sent support for the *Fedayeen* soaring among the Lebanese, previously the most remiss of Arab governments in the eyes of Palestinians. Despite losses estimated between $50 and $100 million, Lebanese popular opinion forced a change of government favorable to the *Fedayeen*.

Egypt bade farewell to the "hated" Johnson Administration in January 1969 with a quasi-official diatribe against a US invitation of the "highest priority" to Russia and other states "to use all their influence to stop the grave increase of Arab terrorist operations." Washington was surprised at Cairo's umbrage in defense of terrorism. Most Americans are deeply imbued with sympathy for the catastrophe suffered by the Jews of Europe under Hitler but they are aware neither of the distinct sense of nationality of the Palestinian Arabs nor of the extent of their losses and dispersion at the hands of Israel. They regard the *Fedayeen* with repugnance and anger.

In contrast to Americans, most of the world's people and governments feel the bonds of sympathy with the Palestinians, including the *Fedayeen*, that are common to the Third World of the colored, the ex-colonized, the weak, the poor. The Palestine Partition resolution of 1947, for example, could not hope for passage by today's UN General Assembly. Paradoxically, the Arabs now demand implementation of that resolution, doubtless as a step toward weakening and eventually eliminating Israel. For twenty years the General Assembly has annually reaffirmed its resolutions prescribing the right of the refugees to choose either repatriation or compensation. Israel's refusal of their rights turns refugees into *Fedayeen*. A brilliant champion of all victims of man, the American journalist I. F. Stone, recently urged his fellow Jews "to recognize that the Arab guerrillas are doing to us what our terrorists and saboteurs of the Irgun, Stern, and Haganah did to the British" and "to admit that their motives are as honorable as were ours . . . "

What has made the struggle for Palestine more unquenchable with every war that Israel wins and every square mile that she conquers is that every new refugee furthers the Palestinization of the Arab world. Just as the fate of the Jews in the Nazi holocaust Judaized the conscience of the Western world and made possible the Zionist establishment of Israel, so the dispossession, dispersion, and sufferings of the Palestinians at the hands of Israel Palestinized the conscience of the Arab world. There has never been an armistice or a cease-fire between Israel and the Palestinians, who have conducted guerrilla warfare from their lands of exile. Israel's reprisals and other raids continue to help the Palestinization of the neighboring countries between wars. Egypt, for example, was laggard, being insulated from the problem by the Sinai Desert. The Palestinization of Egypt's conscience began with the Gaza Raid and it was seemingly completed in 1967, when 39,000 Egyptians became refugees.

There is an erroneous belief in some Western countries, including the United States, that the Arab host Governments callously prevent settlement of the refugees in order to use the discontented thousands in their teeming camps as political pawns. Zionist publicists are active promoters of this mistaken and unrealistic idea. The UN Relief and Works Agency corrects it in a 1968 publication on the refugees entitled *Twice In A Lifetime*. It says:

Although the host Governments have opposed mass schemes of direct resettlement, on the grounds that this would be contrary to the interests and expressed wishes of the refugees themselves, their record in promoting the rehabilitation of the refugees as individuals through education, training, and employment has been notably humane and helpful. They have extended this aid to the refugees in spite of the grave difficulties which already confronted them in providing a livelihood for their own rapidly expanding populations.

In the main, those refugees making their own livelihood in exile have been those from the cities and towns of Palestine who possessed the skills needed in the rapidly modernizing Arab region. They constituted about one-third of the 1.2 million refugees before the 1967 war. The other two-thirds became surplus farm workers in lands already burdened, like most of the Third World, with their own surplus farm workers. Dr. John H. Davis, a Missouri man and an agriculturalist who was Commissioner General of UNRWA before the 1967 war, writes of the plight of the children born in exile to rural refugees:

Because, in general, rural refugee fathers have been unemployed, their sons have had but limited opportunity, if any at all, to learn even the self-discipline of work or the skills of their fathers. Therefore, in competition with the indigenous rural boys, the maturing refugee boy is at a serious disadvantage.... It is for this reason, above others, that they continue to be forced to live the life of dependent refugees.

As a result of the 1967 war there are now 1.5 million Palestinian refugees, two-thirds of the entire nation, and, in addition, 100,000 Syrian and 39,000 Egyptian refugees.

It is with this nation in exile that Israel must make peace, more than with any other, if she is ever to live in tranquillity. Yet it is with the claim of this people to the national home in Palestine from which it was driven, just twenty-one years ago, after immemorial ages of residence, that the fundamental tenets of Zionism are most irreconcilable. The Zionist movement and the State of Israel which is its vital essence assert the right of each and every Jew in the world to return to Zion—the Land of Israel. It is a millennial vision, heroically realized, but in utter disregard of the ancient people who were in full possession under age-old rights unquestioned by any laws or traditions other than those framed since the first World War by and for the Zionists. The right of the Palestinians to return home, reaffirmed every year by the UN, is dismissed in quotation marks by Abba Eban in his history of the Jews, entitled *My People*.

Israel's Zionist mission to be both a haven and a defender for Jews everywhere required that, whatever Israel's size may be, it must have an unassailable Jewish majority. This undeniably racist requirement that Israel must be, in Weizmann's words, as Jewish as England is English, is proudly asserted by Eban: "Israel will continue to be conspicuously non-Arab in its speech, thought, and shape of mind. Its Jewish connections will be stronger than its links with the Arab environment. . . . The question is not whether Israel will change its special nature, but whether the Arabs will come to terms with Israel as it is." When Eban says: "Immigration was the purpose of Israel's existence; sovereignty was the means which served the end," he is speaking of Jewish immigration and only Jewish immigration. It is this mission which has made Israel expanionist and which makes it impossible for her to achieve a reconciliation with the Arabs, whether of Palestine or any other country.

Israel and her friends in the West have been too ready to forget that when political Zionism was born at the turn of the century, the Ottoman province of Palestine was, to paraphrase Weizmann, ethnically as Arab as England was English. The Jewish minority there was smaller proportionately than that in some of the European provinces from which the Zionists emigrated. The destruction of Arab Palestine was the direct result of Zionism's mission. Clearly, just as Germany had to make her peace with the Jews before she could win reacceptance into the Western community, so Israel must make her peace with the Palestinians if she is ever to win acceptance into the Middle East and the Third World. This means acknowledging that their right of return to their native land is fully as valid as the Israeli law that gives all Jews the right of return to the Promised Land. To Israel, the logical outcome of letting the refugees return is national suicide. But if she—and we—are ever to have peace she must somehow share her Promised Land with those whose native land it is. To paraphrase Weizmann again, Israel must risk becoming merely as Jewish as Canada is English—or Belgium is Flemish, or Switzerland French.

Meanwhile, Israel has become a modern Sparta, pugnacious, beset on all sides, and increasingly violent and short-tempered. Indeed, Israel is beginning to Palestinize the conscience of more than the Arab world. De Gaulle's France, for example, shifted markedly toward the Arabs. Israel's raid on Beirut airport indicates that this Palestinization is happening in her own mind for she failed to distinguish between the relatively un-Palestinized merchant-nation of Lebanon and the thoroughly Palestinized remainder of the Arab world, raiding the former as readily as the latter. Her reaction to world criticism of the raid was to see anti-Semitism on all sides and to manifest "scorn and contempt" for the censorious UN. Surely these are symptoms of a sense of isolation that is in danger of feeding upon itself. The urbane Eban himself commented: "The attitude of foreign countries cannot be entirely divorced from the traditional attitude of the non-Jewish world to the Jewish world." If he is right it is a misfortune for civilization and if he is wrong, such paranoia is equally a misfortune. As I. F. Stone said: "How we feel toward the Arabs will determine what kind of Jews we are." How Jews feel toward all non-Jews, not merely Arabs, also will be determinant.

The open partisanship of the Johnson Administration for Israel weakened American links with the Arab world and strengthened Arab ties with the East. The immediate danger is that, the Arab-Israeli arms race having polarized, with the US supplying Israel and Russia supplying the Arabs, a renewal of open war could transform the two nuclear Super-Powers from seconds standing outside the ring into combatants. The possibility that Israeli technology will escalate the arms race to the level of atomic or nuclear bombs, with Russia supplying the Arabs, increases the danger.

Thus far, divided Germany is the only place in the world where local conflict is more threatening to mankind than the Middle East. The reason is that our commitment to West Germany and the Russian commitment to East Germany are far stronger and more specific than our respective commitments to Israel and the Arabs, so much so that an uncontrolled dispute in Germany could lead swiftly to the end of civilization in a nuclear war between us and the Russians. But neither of the Germanies has its own nuclear bomb and both are more amenable to control by their respective superpower patrons than either Israel or the Arabs. Israel has turned a deaf ear to all invitations to join the nuclear non-proliferation agreement. If she obtains her own atomic bomb independently—or if it is confirmed that she has already done so—Russia will be impelled to give Egypt atomic bombs, either outright or at bases under Russian control. The struggle for Palestine will then have become more dangerous to mankind than German yearning for reunification. The Middle East, where civilization was born, will have become the scene where it is most likely to die.

There is also the long-range possibility that the Arabs will become so alienated from the West that they will withhold their oil from the dependent markets of the West. The Middle East has three-quarters of the non-Communist world's proven oil reserves—some 300 billion barrels. Arab wells, producing 9 million barrels a day, supply two-thirds of the imports of Western Europe and Japan. Thus far, there have been no alternative markets for the Arab oil-producing countries to turn to, a factor that has aborted their occasional efforts to embargo the West, such as after the two Suez wars. But Russia is now curtailing her oil exports to supply home needs. And China, ever alert to woo the Arabs, is industrializing with coal instead of oil. If China should convert to oil, as the British have done, it would constitute an immense potential market offering the Arabs the alternative they have occasionally looked for. This could cripple the West. Walter Levy, one of the foremost oil consultants in the US, has said that the complete loss of Arab oil to the West could not be made up from any other conceivable combination of sources for ten years or more.

The new US Administration of President Nixon has shown signs of reviving the policy of "even-handedness" between Israel and the Arabs which was attempted by President Eisenhower and John Foster Dulles. There will again be difficulties in determining just what "even-handedness" means between the irreconcilable claimants to Palestine. Any effort to go beyond this to achieve peace, whether by imposing it or by trying to persuade one Arab State or another to work out a compromise over the heads of the Palestinians, appears impossibly difficult. An imposed peace, for example, although better than nothing, would be torn up by the first side that felt it could get away with it. More immediately the US must learn to live with the dangerous present that has been with us for twenty years and which shows no tendency to recede into the past. Any miscalculation by ourselves or Russia could lead to a nuclear confrontation. As for the Middle East, the question haunting the foreseeable future is not whether the Palestine War will be renewed but when and how and how far it will spread. For there will be more reprises before Israel gives up Zionism or the Arabs forget thee, O Jerusalem.

Not heaven itself upon the past has power;
But what has been, has been, and I have had my hour.
                    —Dryden

Notes

In the main I have identified my sources in the text in the old pre-footnote manner of chronicles so that the reader will not be distracted by impulses to look up how I came by this or that piece of information. Where I have given less than full source identifications in the text it was either because it was stylistically too cumbersome or because the source asked anonymity. I apologize to the scholar-reader for not having pinpointed all my references; it would have added too many pages of notes to an already bulky book. The text and the bibliography should provide enough clues for an assiduous researcher to track down the sources of quotations and information that are unsupported by notes. I have limited my notes to items that might justly raise distracting controversy, doubt, or curiosity. In order further to reduce distraction I have not placed reference numbers in the text but instead have keyed the notes to page, line, and phrase of text. The line references will help the reader locate key phrases more easily when checking back from the notes, bearing in mind that there are 40 or 39 lines to a page. Unless otherwise noted, my treatment of events, speeches, and context is based on press coverage (sometimes my own) or historical accounts accepted widely enough to do without the support of notes.

Money is an important factor in this history, as indeed it is in the whole story of the world. The fluctuations in the purchasing power and in the exchange rates among the world's currencies during the span of this history make any brief table of equivalents seem grossly oversimplified. Bearing that in mind, I offer the dollar equivalents of the main currencies that figure in this story at the beginning and end of the century of Suez.

	£1 Sterling	1 franc	£1 Egyptian
1856	$4.87	$00.193	$4.99
June 1956	$2.80	$00.00255 (free market)	$2.70 (free market)

CHAPTER 1: THE GAZA RAID

p. 5, l. 1: The last night of February ...
My account of the raid is based mainly on General Burns's report to the Security Council, UN Doc. S/3373, particularly its Appendixes I to VII and its maps.

p. 5, l. 3: The weather ...
William H. Haggard of the National Weather Records Center, Asheville, N.C., verified the weather.

p. 5, l. 3: Sunset ...
Tom Southerland of the Princeton Observatory verified the astronomical ephemera.

p. 5, l. 8: The torpid old Arab town of Gaza ...
My descriptions of Gaza are based on many visits.

p. 11, l. 3: ... the opposition of Moshe Sharett ...
Extracts from Sharett's diary published in Israel in 1965, cited in *Le Monde*, 8 March 1966.

p. 11, l. 12: The machine-gunning of an Israeli cyclist ...
Burns report, UN Doc. S/3373, paragraphs 29 to 31.

p. 11, l. 36: In 1950 Israel expelled 3,500 Azazme ...
Burns, *Between Arab and Israeli,* pp. 92–98. Security Council Official Records, 27 October 1953 and 9 November 1953.

p. 12, l. 24: ... Egypt had taken the lead ...
Eric Johnston to author, several times. See also: Burns, *op. cit.,* p. 112.

p. 13, l. 9: During the negotiations ...
Anthony Nutting, *I Saw for Myself,* Doubleday, Garden City, N.Y., 1958, p. 95.

p. 13, l. 12: At a press conference ...
Tom Little, *Egypt,* Benn, London, 1958, p. 268.

p. 13, l. 24: Nasser had said much the same thing ...
Burns, *op. cit.,* p. 18.

p. 13, l. 27: Nasser told me in June 1955 ...
My dispatch from Cairo to *The New York Times* on 2 June 1955, unpublished (see pp. 92–94).

p. 14, l. 8: Crossman ...
New Statesman and Nation (London), 22 January 1955.

p. 14, l. 28: "Neither Egypt ..."
24 October 1954.

p. 14, l. 30: Cairo broadcasts . . .
21 October 1954, Anthony Nutting's statement.

p. 14, l. 34: Cairo Radio's "Voice of the Arabs" . . .
20 October 1954.

p. 14, l. 38: Tom Little . . .
Little, *Egypt*, p. 264. For Nasser's account of assassination attempt, see Nasser, *Egypt's Liberation: the Philosophy of the Revolution*, Public Affairs Press, Washington, 1955, pp. 54–57. The text of Nasser's famous booklet runs from page 11 to page 114 in this edition, which I cite because of its availability in the West. Persons using other editions of *The Philosophy of the Revolution* can calibrate approximate page numbers by noting, for example, that this citation begins on the 44th of 104 pages.

p. 15, l. 7: Nasser has recalled . . .
Burns, *op. cit.*, p. 18. US Ambassador Byroade told me the same.

p. 15, l. 11:As Nasser recalls it . . .
Nasser to author, 17 February 1966.

p. 17, l. 23: The trial itself . . .
Roger Baldwin, *The Cairo Trial*, Land Reborn, February–March 1955, and in letter to me, 30 June 1965.

p. 20, l. 4: Nasser's decision to rearm . . .
Nasser to author, 17 February 1966.

CHAPTER 2: ISAAC AND ISHMAEL

p. 24, l. 25: They contend further . . .
How to Speak to the Arabs; A Maariv Round Table, Middle East Journal, Spring 1964, p. 143ff.

p. 32, l. 7: Jewish statehood . . .
Leonard Stein, *The Balfour Declaration*, Vallentine & Mitchell, London, 1961, p. 523.

p. 33, l. 14: Balfour himself said . . .
Carroll Quigley, *Lord Balfour's Personal Position on the Balfour Declaration*, Middle East Journal, Summer 1968, p. 340ff.

p. 34, l. 8: Lord Balfour himself wrote . . .
Woodward and Butler, Eds., *Documents on British Foreign Policy 1919–1939; First Series, Vol. IV, 1919*, p. 345.

p. 41, l. 2: Weizmann and Ben-Gurion, years before . . .
Christopher Sykes, *Crossroads to Israel*, p. 261 n.

p. 41, l. 16: Of the partition proposal . . .
Ben-Gurion, article in Jewish Observer, 8 May 1959.

p. 41, l. 22: When he proclaimed Israel a state . . .
Ben-Gurion, *In Reply to President Charles de Gaulle*, The New Leader, 29 January 1968.

p. 43, l. 29: Captain Yeruham Cohen . . .
Yeruham Cohen, *The Secret Negev Talks*, Jewish Observer, 13 February 1953, p. 6ff.

CHAPTER 3: FOREMATH

p. 48, l. 30: At Ben-Gurion's reported instigation . . .
The New York Times, 29 December 1960.

p. 48, l. 16: And Ben-Gurion's chief lieutenants . . .
Général d'Armée Marie-Pierre Koenig to author, 26 January 1966.

p. 49, l. 7: "It was difficult to be Prime Minister . . ."
Sharett to author, 26 April 1964.

p. 52, l. 32: Dr. Arieh Loya . . .
Loya to author, 1968.

p. 55, l. 36: Furthermore, after the Deir Yasseen massacre . . .
George Kirk, *The Middle East 1945–1950*, p. 261.

p. 58, l. 30: As for Gaza . . .
Sharett to author, 26 April 1964.

p. 63, l. 20: Israel's response . . .
Eban, interview transcript, Dulles Oral History project, Princeton University Library.

p. 64, l. 8: Dulles noted . . .
Dulles's private papers, Princeton University Library.

p. 72, l. 19: . . . a tactic to stifle criticism . . .
Sykes, *Crossroads to Israel*, p. 247.

p. 72, l. 26: Israelis felt their sovereignty threatened . . .
Dayan disclosed and commented on the memorandum in a lecture to the Asaf Simhoni Memorial Association in Tel Aviv, 7 November 1963. The lecture was published in Haaretz, 17 April 1964, and, with some deletions, in the *Jerusalem Post*, 24 April 1964, under the title *Security Before Sinai*.

p. 74, l. 30: Dayan wrote later . . .
Ibid.

p. 75, l. 16: In Paris on 31 July 1954 . . .
Koenig to author, 26 January 1966.

p. 77, l. 11: Israel remembered the imprisoned . . .
The New York Times, 24 January 1968.

p. 77, l. 36: In his published account . . .
Baldwin, *The Cairo Trial*, Land Reborn, February–March 1955.

p. 78, l. 5: "I cannot say I got any assurances," . . .
Baldwin, letter to author, 30 June 1965.

p. 80, l. 12: He answered . . .
Sharett to author, 26 April 1964.

CHAPTER 4:   THE TURNING POINT

p. 86, l. 1: Dayan, presumably on the basis . . .
Dayan, *Diary of the Sinai Campaign*, p. 5.

p. 87, l. 30: . . . "hopes" and "lively sympathy for Mr. Sharett" . . .
The Lacoutures, *Egypt in Transition*, p. 233.

p. 88, l. 5: When President Eisenhower saw . . .
A US ambassador to author, 13 June 1966.

p. 95, l. 5: . . . Israel asked France to cancel . . .
Bar-Zohar, *Suez Ultra-Secret*, p. 107

p. 96, l. 21: "There has never been anything like it . . ."
The New York Times, 29 August 1955.

p. 105, l. 35: On 22 October Ben-Gurion summoned Dayan . . .
Dayan, *Diary of the Sinai Campaign*, p. 12.

p. 114, l. 19: Heavy bribes . . .
A French ambassador to author, 17 January 1966, and a French Air Force general to author, 26 January 1966.

p. 114, l. 24: As Abba Eban . . .
Eban, interview transcript, Dulles Oral History project, Princeton University Library.

p. 115, l. 7: In addition to talking with Nasser . . .
The New York Times, 9 December 1955.

p. 116, l. 35: Alfred Robens . . .
Calvocoressi, *Suez: Ten Years After*, p. 96.

p. 118, ll. 8 & 9: In mid-April. . . . By mid-October . . .
The New York Times, 15 April 1956, and Eisenhower, *Waging Peace,* p. 677.

p. 121, l. 6: At midnight on 12 April . . .
Bar-Zohar, *Suez Ultra-Secret,* p. 119.

p. 122, l. 25: On 16 June, Sharett submitted . . .
Sharett to author, 26 April 1964.

p. 123, l. 8: Some years later . . .
Ibid.

p. 124, l. 24: The Israeli Intelligence Department . . .
An Israeli intelligence officer to author, 26 May 1964.

CHAPTER 5: A COMMON ENEMY

p. 131, l. 6: Their embarrassment . . .
Alfred Grosser, *La IVe République et sa Politique Extérieur,* Colin, Paris, 1961, p. 175.

p. 134, l. 39: The first clandestine officers' oaths . . .
Jean-Raymond Tournoux, *Secrets d'Etat,* Plon, Paris, 1960, p. 78.

p. 138, l. 7: He recalls having recommended . . .
Peres to author, 4 May 1964.

p. 139, ll. 2 & 3: It provided . . . Several knowledgeable officials . . .
Bar-Zohar, *Suez Ultra-Secret,* p. 76, and author's interviews with a French ambassador,
17 January 1966, and General Koenig, 26 January 1966.

p. 139, l. 11: As Dayan wrote later . . .
Jerusalem Post, 17 April 1964.

p. 141, l. 1: Bar-Zohar, Ben-Gurion's authorized biographer . . .
Bar-Zohar, *Suez Ultra-Secret,* p. 137.

p. 141, l. 21: In July 1955 . . .
Ibid., p. 107.

p. 141, l. 36: As Pineau said later . . .
Pineau to author, 18 January 1966.

p. 143, l. 9: As for Suez . . .
A French ambassador to author, 17 January 1966.

p. 143, l. 37: Peres received extraordinary courtesies. . . .
Bar-Zohar, *Suez Ultra-Secret,* pp. 111/112.

p. 144, l. 28: **Even before the election . . .**
Ibid., p. 112.

p. 145, l. 8: **He kept Nasser's slim book . . .**
Douglas Dillon to author, 6 October 1965.

p. 146, l. 21: **Thomas, as loyal and immodest . . .**
Abel Thomas to author, 21 January 1966.

p. 148, l. 9: **"One French division in Egypt . . ."**
Serge and Merry Bromberger, *Les Secrets de l'Expedition d'Egypte*, Aymon, Paris, 1957, p. 69.

p. 148, l. 13: **On Ambassador Gilbert's advice . . .**
A French ambassador to author, 17 January 1966.

p. 149, l. 2: **It was Nehru . . .**
Pineau to author, 18 January 1966.

p. 149, l. 7: **The meeting . . .**
Both Nasser and Pineau gave the author accounts of their meeting which were essentially complementary. French and Egyptian diplomats furnished additional material supplementing published accounts.

p. 157, l. 35: **Egypt is striving . . .**
In preface to Moustapha al-Hefnaoui, *Les Problèmes Contemporains Posés par le Canal de Suez.* Guillemot et de Lamothe, Paris, 1951.

p. 149, l. 16: **Even at the time of our first meeting . . .**
Tito, speech at Pula, Yugoslavia, 11 November 1956.

p. 149, l. 23: **Nasser says Tito must have misunderstood . . .**
Nasser to author, 17 February 1966.

p. 163, l. 8: **Tsur recalled later . . .**
Tsur to author, 27 April 1964.

p. 163, l. 27: **In 1955 he raised the subject . . .**
Comte de Grailly to author, 6 March 1966.

CHAPTER 6:   THE LION AND THE SPHINX

p. 174, l. 21: **Kitchener's expedition was mounted . . .**
Winston Churchill, *The River War*, Longmans Green, London, 1899, Vol. II, p. 407.

p. 186, l. 7: **"Not a single soldier . . ."**
Lord Moran, *Churchill: Taken from the Diaries of Lord Moran*, Houghton Mifflin, Boston, 1966, p. 617.

p. 187, l. 35: The final agreement . . .
Full text in English published by the Societé Egyptienne de Droit International, 1954.

CHAPTER 7: EDEN FOR AND AGAINST NASSER

p. 194, l. 13: Dulles expressed himself . . .
Dulles's private papers, Princeton University Library.

p. 195, l. 35: "Nuri is in power . . ."
Tom Little, *Egypt*, Benn, London, 1958, p. 257.

p. 196, l. 29: "It is clear that any aggressor . . ."
Nasser to author, 19 August 1954. See *The New York Times*, 20 August 1954.

p. 197, l. 10: "Shabandar? . . ."
Nasser to author, 17 February 1966.

p. 199, l. 9: I began to express . . .
Ibid.

p. 201, l. 34: "This was in April 1955 . . ."
Ibid.

p. 202, l. 5: In keeping with the new understanding . . .
Nasser made his first public reference to the moratorium with Eden on the Baghdad Pact in an interview with Tom Little published in *The Observer* (London) on 25 March 1956. By then Selwyn Lloyd, on 1 March 1956, had suggested a new moratorium and found Nasser receptive, a development that was disclosed in the Cairo newspapers on 12 March 1956. Wilton Wynn, one of the best American correspondents in the Middle East, reported the original "freeze" agreement in his book, *Nasser of Egypt: The Search for Dignity*, Arlington Books, Cambridge, Mass., 1959, pp. 145/6. He told me he learned of it from Clifford Jupp of the British Embassy and Abdel Kader Hatem, then director of the Egyptian government information department. Sir Ralph Stevenson wrote me on 15 April 1966 that while he did not personally recall the moratorium he could "see no reason for President Nasser to make the statement unless he had what he regarded as good reason for doing so." Eden will not comment for publication but is understood privately to have denied making the moratorium pledge. Circumstantial evidence and Nasser's reputation for truthfulness among diplomats and newsmen persuade me to accept his version.

p. 203, l. 6: That same evening . . .
The negotiations culminating in the disastrous Templer mission are described by Eden in *Full Circle* and by Glubb in *A Soldier with the Arabs*, Hodder and Stoughton, London, 1957.

p. 203, l. 18: Accordingly, during the inaugural . . .
Eden, *Full Circle*, p. 383.

p. 204, l. 33: Eisenhower gave the reason . . .
Eisenhower, third draft of *Waging Peace*, seen among Eisenhower papers at Gettysburg.

p. 208, l. 6: The idea was discussed . . .
An Eden cabinet minister to author, 28 February 1966.

p. 213, l. 8: Word quickly reached Eisenhower . . .
Eisenhower, third draft of *Waging Peace*.

p. 214, l. 2: . . . he made a new effort to persuade . . .
Drew Middleton in *The New York Times*, 8 March 1956.

p. 216, l. 27: Eden tried to obtain . . .
Kermit Roosevelt to author, 24 February 1964.

CHAPTER 8:   ENTER, THE BEAR

p. 225, l. 1: It was Nasser who spoke first . . .
Nasser to author, 17 February 1966.

p. 235, l. 14: . . . L. N. Vatolina . . .
Quoted by W. Z. Laqueur in his useful study, *Communism and Nationalism in the Middle East*, Praeger, New York, 1956, p. 262. His book was among my sources of guidance and information for this chapter.

p. 243, l. 22: Nasser later told Keith Wheeler . . .
Time, 14 November 1955.

p. 244, l. 20: "We were desperately weak . . ."
Patrick Seale, *The Struggle for Syria*, p. 235.

p. 244, l. 38: He and Shepilov reached agreement . . .
Nasser to author, 17 February 1966.

p. 245, l. 3: In Paris on 20 July . . .
Bar-Zohar, *Suez Ultra-Secret*, p. 107.

p. 253, l. 24: Rumors of it . . .
Murphy, *Diplomat among Warriors*, p. 377.

p. 254, l. 36: Shipment schedules . . .
Le Monde, 30 September 1955.

p. 260, l. 38: Pineau, in his biography . . .
Christian Pineau, *Nikita Serguéevitch Khrouchtchev*, Perrin, Paris, 1965, pp. 143–145.

p. 261, l. 23: **The Russian ambassador had informed ...**
Barraclough and Wall, *Survey of International Affairs, 1955–1956*, p. 278.

CHAPTER 9: THE PISTOL

p. 266, l. 24: **As William Polk wrote ...**
William R. Polk, *The United States and the Arab World*, Harvard University Press, Cambridge, Mass., 1965, p. 164.

p. 272, l. 16: **Dulles's private memorandum ...**
Dulles's private papers, Princeton University Library.

p. 273, l. 37: **When Byroade and Dulles got the news ...**
A US ambassador to author, 13 June 1966.

p. 275, l. 17: **Dulles's conclusions concerning aid ...**
Dulles's private papers, Princeton University Library.

p. 276, l. 19: **The US shift toward impartiality ...**
Eban, interview transcript, Dulles Oral History project, Princeton University Library.

p. 279, l. 3: **"After the Suez settlement ..."**
The New York Times, 20 August 1954 (Nasser to author, 19 August 1954).

p. 279, l. 13: **"... you Americans do not realize ..."**
The remainder of this quotation did not appear in the published portion of my dispatch, presumably having been deleted for reasons of space.

p. 280, l. 31: **"We had lunch together," ...**
Nasser to author, 17 February 1966.

p. 281, l. 4: **The end of the first story ...**
The Scribe (monthly magazine), National Publications House, Cairo, May 1964, p. 8.

p. 281, l. 29: **"The second story ..."**
Nasser to author, 17 February 1966.

p. 282, l. 31: **... but he did not take the talks as seriously ...**
Kermit Roosevelt to author, 24 February 1964.

p. 283, l. 25: **Another reason ...**
Nasser to author, 17 February 1966

p. 283, l. 32: **There were suspicions ...**
Zakaria Mohyeddin to author, 3 February 1966.

p. 284, l. 7: **He made it reluctantly ...**
My account of Allen's trip is largely based on my notes of interviews with him at the

time, on 3 and 4 October 1955, and subsequently, on 6 July 1966, as well as on published reports.

CHAPTER 10: RENEGE ON THE DAM

p. 303, l. 14: Nasser, in retrospect . . .
Nasser to author, 17 February 1966.

p. 303, l. 19: He said of the British . . .
Nasser, Suez nationalization speech, 26 July 1956.

p. 303, l. 24: Fulfillment of the Western promise . . .
I learned of the peace mission, carried out by Robert B. Anderson, from an early draft of President Eisenhower's *Waging Peace*. The reference was deleted from the published book. Persistent research and questioning of White House, Cabinet, and State Department personnel of the Eisenhower administration brought forth the circumstances of the mission as I have set them down as well as emphatic denials. Since the State Department refuses to declassify the records of the mission, verification is not yet possible. Some of my sources on the Anderson mission seemed indifferent about protecting their anonymity; others were anxious to protect it. On the assumption that casting light on some might penetrate the obscurity of others, I decided to identify none of my sources.

p. 310, l. 17: . . . Eugene Black, on a mission of his own . . .
Most of the information in this chapter from Eugene Black came from an interview with the author on 26 May 1965 and from the transcript of his tape-recorded interview for the Dulles Oral History project at the Princeton University Library.

p. 311, l. 39: Dulles cabled Kermit Roosevelt . . .
Kermit Roosevelt, draft of article entitled "The Ghost of Suez," written in 1963.

p. 315, l. 12: As Allen recalls it . . .
Allen to author, 6 July 1966.

p. 321, l. 30: (Nasser's scoffing to the contrary, . . .)
Churchill, *The River War*, Vol. II, p. 14.

p. 327, l. 24: Nasser believed the renege . . .
Nasser interview with William Attwood, *Look* magazine, 25 June 1957, and Nasser to author, 17 February 1966.

CHAPTER 11: "THIS CANAL BELONGS TO EGYPT"

p. 333, l. 21: In Jerusalem Dag Hammarskjold . . .
Homer Bigart in *The New York Times*, 20 July 1956.

p. 333, l. 28: **Ben-Gurion rejected...**
Burns, *Between Arab and Israeli*, p. 160.

p. 333, l. 37: **"You know, I was ready for it ..."**
Nasser to author, 17 February 1966.

p. 335, l. 34: **By Sunday afternoon ...**
Ibid. The holograph appreciation itself in 1966 was in the custody of Mohammed Hassanein Haikal, editor of *Al-Ahram*, who published a report of it in that paper on 7 October 1966. *The New York Times* described the article on 9 October 1966. Haikal's account contains chronological errors at variance with the careful chronology worked out for me by Nasser.

p. 338, l. 32: **"I went into his office ...**
Yunis to author, 3 February 1966. My interviews with Yunis and Nasser provided information scattered throughout this chapter.

p. 340, l. 32: **The 2d Armored Group ...**
Colonel Taha Magdoub and Egyptian Military Archives staff, 10 February 1966.

p. 342, l. 40: **De Grailly himself says ...**
The Comte de Grailly gave the author his version of the nationalization in an interview on 6 March 1966.

p. 344, l. 12: **In Alexandria as the sun went down ...**
Egyptian newsreels supplemented interviews and press reports in the author's research on the scene in the great square and on the balcony.

p. 344, l. 35: **Nasser began speaking at 7:41.**
The BBC Summary of World Broadcasts gives the times of broadcasts.

p. 350, l. 5: **... he did not laugh at all.**
Osgood Caruthers of *The New York Times* and the Big Three ambassadors in Egypt at the time all told me Nasser did not laugh.

p. 354, l. 4: **Nuri reportedly advised Eden:**
Hugh Thomas, *The Suez Affair*, Weidenfeld and Nicolson, London, 1967, p. 30.

p. 354, l. 24: **Georges-Picot was not admitted ...**
Georges-Picot letter to author, 23 May 1966.

p. 355, l. 14: **Andrew Foster cabled ...**
Foster's cable is among President Eisenhower's papers at Gettysburg.

p. 358, l. 8: **He was badgered so severely ...**
Henri Azeau, *Le Piège de Suez*, Laffont, Paris, 1964, p. 120.

CHAPTER 12: CALL TO ARMS

p. 365, l. 3: The next day he cabled Eisenhower . . .
The Eden–Eisenhower correspondence is in President Eisenhower's papers at Gettysburg. Only a part of it appears in the memoirs of the two men.

p. 368, l. 5: He told me later . . .
Eisenhower to author, 25 November 1964.

p. 368, l. 29: In Paris Pineau summoned . . .
Kamal Abdel Nabi to author, 28/29 January 1966; and Mahmoud Abul Nasr to author, 16 December 1965; and Pineau to author, 28 January 1966.

p. 369, l. 25: There were six members . . .
An Eden cabinet minister to author, 18 March 1966; and Thomas, *The Suez Affair*, p. 41.

p. 370, ll. 12 & 14: . . . no opposition to Eden's war policy. . . . The three Chiefs of Staff . . .
Ambassador Winthrop Aldrich to author, 9 November 1965; and an Eden cabinet minister to author, 18 March 1966.

p. 370, l. 28: The whole cabinet knew . . .
Ibid.

p. 373, l. 10: Nasser returned by train . . .
Egyptian newsreels of Nasser's return are the basis of this description.

p. 375, l. 28: Eden and Macmillan sent . . .
Eisenhower, *Waging Peace*, p. 664.

p. 376, l. 14: "I left on two hours' notice," . . .
Dulles briefing for Latin American ambassadors in Washington, 7 August 1956; text in Dulles's private papers, Princeton University Library.

p. 376, l. 21: Dulles took with him . . .
Dulles's working folder for conference is in his private papers; it contains these items.

p. 384, l. 7: Ten days later Dulles told . . .
Sherman Adams, *Firsthand Report*, p. 251.

p. 387, l. 2: "Had they done it quickly . . .
Eisenhower interview transcript, Dulles Oral History project, Princeton University Library.

CHAPTER 13: PALAVER

p. 392, l. 4: But their main hope . . .
An Eden cabinet member to author, 1 January 1965.

p. 392, l. 17: The French agreed at a meeting . . .
The Brombergers, *Les Secrets de l'Expédition d'Egypte*, p. 263; and *France-Observateur*, 15 November 1956; and Erskine B. Childers, *The Road to Suez*, MacGibbon and Kee, London, 1962, p. 227.

p. 392, l. 23: Summoned from Germany . . .
Stockwell's articles in the *Sunday Telegraph* (see Bibliography) give a valuable chronology of military developments.

p. 392, l. 28: The French accepted . . .
Pineau to author, 18 January 1966.

p. 392, ll. 30/31: De Gaulle . . . warned at the time . . .
Ibid.

p. 392, ll. 34/35: General André Beaufre . . . tried to correct . . .
Beaufre to author, 20 January 1966.

p. 393, l. 36: Egypt was sufficiently alarmed . . .
Egyptian Military Archives, Cairo.

p. 398, l. 29: General Sir Charles Keightley . . .
Keightley, *Operations in Egypt*, Her Majesty's Stationery Office, London, 12 September 1957.

p. 398, l. 38: Before Eden's broadcast Nasser had planned . . .
Aly Sabry to author, 20 August 1956; and Nasser to Hugh Pilcher, *Daily Herald*, (London) 13 September 1956.

p. 402, l. 24: He fought with the BBC . . .
Harman Grisewood, *One Thing at a Time*, Hutchinson, London, 1968, as quoted in *The New York Times*, 25 March 1968. Grisewood was chief assistant to the BBC's Director General at the time of Suez.

p. 404, l. 25: Dulles cabled Eisenhower . . .
Dulles's messages to Eisenhower are among the Eisenhower papers at Gettysburg.

p. 404, l. 28: Lloyd proposed . . .
The verbatim record kept by the London Conference secretariat is incorporated in *The Suez Canal Problem: July 26–September 22, 1956*, US Government Printing Office.

p. 407, l. 13: Eisenhower preferred Gaitskell's approach . . .
Adams, *Firsthand Report*, p. 253.

p. 412, l. 10: He told Nasser at the first meeting . . .
Egyptian Gazette, 20 September 1956.

p. 414, l. 25: The day Menzies arrived . . .
Le Monde, 26 June 1960.

p. 415, l. 32: "I exhausted my energy . . ."
Eden, *Full Circle*, pp. 525–528.

p. 416, l. 11: Menzies' official report said:
Menzies' official report appears in *The Suez Canal Problem: July 26–September 22, 1956*, US Government Printing Office.

p. 417, l. 5: By our conference session . . .
The Sunday Times, (London) 28 February 1960.

p. 417, l. 17: On the contrary, Nasser told Byroade . . .
Byroade to author, 13 June 1966; and Little to author, 2 February 1966.

p. 417, l. 26: He is said to have been equally rude . . .
Thomas, *The Suez Affair*, p. 72.

p. 417, ll. 34/35: Kamel Georges . . . expressed the consensus:
Kamel Georges to author, 18 March 1964.

p. 418, l. 19: "At our last meeting" . . .
Byroade to author, 13 June 1966.

p. 420, l. 9: One key member . . .
An Eden cabinet minister to author, 18 March 1966.

p. 421, ll. 30/31: . . . instructed their consuls . . . to encourage pilots . . .
Ambassador Amin Hilmy II to author, 21 December 1965.

p. 426, l. 18: . . . a "slap in the face" for Nasser.
Eisenhower, third draft of *Waging Peace*, in Eisenhower papers at Gettysburg.

CHAPTER 14: COLLUSION

p. 433, l. 13: . . . Israel requested a big increase . . .
Bar-Zohar, *Suez Ultra-Secret*, pp. 140/141.

p. 433, l. 27: Bourgès-Maunoury asked Peres . . .
Bar-Zohar, *The Armed Prophet: A Biography of Ben-Gurion*, p. 219.

p. 433, l. 32: The Israelis, however, began air and ground . . .
Egyptian Gazette, 10 August 1956.

p. 433, l. 39: The French informed Israel . . .
Dayan, *Diary of the Sinai Campaign*, p. 20.

p. 434, l. 13: If fight you must . . .
Tom Little, *Egypt*, Benn, London, 1958, pp. 291/292.

p. 436, l. 30: "I, personally, do not like very much . . .
Verbatim record of conference, included among Dulles's private papers, Princeton University Library.

p. 438, l. 1: . . . a grim note from Dulles . . .
Dulles's letter to Ambassador Firooz Khan Noon of Pakistan, 21 September 1956, from carbon copy among Dulles's private papers, Princeton University Library.

p. 438, l. 8: Pineau said afterward . . .
Pineau to author, 18 January 1966.

p. 438, l. 22: "It's a terrible thing . . .
Aldrich to author, 9 November 1965.

p. 439, l. 20: Fawzi described the exchange . . .
From Fawzi–Nasser correspondence in the files of Mohammed Hassanein Heikal at *Al-Ahram*, Cairo.

p. 440, l. 9: At all costs Israel must avoid . . .
The Spectator, (London) 6 October 1959.

p. 440, l. 28: But on 23 September he cabled Peres . . .
Bar-Zohar, *Ben Gourion, le Prophète Armé*, Fayard, Paris, 1966, pp. 288/289.

p. 441, l. 13: Peres returned to Israel . . .
Dayan, *Diary of the Sinai Campaign*, p. 24.

p. 441, l. 28: "He must be stopped somehow" . . .
Indianapolis Star, 23 September 1956.

p. 441, l. 37: Dayan took off for Paris . . .
Dayan, *Diary of the Sinai Campaign*, p. 29.

p. 442, l. 31: On the evening of 2 October . . .
Ibid., pp. 31/32.

p. 444, l. 13: Eden was felled that day . . .
An Eden aide to author, 10 May 1964.

p. 444, l. 24: On that same 5 October, as the Security Council . . .
From Nasser-Fawzi correspondence in files of Mohammed Hassanein Heikal at *Al-Ahram*, Cairo.

p. 446, l. 28: One of Eden's senior cabinet colleagues . . .
An Eden cabinet minister to author, 23 February 1966.

p. 446, l. 31: Lloyd and Pineau, in spite of . . .
Pineau to author, 18 January 1966; and an Eden cabinet minister to author, 28 February 1966.

p. 446, l. 36: Bourgès-Maunoury says . . .
Bourgès-Maunoury to author, 2 March 1966.

p. 450, l. 17: Bourgès-Maunoury claims . . .
Ibid.

p. 451, l. 14: Challe reported back . . .
Ibid.

p. 455, l. 3: . . . only Yacov Tsur . . .
A French ambassador to author, 17 January 1966.

p. 455, l. 11: Ben-Gurion rejected . . .
An Israeli cabinet minister to author, 27 April 1964.

p. 456, l. 6: Egypt offered to submit . . .
Aly Sabry to author, 27 October 1956.

p. 456, l. 18: "We are dishonored!"
Jean-Raymond Tournoux, *Secrets d'Etat*, p. 116.

p. 457, l. 13: Pineau said he asked Eden . . .
Pineau to author, 18 January 1966.

p. 457, l. 32: Ben-Gurion insisted on the Sèvres meetings . . .
Bourgès-Maunoury to author, 2 March 1966.

p. 457, l. 38: The war plan . . .
Stockwell to author, 27 February 1966.

p. 458, l. 4: Musketeer Revise was planned . . .
Stockwell article in *Sunday Telegraph* (London), 30 October 1966.

p. 458, l. 26: . . . Beaufre told me: "In the event . . ."
Beaufre to author, 20 January 1966.

p. 458, l. 30: This was not in the Sèvres accord but . . .
Pineau to author, 28 January 1966.

p. 460, l. 8: On 19 October . . .
Le Figaro, 8 November 1966.

p. 460, l. 13: In the occupation of Egyptian territory . . .
Beaufre to author, 24 January 1966.

p. 460, l. 17: At this point Ben-Gurion decided . . .
A French ambassador to author, 17 January 1966.

p. 460, l. 21: Bourgès-Maunoury had hidden . . .
Bourgès-Maunoury to author, 2 March 1966.

p. 460, l. 25: He wrote Eisenhower on 20 October . . .
Cable is in Eisenhower papers, Gettysburg.

p. 460, l. 33: Ben-Gurion, Dayan, and Peres landed, . . .
A French ambassador to author, 17 January 1966.

p. 461, l. 9: The participants in the talks . . .
Pineau to author, 18 January 1966.

p. 462, l. 11: The ministerial talks . . .
Bourgès-Maunoury to author, 2 March 1966.

p. 462, l. 15: Pineau described the villa . . .
Pineau to author, 18 January 1966.

p. 462, l. 16: . . . it was a house of "no color" . . .
Bourgès-Maunoury to author, 2 March 1966.

p. 462, l. 37: Ben-Gurion, too, had asked Pineau . . .
Pineau to author, 18 January 1966.

p. 466, l. 10: France promised, in addition to air cover . . .
Beaufre to author, 20 January 1966.

p. 466, l. 22: The Sèvres accord was signed in triplicate . . .
Pineau to author, 18 January 1966.

p. 467, l. 3: Ben-Gurion made this too look like . . .
Ben-Gurion, *Israel: Years of Challenge*, p. 108.

p. 468, l. 12: Immediately after the cabinet meeting . . .
Nutting, *No End of a Lesson*, p. 105ff.

p. 469, l. 3: The final operational order . . .
Stockwell, *Sunday Telegraph* (London), 30 October 1966.

p. 469, l. 6: Dayan issued his directive . . .
Dayan, *Diary of the Sinai Campaign*, pp. 61 and 210.

p. 471, l. 4: "After the poor crop of Israeli vehicles . . ."
Ibid., p. 68.

p. 471, l. 16: Stockwell decided on a ruse . . .
Stockwell, *Sunday Telegraph* (London), 30 October, 1966.

p. 471, l. 28: Thomas took the opportunity to call on Lloyd . . .
Bar-Zohar, *The Armed Prophet*, p. 234.

p. 472, l. 15: **By 27 October it was common knowledge . . .**
Paul H. Nitze to author, 30 January 1964.

p. 472, l. 22: **The only break in the clam-up . . .**
Dillon to author, 6 October 1965.

p. 472, l. 36: **Chaban-Delmas told me . . .**
Chaban-Delmas to author, 19 January 1966.

p. 473, l. 3: **On 27 October Ben-Gurion summoned . . .**
Ben-Gurion, *Israel: Years of Challenge*, p. 117ff.

p. 473, l. 19: **On the 27th, the invasion force . . .**
D.M.J. Clark *Suez Touchdown*, p. 37ff.

p. 474, l. 4: **As Nasser described it, Amer ordered the plane . . .**
Nasser to author, 17 February 1966.

p. 474, l. 37: **In London, Lloyd dined with and lied to . . .**
Aldrich to author, 9 November 1965; and Aldrich, *The Suez Crisis*, Foreign Affairs, April 1967.

p. 475, l. 6: **Until a few days before the war . . .**
Amin Hilmy II to author, 21 December 1965.

p. 476, l. 6: **The first victims of the war . . .**
Burns, *Between Arab and Israeli*, pp. 304–306.

CHAPTER 15: WAR IN THE SINAI

p. 481, l. 1: **Nasser was watching over a birthday party . . .**
Nasser to author, 17 February 1966, is source of all Nasser quotations in this chapter unless otherwise noted.

p. 481, l. 18: **The first report of the invasion . . .**
Messages cited in this chapter were seen at Egyptian military archives, Cairo. Author has copies of most of them.

p. 481, l. 27: **Wagdy thought the firing . . .**
Major General Mustafa Hassan al-Gamal to author, 3 February 1966.

p. 482, l. 7: **"We realized immediately . . ."**
Akher Saa (Cairo), 5 December 1956. Article is summarized in *The New York Times*, 5 December 1956.

p. 487, l. 28: **But from the outset Pineau was contemptuous . . .**
Pineau to author, 18 and 28 January 1966.

p. 488, l. 7: As Dayan told a BBC interviewer ...
Calvocoressi, *Suez: Ten Years After*, pp. 103/104.

p. 488, l. 21: "As a result of previous preparedness ..."
Keightley, *Operations in Egypt*, is the source for all quotations from Keightley unless otherwise noted.

p. 488, l. 36: Eden quoted the speech ...
Eden, *Facing the Dictators*, Houghton Mifflin, Cambridge, Mass., 1962, p. 20.

p. 490, l. 1: ... the British sought to soften the impact ...
An Eden cabinet minister to author, 18 March 1966.

p. 491, l. 35: At the time of Suez ...
Information on the relative strengths of the two armies comes from the following sources: Dayan, *Diary of the Sinai Campaign*; Nasser's analysis of the war in *Akher Saa*, 5 December 1956; Edgar O'Ballance, *The Sinai Campaign 1956*, Faber & Faber, London, 1959; Erskine B. Childers, *The Road to Suez*, MacGibbon and Kee, London, 1962; with verification and additional detail from the Egyptian military archives and the officers of the Egyptian armed forces historical section.

p. 493, l. 3: Of Israel's sixty Mystères ...
Dayan, *Diary of the Sinai Campaign*, p. 80.

p. 493, l. 4: In addition, there were forty-five French pilots ...
A French Air Force general to author, 26 January 1966.

p. 493, l. 10: And her pilots in training were at home while ...
Nasser to author, 17 February 1966.

p. 495, l. 21: "In order to guarantee fully the junction ..."
Historical Branch, Israeli Army, *The Sinai Campaign*, p. 6.

p. 495, l. 28: Egypt's Eastern Command ...
Information on the Egyptian Eastern Command came from the Egyptian military archives and officers of the Egyptian armed forces historical section.

p. 496, l. 20: Regular army units east of the Canal ...
Dayan, *Diary of the Sinai Campaign*, p. 211.

p. 500, l. 18: Israeli Government sources, in fact, falsely announced ...
The Times, 30 October 1956.

p. 500, l. 34: What is called the Parker Memorial ...
Naum Shoucair, *Tareekh Seena'*, (History of Sinai) Maarif Press, Cairo, 1916.

p. 501, l. 7: As they flew across the frontier ...
For the Israeli side of the action I have relied heavily on both Dayan's *Diary of the Sinai Campaign* and the Israeli Army Historical Branch's *The Sinai Campaign*.

p. 501, l. 17: During the night . . .
A French Air Force general to author, 26 January 1966.

p. 501, l. 20: The Israelis had arranged in advance . . .
Beaufre to author, 20 January 1966.

p. 502, l. 33: The twenty-four casualties . . .
Burns, *Between Arab and Israeli*, p. 181.

p. 503, l. 9: UNTSO tallies from 1 January 1955 . . .
Ibid., pp. 173/174.

p. 503, l. 30: . . . Eisenhower ordered a strong warning . . .
Eisenhower to author, 25 November 1965. Interview transcript is among Eisenhower papers at Gettysburg. My account of Eisenhower's actions is mainly based on this interview and Eisenhower's *Waging Peace*.

p. 504, l. 1: At the UN that evening Sir Pierson Dixon . . .
Eisenhower, *Waging Peace*, p. 75.

p. 504, l. 10: At 4:39 A.M. EST on the 30th . . .
The times of messages are taken from the originals in the Eisenhower papers at Gettysburg.

p. 504, l. 22: Lloyd replied that he thought . . .
Aldrich to author, 9 November 1965; and Aldrich, *The Suez Crisis*, Foreign Affairs, April 1967.

p. 505, l. 8: The ultimatum broke into . . .
The Eden–Eisenhower correspondence is among the Eisenhower papers at Gettysburg.

p. 505, l. 33: Eden had said of it in the House . . .
Hansard, 2 November 1954.

p. 506, l. 28: Eden feels that delaying the message . . .
An Eden cabinet minister to author, 1 January 1965.

p. 507, l. 7: "As I read it I could not believe my eyes . . ."
Hayter, *The Kremlin and the Embassy*, p. 142.

p. 508, l. 5: In Malta that morning . . .
Clark, *Suez Touchdown*, pp. 42, 44–49, and 52.

p. 511, l. 30: Trevelyan had started the day . . .
Dr. Esmat Abdel Megid of the Egyptian Foreign Ministry to author, 25 January 1966.

p. 511, l. 33: . . . Fawzi told Nutting afterward . . .
Nutting, *No End of a Lesson*, pp. 115/116.

p. 512, l. 21: A sea action off Haifa . . .
The account of the *Ibrahim al-Awwal* is drawn from Egyptian military archives and Dayan, *Diary of the Sinai Campaign*, pp. 110–114.

p. 513, l. 15: The myth rests on the misapprehension . . .
This myth appears in Tournoux, *Secrets d'Etat*, pp. 131/132, and Terrence Robertson, *Crisis: The Inside Story of the Suez Conspiracy*, Atheneum, New York, 1965, p. 169.

p. 513, l. 39: The Ibrahim's mission, described by . . .
In a broadcast on 5 November 1956.

p. 518, l. 35: He said he could not continue to serve . . .
Jerusalem Post, 1 November 1956.

p. 519, l. 14: Dulles was assigned to write a first draft.
Emmet John Hughes, *The Ordeal of Power*, p. 219.

p. 521, l. 9: Eden appealed desperately . . .
Keightley, *Operations in Egypt;* Aldrich to author, 9 November 1965; and an Eden cabinet member to author, 18 March 1966.

CHAPTER 16: RETREAT

p. 526, l. 39: "There was a mistake" . . .
Nasser to author, 17 February 1966, an interview from which the Nasser quotations in this chapter are drawn unless otherwise noted.

p. 527, l. 3: Three waves of British bombers . . .
Keightley, *Operations in Egypt*.

p. 527, l. 15: Colonel Amin Haney Hilmy II . . .
Hilmy to author, 21 December 1965.

p. 527, l. 39: The rail and road bridge at Ferdan . . .
In a speech broadcast on 9 November 1956.

p. 528, ll. 18/19: That night . . . French F-84s . . .
A French Air Force general to author, 26 January 1966.

p. 528, l. 24: Nasser conceded . . .
Akher Saa, 5 December 1956.

p. 529, l. 9: Egyptian civilians accepted the claims . . .
Ambassador Raymond Hare to author, 6 July 1966.

p. 529, l. 11: Even with wing-tanks . . .
Keightley, *Operations in Egypt*.

p. 529, l. 12: Allied claims . . .
Thomas, *The Suez Affair*, p. 151, quoting *Air Pictorial*, September 1965.

p. 530, l. 9: "This wasn't so easy" . . .
Stockwell, *Sunday Telegraph*, 6 November 1966.

p. 531, l. 11: When Nasser arrived at General Headquarters . . .
Nasser in *Akher Saa*, 5 December 1956.

p. 531, l. 17: The order to reverse military movements . . .
Unless otherwise noted, the Egyptian military communications in this chapter were translated and copied by the author from originals in the Egyptian military archives with the help of officers of the Egyptian armed forces historical section.

p. 533, l. 6: The colonels of Syria protested . . .
Riad to author, 19 February 1964.

p. 533, l. 33: Mrs. Golda Meir sent an assurance . . .
Burns, *Between Arab and Israeli*, p. 186.

p. 534, l. 8: The plan was brought out . . .
Mohyeddin to author, 3 February 1966.

p. 535, l. 25: The Abu Aoueigila area . . .
My account of the battle of Abu Aoueigila is based on interviews with the Egyptian commander, Colonel Saadeddeen Mutawally, 9 April 1964, and Lieutenant Colonel Mohammed Zohdy, an artillery officer and veteran of the battle, on 9/10 February 1966; Dayan's *Diary of the Sinai Campaign;* the Israeli army's *The Sinai Campaign;* O'Ballance's *The Sinai Campaign 1956;* and a tour of the battlefield in February 1966.

p. 545, l. 39: The Egyptian defenses at Rafah . . .
My account of the battles on the Northern Axis—Rafah, al-Arish—is based on Dayan's and the Israeli army's histories of the Sinai campaign and upon Egyptian military archives material researched with the help of Brigadier General Hassan al-Badry.

p. 548, ll. 15/16: The Israeli military attaché . . . had arranged . . .
Beaufre to author, 24 January 1966, and a French Air Force general to author, 26 January 1966.

p. 551, l. 31: Along with the leaflets . . .
Burns, *Between Arab and Israeli*, p. 183.

p. 552, l. 20: The Israelis regarded the capture . . .
See the *Jerusalem Post*, 5 November 1956.

p. 552, l. 34: Henry Labouisse, the American Director . . .
UN Document A/3212/Add. 1.

p. 553, l. 11: General Burns cited Israel's "record . . ."
Burns, *Between Arab and Israeli*, p. 191.

p. 553, l. 24: After these Arabs had crossed into Syria . . .
Jerusalem Post, 4 November 1956.

p. 553, l. 31: Although Ben-Gurion said afterward . . .
Ben-Gurion, *Israel: Years of Challenge*, p. 120.

p. 553, l. 34: Walter Eytan wrote . . .
In *Israel and the Middle East: Special Issue: Eight Years of Arab Aggression*, Nos. 1–3,
Vol. VIII, Tel Aviv, 1956.

CHAPTER 17: LULL

p. 557, l. 1: Nasser called the withdrawal . . .
Akher Saa, 5 December 1956.

p. 557, l. 16: For this last reason chiefly . . .
Hare to author, 6 July 1966.

p. 557, l. 20: Nasser told me about it nearly a decade later . . .
Nasser to author, 17 February 1966, from which Nasser quotations in this chapter are
drawn unless otherwise noted.

p. 557, l. 36: Hare told me that Nasser was disappointed . . .
Hare to author, 6 July 1966.

p. 558, l. 36: The distribution of arms . . .
Mohyeddin to author, 3 February 1966.

p. 559, l. 6: "I have dedicated my life . . ."
Egyptian Gazette, 27 March 1964.

p. 559, l. 8: Heedless of the dangers . . .
Hare to author, 6 July 1966.

p. 560, l. 22: All of these measures were carried out . . .
The Times, 5 November 1956.

p. 562, l. 1: Eisenhower had told Dulles . . .
White House telephone memorandum, Eisenhower papers, Gettysburg.

p. 562, l. 7: Immediately after the meeting . . .
White House telephone memorandum, Eisenhower papers, Gettysburg.

p. 562, l. 12: Pineau told me afterward that he had made . . .
Pineau to author, 18 January 1966.

p. 562, l. 24: **Speaking from hasty notes . . .**
William B. Macomber to author, 29 January 1964.

p. 563, l. 6: **He told his special assistant . . .**
Ibid.

p. 563, l. 37: **Speaking for Israel . . .**
Eban to author, 27 February 1964.

p. 564, l. 27: **Gaitskell later called it the largest majority . . .**
The Times, 5 November 1956.

p. 565, l. 33: **Eastern Command Headquarters was pulled back . . .**
Egyptian military archives.

p. 566, ll. 7/8: **Ahmed Said, . . . remembered . . .**
Ahmed Said to author, 24 March 1964.

p. 566, l. 23: **From the 2nd of November . . .**
Ibid.

p. 571, l. 38: **. . . Lloyd asked Nutting to help . . .**
Nutting, *No End of a Lesson*, pp. 134 and 137/138.

p. 572, l. 32: **"A dishonest but able performance" . . .**
Sir Harold Nicolson, *The Later Years, 1945–1962*, Atheneum, New York, 1968, p. 314.

p. 572, l. 36: **. . . "Israel agrees to an immediate cease-fire . . ."**
United States Policy in the Middle East: September 1956–June 1957, Department of State Publication 6505, contains excellent documentation on the UN effort to obtain a cease fire. I have relied heavily on it.

p. 574, l. 18: **Israel would not tolerate the presence . . .**
The Times, 5 November 1956.

p. 575, l. 31: **. . . a plan, code-named Penelope . . .**
Beaufre painstakingly clarified the series of supplementary operational plans for the author on 24 January 1966.

p. 577, l. 30: **The paratroopers in Cyprus were alerted . . .**
Sandy Cavanagh, *Airborne to Suez*, p. 109.

p. 577, l. 32: **In London the Cabinet anguished . . .**
An Eden cabinet member to author, 18 March 1966.

p. 578, l. 9: **Stockwell said they brought . . .**
Stockwell, *Sunday Telegraph*, 6 November 1966.

p. 578, l. 23: ... Beaufre wrote afterward, Head canceled ...
Paris Match, 5 November 1966.

p. 578, l. 27: Eden sent a cable ...
From original in Eisenhower papers, Gettysburg.

p. 579, l. 19: In a final flurry of hesitation ...
Keightley, *Operations in Egypt.*

p. 579, l. 40: In essence, the relationship as explained ...
Beaufre to author, 20 and 24 January 1966, and Stockwell to author, 27 February and 9 March 1966.

p. 582, l. 32: Hayter and American Ambassador Charles Bohlen ...
Hayter, *The Kremlin and the Embassy*, p. 154; Bohlen to author, 29 July 1965; Murphy, *Diplomat Among Warriors*, p. 430.

p. 584, l. 4: Andrew H. Berding quotes ...
Berding, *Dulles on Diplomacy*, pp. 115/116.

p. 584, l. 24: At 4 o'clock that Sunday afternoon ...
Stockwell, *Sunday Telegraph*, 6 November 1966.

CHAPTER 18:   PORT SAID

p. 589, l. 5: At 8:20 Monday morning ...
Keightley, *Operations in Egypt;* see also Cavanagh, *Airborne to Suez*, p. 123.

p. 589, l. 7: By 9 o'clock, at Sharm al-Sheikh ...
Historical Branch, Israeli Army, *The Sinai Campaign*, p. 60.

p. 589, l. 10: "You have brought to a successful conclusion ..."
Jerusalem Post, 7 November 1956; see also monitored text of broadcast 7 November 1956.

p. 589, l. 33: An Italian frogman ...
Brigadier General Hassan al-Badri to author, February 1966.

p. 590, l. 22: Egyptian defenses at the straits ...
Colonel Mohammed Wafa' Galal helped me piece together from the Egyptian military archives the Egyptian side of the battle of Sharm al-Sheikh. Keightley's *Operations in Egypt;* Dayan's *Diary of the Sinai Campaign;* and the Israeli Army Historical Branch's *The Sinai Campaign* were the other main sources of my account of the battle.

p. 591, l. 11: The first casualties ...
Colonel Mohammed Dia-eddeen Zohdy helped me reconstruct the Egyptian side of the Damietta incident. The war narratives by Dayan, Keightley, and the Historical Branch of the Israeli army were my main additional sources.

p. 596, l. 19: Stockwell's two essential requirements . . .
Stockwell to author, 27 February 1966.

p. 596, l. 28: "The British allowed their strategy . . ."
Fahmy to author, 9 February 1966.

p. 598, l. 17: Until the first week in September . . .
Brigadier General Salaheddeen Moguy, commander at Port Said, to author, 17 February 1966.

p. 599, l. 8: He was in Ismailiya at 8 P.M. . . .
Ibid.

p. 599, l. 31: "The problem then was . . ."
Brigadier General M. A. H. Butler to author, 12 January 1966. Stockwell, *Sunday Telegraph*, 6 November 1966.

p. 600, l. 6/7: The planes . . . signaled "good morning" . . .
Stockwell, *Sunday Telegraph*, 6 November 1966.

p. 601, l. 24: A French error . . .
Fahmy to author, 9 February 1966.

p. 601, l. 30: Gameel Airfield was defended . . .
Ibid.

p. 602, l. 32: "The showpiece of their performance . . ."
Bernard Fergusson, *The Watery Maze*, p. 404.

p. 603, l. 12: By mid-afternoon Port Said was suffering . . .
My account of the Egyptian side of the Port Said parleys is largely based on an interview with Moguy, 17 February 1966. My interviews with Stockwell and Butler underlie the account of the Allied view of events.

p. 605, l. 5: In an account published in Cairo . . .
In *al-Ahram*, 14 September 1957.

p. 605, l. 22: Nasser was angry . . .
Nasser to author, 17 February 1966.

p. 610, l. 1: Khrushchev told the ambassador . . .
Translated by author from original in Egyptian military archives, Cairo.

p. 613, l. 36: . . . this is the document . . .
Colonel Richard Meinertzhagen, *Middle East Diary 1917–1956*, Cresset, London, 1959, pp. 291/292.

p. 614, l. 13: Shepilov summoned Ambassador Bohlen . . .
Bohlen to author, 29 July 1965.

p. 614, l. 31: Eisenhower's personal reaction . . .
Eisenhower to author, 25 November 1964.

p. 615, l. 9: Mollet's urgent inquiry . . .
Dillon to author, 6 October 1965.

p. 615, l. 14: Eisenhower received "intelligence reports" . . .
Eisenhower, *Waging Peace*, p. 91.

p. 616, ll. 29/30: . . . the Sixth Fleet Commander . . . categorically denied . . .
In *US News and World Report*, 14 December 1956.

p. 617, l. 7: Egypt's main naval effort . . .
My account of Egyptian naval operations is based mainly on the naval headquarters message logs in the Egyptian military archives. Brigadier General Hassan al-Badry greatly assisted my research and added his personal recollections.

p. 617, l. 32: About sixty Egyptian officers were flown . . .
A French ambassador to author, 17 January 1966.

p. 618, l. 11: Douglas Clark, a gunnery officer . . .
Clark, *Suez Touchdown*, p. 63ff.

p. 619, l. 4: A lone Egyptian Mig strafed the British . . .
Cavanagh, *Airborne to Suez*, p. 168.

p. 619, l. 8: Stockwell, however, who was on the scene . . .
Stockwell, *Sunday Telegraph*, 6 November 1966.

p. 619, l. 17: The Egyptians said napalm was used . . .
Fahmy to author, 9 February 1966.

p. 621, l. 4: The only event of military significance . . .
Fergusson, *The Watery Maze*, pp. 399 and 443.

p. 622, l. 40: Eisenhower was fully aware . . .
Eisenhower to author, 25 November 1964.

p. 623, ll. 20/21: Murphy . . . evidently was by-passed . . .
Murphy, *Diplomat among Warriors*, p. 391.

p. 623, l. 26: "Eden's ministry was a dictatorship . . ."
An Eden cabinet minister to author, 23 February 1966.

p. 624, l. 25: The Cabinet insisted . . .
Ibid.

p. 624, l. 27: Another minister put it to me this way . . .
An Eden cabinet minister to author, 23 February 1966.

p. 625, l. 16: The US did not begin operating . . .
Dillon to author, 6 October 1965.

p. 625, l. 22: R. A. Butler, Leader of the House . . .
An Eden cabinet minister to author, 23 February 1966.

p. 625, l. 35: "It was not exactly blackmail" . . .
Ibid.

p. 626, l. 21: Adenauer advised Mollet to accept . . .
Chaban-Delmas to author, 19 January 1966.

p. 627, l. 4: "The question never came up" . . .
An Eden cabinet minister to author, 24 February 1966.

p. 627, l. 20: Excerpts from their talk . . .
Filed among the Eisenhower papers, Gettysburg.

p. 629, l. 18: . . . Eden received a cable from Eisenhower . . .
From copy in Eisenhower papers, Gettysburg.

p. 629, l. 28: General Butler recalled . . .
Butler to author, 12 January 1966.

p. 630, l. 8: "We've now achieved the impossible. . . ."
Stockwell to author, 27 February 1966.

CHAPTER 19:   DISGORGING

p. 635, l. 40/p. 636, l. 1: The Israelis . . . returned nearly 6,000 prisoners . . .
Burns, *Between Arab and Israeli*, p. 246.

p. 636, l. 11: They killed a lone Egyptian soldier . . .
From Uri Dan's broadcast on 6 November 1956.

p. 636, ll. 21/22: The Israelis estimated . . . that 3,000 Egyptians died . . .
Jerusalem Post, 11 November 1956.

p. 637, l. 6: General Burns estimated . . .
Burns, *Between Arab and Israeli*, p. 232.

p. 639, l. 32: Ben-Gurion's biographer and confidant . . .
Bar-Zohar, *The Armed Prophet*, p. 251.

p. 639, l. 35: Oral messages from Washington . . .
Robert St. John, *Ben-Gurion*, Jarrolds, London, 1959, pp. 291/292.

p. 640, l. 12: "He had given in, but..."
Bar-Zohar, *The Armed Prophet*, p. 252.

p. 641, l. 1: Attempting to stave off US pressure...
Ben-Gurion message to Dulles, 18 February 1957, from original in Eisenhower papers, Gettysburg.

p. 641, l. 16: He told me that when his threat of sanctions...
Eisenhower to author, 25 November 1964.

p. 642, l. 1: "My immediate preoccupation after the cease-fire"...
Stockwell, *Sunday Telegraph*, 13 November 1966.

p. 642, l. 6: Keightley kept his full force ready...
Keightley, *Operations in Egypt*.

p. 642, l. 10: The beautiful Madame Beaufre said...
Madame Beaufre to author, 20 January 1966.

p. 642, l. 14: He telephoned Eisenhower at 8:43 A.M....
This account is based on transcripts of the telephone conversations in the Eisenhower papers at Gettysburg.

p. 642, l. 25: The State Department people...
Accounts of how the invitation was withdrawn appear in the following memoirs: Eisenhower, *Waging Peace*, pp. 93/94; Eden, *Full Circle*, p. 630; Adams, *Firsthand Report*, p. 260; and Murphy, *Diplomat Among Warriors*, p. 393.

p. 644, l. 3: US Ambassador Hare... discussed with Nasser...
Hare's report is in the Eisenhower papers, Gettysburg.

p. 648, l. 14: The proposal was raised...
Burns, *Between Arab and Israeli*, pp. 98 and 136/137.

p. 650, l. 40: ... his memorandum on the Rhineland...
Eden, *Facing the Dictators*, p. 376.

p. 652, l. 25: "We had Hungary thrust upon us...."
Washington Post, 19 November 1956.

p. 654, l. 2: "The Western powers are trying to denigrate..."
Ibid.

p. 655, l. 3: Oil already on the way...
Harold Lubell has written a lucid analysis of the Suez oil emergency in a RAND Corporation study for the US Air Force, *Middle East Oil Crises and Western Europe's Energy Supplies*, Johns Hopkins Press, Baltimore, 1963.

p. 655, l. 29: . . . sold their booty of Czech and Soviet small arms . . .
Cavanagh, *Airborne to Suez*, p. 190.

p. 655, l. 32: Terrorism increased . . .
Keightley, *Operations in Egypt*.

p. 657, l. 37: Foster and I at first found it difficult . . .
Eisenhower, *Waging Peace*, p. 122.

p. 659, l. 36: Emissaries like Teddy Kolleck . . .
Teddy Kolleck to author, 4 May 1964.

p. 659, l. 40/p. 660, l. 1: The most quotable . . .
As translated by the *Jerusalem Post*, 16 November 1956.

p. 660, l. 4: This was the directive . . .
Dayan, *Diary of the Sinai Campaign*, pp. 149/150.

p. 660, l. 9: Egyptians at the UN noted . . .
The New York Times, 16 November 1956.

p. 660, l. 15: He asked for a diagnosis . . .
Jerusalem Post, 16 November 1956.

p. 660, l. 34: Another funny coincidence involving Meinertzhagen . . .
Meinertzhagen, *Middle East Diary 1917–1956*, p. 282.

p. 661, l. 16: When Eban called on Dulles . . .
Eban to author, 27 February 1964.

p. 662, l. 13: . . . the Israelis destroyed the many military buildings . . .
Burns, *Between Arab and Israeli*, p. 243.

p. 662, l. 25: An Israeli *aide mémoire* to Hammarskjold . . .
Text in *United States Policy in the Middle East: September 1956–June 1957*, Department of State Publication 6505, pp. 255–259.

p. 663, l. 22: Ben-Gurion wrote in his memoirs . . .
Ben-Gurion, *Israel: Years of Challenge*, p. 151.

p. 664, l. 24: In a very long secret *aide mémoire* . . .
Text taken from copy in Eisenhower papers, Gettysburg.

p. 668, l. 6: . . . those formulations consciously avoided . . .
R. R. Baxter, *The Law of International Waterways*, pp. 161/162.

p. 668, l. 9: Ben-Gurion called his Cabinet . . .
Burns, *Between Arab and Israeli*, pp. 258/259.

p. 668, l. 40: Nasser told me he was impelled . . .
Nasser to author, 17 February 1966.

p. 670, l. 9: The *Fedayeen* were reorganized as special police . . .
Burns to author, 5 May 1965.

CHAPTER 20:   REPRISE

p. 677, l. 18: Brigadier General Mordecai Hod . . .
Randolph S. and Winston S. Churchill, *The Six Day War*. Houghton Mifflin, Boston, 1967, p. 91.

p. 677, l. 25: The Israelis had every last detail worked out . . .
Peter Young, *The Israeli Campaign 1967*, William Kimber, London, 1967, p. 87.

p. 681, l. 6: General Rabin threatened to send a force . . .
The Churchills, *The Six Day War*, p. 29; and Nasser's speech, 22 May 1967.

p. 681, l. 10: Then on 13 May . . .
Nasser's speech, 22 May 1967.

p. 681, l. 12: The Knesset Foreign Affairs and Security Committee . . .
Soviet government statement, 23 May 1967.

p. 682, l. 11: Israeli gunners shelled UN headquarters . . .
The New York Times, 14 June 1967.

p. 682, l. 13: Israeli soldiers had three UNEF Swedes . . .
The New York Times, 15 June 1967.

p. 682, l. 35: James Reston reported from Cairo . . .
The New York Times, 5 June 1969.

p. 683, l. 35: . . . the Sixth Fleet moved to within striking distance . . .
The New York Times, 31 May 1967.

p. 683, l. 40/p. 684, l. 1: Richard Rovere reported . . .
The New Yorker, 24 June 1967.

p. 684, l. 7: But four days later the Russians were worried . . .
Nasser's speech, 9 June 1967.

p. 684, l. 11: Nasser, increasingly fearful . . .
Ambassador Charles Yost, *The Arab-Israeli War: How It Began*, Foreign Affairs, January 1968.

p. 684, l. 13: **He gave a similar assurance . . .**
Secretary General's report, 27 May 1967.

p. 686, l. 2: **. . . Senator Fulbright was the only prominent figure . . .**
The New York Times, 29 May 1967.

p. 686, l. 10: **. . . Johnson deliberately delayed . . .**
James Reston, *The New York Times,* 11 June 1967.

p. 686, l. 12: **. . . the US canceled aid agreements . . .**
The New York Times, 24 June 1967.

p. 687, l. 21: **"An army in a democratic republic . . ."**
The New York Times, 30 May 1967, p. 3.

p. 688, l. 15: **At 7:45 A.M. on 5 June 1967 . . .**
This summary of the war is based on the reporting in *The New York Times* and the excellent book, *The Six Day War,* by the Churchills, father and son.

p. 690, l. 2: **Nasser estimated Egypt had lost 80 per cent . . .**
Nasser interview with William Attwood, *Look* magazine, 19 March 1968.

p. 690, l. 3: **Israel listed 679 dead . . .**
The New York Times, 12 June 1967.

p. 690, l. 19: **. . . Washington was stalling . . .**
James Reston in *The New York Times,* 11 June 1967.

p 690, l. 24: **Whether or not there was any collusion . . .**
Al-Ahram as reported in *The New York Times,* 14 October 1967.

p. 690, l. 26: **Major General Carl von Horn . . .**
Major General Carl von Horn, *Soldiering for Peace,* p. 114.

p. 690, l. 40/p. 691, l. 1: **Cairenes wept openly . . .**
Neal Ascherson in *The Observer,* (London) 25 June 1967.

p. 691, ll. 11 & 13: **. . . Ben-Gurion said, . . . "Nasser is a patriot . . ."**
The New York Times, 18 June 1967.

p. 691, l. 36: **Every victory might be followed . . .**
As broadcast on 2 April 1957.

p. 692, l. 39: **Israel has now reached 90 per cent . . .**
The New York Times, 20 January 1969.

p. 695, l. 15: **The present leaders of the *Fedayeen,* . . .**
The New York Times, 1 January 1969.

p. 695, l. 39: Egypt bade farewell . . .
The New York Times, 20 January 1969.

p. 696, l. 18: . . . I. F. Stone recently urged his fellow Jews . . .
I. F. Stone's Weekly, 13 January 1969.

p 697, l. 17: Because, in general, rural refugee fathers . . .
Dr. John H. Davis, *The Evasive Peace*, pp. 63/64.

p. 697, l. 36: . . . dismissed in quotation marks by Abba Eban . . .
Abba Eban, *My People*, p. 500.

p. 698, l. 4: "Israel will continue to be conspicuously non-Arab . . .
Ibid., p. 499.

p. 698, l. 37: . . . "scorn and contempt" . . .
James Feron in *The New York Times*, 2 January 1969.

p. 698, l. 39: The urbane Eban himself commented: . . .
The New York Times, 5 January 1969.

p. 699, l. 3: As I. F. Stone said: "How we feel . . ."
The New York Times, 19 November 1968.

p. 700, l. 2: Walter Levy . . .
Quoted by Dan Cordtz in his article, *But What Do We Do About the Arabs?*, Fortune, 1 September 1967.

Bibliography

So many books and articles have been published on the two Suez-Sinai wars that the list of titles in English and French alone would fill a respectable volume. In the larger context of the Palestine Problem, the Zionist Archives in New York have published since 1946 some twenty-odd volumes of bibliography. Appending a full critical bibliography here would be like adding water to the sea. In any case, the bulk of what I read had to be rejected or taken at other than face value in the light of the interviews and personal experiences which not only provided a great part of my information but also guided my research and interpretation. In short, a full bibliography in addition to my source notes would not justify the resulting enlargement of the size and cost of this book. But for the serious general reader—layman, politician, diplomat, soldier, and visiting scholar from other fields—I have, after discarding the preponderance of material of narrow relevance or dubious value, selected from what remained some titles I think will best reward further reading. Most of these are writings based on firsthand experience—illuminations from the inside—to which I have added a handful of particularly illuminating works by outsiders.

ILLUMINATION FROM THE INSIDE

Books by Characters in the Story

ADAMS, SHERMAN, *First Hand Report*. Harper & Brothers, New York, 1961.

ALAMI, MUSA, *The Lesson of Palestine*. *Middle East Journal* (Washington), October 1949. (Condensed translation of his book, *'Ibrat Falasteen*, Beirut, 1949.)

BEN-GURION, DAVID, *Israel: Years of Challenge*. Holt, Rinehart & Winston, New York, 1963.

BERDING, ANDREW H., *Dulles on Diplomacy*. Van Nostrand, Princeton, N.J., 1965.

BURNS, LIEUTENANT GENERAL E. L. M., *Between Arab and Israeli*. Obolensky, New York, 1963.

CALVOCORESSI, PETER, *Suez: Ten Years After*. Pantheon, New York, 1967. (BBC interviews)

CAVENAGH, SANDY, *Airborne to Suez*. William Kimber, London, 1965.

CLARK, D. M. J., *Suez Touchdown: A Soldier's Tale*. Peter Davies, London, 1964.

DAVIS, DR. JOHN H., *The Evasive Peace: A Study of the Zionist-Arab Problem*. John Murray, London, 1968. (Former UNRWA chief focuses on refugees)

DAYAN, MAJOR GENERAL MOSHE, *Diary of the Sinai Campaign*. Harper & Row, New York, 1966, also Weidenfeld & Nicolson, London, 1966.

EBAN, ABBA, *My People: The Story of the Jews*. Random House, New York, 1968.

——, *Voice of Israel*. Horizon Press, New York, 1957. (Collection of speeches)

EDEN, SIR ANTHONY (Earl of Avon), *Full Circle: The Memoirs of Anthony Eden*. Houghton Mifflin, Boston, 1960. (The third of three volumes)

EISENHOWER, DWIGHT D., *Waging Peace: 1956–1961*. Doubleday, Garden City, N.Y., 1965. (The second of two volumes of White House memoirs.)

EYTAN, WALTER, *The First Ten Years: A Diplomatic History of Israel*. Simon & Schuster, New York, 1958.

BERNARD EDWARD FERGUSSON, *The Watery Maze: The Story of Combined Operations*. Collins, London, 1961.

GLUBB, LIEUTENANT GENERAL SIR JOHN BAGOT (Glubb Pasha), *A Soldier with the Arabs*. Hodder & Stoughton, London, 1957.

HAYTER, SIR WILLIAM, *The Kremlin and the Embassy*. Hodder & Stoughton, London, 1966.

HISTORICAL BRANCH OF GENERAL HEADQUARTERS, ISRAELI ARMY, *The Sinai Campaign*. Tel Aviv, no date.

HUGHES, EMMET JOHN, *The Ordeal of Power: A Political Memoir of the Eisenhower Years*. Atheneum, New York, 1963.

HURST, H. E., *The Nile*. Constable, London, 1952.

HUSSEIN, KING OF JORDAN, *Uneasy Lies the Head*. Heinemann, London, 1962.

HUTCHISON, COMMANDER ELMO H., *Violent Truce*. Devin-Adair, New York, 1956.

IONIDES, MICHAEL, *Divide and Lose: The Arab Revolt, 1955 to 1958*. Geoffrey Bles, London, 1960.

LEULLIETTE, PIERRE, *St. Michael and the Dragon: Memoirs of a Paratrooper*. Houghton Mifflin, Boston, 1964.

MENZIES, ROBERT GORDON, *Speech Is of Time: Selected Speeches and Writings*. Cassell, London, 1958.

MOLLET, GUY, *Bilan et Perspectives Socialistes*. Librairie Plon, Paris, 1958.

MURPHY, ROBERT, *Diplomat among Warriors*. Doubleday, Garden City, N.Y., 1964.

NAGUIB, MOHAMMED, *Egypt's Destiny*. Gollancz, London, 1955.

NASSER, GAMAL ABDEL, *The Philosophy of the Revolution*. Mondiale Press, Cairo, no date. (Also under title, *Egypt's Liberation: The Philosophy of the Revolution* introduction by Dorothy Thompson). Public Affairs Press, Washington, 1955.

——, *President Gamal Abdel Nasser's Speeches and Press Interviews*. Information Department, Cairo. (Annual publication, of uneven quality, beginning in 1958.)

——, *Majmouaa Khutub wa Tasreehat wa Bayanat, Vol. I*. (Speeches and interviews from 1952 to 1958, available only in Arabic), Information Department, Cairo, no date. (Also of uneven quality.)

NICOLSON, NIGEL, *People and Parliament*. Weidenfeld & Nicolson, London, 1958.

NUTTING, ANTHONY, *No End of a Lesson*. Constable, London, 1967.

REYNIER, JACQUES DE, *A Jerusalem un Drapeau Flottait sur la Ligne de Feu*. La Baconnière, Neuchâtel, Switzerland, 1950. (Eyewitness report of Israel's birth struggles by chief Red Cross representative.)

SADAT, COLONEL ANWAR, *Revolt on the Nile*. Allan Wingate, London, 1957.

UNITED NATIONS RELIEF AND WORKS AGENCY, *Twice in a Lifetime*. Middle East Export Press, Beirut, 1968. (Text and pictorial essay on the refugees.)

VON HORN, MAJOR GENERAL CARL, *Soldiering for Peace*. McKay, New York, 1967.

WEIZMANN, CHAIM, *Trial and Error* (Autobiography), Harper & Brothers for East West Library, London, no date.

Articles by Characters in the Story

ALDRICH, AMBASSADOR WINTHROP W., "The Suez Crisis: A Footnote to History." *Foreign Affairs* (New York) April 1967.

BALDWIN, ROGER N., "The Cairo Trial." *Land Reborn* (New York), February/March 1955. (*Land Reborn* is a defunct periodical of the American Christian Palestine Committee.)

BEAUFRE, GENERAL ANDRÉ, "Suez 1956: Un Succès Militaire qui dédouche sur un Echec Politique." *Figaro* (Paris), 8 November 1966.

BEN-GURION, DAVID, "In Reply to President Charles de Gaulle." *The New Leader* (New York), 29 January 1968.

——, "Israel's Security and Her International Position Before and After the Sinai Campaign." *Israel Government Year Book*, 5720, 1959/60.

——, (Condensed translation of an essay on the achievement of statehood). *Jewish Observer and Middle East Review* (London), 8 May 1959.

CROSSMAN, R. H. S., "Nasser's Plan for Peace." *New Statesman & Nation* (London), 22 January 1955. (An interview.)

DAYAN, MAJOR GENERAL MOSHE, "Israel's Border and Security Problems." *Foreign Affairs* (New York), January 1955.

——, "Security before Sinai," *Jerusalem Post*, 24 April 1964.

EBAN, ABBA, "Vision in the Middle East." *Foreign Affairs* (New York), July 1965.

GLUBB, LIEUTENANT GENERAL SIR JOHN BAGOT, "Violence on the Jordan-Israel Border," *Foreign Affairs* (New York), July 1954.

KEIGHTLEY, GENERAL SIR CHARLES F., "Operations in Egypt—November to December, 1956." Supplement to the *London Gazette* of Tuesday, 10 September 1957, Her Majesty's Stationery Office, London, 12 September 1957.

NASSER, GAMAL ABDEL, "The Egyptian Revolution," *Foreign Affairs* (New York), January 1955.

——, "Nasser Describes 'Foiling' of Israel." *The New York Times*, 5 December 1956. (Greatly condensed version of Nasser's war article in *Akher Saa*, the Cairo weekly magazine, 5 December 1956.)

PINEAU, CHRISTIAN, "Si J'Avais à Refaire l'Opération de Suez." *Le Monde* (Paris), 4 November 1966.

ROOSEVELT, KERMIT, "The Partition of Palestine: A Lesson in Pressure Politics." *Middle East Journal* (Washington), January 1948.

STOCKWELL, GENERAL SIR HUGH, "Suez from the Inside." *Sunday Telegraph* (London), 30 October, 6 November, and 13 November 1966.

SUEZ CANAL COMPANY, *Assemblée Générale des Actionnaires, 98ème Réunion, 12 Juin 1956.* (Last annual report before nationalization.)

WEIZMANN, CHAIM, "Palestine's Role in the Solution of the Jewish Problem." *Foreign Affairs* (New York), January 1942.

YOST, AMBASSADOR CHARLES W., "The Arab-Israeli War: How It Began." *Foreign Affairs* (New York), January 1968.

YUNIS, MAHMOUD, "The Nationalization of the Suez Canal Company." *The Scribe* (Cairo), May 1963.

Documents on the Region and the Period

HUREWITZ, J. C., Ed., *Diplomacy in the Near and Middle East: A Documentary Record; Vol. I, 1533–1914; Vol. II, 1914–*Van Nostrand, Princeton, 1956.

KHALIL, MUHAMMAD, Ed., *The Arab States and the Arab League: A Documentary Record; Vol. I, Constitutional Developments; Vol. II, International Affairs.* Khayat's, Beirut, 1962.

WOODWARD, E. L., and BUTLER, ROHAN, Eds., *Documents on British Foreign Policy 1919–1939; First Series, Vol. IV, 1919.* Her Majesty's Stationery Office, London, 1952, and

BUTLER, ROHAN, and BURY, J. P. T., Eds., *Ibid., Vol. XIII, January 1920–March 1921.* Her Majesty's Stationery Office, London, 1963.

Documents on International Affairs (Annual); *1953*, Ed., Denise Folliot; *1954*, Ed., Denise Folliot; *1955*, Eds., Noble Frankland and Patricia Woodcock; *1956*, Eds., Noble Frankland and Vera King; *1957*, Eds., Noble Frankland and Vera King; *1958*, Ed., Gillian King; *1959*, Ed., Gillian King. Oxford University Press for the Royal Institute of International Affairs, Chatham House, London.

Public Papers of the Presidents of the United States (Annual), *1956* and *1957*. General Services Administration, Washington, D.C.

Summary of World Broadcasts, especially *Part IV: The Arab World, Israel, Greece, Turkey, Persia.* British Broadcasting Corporation Monitoring Service, Caversham Park, Reading, England. (Daily translations of speeches, statements, communiqués, and press commentary, with full texts of the most important items, constituting the contemporary historian's richest trove of dated and timed source material. Its American counterpart is the *Foreign Broadcast Information Service*, Washington.)

Documents on the Suez Canal Crisis and the High Dam

EAYRS, JAMES, *The Commonwealth and Suez: A Documentary Survey*. Oxford University Press, London, 1964.

LAUTERPACHT, ELIHU, Ed., *The Suez Canal Settlement: A Selection of Documents*. Stevens, London, 1960. (Companion to the Comparative and International Law Society selection below.)

SHEPILOV, D. T., *The Suez Problem*. (Selection of his speeches and Soviet Statements), Foreign Languages Publishing House, Moscow, 1956.

Aswan (Special Issue). The Scribe–The Arab Review (National Publications House, Cairo), May 1964.

La Crise de Suez: Etude Chronologique et Documentaire. Orient (Paris) No. 1, January 1957, and

Documents et Notices. Orient (Paris) No. 2, April 1957. (These first two issues of *Orient*, a quarterly edited by Marcel Colombe, are hard to come by but they are worth the trouble.)

The Suez Canal: A Selection of Documents Relating to the International Status of the Suez Canal and the Position of the Suez Canal Company, 30 November 1854–26 July 1956. The Society of Comparative Legislation and International Law, London, 1956. (Useful, although apparently presented to make the case against nationalization.)

The Suez Canal Company and the Decision Taken by the Egyptian Government: Part I, 26 July–15 September 1956, and *Ibid.: Part II, August 1956–May 1957*. Suez Canal Company, Paris, (*Part I*) 1956 and (*Part II*) 1957.

The Suez Canal Problem: July 26–September 22, 1956. Department of State Publication 6392, US Government Printing Office, Washington, October 1956, and

United States Policy in the Middle East: September 1956–June 1957. Department of State Publication 6505, US Government Printing Office, Washington, August 1957. (Companion compilations of documents.)

White Paper on the Nationalization of the Suez Maritime Canal Company. Government Press, Cairo, 1956. (Hard to find but worth it.)

ILLUMINATION FROM THE OUTSIDE

Books

ANONYMOUS, *The Old Testament*, especially Genesis, Exodus, and Joshua.

ANTONIUS, George, *The Arab Awakening*. Hamish Hamilton, London, 1938.

BARRACLOUGH, GEOFFREY, and WALL, RACHEL F., *Survey of International Affairs, 1955–1956*. Oxford University Press for the Royal Institute of International Affairs, Chatham House, London, 1960, and

BARRACLOUGH, GEOFFREY, *Survey of International Affairs, 1956–1958*. Oxford University Press for the R.I.I.A., Chatham House, London, 1962. (Two volumes in a perennial series of great value.)

BAR-ZOHAR, MICHEL, *The Armed Prophet: A Biography of Ben-Gurion* (translated from the French). Barker, London, 1967, and

——, *Suez Ultra-secret* (in French). Fayard, Paris, 1964. (Two works based on privileged access to Ben-Gurion, his papers, and his circle, unfortunately marred by careless and florid writing.)

BAXTER, R. R., *The Law of International Waterways, with Particular Regard to Interoceanic Canals*. Harvard University Press, Cambridge, Mass., 1964.

EPSTEIN, LEON D., *British Politics in the Suez Crisis*. University of Illinois Press, Urbana, Ill., 1964.

FRISCHWASSER–RA'ANAN, HEINZ FELIX, *The Frontiers of a Nation*. Batchworth Press, London, 1955.

KIMCHE, JON and DAVID, *A Clash of Destinies*. Praeger, New York, 1960.

KIRK, GEORGE, *The Middle East in the War*. Oxford University Press for the R.I.I.A., Chatham House, London, 1952, and

——, *The Middle East 1945–1950*. Oxford University Press for the R.I.I.A., Chatham House, London, 1954. (Two volumes in the above-praised perennial series of Surveys.)

LACOUTURE, JEAN and SIMONNE, *Egypt in Transition* (translated from the French). Methuen, London, 1958.

LITTLE, TOM, *High Dam at Aswan*. Methuen, London, 1965.

SEALE, PATRICK, *The Struggle for Syria: A Study of Post-War Arab Politics, 1945–1958*. Oxford University Press for the R.I.I.A., Chatham House, London, 1965.

STEIN, LEONARD, *The Balfour Declaration*. Vallentine-Mitchell, London, 1961.

SYKES, CHRISTOPHER, *Crossroads to Israel*. World, Cleveland and New York, 1965.

United States Foreign Policy, Study No. 13, prepared by the staff of the US Senate Committee on Foreign Relations, in Vol. II of the *Compilation of Studies*, US Government Printing Office, Washington, September 1960.

Articles

BRILLIANT, MOSHE, "Israel's Policy of Reprisals." *Harper's Magazine*, March 1955.

CORDTZ, DAN, "But What Can We Do about the Arabs?" *Fortune*, September 1967.

Periodicals Edited for the General Reader with Special Interests

l'Année Politique: Revue Chronologique des Principaux Faits Politiques, Economiques, et Sociaux de la France, Editions du Grand Siècle, Paris. (Annual since World War II.)

Israel Government Year Book. (Has valuable introductory articles.)

The Listener, London. (Weekly publication of notable BBC broadcasts.)

The Middle East Journal, Washington. (Quarterly publication since 1947 of the

Middle East Institute with regular documentary, bibliography, and chronology sections as well as articles and book reviews.)

Revue Egyptienne de Droit International, Cairo. (Annual publication since 1945 of the Egyptian Society of International Law, Cairo. Owes its existence and much of its excellence to limelight-avoiding Judge Jasper Yeates Brinton of Cairo, an American who was presiding judge of the international Mixed Courts of Egypt until their abolition in 1948.)

United Nations Yearbook. (Annual chronology and summary of the official records of the Security Council, the General Assembly, and other branches and agencies of the UN.)

The parliamentary journals, the diplomatic bulletins, the full UN official records and reports, the press and periodicals of the several countries involved in this history, which were among my best published sources, will be too well known to the specialist and of too little use to the general reader to merit lengthening this bibliography with them.

Index

Abbas Hilmi, Khedive of Egypt, 172
al-Abd, Brig. Gen. Jaafar, 532, 546, 548, 549, 550
Abdullah, King of Jordan, 695
Abercrombie, Sir Ralph, 167
Abraham, 23–24
Abu Aoueigila, Sinai, 108, 467, 492, 496, 591; Sinai invasion (1956), 497, 498, 510, 516, 518, 526, 530, 531, 536–44, 545, 546, 569, 592, 662, 689; Sinai invasion (1967), 689
Abu Kir (vessel), 528, 670
Abu Kir Bay, 167
Abu Nossair, Mohammed, 339
Abu Nuwwar, Maj. Gen. Aly, 532–33
Abu Suwweir, Egypt, 340, 398, 458, 526, 622, 650
Abu Zabel, Egypt, 529, 566
Abul Fath brothers, 409
Abul Fath, Mahmoud, quoted, 187
Acheson, Dean, 372–73
Activism (Israeli): Ben Gurion leadership and, 47, 48, 49–53. 64, 65, 69, 80, 94, 95, 106, 245, 270, 454, 678; of Dayan, 69, 494–95; expansionism and, 71, 72, 102–104, 105, 278, 691–92, 697–98; terrorism and, 60–61, 63, 97, 684–85
Adams, Sherman, 614; quoted, 314, 610, 643, 665, 666
Aden, 335, 374, 409

Adenauer, Konrad, 626
Afghanistan, 667
Africa, 89, 129, 149, 152, 154; Jewish immigrants, 495; Russia and, 228, 582; Suez War (1956) response, 348, 568, 573, 582, 633; Suez War (1967) response, 695. *See also* specific countries
Afrika Korps, 177
Agence France Presse, 351
Ahmed, Hocine Ait, 133
al-Ahram (newspaper), 261, 324, 503
L'Aigle (vessel), 168
Air warfare, 172, 254, 474, 486; al-Auja, 11; on Bedouin refugees, 109; French aircraft sales and, 95, 100, 101, 439; Gaza Strip (1955), 97, 247; helicopters in, 621, 689; Jordan raids, 448, 678; Suez War (1956) attacks, 364, 370, 374, 387, 392, 398, 443, 450, 457–58, 461, 462, 464, 466, 470, 472, 483, 488–89, 492–93, 498, 508, 509, 510, 512, 513, 516, 518, 519, 521, 525, 526–30, 537, 540, 541, 543, 544, 548–49, 550, 558–59, 565, 566, 567, 594, 601, 606–607, 617–19, 634, 658, 687; Suez War (1956) paratroops, 465, 469, 471, 481, 488, 490, 495, 497, 500, 501, 507–508, 509–10, 515, 517–18, 530, 539,

554, 570, 573, 575–77, 578, 579, 599–604, 609, 613, 618, 620–21, 622, 629, 636, 688; Suez War (1956) plane losses, 529; Suez War (1967), 488, 679, 687–89, 690
al-Akhbar (newspaper), 119, 218, 259, 413, 418
Akhbar al-Yom (newspaper), 256
Akher Saa (periodical), 85, 410, 635
Akka (vessel), 527, 528
Akrotiri, Cyprus, 576, 577
Alamein, battle of, 178, 467, 540
Albion (vessel), 471, 527
Aldrich, Winthrop, 322, 342, 426, 438, 447; Lloyd and, 474–75, 504, 573
Aleutians, 230
Alexander, Field Marshal Lord, 374
Alexandria, Egypt, 113, 180, 300, 321, 340; Algerian arms shipments, 456; assassination attempt in, 15–20, 188–89; riots of 1882, 170; sabotage in, 17, 73, 74, 76; Suez Canal nationalization speech in, 341, 342, 344–52, 367, 373; Suez War (1956) and, 382, 393–94, 397, 398, 424, 434, 457–58, 489, 490, 496, 513, 521, 530, 596, 598, 615, 616–17, 618; Suez War (1967) and, 683

Algeria, 39, 41, 100, 136, 139, 218, 260–61, 358, 402, 694; Egypt and, 19, 98, 118, 129–52, 213, 220, 247, 249, 314, 333, 334, 336, 342, 368, 373, 378, 433, 456, 558, 566; FLN cease-fire offer (1956), 414; Suez War (1956) and, 406, 434, 445, 633, 637
Algiers, Algeria, 147, 152, 456
Ali Muntar, Gaza Strip, 552
Allen, George V., 100, 254, 283–89, 326, 346; quoted, 315
Allenby, Edmund, Lord, 172, 173
Almaza airfield, Cairo, 526, 527
Alon, Gen. Yigal, 108
Altalena (vessel), 52
Aly, Rashid, 229
Amer, Maj. Gen. Aly Aly, 343
Amer, Gen. Abdel Hakim, 178, 283, 474, 599, 603, 612; rearmament (1955), 13, 84, 98, 99, 243, 249; Sinai defense and, 111, 119, 481–82, 491, 493–94, 510, 532; Suez Canal nationalization and, 337; Syrian pipelines and, 533
American Baptist Hospital, Gaza, 120, 661
American Civil War, 155
American Council for Judaism, 63
American Revolution, 38, 41
Amery, Julian, 371, 401
Amman, Jordan, 124, 202, 203, 210, 448, 474, 482
Andau Bridge, 643
Anderson, Robert B.; secret peace mission, 307, 308, 309, 310, 313; Canal nationalization and, 413–14
Andrea Doria (vessel), 348–49
Anglo-Egyptian Condominium, 174
Anglo-Egyptian Suez Canal Base Evacuation Agreement, *see* Heads of Agreement
Anglo-Egyptian Treaty of Preferential Alliance (1936), 175–77, 179, 181, 184, 193; abrogation, 180, 188
Anglo-Iranian Oil Company, 180
Anglo-Iraqi *Special Agreement* (1955), 202
Anglo-Iraqi Treaty of Preferential Alliance (1932), 193, 449
Anglo-Jordanian Treaty, 203, 448, 449
Anglo-Turkish boundary agreement (1906), 639
Anti-Semitism, 106–107, 190, 397; Dulles accused of, 276; European, 28, 29, 38–39, 40, 73, 131, 230–31, 232, 251; Suez War and, 672; Zionist charges of, 72, 686, 698–99
Antonius, George, 35
Anwar, Ibrahim, 599, 603

Aqaba, Jordan, 32, 35, 486, 590, 661
Aqaba, Gulf of, 11, 439, 486; Israeli shipping rights, 42, 53, 94, 98, 104, 143, 163, 433, 460, 462, 589, 590, 662, 664–65, 667–68, 669, 675, 676; Suez War (1956), 106, 111, 121, 468, 471, 483, 531, 554, 589, 590, 638, 640, 662, 664–65, 676, 692; Suez War (1967) and, 590, 682–83, 685–86, 692
Arab Empire, 26, 27
Arab-Israeli nonaggression pact proposal (1954), 75
Arab-Israeli War (1948) *see* Palestine War (1948)
Arab League, 40–42, 94, 278, 680; Algeria and, 133, 151; Aqaba shipping and, 590, 675; Baghdad Pact and, 18, 195, 196, 197, 201–205; Britain and, 178–79, 186, 197, 204–205, 393, 403; Egyptian entry, 41–42; military strength, 96, 270–71; Palestine peace treaties and, 67–68, 73
Arab League Collective Security Pact (1950), 88, 197–98
Arab Legion, *see* Jordanian Army (Arab Legion)
Arab News Agency, 282, 307, 414
Arab Rebellion (1936), 50, 53, 54, 55
Arabi, Col. Ahmed, 169, 170, 183, 217, 527
Arabs, 23, 24, 53, 54, 55, 411, 647; Algerian numbers, 132; British pro-Arab policy, 28, 30–31, 434–35, 686; European imperialism and, 40–41, 43, 88, 178, 194, 218, 227–28, 250, 251, 252, 253, 254, 272, 279, 288, 292, 335, 345, 452, 645; infiltration control measures, 61, 69; Israeli arms policy and, 678–69, 699; Palestine claims of, 26–35, 68, 268–69, 692, 694, 697, 698, 700; refugee compensation issue and, 103–104; Russian expansionism and, 227, 230, 232, 250, 611; Suez War (1956) responses, 568, 611, 635, 637, 644, 653; Suez War (1967) responses, 694, 695, 696; unity, Eden and, 178–79
See also specific countries
Ardahan, Turkey, 229, 230
Argov, Meir, quoted, 122
al-Arish, Egypt, 108, 428, 483, 492, 530, 639; Sinai invasion (1956) and, 495, 496, 497, 518, 526, 531, 536, 538, 539, 540, 541, 543, 544, 545, 548, 550, 551–52, 613, 635, 636, 660, 662
Ark Royal (vessel), 471, 527
Arlosoroff, Chaim, 50

Armaments, 1, 6, 270; Algerian, 19, 134, 150, 151, 378, 456; British, 364, 457, 475, 532, 565, 567–68, 596, 657; "dibber" bombs, 689; Egyptian guerrillas and, 531, 534, 536, 558–59, 565, 568, 599, 608, 619, 695; Egyptian requirements, 8, 13, 14, 15, 20, 74, 83–85, 87–88, 89–91, 116, 142–43, 190, 238, 239, 265, 375, 396, 496, 552, 646; Egyptian-Russian deal, 3, 90–91, 96, 98–102, 106, 107, 109, 112–14, 117, 118, 121, 140, 141, 143, 186, 201, 215, 216, 219, 220, 225, 240, 241, 242–55, 256, 258, 259, 261, 281–94, 302, 304, 306, 310, 316–18, 322, 326, 334, 346, 369, 487, 492–93, 557, 610, 617, 686, 695, 699; embargo proposals, 118, 219, 259–60, 293, 564; Iraq, 71, 195, 200, 408; Israeli requirements, 14, 48, 51, 52, 67, 70, 83, 96, 101–102, 106, 115, 130, 134, 143–44, 231, 270, 281, 287, 346, 442, 475, 487, 678–79, 686, 699; Israeli-French deal, 75, 88–89, 95, 98, 100, 101, 112, 113, 114, 116, 117, 121, 125, 135, 137, 138–39, 140, 141–42, 146, 148, 149, 151, 201, 213, 216, 219–20, 245, 249, 253, 288, 289–91, 310, 392, 433, 439, 445, 454, 470–71, 492–93, 494, 573; napalm, 518, 543, 592, 595, 636, 658; nuclear, 186, 187, 236, 237, 239, 240, 610, 611, 614, 615–16, 636, 657, 699, 700; Suez War imbalance, 634, 635, 661, 686; Syrian, 117, 253, 653, 661; UN Emergency Force, 608, 669–70, 682; Western offers to Arabs, 64, 71, 88, 195, 200–205 (*See also* Baghdad Pact)
Armenia, 53, 236
Arriba (newspaper), 434
Asia, 89, 129, 149, 152; Jewish emigrants, 495; Russia and, 225–26, 228, 582; Suez War (1956) response, 568, 573, 582, 633; Suez War (1967) response, 695. *See also* specific countries
Assimilationism, 39, 231
Assiut, Egypt, 545, 566, 603, 606
Associated Press, 285
Aswan, Egypt, 675
Aswan Dam, 174, 299, 300, 301, 321
Aswan High Dam, 114, 186, 203, 204, 213, 216, 251, 280, 288; American renege on, 112, 217, 219, 220–21, 223, 260, 294, 296, 297–327, 333–34, 361, 362; Russia and, 255–56, 260, 294, 297, 301, 302, 304, 306, 311, 315, 316–17, 318, 319–20, 322–

746

23, 335, 347, 361, 401, 675; Sudan permission, 210, 242, 300, 311, 312, 313–14, 323, 347, 675; Suez Canal Nationalization and, 159, 160, 164, 250, 320–21, 346–47, 349, 361, 366, 380
Ataturk, Kemal, 676
Atbara River, 298
Athos (vessel), 456
Atleet, Israel, 513
al-Auja (Nitzana), Sinai, 62, 99, 107–12, 113, 119, 252, 337, 443, 536; routes around, 11–12, 48, 291, 306, 486, 537, 542, 546, 548, 549; al-Sabha and, 102, 107, 108, 110, 116, 202, 253, 648; Suez War (1956) and, 466, 473, 497, 502, 537, 540, 542, 545; withdrawal (1957), 640, 663
Auja al-Masri (Egyptian Auja), Sinai, 538
Aurès Mountains, Algeria, 135, 139, 140, 141
Australia, 373, 385, 402, 403, 417–18; racism in, 412; Sinai invasion and, 519, 564
Austria, 171, 268, 385, 583, 584
Austrian Peace Treaty, 238, 243, 258, 583
Avner, Gershon, 512
Avnery, Uri, quoted, 684–85
Awad, Fawzi, 423
Awlad Aly, Sinai, 540
Ayrout, Father Henri, 559–60
Azar, Samuel, 76–77, 78
Azerbaijan, Iran, 614
al-Azhary, Ismail, 242
Azzam, Abdur Raham, quoted, 40
Azazme Bedouins, 11, 61–62, 108–109

Babylon, 25
al-Badry, Brig. Gen. Hassan, quoted, 569–70, 592, 618
Baghdad, Iraq, 154, 202, 203, 256, 653
Baghdad Pact, 89, 105, 113, 149, 190, 214, 217; Iraq and, 17–18, 19, 71, 77, 193–97, 198–99, 200–201, 207, 210–11, 225, 235, 240, 246, 273–75, 280, 568, 676; Jordan and, 107, 116, 117, 196, 202–205, 207, 210, 252, 255–56, 275, 308, 449; Nasser-Eden moratorium on, 201–203, 204, 205, 207, 208, 210–11, 217; Russia and, 194, 199, 200, 225, 229, 235, 237, 238–40, 243, 252, 259, 275; Suez Crisis (1956) and, 3, 207, 215, 219, 336, 370, 380, 406, 413, 672
Bahrein, 212, 568
Baku, 228
Baldwin, Roger N., quoted, 77–78, 106–107

Balfour, Arthur James, Lord, 24, 31, 32, 33; quoted, 34, 103
Balfour Declaration, 31–33, 37, 51, 53, 103, 239, 266; Arab majority and, 23, 30, 34, 38
Balkan Pact, 236, 245
Banat Yaqoub bridge, Syria, 553
Bandung Conference (1955), 89, 149, 201, 234, 238, 241, 250, 345; on nuclear arms, 239
Bank of England, 624–25
al-Banna, Hassan, (Moslem Brotherhood founder), 16
al-Banna, Maj. Gen. Hassan, 603
Barber, Stephen, 306
Barbour, Walworth, 475
Bar Lev, Col. Haim, 689
Bar-Zohar, Michel, 141, 515; quoted, 140, 164, 433, 460, 639, 640
Barjot, Admr. Pierre, 433, 513, 579
Barraclough, Geoffrey, quoted, 243
Basel, Switzerland, 29
Bat Galim (vessel), 12, 49, 74–75, 198
Batna, Algeria, 135
Baxter, Prof. R. R., 671
Bayar, Celal, 202–203
Beaufre, Gen. André, 392, 406, 460, 621; quoted, 458; Sinai invasion action and, 471, 501, 548, 575; strategy and, 576–77, 578, 579–80, 599, 602, 609, 642
Beerotayim (Bir Ain), Sinai, 109–10
Beersheba, Israel, 5, 77, 94, 111, 486, 545
Bégarra, Joseph, 150
Behr, Edward, quoted, 147
Beigin, Menachem, 52, 94, 640
Beirut, Lebanon, 322, 695, 698
Belgium, 7, 116, 249, 519, 698
Belgrade, Yugoslavia, 152, 321, 414
Belgrave, Sir Charles, 212
Ben Bella, Ahmed, 133, 134; kidnapping of, 456–57, 462, 474
Ben-Gurion, David, 2, 29, 30, 49–53, 72, 334, 449; al-Auja and, 107–108, 111, 112, 143, 202, 252, 253, 306, 333, 453, 466, 502, 536, 640, 663; Anglo-French collusion and, 216, 220, 382, 440, 441, 453, 454, 457, 460–66, 469, 470, 472, 473, 474, 487, 490, 504, 511, 515, 533, 565, 570, 572, 574–75, 590, 611, 638, 642, 654, 658, 659; anti-Semitism and, 72; on Aqaba, 42, 53, 94, 98, 104, 106, 111, 121, 143, 163, 433, 460, 462, 589, 590, 638, 640, 667, 676; on Armistice Agreements, 124, 125, 333, 460, 638, 663, 668; on arms needs of Israel, 678–79; Egyptian-Russian arms deal

and, 98, 99, 101–102, 140, 143, 252, 253–54; Eshkol and, 677, 687; on Foreign Ministry duties, 502, 564; France and, 75, 130, 140, 141, 142, 151, 314, 462, 574–75; Gaza Raid and, 1, 4, 5, 8, 23, 47, 58, 85, 86, 87, 89, 107, 190, 200, 243; on Gaza Strip capture, 553, 570, 662, 663, 664, 666–67; Jordan attacks (1956), 447, 449, 453–54, 460, 504, 687; Lavon and, 78, 79, 80, 137; on Nasser, 3, 9, 104, 107, 676, 691; Qibya and, 57–58, 59, 60; retirement, 10, 11, 12, 47, 48, 58, 65, 70, 76, 137; Russian ultimatum (1956) and, 613–14; Sharett dismissal and, 121–23, 124, 151, 261, 455; Sharm al-Sheikh, 589, 638; Syrian attack (1955), 114–16, 120, 203–204, 564, 683; Suez cease-fire (1956) and, 570, 572–73, 574, 613–14, 633; Suez War (1956) withdrawal and, 637–40, 642, 646, 654, 659, 661–69, 675; on Tripartite Declaration, 270; UN Emergency Force and, 574, 638, 640, 662, 663, 667–68; United States and, 41, 64, 105, 118–19, 268, 269, 278, 289, 303, 304, 309, 454–55, 460, 473, 474, 504, 519, 633, 639–40, 641, 659, 663, 664–68, 675
Bennett, Max, 76
Bennike, Maj. Gen. Vagn, 62, 66, 109; quoted, 10, 60–61
Benson, Ezra Taft, 282
Berbers, 131, 132, 135, 142
Berding, Andrew H., 319, 320, 584
Beria, Lavrenty, 236, 256
Berlin, Germany, 257
Berlin Blockade, 230
Bermuda Conference (1957), 657
Bernadotte, Count Folke, 55, 65–66
Bevan, Aneurin, quoted, 561, 579, 607
Bevin, Ernest, 144, 180
Bigart, Homer, quoted, 125
Biggin Hill, England, 578
Bilbeis Air Academy, Egypt, 429
Billotte, Gen. Pierre, 143, 144
Bir Ain (Beerotayim), Sinai, 109–10
Bir Gifgafa, Sinai, 496, 497, 502, 510, 516, 517, 530
Bir al-Hassana, Sinai, 516, 530, 539, 540
Bir Lahfin, Sinai, 540, 569–70
Bir Rod Salem, Sinai, 497, 502, 530, 532, 540
Birdwood, Lord, quoted, 215
Birobidzhan, Russia, 231
von Bismarck, Otto, quoted, 361

Bitter Lakes, 153, 340, 670
Bizerte, Tunisia, 442
Black, Eugene: quoted, 296, 316, 320, 325, 674; Aswan High Dam and, 256, 305, 307, 308, 309, 310, 311–12, 313, 314, 316, 319, 320, 322, 325–26, 327, 335; on Middle East war danger, 674
Black Hand gang, 62, 108–109
Black Saturday (1952), 73, 180
Black Sea, 225, 226, 267
Blake, William, quoted, 432
Blue Nile, 298, 299
Bohlen, Amb. Charles, 582, 652; quoted, 614
Bolshevik Revolution (1917), 31, 38, 228, 258, 643
Bonham-Carter, Lady Violet, quoted, 629
The Bosporus, 225, 227, 228
Boumedienne, Col. Houari, 134
Bourges-Maunoury, Maurice, 141, 142, 146, 446; Anglo-Israeli collusion and, 392, 433, 440, 441, 442, 450, 451, 460, 461, 462, 471, 472, 574, 626
Bourguiba, Habib, 130
Bouvet (vessel), 475
Boyle, Air Marshal Sir Dermot, 370
Boyle, Edward, 626
Brandeis, Justice Louis D., 663
von Brentano, Heinrich, 626
Bridge of Jacob's Daughters, 67
Brilliant, Moshe, 76; quoted, 58
Brioni, Yugoslavia, 152, 256, 321, 333, 345, 376
Britain, 51, 63, 130, 266–67, 292–93, 334, 699; Algeria and, 148, 213, 434; Arab League and, 178–79, 186, 197, 204–205, 393, 403, 457, 568; Aswan High Dam and, 114, 159, 161, 174, 186, 203, 204, 210, 213, 216, 217, 220–21, 255, 299, 300, 302–303, 306, 307, 310–11, 312, 313, 314, 318, 325, 326, 338, 346, 347, 349, 380; al-Auja and, 108, 466; Baghdad Pact and, 17–18, 19, 105, 107, 117, 190, 193–95, 197, 198–99, 200, 201–202, 203, 204–205, 207, 208, 210–11, 213, 214, 215, 217, 238–40, 246, 273–75, 308, 370, 380, 449; Channel Tunnel project, 153, 672; death penalty abolition issue in, 206, 371; Egyptian arms and, 88, 89, 90, 100, 112, 116, 140, 186, 190, 201, 215, 238, 239, 244, 246, 247, 248, 249–50, 251, 265, 283, 286, 311; Egyptian invasion (1882), 36, 170, 311, 344, 527, 611; Egyptian Protectorate, 35, 36, 37, 39, 72–73, 234, 491; elections of 1959, 657; Gaza Raid and, 1, 85; Israeli-French arms deal and, 95, 100,
116, 118, 121, 134, 135, 139, 148, 216, 433; Jordanian arms and, 203, 204–205, 208–209, 211; Jordan defense (1956), 448, 449, 450, 451, 452, 462, 463, 476, 482, 505, 568, 687; missile bases, 657–58; Napoleon and, 27, 154, 167; Nasser *coup d'état* (1952), 43, 181, 182–83, 567; Palestine Dispute and, 23, 27–28, 30–37, 136, 690; Palestine Mandate of, 9, 29, 34, 35–38, 39, 40, 50, 54, 137, 182, 227, 457, 491; Russia and, 219, 227, 228, 229, 231, 232, 234, 258–59, 267, 425, 428, 446, 506–507, 610–11, 612, 653, 657; Suez Canal base evacuation, 12, 13, 14, 15, 17–18, 19, 38, 48, 64, 70, 71, 73–74, 75, 84, 112, 137, 139, 158, 159, 174–76, 179, 180, 182–88, 190, 195, 200, 217–18, 235, 237, 239, 261, 271, 273, 280, 281, 290, 322, 334, 340, 371, 380, 475, 672; Suez Canal financing and, 156, 167–68; Suez Canal nationalization and, 85, 158, 162, 215, 219, 221, 292, 311, 335–37, 345–46, 348, 353–54, 355–57, 358, 361–87, 391–429, 435, 444–46, 447, 463
   Suez War (1956) and, 2, 188, 207, 215, 217, 219, 221, 227, 273, 300, 348, 364, 369, 371–72, 375–79, 381–84, 385, 387, 391–93, 394, 397–98, 401, 402, 406, 411, 413, 418–19, 420, 422–29, 434, 435, 445, 447, 449–50, 467, 471, 472, 504, 517, 519, 525–54, 556, 558, 559, 560–61, 567, 568, 574, 575–79, 596–630, 633, 635–36, 644, 671–72; French-Israeli collusion, 1, 216, 219–20, 293, 336, 361, 367, 370, 374, 375, 392, 424, 428–29, 433–76, 482–83, 486–90, 495, 498, 500, 503–504, 506–507, 508, 511–12, 514, 515, 520–21, 525, 531, 533, 534, 557, 562, 564, 565, 568–69, 570–74, 575, 576, 596, 607–608, 616, 626–27, 638, 642–43, 646, 652–53, 654, 658–59, 672, 687, 688, 690; UN cease-fire resolution and, 519, 561–65, 570–74, 606, 607–608, 613, 615, 622–23, 624, 625–30, 633; withdrawal, 638, 639, 648, 650–51, 653, 654, 662, 691
   Suez War (1967) and, 686, 690; Tripartite Declaration and, 70, 207, 269–71, 289, 380, 450, 455, 474, 504, 505–506
British Air Force, 382, 488
British Army, 183, 185, 217, 336; Cyprus stations, 334–35, 393; Jewish Legion, 49, 50–51; mobilization (1956), 381–82, 393;
16th Independent Parachute Brigade Group, 599, 601, 609; Tenth Armored Division, 393, 577
British Broadcasting Corporation (BBC), 312, 396, 402, 488, 677; Eden-Gaitskell dispute and, 572
British Colonial Office, 37
British Commonwealth, 373. *See also* specific countries
British Conservative party, *see* Tory party (British)
British Exchequer, 205, 625
British Foreign Office, 18, 32, 33, 110, 187, 202, 205; Aswan High Dam and, 221; Eden's Middle East policy and, 214, 215, 447, 457, 571–72, 626; Glubb dismissal and, 210, 212; Russian-Egyptian arms deal and, 248; Suez Canal nationalization and, 337, 369, 380, 421–22; Suez War (1956) and, 393, 402, 434
British House of Commons, 187, 213–14, 218, 274, 488, 563; capital punishment issue in, 206, 371; collusion inquiry demands, 659; Egyptian bombings and, 560–61, 606–607, 618; Sèvres ultimatums and, 504–505, 506, 507, 520, 521; Suez Canal nationalization and, 369, 375, 379–81, 382, 383, 385, 411, 426, 427–28, 436, 463; Suez War (1956) cease-fire and, 568, 569, 570–71, 606, 627–29, 643; Suez War (1956) withdrawal issue and, 654, 657
British Law Society, 637
British Middle East Command, 577
British Navy, 183, 219, 335, 375, 382; Port Said invasion and, 616, 619
British Parliament, 37, 419, 426, 628. *See also* British House of Commons
British Royal Commission of Inquiry (1936), 41
British War Cabinet (1917), 32
British War Office, 100, 375, 382; Suez War (1956) and, 392, 393, 397, 630
Bromberger, Merry and Serge, 659; quoted, 650
Brown, Vice Admr. Charles R., quoted, 616
Bubastis, 153
Buber, Martin, quoted, 26
Budapest, Hungary, 256, 455, 467, 473; Red Army in, 514, 561, 581, 583, 584
Bugeaud, Marshal Thomas-Robert, 131
Bulganin, Nikolai, 219, 236, 258, 259; arms embargo and, 260; on Lancaster House, 403; Suez

748

Canal internationalization issue
and, 404, 446; Suez War
(1956) and, 428, 610–16, 623
Bulwark (vessel), 471, 527
Bunche, Ralph, 66, 108, 668
al-Bureig, Egypt, 10, 61, 64, 276
Burke, Admr. Arleigh, 395
Burns, Gen. E. L. M., 13, 66, 83,
91, 190, 198, 654; quoted, 8,
10, 47, 48, 67, 69, 75–76, 97,
98, 109, 110–11, 112, 115, 120,
124, 247, 443, 476, 553, 637; on
Anglo-French bombings, 530;
border negotiations (1955), 94,
95, 96, 110, 243, 246, 648;
Emergency Forces command,
574, 608, 648, 649–50, 656,
668, 669–70; prisoner ex-
changes, 636; Sinai invasion
and, 428–29, 443, 470, 493, 496,
502, 553
Burullus, Egypt, 617
Butler, Brig. Gen. M. A. H., 601,
603, 604, 606, 609, 622; quoted,
599, 605, 629
Butler, Richard Austen, 571–72,
625, 657; quoted, 654
Butlin, Billy, 387
Byroade, Amb. Henry A., 90, 94,
98, 99, 244, 271–72, 282, 288;
quoted, 63, 71–72, 246, 248,
278, 290, 312, 418; Aswan High
Dam and, 309, 312–13, 322,
326; Baghdad Pact and, 199,
273, 274; Nasser quarrel, 283,
284, 285, 286
Byzantium, 26

Caccia, Sir Harold, 210, 471, 652
Caffery, Amb. Jefferson, 181, 183,
184, 280
Cairo, 13, 14, 17, 74, 96, 170, 339,
486; Algerian activists in, 132,
133; Arab League and, 42, 197;
al-Azhar mosque, 565, 644;
Black Saturday, 73, 180; British spy trials (1956), 414;
British embassy in, 210, 521,
559, 567; civil discipline
(1956), 559–60; Jewish community, 106–107; Lavon Affair
trials in, 76, 77–78, 79; Pineau
visit (1956), 149–50, 151; Port
Said invasion and, 603, 605,
609, 626; Preferential Treaty
(1936) talks, 175–76; Suez
Canal offices in, 339, 342–43,
344, 348, 350–51, 354–55; Suez
War (1956) and, 364, 382,
393–94, 458, 489, 490, 496, 517,
521, 526, 527, 529, 533, 545,
566, 649; Thant visit (1967),
684, 686; United States embassy in, 316–17
Cairo International Airport, 526,
527, 649

Cairo Radio (and its "Voice of
the Arabs"), 14, 122, 190, 374,
400, 527, 559; Algeria and,
135, 142; Aswan High Dam
and, 221, 334, 335; Baghdad
Pact and, 197, 202, 203, 204,
207; Cairo bombing (1956)
and, 526, 529, 566; on Canal
shipping, 423, 515; on Hussein,
470; jamming of, 408–409;
656; on Port Said invasion,
603, 606, 624; Russian arms
deal and, 248; Sèvres ultimatum and, 511, 514; Swahili
broadcasts, 217
Cairo West airfield, 521, 528
Camp David, 307
Canaan, 24, 443
Canada, 110, 118, 249, 564, 571,
648, 698
Canadian Army, Queen's Own
Rifles, 649
Canberra, Australia, 418
Cape of Good Hope, 75, 155, 167,
168, 375; shipping routes, 416,
655
Carmel, Moshe, 442
Caruthers, Osgood, 116, 119;
quoted, 308, 318
Caspian Sea, 226, 227
Castro, Fidel, 240
Casualties: Algerian rebellion,
131, 142; al-Auja, 11, 107, 466,
502; Fraser expedition, 167;
Gaza bombardment (1956),
120; Gaza Raid, 1, 5–6, 7, 61,
84; Port Said guerrilla action,
655–56; refugee camp raids, 10,
376; reprisal raids, 10–11, 54–
55, 56, 57, 59–60, 61, 62–63,
68–69, 91, 95–96, 97, 109, 110,
114, 115, 120, 204, 243, 246,
276, 403, 428, 440, 448, 503;
riots, 38, 180, 204, 456; Suez
War (1956), 476, 508, 510,
513, 517, 530, 541, 552, 553,
570, 577–78, 592, 595, 596, 600,
601, 604, 605, 607, 616, 619,
620, 635–37, 661; Suez War
(1967), 678, 682, 689–90; Syrian raid (1955), 308
Caterham, England, 417
Catherine the Great, 225
Catroux, Diomède, 139
Catroux, Gen. Georges, 146, 147
Cavanagh, Sandy, quoted, 578,
602, 620, 655
Central Intelligence Agency
(CIA), *see* United States Cen-
tral Intelligence Agency
Central Treaty Organization
(CENTO), 275. *See also* Bagh-
dad Pact
*Centre d'Information du Proche-
Orient,* 140
Ceylon, 385, 406

Chaban-Delmas, Jacques, 472;
quoted, 613, 626
Challe, Gen. Maurice: collusion
and, 442, 450, 451, 452, 454,
457, 471
Chamberlain, Austen, 175
Chamoun, Camille, 252
Charles X, King of France, 131
Charles-Roux, François, 150, 163
Chateau-Jobert, Col. Pierre, 603,
604
Chauvel, Amb. Henri George, 354
Chayla, Count Armand du, 149,
150, 322, 342, 350–51, 358
Chequers estate, England, 450,
471
Childers, Erskine, cited, 636
China, 118, 119, 121, 161, 293,
318–19, 323, 326–27, 695; Civil
War (1949), 230, 241; oil and,
699–700; Pakistan and, 275;
Russia and, 226, 228, 232, 253,
258, 259–60, 261; Shuqairy
and, 680; United Nations and,
239, 259, 333
China, Nationalist, 519
Chinese Navy, 512
Chou en-Lai, 239
Christian Arabs, 9, 26, 27, 28,
226, 227, 559–60
Churchill, Randolph, 578, 677,
687, 688; quoted, 205, 214
Churchill, Sir Winston, 237, 534,
558; quoted, 178, 182, 239, 299,
579; Eden and, 18, 105, 178,
180, 181–82, 202, 238–39, 369,
401, 579, 623; Eisenhower and,
183–84, 186, 265; oil and, 219
Churchill, Winston (son of Randolph), 677, 687, 688
Clark, Capt. D. M. J., 508;
quoted, 572, 618, 619, 620
Clark, William, 396, 411, 419,
427, 626
von Clausewitz, Karl, quoted, 82
Cohen, Capt. Yeruham, 47;
quoted, 43
Cold War, 232, 265, 266, 272,
292–93; Aswan High Dam and,
220–21, 304, 317–18; Baghdad
Pact and, 18, 194, 195, 199,
201, 229–30, 235, 237, 238, 240,
275; Central Intelligence Agency and, 216, 653; China diplomatic recognitions and, 118,
121, 216, 219, 239, 253, 259,
275, 293–94, 315, 318–19, 323,
326–27, 361; coexistence policy
and, 258–59, 260, 261; Eisenhower Doctrine and, 646–48,
676; Hungary and, 580–84,
614; neutralism and, 234, 236,
239, 241, 242, 245–46, 273, 282,
287, 310, 333, 611–12, 644, 646;
nuclear arms and, 237, 240; oil
and, 699–70; Russian-Egyptian

arms deal and, 99, 100, 101, 102, 112, 201, 243–44, 250, 293, 346, 699; Russian-American joint action proposal (1956) and, 614–16, 623; Suez Canal and, 179, 180, 407, 437, 506; Syria and, 653, 661. *See also* Communism

Collusion, *see* Suez War (1956), Anglo-French collusion in

Colombia, 648, 650

Colonialism, *see* Imperialism

Columbia Broadcasting System, 445

Comité Révolutionnaire pour l'Unité et l'Action (CRUA), 133

Commin, Sen. Pierre, 152, 414

Communism, 220, 228, 230, 250; Baghdad Pact and, 194, 195; de-Stalinization and, 256–58, 272, 455, 514, 580–81, 643; Egypt and, 15, 19, 88, 185, 187, 196, 201, 228, 235, 243, 251, 252, 279, 287, 293, 294, 326–27, 334, 346, 644, 645, 647, 653–54, 676; France and, 144; Iran and, 184, 216; Syria and, 653. *See also* Cold War

Communist Information Bureau (Cominform), 258

Communist International (Comintern), 258

Congress of the Communist Party of the Soviet Union, Twentieth, 256–57, 580

Congress of the Peoples of the East, First (Baku), 228

Congressional Record, cited, 314

Constantinople, 2, 28, 168, 265; Russia and, 226, 227, 228

Constantinople Convention (1888), 172, 227, 588; Anglo-French port seizures (1956) and, 475, 580, 588; Israeli shipping restraints and, 75, 171, 362, 383, 670–71; Suez Canal nationalization and, 355, 356, 368, 376, 380–81, 384–85, 386, 399–400, 401, 404, 407, 415, 418, 425, 426–27

Copeland, Miles, 285

Copts, 559

Cornut-Gentille, Amb. Bernard, 507

Cotton, 155, 235, 237, 305, 363; Russian-Egyptian arms deal and, 98, 117, 241, 249, 250, 254, 282, 293, 317, 326

Cotton. Gladys, quoted, 402

Coty, René. quoted, 456

Courtney, David (Roy Elston), quoted, 64

Couve de Murville, Maurice, 342

Crane (vessel), 594

Crimean War, 227

Croly, Herbert, quoted, 46

Cromer, Lord, 321; quoted, 174, 192, 224, 404

Crook, Lieut. Col. Paul, 601

Crossman, Richard H. S., 13, 198; quoted, 14

The Crusades, 27, 40, 225

Cuba, 240, 519

Cunha, Paulo, Foreign Minister of Portugal, quoted, 436, 437

Curzon, Lord, 175, 267, 690, 692; quoted, 173

Cyprus, British forces on, 187, 207, 334–35, 364, 374, 398, 406, 457, 472, 474, 475, 482, 483, 521, 527, 528, 573, 575–78, 599, 600, 606, 607; French on, 393, 413, 472, 474, 501, 573, 576, 600, 655, 658; nationalist movement of, 39, 215, 334–35, 401, 483, 558, 655; radio station, 409, 514, 518, 526, 529, 566, 607, 629–30; Russia and, 227

Czechoslovakia, 54, 59, 230, 232; Russian-Egyptian arms deal and, 90–91, 98–102, 106, 107, 109, 112, 117, 140, 141, 143, 186, 244, 245, 248, 249, 250, 252, 254, 259, 283, 346

Dagania, Palestine, 494

Dahab, Sinai, 590, 592

Damascus, Syria, 136, 322, 474, 533; *coup d'état* plots (1956), 482–83, 653; Israeli threats (1967), 681; Suez cease-fire (1956), 641

Damietta (vessel), 560, 591

Dan, Uri, quoted, 636

Daninos, Adrian, 300, 301

Danube River, 227

Dar, Col. Avraham, 73, 76

Darb al-Haj (road), 486

The Dardanelles, 225, 227

Dardaud, Gabriel, 351

Darius, King of Persia, 349

Davar (newspaper), 50, 100

Davis, Dr. John H., quoted, 697

Davis, John W., 267

Dayan, Maj. Gen. Moshe, 54, 65, 76, 98, 254; Army organization and, 69, 494–95, 687; on the *Bat Galim,* 74; on British defense of Jordan, 449; on Bulganin ultimatums (1956), 613; on collusive aid in Sinai, 658, 659; on Egyptian air warfare, 512, 513, 528–29; on expansion, 22; on *Fedayeen,* 86; France and, 75, 89, 112, 134, 138–39, 140. 216, 289, 306, 441, 442, 460; Gaza Raid and, 8, 86–87; Gaza withdrawal (1957), 668; Lavon and, 48, 79, 80; Qalqilya raid (1956), 448; on reprisal policy, 97; Sinai campaign (1956), 105, 106, 108, 112, 119, 143, 433, 439–40, 441, 442–43;

457, 465, 466, 469–70, 471, 473, 475–76, 483, 486, 487–88, 490, 491, 492, 494, 497, 498, 500, 502, 504, 508, 510, 517, 518, 519, 526, 538, 539, 540, 541–42, 545, 546, 548–49, 550–51, 552, 576, 590, 592, 594–95, 634, 635, 636, 660, 687–88; Sinai campaign (1967), 677, 688–89, 690; Suez Canal attacks and, 576, 609; on Suez War (1956) cease-fire, 570, 573, 624

al-Dayyiqa, Sinai, 537, 538, 539, 542, 689

Dead Sea, 497

Dean, Patrick, 461, 463, 466

Deeb, Fat'hy, 133, 134

Deir al-Balah, 7, 91

Deir Yasseen, 54–55, 476, 553

Denmark, 60, 66, 385

Dervish Empire, 174

Dessouqi, Ibrahim, 617

Deuteronomy, 24

al-Dib, Tewfik, quoted, 436

Dienbienphu, battle of, 134–35

Digwy, Gen. Fuad, 552

Dillon, Amb. Douglas, 145, 367, 472, 562, 616, 625; on Bulganin ultimatum, 612–13, 615

Disraeli, Benjamin, quoted, 168–69, 420

Dixon, Sir Pierson, 505, 507, 568; quoted, 504, 563

Dome of the Rock, Jerusalem, 26, 27

Doty, Robert, 242; quoted, 6

Douglas-Home, Sir Alec, *see* Home, Sir Alec Douglas-

Drome, Lieut. Col. Asher, 635

Druzes, 27, 28, 408

Dryden, John, quoted, 701

Dulles, Allen, 248, 282–83, 367, 472; quoted, 53, 483, 514, 561, 581

Dulles, John Foster, 2, 48, 62, 63, 91, 103, 105, 134, 234, 271–76, 277, 614, 623, 700; Aqaba issue and, 590, 685–86; Aswan High Dam and, 112, 125, 159–60, 219, 220–21, 256, 294, 302, 305, 306, 307, 310, 311–12, 313, 315–16, 317, 318, 319–20, 322, 323–27, 334, 335, 337, 361, 362; on Austrian peace treaty (1955), 243; Baghdad Pact and, 194, 195, 199, 273–75; on British missile bases, 657; on British Suez base evacuation, 12, 184–85; Central Intelligence Agency and, 282–83, 285, 376; China and, 118, 216, 219, 293–94, 315, 318–19, 326, 361; death of, 676; Franco-Israeli alliance and, 151–52, 454; Hungary and, 473, 503, 583, 584; Israeli arms and, 113, 115, 248; Menzies mission and, 412, 415;

Naguib and, 64, 265; NATO and, 183; Russell Middle East study (1954) and, 303–304; Russian arms deal news and, 100, 284–89, 293, 326 Suez Canal nationalization and, 320, 326, 337, 342, 348, 355, 361, 362, 365, 372, 374, 375–79, 384, 385, 386, 387, 391, 393, 395, 396, 402, 404, 405–406, 407, 438–39, 444, 446, 447, 453, 562; SCUA proposal, 419, 425–26, 427, 434, 436, 437, 438–39, 442, 683 Suez War (1956) and, 561–63, 652; Sinai invasion and, 451, 457, 503, 506, 519; on Suez withdrawal issue, 633, 641, 647–48, 664, 665
Dunkirk, battle of, 557, 558

East Germany, 237, 699
Eban, Abba, 8–9, 59, 60; quoted, 22, 63, 86, 114, 674, 698; Anglo-French collusion and, 563–64; captured documents, 459, 659–60; on Egyptian militarism, 660, 661; Eisenhower warning (1956), 454–55; non-aggression pact proposal (1954), 75; on refugees, 697, 698; Suez cease-fire (1956) and, 575; Suez War (1967) withdrawals, 664; on Syria (1967), 681
L' Echo d'Alger (newspaper), 147
Les Echos de Paris (newspaper), 247
Eden, Sir Anthony, 2, 103, 110, 117, 134, 178, 273, 676; Algeria and, 148; on American anti-colonialism, 439; Aswan High Dam and, 310, 313, 314, 316; on Black Saturday, 180–81; compromise peace proposals (1955), 105, 107, 114, 115, 119, 306, 447; Eisenhower visit plans, 642–43, 646; Franco-Israeli collusion and, 434–35, 441, 447, 448, 449, 450–53, 455–56, 457, 459, 460, 461–65, 467–69, 470, 471, 472, 473, 486, 487–89, 504, 505, 506–507, 508, 511–12, 520–21, 533, 534, 562, 564, 568–69, 570–74, 575, 576, 596, 607, 608, 616, 626–27, 642, 652, 654, 658–59, 672, 687, 688; Glubb Pasha and, 206, 207, 208, 209, 210, 212–15, 216, 275, 371, 622, 623; ill health, 206–207, 214, 419, 568–69, 623, 657; Iraq and, 195, 197, 274, 651; Jordan defense (1956), 448, 449, 450, 599; moratorium with Nasser, see Baghdad Pact; Nasser antipathy, 3, 18, 107, 116, 119, 148, 181, 184, 187, 198–221, 238–39, 243, 252, 293, 306,

314, 327, 357, 364, 367, 368, 372, 379, 394–95, 396–97, 419, 420, 434, 435, 442, 447, 452, 486, 568, 569, 578, 585, 596, 622–23, 624, 633, 672; resignation, 657; Russian threats (1956) and, 612, 613, 615, 624; Suez base evacuation and, 12, 175–76, 182, 183, 184, 187, 190, 239; Suez Canal nationalization and, 219, 335–36, 342, 353–54, 355–57, 362–87, 394, 422, 423, 424–26, 435, 436, 445, 446; Suez War (1956) and, 273, 356–57, 364, 367, 368, 370, 371–80, 381–82, 385, 387, 391–92, 393, 394, 397, 398, 401, 402, 406, 407, 411, 413, 418–19, 420, 422–29, 446, 449–50, 457, 459, 463, 471, 472, 486, 487–89, 504, 505, 511, 533, 560–61, 563, 568–69, 577, 578–79, 606–607, 610, 612, 613, 615, 616, 618, 622–30, 633, 645; Suez withdrawals issue, 639, 650, 654; Suez War (1967) and, 687
Eden, Clarissa Churchill, 401
Edgar Bonnet (vessel), 527
Egypt, 27–28, 32, 167–72, 634; Arab League and, 41–42, 133, 179, 196, 197, 278, 675; Aswan High Dam project and, 116, 125, 203, 204, 213, 294, 296, 297–327 (See also Aswan High Dam); al-Auja and, 107–12, 113, 116, 143, 202, 253, 337, 453, 466, 502; Baghdad Pact and, 17–18, 77, 194–205, 207, 238–41, 271, 274–75, 280, 308, 370; Bat Galim incident and, 12, 49, 74–75, 198; Biblical, 24–25, 40, 132; British Preferential Treaty (1936) 175–77, 180, 181, 188, 193; British Protectorate, 35, 36, 37, 39, 172–73, 234, 491; China and, 118, 121, 216, 259–60, 293–94, 315, 318–19, 323, 326–27, 333, 361; collusion against, see Suez War (1956), Anglo-French-Israeli collusion in; Eisenhower Doctrine and, 646–48, 676; Franco-Israeli alliance and, 129, 130, 131, 134, 135, 137, 138, 140, 141–42, 143, 144, 145, 146, 148–52, 201, 245, 288, 290, 291, 370; Gaza Raid and, 1, 5–20, 23, 34, 47, 61, 76, 83–86, 100, 102, 116, 140, 186, 200, 201, 225, 240, 274, 281, 288, 294, 361, 495, 696; Gaza Strip return (1957), 668–69; Israeli peace treaty demands, 114–15, 663, 664–65, 690; Israeli sabotage in, 48, 73, 74, 124, 337, 345, 552; Jewish community in, 106–107, 190, 672; Jordan defense (1956),

447, 448, 449, 450; Jordan waters issue and, 12, 277; Khan Yunis raid and, 96–97, 98, 116, 143; "Liberation Army," 531, 534, 536, 558–59, 565–66, 596, 598, 599, 605, 608–609, 619–20, 622; London Conference (1956), 384–86, 398–99, 401, 403, 405, 406, 411–18, 459–60; neutralism of, 234–35, 236, 239–41, 242, 245–46, 251, 252, 253, 256, 278, 287, 316, 319, 326, 333, 334, 345, 347, 611–12, 644, 645–46; Palestine War and, 9, 41–42, 43, 66, 84, 89, 108, 163, 346; Port Said invasion and, 596–630, 635–36, 637; reprisal policy and, 61, 62, 69, 70, 84, 95–96, 104, 120, 143, 247, 490, 684, 685, 696; revolution of 1952 in, 8, 9, 10, 14, 15, 16, 17, 19, 43, 64, 83, 84, 104, 134, 158, 169, 178, 181, 182–83, 185, 198, 218, 234, 247, 265, 271, 280, 298, 300, 334, 559, 567; Russian war support (Suez, 1956), 610–16; Sèvres ultimatum (1956), 463–65, 471, 488, 489–90, 504, 505, 506, 508, 511, 513, 514, 515, 518, 520, 531; Sinai invasion (1956), 8, 102, 103, 105–106, 121, 143, 291, 346, 428–29, 439–40, 442–44, 447, 448, 457–59, 463–66, 468, 469–76, 480–521, 530–32, 536–54, 589–95, 634, 635–36, 660; Sinai retreat (1956), 497, 509, 517, 521, 525–54, 557, 558, 560, 565, 569, 591, 634; "Six Principles" of settlement and, 445–47, 452, 562, 670; Sudan and, 173–74, 176, 179, 180, 181, 210, 242, 311, 312, 313, 323, 347, 675; Suez Canal construction, 152–55, 167; Suez Canal Conference proposal (1956), 436, 437; Suez (1956) cease-fire and, 564–65, 566, 569–74, 608–15, 622–23, 624, 628, 633; Suez War (1956) relief shipments, 647; Suez War (1956) withdrawals issue, 637–72, 675; Syrian-Saudi Arabian pact, 202, 213, 308, 408; White Paper (1956) on Canal nationalization, 399–400, 404. See also Nasser, Gamal Abdel; Suez War (1956); Suez War (1967); and see specific place names; e.g., Suez Canal
Egyptian Air Force, 558, 592, 644; captured documents, 691; Israeli military strategy (1956) and, 391, 429, 443, 457, 458, 463, 464, 469, 487–88, 489, 634, 688; Port Said attack and, 597, 602, 619; Sinai invasion action,

510, 512, 528–29, 548, 554;
strikes at Israel, 512, 635; Suez
War (1967) and, 688–89
Egyptian Army, 96, 391, 633–34,
644; budget (1954), 13, 14, 15;
Eastern Command, 495–96, 501,
527, 565, 566, 569, 599; Jordanian Army and, 117; mobilization (1967), 679; organization,
495, 552, 634; Port Said invasion and, 596, 598–99, 602–607;
post-Gaza Raid conduct of, 86,
91, 94, 98, 247; rearmament
(1955), 20, 74, 75, 83–85, 98–
101, 110–11, 112, 186, 241, 247,
250, 251, 491; Sinai invasion
(1956) and, 442, 450, 465–66,
482, 487, 489, 490, 491, 492,
508–509, 510, 515–17, 518, 530,
531, 532, 537–44, 590–94, 634;
Sinai retreat (1956), 525–54,
557, 558, 560, 565, 569; Sinai
retreat (1967), 689–90; Suez
Canal nationalization and, 339,
340, 353, 393–94; surplus
stores, 660–61; Third Infantry
"captured orders," 459, 551,
613–14, 635, 659–60
Egyptian Army Engineers, 527
Egyptian Chamber of Deputies,
399
Egyptian Commerce Ministry, 158
Egyptian Defense Ministry, 110
Egyptian Information Department,
411
Egyptian-Israeli MAC, 66, 67, 77,
83, 108, 109, 685
Egyptian-Syrian-Jordanian Joint
Command, 447, 448, 467, 474,
681; Sinai invasion (1956) and,
482, 502, 503, 514–15, 532–33,
644
Egyptian National Bank, 357, 394
Egyptian National Guard, 532,
534, 546, 551, 552, 569, 590;
Port Said invasion and, 598,
601, 612
Egyptian Navy, 339, 512–15, 670
Egyptian Petroleum Authority,
338, 351
Egyptian Revolution Command
Council (Revolutionary Junta),
16, 17, 78, 134, 534; Russian
arms deal and, 90, 242, 249;
Suez Canal nationalization and,
337, 341, 342, 344
Egyptian State Broadcasting Company, 249, 566
Egyptian Suez Canal Authority,
339, 362, 382, 459; pilots and,
420–24
Egyptian-Syrian Defense Alliance
(1966), 678, 679, 681, 683
Egyptian War Ministry, 660
Eisenhower, Dwight D., 1–2, 3, 48,
63, 64, 105, 117, 216, 271, 278,
310, 370, 379, 406, 460, 514,
582, 676, 700; Aqaba issue and,
590, 685–86; Aswan High Dam
renege and, 302, 305, 307, 309,
313, 314, 315, 316, 317, 318,
319, 320, 322, 323, 324, 325–26,
327; Baghdad Pact and, 204,
214, 275; Bermuda Conference
(1957) and, 657–58; British
Suez base evacuation and, 183–
84, 186; Egyptian arms and,
74, 75, 87–88, 90, 91, 243–44,
265, 281–82, 284, 290–91, 293,
294, 316, 646; on Hungarian intervention (1956), 583, 628;
Jordan water proposals and, 12,
115–16, 276, 303; Nasser appeal
to, 557, 612; Russian joint-action
proposal (1956) and, 614––16;
Suez Canal nationalization and,
320, 357, 365, 367–68, 374–75,
394–95, 402, 405, 406–407, 412,
413–14, 416–17, 420, 446; Suez
War (1956) and, 368, 371, 372,
375, 376–77, 378, 387, 418–19,
422, 449–50, 451, 454, 457, 469,
472, 473, 474, 475–76, 503–505,
506, 519–20, 554, 557, 562, 578,
610, 612, 614–15, 622–23, 627–
28, 629, 633, 642, 652–53, 685;
Suez withdrawals issue and,
124, 633, 639–40, 641, 647–48,
654, 663, 665–66, 668, 669
Eisenhower Doctrine, 646–48, 665,
676
Ekron airfield, Israel, 501, 512
Elath, Amb. Eliahu, 12, 59
Elath, port of, 42, 64, 163, 486,
573; Sharm al-Sheikh capture
and, 589, 591, 592, 638
Elath (vessel), 513
Eliot, T. S., quoted, 192, 296
Elizabeth II, Queen of England,
381, 463, 628
Ely, Gen. Paul, 433, 442
England, *see* Britain
English Channel, 153, 387, 672
EOKA of Cyprus, 39, 334–35,
483, 655
Episkopi, Cyprus, 577
Eshkol, Levi, 65, 674, 677, 681,
683; Suez War (1967), 687,
690
Espionage, 11, 48, 75, 106, 136,
171, 589; American, 216, 248,
282–83, 285, 320, 407–408, 472,
483, 615, 653; British, 414, 457,
468, 472, 598; Egyptian, 85,
124, 334–35, 467, 482–83, 681;
executions for, 17, 19, 76–78,
198, 232, 552; Israeli, 690. *See
also* Terrorism, sabotage and
Ethiopia, 174, 298, 385, 406, 415,
437
Eugénie, Empress of France, 155,
168
Euphrates River, 24, 196, 692
European Defense Community,
290
Ewer, W. N., 218
Executions, 61, 152, 232, 236;
British death penalty issue, 206,
371; Egyptian, 15, 17, 19, 76–
78, 189, 198, 552
Exercise Boathook, 471, 473, 488,
508
Exodus, Book of, 24, 25
Exodus 1947 (vessel), 136
Expansionism, 22, 32; Israeli
state, 34–35, 37, 40–41, 43, 52,
53, 71, 72, 89, 91, 102–105, 106,
130, 269, 276, 278, 289, 304,
346, 447–48. 466, 471, 553–54,
589, 595, 679, 698; Israeli Suez-
Sinai conquests, 35, 40, 637–41,
661, 690, 691–92, 694, 696;
Ottoman Empire collapse and,
31, 227, 228; Palestine War
and, 9, 35, 42; Russian, 39, 88,
225–30, 232. *See also* Imperialism
Eytan, Walter, 8, 91; quoted, 105,
108, 233, 447–48, 553–54
Ezzat, Ibrahim, 122

Fahmy, Brig. Gen. Abdel Rahman,
quoted, 596, 598
Faisal I, King of Iraq, 34–35, 193,
275, 342; quoted, 36
Farouk, King of Egypt, 73, 160,
177, 132, 240; cotton policy,
282; exile, 9, 43, 154, 181, 300,
352; Nasser and, 78, 134, 163,
178, 181, 218; Tiran, 589
Fatah, 695
Faure, Edgar, 113, 139, 140, 141,
143
Fawzi, Mahmoud, 150, 162. 210.
234, 283, 649; Canal nationalization and, 344, 439, 444–45,
452, 511
Fayid, Egypt, 340, 496, 501, 502
Fedayeen, 70, 84, 85–86, 97, 98,
102, 104, 143, 462, 519; Israeli
reprisal policy and, 694–95;
"Kilo 95" and, 95–96; Negev
(1956), 120–21; officials murdered, 124, 337; police service,
670; Suez War (1956) and,
467, 474, 481, 502, 551, 552,
553, 573. 661, 662
al-Ferdan Bridge, Egypt, 496,
502, 527–28
Fergusson, Brig. Gen. Sir Bernard, 514; quoted, 602, 607
Festing, General Sir Francis,
quoted, 185
Finance: for Aswan High Dam,
116, 160, 161, 216, 217, 220–21,
255, 256, 260, 288, 292, 301–
327, 335, 337, 338, 346–47, 349,
361, 366, 380, 381, 396, 675;
British sterling, 336, 363–64,
369, 394, 422, 491, 623, 624–25,

752

626, 651; Egyptian military budget (1954–1955), 13, 14, 15, 244, 254, 281, 291, 316–17, 396; Egyptian nineteenth century debts, 168; Israeli budget (1957), 663–64; for Israeli-French arms deal, 118; for Jordan River diversion, 60; Saudi Arabian, 203, 204, 207, 213; Suez Canal clearing (1956), 670; Suez Canal construction, 154–56; Suez Canal earnings, 153, 157, 160, 161–62, 163, 321, 349, 350, 352, 357, 366, 397, 415, 416, 425; Suez Canal nationalization compensation, 365–66, 397, 671; Suez War costs (1956), 374, 672; Suez War relief aid, 647, 686; Suez War reparations, 671–72; Zionist, 269, 347, 665

Finland, 258, 445

Fleming, Ian, 654

FLN (Front de Libération Nationale), *see* National Liberation Front (Algerian)

Flux, J. B., 414

Foreign Affairs (periodical), 14, 86, 679

Foster, Andrew, 354, 357, 365, 367; quoted, 355–56

Foster, William C., 84, 280

Fourteen Points (Wilson), 266

France, 30, 76, 174, 227, 244, 250, 266, 272, 409; Algerian independence and, 40, 98, 100, 118, 129–52, 213, 218, 247, 249, 260–61, 314, 330, 336, 342, 358, 368, 373, 378, 402, 414, 433, 434, 456–57, 558, 633, 637, 694; Arab State relations, 27, 28, 29, 568, 646, 698; Aswan High Dam and, 221; Baghdad Pact and, 18–19, 194, 213, 336; Crimean War and, 227; elections of 1956, 143–44; Israeli arms sales, 75, 88–89, 95, 98, 100, 101, 112, 113, 114, 116, 117, 121, 125, 135, 137, 138–39, 140, 141–42, 146, 148, 149, 151, 201, 213, 216, 219–20, 245, 249, 253, 288, 289–91, 310, 392, 433, 439, 445, 454, 470–71, 492–93, 494, 573; *Maquis* of, 695; Suez Canal and, 85, 121, 143, 148, 149, 150, 153, 154, 155, 156, 157, 158, 163, 167, 171, 179, 184, 336, 340, 342, 346, 350–51, 353, 355, 356, 358, 361, 367, 368–69, 373, 385, 415, 435, 438, 446, 447
Suez War (1956) and, 2, 148, 151, 291, 348, 378, 383–84, 391–93, 398, 406, 413, 418, 420, 422, 425, 445, 447, 463–65, 466, 471, 472, 501, 525–54, 558, 560, 561, 574, 596–630, 633, 635–36, 644;

Anglo-Israeli collusion in, 1, 216, 219–20, 293, 336, 367, 370, 374, 375, 392, 424, 428–29, 433–76, 486–90, 495, 498, 500, 503–504, 506–507, 508, 511–12, 515, 520–21, 525, 531, 533, 534, 557, 562, 564, 565, 568–69, 570, 575, 576, 596, 616, 626–27, 638, 642–43, 646, 652–53, 654, 658–59, 672, 687, 688; cease-fire and, 519, 561–65, 573, 574–75, 615, 622, 623, 626–27; reparations, 671–72; Russian threat and, 612–13, 615, 623; Sinai action, 487, 489, 513, 521, 658; withdrawals, 638, 640, 648, 650–51, 653, 654, 655, 656, 662, 691
Suez War (1967), 686;
Tripartite Declaration (1950) and, 70, 269–70, 289, 455, 474

Fraser, Gen. A. Mackenzie, 167, 345

de Freitas, Geoffrey, 607

French Air Force, 442, 509

French Army, 134–35, 144, 148, 392; draft (1956), 151; Second Colonial Parachute Regiment, 600–601, 609

French Chamber of Deputies, 342, 358

French Council of Ministers, 146

French Defense Ministry, 75, 134, 135, 138, 139, 140, 141, 433, 441; Israeli liaison with (1956), 576, 658

French Foreign Legion, 142

French Foreign Ministry, 136, 137, 145, 373, 658

French Interior Ministry, 141, 146

French Ministers' Cabinets, 146

French National Assembly, 133, 143, 144, 150, 151–52; 290; Suez Canal nationalization and, 342, 358, 383, 440

French Navy, 616, 617, 618

French Socialist Party, 144, 145, 146, 152, 414

Fulbright, Sen. J. William, 590, 686; quoted, 279, 310, 316, 317, 324, 326, 556

Gaitskell, Hugh, 560; quoted. 214, 383, 409, 520, 564, 571, 606, 628–29, 643; collusion charges, 520, 571, 572, 616, 658; Suez Canal nationalization and. 372, 393, 400, 407, 424, 427–28; Suez War cease-fire and, 568, 571, 628–29, 643

Galilee, 41. *See also* Kinneret

da Gama. Vasco, 154, 155

Gamal. Col. Mustafa, 539

Gameel airport. Egypt, 577, 589; Port Said invasion and, 600, 601, 602, 603, 612, 619

al-Gamhouriya (newspaper), 14, 248, 417; on Canal nationalization, 362, 406

Gandhi, Mahatma Mohandas, 26, de Gaulle, Gen. Charles, 130, 369, 392, 441, 698; Algeria and, 148; Challe and, 450; Sinai invasion and, 487; Suez War (1967) and, 686

Gaza, Palestine, 5, 10, 12, 67, 247; bombardments, 120, 151, 260, 551, 682; capture, 552, 553, 661; routes to, 486, 546; sabotage in, 124

Gaza Emergency Hospital, 120

Gaza Raid (1955), 1–2, 4, 5–20, 23, 34, 47, 80, 115, 116, 120, 140; Baghdad Pact and, 200, 240–41; Egyptian arms in, 244; Egyptian responses to, 69, 83–96, 100, 102, 107, 186, 201, 225, 239, 240, 243, 247, 252, 271, 274, 278–79, 281, 288, 294, 361, 495, 696; as reprisal, 57, 58, 76, 83, 678

Gaza Strip, 11, 24, 42–43, 91, 246, 492; Egyptian return (1957), 668–69; Israeli capture (1956), 103, 468, 469, 482, 490, 525, 548, 551–54, 569–70, 636, 661–68; Israeli withdrawal issue, 654, 661–63, 664, 665–68; refugees in, 10, 20, 42, 61, 83, 486, 554, 608, 662, 664; UNEF withdrawal, 682; vulnerability of, 92–93, 97, 247, 433, 440, 486, 496, 546, 552

Gazier, Albert, 450–51, 454

General Armistice Agreements (1949), 8, 13, 17, 70, 87, 95, 104; al-Auja and, 11, 111, 119, 306; Ben Gurion on, 124, 125. *See also* Palestine War, armistice

Genesis, Book of, 23–24

Geneva Conference (1954), 134, 136

Geneva Conference (1955), 91, 112–13, 243–44, 245, 258

Geneva Conference, proposed (1956), 451, 453, 460, 490

Genghis Khan, 225

Georges, Kamel, quoted, 417

Georges Leygues (vessel), 466, 548

Georges-Picot, Jacques, 161–62; quoted, 160, 163, 420; Suez Canal nationalization and, 354, 420, 421, 422, 423

Georgia, USSR, 236

Germany, 30, 76, 141, 171, 392, 402; Aswan High Dam and, 300, 301; nationalism and, 237, 699; Nazi, 38–39, 136, 144–45, 177, 178, 228–29, 268, 698; Turkey and, 28, 31, 33, 49, 227,

229. *See also* East Germany and West Germany
Gero, Erno, 580–81
al-Gezira, Cairo, 567
Ghaleb, Brig. Gen. Abdel Hamid, 281
Ghaleb (vessel), 159
Ghali, Boutros, 157
Ghali, Waguih, quoted, 156–57, 432, 556
Gharandal, Jordan, 428, 440
Giap, Gen. V. Nguyen, 130
Gilbert, Amb. Pierre-Eugène, 136, 137, 143, 148, 472, 576
Gilles, Brig. Gen. Jean, 602, 605, 606
Gilroy, Harry, 94, 107, 110; quoted, 95
Givli, Col. Benjamin, 78–79, 546, 549
Glubb Pasha, 61, 203, 495, 694–95; quoted, 57, 117; expulsion, 148, 150, 206, 207, 208–13, 216, 275, 293, 314, 371, 407, 622, 623
Gomulka, Wladyslaw, 257, 455, 467, 473, 514, 582, 652
Gordon, Gen. Charles George, 174
Goodpaster, Col. Andrew, 367
Gorse, Georges, 149, 150–51
Gottwald, Klement, 232
Gove, J. G., 414
Graham, Maj. David, 621–22
Grailly, Count Jean de, 342–43, 344, 350–51, 354–55, 357, 358, 422
Grange, Alphonse, 343, 350
Grantham, Admr. Sir Guy, 471
Granville, Lord, 170–71
Great Britain, *see* Britain
Greece, 183, 229, 230, 267; Balkan Pact and, 236, 245; Nazi resistance, 558; Suez Canal nationalization and, 385, 401, 422, 423, 436
Green, Avigdor, 49
Griffiths, James, quoted, 561
Gruenther, Gen. Alfred M., 462; quoted, 615–16
Gyor, Hungary, 584

Haaretz (newspaper), 115
Habbaniya, Iraq, 201
Hadassah Hospital, Mount Scopus, 55
Hafez, Col. Mustafa, 124, 337, 345
Hafez, Suleiman, 567
Haganah (Israel Defense Forces), 50–51, 53, 54, 55, 57, 136, 494, 679, 691, 696. *See also* Israeli Army
Hagar, 23
Haifa, Israel, 64, 76, 475, 515, 532; sea attack (1956), 512–13
Hammarskjold, Dag, 60, 93, 447, 451, 463, 681; quoted, 62, 444–45, 649; al-Auja and, 111, 112,

333, 337, 648; Middle East missions (1956), 119–20, 124–25, 151, 333, 337; Sinai invasion and, 428, 518, 564–65; Suez cease-fire (1956) and, 573, 574, 575, 607–608, 628, 650; Suez War withdrawal issue and, 662, 664, 667, 669; Syrian raid (1955) and, 116, 308
Harding, Field Marshal Sir John, 198, 199
Harding, Warren Gamaliel, 266
Hare, Amb. Raymond A., 644, 646; quoted, 557–58, 567
Harkavi, Col. Yehoshafat, 78, 124, 148, 337
Harman, Avraham, 659
Harpaz, Col. Yosef, 538
Harper's Magazine, 58, 76
Harrison, Earl G., quoted, 268
Hashemite dynasty, 193, 207
Hatem, Col. Abdel Kader, 566
Hatseva (Ain Hasb), Israel, 497, 501
Hatzor, Israel, 470
Havlagah policy, 53–54
Hawthorne, Nathaniel, quoted, 192
Hayter, Amb. Sir William, 259, 610; quoted, 506–507, 582, 612
Head, Anthony, 74, 186, 217, 447, 560, 578; quoted, 382, 521, 618, 658
Heads of Agreement (and Anglo-Egyptian Suez Canal Base Evacuation Agreement), 218, 451, 475; abrogation, 672; Baghdad Pact and, 17, 18, 19, 71, 190, 196; collusion and, 475; Eisenhower and, 280, 281; Franco-Israeli alliance and, 75, 139; Moslem Brotherhood and, 15, 73, 188–89, 235; signing of, 12, 13, 14, 74, 184–88, 279; Suez Canal nationalization and, 158, 380, 381, 399. *See also* Suez Canal; British base evacuation
Healey, Dennis, quoted, 568
Hebrew language, 29–30, 49, 53, 495
Hebrew University, 62
Hebron, 27, 62, 486
Hedjaz, Kingdom of the, 35
Hefnaoui, Mustafa, 339
Heikal, Mohammed Hassanein, 256, 320, 410; quoted, 306–307, 413
Heitan Defile, 500, 509, 516–17, 530, 541, 548
Heliopolis airport, Cairo, 526
Hell's Canyon Dam, Oregon, 310
Henderson, Amb. Loy, 415, 416
Henriques, Col. Robert, quoted, 440
Herbaut, Pierre, 414
Herbert, Sir Edwin, 637
Herodotus, quoted, 297, 349
Herut (Freedom) party, 52, 94,

97, 453–54
Herzl, Theodore, 29, 30, 33, 40, 230, 639
High Dam, *see* Aswan High Dam
Hightower, John, 285
Hill 168, Sinai, 543
Hill 209, Sinai, 537, 538
Hill of Evil Counsel, 67
Hilmy, Col. Haney Amin II, 527, 528; quoted, 475, 568
Histadrut (labor federation), 50, 79
Hitler, Adolf: Jewish persecution, 38–39, 50, 136, 696 (*see also* Nazism); Nasser analogy, 145, 178, 367, 369, 370, 375, 383, 394, 397, 400, 409, 410, 415, 442, 574, 676, 684
Ho Chih Minh, 130, 558
Hochtief and Dortmund firm, 301
Hod, Brig.-Gen. Mordecai, 679; quoted, 677
al-Hodeiby, Hassan, 15, 189
Home, Sir Alec Douglas-, 354, 659
Hommel, Col. R., quoted, 110
Hoover, Herbert, 304
Hoover, Herbert, Jr., 563, 614, 639, 642, 643, 652; Aswan High Dam and, 284, 285, 286, 304–305, 306, 307, 308, 309, 310, 314, 315, 316, 323, 325; Suez Canal nationalization and, 355, 367, 377
von Horn, Maj. Gen. Carl, quoted, 690
Hourani, Albert, quoted, 218, 293
Huc, Capt., quoted, 7
Hughes, Emmet, 519
Hull, Cordell, quoted, 365
Humphrey, George, 307, 625, 665
Hungary, 76, 102; London Conference (1956), 385; revolt, 119, 256, 257, 334, 348, 406, 455, 467, 470, 473, 503, 514, 557, 561, 580–84, 610, 613, 614, 628, 629, 643, 652, 666, 686
Hurewitz, Prof. J. C., 376
Hurst, H. E., 299; quoted, 298
Husan, Jordan, 440, 448
Hussein, King of Jordan, 205, 219, 252, 72, 695; assassination rumor (1956), 470; British appeal (1956), 448, 599; Egyptian alliance (1957), 52, 686–87; Glubb Pasha and, 117, 148, 203, 207, 208–13, 275; Iraq appeal (1956), 533; Shuqairy and, 680; on Suez nationalization, 364
Hussein, Sherif of Mecca, 30, 31, 33, 34, 35
Hussein Kamel, Sultan of Egypt, 172
Hussein, Amb. Ahmed, 294, 302, 315, 321–22, 325
Hussein, Kamaleddeen, 534, 565–66, 584–85, 605

Hussein, Cmdr. Shakr, 591
Hussein-McMahon Agreement, 30–31, 32, 33–34, 37
Hutchison, Cmdr. Elmo H., 62
Huweitat, 32
Hylton-Foster, Harry, 428

Ibn al-Aas, Amr, 154
Ibn Saud, King of Saudi Arabia, 35
al-Ibrahim, Shaikh, of Algeria, 134
Ibrahim, Hassan, 302
Ibrahim al-Awwal (vessel), 512–14, 661
Ihud (Unity) party of Israel, 52
Immigration, *see* Migration
Imperialism, 18, 39, 182; American anti-colonialism and, 438–39; Arab view of, 40–41, 43, 88, 178, 194, 218, 227–28, 251, 252, 253, 254, 272, 279, 288, 292, 335, 345, 452, 645; Cold War, 646–48; French, 130, 136, 230; Russian, 225–26, 228–30; Suez Canal and, 158, 167–74, 362, 412. *See also* Expansionism
India, 149, 155, 159, 167, 168, 265, 663; Baghdad Pact and, 198; independence, 179; Russia and, 226, 232; Suez Canal nationalization and, 362, 364, 385, 402, 405, 406, 459, 463; Suez War cease-fire and, 573; Suez War collusion and, 562, 568
Indochina, 130, 132, 134–35, 139, 146, 186, 230, 384
Indonesia, 385, 404, 406, 558, 667
Infiltration, 9–10, 11, 105, 130; reprisal policy and, 56, 57, 58, 60, 61, 68–69, 75–76, 78, 87, 694–95; UNEF and, 669–70, 680
Inshas airfield, Cairo, 526
Institut d'Egypte, 300
International Chamber of Shipping, 384
International League for the Rights of Man, 77
International Monetary Fund, 625
Intisar (vessel), 134
Ionides, Michael, 37; quoted, 569
Iran, 141, 180, 184, 385, 415, 419; Baghdad Pact and, 196, 197, 202, 238, 406; CIA in, 216, 304, 327; Russia and, 227, 229, 230, 267, 275, 614; Sinai invasion and, 519
Iraq, 23, 175, 216, 230, 251, 334, 346, 353, 409, 442, 672; Arab League organization and, 41–42, 179; arms purchases, 71, 141, 219; Baghdad Pact and, 17–18, 19, 71, 77, 193–97, 198–99, 200–201, 207, 210–11, 225, 235, 240, 246, 273–75, 280, 568, 676;

French relations (1956), 568; Jordan defense (1956), 95, 213, 448–49, 450, 460, 462, 470, 474, 504, 533; Jordan riots (1955) and, 207–208; oil stoppage, 651; Palestine War and, 9, 66, 71, 447–48; Rashid Aly regime in, 229; revolution of 1958, 676; Russia (1959) and, 611; Sinai invasion (1956) and, 443, 463, 504, 653; Suez Canal nationalization and, 354, 364; Suez War (1967) and, 685, 689; Syrian revolt (1956) and, 407–408, 483, 532, 653; UN Israeli sanctions vote, 667
Iraq Petroleum Company, 533, 568
Iraqi Air Force, 689
Irgun Zvai Leumi, 51, 52, 54, 55, 94, 696
Isaac, 23, 24, 26
Ishmael, 23, 24, 26, 694
Ismail, Khedive of Egypt, 154, 156, 168–69
Ismail, Brig. Gen. Hafez, 533
Ismailya, Egypt, 163, 170, 283, 486, 565, 650; *Akka* at, 527; al-Auja road, 536, 537; Canal offices in, 339, 342, 343, 344, 347–48, 351, 354, 357–58, 421, 436; capture plans (1956), 451, 458, 464, 467, 468, 497, 518, 596, 599, 613, 622, 642; Eastern Command headquarters in, 495, 496, 599, 605; Liberation Army in, 534, 584–85, 605
Israel: Algeria and, 129, 130, 131, 134, 135, 136, 142, 143, 145–46, 148, 151, 152, 249, 314; Anglo-French Canal port seizures and, 576, 580, 624; Anglo-French collusion and, 1, 216, 219–20, 293, 336, 361, 367, 370, 374, 375, 392, 424, 428–29, 433–76, 482–83, 486–90, 495, 498, 500, 503–504, 506–507, 508, 511–12, 514, 515, 520–21, 525, 531, 533, 534, 557, 562, 564, 565, 568–69, 570–74, 575, 576, 596, 607–608, 616, 638, 642–43, 646, 654, 658–59, 672, 687, 688 (*see also*, infra, Israel: Sèvres ultimatum); Aqaba users association proposal, 439, 683; Aswan High Dam and, 114, 125, 220, 304, 306–308, 309, 346; al-Auja and, 107–12, 113, 116, 119–20, 143, 202, 252, 253, 291, 306, 333, 337, 453, 536, 648; Baghdad Pact and, 18, 196, 198, 200, 201, 202, 203–204; borders, 8, 9, 10, 11, 12, 13, 14, 19, 35, 41, 56, 60–61, 68, 75, 86, 91–92, 94, 95, 96, 99, 103, 105, 110, 119, 121, 190, 200, 204, 208, 245, 246, 247, 270, 277, 303, 304,

403, 440, 474, 476, 503, 669–70, 680, 690, 691, 692, 696; British Suez base evacuation and, 17, 37, 64, 71, 73–74, 75, 112, 137, 180, 184, 188, 190, 290; China and, 118, 259, 294; Egyptian peace treaty demands, 114–15, 663, 664–65, 690; elections of 1955, 79, 94, 95, 122, 245; Gaza Raid and, 1, 5–20, 23, 34, 47, 80, 83–86, 89, 100, 115, 116, 200, 225, 247, 281, 288; Jordan River and, 12, 60, 63, 64, 65, 105, 116, 119, 233, 276–77, 289, 690; Jordan raids (1956), 440, 441, 447, 448–49, 450, 451, 452, 453–54, 459, 462, 463, 464, 467, 470, 475, 476, 482, 505, 533, 568; Khan Yunis and, 96–97, 98, 116, 143, 247, 552, 554, 569; Palestine War armistice and, 9, 41–42, 67–68, 69–70, 72, 124, 125, 306, 333, 447–48, 449, 460, 638, 663, 668, 690; refugee return issue and, 103–104, 105, 346, 696, 697–98; reprisal policy of, 53–69, 70, 71, 76, 83, 85, 87, 91, 97, 109, 114, 115, 242–43, 276, 428–29, 440, 448, 482, 553, 678, 680, 694–95, 696, 698; Russia and, 37, 73, 98–99, 102, 112, 113, 119, 225, 226, 229, 230–34, 236, 246, 250, 252, 260, 269, 287, 455, 610–11, 663, 683–84; Sèvres ultimatum (1956), 463–65, 466, 504, 505, 506, 508, 511, 514, 515, 520; Sinai attack threats (1955), 99–100, 101, 102, 103, 105–106, 107, 108, 112, 119, 140–41, 143, 245, 289, 306, 307, 309, 392, 536; Sinai invasion (1956), 2, 121, 143, 151, 346, 348, 364, 428–29, 439–40, 442–44, 447, 448, 450–51, 457, 463–66, 468, 469–76, 480–521, 530–32, 536–54, 558, 569, 572–73, 589–95, 624, 640, 658, 660, 661, 675; Suez Canal nationalization and, 85, 105, 112, 163–64, 171, 336, 362, 383, 433, 439; Suez War (1956) cease-fire, 519, 561–65, 569, 570, 572–75, 607–608, 623–24, 628, 633; Suez War (1956) withdrawals issue, 637–44, 646, 648, 650, 651, 654, 661–69, 670, 675, 691; Suez War (1967), 488, 634, 676–97; United States economic aid, 663, 665, 686, 694; water resources, 692, 694; World Court and, 676–71, 685–86; Zionist state establishment, 28–40, 41, 47, 50, 52–53, 65, 71–72, 102–104, 136, 137, 163, 180, 182, 229, 230, 231, 232, 251, 266, 268–69, 275–76, 278, 346, 692, 696, 697–98

Israeli Air Force, 439, 443, 462, 465, 469–70; Sinai invasions, 509–10, 549, 595, 687–89
Israeli Army, 48, 50, 51, 101, 103, 139, 249; Armored Corps, 96, 97, 496, 497–98, 507, 537, 539, 540–43, 545, 547, 549, 550, 594, 595, 689; al-Auja and, 109–10, 111; Central Command, 497, 498; Churchill on, 239; Elath campaign (Palestine War), 42; mobilization (1956), 442–43, 454, 469, 471, 472, 473, 474, 491, 492, 511–12, 658; mobilization (1967), 679–80, 681, 686; Ninth Infantry, 471; Northern Command, 79, 497; organization, 491–92, 494–95, 517, 634; reprisals and, 53–69, 91, 96–97; Sinai invasion (1956), 481, 486, 489, 491, 492, 497–503, 507–508, 515–17, 518, 525–54, 589, 634, 635, 687–88; Sinai invasion (1967), 689–90; Southern Army Command, 5–20, 486, 497, 545; 202nd Paratroop Brigade, 495, 497, 500, 501, 507, 508, 510, 515–17
Israeli Border Police, 476
Israeli Defense Ministry, 51, 65, 658, 679; Ben Gurion return to (1955), 47, 78, 79–80, 105, 140–41, 200, 204; Dayan return to (1967), 687; France and, 48, 75, 101, 116, 137, 138, 139, 140; reprisal policy and, 57–58, 59; sabotage orders, 17, 73, 74, 76, 78, 83
Israeli Foreign Ministry, 8, 47, 51, 96, 447–48, 459; Anglo-French collusion and, 473, 563–64, 658; Baghdad Pact and, 200; French relations, 75, 101, 136, 137, 138, 658; Jordan water project, 60; Khan Yunis and, 97; Russia and, 73; Sharett resignation, 50, 121–23; Sinai invasion and, 502, 658; Suez cease-fire and, 574
Israeli Intelligence Department, 73, 74, 78, 124, 690
Israeli Knesset (Parliament), 9, 72, 73, 80, 94, 105–106, 121, 678, 691; al-Auja and, 107, 306; Egyptian spy trials and, 77; Elath and, 42; Kafr Kassem massacre and, 476; Qalqilya and, 454; reprisal policy and, 58–59, 62, 87; Russian-Egyptian arms deal and, 102; Sharett resignation, 122; Suez War withdrawals issue and, 637–38, 640, 662, 666; Syrian attack (1967) and, 681
Israeli Navy, Haifa base, 512–13
Italy, 115, 133, 171, 174, 250, 385, 437
Ivan the Terrible, 225

Jabotinsky, Vladimir, 29, 51, 52
Jacob, 632
Jaffa (vessel), 513
Jamal, Jules, 617
Japan, 228, 385, 437, 688, 699
Japanese Peace Treaty (1951), 379
Javits, Sen. Jacob K., 641
Jean Bart (vessel), 617, 618
Jebb, Amb. Sir Gladwyn, 454
Jebel Aida, 590
Jebel Dalfa, Sinai, 537, 538, 540, 542, 543
Jebel Halal, Sinai, 537
Jebel Libni, Sinai, 495–96, 539, 540
Jebel Nizaa, Sinai, 537, 543
Jebel al-Sabha, Sinai, 102, 108, 110, 202. See also al-Sabha, Sinai
Jebel Wugeir, Sinai, 537
Jerusalem, 486, 572, 700; internationalization proposals, 234; Israeli capture, 41, 52, 449; 690, 692; Moslem associations of, 26–27; reprisals in, 55; UNTSO headquarters, 66–67; Western consulates, 120, 233, 456
Jerusalem Post (newspaper), 58, 97, 515, 560; on Dulles, 63, 64, 276; on Jordan, 449; on Qibya, 59; on Sinai, 639, 660; on Syrian reprisals, 639, 660
Jesus, 26, 27
Jewish Agency, 37, 50, 137
Jews, 23–26, 27, 32; assimilationism and, 39, 231; Egyptian community, 106–107, 190, 672; nationalism and, 28, 29–40, 268–69, 698–99 (See also Zionism); Oriental, 495; persecutions of, 28, 38–39 (see also Anti-Semitism); Russian population, 230–31, 232
Joffe, Col. Avraham, 554
Johnson, Lyndon B., 310, 324, 665, 666, 695, 699; Israeli water resources and, 692; Suez War (1967) and, 684, 685, 686
Johnston, Eric, 198, 285; Jordan waters proposal (1953) and, 12–13, 60, 115–16, 255, 276, 277, 289
Jordan, 34, 48, 66, 95, 103, 219, 334, 335, 346, 370, 486; Baghdad Pact and, 107, 116, 117, 196, 202–205, 207, 210, 252, 255–56, 275, 308, 449; bus massacre (1954) and, 62; Glubb Pasha expulsion, 148, 150, 206, 207, 208–13, 216, 275, 293, 314, 371, 407, 622, 623; Israeli reprisals (1956) in, 291, 440, 441,

447, 448–49, 450, 451, 452, 453–54, 459, 460, 462, 463, 464, 467, 470, 474, 475, 476, 482, 503, 505, 533, 568; Jordan water project and, 65, 277; measures against infiltration, 61, 694–95; Nahhaleen, 62–63, 233; Qibya raid (1953) and, 10–11, 56–60, 64; Russia and, 73, 209, 233; Suez Canal nationalization, 364; Suez War (1956) and, 398, 428–29, 440, 443, 447, 448, 474, 492, 502, 503, 504, 514–15, 532–33, 568, 617, 644, 672; Suez War (1967) and, 52, 536, 678, 680–81, 685, 686–87, 689, 690; West Bank annexation, 269–70
Jordan River, 67, 105, 208, 443, 635, 690; Israeli diversion project, 60, 63, 64, 65, 116, 119, 233, 276–77; Johnston Plan for, 12–13, 60, 115–16, 255, 276–77, 289, 302, 303
Jordanian Air Force, 689
Jordanian Army (Arab Legion), 56, 57, 61, 117, 694–95; Glubb and, 208, 209–10
Jordanian-Israeli MAC, 66, 67, 443
Joseph, 24
Joshua, 24, 25, 38, 40
Joshua, Book of, 24, 25, 694
Judean Hills, 56

Kabrit, Egypt, 340, 526
Kabylia, Algeria, 148
Kadar, Janos, 580, 581, 583, 584
Kafr Kassem, Israel, 476, 533
Kaissouny, Abdel Moneim, 162, 255, 364; Aswan High Dam and, 302, 303, 307, 316, 335
Kalinin, Mikhail, 231
Kalinin Declaration, 231
Kantara, Egypt, see Qantara
al-Kap, Egypt, 491, 528, 596, 629, 651
Karachi, Pakistan, 148–49, 211, 216
Kars, Turkey, 229, 230
Keightly, Gen. Sir Charles, 398, 448; quoted, 488, 521, 526, 528, 530, 602, 616, 618, 619–20, 621; Port Said attack and, 577–78, 579, 580, 599, 600, 602, 605, 606, 616, 618–20, 621, 623, 627, 635–36, 642, 654
Kennedy, John F., 685
Kennedy, Robert, 694
Kenya, 29, 32, 39
Kersaint (vessel), 475, 512–13
Kesalon, 62
Ketziot, 11–12, 109
Kfar Etzion, 62
al-Khalidy, Hussein Fakhry, quoted, 695
Khallaf, Capt. Showqi, 527

Khan Yunis, Gaza Strip, 83, 96–97, 98, 116, 120, 143, 247, 486, 495; Sinai invasion (1956) and, 552, 554, 569
Khartoum, Sudan, 174, 182
Khider, Mohammed, 133, 150, 152, 414
Khrushchev, Nikita S., 2, 145, 220, 235–36, 244, 245, 253; admits inability to help Egypt, 609–10; Algeria and, 260–61; 'bury you" comment, 652, 653–54; deposition of, 583, 676,; de-Stalinization policy of, 256–58, 514, 580; Eden and, 219, 243, 258–59, 578, 652; Nasser and, 118, 240, 243, 260, 261, 293, 323, 609–10, 611, 654, 675, 676; Polish crisis (1956), 455, 582; Suez Canal nationalization and, 377; Warsaw Pact and, 237–38
Kilmuir, Lord, 369, 412, 657; quoted, 205, 221, 354, 560, 659
"Kilo 95", 67, 94, 115; attack, 95, 98
Kimche, David, quoted, 42, 108
Kinglake, Alexander, quoted, 166
Kinneret, Galilee, 114–16
Kiouane, Abderrahmane, 414
Kirkpatrick, Ivone, 434, 504
Kiselev, Amb. Yevgeni D., 401, 444, 609, 610; quoted, 335
Kitchener, Lord, 174, 299
Knowland, Sen. William F., 665, 666
Koenig, Gen. Marie-Pierre: Israeli arms and, 75, 134, 138–39, 140, 141, 142, 143, 146, 290
Kolleck, Teddy, 659
al-Kony, Amb. Mohammed, 610
The Koran, 26–27
Korean War, 230, 241, 271, 272, 282, 426, 563; Russia and, 614–15; Uniting for Peace resolution, 518–19, 562
Korean Armistice (July 1953), 237
Krim, Abdel, 132
Krim, Belkacem, 133
Kubba, Mohammed Mahdi, quoted, 364
Kubri al-Kubba, Cairo, 341–42, 243
Kuntilla, 110, 116; Sinai invasion action, 481, 497, 501, 591
Kurds, 266

Labor party (British), 179–80, 182, 206; Baghdad Pact and, 202; Egyptian bombings (1956) and, 560–61, 606–607; Sinai invasion and, 505, 520, 556, 654, 658, 659; Suez Canal nationalization and, 371, 372, 383, 393, 400, 426, 428; Suez cease-fire (1956) and, 568, 571, 572, 628–29, 643, 657
Labouisse, Henry, cited, 552, 553

Lacey, Brigadier John H. S., 217
Lacoste, Robert, 146, 147; quoted, 148
Lake Manzala, 598, 600, 604, 641
Lake Mariotis, 167
Lake Timsah, 527
Lake Victoria, 299, 300
Lampson, Amb. Sir Miles, 175, 176, 177, 178, 181, 182
Lane, Edward William, quoted, 480
Lange, Halvard, quoted, 437
Lansing, Robert, 266
Latakia, Syria, 617, 653
Latif, Mohammed Abdel, 189
Latin America, 695
Lavon, Pinhas, 65, 76, 78, 79, 80, 137, 679
Lavon Affair, 48, 52, 73, 74, 75, 79, 80, 187; executions, 76–78
Law of Return, 41, 104, 697–98
Lawrence, T. E., 31, 32, 193, 266
League of Nations, 176, 227; Mandate for Palestine, 34, 35–36, 54
Lebanese-Israeli MAC, 66
Lebanon, 27, 28, 34, 151, 270, 413, 692, 694; Baghdad Pact and, 196, 202, 252; French Mandate, 35, 130, 136, 137; Israeli raid (1968), 695, 698; Israeli sanctions resolution, 667; Jordan waters proposal, 12, 277; Palestine War and, 9, 66; Russia and, 229; United States Marines in, 676
Lehmann, Sen. Herbert H., 276
von Leibnitz, Gottfried Wilhelm, 154
Leith-Ross, Sir Frederick, 396; quoted, 294
Lenin, Vladimir Ilyich, 256, 258
Lennox-Boyd, Alan, 369
Le Père, Jacques-Marie, 154
de Lesseps, Ferdinand, 128, 152, 153, 155, 156, 167, 168, 321; British invasion of Egypt (1882) and, 170; Nasser code signal, 341, 343, 344, 347, 348, 349, 351; Port Said and, 598, 656; Suez Canal Company concession, 385
de Lesseps, Mathieu, 155
Leulliette, Pierre, 642; quoted, 600, 601, 620–21, 655, 656
Levy, Walter, quoted, 700
Liberia, 385, 439
Libya, 174, 265, 419, 442; Suez War (1956) and, 335, 393, 398, 577
Lidice, Czechoslovakia, 55, 59
Lima, Peru, 355, 375
Limassol, Cyprus, 584, 600
Lindsay, Sir Ronald, quoted, 264
Litani River, 277, 692
Little, Tom, 282, 307, 414, 417; quoted, 14–15, 178–79, 197

Llandudno, Wales, 449, 450
Lloyd, Selwyn, 116, 117, 119, 190, 205, 217, 259, 390, 676; Aswan High Dam and, 313, 314, 338; British monetary crisis (1956) and, 625; collusion and, 215, 216, 220, 424–25, 434, 441, 451, 452–53, 454, 457, 459, 461–65, 468, 471, 474–75, 504, 508, 520, 573, 590, 607–608, 652–53, 657–58; Glubb dismissal and, 210–12; Nasser meeting, 210–12; Suez base evacuation and, 218; Suez Canal nationalization and, 354, 355, 356, 369, 374, 375, 378, 402, 404, 406, 411, 422, 426, 436–37, 439, 444–46, 449–50, 463; Suez withdrawal issue and, 654, 662; turns against Nasser, 215; United Nations Emergency Force and, 568, 571–72, 607–608
Lloyd George, David, 32, 36
Lloyd's of London, 428, 429, 446
Lodge, Amb. Henry Cabot, Gaza withdrawal issue and, 653, 654, 665, 666, 667–68; Sinai invasion and, 504, 507
London, England, 397, 403
London Conference (August 1956), 323, 384–86, 387, 390, 391, 400, 401–405; Nasser on, 398–99; negotiating mission, 411–18, 420, 424, 425, 426, 436, 459–60; Second London Conference (September 1956), 436, 437
London Daily Express (newspaper), 400
London Daily Herald (newspaper), 206, 218
London Daily Mail (newspaper), 400
London Daily Mirror (newspaper), 206, 400
London Daily Telegraph (newspaper), 205–206, 377, 409, 438
London Economist (periodical), 307
London Evening Standard (newspaper), 578
London Financial Times (newspaper), 365–66
London Jewish Observer (periodical), 410
London News Chronicle (newspaper), 306, 412
London Observer (newspaper), 323, 658
London Sunday Times, 409
London Times (newspaper), 162, 187, 217, 220, 247, 251, 292; on Aswan High Dam and, 659; on Egyptian oil nationalizations, 560; on Suez Canal nationalization, 360, 362–63, 378, 394, 395–96, 400, 419–

20, 426, 428, 463; on Suez War (1956), 520–21, 607, 629
Longgood, William, 114
Lorenz, Konrad, quoted, 524
Lourie, Arthur, quoted, 96
Lovers of Zion, 49
Loya, Dr. Arieh, quoted, 52–53
Luke, 296, 524
Lundstrom, Gen. Aage, 65–66
Luns, Dr. Joseph M.A.H., Foreign Minister of the Netherlands, quoted, 436
Luxor, Egypt, 521, 528, 688
Lydda, Israel, 470, 528

McCarthy, Sen. Eugene, 694
McCarthy, Sen. Joseph, 280
Macomber, Amb. William B., Jr., 563
McDonald, Amb. James G., 269
MacDonald, Ramsey, 174
Macedonia, 25
McLachlan, Donald, quoted, 205–206
McMahon, Sir Henry, 30, 33, 34
Macmillan, Harold, 113, 203, 205, 214, 401, 507, 625; premiership, 626, 657–58, 659; Suez Canal nationalization and, 336, 369–70, 374, 375, 378, 441
Madoc, Brig. Gen. R. W., 621
Maghrib Office, Cairo, 133
Magnes, Judah, 51, 52
Maher, Aly, 177, 181
Makarios, Archbishop, of Cyprus, 215
Makins, Sir Roger, 307, 425, 471
Malaya, 230
Malenkov, Georgi M., 235, 237, 240; quoted, 236
Maleter, Col. Pal, 581
Malta, 180, 335, 369, 512; Suez War (1956), 374, 387, 406, 457, 465, 468, 471, 473, 475, 508, 527, 568, 572, 575, 588
Manchester Guardian (newspaper), 397, 421, 628, 658
Mandates system, 29, 34–38, 50, 54, 227
Mandelbaum Gate, Jerusalem, 64, 67
Manjin, Louis, 442, 460–61
Mankabad, Egypt, 177
Manshiet al-Bakry, Cairo, 339
Mapai (Socialist) party, 49, 52, 58, 65, 72, 97, 677; elections of 1955 and, 79–80, 94; Kinneret raid and, 115; Russia and, 73; Suez War collusion and, 440
Marauders, *see* Infiltration; *Fedayeen*
Mareri, Count Vicente, 621, 622
Marlowe, John, quoted, 360
Marshall Plan, 183, 302
Martino, Gaetano, Foreign Minister of Italy, quoted, 437

Marx, Karl, quoted, 46
Marzouk, Moussa Lieto, 76–77, 78
Massu, Gen. Jacques, 622
Mau Mau, 32, 39
Mecca, 26, 30, 31, 89, 154, 486
Medina, 26, 154
Mediterranean Sea, 56, 196, 290–91, 456; Russia and, 225, 226, 580, 612; Sinai and, 11, 483, 486; Suez Canal and, 153, 154, 179, 298, 356, 375, 382
Mein Kampf (Hitler), 145, 409, 410, 415
Meinertzhagen, Col. Richard, 551, 613, 660; quoted, 459
Meir, Golda, 79, 122, 441; collusion and, 473, 511, 533, 573; Suez War withdrawals issue and, 639, 667
Meknes, Morocco, 456
Menderes, Adnan, 197, 199
Mendès-France, Pierre, 139, 146
Menes, 297
Mennessier, Pierre, 351, 352, 353, 354
Menon, V. K. Krishna, 403, 404
Menzies, Robert: mission to Nasser, 402, 411–18, 420, 424, 425, 426, 436, 446, 459–60
Mesopotamia, *see* Iraq
Metulla, 67
Mexico, 365
Middle East, 14, 22, 33, 36, 692; arms race, 1, 100, 117–18, 253, 254, 259, 270, 287, 293, 494, 686, 699; Defense Pact proposals, 64, 70, 71, 180, 194, 225, 230, 234, 238, 242, 268, 271, 273, 274, 279, 280–81; Northern Tier of, 18, 225, 253; Russian power in, 672; United States power in, 265–68, 271, 272, 439, 503, 613, 615, 628, 642, 646–48, 665, 685. *See also* specific countries
Middle East Emergency Committee, 407, 651
Middleton, Drew, 205; quoted, 214
Migdal-Ashkelon, Israel, 247
Migration: Algerian French, 40; American Jews, 266; Arab country Jews, 52–53, 57, 130–31; Bedouin, 61–62; Birobidzhan, 231; Zionist, 28–29, 34–35, 37, 38–39, 40–41, 50, 51, 71, 72, 102, 104, 105, 136, 231, 269–69, 346, 347, 495, 677, 697–98. *See also* Population; Refugees
Mikoyan, Anastas, 444, 514, 581, 582, 583
Milner, Alfred, Lord, 321
Minost, Etienne, 354
Minya, Egypt, 566, 617
al-Misri (newspaper), 187

Mitla Pass, 444, 466, 483, 486, 489, 591; invasion action (1956) at, 507–508, 509, 510, 511, 512, 515–18, 526, 538, 548, 634; paratroop drop (1956), 465, 469, 471, 481, 489, 490, 495, 497, 498, 500, 501, 502, 636, 658
Modern Egyptians (Lane), 480
Moguy, Brig. Gen. Salaheddeen, quoted, 604, 612, 619; Port Said invasion and, 599, 603, 604, 605, 609, 612, 619, 621–22
Mohammed, 26
Mohammed V, King of Morocco, 130, 132, 142, 146, 456
Mohammed Aly, Ruler of Egypt, 27, 28, 157, 167, 174, 639; Suez Canal and, 154, 155, 168, 170
Mohammed Said, Ruler of Egypt, 155, 168
Mohyeddin, Zakaria, 76, 333, 533–34, 690; American mission (1967), 685; Port Said invasion and, 598
Mollet, Guy, 2, 3, 116, 121, 135, 144–47, 148, 213, 314, 672, 676; Algerian secret talks, 149–50, 152, 220, 414; Ben Bella kidnapping, 456–57, 462; Eisenhower visit proposed, 642; Jordan defense (1956) and, 450, 452; on Nasser's book, 145, 409, 410; Russian threat (1956) and, 612–13, 615; Suez Canal nationalization and, 358, 375, 381, 382, 391–92, 393, 420, 422, 425–26, 428, 446, 447; Suez invasion (1956) and, 459, 472, 506, 515, 568, 610–11, 612–13, 616, 623, 626–27, 633
Molotov, Vyacheslav, 112, 115, 248, 261, 507
Monckton, Sir Walter, 447, 468, 572
Le Monde (newspaper), 375, 409, 651
Mongol empire, 225–26
Montefiore, Sir Moses, 27–28, 29, 39
Montreux Convention (1936), 229
Moorhouse, Lieut. Anthony, 656
Moria (vessel), 445
Morocco, 98, 171, 261, 456; independence, 130, 131–32, 133, 134, 142, 146, 149; Russia and, 228
Morris, James, 251, 292, 658
Morrison, Herbert, 372, 383
Morse, Sen. Wayne, 310
Moscow, 225, 232, 652
Moses, 24, 25, 26, 29, 443
Moslem Brotherhood, 104, 178; British Suez base evacuation and, 73, 182, 185, 187; on Hitler, 397; Nasser assassination attempt of, 14, 15–16, 17, 18, 19, 77, 78, 188–89, 235

Moslems, 9, 26–28, 36, 40, 89, 169; Cairo vigilantes, 559–60; North African, 130–31, 135, 136–37, 142, 152; political leadership and, 265; Ramadan festival, 241–42; Russia and, 231, 250–51
Mossadegh, Mohammed, 180, 216, 304, 327
Mostarod, Egypt, 337, 339, 345, 367
Mount Scopus, 55
Mount Sinai, 483
Mountain of Graves, 67
Mountbatten, Louis, Lord, 354, 370, 397
Mukassar al-Fanageel dunes, Sinai, 537, 544, 545
Murphy, Robert, 367–68; quoted, 316, 319, 325, 372, 374, 375, 377, 379, 412, 427, 446, 454, 582, 610, 623
Murrow, Edward R., 159, 445
Mussolini, Benito, 174, 383, 394, 442, 578
Mustafa, Col. Salah, 124, 337, 345
Muste, A. J., quoted, 632
Mutawally, Col. Saadeddeen, 538, 539, 543–45, 569; quoted, 541, 634
Myerson, Golda, see Meir, Golda

Nabi, Amb. Kamal Abdel, 368–369
Nabulsi, Suleiman, 449, 568
Naggar, Georges, 560
Naguib, Maj. Fuad, 605
Naguib, Mohammed, 73, 163, 182; Egyptian revolution and, 15, 16, 19, 64, 104, 185, 189–190, 198, 235, 252; Eisenhower and, 74, 265, 305
Nagy, Imre, 257, 455, 470, 473, 514, 580–584
Nahals, 40, 51, 226
Nahhaleen, Jordan, 11, 62–63, 71; Russia and, 233
Nahhas, Mustafa, 176, 177, 180, 181, 188; Russia and, 234
Nahmias, Josef, 141
Nahum, Grand Rabbi Chaim, 106
Nakhl, Sinai, 481, 486, 497, 508, 510
Napoleon Bonaparte, 137, 153, 155, 176, 226; quoted, 128, 298, 633; Britain and, 27, 154, 167
Narkis, Col. Uzi, 548
Nasheet, Admr. Mahmoud, 617
Nasir (vessel), 617–18
Nasser, Abdul Hameed, 481
Nasser, Gamal Abdel, 2, 51, 115, 177–78, 236, 474, 590; Algeria and, 19, 98, 118, 129, 130, 133–34, 135, 138, 139, 145, 148–49, 150–51, 152, 213, 220, 249, 314, 333, 334, 336, 368, 373, 378, 456; Anglo-French bombings (1956) and, 525, 526–27, 528, 530, 531, 548, 557, 565, 567, 598; Aswan High Dam and, 116, 125, 210, 216, 217, 219, 220–21, 242, 255–56, 260, 288, 292, 294, 297–327, 333–34, 335, 361, 675; Baghdad Pact and, 18, 89, 194–205, 207, 210, 215, 217, 225, 238–41, 243, 246, 252, 271, 274, 370; clandestine radio attacks on, 408–409, 529; coup d'état (1952), 9, 181, 182–83, 234, 247, 410, 493; Eden antipathy to, 3, 214, 215–21, 293, 314, 353, 357, 364, 367, 368, 372, 379, 394–95, 396–97, 419, 420, 434, 435, 442, 447, 452, 486, 568, 569, 578, 585, 596, 622–23 624, 633, 672; Gaza Raid and 1, 8, 13, 15, 20, 23, 58, 59, 83–97, 102, 107, 116, 140, 200, 247, 252, 278–79; 361; on Gaza Strip return (1957), 668–69; Glubb Pasha dismissal and, 210, 211–12, 213, 314, 622, 623; on guerrilla warfare, 531, 534, 536, 558–59, 565–66, 598; Heads of Agreement negotiations, 184, 185, 186, 188, 190, 235, 279; Khan Yunis and, 98, 116; Lavon Affair executions and, 76, 77; Menzies mission (1956) to, 411–18, 420, 446; moratorium with Eden, see Baghdad Pact; Naguib and, 15, 16, 19, 64, 73, 104, 182, 189–90, 198, 235, 252; New York Times interview unpublished, 92–94; Palestine War and, 43; peace efforts of, 12–14, 15, 47, 91–94, 95, 107, 111, 119, 198, 218, 245, 306, 309, 333, 391, 436, 437, 444, 445–47, 644–45, 684–85; political survival of, 676–77, 690–91; Port Said attack (1956) and, 584–85, 596, 598, 605, 609, 622–23, 624, 644; resignation offer (1967), 690–91; Russian arms deal announcement, 99–102, 109, 113–14, 142–43, 225, 238, 240–55, 259, 261, 282–94, 306; Sinai invasion and, 481–82, 483, 490, 491, 494, 496, 501–502, 510–11, 514, 515, 521, 525, 531–32, 550, 557; Suez Canal nationalization, 3, 85, 88, 112, 121, 149, 150, 156–64, 167, 215, 219, 221, 250, 292, 294, 311, 320–21, 322, 323, 326, 327, 333–58, 361–87, 391–92, 393, 394–95, 398–400, 402, 405, 407, 419, 425, 426–29, 433, 437, 444–45, 446, 490, 622–23; Suez War (1956) withdrawal issue and, 643–44; Suez War (1967) and, 680–85, 686, 690–91; threats to Israel, 638–39, 684; UNEF refusals, 649–50, 681–83

Natanson, Philip, 74
Natanya, Israel, 689
National Jewish Post (periodical), 59
National Liberation Front (Algerian), 19, 39, 132–33, 142, 148, 334; Ben Bella kidnapping and, 456; secret talks (1956), 150–51, 152, 220, 414
Nationalism, 2, 130, 647; Algerian, 19, 129, 132–34, 137, 138, 141, 142, 144, 146, 147, 148, 149, 152, 456; Arab, 27–31, 34, 35, 36, 38, 39, 40, 129, 200–201, 203, 204, 208, 239, 305, 346, 357, 395, 404, 411, 434, 599, 610, 637, 644, 645; Armenian, 53; Cypriote, 39, 215, 334, 401, 558, 655; Egyptian, 36, 43, 157–58, 159, 162, 169–70, 172–73, 174, 176–77, 187–88, 193, 288, 292, 310–11, 314, 318, 326, 345, 368, 373, 412, 533–34, 536, 558–59, 565–68, 569, 644–45, 654, 676; Hungarian, 256, 257, 334, 455, 470, 514, 580–84; Iraqi, 193, 653; Jordanian, 208–209, 448, 449; Palestinian, 34–35, 37, 42, 692, 694–99, 700; Red Army and, 237–38; Sudan, 180, 181; terrorism and, 39, 148, 152, 157, 655, 694–95, 696. See also Zionism
Nazism, 38–39, 55, 135, 136, 144, 268; Nasser and, 138, 145, 177, 178, 415, 684; resistance to, 558, 695, 696; Russia and, 228–29, 231, 258
Near East Arab Broadcasting Station on Cyprus, 514
Near East Arms Committee, 141
Nechos, Pharaoh, 153, 349
Negev, 5, 66, 99, 163, 494; Ben-Gurion in, 12, 47, 70; bus massacre (1954), 11, 61, 109; Jordan River diversion, 60, 64, 116
Nehru, Jawaharlal, 149, 152, 234, 321, 568; Baghdad Pact and, 198, 240; on collusion, 562; neutralism and, 241, 242, 333; Suez Canal nationalization and, 362, 364, 402
Nelson, Horatio, Lord, 167
Ness-Ziona, Israel, 112
Netherlands, 171, 385, 436, 558
Neuberger, Sen. Richard, 310
New Delhi, India, 149
New Statesman (periodical), 14
New York City, 51, 77, 454, 641
New York Evening Post (newspaper), 59
New York Journal-American (newspaper), 93
New York Stock Exchange, 350
The New York Times (newspaper), 58, 107–108, 110, 242; on Anglo-French-Israeli collu-

sion, 658 ; on Aswan High Dam, 307–308, 318, 323, 324 ; de-Stalinization text, 257 ; on Eden, 205, 214 ; on Gaza Raid, 6 ; on Israeli-French arms deal, 289 ; on Javits, 641 ; on Jordan (1968), 695 ; Nasser peace efforts and, 92–94 (unpublished interview), 116, 119, 245 ; on Russian arms deal, 246, 247 ; on Suez Canal nationalization, 348–49 ; on Suez War (1967), 674, 682

New York *World-Telegram and Sun* (newspaper), 93, 115

New Yorker (periodical), 684

New Zealand, 373, 385, 403, 564

Newfoundland (vessel), 560, 591, 594

Newsweek (periodical), 91

Nicholas I, Tsar of Russia, 227

Nicolson, Harold, quoted, 390, 572, 654

Nicolson, Nigel, 505

Nicosia, Cyprus, 577, 600

Nile River, 153, 155, 170, 174, 296, 567 ; Aswan High Dam and, 242, 297–99, 313, 323, 675 ; Barrage, 154 ; Pharaoh Nechos and, 349

Nitzana, *see* al-Auja (Nitzana)

Nixon, Richard, 307, 700

Nizameddeen, Maj. Gen. Tawfeeq, 532–33

Noon, Firooz Khan, 437

North Africa, 130–31. *See also* specific countries

North Atlantic Treaty Organization (NATO), 48, 118, 141, 183, 184, 195, 253 ; Aswan High Dam project and, 216, 310 ; Russia and, 194, 229, 230, 237–38, 240, 245, 267, 581, 652 ; Suez Canal nationalization and, 348, 367, 402, 413 ; Suez War (1956) and, 2, 454, 521, 561, 613, 615, 652

North Vietnam, 558

Norway, 356, 385, 437, 648, 650

Nursella, Lieut. Col. Jacob, quoted, 96

Nutting, Anthony, 648 ; on collusion, 441, 447, 450–53, 454, 461–62, 468–69, 504, 572, 659 ; on Eden-Dulles antagonism, 439 ; on Eden view of the United Nations, 424–25 ; on Eden *vis à vis* Nasser, 214, 215, 314, 357, 367, 420 ; on Glubb dismissal, 212–13 ; *Heads of Agreement* and, 74, 187, 190 ; on Israeli shipping restraints, 383, 682 ; resignation (1956), 571–72, 574, 626, 659

O'Ballance, Maj. Edgar, quoted, 497

Ocean (vessel), 621

Oil, 179, 196, 259 ; China and, 699–700 ; clandestine propaganda on, 411, 426 ; Egyptian nationalizations, 560 ; Iran nationalization, 180 ; Israel, 98 ; pipeline cuts, 403, 408, 533, 568, 651 ; rationing, 643, 655, 672 ; Saudi Arabian, 203, 655 ; shipping costs, 416 ; Suez Canal nationalization and, 161, 163, 219, 292, 336, 338, 354, 357, 362, 366, 367, 377, 419 ; United States and, 2, 265, 266–67, 278, 279, 282, 304–305, 377, 407, 452, 568, 651, 652, 654, 655, 666

Omar, Caliph, 26, 27

Omdurman, Sudan, 182

Operation Amer, 514

Operation Beisan, 515, 532

Operation Horeb, 108

Operation Joab, 89

Operation Kadesh, 443–44, 469, 473, 595. *See also* Sinai Peninsula, Israeli invasion (1956)

Operation Musketeer, 398, 406, 424, 543, 577 ; collusion in, 433–34, 441, 451, 460, 508, 575 ; supplementary strategies, 576

Operation Musketeer Revise, 457–58, 459, 465, 469, 579–80

Operation Nursery, 411

Operation Omelette, 576

Operation Penelope, 575

Operation Telescope, 576, 577, 579–80, 599

Oran, Algeria, 133

Orbach, Maurice, 87

Ordzhonikidze (vessel), 258

Organisation Secrète (O.S.), 132–33

Osborne, John, 656

Ottoman Empire, 23, 27, 28, 31, 49 ; Russia and, 226–27, 228, 232. *See also* Turkey

Ouamrane, Omar, 133

Oued Zem, Morocco, 142

Pace, Eric, quoted, 695

Pakistan, 141, 148–49, 385 ; Baghdad Pact and, 71, 198, 202, 235, 240, 275, 406 ; SCUA and, 437–38 ; United Nations Israeli sanctions resolution, 667

Palestine, 23–43, 50, 437 ; colonists' reprisal raids on marauders, 9–10, 53–54, 494 ; Naguib in, 15 ; refugee numbers, 697 ; Sinai and, 639 ; Suez War (1967) and, 690 ; United Nations resolutions on, 65, 103, 105, 114, 179, 200, 231, 306

Palestine Dispute, 23, 27–28, 30–37, 136, 179, 228

Palestine Liberation Organization, 680

Palestine Mandate (British), 9, 29, 34, 35–38, 39, 40, 50, 54, 137, 182, 227, 457, 491

Palestine War (1948), 35, 51, 88, 89, 637, 700 ; armistice, 9, 42, 52, 56, 65–66, 67, 69–70, 71, 72, 75, 93, 95, 96, 104, 105, 106, 108, 289, 306–307, 333, 334, 337, 447–48, 449, 460, 466, 494, 536, 564, 573, 589, 638, 668, 671, 690 ; Aswan High Dam and, 300, 303–304, 305, 308 ; Israeli shipping restraints and, 163, 333, 640 ; reprisals, 55–56, 58, 62 ; Russia and, 231 ; Suez War (1967) and, 42, 690, 691, 692 ; United Nations peace efforts (1956), 564, 571 ; United States peace efforts (1955), 303–10

Palmer, Prof. Henry, 500

Palmerston, Lord, 27, 28, 39, 167

Panama, 375, 385, 445

Panama Canal, 153, 368

Paris, 29, 113

Paris Bourse, 342, **350**

Paris, Treaty of, 227

Paris *Libération* (newspaper), 421

Parker, Col. A. C., 501

Parker Memorial, 486, 500–501 ; battle of, 509, 516, 517, 526, 539, 592, 636

Pearl Harbor, Hawaii, 688

Pearson, Lester, 110, 564, 648

Peel Commission, 41

Pelusium, 152, 153

Perdrizet, Brig. Gen. Maurice, 470

Peres, Shimon, 65, 164, 442, 494 ; quoted, 82, 101–102, 687 ; France and, 48, 75, 89, 101, 112, 121, 134, 138–39, 140, 141, 143–44, 151, 289, 290, 392, 433, 440–41, 460, 466, 469 ; Lavon and, 79, 80

Peron, Juan, 163

Persan-Beaumont airport, France, 461

Persia, 25, 153, 226, 227, 266, 692. *See also* Iran

Persian Gulf, 26, 28, 196, 216, 230, 655

Persian Gulf Command, 267

Peru, 355, 374, 375, 519

Petrograd, Russia, 31

Philippeville, Algeria, 142

Philippines, 230

The Philosophy of the Revolution, (Nasser), 145, 176–77, 409, 410–11, 414, 445 ; on Palestine refugees, 536

Phleger, Herman, 377, 378, 614

Pinay, Antoine, 142

Pineau, Christian, 145, 146, 260–61, 414–15, 676 ; quoted, 141, 213, 462, 471 ; American mission (1956), 151–52 ; Anglo-

760

Israeli collusion and, 392, 440, 441, 452, 453, 457, 458, 459, 461–65, 466, 472, 487, 562, 568, 574, 576, 626–27, 659; on Dulles, 326; Nasser visit (1956), 148–51, 216; Suez Canal nationalization and, 358, 367, 368, 374, 378, 384, 386, 393, 422, 436, 438, 444, 445, 446

Pirandello, Luigi, 411; quoted, 390

Pittuck, Charles, 414

Poland, 28, 37, 49, 102, 250; crisis of 1956, 119, 455, 467, 473, 557, 582, 643, 652; nationalism, 257, 334, 406, 514, 581

Polish Communist Party, Central Committee, 582

Polk, William, quoted, 266

Population: Algeria, 132; Aswan region, 675; Egypt, 298, 300, 367; Franco-Algerian, 40; Gaza Strip, 486, 553, 554, 662; Jewish community in Egypt, 106; Palestine Arabs (1919), 34, 37, 41; Palestine Zionists (1917), 30; Palestine Zionists (1947), 65; refugee numbers, 10, 42–43, 103, 696, 697; refugee return issue and, 35, 103–104, 697; Russian Jews, 230–31; self-determination principle and, 36, 37; Sinai, 483, 486

Porkkala Naval Base, Finland, 258

Port Fuad, Egypt, 460, 560, 577, 579, 602, 603, 620–21, 635

Port Said, Egypt, 153, 168, 170; canal offices in, 339, 343–44, 348, 352, 423; guerrilla operations in, 534, 536, 598, 619–20, 622, 641–42, 655–56; Suez War (1956), 393, 397–98, 424, 434, 451, 458, 460, 464, 465, 467, 475, 488, 489, 490–91, 508, 525, 526, 530, 554, 568, 569, 570, 575, 577–78, 579, 584–85, 589, 595–630, 635–36, 637; Suez War withdrawals, 639, 653, 654; UNEF in, 545, 642, 650–51, 656

Port Tewfik, see Suez

Portsmouth, England, 193

Portugal, 385, 436

Poujadists, 144

Poznan riots, Poland, 257

Prague, Czechoslovakia: Egyptian mission (1955), 90, 98–99

Pravda (newspaper), 90, 187, 244, 261

Press, 13; Arabic, 14, 55, 93, 120, 121, 197, 200, 203, 207, 217, 311, 333, 335, 338, 505; British, 35, 95, 259, 369, 421, 435, 506, 518, 569; clandestine, 409, 411, 426; French, 421, 560; Israeli, 51, 55, 58, 59, 75, 87, 97, 476, 661, 684; Russian, 235, 250; United States, 653. *See also* specific journals

Prinkypo, Greece, 274

Procopius, 460, 590

Psalm 105, quoted, 632

Pyramid of Cheops, 301

al-Qadi, Brig. Gen. Anwar, 538, 539, 540, 544

Qadry, Col. Abdel Raheem, 599

Qalqilya, Jordan, 448, 454

Qantara, Egypt, 486, 497, 545, 546, 570, 598, 636; cease-fire and, 642

Qastina, Israel, 512

Qibya, Jordan, 233; raid, 8, 10–11, 55, 56, 57–60, 62, 63, 64, 276

Queen of Sheba (vessel), 669

Qussaima, Sinai, 62, 108, 428, 492; Sinai invasion, 497, 498, 536–37, 538, 539, 542, 543, 544, 545, 662

al-Quwwatli, Shukry, 149, 448, 514, 610, 617

Rabat, Morocco, 132

Rabin, Maj. Gen. Itzhak, 681

Radio Ankara, 203

Radio Cairo, see Cairo Radio

Radio Free Egypt, 246

Radio Free Europe, 583

Radio Free Iraq, 246

Radio Israel ("Voice of Israel"), 91, 96, 551

Radio Liberation, 583

Radio Moscow, 401, 583, 611

Radio "Voice of Britain," 514, 518, 529, 566, 607, 629–30

Radio Warsaw, 643

Rafah, 83, 428, 486, 492, 496, 648; Sinai invasion, 497, 526, 531, 532, 537, 538, 539, 540, 541, 543, 545–46, 548–51, 553, 592, 634; withdrawal issue, 662, 668

Rafi party (Israel), 52, 677

Raghab, Gen. Hassan, 254

Rahwa, Jordan, 428, 440

al-Rais, Munir, 668

Rakosi, Matyas, 580–81

Ramat David, Israel, 512

Ramat Gan, Israel, 77

Ramat Rahel, Israel, 440, 441

Ramla, Israel, 441

Ras Gharib, Egypt, 591

Ras al-Naqb area, Sinai, 481, 498, 591, 592, 669

Ras Naqura, 67

Ras Nasrani, Sinai, 589, 590, 594, 595, 669

Ras al-Sudr, Sinai, 592

Rasheed (vessel), 590, 591

Raswa Channel, Port Said, 577, 579, 598, 601, 602, 613

Red Army, 237, 287, 455, 467; in Hungary, 514, 561, 581–84

Red Cross, 54, 689

Red Mesa, 537, 538

Red Mogen David, 474

Red Sea, 153, 154, 167, 179, 298, 349, 580, 638

Refugees, 64, 101, 304; Bedouin, 61–62, 108–109; al-Bureig camp, 276; Egyptian Jews, 106; Gaza Raid and, 20; Gaza Strip numbers, 10, 42, 83, 486; Gaza Strip responsibility, 42, 554, 662, 664; Hungarian revolt (1956), 584, 643; from Nazism, 38–39, 50, 57, 72, 268; Palestine War, 9, 35, 42–43, 56, 72, 486, 536; repatriation issue, 43, 103–104, 105, 111, 260, 269, 306, 346, 685, 696–97; reprisal strategy and, 55, 61; Suez War (1956) actions against, 476, 532, 552–53; Suez War (1967), 696; Zionist State establishment and, 22, 41

Rehovot, Israel, 94, 96

Reprisal raids, 9–10, 53–69, 76, 87, 91, 243, 276, 277, 494; *Fedayeen*, 70, 84, 85, 95–96, 120–21, 143, 247, 303; French North Africa, 142, 148, 152; Khan Yunis, 96–97, 143; Kinneret, 114–16; Palestinian nationalism and, 694–96, 698–99; Suez War (1956) and, 428–29, 440, 448, 474, 496, 552–54, 688; Suez War (1967) and, 678. *See also* place names

Republican party (USA), 271, 276, 406, 641, 665

Reston, James, quoted, 504, 682

Revisionist party (Zionist), 51

de Reynier, Jacques, cited, 54–59

The Rhineland, 650–51, 687

Rhodes, Palestine armistice talks on, 9, 42, 66

Riad, Mahmoud, 533

Riad, Mohammed, 343, 353, 603, 657

Richmond, Virginia, Eisenhower in, 503

Rifai, Samir, 209–10

Riff Mountains, 132

Riley, Brig. Gen. William E., 66

Rishon Le-Zion, Israel, 87

Robens, Alfred, 417; quoted, 116

Roberts, Chalmers, 658; quoted, 573–74

Rokossovsky, Marshal Konstantin, 455

Rome, 25, 26, 152, 414, 617

Rommel, Field Marshal Erwin, 177, 178

Roosevelt, Kermit, 283, 285, 286, 311–12
Rose al-Youssef (periodical), 122
de Rothschild, Baron Edmond, 29, 39
Rothschild, Baron Lionel Walter, second Lord, 32–33
Rouchdy, Ahmed, 78
Rountree, William, quoted, 451
Rovere, Richard, cited, 683–84
Rumania, 237
von Runstedt, Field Marshal Karl, 124
Rushdy, Col. Hassan, 603, 604, 605
Russell, Sen. Richard, 666
Russell, Francis H., 303
Russia, 1, 28, 49, 148, 171, 179, 209, 219, 224–61, 334, 406, 700; Aswan High Dam and, 255–56, 260, 294, 297, 301, 302, 304, 306, 311, 315, 316–17, 318, 319–20, 322–23, 335, 347, 361, 401, 675; Baghdad Pact and, 194, 199, 200, 225, 229, 235, 237, 238–40, 243, 252, 259, 275; de-Stalinization policy, 256–58, 261, 272, 455, 514, 580–81, 643; Egyptian arms deal, 3, 90–91, 96, 98–102, 106, 107, 109, 112–14, 117, 118, 121, 140, 141, 143, 186, 201, 215, 216, 219, 220, 225, 240, 241, 242–55, 256, 258, 259, 261, 281–94, 302, 304, 306, 310, 316–18, 322, 326, 334, 346, 369, 487, 492–93, 557, 610, 617, 686, 695, 699; expansionism, 39–40, 88, 225–30, 232, 267, 273, 611; Hungarian revolt suppression, 580–84, 643, 652, 666, 686; Israel and, 37, 73, 98–99, 102, 112, 113, 119, 225, 226, 229, 230–34, 236, 246, 269, 455, 660, 661, 663, 678, 683–84; oil export, 699; revolution in, 31, 38, 228, 258, 643; Suez Canal nationalization and, 323, 367, 377, 384, 385, 401, 403–404, 405, 406, 407, 419, 428, 433, 437, 444, 446; Suez War (1956) and, 372, 375, 425, 428, 467, 473, 487, 503, 505, 506–507, 519, 557, 562, 563, 580, 582, 608, 629, 652; Suez War cease-fire (1956) and, 570, 608–15, 623, 628, 641, 644; Suez War relief shipments, 647; Suez War withdrawals issue and, 639; Suez War (1967) and, 683–84, 685, 686
Russian Army, *see* Red Army
Russian Foreign Ministry, 248
Russo-Japanese War, 228
Ruwafa Dam, Sinai, 538, 539, 541, 636

al-Sabha, Sinai, 102, 108, 110, 202, 253, 291, 648; prisoners, 513; Sinai invasion and, 538
Sablier, Edouard, 140
Sabotage, *see* Terrorism, sabotage
Sabry, Aly, 84, 149, 280–81, 590; Aswan High Dam and, 300, 323, 335; Suez Canal nationalization and, 377, 381, 403
Sabry, Hassan, 177
Sadat, Col. Anwar, quoted, 177–78, 373–74, 417
Sadeh, Isaac, 54
Safad, 27
Said, Ahmed, 409; quoted, 566–67
al-Said Nuri, Premier of Iraq, 219, 236, 353, 452, 672; Arab League organization and, 41–42, 179; Baghdad Pact and, 18, 19, 193, 195–97, 199, 200–201, 203, 207, 215, 240, 246, 252, 273–75, 280, 342, 568; Jordan defense (1956), 448, 449, 450; nationalist revolt (1956) against, 653; Palestine settlement proposal, 447–48; Suez Canal nationalization, 364, 419
Saidis, 493
St. Laurent, Louis, quoted, 564
de Saint-Simon, Henri, 154
Salaheddeen, Mohammed, 234; quoted, 157–58
Salem, Maj. Gen. Ahmed, 467
Salem, Gamal, 248
Salem, Maj. Salah, 243, 344, 534, 565–66; quoted, 244
Salisbury, Lord, 354, 369, 370, 375; quoted, 169, 657
Samson's Tomb, 5
al-Samu, Jordan, 678
Sanafir Island, 589, 591, 682
Santayana, George, quoted, 674
Sarah, 23
Sarraj, Col. Abdel Hameed, 653, quoted, 533
Saud, King of Saudi Arabia, 149, 419, 448
Saudi Arabia, 89, 213, 334, 439, 442, 448, 528, 644, 655; Baghdad Pact and, 113, 198, 202, 203, 204, 207, 253
Savary, Alain, 456
Schmidt, Dana Adams, quoted, 289
Scorpions' Pass, Negev, 61–62, 109
Sde Boker, Negev, 12, 47, 79, 98, 137, 467, 654
Sea of Galilee, 67, 115, 116, 277. *See also* Kinneret
Seale, Patrick, 244, 407
de Sérigny, Alain, 147
Setero (vessel), 445
Sèvres, France, 454, 457, 458, 461–62, 469, 581; accord, 465, 466, 654, 659; Israeli strategy decisions, 468, 473, 489, 495, 503, 508, 590; ultimatums, 463–

65, 467, 471, 488, 489–90, 504, 505, 506–507, 508, 511, 513, 514, 515, 518, 520, 531. *See also* Suez War (1956), Anglo-French-Israeli collusion in
Shabander, Musa, 197
Shakespeare, William, quoted, 296, 674
Sharaf, Capt. Wagdy, 481
Sharett, Moshe, 12, 14, 30, 112, 679; American mission (1955), 114; Aqaba and, 163, 590; on Arab arms supply, 71, 101, 113; Ben-Gurion conflict, 11, 13, 47–48, 49, 50, 52, 53, 59, 65, 102, 104, 105, 106, 111, 113, 114, 115, 121–23, 124, 137, 143, 151, 261, 334, 455; British Suez base evacuation treaty and, 74; on bus massacre (1954), 62; on Eden compromise peace proposal, 306; on Egyptian control of Gaza Strip, 91, 92, 93, 246; on Egyptian spy executions, 19, 77, 79; election of 1955 and, 79, 94; Gaza Raid and, 23, 47, 58, 80, 85; on Russia, 73
Sharm al-Sheikh, Sinai: captured Egyptian arms at, 661; Israeli attack (1956), 468, 492, 497, 498, 531, 554, 565, 569, 572–73, 575, 589–95, 624, 634, 635; Israeli withdrawal, 638, 667, 669; UNEF withdrawal (1967), 682
Sharon, Col. Ariel, 510, 515–16, 517, 526, 548, 689
Sharqiya, Egypt, 534
Shatt, Egypt, 481
Shawcross, Sir Hartley, 372
Shepilov, Dmitri, 444; Aswan High Dam offer, 322–23, 335; Egyptian arms deal and, 90–91, 244, 245, 250, 261; London Conference (1956) and, 401, 403, 404–405, 412–13; United States joint action proposal (1956), 614–15
Shertok, Yaakov, 49
Shipping: Algerian arms, 134, 456; Anglo-French bombing of, 527–28; Anglo-French Canal closing and, 580, 629, 644, 645, 655, 670; Aqaba Straits, 42, 53, 94, 98, 104, 106, 111, 121, 130, 143, 163, 433, 439, 460, 462, 589 638, 640, 661, 662, 664–65, 667, 669, 675, 676, 682–82, 685–86, 692; British arms (1956), 471, 473, 475, 488; British regulation of, 170, 172; Canal transit restrictions, 12, 49, 73, 74–75, 87, 104, 105, 111, 121, 125, 130, 143, 163, 170–71, 218, 232, 233, 333, 362, 383, 444, 445, 453, 670–71; flags of convenience, 385, 445; Napoleonic

trade routes, 163; pilots, 161, 162, 353, 355, 356, 358, 392, 420–24, 425, 428, 433, 434, 435–36, 437, 458, 496; propeller-driven, 154–55; Sinai invasion and, 501, 502, 505, 509, 515; Suez Canal boycott measure and, 415, 416; Suez Canal nationalization and, 340, 353, 355, 356, 357, 358, 362–63, 368, 369, 373, 377, 382, 392, 394, 396, 399–400, 407, 413, 422–23, 424, 429, 435–36, 445–46, 450; Suez Canal volume, 153, 168, 366, 384–85, 399, 422, 423; Suez War (1967) and, 691; Turkish Straits naval rights, 229, 236. *See also* specific vessels

Shuaiba, Iraq, 201

Shuqairy, Ahmed, 680

Siberia, 40, 226, 231

Sidky, Ismail, 180

Siegfried, André, quoted, 130

Simhoni, Col. Asaf, Sinai invasion (1956), 497, 498, 518, 538, 539, 545, 635

Sinai Peninsula: demilitarization proposals, 662; UN Emergency Force stationed in, 574; French air attacks, 658; invasion threats (1955), 99–100, 101, 102, 103, 105–106, 107, 108, 110, 112, 119, 140–41, 143, 245, 289, 306, 307, 309, 346, 536; Israeli invasion (1956) of, 103, 121, 291, 346, 364, 392, 428–29, 433, 439–40, 442–44, 447, 448, 450–51, 457–59, 463–66, 468, 469–76, 480–521, 525, 530–32, 536–54, 558, 569–70, 594–95, 608, 624, 634, 635, 636, 640, 660, 675; Israeli invasion (1967), 640, 677, 681–82, 687–90; Israeli withdrawal issue and, 637, 638, 639, 640, 650, 654, 661; Suez Canal nationalization and, 340, 393–94, 439

Sirhan, Sirhan, 694

"Six Principles" of Suez settlement, 445–47, 449, 452, 562, 670

Slade-Baker, J. B., 247, 250, 283

Slansky, Rudolph, 232

Smallholders party (Polish), 583

Solod, Amb. Daniel, 90, 91, 243; quoted, 255, 318; Aswan High Dam and, 302, 318

Solomon, 26, 29

Soummam Valley, Algeria, 406

Soustelle, Jacques, 131, 139, 143, 146–47; quoted, 129, 140, 141

Southeast Asia, 692

Southeast Asia Treaty Organization, 48, 148–49, 195, 216, 229, 230, 238, 267, 413; Bangkok Conference (1954), 198, 199;

Karachi Conference (1956), 211, 216

Soviet Union, *see* Russia

Spain, 131, 132, 171, 368, 385, 434

Spanish-American War, 368

Spears, Gen. Sir Edward, 130, 136

Stack, Sir Lee, 173, 174

Stalin, Joseph, 73, 178, 228, 229, 230, 237, 240, 272; death of, 232, 233, 236 238, 256–57, 280

Stalingrad, battle of, 178

Stern Gang, 51, 54, 696

Stevenson, Adlai, 406, 641

Stevenson, Amb. Sir Ralph Skrine, 396; quoted, 246, 395; Egyptian arms and, 90, 201–202

Stockholm (vessel), 348–49

Stockwell, Gen. Sir Hugh, 656; quoted, 398, 424, 458, 460, 530, 578, 596, 619, 630, 642, 650; collusion and, 392–93, 397, 441, 451, 471, 488, 575; Port Said attack (1956), 406, 457, 580, 584, 596, 599, 600, 602, 606, 619, 621, 622, 627, 629, 630, 642

Stone, I. F., quoted, 22, 696, 699

Strijdom, Johannes, quoted, 373

Sudan, 90, 173–74, 176, 179, 299; Aswan High Dam and, 210, 242, 300, 302, 311, 312, 313–14, 323, 347, 675; independence, 180, 181; Israel sanctions vote, 667

Sudan Agreement (Anglo-Egyptian), 181

al-Sudr, Sinai, 518, 636

Sudr al-Heitan, Sinai, 481

Suez (and Port Tewfik), Egypt, 339, 343–44, 348, 352–53, 486, 497, 639; capture plans (1956), 451, 464, 467, 468, 481, 596, 613, 622; Liberation Army in, 534, 566

Suez, Gulf of, 152, 483, 486; *Damietta* in, 560, 591

Suez Canal, 128, 152–56, 167–73, 298; Anglo-French port seizures (1956), 580, 589–630, 644; Anglo-French ultimatum (1956) on, 463–65, 467, 511; bridges, 496–97, 527, 544; British base evacuation, 12, 13, 14, 15, 17–18, 19, 38, 48, 64, 70, 71, 73–74, 75, 84, 112, 137, 139, 158, 159, 174–76, 179, 180 182–88, 190, 195, 200, 217–18, 235, 237, 239, 261, 271, 273, 280, 281, 290, 322, 334, 340, 371, 380, 475, 672; internationalization proposals, 170–71, 184, 321, 37, 382, 384, 385–86, 404, 405–406, 412–13, 415–16, 418, 419, 424, 425–27, 429, 434, 436–39, 444 459, 463, 649; Israeli closing of, 691; nationalization, 3, 85, 88, 105, 112, 121, 143, 149, 156–64, 167, 215, 219, 221, 250, 292,

294, 311, 320–21, 322, 323, 326, 327, 333–58, 361–87, 391, 393, 394–95, 398–400, 402, 419–20, 421, 425–29, 433, 435–36, 441, 445–47, 450, 452, 490, 519, 529, 534, 562, 571, 596, 610, 622–23, 628–29, 633, 671; Operation Musketeer Revise plan for, 458; repairs (1956–57), 645, 651–52, 670; Sinai invasion and, 433, 439–40, 443–44, 450, 451, 469, 475, 481, 489, 490, 491, 496, 501, 502, 505, 506, 507, 509, 511, 512, 515, 518, 525, 526, 531, 569, 570; transit restraints, 12, 49, 73, 74–75, 87, 104, 105, 111, 121, 125, 143, 163, 171, 218, 232, 233, 333, 362, 383, 444, 445, 453, 638, 640 662, 663, 665, 668, 670–71

Suez Canal Company, 112, 150, 152, 153; British control, 168–72, 366, 425; concession, 156–64, 168–69, 321, 322, 380–81, 385–86, 399; management methods, 416, 445; medical records, 349; pilot walkout, 420–24, 435, 458; seizure, 320, 335–58, 362–63, 377, 395, 404, 672; seizure compensation, 365–66, 385, 397, 671

Suez Canal Zone: bombings, 527–28, 530; British domination, 36, 38; Liberation Army command, 566; port seizures (1956) and, 576, 577–78, 580, 584–85, 596–630; United Nations Emergency Force and, 640, 649–50, 656–57. *See also* specific place names

Suez Canal Users Association (SCUA), 419, 424, 425–27, 429, 434, 436–39, 441, 442, 683; Indian proposals, 459–60; naming of, 436–37; Nasser concessions on, 444, 446

Suez Crisis, 1–4, 20, 23, 134, 164, 361–87. *See also* Suez Canal, nationalization of; Suez War (1956)

"Suez Rebels," *see* Tory party (British), Suez Canal and

Suez War (1956), 2, 66, 70, 92, 106, 107, 123–24, 253, 254, 256, 480–630; Anglo-French-Israeli collusion in, 1, 9, 141, 216, 219–20, 293, 336, 361, 367, 370, 374, 375, 392, 393, 398, 415–16, 418, 420, 424, 428–29, 433–76. 482–83, 486–90, 495, 498, 500, 503–504, 506–507. 508, 511–12, 514, 515, 518, 520–21, 525, 531, 533, 534, 557, 562, 564, 565, 568–69, 570, 575, 576, 596, 607–608, 616, 626–27, 638, 642–43, 646, 652–53, 654, 658–59, 672, 687, 688, 690; Anglo-French military strategy in, 392, 397–

98, 406, 411, 424, 434, 441, 451, 457–58, 459, 460, 461–62, 463, 464, 465, 468, 482, 483, 487, 488, 489, 490, 525–26, 531, 565, 569, 575–78, 579–80, 595–96, 599–601, 620, 621, 622, 629–30, 642; cease-fire, 42, 466, 491, 507, 564–65, 568, 569, 570–74, 583, 606, 607–608, 612, 622–23, 624–30, 633, 641–42, 692; Egyptian retreat from Sinai, 497, 509, 517, 521, 525–54, 557, 558, 560, 565, 569, 591, 634; guerrilla strategy in, 531, 533–34, 536, 558–59, 565–66, 568, 596, 598, 599, 603, 605, 608–609, 619–20, 622, 641–42; Israeli military strategy in, 42, 98, 442–43, 447, 448–49, 450–51, 453, 457, 461, 462, 464, 465, 468, 469–70, 482, 483, 486, 487–88, 490, 495, 496–98, 500, 526, 536, 538, 539, 540–41, 565, 569, 570, 571–72, 576, 591–95, 624, 630, 634, 635, 676–77, 687–88; prisoner exchange, 635–36; relief supplies, 647; Russian inability to help Egypt, 609–10; Russian rocket threats, 610–15, 623; Sèvres ultimatums, 463–65, 488, 489–90, 518, 520; Sinai invasion action, 79, 480–521, 525, 530–32, 536–54, 558, 569–70, 589–95, 596, 624, 634, 635, 636, 677; Suez Canal nationalization issue in, 348, 361, 364, 367, 369, 371–79, 381–82, 385, 386–87, 391, 394, 401, 402, 407, 411, 418–19, 420, 422–29, 435, 441, 444–45, 446, 453, 464, 519, 529, 534, 571, 596, 610, 622–23, 628–29, 633; United Nations Emergency Force and, 107, 110, 561, 563, 564, 568, 570, 571, 573, 574, 575, 578, 607–608, 614, 628, 629, 640, 675; war reparations, 671–72; withdrawals, 53, 633–72, 675–76
Suez War (1967), 3, 67, 254, 310, 676–97; air strategy and, 488, 634, 677, 679, 688–89, 690; Aqaba issue and, 42, 439, 590, 682–83, 685–86, 692; al-Auja and, 110, 253; cease-fire, 686, 690, 691; Egyptian prisoners, 77; refugees, 536, 696–97; Sinai invasion, 40, 42, 640, 669, 677, 687–90; Tripartite Declaration and, 270, 686; United Nations Emergency Force and, 638, 681–83, 685, 692
Suleiman, Maj. Ezzat, 133
Sulzberger, Cyrus, 94, 247
Summit Conference (Geneva, 1955), 91, 112–13, 243–44, 245, 258, 282
Surcouf (vessel), 475

Suslov, Mikhail A., 237, 581, 583, 643
Sweden, 65, 385, 415, 690
Sweetwater Canal, 153, 155, 298, 380–81, 398; Suez War (1956), 460, 598
Switzerland, 689
Swinburn, James, 414
Sykes, Christopher, quoted, 32, 34
Sykes, Sir Mark, 32, 175
Sykes-Picot Agreement, 31, 32, 35, 36, 228
Syria, 27, 28, 149, 413, 617, 639; Algeria and, 151; Amer visit (1956), 473; arms (1956), 653, 661; Baghdad Pact and, 71, 196, 198, 202, 203, 204; Egyptian alliance, 101, 113, 116, 202, 203, 204, 213, 253, 345, 408, 448, 678, 683; French Mandate, 35, 130, 136, 137; Israeli raids on, 12, 103, 107, 114–16, 117, 120, 203–204, 253, 277, 291, 308, 346, 553, 564, 679, 683; Jordan alliance (1956), 447, 448, 467, 474, 482, 503, 678; oil pipelines and, 403, 408, 533, 568, 651; Palestine War and, 9, 66; refugee numbers, 697; revolt attempted in (1956), 407–408, 482–83, 532; Russia and, 229, 233, 253, 610, 678; Sinai invasion (1956) and, 482–83, 492, 514–15, 532–33, 644; Suez War (1967) and, 536, 681, 682, 683, 684–85, 689, 690; in United Arab Republic, 676; Vichy French in, 494; United States flights (1956) over, 615
Syrian Air Force, 689
Syrian-Israeli MAC, 66, 67
Szolnok, Hungary, 583

al-Tahreer (periodical), 158
Tailyour, Lieut.-Col. N. H., 621
Tamazin, Lieut. Comdr. Hussan Rushdy, 512–13
Tankus, Commodore Shmuel, quoted, 513–14
Tarabin Bedouins, 466–67
Taret Um Basseess, Sinai, 538
TASS, news agency, 250
Taya, Auda Abu, 32
Tchikov, Anatoly, 608–609, 616, 621
Teheran, Iran, 217
Tel al-Kebir, 170, 172, 183, 217
Tel Aviv, Israel, 53, 87, 475, 532; British Embassy, 515; riots of 1967, 678; Soviet Legation, 73, 232, 611; United States Embassy, 137–38, 515
Templer, Gen. Sir Gerald, 354, 578; Mission of, 203, 204–205, 207, 208, 210, 370, 599, 617
Tennessee Valley Authority, 60
Terrapin, 392, 397, 424, 434, 441; paratroop action and, 579

Terrorism, 558–59; Algerian, 39, 131, 148, 152, 694; British Suez base evacuation issue and, 183, 185–86; Cairo Black Saturday, 180; guerrilla, 10, 531, 533–34, 536, 558–60, 565–66, 568, 596, 598, 599, 603, 605, 608–609, 619–20, 622, 641–42, 694, 696; Havlagah policy and, 53; Mau Mau and, 32, 39; Morocco, 142, 456; Moslem Brotherhood, 15–16, 17, 19, 73, 77, 182, 188–89; Nazi, 38–39, 55, 696; nuclear, 186, 684, 699; reprisals and, 10, 54–69, 87, 96–97, 120, 247, 448, 685, 694–95; sabotage and, 48, 73, 74, 75, 76, 124, 152, 171, 187, 190, 198, 337, 655–56; Zionist, 39, 51, 52, 65–66, 696
Tewfik, Khedive of Egypt, 169
Thackeray, William, quoted, 588
Thamad, Sinai, 497, 501, 508, 510, 591
Thant, U, 681, 684, 685, 686
Theseus (vessel), 394, 621
Thomas, Abel, 141, 146, 433, 461, 471
Thomas, Hugh, quoted, 219, 625
Thomas, Lowell, 266
Thompson, Dorothy, quoted, 410
Thorneycroft, Peter, 369
Tiberias, Israel, 27
Tibet, 230
Tigris River, 196
Tildy, Zoltan, 583
Time (periodical), 243
The Times. See London Times
Tiran Island, 589, 590–91, 682
Tiran, Straits of, 105, 440, 460, 468, 469, 492; Israeli withdrawal, 662, 667–68, 669; Nasser's mine bluff (1967), 685; Sharm al-Sheikh and, 589, 590, 494, 638; United Nations Emergency Force withdrawal (1967), 682–83, 685
Tirat Yehuda, Israel, 57
Tito, Marshal, 234, 236, 245, 251, 320; quoted, 119, 159; Aswan High Dam and, 256, 319, 323; Brioni meeting, 152, 321, 333
Titus, Emperor of Rome, 25
Tobbal, Lakhdar Ben, 134
Togliatti, Palmiro, 257
Tolkovski, Gen. Dan, 140
Tomb of the Martyrs, Port Said, 637
Tor, Sinai, 592, 595
al-Toudy, Brig. Gen. Mohammed Fuad, 342, 343
Tournoux, Jean-Raymond, quoted, 461, 615
Tory Party (British), 148, 180, 205–206, 214, 370, 599; Khrushchev and, 259; Suez Canal and, 182, 186, 187, 218, 219, 371, 377, 395, 401, 426, 449;

Suez War (1956) and 371, 401, 441, 449–50, 505, 569, 570, 571, 572, 606, 623, 625–26, 628, 659, 672; Suez withdrawal issue and, 654, 657, 675–76

Trans-Arabian Pipeline (TAP-line), 568, 651, 655

Trans-Jordan, 9, 35. *See also* Jordan

Trevelyan, Amb. Sir Humphrey, 100, 248, 283, 306, 599; Glubb dismissal and, 211, 212; Suez Canal nationalization and, 322, 344–45, 511

Trieste, 115

Tripartite Declaration (1950), 70, 119, 137, 269–71, 278; Eden on, 190, 207, 450, 505–506; Eisenhower Doctrine and, 647; Franco-Israeli alliance and, 139, 141, 288, 289, 433, 454; Suez War (1956) and, 380, 450, 455, 474, 503, 504; Suez War (1967), 686

Tripoli, Syria, 533

Trotsky, Leon, 228

Truman, Harry S, 48, 63, 183, 267, 268, 269, 280, 441; Byroade and, 271–72

Truman Doctrine, 183, 229, 267

Tsur, Amb. Jacob, 164, 455; quoted, 163

Tunis, Tunisia, 290, 456

Tunisia, 442; independence, 130, 131–32, 133, 134, 136, 139, 146, 149; United States and, 261, 290

al-Tunsi, Lieut., 351

Turkey, 23, 27, 30, 49, 167, 169, 177, 178, 183, 345, 409, 698; Arab Revolt, 28, 29, 31, 32, 33, 193; Ataturk and 676; Baghdad Pact and, 17–18, 71, 196, 197, 198–99, 200, 202–203, 225, 238, 273, 406; British Agreement to withdrawal from Egypt (1887), 179; Russia and, 225, 226–27, 229, 230, 235, 236, 238, 245, 267, 615; Sinai Peninsula and, 639; Sudan and, 174; Suez Canal and, 154, 167, 168, 171, 172, 184, 186, 385; United States and, 266, 271, 273

Turkey-Pakistan pact (1954), 194–95, 235

Turkish Army, 49

Turkish Straits, 225, 227, 228, 229, 236, 404

Twice in a Lifetime (United Nations Relief and Works Agency), 696–97

Tymbou, Cyprus, 576, 577, 600

Tyne (vessel), 584, 606, 622, 627

Um Qataf, Sinai: Sinai invasion, 536–37, 538, 539, 540, 541, 542–43, 544, 545, 548, 550, 551, 594, 634, 635; Suez War (1967) and, 689

Um Rashrash, 42

Union of South Africa, 313, 373 590

Union of Soviet Socialist Republics, *see* Russia

United Arab Republic, 149, 676

United Jewish Appeal, 114

United Kingdom, *see* Britain, also specific countries

United Nations, 24, 48, 54, 89, 268; Algeria and, 136; arms embargo, 118, 219, 253, 259–60, 293; Charter, 230, 347, 380, 418, 451, 511, 518, 520, 561, 562, 614; China exclusion from, 239, 259, 333; Egyptian peace efforts and, 92, 93, 306, 437; Farouk and, 132; Israeli sanctions threat (1957), 665–67; Israeli sovereignty and, 37, 72, 92, 102, 111, 138, 665–67; Israeli Syrian raids and, 553; on Jerusalem, 233, 234; Palestine War and, 9, 41, 52, 56, 67–68, 70, 91; Port Said evacuations, 616–17; post-Gaza Raid riots and, 20, 83, 84; refugee repatriation issue and, 43, 103, 697; Sudan and, 180; Suez Canal salvage operation, 651–52; Suez War (1956) and, 368, 383, 424–25, 427, 428, 441, 444, 453, 459, 488, 518–19, 520, 525, 534, 548, 552, 557–58, 561–65, 568–69, 607, 611, 614, 623, 629, 639, 642, 643, 653; Suez War (1967) and, 684, 685, 686, 690; Tunisia and, 136. *See also* specific agencies

United Nations Emergency Force, 656; Egyptian withdrawal (1967) request, 681–83, 685, 692; General Assembly creation of, 561, 563, 564, 568, 570, 571, 573, 607–608, 614; Israeli refusal of, 107, 110, 638, 642, 648, 649, 662, 663, 664, 675, 681; organization and establishment of, 574, 575, 578, 607–608, 628, 629, 640, 642–43, 648–49, 669; Tiran Straits, 667–68, 682

United Nations General Assembly, 118, 383, 648–49, 650; Hungarian crisis (1956) in, 583; Palestine Partition Resolution (1947), 41, 43, 65, 103, 105, 114, 179, 200, 231, 260, 306, 696; Suez War cease-fire resolutions (1956), 519, 561–65, 568–69, 570–71, 572–75, 583, 606, 607–608, 624, 625–30, 633; Suez War (1956) withdrawals issue, 638, 662, 663, 664, 665–67

United Nations International Law Commission, 668

United Nations Military Observers: al-Auja, 109, 110, 112, 333, 473, 502; Gaza bombardment (April 1956), 120; Gaza Raid, 5, 6, 7–8; Israeli disregard for, 96, 97–98, 110, 670; Port Said (1956), 655, 656; Qibya, 57; Sinai invasion (1956), 428, 443, 570

United Nations Mixed Armistice Commissions, 62, 66–67, 68, 69, 70, 72, 75; Gaza Raid and, 8; Israeli boycotts of, 91, 243, 443, 685

United Nations Relief and Works Agency: al-Bureig and, 10; Gaza Strip refugees and, 43, 552, 553, 696–97

United Nations Security Council, 98, 116, 179, 571; al-Auja and, 111, 119, 333; Bat Galim and, 74, 75; al-Bureig attack (1953) and, 10; censure of Israel (1966), 678; France in, 130; Gaza bombardment (April 1956) and, 260; Gaza Raid, 8, 85, 87, 89, 140; Hungarian uprising and, 470; Israeli shipping and, 232, 663; Nahhaleen and, 62, 233; Palestine War and, 65, 93; Qibya and, 60, 233; Russian cease-fire draft resolution (1956), 614; Sinai invasion, 466, 487, 503, 504, 505, 506, 507, 518–19, 520, 525, 563; Suez Canal nationalization and, 355, 357, 383, 413, 415, 425, 428, 438, 441, 444, 445, 451, 490, 502, 534; Syrian reprisals issue in, 564; Vyshinsky speech (1954), 73, 233

United Nations Truce Supervision Organization, 62, 65–67, 70, 137–38, 233, 574, 608, 638, 690; al-Auja and, 109, 110–11; al-Bureig raid and, 10; Gaza Raid and, 8, 69; Qibya, 57, 59, 60

United States, 17, 30, 37, 38, 40, 41, 48, 73, 76, 181, 253, 700; Algeria and, 148, 260–61; Anglo-French-Israeli collusion and, 451, 452, 454, 471–72, 473, 474–75, 476, 486, 487, 488, 503–504, 506, 533, 568, 569, 573–74, 642–43, 652–53, 658; Aswan High Dam and, 112, 114, 116, 125, 159, 160, 161, 203, 204, 213, 216, 217, 219, 220–21, 223, 255, 260, 280, 288, 294, 296, 297–327, 333–34, 337, 346–47, 349, 361, 362; Baghdad Pact and, 18, 194, 195, 197, 199, 200, 201, 203, 204, 214, 217, 229, 235, 271, 273–75, 280; British colonialism and, 438–39, 506;

British sterling crisis (1956) and, 625, 626; British Suez base evacuation and, 183, 184, 271, 280, 281; Egyptian arms and, 84, 87–88, 89–90, 91, 100, 106, 112–14, 118, 140, 186, 201, 241, 243–44, 245, 247–48, 249–50, 254, 265, 280–94, 302, 316–18, 646; Egyptian *rapprochement* (1954), 73, 74, 75, 105, 241; elections (1956), 454–55, 472, 506, 558, 627, 628, 641, 642; elections of 1968, 694; *Fedayeen* and, 694, 695–96; Gaza Raid and, 15, 85, 115, 200, 278–79, 281; Hungarian crisis (1956) and, 473, 503, 581, 582–84, 610, 614, 628; Indochina and, 134; Israeli alliance proposal, 232–33, 245; Israeli arms and, 114, 115, 116–18, 135, 138, 139, 141, 143, 144, 213, 287, 288, 289–91, 433, 475, 686, 699; Jordan Valley project, 12–13, 60, 63, 65, 115–16, 276–77, 302; Korean intervention, 563; Nasser public image in, 92–94, 279–80, 287, 288, 307, 314, 318, 326–27, 445, 455, 644, 654; peace efforts (Anderson mission), 303–10; reprisal raids (1956) and, 120–21; Russian joint action proposal (1956), 612, 613, 614–16, 623, 644; Suez Canal nationalization and, 320, 327, 336, 345–46, 347, 348, 355–56, 365, 367–68, 374–75, 384, 385, 387, 393, 394–95, 402, 403, 405–406, 407, 412, 413–18 422–27, 435; Suez War (1956) and, 2, 151–52, 364–65, 368, 391, 393, 407, 418–19, 427, 441, 449–50, 451, 454–55, 457, 468–69, 491, 503–506, 519–20, 533, 548, 557–58, 561–63, 576, 578–79, 611, 616–17, 622–23, 625, 627–28, 633, 652–53, 685–86; Suez War (1956) withdrawals issue and, 633, 639–40, 641, 646, 647–48, 650–51, 654, 659, 663; Suez War (1967) and, 683–84, 685–86, 690; Syrian revolt plots (1956) and, 407–408, 483, 532; Tripartite Declaration (1950) and, 70, 137–38, 139, 269–71, 278, 289, 455, 474, 503, 504, 505, 647, 686; Yugoslavia and, 245
United States Air Force, 621
United States Central Intelligence Agency (CIA), 216, 304, 327; Anglo-French-Israeli collusion and, 472, 573; clandestine radio of, 409; Russian arms deal and, 248, 282–83; Russian threats and, 615; Suez Canal nationalization and, 376; Syrian *coup-d'état* plots and, 653

United States Congress, 266, 305, 320, 323, 324, 685; elections of 1956, 641; on sanctions against Israel, 665–66; Suez Canal nationalization and, 368, 376, 384, 407, 519. *See also* United States Senate
United States Department of Justice, 407
United States Department of State: Anglo-French-Israeli collusion and, 573, 642–43, 658; Aswan High Dam and, 302, 304, 312, 314, 315–16, 317, 324–27, 347; Baghdad Pact and, 18; Egyptian arms and, 90, 100, 106, 245, 248, 253, 254, 265, 281–89, 294; Menzies mission and, 415; peace efforts (1955), 303–304, 308; reprisal policy and, 63, 71, 684; Suez War (1956) and, 474, 561–63, 653; Zionism and, 266
United States Federal Reserve Bank, 625
United States Information Service, 17, 74
United States Marine Corps, 66, 110, 676
United States Mutual Security Act, 200–201, 280–81, 324
United States National Security Council, 396, 407, 561, 562
United States Navy, 395; Sixth Fleet, 121, 472, 513, 515, 557, 616–17, 683, 685
United States Senate, 292; Appropriations Committee, 319, 324; Foreign Relations Committee, 306, 308, 309, 316, 447
United States Treasury, 377, 625, 665

Vatolina, L. N., quoted, 235
Verdi, Giuseppe, 156
Victoria, Queen of England, 168, 174
Vietnam War, 39, 61, 148, 558, 674, 676, 692; guerrilla strategy of, 694; helicopter use in, 621; nuclear threats and, 684
Villacoublay, France, 460, 461, 469
"Voice of the Arabs," *see* Cairo Radio
"Voice of Israel" (*Kol Yisroel*), *see* Radio Israel
Volga River, 225
Vyshinksy, Andrei Y., 73, 233

Wadi Arish, Sinai, 483, 537, 538, 540
Wadi Halfa, Sudan, 311
Wadi Jirafi, Sinai, 481
Wadi Mileiz, Sinai, 502, 510, 516
Wadsworth, Amb. James J., quoted, 85

Wafd party (Egypt), 177, 187
Wailing Wall, Jerusalem, 690
Wall, Rachel, quoted, 243
Wall Street Journal (newspaper), 418
Waller, Ian, quoted, 214
al-Wardani, Ibrahim, 157
Warsaw, Poland, 455
Warsaw Pact, 237–38, 581–82, 583
Washington, George, quoted, 183, 264
Washington Post (newspaper), 573–74, 658
Waterhouse, Capt. Charles, 186, 371
Weizmann, Chaim, 33, 51, 230, 589, 698; Faisal and, 34–35; Jordan River and, 276–77, 690, 692; on refugees, 41
Weizman, Brig. Gen. Ezer, 677
Wejh, Saudi Arabia, 591
West Germany, 237, 385, 626, 699
Western Galilee, Israel, 41
Westlake, Peter, 448
Wheat, 647
Wheeler, Keith, 243
Wheeler, Lieut. Gen. Raymond A., 651
White, William S., quoted, 324
White Highlands, Kenya, 32
White Nile, 298, 299
Willcocks, Sir William, quoted, 296, 300
Wilson, Harold, quoted, 369, 625
Wilson, Woodrow, 30, 36–37, 266
Wingate, Orde, 10, 54, 491, 494
Wolseley, Gen. Sir Garnet, 170, 183, 527
World Bank, 220, 255, 256; reports on Aswan Dam project, 301, 302–303, 305–306, 310, 311, 312, 313, 314, 316, 317, 326, 346, 347
World Court, 363, 385, 670–71; Aqaba and, 98, 590, 664, 668, 685–86
World War I, 40, 41; Arab nationalism and, 35, 36, 39, 697; Ben-Gurion in, 49; Eden and, 175, 488; Gaza in, 552; Ottoman Empire and, 23, 28, 29, 30, 31, 32, 172, 178, 193, 226–27; United States and, 265, 266
World War II, 10, 29, 38–39, 54, 534, 558; Ben Bella in, 133; Eden and, 370, 394, 406, 488, 574, 623, 650–51, 687; Egypt and, 177–78, 179, 183, 363, 467, 540; France and, 36, 129, 130, 135, 136, 138, 144–45, 227, 460, 695; Pearl Harbor attack, 688; Russia and, 229, 231, 258, 266, 267, 582
World Zionist Organization, 29, 72, 114

Yad Mordecai, Israel, 87
Yadin, Yigal, 677
Yarmuk River, Jordan, 277
Yassa, Brig. Gen. Sami, 537–38, 539
Yazid, M'hammed, 414
Yemen, 73, 198, 676, 686
Yoffe, Col. Avraham, 591, 592, 595, 689
Yost, Amb. Charles W., 680; quoted, 679
Yotvat (Tiran), *see* Tiran
Young, Sir George, 421–22, 434; quoted, 221
Young, Brig. Gen. Peter, quoted, 677
Younger, Kenneth, 383
Yugoslavia, 115, 119, 159, 321, 446; Algerian talks in, 152; Budapest crisis (1956) and, 584; Nazism and, 558, 695;

Russia and, 236, 245, 256, 258, 319; Sinai invasion and, 518, 519
Yunis, Mahmoud, 337–42, 347–48, 351, 352, 353, 354; quoted, 338, 339, 343, 357, 358; pilot shortage and, 421, 422–24, 436

Zafir (vessel), 617–18
Zagazig, Egypt, 153, 565, 599
Zaki, Col. Raouf Mahfouz, 591, 594
Zamálek, Cairo, 567
Zarb, James, 414
Zhukov, Georgi K., 514, 582, 610
Zinoviev, Gregory, 228
Zionism: activist, 47, 697–98 (*See also* Activism); Anglo-French-Israeli collusion and, 658; Arab view of, 35, 40–41, 250, 696, 698; Biblical bases of, 23–24,

25, 41, 662, 690, 692; British sponsorship of, 27–28, 29, 30–40, 51, 137, 182, 229, 230, 231, 239, 266, 268, 269, 346, 452, 639, 690; French, 130–31; Israeli charter of, 72; language and, 29–30, 495; Nazi persecution and, 38–39, 231, 268, 684, 696; Palestinian nationalism and, 34–35, 692, 694–99, 700; Russia and, 39–40, 230–31, 611; United States and, 37, 265, 266, 268–69, 275–76, 278, 305, 314, 347, 454, 641, 646, 659, 664, 665, 685–86, 694, 696, 700
Zionist Conference (New York City), 51
Zionist Congress (Basel), 29, 50
Zionist Executive, 50
Zohdy, Lieut. Col. Mohammed, quoted, 542, 543
Zorin, Valentin, 641